VOLUME 13 PART 2 OF 2

Plains

RAYMOND J. DeMALLIE

Volume Editor

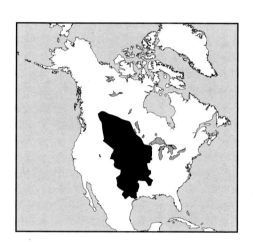

SMITHSONIAN INSTITUTION

WASHINGTON

2001

Library of Congress Cataloging in Publication Data

Handbook of North American Indians.

    Bibliography.
    Includes index.
    CONTENTS:

        v. 13. Plains.

    1. Indians of North America.
I. Sturtevant, William C.

E77.H25   970'.004'97   77-17162

For sale by the U.S. Government Printing Office
Superintendent of Documents, Mail Stop: SSOP, Washington, DC 20402-9328

ISBN 0-16-050400-7

Plains Volume Planning Committee

Raymond J. DeMallie, Volume Editor

Douglas R. Parks, Associate Volume Editor

William C. Sturtevant, General Editor

W. Raymond Wood, Coordinator for Prehistory Chapters

Loretta Fowler

George Frison

Ives Goddard

Mildred Mott Wedel

Waldo R. Wedel

Contents

This map is a diagrammatic guide to the coverage of this volume; it is not an authoritative depiction of territories for several reasons. Sharp boundaries have been drawn and no area is unassigned. The groups mapped are in some cases arbitrarily defined, subdivisions are not indicated, no joint or disputed occupations are shown, and different kinds of land use are not distinguished. The simplified ranges shown are a generalization of the situation in the early 19th century, with those to the east showing earlier locations. Movements and changes in range were common and continual in this area, and territories at earlier and later dates were substantially different. Not shown are groups that came into separate existence later than the map period for

their areas. For more specific information see the maps and text in the appropriate chapters.

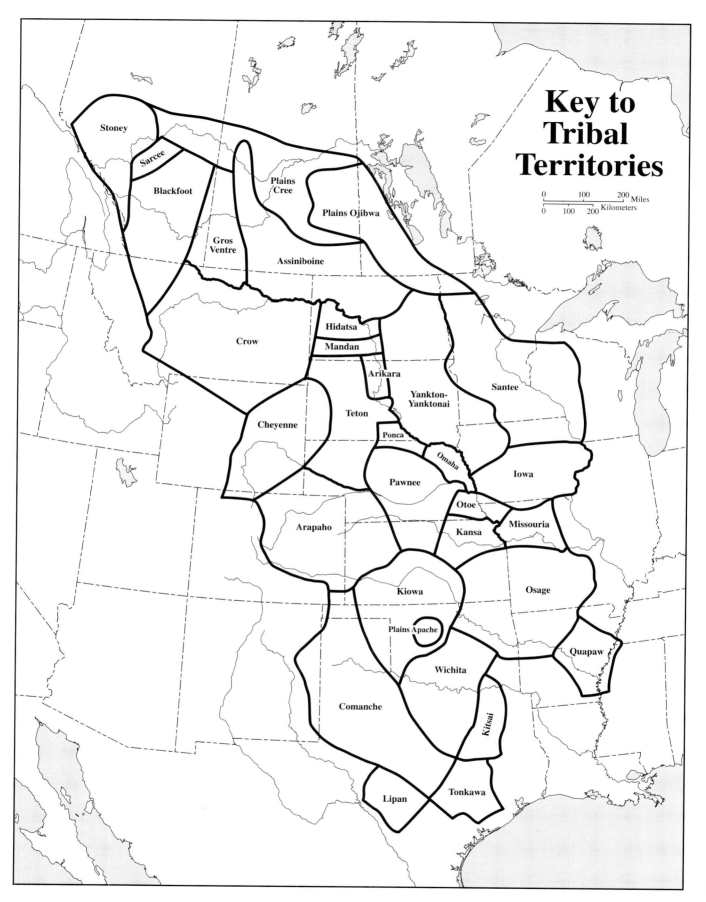

Key to Tribal Territories

0   100   200 Miles
0   100   200 Kilometers

Stoney

Sarcee

Blackfoot

Plains Cree

Plains Ojibwa

Gros Ventre

Assiniboine

Crow

Hidatsa

Mandan

Arikara

Yankton-Yanktonai

Santee

Teton

Cheyenne

Ponca

Omaha

Iowa

Pawnee

Otoe

Missouria

Arapaho

Kansa

Kiowa

Osage

Plains Apache

Quapaw

Wichita

Comanche

Kitsai

Lipan

Tonkawa

ix

Technical Alphabet

Consonants

		bilabial	labiodental	dental	alveolar	alveopalatal	velar	back velar	glottal
stop	vl	p		t	t		k	q	ʔ
	vd	b		d	d		g	ġ	
affricate	vl			θ̂	c	č			
	vd			δ̂	ʒ	ž, ǰ			
fricative	vl	φ	f	θ	s	š	x	x̣	h
	vd	β	v	δ, ð	z	ž	γ	γ̇	
nasal	vl	M		N			N̦		
	vd	m		n			ŋ	ŋ̇	
lateral	vl				ł				
	vd				l				
semivowel	vl	W					Y		
	vd	w					y		

vl = voiceless; vd = voiced

Other symbols include: λ (voiced lateral affricate), ƛ (voiceless lateral affricate), ʕ (voiced pharyngeal fricative), ḥ (voiceless pharyngeal fricative), r (medial flap, trill, or retroflex approximant).

Vowels

	front	central	back
high	i (ü)	ɨ	u (ɨ)
	ɪ		ʊ
mid	e (ö)	ə	o
	ɛ		ɔ
		ʌ	
low	æ	a	a

Unparenthesized vowels are unrounded if front or central, and rounded if back; ü and ö are rounded; ɨ is unrounded. The special symbols for lax vowels (ɪ, ʊ, ɛ, ɔ) are generally used only where it is necessary to differentiate between tense and lax high or mid vowels. i and a are used for both central and back vowels, as the two values seldom contrast in a given language.

Modifications indicated for consonants are: glottalization (ṫ, k̇, etc.), retroflexion (ṭ), palatalization (tʸ, kʸ, nʸ, lʸ), labialization (kʷ), aspiration (tʰ), length (t·). For vowels: length (a·), three-mora length (a:), nasalization (ą), voicelessness (A). The commonest prosodic markings are for stress: á (primary) and à (secondary), and for pitch: á (high), à (low), â (falling), and ǎ (rising); however, the details of prosodic systems and the uses of accents differ widely from language to language.

Words in Indian languages cited in italics in this volume are written in phonemic transcription. That is, the letters and symbols are used in specific values defined for them by the structure of the sound system of the particular language. However, as far as possible, these phonemic transcriptions use letters and symbols in generally consistent values, as specified by the standard technical alphabet of the *Handbook*. Deviations from these standard values as well as specific details of the phonology of each language (or references to where they may be found) are given in an orthographic footnote in each tribal chapter.

No italicized Indian word is broken at a line end except when a hyphen would be present anyway as part of the word. Words in italicized phonemic transcription are never capitalized. Pronunciations or phonetic values given in the standard technical alphabet without regard to phonemic analysis are put in square brackets ([]) rather than in italics. Pointed brackets (⟨ ⟩) indicate an exact, unnormalized spelling or transcription. The glosses, or conventional translations, of Indian words are enclosed in single quotation marks.

Indian words recorded by nonspecialists or before the phonemic systems of their languages had been analyzed are often not written accurately enough to allow respelling in phonemic transcription. Where phonemic retranscription has been possible the citation of source has been modified by the label "phonemicized" or "from." Words that could not be phonemicized have in some cases been "normalized"—rewritten by mechanical substitution of the symbols of the standard technical alphabet. Words that have not been normalized sometimes contain letters used according to the values of other technical alphabets or traditional orthographies. The most common of these are ä for the *Handbook*'s a; c for š; ć for č; ch for š (in French sources) or for x or h (in German sources); eñ for ę; ğ or ġ for γ; ħ or ħ for x; j for ž, ǯ, or y; ⁿ or ŋ for nasalization; ň for ŋ; oñ for ǫ; 8 for French ou; q for x; ś for š; tc and tj for č; ź for ž; ' for ʔ; ' or ̣ for glottalization; and ' for h (or nondistinctive aspiration). All nonphonemic transcriptions give only incomplete, and sometimes imprecise, approximations of the correct pronunciation.

Nontechnical Equivalents

Correct pronunciation, as with any foreign language, requires extensive training and practice, but simplified (incorrect) pronunciations may be obtained by ignoring the diacritics and reading the vowels as in Italian or Spanish and the consonants as in English. For a closer approximation to the pronunciation or to rewrite into a nontechnical transcription the substitutions indicated in the following table may be made.

Technical	Nontechnical	Technical	Nontechnical	Technical	Nontechnical
æ	ae	M	mh	Y	yh
β	bh	N	nh	$\check{z}$	zh
c	ts	η	ng	$\mathfrak{z}$	dz
$\check{c}$	ch	N	ngh	$\check{\mathfrak{z}}$	j
δ	dh	$\mathfrak{o}$	o	$\mathfrak{P}$	'
$\hat{\delta}$	ddh	θ	th	$\acute{k}, \dot{p}, \dot{t}$, etc.	k', p', t', etc.
ε	e	$\hat{\theta}$	tth	$a\cdot, e\cdot, k\cdot, s\cdot$, etc.	aa, ee, kk, ss, etc.
γ	gh	ϕ	ph	a, e, etc.	an, en, etc.
$\dot{t}$	lh	$\check{s}$	sh	k^y, t^y, etc.	ky, ty, etc.
λ	dl	W	wh	k^w	kw
$\check{\lambda}$	tlh	x	kh		

English Pronunciations

The English pronunciations of the names of tribes and a few other words are indicated parenthetically in a dictionary-style orthography in which most letters have their usual English pronunciation. Special symbols are listed below, with sample words to be pronounced as in nonregional United States English. Approximate phonetic values are given in parentheses in the standard technical alphabet.

ŋ:	thi**ng** (η)	ä:	f**a**ther (a)	ə:	**a**bout, gall**o**p (∂)	ō:	b**oa**t (ow)
θ:	**th**in (θ)	ā:	b**ai**t (ey)	ĭ:	b**i**t (ι)	o͝o:	b**oo**k (υ)
δ:	**th**is (δ)	e:	b**e**t (ε)	ī:	b**i**te (ay)	o͞o:	b**oo**t (uw)
zh:	vi**si**on ($\check{z}$)	ē:	b**ea**t (iy)	ô:	b**ou**ght ($\mathfrak{o}$)	u:	b**u**t (Λ)
ă:	b**a**t (æ)						

ˈ (primary stress), ˌ (secondary stress): elevator (ˈeleˌvātər) (éləvèytər)

Conventions for Illustrations

- Native settlement
- Abandoned settlement
- Non-native or mixed settlement
- Abandoned settlement
- ▲ Modern reservations or archeological sites
- × Battlefield
- Rapids
- Dam
- + Mountain peak
- Mountain pass

Arapaho Tribe

Livingston Settlement

Black Hills Geographic feature

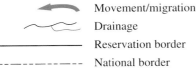 Movement/migration

Drainage

Reservation border

National border

State border

Railroad

Indian reservations and reserves

Precontact territory

Water

Credits and Captions

Credit lines give the source of the illustrations or the collections where the artifacts shown are located. The numbers that follow are the catalog or negative numbers of that repository. When the photographer mentioned in the caption is the source of the print reproduced, no credit line appears. "After" means that the Handbook illustrators have redrawn, rearranged, or abstracted the illustration from the one in the cited source. Measurements in captions are to the nearest millimeter if available; "about" indicates an estimate or a measurement converted from inches to centimeters. The following abbreviations are used in the credit lines:

Amer.	American	Lib.	Library
Anthr.	Anthropology, Anthropological	ms.	manuscript
		Mus.	Museum
Arch.	Archives	NAA	National
Arch(a)eol.	Arch(a)eology		Anthropological
Coll.	Collection(s)		Archives
Dept.	Department	Nat.	Natural
Dev.	Development	Natl.	National
Div.	Division	neg.	negative
Ethnol.	Ethnology, Ethnological	no.	number
		opp.	opposite
fol.	folio	p.	page
Ft.	Fort	pl(s).	plate(s)
Hist.	History	Prov.	Provincial
Histl.	Historical	Res.	Reservation (U.S.)
Inc.	Incorporated		Reserve (Canada)
Ind.	Indian		
Inst.	Institute	Soc.	Society
Lab.	Laboratory	St.	Saint
		U.	University

Metric Equivalents

100 cm = 1m	10 cm = 3.937 in.	1 km = .62 mi.	1 in. = 2.54 mi.	25 ft. = 7.62 m
10 mm = 1cm	1 m = 39.37 in.	5 km = 3.1 mi	1 ft. = 30.48 cm	1 mi. = 1.60 km
1,000 m = 1km	10 m = 32.81 ft.	10 km = 6.2 mi	1 yd. = 91.44 cm	5 mi. = 8.02 km

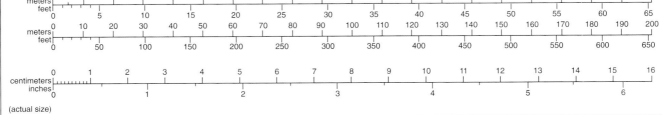

Preface

This is the twelfth volume to be published of a 20-volume set planned to give an encyclopedic summary of what is known about the prehistory, history, and cultures of the aboriginal peoples of North America north of the urban civilizations of central Mexico. Volumes 5–12 and 14–15 treat the other major culture areas of the continent.

Some topics relevant to the Plains area are excluded from this volume because they are more appropriately discussed on a continent-wide basis. Readers should refer to volume 1, Introduction, for general descriptions of anthropological and historical methods and sources and for summaries for the whole continent of certain topics regarding social and political organization, religion, and the performing arts. Volume 2 contains detailed accounts of the different kinds of Indian and Inuit (Eskimo) communities in the twentieth century, especially since 1950, and describes their relations with one another and with the surrounding non-Indian societies and nations. Volume 3 gives the environmental and biological backgrounds within which Native American societies developed, summarizes the early and late human biology or physical anthropology of Indians and Eskimos, and surveys the very earliest cultures. (Therefore the Paleo-Indian or Early Man period in the Plains receives major treatment in volume 3 rather than in this volume.) Volume 4 contains details on the history of the relations between Whites and Native American societies. Volume 16 is a continent-wide survey of technology and the visual arts—of material culture broadly defined. Volume 17 surveys the Native languages of North America, their characteristics, and historical relationships. Volumes 18 and 19 are a biographical dictionary; included in the listing are many Plains Indians. Volume 20 contains an index to the whole, which will serve to locate materials on Plains Indians in other volumes as well as in this one; it also includes a list of errata in all preceding volumes.

Preliminary discussions on the feasibility of the *Handbook* and alternatives for producing it began in 1965 in what was then the Smithsonian's Office of Anthropology. (A history of the early development of the whole *Handbook* and a listing of the entire editorial staff will be found in volume 1.) By 1971 funds were available and plans had advanced to the point where the details of the *Plains* volume could be worked out. In 1971 William W. Bittle agreed to serve as editor for the volume, and met with a planning committee (Robert E. Bell, Donald Lehmer, Beatrice Medicine, Abraham P. Nasatir, William W. Newcomb, Jr., and Symmes C. Oliver) to organize the contents and choose the authors to be invited.

Many draft manuscripts were received, but work on this volume proceeded very slowly. Editorial attention was devoted to other volumes in the series, which advanced more rapidly.

After Bittle's resignation in 1983, Raymond J. DeMallie was appointed volume editor. In 1985 a new planning committee (listed on p. [v]) met in Washington with Sturtevant and Goddard to revise the outline of chapters and select a new list of authors. Many of the chapter topics and their authors in the 1971 plan were still appropriate and were carried over into the newly planned volume.

In September 1986 the Volume Editor contacted all authors to inform them that work on the *Plains* volume was imminent. Between February and August 1987 the Volume Editor sent each new author a brief description of the desired contents of the chapter. Authors remaining from the 1971 plan were sent new suggestions for revising and updating their chapters. Also sent each author was a "Guide for Contributors" prepared by the General Editor, which described the general aims and methods of the *Handbook* and the editorial conventions. One convention has been to avoid the present tense, where possible, in historical and cultural descriptions. Thus a statement in the past tense, with a recent date or approximate date, may also hold true for the time of writing.

Work on the *Plains* volume proceeded so slowly after 1987 that in 1992 other volumes in the series had to be given priority. Finally, in 1998 intensive work to complete the *Plains* volume was initiated. The contents of this volume reflect the state of knowledge in the 1990s, rather than in the early 1970s when planning first began.

As they were received, the chapter manuscripts were reviewed by the Volume Editor, the General Editor and his staff, and usually one or more referees, who frequently included a member of the Planning Committee and often authors of other chapters. Suggestions for changes and additions often resulted. The published versions frequently reflect more editorial intervention than is customary for academic writings, since the encyclopedic aims and format of the *Handbook* made it necessary to attempt to eliminate duplication, avoid gaps in coverage, prevent contradictions, impose some standardization of organization and terminology, and keep within strict constraints on length. Where the evidence seemed so scanty or obscure as to allow different authorities to come to differing conclusions, authors have been encouraged to elaborate their own views, although the editors have endeavored to draw attention to alternative interpretations published elsewhere.

The first editorial acceptance of an author's manuscript was on January 16, 1992, and the last on November 14, 2000. Edited manuscripts were sent from the Washington office to authors for their final approval between May 8, 1998, and December 15, 2000. These dates for all chapters are given in the list of Contributors.

Linguistic Editing

As far as possible, all cited words in Indian languages were referred to consultants with expert knowledge of the respective languages and rewritten by them in the appropriate technical orthography. In some cases a chapter author served as the linguist consultant. The consultants and the spelling systems are identified in the orthographic footnotes, most of which were written by Douglas R. Parks, others by the Linguistic Editor, Ives Goddard; all were edited by Goddard.

Statements about the genetic relationships of Plains languages have also been checked with linguist consultants, to ensure conformity with recent findings and terminology in comparative linguistics and to avoid conflicting statements within the *Handbook*. In general, only the less remote genetic relationships are mentioned in the individual chapters. The chapter "The Languages of the Plains: Introduction" discusses the wider relationships of those languages, and further information will be found in volume 17.

The Linguistic Editor served as coordinator and editor of these efforts by linguist consultants. A special debt is owed to these consultants, who provided advice and assistance without compensation and, in many cases, took time from their own research in order to check words with native speakers. The Linguistic Editor is especially grateful to Jean Charney, Eung-Do Cook, Raymond J. DeMallie, Donald G. Frantz, Randolph Graczyk, A. Wesley Jones, John E. Koontz, Wayne Leman, Mauricio Mixco, John D. Nichols, Douglas R. Parks, David H. Pentland, Robert L. Rankin, Willem J. de Reuse, David Rood, Scott Rushforth, Allan R. Taylor, Laurel Watkins, and H.C. Wolfart.

In the case of words that could not be respelled in a technical orthography, an attempt has been made to rationalize the transcriptions used in earlier anthropological writings in order to eliminate phonetic symbols that are obsolete and diacritics that might convey a false impression of phonetic accuracy.

Synonymies

Toward the end of ethnological chapters is a section called Synonymy. This describes the various names that have been applied to the groups and subgroups treated in that chapter, giving the principal variant, self-designations, the names applied to the groups in neighboring Indian languages, and the spellings used in European languages—English, French, and Spanish. For the major group names, an attempt has been made to cite the earliest attestations in English.

Throughout the ethnographic chapters more space has been devoted than in other volumes to presenting tribal synonymies that are as full and detailed as possible. The published literature is so replete with errors that accurate synonymies for Plains ethnonyms are a critical need. All synonymies were written by Douglas R. Parks to insure comparability of scope and detail. He provided linguistic forms, based on field elicitation, for Arikara, Assiniboine, Iowa-Otoe, Hidatsa, Mandan, Pawnee, Ponca, Sioux, Stoney, and Wichita. Parks wishes to acknowledge the following individuals who also provided data for the synonymies: Alice J. Anderton (Comanche); James Armagost (Comanche); Timothy A. Bernardis (Crow); Wallace L. Chafe (Caddo, Seneca); Jean Charney (Comanche); Eung-Do Cook (Sarcee, Stoney); David Costa (Illinois, Miami); Loretta Fowler (Arapaho); Donald G. Frantz (Blackfoot); Louanna Furbee (Iowa-Otoe); Talmy Givón (Ute); Ives Goddard (Arapaho); James Good Tracks (Iowa-Otoe); Randolph Graczyk (Crow); Robert Hollow (Mandan); A. Wesley Jones (Hidatsa); Thomas W. Kavanagh (Comanche); Geoffrey Kimball (Koasati); John E. Koontz (Omaha-Ponca); Wayne Leman (Cheyenne); G. Hubert Matthews (Crow); Wick R. Miller (Eastern Shoshone); Ken Miner (Winnebago); Mauricio Mixco (Mandan); John D. Nichols (Ojibwa); David H. Pentland (Plains Cree); Carolyn Quintero (Osage); Robert L. Rankin (Omaha-Ponca, Quapaw, Osage, and Kansa); Richard Rhodes (Ojibwa); David Rood (Wichita); Zdeněk Saltzmann (Arapaho) ; David Shaul (Eastern Shoshone); Demetri Shimkin (Eastern Shoshone); Allan R. Taylor (Blackfoot); Sarah G. Thomason (Salish); Randolph Valentine (Ojibwa); Paul Voorhis (Kickapoo); Laurel Watkins (Kiowa); H.C. Wolfart (Plains Cree).

These sections should assist in the identification of groups mentioned in the earlier historical and anthropological literature. They should also be examined for evidence on changes in the identifications and affiliations of groups, as seen by their own members as well as by neighbors and by outside observers. Questionable ethnonyms, and those not identifiable with a known tribe, are presented in the chapter "Enigmatic Groups."

Radiocarbon Dates

Authors were instructed to convert radiocarbon dates into dates in the Christian calendar. Such conversions have often been made from the dates as originally published, without taking account of changes that may be required by developing research on revisions of the half-life of carbon 14, long-term changes in the amount of carbon 14 in the atmosphere, and other factors that may require modifications of absolute dates based on radiocarbon determinations.

Binomials

The scientific names of animal and plant genera and species, printed in italics, have been checked to ensure that they reflect modern usage by biological taxonomists. Especially the plant names (but also most of the animal names) submitted in the chapter "Environment and Subsistence" were taken as standard. Binomials in other chapters have been brought into agreement with those in that chapter, or if they do not appear there, have been revised in consultation with curators in appropriate departments of the National Museum of Natural History.

Bibliography

All references cited by contributors have been unified in a single list at the end of the volume. Citations within the text, by author, date, and often page, identify the works in this unified list. Cesare Marino, the *Handbook* Researcher, served as bibliographer. Wherever possible, he resolved conflicts between citations of different editions, corrected inaccuracies and omissions, and checked direct quotations against the originals. The bibliographic information has been verified by examination of the original work or from standard reliable library catalogs (especially the National Union Catalog, the published catalog of the Harvard Peabody Museum Library, and the OCLC/PRISM on-line catalog). The unified bibliography lists all the sources cited in the text of the volume, except personal communications, and works consulted but not cited in the chapters. In the text, "personal communications" to an author are distinguished from personal "communications to editors." The sections headed Sources at the ends of most chapters provide general guidance to the most important sources of information on the topics covered.

Illustrations

Authors were requested to submit suggestions for illustrations: photographs, drawings, maps, and lists and locations of objects that might be illustrated. To varying degrees they complied with this request. Yet considerations of space, balance, reproducibility, and availability often required modifications in what was submitted. Much original material was provided by editorial staff members from research they conducted in museums and other repositories and in the published literature. Locating, collecting, and selecting suitable photographs, drawings, and paintings was the responsibility of the Illustrations Researcher, Joanna Cohan Scherer. Selection of and research on suitable artifacts to be photographed or drawn was the responsibility of the Artifact Researchers, Ernest S. Lohse, Thomas W. Kavanagh, and Christine A. Jirikowic during the initial period of volume preparation and Brenda G. McLain and Scherer during the later stages. During the final two years of volume preparation Candace S. Greene contributed valuable artifact research to many chapters in addition to the one she authored. All drawings are credited.

Maps for the "Key to Tribal Territories" and "Introduction" were produced by David Swanson of Equator Graphics, Inc. and for "Environment and Subsistence" by Roger Thor Roop. Maps for 23 tribal chapters were produced by Catherine Spencer while all others were by Daniel G. Cole of the Smithsonian Automatic Data Processing office. Digital sketch maps were created using information from the chapter manuscripts, from their authors, and from other sources. Final production (of all maps) was the responsibility of David Swanson, Alex Tait, and Dana Gantz of Equator Graphics, Inc.

Layout and design of the illustrations were the responsibility of the Scientific Illustrators, Catherine Spencer (1998–1999) and Roger Thor Roop (1999–) in coordination with Scherer. Captions for most illustrations were composed by Scherer; others were written by Lohse, Kavanagh, Jirikowic, McLain, Greene, Spencer, and Roop and for maps by Cole, with several by Swanson and Spencer. Native place-names in map captions were supplied by authors and edited by the Linguistic Editor and his consultants. All illustrations, including maps and drawings, and all captions have been approved by the Volume Editor, Technical Editor, and the authors of the chapters in which they appear.

The list of illustrations was compiled by Joanna Cohan Scherer.

Acknowledgements

During the first few years of this project, the *Handbook* editorial staff in Washington worked on materials for all volumes of the series. Since intensive preparation of this volume began in 1998, especially important contributions were provided by: the Editorial Liaison and Staff Coordinator, Paula Cardwell; the Production Manager and Manuscript Editor, Diane Della-Loggia; the Researcher and Bibliographer, Cesare Marino; the Scientific Illustrators, Catherine Spencer (1998–1999) and Roger Thor Roop (1999–); the Illustrations Researcher, Joanna Cohan Scherer; the Assistant Illustrations Researcher, Vicki E. Simon (1999–); the Artifact Researchers, Ernest S. Lohse (1985–1989), Thomas W. Kavanagh (1990–1992), and Christine A. Jirikowic (1994–1995); Brenda McLain (1998), Assistant Illustrations Researcher and Artifact Researcher; the Administrative Specialist, Melvina Jackson (until February 2000). Alex Young, Peta Joy Sosnowski, and Terrilee Edwards-Hewitt served as bibliographic assistants at various stages of volume preparation. Barbara Watanabe provided valuable back-up research assistance and technical support during critical periods of reduced staffing while Gabrielle Lawson provided additional typing. Between 1985 and 2000, the Illustrations Researcher was assisted at various times by Catherine J. Adams, Peggy Albright, Rosa Anchondo, Rebecca Blom, Amber Breiner, Monika Carothers, Christian Carstensen, Erica Davis, Francis Galindo, Billie Gutgsell, Jason Jones, Meredith Kilduff, Colleen Lodge, Timothy McCleary, Wendy Niece, Courtney O'Callaghan, Elizabeth Noznesky, Lynn Spriggs, Sarah Trabucchi, Laura Woodson, and Layla Wuthrick as interns, volunteers, or assistant illustrations researchers.

Candace S. Greene was assisted by Lea Foster and Marit Munson. Donald Tenoso (Hunkpapa Lakota) of the American Indian Program, National Museum of Natural History, helped document certain illustrations. Scientific Illustrators Karen B. Ackoff (until 1997) and Norman J. Frisch (Brockport, New York) prepared some drawings. Thanks are due to the many others (including student interns and volunteers) who provided assistance with the illustrations research effort at different stages of volume preparation. The index was compiled by Lee Gable of Coughlin Indexing Services, Inc.

Carolyn Rose served as Managing Editor in addition to her other duties as Deputy Chair and (since January 2000) Chair of the Department of Anthropology, National Museum of Natural History. She was particularly helpful in guiding the *Handbook* staff to work within an accelerated production schedule.

Throughout, Ives Goddard was of particular assistance on matters of historical and geographical accuracy. He served as Technical Editor as well as the *Handbook* Linguistic Editor and advisor to the General Editor.

Special thanks are owed to Stanwyn Shetler, Jerry Harasewych, and Phillip Angle, National Museum of Natural History, who were of particular assistance regarding scientific names of plants and animal genera and species.

Beyond the members of the Planning Committee and those individuals acknowledged in appropriate sections of the text, the Volume Editor would especially like to thank two individuals for their contributions to the volume—Douglas R. Parks who was asked by DeMallie to serve as Associate Volume Editor and to prepare the synonymies for the tribal chapters and Joanna Cohan Scherer who coordinated the majority of the illustrations for the volume. The Volume Editor also thanks W. Raymond Wood who graciously agreed to review final versions of the prehistory chapters after failing health prevented Waldo Wedel from continuing in his role as advisor in archeology. Special thanks are owed to the Volume Editor's research assistants, Lee Irwin (1989–1990) and Dennis M. Christafferson (1999–2000), who helped to finalize many of the chapters. Thanks also to Wallace E. Hooper, who oversaw the preparation of electronic files in Bloomington. Finally, DeMallie expresses his gratitude to graduate students at Indiana University who assisted him in editorial work on the volume: Christina E. Burke, Brenda Farnell, Erik D. Gooding, Jason Baird Jackson, Michael B. Moore, Mindy J. Morgan, and Joseph Sweeney. Other colleagues who provided support and advice include Carolyn R. Anderson, Morris W. Foster, Louis Garcia, Richard B. Henne, David Reed Miller, Jacqueline Peterson, David Smyth, Daniel C. Swan, and Arok Wolvengrey.

The following contributors to the volume would like particularly to acknowledge the support of various individuals and scholarly institutions that helped to make their research possible. Dennis Christafferson thanks Christina E. Burke and Mindy J. Morgan. Ian Dyck and Richard E. Morlan thank David A. Meyer, Rod Vickers, Ernest G. Walker, and the Canadian Museum of Civilization (especially the library staff). Ian A.L. Getty thanks Gerald Kaquits.

Acknowledgement is due to the Department of Anthropology, National Museum of Natural History, Smithsonian Institution (and to its other curatorial staff), for releasing Sturtevant and Goddard from part of their curatorial and research responsibilities so that they could devote time to editing the *Handbook*. The Department is also owed thanks for supporting the participation of Chair Carolyn Rose and Researcher Candace S. Greene. DeMallie acknowledges the support of Indiana University, Bloomington, especially George E. Walker, Vice-President for Research and Dean of the University Graduate School; the American Indian Studies Research Institute; and the Department of Anthropology.

Preparation and publication of this volume have been supported by federal appropriations made to the Smithsonian Institution.

February 11, 2001

William C. Sturtevant
Raymond J. DeMallie

Gros Ventre

LORETTA FOWLER AND REGINA FLANNERY

Language and Territory

The Gros Ventre ('grō₁vän(t)) spoke an Algonquian language, closely related to Arapaho.* When and where the two peoples separated is unknown (Kroeber 1908:145–147; Mooney 1896:954–955; Salzmann 1969:308).

In the mid-eighteenth century the Gros Ventre were located on the Canadian plains between the North Saskatchewan and South Saskatchewan rivers. They were gradually pushed south, and by the mid-nineteenth century they had moved into northern Montana. In 1988 about half the 2,300 enrolled Gros Ventres lived on Fort Belknap Reservation in Montana, which they shared with some 1,500 Assiniboines (fig. 1).

Historical Identification

The Gros Ventres cannot be identified with certainty on early eighteenth-century maps. The first unequivocal mention of them was in 1772 when Cocking (1908:110–111) met the Gros Ventre on their home ground between the forks of the Saskatchewan and identified them as the Waterfall Indians, one of five allied peoples known to western Crees as Archithinue, the others being the three Blackfoot groups and the Sarcee. In the 1730s and 1740s, "earchithinues" traded with the Cree and also were at war with the Cree and Assiniboine (Isham 1949:87, 113–115). In 1751 the Cree and Assiniboine were at war with the Hyactchejlini (Archithinue), Brochets (unidentified), and the Gros Ventres (Le Gardeur de Saint-Pierre 1887:clx). These Gros Ventres may have been the Algonquian-speaking Waterfall Indians or the Siouan-speaking Hidatsa (Kehoe and Kehoe 1974; Wood and Thiessen 1985); in 1784 the people known to the French as Gros Ventres were identified as the Waterfall or Fall Indians (Umfreville 1790:197).

*The phonemes of Gros Ventre are: (voiceless unaspirated stops and affricates) t, c, č, k, ʔ; (voiceless spirants) θ, s, h; (voiced stop and resonant) b, n; (semivowels) w, y; (short vowels) i, e, ɛ, ɔ, o, u; (long vowels) ii, ee, ɛɛ, ɔɔ, oo, uu; (extra-long vowels) iii, eee, ɛɛɛ, ɔɔɔ, ooo, uuu; (long diphthongs) ei, ou; (extra-long diphthongs) eei, oou; (unstressed, low pitch) v, vv, vvv; (stressed, high pitch) v́, v́v́, v́v́v́; (falling pitch) v́v, v́vv. The i-quality vowels are pronounced [i] after c, s, and w.

The analysis and transcription of Gros Ventre follows the narrow phonemic system of Taylor (1994).

History to the 1870s

English fur traders pushed into the interior of Canada from Hudson Bay after 1670, with the Woods Cree and Assiniboine serving as middlemen in trade with peoples west of Lake Winnipeg. French traders established Fort à La Corne in 1753, a few miles below the forks of the Saskatchewan, possibly in Gros Ventre country. The English attempted to compete by sending Anthony Henday (also spelled Hendry) and Matthew Cocking to convince the westerly peoples to come to the Hudson's Bay posts.

In 1754–1755 Henday met with the Archithinue on their home ground, between the north and south branches of the Saskatchewan. They have been variously identified as Gros Ventre and as Blackfoot (see Wissler 1936:5; Lewis 1942:16). The Archithinue were exchanging furs for trade

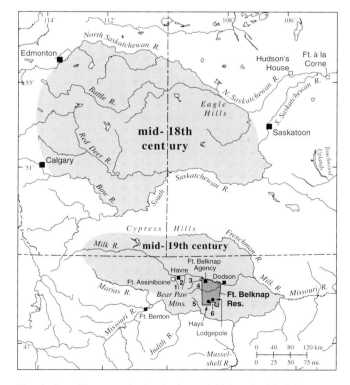

Fig. 1. Gros Ventre territories in the mid-18th and mid-19th centuries with Ft. Belknap Res. 1, Beaver Creek; 2, Clear Creek; 3, Snake Creek; 4, Peoples Creek; 5, Cow Creek; 6, Little Rocky Mts.

goods with Cree and Assiniboine middlemen, and at other times they fought with these same middlemen. According to Henday the Archithinue were found in bands of 70–127 tepees during the spring; in the fall several bands came together to form a camp of over 300 tepees, which were set in two parallel rows. In the winter they moved farther west into higher country. They were skilled in hunting buffalo on horseback and had asses as well as packhorses. They used hair ropes and buffalo skin saddles with stirrups; apparently they had been equestrian for at least a generation. The Archithinue, "under proper discipline," had a "Great Leader . . . attended by 20 elderly men." This head chief was apparently wealthy in horses, for he had a tepee that seated 50 people (Hendry 1907:337, 339).

In 1772 when Cocking met 28 tepees of Gros Ventre on the Saskatchewan plains near Eagle Hills at one of their buffalo pounds, it was early December and the Gros Ventre had already separated into bands for the winter. The leader spoke Assiniboine, and the Gros Ventre were on friendly terms with some bands of Assiniboine, to whom they traded horses, hide clothing, and skins, meeting them in early spring at the forks of the Saskatchewan. The Gros Ventre had many riding and pack horses and were expert mounted hunters, driving the buffalo into pounds. They grew tobacco; made "earthen vessels"; and they made fire with a "black stone" used as flint, a kind of "ore" as steel, and moss as tinder (Cocking 1908:109–112).

In 1778 the Hudson's Bay Company built Hudson's House on the North Saskatchewan and began to trade there regularly with the Gros Ventre (Fowler 1987:41–42). Both the Hudson's Bay Company and the North West Company built other posts on the North and South Saskatchewan rivers. White traders courted them with gifts and special privileges in order to facilitate trade (Fowler 1987:34–40). Gros Ventre traded provisions, wolf skins, and horses for guns, gunpowder, cloth, metal tools, liquor, and Euro-American tobacco. Competition for trade precipitated a period of intense warfare, and although the Gros Ventre still were allied with the powerful Blackfoot, they bore the brunt of attacks from Plains Cree and Assiniboine, for their territories were contiguous. High casualties, compounded by the effects of epidemics introduced by Euro-American traders, began to take a heavy toll. The Gros Ventre were weakened by smallpox in 1780–1781 and 1801–1802.

In the late 1770s and 1780s, the traders had friendly relations with the Gros Ventre. In 1793 Hudson's Bay man William Tomison characterized them as a "peaceable People" and his colleague James Bird thought them "the most rational and inoffensive" people in the Saskatchewan area (Fowler 1987:43). But as the Gros Ventre were increasingly pressed by the well-armed Plains Cree and Assiniboine, whom they viewed as allies of the traders, relations with the traders deteriorated. In 1794–1795 the Gros Ventre attacked three trading posts on the Saskatchewan. Subsequently the Gros Ventre were portrayed as especially hostile and dangerous to traders.

Pressed by the well-armed Cree and Assiniboine, whom they viewed as allies of the traders, in 1794–1795 the Gros Ventre attacked three trading posts on the Saskatchewan. The conflict only worsened their predicament; after 1795 bands of Gros Ventre began moving south, and in 1801 and subsequent years they were observed living with the Arapaho (Fowler 1982:17, 1987:45–47; Gregg 1845, 1:81–86, 95). By 1830, the last of the Gros Ventre bands, together with their Piegan Blackfoot allies, had retreated or been drawn south of the Cypress Hills (Fowler 1987:41–48). There the Gros Ventre established a territory that reached from the Judith River and the Bear Paw Mountains on the west, down the Missouri to the mouths of the Milk and Mussellshell rivers on the east.

At first the Gros Ventre and their Piegan allies clashed with trappers in the upper Missouri area. After 1831, relations improved and Gros Ventres traded peacefully at the American Fur Company posts on the upper Missouri. There they grew rich in horses and trade goods and escaped the smallpox epidemic of 1837 with only 200 deaths, a small loss compared with other tribes (Fowler 1987:48–52).

When the United States negotiated a treaty in 1855 (fig. 2) the Gros Ventre and their Blackfoot allies agreed to allow military posts and travel in their country (Kappler 1904–1941, 2:736–740). American citizens moved into the upper Missouri area in larger numbers, settling to the southwest of Gros Ventre territory around Fort Benton. The Gros Ventre and the U.S. Army were never in conflict (Fowler 1987:47–50). Pressure to confine Montana Indians to small areas removed from regions of non-Indian settlement increased in the 1870s and 1880s. Despite the guarantees of the Treaty of 1855, a series of executive orders drastically reduced Indian lands (Ewers 1974:141–143, 147).

Gros Ventre bands began going more regularly to Fort Belknap Agency for food and supplies in the 1870s when the number of buffalo in their territory began to decline. They camped within a few miles of the agency, remaining in large groups to better defend themselves from Blackfoot and Yanktonai Sioux raiders and moving away to hunt for a few days at a time. From 1878 until 1890 they camped in three or four large bands along Cow, Peoples, Beaver, Snake, and Clear creeks; in the early 1880s a few smaller bands (about 40 tepees altogether) periodically went south of the Missouri into Crow country (Lincoln 1881, 1881a, 1883, 1884a; O'Hanlon 1881; McClure 1882; Barr 1884). After signing the Agreement of 1887 (ratified the next year), by which they ceded most of their territory to the United States, the Gros Ventre were relocated on a reduced reservation in 1890 with some bands of Assiniboine.

Culture from Contact to 1878

The Gros Ventres probably obtained their first horses from mounted tribes to the southwest or south at least within the second quarter of the eighteenth century (Ewers 1955:11, 18). By the early nineteenth century, wealth differentials

Fig. 2. Gros Ventre leaders. left, Woh-se Im-meh-ca-tan, Bear's Shirt, at the 1855 treaty council where Isaac Stevens, the U.S. Representative, unsuccessfully tried to promote him as head chief. Instead, 8 "principal chiefs" including Bear's Shirt were chosen to sign the treaty. center, Mexkemauastan or Stirring Iron. He holds a gun in a case, and a bow and arrow quiver is hanging over his back. He wears shell and bead ornaments in his ears and in his hair. His top knot marks him as keeper of the sacred pipe (Kroeber 1908:273). He also wears a red painted buffalo robe over fringed leggings. Watercolor by Karl Bodmer, 1833. right, Ac-kyo-py, Woman That Sets, a war chief of the Gros Ventre. left and right, Pencil drawings by Gustav Sohon, 1855.

were observed and commented upon (Fowler 1987:36), but communal sharing began to be undermined soon after the Gros Ventre became fully equestrian (see Ewers 1955:314–16). Men wealthy in horses attracted younger kinsmen and horse-poor followers. Leadership was associated with distribution of food and horses, and both political and ritual authority had to be validated by gifts (Flannery 1953:32, 82). Warfare probably received more emphasis because of the desire to raid other peoples for horses and to protect the Gros Ventre herds. The mobility and trading advantage brought by horse ownership also may have been a factor in the development of a rich ceremonial complex that underpinned the Gros Ventre status and political system.

Subsistence

Social organization, work activity, and hunting technology varied with the season. Before they had large numbers of horses, or later when they were in short supply, Gros Ventres hunted buffalo by impounding them (Curtis 1907–1930, 5:111; Flannery 1953:56–57; Kroeber 1908:148–149). When horses were plentiful, at the first sign of spring most or all Gros Ventre families—grouped into bands of approximately 300 to 500 people—congregated in anticipation of the northward migration of the buffalo. Men with trained "buffalo horses" joined in making "runs" on the herd, shooting with bow and arrow. During summer the bands separated from time to time, the men going out in smaller

hunting parties, but during the important ceremonies (the sacred lodges), the bands came together and camped in a circle. This was also a season for raiding other tribes, and war parties left frequently. In the fall the bands again came together and men made buffalo runs. In the winter the bands separated into smaller groups that camped along wooded water courses. Small hunting parties and individuals stalked deer, elk, and antelope. Men made bows, arrows, war clubs, shields, and ceremonial equipment and took responsibility for hunting, skinning, and butchering game and for obtaining and caring for horses (Flannery 1953:53–58, 69–70).

Women's activities varied seasonally as well. They collected plant food, prepared food for consumption and storage, set up the tepees (using a three-pole foundation) (fig. 3) and moved camp, cared for children, collected firewood and water, and made clothing and other household equipment. In the spring they collected roots and berries and preserved large quantities of food for use during the summer ceremonies. Since the hair on the buffalo hides was not so thick in the spring and summer as it was in the fall, these seasons were spent making tepee covers (which usually were replaced every three years), moccasins, parfleches, bags, and ropes. During the summer the women moved camp six or seven times to allow the hunters to follow smaller herds of buffalo. In the fall the women dried and stored large quantities of meat for use during the winter months. They made pemmican by pounding dried meat

73). In the fall and winter, women made clothing, primarily from deer hide—men's moccasins and hip-length leggings, loincloths, and shirts, and women's one-piece, full-sleeved dresses, and women's moccasins and knee-length leggings (Curtis 1907–1930, 5:111–112).

Ordinary clothing was unornamented, but families with the means had special clothing for ceremonial occasions. Designs were painted or embroidered with dyed porcupine quills (fig. 4) or glass beads obtained in trade, and powdered mica glistened when spread over a robe. Polished deer hooves dangled from robes, leggings, and garters as tinklers. Elk teeth and dentalia were used principally for decoration of girls' and women's dresses, even into the twentieth century (fig. 5).

Hair from slain enemies was worn as fringe on clothing and footgear by men who had taken scalps. Furs such as mink, otter, or muskrat were used as trimmings (Flannery 1953:61–63). Although influenced by surrounding peoples in style of decoration, the Gros Ventre designs were most similar to the Arapaho (Kroeber 1908:152).

Fig. 3. Raising a tepee at Hays, Fort Belknap Res., Mont. top, Women placing the poles for the framework. center, Laying on the canvas cover. bottom, The painted canvas cover almost in place. The man on the right is making a ladder to be used in placing the pegs. Photographs by Richard A. Pohrt, 1937.

with grease and berries. At least two women were needed to process one man's kill; one buffalo cow yielded 45 pounds of dried meat or 55 pounds of pemmican.

Clothing and Adornment

In the fall the buffalo hides were in prime condition; this was the robe-making season. Hides were scraped, tanned, and sometimes decorated (Flannery 1953:54–55, 58–66, 70–

680

Mus. für Völkerkunde, Berlin: IV-B-200.
Fig. 4. Girl's quilled bison robe. The body of the robe has 68 vertical and 6 horizontal stripes made of flattened porcupine quills in white, yellow, light brown, dark brown, and black; the tail end and all 4 legs are each decorated with 5 quilled stripes, while the head area has 5 groups of the same type; these groups are crossed with rows of tufts of red wool yarn. Collected by Maximilian, Prince of Wied, before 1844; length 210 cm.

FOWLER AND FLANNERY

top, Mont. State U., Mus. of the Rockies, Bozeman: 83.13.645; center, Colo. Histl. Soc., Denver: J-19797; bottom, Catholic U., Dept. of Anthr., Washington.

Fig. 5. Prominent individuals. top, front row: Blackbird, a noted doctor; Lame Bull, a leader in the age-grade organization, a Keeper of the Flat Pipe, and a spokesman to U.S. officials; unidentified man, possibly Standing Bear, in striped cloth shirt; and Sitting on High, who was Keeper of the Feathered Pipe. back row: Mrs. Blackbird; unidentified woman; unidentified man; Curly Head, Keeper of the Feathered Pipe, 1910–1938, wearing a fur sash decorated with round disks; probably Tom Badroad, wearing fur-wrapped braids, cloth vest, and watch chain; and unidentified man with a line painted diagonally across his face, wearing a Hudson's Bay Company blanket and a vest with beaded studs. Photograph by Dan Dutro at a camp between the Milk and Missouri rivers, near Ft. Boston, an area where the Gros Ventre often hunted, 1887. center, White and Yellow Cow (b. 1842 or 1846) wearing beaded moccasins and carrying a lance. He was a warrior and headman, and often identified as a "principal chief" during the late 1870s–1890s. His wife, Singing Bird, wears a dress ornamented with dentalia and holds a pipe. Photograph by William H. Jackson, copyright 1907. bottom, Elders who were consultants on traditional culture to John Cooper and Regina Flannery. left to right, Thick (b. about 1870, d. 1950s), wearing false braids for this photo, a singer of Sun Dance and Grass Dance songs whose father pledged the last Sun Dance in 1885; Tom Main (b. 1890, d. 1952), a skilled interpreter, a member of the business council frequently sent to Washington; The Boy (b. about 1872, d. 1957), a singer and officer in the Grass Dance, wearing a medal, probably his father Lame Bull's, and holding a feather fan, also a member of the business council; and John Buckman (b. about 1875, d. 1949), Grass Dance singer and member of the business council. Photograph by John M. Cooper, Hays, Mont., 1938.

Social Organization

Closely related families camped together year round, joining other more distantly related families to form a group or band whose name changed frequently. Some bands tended to group together, camping within a few miles of each other during the winter and spring and occupying contiguous places in the camp circle during the summer. The exact order of the bands in the camp circle changed over time. At any one time during the nineteenth century the Gros Ventre had 10–12 such bands, some of which were large enough and successful enough to remain together throughout most of the mid-century (Flannery 1953:25–29; Kroeber 1908: 147–148; Curtis 1907–1930, 5:112, 153). Traveling over the same country along the Milk River and sometimes camping near each other were the prosperous Upper Quarters (ʔitiyɔ́ɔɔ́ʔɔ́nɔh) and Frozens (nííʔɔcích), and occasionally joining them were less prosperous bands. The Plenty Bad (wanasutasuts) and Tendon (ʔichʔícinɔh) bands wintered together farther south in the Fort Benton and Bear Paws area and associated closely with each other. South of the Missouri were the Slippery Travois Poles (wɔɔθɔ́ɔ́θɔ́ɔʔinɔ́tééch) and with them at times, the Coffees (table 1). Band leaders (ninaninanaa 'he who takes us around') had great influence in decisions about the movements of the band but did not have directive authority (Flannery 1953:28–29, 31–34; Curtis 1907–1930, 5:112).

Usually a child resided with his father's band, as a wife resided with her husband's group unless her family was more prosperous. Bands were exogamous, and incest taboos were applied to blood and intergenerational affinal

Table 1. Band Name Synonymy

Curtis 1907–1930, 5:153; Taylor 1994	Kroeber 1908:148	Flannery 1953:25–31
1. Gray Ones (*ninííky²íhch*)	Gray Ones, or Ash Colored	Grays
2. Slippery Travois (*wɔɔθɔ́ɔθɔ́ɔ²inɔ́téέch*)	Tent Poles Worn Smooth, Ugly Ones	Slippery Travois Poles, Slick Runners, Fast Travelers
3. Water Their Horses Once (*kyɛɛθéi² béénhɔ́ɔθibyééch*)	Those Who Water Their Horses Once A Day	Water Horses Once A Day
4. Forequarters (*²itiyɔ́ɔ²ɔ́nɔh*)	Buffalo Humps, Those Who Do Not Give Away	Upper Quarters
5. Frozen Meat (*níí²ɔcích*)	Frozen, Plumes	Frozen, Plumes, Those Who Wear Feathers On The Head
6. Round Neck Fascia (*²ich²ícinɔh*)	Tendons	Tendons
7. Blood Men (*bɔ²ɔ́ɔ́ciinén²* sg.)	Bloods	Bloods
8. Night Hawk (*cííθoouh*)	Night Hawks	Night Hawks
9. Black Horn (Watǎnníntibǎts)		Black Horns
10. Queer Crowd (Wanasétasǐts)		Plenty Bad
11.	Coffee	Coffees
12.	Opposite Assiniboine, Middle Assiniboine	Same As Assiniboine

relationships as far as they were known. Relatives were categorized in two ways. Those toward whom "respect" and sometimes avoidance was expected were ego's parents (including their siblings and siblings' spouses), parents-in-law, and siblings of the opposite sex (including children of parents' siblings). Those toward whom freedom of behavior was allowed were ego's grandparents (and grandchildren), siblings of the same sex, and in-laws of the same generation. Sexual joking was expected between same generation in-laws of different sex (in fact, they not infrequently married) but prohibited between same-sex in-laws (Flannery 1953:29–31, 107–126; Kroeber 1908:147).

Household composition varied. A prominent man with a large herd of horses usually had more than one wife and might also have younger male relatives living with him. He could afford a large tepee composed of 25 skins. Several households clustered around a prominent man, borrowing horses and sharing in his bounty. Elderly women, with their granddaughters or nieces whom they trained in women's tasks, often occupied their own tepees nearby. Less prominent men, lacking a surplus of horses, had smaller households. The average-size tepee was made of 14–17 skins (Flannery 1953:71). Households comprising each band relied on mutual help, men often hunting collectively and women working in groups.

Between the 1830s and 1880s the composition of the family was probably affected by the Gros Ventres' heavy participation in the robe trade. One woman could dress only 20 robes a season; the more wives a man had the better trade he could make (Flannery 1953:72–73). Polygyny was common during this period, and girls were often married at 10–11, before puberty, usually to a prominent, older man

and preferably to a man already married to one or more of the girl's sisters.

Gros Ventres believed that menstruation occurred subsequent to sexual relations and that for conception to occur, sexual relations must continue over a period of time (Flannery 1953:127). Young girls were not consulted about their marriages, but as a woman aged she had more control over her marital situation.

A man in his twenties usually married a woman mature enough to be able to run a household, who owned property of her own and who could help him get established. Marriage was legitimized by the groom's gift of horses and other property to the bride's family (Flannery 1953:127, 157–159, 171–181).

Religion and Political Organization

All supernatural power was believed to emanate from The One Above, called *niibh²íinɛɛ²ééč²* 'he who makes or does (by thought or will)', or *²ihkéb²ɛ níh²ɔɔtɔh* 'the Nih'atah above'. (Nih'atah [*níh²ɔɔtɔh*] is the Gros Ventre culture hero, whose name is also used to mean 'spider' and 'White man'.) This being—not anthropomorphized—was the ultimate source of life and of the power possessed both by lesser supernatural beings and by humans. Because The One Above endowed humans with the ability to think, they, like supernatural beings, could cause things to happen, both good and bad, through thought, a concept that was the basis of Gros Ventre religion (Cooper 1957:2, 4, 7, 365–370).

The One Above delegated supernatural power of varying kind and degree to *bɔh²ɔ́ɔɔ²* 'thunder', sun, "water monsters," animals, birds, insects, reptiles, mountains and rocks, and "false persons"—beings with no human body, such as whirlwind and ghosts (ancestral and nonancestral). Their power included the ability to cure, to assure success in particular ventures, to foretell, and to harm (Cooper 1957:21).

No creation or origin story was known by Gros Ventres living in the nineteenth century, although three culture hero traditions were recorded. The story of the culture hero and trickster Nih'atah tells how he gave the ancestors of the Gros Ventres the wherewithal to achieve independence and taught them how to pray with a pipe, how to conduct the sweatlodge, and how to sacrifice bits of flesh—all prayer-sacrifices to The One Above. The story of how Earthmaker, primordial keeper of the Gros Ventres' tribal medicine bundle, the Flat Pipe, recreated the world after a deluge probably represents a subsequent era. Floating on top of the water with the Flat Pipe, Earthmaker sent a waterbird and a turtle below; from the mud they brought up to him, he formed the earth and shaped a man and woman. He also taught the Gros Ventres the Flat Pipe rituals, how to plant tobacco, and taught them to sing (the song was Earthmaker's first utterance when alone on the water). The story of He Who Starved To Death recounts how a young Gros Ventre man acquired supernatural assistance in order to lure horses out of a lake and thus bring them to the Gros Ventre. He added new elements to the Flat Pipe ceremony (Kroeber 1907; Cooper 1957:19, 22–23, 79, 429–446).

Humans tapped supernatural power by communicating with The One Above through prayer or particularly earnest wish-thought. Prayers expressed homage or atonement for ritual errors or neglect (not for moral delinquency), or made petition for assistance. Gros Ventres prayed with words and thought, often using a pipe, smoke, steam, or singing to convey prayers. They petitioned The One Above to intervene directly or to compel lesser supernatural beings to offer them aid. Acts of sacrifice, which expressed the supplicant's sincerity, often accompanied prayers. Offerings included food (especially pup), tobacco or a filled pipe, property, or flesh. Sacrifice was often made as the result of a vow. In return for supernatural assistance one might offer property, or, in a particularly grave matter, one might sacrifice a finger-joint or a bit of one's own flesh or offer one's suffering and literally one's body through self-torture (Cooper 1957:370–372, 382–398; Horse Capture 1980a). Rites of prayer-sacrifice were either for the tribe as a whole (Pipe rituals and sacred lodges) or for specific individual purposes (acquisition of individually owned power).

The two tribal medicine bundles were symbols of the power of creation and of the Gros Ventres' place in the universe. They represented the Gros Ventres' special relationship with The One Above, a relationship that was the basis for health and happiness. The Flat Pipe bundle was made up of a sacred pipe, turtle shell, duck (or grebe) pelt,

native tobacco, and other ritual articles all enclosed in many wrappings and contained in an elkskin outer cover tied with three thongs. The pipe was carved of one piece of wood with a low, round flaring bowl and a tapered stem with a ring carved round the middle to which is attached a string ornament, and its proximal end carved in the shape of a duck's bill (see Ewers 1986:185–186 for this pipe's similarity to the Mandan flat pipe). Three seasonal Flat Pipe rites were essential to the people's prosperity, both ensuring and sanctioning success in the hunt, horse raid, and battle, and in the pursuit of wealth (Cooper 1957:33, 69–76).

The Feathered Pipe bundle, wrapped in an elkskin and tied with four thongs, contained a sacred pipe carved from one piece of dark stone with three or four humps on the upper surface of the stem, which was wrapped in buffalo hair; an eight-inch long stone human effigy carving; a feathered stick; a whistle; many dried bird skins; and other ritual objects. Rites of the Feathered Pipe controlled stormy weather and brought success in life. The bundle, given to the Gros Ventre by The One Above through Thunder, miraculously appeared during a storm to Man Whistles, probably in the mid-eighteenth century (Cooper 1957:140–145, 153; Horse Capture 1980a:104–106).

Priests, called keepers, were trained to care for and perform the bundle rituals. In the nineteenth century a new keeper was chosen every few years by the exkeepers. In earlier times the keepership was said to have been hereditary in one band. Individuals would vow to make a prayer-sacrifice in a pipe bundle ritual, to cover one of the bundles with gifts, or to sponsor a sweat ceremony for one or the other.

Gros Ventre concepts of authority were based on their ideas about proper relations with the supernatural, and many authority roles were legitimized by participation in an age-group system through which sacred knowledge was attained in a series of sacred ceremonies or lodges. Men took on new kinds of leadership responsibilities as they aged. The Gros Ventre organized their entire social system largely in terms of this age-group system, the central symbol of which was the offering of a pipe. In political affairs, pipe bundle keepers and exkeepers, who were regarded as holy and powerful, used their authority to generate consensus and cooperation and resolve conflict. In the age-grade lodges (and the Sacrifice Lodge), a man vowing to join sought out an older man who had already received the sacred knowledge associated with it; by offering him an ordinary black stone pipe, he petitioned him to become his "grandfather," that is, his instructor during the ceremony. The grandfather, who had an obligation to accede to the request, represented the pipe bundle keeper; the pipe represented the tribal pipe bundle. This established a sacred bond between grandfather and grandson symbolized by reciprocal gift-giving. They and their wives were supposed to treat each other with great respect, never to quarrel, and to do any favors asked of one another. Each could dissuade the other from violence (Cooper 1957:59–62, 68–69, 84–86, 176–179).

The age-group system was based on each man's membership in one age-set, one society, and progressive initiation into the graded series of lodges. When a boy reached the age of 15–16 he and others of about the same age formed a named age-set. Subsequently, they decided as a body to join one of the two men's societies, the Wolf or Star moiety (fig. 6). Membership in the age-set and moiety was for life, and men in the same set were bound to aid one another in all endeavors (Flannery 1953:36–43; Curtis 1907–1930, 5:113).

Members of a newly formed age-set might make a vow to The One Above to join the Fly Lodge, the first in the series of age-graded or sacred lodges. There were several age-sets each year whose members were eligible to join each of the lodges. The next in the series, the Crazy Lodge, conveyed sacred knowledge of a higher order. A man joined with his wife (or an appropriate substitute, not a kinswoman), for much of the supernatural power conveyed in the lodge was transferred from the grandfather to the novice's wife through symbolic sexual intercourse, then from wife to husband. This power had to do with fertility. The rite was a prayer-sacrifice in which a man gave away property and symbolically offered or sacrificed his wife by sending her alone to meet with the grandfather. After initiation into the Crazy Lodge, the age-set members (again, with the aid of their wives) were eligible to join successively the Kit Fox and Dog Lodges, which conveyed curative power and long life, respectively, as well as success in war. As elders, men were eligible to join the last grade in the series, nannanehao'we, which conveyed the power to attract buffalo. There was only one women's lodge, benohteao'we, and all adult women were able to vow to sponsor or join it. They petitioned an older woman to instruct them as their "grandmother" (Cooper 1957:173–174, 200–217, 228–229, 233–237, 242–244).

Power might come to males as a result of a vision quest. A man seeking power fasted alone, concentrating his thought

Fig. 6. Dance rattle of the Star Society moiety. Although Star Dancers' bodies were decorated, they used no distinctive regalia except rattles. This rattle includes a yellow-painted rawhide tube, bent to form a hoop, and fastened to a stick handle. The handle is covered with dark-blue cloth with dyed green and yellow feathers. At the top is an eagle feather, with the white portion reddened and a yellow-green stripe on black along the quill (Kroeber 1908:234–237). Collected by Alfred L. Kroeber, Ft. Belknap, Mont., 1901; length 23 cm.

and making offerings for one or more days on top of a promontory. He might induce a supernatural being—usually a quadruped, bird, snake, rock—to impart powers in matters of war, accumulation of wealth, or curing. Along with power the petitioner received instructions, a song associated with the power, and an object that symbolized or served as a vehicle of the power. The power was permanently transferred unless the recipient violated the rules associated with it. The object or objects often were kept in a hide bag, but not infrequently the recipient swallowed the power object when he first was given it, and it remained in his body until he forfeited his power by violating the instructions, or until just before his death, when it came out from his mouth. Power in gambling or sexual affairs was obtained by fasting in the brush and timber along streams (Cooper 1957:264–291, 298).

Many men attempted a quest but few succeeded. In fact, Gros Ventres thought such power was inherently dangerous and necessitated too many restrictions; parents discouraged children from seeking it, urging other methods of prayer-sacrifice to attain fame and fortune. Individuals often refused power when it was offered. Power and the instructions for its use could also be acquired by men or women in a dream, in which a supernatural being offered power on its own volition or in response to an individual's prayer. It could also be purchased or, more usually, might be acquired as a gift from the original owner. The majority of men and women probably possessed some kind of power, but few succeeded in getting really significant power (Cooper 1957:265–274, 292–298).

Curing

The Gros Ventre believed that illness resulted from physiological or supernatural causes, although the line between the two was often blurred. Supernaturally caused illnesses included those due to the breach of taboos (violation of the supernatural helper's instructions, for example) or to the malevolence of particular supernatural beings, or humans who harmed others either through doctoring power or concentrated hostile thoughts. Malevolent nonhumans or humans commonly caused illness by projecting small objects into the victim's body. As the individual's condition worsened the Gros Ventre believed his soul left his body, getting progressively farther away until he eventually died (Cooper 1957:23, 310–313).

Preventives and treatments usually were a combination of natural and supernatural remedies. Preventives included a daily plunge into a stream or roll in the snow and adherence to taboos. Persons who were ill would avoid contact with women during menses and in labor. Remedies were of three types. First, there were domestic treatments, which included herbal curatives for colds, stomach disorders, dysentery, urinary problems, eye irritations, headache, hay fever. Bloodletting (for dizziness or body aches), lancing of gums and boils, massage, and thermotherapy (for rheumatism, for example) were commonly used. Encouraging words and well-meaning wish-thoughts were considered necessary to all successful treatments. Second, some remedies were owned by individuals but used primarily within the family. In earlier times, only the Flat Pipe keepers had the right to use some herbs, such as sage and peppermint. Third, there were supernatural remedies owned and used only by those with a great amount of doctoring power. They expected to receive payment for their services, and while they used herbal remedies, massage, the sweatbath and other remedies also used by lesser practitioners, they were skilled in psychotherapy and legerdemain as well. Most used the technique of "sucking out" foreign objects that caused illness. There were general practitioners but most were specialists, for example, in extractions of arrowheads, bullets, or tumors; in curing facial paralysis; in treating rattlesnake bites; or in preventing or promoting conception (Cooper 1957:313–328).

Warfare

Much of the focus of religious rituals and individuals' use of power was on success in battle. After 1780 the Gros Ventres were pressed by their more numerous enemies and suffered disproportionate population loss. The Gros Ventre's men's moiety system was unique on the Plains. With the age-group system, it helped unify men from different bands and encouraged bravery. The Wolf and Star moieties competed in the acquisition of war honors and in display of generosity (Fowler 1987:30,38,51–52). Individuals selected an "enemy-friend" (tsaasenetedja) from the opposite moiety, these two competitors challenging each other to excel in battle and in generosity. Giving a gift of a horse, weapon, or other trophy stolen from the enemy initiated the relationship. Whatever one enemy-friend did or said to the other, from teasing and jokes to the most humiliating exposure of misdemeanors, had to be borne with equanimity. Thus the relationship functioned as a means of social control. The competitive fervor, as well as the encouragement of bravery by moiety songs to honor brave deeds, stimulated military vigilance. As members of the same moiety, different age-sets cooperated with one another. Since grandfathers were usually if not always selected from the opposite moiety, this relationship worked to prevent moiety competition from getting out of hand (Cooper 1957:205; Flannery 1953:36–43, 101–106).

Recognition for bravery was granted for any accomplishment that involved risk of life at the hands of the enemy. The most prestigious war deeds were the capture of a horse (especially a tethered one), taking of a scalp, striking or killing an enemy, capture of a weapon or other trophy, and assistance to another Gros Ventre in danger. War parties set out to steal horses or avenge loss of Gros Ventre life. Sometimes enemy women and children were taken captive and were incorporated into the band. War parties were led by men with well-established reputations for bravery.

Before leaving camp, young men would sing the "men's song," and many other songs that either recognized bravery or were associated with war power were sung during the expedition (Hatton 1990). When they were close to the enemy the leader proposed a plan of attack, but if all were not in agreement, the party might split. A member of the party who had an ancestral ghost helper might be asked to call on the helper for advice. When the war party returned to camp, if no Gros Ventre lives were lost, victory songs honored specific achievements. War trophies were given to the women, and they and the war party danced to victory songs. Gros Ventre men who established impressive war records were called "chiefs" (*néékyɛɛʔ* sg.); there were several in each band. War exploits were symbolized in designs on clothing and tepee linings, and a few prominent men were entitled to paint their war records on their tepees even into the twentieth century (Kroeber 1908:191–192, 196; Flannery 1953:88–102).

The Gros Ventres had an oral tradition of a "head chief," chosen to preside over tribal councils (Flannery 1953:34). Eagle was described by traders as head chief in the 1840s (Fowler 1987:35, 39). In the 1860s Sits Like a Woman was recognized as head spokesman; but after Congress failed to ratify the treaty agreements of 1865 and 1868 the intermediary role seems to have become less important (Fowler 1982:84–86, 90).

History, 1878–1987

Once they had settled near the Fort Belknap Agency, the Gros Ventres began raising cattle and horses enthusiastically, and many began to grow hay and grain; yet they continued to view the generous distribution of property as a means to maintain authority and validate status. Rituals that impressed the agents as "uncivilized" were transformed or replaced by less objectionable ones that expressed prereservation values and ideas about the supernatural (Fowler 1987:132–133).

1878–1901

Gros Ventres handled their new circumstances by seeking help from The One Above through prayer-sacrifice. They sponsored lodge ceremonies and pipe ceremonies, but the age group system was not fully operative. A few men in their 50s and 60s had completed the series (except for the Drum Lodge, which had been discontinued in the first half of the nineteenth century).

The Gros Ventres were also introduced to new religious rituals, first in 1891, when the Northern Arapahoe in Wyoming introduced them to the Ghost Dance. The Gros Ventre held Ghost Dances between 1891 and 1893, but they did not become fervent believers. The Arapahoe transferred the associated hand game bundle ritual to several Gros Ventre men, and this ceremony was held frequently until

685

the 1930s (Cooper 1957:252–256, 402; Fowler 1987:58–60). An individual who was ill or whose relative was ill or who had some other serious difficulty could vow to The One Above to make a prayer-sacrifice, in the form of paying the expenses of the hand game ceremony, in return for aid. The petitioner presented a gift to the owner of a bundle and requested him to conduct the ceremony. The owner of the bundle would pray for the petitioner during the ritual. The game itself involved two teams, usually one comprised of men and the other of women. Small disks were held by one team while the other team attempted to guess their location. There was no gambling involved; the winning team, if the ceremony had been correctly performed, was that of the petitioner.

Christianity was introduced to the Gros Ventres by Jesuit missionaries who built Saint Paul's Mission (in the present community of Hays, Montana), in the foothills of the Little Rockies and established a boarding school there in 1887 (Palladino 1894:197–203). The missionaries made little headway until the 1890s, when several school children and a few adults had conversion experiences. Such conversions were consistent with Gros Ventre supernatural beliefs. In each case, the individual had a dream or an encounter with a supernatural being during a vision quest in which he was instructed to follow the teachings of the Jesuits (Fowler 1987:56, 146–147). Some of the basic components of Roman Catholicism were compatible with Gros Ventre religious belief, for example, the concept of a supreme being and of prayer-sacrifice.

Moreover, the Jesuits' efforts to establish the mission and the school were facilitated by the Gros Ventres' need to convince the Indian agents that they were moving toward "civilization." By 1889 half the Gros Ventre children were in school at Saint Paul's (Junkin 1889); some went to the government boarding school after it was established in 1891. Lodge ceremonies, including the Sacrifice Lodge or Sun Dance, last held in 1885, were gradually curtailed (Fowler 1987:56, 63, 65, 68, 70–71).

Pursuit of prominence remained an all-consuming goal of most Gros Ventres despite the obstacles of reservation life. With the extinction of the buffalo and the termination of intertribal warfare, the traditional avenues to prominence were no longer open. Gros Ventre men who had reputations for bravery and who had acquired large horse herds continued to receive public recognition. Horses could be sold and the proceeds used to support followers. Cattle also became a means to attain prominence; they were important as food and their hides could be sold.

Prominent men were able to build on or solidify their social rank well into the second decade of the twentieth century. They obtained help from the Indian agent, who had the authority to issue cattle and establish communal gardens under the management of Gros Ventre leaders, by offering to assist him in his programs and in preventing intertribal hostility. Men born too late to have gone on war parties might attain prominence by obtaining assistance from the agent or by working for wages as herders and laborers (Fowler 1987:61–65).

Before 1890, the Gros Ventre built one-room log cabins, many with fireplaces and chimneys, which stood alongside their canvas tepees and were used during the winter (Lincoln 1884b, 1885). They hunted antelope and deer and continued to gather roots and berries, but as early as 1885 the agent attributed only one-eighth of their subsistence to foraging (ARCIA 1885:129–132). Thereafter, game became increasingly scarce. The agent issued rations once a week, but gradually the number of recipients decreased as the federal government tightened eligibility requirements to include only the old and sick (Bridgeman 1902). The camp headman was expected to provide food for his group even at the cost of impoverishing himself. He distributed produce from his garden, sold off stock, and lent his horses to Indian freighters.

In the 1890s, after ceding most of their land, the Gros Ventre were left with an area about 25 by 40 miles, only half the size required for every head of household to make a living in agriculture. This they shared with the Assiniboine. The agency had to be moved east, and by 1890 the Gros Ventre bands were resettled in four large camps along the headwaters of Peoples Creek (U.S. Census Office 1894:358). Later they dispersed into many smaller ranches (ARCIA 1897:170–173). Most families used 20–40 acres for stock, tended gardens of 2–12 acres, and grew hay (ARCIA 1896, 2:192–194, 1899, 2:256–257).

Much of Gros Ventre ritual life still revolved around the distribution of wealth. The two men's moieties persisted until around 1900. The Wolfmen had replaced their Wolf Dance with the Grass Dance (fig. 7), purchased from the Assiniboine about the time of reservation settlement (Kroeber 1908:234–239, 268; Flannery 1946). The moieties held dances at which they competed against one another in the display of generosity. Prominent families were expected to host "tea" or "house" dances to which neighboring camps were invited to feast and receive gifts. Individuals gave away horses and other property to honor their children (fig. 9) or other relatives and to demonstrate their worthiness for a ceremonial office.

Prominent men were expected to give a substantial gift to the bride's family when they married. The Bureau of Indian Affairs outlawed polygyny, but agents did not force men already in polygynous unions to separate from their wives. While there was a gradual end to polygyny, marriages, particularly girls' first marriages, were still arranged by their male relatives probably until the twentieth century (Amadeus 1895; Flannery 1941:33–37, 1953:175–176; Fowler 1987:61–66; Kroeber 1908:180).

Prominent men frequently dealt with the agent on behalf of the Gros Ventres and negotiated payments from cattlemen wishing to take herds across the reservation. At Fort Belknap, Gros Ventre leaders sought to defend tribal interests in contests with the Assiniboine, once allies but, because of federal policy that resulted in intertribal rivalry,

686

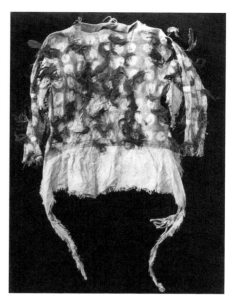

Fig. 7. left, Bill Jones (b. about 1827) with scalp lock and shield singing outside Grass Dance circle. The painted figures on his horse are probably symbols of his war exploits. He was a keeper of one of the sacred pipes (Kroeber 1908:233, 273). The Sun Dance lodge is in the background on right. The women spectators on left wear skirts with what appears to be ribbon appliqued stripes. Photograph by Sumner Matteson, Ft. Belknap, Mont., at the Grass and Sun Dance, July 1905–1906. right, Dog Lodge shirt originally owned by Bill Jones. Membership in the Dog Lodge, fourth in the series of age-grade men's ceremonies, was conferred as the result of the pledge of an individual in the hope of deliverance from death or danger (Kroeber 1908:228). During society rituals the 2 most honored men, called "shaggy dogs," wore deerskin shirts such as this one. The neck is edged in red flannel, the shirt was painted yellow then stained brown, and there are 225 yellow circles, edged in white quillwork with crow feathers attached to the center of each. Other parts of the shaggy dog outfit included a necklace of bear claws, a headdress of owl feathers, a forked-stick hoof rattle, and a wooden whistle (Kroeber 1908:252–254). Collected by Clark Wissler, Ft. Belknap, Mont., 1903; length 77 cm.

Fig. 8. Recreation of a Crazy Dance ceremony called Flight of Arrows. The initiates, who have received ceremonial knowledge, medicine, or powers, shoot arrows up into the air and remain motionless as the arrows fall around them (Curtis 1907–1930, 5:116). Among the powers acquired were the abilities to walk on hot coals and to shoot arrows treated with medicine that induced paralysis in humans or animals. The Crazy Men exhibited "backward talk" and "contrary" behavior during the 4-day and 4-night ceremony, saying and doing the opposite of what was expected. Photograph by Edward S. Curtis, before Nov. 1908.

there in the Little Rockies trespassing miners had found gold. Led by the highest ranking men of the age-grade system, the majority of the Gros Ventres wanted to retain the mountains and develop the mineral resources themselves. The Assiniboines, joined by only a few Gros Ventres, approved the cession by a slight margin, and the reservation lost an immensely valuable resource for small compensation. Of equal importance, the Gros Ventres' ability to achieve consensus and enforce cooperation was impaired; the authority of the age-grade leaders and the exkeepers, who had opposed the cession, was effectively challenged (Fowler 1987:60–61, 66–71).

1902–1937

In the early twentieth century only a minority of adults participated in the pipe bundle rituals. Flat Pipe seasonal rituals, which largely reflected the concerns of a hunting way of life, were discontinued. The last official keeper died in 1924; then the Flat Pipe was taken into the custody of an elderly man who performed at least two ceremonies, one for Gros Ventre soldiers in the Second World War. Feathered Pipe prayer-sacrifice ceremonies continued until the death of the last official keeper in 1938, when another elder took charge of the bundle. Gros Ventres who had been educated at Saint Paul's Mission were rarely involved. Still, the Gros Ventres felt the pipe rituals to be

competitors after reservation settlement. In 1895 business interests in Montana demanded that the Fort Belknap Indians cede part of the southern end of the reservation, for

Fig. 9. White Plume and wife (shrouded in center) giving away the horse and belongings of their son who had disappeared during the winter of 1904–1905 and was later found dead. Photograph by Sumner Matteson during the Grass Dance, probably July 1905–1906.

central to their identity as a people (Fowler 1987:74–75, 94–95, 97, 110, 142–143). Evidence of the Gros Ventres' belief in the ability of wish-thought to cause harm appeared in frequent accusations that illness or misfortune were caused thus and by occasional reliance on the few elders with doctoring power (Cooper 1957:356–357, 365–370; Fowler 1987:75–76, 94–95; Horse Capture 1980a:58).

The quest for prominence remained a focus of Gros Ventre life. The first generation that grew to adulthood on the reservation was bilingual and Roman Catholic, yet determined to achieve social prominence. This goal was more difficult to achieve, for most of the Gros Ventres' cattle was stolen between 1901 and 1910 (Sample 1900; C. Davis 1913). And in 1917 the federal government began a campaign to reduce the size of the herds of horses Gros Ventres were raising for sale (Foley 1975:196–231). From 1913 to 1928 the Indian Office leased most of the reservation grazing land below the market value to non-Indian stockmen. Farming equipment was no longer issued at the agency but had to be purchased. Nonetheless, many Gros Ventre men got a start in ranching by inheriting stock and equipment from relatives or by marrying widows with stock or property. In fact, because the federal government allowed women to inherit equally with male siblings and to inherit from their husbands, women generally owned more property than in prereservation times. Thus wealth differentials persisted, and prominent families were responsible for aiding the needy as well as for heavy ceremonial obligations (Fowler 1987:85).

About 1900 began a florescence in Gros Ventre ritual life. Young people built a dance hall in Hays, started a Christmas–New Year's dance, and organized the summer Hays Fair, which featured Indian dancing and games, horse races (fig. 10), tugs of war and sham battles with the Assiniboines, rodeo events, a carnival, and competition with neighboring Whites (Flannery 1947; Fowler 1987:76, 78–79, 83–89, 109, 157–161).

A group of Gros Ventres led by Stiffarm, an elderly man known for his war and doctoring power, went to Crow Agency and returned with ideas about how to perpetuate their moiety organization in a new form. They organized Hays into moieties based on residence, the Black Lodges north of the dance hall, and the Mountain Crows south of the hall. Named after the Crow tribal divisions, the moieties competed in the sponsorship of community activities. The Grass Dance was transformed from a men's moiety dance to a more elaborate performance that involved the entire community. Grass Dance officers (22 men and 8 women), each with specific regalia and particular roles, compelled people to attend and to dance, and this authority

Fig. 10. Early 20th century activities. left, Paul Horse Capture (wearing crow belt) and Dan Sleeping Bear, participants in the Crow Belt ritual of the Kettle Dance, re-enacted at the Hays Fair, Mont. Horse Capture wears false braids and holds a fan. Sleeping Bear wears a hair roach and holds a metal studded mirror. Both wear dance bustles. Photograph by Sumner Matteson, July 1905–1906. right, Assiniboine and Gros Ventre horse race. Photograph by William Henry Jackson, 1907.

obligated them to donate livestock and valuable property to the gathering. Regalia was transferred much like a sacred bundle: the recipient gave substantial property to the former owner and the spectators. In the 1920s the ceremony became abbreviated, then ceased to be performed.

Prominent men, all generous donors and participants in ritual life, were selected for a business council, organized in 1904 (fig. 11). The Bureau of Indian Affairs agent called together a group of Gros Ventre and Assiniboine headmen twice a year to approve land leases. Their influence was limited, but using literate Gros Ventre as scribes, Gros Ventre leaders protested agency abuses and successfully called for investigations. About 1909 the agent insisted that the Fort Belknap Indians hold elections for council members (Logan 1908). By about 1918 the elected Gros Ventre council consisted by and large of young bilingual boarding school graduates. Their goals included allotment and the filing of a claim against the federal government for violation of the 1855 treaty, which they won in 1935. The selection of councilmen, by voice vote in general meetings, was greatly influenced by elders, and councilmen validated their new positions by giving away property. Six Gros

Fig. 11. Jerry Running Fisher, a spokesman during the early reservation days. He was captain of Indian police until 1908 and went to Washington as a Gros Ventre delegate in 1894 regarding the cession of some Ft. Belknap land. He was a member of the business council in the first decade of the 20th century. He also worked with the photographer Edward S. Curtis, who reported that he fasted for war power and had an outstanding military career as a result (Curtis 1907–1930, 5:121). He successfully led 14 war parties, one of which returned with 300 horses. Photograph by a Bureau of American Ethnology photographer, Washington, 1894.

Ventres (and six Assiniboines chosen in the Assiniboine settlements) comprised the elected business council. Decisions were made by consensus. By the early 1930s most of the Gros Ventre councilmen were elderly (Fowler 1987:79–84).

In order to protect the tribe's land from sale to Whites and to gain control over their own affairs, Gros Ventre leaders worked to have the reservation allotted. They enlisted the support of most of the Assiniboines, and, after 10 years of lobbying to have the reservation allotted in plots large enough so that no surplus land would be available for sale, they were successful in 1923 (Fowler 1987:89–94). By 1927, 57 percent of allotted grazing land was leased, providing money for the allottees (J.T. Marshall 1927).

The Gros Ventres at Hays voted to accept the Indian Reorganization Act on October 27, 1934. Federal officials assured the Gros Ventre that they would have greater economic aid and more authority in reservation affairs and that they would not lose tribal identity by forming a joint government with the Assiniboine. On October 20, 1935, Fort Belknap voters approved a constitution and by-laws, which provided for the Gros Ventre and Assiniboine each to elect six of their number as councilmen. The Bureau of Indian Affairs insisted on Fort Belknap adopting a charter of incorporation before they received any aid, but the Gros Ventre opposed incorporation as the Fort Belknap Community because they believed that their status as a federally recognized tribe would be jeopardized. Although in 1933, only 7 percent of reservation adults were of mixed Gros Ventre–Assiniboine ancestry, the government insisted that the two tribes were intermarried to the extent that tribal distinctions were eroded. Despite Gros Ventre opposition, the charter was accepted in a reservation-wide vote, August 25, 1937 (Fowler 1987:95–97).

1938–1964

The Indian Reorganization Act raised expectations of economic rehabilitation and political autonomy, but federal officials ignored or violated the new constitution, and the economic aid was not adequate. The tribal council pursued a claim against the United States to compensate for the low price paid for the 1888 land cession. Filed in 1951, the claim was won in 1964 (Fowler 1987:96–105).

In the 1950s several young veterans replaced older Gros Ventres on the council, but they also were not able to improve economic conditions. The turnover on the council was high. In the 1940s federal officials encouraged the council rather than the moieties to sponsor dances; when the council's funds were drastically reduced in the 1950s, community celebrations began to wane (Fowler 1987:101–102, 107, 109–110).

By 1942, 35 percent of the Gros Ventre had left Hays for urban areas (Flannery 1953:107), but the community's economic decline, aggravated by population increase, began in the 1930s. In 1936 a forest fire in the Little Rockies destroyed the timber industry and severely damaged the livestock industry. Ranchers were already in difficulty due to a long period of drought in the mid-1930s (Foley 1975:422–23). Work relief programs were curtailed as federal resources were devoted to the war effort (Fowler 1987:102). After the war agriculture became increasingly mechanized, which reduced job opportunities and drove Gros Ventre ranchers, who lacked the capital to mechanize, out of business.

In 1922 a township had been established at Hays as part of the allotment agreement, and restaurants, pool halls, rooming houses, and stores were built. Several Whites and Métis (French-Chippewas) lived at Hays in the 1930s, and there were several intermarriages with Métis. Improved roads, automobiles, and radios increased exposure to the wider society. These conditions, coupled with the government's introduction of the concept of per capita shares in tribal assets as a result of mineral and claim payments and land allotments to individuals, contributed to more constricted sharing networks and the decline of large-scale public redistributions. By the 1950s the nuclear family was the unit of production, but recognition of ties with and obligations to classificatory siblings, parents, and grandparents persisted. The Black Lodge–Mountain Crow moiety organization disbanded by 1942 (Fowler 1987:106, 108–110; Flannery 1953:119).

During the 1940s and 1950s intermarriage with non–Gros Ventres increased, especially among off-reservation Gros Ventres. In 1959 the Fort Belknap tribes passed a referendum that required an individual to be one-fourth Gros Ventre (or one-fourth Assiniboine or one-fourth combined Gros Ventre-Assiniboine) ancestry to be enrolled at Fort Belknap. There was no residency requirement (Fowler 1987:114). The Gros Ventre also recognized that their community was no longer autonomous in relation to Assiniboines, and in 1964 the business council electoral process was changed to provide for election at large of 12 delegates—six Gros Ventres and six Assiniboines (Fowler 1987:105). Pipe bundles continued as a symbol of identity, though no one felt qualified to conduct the ceremonies. Gros Ventres living off the reservation frequently returned for dances jointly organized with Assiniboines, a Memorial Day ceremony in the Hays cemetery, or to conduct tribal business.

Political Organization, 1965–1987

The Great Society programs of the late 1960s and 1970s brought about new jobs and housing at Fort Belknap. Gros Ventres (and Assiniboines) were hired in managerial and teaching as well as in skilled and unskilled positions; for the first time, women were hired in large numbers in clerical, health, and education fields. Scholarships for Native Americans and educational benefits for Vietnam veterans resulted in large numbers of young Gros Ventres attending college. The tribal government employed many individuals (Fowler 1987:16). Transfer payments were another source of income. Several Gros Ventre men had small ranching and farming operations, and elderly people derived some income from leasing their allotted land (Fowler 1987:17).

Besides the 1937 claim payment, the Gros Ventres received three other large payments for the settlement of claims against the federal government, in 1967, 1972, and 1983. Individuals used this money for consumer goods. In order to have received the payments, one had to be of one-fourth Gros Ventre ancestry. In 1984, 2,236 Gros Ventres were so enrolled (table 2). (There were 1,437 Assiniboines enrolled and 421 Gros Ventre–Assiniboine). With the high incidence of intermarriage, only 17 percent of persons born 1955–1984 were enrolled as one-half or more (Fowler 1987:129–130).

In 1984, virtually all houses at Fort Belknap had electricity and plumbing. Most units were built in projects, the largest of which is at the agency and at Hays. There were 1,082 Gros Ventres living on the reservation, 44 percent at the agency and 52 percent in Hays (Fowler 1987:14). The result of new jobs and housing was a migration back to the reservation. This, coupled with a high birth-death ratio (6:1 in 1983), strained reservation resources. Gros Ventres who had incomes shared with those who did not. Fort Belknap remained an economically depressed community. The median household income on the reservation in 1979 (at the peak of the job programs) was $6,486; the median in Montana was $15,420. In 1965, before the federal poverty programs were instituted, the rate of unemployment was 77 percent; in 1979, 44 percent; in 1981, 70 percent (Fowler 1987:16–17, 118, 120–121).

The economic problems of Fort Belknap stem from several factors. The reservation's 652,594 acres are not sufficient for any but a few to make a living in agriculture, even though 95 percent of the land is still in trust, 63 percent owned by individuals. Lack of capital is another obstacle. There is no local industry and no minerals that can be developed on the reservation. Thus, the tribes are dependent on the federal government for economic development, and these funds are uncertain (Fowler 1987:13, 16–18).

Federal economic and social programs of the 1960s and 1970s strengthened tribal government. The Indian Self-Determination and Education Assistance Act of 1975 enabled the business council to contract with the federal government to operate reservation programs formerly run by the Bureau of Indian Affairs. In the 1980s, Bureau positions were filled primarily by Gros Ventres and Assiniboines, and the reservation superintendent was selected by the business council. Beginning in the 1960s, women began to be elected regularly to the council (Fowler 1987:115–116, 119).

Among the Gros Ventres, prominence became associated with a college degree as well as a successful ranching operation, for persons with higher education were in

Fig. 12. Life in the 1980s–1990s. top left, Joe Ironman (b. 1939), keeper of the Feathered Pipe; he performed ceremonies for many gatherings. top right, Joe Ironman overseeing the move of the Feathered Pipe bundle from Hays to Lodgepole, Mont., 1994. center left, John Capture (b. 1911, d. 1997), historian and statesman, 1985. center right, Jeanette Warrior (b. 1904, d. 1998), seated, with Mary Ereaux Kuntz, at a Ft. Belknap Wellness Women's conference, 1994. Warrior was the caretaker of the Flat Pipe from the late 1950s–1993, after her husband's death. bottom left, Theresa Walker Lamebull (b. 1907) in 1994, a fluent speaker of Gros Ventre and a major contributor to the Gros Ventre dictionary compiled and edited by Allan R. Taylor (1994, 1:iii). top left and right, center left and right, and bottom left, Photographs by Jessie James-Hawley, Ft. Belknap Res., Mont. bottom right, George Horse Capture, Jr., and Robert Walker, Sr., at the signing of the deaccession papers for repatriation of skeletal remains of 2 Gros Ventre individuals collected in the 19th century. The Smithsonian Institution representative Thomas W. Killion is on the right. Photograph by Jane Beck, Washington, D.C., 1998.

Table 2. Gros Ventre Population, 1805–1998

Year	Population	Source
1805	2,100–2,400	Larocque 1910:47
1823	4,200	Chesterfield House Report 1822–1823
1830	2,800–3,200[a]	Rowand 1830
1835	4,000–5,000	Bradley 1917:153
1855	2,970	Fowler 1987:51
1860	2,100[b]	ARCIA 1860:84
1879	1,135	ARCIA 1879:98
1895	624	ARCIA 1896:568
1925	594	Fowler 1987:102
1935	725	Fowler 1987:102
1964	1,873	Fowler 1987:102
1984	2,236	Fowler 1987:130
1998	3,078	Arthur Stiffarm, communication to editors 1998

[a]Perhaps only the bands trading in British territory.

[b]400 men, 700 women, 1,000 children.

a position to help others (Fowler 1987:117–121). In 1980, six percent of reservation residents were college graduates.

The two sacred pipe bundles were in 1988 in the care of Gros Ventre individuals on the reservation, and there were efforts to revive pipe bundle ceremonies in some form. Several Gros Ventres traveled to other reservations to participate in Sun Dances and occasionally attended Assiniboine hand games or spirit lodges on Fort Belknap. Some youths fasted for a vision; at least one used doctoring power. A few Gros Ventre youths attended and sponsored Peyote meetings (Fowler 1987:150–156). All ceremonies were conducted in English; only a small number of elders spoke the Gros Ventre language in the late 1980s.

The giveaway ceremony became the nucleus of several rites. As in earlier times, Gros Ventres distributed property—stock, dress goods, food, cutlery—to validate authority and status, as well as to reaffirm kinship ties. One type was the public naming ceremony, in which a link was established between the person named and the namesake, an ancestor who was part of the Hays community. Held one year after the death of a loved one, the idea for the memorial giveaway was borrowed from the Assiniboine.

Three intertribal powwows were held each summer. At the powwows, giveaways were held to honor relatives and to transfer powwow offices. These positions—for men and women—had associated regalia, some with sacred connotations (Fowler 1987:163–185). Powwow songs expressed values of generosity and bravery. At all these events, the Hays Singers, whose Gros Ventre origin can be traced to the early reservation era, were an essential part. Since the 1970s, they have been a "mixed drum"; women sat at the drum and sang with the men (Hatton 1986:208, 214).

Synonymy†

The Gros Ventre name for themselves is ʔɔɔʔɔ́ɔ́ɔniinénin̩ɔh (sg. ʔɔɔʔɔ́ɔ́ɔniinénʔi), which is generally said to mean 'white clay people' (Taylor 1983a), an etymology that refers to lime or chalk used for cleaning buckskin. This etymology has been questioned (Kroeber 1908:145), and some Gros Ventre have claimed that the name refers to 'mounds of earth used to turn buffalo when driving them into a corral' (Curtis 1907–1930, 5:154). The native designation appears in various forms: A-lân-sâr, 1804–1805 (Lewis and Clark in Moulton 1983–, 2:432), Ahni-ninn (Maximilian 1839–1841, 1:530), Ahnenin (Latham 1860:276), Ahahnelins (Morgan 1871:226), Aä′ninĕna (Mooney 1896:955), Haāninin (Kroeber 1908:145), and aa′ni (Sifton 1977).

Gros Ventre is a French translation of forms that appear in many northern Plains languages. One variant reputedly refers to 'beggars': Arapaho hitóu·nénnoʔ (pl.) (Ives Goddard and Loretta Fowler, personal communications 1990). The Cheyenne name is hestóetaneoʔo, perhaps meaning 'meat begging men' (Curtis 1907–1930, 6:158; Glenmore and Leman 1985:201; recorded as His-tuu-i'-ta-ni-o in Hayden 1862:290), Hīstúitä′n-eo (sg. Hīstúitä′n-eo) (Mooney 1907:422), and may be a borrowing of the Arapahoe term with its Arapahoe meaning (Petter 1913–1915:582). A closely related variant designates a 'belly': Kiowa bót-k′yà-gɔ 'belly man' (Laurel Watkins and Parker McKenzie, personal communication 1979); Shoshone sop′-pe-ne′-ah 'big bellies' (Ballou 1880–1881) or s:ap 'paunch' (Shimkin 1947:251); Hidatsa e·rihtías 'big belly' (Parks 1987) or e·rihtías ruxpá·ka 'big belly people' (James 1823, 2:lxxxiv; Curtis 1907–1930, 4:186); Mandan pe·šiaxté 'big belly' (Parks 1987).

There is no consensus on the sign language designation. One is described as a sweeping pass with both hands in front of the abdomen, conveying the notion of 'always hungry, beggars' (Mooney 1896:955), while a closely related one is a sweep with open right hand in an arc from the chin to the waist, indicating a large belly (Hadley 1893; Kroeber 1902–1907, 1:6). The sign used by the Crow, while differing in form from other descriptions, means 'big belly' (W.P. Clark 1885:67, 193). Another description of the sign is of both hands in front of the stomach and curved, as if holding a ball six inches in diameter, said to represent the paunch of a buffalo and not the belly of a human (Scott 1912–1934). Mallery (1881:462) gives two signs for the Atsina, whom he also calls Lower Gros Ventre: one connotes 'corn shellers' and the other 'tattooed breast'. The former, in fact, refers to Arikara or more likely Hidatsa, while the latter is the sign for the Northern Arapahoe.

French and English translations of the 'belly' designation are the most common in the historical literature as well as in contemporary usage. French Canadian traders,

†This synonymy was written by Douglas R. Parks.

who consistently employed the name for the tribe through-out the eighteenth and nineteenth centuries, were using Gros-Ventres at least as early as 1751 (Le Gardeur de Saint-Pierre in Margry 1876–1886, 6:640). Some early writers maintained a version of the French form in English works, for example, Grosse Ventres (Brown 1817:212), Gros-Vents (Kane 1859:366); and Grovan (Bonner 1856:162). Others used variants of the English translations—Big-bellys (Gass 1807:76), Big bellied (Mackenzie 1801:lxiv), and Great Belly Indians (Massachusetts Historical Society 1810:111). Sometimes French Canadians also referred to them as Panse or Gens de Panse, 1804–1805 (Tabeau 1939:161), with English writers using its translated form Paunch (Hayden 1862:343).

Because the Hidatsa living on the middle Missouri River were also called Gros Ventres by French Canadian traders, a name that was used in North and South Dakota in the late twentieth century, some writers have distinguised between the two unrelated tribes by referring to them as Gros Ventres of the Missouri (Hale 1846:220), Gros Ventres of the Prairie, or Prairie Gros Ventres (Brackenridge 1814:79; McCoy 1836–1838:47; Clark 1885:197–199; Curtis 1907–1930, 5:103), which are sometimes given in their French forms, *Gros Ventres des Plaines* (de Smet 1848:253) and *Gross-ventres* of the *Prairie* (Schermerhorn 1814:36). Because the Gros Ventre and Blackfeet traded at Fort de Prairie, one of two North West Company trading posts on the Saskatchewan, the Gros Ventre were also referred to as Gros ventre of the Fort Prairie (James 1823, 2:lxxxiv). Similarly, because Hidatsa were also known as Minitaree ('water people') in the eighteenth and nineteenth centuries, the Algonquian-speaking Gros Ventre have by analogy been referred to as Minnetarees of the Prairie (Gallatin 1848, 2:21; Latham 1854, 6:85; Hayden 1862:344; Curtis 1907–1930, 18:157), Minnitarries of the north (Lewis and Clark in Moulton 1983–, 5:226), and Minetaries of Fort de Prairie (Lewis and Clark in Moulton 1983, 4:211, 216).

Another common designation for the Gros Ventre that occurs primarily among English traders in the late eighteenth and early nineteenth centuries is the Plains Cree name for the tribe, *pa·wistikowiyiniw* 'falls people, rapids people' (or its Woods Cree equivalent), which is said to derive from their residence along the rapids of the South Saskatchewan River (Maximilian in Thwaites 1904–1907, 23:70; H. Christoph Wolfart, personal communication 1987; Curtis 1907–1930, 5:103, 18:157). The same name occurs in Assiniboine *xaxáthuwą* 'flowing water village' (Parks and DeMallie 198). Frequently citations are renderings of the Cree form or its Ottawa-Ojibwa equivalent, for example, Bahwetego-weninnewug, Bahwetig, Bowwetegoweninnewug (Tanner 1830:63, 64, 315); Paw-is-tick I-e-ne-wuck (Harmon 1820:78); Pawaustic-eythin-yoowuc (Franklin 1824:169); and Powestic-Athinuewuck (Cocking 1908:110–111). Others are translations, as Waterfall Indians (Cocking 1908:110–111), Fall Indians (Graham 1969; Umfreville

1790:197), Rapid Indians (Harmon 1820:78), and the French version Gens des Rapides (Curtis 1907–1930, 5:103) or Gen de rapid (Lewis and Clark in Moulton 1983–, 3:433). Although all sources on the Plains sign language concur that the sign for the Gros Ventre refers to a 'belly' or 'gut', it has been suggested that this designation may have arisen out of a misreading of the sign for 'falls', which is similar to 'belly' and in fact has a Cree source (Scott 1912–1934; Taylor 1983a:432).

Other early designations sometimes used for the Gros Ventre are based on the Plains Cree term *ayahciyiniw* or its Woods Cree equivalent, meaning 'stranger, foreigner', and by extension 'enemy', and a generic name for the Blackfoot confederacy, of which the Gros Ventre were a member. Its rendering as archithinues in 1754–1755 is thought to be a reference to the Gros Ventre (Hendry 1907, 1:328–351; Flannery 1953:3).

As early as the mid-nineteenth century the Blackfoot form of the name, *atsí·na* (Frantz and Russell 1989:376), was used to designate the tribe: Achena (de Smet 1848:253), Atsina (Latham 1854, 6:86), Azäna (Maximilian 1839–1841, 1:530). It was also a self-designation (Hayden 1862:344). During the late nineteenth and twentieth centuries, its anglicized form, Atsina, was favored as a designation, particularly by ethnologists and linguists seeking to differentiate the Gros Ventre from the Hidatsa (Grinnell 1905; Curtis 1907–1930, 5:103; Mooney 1907:113; Taylor 1983a:430). Although the etymology of the Blackfoot name has been cited as 'gut people' (Grinnell 1892:244) or 'big eaters' (Curtis 1907–1930, 18:186), there is apparently no linguistic basis for these interpretations; the term, in fact, seems to be a loanword derived from Plains Cree *ayahciyiniw* (Taylor 1983a:430–431).

Early sources occasionally refer to the Gros Ventre as Pâh-kees (Lewis and Clark in Moulton 1983–, 5:80, 91; cf. James in Thwaites 1904–1907, 17:299), a rendition of the Shoshone term *pakihiʔi*, literally 'stiff hardened blanket', denoting the rawhide armor worn by the Eastern Shoshone's northern enemies, the Blackfoot, Arapaho, Gros Ventre, and Assiniboine. In the early nineteenth century the term was a generic designation for all four tribes, but over time its usage has narrowed to mean only the Piegan Blackfoot (Sven Liljeblad, personal communication 1987).

A late eighteenth-century name that apparently designates the Gros Ventre is cited in several forms: Chiouitounes and Chioutoumes, 1795–1796 (Truteau in Parks 1992), Shivitauns (McKay in Nasatir 1952, 2:494), Shiveytoon (Massachusetts Historical Society 1810:24). It has been incorrectly identified as Sisseton (Hodge 1907–1910, 2:582) and Shoshone (Nasatir 1952, 1:245). This group may also be the one mentioned in 1804, rendered Squihitanes and Skihitanes (Tabeau 1939:154–155). The last form seems to be ultimately the same as the Sioux *skútani* 'Gros Ventre' (Mooney 1896:955), perhaps related to Sioux *škútani*, given as 'Kootenai' (Riggs 1890:446; Buechel 1970:465).

A unique designation is the Crow term *api·wišé*, literally 'hairy nose' (Randolph Graczyk, personal communication 1987; Curtis 1907–1930, 4:180; W.P. Clark 1885:193). The Cheyenne reportedly used an alternate term E-tá-ni-o 'people' (*hetaneoʔO* 'men') for Gros Ventre (Hayden 1862:290; Glenmore and Leman 1985). Two terms used by Plateau tribes are the Flathead name Sĭnkaiyóskaischi (*snq̓eʔewssqesčínt*, literally 'two tent poles people') and its Spokane variant Sĭkaióskaischí (Curtis 1907–1930, 7:165; Sarah G. Thomason, personal communication 1987). The Mandan Háⁿ-oti (*xǫh oti*) 'grass lodge' has been identified as a name for the Gros Ventre (Curtis 1907–1930, 5:147; Hollow 1970) but more likely referred to the Eastern Shoshone (cf. the Sioux form *pʰeží wokʰéya otʰí* 'grass lodge dwellers' in Buechel 1970:440, 733).

Bands

Lists of Gros Ventre band names suggest 10–12 bands (table 1). In addition, Flannery (1953:25–31) obtained two names—Buffalo Overloaded and Poor Grays—thought to be primary bands, as well as five additional names that may have been either primary bands or their alternate designations—Yellow Tail Feathers, Saw-whet Owls, Red Eagles, Torn Leggings, and Traders. Kroeber (1908:148) lists a primary band, Fighting Alone, which does not occur in the other two lists. Because bands frequently had alternate names, changed their names, or merged with other bands, and because these lists were obtained during the reservation period, it is impossible to provide a complete sorting of names for any given period.

Sources

The journals of fur traders in the late eighteenth and early nineteenth centuries frequently mention the Gros Ventre but provide little information on their culture and society. Fowler (1987) synthesizes and interprets much of the information from these and other unpublished sources on the pre-reservation period. Ewers (1974) summarizes what is known about federal relations with the Gros Ventre prior to and during the treaty era. J.F. Taylor (1989) discusses population, 1800–1880.

Kroeber's work is the first reconstruction of Gros Ventre nineteenth-century social life (1908) and the first collection of mythology (1907). Curtis (1907–1930, 5) gives some additional information, primarily biographical sketches of men. Cooper's (1940, 1944, 1957) and Flannery's (1941, 1944, 1946, 1953, 1960) studies in the 1930s and 1940s are rich sources on the belief system, ritual life, economics, family life, women, and the life cycle. Interviews with elderly Gros Ventres in the 1930s focus on mythology and prereservation culture (Gone 1941–1942; Horse Capture 1980a).

Fowler's (1987) study is the main source on culture and history since the reservation period. There are also studies of the Grass Dance (Flannery 1947), politics (Fowler 1982, 1984), and ritual life (Dusenberry 1961, 1963). The Fort Belknap tribes published collections of oral history dealing with nineteenth-century warfare and with reservation history (Fort Belknap Education Department 1982, 1982a). There are histories of federal-Indian relations on Fort Belknap Reservation (Barry 1974; Foley 1975) and a history of the Sisters of Saint Francis's work among the Gros Ventre since the 1930s (Hartmann 1984).

Studies of the language include Kroeber (1916), Sifton (1895, 1895a, 1895b), Salzmann (1969), Goddard (1974), and Taylor (1967, 1983, 1983a, 1994). Flannery (1946) obtained information on men's and women's speech.

Records of songs collected in 1940 are on deposit in the Department of Anthropology, Catholic University of America, Washington, D.C. A few of the songs were transcribed (Kilpatrick 1946). Gros Ventre songs and their cultal context are discussed by Hatton (1986, 1990).

The major museum collection of Gros Ventre material is at the American Museum of Natural History, New York (Kroeber 1908).

Crow

FRED W. VOGET

Language and Territory

The Crow ('krō), who speak a Siouan language,* were most closely related in language and culture to the Hidatsa, from whom they separated just prior to the historic period. By the early nineteenth century, the Crow comprised two divisions, Mountain Crow, and River Crow; about 1850, a third division, the clan-based Kicked in the Bellies, formed out of the Mountain Crow (Lowie 1912:183–184). In the 1820s, the Mountain Crow hunted about the Bighorn, middle Yellowstone, upper Tongue, and Powder rivers and into the Bighorn, Absaroka, Beartooth, and Wind River mountain ranges. River Crow ranged over the lower Yellowstone and north along the Marias and Milk rivers, turning to the Judith Basin for fall and winter hunting (fig. 1). The bands usually united for spring and summer hunting.

Origins

In 1862 fur trader Robert Meldrum, who had lived with the Crow since 1827 and was married to a Crow woman, stated that tribal traditions placed their original home near the Bear Paw Mountains and at the Three Forks of the Missouri River, and that the Crow had no knowledge of earlier migrations or of the details of their separation from the Hidatsa (L.H. Morgan 1959:167, 197). Oral traditions recorded later provide a variety of legendary accounts concerning the separation of the Crow from the Hidatsa, most

*The phonemes of Crow are: (voiceless stops and affricate) *p, t, č, k, ʔ*; (voiceless spirants) *s, š, x, h*; (voiced stops and resonants) *w* ([m], [b], [w]), *r* ([n], [d], [l] ~ [r]); (short vowels) *i, e, a, o, u*; (long vowels) *i·, e·, a·, o·, u·*; (diphthongs) *ea, ia, ua*; (high pitch) v́, v́·, v́v̀, (falling pitch) v̂·, v̂v. Long consonants are analyzed as geminates. The voiced consonants (*w* and *r*) are pronounced [b], [ᵐb], or [m] and [d], [ⁿd], or [n] word-initially; [b] and [d] following a consonant other than a voiced consonant or *h*; [w] and [l] (or conservatively [r], a tap) between vowels; and [m] and [n] elsewhere. The voiceless oral stops and affricate are aspirated word-initially, word-finally, and after a stop; between vowels they are lax, unaspirated, and often voiced. The oral spirants are lax intervocalically, where *š* is often voiced, and *s* is sometimes voiced. *k* is palatalized after *i(·)(h), e(·)(h), č,* and *s*. This phonemic inventory follows the analysis of Graczyk (1991:37–48); additional details are in Kaschube (1967:5–12) and Gordon (1972).

In the practical orthography used by the tribal bilingual program (Medicine Horse 1987) these phonemes are spelled: p, t, ch, k, ʔ; s, sh, x, h; m/b/w, n/d/l; i, e, a, o, u; ii, ee, aa, oo, uu; ea, ia, ua; (high pitch) v́ and v́v̀ (or v' and vv'), (falling pitch) v̀v (or v'v). The sequence *šš* is written ssh, *čč* is tch, and *šč* is sch.

of which begin with a confrontation between two chiefs, one of whom leads his followers off to the west (Curtis 1907–1930, 4:38–39; W. Matthews 1877:39; W.P. Clark 1885:196; Lowie 1918:272–275). Historically, the process of separation was likely a gradual one, beginning in the late 1600s. The suggested date of 1750–1775 for the separation of the two tribes is much too late and may represent the end of the process (Denig 1961:137; Hayden 1862:391; J.H. Bradley 1896–1923, pt.1:179; W.R. Wood and A.S. Downer 1977; L.B. Davis 1979). Linguistic evidence suggests an earlier date for the separation between the Crow and Hidatsa languages, perhaps ranging from 1500 to 1600 (Hollow and Parks 1980:80).

The ancestral Crow probably represented at least two major groups, one associated with the Awatixa Hidatsa, believed to be the ancestors of the Mountain Crow, the other associated with the Hidatsa proper, believed to be the ancestors of River Crow (Bowers 1965:482–486; Curtis 1907–1930, 4:43). One earthlodge site (the Hagen site) and many temporary campsites, identified by the presence of "Mandan tradition" pottery and found throughout north-central and northeastern Wyoming, have been attributed to the ancestral Mountain Crow and dated from the beginning of the sixteenth century until well into the eighteenth century (Mulloy 1942; Frison 1976, 1978, 1979).

History

Trade Middlemen, Early 1700s–1800

The Crow probably obtained horses by 1730 (Haines 1938:430, 436; Jablow 1950:15). According to nineteenth-century traditions, these first horses were obtained in trade from the Comanche (L.H. Morgan 1959:197) and the Nez Perce (J.H. Bradley 1896–1923, pt.3:220); the Eastern Shoshone must also have been a major provider of horses to the Crow (Haines 1938:436). After they were mounted, the Crow drove the Eastern Shoshone from the Yellowstone country, where they could find good winter grazing for their horse herds (L.H. Morgan 1959:197).

With horses the Crow obtained buffalo hides sufficient to double and even triple the size of their tepees. They developed a whole new lore about horses, from breaking and riding to daily care and medicines to make them fast and long-winded runners. Horses became prime currency in the search for wealth, status, and spouses.

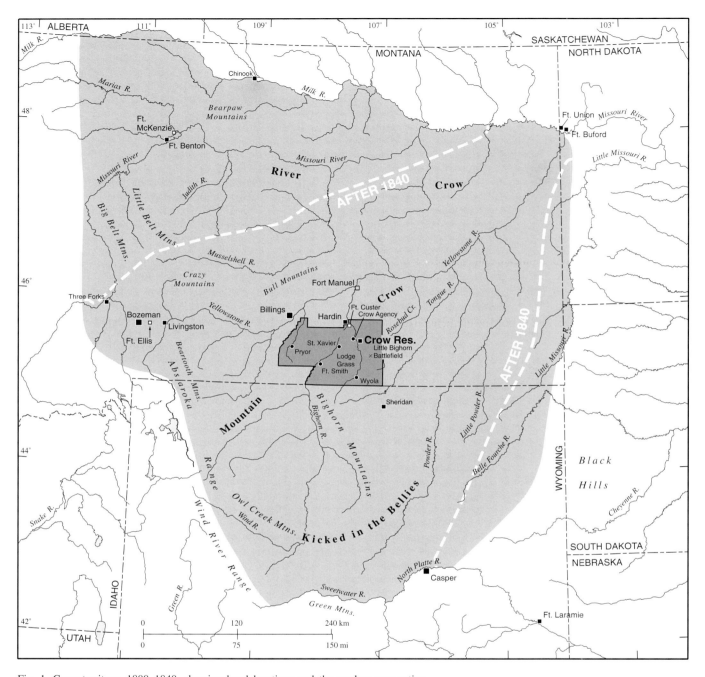

Fig. 1. Crow territory, 1800–1840, showing band locations and the modern reservation.

The new economic opportunities provided by horses doubtlessly intensified individual competition, which became integral to Crow culture (Leonard 1934:232–233). Sacred power was important to success, and new opportunities fed the desire for private ownership of medicines, especially for war and horse raiding (Wildschut 1975:172–173). Major ceremonies—the Sacred Sweat, Tobacco, and Sun Dance—probably were given their basic forms through vision revelations and dreams between 1725 and 1770.

The Crow trade network linked them to the western and eastern limits of the continent (vol. 4:352). Besides horses,

western tribes brought salmon oil and pemmican, root flour and berry cakes, Indian hemp and twine, composite horn and sinew-backed bows, arrows, clothing, shells, and cylindrical greenstone for pipes. In return, they bartered for eagle feather warbonnets of Sioux manufacture, Crow buffalo robes, catlinite pipes, buckskin clothing, and Anglo-European goods (Teit 1930:113–114).

In 1805, the Mountain Crow were joined enroute to the Missouri River villages by 20 lodges of Eastern Shoshone (or Comanche) traders who brought Spanish bridles, axes, beads, and blankets to trade for buffalo and deer skins

(Wood and Thiessen 1985:189). The Eastern Shoshone trade was an important secondary center in the Crow network. The Missouri River trade was carried on through an adoption and dance ceremony in which each group traded collectively. In 1805 the Hidatsa laid out 200 guns, 100 rounds of ammunition for each of them, 100 bushels of corn, various axes, kettles, and cloth goods. In turn, Crow put out 250 horses, bundles of buffalo robes, buckskin leggings, shirts, as well as moccasins, pouches, bows and arrows, and lances (C. Mackenzie 1889–1890:346). The Crow carried on a similar trade with the Mandan.

The interrelationship of horse and trade was critical, for the dynamics of horse raiding and trade intensified intertribal cultural exchanges in the late eighteenth century. The Mandan, Hidatsa, and Arikara villages became primary trade centers; and secondary centers linked the Mountain Crow with the Nez Perce, Flathead, and Northern Shoshone. The Mountain Crow in their western location were in a better position than the River Crow to transmit traits characteristic of tribes of the Upper Missouri region to the Great Basin and Plateau areas, and to borrow elements from both, but particularly from their principal trading partners, the Nez Perce. This would hold especially if the River Crow early in the trade served as middlemen between the Mountain Crow and the Mandan and Hidatsa (C.F. Taylor 1981).

In their westward migrations, locations, and trade contacts, the Crow transmitted craft techniques and designs that influenced Plateau and Northern Plains art styles (Feder 1980; Lessard 1980; C.F. Taylor 1981). The location between two culture areas may have stimulated Mountain Crow to become the quality producers and innovators in craftwork for which the Crow became famous. A flair for ceremonial dress and horse decorations instilled a preference for stylish complex designs and decorative items like beaded horse collars and lance cases. Beadwork during the "classic phase," about 1850–1900, generally continued earlier quillwork designs, but patterns increasingly reflected the painted geometric decoration of parfleches.

Decoration expressed sacred associations of power and protection as well as military honors. Hide fringes, paints, porcupine quills, beads, feathers, and tufts of human or horse hair were basic media for artistic expression. Medicine bundles sometimes included a rudimentary carved human figure or effigy cut from hide and stuffed with hair and sweetgrass. Women painted and embroidered domestic objects and clothing with geometric designs while men drew representations of their war exploits and animal or bird tutelaries on tepee covers, wind screens, robes, and hides for calendar counts (Lowie 1922a). After 1850 beads gradually supplanted quills until little quillwork was done after 1890 (Wildschut 1959:40).

Mountain Crow borrowed bandolier bags, a cradle form, incised rawhide decoration, and possibly a diamond motif from Great Basin or Plateau sources. They in turn contributed the "Crow stitch," geometric designs, and double lane quill-wrapped horsehair motifs, and passed along the dis-

tinctive rosette and hourglass-broken circle forms. Combinations of local forms with Crow designs, or vice versa, marked the beginnings of a regional Western Plains and Plateau style complementary to the Upper Missouri style (Lessard 1984). The presence of female war captives, a desire to imitate a pleasing form and design, and economic incentives to imitate fashionable trade items may have combined to regionalize the art.

Fur Trade, Diplomacy, and War, 1800–1870

Although the Crow did not materially alter their subsistence cycle or abandon trade with the Missouri villagers to accommodate the fur trade, they committed themselves more than other Plains tribes to the trapping of beaver (Denig 1930:411, 538). During the first two decades of the nineteenth century Manuel Lisa made a determined effort to acquire the Crow and Flathead fur trade with posts at the mouth of the Bighorn River and at the Three Forks of the Missouri (Oglesby 1963:54; Phillips 1961, 2:262). However, Blackfoot and Gros Ventre war parties frustrated Lisa's trade, and a Crow presence was needed at all times to protect post hunters and trappers. The Crow also assisted Flathead in routing Blackfoot in 1808 at Three Forks (Phillips 1961, 2:262).

In 1825 the Crow visited the Mandan villages to meet with Gen. Henry Atkinson. Angered by the training of cannon on the Crow encampment, the River Crow chief, Rotten Belly (*e·rápuaš* 'sore belly'), had his men stop up the mouths of the cannon; and the Mandan had to intervene to prevent escalation of the encounter (Curtis 1907–1930, 4:47–48). Long Hair, with 15 Mountain Crow chiefs, signed a treaty of peace and friendship with the United States (Kappler 1904–1941, 2:244–246), but Rotten Belly, representing the River Crow, did not sign. In 1834 Rotten Belly laid siege to Fort McKenzie, situated on the north bank of the Missouri River about six miles above the mouth of the Marias River. The untimely arrival of Blackfoot lifted the siege and in the Crow withdrawal, Rotten Belly made a suicidal run against an intercepted Blackfoot war party (Denig 1961:172–184). The failure at Fort McKenzie and Rotten Belly's death may have led the River Crow to withdraw their range to the Musselshell River.

Fort Union, established in 1829 by the American Fur Company, withstood Blackfoot raiders and became a primary trading center for Assiniboine, Plains Cree, and Crow (Kurz 1937:123, 225). This post, as well as the annual fur trade rendezvous (1829–1839)—many of which were located in or near Mountain Crow territory along the flanks of the Wind River Mountains (vol. 11:504) or about the headwaters of the Bighorn and Powder rivers—gave Crow improved opportunities for trade (Phillips 1961, 2:265).

The presence of traders intensified warfare as tribes sought to interdict the arming of enemies, to plunder horses, and to drive other tribes from favorable trade and food areas. The Crow were targets because they possessed numerous and quality horses, trade goods, and lands rich in buffalo and other game. Out of self-interest traders encouraged intertribal peace or war. Trader Edwin Denig, married to an Assiniboine, persuaded Crow and Assiniboine around 1849 to end "half a century of bloody warfare" (1930:404). The peace conferred mutual benefits. The Assiniboine permitted the Crow to locate in Assiniboine territory in the winter and to hunt buffalo, while the Crow gave horses each year and some of their kill to the Assiniboine. In 1851 the Crow signed the Fort Laramie treaty, which defined tribal boundaries and promised intertribal peace. In return, the Crow were to receive annual distributions of merchandise (Kappler 1904–1941, 2:594–596).

On entering agreements chiefs commonly warned that their young men were difficult to control. Ambitious warriors frequently turned alliances into brittle affairs; and Crow from time to time skirmished with their Nez Perce, Flathead, and Eastern Shoshone trading partners. Termination of the longstanding Blackfoot–Gros Ventre alliance in 1861 gave the Crow an opportunity to contain the Piegan by allying themselves with the disgruntled Gros Ventre. However, the new allies were unable to best the Piegan in battle at the Cypress Hills in 1866 (Ewers 1958:243).

In August 1864 in the Pryor Mountains the Crow beat back an attempt by a combined force of Teton Sioux, Arapaho, and Cheyenne who had boasted that they would drive them out of their lands (Curtis 1907–1930, 4:91–92). During this period, Crow leaders realized that the White men were their best allies against their traditional enemies, as revealed to Plenty Coups in a vision quest (Linderman 1930:173–174). In 1868 the government again assembled the Crow and other tribes at Fort Laramie and in this instance promised civilization in exchange for their lands. The Crow surrendered title to upwards of 38,000,000 acres of which 8,000,000 acres were to be set aside for their exclusive use (Kappler 1904–1941, 2:1008–1011). The treaty promised an agency headquarters, with school and other services under the supervision of a resident Indian agent (fig. 2). The Crow were encouraged to take up farming, and agency residents would receive rations and clothing. In return, they were to compel their children to go to school and to submit to regulations set forth by the agent.

Prelude to Reservation Life, 1870–1883

The first step toward reservation life was taken in 1870 when the Mountain Crow were required to report to the Fort Parker Agency at Mission Creek, near Livingston, Montana, and the River Crow to Milk River Agency, near Chinook, Montana. They maintained a seasonal hunt for buffalo and pelts for trade, with calls at the agency for head counts and distributions. In 1875 the Crow were consolidated at a new agency on Rosebud Creek at Absarokee, where they were more easily recruited for army service. Crow scouts served Lt. Col. George A. Custer at the Battle

of the Little Bighorn in 1876. Subsequently, they were recruited to scout for the army in campaigns against the Nez Perce (vol. 12:435), the Sioux, Cheyenne, and Bannock, and from the establishment of Fort Custer in 1877 until near 1890, Crow scouts were busy with Piegan, Assiniboine, Plains Cree, and Sioux horse raiders as well as cattle rustlers (Marquis 1928:252–319).

By an agreement in 1880 (22 Stat. 42), the Crow sold to the government the western portion of their reservation—some 1,500,000 acres—and moved in 1883–1884 to the present Crow Agency near Hardin, Montana. Following the lead of band and clan leaders, the Crow settled in five districts, Black Lodge (Crow Agency), Reno, Chiefs' Creek (Lodge Grass or Valley of the Chiefs), Big Horn (St. Xavier), and Pryor. Mountain Crow settlements were principally south of Crow Agency at Reno, Pryor, and Upper Big Horn. River Crow settled north of Crow Agency at Black Lodge, along the lower Little Bighorn and Bighorn rivers. The Kicked in the Bellies settled in Lodge Grass and Wyola districts. Agency subdistricts were set up at each of these locations and became the basis for political action under chiefs and outstanding warriors (Hoxie 1984a:77). Clans did not influence settlement since they were scattered throughout the Mountain and River Crow bands.

Culture, 1780–1882

Subsistence

Buffalo were the major source of meat, but in winter especially, elk, deer, antelope, mountain sheep, and bear were hunted. Buffalo, elk, and deer were hunted by the surround, precipice jump, and impoundment methods. Men possessing buffalo medicine were selected to direct hunts (Curtis 1907–1930, 4:112–114). A man's average kill was four or five buffalo, but successful hunters might kill 15 buffalo in one hunt, identifying their kill by the marks on their arrows.

Women cut meat into thin strips following the grain and draped it over pole frames for sun drying. They pounded the dried meat with stone mauls and made pemmican by mixing it with fat and pulverized dried berries and fruits, especially chokecherries. Fire was produced by hand twirling a compound sagebrush or wild grape drill set in a cottonwood or driftwood hearth sprinkled with pulverized buffalo dung or rotten bark tinder (Lowie 1922:214–215). Buffalo chip punks were used to carry live coals from camp to camp. Hot stones were dropped in a rawhide "kettle" filled with water to boil meat. Women commonly set up a small log tepee for cooking and used hide shelters as windbreaks when sewing or working hides.

Technology

Eating bowls were crafted from box elder. Spoons, dishes and cups were fashioned from mountain sheep and buffalo horn, shaped by softening in hot water. Buffalo shoulder

Fig. 2. Delegation to Washington, 1873, to protest the removal of Indian Agent Fellows D. Pease and to follow up on promises made by Gen. William Tecumseh Sherman during the Treaty of 1868 (*Evening Star*, Oct. 21, 1873). left to right, back row: Eche-has-ka or Long Horse; Ella-causs-se or Thin Belly; Bernard Prero, interpreter; Blackfoot's wife; Agent Pease; Iron Bull's wife wearing elktooth dress; Pierre Shane, interpreter; Mo-mukh-pi-tche. middle row: Se-ta-pit-se or Bear Wolf (Packs the Bear); Te-shu-nzt or White Calf; Blackfoot or Kam-ne-but-se or Sits in the Middle of the Land, a principal chief of the Mountain Crow; Che-ve-te Pu-ma-ta or Iron Bull, a principal chief of the Mountain Crow; Pish-ki-ha-di-ri-ky-ish or One Who Leads the Old Dog; Perits-har-sts or Old Crow. front row: Stays with the Horses, Bear Wolf's wife, wearing elktooth dress; Ish-ip-chi-wak-pa-i-chis or Good Medicine Pipe, Old Crow's wife. Photograph by Henry or Julius Ulke, Washington, D.C., 1873.

blades also served as dishes (Linderman 1932:33). A buffalo paunch held water, and the pericardium served as a canteen. During the historic period no pottery was manufactured, but steatite bowls holding some two gallons were made. Dried meat was stored in rectangular rawhide parfleches decorated with rectangles and triangles painted in traditional red, blue, yellow, and green (Mason 1926:399). Women gathered prairie turnips using a digging stick about two and one-half feet long, padded with buffalo hair and leather (Marquis 1928:158–159).

The strongest bows were made of elk or sheep horn laminations spliced and glued in place along with bands of sinew taken from the neck and shoulder of buffalo. Wood bows were made of cedar, ash, and hickory. Specialists shaped arrows out of chokecherry, straightening the shaft with grooved stones or mountain sheep horn perforated with four graduated holes. Quivers were made of otter, mountain sheep, or buffalo calf skins to which a sheath for the bow was attached (Belden 1870:107, 112; Lowie 1922:230–232; Laubin and Laubin 1980).

Women were the primary processors of raw materials for domestic use. Moistened hides were staked on the ground, and a buffalo foreleg fitted with a serrated bone chisel was used to chip off the flesh. Hair was removed with an elkhorn adz; and for use as tepee covers both sides were smeared with a mixture of buffalo brains, liver, grease from bone soup, floral balls from sage, and prairie chicken or sage hen droppings to whiten the hide. After applying rich buffalo belly fat, much alternate wetting, kneading, drying, scraping, and pulling through a sinew loop remained to soften the hide. Fifteen to 20 tanned buffalo hides, often painted and decorated with quillwork, were sewn together and drawn over 14–30 pine poles to construct the tepee, which was raised on a four-pole foundation (Campbell 1927:87–88; Lowie 1922:222–225; Wissler 1941:37–38; Laubin and Laubin 1977:217–224). About 8 to 16 persons occupied a tepee.

Women owned the tepee and relied on special lodge-cutters to supervise making of the cover. Rawhide containers and personal luggage placed around the base kept an inside liner in place. Sparse furniture included backrests and hide walls that separated bed spaces, where buffalo robes served as mattresses and blankets. A hide screen painted with the warrior's exploits protected a central fire from draft. The entrance faced east, away from prevailing winds, permitting the medicine owner to step forth at break of day and greet Sun with prayer (Lowie 1922:224; Marquis 1928:149–154).

Clothing and Adornment

According to weather and task, men put on breechcloth, skin-tight leggings extending from ankle to hip, a shirt with fringed front and attached sleeves, one-piece moccasins decorated with quills or beads, fur mittens and cap, and a buffalo robe with quilled or beaded mid-seam, sometimes painted with war exploits. Clothing was made from skins of antelope, big horn sheep, and deer (Curtis 1907–1930, 4:22–23; Larocque 1910:66–67; Wildschut 1959:4–10). Elk, deer, and mountain sheep skins were smoked with buffalo dung or rotten wood, giving a brownish color and preventing clothing from becoming stiff after being wet (Lowie 1922:225–226).

In 1805 women wore leggings reaching to mid-thigh, held by a garter below the knee and heavily decorated along the seams with their favorite blue beads (Larocque 1910:67–68). They crafted dresses from two elk hides, or preferably, large antelope or big horn sheep skins, fringed at the bottom and garnished along the edge with porcupine quills. Arm-length sleeves attached at the shoulder were left open above the ribs to allow suckling. Women did not paint their robes but decorated them and their moccasins with quills. Boys up to 10 years went naked (Larocque 1910:68).

By the 1850s Crow women were making cloth dresses patterned after skin clothing and sewing cloth leggings for their men. They also copied European patterns, fashioning coats and capotes out of striped Mackinaw blankets (Kurz 1937:259). By the 1870s annuity distributions resulted in a mix of skin and cloth clothing. Buckskin leggings competed with scarlet or blue cloth leggings, and feather headdresses with felt hats, including the high-crowned, wide-brimmed "reservation hat" typical of late nineteenth-century Crow men. Breechcloths and moccasins alone were standard along with a wooden or elkhorn whip (Dunraven 1876:85–86).

The Crow rose with the sun and bathed winter and summer as a family before eating (Curtis 1907–1930, 4:6; Larocque 1910:68). They were fastidious about personal appearance, plucking facial and body hair, including eyebrows and pubic hair (Larocque 1910:56). Until the 1950s older men carried tweezers to eliminate beard hair.

In the early nineteenth century both males and females divided the hair in the middle and let it hang loose at shoulder length, painting the part red. In 1833 Maximilian (Thwaites 1904–1907, 23:266) noted that Crow mixed aromatic castor with red paint, which was rubbed over their bodies, faces, and hair (Belden 1870:146; Lowie 1922:228–229). A porcupine tail mounted on a handle served as a hairbrush, and by the 1840s young men sported a special pouch slung over the wrist for mirror, paint, and comb (Belden 1870:146; Wildschut 1959:36). The style of wearing the hair in braids was said to have been borrowed from the Nez Perce in the 1870s (Curtis 1907–1930, 4:22; Lowie 1935:83; Voget 1939).

Paint was made by boiling chokecherry gum and buffalo hoofs until jelled, then adding colored earths. For use, the dried paint, cut in squares, was mixed with water or grease in shallow bowls (Linderman 1930:135–136). Tattooing was not in vogue among Crow, and only a few men and women had arm or facial tattoos (Curtis 1907–1930, 4:175). Crow men shaped the upsweeping roach of their hairstyle using a hot stick as a curling iron. Long hair had medicine properties, and to achieve a "medicine train" men added strands of natural and horse hair matted with balls of pitch pine (Denig 1961:155; Larocque 1910:66–67).

Transport

Horses were the major transport, and Crow were known as superb riders who paid as much attention to decorating their horses (fig. 3) as themselves. They mounted from the right, and, while riding bareback or with a soft hide was common, saddles must have come into use when horses were first introduced. In 1805 Larocque (1910:64) noted the high pommel and cantle of women's saddles, which reached as high as the shoulders and the lower chest. Men's saddles were not so high, and the Spanish design was replaced with a two-cushion pad saddle (Kurz 1937:pl. 9). A soft hide tanned with the hair on served as a saddle blanket, but for dress the Crow draped red flannel over the saddle as lining for a mountain lion skin (Maximilian in Thwaites 1904–1907, 22:346). Pommel, cantle, bridle, stirrups, crupper, and saddle blankets were all decorated; and beaded horse collars were introduced in the 1850s (Wildschut 1959:24–28). The man's riding and pack saddle probably was introduced in the 1870s, a possible invention of the Kiowa (Ewers 1955:92–93).

Five horses were needed to take care of a family's baggage, and another five for riding and hunting. Women packed horses with domestic equipment and the travois was used only for moving the sick or wounded. One or two horses carried the lodge cover and another the lodge poles. Separate sacks held 40 to 50 pegs for the tepee, 8 to 10 for staking horses, and some 70 for staking hides. Infants were strapped to saddle horns and held tight within the buckskin

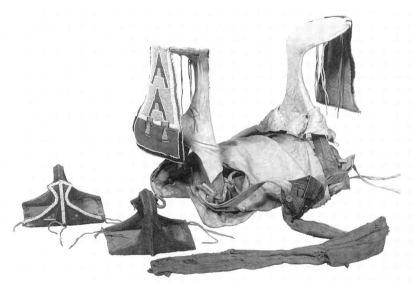

Fig. 3. Transportation. top, Men dressed for a ceremony or a social dance, Hoop on the Forehead (far right) and 2 others in a wagon pulled by a horse decorated with a painted hand print and lines on the rump. The designs on the horse represent coups or war honors achieved by the owner. Photograph possibly by Fred Miller, 1898–1910. bottom left, Woman's pack saddle with stirrups. The frame is covered with rawhide and has a rawhide pad underneath. The pommel and cantle have a soft skin slip cover with beaded cloth pendants. The pendants are decorated with blue, white, yellow, and green beads on red fabric. The girth is made of old Levis. Collected by Dr. W.J. Hoffman before 1892; length of sidebars 44.5 cm. bottom right, Decoration on truck fender, Crow Fair, Mont. The handprint is red and the dots are black. Photograph by Michael Crummett, 1979.

casing of their cradleboards. A woman tied her husband's shield and medicine bundle to the pommel.

Crow had no water transport other than pole rafts and makeshift circular bullhide boats constructed to ford streams and to ferry baggage across.

Social Organization

Crow society was organized politically into territorial units (bands, tribe) crosscut by kinship units (clans and families) and by functional associations (military, religious, curing, and horse wealth societies). There were no social classes. Membership in matrilineal clans conveyed basic civil rights and obligations. Clans had their own chiefs, determined marriage through exogamy, and obligated clan members to aid, revenge, and mourn as brothers and sisters. Historically, the number of clans varied but during the nineteenth century numbered 12 or 13 (table 1), with two or three clans forming unnamed phratries that cooperated with one another in hunting, feasting, mutual aid, and supplying spouses.

701

Every Crow belonged to his mother's clan but was also born as a "child" of his father's clan. Establishment of a family united the father's and mother's clans in reciprocities that conveyed health, longevity, and success to a child's career, especially males. Clan fathers bestowed good luck blessings obtained in dreams, and in return were feasted by the child and his maternal kin and given choice meats, moccasins, robes, beadwork, and horses. Clan fathers usually had a stock of dream blessings for the naming of children, to honor a boy's first kill of deer or buffalo, or on any occasion when a change of luck was called for. "Fathers" included not only the men of the father's clan but also adopted "medicine fathers" who instructed the individual in ceremonies or who sold their "sons" a medicine bundle or other sacred object (Lowie 1935:18–19). The exchange of sacred power and protection for material wealth was crucial to the structuring and continuity of Crow society, expressed in the giveaway (Voget 1987:207–216).

Kinship terminology reflected reciprocities between the mother's and father's matrikin by stressing a respect relationship between a "child" and the members of his father's matrilineage, all of whom, from elder to infant, were addressed and treated as special fathers and mothers. Through public ridicule, joking relatives—children of the father's clan—tried to shame anyone who carried out objectionable deeds (Lowie 1935:222).

The other important kinship reciprocity was between a woman's brother and her children. A mother's brother was like an older brother to the child, and he was expected to help his younger brother to get a horse and saddle, watch out for him on his first war foray, and teach him traditional Crow behavior. Reciprocally, a mother's brother's children were sons and daughters; were a younger brother to marry

Table 1. Crow Clan Names

L.H. Morgan (1877)	Curtis (1907–1930, 4)	Lowie (1935:9)	Frey (1987), Medicine Horse (1987:15–16)
A-che-pä-be'-cha Prairie Dog			čihpawa·íčče 'do good prairie dog'[a]
E-sach'-ka-buk Bad Leggins			
Ho-ka-rut'-cha Skunk			
Ash-bot-chee-ah Treacherous Lodges	Ashbatshúwa Backbiter Lodge	acbatcu'a	ašwatšua 'mean lodge'
Ah-shin'-nä-de'-ah Lost Lodges	Ashidhadhío Newly Made Lodge	acirārī'o	ašhira·río· 'newly made lodge'[a]
Ese-kep-kä-buk Bad Honors	Ashkyŭpkaviya Bad Coups	ackya'pkawi`a	aškápkawi·a 'bad war deeds'[a]
Oo-sä-bot'-see Butchers	Úsawatsiya Never Shoots, Packs Game	ū'sawatsi`a	ú·ssa·wa·či·a 'packs without shooting'
Ah-hä-chick Moving Lodges			
Ship-tet'-zä Bear's Paw			
Ash-kane'-na Blackfoot Lodges	Ashkyámně Piegan Lodge	ackyā'mne	aška·wre 'Piegan'[a]
Boo-a-dä'-sha Fish Catchers			
O-hot-dū'sha Antelope			
Pet-shale-ruh-pä'-ka Raven			
	Ashíoshě Burnt Mouth	acī'oce	aší·o·še 'burnt lip lodge'[a]
	Úwutashě, Greasy Mouth	ū'wutace`	û·wu·tašše 'greasy mouth'[a]
	Bidikyóshě Whistle Water	birikyō'oce	wirikô·še 'whistling water'[a]
	Ashħats'ě (meaning unknown)	acxatse`	ašxáhče 'streaked lodge'
	Ashitsítě Big Lodge	acitsi'te	aššiččíte 'big lodges'[a]
	Ishidetě Not Mixed		
	Adhidhěpiyo Kick Belly	ē`rarapī'o	e·rarapí·o 'Kicked in the Belly'
		xu'xkaraxtse	xúhka·laxče 'tied in a bundle'[a]
		acpénuce	ašpe·rru·še 'eat filth'

702   [a]Clans that survived into the late 20th century (Medicine Horse 1987; Frey 1987:40).

the widow of his mother's brother according to the levirate, they became so in fact. A father's brother was a father, and a mother's sister was a mother, and their children respectively were brothers and sisters, the kin terms differentiating between older and younger (Lowie 1912:207–212, 1917:53–82, 1935:18–32; L.H. Morgan 1871). A group of brothers united for hunting and warfare, and marital residence tended to be patrilocal.

Men and women used different terms of address and reference for most relatives, and terminology was more sensitive to social than to biological contexts. Children referred to a father's special friend (*i·rápa·če*) as "father," and two men married to sisters addressed each another by the "friend" term (Lowie 1912:212). A woman referred to her mother's brother's children as "son" and "daughter" and they called her "mother."

Games and Amusements

Crow generally enjoyed the excitement of betting. The hand game in which elk tooth counters were hidden in the hand was a favorite (fig. 4), with each side employing medicine to win (Lowie 1922:235–236). Women were dice players, throwing marked sticks in sets of four or bouncing marked plum stones in a bowl (Lowie 1922:238–239). In spring women used a hide ball stuffed with animal hair to play shinny. Men practiced archery in competitions, threw arrows at targets (fig. 4), and hurled javelins at rolling hoops. Foot and horse races were also gambling favorites.

Winter ice brought sliding and pushing competitions between men's societies. Young men slithered buffalo rib snow snakes across the ice, pulled their girlfriends on buffalo skulls or sleds, or coasted on buffalo hide and rib toboggans. Boys spun conical tops on the ice (Lowie 1922:247–249; Nabokov 1967:5).

Life Cycle

A woman gave birth kneeling on a pile of robes. With elbows supported, she grasped two poles set up over where her pillow was placed during sleep (Lowie 1935:33–34). A midwife grandmother cut the umbilical cord at three fingers' breadth and the baby was washed, greased, and wrapped in a soft robe. Feeding was on demand, and the infant, except for cleaning, was not released from the cradleboard until able to sit up (Voget 1939). After two days the infant's ears were pierced and on the fourth day a clan father brought him under protection of his medicine, raising him three times in protective cedar incense and on the fourth time naming him after a dream or coup. When the child walked, the namer would claim a horse.

Crow courted in secret and some youths played wooden flageolets to signal a meeting. Older female relatives usually tried to learn how many horses to offer for marriage, for the most honorable marriage was called "paying for her" (Lowie 1917:75). Girls were taught not to shame brothers by bear-

top, Eastern Wash. State Histl. Soc., Cheney Cowles Mus., Spokane: MS 1204.12.2.

Fig. 4. Games. top, Girls imitating adult activity, playing "house" with tepees and tents. Photographed at Crow Agency, Mont., 1898–1910. center, Hand game, known as "hiding," a time of intense competition between clans and districts (Voget 1984:37). Jack Covers Up (left) conceals an elk tooth in one hand. The man keeping score is beside a drummer. The men on the left wear reservation-style hats with beaded bands. Photograph by Fred Voget, 1940. bottom, Arrow-throwing tournament with districts competing against one another. left to right: Jerome White Hip, unidentified man, Carlson Goes Ahead, unidentified man in background, Calvin Birdinground, Roy Old Crane, Marvin Falls Down, Mike Fitzpatrick, Jr., Ben Stands, and Ronald Falls Down. Photograph by Kathleen Westcott, Lodge Grass, Mont., 1979.

ing children out of wedlock. Crow women practiced abortion, using simple pressure, jumping, and blows to the abdomen (Denig 1930:521).

Older brothers had the right to approve a sister's marital choice, and parents sometimes rewarded a son's friend by offering a daughter in marriage. Elopement was an alterna- 703 tive. Marriage conveyed to a man rights to his wife's sisters, and for family harmony men preferred marrying sisters when adding spouses. If a man's wife died soon after marriage, a sister was offered as a substitute.

Strong gift reciprocities and respect behavior between sisters-in-law and between brothers-in-law strengthened family relationships. A man treated his wife's brother's wife with the same respect accorded his sister. He must not be with her alone and should not hold her hand or embrace her affectionately. His brothers' wives (sisters-in-law) were open to all manner of sexual repartee and body touching, for they were potential spouses. A man was not to stare at, touch, speak to, or eat with his mother-in-law, and he was equally respectful toward his father-in-law. Men of distinction could eliminate in-law avoidance by making a public announcement through a herald and giving his mother-in-law a horse. In turn she dressed him up with a new outfit.

Either husband or wife could initiate divorce, but adultery penalized the woman more heavily, especially if the liaison happened while the husband was on the warpath. During the spring reorganization of the men's societies, members counted liaisons with the wives of competitors as coups. Winners took the wives of losers and paraded them on horses that had been ridden to rescue a warrior from the enemy. Such wives were soon turned out by the losing husbands, since a man's honor merged with that of his society, which disapproved his taking back an abducted wife.

Crow used circumlocutions to refer to the dead; for example, "He is not here" (Lowie 1917:82; Marquis 1928:169). They never took the body out a lodge entrance for fear that the ghost would return and take another of the household. A dead person was dressed in his best, painted, and wrapped in the upper portion of the tepee cover. A chief was placed on a four-pole scaffold in a tepee (fig. 5) decorated with red stripes and scalps. His lance, decorated with wolf skin, stood outside the entrance along with streamers from the mane and tail of his favorite horses (Bushnell 1927:79; Lowie 1935:67). Crow anciently buried their dead in rockshelters or caves and took over scaffold and probably tree burial from the Hidatsa around 1825 (Curtis 1907–1930, 4:179).

When a warrior was killed by the enemy the whole camp mourned. The corpse was put on view and a herald invited people to come and smoke with their friend (Curtis 1907–1930, 4:36–37). Women displayed grief by puncturing the skin of their heads with arrow points, making a full circle, and wives and close relatives jabbed thighs and arms as was customary for men. Relatives gathered at a log to cut off finger tips or joints, leaving the wound to bleed for a day (Belden 1870:160; Lowie 1912:226–228). Hair was cut short also. Close relatives disposed of the corpse and extended their mourning for a full year or until an enemy had been killed. The deceased's tepee and domestic articles were given away, together with property contributed by a man's military society (Curtis 1907–1930, 4:33–36).

Fig. 5. Grave of a Crow chief. A scaffold burial is inside the disintegrating tepee, which is made of hides. Photographed before 1902.

Warfare

A man began his martial career at age 14 to 16 when he joined the Hammer Owners who were organized in imitation of men's societies. Youths individually accompanied war parties as errand boys and looked forward to an invitation to join one of the men's military societies. During the late prereservation period there were four main societies: Lumpwoods, Foxes, Muddy Hands, and Big Dogs, although earlier in the nineteenth century there were a larger number (table 2). These societies shared power with the chiefs since one was selected yearly as camp police (*akíssatre·*) to control hunts and direct camp movements and to mediate personal conflicts by thrusting a medicine pipe between the fighters. They had authority to arrest poachers before a hunt, whip them, kill their horses, and confiscate their kill without retaliation. As a retired warrior a man was inducted into the Bull Owners society and felt free to offer wise counsel at public gatherings (Lowie 1913a:143–217, 1935:172–206; Curtis 1907–1930, 4:13–20, 177).

The ambitious strove to become pipe holders, the acknowleged leaders of war parties. Beyond this, to enter the ranks of the chiefs (*wače·íčče* 'good men'), a man completed four prescribed deeds: wrested a weapon from an enemy, struck first coup on an enemy, captured a horse picketed before a tepee in an enemy camp, and led a war party that took horses or scalps without loss of life.

Pipe holders were entitled to wear shirts with ermine strips and scalps or horsehair substitutes. Wolf tails at a

Table 2. Crow Men's Societies

Crow Name	English Name
íáxuhke	Kitfox
waraxíšše	Lumpwood
wiškisâ·te	Big Dog
iščišipîa	Muddy Hand
wû·pčake·	Hammer Owner
čî·rapake·	Bull Owner
wiškawa·râ·xe háčkite	Long Crazy Dog
wiškawa·râ·xe akšê·wia	Crazy Dog Who Wishes to Die
ičču·sê· čirašsu·čé	Half-Shaved Head
í·šipia	Muddy Mouth
wiškíáte	Little Dog

SOURCES: Lowie 1913a:155; phonemicized from a retranscription by Randolph Graczyk (personal communication 1994).

man's moccasin heels indicated a first coup (Curtis 1907–1930, 4:11–13; Lowie 1912:230–238, 1935:215–236). A warrior's image was sensitive to ridicule, and to die in a suicidal run at the enemy as a "Crazy Dog Wishing To Die" was preferable to humiliation (Curtis 1907–1930, 4:13–14; Lowie 1913a:193–196, 1917:83–84).

In frenzied grief for tribal members slain, Crow sometimes mutilated the enemy dead, cutting off their heads, hoisting them on poles, and finally hurling them against rocks or trees (Leonard 1934:245–246). Enemy scalps were raised on poles, and mourners joined in the victory dance.

Before the introduction of firearms, weapons included bow and arrows, war club, knife, lance, and medicine shield (fig. 6); and a medicine bundle and pipe for prayer was indispensable for protection (fig. 7). Dreams prophetic of success motivated war parties and before engaging the enemy the leader used his medicine to confirm in vision that the promised success still held. According to Two Leggings, horse raids were sometimes led by a man with blackbird medicine, who would attach the skin of a blackbird to his head (Nabokov 1967:152). The leader of a war party was in complete control and took charge of distributing the booty. Raiding parties were small, but revenge expeditions under an outstanding chief could number several hundred, including mourners (Curtis 1907–1930, 4:83–91). In enemy territory the Crow built log tepees or rectangular forts out of dead wood for protection against surprise (Voget 1987:1–18).

The Crow entrusted leadership to those whose military exploits and dreams demonstrated that they were favored directly by spirits or by powerful medicine fathers. An informal council of elders noted for their medicine powers usually nominated for public acclaim one chief who became chief of the camp (ašwače·íčče). When moving camp, he was called 'he leads the moving band' (akdá·lo·čiale·) (Curtis 1907–1930, 4:9, 177); the chief carried a sacred pipe and led the procession to the new encampment and no one was allowed to go before him. In a consultation of chiefs, a prayerful smoking of the pipe indicated agreement and

top left, Smithsonian, Natl. Mus. of the Amer. Ind.: 11/7680 (neg. 29656); bottom left, Field Mus., Chicago: 71736 (neg. 111348); Smithsonian, Dept. of Anthr.: center, 361,768; right, 361,361 (neg. 72-7540).

Fig. 6. Shield covers and lances. Supernatural powers were obtained through visions and the objects and designs empowered by those visions could be transferred to others. This resulted in the reproduction of basic designs with variations dependent on the personal choices and visions of the owners. top left, Shield cover reportedly owned and designed by Rotten Belly (d. 1834), head chief of the River Crow, who was given the shield by the moon in a vision (Wildschut 1960:71). The base color is red; the black figure with disproportionately large ears and red stripes represents the moon. To its right is a sandhill crane's head and neck wrapped in red flannel and hung with strips of fur and hawk feathers; a single golden eagle feather and a deer's tail are tied on the left. Collected by William Wildschut before 1923; diameter 61 cm. bottom left, Shield cover owned originally by Old He Dog and later by Wraps Up His Tail. The design by Old He Dog included a black field with a white figure representing a spirit appearing in his vision. To the left of the figure is "the star always near the moon," identified as Jupiter. A sandhill crane's head with military buttons for eyes and 3 golden eagle feathers complete the design. After Wraps Up His Tail acquired it he prayed for medicine and saw a red skeleton spirit; the shield cover was modified accordingly. Collected by S.C. Simms, 1902; diameter 60 cm. center and right, Wooden lances adorned with feathers and iron points. Collected by Victor J. Evans before 1930; length of right, 120 cm.

brought about consensus in decision making. Chiefs had no judicial functions in settling murders or other disputes involving families or clans (Curtis 1907–1930, 4:9, 11, 177).

Mythology

Crow mythology reveals close affinity with their Hidatsa relations, and secondarily with the Assiniboine and Arapaho (Lowie 1918:10–13). Origin myths were of the earth diver type, in which Old Man (*isâ·hkaxa·ria*) shaped the earth out of mud brought from below flood waters by Helldiver (the pied-billed grebe). The Crow identified Old Man with Sun (*áxxa·še*), and some also identified him with Old Man Coyote (*isâ·hkawuatte·*); others considered them separate beings (Lowie 1918:14–19).

According to Iron Bull, after making the world, Old Man blew some dry earth from his hand, creating First Man, First Woman, and a flock of crows. Old Man taught them how to live and First Man chose to name his people "Crow," after the birds. Then Old Man placed them in their Yellowstone homeland surrounded by enemy tribes, whom they were destined to fight. Old Man struck a tree, and White men emerged like mice from a hole. He told the Crow not to fight the White men, who would teach them to make iron. After touring their land with the Crow, Old Man told them that they should pray to him and make offerings of white buffalo hides, blacktail deerskins, and white-tail hawk feathers, and in return he promised them help (W.P. Clark 1885:136–138).

Religion

Sun, addressed in prayer as "father," was considered the most powerful spirit being, to whom fasters never failed to pray and make flesh offerings (Lowie 1918:319, 1935:243–244, 252). Prayers were also offered to First Maker (*i·číhkwa·hire*), The One Above (*wâ·kukkure*), and Old Man Coyote. Morning Star, Buffalo, Thunderbird, Eagle, and Dwarf People were addressed in prayer but if these beings had evil intentions, a human aided by a powerful medicine helper could defeat them.

Medicine power (*wa·xpê·* 'sacred, having power') was essential for success in life. Such power transcended ordinary human ability and reflected the inherent but hidden presence of the many spirit beings. Human figures seen in dreams or visions changed into animals, birds, insects, and snakes that bestowed medicine power in exchange for offerings. In the vision quest the supplicant fasted and offered a finger joint or strips of flesh to induce a spirit being to adopt him as a son and to give him rights to a medicine song, body painting, and various power objects to be kept in a medicine bundle. The visionary addressed the spirit as "father," assimilating the relationship into the general structure of Crow kinship (Lowie 1918:315–343; Curtis 1907–1930, 4:52–54).

Alternatively, an individual might borrow a clan father's medicine four times, repaying him with horses, choice meat, and other wealth, after which the adopted "child" became an owner of the medicine. On some occasions such a

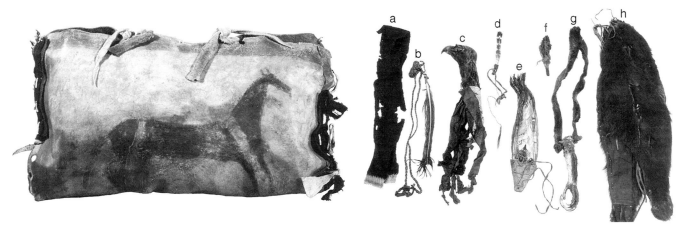

Smithsonian, Natl. Mus. of the Amer. Ind.: 14/6481 (negs. 11219, 11220).

Fig. 7. War medicine bundle that belonged to Two Leggings, River Crow chief. It was made by Weasel Moccasin, who transferred it to Wolf Chaser, who in turn gave it to his younger brother, Two Leggings, when he started to go on war expeditions (Wildschut 1960:51). left, Bundle cover. Weasel Moccasin saw a vision of a black horse in the sky, struck by lightning, which he represented with zigzag streaks in red. The Thunderbird that gave the bundle to him is represented on the cover as the lightning ending in eagle claws and is also represented in the bundle as the eagle head, claws and feathers. right, Bundle contents. a, Strip of blue cloth representing good luck. b, Feather necklace and herb bag tied around the horse's neck to make it run faster and easier. The herbs were used as medicine for the horse to renew the animal's strength. c, Eagle head hung with colored ribbons representing the sky. It was tied to the owner's chest when going into battle, imparting the power of flight, vision, and noiseless yet swift approach. d, Eagle plume attached to a hawk feather that was tied to a horse's tail to make the animal light and fast. e, Eagle feather, worn attached to the back of the head to give the eagle power. f, Swallow, which gave the power to evade the enemy. g, Otterskin strip with an eagle foot attached worn over the left shoulder and under the right arm. The eagle foot symbolizes the lightning and gives the owner the power to pounce on its enemy. h, Bear hair and claws used to fasten around the horse's neck to keep the animal fat and in prime condition (Wildschut 1960:52). Collected by William Wildschut, 1922; width of case 45.7 cm.

medicine father might have sexual relations with the son's wife as part of the transference of ritual power (Voget 1984:40). A dream or vision confirmed the transfer of power and the right of the new owner to become the caretaker of the medicine (Frey 1987:81ff., 95).

Use of medicine bundles, in both private and public ceremonies, was motivated by the pragmatic needs to prolong life, have plenty to eat, forestall and heal disease, increase wealth and population, and gain victories over the enemy. Crow religious organization was diffused among owners of medicine bundles, informal associations of those possessing the same medicine, and society members who had purchased a share in medicines through adoption. The Cooked Meat Singing ceremony brought together those with Rock medicines while Bear Song dancers gathered to dramatize the spirit that dwelt within their bodies. Tobacco, Horse Dance, and Sacred Pipe were adoptive purchase societies (Lowie 1919a, 1922b, 1924). Although medicines for each of these societies were specialized, all promised good luck in war, health, and wealth.

The Tobacco society was by far the most prominent. No Vitals, the legendary leader of the Crow at the time of their separation from the Hidatsa, received (or was told to seek) the gift of tobacco at Devils Lake, in eastern North Dakota (Curtis 1907–1930, 4:44–45, 62). At the creation, Morning Star transformed himself from a human into the sacred tobacco plant, which would help the Crow to overcome their enemies. They were instructed to raise it and were told that their destiny was linked to tobacco and its worship (Denig 1961:189).

After death, some souls were believed to journey to a Crow encampment where life resembled that of the living. Others became ghosts, who appeared as whirlwinds or who gave the call of an owl. Ghosts might bestow a curse by stealing a lock of hair or might give a blessing through a vision. Certain medicine men and women had ghost power enabling them to find lost persons or property (Curtis 1907–1930, 4:60; Lowie 1935:69–70).

Ceremonies

Fall and spring were major ceremonial seasons. In September or October, following a dream instruction received by the owner of a Rock medicine, a Crow band feasted on buffalo meat and pemmican. Through this Cooked Meat Singing they expressed their good feelings and prayed for plenty and happiness in the next year. Bear Song performers also demonstrated their medicine power for the coming year by producing from their mouths horse and buffalo tails, bear teeth, and eggs—signs of their in-dwelling spirits. Spring was the time to unite for Tobacco planting, followed by adoption rites. Spring thunder signaled a reawakening and the time to open medicine bundles during full moon ceremonies.

Sun Dances, pledged by mourners seeking revenge against an enemy tribe, usually took place in late spring or summer. The ceremony shared basic elements with many Plains tribes, but the Crow Sun Dance (*aškíššírissu·a* 'temporary-lodge dance') was a considerably modified version of the Hidatsa Hide Beating ceremony (Bowers 1965:308–323; Spier 1921; Voget 1984:79). The entire tribe united to focus their medicine powers to gain victory over the enemy. To achieve this, pledger and people placed themselves under direction of an owner of a powerful Sun Dance bundle, which contained the Sun Dance manikin that was central to the ceremony. The "whistler" (pledger) danced before the manikin, which was displayed in a hoop decorated with eagle feathers and tied to a cedar tree. He danced in place on a bed of white clay and blew prayer wishes through an eagle-bone whistle. Young men pierced themselves or dragged buffalo skulls in the hope of receiving medicine power. When the pledger saw the manikin turn black, he knew his revenge had been granted and the ceremony ended (Curtis 1907–1930, 4:67–83; Lowie 1915b:7–50, 1935:297–326; Voget 1984:77–128).

No religious ceremony, vision quest, mourning fast, or war party was undertaken without a Sacred Sweat. Men of a war party sought out renowned warriors who in a vision quest had received the gift of Sun's most powerful sweatlodge made of 104 willows. All medicines had to be protected from menstruants to avoid offense to a medicine father, and some women withdrew to a makeshift shelter during menstruation.

In Crow belief disease was caused by spirits angered by breaking of a taboo, and by malevolent ghosts or humans. Healers applied herbs, massaged, and sucked bad substances from patients using tubular pipes. Others specialized in healing wounds. Sorcery was practiced with imitative magic and spells (Lowie 1935:62–65).

Culture, 1883–1980s

The old life came to a sudden end, filled with hunger, fruitless searches for buffalo, and removal to the reservation. With the establishment of Crow Agency in 1883, rules forbade horse raids, scalp and war dances, and the Sun Dance. To hunt off the reservation required a pass from the agent. Indian police, answerable to the agent, picked up anyone breaking rules and took them to the Court of Indian Offenses for trial, where offenders were punished with fines, restriction of rations, or compulsory labor (C.C. Bradley 1972:45–49).

Life was focused on convivial get-togethers and competitive recruitment of Hot Dance and Crazy Dog societies—both purchased from the Hidatsa around 1875—and the reliving of war experiences (vol. 4:177) when Cheyenne and Sioux arrived to barter beaded vests, gauntlets, and hard-soled moccasins for horses (Lowie 1935:206–214; Wildschut 1959:11–12, 21–23). In the early reservation years a few young men continued to sneak out on horse raids or to pursue Piegan raiders. In 1887 Wraps Up His Tail aroused the young men with the claim that he had a sword with power to kill soldiers at a distance. However, the Crow remained virtually unmoved by the Ghost Dance religion.

By 1886, 250 Crows farmed individual allotments, but the system introduced by the Dawes Severalty Act of 1887, which scattered the land holdings of husband, wife, and children, created dependency rather than a solid family economy (C.C. Bradley 1972:62). The 160 acres alloted a family head could support no more than 16 head of cattle. Inheritance laws further diffused holdings in multiple heirship, and consequently lease income arranged through the Indian agency became basic to family economy.

By 1905 government boarding schools at Crow Agency and Pryor accommodated some 225 pupils. Between 1886 and 1907 Roman Catholic mission schools were established at Saint Xavier, Pryor, Lodge Grass, Crow Agency, and Wyola (Watembach 1996), and the Baptist Home Mission School opened in Lodge Grass in 1903 (C.C. Bradley 1972:83–91). Beginning in 1883 Crow children also were sent to Carlisle Indian School in Pennsylvania.

By the 1890s, the most visible changes in Crow culture occurred in technology; only women's skills in food processing, crafting of skin clothing, and beadwork remained (fig. 8). Social organization and religion changed more slowly and were crucial in forging an adaptive reservation culture that accommodated traditional institutions both to local American culture and to Crow social ends and procedures. Pragmatically, they applied dream blessings of paternal clansmen to the school and athletic achievements of their children. An honor achieved required a giveaway, with maternal clan members distributing gifts to a child's clan fathers and mothers.

The Tobacco society (fig. 9) continued to be the focal point for maintenance of Crow identity (Curtis 1907–1930, 4:64; Lowie 1919a:135). Adoption into the Tobacco worship remained highly prestigious, calling for a vast expenditure of blankets and other wealth. Additions to the reservation culture emphasized the continuing importance of traditional religion and medicine healers. Peyotism was brought from the Northern Cheyenne in 1910 (Kiste 1965), and in 1941 the Eastern Shoshone Sun Dance was introduced. Both became important religious forces, including women as well as men in their ceremonies.

Secular dances, such as the Push Dance, invented by Crows around 1900, were firmly established in the social dance repertoire. Imported dances stressing adoption or payment to an owner for performance—Woman Chief's dance, introduced by a Gros Ventre woman married to a Crow; Long Lodge, purchased from the Nez Perce; Elk Lodge, purchased in association with the Eastern Shoshone Sun Dance—each flourished for a decade or two, then faded (Voget 1987a). The Crow Fair, initiated in 1904 (fig. 10) to encourage farming and education, developed into an annual fall event celebrating the start of the Crow new year. The fair featured Indian dance and dress competitions, rodeo events, and horse racing.

In the early 1900s the Crow were receiving the last of the original allotments and were giving up formal matrilineal descent and inheritance and taking on English sur-

Fig. 8. Women's activities. left, Cutting up meat from cattle issued on ration day at Crow Agency, Mont. Photograph by Henry R. Locke, © 1895. top right, Beading a floral design. Photograph by Charles J. Belden, probably 1920s. bottom right, Ration ticket bags with beaded designs. Length of left 16.2 cm, other to scale; collected by George A. Dorsey before 1903.

top, Smithsonian, NAA: 3434-e-2; bottom, Amer. Mus. of Nat. Hist., New York: 50.1/3958 a–b.

Fig. 9. Tobacco Society. top, Interior of the society's ceremonial tepee, which was made of the covers of 2 ordinary-size tepees. Identifications: 1, Sees Pretty; 2, Knows Horses; 3, Old Nest; 4, Black Bird; 5, Knows Otter; 6, Bird in the Cloud; 7, See Buffalo; 8, Medicine Tail; 9, Packs Hat; 10, Packs Arrows; 11, Bear in the Middle; 12, Long Bear with drum (his short hair indicates mourning); 13, unidentified boy; 14, Black Tail; and 15, Stops. Photographed 1890–1895. bottom, Moccasins made of hide, with beaded designs on the vamp and carved dewclaws attached to the outside edges. The beaded design may represent tobacco seeds. Collected by Robert Lowie, 1910; length 24.5 cm.

names and legalities. Between 1916 and 1920 the Crow drew up a list of enrolled members, in the process adopting Indians from various tribes who were married to Crow and resided on the reservation. They also sent volunteers to World War I and sold off many horses to aid agricultural production. After World War I the Crow distributed all unalloted farming and grazing land to thwart opening the reservations to non-Indian settlement. Individual allottees averaged 900 acres, but the Crow Act of 1920 created a class of unallotted landless Crow born after December 1921 (C.C. Bradley and S.R. Bradley 1974:23). Robert Yellowtail, who negotiated on the land issue, was reservation superintendent 1934–1945.

In 1948 the Crow adopted a constitution specifying a form of government based on a general council. Tribal government was formalized with a tribal chairman and other officers. The executive council was made up of two representatives from six districts and two for off-reservation Crow. Any male of 21 years and any female of 18 years could vote and take part in the general council. In the 1990s the voting age for males was lowered to 18. Women began to play a greater role in politics after World War II, and in 1955 two women were elected tribal delegates.

During World War II the Crow pledged their resources and sacrificed themselves in the Sun Dance to safeguard their "soldier boys" and to bring victory over the "Iron Hats" (Germans). Crows also served in the Korean and Vietnam wars (fig. 11). These years marked a watershed in Crow relations with non-Indians, which resulted in striking changes to their reservation culture. Some veterans urged the Crow to begin economic development of their reservation. In a political struggle that divided the tribe, the Crow sold Bighorn canyon land for the Yellowtail Dam (completed in 1965) to generate per capita payments and to further economic development. The land sale produced

709

Fig. 10. Crow celebrations. top, 4th of July processional. Photograph probably at Lodge Grass, Mont., by William A. Petzoldt, 1904. left center, Business committee at Crow Fair. left to right: Frank Shane or Joe Cooper; Frank Shively or Will Cashen; possibly Holds the Enemy; Two Leggings; chief Medicine Crow; possibly See with His Ears; Birds All Over the Ground or High Fish; Plenty Coups; and Spotted Jack Rabbit. Photograph by Norman A. Forsyth, about 1907–1908. right center top, Crow dance at Crow Fair, with drummers to the right. right center bottom, Food line at giveaway. right center, Photographs by Fred Voget, Crow Res., Lodge Grass, Mont., 1940. bottom left, Family blessing a Pendleton blanket by dancing over it before it is "thrown away." left to right: Dennis Beaumont; 2 unidentified children; Phillip Beaumont, Jr., holding a money tree; Ronnie Beaumont; Hugh Little Owl; and Dallas Bird Hat. Photograph by Michael Crummett, Crow Agency, Mont., 1977. bottom right, War Bonnet Dance at Crow Fair, celebrating the accreditation of Little Big Horn College. Photograph by R. Landsman, 1990.

$2,500,000 in 1958 with another $2,000,000 judgment added in 1964.

In 1962 the Crow received a $10,500,000 judgment for land acknowledged in the 1851 treaty, but not credited them in the 1868 treaty. With capital available they established an Industrial Development Commission, but the motel and carpet mill they financed were not successful. Reservation economy remained depressed for lack of investment capital and economic planning. In 1965 the majority of resident ranchers who owned over 100 head of cattle were non-Indian men married to Indian women (Bureau of Indian Affairs 1968:20).

The summer All American Indian Days powwow, originally held in association with the Sheridan, Wyoming, rodeo, attracted visitors from throughout the country. In 1954 over 3,000 Indians were present; at this time the Cheyenne performed a part of their Crazy Dog Society, and the Crow revived their Sacred Pipe ceremony.

Beginning in the 1970s clan exogamy was not always observed, along with mother-in-law and son-in-law respect-avoidance and brother-sister respect, but primary kinship reciprocities remained. Brothers-in-law still exchanged expensive gifts, notably horses and gear, and sisters-in-law gave beadwork to one another. At marriage, a son-in-law was outfitted with a horse, saddle, bridle and buckskin clothing and parade gear, while a daughter-in-law was provided with an elk-tooth dress, blankets, and home equipment, including a tepee.

The giveaway, centered on the health and luck of a paternal clan "child," was the central institution that drew clan members actively and respectfully into kinship reciprocities and conveyed a primary functional importance to clans. Crows earned a reputation for putting on some of the most lavish giveaways on the northern Plains. Distinctive "money trees" appeared at grand giveaways when the grass dance, which the Crow called the Hot Dance, was performed. A man might contribute a money tree to a relative holding a giveaway, attaching one dollar bills to the leafy branches of small chokecherry or cottonwood trees. This uniquely Crow form of giveaway has been practiced off and on since the 1940s.

Kinship terminology accommodated to the American system, and usages combined the patterns of Crow and English

Fig. 11. Warriors and flags. left, Encampment at Lodge Grass, Crow Res., Mont., probably July 4th celebration. Painted tepees with tepee on right, belonging to White Man Runs Him, decorated with a magpie design. The woman on left, wearing a feather bonnet, holding an unidentified flag, may be participating in a ceremony honoring war dead. Women were associated with the strong warrior heritage and often participated in public gatherings honoring soldiers. Photograph by Elsa Spear Byron, 1925. right, Color guard at the Crow Fair parade. William Gros Ventre, World War II veteran, who earned medals, holds the Crow tribal flag, which displays Tobacco Society medicine bundle, sweatlodge, tepee, 2 war bonnets, Big Dipper, Four Sacred Arrows, the sacred pipe, and the sun coming up over the mountains. His Indian names are Rides a Black Horse, the name from his youth, and Bear Protector, the name given by his paternal clan uncles (Charlene James, communication to editors 1995). Next to him is Carson Walks Over Ice, a veteran of the Vietnam war, also known as Buffalo Chief. Photograph by Rachel O'Conner, Crow Fair Grounds, Crow Agency, Mont., 1992.

terminology. By the 1980s Crow referred to mother's brothers and sisters as uncles and aunts, while designating paternal relatives as "clan" uncles and aunts. The distinctive lineal pattern of traditional Crow kin terminology was not always followed; cousins were all called brother, sister, or cousin. A man's sister's children were nephews and nieces, and brother's children were sons and daughters.

Possession of mystical power bestowed by a spirit person or a creator being continued to be central to the Crow orientation to life. Until the 1950s the reservation comprised a multi-religious Christian and traditional community where individuals shifted loyalties and participations in a pragmatic search for mystical influence to resolve immediate personal and family problems.

In the 1980s, Sun was addressed as "Grandfather," and was distinguished from The One Above, First Maker, and the Christian God, called The Maker of Everything (akba·tatdía). Forty to 50 percent of the population participated in the Native American Church (Stewart 1987).

Evangelical Christianity, introduced to the Crow reservation in the 1920s, flourished during the late 1980s when evangelical churches were established in the Pryor, Black Lodge, Wyola, and Reno districts. Some Crow Pentecostals refused to participate in kinship reciprocities and giveaways, they opposed bilingual programs and the teaching of Crow studies in the community college, and they mustered strong opposition to political figures who conformed to traditional Crow expectations.

Most Crows continued to defer to respected elders to direct them to right decisions. The clan father-child relationship formalized the highly respected counselor role of father's clan members, who encouraged proper behavior for a "child." At every turn in health or career, an individual gave gifts and feasts to clan uncles and aunts for their blessings, and they in return honored their nephews and nieces with public prayers and praise songs (Voget 1980, 1984:18–33, 208–209, 1987).

Competition sustained clan identity, in combination with the district rivalries that succeeded band rivalries. In the 1980s, hand games and arrow throwing were the most important of these competitions. The hand game, or "hiding," maintained a singular popularity as a competition among districts. Two male players each hid an elk tooth, while two female players each hid bone hairpipes, about three to four inches long, one marked with black tape. Opponents sought to guess the location of the counters hidden in the hands. Fourteen wooden tallies about 18–20 inches long were placed midway between the two teams, and when one team took all the tally sticks, the game was over. When a team's guessers correctly picked the hands holding the two elk teeth and the two unmarked bones, their opponents surrendered both the elk teeth and the bones and tried their luck at guessing. If a team made a wrong choice, their opponents won one of the tally markers.

The Crow fielded seven teams (Lodge Grass, Black Lodge, Big Horn, Pryor, Wyola, Reno, and No Water) that

competed from October until tournament competition in April and May. In the championship tournaments each district had its own team uniforms and colors.

Other occasions for giveaway, respect, blessing, and wealth exchanges were furnished by a social and ceremonial calendar that included the entire year. The two dancing societies, the Night Hawks and Big Ear Holes or Rees (Arikaras), offered cash and gifts to new members.

Litigation over rights guaranteed by treaties was a constant in Crow political action. In 1981 the U.S. Supreme Court denied that by treaty the Crow owned the bed of the Bighorn River. Since the riverbed was held to belong to Montana, the Crow therefore could not prohibit nonmembers from hunting and fishing within the reservation.

In 1980, with the aid of Montana State University in Bozeman, the Crow tribe established Little Big Horn College at Crow Agency. The appointment of a tribal historian following World War II as well as the initiation of a bilingual program and establishment of an archives in association with the college stimulated collection, codification, and interpretation of materials relevant to Crow culture and history. Oral history compiled by tribal historian Joseph Medicine Crow (1979:67–69) placed Crow history in a religious context, linking the separation of the Crow from the Hidatsa with fulfillment of a divine promise.

The 1990s†

In July 1998, there were 2,282,000 acres within the exterior boundaries of the Crow reservation of which 455,809 were tribal trust lands, 1,013,710 were allotted to tribal individuals in trust, and 709,167 acres were fee (deeded) land. The fee land includes 46,625 acres held by the state of Montana and 28,105 acres owned by the Crow tribe while approximately 95 percent of the remainder is owned by non-Indians (Vianna Stewart, Michael Caprata, and Donna McCurdy, personal communications 1998; Bureau of Indian Affairs. Crow Indian Agency. Land Services Office 1998; Crow Tribe of Indians and United States of America 1994:10; Big Horn County (Montana). Assessment Appraisal Office 1998:3). Indians were the majority population in Big Horn County, where the County sheriff, attorney, and two of the three commissioners were enrolled members of the Crow tribe in 1998.

Political and Economic Situation

One of the major developments of the 1990s was the expansion and continuity of the tribal government, fueled by political and economic factors. It began with the 1988 U.S. Supreme Court decision *Montana* v. *Crow Tribe of Indians*, which directed that $30 million in 1983 to 1988 protested taxes go to the tribe after the court held that the state of Montana could not tax Crow coal. However, the tribe received a setback in 1998 in *Montana et al.* v. *Crow*

†This section was written by Timothy A. Bernardis.

Tribe of Indians et al. when the Supreme Court ruled that the 1976 to 1982 coal taxes paid to the state amounting to $58 million plus hundreds of millions in interest would not be returned to the tribe. In the early 1990s, the tribe began to administer several federal programs, including some formerly administered by the Bureau of Indian Affairs. In 1993, the tribe levied a railroad and utility property tax and established a casino that provided about 60 jobs in 1998 (Denis Adams, personal communication 1998).

The next great influx of dollars began in 1995 with the 1994 settlement of the 107th meridian boundary dispute which resulted from an 1891 federal surveying error leaving some 36,000 acres with great coal reserves outside of the eastern boundary of the Crow reservation with some acreage included instead within the adjacent Northern Cheyenne reservation. As compensation, Congress passed a complicated agreement with the Crow tribe that involves the restoration and exchange of some land and subsurface rights as well as the establishment of a trust fund of up to $85 million. The interest from the trust is to be used for education, land acquisition, economic development, youth and elderly programs, or other tribal purposes (Crow Tribe of Indians and United States of America 1994:15; United States Congress 1994). In May 1998, the tribe signed a contract for a new coal mine on the reservation that could bring in millions including royalties, taxes, and jobs for tribal members (J. Powers 1998:1). Coal taxes on the existing mine brought in large sums.

In the 1960s, tribal employees numbered approximately 10 with a budget mostly for salaries (Denis Adams, personal communication 1998). In the late 1980s, the budget was $200,000–300,000. The fiscal year 1998 budget was approximately $9 million with another $8.8 million in federal programs, and $1.6 million in 107th meridian settlement interest. In addition, the BIA administered another $1 million in tribal land acquisition funds, and enrolled tribal members received approximately $3 million a year in per capita payments from coal royalties and tribal agricultural and oil and gas leases (Crow Tribe of Indians. Finance Department 1998; Loren Old Bear, personal communication 1998). The tribe was by far the largest employer on the reservation and county with approximately 700 employees in 1997 (Little Big Horn College 1997a:1).

Though employment of Crow tribal members increased, it was almost entirely public sector and many of the jobs were low-paying. Per capita income was $4,243 in 1989 (Tiller 1996:400).

In 1997, 15 of 245 businesses in Big Horn County were owned and operated by Crows (Little Big Horn College 1997a:2). Agriculture has historically been the economic mainstay of the area. On reservation trust land in 1997, only 74 of 765 farmers were Indians, while Indian ranchers numbered 60 compared to 116 non-Indians (Bureau of Indian Affairs. Crow Indian Agency 1997:21).

The tribal government granted strong powers to the chairman in 1990. Tribal factionalism, though reduced, remained a factor of everyday life, particularly at election time (Young 1994:A1; Anonymous 1997:1).

Cultural and Social Situation

In 1996 language fluency in Crow was estimated at 60 percent of the tribe (Little Big Horn College 1997c:8). In 1995, 85 percent of those 40 and older were fluent (Sharon Peregoy, personal communication 1998); 25 percent of children ages 3–18 spoke the Crow language as their primary language.

The importance of the extended family remained, though relatives were more geographically scattered across the reservation than in previous decades due to district intermarriage and diverse land holdings. The clan system was still fairly strong. The network of clan kinship obligations and responsibilities was observed, especially in regard to giveaways, but also through clan feasts and everyday behavior such as showing respect to clan fathers and mothers, asking for their prayers and guidance, and teasing the children of one's father's clan.

Beginning in the Depression of the 1930s, many Crows moved off their land into towns. In the 1990s, only about one-third of Crow families remained living on the land (John Doyle, personal communication 1998); many raised horses and cattle, and a few farmed. Common land use activities included hunting, picking berries, gathering wood, and cutting sweatlodge frames and tepee poles. Some gathered plants for medicines, foods, roots, and tobaccos. Some fasted, including women. Tribal rituals included the Beaver Dance (Tobacco Society), sweatlodge, "feeding" the river to protect the family, and the Parade Dance at Crow Fair in which the dancers saluted the holy places in the mountains.

The Crow people in the 1990s followed a sociocultural seasonal cycle (Voget 1995:168–201; McCleary 1997:5–6). Winter began with the Christmas and New Year's dances and was the time for storytelling, district hand games, and basketball. Crow high school basketball teams won several state titles in the 1980s–1990s. Preliminary Sun Dance preparations also take place in winter.

The spring brings the championship hand game tournaments, the construction of sweatlodges, graduations, Memorial Day graves decoration, arrow throwing games, and Tobacco Society adoption ceremonies. Interest in the arrow tournaments has waned while Tobacco Society adoptions have increased in the late 1990s (Barney Old Coyote, personal communication 1998).

Summer activities included Sun Dances, fasting, Christian camp meetings and revivals, berry picking, horse racing, rodeos, powwows, and tepee pole cutting. These activities culminate in the gathering of virtually the entire tribe for the annual Crow Fair Celebration, Rodeo, and Race Meet held in August. In the 1990s there was an average of five Sun Dances each summer (Barney Old Coyote and John Pretty On Top, personal communications 1998). The Teton Sioux–style Sun Dance first brought in the late 1980s increased the number of dancers and has even been combined with the Shoshone-Crow style to create a hybrid Sun Dance. Crow Fair has witnessed an increase in attendance of both Crows and visitors with 1,000 to 1,400 tepees in the camp and 20,000 to 30,000 visitors (Bryan 1996:88; Stillman 1994:A6).

Dance society activities continued in the 1990s, especially in the Lodge Grass district. New Way/Christian style Peyote meetings were few with the native Tepee Way assuming dominance. There were about 100 Peyote meetings a year across the reservation. An old ceremony that was revived in the 1980s in the Lodge Grass district and in the 1990s in the Black Lodge district was the Daytime Dance, a part of the historic Grass Dance movement. It celebrates the good fortune of honored individuals with prayers and wishes that those in attendance experience the same good fortune (Barney Old Coyote, personal communication 1998).

In 1998, there were 195 tribal members with associate of arts degrees, 303 with bachelor's degrees, 63 with master's degrees, and 11 with doctorates (Little Big Horn College. Rural Systemic Initiative Program Office 1998). Between 1985 and 1997, 75 percent of the Crow Indian adult population took courses at Little Big Horn College (1997:5, 1997a:1). In 1995, 85 percent of graduates worked on the reservation. Awarded accreditation in 1990 and nationally prominent among the tribal colleges, by 1998 the college had awarded 189 associate of arts degrees while serving many who have gone on to four-year institutions. Of greater importance has been the mission of the college to provide education "in areas that reflect the developing economic opportunities of the Crow Indian reservation community" and its commitment to the "preservation, perpetuation, and protection of Crow culture and language" (Little Big Horn College 1997:9). Some classes and many college services are conducted entirely in the Crow language.

Population

A review of figures supplied by Larocque (W.R. Wood and T.D. Thiessen 1985), Lewis and Clark (Thwaites 1904–1905), Curtis (1907–1930, 4), Leonard (1934), Maximilian (Thwaites 1904–1907, 22–23), and Denig (1961) suggests a population between 8,000 and 10,000 before the smallpox epidemics of 1781. Kroeber's (1939) figure of 4,000 is far too low. Between 1830 and 1870 Crow population approximated 5,000. Population declined from 3,500 in 1881 to 1,826 in 1905 and 1,679 in 1930. By 1937 their number increased to 2,175 and to 2,781 in 1950 (U.S. Congress. House. Committee on Interior and Insular Affairs 1953:796).

By 1970 about one-half of the resident population of 3,161 (1,521 males, 1,620 females) lived along creeks and valleys with the remainder concentrated in small towns (Crow Agency, 1,000; Lodge Grass, 806; Wyola, 125). In 1985 enrollees numbered 7,300 of whom 4,500 were residents, leaving some 2,900 living in adjacent towns (Hardin,

714

Billings, Sheridan) and in cities. In 1998 there were 9,814 enrolled members of the Crow Tribe, 7,514 living on or near the reservation (Crow Tribe of Indians. Per Capita Development 1998).

Synonymy‡

Although the origin of the designation Crow is obscure, the names 'raven' and 'crow' have been used interchangeably as a tribal designation since the late eighteenth century. In the twentieth century, the name Crow is used by the Crow themselves in English.

Among other tribes the Crow are most commonly designated as 'crow' or 'raven'. In the Teton, Yanktonai, and Santee dialects of Sioux, the name is $k^h a \gamma i \ wi\check{c}^h a\check{s}a$ 'crow man' (Curtis 1907–1930, 3:141; Buechel 1970:283; S.R. Riggs 1890:260). In the Yankton dialect as well as in Assiniboine, the name is $k^h a \gamma i \ t^h oka$ 'raven enemy' (J.P. Williamson 1902:42; Parks and DeMallie 1988:217), an Assiniboine recording of which is Cawrie or Caunzie, 1809 (Gough 1988–1992, 2:393). The Omaha name is $kkaye \ nia\check{s}iga$ 'crow people' (Fletcher and La Flesche 1911:102, phonemicized); in Ponca one designation is $ka\acute{g}i \ wit\check{s}\grave{a}sa$ 'crow man', a usage borrowed from Sioux (J.H. Howard 1965:134). Two early nineteenth-century recordings indicate that the Hidatsa referred to the Crow, or perhaps to only one division, as 'crow people': Pa-rees-car, phonemicized $p\acute{e}\cdot ricka$, the name of one of four bands, 1804–1805 (Lewis and Clark in Moulton 1983–, 3:428); and par-is-ca-oh-pan-ga, phonemicized $p\acute{e}\cdot ricka \ ruxp\acute{a}\cdot ka$ 'crow people' (E. James 1823, 2:lxxxiv).

Among Plains Algonquian–speaking tribes the same meaning occurs as Arapaho $h\acute{o}u\cdot n\acute{e}nn\acute{o}^{\gamma}$ (sg. $h\acute{o}u\cdot n\acute{e}n$) 'crow, raven people' (Salzmann 1983:72), rendered a-i-nun' 'Crow people' (Hayden 1862:326); Gros Ventre $^{\gamma}\acute{o}\acute{o}\acute{u}n\acute{e}nin\jmath$ (sg. $^{\gamma}ooun\acute{e}n^{\gamma}i$ 'crow person') (Allan R. Taylor, personal communication 1987); Cheyenne $\acute{o}oetaneo^{\gamma}o$ 'crow, raven people' (Glenmore and Leman 1985:202; Petter 1913–1915:582); and Plains Cree $ka\cdot hka\cdot kiwace\cdot n$, compounded of 'raven' and one or more obscure elements (H. Christoph Wolfart, personal communication 1987), cited as Cahcahkewahchow, 1809 (Henry in Gough 1988–1992, 2:393). It occurs as Ojibwa Cacawguieohninnewog (pl., with the addition of $ininiw$ 'man' and $-ak$ 'pl.'), 1809 (Henry in Gough 1988–1992, 2:393) and as eastern Algonquian Fox $ka\cdot ka\cdot kiwaki$ (sg. $ka\cdot ka\cdot kiwa$) (Ives Goddard, personal communication 1993), cited also as Kokokiwak (Gatschet 1882 in Hodge 1907–1910, 1:369). A related form documented for Cree is Kakakoschena, which is given in French as gens de la Pie 'magpie people', 1757 (Bougainville in Thwaites 1903:189).

The Pawnee and Arikara names for the Crow are, respectively, $tuhk\acute{a}\cdot ka^{\gamma}$ and $tUhk\acute{a}\cdot ka^{\gamma}$ 'raven village' or 'crow village' (Parks 1965–1990, 1970–1990). The Kootenai name

‡This synonymy was written by Douglas R. Parks.

is kokṳmkántĭk 'ravens' (Curtis 1907–1930, 7:168). Other names that derive from the term for crow or raven include Kiowa kɔ́ɔ́-k̓yàgɔ̀ (cf. kɔ́ɔ́- 'crow') (Laurel Watkins, personal communication 1979) and Sarcee čosuwá (cf. čosí 'crow') (Eung-Do Cook, personal communication 1990).

'Crow' or 'raven' is the most common designation found is early historical accounts. French Canadian traders referred to the people as Gens des Corbeaux 'raven people'. Examples are nation du Corbeau and Corbeaux, 1795 (Truteau in Parks 1992); Corbeaux (crows), 1796 (Mackay in Quaife 1916:194); Corbeaux, 1805 (Tableau in Abel 1939:160; McKenzie in W.R. Wood and T.D. Thiessen 1985:246); and Cor beaux, 1804–1805 (Lewis and Clark in Moulton 1983–, 3:427). The Spanish form of the name occurs in early nineteenth-century documents; for example, Cuerbos, 1804 (Loisel in Nasatir 1952, 2:739). In English accounts both 'crow' and 'raven' occur, frequently interchangeably (see Nicholas Biddle notes from William Clark in D.D. Jackson 1962:525); for example, Crow and Raven or Ravin nation, 1804–1805 (Lewis and Clark in Moulton 1983–, 3:161, 234, 427); Crows, Crowes, Cro, 1821–1822 (Fowler in Coues 1898:63, 73, 94). In treaties with the U.S. government, beginning in 1825, the designation is Crow (Kappler 1904–1941, 2:244).

The gesture for Crow in the Plains sign language is an imitation of flapping wings, representing a bird in flight. Although there are several variants of this sign, the most common one is to bring the hands, opened flat, to the height of the shoulders, and then move the extended palms up and down (Mallery 1881:458; W.P. Clark 1885:132–133; H.L. Scott 1912–1934).

The Crow name for their tribe is apsâ·ro·ke (H.L. Scott 1912–1934; Medicine Horse 1987:15), in the practical orthography Apsáalooke, apparently a generalization of a former band name. Although the word has no known etymology (Scott 1912–1934), it has been translated historically as a reference to a bird: Ap-sah-ro-kee 'sparrowhawk people' (Beckwourth in Bonner 1856:298); Atsharoke and Aabsaroka 'crow' (de Smet 1843:51; in Chittenden and Richardson 1905, 1:238); and Aub-sa'-ro-ke 'anything that flies' (Hayden 1862:392). Other renditions of the name are Apsarechas, 1805 (Wood and Thiessen 1985:206); Apsaruka (Maximilian 1843:174); Arp-Sar-co-gah, 1804–1805 (Lewis and Clark in Moulton 1983–, 3:427); Äpsárräkä (Everette in Pilling 1885:942); Hapsaroke (Burton 1861:151); Up-sa-ro-ka (Long in E. James 1823, 2:lxxix); and Upsàraukas (Browne in Beach 1877:83). The designation was also borrowed into Eastern Shoshone, in which it was recorded as Hapsa-ro-kay (Gebow 1868:8), Up sa ro ka (G.W. Hill 1877:101), and Ap sair e ca (Moore 1860 in Tidzump 1970:109). It was borrowed into Teton Sioux as psáloka (Buechel 1970:446, phonemicized).

Perhaps the earliest European recording of a name for the Crow is Beaux Hommes, or Handsome Men, 1744 (La Vérendrye in Burpee 1927:409), which is the French rendition of the Plains Cree name cited as Owilinioek, 1757

(Bougainville in Thwaites 1908:189). That form is probably phonemicized as owe·liliniwak 'well-arranged people' (David H. Pentland, personal communication 2000), a reference to the Crow reputation for handsome grooming and clothing. The same name for the Crow occurs as Gros Ventre ʔóounénnɔh (sg. ʔóounénʔi) (A.R. Taylor 1994, 1:190), first recorded as HOw win nin nin (with initial H and final syllable nin crossed out in the manuscript) (Fidler 1800–1801: fo.17 br). A subsequent, late eighteenth-century designation current among Canadian traders was Rocky Mountain Indians (David Thompson, François-Antoine Larocque, Charles McKenzie in W.R. Wood and T.D. Thiessen 1985:114, 206, 292).

Several tribal designations for the Crow refer to their hairstyle. Both Osage hpe-kázạce and Kansa ppe-gázạǰe designate the Crow as well as the Nez Perce, and perhaps Sahaptins in general, referring to the way in which the hair was braided on either side of the forehead (Robert L. Rankin, personal communication 1993). The Osage name has been misanalyzed as comprising an unknown element plus the form for 'upland forest' (La Flesche 1932:127). The Comanche designation is aʔa·ni· 'horns' (Casagrande 1954–1955, 2:231; Robinson and Armagost 1990:11), recorded as Áa (sg.) (Curtis 1907–1930, 19:229), and apparently also refers to the Crow hairstyle. The same name occurs in Eastern Shoshone, recorded there as Ah' ne (Ballou 1880–1881), Aah (G.W. Hill 1877:101), and Ah (G. Stuart 1865:25).

The designations referring to the Crow hairstyle are reflected in a variant Plains sign language designation for the tribe, in which the sign for a flying bird was followed by a sign with the hand, fingers closed, placed in front of the forehead and raised vertically several inches to imitate the upright forelock of Crow men (H.L. Scott 1912–1934).

Several tribal names are of limited provenience and are etymologically obscure. The Plains Apache name tá-dí-kʰạ̀ has no known etymology (Bittle 1952–1953). The Blackfoot designation has two variants, issapówa and ssapó (Frantz and Russell 1987:97; Allan R. Taylor, personal communication 1993). This form, which through folk etymology has been incorrectly translated as 'gut' (Curtis 1907–1930, 18:187) or 'marrow gut people' (H.L. Scott 1912–1934), actually has no known etymology (Allan R. Taylor, personal communication 1993). The Nez Perce designated the Crow Ishúhẽ (no meaning) but gave them the nickname Tsáplĭshtake 'pasted on', a "reference to the custom of increasing the length of the hair by attaching other strands of hair with gum" (Curtis 1907–1930, 8:163). The designations of several Plateau tribes were the same, all with no known meaning: Flathead Stĕ́chi, Spokane Stắmchi, Kalispel Stĕ́chi (Curtis 1907–1930, 7:165); Salish Stĕ́ămtshi (W.J. Hoffman 1886:371); Kalispel Stèmchi (Giorda et al. 1877–1879, 2:81); Okanagan Stimk (Gatschet 1884 in Hodge 1907–1910, 1:379).

The Mandan called the Crow hreró·ka (Maximilian in Thwaites 1904–1907, 24:249; Parks 1987, phonemicized), a term given in the nineteenth century as one division of the tribe. The Hidatsa used the same name, Haideróhka and Haideróhke 'those who dwell in the middle', which was recorded as designating both the name of the Crow tribe and one of its divisions (Maximilian in Thwaites 1904–1907, 24:275).

In the late nineteenth and twentieth centuries the Hidatsa name for the Crow was *kixa ihcá* 'paunch pouter' (W. Matthews 1877:220; Parks 1987; A. Wesley Jones, personal communication 1993).

Divisions

• RIVER CROW   The native name of the River Crow is *wirrê·sape·re* 'dung on the river bank' (Randolph Graczyk, personal communication 1994), which appears variously as Mine-set-peri, 1850 (Culbertson 1952:137); Mĭnĕsupĕ′rik (translated as 'those who defecate under the bank') (H.L. Scott 1912–1934), Minneh-sup-pay-deh (Anonymous Crow vocabulary cited in Hodge 1907–1910, 1:867), Binĕsŭpĕdĕ (Curtis 1907–1930, 4:8), and minésepēre (Lowie 1935:4). One source gives the English equivalent as Sap-suckers, 1850 (Culbertson 1952:137).

In the late twentieth century the River Crow are designated *pe·lačči̇wiraxpâ·ke* 'raven people' (Medicine Horse 1987:16). This designation for one division extends back at least to the late eighteenth century, when the name Pa-rees-car (Crow *pe·račč*é 'raven', Hidatsa *pé·ricka*) was recorded as one of four divisions of the Crow (Lewis and Clark in Moulton 1983–, 3:428). A variant is Crow People, probably a translation of the Hidatsa name (Culbertson 1952:137).

Apparently another designation for the River Crow specifically is the native name cited variously as Hey-re-ro-ka (Hidatsa form) and Hen-ne-no-ta or Hen ne no ka (Crow form), 1805 (McKenzie in W.R. Wood and T.D. Thiessen 1985:248–249); Ererokas and Erreroka, 1805 (Laroque in W.R. Wood and T.D. Thiessen 1985:170, 172); and Haideróhka and Haideróhke 'those who dwell in the middle' (Hidatsa forms; Maximilian in Thwaites 1904–1907, 24:275). It may be the division that Lewis and Clark recorded as Noo′-ta (Moulton 1983–, 3:428). In the twentieth century the name is the Mandan designation for the Crow.

• MOUNTAIN CROW   The English designation Mountain Crow as a divisional name extends to the early nineteenth century, when it appears as Crow Mountain Indians, 1811 (Henry in Gough 1988–1992:463) and later as Mountain Crows (F.D. Pease in ARCIA 1871:420), probably a variant form of Rocky Mountain Indians (see above). The Crow name of the division is *ašarahó* 'many lodges' (Randolph Graczyk, personal communication 1994), which has been recorded as ac'araho (Lowie 1935:4). The English translation Many Lodges has been used as a designation for the division (Curtis 1907–1930, 4:8; Lowie 1913a).

Another frequently recorded Crow divisional name is a rendition of *kixa ihcá* 'paunch pouters' (Hidatsa form; Crow form no longer known), which refers to a legendary quarrel over a buffalo paunch that led to a division of the Crow from the Hidatsa and is associated with the Mountain Crow (H.L. Scott 1912–1934). Examples of the name are Keigh-chy-ta and Kegh chy ta, 1805 (McKenzie in W.R. Wood and T.D. Thiessen 1985:249); Kee-hât-sâ, 1804–1805 (Lewis and Clark in Moulton 1983–, 3:427–428); Kee the resas, 1805 (Laroque in W.R. Wood and T.D. Thiessen 1985:206); and Gihchaitsá (Maximilian in Thwaites 1904–1907, 24:275). The English rendition Paunch Indians and the French equivalent Gens des panse were also used, along with the Crow form cited as Al-la-ka-we-ah, 1804–1805 (Lewis and Clark in Moulton 1983–, 3:428).

The name of the Mountain Crow in Kalispel is Skois'-chint (Giorda et al. 1877–1879, 2:81).

• KICKED IN THE BELLIES   In the late nineteenth century, and perhaps earlier, the Kicked in the Bellies (*e·rarapí·o*, also recorded as ērarapī′o), lived apart from the other two bands and was in the process of becoming a third division (Curtis 1907–1930, 4:8–9; Lowie 1935:4). The name *e·rarapí·o* is preserved in the late twentieth century as the name of the Lodge Grass district on the Crow Reservation (Tushka 1979:69). One source refers to this group as the Whistle Water clan (Curtis 1907–1930, 4:43), the modern Crow form of which (*wirikô·še*, Medicine Horse 1987:15) is different from earlier recordings.

Other band names that appear in historical sources but are unidentifiable are Ashcabeaber (Larocque in W.R. Wood and T.D. Thiessen 1985:206); and A-hâh′-âr-ro′-pir-no-pah and E-hârt′-sâr (Lewis and Clark in Moulton 1983–, 3:428). E-hârt′-sâr is also the name of the Hidatsa, suggesting that there was a Hidatsa division associated with the Crow in the early nineteenth century.

Sources

The most thorough description of Crow society and culture is in Lowie's monographs, summarized in Lowie (1935). Curtis's (1907–1930, 4) excellent description includes accounts of hunts, war parties, and a Sun Dance, and biographical sketches of tribal chiefs. Besides Curtis's classic images, other important photographic works on the Crow include those of Fred E. Miller (O'Connor 1985) and Richard Throssel (Albright 1997). Simms (1903, 1904) presents Crow myths and describes the cultivation of sacred tobacco.

Frison (1976, 1978, 1979) summarizes archeological evidence relative to an early occupation of the Yellowstone-Bighorn region by the Crow, while Mulloy (1942) describes a site on the Yellowstone that he considered transitional in their westward migration. W.R. Wood and A.S. Downer (1977), L.B. Davis (1979), Byrne (1978), and C.F. Taylor (1981) assess evidence with regard to Crow migrations. Studies of Crow history include Hoxie (1995), Bernardis (1986), Algier (1993), Bearss (1970), and C.C. Bradley and S.R. Bradley (1974).

Larocque's sketch of Crow culture in 1805 is the first, and it is evident that he traveled with the Mountain Crow (1910,

1985). Maximilian (1843; in Thwaites 1904–1907, 22–23) supplies details of Crow religion and military organization in 1833–1834, while Leonard (1934) reports a battle with the Blackfoot, mutilation of enemy dead, mourning, and burial. Denig (1930, 1953, 1961) describes the Crow around 1850. Kurz (1937) adds cultural detail and drawings of horse gear and Indian dress. W.P. Clark's (1885) study of sign language includes a sketch of Crow history. The diary of Lt. James J. Bradley (1896–1923), who was with the Crow scouts during the military campaign against the Sioux in 1876, contains information on intertribal relations. Dunraven (1876) offers observations during the transition to reservation life, as does Wagner and Allen (1987).

Biographies of Chief Plenty Coups (vol. 17:255) and of Pretty Shield, a woman (Linderman 1930, 1932), convey insights into Crow life, while Wildschut's account of Two Leggings (Nabokov 1967) is indispensable for understanding the quest for chieftaincy. Voget (1995) gives the story of a Crow woman on the reservation. Marquis's (1928) biography of a White man married to a Crow woman describes the Crow before and during the transition to reservation life. James Beckwourth's (1856) autobiography reveals aspects of Crow life and warfare.

L.H. Morgan (1871, 1877) was the first to record Crow kinship terms and to note their matrilineal descent. His edited journals (Morgan 1959) contain valuable data on the Sun Dance as well as a list of Crow clans and notes on Crow ceremony and customs. Voget (1980) analyzes the persistence of Crow social organization and culture. Old Horn and McCleary (1985) summarize social organization. Real Bird (1997) discusses the clan system.

Lowie (1960 and 1960a) presents a collection of Crow texts and a Crow word-list. Lowie's (1941) linguistic analysis is supplemented by Kaschube (1967) (vol. 17:53). Pierce (1954) and G.H. Matthews (1979) explored Hidatsa-Crow glottochronology. Discussion by Kaschube (1954), Hamp (1958), G.H. Matthews (1959), and Gordon (1972) produced tentative rules governing pitch accent in Crow. Read (1978) analyzed the influence of social factors on language persistence. The U.S. Department of Education at Crow Agency has produced bilingual materials and a dictionary (Medicine Horse 1987). Early Crow language works by Jesuit missionaries are listed in Carriker et al. (1976:25–28).

Wildschut (1959) corrected Lowie's analysis of Crow art based on pieces wrongly assigned and added measurably to the history of Crow art. A special issue of *American Indian Art* (1980, no. 6) includes descriptive analyses of Crow design. Lessard (1984) and P.J. Powell (1988) describe art collections. Logan and Schmittou (1998) analyze art style.

Wildschut (1960) is the most comprehensive description of Crow medicine bundles. Nabokov (1988) discusses the Tobacco Society. Astronomical knowledge is explored by McLeary (1997). Campbell (1927) is basic for the Crow tepee, supplemented by Laubin and Laubin (1977). Laubin and Laubin (1980) is a well-illustrated history of Indian archery. Ehrlich (1937) surveyed mythology for descriptions of Crow culture and extracted a wide range of custom, belief, and technology. Linderman (1931) relates Old Man Coyote stories. Heidenreich (1971) described and analyzed verbal and visual "images" of the Crow expressed in nineteenth-century writings and paintings.

C.C. Bradley (1972) uses archival sources to describe Crow experiences from 1880–1920. Frey (1987) interprets the Crow world view and its influence on life in the 1980s. Voget (1984, 1987) investigates the transmission of the Eastern Shoshone Sun Dance to the Crow in 1941 and the importance of the giveaway. Crow concepts of history are presented by Belue (1991), Old Coyote and Old Coyote (1985), Old Coyote and Smith (1992), and Medicine Crow (1992). Fitzgerald (1991) presents the autobiography of Crow medicine man and Sun Dance reader Thomas Yellowtail (b. 1903, d. 1993). Crummett (1993) is a photographic and textual account of the fiftieth anniversary Crow Sun Dance held in 1991.

Important Crow collections are found in the National Museum of the American Indian and the Department of Anthropology, National Museum of Natural History, Smithsonian Institution; American Museum of Natural History, New York; Museum of the Plains Indian, Cody, Wyoming; Field Museum of Natural History, Chicago. Pieces are found in other museums including The Denver Art Museum; Milwaukee Public Museum; Los Angeles County Museum of Natural History; Little Bighorn National Monument, Montana; Linden Museum, Stuttgart; and the Museum für Völkerkunde, Berlin. Documents from Plenty Coups, the last Crow chief, are in the Plenty Coups Museum, Pryor, Montana.

Sioux Until 1850

RAYMOND J. DeMALLIE

The Sioux (sōō) tribes share common language, history, social organization, and culture. For a century after their first mention by Europeans in 1640 (JR 18:231), the Sioux lived in an area stretching from Mille Lacs to the Missouri River (fig. 1). By the early nineteenth century three divisions were recognized, reflecting geographical, linguistic, and cultural distinctions—Santee, Yankton and Yanktonai, and Teton. This chapter presents the common cultural and historical background of all three groups until 1850.

Language

The unity of the Sioux as a people is most fundamentally reflected in language.* Despite dialectal differentiation represented in systematic sound differences and local vocabularies, all Sioux speakers were intelligible to one another. The Santee and Yankton-Yanktonai called themselves *dakʰóta* while the Teton used the form *lakʰóta*. This difference in pronunciation reflects the systematic sound change that is most frequently used to characterize the differences among the speech of the three divisions: Santee *d* corresponds to Yankton-Yanktonai *d* and *n* and Teton *l*. The speech of the Yankton-Yanktonai, while frequently designated an "*n*" dialect, uses *d* in various contexts, including at the beginning of words. Therefore the historical self-designation of the Yankton-Yanktonai was *dakʰóta*, although some writers incorrectly used "Nakota" to designate this division (Hodge 1907–1910, 2:376; J.H. Howard 1966a) and by the late twentieth century, many Sioux themselves, when speaking in English, used "Nakota" as the designation for the Yankton-Yanktonai. However, the form *nakʰóta* is

*The phonemes of Sioux are: (voiced stops) *b, d, g*; (voiceless unaspirated stops and affricates) *p, t, č, k, ʔ*; (voiceless aspirated stops and affricate) *pʰ, tʰ, čʰ, kʰ*; (glottalized stops and affricate) *ṗ, ṫ, č̇, k̇*; (voiceless spirants) *s, š, x, h*; (voiced spirants) *z, ž, γ*; (glottalized spirants) *ṡ, ṧ, ẋ*; (nasals) *m, n*; (lateral resonant) *l*; (voiced semivowels) *w, y*; (oral vowels) *i, e, a, o, u*; (nasal vowels) *į, ą, ų*; (primary stress) *v́*. The Santee-Sisseton and Yankton-Yanktonai dialects have *d*, which the Teton lacks. Teton has *l*, which the other dialects lack. This phonemic analysis follows Boas and Deloria (1941). For a description of dialectal differences see Parks and DeMallie (1992).

A slightly different phonemic analysis and transcription for Teton (Lakhota) is in "Sketch of Lakhota: a Siouan Language" (vol. 17). There the glottalized spirants are treated as clusters with glottal stop, and the phonetic velar nasal [ŋ] is written (as ň) although it is an allophone of *k*. Both analyses write *g* as a phoneme, for practical reasons and because of pattern symmetry, but it, too, is an allophone of *k*.

properly the self-designation of the Assiniboine and Stoney, who were close relatives to the Sioux, but politically and ethnically separate from them since before the start of the eighteenth century, if not prehistorically (Parks and DeMallie 1992:240–244). The Santee, Yankton-Yanktonai, and Teton spoke three distinct dialects and therefore constituted three distinct social groups. Nonetheless, extensive intermarriage and close associations blurred precise dialect boundaries, and individuals' speech reflected family history and life experiences.

Anthropologists, following government administrators, generally grouped all three Sioux divisions under the designation "Dakota" (see, for example, Dorsey 1897:215; Wissler 1912a; E.C. Deloria 1944; J.H. Howard 1966a; Holder 1970). This gave rise to the forms "Santee Dakota," "Yankton Dakota," and "Teton Dakota" as labels for the three divisions. Scholars tended to minimize use of the term "Sioux" both because it had a foreign origin in an Ojibwa ethnonym and because it was said to mean "snake" and therefore had pejorative connotations. The form "Lakota" could be used by anyone writing exclusively about the Teton (Standing Bear 1928; Grobsmith 1981), while those writing only about the other divisions could use "Dakota" (W.D. Wallis 1947; Landes 1968). However, a cover term for all three divisions remained problematical. Some anthropologists abandoned use of Dakota in favor of Sioux (Hassrick 1964; Nurge 1970; Powers 1972, 1977), recognizing *Sioux* as the most common English designation used by the Sioux and non-Indians alike, as well as serving as the tribal name of most of the reservation groups during the late-nineteenth and twentieth centuries. Therefore, in this volume the term *Sioux* is used in preference to *Dakota*.

Origins

Linguistic reconstruction based on a comparison of terms for natural species in relation to their geographical distribution places the homeland of the proto-western Siouans (Sioux, Dhegiha, and Chiwere groups) west of Lake Michigan, in the area of southern Wisconsin, southeastern Minnesota, northeastern Iowa, and northern Illinois (Munson 1975). Sioux traditions recorded in 1839 recounted an origin near "the northern lakes east of the Mississippi," with the Teton moving westward, followed by the Yankton and Yanktonai, and finally the Santee (J.N. Nicollet in DeMallie 1976:253–254). According to a tradition of the

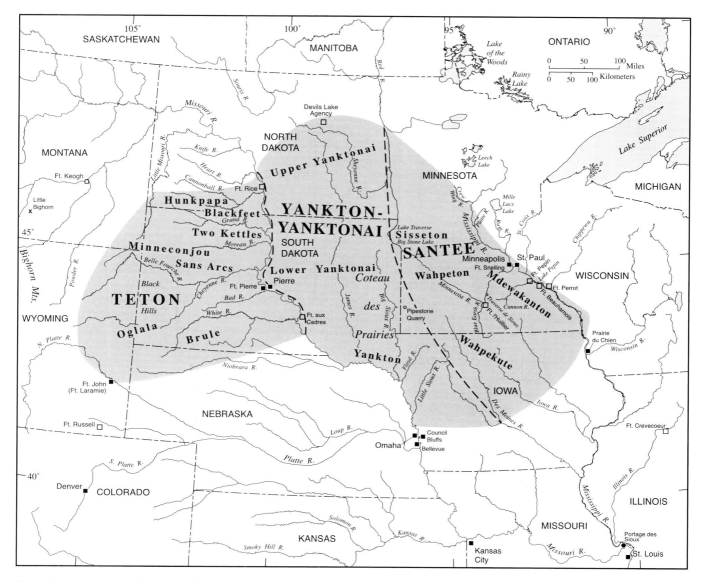

Fig. 1. Sioux territory, early to mid-19th century. Boundaries between the divisions suggest areas of greatest use.

Mdewakanton group of Santee recorded in the midnine-teenth century, "their fathers left the lakes around the head-waters of the upper Mississippi" and moved downstream to the region of the Minnesota River, *"because plenty of buffalo were there"* (ARCIA 1849:1006)

Oral tradition also reported that the Assiniboine split off from a band of Yanktonai (S.R. Riggs 1893:188), but on the basis of linguistic similarities and differences the Assini-boine were no more closely related to any one of the Sioux groups than to the others, suggesting that the split be-tween the Assiniboine-Stoney and the Sioux took place before or at the same time as the differentiation of the three Sioux dialects (Parks and DeMallie 1992:247–248).

Archeology adds nothing to the question of Sioux ori-gins. Sites identified with the prehistoric Sioux in Minne-sota, on the northeastern periphery of the plains, are classified as belonging to the Woodland tradition (Eggan

1952:41; Winchell 1911:385, 408), as are early contact sites (D.A. Birk and E. Johnson 1988).

External Relations Until 1750

In the mid-seventeenth century Sioux territory stretched from the coniferous forests around Mille Lacs, through the deciduous forests and open grassland-forests that fol-lowed the Mississippi and Minnesota rivers, and across the tall-grass prairies of western Minnesota and eastern North and South Dakota to the Missouri River (H.H. Tanner 1987:14, 58). In the heavily forested areas deer were the principal game, but most of Sioux territory was buffalo country. In 1660 the explorer Pierre-Esprit Radisson (1961:134, 142) called the Sioux "the nation of the Beef," because they made their livelihood by hunting buffalo.

719

The eastern Sioux groups at this time hunted buffalo to the south, in the mixed grassland-forest area east of the Mississippi. There they warred with the Illinois, Fox, and other Central Algonquian tribes, all of whom had access to guns supplied by traders, and all of whom depended on the buffalo. This warfare may have caused the Sioux to hunt west of the Mississippi, where they came into conflict with the Iowa, forcing the latter southward. Later the Sioux and the Iowa allied to fight their common enemy, the Fox. The Cree, moving south from their territory north of Lake Superior, and armed with guns from the Hudson's Bay traders, came into contact with the Sioux and Assiniboine. The Assiniboine decided to ally with the Cree to gain access to guns, but the Cree and Sioux kept up a desultory warfare in which, according to Radisson (1961:94), few were killed on either side.

Relations between the Sioux and remnant Ottawa and Huron groups, also driven west by the Iroquois, are well documented by Nicolas Perrot (Blair 1911–1912, 1:159–162), a fur trader with Indians 1665–1699. The refugees settled at Isle Pelée (Prairie Island) in the Mississippi River at the head of Lake Pepin. At first they engaged in trade with the Sioux, but about 1665 the Huron and Ottawa began to war on them in an attempt to expand into Sioux territory. However, the Sioux greatly outnumbered the Huron and Ottawa and drove them back to Lake Superior. Warfare continued until 1672 when a war party said to number 1,000 Huron, Ottawa, Fox, and Potawatomi was defeated by the Sioux (Perrot in Blair 1911–1912, 1:187–190).

In the mid-seventeenth century some Chippewa began to move west from Sault Sainte Marie, to the southern shore of Lake Superior. At first they warred with the Sioux, but later they made peace, sealed by intertribal marriages (Bacqueville de la Potherie in Blair 1911–1912, 1:279). The Sioux allowed the Chippewa to hunt in their territory and in return Chippewa served as trade middlemen with the French. Although this peace continually erupted into warfare, conflicts were temporary and were at a band, rather than tribal, level.

During this period Chippewa society was transforming from an amorphous network of bands into a more tightly structured political system based on patrilineal clans (H.E. Hickerson 1970). The Midewiwin or Medicine Lodge developed as a means of integrating the Chippewa bands into a religious and social network. The easternmost bands of Sioux were affected by these developments and in time adopted the Medicine Lodge along with many cultural traits from their Chippewa neighbors, giving a distinctly Woodlands cast to Santee Sioux culture.

The Sioux lacked direct access to European traders. In 1662 they told Radisson (1961:138) that their doors were always open to him because it was the European traders who "kept them alive" by their merchandise. Guns were essential (fig. 2) to maintain the balance of power among the tribes, and the Sioux were quickly coming to depend on manufactured items—particularly metal goods—for many everyday needs. In 1679 Daniel Greysolon Duluth "planted his majesty's arms" at three Santee villages, declaring himself to be the first Frenchman to visit there (Hennepin 1880:375; Margry 1876–1886, 6:22). Duluth had been sent from New France to establish peace among the tribes on the Upper Mississippi and to establish trade with the Sioux. In 1680 Louis Hennepin, a Recollect priest, and two companions set out from Fort Crèvecoeur, in Illinois, to visit the Sioux. By Hennepin's own account ([1683] 1880:198, 376), the three were taken prisoner by the Sioux and traveled with them until they were rescued by Duluth. Perrot built the first French trading post for the Sioux at Lake Pepin in 1686 and visited the Midwestern tribes attempting to negotiate peace (Bacqueville de la Potherie in Blair 1911–1912, 1:365–367; Folwell 1921–1930, 1:36–37). The post, which became known as "the post of the Nadouessioux," was an important trade center for the Sioux but did little for the cause of intertribal peace.

By providing the Sioux with direct access to trade goods, Perrot's post undercut the Sioux alliance with the Chippewa. Hostilities between them increased as they contested for hunting grounds northeast of the Mississippi River. At the same time warfare with the Fox and other Midwestern tribes intensified.

By the late 1680s the trader and adventurer Pierre-Charles Le Sueur continued trade with the Sioux at Lake Pepin and attempted to maintain intertribal peace. In 1695 he built a new post on Isle Pelée (M.M. Wedel 1974a:159–160). That year Le Sueur escorted a Sioux chief to Montreal who begged the governor to send them more traders (Margry 1876–1886, 6:83). However, in 1696 the government of France closed all its posts west of Michilimackinac (Kellogg 1925:257; Edmunds and Peyser 1993:28). Although illegal coureurs de bois continued the Indian trade, the volume of trade goods diminished.

In 1700 Le Sueur built Fort l'Huillier on the Blue Earth River, a tributary of the Minnesota, to mine what he mistakenly believed to be copper (Margry 1876–1886, 6:69; M.M. Wedel 1974a:162). Some of the Sioux living east of the Mississippi, assuming that Le Sueur had come to trade, were incensed that he located his post west of the river. In retaliation, they robbed two French hunters and fired on the post. The western Sioux disclaimed any responsibility, declaring that they should not be made to suffer for the actions of a "single village that had no good sense," a clear indication of village autonomy and the lack of any overarching political organization. Eventually Le Sueur received beaver pelts from the eastern Sioux in payment for the robbery (Margry 1876–1886, 6:80–81). The post was abandoned in 1702, and for over two decades the Sioux lacked direct contact with the French.

During this period Sioux depended alternately on Chippewa and Fox trade middlemen. In 1714 and again in 1721 the Fox made peace with the Sioux, in part to enlist their support against the Chippewa, who were pushing southwest from Lake Superior, but also for purposes of trade

top, Smithsonian, Dept. of Anthr.: 387,266 (neg. 38,8111B); bottom left, 395,590 (neg. 86-11786); bottom center: 23,725 (neg. 72-11305B and 72-11305); bottom right: 1,935 (neg. 81-11353).

Fig. 2. Firearms. A good supply of firearms gave the Sioux a military advantage over tribes with limited access to such trade, but required the continuing production of surplus hides and meat to trade for powder and lead. The muzzle-loading flintlock was the most common type of weapon through the 1850s and continued in use well after that date. Ammunition for it consisted of lead shot in various forms, often Native-made from lead acquired in trade, hide patches to make the shot fit the bore of the gun, and gun powder. A shot pouch to carry these items, usually with a powder horn attached, was a ubiquitous accessory. top, Northwest trade gun made by the British firm of Parker Field and Co., dated 1868. Length 116 cm. bottom left, Shot pouch with powder container made of cowhorn, buckskin patches strung on a thong, and two forms of lead shot. Collected by Rev. E.W.J. Lindesmith at Ft. Keogh, Mont., in 1881. Pouch 18 cm square. bottom center, Front and side views of a shot mold incised with figures of a snake, a thunderbird, and an elk or deer. Molten lead was poured on a screen inserted in the opening; running a stick against the notches in the handle created a vibration that caused drops of lead to fall into a container of water. Collected at Devils Lake Agency, Dak. Terr., in 1876 by Paul Beckwith. Length, 58.5 cm. bottom right, Shot pouch and shoulder strap made of hide covered with red cloth and beadwork. Collected by G.K. Warren, probably from the Brule in Nebr. in 1855 (J.A. Hanson 1996). Width of pouch, 24 cm.

(Edmunds and Peyser 1993:77–78, 94). In 1726, representatives of the French negotiated a peace between the Chippewa and the Sioux, and in the following year they sent to the Sioux a party of traders and two Jesuit priests who established Fort Beauharnois on Lake Pepin (Edmunds and Peyser 1993:106; Kellogg 1925:308–311). As the French intended, these actions undermined the alliance between the Sioux and the Fox, but the opening of direct trade also undercut the peace with the Chippewa (H.E. Hickerson 1962:69–70).

During the 1730s the explorer Pierre Gaultier de Varennes, sieur de la Vérendrye, financing his search for the Western Sea by trading with the Indians, built posts west and north of Lake Superior. La Vérendrye allied himself with the Chippewa and Cree, and in 1734 his eldest son accompanied a Cree war party against the Sioux. The Sioux were angered that the French provided firearms to their enemies. In 1735 the Mdewakanton began hostilities against coureurs de bois and travelers. In spring 1736 a Sioux war party killed and scalped two Frenchmen, bringing the scalps to Fort Beauharnois where they danced the scalp dance for four days (Thwaites 1906:269–270). That summer a war party of Sioux, seeking the Cree, discovered on an island in Lake of the Woods a party of Frenchmen including the younger La Vérendrye, a Jesuit missionary, and 20 voyageurs. They were all killed and most were scalped, decapitated, and the heads placed on beaver skins (La Vérendrye in Burpee 1927:218–219, 263–264). Escalating warfare between the Sioux and the Chippewa, in which the French, being allied with both tribes, were caught in the middle, and Sioux threats against the French at Fort Beauharnois, led to the abandonment of the post in spring 1737 (Thwaites 1906:270–274).

By 1736 most of the Sioux lived west of the Mississippi. That year the number of Sioux men living east of the Mississippi was 300 compared with 2,000 Sioux on the prairies (Thwaites 1906:247–248). Warfare with the Chippewa had forced the Sioux to abandon their remaining villages around Leech Lake and Mille Lacs, but this did not put an end to the hostilities. An intermediate zone between the Sioux and Chippewa became a contested area that both tribes used for hunting. In the absence of human habitation, white-tailed deer flourished in this area (H.E. Hickerson 1970:64–79; H.H. Tanner 1987:58). Chippewa traditions recounted many victories in the removal of the Sioux west of the Mississippi, and historical accounts have usually attributed the success of the Chippewa to being better supplied with firearms; however, French documents do not corroborate such accounts. Most of the Sioux had already been drawn to the Mississippi and Minnesota river valleys by the availability of buffalo and the advantages for trade with the French (DeMallie 1971:99–101; G.C. Anderson 1980:26–27).

Culture in the Seventeenth and Early Eighteenth Centuries

The division of the Sioux into Santee, Yankton, and Teton, based on dialect and geographical location, was not noted in seventeenth- and eighteenth-century French documents. Instead, the French distinguished only between the Sioux of the East and the Sioux of the West, reflecting their geographical location in relation to the Missisippi River. Judging from the band names given in these accounts, the Sioux of the East were all members of what was later termed the Santee division, while the Sioux of the West represented all three divisions: Santee, Yankton, and Teton.

In 1695, Le Sueur returned to Montreal, taking a Sioux chief and a Chippewa chief. The Sioux leader laid 22 arrows at the foot of the governor of New France, asking that traders be sent to all the 22 villages of the Sioux (M.M. Wedel 1974a:160). Twenty-two Sioux villages are shown on the 1697 map by Jean-Baptiste Louis Franquelin from information provided by Le Sueur (fig. 3). A list of the village names written on the border of the map includes a twenty-third village name, without locating it on the map. Eleven of these villages are indicated as Sioux of the East, 12 as Sioux of the West. Extracts from Le Sueur's journal named 20 Sioux villages (Delisle 1702), noting that they all spoke the same language, of which seven were Sioux of the East and 13 were Sioux of the West. Among the western groups are four given on the Franquelin map as Sioux of the East (table 1). M.M. Wedel (1974a:166) hypothesized that these were villages that moved to be near Le Sueur's fort on the Blue Earth River, although there was evidently much fluidity in village locations and composition during this period.

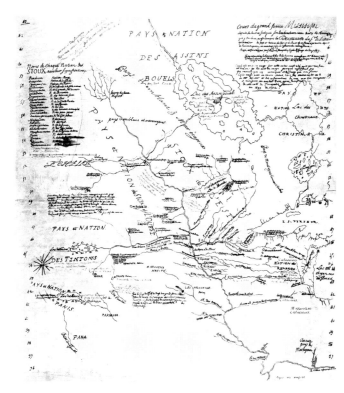

Fig. 3. Northern portion of a map depicting the upper Mississippi River drawn in 1697 by Jean-Baptiste Louis Franquelin with additions in red made in 1699 and 1702 by Claude and Guillaume Delisle on the basis of information dictated by Pierre-Charles Le Sueur. The map labels the "Sioux of the East" and the "Country of the Sioux of the West" on either side of the Mississippi River, the "Country and Nation of the Assinibouels" (Assiniboine) north around present Lake Winnipeg, and the "Country and Nation of the Tintons" (Teton) around present Big Stone Lake. This was the first map to depict the territory of the Sioux. Tracing by Pierre Margry, 1845–1851; original not known to exist.

The Sioux of the East

The territory of the Sioux of the East shown on the 1697 Franquelin map is entirely east of the Mississippi River. Their villages were located around Mille Lacs and on the eastern tributaries of the Mississippi from the Platte to below the mouth of the Crow Wing rivers. Toward spring, the winter camps began to break up as the men set off in small groups to hunt, taking their families with them. An intertribal gathering in the spring was first referred to by the Jesuit Paul Le Jeune in 1640 (JR 18:233). The Feast of the Dead, witnessed by Radisson and Médart Chouart, sieur des Groselliers, in the early spring of 1662, was clearly held during a period of suspended hostilities between warring tribes. Radisson estimated the camp at over 1,500 people from "eighteen several nations," both Siouans and Algonquians. Later, another 1,000 people arrived. Radisson exhorted the Sioux to cease their war with the Cree and convinced them, instead, "to lead them [the Cree] to the dance of union, which was to be celebrated at the death's feast and banquet of kindred." During 14 days of festivities

722

Table 1. Sioux Village Names from Pierre-Charles Le Sueur, 1699–1702

Village Name	French Designation	Retranscription
Sioux of the East		
1. Psinchaton[a]	Nation Rouge 'red nation'; vill.[age] de la folle avoine rouge 'nation of red wild rice'	*psįšátʰų* 'red wild rice village'
2. Ouacpeton[a, b]	Nation de la feuille 'nation of the leaf'	*waxpétʰų* 'leaf village'
3. Ouiatspouiton, Oüiatespouitons[a]	Nation du foyer 'nation of the fireplace'; vill.[age] dispersé en plus[ieu]rs petites bandes 'village dispersed into several little bands'	*oyáte sbútʰų* 'village of people divided into small groups' [?]
4. Psinounaton, Psinoumanitons	N[ation] de la jambe a la folle avoine 'nation who go on foot for wild rice'; vill.[age] des chercheurs de folle avoine 'village of the wild rice gatherers'	*psįʔómanitʰų* 'village that goes on foot for wild rice'
5. Tangapsinton[a]	N[ation] de la grande foll'avoine 'nation of the big wild rice'; vill.[age] de la Crosse 'lacrosse village'	*tʰakápsinčatʰų* 'village at the ball ground'
6. Ouadebaton	N[ation] de La riviere 'nation of the river'	*watpátʰų* 'river village'
7. Songatsquiton, Songasquitons	N[ation] des hommes forts 'nation of strong men'; Vill.[age] du fort 'village of the fort'	*čʰúkašketʰų* 'fortified village'
8. Ocatameneton	N[ation] des Lacs 'nation of the lakes'; vill.[age] de[s] gens qui sont seuls sur la pointe d'un lac 'village of people who are alone on a point in a lake'	[?]
9. Mantanton	N[ation] de la Grosse Roche 'nation of the big rock'; village d'un grand lac qui se decharge dans un petit 'village of big lake that discharges into a small one'	[?]
10. Quiocpeton, Quioepetons	N[ation] renfermée, Nation enfermée 'enclosed nation'; vill.[age] de la decharge d'un lac dans une R.[ivière] 'nation at the discharge of a lake into a river'	*kʰiyúšpatʰų* 'divided village' [?]
11. Mendeouacanton	N[ation] du Lac 'nation of the lake'; village du lac d'esprit 'village of spirit lake'	*mdewákʰątʰų* 'sacred lake village'
Sioux of the West		
12. Chaienaton[c]	N[ation] des hommes accomplis 'nation of accomplished men'	*šahíyenatʰų* 'Cheyenne village'
13. Ouasicouteton	N[ation] du pein percé 'nation of the pierced pine'; vill.[age] de gens qui s'exercent a tirer dans un grand pin 'village of people who practice shooting in a large pine forest'	*wazíkʰutetʰų* 'pine shooter village'
14. Ouidaougeounaton[c]	N[ation] de l'Isle pleine 'nation of the full island'	*wíta . . . atʰú* 'village . . . on island'
15. Mechemeton[c]	N[ation] des errans 'nation of the wanderers'	*ícimanitʰų* 'village of travelers' [?]
16. Hoĥetôn; Hocheton[c]	N[ation] des Mors 'nation of the bit'[d]	*hóhetʰų* 'Assiniboine village'
17. Onghetgechaton, Onghetgéodatons	N[ation] de la fiante 'nation of the dung'	*ųkčékčedątʰų* 'cactus village'
18. Ouidachenaton[c]	N[ation] des Isles pelees 'nation of bald islands'	*wítašnatʰų* 'bald island village'
19. Menostamenaton[c]	N[ation] de la Pomme de terre 'nation of the potato'	*mnó ostąmnatʰų* 'rotten wild potato smell village'
20. Tinton	N[ation] des Prairies 'nation of the prairies'	*tʰítʰųwą* 'prairie village'
21. Isantiton[c]	N[ation] de la Cabane au Couteau 'nation of the lodge on the hill'	*isątʰitʰų* 'knife lodge village'

Village Name	French Designation	Retranscription
22. Hehancton; Hinhanetons	N[ation] de la Pierre 'nation of the stone'[c]	*iháktʰų* 'end village'
23. Touchouaccinton Touchououacsintons	N[ation] de la Perche 'nation of the pole'	*tʰošú . . . tʰų* 'lodgepole . . . village'
24. Psinoutanguienton, Psinoutanghihintons	vill.[age] de la grande folle avoine 'village of the big wild rice'	*psihútʰakiyatʰų* 'very large-stemmed wild rice village'
25. Ouacpecouteton	vill.[age] des gens qui s'exercent a tirer sur des fueilles 'village of people who practice shooting at leaves'	*waxpékʰutetʰų* 'leaf shooter village'
26. Inhanctonouanan, Hinhanetonsouanons	vill.[age] de la pierre separée des autres 'village of the stone separated from the others'	*iháktʰųwąna* 'little end village'
27. Titangongihatons, Titanghaongiaton[f]	vill.[age] de la grande cabane 'village of the big lodge'	*tʰitʰąka . . . tʰų* 'big lodge . . . village'

SOURCE: C. Delisle and G. Delisle 1699-1702 (map); C. Delisle 1702 (Le Sueur memoir). Nos. 1-26 are listed on the upper left of the map; significant alternate spellings from the map and the memoir are noted. Bracketed question marks indicate conjectural forms.
  [a] Given as Sioux of the East on the map, but as Sioux of the West in the memoir.
  [b] Listed on the map but not located on the map.
  [c] Listed on the map but not given in the memoir.
  [d] "Bit" apparently refers to devil's bit, a type of plant of the genus Scabiosa; perhaps the blazing-star, used by Plains Indians as medicine to make horses swift (M.R. Gilmore 1919:133-134).
  [e] "because of a quarry of red stones that they have near them in the middle of a prairie" (C. Delisle 1702:fol. 52).
  [f] Not listed on the map but listed in the memoir.

Radisson mentions "plays, mirths, and battle for sport," games and physical contests, dances, and a feast made "to eat all up. To honnor the feast many men and women did burst." Further, he wrote, they visit the "bones of their deceased friends, for they keep them and bestow them upon one another" (Radisson 1961:136–142). Radisson reported that the Feast of the Dead was celebrated every seven years. Later in the spring, the Sioux returned to their summer villages in the Mille Lacs area.

The Sioux of the East lived in small scattered villages, each comprised of only five to six families, located on both sides of the Mississippi. Their territory was "nothing but lakes and marshes, full of wild oats [rice]." The inaccessibility of the summer villages protected them from their enemies (Perrot in Blair 1911–1912, 1:166–167). Le Sueur noted that their canoes were small and covered with birch bark; they were more easily maneuvered in the marshes and small lakes than were the larger canoes of their enemies (M.M. Wedel 1974a:170).

In addition to these small villages, the Sioux of the East had larger ones to which they returned annually. In 1662, Radisson described one such village as a palisaded town comprised of large lodges, some covered with skins and others with mats. He was told it housed 7,000 people. Lacking wood, they used moss for fires. The Sioux dwellings at the Feast of the Dead were round and constructed "with long poles with skins over them" (Radisson 1961:136). The tent poles were not carried from place to place but were gathered anew at each camping site by parties of young men. Women transported the tent coverings on their backs and were able to set the lodges up in less than half an hour (Raddison 1961:138).

Le Sueur described the Sioux dwellings as made from "several buffalo hides, dressed and sewn together and they take them wherever they go[;] in each dwelling there are usually two or three men with their families" (M.M. Wedel 1974a:165). On the occasion of a feast held at Le Sueur's fort on December 1, 1700, the Sioux joined together four individual lodges to make one large structure that accommodated the 100 men who participated. Le Sueur also noted the use of buffalo robes as carpets inside the lodges.

An anonymous early- to mid-eighteenth century French memoir (E.D. Neill 1890:236) described the lodges of the Sioux of the East, stating that they were made "in sugar loaf shape [conoidal], covered with skins dressed and smoothed, painted with various designs such as sun, calumets, arrows, etc." These lodges were 12–15 feet high, and 60–80 feet in circumference; each housed 12–15 people. The fire was built in the middle. There was only one door, covered by a bear skin.

Taken together, the evidence suggests that the Sioux of the East were living in tepees, usually constructed with buffalo hide covers, much like those of the nineteenth century. The most significant difference appears to be that since transporting them was difficult, each woman carried a portion of a tent cover, several women joining their portions to form multifamily dwellings. No mention is made during this period of the use of dogs as beasts of burden.

When the Sioux returned to their village sites in the spring, they opened cache pits in which surplus wild rice from the last harvest was stored. Wild rice provided them nourishment throughout the year (M.M. Wedel 1974a:170).

According to Le Sueur the Sioux of the East did not cultivate the ground and Hennepin, who was with them in 1680, mentioned only the cultivation of native tobacco. However, Radisson (1961:143) wrote: "They sow corn, but their harvest is small. The soil is good, but the cold hinders it, and the grain very small." Evidence from the *Jesuit Relations* is also conflicting. In 1642 mention is made that the Sioux "harvest Indian corn," but in 1670–1672 the opposite is stated, that the Sioux "know not what it is to till the soil for the purpose of sowing seed" (JR 23:225, 55:169). From the evidence it seems likely that only some of the Sioux of the East practiced horticulture, and only on a limited scale. Tobacco may well have been the most important crop.

During the summer, when the buffalo congregated in large herds, the Sioux gathered together for communal hunts. The hunts were extremely important for they provided the surplus meat to be dried for winter use, as well as the hides for their lodge coverings. When scouts returned after locating a herd, the hunters and their families traveled as quickly as possible by canoe to get near the buffalo, then marched overland on foot, leaving some old men behind to guard the canoes and watch for enemies. Hennepin (1903, 1:290) reported that sometimes 100 to 120 buffalo were killed in a single hunt. The hunters circled the herd and kept the animals milling while they killed as many as possible with arrows. Apparently fire was also sometimes used to encircle the herd. After the kill the buffalo were skinned and butchered, the meat preserved by drying in the sun, the hides cared for, and everything cached; then the group was ready to search for another herd.

Because of the large size of the buffalo herds during the summer, and the long distances between them, it would have been disastrous if careless hunting by a single individual or a small group frightened the herd away before the communal hunt. The hunts were therefore controlled by the chiefs for the common good, and anyone who went hunting before the buffalo surround took place was liable for punishment. These sanctions were strictly enforced by appointed police. Hennepin (1903, 1:279–280) described them as carrying clubs, overturning the lodges of the offenders, and confiscating their food.

After the communal hunts, the Sioux of the East returned to their villages in the lake country for the harvest season. Wild rice stalks were tied in bundles to protect the grain from wild fowl; when ripe, the bundles were untied and the grain beaten with clubs to fall into birchbark canoes. The wild rice was then dried, threshed, and winnowed, and part of it was stored in the underground caches (Radisson 1961:139–140; Hennepin 1903, 1:224). Whatever corn was grown was probably eaten as soon as it ripened. Various roots, fruits, and berries were gathered and eaten fresh, or preserved by drying (Hennepin 1903, 1:256; Bacqueville de la Potherie in Blair 1911–1912, 2:73).

As winter approached, the Sioux of the East moved their camps northward into the wooded areas. There they trapped beaver, hunted deer, and fished (Radisson 1961:143; Hennepin 1903, 1:230, 256).

The Sioux of the West

The Sioux of the West were first mentioned in 1679–1680. According to Hennepin (1903, 1:223), the Sioux of the East told him that 50–75 miles above the falls of Saint Anthony (present Minneapolis), during certain seasons, lived the "Nations *Tintonha,* that is, *The Inhabitants of the Meadows.*" While living with the Sioux of the East he met some of these Sioux of the West, whom he characterized as a people allied with them, "with whom they had danced the calumet" (Hennepin 1903, 1:266–268). He learned that the visitors had walked four "moons" (months) in order to reach the Sioux of the East. They told him that in the western country there were few forests, and that sometimes they made fires out of dry buffalo dung over which they cooked their food in earthern pots, since they had no metal ones.

In 1700–1701 Le Sueur provided more detail on the Sioux of the West. He said that they lived "only by the hunt" and roamed on the prairies between the upper Mississippi and the Missouri rivers where canoes were not needed. They practiced no horticulture and did not gather wild rice. They had no fixed villages. All their travel was by foot (M.M. Wedel 1974a:165–166).

Social Organization

During the late seventeenth and eighteenth centuries the picture of Sioux society that emerges from the literature is one of small village groups held together by common language and customs. The number of villages was variously reported as 40 in 1660 (JR 46:69), 20–23 in the 1690s (Le Sueur in M.M. Wedel 1974a:163), and 20–27 in the early eighteenth century (E.D. Neill 1890:235). According to Le Sueur, there was at least some territoriality, the eastern and western groups recognizing the Mississippi River as the boundary between them. Le Sueur noted that the Sioux of the East were the "masters of all the other Sioux and the Ioways and Otos because they are the first with whom we traded and to whom we gave arms so that they are rather well armed" (M.M. Wedel 1974a:166).

Sioux villages were bands that traveled about independently of one another. The small communities described by Perrot (in Blair 1911–1912, 1:166), consisting of only five or six families, may be taken as a lower limit. The dispersion of the Sioux of the East into many small villages probably related to the need for each extended family to have access to a large enough area of the wild rice marshes to make the harvest profitable. At other times of the year, particularly during the spring gatherings and summer buffalo hunts, several villages came together. The buffalo-hunting party of Sioux of the East that Hennepin (1903, 1:272) accompanied in

July 1681 numbered 250 men (80 lodges, housing 130 families). Trading posts also served as a resource around which the Sioux gathered. The Yanktons who wintered with Le Sueur at his fort on the Blue Earth River numbered 150 lodges; the Wahpekute Santees, 60 lodges. The next spring, May 1701, Le Sueur wrote that there were 200 lodges camped near the fort (M.M. Wedel 1974a:170).

There were no indications of any type of unilineal organization. Boys were named after elders of the father's family, while girls were named after the mother's family (Neill 1890:237). Radisson (1961:137) observed status distinctions differentiating young men from elders. He described a formal procession, led by young men whose faces were painted and who wore crow skins at their belts, clearly the prototype of the "crow belt" bustles worn by some of the nineteenth-century men's societies. The elders followed, their faces unpainted, and carrying their pipes.

Two types of chiefs were recognized. Council chiefs were the village leaders, while war chiefs were both leaders in war and conjurors, prophets of the future who were called "those who seek after truth in the dark," according to the anonymous memoir (E.D. Neill 1890:230, 238). The families of chiefs apparently had higher status than others. Sometimes the daughter of a chief would marry much later than the usual age (E.D. Neill 1890:229). Hennepin (1903, 1:214) reported that hunters took the best part of the game that they killed and presented it to the chief as an offering to the sun. Chiefs, however, did not possess any coercive authority. For example, when Hennepin (1903, 1:271–272) asked a chief to bring his band and travel with him to meet Duluth, the chief "heard my Proposal, and was willing to embrace it; but those of his Band wou'd not let him."

There were two other types of medicine men. "Those who strive against death" were old men who were conjurors (apparently in matters not involving war) and curers, doubtless religious curers. "Those who dress wounds" were more strictly herbalists and healers (E.D. Neill 1890:230).

Hennepin (1903, 2:653) reported the existence of men among the Sioux who, from the time they were youths, wore women's clothing, never married, and performed women's work. Such men, believed to be sacred, played essential roles in ceremonies and councils.

Kinship and the Life Cycle

What little information appears in seventeenth- and eighteenth-century accounts concerning the Sioux kinship system accords with the pattern documented in the nineteenth century. The father and father's brother were classed together, as were mother and mother's sister. Father's sister and mother's brother were called by aunt and uncle terms (E.D. Neill 1890:229).

Polygyny was commonly practiced. A Sioux man was not considered worthy of marriage until he had killed an enemy (M.M. Wedel 1974a:165). Marriage was preceded by a period of courtship lasting perhaps three months (E.D. Neill

1890:229). During this time the man visited the girl nightly, making presents to her parents. Sexual relations were not permitted during courtship. If the union was approved, one night the man would arrive at the girl's lodge, fire his gun at the doorway, then hand it to one of her near relatives (evidently as gift). Then he led the girl away (E.D. Neill 1890:229). According to Radisson (1961:142–143), "the maidens have all manner of freedom, but are forced to marry when they come to the age," and he reported that women were respected according to the number of children they had borne.

Sometimes a man terminated a marriage by sending his wife back to her parents' lodge. One man might offer his wife sexually to another man as proof of friendship, and refusal of this offer was taken as an insult. In the case of adultery, the husband might cut off his wife's nose, ears, or hair. A wronged husband might give a feast in honor of the guilty man; "They do this so as to kill him" (E.D. Neill 1890:229). Radisson (1961:142) also mentions cutting off the nose or "crown of the head" of a man as punishment for adultery.

In the case of murder, the victim's nearest relatives were obliged to revenge the death. This might result in a brawl during which several more men were killed. Before such a quarrel developed into a blood feud, however, the elders of the two families would agree to put an end to it. The last murderer would undergo a ritual of forgiveness, and doubtless of adoption into the family of his victim (E.D. Neill 1890:234).

The dead were either placed on scaffolds or buried in the ground. If a person died while on a journey, the body might be burned and the ashes preserved. The dead were greatly respected and probably feared. After a man's death a "Crow feast" was held at which the participants emulated the call of that bird as well as its habits, eating without using their hands. The purpose was to send the soul of the deceased to the country of souls (E.D. Neill 1890:233, 229–230). Both Radisson (1961:142) and Hennepin (1903, 1:241, 255) recorded that the bones of the dead were sometimes preserved, honored, and carried on war expeditions. According to Le Sueur, a person was believed to possess three souls. After death the good soul went to the warm country, the bad soul to the cold country, while the third remained with the body (M.M. Wedel 1974a:165).

Peacemaking and Adoption

Adoption ceremonies involving the red pipestone calumet or feathered "reed" played an important part in intertribal relations during this period. According to Perrot, when the pipe was "sung" for a person of another tribe, "they render him who has had that honor a son of the tribe, and naturalize him as such" (Blair 1911–1912, 1:185). The calumet ceremony was held to be a very sacred ritual, compelling the suspension of hostilities between the groups involved, since the person of another tribe was adopted not just as an individual but as a representative of his tribe. Regarding the calumet itself, Perrot wrote that the Sioux "believe that the sun gave it to the Panys [Pawnees], and that since then it has been communicated from village to village as far as the Outaouas [Ottawas]" (Blair 1911–1912, 1:186). The calumet was thus a symbol of peace; it was presented to travelers to give them safe passage among the Midwestern tribes. Hennepin (1903, 1:228, 236–237) noted that a calumet was also symbolic of war; men who wished to fight the enemy danced the calumet of war.

Hennepin (1903, 1:251–252, 2:476–477) described a formal adoption ritual. The Sioux took Picard du Gay, one of Hennepin's companions, attached feathers to his hair, placed a gourd rattle in his hand, and had him sing. Individuals adopted in this manner, Hennepin wrote, were "cherished as if they were natural relatives" and were called by kin terms. Captives were adopted to take the place of deceased relatives; Hennepin and his two companions were adopted by two of the chiefs in place of sons who had been killed in battle. Hennepin reported that he was called "brother" by the chief of one village, "uncle" by another man, and so on. Once adopted, he was integrated into the entire kinship network.

History, Mid-Eighteenth to Early Nineteenth Centuries

During the eighteenth century all the Sioux divisions shifted their territory westward. Among the factors involved in this movement were pressures from the better-armed Chippewa and Cree; the need to follow the buffalo herds, whose range was contracting steadily westward; and the attraction of traders on the Des Moines, Mississippi, and Missouri rivers (S.R. Riggs 1893:168–182; G.C. Anderson 1980). The writings of Jonathan Carver concerning his 1766–1767 journey, during which he wintered with a Sioux village on the Minnesota River, reported ongoing hostilities between the Sioux and Chippewa, despite periodic attempts to insure a truce (J. Parker 1976).

Trade opportunities for all the Sioux increased after 1763. English traders from Michilimackinac visited the Mississippi and Des Moines rivers, competing with Spanish traders from Louisiana. In 1774 Peter Pond, an independent trader, reported that the Midwestern tribes and resident French traders met at Prairie du Chien in the fall and spring for festivities that included ball games. Boats arrived from Louisiana with trade goods, including wine, ham, and cheese to supply the French and trade with the Indians. Pond spent the winter trading with the Sioux on the Minnesota River and the next spring, at Prairie du Chien, he presented them with three wampum belts that he brought from Michilimackinac. Some of the Sioux chiefs returned with Pond to Michilimackinac where, with a number of Chippewa chiefs, they signed a treaty that set the Mississippi River as the boundary between the two tribes' hunting grounds (Gates 1965:45, 50).

Traders from Hudson Bay and Montreal came to Red River and to the Mandan and Hidatsa villages on the Upper Missouri (W.R. Wood and T.D. Thiessen 1985). French voyageurs from Saint Louis also carried trade directly to the Indian villages on the Missouri. Jean-Baptiste Truteau, for example, spent several years on the Des Moines trading with the Yankton. In the 1790s, trade expeditions organized in Saint Louis, including one led by Truteau, brought manufactured goods up the Missouri River as far north as the Mandan (Parks 1993).

Yet the majority of trade goods reaching the Sioux did so through Indian middlemen. By the late eighteenth century a gathering took place each May on the James River, where the Santee, Yankton, and Yanktonai brought large quantities of trade goods, including guns and ammunition, as well as catlinite pipes and walnut bows, to give to the Teton in exchange for horses, tepee covers, buffalo robes, and antelope skin clothing (Lewis and Clark in Moulton 1983–, 3:412–413; Tabeau in A.H. Abel 1939:121–122). This trade fair seems to have supplanted older spring gatherings farther east on the Minnesota River, as reported by Carver in 1767 (J. Parker 1976:116–117). According to the trader Pierre-Antoine Tabeau, as many as 1,200 lodges came together at these gatherings. However they were obtained, by the late eighteenth century the material culture of the Sioux was heavily dependent on European manufactured goods.

This westward movement of the Sioux brought about cultural changes, many of which developed from contact with other tribes, including the Cheyenne and the Arikara. The Cheyenne, or at least some of them, still lived in earthlodges on the Sheyenne River when pressure from the westward-moving Sioux pushed them to the Missouri. The Cheyenne, according to Carver, had horses in 1766 (J. Parker 1976:137–138), but he makes no mention of them among the Sioux. Pond, however, mentions that the Yankton and other Sioux on the prairies in 1774 had a great many horses, used for both hunting and carrying baggage (Gates 1965:57–58). The adoption of horses by the Sioux during this period was a crucial innovation that fit into the old nomadic buffalo-hunting economy and can be characterized as an intensifier of earlier cultural patterns (Wissler 1914a). Horses were the major factor shaping changes in Sioux culture (fig. 4). During this time the Sioux developed cultural traits that became central to Plains culture, doubtless incorporating old elements with new ones borrowed from other tribes. These included the intertribal pipe adoption ceremony and the Sun Dance (Truteau in Parks 1993).

Santee

After the Santee abandoned the Mille Lacs region in the mid-eighteenth century, the Mdewakanton settled on Rum River, and only a few years later, still under pressure from the Chippewa, they moved the last of their villages to the Mississippi and lower Minnesota rivers. The Wahpeton built their villages on the Minnesota, beyond the Mdewakanton. The Sisseton moved farther up the Minnesota to Big Stone Lake and Lake Traverse, where by 1800

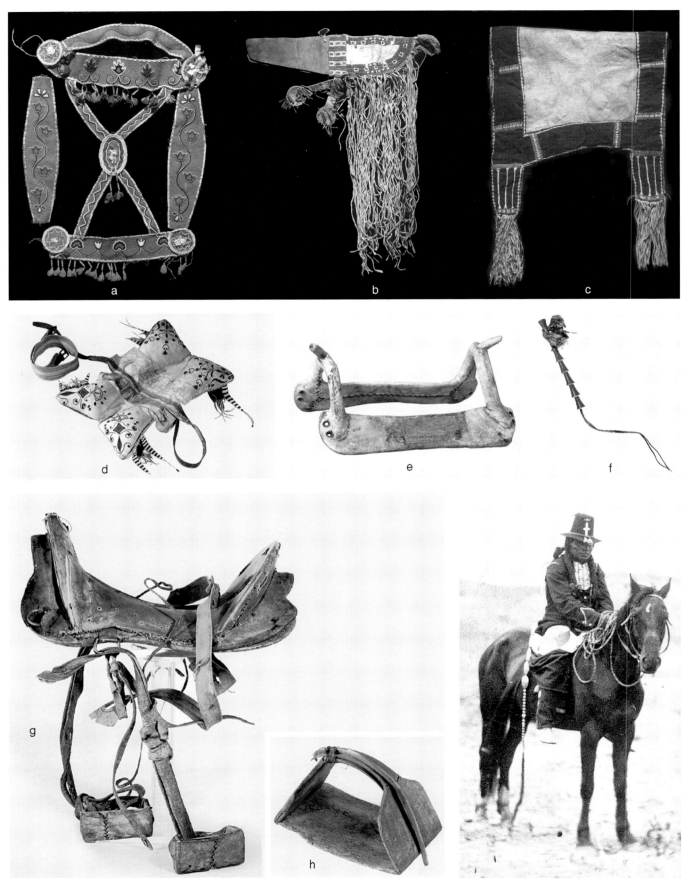

a

b

c

d

e

f

g

h

728

Smithsonian, Dept. of Anthr.: g, 59,741 (neg. 58892A); h, 12,567 (neg. 74-2878); a, 1,918 (neg. 81-11369); b, 1,936 (neg. 81-11372); c, 1,957 (neg. 81-11370); d, 1,942 (neg. 79-3834); e, 76,883 (neg. 74-2881); f, 1,908 (neg. 81-11335); bottom right, The British Mus., Mus of Mankind, London: MM016335, album 38/78.

Fig. 4. Horse gear. Trade materials were often incorporated into Native-made items. Horses were the main form of wealth in Sioux society, and horse gear was often highly decorated. a, Beaded headstall of red flannel. b, Crupper of beaded hide with long fringes and pendants with metal cone tinklers that hung on the flanks of the hose on each side. c, Saddle blanket of hide bordered with beaded bands of blue flannel. f, Carved wooden quirt. Three main types of saddles were used, although riders sometimes went bareback. The soft pad saddle (d) was made of tanned hide stuffed with buffalo hair and was often highly decorated. This example has a commercial cinch and buckle suspended from a section of painted rawhide cut from an old parfleche. The hard saddle (e) had wooden side pieces and an arched pommel and cantle covered with tightly stretched rawhide. It was placed on top of a saddle blanket and the seat padded with a blanket or buffalo robe. The arched pieces of this pack saddle are made of elk antler. Commercial saddles (g) acquired through trade or capture were often modified. This cavalry saddle, which was captured at the Battle of the Little Bighorn, was stripped of brass and refitted with Indian stirrups. Stirrup (h) made of wood tightly encased in rawhide. bottom right, Oglala man at the Ft. Laramie Treaty Council, Wyo. Terr. The horse is equipped with a Native-made braided rawhide rope and a manufactured halter. No saddle is visible. The rider wears a U.S. army coat, military hat with German silver cross, long hair ornament of German silver disks and a hairpipe breastplate (DeMallie 1981:56). Photograph by Alexander Gardner, 1868 (cropped). a–d, f, Collected by G.K. Warren, probably from the Brule in Nebr. in 1855; e, collected by Charles Ridley at Ft. Russell, Wyo., around 1876; g, collected by A.M. Hawes before 1882; h, collected by J.A. Allen at Ft. Rice, Dak. Terr., 1873. a, Width 31 cm; b, length without fringe 73 cm; c, width 73 cm; d, length at center 47 cm; e, length 40 cm; f, length of handle 50 cm; g, length about 47 cm; h, width 23 cm.

they were joined by most of the Wahpeton, probably due to scarcity of buffalo to the east. The Wahpekute moved farther south, building villages on Cannon River and at Traverse des Sioux, on the Minnesota, beyond the Wahpeton (S.W. Pond 1908:320–321; G.C. Anderson 1980:34). The locations of these groups, and many of their village sites, remained relatively stable from the 1760s until 1851, when, by treaty, the Santee sold most of their lands to the United States.

The Santee lost some of the best wild rice areas to the Chippewa, but the grain was still plentiful in their territory. In 1776 Carver commented on the vast quantities found along the lower Minnesota (J. Parker 1976:95). Pond reported in 1774 that the Mdewakanton, living near the mouth of the Minnesota, raised "plenty of corn" (Gates 1965:56). After the spring planting they set off on a buffalo hunt, returning in the fall to harvest both the corn and the wild rice. The Santee bands did not occupy their village sites along the rivers year-round; Carver wrote that the Santee never stayed more than a month in any one place, but traveled about to hunt, living in hide tents. In a sketch he depicts a Santee "tent" lacking the characteristic wind flaps of Plains-style tepees (fig. 5.).

Trade with the Sioux was curtailed during the American Revolution but increased after 1785 when trading companies formed at Mackinac Island and traders established posts in Sioux country and married Sioux women. These men and their mixed-blood children served as interpreters and culture brokers (Wozniak 1978). The increase in trade stimulated a corresponding increase in warfare between the Sioux and Chippewa. The British brought leaders of both tribes to Mackinac in 1786, but the treaty they signed there had little effect. Trade slackened after the American embargo against British traders in 1807, again bringing about a period of decreased hostilities between the Sioux and Chippewa (G.C. Anderson 1980:29–34).

Lewis and Clark reported in 1804 that the Santee obtained horses from the Teton at the spring trade fair on the James River (Moulton 1983–, 3:412–413), but horses remained scarce among the Santee on the Minnesota River. In 1823 Sioux were using dogs for transport (Keating 1825, 1:453),

although the Mdewakanton did not, apparently considering them sacred (S.W. Pond 1908:359). When the Santee sold their lands to the United States in 1851, much of the money they received was immediately used to buy horses (D. Robinson 1904:214–215).

In 1804 the Santee received all their trade goods from the British at Michilimackinac. Traders went to the Santee in their winter camps and spent the season with them, urging them to hunt for furs. In return for manufactured items the Santee traded beaver, otter, fox, mink, black bear, raccoon, fishers, and muskrat, as well as a larger quantity of deer hides (Moulton 1983, 3:408–412). In 1805 the Sisseton and Wahpekute were also reported to trade buffalo robes, the former in large numbers (Pike in Coues 1895, 1:346–347).

At the beginning of the nineteenth century the Mdewakanton and Wahpekute were the only Sioux groups living in forested areas. The lifeway of the Mdewakanton, on the lower Minnesota River and adjacent Mississippi, was adapted to the woodlands and resembled that of the Southwestern Chippewa, with whom they had been on a band-by-band basis alternately at peace and at war since the 1670s. Unlike the other Santee groups, the Mdewakanton stayed in the east and as the buffalo herds retreated westward, they specialized in the hunting of deer. By adopting the hunting patterns of their Chippewa neighbors the Mdewakanton were in continual conflict with them, leading to perpetual violations of the truce between them. In 1804 the Mdewakanton were also reported to be at peace with the Sauk, Fox, and other tribes east of the Mississippi, below the Chippewa (Lewis and Clark in Moulton 1983–, 3:410).

At this time the Mdewakanton were the only Santee tribe cultivating corn, and according to Tabeau, only two of the four bands practiced horticuture (Lewis and Clark in Moulton 1983–, 3:410; A.H. Abel 1939:103). Pike mentioned that the Mdewakanton depended primarily on wild rice, cultivating only a very small quantity of corn and beans. They were also the only Sioux who at the turn of the nineteenth century still used canoes (Coues 1895, 1:344).

Of all the Sioux, the Mdewakanton on the Minnesota and Mississippi were the most familiar with Whites and were also the best supplied with trade goods. After the War of

Fig. 5. Early depictions of Sioux daily life and ceremonies. top left, *A Man & Woman of the Naudowessie*. The man wears a breechcloth, feathered headdress, and necklace with triangular pendant. The woman wears a fringed short garment and may have tattooing or painted decorations around her neck. The structures in the background are the first representation of Sioux tepees. Engraving based on the original drawings (J. Parker 1976:96) by Jonathan Carver, 1766–1767. top right, Self-sacrifice in the Sioux Sun Dance. Oil painting by George Catlin, near Ft. Pierre, Mo. Terr., 1832. bottom left, Sioux women guarding a cornfield from birds. Horticulture, from planting to harvesting, was an activity of the women. The woman on the nearer scaffold, with a sun shade, appears to be banging on an object while the woman near the tepee is waving a piece of cloth or skin. Watercolor by Seth Eastman, 1850. bottom right, Hunters cooking and eating meat. The men are wearing fringed buckskin shirts, breechcloths and are armed with bows, quivers, and a rifle. The man on the left is skinning a carcass. Watercolor by Heinrich Balduin Möllhausen, 1851.

1812, American traders based at Prairie du Chien began to send their goods to them. Some of these traders had previously operated out of Mackinac Island. The Mdewakanton depended heavily on this trade, not only for guns, powder, and lead but also for metal kettles (native pottery making having died out), cloth and blankets, as well as food, including delicacies such as mustard and onions (Tabeau in A.H. Abel 1939:122–123). They also used trade goods, along with supplies of wild rice and corn, to trade with Sioux groups to the west for horses, buffalo meat, and buffalo robes. Although they were completely armed with guns (Pike in Coues 1895, 1:344), this fact gave them no special advantage over other Sioux groups. In 1827 a Mdewakanton chief remarked to Indian agent Lawrence Taliaferro that his people would starve without traders: "The Sioux of the plains say they can jump on their horses & with their bows and arrows they can kill what they want and do not want your assistance. We my Father cannot do this" (quoted in H.E. Hickerson 1970:108).

The Sisseton, western Wahpeton, and Wahpekute, who lived on the prairies near the head of the Minnesota River, developed a lifeway closer to that of the western Sioux groups. They made their livelihood principally by hunting buffalo, using some of the surplus hides and dried meat to trade with the Mdewakanton and eastern Wahpeton for wild rice and trade goods. At the turn of the nineteenth century, according to Truteau (Parks 1993), the valley of the Big Sioux River was an important buffalo-hunting ground for the Santee. Because the Sisseton trapped many fur-bearing animals in the small lakes that dotted the prairie in their territory, they were able to purchase proportionally more trade goods than the other groups. According to Lewis and Clark (Moulton 1983–, 3:411–413), both the Sisseton and Wahpekute used much of the merchandise they received from the traders to exchange with the Teton for horses at the James River trade fairs.

Culturally, the western Santee groups were nearly identical with the neighboring Yankton and Yanktonai, and some bands lived together and were intermarried. They were even reported to have held Sun Dances, though infrequently (S.W. Pond 1908:418). Nonetheless, the western Santee shared both dialect and identity with the Mdewakanton and eastern Wahpeton.

Yankton and Yanktonai

During the mid-eighteenth century the Yankton and Yanktonai lived on the Coteau des Prairies between the Minnesota and James rivers and west to the Missouri River. Yankton territory included the lower Sioux River and the heads of the Floyd's, Little Sioux, and Des Moines rivers. Yanktonai territory was to the north, from Big Stone Lake and Lake Traverse to the Missouri (Lewis and Clark in Moulton 1983–, 3:413–414; H. Atkinson 1826:8–9).

When Peter Pond built a trading post on the lower Minnesota in the autumn of 1774 he was soon visited by a group of Sioux he called Yanktons (but probably Yanktonai) who said that they had traveled 200 miles downstream to request him to come trade with them. Pond agreed, and taking a stock of goods by canoe, he traveled upriver for nine days before reaching their camp. As the first trader ever to visit them, Pond was treated as an honored guest; before the trade began he was ritually carried into a lodge on a beaver robe and feasted. The chief appointed police armed with spears to keep order during the trade (Gates 1965:52–55).

Pond was the first writer to describe the Yankton-Yanktonai. They lived in hide tepees 14 feet in diameter and had a great many horses and dogs, which they used for moving camp. Because wood was scarce, they used dried buffalo dung for fuel. They were continually at war with their neighbors and kept constant lookout parties when they traveled. Men carried rawhide shields, an innovation that apparently spread along with horses, and wore shirts made of several layers of hide that provided protection from arrows (Gates 1965:57–58).

Thirty years later Lewis and Clark (Moulton 1983–, 3:413–414) reported that the Yanktonai were at war with the tribes to the north—the Assiniboine, Cree, Plains Ojibwa, and Mandan—but were at peace with the Arikara, with whom they doubtlessly exchanged European trade goods, buffalo meat, and hides for corn and other garden produce and horses. The Yankton warred with the Arikara but were at peace with the Omaha and Ponca. In 1803, Tabeau mentioned that the Yankton "had already [i.e., previously] been tillers of the soil" (A.H. Abel 1939:169), and the next year Lewis and Clark wrote that none of the Yankton planted crops. It is likely that some of the Yanktons experimented briefly with horticulture, emulating the Cheyenne, Arikara, or Omaha-Ponca. Lewis and Clark reported that the Yanktonai did not carry on a regular trade with Whites and were little acquainted with them; the Yankton regularly received goods from a trader on the Des Moines River. They also traded with Pierre Dorian, originally from Spanish Louisiana, who married a Yankton woman and settled on

the Missouri in the late eighteenth century; his son served as interpreter for Lewis and Clark (Moulton 1983–, 3:21–23). Both Yankton and Yanktonai traded on the James River (H. Atkinson 1826:8–9).

Teton

The Teton were in the forefront of the westward movement of the Sioux. By the mid-eighteenth century the western Santee, Yankton, and Yanktonai, as well as the Teton, were all hunting on the prairies east of the Missouri River. The numerous villages of the Arikara, who were rich in horses, controlled the Missouri below the Cheyenne River. Two bands of the Oglala Teton tried settling with the Arikara and raising corn. When hostilities broke out between other Sioux groups and the Arikara, one Oglala band sided with the Arikara, the other with the Sioux; later the Oglalas reconciled, but abandoned horticulture (Tabeau in A.H. Abel 1939:104). At about this time the more southerly Teton tribes, the Oglala and Brule, crossed the Missouri around the mouth of White River.

From 1771 to 1781 a series of smallpox epidemics decimated the Arikara, reducing their population by three-fourths and the number of their villages from more than 30 to two, which were located just below the mouth of the Cheyenne River. This opened the way for the more northerly Teton tribes, the Minneconjou and Saone, to cross the Missouri. In 1796 the Arikara abandoned their last two villages and soon built three new ones upriver, above the mouth of the Grand, known to the Sioux thereafter as the Arikara River (Truteau in Parks 1993).

The displacement of the Arikara left the way clear for the Teton, who by the end of the eighteenth century were fully mounted. A year name in American Horse's winter count for 1775–1776 is interpreted to commemorate the discovery of the Black Hills (Mallery 1886:130). In 1804–1805 Lewis and Clark reported that the Teton lived on both sides of the Missouri River (Moulton 1983–, 3:415–417). By 1833 the Teton had withdrawn from the east side of the Missouri, although some Teton were still hunting in the James River country in the 1860s (Denig 1961:16–28).

Horses allowed the Teton great mobility. During the spring some bands traveled from their winter camps along the Missouri east to the James River for the annual reunion with Sioux from the other divisions. Most of the spring and summer, from April to August, the Teton hunted buffalo on the plains west of the Missouri. They formed a barrier that prevented the Arikara from hunting buffalo, then went to the Arikara villages to trade buffalo meat and robes for corn, beans, pumpkins, tobacco, and horses. Because horticultural produce was important to the Teton, when harvest time came, they made temporary truces with the Arikara to facilitate trade (Tabeau in A.H. Abel 1939:131). During the winter the Teton returned to winter in the wooded areas along the Missouri; when the weather was coldest the buffalo also sought shelter there, providing the people with meat. Then in the spring the buffalo herds migrated west onto the plains and the Teton followed them.

Traders from Spanish Louisiana began to reach the Teton on the Missouri in the late eighteenth century. The traders were headed for the Mandan and Hidatsa villages because these tribes provided higher-quality beaver pelts than tribes farther down the Missouri. The Omaha, Ponca, and Sioux each watched the river carefully, attempting to stop traders from going upriver in order to monopolize the trade for themselves and prevent trade goods, particularly guns and ammunition, from reaching their enemies. In 1796 Truteau barely escaped losing his trade goods to a band of Teton, and the next spring he in fact lost most of the robes and furs he had obtained in trade from the Arikara and Cheyenne to the Teton, whose untimely arrival forced him to abandon his goods and flee for his life (Parks 1993).

During the first decade of the nineteenth century traders from Spanish Louisiana established posts on the Missouri for the Teton. Régis Loisel's post, Fort aux Cedres, built about 1802, was located at Cedar Island. In the winter of 1804 he traded there with the Brule, while Hugh Heney traded with the Oglala and northern Tetons at a post built near the mouth of the Cheyenne (A.H. Abel 1939:24–25, 72–73). Tabeau's account of the trading process among the Brule was very similar to Pond's account of the Yankton. The trade was under the patronage of a chief named The Partisan who appointed two police to guard the merchandise and keep order during the trading. When some Sioux from the Minnesota River arrived at Loisel's post and incited the Tetons by claiming that mechandise was more plentiful and traded more cheaply by the British traders on the Minnesota, and otherwise disparaged the French traders, The Partisan stopped the trading. He and other leaders, accompanied by two police painted black and wearing crow-skin bustles—just as described by Radisson more than a century before—entered the trading house and refused to let anyone leave or enter. After making threatening speeches the leaders accepted Loisel's payment of a barrel of whiskey and other presents and the trade continued as before (A.H. Abel 1939:114–115). European trade with the Teton during the late eighteenth and early nineteenth centuries was always tense with the possibility of violence. Lewis and Clark concluded that the Teton could be contemptuous of the Missouri River traders because they had a regular supply of British trade goods from the Minnesota River and believed "the more illy they treat the traders the greater quantity of merchandise they will bring them" (Moulton 1983–, 3:418).

History, Early to Mid-Nineteenth Century

During the first half of the nineteenth century the westward movement of Sioux groups continued. The Teton, allied with the Cheyenne and Arapaho, pressed westward, driving the Kiowa and Crow from the Black Hills area and claiming it as their own (DeMallie 1980:44–45; R. White 1978:338). The Yankton and Yanktonai, too, shifted their focus to the Missouri River, though they continued to live on the east side. Well mounted, and with bountiful supplies of buffalo, this was the period in which the classic western Sioux culture developed, shaping stereotypes that ultimately would define the Indian in American popular culture (fig. 6).

Treaties

After the purchase of Louisiana by the United States in 1803, the establishment of formal relationships with Indian

Smithsonian, NAA: left, 86-4812; right, 3184-a.

Fig. 6. The Plains Indian as representative of all Indians. The classic Indian image in the 19th century was one wearing a feathered headdress and fringed buckskin garments. This stereotype was used on the Indian head nickel as well as the $5 silver certificate issued in 1899 (left). right, Running Antelope, Hunkpapa Sioux (b. 1821, d. 1896–1897), whose photograph was used for the portrait on the certificate (Daniel 1969). He is wearing a fringed buckskin shirt decorated with quillwork, a peace medal (probably the Andrew Johnson medal issued in 1865), and eagle feathers and holds an eagle-wing fan and pipe with plaited quillwork. On the silver certificate the artist showed him wearing a war bonnet associated with Plains chiefs. Photograph by Alexander Gardner, Washington, D.C., 1872.

732

tribes became an integral part of the government's need to explore and exploit the new territory. On their trip up the Missouri River in 1804 Lewis and Clark met with representatives of the Yankton, Yanktonai, and Teton tribes and presented to chiefs peace medals bearing the likeness of George Washington, and United States flags as tokens of the new political order. This continued the practice of the British, French, and Spanish. The medals and flags had great significance to the Sioux both as affirming the status of chiefs and as sources of power in their own right.

To protect the territorial interests of the United States against Great Britian, a military expedition under Lt. Zebulon M. Pike ascended the Mississippi River in 1805 and signed the first treaty with "the Sioux Nation of Indians" (Kappler 1904–1941, 2:1031). Under its terms the Mdewakanton ceded to the United States two areas of land along the Mississippi for the construction of military posts. One of these areas was at the juncture of the Minnesota and Mississippi rivers, where Fort Saint Anthony (later Fort Snelling) was erected in 1819.

The War of 1812 divided the Sioux. The eastern Sioux were loyal to the British and a considerable number of them fought with British troops against the Americans. The Sioux on the Missouri River, however, tacitly sided with the United States, largely because of the influence of the traders (D. Robinson 1904:92–93). In summer 1815, after the conclusion of the war, representatives of Midwestern tribes were invited to Portage des Sioux where they signed treaties of peace and friendship with the United States. The Teton and Yankton each signed a copy of the treaty and two groups of Santees also signed; in 1816 a third group of Santees signed a similar treaty (Kappler 1904–1941, 2:112–115, 128–129). These treaties were significant because they specified that the Indian signers acknowledged themselves and their tribes to be under the sole protection of the United States. This was the first extension of federal jurisdiction over the Sioux.

In 1825 a military expedition up the Missouri River led by Gen. Henry Atkinson and Indian Agent Benjamin O'Fallon signed four more treaties with the Yankton, Yanktonai, and Teton (Kappler 1904–1941, 2:227–236; H. Atkinson 1826). In addition to peace and friendship, these treaties specified that the Sioux acknowledged living within the United States, recognized its supremacy, and claimed its protection. The treaties also gave the right to the United States to regulate all trade and intercourse with the Indians. While the Sioux at the time could not have understood those articles, they became law and established the basis on which future relations between the Sioux and the federal government would unfold.

Other treaties from this period had more specific purposes. In 1830 at Prairie du Chien the Santee and Yankton signed a treaty jointly with the Sauk and Fox, Omaha, Iowa, Otoe, and Missouria (Kappler 1904–1941, 2:305–310), the

Fig. 7. Ft. Pierre, Nebr. Terr., an American Fur Company post established in 1832. It was important in fur trade with the Sioux and then became a military fort in 1855. In the Sioux camp are decorated tepees and skin preparation in progress. On the other side of the fort Indian women play shinny. Painted portals depicting trading and buffalo hunting appear over the gates of the fort (Ewers 1972a:106–107). Watercolor by Frederick Behman, before April 1855.

ostensible purpose of which was to end intertribal warfare. It was significant for the Sioux and the Sauk and Fox in that they surrendered to the United States two 20-mile wide strips of land separating their territories from each other. For the first time the Sioux were to receive annuities, payable over a 10-year period in money or goods (R.W. Meyer 1967:50–51). This treaty was the first of many in which promised annuities became more and more important to the Indians' survival. Treaties in 1836 and 1837 further eroded Santee and Yankton lands (Kappler 1904–1941, 2:466–467, 479–482, 493–497).

Interaction with Whites

The nineteenth-century westward movement of the Sioux resulted not only from the dwindling of the buffalo herds in the east but also from the pressure of rapidly developing White settlement. By 1849, across the river from Fort Snelling, the town of Saint Paul, which had begun a decade before as a squatter's cabin where illegal alcohol was traded to the Sioux, had become the capital of the new Minnesota Territory. Saint Paul was reported to have as many as 910 residents, and the White and mixed-blood population of the entire territory was about 4,500 (Folwell 1921–1930, 1:220, 250, 351–352). In Minnesota the Sioux began to have a great deal of contact with Whites, including traders, missionaries, military officers, soldiers, and their first Indian agent, Lawrence Taliaferro, who served 1819–1839, headquartered at Fort Snelling. Individual Whites loomed large in shaping the course of relations between the Sioux and the United States, many of whom, like Taliaferro, married Sioux women.

The work of missionaries among the Sioux during this period, most of which was centered in Minnesota, had long-term significance. In addition to introducing the Sioux to Christianity, the missionaries focused on education. In 1834 the Congregational missionaries Samuel W. Pond and Gideon H. Pond devised an orthography for writing the Sioux language that was adopted as an integral part of mission work. Utilized first in the schools and churches, the foundations for native-language literacy were established in the 1840s. Newspapers, Bible translations, and other printed material spread literacy rapidly among the Sioux, making it a major force in the second half of the nineteenth century (S.R. Riggs 1880; Parks and DeMallie 1992a:122–123).

On the Missouri, fur traders married to Sioux women provided the main contact with White culture, and until midcentury many Indians in the region had little familiarity with Whites. In 1819 the Upper Missouri Agency was established to oversee the Sioux and other tribes of the region. The agency was located at various times at Council Bluffs, Iowa, and at Bellevue, Nebraska. In 1824 a sub-agency for the Sioux was located near the Big Bend, in central South Dakota, and in 1837 it became independent and was renamed the Upper Missouri Agency. During the 1840s the agent was not resident and only made annual

visits by steamboat (E.E. Hill 1974:184–187). The agents were former fur traders, who were well known to the Sioux.

The beginning of commercial steamboat traffic in 1830 made trade goods available to the tribes of the Upper Missouri in larger quantities than ever before, but the effects of that traffic proved to be disastrous to the Indians. The steamboats consumed great quantities of wood, drove game animals away from the river, and brought diseases. The smallpox epidemic of 1838, spread by steamboat, took a heavy toll on the population of the Hunkpapa and other Sioux along the Missouri (Denig 1961:28).

Then, in 1849, following the discovery of gold in California, floods of emigrants in unfathomable numbers followed the California and Oregon Trail along the Platte River, crossing the hunting grounds of the Brule and Oglala, whose populations were decimated by disease (Denig 1961:14, 20, 22). That year the government bought Fort John, a trading post on the Platte that was garrisoned and renamed Fort Laramie (vol. 4:372–373), to serve as a supply depot and, in theory at least, to protect overland travelers. The establishment of a military post among the Teton inevitably signaled the beginning of another period of change that would, by the end of the century, transform the social order of the western Sioux.

Organization of Society

During the early nineteenth century the Sioux, as they followed the buffalo herds, put pressure on all the neighboring tribes. Sioux expansion eventually pushed even their allies, the Cheyenne, west and south, beyond the Black Hills, and Sioux war parties kept the hunting expeditions of the Village tribes, including the Arikara, Mandan, Hidatsa, Pawnee, and Omaha, in constant jeopardy. As the Sioux tribes expanded the territory in which they hunted, clearly reflecting the mobility enabled by the increase in horses, the divisions began to lose touch with one another. Tabeau reported in 1803 that the Santee on the Minnesota, the Yankton on the head of the Des Moines, and the Sioux on the Missouri "regard each other as strangers" (A.H. Abel 1939:104). An 1829 report stated that the annual meeting on the James River, "at which they arranged the business of the tribe," was fast disappearing, "and the different bands have less and less connexion every year" (ARCIA 1829:101).

It was the band structure that allowed the Sioux to maintain stability in their day-to-day lives while at the same time adapting to rapid changes brought about by the western migration. The band structure, shared by all the Sioux tribes, was based on the *tʰiyóšpaye* 'lodge group', a term that designated an extended family or group of extended families (E.C. Deloria 1944:40–42; DeMallie 1971:110–113). The lodge group was the minimal social unit that stayed together throughout the year; sometimes two or three lodge groups associated during the summer but split up during the winter, to find shelter and forage along different creek bottoms. These lodge groups, which can be designated "bands," probably averaged 10–20 families, around 100 people. Bands were kinship units, whose members were ordinarily but not always related to one another through a network of men; women tended to marry outside the band. The kinship system was bilateral and is classified as the Dakota type (see "Kinship," this vol.). Each band was named, most commonly with a nickname, but relatively new bands were sometimes designated by the name of the leader. Each band had a recognized leader (itʰą́cʰą). Band leaders, called "chiefs," in English, tended to inherit their position from their fathers, but the position of chief required both ability as a leader and the consent of the band council. Generosity was an important qualification for a chief; acquiring goods from White traders enhanced a chief's prestige by increasing his ability to give. Although residence tended to be patrilocal, families could leave to join other bands if they were dissatisfied with the actions of the chief. New bands were formed by fission, sometimes when a group of disgruntled families left to follow a new leader, or sometimes when, after the death of a popular leader, a large band split into two or more under the leadership of the deceased chief's sons.

Inevitably, there was competition among chiefs, which was exacerbated by the Euro-American need to recognize certain men as chiefs through whom the government could deal with their tribes. Although chiefs had no power to compel their followers' actions (A.H. Abel 1939:104–105), they spoke for the band, using the first person to symbolize the fact that their voice represented not just themselves but all their people. But when they spoke, they represented the consensus of the council, the group of adult men who met together in the council lodge (tʰiyótʰipi) to discuss matters of common interest. The chief's only power in the council was persuasion; hence skill as an orator was a valued quality for a chief. Family status mattered, too. The more "brothers" (brothers and parallel cousins) a chief had, the greater his ability to control the council. Chiefs enforced the decisions of the council by appointing camp police (akíčʰita), young men charged with carrying out such tasks as maintaining order during ritual events and visits of White traders and policing communal hunts. The chief and the council, however, always struggled against the cultural tenet that all men were autonomous and no one had the right to infringe upon an individual's freedom. Both Truteau (Parks 1993) and Tabeau (A.H. Abel 1939:105–106) witnessed this among the Teton, when a single individual subverted the decision of a chief.

The bands were organized into named tribes, which in turn comprised the three highest-level social divisions, the Santee, Yankton, and Teton (tables 2–5). There was no Sioux word that specifically differentiated these levels of social organization. The word oyáte 'people' designated tribes but also could refer to any social grouping, or to the Sioux as a whole. In 1766 Carver listed 11 Sioux "bands" (using the term band to designate what are here called tribes, a common practice in the historical literature), but the Sioux told him "that they knew not how many bands they had to the westward which they was not acquainted with for they say that the people as far as the great waters, pointing to the west, spake their tongue" (J. Parker 1976:101).

A clearer picture of Sioux society emerged in the early nineteenth century. Tabeau reported that "The entire Sioux nation is divided first into five principal tribes" (A.H. Abel 1939:102). Lewis and Clark in their journals present a list of 12 tribes, given by Pierre Dorian, but one of their two summary charts lists only 9, the other 10 (Moulton 1983–, 3:27, 28, 32–33, 408–420). Edwin T. Denig, a fur trader among the Sioux on the Missouri in 1833, prepared two lists of Sioux "bands" living on both sides of the river; one gave 14 names, the other 12 (Denig 1930:435; Ewers 1961:14–15). In 1823, a member of the military expedition under Maj. Stephen H. Long, sent to explore the Upper Mississippi and its tributaries, listed 14 "villages or parties" of the Sioux. This information came from Joseph Renville, a trader of French and Mdewakanton parentage, who explained that the traders classified the Sioux into "two great divisions," each comprising seven groups. The first division was the "gens du lac" (the Mdewakanton villages) and the second was the "gens du large," or "roving" Sioux, who included all the rest (Keating 1825, 1:394–396; S.R. Riggs 1869:153–154).

The Sioux classification of their divisions differed from that used by the traders. Renville explained that the Sioux designated themselves "the nation of seven (council) fires," ocʰétʰi šakówį 'seven fireplaces', referring to the organization that "formerly prevailed among them." Four of the Seven Fires were Santee groups, the Mdewakanton, Wahpeton, Sisseton, and Wahpekute; the others were the Yankton, Yanktonai, and Teton (Keating 1825, 1:393–394). Renville interpreted the Seven Fires as a political alliance: "When they lighted the common calumet at the General Council Fire, it was always among the Mende Wahkantoan, who then resided near Spirit Lake, and who were considered as the oldest band of the nation" (Keating 1825, 1:442). Joseph N. Nicollet, mapping the Upper Mississippi in 1838–1839, recorded the name "Seven Nations" oyáte šakówį 'seven peoples' in addition to the "Seven Fire Places" (E.C. Bray and M.C. Bray 1976:255). Riggs (1852:vii) also mentioned the Seven Council Fires, but he, too, worked directly with Renville.

In 1849, Alexander Ramsey, governor of Minnesota Territory, wrote that the Sioux were divided into independent "sub-tribes," which he designated "the Seven Grand Council-Fires," each further subdivided into a number of bands. Ramsey quoted a report by Thomas P. Moore, agent for the Upper Missouri Agency, that "Each band claims the exclusive use of certain portions of their common territory," and concluded that "a common origin, language, customs, and country, with a perpetual tacit alliance for offence and defence against all other nations," was "their only bond of union" (ARCIA 1849:1014). Accounts throughout the nineteenth century reveal the use of the number seven and the symbol of the fireplace (or council fire) as a metaphor for the

Table 2. Sioux Tribal Names

Tabeau 1803-1804 (A.H. Abel 1939:102)	Lewis and Clark 1804-1805 (Moulton 1983-, 3:408-419)	Keating 1823 (1824, 1:396)
SANTEE		
people of the lakes	Min-da-war-car-ton	Mendewahkantoan
people of the leaves	Wah-pa-tone	Wahkpatoan
	Wâh-pa-coo-tar	Wahkpakota
Seissitons	Sis-sa-tone	Miakechakesa (or Sisitons)
		Kahra (a band of Sisitons)
YANKTON		
Hyinctons	Yanktons of the N.[a]	Yanktoan
YANKTONAI		
	Yank-tons-Ah-nah[a]	Yanktoanan
TETON		
Titons		Tetoans
	Teton Bois rouley	
	Teton-O-kan-dan-das	
	Teton-Min-na-Kine-az-zo	
	Teton-Sah-o-ne	
	Se ah sap pas	
	Wo hai noom pah	

[a]Lewis and Clark incorrectly reversed the designations for the Yankton and the Yanktonai.
[b]Nicollet translates as 'I killed by mistake, without wishing it'.

Table 3. Santee Band Names

Pierre-Antoine Tabeau, 1803-1804 (A.H. Abel 1939:103)	Lewis and Clark, 1804-1805 (Moulton 1983-, 3:419)	William Keating (1824, 1:396; 399-403)	Joseph N. Nicollet, 1838-1839 (DeMallie 1976:255-256)
MDEWAKANTON	MDEWAKANTON	MDEWAKANTON	MDEWAKANTON
1. Kiouxas	1. Kee-uke-sah	1. Keoxa	1. Kiuksa or Kiuksapi, those who cut themselves in half; village of Wapasha
2. Tintatons	2. Tin-tah-ton		2. Tinta ottonwe, village of the prairie; village of Six
		3. Taoapa	
4. Mindewacantons	4. Mindawarcarton		
5. Matatons	5. Mah-tah-ton		
		6. Eanbosandata	6. Rheminicha, the village of Lake Pepin, or of La Grange Mountain
		7. Kapoja	7. Kap'oje, the light ones, Little Crow's band
		8. Oanoska	8. Hohaanskae, village of the long avenue; village of Black Dog
		9. Tetankatane	9. Tanina ottonwe, the old village; village of Penichon
		10. Weakaote[a]	
			11. Rheatan ottonwe, village of the end (Lake Calhoun)
			12. Village at Pine Bend (associated with no. 7)

Denig 1833 (1961:14-15)	Nicollet 1838-1839 (DeMallie 1976:254-259)	Retranscription
SANTEE	Issan-a ti, village on the cutting stone	*isą́ʔatʰi* 'dwell at knife'
Midewahconto	Mdewakantonwan-nan	*mdewákʰatʰųwą* 'sacred lake village'
	Warhpetonwan-nan	*waxpétʰųwą(ną)* '(little) leaf village'
Esan tees	Warhpekute	*waxpékʰute* 'shoot at leaves'
	Sisintonwan-nan	*sisítʰųwą(ną)* '(little) [. . . ?] village'
		kʰągí 'crow' [?]
YANKTON		*ihą́ktʰųwą* 'end village'
Lower Yancton	Itokarh-ihantonwan	*itókax ihą́ktʰųwą* 'sound end village'
YANKTONAI	Ihanktonwan-nan	*ihą́ktʰųwąną* 'little end village'
Pah Baxah (Tête Coupees)	Pamaksa	*pʰábaksa* 'cut head'
Gens des Perches	Onkpati	*hų́kpatʰi* 'lodge at camp circle entrance'
Wahzecootai		*wazíkʰute* 'shoot at pine'
TETON	Titonwan	*tʰítʰųwą* 'prairie village'
Se chong hhos	Sichanr̄us	*sičʰą́ɣu* "burned thigh"
Ogallalahs	Oglalas	*oglála* 'scatter one's own'
Min ne con zus	Minikanye oju	*mnikʰówožu* 'plant by water'
	Saonis	*sa'óni* '[?]'
Se ah sap pas	Sia-sappâ	*sihásapa* 'blackfeet'
Wo hai noom pah	Wanonwakteninan^b	*oʔóhenųpa* 'two boilings'
Etas epe cho	Itazichonan	*itʰázipčʰo* 'without bows'
Honc pap pas	Onkpapa	*hų́kpapʰa* 'head of camp circle entrance'

Joseph N. Nicollet, 1838-1839 (DeMallie 1976:257-258)	Stephen R. Riggs, 1852 (1893:156-159)	James Owen Dorsey (1897:215-217)	Retranscription
MDEWAKANTON	MDEWAKANTON	MDEWAKANTON	MDEWAKANTON
1. Keyooksā, the mingled people	1. Ki-yu-ksa, Breakers of custom or law	1. Kiyuksa, Breakers (of the law or custom)	1. *kʰiyúksa* 'break in two'; *wápahaša* 'red standard'
2. Tintatoan, the people of the plains or prairies, Six village	2. Tiⁿ-ta-toŋ-we, Prairie Villagers	2. Tiⁿta otoⁿwe, Village on the Prairie	2. *tʰitá otʰų́we* 'village on the prairie'
3. Band or people of the Eagle's Head			3. *tʰewápa* 'lotus'
			4. *mdewákʰatʰųwą* 'sacred lake village'
			5. [?]
6. Iyanmobondata, people of the standing rocks	6. Ḣe-mni-ćaŋ, Hill-water-wood	6. Qe-mini-tcaⁿ, or Qemnitca, hill covered with timber that appears to rise out of the water	6. *iyą bosdáta* 'erect rock' (Castle Rock); *xemnícʰą* 'bluff water wood' (Barn Bluff)
7. Kapozha, Little Crow's band	7. Ka-po-źa, Light ones	7. Kaṗ'oja, Unimcumbered with much baggage	7. *kaṗóža* 'light (in weight)'
8. Marhayouteshni, those who do not eat geese, Black Dog village	8. Ma-ġa-yu-te śni, They who do not eat geese	8. Maxa yute cni, Eat no geese	8. *hoháska* 'long camp enclosure'; *maɣá yútešni* 'does not eat geese'
9. Oyateshitsha, the bad people, Penichon village	9. Oyate-śića, Bad people	9. Oyate citca, Bad Nation	9. *tʰitʰą́ka tʰaníná* 'old big lodge'; *tʰanín otʰų́we* 'old village'; *oyáte šíča* 'bad people'
			10. [?]
	11. Ḣe-ya-ta-toŋ-we, Black Villagers	11. Qeyata otoⁿwe, Village back down from the river	11. *xeyáta otʰų́we* 'upland village'
12. Band at Pine Bend			

Table 3. Santee Band Names (continued)

Pierre-Antoine Tabeau, 1803-1804 (A.H. Abel 1939:103)	Lewis and Clark, 1804-1805 (Moulton 1983-, 3:419)	William Keating (1824, 1:396; 399-403)	Joseph N. Nicollet, 1838-1839 (DeMallie 1976:255-256)
WAHPETON	WAHPETON	WAHPETON	WAHPETON
1. Warhpetons	1. Wah-pa-tone	1. Wahkpatoan	
2. Otherhatons	2. O-ta-har-ton		
			3. Mede iedan
			4. Inyan chèaka, the barrier of stone
			5. Mede iyantankiake, the village of Big Stone Lake
WAHPEKUTE	WAHPEKUTE	WAHPEKUTE	WAHPEKUTE
1. Warpecoutais[b]	1. War-pa-coo-ta		
	2. Mi-ah-kee-jack-sah[c]		
			3. Tasagie, Cane (chief's name)
			4. Wanmedi sapa, Black War Eagle (chief's name)
SISSETON	SISSETON	SISSETON	SISSETON
1. Karhes	1. Caw-ree	1. Kahra (Wild Rice)	
2. Mayakidjaxes		2. Miakechakesa	2. Mayakichakse, village of the cut point
	3. Sissatone		
			4. Oyuwanrhe, détour; formerly Mayaskadan
			5. Waziata Sisiton, the Sisitons of the North (Lake Traverse)

Joseph N. Nicollet, 1838-1839 (DeMallie 1976:257-258)	Stephen R. Riggs, 1852 (1893:156-159)	James Owen Dorsey (1897:215-217)	Retranscription
WAHPETON	WAHPETON	WAHPETON	WAHPETON
	1. Wah-pa-ton-wan		1. waxpétʰų 'leaf village'
	2. Oteḣatoŋna	2. Oteqi atoⁿwaⁿ, Village in the Thicket	2. otʰéxi atʰúwą 'village at the thicket'
3. Village at Lac qui Parle			3. mdéʔiyedą 'talking lake' (Lac Qui Parle)
4. Village at Little Rapids		4. Iⁿyaⁿ-tceyaka atoⁿwaⁿ, Village at the Rapids	4. iyątʰeyaka atʰúwą 'village at stone dam' (Little Rapids)
			5. mdéʔiyątʰąka 'big stone lake'
6. Tizapta, people of the five lodges[c]			6. tʰizáptą 'five lodges'
	7. Ta-ka-psin-tona	7. Takapsin toⁿwaⁿna, Village at the Shinney ground	7. tʰakápsitʰųwąna 'little ball-ground village'
		8. Wiyaka otina, Dwellers on the Sand	8. wiyáka otʰína 'little dwellers on the sand'
		9. Wita otina, Dwellers on the Island	9. wíta otʰína 'little dwellers on the island'
		10. Wakpa atoⁿwaⁿ, Village on the River	10. wakpá atʰúwą 'village on the river'
		11. Tcaⁿkaxa otina, Dwellers In Log (huts?)	11. čʰąkáɣa otʰína 'little dwellers in log (cabins)'
WAHPEKUTE	WAHPEKUTE	WAHPEKUTE	WAHPEKUTE
1. Warhpekutes, those who shoot at the leaf	1. Waḣpekute, Leaf-shooters	1. Waqpe-kute, Shooters among the leaves	1. waxpékʰute 'leaf shooters'
			2. mayá kʰičákse 'bank cut in two'
			3. tʰaságye 'his cane'
			4. wąmdí sápa 'black eagle'
SISSETON	SISSETON	SISSETON	SISSETON
3. Sissintonwan, Sissinthonwannan			2. mayá kʰičákse 'bank cut in two'
			3. sisítʰųwą 'Sisseton'
4. Sissitoan			4. oʔíyuweɣe 'ford' (Traverse des Sioux); mayáskadą 'little white bank'
5. Sissitons of Lake Traverse			5. wazíyata sisítʰų 'north Sisseton'
	6. Ti-zaptaŋna, Five Lodges	6. Ti zaptaⁿ, Five lodges	6. tʰizáptą 'five lodges'
	7. Okopeya	7. Okopeya, In Danger (offshoot of no. 6)	7. ókopʰeya 'visible through an opening'
	8. Ćan-śda-ći-ka-na, Little place bare of wood		8. čʰąšdá číkʔana 'little treeless (place)'
	9. Amdo-wa-pus-kiya, Dryers on the Shoulder	9. Amdo wapuskiyapi, Those who lay meat on their shoulders to dry it during the hunt	9. amdó wapúskʰiyapi 'caused to dry on the shoulder'
	10. Basdeće śni	10. Basdetce cni, Do not split (the body of a buffalo) with a knife (but cut it up as they please)	10. basdéčešni 'split not'
	11. Kapoźa	11. Kap'oja, Those who travel with light burdens	11. kapóža 'light'
	12. Ohdihe	12. Ohdihe (offshoot of no. 14)	12. ohdíhe 'fallen in'

Table 3. Santee Band Names (continued)

Pierre-Antoine Tabeau, 1803-1804 (A.H. Abel 1939:103)	Lewis and Clark, 1804-1805 (Moulton 1983-, 3:419)	William Keating (1824, 1:396; 399-403)	Joseph N. Nicollet, 1838-1839 (DeMallie 1976:255-256)
SISSETON	SISSETON	SISSETON	SISSETON

aPerhaps identical with the Wahpeton village of the same name (no. 8).

bTabeau list this band as Sisseton.

cLater accounts classify this band as Sisseton.

dNicollet identifies Eagle Head (*xuyá pʰá*) as the chief of the band living near Lotus Lake (*tʰewápa mdé*) (E.C. Bray and M.C. Bray 1976:44); this band broke off from no. 2 (S.W. Pond 1908:322).

eLater accounts classify this band as Sisseton.

Table 4. Yankton and Yanktonai Band Names

Pierre-Antoine Tabeau, 1803-1804 (A.H. Abel 1939:103)	Lewis and Clark, 1804-1805 (Moulton 1983-, 3:419-420)	Joseph Nicollet, 1838-1839 (DeMallie 1976:256-257)	Joseph Nicollet, 1838-1839 (DeMallie 1976:258-259)
YANKTON	YANKTON	YANKTON	YANKTON
1. Sitchanrhou-Yincton	1. Yanc-ton, sa-char-hoo		
2. Tacohimboto	2. Tar-co-im-bo-to		2. Taku ibotto, those who hit themselves with something
3. Seascapé			
			4. Oyurhpe wanitcha, those who never rest
			5. Amdowapuskia, those who dry their booty on the shoulders
UPPER YANKTONAI	UPPER YANKTONAI	UPPER YANKTONAI	UPPER YANKTONAI
1. Saone-Yinctons	1. Sah-own	1. San Chihiapi, people who whiten themselves; also, still called Sanyoda	
2. Kiouxas-Yinctons	2. Kee-uke-sah		2. Kiuksa, the breakers
3. Raharhatons	3. Hah-har-tones		
4. Passandoucas			
5. Wasicoutais		5. Wazikute, those who shoot in the pines	5. Wazikute, those who shoot at the pines
	6. Za-ar-tar		

Joseph N. Nicollet, 1838-1839 (DeMallie 1976:257-258)	Stephen R. Riggs, 1852 (1893:156-159)	James Owen Dorsey (1897:215-217)	Retranscription
SISSETON	SISSETON	SISSETON	SISSETON
		13. Itokaq tina, Dwellers at the South (offshoot of no. 10)	13. *itókaxtʰina* 'little south dwellers'
		14. Wita waziyata otina, Village at the North Island	14. *wíta wazíyata otʰína* 'little dwellers on north island'
		15. Kaqmi otoⁿwaⁿ, Village at the Bend	15. *kaxmí atʰų́wą* 'village at the bend'
		16. Mani ti, Those who camp away from the village (offshoot of no. 15)	16. *manín tʰí* 'camp away (from the village'
		17. Keze, Barved like a fish-hook (offshoot of no. 15)	17. *kʰezé* 'barb of a fishhook'
		18. Tcaⁿ kute, Shoot in the woods, a name of derision	18. *čʰąkʰúte* 'shoot at wood'

Stephen R. Riggs, 1852 (1893:160-161)	James Owen Dorsey (1897:260)	Retranscription
YANKTON	YANKTON	YANKTON
		1. *sičʰą́yu ihą́ktʰųwą* 'Burned Thigh Yankton'
		2. [?]
		3. *sihásapa* 'black foot'
		4. *oyúxpe waníča* 'never unloaded'
		5. *amdó wapúskʰiya* 'caused to dry on the shoulder'[a]
	6. Tcaⁿ kute, Shoot in the Woods	6. *čʰąkʰúte* 'shoot at wood'
	7. Tcaxu, Lights or Lungs	7. *čʰayú* 'lung'
	8. Wakmuha oiⁿ, Pumpkin Rind	8. *wakmúha oʔį* 'gourd earring'
	9. Iha isdaye, Mouth Greasers	9. *ihá isdáye* 'greasy lip'
	10. Watceuⁿpa, Roasters	10. *wačʰéʔupa* 'roasters'
	11. Ikmuⁿ, some animal of the cat kind	11. *ikmų́* 'cat'
	12. Oyate citca, Bad Nation	12. *oyáte šíča* 'bad people'
	13. Wacitcuⁿ tciⁿtca, Sons of White Men, the Half-breed "band" (a modern addition) Earring	13. *wašíčų čʰįčá* 'white man's child'
UPPER YANKTONAI	UPPER YANKTONAI	UPPER YANKTONAI
		1. *saʔóni ihą́ktʰųwą* 'Saone Yankton'; *sąʔíčiyapi* 'whiten themselves'
2. Kiyuksa, Dividers or Breakers of Law	2. Kiyuksa, Breakers (of the law or custom)	2. *kʰiyúksa* 'break in two'
		3. *xaxátʰų* 'falls (Ojibwa) village'
		4. [?]
5. Waxikute or Ćaŋona, Pine Shooters	5. Tcaⁿona, Shoot at Trees	5. *wazíkʰute* 'shoot at pine'; *cʰąʔóna* 'little tree shooter [?]'
		6. [?]

741

Table 4. Yankton and Yanktonai Band Names (continued)

Pierre-Antoine Tabeau, 1803-1804 *(A.H. Abel 1939:103)*	*Lewis and Clark, 1804-1805* *(Moulton 1983-, 3:419-420)*	*Joseph Nicollet, 1838-1839* *(DeMallie 1976:255-256)*	*Joseph Nicollet, 1838-1839* *(DeMallie 1976:258-259)*
UPPER YANKTONAI	UPPER YANKTONAI	UPPER YANKTONAI 7. Pamaksa ewichakiapi, those who cut their heads 8. Watapaatidan, those who put their lodges on the rivers; also called Toshu henduapi, those who bring the poles of lodges	UPPER YANKTONAI 7. Phabaksa, the cutters of heads
LOWER YANKTONAI 1. Hont-patines	LOWER YANKTONAI 1. Hone-ta-par-teen 2. Hone-ta-par-teen-wax	LOWER YANKTONAI	LOWER YANKTONAI 1. Onkpati, those who camp at the end

[a]Later sources classify this band as Sisseton.
[b]Based on Dorsey's mistaken assumption that the Assiniboine were an offshoot of the Yanktonai.

Table 5. Teton Band Names

Pierre-Antoine Tabeau, 1803-1804 *(A.H. Abel 1939:104)*	*Lewis and Clark, 1804-1805* *(Moulton 1983-, 3:420)*	*Joseph Nicollet, 1839* *(DeMallie 1976:259-260)*	*F.V. Hayden* *(1862:375-376)*
BRULE 1. Issanhati 2. Watchihoutairhe 3. Tchocatonhan 4. Woisage	BRULE 1. E-sah-a-te-ake-tar-par 2. War-chink-tar-he 3. Choke-tar-to-womb 4. Oz-ash 5. Me-ne-sharne	BRULE 3. Chokatowanyans, Brulés proper, those of the middle village 4. Wazazi, Osage 5. Minishanan, little band of Red Water 6. Kiuksa, those who divide, who separate	BRULE 4. wa-źá-za, Band rubbed out 7. wa-ći'-ōm-pa, The band that roasts meat 8. a-á-ko-za, Big ankle band 9. wam-bi-li'-ne-ca, Orphan band 10. si-ćá-wi-pi, Band with poor guns or bows

742

Stephen R. Riggs, 1852 (1893:160-161)	James Owen Dorsey (1897:260)	Retranscription
UPPER YANKTONAI	UPPER YANKTONAI	UPPER YANKTONAI
7. Pabakse, Cut Heads	7. Pa baksa, Cut Heads	7. *pʰábaksa* 'cut head'
		8. *watpá atʰídą* 'little dwellers at the river'; *tʰošúheyųpi* 'travois'
	9. Takini, Improved in condition, as a lean animal or a poor man	9. *tʰakíni* 'revived'
	10. Cikcitcena, Bad ones of different sorts	10. *šikšíčena* 'little bad ones'
	11. Bakihoⁿ, Gash themselves with knives	11. *bakíhų* 'cut or gash oneself'
	12. Name forgotten (probably an offshoot of the Wazi-kute now known as the Hohe, or Assiniboin)[b]	
LOWER YANKTONAI	LOWER YANKTONAI	LOWER YANKTONAI
1. Huŋkpatina		1. *húkpatʰina* 'little camp at camp circle entrance'
		2. *húkpatʰina wazíyata* 'northern little camp at camp circle entrance'
	3. Saⁿ ona, Shot at something white	3. *sąʔóna* 'little whitish shooter [?]'
	4. Pute temini, Sweat Lips	4. *pʰutétʰemni* 'sweaty lip'
	5. Cŭⁿ iktceka, Common Dogs, Dogs	5. *šųkíkčeka* 'common dog'
	6. Taquha yuta, Eat the scrapings of hides	6. *tʰaxúha yúta* 'eat hide scrapings'
	7. Iha ca, Red Lips	7. *ihá ša* 'red lip'
	8. Ite xu, Burnt Face	8. *itéɣu* 'burned face'
	9. Pte yuta cni, Eat no Buffalo (cows)	9. *pté yútašni* 'doesn't eat buffalo cow'

James Owen Dorsey (1897:261-263)	James Owen Dorsey (1897:261-263)	Retranscription
BRULE	BRULE	BRULE
	1. Isaⁿyati, Santees	1. *isą́ʔatʰi* 'camp at knife' (Santee)
		2. [?]
3. Tcoka towela, Blue spot in the middle		3. *čʰoką́tʰųwąą, čʰoką́tʰųwela* 'middle village'
	4. Wajaja, Osages (?)	4. *wažáže* 'Osage'
		5. *mnišána* 'little red water'
	6. Kiyuksa, Breaks, or Cuts, in two His own (custom, etc.)	6. *kʰiyúksa* 'break in two'
7. Watceŭⁿpa, Roasters	7. Watceŭⁿpa, Roasters	7. *wačʰéʔųpa* 'roasts meat'
8. Iyak'oza, Lump, or wart, on a horse's leg		8. *iyák̓oza* 'swollen knuckles (of a horse)'
		9. *wabléniča* 'orphan'
		10. *šíča wípʰe* 'bad weapons'
11. Ciyo taṅka, Big Prairie Chicken, or Grouse		11. *šiyó tʰą́ka* 'big prairie chicken'
12. Ho-mna, Fish Smellers		12. *hómna* 'fish odor'
13. Ciyo subula, Sharp-tailed Grouse		13. *šiyó swúla* 'small prairie chicken'
14. Kañ-xi yuha, Raven Keepers		14. *kʰąɣí yuhá* 'raven keeper'
15. Pispiza witcaca, Prairie Dog People		15. *pispíza wičʰáša* 'prairie dog people'

743

Table 5. Teton Band Names (continued)

Pierre-Antoine Tabeau, 1803-1804 (A.H. Abel 1939:104)	Lewis and Clark, 1804-1805 (Moulton 1983-, 3:420)	Joseph Nicollet, 1839 (DeMallie 1976:259-260)	F.V. Hayden (1862:375-376)
BRULE	BRULE	BRULE	BRULE
OGLALA	OGLALA	OGLALA	OGLALA
1. Okondanas	1. O-kan-dan-das		1. ōg-lá-la
2. Chihaut	2. She-o		
		3. Onkp'hatinas, lodges at the end of the circle	
		4. K̄u-Inyan, he gives the rock	
		5. Oyur̄pe, those who put down (the burden that they carry)	
			6. min-i-shá, Red water
			7. pe-hi'-pte-ći-la, Short hair band
			8. pa-ha-hi'-a, Those who camp at the end

James Owen Dorsey (1897:261-263)	James Owen Dorsey (1897:261-263)	Retranscription
BRULE	BRULE	BRULE
16. Walexa uⁿ wohaⁿ, Boil food with the Paunch-skin	16. Walexa oⁿ wohaⁿ, Boils with the Paunch-skin	16. *waléγa ų́ wóhą* 'boil using bladder'
17. Cawala, Shawnees (the descendants of a Shawnee chief adopted into the tribe)		17. *šawála* 'Shawnee'
18. Ihañktoⁿwaⁿ, Yanktons (so called from their mothers, not an original Sitcaⁿ-xu gens)		18. *ihą́ktʰųwą* 'Yankton'
19. Naqpaqpa, Take down leggings (after returning from war)		19. *naxpáxpa* 'leggings hanging down'
20. Apewaⁿtañka, Big Mane, so called from horses		20. *apʰéyohą tʰą́ka* 'big mane (of a horse)'
	21. Sitcaⁿ-xu, Burnt Thighs (proper)	21. *sičʰą́γu* 'burned thighs'
	22. Kak'exa, Making a grating noise	22. *kaǩéγa* 'making a grating sound'
	23. Hiⁿhaⁿcuⁿ-wapa, Towards the Owl Feather	23. *hįhą́šų wapʰáha* 'owl feather headdress'
	24. Cūñkaha nap'iⁿ, Wears a Dog-skin around the Neck	24. *šų́kaha napʔį́* 'dog (wolf) skin necklace'
	25. Hi-ha kaⁿhaⁿhaⁿwiⁿ, Woman the Skin of whose Teeth Dangles	25. *ihákąhąhą wį* 'dangling lip woman'
	26. Hūñku wanitca, Without a Mother	26. *hų́ku waníča* 'lacking mother'
	27. Miniskuya kitc'ŭⁿ, Wears Salt	27. *mniskúyakičų* 'wears salt'
	28. Ti glabu, Drums in his own Lodge	28. *tʰí glabú* 'makes his noise in the lodge'
	29. Wagluqe, Followers, commonly called Loafers	29. *wágluxe* 'lives with wife's relatives'
	30. Wagmeza yuha, Has Corn	30. *wagméza huhá* 'owns corn'
	31. Oglala itc'itcaxa, Makes himself an Oglala	31. *oglála ičíčaγa* 'makes himself Oglala'
	32. Tiyotcesli, Dungs in the Lodge	32. *tʰiyóčʰesli* 'defecates in the lodge'
	33. Ieska tciⁿtca, Interpreter's sons (Half-breeds)	33. *iyéska čʰičá* 'interpreter's child'
	34. Ohe noⁿpa, Two Kettles or Two Boilings	34. *oʔóhe núpa* 'two boilings'
	35. Okaxa witcaca, Man of the South	35. *okáγa wičʰáša* 'south man'
	36. Waqna, Snorts	36. *waxná* 'groans'
OGLALA	OGLALA	OGLALA
	1. Oglala, Scattered his own	1. *oglála* 'scatter one's own'
		2. *šiyó* 'prairie chicken'
		3. *hų́kpatʰina* 'little camp at camp circle entrance'
		4. *ǩú įγa* 'gives rock'
5. Oyuqpe	5. Oyuqpe, Thrown Down, or Unloaded	5. *oyúxpe* 'unloaded'
		6. *mnišá* 'red water'
	7. pe cla ptetcela, Short Bald Head	7. *pʰešlá ptéčela* 'short bald head'
8. Payabya	8. Payabyeya, Pushed aside	8. *pʰayábya* 'pushed aside [?]'
9. Wajaja		9. *wažáže* 'Osage'
10. Kiyuksa, Breaks his own (custom?)		10. *ǩiyúksa* 'break in half'
11. Tapicletca	11. Tapicletca, Spleen of an animal	11. *tʰapʰíšleča* 'spleen (of animal)'
12. Ite citca, Bad Face, or Oglala qtca, Real Oglala	12. Ite citca[a], Bad Face	12. *itéšiča* 'bad face'
13. Wagluqe	13. Wagluqe[b], Followers or Loafers	13. *wágluxe* 'lives with wife's relatives'
	14. Wablenitca, Orphans	14. *wabléniča* 'orphan'
	15. Pe cla, Bald Head	15. *pʰešlá* 'bald head'
	16. Tceq huha toⁿ, Kettle with Legs	16. *čʰéxhuhatʰų* 'kettle with legs'
	17. Tacnahetca, Gopher	17. *tʰašnáheča* 'gopher'
	18. I wayusota, Uses up by begging for, "Uses up with the Mouth"	18. *í wayúsota* 'use up by mouth'
	19. Wakaⁿ, Mysterious	19. *wakʰą́* 'sacred'
	20. Iglaka teqila, Refuses to Move Camp	20. *igláka tʰexíla* 'unwilling to move camp'

745

Table 5. Teton Band Names (continued)

Pierre-Antoine Tabeau, 1803-1804 (A.H. Abel 1939:104)	Lewis and Clark, 1804-1805 (Moulton 1983-, 3:420)	Joseph Nicollet, 1839 (DeMallie 1976:259-260)	F.V. Hayden (1862:375-376)
OGLALA	OGLALA	OGLALA	OGLALA
SANS ARCS	SANS ARCS	SANS ARCS	SANS ARCS 1. ta-shunk'-e-o-ta, Plenty of horses 2. min-i-shá, Red water band
HUNKPAPA	HUNKPAPA	HUNKPAPA	HUNKPAPA 1. hunk'-pa-pa, (meaning unknown) 2. ta-ló-na-pi, Fresh meat necklace band 3. ćé-ḣa-na-ka, Half-centre cloth band 4. ći-o-hó-pa, Sleeping kettle band 5. ćaŋ-ho-ham'-pa, Band with bad backs
MINNECONJOU 1. Minican-hojou 2. Tacohiropapais	MINNECONJOU 1. Min-na-kine-az-zo 2. Tar-co-eh-parh	MINNECONJOU	MINNECONJOU 1. min-i-kaŋ́-źu, Band that plants near the river 3. wak-pó-ki-an, Flying river band 4. i-na-há-o-wīn, Stone ear-ring band 5. wa-ḣa-lé-zo-wen, Striped snake ear-ring band 6. shunk'-a-yu-tēsh-ni, Band that eat no dogs
BLACKFEET	BLACKFEET	BLACKFEET	BLACKFEET 1. si-há-sa-pa, Blackfeet 2. ći-hú-pa, Jawbone band 3. pa-á-bi-a, Those who camp at the end

James Owen Dorsey (1897:261-263)	James Owen Dorsey (1897:261-263)	Retranscription
OGLALA	OGLALA	OGLALA
	21. Ite citca etaⁿhaⁿ, Part of the Bad Face "Face Bad From"	21. *itéšiča etáhą* 'out of bad face'
	22. Zuzetca kiyaksa, Bit the Snake in Two	22. *zuzéča kʰiyáksa* 'bite snake in two'
	23. Watceoⁿpa, Roasters	23. *wačʰéʔųpa* 'roasts meat'
	24. Watcape, Stabber	24. *wačʰápʰe* 'stabber'
	25. Tiyotcesli, Dungs in the lodge	25. *tʰiyóčʰesli* 'defecates in the lodge'
	26. Ieska tciⁿtca, "Interpreter's" sons, Half-breeds	26. *iyéska čʰičá* 'interpreter's child'
SANS ARC		SANS ARC
		1. *tʰašų́ke óta* 'many horses'
2. Itaziptco qtca, Real Itaziptco, or Mini-ca-la, Red Water		2. *mnišá(la)* '(little) red water'; *itázipčʰo xčá* 'real without bows'
3. Cina luta oiⁿ, Scarlet Cloth Earring		3. *šiná lúta oʔį* 'scarlet blanket earring'
4. Woluta yuta, Eat dried venison, or buffalo-meat, from the hind quarter		4. *wóluta yúta* 'eat dried buffalo round'
5. Maz pegnaka, Wear (pieces of) Metal in the Hair		5. *máspʰégnaka* 'metal headdress'
6. Tatañka tcesli, Dung of a Buffalo-bull		6. *tʰatʰą́ka čʰeslí* 'buffalo bull dung'
7. Cikcitcela, Bad ones of different sorts		7. *šikšíčela* 'little bad ones'
8. Tiyopa otcaⁿnůⁿpa, Smokes at the Entrance of the Lodge		8. *tʰiyópa očʰą́nųpa* 'smokes at the doorway'
HUNKPAPA		HUNKPAPA
		1. *hų́kpapʰa* 'head of camp circle opening'
2. Talo nap'iⁿ, Fresh-meat Necklace		2. *tʰaló napį́* 'raw meat necklace'
3. Tcegnake okisela, Half a Breech-cloth		3. *čʰégnake okʰísela* 'little half breech cloth'
4. Tce oqba		4. *čʰé oxpá* 'drooping penis'
5. Tcañka oqaⁿ, Sore Backs (of horses), not the original name		5. *čʰąká oẋą* '[over]worked back' [?]
6. Tinazipe citca, Bad Bows		6. *itázipčʰo šíča* 'bad bows'
7. Kiglacka, Ties his Own		7. *kʰigláška* 'ties his own in the middle [?]'
8. Cikcitcela, Bad ones of different sorts		8. *šikšíčela* 'little bad ones'
9. Wakaⁿ, Mysterious		9. *wakʰą́* 'sacred'
10. Hůⁿska tcaⁿtojuha, Legging Tobacco-pouch		10. *hųská čʰątóẋuha* 'legging tobacco bag'
MINNECONJOU	MINNECONJOU	MINNECONJOU
		1. *mnikʰówožu* 'plant at water'
		2. [?]
3. Wakpokiⁿyaⁿ, Flies along the Creek	3. Wakpokiⁿyaⁿ, Flies along the Creek	3. *wakpókįyą* 'flying along river'
4. Iⁿyaⁿ-ha oiⁿ, Mussel-Shell Earring	4. Iⁿyaⁿ-ha oiⁿ, Mussel-Shell Earring	4. *íyąho oʔį* 'shell earring'
5. Wagleza oiⁿ, Water-snake Earring	5. Wagleza oiⁿ, Water-snake Earring	5. *wagléza oʔį* 'garter snake earring'
6. Cůñka yute cni, Eat no Dogs	6. Cůñka yute cni, Eat no dogs	6. *šų́ka yútešni* 'doesn't eat dog'
7. Uñktce yuta, Eat Dung	7. Uñktce yuta, Eat Dung	7. *ųkčé yúta* 'eats dung'
8. Glagla hetca, Slovenly	8. Glagla hetca, Slovenly	8. *glaglá héčʰa* 'unkempt kind'
9. Cikcitcela, Bad ones of different sorts, or Very Bad	9. Cikcitcela, Bad ones of different sorts, or Very Bad	9. *šikšíčela* 'little bad ones'
	10. Nixe tañka, Big Belly	10. *niɣé tʰą́ka* 'big belly'
	11. Waⁿ nawexa, Broken Arrows	11. *wą́ nawéɣa* 'arrow broken by foot'
BLACKFEET	BLACKFEET	BLACKFEET
1. Siha sapa qtca, Real Black Feet	1. Siha sapa qtca	1. *sihá sápa* 'black foot'
		2. *čʰehúpa* 'jawbone'
		3. *pʰayábya* 'pushed aside [?]'
4. Kaⁿxi cůⁿ pegnaka, Wears Raven Feather in the Hair	4. Kaⁿxi cůⁿ pegnaka	4. *kʰaɣí šų́ pʰégnaka* 'crow feather headdress'

Table 5. Teton Band Names (continued)

Pierre-Antoine Tabeau, 1803-1804 (A.H. Abel 1939:104)	Lewis and Clark, 1804-1805 (Moulton 1983-, 3:420)	Joseph Nicollet, 1839 (DeMallie 1976:259-260)	F.V. Hayden (1862:375-376)
BLACKFEET	BLACKFEET	BLACKFEET	BLACKFEET
TWO KETTLES	TWO KETTLES	TWO KETTLES	TWO KETTLES
1. Waniwacteonilla	1. Wah-nee-wack-a-ta-o-ne-lar	1. Wanonwakteninan, I killed by mistake, without wishing it	1. wak-to-ni'-la, The band that kill no people

unity of the Sioux as a people. There is no evidence for the historical existence of the Seven Council Fires as a political alliance or for a level of social integration greater than the tribe (DeMallie 1986:20–21).

Population

The first estimates of the Sioux population are 7,000 men, given by Radisson (1961:142), who visited the Sioux of the East in 1662, and 8,000–9,000 men given by Hennepin (1903, 1:226), who was among the Sioux of the East in 1680. Le Sueur, in the 1690s, estimated the population of the Sioux of the East at 300 dwellings (600–900 families) and the Sioux of the West at over 1,000 dwellings (more than 2,000–3,000 families). In 1702 Le Sueur's estimate of the Sioux was 4,000 families (M.M. Wedel 1974a:163, 165, 166). An estimate from 1778 gives the Sioux population as 10,000 (Thomas Hutchins in Schoolcraft 1851–1857, 6:714). In 1804–1805 Lewis and Clark gave a total of 8,410 (Moulton 1983–, 3:410–417), but Pike gave 21,675 (D.D. Jackson 1966, 1:222) (table 6).

Table 6. Sioux Population, 1804-1805 to 1868

	1804-1805 (Lewis and Clark in Moulton 1983-, 3:408-417)	1805 (Pike in D.D. Jackson 1965, 1:220-222)	1820 (Morse 1822:365)	1823 (Long in Keating 1825,1:396)	1833 (Denig 1961:14-15)[a]	1849 (Ramsey 1849: 1015-1023)	1856 (Warren 1856:16)[b]	1868 (ARCIA 1868: 812-813)
Santee								
Mdewakanton	1,200	2,105	1,650	1,500		220		1,340
Wahpekute	500	450	1,250	800		800		
Wahpeton	700	1,060		900		1,500		1,637
Sisseton	800	2,160	1,950	2,500		3,800		3,500
Yankton	700	4,300	1,000	2,000	1,500	3,200	2,880	2,500
Yanktonai	1,600		2,500	5,200	2,000	4,000	6,400	4,650[c]
Teton		11,600		14,400		6,000		
Brule	900		1,500		2,500		3,840	12,485[d]
Oglala	360		2,250		1,500		2,880	
Minneconjou	750				1,300		1,600	3,060
Saone	900		1,500					
Blackfeet					1,100		1,280	1,200
Two Kettles					500		800	750
Sans Arcs					500		1,360	720
Hunkpapa					750		2,920	3,000
Total	8,410	21,675	13,600	27,300	11,650	19,520	23,960	34,842

[a]Based on Denig's estimate of 5 people per lodge.
[b]Based on Warren's estimate of 8 people per lodge.
[c]Lower Yanktonai 2,250; Upper Yanktonai 2,400.
[d]Brule and Oglala on the Platte River 7,885; Lower Brule 1,600; Oglala on the Missouri River 3,000.

James Owen Dorsey (1897:261-263)	James Owen Dorsey (1897:261-263)	Retranscription
BLACKFEET	BLACKFEET	BLACKFEET
5. Glagla hetca, Untidy, Slovenly, Shiftless	5. "There is no band called Glagla hetca."	5. *glaglá héčʰa* 'unkempt kind'
6. Wajaje (Kill Eagle's band, named after the band of Kill Eagle's father he being a Wajaja of the Oglala	6. Wajaje	6. *wažáže* 'Osage'
7. Hohe, Assiniboin	7. Hohe	7. *hóhe* 'Assiniboine'
8. Wamnuxa oiⁿ, Shell Ear-pendant	8. Wamnuxa oiⁿ	8. *wamúxʔa oʔį* 'cowrie shell earring'
	9. Ti zaptaⁿ, Five Lodges	9. *tʰizáptą* 'five lodges'
TWO KETTLES		TWO KETTLES
		1. [?]
2. Oohe noⁿpa, Two Boilings		2. *oʔóhe núpa* 'two boilings'
3. Ma waqota, Skin Smeared with Whitish Earth		3. *há waxóta* 'skin streaked grayish'

Synonymy†

The name Sioux derives from the early Ottawa designation *na·towe·ssiwak* (sg. *na·towe·ssi*) 'Sioux', which was borrowed into French as Nadoüessioüak and adapted as Nadouessioux, with the French plural -*x* substituted for the Ojibwa plural -*ak* (Goddard 1984:105; Baraga 1878–1880, 2:264). The name was shortened to Sioux, the last syllable of the longer form, a type of abbreviation that was common French practice. The Ottawa name *na·towe·ssi* is derived from Proto-Algonquian **na·towe·wa* 'Northern Iroquoian', which in several Algonquian languages also means 'eastern massasauga (*Sistrurus*)', a small rattlesnake. The name **na·towe·wa* appears to be related to a Proto-Algonquian element **-a·towe·* 'speak a (foreign) language', suggesting that the meaning 'massasauga' is secondary (Pentland 1979; Goddard 1984:105). Alternatively, Siebert (1996) argued that the original form was **na·tawe·wa* 'massasauga' (literally 'seeker of heat') and was later extended to designate Northern Iroquoians. The translation of Ottawa *na·towe·ssi* and hence of *Sioux* as 'snake; enemy' (Hodge 1907–1910, 1:376, 379, 2:577) is a misrepresentation based on the alternate meaning of the related name **na·towe·wa*; the name *Sioux* never meant 'snake'.

The earliest French recordings of the Ottawa name are exemplified by Nadvesiv, 1640 (Le Jeune in JR 1896–1901, 18:231); Naudouisioux and Naudouisses, 1642 (Raymbault in Brackett 1877:466); Nadoüessis, 1642, Nadouesiouek, 1656, Nadouechiouek, 1658, Nadwechiwec, 1660, Nadoüechiowec, 1660, Natwesix, 1661, Nadoüessioüax, 1665, Nadouessiouek, 1665, Nadoüecious, 1670, and Nadoüessious, 1670, Nadoussiens, 1677 (JR 1896–1901, 23:225, 42:221, 44:249, 45:237, 46:67, 143, 49:241, 249, 54:223, 229, 60:211); Nadouags, Nadouagssioux, Nadouaissious, Nadouaissioux, and Nadouayssioux (Bacqueville de la Potherie 1753, 2:49, 147, 179, 62, 56); Nadoüessans and Nadoüessious, 1679–1681 (La Salle in Margry 1876–1886, 1:481); Nadoussieux, 1681 (Du Chesneau in NYCD 1853–1887, 9:153); Nadouesioux, 1689 (Perrot in Margry 1876–1886, 5:33); Nadoessious, 1697 (La Chesnaye in Margry 1876–1886, 6:6); and Nadouesans and Nadoussians (Hennepin 1698, 1:map, 178).

Later renditions of the name include: Nadonessis (Lahontan 1703, 1:301); Nadouessons (Coxe 1741:42); Nottoweasses, 1759 (Croghan 1831:146n); Naudowessies and Nawdowessie (Carver 1778:56, 59); Naudawissees, 1790 (Umfreville 1954:101); Nauduwassies, 1812 (Schermerhorn 1814:39); Naddouwessioux and Naddouwessces (Brackenridge 1815:77); Nadiousioux (Keating 1824, 2:323); Nadowassis (Maximilian 1843:148); Nadonaisioug, Nadonechiouk, Nadouesciouz, and Nadsnessiouck (Domenech 1860, 2:26); Nadouessies and Nadouwesis (Hayden 1862:380); Nad8echi8ec (Charlevoix 1866–1872, 3:31); and Mattaugwessawacks (Sproat 1868:188, a misprint). For other spellings see Hodge (1907–1910, 1:379–380).

Cognates of the Ottawa name occur as designations for Sioux in other Algonquian languages: Arapaho *nó·tinéihinóʔ* (sg. *no·tínei*) (Ives Goddard, personal communication 1990), cited earlier as Nat-e-ne'-hin-a 'cut-throats' (Hayden 1862:326), an interpretation derived from the sign language designation; Natenéhima (Mallery 1878:352); and Natni (Mooney 1896:1057); also as Potawatomi Nátuessuag (sg. Nátuesse), mistranslated 'small snakes' (Gatschet 1878, 1879:78).

The earliest occurrences of the shortened French form Sioux (sg. Siou) begin in the seventeenth century: Siroux and Scioux, 1665–1699 (Perrot 1864:55, 385); Sioux, 1687 (Morel in Margry 1876–1886, 5:32); Cioux, 1693 and Ciou, 1695 (NYCD 1853–1887, 9:570, 611); Scious, 1702 (JR 1896–1901, 65:173; 66:31); Siou, 1703 (Lamothe Cadillac in Margry

†This synonymy was written by Douglas R. Parks.

1876–1886, 5:329); Sieux (Coxe 1741:20); Siouxes (Bacqueville de la Potherie 1753, 4:33); Sous, 1761 (Gorrell in Draper 1855:26); La Sues and Sue, 1765 (Croghan 1831:38); and Siooz (Jefferys 1776:map 8). By the nineteenth century, Sioux had become the common Euro-American designation but continued to be spelled variously; for example, Scieux, 1801(Henry in E.D. Neill 1885:453); Soos, Sous, Soues, Sisouex, Sceouex, Scioux, Souix, and Seauex, 1804–1805 (Lewis and Clark in Moulton 1983–, 3:8, 11, 20, 22, 24, 32, 408, 234); Siowee (Ordway in Moulton 1983–, 9:45); Saoux, 1812 (Schermerhorn 1814:12); Sciou (E.D. Neill 1858:149); Saux (Hurlbert in P. Jones 1861:178); Chi8 (Charlevoix 1866–1872, 3:31); and Sioxes (Poole 1881:153).

The name Sioux was borrowed from French as Menominee *si·y* (*si·yu·hkiw* 'Sioux woman') (Bloomfield 1975:243) and Michif *syoo* (Laverdure and Allard 1983:298), and from English as Fox *so·ha* (Ives Goddard, personal communication 2000), Kansa *su* (Gatschet 1878:27 in Hodge 1907–1910, 1:380), and Quapaw *sú* (Robert L. Rankin, personal communication 1987).

The Sioux name for themselves is Santee-Sisseton and Yankton-Yanktonai *dakʰóta* and Teton *lakʰóta*, generally interpreted as meaning 'feeling affection, friendly' (Riggs 1890:106) or 'united, allied' (Keating 1825:337, 393; S.R. Riggs 1893:183). The term was first documented as a self-designation in 1804–1805, when William Clark (Moulton 1983–, 3:27, 32) wrote that "This nation call themselves— Dar co tar. The french call them Souex." The Stoney used the cognate form *nakʰóta* for Sioux and Assiniboine (Laurie 1959a:93), while the Crow borrowed it as *dakkó·te·*, a less frequently used designation (Medicine Horse 1987:15; Randolph Graczyk, personal communication 1989), cited previously as Ma-koʹ-ta (Hayden 1862:402). In English the name Dakota has been used for the Santee-Sisseton division and for the Sioux as a whole (Hodge 1907–1910, 1:376).

Early in the twentieth century the form *nakʰóta*, used as a self-designation by both the Assiniboine and Stoney, was incorrectly attributed to the Yankton and Yanktonai as well (Hodge 1907–1910, 1:376), and the assertion that the Yankton and Yanktonai used the form *nakʰóta* was repeated by anthropologists and linguists until by 2000 it had become entrenched in the literature. It had also become a symbol of self-identification for Yankton and Yanktonai young people that distinguished them from the Santee-Sisseton and Teton, even though the actual self-designation in Yankton and Yanktonai is *dakʰóta* (Parks and DeMallie 1992).

Examples of variant spellings of Dakota are: Dacorta, 1805 (William Clark in D.D. Jackson 1962:536); Dacota (Keating 1824, 2:245); Dahcotah (Tanner 1830:18); Dahcotas (Gallatin 1836:121); Dakotha (de Smet 1848:264); Docota (Drake 1848:vii); and Dacotah (Howe 1851:357). Several early recordings of the name, all written in Santee country, reflect a prenasalized dental stop [^{n}d], which was characteristic of Santee (and perhaps Yankton-Yanktonai) speech in the nineteenth century and was sometimes heard by Euro-Americans as an n: Narcotah (Schoolcraft 1821:291), Ndakotahs

(Nicollet 1843:10), and Nahcotah (Featherstonhaugh 1847, 1:223). Sometime in the mid- to late-nineteenth century the sound lost its prenasalization (although it survived in one dialect of Assiniboine in the late twentieth century).

Spellings of Lakota include La-cotahs (Ruxton 1849:112) Lahcotah (Hyer and Starring 1866), and Lacota (L.H. Morgan in Beach 1877:220).

A designation for the Sioux occasionally used by the French in the seventeenth century appears as Nacion qu'on nomme du Boeuf, 1662 (JR 1896–1901, 47:148) and Nation of the Beef (Radisson 1961:134, 136), probably actually 'buffalo nation'.

The Ojibwa called the Sioux *pwa·nak* (sg. *pwa·n*) (Baraga 1878–1880, 1:231, 2:97; Nichols and Nyholm 1995:39 retranscribed), which was *pwa·rak* (sg. *pwa·r*) in seventeenth-century Ojibwa-Algonquin and *pwa·lak* (sg. *pwa·l*) in Old Ottawa; these forms appear as Ponarak (for Pouarak), 1656 (JR 1896–1901, 42:221); Poulak and Poualak, 1658 (JR 1896–1901, 44:247, 296); Pouanak (Tailhan in Perrot 1864:232); Booines (Keating 1824, 1:389); Bwoinug and Bwoirnug (Tanner 1830:144, 316); and Boin-acs and Bevanacs (ARCIA 1849:70); Wanak, 1853 (Belcourt 1872:235); Bewanacs (Lapham, Blossom, and Dousman 1870:15); and Poualac (Mallery 1878:352). This name is from Proto-Algonquian *pwa·θa, used for various foreign tribes.

The cognate in Cree, including the Plains dialect, is *pwa·tak* (sg. *pwa·t*), which frequently occurs with the diminutive suffix as *pwa·tis* (H. Christoph Wolfart, personal communication 1987). Previous citations of the Cree form are Pwâtak (Pwât) (Lacombe 1874:547), and Poatŭk (Poatá) (Curtis 1907–1930, 18:158), which in the early fur trade literature appears as either Poet or a close variant of it in the name for Assiniboine.

A nineteenth-century folk-etymology of Ojibwa *pwa·n* erroneously connected it with Ojibwa *apwe·* 'to roast' and *apwa·na·kk* 'roasting stick', assuming a reference to the Sioux custom of torturing foes (W.W. Warren 1885:36). Examples are: Abbwoi-nug (Tanner 1830:57); Ab-boin-ee Sioux or Roasters (ARCIA 1850:83); Aboinug, Abwoinug, and O-bwah-nug (Schoolcraft 1851–1857, 2:141, 5:39, 193); and Ab-boin-ug and Ab-oin (W.W. Warren 1885:36, 162).

A widely distributed name for Sioux occurs among Algonquian languages as Miami-Illinois *ša·ha* (Gatschet 1895) and *aša·haki* (sg. *aša·ha*) (Gravier 1700–1710; Le Boullenger 1725, phonemicized); Fox *aša·ha* (Goddard 1994a:19, 275); Kickapoo *wasa·ha* (Paul Voorhis, personal communication 1989); and Shawnee *šaha·ki* (sg. *šaha*) (Voegelin 1938–1940, 8:318). The same name appears in Dhegiha-Chiwere Siouan languages as Winnebago *ša̜·há̜* (Kenneth Miner and Josephine White Eagle, personal communications 1987); Omaha *ša̜* (Dorsey 1890:339; Fletcher and La Flesche 1911:102; retranscribed) from Pre-Omaha *šahá* (John Koontz, personal communication 1987); Ponca *ša̜·* or *šá̜* (Parks 1988; J.H. Howard 1965:133); Kansa *šahá̜* (Rankin 1987:128); Iowa and Otoe *šáha̜* or *šá* (Dorsey 1878–1881, retranscribed) or *šá̜ha̜* (G.H. Marsh 1936; Parks 1988).

In contrast, Quapaw *šahá* (Dorsey 1882–1894, retranscribed), Arikara *ša·hé?*, and Pawnee *sa·he* (Skiri *sáhi*) designate the Cheyenne.

In the Plains sign language the gesture for Sioux is to draw the hand, extended and flat, palm down, across the throat from left to right, as if cutting it; a variant used by the Sauk, Fox, Kickapoo, and Sioux, is to draw the forefinger of the left hand from right to left across the throat (Mallery 1881:467; W.P. Clark 1885:341; H.L. Scott 1912–1934). The standard interpretation is that it represents slitting the throat or cutting a head off, said to be a trait of the Sioux.

The standard interpretation of the sign language gesture is a common designation for Sioux that occurs primarily among tribes living west of them and invariably translates as 'head-cutters, decapitators' or 'cut-throats'. Names among Plains tribes with this meaning are the following: Osage *ppápaxǫ* (Carolyn Quintero, personal communication 1999; Francis La Flesche 1932:124) and *ppápawaxǫ* (Robert L. Rankin, personal communication 1990); Caddo *ca ba?kuš* or *ba?kuš* (Gatschet in Hodge 1907–1910, 1:378, phonemicized; Wallace L. Chafe, personal communication 2000), cited also as Tsaba'kosh (Mooney 1896:1057); Kitsai Niakĕtsikûtk (Mooney 1893); Comanche *papiciminani* (sg. *papicimina*) (Robinson and Armagost 1990:75, 96; Casagrande 1954–1955:231; Curtis 1907–1930, 19:229), cited also as Túyĕtchískĕ (ten Kate 1884:9); and Crow *akparea·šú·paško* (Medicine Horse 1987:15; Randolph Graczyk, personal communication 1987), cited previously as mar-an-sho-bish-ko (James 1823, 2:lxxix), barashū'-gi-o (Hayden 1862:402), and Minishúpsko (H.L. Scott 1906 in Hodge 1907–1910, 1:378; Randolph Graczyk, personal communication 2000). The same designation occurs as the name of an Arikara men's society, *pahnIšúkAt* 'cut-throat', a reference to the Sioux (Lowie 1915:670; Parks 1999).

Names with the same meaning among tribes west of the Rocky Mountains are: Flathead Noxtu' 'Sioux; Cree' (Teit 1930:302), also recorded as Nhutú (Curtis 1907–1930, 7:166), phonemicized as *n-x^w'tu* (Sarah G. Thomason, personal communication 1998); Salish Nŭqtu' (W.J. Hoffman 1886a:371) or Nuktúsĕm, translated as 'cut-throats' (Gatschet 1884 in Hodge 1907–1910, 1:380); Okanagan Nxtúsum (Gatschet 1884 in Hodge 1907–1910, 1:380); Nez Perce *?isequ·lkt* (Aoki 1994:597), cited previously as Isăkúlkt (Curtis 1907–1930, 8:163); Kootenai khtuhtamá'ka (Curtis 1907–1930, 7:168); and Yakima Píshakulk (Mooney 1892 in Hodge 1907–1910, 1:380). In Eastern Shoshone it is *pampiciminah* (Tidzump 1970; David Shaul, personal communication 1989), cited also as Pain-pe-tse-menay (Gebow 1868:18) and as Pambizimina and Papitsinima (Mooney 1896:1057). An unattested Ute cognate is given as Pámpe Chyimina 'hand cutters' (Burton 1861:124; Talmy Givón, personal communication 2000).

The name occurs in English sources as Cutthroats (Marcy 1866:33, where erroneously given as the translation of Dakota) and in French as Coupe-gorges (Blackmore 1869:301; Burton 1861:95).

Perhaps derived in meaning from the preceding names is Kiowa *k'ól-p^hǎ-hɔ́* 'necktie people' (Laurel Watkins, personal communication 1979), recorded also as K'odalpäk'iñago 'necklace people' (Mooney 1896:1057) and Go/-dlp'äk'i 'bead necklace people' (La Barre 1935), and given in translation as 'neckless people' by H.L. Scott (1912–1934).

Another name for Sioux is Arikara *sanánat*, also cited as sun-nún-at (Hayden 1862:357), and its Pawnee cognate *carara·t*, also cited as Chah'-ra-rat (Grinnell 1889:92), both of which have the general meaning 'enemy' as well as the specific designation 'Sioux' (Parks 1999c, 1999a, 1999b; Curtis 1907–1930, 5:152). Similar to it in form is Plains Apache *cànnànà·*, which has no known underlying meaning (Bittle 1952–1953) and may be a borrowing of the Pawnee or Arikara name.

Two tribes refer to the Sioux as 'downriver (or southern) Assiniboine': Piegan Pinápǐ-sĭnna (Curtis 1907–1930, 6:155) and Gros Ventre *nɔ́ɔ́wunɔ́ɔ́kinéíhinɔh* (sg. *nɔ́ɔ́wunɔ́ɔ́kinéíh*) 'southern Assiniboine' (Allan R. Taylor, personal communication 1987), cited also as náwinatyiné 'downriver Assiniboine' (Curtis 1907–1930, 5:154). The cognate Blackfoot term for Sioux is *pina·pisina·* 'downstream or east Cree' (Frantz and Russell 1989:434; Allan R. Taylor, personal communication 1987). The name kaí'spa 'parted hair', which is also the sign language gesture for 'woman', is attributed to the Blood (Curtis 1907–1930, 18:187) and to the Sarcee (E.F. Wilson 1889:243). A Seneca designation for the Sioux, apparently also used by other northern Iroquoians, is Wä-sä-sa-o-no and Wä-sä'-seh-o-no (L.H. Morgan 1870:52n, 1851:268), phonemically *wasáse·onǫ?* 'war dance people', formed from *wasa·se?* 'war dance' (Wallace L. Chafe, personal communication 2000), which is a borrowing of the Osage name for themselves. Other descriptive names with no known explanation are: Hidatsa *ita·hácki* 'long arrow' (W. Matthews 1877:159; Curtis 1907–1910, 4:186; A.W. Jones 1979:131), cited also as It-ans-ke (E. James 1823, 2:lxxxiv); Mandan *xǫhnú·mǫk* 'grass man' (Curtis 1907–1930, 5:148; Parks 1991a; Mauricio Mixco, personal communication 2000); and Wyandot Yuⁿssáha 'birds' (Gatschet 1879 in Hodge 1907–1910, 1:380).

Names with no known etymology are Cheyenne *ho?óhomo?eo?o* (sg. *ho?óhomo?e*) (Glenmore and Leman 1985:201), cited previously as Hóh-otann (Maximilian in Thwaites 1904–1907, 24:222), Ohó-homo 'those on the outside' (ten Kate 1884:8), Ohoomeo (sg. Ohoomoe) (Petter 1913–1915:583), and Hoóhomoéo (Curtis 1907–1930, 6:158); and Wichita *wá·k^wicinn* (Parks 1987; David S. Rood, personal communication 1987).

Santee-Sisseton

The name Santee was used by Sioux groups living along the Missouri River to designate the four tribes comprising the Eastern Sioux (Mdewakanton, Wahpekute, Wahpeton, and Sisseton). The native form, which has two variants in Santee and Teton, *isą́?at^hi* and *isąyat^hi*, is derived from   *751 isą́* 'knife' + *at^hí* 'to encamp at', that is, 'camp at knife (quarry)' (S.R. Riggs 1890:206–207; Buechel 1970:233). Although the source of the name is obscure, it may be a reference to the Santee camps at what is now Pipestone National Monument, Minnesota, or to their former residence at Knife Lake (S.R. Riggs 1890:206).

Santee is an anglicization of the Sioux name, and most historical citations are renditions of it. Early French spellings are: Izatys, 1678 (Dulhut in Margry 1876–1886, 6:22); Issaqui and Issaquy, 1697 (La Chesnaye in Margry 1876–1886, 6:6); Issati and Issatrians (Hennepin 1698:99, 174); Isantiton, 1700 (De l'Isle in E.D. Neill 1858:164). An early English spelling is Hizantinton (Jeffreys 1776:map 5). Two of those forms (Isantiton and Hizantinton) suggest that an eighteenth-century variant of *isą́ʔat^hi* was *isą́ʔat^hit^hųwą*, which has *t^hųwá* 'village' as a final element of the compound, the common Sioux designator for a tribe or division.

American renditions of Santee are exemplified by: Esantees, 1833 (Denig 1961:15); Santas (S. Parker 1842:45); Isanati and Es-sah'-ah-tee (Ramsey in ARCIA 1849:78); Isanyate, Issanti, and Santie (Seymour 1850:17, 86, 152); Isanties and Esanties (S.R. Riggs 1852:92); Isantie Dakotas and I-saŋ'-tis (Hayden 1862:map, 371); Isaunties (L.H. Morgan 1870:44); Santee Sioux (Poole 1881:31). Other variants are in Hodge (1907–1910, 2:892–893).

The Sioux form of the name was borrowed into surrounding languages as Arikara *sá·tI* (Parks 1999c), Mandan *isáhti* (Parks 1982), and Hidatsa I-tsá'-ti (W. Matthews 1877:161).

Other historical forms refer to the Santee as Sioux with a modifier, generally geographical. Eastern Sioux is the most common: Sioux orientaux, 1665–1699 (Perrot 1864:232n); Scioux of the East, 1700 (Le Sueur in E.D. Neill 1858:170); Sioux de L'Est, 1700 (Le Sueur in Margry 1876–1886, 6:78); Eastern Sioux (Jefferys 1761, 1:45); E. Scihous (Coxe 1741:map). Others refer to their sedentary life or their woodlands residence: Nad8esseronons sédentaires and Sioux orientaux ou sédentaires (Tailhan in Perrot 1864:232, 340); Scioux of the Woods, 1736 (Chauvignerie in Schoolcraft 1851–1857, 3:557); Sioux of the Woods (W. Smith 1766:70); 1766:70); Saux of the Wood (Trumbull 1851:185); Siouxs of the river St. Peter's (Treaty of 1815 in Kappler 1904–1941, 2:114); Sioux of the River (Seymour 1850:135); and Dacotas of the St. Peter's (G.K. Warren 1856:17). Two geographical references are Lower Sioux (ARCIA 1858:52) and Upper Dakotas, 1851 (Ramsey 1872:49).

The Cheyenne call the Eastern Sioux tribes *náhtovonaho* (Glenmore and Leman 1985:201), cited also as Nàtovona (Petter 1913–1915:583). The Menominee call them *wi·kwana·skiw* (Bloomfield 1975:281).

• MDEWAKANTON Mdewakanton, the self-designation of this tribe, is derived from *mdé* (later *bdé*) 'lake' + *wak^hą* 'holy' + *t^hųwą* 'village', that is, 'holy lake village', a reference to its residence by an unspecified lake, frequently said to be Mille Lacs.

Most historical citations reflect the Sioux form. Early French and English examples are: Menchokatonx, 1689 (Perrot in E.D. Neill 1858:144); Menchokatoux, 1689 (Perrot in E.D. Neill 1881:93); Manchokatous, 1689 (Perrot in Margry 1876–1886, 5:34); Mencouacantons, 1700 (Pénicaut in McWilliams 1953:47); Mendeouacantons and Mandeouacantons, 1702 (Le Sueur in Margry 1987–1886, 6:80, 81); Mendouca-ton, 1700 (La Harpe in B.F. French 1851:27); Mawtawbauntowahs (Carver 1778:60); and Winde-wer-rean-toon, 1795 (Arrowsmith 1814:map).

Later citations are: Mindewacantons, 1803–1804 (Tabeau 1939:103); Mindawarcarton and Min'-da-wâr'-câr-ton, 1806 (Lewis and Clark 1809:28, 30); Minowakanton (Lewis and Clark 1814, 1:145); Minoway-Kantong and Minoway-Kautong (Schermerhorn 1814:40); Menowa Kautong (Boudinot 1816:127); Minow Kantong and Mendewacantongs (Schoolcraft 1821:286; 307); Mende Wahkan toan (Keating 1824, 1:396); Me-da-we-con-tong (Treaty of 1825 in Kappler 1904–1941, 2:254); Munday Wawkantons (Snelling 1830:231); Mende-Wakan-Toann, 1833 (Maximilian 1843:149); Mdewakantonwan-nan 'village of Spirit Lake' and Mendewakantoan, 1839 (Nicollet in DeMallie 1976:255, 257); Medawakantons (ARCIA 1839:494); Med-ay-wah-kawn-t'waw and Mede-wakant'wan (Ramsey in ARCIA 1849:1014); Mundaywahkanton (McKenney and Hall 1846–1854, 1:303); Medawakantwan (N.H. Parker 1857:140); M'daywawkawntwawns (E.D. Neill 1858:144n); Midewakantonwans (Domenech 1860, 2:26); and Mediwanktons (Keane 1878:521). Other variants are in Hodge (1907–1910, 1:828).

The Mdewakanton were also designated by the name Sioux with a geographical modifier. The most common name was Sioux of the Lakes, cited as people of the lakes (Tabeau 1939:102; Nicollet in DeMallie 1976:257), Gens de Lake (Lewis and Clark in Moulton 1983–, 3:410), People of the Lake (Lewis and Clark 1814, 1:145), Gens de Lac (Z.M. Pike 1810:93), Gens De Lai (Schermerhorn 1814:40), Gens du Lac (Keating 1824, 1:380), and Siouxs of the Lakes (Treaty of 1815 in Kappler 1904–1941, 2:113), as well as Sioux of the River (Seymour 1850:133), the latter a reference to the St. Peter's (Minnesota) River.

• WAHPEKUTE The native self-designaton *waxpék^hute*, anglicized as Wahpekute, is derived from *waxpé* 'leaf' + *k^huté* 'to shoot', that is, 'leaf shooter(s)', the significance of which is obscure. Historical citations of the name in English and French translation include: Leaf Beds (Coyner 1847:70); people of the leaves, 1803–1804 (Tabeau 1939:102); People of the Leaves detached, 1806 (Z.M. Pike in Schoolcraft 1851–1857, 3:563); People of the Broad Leaf (S.R. Brown 1817:209); those who shoot at the leaf, 1839 (Nicollet in DeMallie 1976:256); Gens des Feuilles-tirées (Schoolcraft 1851–1857, 3:563); Gens de Feuilles-tirées (Burton 1861:117); and People of the Shot Leaf (H.H. Sibley 1874:250).

Most historical citations are versions of *waxpék^hute*: Afrahcootans (Carver 1778:80); Warpecoutais, 1803–1804 (Tabeau 1939:103); Sioux Wahpacoota and Wâh'-pa-coo-ta, 1806 (Lewis and Clark 1809:28, 30); Wachpecoutes (Z.M. Pike 1810, 1, append.:25); Washpeconte (Z.M. Pike 1811:128);

Washpecoate (Schermerhorn 1814:41); Washpecoutongs (Schoolcraft 1821:307); Wahpakotoan and Wahkpakota (Keating 1824, 1:378, 386); Wappacoota (Treaty of 1825 in Kappler 1904–1941, 2:254); Wahch-Pekuté and Wahch-Pe-Kutch (Maximilian 1843:134, 149); Warpekutey and Warpekute (Nicollet 1843:map, 13); Warhpekute, 1839 (Nicollet in DeMallie 1976:256); Wahpacootay Sioux (ARCIA 1849:114); War-pe-kintes and Wark-pay-ku-tay (Ramsey in ARCIA 1849:74, 82) Wahpekutes (G.K. Warren 1856:15); Wapakotah (Schoolcraft 1851–1857, 6:707); Wha-pa-ku-tahs (Cullen in ARCIA 1857:79); Waakpacootas (Domenech 1860, 2:26); and Wahpeconte (Burton 1861:117).

The Ojibwa name for the Wahpekute was recorded as Anibishiwininiwak (Gatschet in Hodge 1907–1910, 2:891), meaning 'leaf people'.

• WAHPETON   The name Wahpeton is an anglicization of Sioux *waxpéthuwą* 'leaf village', comprised of *waxpé* 'leaf' + *thuwá* 'village'. The reference is obscure.

Most historical citations to the Wahpeton are renditions of the native term itself. English and American renditions are: Wawpeentowahs (Carver 1778:80); Warhpetons, 1803–1804 (Tabeau 1939:103); Sioux Wahpatone and Wâh′-pa-tone, 1806 (Lewis and Clark 1809:28, 30); Washpetong and Washpotang (Schermerhorn 1814:40, 41); Wahpetongs (Schoolcraft 1821:307); Wahkpa-toan (Keating 1824, 1:378); Wappitong (Treaty of 1825 in Kappler 1904–1941, 2:254); Wapintowaher (Balbi 1826:55); Wah-pee-ton (ARCIA 1839:431); Warpetonwans, Warhpetonwan-nan, and Warhpeton, 1839 (Nicollet in DeMallie 1976:254, 256, 257); Warpeton (Nicollet 1843:13); War-pe-t′wans, Wark-pey-t′wawn, and War-pe-ton-wan (Ramsey in ARCIA 1849:74, 83); Wahpe-tonwans (G.K. Warren 1856:15); Wahpatoan Sioux (ARCIA 1856:38); and Wabipetons (Keane 1878:542, a misprint). Additional spellings are in Hodge (1907–1910, 2:892–893).

French citations that are translations of Wahpeton are Village de la feuille (Le Sueur in Margry 1876–1886, 6:87); people of the leaves, 1803–1804 (Tabeau 1939:102); Gens des Feuilles (Z.M. Pike 1810:93); and Gens de Feuille (Z.M. Pike 1811:110). English renditions are Leaf Nation (William Clark in Coues 1893, 1:101n); People of the Leaves, 1806 (Z.M. Pike in Schoolcraft 1851–1857, 3:563); Sioux of the Leaf, and perhaps Sioux of the Broad Leaf (Treaty of 1816 in Kappler 1904–1941, 2:128); Leaf (Drake 1848:viii); and Leaf Villagers (Mazakootemane 1880:83).

Early French references to the Wahpeton are renditions of the Sioux name *watpáthuwą* 'river village', that is, 'river people'. Forms illustrating this usage are: Houebaton (Crepy, Carte de l'Am. Sept. in Hodge 1907–1910, 2:892); Houetbatons, 1678 (Du Lhut in Margry 1876–1886, 6:22); Oetbatons, 1697 (La Chesnaye in Margry 1876–1886, 6:6); Ouadebatons, 1679–1681 (La Salle in Margry 1876–1886, 1:481); Oua de Battons (Hennepin 1698:map); Quioepetons and Quiopetons, 1700 (Le Sueur in Margry 1876–1886, 6:86; Le Sueur in E.D. Neill 1858:170); Ouyopetons, 1700 (Pénicaut in Margry 1876–1886, 5:414); Ouadbatons, 1700

(Lahontan 1703, 1:231); and Ouatabatonha, 1722 (Pachot in Margry 1876–1886, 6:518); and Ovadebathons (Coxe 1741:map). Citations that are English translations of the French forms are Men of the River (Hennepin 1698:184) and River People (Hennepin in E.D. Neill 1902:208).

• SISSETON   The Sioux form of the anglicized name Sisseton is *sisíthuwą*, which is composed of a now meaningless stem *sisí* + *thuwá* 'village'. Numerous folk-etymologies for the name have been given: Nicollet (DeMallie 1976:256, 258) in 1838–1839 gave three interpretations: 'those who go on foot'; 'those impregnated with fish smell', based on a stem *sisí-*; and 'those who make their village in cleared, treeless level areas', based on another stem *sisí-*. S.R. Riggs (1890:434–435, 1893:158, 184–185) reported two interpretations: 'swampy villagers', based on a putative stem *sisí* 'swampy land; putrid odor of dead fish'; and 'villagers who live on heaps of fish scales and entrails', derived from the stem *sisí-* 'besmeared, slimed, as with fish'. Other interpretations are 'swamp villagers', 'village of the marsh', and 'fish scales village' (Ramsey in ARCIA 1849:1021; G.K. Warren 1856:15; Black Thunder et al. 1975:52); however, the meaning of *sisí* remains obscure.

Nearly all historical citations of the name are renditions of the native form. Examples include Shahsweentowahs (Carver 1778:60); Seissitons, 1803–1804 (Tabeau 1939:102); Sisatoone, 1795 (Arrowsmith 1814); Se-si-toons and Sou si-toons (Lewis and Clark in Moulton 1983–, 3:28, 33); Sissatones, 1806 (Lewis and Clark 1809:24); Cisitons (William Clark in D.D. Jackson 1962:309); Sisatoone (Biddle in D.D. Jackson 1962:536); Sussitongs (Z.M. Pike 1810:49); Saussetons (Z.M. Pike in Schermerhorn 1814:40); Sessatone (Brackenridge 1815:78); Sissitongs (Schoolcraft 1821:307); Sisi toan (Keating 1824, 1:378); Sistons and Schahswintowaher (Balbi 1826:55); Sissitonwan-nan, Sissitoan, and Sissitons, 1839 (Nicollet in DeMallie 1976:256, 258); Sussetonwah and Sesetons, 1847 (Prescott in Schoolcraft 1851–1857, 2:168, 185); Sihsitwans, Sisetwans, Si-si-ton-wans, and Se-see-t′wawns (Ramsey in ARCIA 1849:72, 84); and Se-see-toans (ARCIA 1858:15). For other variants see Hodge (1907–1910, 2:582).

Yankton and Yanktonai

The Teton designated both the Yankton and Yanktonai tribes by the name *wičhíyela*, which in Yankton-Yanktonai is *wičhíyena* (Nicollet in DeMallie 1976:254). There is no satisfactory etymology for the word, despite a variety of explanations: 'our people, those who are ours' (Nicollet in DeMallie 1976:254), 'first nation' (G.K. Warren 1856:15), 'those who speak like men' (J.H. Howard 1966a:3). The form appears to be made up of *wičhá* 'man; object plural; collective subject plural' + *iyá* 'to speak' + *-lal-na* 'diminutive', the combination of which allows various interpretations. The Santee and other non-Sioux tribes did not use this name, but referred to the Yankton and Yanktonai by their own names for themselves, *ihákthuwą* and *ihákthuwąna*, respectively (G.K. Warren 1856:15;   *753*

S.R. Riggs 1890:571; Curtis 1907–1910, 3:142; Buechel 1970:581). In the Plains sign language the two tribes were not distinguished from other Sioux, although the Teton apparently used a compound sign, the gesture for 'Sioux' followed by one for 'pierced nose', to designate both the Yankton-Yanktonai and the Santee-Sisseton (W.P. Clark 1885:410).

• YANKTON   The name Yankton is an anglicization of the self-designation *ihą́ktʰųwą* 'village on the end' (*ihą́ke* 'on the end' + *tʰųwá* 'village'), the significance of which is uncertain.

Historical renderings of Yankton fall into two general groups, based on the initial letter of the word. Forms with an initial h, generally French renditions, are exemplified by the following: Hanctons (Hennepin 1698:map); Hinhanetons, 1702 (Le Sueur in Margry 1876–1886, 6:87; Alcedo 1786–1789, 2:362); Hanetones (Barcia 1723:238); Hanctons Sioux, 1795–1796 (Truteau in Parks 1993); Honctons (Bacqueville de la Potherie 1753, 2:map); Hinkaneton (Morse 1798:map in Hodge 1907–1910, 2:989); Hyinctons and Yinctons, 1803–1804 (Tabeau 1939:102–103); and Hannetons (McKenny and Hall 1846–1854, 3:80). Spellings with an initial y are characteristic of the American period: Yanktown Souise, 1804–1806 (Ordway in Moulton 1983–, 9:75); Yonktin (Gass in Moulton 1983–, 10:274); Yanctongs (Z.M. Pike 1810:49); Yentonas, 1812 (Luttig 1920:56); Yengetongs (Schoolcraft 1821:308); Yancton, 1815 (Kappler 1904–1941, 2:115; E. James 1823, 1:179); Yank toan (Keating 1824, 1:394); Yanctonas (ARCIA 1839:497); Yanktau-Sioux (Sage 1846:54); Yanka-taus (Ruxton 1849:111); Yanktown (Culbertson 1851:86); Yanctorinans (ARCIA 1854:295); and Yanctowah (Boller 1868:29). Two recordings have initial j (pronounced as y): Jantous and Jantons (de Smet 1843:23, 1848:264).

American renditions of *ihą́ktʰųwą* are ihantonwan in Itokarh-ihantonwan 'southern Yankton', 1839 (Nicollet in DeMallie 1976:257); Ihanktonwans (ARCIA 1845:564); Ihank'-t'wans, Ihanketwans, and E-hawn-k'-t'-wawns (Ramsey in ARCIA 1849:72, 85, 86); and Ihanktonwe (S.G. Boyd 1885:55). Misprints include Shan-ke-t'wans, Shank't'wannons, and Shank-t'wans (Ramsey in ARCIA 1849:74, 75, 78).

Tribes living near the Yankton borrowed *ihą́ktʰųwą* as Omaha-Ponca Ihañk'-toⁿwaⁿ (Dorsey 1883–1891) and *ihą́ttąwį* (Fletcher and La Flesche 1911:102; J.H. Howard 1965:134; phonemicized); Mandan *ihątu* (Hollow 1970:85); Pawnee Ihā́'tawa kátaxka (i.e., *ihą́ktawa kátahka* 'Yankton enemy') (Gatschet in Hodge 1907–1910, 2:989). The Assiniboine and Yanktonai used the form *ihą́ktʰųwą* (Parks and DeMallie 1999; Curtis 1907–1930, 3:142). An anomalous form is Omaha-Ponca žą́ata nikacįga (*žąatta nikkašįga*) 'people who dwelt in the woods' (Dorsey 1884:212).

During the early American period the tribe was occasionally referred to as Siouxs of the Grand Détour or Great Bend, 1796 (McKay in Quaife 1916:194); Yanctongs of the South, 1805 (Pike in Coues 1895, 1:343); South Yanktons (Prescott in Schoolcraft 1851–1857, 2:169); Lower Yancton, 1833 (Denig 1961:15; Hayden 1862:371); as well as Yanktons of the River De Moin, 1807 (William Clark in A.R. Woolworth 1974:56). Clark (Moulton 1983–, 3:413–414) transposed the

names for Yankton and Yanktonai in his chart of Missouri River tribes, giving Yanktons of the N[orth] for Yankton of the South and Yank-tons-Ah-nah [Yanktonai] for Yankton. The geographical modifiers served to distinguish the tribe from the Yanktonai.

• YANKTONAI   Yanktonai is an anglicization of the self-designation *ihą́ktʰųwąna* 'little village on the end', which is identical in form with the Yankton name but has the diminutive suffix *-na* added to it. The significance of the designation is unknown, despite interpretations such as 'fern leaves' (Keating 1824, 1:378) and 'lesser people of the further end' (Ramsey in ARCIA 1849:86). The name occurs in the same form in Santee-Sisseton (S.R. Riggs 1890:185) and Assiniboine (Parks and DeMallie 1999). In the Assiniboine spoken on the Fort Belknap Reservation *ihą́ktʰųwąna* came to signify the Sioux on the Fort Peck Reservation as well as Sioux generally (Parks and DeMallie 1999).

References to the Yanktonai occur almost exclusively during the American period. Forms that directly reflect the modern spelling of Yanktonai are: Hanctonnants, 1795–1796 (Truteau in Parks 1993); Yank-tons-Ah-nah (William Clark in Moulton 1983–, 3:414, misidentified as Yankton of the Des Moines River); Yangtons Ahnah (Bradbury 1817:83); Yanktoanan (Keating 1824, 1:378); Yanctonie (H. Atkinson 1826:6); Yanktonans and Yanktoanons (Maximilian 1843:149); Yank-ton-ees and Yank-ton-us (Prescott in Schoolcraft 1851–1857, 2:169n); Yanktonians and Yanktonnan (Culbertson 1851:89, 151); Yanktonais (G.K. Warren 1856:15); Yanctonais (Harney in F. Pierce 1856:1); Yanctonees (ARCIA 1856:7); Yanctonnais (ARCIA 1858:15); Yanktonaias (Corliss 1874:107); and Yanktonias-Sioux (T.S. Williamson 1880:285). Three forms with initial j for y are Jantonnees and Jantonnois (de Smet 1843:23, 37n), and Jantonnais (de Smet 1848:264).

Historical spellings that directly reflect the Yanktonai form are: Ihanktonwannan, 1839 (Nicollet in DeMallie 1976:254, 258); Ohantonwanna (ARCIA 1845:566); E-hawn-k'-t'-wawn-nah, Ihan-k'-tow-wan-nan, and Ihank'-t'wan-ahs (Ramsey in ARCIA 1849:85, 86); Eyank-ton-wah (Schoolcraft 1851–1857, 2:169); Ihanktonwannas (G.K. Warren 1856:15); Ihanktonwanna Dakotas (Hayden 1862:map); Ehanktonwanna (Lynd 1864:59); and E-hank-to-wana (Brackett 1877:472).

In the early American period the Yanktonai were distinguished from the Yankton by referring to them as Yanktons of the North (Lewis and Clark in Moulton 1983–, 3:412); Yanctongs of the North, 1805 (Pike in Coues 1895, 1:343); yanktons of the Plains, 1806 (William Clark in D.D. Jackson 1978:309–310); Yanktons of the plains or Big devils, 1810 (Biddle in D.D. Jackson 1978:536); and North Yanktons (Prescott in Schoolcraft 1851–1857, 2:169n); as well as Sieoux of the North, 1807 (William Clark in D.D. Jackson 1962:414).

Although there were numerous bands or semi-autonomous villages of the Yanktonai, four divisions stand out as major groups—Hunkpatina, Wazikute or Chanona, Kiyuksa, and Pabaksa or Cuthead.

DeMALLIE

The name *húkpatʰina* is a self-designation comprised of *húkpa* 'entrance of a camp circle' + *tʰi* 'to dwell' + *-na* 'diminutive', hence 'dwellers at the camp circle entrance'. It occurs as Santee *húkpatʰidą* (S.R. Riggs 1890:158) and Teton *húkpatʰila* (Buechel 1970:189). The name also occurs as *húkpatʰi*, without the diminutive suffix, in all dialects.

Historical renditions of *húkpatʰina*, as well as the Santee and Tetons forms, are: Hont-patines, 1803–1804 (Tabeau 1939:103); Hone-ta-par-teen and Hont-ta-par-teen-was (William Clark in Moulton 1983–, 3:419–420); Hone-ta-par-teen-waz, 1806 (Lewis and Clark 1809:34); Amkepatines and Unkepatines (de Smet 1843:23, 3n); Hunkpatidan (Schoolcraft 1851–1857, 1:248); Honcpatela band (F. Pierce 1856:11); Hunkplatin (Brown in ARCIA 1859:92); and Uncpatina (Alderson in ARCIA 1874:266). Examples of *húkpatʰi* are Hen-ta-pah-tus and Hen-tee-pah-tees (Prescott in Schoolcraft 1851–1857, 2:169n); Hunk-pate (ARCIA 1858:71); and Unc-pah-te (ARCIA 1867:231).

The Hunkpatina were also designated Lower Yanktonai (Robinson 1879 in Hodge 1907–1910, 1:580), cited also as Lower Yanctonais (ARCIA 1866:371) and Lower Yanktonnais (ARCIA 1878:27).

The name of an Upper Yanktonai division, *wazíkʰute* is a compound of *wazí* 'pine' + *kʰuté* 'to shoot at', hence 'pine shooters'. Early French citations and their translations of the name include Ouapeontetons 'village of those who shoot in a great pine', 1700 (La Harpe in Shea 1861:111); and Ouasicontetons 'village of those who shoot in a large pine', 1702 (Le Sueur in Margry 1876–1886, 6:87). They indicate that the name formerly was *wazíkʰutetʰuwą*, from which the noun *tʰuwá* 'village' was subsequently dropped.

Later references to this division include Wasicoutais, 1803–1804 (Tabeau 1939:103); Siouxs who shoot in the Pine Tops (Treaty of 1816 in Kappler 1904–1941, 2:128); Wahzecootai (Gens des Pin), 1833 (Denig 1961:15); Wazikute, 1839 (Nicollet in DeMallie 1976:258); Those that Shoot in the pines (Culbertson 1851:141); Wah-zu-cootas (Schoolcraft 1851–1857, 2:169); Wa-ge'-ku-te, Gens des Pin, and Pine-Band (Hayden 1862:371); Shooters in the Pines (B. R. Cowen 1873:5); and Wazi-kute 'shooters among the pines' (Dorsey 1897:218).

Another name of this band was reputedly *čʰąʔóna* 'shoots the tree', comprised of *čʰą* 'tree' + *ó* 'to shoot, hit' + *-na* 'diminutive'. Citations of it are Tcaⁿ-ona (Dorsey 1897:218) and Pole people (Culbertson 1851:141).

The name of the Kiyuksa is the verb *kʰiyúksa* 'divide, break in two', the significance of which is obscure (see Kiyuksa division of the Oglala). Citations of the form include Kiouxas-Yinctons, 1803–1804 (Tabeau 1939:103); Kee-uke-sah, 1806 (Lewis and Clark 1809:34), Ku-ux-aws (Prescott in Schoolcraft 1851–1857, 2:169), and Kii-ark-sar (Corliss 1874:106).

The designation of the Pabaksa or Cuthead division is *pʰábaksa* 'to cut off the head; cut head', the significance of which is not known. The native name is reflected in the following citations: Pah Baxah (Tête Coupees), 1833 (Denig 1961:15); Pah Baxa (ARCIA 1850:109); Pah-bax-ahs (Schoolcraft 1851–1857, 2:169); Pabaska Sioux (ARCIA 1906:482). English citations are Cut Beards (ARCIA 1850:109), Cut heads (Culbertson 1851:141), and Yanctonnais Cutheads (ARCIA 1858:53). French versions are Tete Coup (William Clark 1832:63), Tetes Coupes (Culbertson 1851:141), and Tête-Coupées (Hayden 1862:371).

Teton

The name *tʰítʰuwą*, from which English Teton is borrowed, is a term used by other Sioux groups to designate this division (S.R. Riggs 1890:470; Buechel 1970:490). The etymology of *tʰítʰuwą* is obscure, despite numerous explanations. Le Sueur, 1702 (Margry 1876–1886, 6:8) gave the name as formerly Tintagaoughiatons 'village of the big cabin'. Nicollet (1843:67; DeMallie 1976:254, 257, 259) recorded several derivations: Ti tanka (*tʰitʰąka* 'big lodge'), the site of a former residence at Big Lodge Lake on the Big Sioux River; Tinta ottonwe 'village of the prairie'; Tintotowan 'people of the prairies'; and Tintonwanyan 'people who have for a long time made villages on the big prairies', abbreviated to tintonwans 'village with lodges'; titonwan 'people whose headdress is elevated like a lodge'; and Titon 'to possess a cabin'. S.R. Riggs (1890:470, 1893:186), who cited the full name as *tʰítatʰuwą*, derived it from Santee *tʰíta* 'prairie' + *tʰuwá* 'village', hence 'prairie dwellers', assuming that nasalization of the vowel in the first syllable was lost and the second syllable *ta* was dropped. (The form *tʰíta* does not occur in the Teton dialect [Buechel 1970:490].)

Most early European recordings of Teton indicate that the vowel in the initial syllable of the name was nasalized: Tintonha, 1679–1681 (La Salle in Margry 1876–1886, 1:481); Tinthona (Hennepin 1698:map); Thintohas (Barcia 1723:238); Tinthenha 'gens des prairies' (Baqueville de la Potherie 1753, 2:map); Tintons (Carver 1778:80); Thuntotas and Tintones (Alcedo 1786–1789, 3:218, 5:137). Later forms include Tintoner (Balbi 1826:55), Tintinhos and Ten-ton-ha (Ramsey in ARCIA 1849:72, 85), Thinthonha and Tinthonha (Shea 1852:112, 113), Tentouha (McKenney and Hall 1846–1854, 3:80), Tintonwans (E.D. Neill 1858:52), and Tindaw and Tinthow (Ladd 1891:67). Two citations of Teton have an initial vowel a, as in Atintons, 1688 (Lahontan 1703, 1:231) and Anthontans (Coxe 1741:50), reflected later in Atentons and Atintans (Lahontan in Ramsey 1849:1008, 1021) and Atrutons (Ramsey in ARCIA 1849:72).

Later spellings, generally American, lack an n in the first syllable: Titoba, 1722 (Pachot in Margry 1876–1886, 6:518); Titons, 1803–1804 (Tabeau 1939:102); Tetons, Tetongues, and Teton Seaux (Lewis and Clark in Moulton 1983–, 3:104, 106, 191, 415–420); Tinton and Teeton (Gass in Moulton 1983–, 10:44, 272); Titons (Schermerhorn 1814:41); Titones (Boudinot 1816:129); Tetons, 1811 (Hunt and Stuart in Rollins 1935:map); Ti toan (Keating 1824, 1:378); Titons and titonwan, 1839 (Nicollet in DeMallie 1976:254, 259); Tee-twawn, Teetwans, Ti-t'-wawn, Ti-twans, and Tit'wan, and

Tetans (Ramsey in ARCIA 1849:69, 72, 85); Tieton (ARCIA 1856:41); and Teetonwan (Lynd 1864:59). For additional spellings see Hodge (1907–1910, 2:737).

Other historical references to the Teton are designations comprised of Sioux and a geographical modifier: Scioux of the West, which includes all the Sioux west of the Mississippi River, 1700 (Le Sueur in E.D. Neill 1858:170); Scious of the Prairies, 1736 (Chauvignerie in Schoolcraft 1851–1857, 3:557); West Schious (Coxe 1741:map); Sioux des prairies, 1756 (Bossu 1771, 1:182); Sioux occidentaux (Tailhan in Perrot 1864:232); Sioux of the Savannas and Western Sioux (Jefferys 1761, 1:45); Sioux of the Meadows (W. Smith 1766:76); Nadooessis of the Plains (Jefferys 1776:map 8); Prairie Indians (Ramsey ARCIA 1849:72); and Sioux of the Plain (Seymour 1850:135). Ojibwa Mascoutens (*maškode·ns* 'little prairie people'), apparently the name for an extinct Algonquian tribe living on the prairies of southern Michigan, Wisconsin, and northern Illinois, and perhaps extended to other indefinite Algonquian tribes living in that area (see vol. 15:668–672), was occasionally also used by the French to modify Nadouessiw, as in Maskoutens-Nadouessians (Hennepin 1698:132) and Mascouteins Nadouessi (Tailhan in Perrot 1864:196). One designation refers to the Teton lifeway: Sioux nomades (Perrot 1864:232).

• BRULE   The French designation *brulé* 'burnt' is a partial translation of this division's self-designation *sičháɣu* 'burnt thigh' (S.R. Riggs 1852:xvi, 1893:187; Buechel 1970:453). American citations of the French traders' form are: Tetons Brulès (Farnham 1843:32); Broulè Sioux (Schoolcraft 1851–1857, 5:494); Bruleés, 1833 (Denig 1961:14); Brulees (Hayden 1862:371; ARCIA 1854:295); Brulies (Hoffman in F. Pierce 1855:3); Brulé Dakotas (Hayden 1862:map); and Brulé Sioux (Shindler 1869:19). A rendering in English translation is Burnt (de Smet 1843:37).

Recordings that directly reflect Teton *sičháɣu* include: Sitchanrhou-Titons, 1803–1804 (Tabeau 1939:103); Che che ree (Lewis and Clark in Moulton 1983–, 3:27); Se chong hhos (Denig 1961:14); Sichanṛus, 1839 (Nicollet in DeMallie 1976:259); Sichangus (G.K. Warren 1856:16); Sicaugu (Hind 1860, 2:154); Se-ćang'-ćos (Hayden 1862:371); Ceetshongos (Corliss 1874:106); Ishango (Brackett 1877:466); Si-chan-koo, 1877 (W.H. Jackson in T. Donaldson 1887:62); Si-Chun-goo (W.P. Clark 1885:83); and Sitcan-xu (Coues 1893, 1:130). Renditions in English translation are burned thighs (Nicollet in DeMallie 1976:259), Burnt-Thighs (Hayden 1862:371), and Burnt Hip Brulé, 1879 (Robinson in Hodge 1907–1910, 1:168).

The name was translated into Cheyenne as Vonetonháes (Petter 1913–1915:583).

The name Burnt Thigh is reflected in the Plains sign language, in which one variant of the sign for Brule is made by rubbing the upper and outer part of the right thigh with the right hand open and fingers pointing downward, while another is made by brushing the palm of the right hand over the right thigh, moving from near the buttock forward. The gesture represents a burnt thigh, reputedly given the tribe

after a prairie fire in which some Brules were caught and either burned to death or were badly burned about the thighs (Mallery 1881:468; W.P. Clark 1885:83; H.L. Scott 1912–1934). Another account describes the sign as first laying one's flat right hand on the thigh and then raising it, making the gesture for fire (Hadley 1893:33).

At the beginning of the nineteenth century the Saint Louis trader Regis Loisel and Lewis and Clark designated the division by Bois Brûlé 'burnt wood', a French term that was more properly used for the offspring of coureurs de bois and Indian mothers during the fur trade period (Robinson 1904:49). Since there was also a Yankton division named *sičháɣu* and extensive intermarriage between its women and the French, resulting in common use of the term *bois brulé* for the resultant mixed-blood population, it appears that Loisel and Lewis and Clark may have either confused the names or, following local usage, generalized Bois Brûlé to both the Yankton and the Teton *sičháɣu*, 1806 (Lewis and Clark 1809:21). Perhaps also contributing to the use of Bois Brûlé was the name of the terrain around the Big Bend of the Missouri where the Brule and Yankton lived, known to the voyageurs as *les côtes brûlées* 'burnt bluffs' or *collines brûlées* 'burnt hills' (Nicollet 1843:40). Examples of this designation are: Bois Brule, 1804 (Loisel in Nasatir 1952, 2:739); Bois ruley, Bauruly, Bous roulee, Teton Bous rouley (burnt woods), and Tetons Bois Brûlé (Lewis and Clark in Moulton 1983–, 3:27, 118, 119, 415, 418); Bob Brulee (Ordway in Moulton 1983–, 9:48); Babarolé (Gass in Moulton 1983–, 10:50); and Debois-B-ruly (Whitehouse in Moulton 1983–, 11:67). Renditions in English are exemplified by Burning Woods (Whitehouse in Moulton 1983–, 11:67) and Tetons of Burnt Woods (William Clark in D.D. Jackson 1962:309, 536). Later citations based on the Lewis and Clark forms are Tetons of the Burnedwood (M'Vickar 1842, 1:148), Burnt-woods (Ruxton 1849:111), and Tetans of the Burnt Woods (Ramsey in ARCIA 1849:85).

The Lower Brule are known by the designation *kʰútawičʰaša*, or more commonly Teton *kʰúlwičʰaša*, 'below man' (Buechel 1970:319), a reference to their living downstream on the Missouri from the Upper Brule. Variant forms of the name are *kʰúnwičʰaša* (Dorsey 1897:218, phonemicized) and Yankton *kʰúdwičʰaša* (*Iapi Oaye* 1884, 12(12):91, phonemicized). The name was also recorded as Coutah-wee-cha-cha (Corliss 1874:106). The English translation of the name occurs as Lower Brulé (Treaty of 1865 in Kappler 1904–1941, 2:885) and Lowland Brulé (Dorsey 1897:218).

The Upper Brule designation is *xeyátawičʰaša* 'upland man', a reference to their living upstream, away from the Missouri Valley (Dorsey 1897:218, phonemicized). Translations of the name include Upper Platte Indians (ARCIA 1866:209), Northern Brule (ARCIA 1875:178), and Highland Brulé and Highland Sicangu (Robinson to Dorsey, 1879, in Hodge 1907–1910, 1:679).

• OGLALA   Oglala is the self-designation of this division, which occurs as Teton *oglála*, Santee-Sisseton *ohdáda*, and Yankton-Yanktonai *okdáda* 'to scatter one's own', derived from *okála* (Santee *okáda*)'to scatter' (Buechel 1970:370; S.R. Riggs 1890:349; 1893:187; Dorsey in Hodge 1907–1910, 2:110). The significance of the name is unknown. It was borrowed as Omaha-Ponca *ubðaða* (Dorsey 1883–1891, phonemicized) and Cheyenne Okanan (Petter 1913–1915:583).

Historical references to the Oglala are almost exclusively variant spellings of the native name in one of its dialectal forms, depending on source. Renditions that reflect the Teton form are: Augallalla (H. Atkinson 1826:6); Angallas (William Clark 1832:63); Ogallalahs, 1833 (Denig 1961:14); Ogabllallas (ARCIA 1838:471); Ogallallahs (S. Parker 1840:65); Ogalallahs (M'Vickar 1842, 1:86); Ogallallees (de Smet 1843:37n); Ogallah (Culbertson 1851:142); Oglallahs (Frémont 1854:57); Ogellahs, Ogellalah, and Ogeelala (Schoolcraft 1851–1857, 1:523, 4:252, 5:494); Oglala Dacotas (G.K. Warren 1856:19); Ogolawlas (N.H. Parker 1857:141); O-ga-la'-las (Hayden 1862:371); O'Gallala (Treaty of 1865 in Kappler 1904–1941, 2:906); and Ogillallah (Parkman 1883:113).

Renditions that reflect Yankton or Yanktonai forms are: Occononas, 1795 (Truteau in Parks 1993); Okondanes, Okondanas, and Okendanes (Tabeau 1939:72, 103, 239); Tetons Okandandas and Teton O-kan-dan-das (William Clark in Moulton 1983–, 3:418, 420; Biddle in D.D. Jackson 1962:536); Arkandada (Brackenridge 1815:78); Okanandans (Bradbury 1817:90); Ok'udada 'he throws at someone' (Nicollet in DeMallie 1976:259); and Teton Okandandes (Ramsey in ARCIA 1849:87).

An anomalous designation for Oglala is Cheyenne *hotóhkEsono* 'little stars' (Glenmore and Leman 1985:201), cited earlier as O-tōh'-sōn (Hayden 1862:290) and Hotoxkson (Petter 1913–1915:583).

The Plains sign language gesture for Oglala is made first by the sign for 'Sioux' followed by the sign for 'dirt, dust, or ashes'; then, holding the right hand closed, back side out, about six inches in front of the face, while moving the hand toward the face, suddenly extend and separate the thumb and fingers with a partial snap. This sign is said to commemorate a quarrel in which the antagonists threw dirt or ashes in each other's faces (Mallery 1881:468; W.P. Clark 1885:272–273; H.L. Scott 1912–1934). Another reported sign, which represents facial pock marks resulting from a smallpox epidemic, is made by holding the fingers and thumb of the right hand separated and straight and then touching them over the face to indicate dots (Mallery 1881:468).

• MINNECONJOU   The name Minneconjou, the self-designation of this tribe, is Teton *mnik^hówožu* or *mnik^hó²ožu* (Buechel 1970:338) and Santee-Sisseton *mínik^hayewožu* or *mínik^hayewožupi*, also pronounced *mínik^hó²ožu* (S.R. Riggs 1890:315; Dorsey 1897:220). The standard etymology, which derives the name from *míni* 'water' + *k^haye* 'near' + *wožu* 'to plant' (+ *pi* 'plural'), hence 'planters by the water' (S.R. Riggs 1852:xvi, 1890:315, 1893:187), is likely a folk-etymology since historical recordings often suggest different phonemic forms of the name.

Historical citations of the name, all from the American period, reflect the native name: MineKanhini-yojou, Minican-hiniyojou, and Minican-hojou, 1803–1804 (Tabeau 1939:103–104); Teton-Min-na-Kine-az-zo and Tetons Minnakineazzo (Lewis and Clark in Moulton 1983–, 3:416–418, 420); Memacanjo 'make fence on the river' (William Clark in Coues 1893, 1:101n); Min-na-kenozo, 1810 (Biddle in D.D. Jackson 1962:536); Minikiniad-za (Brackenridge 1814:78); Tetons Mennakenozzo (Keating 1824, 1:381); Tetons Minnekincazzo (Farnham 1843:32); Minne Con-ojus, 1834 (J.L. Bean in W.M. Anderson 1967:106n); Mee-ne-cow-e-gee (Catlin 1844, 1:211); Minikanye oju or Minikanoju,1839 (Nicollet in DeMallie 1976:260); Minecosias (Sage 1846:285); Minnake-nozzo (Coyner 1847:70) Mini-con-gaha (Culbertson 1851:142); Minecogue, Minnecowzues, and Minnecaushas (ARCIA 1854:285, 295, 301); Mini-kan-jous and Minnikan-jous, 1855 (G.K. Warren 1875:48); Minikanyes (G.K. Warren 1856:16); Men-i-cou-zha and Minicoughas (Hoffman in F. Pierce 1855:3, 4); Minne Coujoux Sioux (ARCIA 1855:79); Minnecarguis (ARCIA 1856:68); Minnecogoux (ARCIA 1859:120); Min-ne-kaŋ'-zu and Mi-ne-kaŋ'-žus (Hayden 1862:371, 374); Monecoshe Sioux (ARCIA 1864:228); Minnecongou (Gale 1867:226); Minnecongew (Boller 1868:29); Minnekonjo (ARCIA 1877:247); Minneconjoux (Stanley in Poole 1881:232); Minnicongew (Parkman 1883:126); and Minikan oju, 1884 (Cleveland in Hodge 1907–1910, 1:868). For other spellings see Hodge (1907–1910, 1:868–869).

The only recorded Plains sign language gesture for Minneconjou is a composite of the sign for 'Sioux', followed by 'to farm', 'close', and 'water' (W.P. Clark 1885:256).

• SAONE   The Saone, the fourth major Teton tribe in the early nineteenth century, by the mid nineteenth century had broken up into four separate tribes—Sans Arcs, Two Kettles, Blackfeet, and Hunkpapa. Two other groups that were probably Saone but were no longer recognized in the twentieth century were the His Bad Heart and Wanonwakteninan. The Minneconjou were also sometimes treated as a Saone band (Nicollet in DeMallie 1976:260; Hodge 1907–1910, 2:464).

The name Saone was undoubtedly a self-designation, but the precise form of the word and its significance are no longer known. Nicollet (DeMallie 1976:259) translated the name as 'whitish people, whose robes are always well whitened with white earth', comprised of sa [*są*] 'whitish' and a putative verb stem oni 'to rub', but that etymology is not satisfactory. S.R. Riggs (Hodge 1907–1910, 2:464) wrote that the name was Sanoni-wicasa (that is, *są²óni wič^áša* 'Sanoni man') and was a nickname that the Brule and Oglala formerly applied to the Sans Arcs, Minniconjou, and Hunkpapa. His spelling, however, does not accord well with other contemporary and previous renditions.

Historical citations of the name are: Chaony and Chahony, 1795–1796 (Truteau in Parks 1993); Saones-Titons (Tabeau 1939:103); Teton-Sah-o-ne and Tetons

757

Sahone (William Clark in Moulton 1983–, 3:417, 418); Tetons Sa-one (Biddle in D.D. Jackson 1962:536); Sa-hone (Brackenridge 1815:78); Sahonies (Bradbury 1817:90); Sa-ho-ne (E. James 1823, 1:179); Sioune and Siouones of the Fire-hearts band (Treaty of 1825 in Kappler 1904–1941, 2:230, 232); Saones (William Clark 1832:63); Saonis, 1839 (Nicollet in DeMallie 1976:259–260); Sowanné, 1834 (J.L. Bean in W.M. Anderson 1967:106n); Sawons (ARCIA 1838:471); Siones (S. Parker 1838:43); Saonies (Nicollet in DeMallie 1976:259); Sowans (ARCIA 1842:59); Saoynes (de Smet 1843:37n); See-oo-nay (its pronunciation), Sioane, and Sionne, and Teton Saone (Ramsey in ARCIA 1849:69, 84, 85); and Sahohes (Schoolcraft 1851–1857, 3:81).

• SANS ARCS   Sans Arcs is the French translation of Teton and Santee *itázipč^ho* 'without bows', the self-designation of this tribe, which is a shortened form of *itázipa* 'bow' + *č^óla* 'lacking, without', in which the diminutive suffix *-la* has been dropped (S.R. Riggs 1852:xvi), though it does appear as *-na*, a Yankton form, in two early recordings below. The full Santee form is *itázipa-č^ódą* (S.R. Riggs 1893:187, phonemicized). The name was translated into Cheyenne as Ma'-i-sin-as (Hayden 1862:290), cited also as Maesenas 'one without a bow' (Petter 1913–1915:583).

Many historical citations of the name are renditions of its Sioux form: Hitasiptchone and Hitachiptchone or Hitachiptchone (Tabeau in A.H. Abel 1939:104); Etas epe cho, 1833 (Denig 1961:15); Ee-ta-si-shov, 1833 (Catlin 1841, 1:223); Itazichonan, 1839 (Nicollet in DeMallie 1976:260); Itahzipchois and Itasipchos (Warren 1856:16); Itazipko (Burton 1861:119); Taze-char and Taze-par-war-nee-cha (the latter *tazípa-wanič^a* 'lacking bow') (Corliss 1874:106); and Itazipcoes (Keane 1878:516). Other references are variants of the French form: Sans Arcs (Schoolcraft 1851–1857, 3:629); Sansarcs Dakotas (Hayden 1862:map); and Sarsarcs (Cleveland 1875:4 in Hodge 1907–1910, 2:453, misprint). Variant English translations are: Lack-Bows (de Smet 1843:37n); Nobows (Hoffman in F. Pierce 1855:3); Bowpith (G.K. Warren 1856:16); and Without Bows (Hayden 1862:371).

The gesture for the Sans Arcs in the Plains sign language is a composite one, comprising the signs for 'Sioux', for 'bow' and for 'wiped out' (W.P. Clark 1885:325).

• TWO KETTLES   The name Two Kettles is an English translation of the self-designation *o'óhenųpa* 'two boilings', composed of *o'óhe* 'cooked (food) by boiling in a kettle' + *nųpa* 'two', a reference to two kettles of cooked food (Buechel 1970:399; Dorsey 1897:220; S.R. Riggs 1852:xvi, 1893:161; forms retranscribed).

Citations of the name that reflect the Sioux form are: Wo hai noom pah, 1833 (Denig 1961:15); Oohenoupa (Hind 1860, 2:154); Ohenonpa Dakotas and Wo-he-nōm'-pa (Hayden 1862:map, 371); Ohanapa (Brackett 1877:466); Ohenonpas (Keane 1878:527). References in English translation include: Two Cauldrons (de Smet 1843:37n); Two Rille band (ARCIA 1846:296); Kettle band (Culbertson 1851:142); Three Kettles (ARCIA 1856:68); Two Kettle (Gale 1867:226); and Two Boilings or Two Kettles (S.R. Riggs 1893:161). The name was translated into Cheyenne as Nixaoxcexháes 'two cookings' (Petter 1913–1915:583).

The Plains sign language gesture for the Two Kettles is a composite one, comprising the sign for 'Sioux' followed by that for 'kettle', and then a repetition of these motions to indicate that another kettle is beside the first one (W.P. Clark 1885:384).

• BLACKFEET   The name Blackfeet is an English translation of the self-designation *sihásapa* 'black foot', composed of *sihá* 'foot' + *sápa* 'black', the significance of which is unknown (Buechel 1970:454; S.R. Riggs 1890:434; 1893:161).

Historical citations of the name that reflect the Sioux form are: Se ah sap pas or Blackfeet, 1833 (Denig 1961:14); Sia-sappâ, 1839 (Nicollet in DeMallie 1976:260); Sísapapa (Blackmore 1869, 1:302; misprint); Se-ä'-sä-pä (L.H. Morgan 1871:284); Se-ash-ha-pa and Si-há-sa-pa (Brackett 1877:466). Variant spellings of the English translation are: Blackfoot Sioux, 1833 (Catlin 1844, 1:223); Black-feet Scioux (de Smet 1843:23); Blackfeet (Culbertson 1851:105); Blackfeet Dakotas (Hayden 1862:290); Blackfoot Dakotas (L.H. Morgan 1870:44); Blackfeet Tetons (Corliss 1874:107); and Blackfeet Sioux (Stanley in Poole 1881:232). The name appears in Cheyenne as Mōh̄-ta'-awa-ta-ta'-ni-o (Hayden 1862:290), cited also as Moxtavàtataneo (pl.) (Petter 1913–1915:583).

There are several signs in the Plains sign language recorded for the Blackfeet. One is to pass the flat right hand along the outer edge of the foot from the heel to beyond the toes; another is to pass the right hand quickly over the right foot from the great toe outward while turning the heel as if one were brushing something from it; a third is to pass the thumb and index finer of the right hand, widely separated, over the lower leg, from immediately below the knee almost down to the heel (Mallery 1881:467). The significance of those signs is not explained. Yet another reported variant is a composite of the sign for 'Sioux' followed by that for 'Blackfoot' (W.P. Clark 1885:73).

• HUNKPAPA   The name Hunkpapa is an anglicization of the self-designation *hųkpap^ha*, presumably *hųkpa* 'entrance of a camp circle' + *p^ha* 'head', hence '(at) the entrance head', said to be a reference to their assigned location in the Teton camp circle (Nicollet in DeMallie 1976:261; S.R. Riggs 1852:viii, 1890:158, 1893:162). A variant of the name is *hųkpap^haya* (Buechel 1970:189; E.C. Deloria 1932:x), which has an unexplained final syllable *ya*.

All historical citations of the name reflect the form *hųkpap^ha*: Hont-papas, 1803–1804 (Tabeau in A.H. Abel 1939:104); Honk pa pa (Ex. Doc. 56, 18th Cong., 1st sess., 1824:9 in Hodge 1907–1910, 1:580); Hunkpapas (Treaty of 1825 in Kappler 1904–1941, 2:235); Honc pap pas, 1833 (Denig 1961:15); Oncpapa, 1833 (Catlin 1844, 1:223); Onkpapa, 1839 (Nicollet in DeMallie 1976:261); Hankpapes (S. Parker 1840:44); Arrapapas (William Clark 1832:63); Ampapes (de Smet 1843:23); Ampapa (de Smet 1848:264); Hunkappas (Ramsey in ARCIA 1849:86; misprint); Onchpa-pah (Culbertson 1851:141); Onkpapah (Schoolcraft

Fig. 8. Early portraits of Sioux men. top left, Sioux man, drawn about 1700, the first depiction of a Sioux, exhibiting either tattooing or body paint that includes fanciful figures of sun and moon. He wears a breechcloth and feather headdress, is smoking a pipe, and holds what may be a war club. top center, Yanktonai Chief Wanata, wearing a breechcloth, moccasins, and a feather headdress and holding a musket. Watercolor by Peter Rindisbacher, 1820. top right, Black Rock, a Minneconjou chief. He wears a horned, ermine-skin-decorated, feathered war bonnet and buffalo rope with painted pictographs representing war exploits. Oil painting by George Catlin, Ft. Pierre, Mo. Terr., 1832. bottom left, 2 views of a Teton man wearing a fur and feather headdress, earrings of large beads or metal balls, and a peace medal "Van Buren 1837" (R. Stewart, J.D. Ketner, and A.L. Miller 1991:92). Pencil on paper sketches by Charles Wimar, Ft. Pierre, 1858. bottom right, Blue Medicine, a medicine man of the Prairie Village band of Mdewakanton Santee. His face is painted with turquoise blue-green paint, and he wears multiple necklaces and a mirror. His turban is made of red cloth decorated with beads, and he wears a roach with eagle feather. He holds a drum of deerskin, a rattle made of antelope hoofs, and a globular drum beater. Oil painting by George Catlin, Ft. Snelling, Mich. Terr., 1835.

1851–1857, 5:494); Honepapas and Aukpapas (ARCIA 1854:295, 297); Oak-pa-pas (Hoffman in F. Pierce 1855:3); Unkpapas (G.K. Warren 1856:16); Unc Papas (ARCIA 1856:7); Unkpapa Dakotas (Hayden 1862:map); Oncapapas (Corliss 1874:107); Uncpappas (Keane 1878:541); and Onkpahpah (Treaty of 1865 in Kappler 1904–1941, 2:901). For other spellings see Hodge (1907–1910, 1:580).

In the Plains sign language the designation for Hunkpapa was a composite one, comprised of, in sequence, the signs for 'Sioux', 'encamp', 'ends of an incomplete camp circle,' where the Hunkpapa had their designated place (W.P. Clark 1885:385).

Sources

The earliest information on Sioux culture appears in the *Jesuit Relations*, where the Sioux are first mentioned in 1640 under the name Naduesiu by the explorer Jean Nicollet (JR 18:231). Radisson's account from 1662 (1885, 1961) provides the ethnographic baseline for the Santee. The writings of Nicolas Perrot offer much additional information (Bacqueville de la Potherie 1722; Perrot 1864; Perrot and Bacqueville de la Potherie in Blair 1911–1912). Accounts of the travels of Father Louis Hennepin (1880, Delanglez 1941) and the explorers Daniel Greysolon Duluth (Margry 1876–1886, 6:20–37; Shea 1880:374–377) and Henry de Tonty (Winchell 1911:524–525) to the Santee in 1679–1680 give the first reliable information on the locations of Sioux groups.

The reports from Pierre-Charles Le Sueur in 1699–1702 are important for locations and ethnographic details (C. Delisle 1702; Margry 1876–1886, 6:55–92; M.M. Wedel 1974a; McWilliams 1953). An anonymous French memoir on the Sioux that may date as early as 1720 or may be as late as 1750 provides considerable detail on Santee social life (Neill 1890). Reports of the explorations of La Vérendrye and his sons provide data from the northern plains (Burpee 1927).

The journals of Jonathan Carver for 1766–1767 with a group of Santees (J. Parker 1976) present the fullest ethnographic description of the Sioux during this period. The journal of Peter Pond (Gates 1965:18–59) provides valuable detail, particularly relating to the Yankton, in 1774. The writings of Jean-Baptiste Truteau provide material on locations and identities of Sioux groups and the first detailed ethnographic descriptions of the Yankton and Teton (Parks 1993; Nasatir 1952, 1:257–311, 2:376–382).

The most extensive account of the Sioux, focused on the Teton, is that of Pierre-Antoine Tabeau, who spent 1803–1804 as a trader on the Missouri River in present South Dakota (A.H. Abel 1939). Invaluable, particularly for information on tribal divisions and locations, are the writings of Meriwether Lewis and William Clark, 1804–1805 (Moulton 1983–, 3) Zebulon M. Pike, 1805–1806 (Coues 1895; D.D. Jackson 1966), and Henry Atkinson (1826). The ethnographic descriptions from the Long expedition (Keating 1825) and the volume by Mary Eastman (1849) are extensive. The artist George Catlin (1844) reported on his visits to most of the Sioux groups, 1832–1836, and made a valuable visual record, including portraits (fig. 8) and depictions of ceremonies (fig. 5). A German artist (H. Lewis 1967), depicted the Santee, 1846–1849. Frank B. Mayer (1932) and Johann B.

Wengler (Feest and Kasprycki 1999) sketched Santee at Little Crow's Village in 1851.

The writings of Philander Prescott, a fur trader and later superintendent of farming for the Mdewakanton, his wife's people, are rich ethnographic sources (Prescott in Schoolcraft 1851–1857, 2:168–199, 3:225–246, 4:59–72; D.D. Parker 1966), as are the reminiscences of Jack Frazer, a mixed blood among the Santee (H.H. Sibley 1950). The Congregational missionaries Samuel W. Pond (1908) and Stephen Return Riggs (1869, 1880, 1893) wrote reminiscences that are basic sources on Santee culture and that chronicle the development of the Dakota Mission in Minnesota.

The Roman Catholic missionary Augustin Ravoux (1890a) ministered on the Minnesota and Missouri rivers. The writings of Pierre-Jean de Smet, S.J. (1905), provide ethnographic material and an account of his missionary activities among the Yankton and Teton Sioux from 1839 through the 1860s.

The narrative of Paul Wilhelm, Duke of Württenburg (1973), who traveled up the Missouri into Sioux country in 1823, includes ethnographic detail. Three other travel accounts present original observations on the Sioux in Minnesota: Beltrami (1824, 1828), Arese (1934), and Featherstonhaugh (1847). Nicollet, assigned to map the Upper Mississippi River 1836–1839, described all the Sioux divisions (Nicollet 1843; M.C. Bray 1970; E.C. Bray and M.C. Bray 1976; DeMallie 1976). Denig (1930, 1961) described the Missouri River tribes. Francis Parkman's diary (Wade 1947, 2:385–510) and narrative of his experiences traveling with an Oglala Teton camp in 1846 (Feltskog 1969) are invaluable.

In addition to Catlin's paintings (Truettner 1979), other visual documentation includes works by Peter Rindisbacher (fig. 8), of the Minnesota Sioux in the 1820s (Josephy 1970); Karl Bodmer, of Yankton and Teton Sioux near Fort Pierre in 1833 (D.C. Hunt and M.V. Gallagher 1984); Alfred Jacob Miller, of Teton Sioux at Fort Laramie in 1837 (R. Tyler 1982); and Seth Eastman (fig. 5) (Boehme, Feest, and Johnston 1995), of the Santee around Fort Snelling in the 1840s.

Contemporary government documents, including the *Annual Reports of the Commissioner of Indian Affairs* (ARCIA 1849–), provide essential documentation of the American period; for a guide, see S.L. Johnson (1977). A particularly useful account is the overview of Indians in Minnesota Territory written by Ramsey (1849).

The historical literature on the Sioux is vast; Hoover (1979) and Marken and Hoover (1980) provide partial guides. Studies of Sioux migrations include those of R. White (1978) and G.C. Anderson (1980). S.R. Riggs (1893:155–194), D. Robinson (1904), Winchell (1911), and Hyde (1937) are also valuable, if used critically, as are the reports to the Indian Claims Commission (Champe 1974; H.E. Hickerson 1974; Hurt 1974; A.R. Woolworth 1974).

Santee

PATRICIA C. ALBERS

The twentieth-century Santee (săn'tē) or Eastern Sioux are descendants of four Sioux tribes, the Mdewakanton, Wahpekute, Sisseton, and Wahpeton, who lived in southern Minnesota when first met by Europeans in the late seventeenth century. Although these tribes have been frequently treated together as a single ethnic group, their members never acted as a cohesive political body and did not follow culturally uniform traditions. Even the name that is commonly given to them, Santee, has not been widely used by the people themselves; the Sisseton and Wahpeton did not call themselves Santee, but assigned this name to its original bearers, the Mdewakanton and Wahpekute. It was the Teton Sioux who employed the term Santee in an inclusive fashion for the Eastern Sioux, and scholars and government officials later adopted this extended usage (Albers and James 1986:12–13).

Territory and Environment

In 1763, when the British gained control over the Great Lakes fur trade, the Santee were consolidating their territorial holdings in southern Minnesota as well as adjacent portions of Wisconsin, Iowa, and South Dakota (fig. 1). This new homeland was situated in a transitional ecological zone that spanned deciduous forests and tall-grass prairies. There, the Santee evolved diverse lifeways that linked them to the Plains as well as the Woodlands. Those who migrated to the forested valleys of the Mississippi and lower Minnesota rivers reflected a Woodlands focus, but those who settled on the prairies west of Lac qui Parle shared the horse and buffalo culture of their Teton and Yankton-Yanktonai relatives.

By the early 1800s, the names Mdewakanton, Wahpekute, Wahpeton, and Sisseton functioned largely as ethnic references; since the Sioux who identified with these tribal names regularly intermarried, collaborated in subsistence, warfare and ceremony, and shared access to one another's lands, they were not exclusive social or cultural groupings (S.W. Pond 1908:320–322). The Sisseton and Wahpeton occupied overlapping territories that followed the course of the Minnesota River from its headwaters beyond Lake Traverse to a point just south of its confluence with the Mississippi. The vast majority of the 1,500 Wahpeton lived along the lower reaches of the Minnesota River, while most of the 2,500 Sisseton stayed in areas west of Lac qui Parle. The Wahpekute numbered no more than 600 people. Their principal areas of residence extended from the Cannon River southwest to the Blue Earth River, although some ranged as far west as Spirit Lake in Iowa. With the exception of one small group who moved to Lac qui Parle, the 2,000 Mdewakanton were concentrated in fairly stable locations along the Mississippi and lower Minnesota rivers.

External Relations

The Santee Sioux were also connected to Sioux groups farther west. In fact, the Sisseton and Wahpeton living near Lake Traverse were more closely tied socially and culturally to the Yanktonai than they were to the Mdewakanton along the Mississippi. For nearly a half-century, the Sisseton and Wahpeton served as middlemen in an active trade with the Teton and Yankton-Yanktonai, exchanging trade goods for horses and hides at prearranged locations along the James River. This traffic declined when the Teton established connections with traders on the Missouri, and it was reduced even more during the War of 1812 when antagonisms developed between the Teton, who were loyal to the Americans, and the Sisseton-Wahpeton, who supported the British (Lewis and Clark in Thwaites 1904–1905, 6:93–98; S.W. Pond 1908:485; Tabeau 1939:121–122; E.C. Bray and M.C. Bray 1976:177).

While the Santee did not always agree with their western relatives on matters of trade, they generally sided with them against the territorial incursions of their mutual enemies, the Chippewa, Cree, Assiniboine, Sauk and Fox, and Pawnee. Of these tribes, the Chippewa and Sauk and Fox were the most serious threats. Relations with neighboring Menominee, Winnebago, Iowa, and Omaha, in contrast, tended to be neutral, and even though warfare was occasionally waged against these tribes, it was not so enduring nor bitter (Stipe 1968:240–254; Hickerson 1965, 1970; Albers and Kay 1987:60).

Since warfare between the Santee and their neighbors interfered with fur production, the British and later the Americans attempted to halt this fighting by sponsoring peace-keeping councils. These pacification measures, including the treaty of 1825, established boundaries between groups along the upper Mississippi, and they provided brief interludes of quiescence, when Sioux joined with their foes in subsistence, ceremony, and recreation. In the long run, White intervention did little to quell intertribal enmities. Instead, it tended to exacerbate them by transforming

761

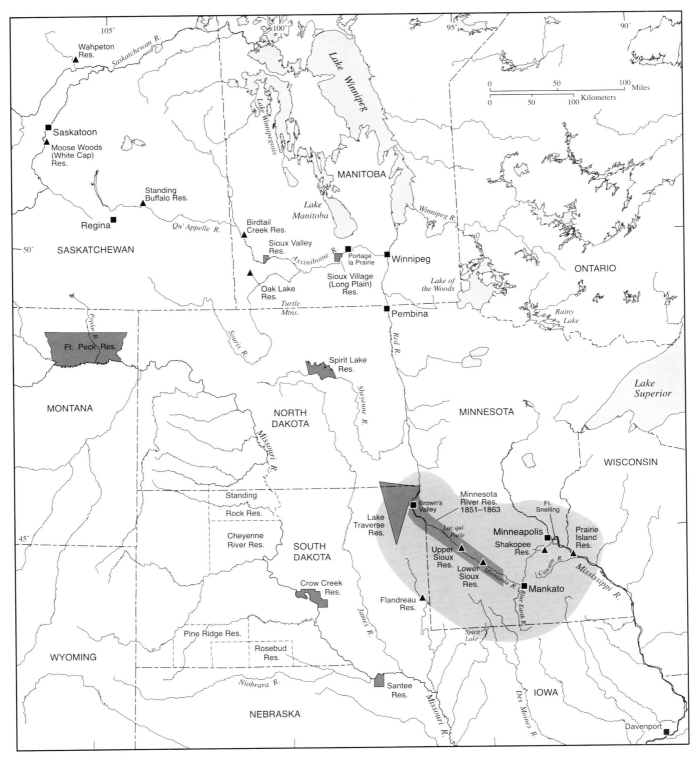

Fig. 1. Early 19th-century territory of the Santee Sioux and the modern reservations and reserves they occupy either alone or with other tribes. The portion of the Minnesota River reservation north of the river was ceded to the federal government in 1858.

what were once amorphous buffer zones into concrete territories (Stipe 1968:250–253, 259).

The British and Americans were hardly effective agents of peace, since they were engaged in warfare between themselves and often commissioned native peoples to fight their

battles. The Santee remained loyal to their British traders and even provided them military support (Elias 1988:6–24). They were not above courting Americans who came to their lands, and, in 1805, when the party of Zebulon Pike arrived in Santee territory to assess its resource potential and to gain the allegiance of its people, the Mdewakanton entered into a treaty and surrendered a small parcel of land to the United States (R.W. Meyer 1967:14; Hickerson 1974:70–112; G.C. Anderson 1984:77–102).

Between 1763 and 1819, the Santee incorporated traders as well as diplomats into their kinship networks and used these ties to gain an edge in their commercial and diplomatic dealings with Whites (Wozniak 1978; G.C. Anderson 1984; Whelan 1987). Economically and politically this was a prosperous period for the Sioux, a time when they were able to achieve unparalleled wealth through the presence of competing avenues of Euro-American trade and gratuitous provisioning (G.C. Anderson 1984:58–76). After the United States erected a military garrison in 1819 on land ceded by the Mdewakanton, British influence in the region came to an end and Sioux interests became increasingly subordinate to those of the United States (Dickson and Grignon 1888:271–315; Coues 1895, 1:82–87; D. Robinson 1967:83–108; G.C. Anderson 1984:103–149).

Culture, 1763–1829

Subsistence

Before relinquishing major portions of their territory in 1830, the Santee were a nomadic people who drew the bulk of their livelihood from foraging pursuits. There was a marked pattern of variation in their subsistence strategies, reflecting the ecological diversity of the lands they occupied (Spector 1985). Some variation was a consequence of differences in the concentration of big game species. Buffalo, once available in all regions of Santee Sioux occupation, began to decrease during the early nineteenth century and had disappeared from areas east of Lac qui Parle by the 1840s (Stipe 1968:131–132). Although buffalo remained a meat staple for the Sisseton and Wahpeton, deer were the most abundant and reliable source of big game for the eastern groups (Hickerson 1970:106–119). All big game species were procured throughout the year by individuals, alone or with companions; and in certain seasons, they were sought out by larger groups of hunters. Collective hunts for deer took place in late fall, and the primary method of securing them was a simply organized surround procedure. In contrast, communal buffalo hunting occurred in late summer or any time a herd was spotted. The Mdewakanton and other Sioux lacking horses hunted afoot and employed driving as well as impounding techniques, whereas the equestrian Sisseton and Wahpeton followed chase methods characteristic of other Plains hunters (S.W. Pond 1908:360–370; Landes 1968:62–85; Stipe 1968:130–132).

Waterfowl, food staples in fall and spring, were procured in collective drives or by solitary hunters (S.W. Pond 1908:345, 374; T. Hughes 1929:279; Landes 1968:191–193). Fishing, which involved spearing and netting techniques, was an important task in early summer and a supplemental one in other seasons (S.W. Pond 1908:346, 356; J.H.

top, Minn. Histl. Soc., St. Paul:E91.31/P52 (neg. 7267-A); bottom, Smithsonian, Dept. of Anthr.: 72,311 (neg. 77-13301).

Fig. 2. Women and children. top, Camp. Between the canvas tents is a Red River cart. Photograph by William H. Jacoby, Blue Earth, Dak. Terr., 1868–1878. bottom, Cradleboard. Like the Woodlands tribes to their east, the Santee used cradles with solid wood backs to which the child was secured with soft hide wrappings for carrying on the mother's back. A projecting hoop protected the child's head if the cradle fell, while designs on the board and cover invoked spiritual protection. Figures of Thunderbirds and deer are worked on the cover in porcupine quillwork between lines of geometric figures. Collected by George Catlin, 1832–1839, probably near the Falls of Saint Anthony, Minn. Length 77 cm.

Howard 1960:251; Landes 1968:192). Birds and small mammals were secured through stalking and trapping methods (S.W. Pond 1908:370–373; Landes 1968:187–191; Stipe 1968:135–140).

Gathering furnished additional sources of food in Santee diets, and when game was unavailable, it was a primary method of food procurement (Stipe 1968:126). From late spring through early fall, the Sioux picked fruit, dug for wild beans and tubers, and collected acorns and other nuts (S.W. Pond 1908:344, 373-374; Landes 1968:202–204). In fall they gathered wild rice, and in spring maple sap was tapped (S.W. Pond 1908:369; E.C. Deloria 1967:102–112; Landes 1968:202–204).

During the early nineteenth century, horticulture was still a secondary occupation among the Santee. Not all local groups cultivated, and those who did so appear to have planted at irregular intervals (Stipe 1968:141–142). The major crop was corn, but squash, beans, and tobacco were also domesticated (S.W. Pond 1908:342–345; Skinner 1919c:167). Crop yields were usually small, and rarely lasted more than a few weeks (S.W. Pond 1908:342).

Technology

Although all Santee were engaged in the production of furs and hides for the Euro-American trade, they varied in the extent to which they depended on it. The Mdewakanton and others who exploited a forest ecosystem drew most of their tools, including traps, guns, and axes, from this trade, whereas the prairie-based Sisseton and Wahpeton still produced their basic hunting weapon, the bow and arrow (Stipe 1968:168–178). Despite an increasing reliance on trade goods, the Sioux continued to produce many of their own artifacts.

In technology, as in other areas of production, there were important local differences. The Mdewakanton and other eastern groups relied more on the use of wood, bark, and

plant fibers in the fabrication of artifacts, and they erected gable-roofed, bark houses for summer habitation (fig. 3) as well as conical-shaped bark lodges in other seasons. Their clothing styles and floral beadwork designs also reflected their Woodlands affiliations (fig. 4). The Sisseton and Wahpeton, by contrast, depended more heavily on hide for constructing artifacts and dwellings, which took the form of the classic Plains tepee (fig. 3) and were made for year-round occupancy. In addition, the costumes and geometric art styles of these Sioux fell within a Plains sphere of influence (Wissler 1904; S.W. Pond 1908:347–359; Winchell 1911:409–505; F.H. Douglas 1932a; Densmore 1954; Hurt 1953a; J.H. Howard 1960:253–255; Stipe 1968:168–178; McDermott 1973).

Notwithstanding local variations, the division of labor among the Santee was fairly uniform. Males were primarily responsible for hunting, but they assisted in gathering activities as well (H.H. Sibley 1950:34). The care of horses and weapon-making were also male tasks. Women played a central role in production, not only in the processing of game secured by men but also in their own foraging efforts. They trapped small birds and mammals, offered supplemental help in collective drives, and a few were even proficient big game hunters (Landes 1968:165–166, 191). Plant gathering and cultivation, however, were their most important subsistence occupations. In addition, the fabrication and repair of clothing, housing, and domestic utensils were female tasks (Landes 1968:162–204).

In the early 1800s, the Santee were an egalitarian people. Even though the fur trade provided individuals a means to advance themselves materially, strong obligations to share counterbalanced inequalities in wealth accumulation (S.W. Pond 1908:97–98; Landes 1968:110). By the standards of

Minn. Histl. Soc., St. Paul:left, E91.31/P8 (neg. 999), right, E91.31/P14, (neg. 583).

Fig. 3. Habitations. left, Mdewakanton elm-bark houses with drying platforms. Women are cutting and hauling firewood and cooking. Ink wash by Robert O. Sweeny, about 1861–1862. right, Canvas tepees in camp near frame house (background) of John Stevens, in present Minneapolis, Minn. Daguerreotype attributed to Tallmadge Elwell, 1852–1854.

764

top left, Oberösterreichisches Landesmuseum, Linz, Austria: top right, Smithsonian, Dept. of Anthr.: left, 2473; right, 5442 (neg. 99-20,262); bottom left, Minn. Histl. Soc., St. Paul: E91.l/p19 (neg. 7266-A); bottom right, Harvard U., Peabody Mus., Cambridge, Mass.: 41-72/10/74 (neg. 22846).

Fig. 4. Men's headgear and adornment. top left, Man on left wearing headband and feather headdress; man on right wearing roach headdress with eagle feathers and head decorations of ribbons and metal disks. Both individuals also have face paint or tattooing. Watercolor by Johann Baptist Wengler, probably at the Mdewakanton village of Kaposia, home of Little Crow's band, 1851 (computer enhanced). top right, Incised elk antler spreaders, each with the figure of a horned head representing a spirit being. The spreader gave shape to the roach headdress and the sockets held eagle feathers ("Otoe and Missouria," fig. 8, this vol.). left, collected before 1841; right, collected by John Varden before the 1850s. Length of right 27 cm; other to same scale. bottom left, Camp with canvas tepee, probably Sisseton or Wahpeton. The boy on left holds a bow and blunt arrows probably used in hunting birds. The 2 men in the center wear cloth hoods decorated with trade fringe and serrated-edge ribbon and Hudson's Bay Company blankets. Photograph by William H. Jacoby, Ft. Abercrombie, Dak. Terr., 1868 1878. bottom right, Eta Keazah or Sullen Face, Mdewakanton, wearing wool hood decorated with ribbon appliqué edged with white glass beads. Painted while he was a prisoner at Ft. Snelling, Minn. (McDermott 1961:51). Oil painting by Seth Eastman, 1844.

neighboring Plains tribes, the Santee were not wealthy. They had few horses, and after 1820, a diminishing reserve of trade wealth. During a time when most Plains populations were reaping the benefits of a burgeoning hide and horse traffic, the basis of Santee wealth—the fur trade—was in a state of decline (Stipe 1968:222).

Social and Political Organization

With few exceptions, the kinship system of the Santee followed the pattern of other Sioux. Genealogical ties were extended widely, facilitating the development of large and ramified social networks. However, clans did not exist (Stipe 1971).

The far-ranging Sioux social networks were maintained in each generation not only through the bilateral extension of kin terms to the fourth collateral line but also through the prohibition of marriage among all recognized consanguines. Most marriages were arranged by parents or other close relatives, but unions arising from elopement and capture were not uncommon. Monogamy was the most prevalent form of marriage; polygamy was practiced by older and influential men. Marital bonds tended to be brittle, and even though adultery was punished, divorce was obtained easily by both sexes. Stigmas were not attached to the divorced or the widowed, who usually remarried. Levirate and sororate were optional (M.H. Eastman 1904:103–109; S.W. Pond 1908:455, 463–468; W.D. Wallis 1947:30–31; E.C. Deloria 1967:13–15; Landes 1968:95–118, 138–153).

Santee social networks were supported through a variety of voluntary associations. Sometimes, these associations

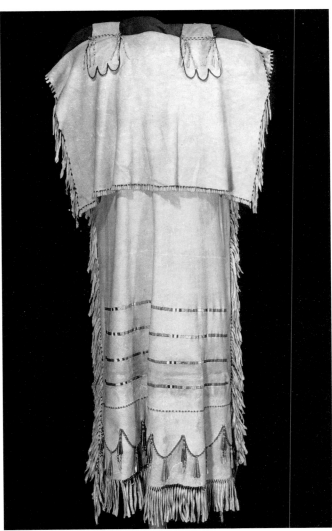

left, Oberösterreichisches Landesmuseum, Linz, Austria: a, The Brooklyn Mus., N.Y.:50.67-2; b, Smithsonian, Dept. of Anthr.:21,670 (neg. 99-20267).

Fig. 5. Women's and men's clothing. top left, Mdewakanton group. The man is wearing cloth shirt, leggings, moccasins, hair roach, and multiple bead necklaces and holds a pipe and lance. The women are wearing cloth clothing, moccasins, and multiple necklaces. Watercolor by Johann Baptist Wengler, probably at the Mdewakanton village of Kaposia, 1851. right and bottom left, Dress and moccasins. By the 1830s Indians near the fort dressed exclusively in clothing made of trade cloth, using buckskin only for their moccasins. Skin garments were found only among more westerly groups, such as the Sisseton, who had limited access to trade goods (Feder 1964:16). The dress is made of 2 pieces of skin folded over at the top and seamed on the sides with shoulder straps. It is decorated with bands of porcupine quillwork, bead edging, metal cones, and fringes. Collected by Dr. Nathan Sturges Jarvis, at Ft. Snelling, Minn., 1833–1836. Length 132.1 cm. The buckskin moccasins are gathered and seamed around a U-shaped vamp embroidered with floral porcupine quillwork. Collected by Dr. J. Frazier Boughter, before 1872. Length 25 cm.

developed into special friendships in which reciprocal responsibilities became as compelling as those among siblings of the same sex and generation (S.R. Riggs 1893:196–197; S.W. Pond 1908:487). In addition, special bonds were created through adoption to replace deceased kin (E.C. Deloria 1967:9–10).

In Santee social formations, households were basic provisioning units. They centered around a couple and their offspring, although other combinations of relatives also lived together. Each household occupied a separate domicile, but in the large bark houses several households stayed in the same dwelling. Households never existed in isolation but formed larger domestic groupings (t^{h}iyóšpaye or bands or villages) that were minimal and sometimes maximal social units. The members of these bands were interdependent, pooling labor as well as provisions (Prescott 1854:676; S.R. Riggs 1893:204–205; S.W. Pond 1908:353–354; Landes 1968:29, 122–133).

The t^{h}iyóšpaye, in turn, formed larger territorial groupings that were named from some peculiarity of their location, appearance, or character. These local groupings were not stable in their size and composition nor enduring over time. They could be enlarged by the addition of distantly related peoples and diminished through gradual attrition or sudden segmentation in their ranks. A few even disappeared, with their followers reconstituting alliances among other extant or emergent groups. Although some local groups did maintain fixed identities and locations, the lands they used were not owned nor were they marked by clear-cut boundaries. Except for restrictions that developed in relation to trapping sites, there was considerable flux in the territorial attachments of households and t^{h}iyóšpaye (Stipe 1968:120–123, 180–181).

In the forested valleys of the Mississippi and lower Minnesota rivers, the settlements of local groups took the form of semisedentary villages. After 1800, these villages were organized in the least productive seasons, and except for groups who practiced horticulture, they had little to do with subsistence. Instead, villages functioned as nuclei for the gathering of people to carry on trade, ceremony, and recreation. Summer villages contained between 250 and 500 residents, and they were inhabited at intermittent intervals from the spring through fall trapping seasons. In the course of a single season, their size could double when ritual events were hosted and decrease when inhabitants left to visit other villages or forage in outlying areas (S.W. Pond 1908:373–375; Landes 1968:33–34,45–47). Winter villages, in contrast, were usually smaller in size and rarely endured for an entire season. When food ran out, the village dispersed and its domestic groups led an independent nomadic existence for the rest of the winter (S.W. Pond 1908:486).

On the western prairies beyond Lac qui Parle, local groups appeared as nomadic bands. Like the villages, the western bands acted as units in political, ceremonial, and recreational affairs. Yet, they differed from the villages not only in relation to the mobile nature of their settlement patterns but also in terms of their productive orientation. Bands were subsistence units, and their internal organization was well suited to the collective pursuit of buffalo. Although band size fluctuated according to season and circumstance, it averaged around 250 people. Residence in band settlements was continuous from late spring through early fall, but during other seasons bands broke into smaller groupings (S.R. Riggs 1893:200–210; Lowie 1913:131–137; Skinner 1919c:173–174).

Each Santee band and village had civil leaders who represented the interests of their followers to Euro-American traders and government officials. In addition, the civil leaders negotiated disputes with neighboring groups, and they arbitrated internal conflicts. In both bands and villages, these leaders had no real authority. They led by persuasion and their power was only as great as their ability to represent their followers' interests and to achieve consensus among them. To these ends, leaders organized councils to which the representatives of resident families were invited. The councils made decisions on a variety of issues, but when their deliberations required collective action, unanimity of opinion was necessary. These councils were also authorized to appoint akíč^{h}ita 'soldiers' (sometimes including women) to police community functions. Since the Santee did not maintain permanent police forces in their settlements, soldiers were chosen informally each time an activity emerged that required their services. It was only among the western bands that soldiers were formally organized, no doubt because they were called upon more often to police community functions such as collective buffalo hunts. Importantly, the influence of civil leaders and their accompanying support structures was suspended as soon as bands and villages dissolved and their members formed other residential arrangements.

Although the civil leaders of bands and villages performed similar functions, they came to power in different ways. The civil leaders of the eastern villages inherited their positions, and there is overwhelming evidence to indicate that this ascribed pattern developed in postcontact times as a direct outcome of Europeans appointing individuals to intervene in trade and diplomacy. Leaders of the western bands, on the other hand, achieved their positions on the basis of their accomplishments and generosity. Yet, even among some of these groups ascription played a role in leadership selection (Prescott 1852:182, 1854:69; E.D. Neill 1872a:290–291; S.R. Riggs 1893:200–210; S.W. Pond 1908:282, 382–385; C.C. Wilson 1908; Lowie 1913:131–137; T. Hughes 1927; Landes 1968:66–94; Stipe 1968:214–221, 236; G.C. Anderson 1984, 1986).

Villages and bands were also focal points for mobilizing war parties, which were organized and conducted through a political apparatus that was separate from the civil authority. War leaders achieved their positions through their skills and supernatural powers, and they initiated raids for reasons of revenge or visionary insight. During a raid's duration, the war leader maintained absolute authority and invested select soldiers with policing responsibilities. While military powers were normally suspended at the end of a raid or defensive skirmish, some war leaders exercised considerable influence in local affairs, either as individual personalities or in special positions supporting the civil leadership (Prescott 1854:62; S.W. Pond 1880; S.R. Riggs 1893:219–223; M.H. Eastman 1904:xviii; Lowie 1913:131–139; Skinner 1919c:172–173; Landes 1959, 1968:204–224; Stipe 1968:240–245).

Unlike the Sisseton and Wahpeton, whose bands functioned as communal hunting units, the village-based Sioux established separate social formations for collective hunts. From October to December, the deer-hunting season, village groups were divided into nomadic encampments, numbering between 50 and 100 people. Similar settlements were formed on an intermittent and less enduring basis for other big-game hunting and for collective waterfowl drives. Even the westerly located bands broke into smaller encampments for hunting deer. All forms of communal hunting, whether organized around band units or smaller encampments, were supervised by special hunt leaders, who acquired their positions on the basis of their talents and supernatural powers. In locating the game and in directing movements on the hunt, the absolute authority of a hunt leader was enforced by soldiers selected for the occasion. The men who were hunt leaders were not the same individuals as the civil authorities (S. Pond 1908:360–370; Landes 1968:170–188).

In addition to hunting encampments, the Santee developed settlements for tapping maple sap and for harvesting wild rice. The spring sugaring camps were in existence from March to May, and they were organized around related females who shared usufruct rights over maple groves. These women, their dependents, the aged, and a few adult men who stayed for defense purposes made up the camp. The remaining males spent their time at trapping sites, often located more than 20 miles from the sugaring encampments. In the early fall months, small encampments were scattered at close intervals along wild rice beds and, as in spring, some of the men left these sites to work their trap lines. Like the domestic groupings that were offshoots of the summer and winter settlements, the formations that emerged around wild rice and maple sugar gathering were not associated with elaborate supervisory structures. Leadership was informal and provided by local family elders (M.H. Eastman 1904:60–61; S.W. Pond 1908:369–375; E.C. Deloria 1967:10–13; Landes 1968:194–201; A.R. Woolworth and N.L. Woolworth 1980:80–85).

The final type of settlement found among the Santee was the large, multiband encampment. These encampments, which numbered as many as 1,000 people, were formed for buffalo hunts, trade fairs, and Sun Dances. The supervisory structures for each of these activities was different, but their underlying principles of organization were the same. In the case of the communal buffalo hunt, special hunt leaders were chosen from among participating bands to form a council that was responsible for coordinating hunt activity and directing camp movement. Soldiers were appointed by this council to keep order, and they were given

rights to punish anyone who disobeyed council directives or violated customary hunt procedure. The council and their representatives exercised total authority over the buffalo hunt encampment, but their powers were suspended at the completion of each hunt (S.R. Riggs 1893:202–204; Lowie 1913:131–137). Although these large encampments were commonly organized by Sisseton and Wahpeton in association with the Yankton and Yanktonai, they were not found among the more easterly located groups, whose nineteenth-century lands were peripheral to the buffalo range (Lynd 1864:156–157; Landes 1968:163–164).

Belief and Ceremonies

In the early nineteenth century, the Santee adhered to a rich and varied belief system, which included features unique to them as Sioux but which also involved an amalgamation of traditions associated with neighboring Woodlands, Prairie, and Plains populations. Basic to Sioux belief was the notion of a pervasive life-giving power, wak^{h}á. All things and happenings were potential repositories of this power which was granted ultimately through contact with various spiritual beings. Whatever their specific character, spirits influenced the destinies of humans in myriad ways (Prescott 1853:229; G.H. Pond 1854; S.W. Pond 1908:410–415, 425).

The Sioux received power and guidance for the well-being of society and for the success of its individual members through innumerable ritual acts. One of the more important ones was the vision experience. Visions in which spirits appeared were sought in isolation or in ceremony, and they came involuntarily in dreams or as apparitions. Males as well as females received power in visions. Those with the strongest powers were the shamans or medicine people. In hunting, curing, warfare, and gambling, the shaman and leader was one and the same person. Just as skill signified power, so power bestowed talent. In theory and in fact, the two were inseparable (G.H. Pond 1867:238–250; Lynd 1864:160–161; Prescott 1894:484; S.W. Pond 1908:403–408,420–21; Skinner 1919c:117; W.D. Wallis 1947:78–223; Landes 1968:48–66).

The medicine men and women with therapeutic powers cured many kinds of illnesses caused by things such as failure to fulfill a visionary command or to propitiate a spirit; violation of a customary or personal taboo by oneself, a relative, or an ancestor; and the envy or sorcery of another person. Sorcery as a cause of illness or other misfortune appears to have been much more developed among Santee than among other Sioux groups. There were also mundane reasons for sickness that were dealt with through herbal remedies. Relationships between curers and their patients were contractual ones, which mirrored encounters between humans and their supernatural benefactors (Andros 1883; Gilmore 1919; G.H. Pond 1854; S.W. Pond 1908:474–477; W.D. Wallis 1923, 1947:78–110; R.S. Wallis and W.D. Wallis 1953; Howard 1960:225–256; Landes 1968:41–47, 56–59, 65).

While many visions offered power for individuals only, others carried messages of wider significance. The Santee followed numerous ceremonies that were initiated on the basis of a visionary command. Some of these were restricted to individuals sharing the same kinds of power, as the Elk, Buffalo, and Double Woman dreamers. In contrast, there were ceremonies in which only the leader was required to have supernatural sanction. The *heyókʰa* 'clown' as well as Raw Fish and Dog Liver Eaters' dances were of this order. The Sun Dance, which was found only among Sisseton and Wahpeton, can also be included here because participation was determined either by a dream or through personal dedication. Ceremonies based on visionary directive were held intermittently, and their range of support appears to have varied over time and place (Fletcher 1887; M.H. Eastman 1904:243–268; J.H. Howard 1955b; S.W. Pond 1908:415–418; Skinner 1919b, 1925b; W.D. Wallis 1921, 1947:58–67; Lowie 1913:117–129).

Among the Santee, most societies, including those of warriors, were organized informally. One exception was the Midewiwin society, *wakʰą́ wačʰípi*, admittance to which was based on family connections, payment, and the exercise of good deeds. As among neighboring Woodlands populations, the rituals of this society were the most widely supported and regularly held. Aside from its purely propitiatory functions, the Midewiwin served as an important medium for curing, self-renewal, and feasting the dead (G.H. Pond 1867:222–226; S.W. Pond 1908:409–412; Skinner 1920:262–305; W.D. Wallis 1947:69–75; Landes 1968:57–60).

In addition to the ceremonies sponsored by nonkin associations, Sioux families held a variety of rituals that marked life cycle transitions. The most elaborate ones were associated with death (Lynd 1864:158–159; S.W. Pond 1908:478–485; W.D. Wallis 1947:31–35; Landes 1968:153–160). Most other rituals marking life cycle events were given by parents in honor of their children. Ceremonies were held when a child first walked, at a girl's menarche, a young man's first successful hunt or coup, and in late adolescence to celebrate female as well as male chastity and role mastery (Fletcher 1887:260; W.D. Wallis 1947:27; Landes 1968:40–42). In addition, there were rituals that guided a child's socialization. For boys, there was the vision quest, which following a Woodlands tradition, began in early childhood (C.A. Eastman 1902:102–112; Skinner 1919c:170). Girls, in contrast, did not usually quest for visions; their time of ritual fasting and seclusion came at the start of menses (W.D. Wallis 1947:35–36).

Values

Like other Sioux, the Santee were indulgent with their children and reared them in a permissive fashion. Each child was named and treated differently according to its gender and birth order position. Nevertheless, all children were taught to be self-reliant and at the same time responsible to others. The Sioux respected each person's individuality, and they believed that forced compliance to adult demands damaged a child's will. A sense of collective responsibility was instilled in children not only by admonishing them to share but also by teasing and shaming them when they were selfish (S.R. Riggs 1855, 1893:210–219; S.W. Pond 1908:459–462; R.S. Wallis 1954; R.S. Wallis and W.D. Wallis 1955; E.C. Deloria and J. Brandon 1961:12–13; C.A. Eastman 1902).

Although the Santee have been described as a people whose values and behavior were communalistic rather than individualistic (Landes 1968:42), it is clear that both value orientations were present but actualized differently over time and place (Albers 1982:262). Fur trapping, for example, was a highly privatized pursuit, whose products were individually owned and not subject to the rules of sharing that governed many other goods. Buffalo hunting, in contrast, involved a high degree of cooperation, and its products were widely shared. Meat was apportioned equally among the hunt participants who, in turn, distributed shares to nonproducing segments of the populace. Hides were given to the ones who led the hunt and to those who killed the animals, but no hunter could accumulate a hide surplus until everyone's needs were met (Landes 1968:164–165, 173–174, 186). The historic subsistence patterns of the Santee may have given them more opportunities to act in a collective way than their Chippewa neighbors (Barnouw 1950), but men as well as women still held autonomy in many of their own affairs. Indeed, Santee females had a variety of independent avenues in which to exercise influence within domestic as well as community settings (Albers 1983, 1985, 1989).

History: 1830–1879

Treaties

During the middle decades of the nineteenth century, the Santee moved from a state of self-sufficiency and autonomy to one of destitution and dependence. In 1830, they signed the Treaty of Prairie du Chien whereby all their lands between the Des Moines and Missouri rivers, along with a small tract in Iowa separating them from the Sauk and Fox, were ceded to the United States (Kappler 1904–1941, 2:305–310). Under the treaty of 1837, signed in Washington, the Mdewakanton relinquished their territory east of the Mississippi River (Kappler 1904–1941, 2:493–494; Textor 1896:67–68; R.W. Meyer 1967:50–61; Hickerson 1974:114–157, 214–220; G.C. Anderson 1984:133–135).

It was not long after these treaties were signed before White settlement approached Sioux borders and placed a severe strain on the region's already dwindling game base. Even though the depletion of game was noted as early as 1820, it became more serious in subsequent decades, when reports of hunger and starvation grew at an alarming rate (R.W. Meyer 1967:63, 75; Stipe 1968:128–129, 131–132;

Hickerson 1970:117–119). By the 1840s, the game scarcity was accompanied by a recession in the demand for furs and an inflation in the price of trade goods. These changing circumstances made it increasingly difficult for Sioux to cancel outstanding debts to traders. Insolvency with the trade was forestalled by using land-sale monies instead of peltries to cover debts. Soon, traders were advancing credit on the basis of future land cessions rather than anticipated fur yields, and they were playing an important role in the outcome of treaty deliberations. Between 1837 and 1853, a large portion of the treaty funds awarded to the Santee was paid to the traders. This left only a small amount for annuities, which were insufficient to compensate for land losses, much less to sustain a livelihood. By the end of the 1840s, many Sioux, especially those living in regions east of Lac qui Parle, were destitute and dependent on the extension of traders' credit and federal annuities for much of their subsistence (S.W. Pond 1908:68–69; R.W. Meyer 1967:24–132; Stipe 1968: 25–33, 73-88, 135–141).

Severe destitution weakened Sioux bargaining powers when negotiations were again convened for the further sale of land. In 1841, they were convinced to sign a treaty whereby some of their territory would have been ceded to accommodate tribes from the East, but the Senate failed to ratify it (R.W. Meyer 1967:72–75). Not long after, plans were underway to bring about the surrender of all Sioux lands in Minnesota. While attempts to negotiate a land sale failed in 1849, ones in 1851 succeeded in getting the Sisseton and Wahpeton and the Mdewakanton and Wahpekute to sign, respectively, the treaties of Traverse des Sioux (vol. 4:50) and Mendota. Under the provisions of the 1851 treaties, the Santee ceded all their land in Minnesota and Dakota Territory. In return, they were to receive financial compensation and a reservation, the final location of which had not been specified (R.W. Meyer 1967:72–91; G.C. Anderson 1984:177–202). Nevertheless, efforts began in 1853 to remove them to a proposed reservation along the upper Minnesota River. Congress belatedly approved Sioux title to this site in 1860, but in 1858, the United States negotiated another treaty (fig. 6) whereby the Santee were compelled to surrender over half the lands set aside for their reservation (R.W. Meyer 1967:103–104).

During the years of treaty negotiation, government agents in collaboration with traders and missionaries introduced Euro-American farming techniques to the Santee. While most Sioux were not interested in agriculture, it was adopted by a few local groups on an experimental and transient basis. At the same time, many Sioux were exposed to Christian evangelism; however, only a small portion of the Santee pursued formal education or converted to Christianity before their settlement on a reservation in 1853. Many of the Christian Sioux were descendants of Euro-American traders, and they lived in permanent settlements adjoining trading compounds (R.W. Meyer 1967:48–132; Stipe 1968:142–147, 205–213; Forbes 1977; Wozniak 1978; G.C. Anderson 1984:142–143).

Reservations

During its short history, the Sioux reservation along the Minnesota River was fraught with many difficulties, not the least of which was an inadequate means of provisioning its residents. This forced most Santees to continue living in their former locales, returning to the reservation only to collect annuities. Unable to survive outside the reservation through traditional means of livelihood, many were reduced to begging and a few were driven to plundering in nearby White communities. By 1856, however, a growing number had established more permanent reservation settlements (R.W. Meyer 1967:88–108; Stipe 1968:147–67, 205–213; G.C. Anderson 1984:203–224).

Of those living on the reservation, some survived primarily on their annuities and traders' credit, but a few began to practice agriculture seriously. Along with adopting European farming methods, living in European-American style houses and wearing a Euro-American style of dress, more Santees became Christians. Some of them played a critical collaborative role in the work of missionaries who published Bible translations and other material in the Dakota language (vol. 4:438) (S.R. Riggs 1872, 1890, 1893). Most of those who farmed could not sustain themselves through agriculture, for drought and the demands of nonproducing relatives mitigated against crop surpluses. In addition, many acculturated Sioux became stigmatized by the majority who continued their indigenous way of life. They also pursued divergent political interests, and factionalism emerged (R.W. Meyer 1967:88–108; Stipe 1968:147–167, 205–213; Forbes 1977).

After 1858, reservation conditions steadily worsened. The kinship ties that connected the Santee with White traders and diplomats had begun to erode, creating a social vacuum between the two populations (G.C. Anderson 1986:226–260). In addition, poor accounting of annuity funds, delays in their payment, and the siphoning of these monies to pay off traders' debts were among many factors that contributed to Sioux embitterment. Although skirmishes between Sioux and Whites had been frequent in occurence throughout the reservation era, it was not until August 1862 that a relatively minor incident erupted into the Sioux Conflict. The hostilities involved only a portion of the Santee, mostly Mdewakanton and Wahpekute, who succeeded in pillaging White settlements and killing many inhabitants. By the fall of 1862, American military forces had broken the Sioux offensive, and in subsequent months, they retaliated against all Santees regardless of their culpability for the hostilities. Whites sought retribution in the indiscriminate killing of Sioux at battles waged in Minnesota and later in Dakota Territory as well as in the hanging of 38 prisoners at Mankato (vol. 4:169). More died in the Conflict's aftermath from disease and starvation, either as prisoners or as refugees who fled Minnesota to escape capture (R.W. Meyer 1967:88–154). Shortly after, Minnesota's White residents pressured Congress to enact

770

Fig. 6. Delegation from the Sisseton and Wahpeton Sioux to Washington in 1858. The delegation signed a treaty ceding land north of the Minnesota River and alloting land south of it (Kappler 1904–1941, 2:785–789). left to right, standing: Akepa, Wahpeton; Scarlet Plume or Wamdupidutah, Sisseton; Red Iron or Muzzahshaw, Sisseton; John Other Day or Umpedutokechaw, Wahpeton; Little Paul or Mazzakootemanee, Wahpeton; and Charles E. Crawford; seated: Iron Walker or Mazzomanee, Wahpeton; Stumpy Horn or Hahhutanai, Sisseton; Sweet Corn or Ojupi, Sisseton; and Extended Tail Feathers or Upiyahideyaw, Wahpeton. Photograph by Charles DeForest Fredericks, New York City, June 25–July 2, 1858.

legislation that would prevent the surviving Sioux from establishing claims to their reservation land in Minnesota and, directly following, that would establish provisions for the permanent exile of most Santees from the state. Congress obliged these demands in March 1863 by passing a bill under which the United States abrogated its treaty obligations with the Santee (R.W. Meyer 1967:139–141).

Immediately after this legislation was passed, efforts were begun to remove the Santee from Minnesota. The first group, most of whom were Mdewakanton and Wahpekute imprisoned in camps at Fort Snelling (fig. 7) and Mankato, were taken to Crow Creek on the Missouri River. In 1866, these prisoners, along with those incarcerated at Davenport, Iowa, were moved to a site along the Niobrara River in Nebraska. Within a few years, they were transferred again to a location on the Missouri that became known as the Santee Reservation (R.W. Meyer 1964, 1967:137–168). Dissatisfied

with the situation at Santee, a few residents left in 1869 to establish homesteads in Dakota Territory, forming the nucleus of what later became the Flandreau Agency (R.W. Meyer 1967:343–357; C. Allen et al. 1971).

The majority of Santee, including most of the Sisseton and Wahpeton, escaped capture and spent the years after 1862 on the northeastern Plains. In 1867, some of them, threatened by starvation, signed a treaty with the United States that led to the formation of the Devils Lake (now Spirit Lake) Reservation in North Dakota and the Lake Traverse Reservation (Sisseton and Wahpeton) in South Dakota. Like the Santee Reservation, the Lake Traverse Reservation developed a discontented element who formed a splinter settlement at Brown's Valley in Minnesota. There was also a mixed population of Santees who joined forces with Teton and Yanktonai and remained unattached to a reservation until 1873, when most of them were settled on

Fig. 7. Prisoners at Ft. Snelling, Minn., with Bishop Henry B. Whipple. left, First communion and confirmation by Bishop Whipple of some of the 1,700 Mdewakanton, Wahpekute, and Wahpeton Sioux prisoners at Ft. Snelling. center, Leather-covered wooden saddle with horse effigy pommel and tack decoration. Family tradition reports that it was a gift to Bishop Whipple from the Santee chief Cut Nose in 1888 in appreciation of assistance to the tribe in legal negotiations. Length 77 cm. right, Teenage boy in the prison compound wearing multiple necklaces, finger-woven sash, and beaded moccasins. He holds a bow and arrow. left (cropped) and right, Photographs by Benjamin F. Upton, April 1863.

the Fort Peck Reservation in Montana. A few ended up on the Standing Rock Reservation, North Dakota (R.W. Meyer 1967:198–203, 220–224; Black Thunder et al. 1975; D.R. Miller 1987:100–148).

A sizable number of Santees fled to Canada and remained there. In 1873, Sissetons, Wahpetons, and a few Mdewakantons settled on the Sioux Valley (Oak River) and Birdtail Creek reserves in Manitoba (fig. 1). The Oak Lake Reserve was established in 1878 for Wahpekute and also Yanktonai. Other Wahpekutes who were granted a reserve in Manitoba's Turtle Mountains surrendered it in 1907 and moved to Oak Lake. A few Wahpetons lived in the vicinity of Portage La Prairie where they purchased land for settlement in 1898, but in 1904, some of them were relocated on the Long Plains Reserve. Most of the Sissetons and Wahpetons in Saskatchewan were settled on the Standing Buffalo Reserve in 1877 and the White Cap (Moose Woods) Reserve in 1881. Finally, a small number of Wahpetons moved north where they were settled on the Wahpeton (Round Plains) Reserve in 1894 (Laviolette 1944; R.W. Meyer 1968; A.B. Kehoe 1975; Elias 1988).

Most of the Santees were exiled from Minnesota, but a few remained under the protection of sympathetic Whites. In later years, more returned to Minnesota where they, along with those who never left, formed several independent communities. The ones at Prairie Island, Prior Lake (Shakopee), and Morton (Lower Sioux), populated largely by Mdewakantons, and another at Granite Falls (Upper Sioux), established by Sisseton and Wahpetons, eventually achieved trust status (R.W. Meyer 1967:258–293).

Whatever unity the Santee may have had in their Minnesota homeland was destroyed after 1862 when they were dispersed and eventually resettled in widely scattered trust communities in Minnesota, North Dakota, South Dakota, Montana, Manitoba, and Saskatchewan. By 1879, when most Santee were permanently relocated outside Minnesota, their lives became orchestrated by the policies of the United States and Canadian governments. The Canadian Sioux tended to retain more of their indigenous culture, including language and ceremony, not only because they were settled on reserves at a later date but also because the Canadian government was not so forceful in its attempts to assimilate them (R.W. Meyer 1968; A.B. Kehoe 1970a; J.H. Howard 1984; Elias 1988). Despite the fact that Santees followed divergent paths in their early reservation adaptations, they all responded to White acculturative pressures in a selective way. By the early twentieth century, many aspects of their indigenous culture had disappeared but other features persisted and flourished.

History, 1880–1930

During the twentieth century, the Mdewakanton, Wahpekute, Sisseton, and Wahpeton became nearly indistinguishable from their Yankton, Yanktonai, and Teton relatives. Similar living conditions, coupled with high rates of intermarriage, erased many of the cultural differences and the divisional and tribal names came to have little significance except as historical markers. Santee more commonly identified themselves and neighboring Indian populations in terms of

Fig. 8. Citizenship. United States Indian Inspector James McLaughlin (vol. 4:663–664) speaking at the ceremony at which 17 Santees became citizens. The plow symbolized civilization. Photograph by Charles E. Burton, superintendent of the Santee government school and Santee agent from 1914 to 1917 (R.W. Meyer 1967, 1993:297–305), May 17, 1916.

community, state, or national affiliations (Feraca and Howard 1963; Albers 1974:43–75).

Economy

During the late nineteenth century, the major policy directive of both Canada and the United States was to encourage farming in Santee communities (vol. 4:51). The desirability of agriculture was accepted when it was reintroduced and later attempts at farming were fairly successful. Some even produced surpluses for sale to outside markets. By the twentieth century, Sioux involvement in agriculture began to wane, especially in the United States. The Canadian Sioux also experienced declines in agriculture, but sizable attritions in the number who farmed did not occur until after World War II. In the late 1980s, a small segment of the Santee practiced farming, and of those who still farmed, only a minority produced cash crops on a full-time basis while the rest raised livestock or cultivated garden-sized plots for their own consumption (R.W. Meyer 1967:155–293, 1968; A.B. Kehoe 1970a:152–167; Elias 1988:55–130).

The withdrawal of the Santee from agriculture was a consequence of many factors, not the least of which was the precariousness of northern plains farming. Over time, the viability of cash-crop production was reduced by an increasingly mechanized and competitive agribusiness. Not only did the Sioux lack necessary equipment, but also they had no collateral to secure capital for improvements and expansion. In the United States, the passage of the Dawes Severalty Act and other land legislation accelerated agricultural decline by opening up avenues for the early and continued loss of reservation lands. By the 1950s, much of the Sioux land base in the United States had been sold and what remained became so entangled in heirship complications to be of little value to its owners (McNickle 1946).

Fig. 9. Native language literacy. Front page of *Iapi Oaye* (Word Carrier), vol. 49, no. 4, April 1920, the Santee Normal Training School paper, published by Frederick B. Riggs, Santee, Nebr. The school was begun in the winter of 1870–1871 by his father Alfred L. Riggs, a missionary, and the bilingual monthly paper was started in 1871. The school, which educated Sioux from all divisions, reached its maximum influence in the 1890s. A.L. Riggs refused the government's attempt to eliminate the use of native language in the school and teach English exclusively and thus lost government financial assistance in 1893, but the school continued until 1936. The influence of native language instruction at the school is demonstrated by the continued publication of *Iapi Oaye*. A photograph of Angel DeCora, Winnebago artist and educator (McAnulty 1976), and some of her illustrations are on the front page.

While a few reservations did regain corporate land holdings under the Indian Reorganization Act, this did not bring about a mass return to farming. As the Canadian Sioux situation demonstrated, even when lands were collectively held, they were not productively useful unless there was an improved technological base and sufficient capital assets to compete in the modern market. As a result of these and other factors, the vast majority of Sioux ended up leasing their lands to Whites (R.W. Meyer 1967:155–357, 1968:177–181, 1975; Elias 1988:109–130).

Even before farming declined, the Santee began to turn to other livelihoods. Hunting, fishing, and gathering were the primary subsistence activities of several small bands in Canada, providing supplemental sources of food in most other Sioux communities as well. Trapping, woodcutting, and craftwork (figs. 10–11) were also undertaken in the early twentieth century. Beadwork, basketry, quilting, rug-making and stone carving were among the crafts important for the Sioux (Landes 1968:161–213; A.B. Kehoe 1970a:160; Albers and Medicine 1983; J.H. Howard 1984:59–78; Elias 1988:31–37, 50–53, 111–117, 155–167, 181–182; Martin, Alex, and Benton 1988).

Income from leasing combined with subsistence farming, foraging, and piece-meal labor never offered the Santee more than a marginal basis of existence. As a result, an increasing number turned to wage labor or various forms of government assistance after 1900. Except in some areas of Canada, the job situation was dismal with most Sioux never able to acquire more than transient or poorly paid forms of work (McNickle 1946; R.W. Meyer 1967:294–357; A.B. Kehoe 1970a:167–168; Albers 1974:110–120; Elias 1988:31–37, 162–167, 215–219).

Community

In both Canada and the United States, the early conditions of reservation living created a sense of group exclusiveness that had not been present in prereservation times. Land ownership coupled with restrictive rules of reservation membership led most Santee to marry and remain in the communities in which they were enrolled. Whether lands were alloted in severalty as in the United States or held in common as in Canada, there was a growing tendency for domestic groups to form around persons holding land rights. Since early federal land and provisioning policies in the United States favored men, and since reserve membership was determined patrilaterally in Canada, an agnatic bias in residence developed (L. Wilcox 1943:34–70; R.W. Meyer 1967:155–272; Albers 1983:182–186; Elias 1988).

Despite this change, certain features of Santee social organization did persist. Domestic groups, consisting of a series of related households, continued to act as cooperative units in provisioning. These residentially based groupings became important sources of support and collaboration in subsistence, politics, ceremony, and recreation (L. Wilcox 1943:14–70; R.W. Meyer 1967:155–272; Landes 1968:104–110; A.B. Kehoe 1970a:164-165; Albers 1974:180-182; J.H. Howard 1984:84–87).

Religion

While some Sioux were deeply committed Christians, expressed in, for example, Roman Catholicism or the evangelical All Nations Revival in Canada, others' involvement in church affairs was nominal. In the late twentieth century, when Sioux subscribed to Christian tenets, symbolism, and ceremony, these were often embedded in an ontological scheme that was peculiarly Sioux. Syncretization has also taken place in the Native American Church (Albers 1974:397–399; J.H. Howard 1984:100–181).

While most Sioux no longer solicited visions in isolated quests or ceremonies, dreams with portents of power were still used as a sign of creativity in beadwork, dancing, gambling, curing and other talents. Medicine people with special curing skills practiced their art in many Santee communities, but the number declined (W.D. Wallis 1947:78–223; Albers 1968–1976; J.H. Howard 1984:135–179).

left, Smithsonian, NAA: 88-8763; right, Smithsonian, Dept. of Anthr.: 2,622 (neg. 92-6887).

Fig. 10. Pipes. Pipe carving, a tradition among the Sioux, continued as an economic activity throughout the 20th century. Pipe bowls were usually carved of catlinite, a red stone quarried primarily from a single site near Pipestone, Minn. left, William Jones from Flandeau, S. Dak., renowned as a skillful carver specializing in pipes with carved eagle claws. A completed pipe stem is leaning on his knee. His grandchildren are with him. Photograph by Dr. H.M. Whelpley, 1902. right, Effigy pipe depicting a chief, identified by the peace medal on his chest, distributing liquor to a follower. It is made of catlinite with geometric designs and buffalo hoof prints inlaid in lead (Ewers 1978a). Collected prior to 1841. Length 20.8 cm.

top, Minn. Histl. Soc., Sibley House Historic Site, Mendota, Bishop Whipple Coll.:SH 1480J; bottom, Minn. Histl. Soc., St. Paul: DAR A79:15: 180, 181, 186.

Fig. 11. Lace making. This cottage industry flourished from 1890 until the 1930s as a means for women to earn income. At Birch Coulee, Minn., the lace school was started by deaconess Sybil Carter with the support of the Episcopal Bishop Henry Whipple (K.C. Duncan 1980). top, Janette Crooks, Mdewakanton from Birch Coulee, displaying her Battenburg lace embellished with Indian motifs of tepees and birds. Photograph by N.B. Andersen Studio, Redwood Falls, Minn., 1894–1920. bottom, Lace squares and lace-edged linen doily. The floral patterns are based on European designs, but a tepee has been incorporated into one square. Collected by Bishop and Mrs. Henry Whipple in Minn. around 1900. Diameter of doily, 37 cm. Other pieces to same scale.

continued to hold rituals until the 1930s. As most of the older religious associations disappeared, they were replaced either by Christian groups, some of which were patterned after indigenous societies, for example, the Saint Joseph and Saint Mary's societies of the Catholic Church, or by native-based groups. Since the early twentieth century, the Native American Church gained a small following in several Santee communities. At the beginning of the twentieth century the *wóyaka tʰéča* 'new tidings', the Canadian Sioux derivative of the Ghost Dance, was introduced at Round Plains, where it was supported until the 1950s (Wilcox 1943:49–66; W.D. Wallis 1947:78–223; Hurt 1960; A.B. Kehoe 1968, 1970a:160, 166, 1989:41–49; Albers 1974:336–337, 401–404; J.H. Howard 1984:131–137, 139–143, 173–180).

The Omaha Dance society, an organization dedicated to helping the needy, flourished in many Santee communities until the 1920s. American Legion Posts and other veterans' associations had a small following, but they were not so actively supported as those on Teton, Yankton, and Yanktonai reservations (Skinner 1919b:173; W.D. Wallis 1947:117–120; Albers 1974:21–22; J.H. Howard 1988:144–169).

The powwow was the most popular ritual activity, and it was sponsored not only by formal societies, such as Omaha clubs, but also by entire communities. While powwows sponsored by small reserve or reservation communities drew participants from immediately surrounding areas, those held in agency towns, including Fort Totten Days at Devils Lake Reservation and the Poplar Oil celebration at Fort Peck Reservation, attracted people from all over the United States and Canada. The ceremonial activities in small community powwows followed traditional norms, whereas those in the large agency powwows represented a unique blending of indigenous traditions with features of White fairs and rodeos (Corrigan 1970; A.B. Kehoe 1970a:162, 165; Albers 1974:363–397).

Honorings were one of many traditional ritual complexes that persisted among Santee. Extended families were expected to honor the achievements and life-cycle transitions of their members through feasting and gift-giving. While family honorings were often held at the time of a community powwow, many others were given at independently sponsored celebrations. Family "doings" celebrated a child's naming, 25th or 50th wedding anniversary,

In the United States, most of the older religious societies ceased to function in the early twentieth century, but in Canada, the Medicine Dance and various dream associations

college graduation, or entrance into military service. The most elaborate honoring celebrations were given for the deceased. In the modern context, honoring ceremonies were one of the most important vehicles for transmitting traditional values of generosity, respect, and achievement (Albers 1974:330–350; Albers and Medicine 1983).

Self-reliance, sharing, and noninterference continued to be valued by the Santee, and they were the behaviors reinforced in socialization practices. Sioux parents and grandparents were still indulgent with children and reared them in a permissive fashion. However, the traditional values instilled in children and the ways in which they were raised at home were often at odds with educational patterns that prevailed in White-dominated school systems (Harkins 1969; A.B. Kehoe 1970a:154–158; Ahler 1974, 1985).

Sources

There is a rich documentary record on the Santee from British domination over the fur trade in 1763 to the Conflict of 1862 (Winchell 1911; R.W. Meyer 1967; Stipe 1968; Wozniak 1978; G.C. Anderson 1984, 1986). The Minnesota Historical Society (1969) published an extensive bibliography. Collections of manuscripts and other primary source material from this era are in the State Historical Society of Wisconsin, Madison; the Minnesota Historical Society, Saint Paul; and the National Archives, Washington, which holds important records as well as correspondence from the Saint Peter's Agency between 1824 and 1870.

Jonathan Carver's journal (J. Parker 1976) provides the only solid ethnographic information on the Santee under the British regime. The most comprehensive source on Santee culture during the American period is the writings of Samuel W. Pond (1880, 1908). Other primary sources of special merit include William Keating (1825), Gideon H. Pond (1854, 1889), Stephen R. Riggs (1841, 1855, 1880, 1889, 1890, 1893, 1918), Charles A. Eastman (1902, 1907, 1911), Mary H. Eastman (1849), Thomas Hughes (1927), Joseph Nicollet (M.C. Bray 1970; E.C. Bray and M.C. Bray 1976), Philander Prescott (1852, 1853, 1854), James Lynd (1864), and Edward Neill (1872, 1872a). Additional material is listed in the Minnesota Historical Society bibliography (1969); see also Marken and Hoover (1980), and Hoover and Zimmerman (1993).

The most comprehensive cultural description comes from the work of Wilson D. Wallis (1921, 1923, 1947)

predominantly on the Wahpeton, and Ruth Landes (1959, 1968) on the Mdewakanton. Ethnographic information can be found in other sources (L.H. Morgan 1871, 1959; Dorsey 1880c, 1891; Fletcher 1887; Jenks 1893; Lowie 1913; Gilmore 1919; Skinner 1919c, 1920, 1921, 1925a; Bushnell 1922, 1927; L. Wilcox 1943; Hurt 1953a; R.S. Wallis 1954, 1955; R.W. Wallis and W.D. Wallis 1953; Landes 1959, 1968; J.H. Howard 1960, 1966, 1970b, 1972a; Fugle and Howard 1962; E.C. Deloria and J. Brandon 1961; E.C. Deloria 1967; Stipe 1968; A.R. Woolworth and N.L. Woolworth 1980; Spector 1985; Whelan 1987).

Except for general historical accounts (R.W. Meyer 1967; Elias 1988), information on early reservation culture is limited. The most complete information, historically as well as culturally, is found on the Santee who migrated to Canada (W.D. Wallis 1921, 1923, 1947; Laviolette 1944; R.S. Wallis 1954, 1955; A.B. Kehoe 1956, 1970, 1975, 1989; Hawthorne et al. 1967; R.W. Meyer 1968; Corrigan 1972; Albers 1974; J.H. Howard 1984; Elias 1988). In the United States, historical and cultural data on the Mdewakanton and Wahpekute, on the Santee Reservation in Nebraska and at the Flandreau Reservation in South Dakota, can be found in a variety of sources (Whipple 1899; Minnesota Governors' Human Rights Commission 1948, 1949, 1952, 1965; M.B. Riggs 1928; C. Kelsey 1956; Leach 1959; Fugle and Howard 1962; R.W. Meyer 1961, 1964, 1967; Landes 1968; Harkins 1969; Harkins, Zemian, and Woods 1970; Gunther 1970; C. Allen et al. 1971; Cash and Hoover 1971). Material on Sisseton, Wahpeton, Mdewakanton, and Wahpekute who settled on the Devils Lake and Lake Traverse reservations are included in various writings (J. McLaughlin 1910; McCaskill and McNickle 1942; Wilcox 1943; N.L. Woolworth 1961; Fay 1967; R.W. Meyer 1967; Wertenberger 1967; Albers 1968-1976, 1974, 1982, 1983, 1985; Cash and Hoover 1971; Black Thunder et al. 1975; Ahler 1974, 1985; Garcia 1977, 1979; Lang 1982, 1989; J.H. Howard 1984; M.J. Schneider 1986; Martin, Alex, and Benton 1988). Finally, there is a small body of data on Santee who settled at Fort Peck (J.H. Bradley 1927; Feraca and Howard 1963; Albers 1974; D.R. Miller 1987).

Museums that preserve collections of Santee material culture include the American Museum of Natural History, New York; Denver Art Museum; Fort Peck Tribal Museum, Montana; Milwaukee Public Museum; Minnesota Historical Society; and the Pipestone National Monument, Minnesota.

Yankton and Yanktonai

RAYMOND J. DeMALLIE

Territory

In the mid-nineteenth century the Yankton ('yǎŋktən) and Yanktonai ('yǎŋktə,nā) lived on the prairies east of the Missouri River, from Painted Woods on the north (near present Washburn, North Dakota) to the mouth of the Big Sioux River on the south (near present Sioux City, Iowa), extending northeast beyond Devils Lake to the Red River. Although the entire area was jointly claimed by both groups, they occupied different parts of it (fig. 1). The Yankton lived in the area south of East Medicine Knoll Creek, a tributary of the Missouri downstream from Fort Pierre. The Yanktonai occupied the area to the north, but they in turn were divided into two geographically distinct groups, the Upper and Lower Yanktonai, the names referring to their locations relative to the Missouri River (Denig 1961:30, 36; A.R. Woolworth 1974:113, 159, 163–164; J.H. Howard 1976:5–6).

The Yankton hunted frequently west of the Missouri, on the Niobrara and White rivers, in association with the Brule Teton (Denig 1961:36; A.R. Woolworth 1974:145, 159; F.V. Hayden in G.K. Warren 1856:74). The Yanktonai, based on evidence from a winter count (pictographic calendar), sometimes hunted west of the Missouri along the Heart River to the Killdeer Mountains, North Dakota (J.H. Howard 1976:5–6).

Social Divisions

The Yankton and Yanktonai spoke a single dialect of the Sioux language, with minor differences among groups, and in the nineteenth century considered themselves to be a single people. In the camp circle of the mythical Seven Council Fires, the Yankton and Yanktonai occupied facing positions at the north and south sides of the entrance to the camp circle (J.R. Walker 1980:17).

The seven bands of the Yankton formed a single tribe that, by the mid-nineteenth century, was divided into two groups with approximately equal populations, referred to as the Lower Yankton (in four bands) and the Upper Yankton (in three bands). All the bands joined together for the Sun Dance and tribal buffalo hunts. The Yanktonai were also divided into two groups that, through separation, essentially became separate tribes, the Lower Yanktonai (a single band) and the Upper Yanktonai (three bands). One of the Upper Yanktonai bands, the Cutheads, is frequently treated in the historical literature as an independent group, either separate from or synonymous with, the Upper Yanktonai (S.R. Riggs 1893:160, 162; J.H. Howard 1976:5). (For band names, see table 4 in "Sioux Until 1850," this vol.)

Because the Yankton and Yanktonai were so geographically dispersed, the history of each division was unique. The Yankton settled on Yankton Reservation on the east side of the Missouri River at the southern end of Sioux territory. About half the Lower Yanktonai settled at Crow Creek Reservation, on the east side of the Missouri below the Big Bend; many moved to the northern part of Standing Rock Reservation; some moved to Fort Peck Reservation. The Upper Yanktonai also split up: part joined the Lower Yanktonai at Standing Rock; part went east to Devils Lake (now Spirit Lake) Reservation, in eastern North Dakota; and part went west to Fort Peck Reservation, in Montana. Some Yanktonai families, whose history is not well documented, moved with Santee bands to Canada, where they settled on reserves in Manitoba and Saskatchewan.

History, 1850–1880

Yankton

In 1851 the Yankton were represented at the Fort Laramie treaty council by Smutty Bear (b. about 1790, d. 1865), who signed the treaty with five chiefs of the Teton (Kappler 1904–1941, 2: 594–596). At the council, Big Yankton (possibly another name for Smutty Bear) complained about the destruction of grass and trees by travelers on the Overland Trail and the consequent scarcity of game (*Missouri Republican,* Nov. 2, 1851). In 1853 the Yankton suffered an attack of cholera while hunting west of the Missouri, another consequence of the overland migration (de Smet in Chittenden and Richardson 1905, 4:1283). That same year, three Yankton chiefs—Smutty Bear, Struck by the Ree, and Standing Medicine Cow—signed the amendment to the 1851 treaty and received the first shipment of annuity goods (H.H. Anderson 1956a:213).

In 1851, when Agent James H. Norwood arrived at Fort Pierre, he found the Yanktons to be in need because of the scarcity of buffalo. He purchased food for them and broke land for them to plant. When Agent Alfred D. Vaughan distributed annuity goods at the mouth of Vermillion River in June 1853 he reported that the Yanktons numbered 375 lodges who lived on both sides of the Missouri from the mouth of the White River to Fort Pierre, and hunted east to

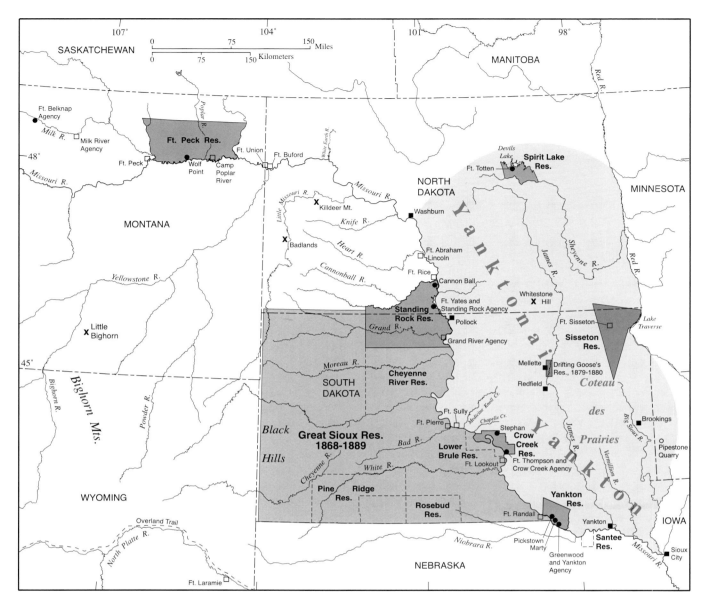

Fig. 1. Mid-19th-century territory of the Yankton and Yanktonai with the Great Sioux Reservation and modern reservations that are occupied alone or with other tribes.

the James River. Some were planting gardens, but he reported that they subsisted primarily on wild vegetables and fruits. The next year the Yankton received agricultural implements as a part of their annuity goods and asked for men to teach them how to farm (A.R. Woolworth 1974:158; ARCIA 1853:353, 1854:287).

When Gen. William S. Harney called all the Sioux to a council at Fort Pierre in 1856, he appointed Struck by the Ree (b. 1804, d. 1888) as head chief. Asked to name nine other chiefs for the Yankton, Struck by the Ree selected Smutty Bear, Standing Medicine Cow, Bear Lies Down, Dog's Claw, Handsome Young Man, Sitting Crow, Quick to Fly, White Buck Elk, and Sailing Hawk (F. Pierce 1856:26). Together, they represented the major constituencies in the tribe. In June 1857, Agent A.H. Redfield traveled up the

Missouri and first arrived at the village of Feather in the Ear, a Yankton chief, numbering 100 lodges, which was located on the north bank, above the mouth of the Big Sioux. The main Yankton village was Struck by the Ree's, located just above the James (the site of present Yankton, South Dakota). A few miles upriver was Smutty Bear's village. Redfield did not visit the village of Mad Bull, on the Vermillion River. The bands living in these four villages were the Lower Yankton. Game was scarce and the people suffered from hunger; they raised corn and other vegetables but not in sufficient quantities to support themselves year-round. They complained to the agent that they deserved to receive part of the money paid to the Santee for the cession of lands to the government, since they had joint interest in them (ARCIA 1857:123–125, 137).

As he continued up the Missouri, Redfield met the Upper Yankton, who lived by hunting and had not yet attempted to plant corn. At Fort Randall, Redfield met 20 lodges and passed a camp of 30–40 lodges near Old Fort Lookout. A few miles above, on the other side of the Missouri, the agent met a small party led by Standing Medicine Cow. He had nothing to give them, explaining that all the annuities had been delivered at Struck by the Ree's village. Because he restricted his travel to the steamboat route on the Missouri, Redfield did not meet the other two Upper Yankton bands under Little Swan and Pretty Boy (A.R. Woolworth 1974:189).

In 1857 hostilities erupted between Smutty Bear's band and settlers moving into the area of the Big Sioux River. The next year the Yankton drove off settlers from the town of Medary, near present Brookings, South Dakota, and burned the buildings. These actions reflected the growing tension between the Yankton and the Whites who were rapidly encroaching on their territory. In December 1857 a delegation of Yankton leaders, including Charles Picotte, a half-blood who served as interpreter, went to Washington (fig. 2) where the next April they signed a treaty ceding all of their land to the government in exchange for a reservation on the Missouri near Fort Randall and annuities for 50 years. The Upper Yankton chiefs, who were opposed to the land sale, did not join the delegation, but Picotte signed as their legal representative. The Yankton as a whole opposed the treaty and blamed Struck by the Ree and Picotte for the loss of their lands (D. Robinson 1904:245–249; Kappler 1904–1941,2:776–781).

• YANKTON RESERVATION In July 1859 Agent Redfield arrived at the site selected for the agency, later named Greenwood. Almost all the Yankton were present, numbering nearly 2,000 people. After distributing the annuities, the agent held a council with the chiefs to select the soldiers, prescribed by Harney's treaty in 1856, who were to act as tribal police, maintaining order and preventing the introduction of alcohol. The chiefs themselves decided on whipping as the punishment for drunkenness. A sawmill was set up and rapid progress was made in constructing agency buildings (ARCIA 1859:121–123). The next summer the Lower Yankton planted some 200 acres and raised a good crop of corn. Redfield planted 160 acres at the agency, but when the Upper Yankton, who had refused to plant, returned from their summer hunt in mid-September, the chiefs and their soldiers were unable to prevent them from raiding the agency garden and carrying off all the corn, potatoes, and turnips, leaving only the rutabagas. Within a month, all the Upper and many of the Lower Yankton had left to hunt buffalo and were not expected to return until spring. In spite of this, 12–15 Lower Yanktons had built log houses, some with shingle roofs, others with sod (ARCIA 1860:86–90).

In fall 1861, the new agent, Walter A. Burleigh, broke 100-acre fields for each band, including those of the three Upper Yankton. Each band selected a location in which to settle, and one and one-half story houses were constructed for each band chief as an incentive to keep them on the reservation. The agent purchased 100 cows, which he distributed among the bands. He reported an unusual

Fig. 2. Yankton leaders. left, left to right, Struck by the Ree, the interpreter Charles Picotte, and Smutty Bear, part of the delegation of 15 Yanktons who visited Washington in 1857–1858. Photograph by McClees Studio, Washington, 1858. center, Ball-headed war club with a spike made from a knife blade. Four pairs of bear tracks are painted on the handle. The club belonged to the Yankton leader Man With Legs Wide Apart (Cha-chine-na). Collected by A.B. Campbell on the Yankton Res., Dak. Terr., 1868. Length 60 cm. right, Flying Pipe from Yankton Res., Dak. Terr. He is wearing a quilled buckskin shirt with horsehair decorations and buckskin leggings and moccasins. He holds a pipe tomahawk decorated with metal studs and feather fan. His earrings are made of dentalia, beads, and shell. He was a member of a delegation of 45 Yankton, Santee, and Teton from the Missouri River who visited Washington in Feb. 1867. Photograph by A. Zeno Shindler, Washington, 1867.

amount of sickness among the Yankton and noted their surprise at the success of the agency physician's treatments (ARCIA 1861:118–121). The agent's reports during the next several years include statistics on the increasing number of acres farmed, but in 1863, 1864, and 1865 the crops were destroyed by drought and grasshoppers. When the Peace Commission visited the Yankton in 1865, Struck by the Ree expressed regret over selling their land. "I am getting poorer every day," he said (Board of Commissioners 1865:3). West of the Missouri the only game were antelope and ducks; to get buffalo they had to hunt east of the James River. But even though the Yankton had provided Gen. Alfred Sully with 50 young men as scouts in 1864, who had never been paid for their service, the army now forbade them to cross the James, to prevent them from coming in contact with White settlers. The commissioners, moved by conditions on the Yankton Reservation, gave them written permission to hunt east of the James as far as the Coteau des Prairies, and requested that food be purchased for them to prevent starvation (Board of Commissioners 1865:5).

During the succeeding years the Yanktons' efforts at agriculture increased in scope but with no better success. Oxen and machinery were never in plentiful enough supply, and drought, hail, and grasshoppers destroyed the crops repeatedly. The agents' annual reports describe abundant harvests in 1866 and 1867, but each year from 1868 to 1872 and in 1874 the crops failed. At the same time, buffalo hunting was becoming a less and less productive source of livelihood; the last mention of a tribal hunt in the annual reports was in 1866. Some number of Yanktons, led by the son of Struck by the Ree, fled the reservation and in 1871 were hunting buffalo in eastern Montana (DeMallie 1986:30). Although a few probably stayed at the new Fort Peck Reservation, most eventually returned to the Yankton Reservation, and may represent the influx of population reported there in 1877 (ARCIA 1877:75).

The Yankton had been promised a school in the 1858 treaty, and their chiefs had repeatedly asked that their children be educated, but no school was established until 1870, when mission work began on the reservation. The Presbyterian minister, John P. Williamson, was fluent in the Sioux language and reported in 1870 that his school had enrolled 83 students; in the same year, Joseph W. Cook, the Episcopal missionary, reported 25 students. Both mission schools developed rapidly and although the agents complained that the Indians' travels—necessary to find food to survive—were detrimental to the attempts to educate the children, native-language literacy began to flourish. From 1871 to 1876 Williamson printed the *Iapi Oaye,* a Sioux language newspaper, at Yankton Agency ("Santee," fig. 9, this vol.).

In 1876 the agent reported that the reservation was divided between non-Christian and Christian parties, with the mixed-bloods (who came to form an eighth band) belonging to the Christian party. There was no ill feeling between the two groups, although the Christian men dressed in White clothing while men of the other party were still painting their faces and wearing blankets (ARCIA 1876:40).

The climate took a turn for the better, and crops were reported to be good in 1873 and 1875–1880. Periodic attempts were made to introduce cattle raising, but they met with failure; in every case, the Yankton ended up eating their cattle to survive. Similarly, various attempts were made to introduce wheat and oats, sheep raising, and even an orchard, with limited success. When the Yankton settled on their reservation only women worked the fields, but by 1875 a large proportion of the able-bodied men were laboring in the fields or at other pursuits, reflecting an important cultural change and acceptance of a new way of life (ARCIA 1875:257).

Gradually the communities abandoned tepees and built houses: 150 by 1872, 391 by 1880. Fevers and other diseases crippled the Yankton and limited population growth. A measles epidemic in 1873 claimed more than 100 lives, and a detailed physician's report in 1880 noted 84 deaths in the previous year, more than 16 percent of the population. The two largest causes of death were tuberculosis (27 cases) and scrofula (30 cases). The same year there were 93 births (ARCIA 1873:239, 1880:59–60).

By 1880 the Yankton had a longer experience with reservation life than any of the Yanktonai or Teton. Yet, despite massive amounts of government expenditures, they were still far from self-sufficient. Their way of living had changed dramatically, and increasingly they accepted the outward forms of White agrarian culture, together with Christianity mediated through native-language translations of Christian texts and hymns. School attendance improved and the first students were sent East to the Indian boarding school at Carlisle, Pennsylvania. With the end of tribal hunts, the former bands had coalesced into communities and as early as 1878 some of the Yankton began moving to individual farmsteads in preparation for the allotment of land to individuals (ARCIA 1878:46).

Yanktonai

Although the Yanktonai were not parties to the 1851 treaty and none of their chiefs signed (or presumably was asked to sign) the 1853 ammendment, treaty annuity goods were distributed to the Yanktonai bands as they were to the Yankton and Teton. In 1855 Agent Vaughan distributed goods to Little Soldier's band of Upper Yanktonai who had built a village of 12 earthlodges on the east bank of the Missouri, near present Pollock, South Dakota. They told him this was their first attempt to establish a permanent village and grow corn. The agent visited them again the next year. Above them lived Two Bears's band of Lower Yanktonai, to whom he also distributed goods (ARCIA 1855:392, 1856:629; H.H. Anderson 1960).

At the Fort Pierre council in 1856, General Harney recognized the two head chiefs, each with nine subordinate chiefs, who in subsequent decades were the prominent leaders among the Yanktonai. Black Catfish was appointed head chief of the Upper Yanktonai (called at this council "the band that wishes the life"); in turn, he selected as chiefs Fool Heart, Red Bull, Paints Himself Red, Soldier, Medicine Bear, Yellow Robe (also called Nest that Wears a Face), "The one who has his lodge inside of the ring," "The buck elk who wears the medicine face," and "The one that runs close by." Two Bears was appointed head chief of the Lower Yanktonai; his chiefs were Bone Necklace, "The man who killed the Mandan chief," White Bear, Mad Bear, The Buck, "The man that has the arrow broke in him," Running Bear, Lousy, and Little Soldier (F. Pierce 1856:25–26). Big Head, a leading Upper Yanktonai chief, was hostile to the Whites, refused to accept treaty annuities, and did not attend the council; Harney vowed to destroy his band, but failed to carry out the threat.

The Fort Pierre treaty established peace between the Sioux on the Missouri and the United States, but military surveys of Sioux country and increasing steamboat traffic on the Missouri in the years before the Civil War caused increasing tension. When hostilities finally occurred, they arose from the Minnesota Sioux Conflict of 1862. Intent on punishing the Santee, the army paid little attention to guilt or innocence; both military and civilian authorities were determined to drive all the Sioux out of Minnesota. Army forces under Gen. Henry H. Sibley tracked the fleeing Indians westward while Gen. Sully went up the Missouri to cut them off from the west. On September 3, 1863, Sully attacked a village of some 400 lodges of Santees, Yanktonais, and Cutheads, with smaller numbers of Blackfeet and Hunkpapa Tetons, at Whitestone Hill (near present Ellendale, North Dakota). Big Head was captured with some 150 others, all of whom were eventually sent to Crow Creek Agency (G.W. Kingsbury 1915, 1:290–298).

The next summer Sully carried the war west of the Missouri, still tracking the remnant groups from Minnesota. On July 28, 1864, his forces attacked a village at Killdeer Mountain estimated at 1,600 lodges, composed of Hunkpapa, Sans Arc, Blackfeet, and Minneconjou Tetons, as well as Yanktonais and a small group of Santees; fighting continued in the badlands of western North Dakota (G.W. Kingsbury 1915, 1:356–361). Sully then established Fort Union, the old trading post at the mouth of the Yellowstone, as a military post; in 1866 it was moved a short distance downstream and renamed Fort Buford. Also in summer 1864, Fort Wadsworth (renamed Fort Sisseton in 1876) was established (Prucha 1964:63, 108, 113). The two posts provided an ongoing military presence in northern Sioux territory.

The Peace Commissions of 1865–1868 met with all the Sioux along the Missouri River, signing treaties with each of the Teton and Yanktonai groups regardless of whether they had been engaged in the recent hostilities. For the Yanktonai, who had not been present at the 1851 treaty council, these were the first treaties they signed for which they received annuities. By the terms of the 1865 treaty, the Indians were to receive an annuity of $30 per lodge, payable for 20 years, and additional annuities, supplies, and assistance when they chose to settle permanently and take up agriculture. In return, the Sioux bound themselves to refrain from warfare and to "withdraw from the routes overland already established, or hereafter to be established, through their country" (Kappler 1904–1941, 2:903–904). The records of the commission, however, reveal that the Indians protested these overland routes as well as the continuation of steamboat traffic on the Missouri, both of which contributed to the scarcity of buffalo; they "touched the pen" to the treaty not to assent to its terms, but to object to them. Nonetheless, the treaties, once ratified by the United States Senate, became law (V. Deloria and DeMallie 1975; Talks and Councils 1910; DeMallie 1980).

The 1868 treaty terminated warfare over the Bozeman Trail, defined the boundaries of a reservation that comprised present South Dakota west of the Missouri, and left the area of northeastern Wyoming and eastern Montana as "unceded Indian territory." By the terms of the treaty, the Teton and Yanktonai gave up claims to all other lands, except previously established reservations east of the Missouri (Kappler 1904–1941, 2:998–1007). Two Bears, the Lower Yanktonai chief, voiced objection to this provision of the treaty: "You are going to put all the tribes together, and I do not approve of it. . . . Our country is over on the other side of the river. We are Yanctonais" (V. Deloria and DeMallie 1975:139). All the Yanktonai, as well as many of the Teton and the Yankton, depended on hunting buffalo on the James River. However, a treaty signed in 1867 by the Sisseton and Wahpeton surrendered to the United States the area between the James and the Red rivers (west and south of the Sheyenne) in exchange for reservations at Lake Traverse and Devils Lake (Kappler 1904–1941, 2:956–959). The Yanktonai, though they claimed rights to this territory, were not consulted and objected to the 1867 treaty. The 1868 treaty, although the wording does not make it explicit, effectively surrendered the rest of Yanktonai territory, the area from the Missouri to the James. One intention of the 1868 treaty was to prevent access to the remaining buffalo herds east of the Missouri, thereby forcing the Yankton, Yanktonai, and Teton to congregate at agencies on the new reservation and take up agriculture.

• CROW CREEK RESERVATION   In 1863 the military post of Fort Thompson was built at the mouth of Crow Creek, on the east side of the Missouri below the Great Bend, to oversee the Santee refugees from Minnesota. When the Santee moved to a new reservation in Nebraska in 1866, the Crow Creek Agency (officially called Upper Missouri Agency until 1874), was assigned to the Lower Yanktonai (on the east side of the river) and the Lower Brule (on the west side). Some Two Kettles Teton also lived at Crow Creek until 1868 (E.E. Hill 1974:185). In 1865, the Lower Yanktonai chief Bone Necklace told the peace commissioners at Fort Sully that he wanted to settle at Chapelle Creek,   *781* above the Big Bend, and although he finally settled at Crow Creek, it was obviously against his wishes (Board of Commissioners 1865:110). In February 1866, the 500–600 Sioux camped at the agency, including Tetons, Yanktons, and Yanktonais, were starving, rations being in very short supply. By March all had left except The Buck's Lower Yanktonai band, numbering 8 lodges, who were about to leave to retrieve food stores from a cache "on the prairie," presumably on the James River (ARCIA 1866:163–164). In 1867, Running Bear pointed out that some of the Lower Yanktonai were still on the James and that his people had planted there for 12 years. "Must they all come here?" he asked (Fort Philip Kearny Commission 1867:June 5).

By 1868 the Lower Yanktonai were geographically divided. About half of them, under the leadership of Two Bears, moved to the Grand River Agency, while most of the rest, led by Bone Necklace, settled at Crow Creek. A few remained on the James River. That year some of the Lower Yanktonai planted gardens at the agency, but Agent J.R. Hanson reported 75 percent of the crop was lost to grasshoppers; he commented that it was a poor location for farming, a theme that would be repeated by the Crow Creek agents for decades. At the same time, Hanson reported that buffalo had almost entirely disappeared from the area (ARCIA 1868:650). With inadequate rations provided by the government, the Indians had no choice but to leave and hunt for buffalo on the James.

Annual changes of agents did little to develop the agency, which moved into the buildings of Fort Thompson when it was abandoned by the army in 1871. That year Agent Henry F. Livingston reported 1,000 Lower Yanktonai on the reservation, as well as many transients. Illegal White traders had begun to introduce "intoxicating liquors." Rations were ample, and the Indians were well supplied with horses and mules. They planted 150 acres, but 75 percent of it was lost to drought (ARCIA 1871:519–520). Some years crops were better than others, but the Indians preferred cattle raising, and the agent considered it a more realistic means of support.

In 1871 all the Indians lived in tepees; by 1874 there were 100 houses, and 40 more were built the next year. Most were built by the Indians themselves using cottonwood logs; windows and doors were manufactured at the agency. Most houses were roofed with sod. In 1875 Livingston recommended that no more canvas be issued for tepee covers in order to force the rest to build houses (ARCIA 1874:252, 1875:283)

In 1874 Livingston selected 30 families who were farming and gave each a yoke of oxen and a cow, later reporting that none had been killed for food. In 1877, the agent's final report noted a change in attitude toward work. In 1871, the men were opposed to any kind of manual labor; by 1877 most were laboring to some extent, cultivating, cutting wood, hauling freight, cutting hay, and herding livestock. An Episcopal mission was established in 1872 and the first school was opened, despite protests from the chiefs. In 1875

a girls' boarding school was constructed at the agency, and two day schools were operating in the camps; by 1877 the average attendance was 62. A church and home for the mission staff were constructed in 1875; Sunday services, in Dakota and English, were well attended (ARCIA 1872:263, 1874:253, 1875:238, 1877:54).

In 1878 the reservation was turned over to military control, which lasted three years. The acting agent, Capt. William G. Dougherty, found 751 Lower Yanktonais at the agency on his arrival in March; in 1879 he reported 900. Traditional religion and healing were still practiced. Sun Dances were not held, but some of the people attended them elsewhere. Polygyny and marriage by purchase continued to be practiced. The chiefs retained control at the time of his arrival. For example, plowed land was assigned to the chiefs to be allotted to their individual band members. Dougherty sought to lessen their influence by allotting gardens in the agency fields directly to individuals. Still, he complained in 1878 that the Indians had eaten most of the seed potatoes, that they harvested what crops they did manage to raise before they were fully ripe, and that many crops were stolen from the fields by others who had not raised them (ARCIA 1878:24–25, 1879:24–26).

In 1878 the chiefs were still opposed to the schools, sometimes sending their *akíčhita* (camp soldiers) to disrupt them, but by 1879 the principal chief, presumably White Ghost, the son of Bone Necklace, decided to support the schools. In August 1878 an Indian police force consisting of one captain, one sergeant, and eight privates was established, again over the initial protest of the chiefs. By 1880 the police had been accepted and positions on the force were sought after. Dougherty found the police efficient and used them to carry messages throughout the reservation, guard freight at the river landing, and recover stray animals. The 1879 annuities included large amounts of civilian clothing, and many of the Indians chose to wear that instead of traditional dress (ARCIA 1879:27, 1880:26).

One band of Lower Yanktonai, called *phuté themní* 'sweating lips', refused to settle at Crow Creek Reservation. Under their chief, Drifting Goose, they hunted between Lake Traverse and the Missouri River, and from about 1859 to 1880 they maintained an earthlodge village on the James River. They spent the summers there, growing corn, fishing, hunting, and gathering; in the winter they traveled on hunts and visited the agencies. Some of the band had served as army scouts in 1864, and although they did not oppose the government, they also did not recognize any treaty. However, the area in which they lived, by the terms of the 1868 treaty, was opened to White settlement. After increasing conflicts with surveyors and settlers in the late 1870s, and Agent Dougherty's threat to bring them to Crow Creek by force, Drifting Goose petitioned the government, traveled to Washington, and made an impassioned speech at the Indian Bureau on behalf of his band. Unexpectedly, President Rutherford B. Hayes issued an executive order in 1879 that set aside a small reservation for Drifting Goose's people, to be under the supervision of the agent at the Sisseton Reservation. Most of the land, however, proved to have already been settled by Whites and the army refused to remove them. In the end, Drifting Goose had no choice but to take his people to Crow Creek, where they arrived June 30, 1880, the last Yanktonai group to be settled on a reservation. The next month another executive order restored the reserved land to the public domain (J.H. Howard 1976:12–15; Kappler 1904–1941, 1:895–896; ARCIA 1879:24–25, 1880:27).

As at all the Sioux agencies, continuation of the Grass Dance was a controversial issue at Crow Creek. At the behest of William H. Hare, the Episcopal bishop, the dances were for a time entirely outlawed. This, however, created enmity between the Christian and non-Christian Indians, which was only resolved by allowing the dances to resume, though limited to Saturday afternoons and evenings. In his 1881 report the agent mentioned that a recent attempt had been made to revive an "immoral dance" given up two years previously; this was "promptly suppressed by the police, attended by a characteristic 'knock down and drag out' of the principal offenders" (ARCIA 1880:28, 1881:29).

The Episcopal schools closed in 1879, and the boarding school reopened in 1880 as a government school. In 1881 an Episcopal missionary was again assigned to Crow Creek (ARCIA 1880:28, 1881:32).

Dougherty's reports provide useful statistics on the population. In 1879–1880 there were 27 births and 14 deaths; the next year 45 births and 38 deaths. An additional 140 people were transferred from other agencies in 1880–1881, mostly from Standing Rock, bringing the reservation population to 1,061. The agent wrote, "The dissolution of the tribal government and existence and establishment of the household or family, as the unit of society, are now accomplished facts" (ARCIA 1881:26). During the year 173 individuals had taken land in severalty (usually 320 acres), and 97 individuals had been engaged in farming,

The situation at Crow Creek looked promising in 1881 (fig. 3). Ample rations were issued weekly to supplement what the Indians could raise; there was no crime; and all able-bodied men were engaged in labor. Dougherty optimistically predicted that within five years, the younger generation would become entirely self-sufficient (ARCIA 1881:32).

• DEVILS LAKE RESERVATION Devils Lake and Lake Traverse reservations were created in 1867, after the treaty with the Sisseton and Wahpeton Sioux. According to an estimate by the trader Joseph R. Brown (1867), 250 families of Cuthead Yanktonais were willing to join the Sisseton and Wahpeton at Devils Lake. Government appropriations, however, only covered the cost of establishing an agency at Lake Traverse, where the larger number of Sisseton and Wahpeton chose to settle. From 1867 through 1869 Fort Totten, the military post at Devils Lake, provided the Indians there—as many as 681 in 1868—with rations. The agency at Devils Lake was not established until 1871, when a resident agent was provided. The population consisted of only about 700 Sissetons and Wahpetons (ARCIA 1867:245, 1868:654–655, 1869:331).

Amon Carter Mus., Ft. Worth, Tex.: 34.69.

Fig. 3. Crow Creek Agency, Dak. Terr. Individuals in foreground from left to right: Mark Wells, mixed blood interpreter; White Ghost; Drifting Goose; Wizi; Surrounded; Whipper; Burnt Prairie; and Wallace Wells, farm instructor. Agency buildings, Episcopal Church, and frame houses with their fenced yards and gardens are in contrast to the scattered Indian tepees with drying racks and cooking fires. Painted by a local carpenter, the picture has been interpreted as a commentary on the benefits and prosperity of assimilation (Schimmel 1991:184–185). Oil painting by William Fuller, who identified by number buildings and individuals, 1884.

The reservation experience of the Devils Lake Sioux differed little from that of the other Sioux agencies. Crops provided some subsistence, but never enough to last the winter; early frosts and grasshopper infestations limited productivity. There were no buffalo in the area. The first missionary, a Roman Catholic priest, spent the winter of 1871–1872 at Devils Lake, and the next year a brick boarding school was built, which opened in 1874 staffed by the Sisters of Charity (Grey Nuns) from Montreal. Initial opposition was overcome and the school was filled to capacity, 35–70 students, for the rest of the decade. In 1874 an agency building was constructed (ARCIA 1872:258–260, 1874:238–239).

From the start, some of the Cuthead Yanktonai went to Devils Lake seeking rations, but were unwilling to settle on the reservation. The Devils Lake agents insisted that men engage in some kind of labor for the agency in order to draw rations (ARCIA 1871:536), but the Cutheads preferred to travel back and forth to the Missouri, visiting their Yanktonai relatives at Crow Creek, Standing Rock, and Fort Peck. They visited Devils Lake in large numbers in the summer of 1874 and the next summer they returned, camping at Crow Hill on the western part of the reservation. Under the leadership of Wanata, son of the early nineteenth-century chief Charger (*waʔánata*) (fig. 5), this group of Cutheads did return, and most eventually settled at Crow Hill (ARCIA 1874:239, 1875:239; J. McLaughlin 1910:15).

In 1876 James McLaughlin, an exceptionally capable administrator, was appointed agent and remained for six years. During this period the reservation population was relatively stable: 1,071 in 1876, 1,046 in 1879, 1,089 in 1880. The Cuthead probably numbered no more than 300. McLaughlin's figures show that births exceeded deaths: 71 to 51 in 1877, 72 to 71 in 1879, 62 to 49 in 1880. Mortality rates were highest from birth to age 4; among adults, the primary cause of death was tuberculosis. Other diseases noted in 1876 were scrofulous tumors, pulmonary diseases,

and rheumatism. His reports document increasing numbers of acres farmed; by 1878 nearly every family had its own field. Most lived in log cabins. From a modest beginning of 50 cattle in 1877, the number doubled in two years. Men hauled freight, cut timber, and put up hay both for the agency and on contract for Fort Totten, and they produced large quantities of lumber and fencing at the agency sawmill. The Benedictines established a Roman Catholic mission in 1879, and the Presbyterians sent a mixed-blood Santee missionary in the same year (Pfaller 1978:45). There was no crime. A police force (fig. 6) was established with some initial opposition, but in 1880 McLaughlin reported that it was growing in popularity and influence and that men were anxious to serve on it (ARCIA 1876:25–27, 1877:55–57, 1878:27–28, 1879:28–29, 1880:29–30).

As for Indian customs, McLaughlin noted the continuation of polygynous marriages and the healing sings of medicine men. By threats he ended performances of the Midewiwin, the last being held in 1878. The more private Sacred Feast of the Midewiwin continued, though in 1881 he wrote that it was no longer popular. The Sun Dance was also no longer performed. Grass Dances continued, held only at times that would not interfere with farm labor. Most injurious, in his opinion, were intertribal visits. Devils Lake was a crossroads; in 1876 McLaughlin noted five visiting parties of Chippewas and one of Mandans and Hidatsas. Each visit involved dancing, feasting, and the lavish exchange of presents. Although he complained about it, such ritual visiting was an established part of reservation culture. In 1878, to smooth over hostilities with the Arikara, in which two children of a mixed-blood at Devils Lake had been killed, McLaughlin himself led 600 Devils Lake Sioux, Cutheads, Sissetons, and Wahpetons, to Fort Berthold to sign a formal peace agreement. The party returned home loaded with presents; the bereaved father received some 50 ponies (ARCIA 1878:28, 1880:30, 1881:35; J. McLaughlin 1910:154–259; Pfaller 1978:40, 53–54).

Smithsonian, NAA: left, 54720-B; right, 54,725.

Fig. 4. Agriculture at Crow Creek Res., S. Dak. left, Wagons and plows ready for issue. According to the Crow Creek and Lower Brule Agent Fred Treon, 486 wagons and 486 plows were sent to the agency under the Sioux agreement of 1889. They were shipped disassembled and had to be put together by the Indians before distribution (ARCIA 1895:276). Photographed about 1894. right, John Bear mowing with a 2-horse mower. Photographed about 1894.

top left, Smithsonian, Dibner Lib.: J.O. Lewis 1835–1836; top right, Natl. Mus. of Scotland, Edinburgh: 1942.1; bottom left, Newberry Lib., Chicago: BOD 29; Smithsonian, NAA: bottom center, 3579-a, bottom right, 3581-a-1.

Fig. 5. Men's clothing, body decorations. top left, Wanata, Cuthead Yanktonai. He is wearing a shirt with hair fringes, moccasins, a bear-claw necklace, feather headdress, and a painted buffalo robe. The artist depicted face paint around one eye. Lithograph based on original by James Otto Lewis, painted at the Treaty of Prairie du Chien, 1825. top right, Shirt acquired from Wanata, before 1844, adorned with quillwork and locks of human hair. Scenes of his war victories are painted on the shirt (details on right). Length 134 cm. bottom left, Horned Rock, also known as Little Soldier, Yankton. He has body paint or tattooing and wears a cloth turban, metal ball-and-cone earrings, and a buffalo robe. His cropped hair was probably the result of his being in mourning at the time (Bodmer 1984:187). Watercolor drawing by Karl Bodmer, 1833. bottom center, Standing Medicine Cow, Lower Yanktonai chief. He is wearing a cloth shirt, beaded cloth leggings and moccasins, a beaded bear-claw necklace; his braids are wrapped in fur, and he wears a hide robe with quillwork. He holds a catlinite pipe decorated with metal studs. Photograph by A. Zeno Shindler, Washington, 1867. bottom right, Not Afraid of Pawnee from Yankton Res., S. Dak. He is wearing a buckskin shirt decorated with quillwork. In his hair he wears eagle-tail feathers and a head ornament. Photograph by Thomas W. Smillie, Washington, 1904.

• STANDING ROCK RESERVATION In 1869 the Lower Yanktonai under Two Bears and Upper Yanktonai under All Over Black and Big Head (son of the older chief, who had died), together with the Hunkpapa and Blackfeet Teton, settled at the new Grand River Agency, on the Missouri at the mouth of the Grand. There they received daily rations of beef, bacon, flour, and corn. By 1871 the agent reported 365 lodges of Lower Yanktonai and 100 lodges of Upper Yanktonai. With the end of buffalo hunting, the Sioux had no way of renewing their lodge covers, and in 1871 the agency issued them duck cloth for that purpose. That summer the Lower Yanktonai planted gardens on the east side of the Missouri, about 40 miles above the agency. Some 200 acres were broken for them and the Indians were given seeds to plant corn, squash, pumpkins, and melons. Most work was done by women, men considering physical labor degrading. The next year the Upper Yanktonai also planted, selecting a site 30 miles above the agency, on the west side of the river. Each band had a separate farm, and the garden plots within them were allotted to families and demarcated by rows of turf. In 1873 the agency was moved 50 miles upriver, and in 1874 the name was changed to Standing Rock, after a local landmark (ARCIA 1869:318–319, 1870:686–687, 1871:525–526, 1872:262–262, 1873:230–231; E.E. Hill 1974:68–69).

The Standing Rock agent in 1875 reported 2,730 Lower Yanktonais and 1,473 Upper Yanktonais, but in 1877 the population dropped to only 768 Lower Yanktonais and 462 Upper Yanktonais (ARCIA 1875:244, 1877:71–72). Though neither set of numbers is necessarily accurate, they do suggest the extent of depopulation that occurred at the agencies during the Sioux War of 1876–1877. For those who remained, the agents reported steady progress. Both groups of Yanktonai settled along the Missouri from the agency north to the reservation boundary at the Cannon Ball River, although Two Bears's band continued to live on the east side of the river, across from Standing Rock.

The agents strove to assimilate the Indians to White culture. The construction of an agency sawmill allowed for the cheap production of lumber; by 1874 the agency was producing coffins, a cemetery was established, and the Indians were persuaded to bury their dead instead of placing them on scaffolds. In 1877 Two Bears, like the

Smithsonian, Natl. Mus. of the Amer. Ind.:20171.

Fig. 6. Policemen and chiefs, Yanktonai. seated left to right: unidentified White man; Ecanazeka (Sisseton); unidentified interpreter; unidentified Indian holding pipe; Left Hand Bear; Indian Agent John H. Waugh and 2 children. standing left to right: Tyakmani; Jim; Swift Bear; Oyesna or Abraham; Thomas; Canpocksa; Sanica; Iron Feather; Louis Lange; Mike; and unidentified policeman. Photographed at Devils Lake Res., N. Dak., about 1893.

Blackfeet chief John Grass, bought a mowing machine for his band using the proceeds from the sale of hides taken from the cattle slaughtered for rations. Putting up hay was essential to prevent the wholesale destruction of cottonwoods near the agency, which the Indians cut down to use the bark as winter feed for their horses. In 1875 the agency chiefs went to Fort Abraham Lincoln where they met the leaders of the Arikara, Mandan, and Hidatsa from Fort Berthold Reservation. They signed a treaty to end the mutual horse stealing and other hostilities between them. The next year Martin Marty, a Benedictine priest, began mission work at Standing Rock, building on the foundation laid over many years by the visits of Father Pierre-Jean de Smet. The Benedictines opened a boarding school at Standing Rock in 1877 with a class of 30 boys (ARCIA 1874:246–248, 1875:244–248, 1876:38–40, 1877:72–75).

• FORT PECK RESERVATION   In autumn 1869, more than 1,000 Yanktonai arrived at Fort Buford and told Lt. Col. Henry A. Morrow, the commanding officer, that they were not bound by any treaty, but they were at peace and wanted to receive annuities like the other Sioux. Morrow prepared petitions to send to Washington that were signed by chiefs of three bands: Cuthead (Medicine Bear, Thunder Bull, and His Road to Travel), Wazikute (Shoots the Tiger, Afraid of Bear, Catches the Enemy, and Heart), and tʰakíni (Calumet Man, Afraid of Bull, Long Fox, Eagle Dog, and Standing Bellow); with them was a band of Sisseton (Brave Bear and Your Relation to the Earth). Morrow encouraged them to winter near the fort and promised that the army would feed them until the government could prepare a treaty (DeMallie 1986:28–29). In fact, Medicine Bull and Thunder Bull had both signed the 1868 treaty but perhaps they did not feel bound by it because the reservation it established was on the other side of the Missouri River from their own territory.

The westward movement of the Upper Yanktonai initiated a major migration of the Sioux. Buffalo were rapidly becoming extinct everywhere but in the region of Montana between the Missouri and the Milk rivers. In 1868, Thunder Bull had told the commissioners: "Our country . . . is ruined . . . our game is giving out" (DeMallie 1986:29). The Upper Yanktonai had long been associated with the Lower Assiniboine; the peace commissioners in 1866 had met with the two tribes jointly on the Missouri above the White Earth River, and in the winter of 1869 they were again camping together at Fort Buford. By the next June, there were 2,500 Upper Yanktonai near Fort Buford, and Lt. Col. Morrow speculated that they intended to drive the Assiniboine away, meaning the Upper Assiniboine, with whom the Yanktonai had always maintained a hostile relationship. In August 1870, 375 lodges of Lower Yanktonai under Black Eye were camped at the mouth of Poplar River. In spring 1871, Agent A.J. Simmons at Milk River, the Assiniboine and Gros Ventre agency, reported that 250 lodges of Sioux, including Yanktonais, Yanktons, Tetons, and Santees, were camped 20 miles below the agency: "They have come in force with their whole

Fig. 7. Council with Yanktons. The speaker wears a finger-woven turban, bear-claw necklace, and Hudson's Bay Company blanket. Although the photographer identified the group as Yanktonai, the dress of the men indicates they were Yanktons (J.H. Howard 1966:pl. 21). Photograph by Stanley J. Morrow, Yankton, Dak. Terr., 1868–1870s.

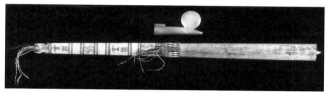

Fig. 8. Important transactions required the ceremonial smoking of tobacco, and elaborately decorated smoking equipment was an essential accessory for men of importance. top left, Yellow Earth or John Lone-Dog, Yanktonai, from Ft. Peck Res., Mont. He is wearing buckskin leggings and shirt and holds a tobacco pouch decorated with beadwork and quillwork. His moccasins and pipe stem are quilled, and he wears a hairpipe breastplate. Photograph by DeLancey Gill, Washington, 1903. top right, Beaded pipebag; collected by J. Frazer Boughter on the Yankton Res., Dak. Terr., before 1875. Length without fringe 50 cm. bottom, Catlinite pipe bowl and accompanying pipe stem wrapped with plaited quillwork in red, black, and white. Acquired from Red Thunder, Yanktonai, by Moses Austice before 1850. Length of stem 92 cm.

encampment asserting *they have come to stay.*" Standing Buffalo, a Sisseton chief, told Simmons that "their country below was burnt and dead," and that they had come to hunt buffalo: "Their country was wherever the buffalo ranged" (DeMallie 1986:30). The son of Struck by the Ree also visited Simmons, and the agent learned that 200 more lodges of Yanktons were on their way. Simmons requested and received permission from his superiors to provide the newcomers with food, fearing that otherwise they would join the Tetons who were hostile toward the government.

In 1872, delegations of Sioux traveled to Washington. Among the leaders of the Montana Sioux making the trip were the Upper Yanktonais Medicine Bear, Afraid of Bear, Black Eye, and Black Catfish; from Grand River, Big Head, Black Eye (a second man of that name), and Big Razee, representing the Upper Yanktonai, and Two Bears, Red Bear, and Bull's Ghost representing the Lower Yanktonai. The outcome of these delegations was a decision to allow those Sioux who wished to stay in Montana to enroll at the new Milk River Agency (renamed Fort Peck in 1874), which would also be home to the Lower Assiniboine. This was a victory for those who did not want to return to the agencies lower on the Missouri. It undermined the policy of the 1868 peace commission to consolidate the Sioux on a single reservation and forced the army to build up its defensive strength in Montana (DeMallie 1986: 32, 34, 36). The agency buildings were constructed in 1873 and in 1874 the agent reported issuing supplies to over 5,000 Sioux, including

2,266 Upper Yanktonais and 460 Lower Yanktonais as well as Santees, Sissetons, and Hunkpapa Tetons (ARCIA 1874:266). Doubtless some of those people were also Yanktons. In 1877 the agency was moved 75 miles downstream to the mouth of Poplar River.

The Sioux at Fort Peck were still living in tepees and setting out on summer and autumn buffalo hunts, which the agent encouraged since he did not have the funds to feed them year round. In the aftermath of the Battle of the Little Bighorn, the government had forbidden the sale of ammunition to Indians, so they turned to the illegal Métis traders. From January to April 1878, several hundred Métis with 75 Red River carts established a winter camp on the Milk River, hunting buffalo and trading ammunition and whiskey to the Sioux and Assiniboine (DeMallie 1986:43). 787

In spring 1878, while a group of Yanktonai was hunting buffalo, their horses were stolen by the Upper Assiniboine. Although Black Catfish, Black Tiger, and Thunder Bull harangued the camp, they were unable to prevent a war party from attacking Fort Belknap Agency. The Upper Assiniboines at Fort Belknap were better armed and fought off the attack, with four Sioux killed and three wounded. Agent Wellington Bird, at Fort Peck, blamed part of the trouble on the lack of a strong leader. Medicine Bear, the most prominent chief, was growing old, and in 1878 there were more than 50 chiefs at Fort Peck, none of whom had a following of over 20 lodges. Bird commented, "the biggest chief seems to be the one who can secure the largest amount of annuity goods or rations" (ARCIA 1878:91–92). In spring 1879 the agent reported that some of the Yanktonai leaders, including Medicine Bear, Afraid of Bear, and Thundering Bull, were making progress in farming, but others, notably Black Catfish and Black Tiger, used their soldier lodges *(akíčʰita)* to prevent members of their bands from farming (DeMallie 1986:45).

During the winters of 1878 and 1879 large numbers of Métis again trespassed on the reservation. Bird wrote, "They are destroying the Buffalo as rapidly as an unlimited supply of Ammunition in their hands can do it, and our Indians with good reason complain bitterly" (DeMallie 1986:44). In addition, Canadian Assiniboines and Plains Crees, as well as Blackfoot and Plains Ojibwas flocked to the Milk River area, the last hold-out of the buffalo herds. Even Sitting Bull's Hunkpapa band, who had sought refuge in Canada after the Battle of the Little Bighorn, returned south of the border in search of buffalo.

In fall 1879 the Fort Peck Sioux made a successful hunt south of the Missouri, then returned to the agency in November. The agency population began to swell as more and more of the non-agency Sioux, unable to find sufficient buffalo and harassed by Col. Nelson A. Miles's forces, went to Fort Peck asking for rations. Many were Tetons, including Hunkpapas from Canada, and their comings and goings kept the agency in constant turmoil. In the autumn of 1880 two companies of troops were sent to Fort Peck, where Camp Poplar River was established to maintain order and keep non-agency Indians away. As the Sioux went in to surrender, they were sent on to Fort Buford. There, in July 1881, Sitting Bull himself surrendered, bringing an end to the Sioux wars with the United States (DeMallie 1986:46–54).

Meanwhile, the Fort Peck Sioux continued to adapt to reservation life. In 1880, the new agent, N.S. Porter, established a police force. The Yanktonai chiefs, relenting their earlier opposition, selected 20 men to serve. Porter appointed Stab Plenty as captain, who only the previous year, as a member of the soldier lodge, had physically assaulted those men who attempted to work in the fields. He took his new assignment equally seriously (ARCIA 1880:113). The Sioux increased their commitment to farming; they planted 250 acres in 1881 and returned from a successful summer buffalo hunt to find an abundant harvest. By the end of 1881, the Fort Peck Sioux were doing well. They were the last of the Yankton and Yanktonai to live by buffalo hunting, but with the fast-dwindling herds, it was a way of life that could not be sustained much longer.

The annual winter invasion of Indian hunters continued, aggravated by a huge influx of White hide hunters. The army was unwilling to mount a major campaign to protect the last of the buffalo. In October 1881 a detachment of troops drove off Métis and Plains Cree hunters from the Milk River. By January 1882 they had returned, and not until April were more soldiers sent to eject them. In July the army scattered another large party of Plains Cree and Métis hunters (DeMallie 1986:55–56).

In 1881–1882 the Fort Peck Indians' winter hunt failed. By summer the shortage of food supplies at the agency was critical; drought destroyed the crops. Agent Porter sent the Indians away to search for buffalo. In the winter of 1882–1883 the Fort Peck Indians camped along the Missouri west of Wolf Point and hunted buffalo on the Milk River for one last successful hunt. They returned to the agency in the spring and planted 1,000 acres. The summer hunt was unsuccessful; Agent S.E. Snider wrote in his annual report, "The buffalo are a thing of the past" (ARCIA 1883:103). When the Indians returned to the agency they found that their crops had again been destroyed by drought. During the winter of 1883–1884 government rations were insufficient to keep them from starvation. Some died, and disaster was averted only by the issuing of army supplies from Camp Poplar River. The Indians at Fort Peck faced a period of baffling and disorienting change. The buffalo disappeared more abruptly than anyone could have imagined. In summer 1884, the ban on the Sun Dance was enforced for the first time, signaling the immensity of the changes they faced (DeMallie 1986:56–59).

Culture

Sioux culture in the mid-nineteenth century was largely consistent across the three divisions, each one characterized by distinctive styles and local variations in traditions and customs. Yankton culture, in particular, as a result of long and close association, resembled that of the Teton, while the Yanktonai shared more traits with the Santee and the neighboring Plains Ojibwa and Plains Cree. At the same time, despite periodic hostilities, both the Yankton and Yanktonai were strongly influenced by the Village tribes of the Missouri River, especially the Arikara, Mandan, and Hidatsa. Medicine Bear, the Upper Yanktonai chief, was a Mandan captive raised by the Sioux, who reestablished contacts with his mother's people and whose band sometimes hunted buffalo with them. The Yankton had longstanding relations of friendship with the Ponca, who by tradition gave them land in exchange for protection, and more intermittently with the Omaha (E.C. Deloria 1954a: Introduction, 1967a:26; J.H. Howard 1966:11, 17).

Unlike the Teton, but much like some of the Santee groups, the mid-nineteenth-century Yankton had permanent villages where they planted gardens, largely abandoning them during the summer buffalo hunts and returning in time for the harvest. Ten Yankton village sites have been identified on the north and east side of the Missouri, from the mouth of the Big Sioux at present Sioux City, Iowa, to above the confluence of the Niobrara, at present Pickstown, South Dakota; three additional sites have been identified on the James River, from a short distance above its mouth upstream to present Redfield, South Dakota (J.H. Howard 1972c:295–299). In 1857, Agent Redfield, visiting the Yanktons, wrote that "they reside chiefly in fixed habitations, mostly earth lodges, though I observed some quite good log-houses at the village of the 'Smutty Bear'" (ARCIA 1857:124).

Five Yanktonai earthlodge village sites have also been identified. Three were on the Missouri: one north of Fort Yates, North Dakota; Little Soldier's village, farther downstream; and one near present Fort Thompson, South Dakota. Two were on the James River: one was a former Yankton village site at present Redfield, South Dakota, known historically as the Dirt Lodges and thought to be the site of the early nineteenth-century trade fairs; the other, Drifting Goose's village, was on present Armdale Island, in the vicinity of Mellette, South Dakota (J.H. Howard 1972c:300, 1976:8). A military expedition described Drifting Goose's village in 1863 as consisting of 15 earthlodges of varying sizes arranged in a circle 165 feet in diameter with "a medicine pole and lookout station in the center." Some 40 acres of gardens were cultivated by women, at least half in corn and the rest in beans, peas, turnips, and potatoes. The river nearby was dammed with a fish trap (G.W. Kingsbury 1915, 1:306–307).

The Yankton and Yanktonai had a number of distinctive cultural characteristics associated with their permanent villages. Poorer families were said to have constructed elongated, dome-shaped lodges covered with hide, similar to the mat- or bark-covered winter lodges of the Central Algonquian tribes. While on hunting trips, tepees were used, built on a three-pole foundation. Hide-covered bull boats were used for river travel. Both the Yankton and Yanktonai made small clay pots, said to have been of high quality; larger pots were obtained in trade with the Arikara and Mandan. Wooden mortars were set into the earthlodge floors for pounding corn. The Yanktonai were also said to have made baskets of willow shoots in the manner of the Arikara and Mandan (J.H. Howard 1976:8–9). Large caches some six feet deep stored dried meat, corn, and other vegetables, packed in rawhide bags (E.C. Deloria 1967a:23–25).

Subsistence

The Yankton and Yanktonai subsisted largely on buffalo meat. A unique method of drying meat was described for the Yankton. First the meat was cut into thin sheets of even thickness, braced with thin sticks to keep it spread out, and hung on drying racks for a day. Next, leafy elm branches were cut and laid on the ground and the meat placed on top, followed by another layer of branches and a covering of hide or canvas. A person then trampled on the meat, in the same fashion as the Santee trampled on wild rice to remove the chaff, which broke down the fibers, flattened the meat, and pressed out moisture. Then the meat was again hung out to dry and afterward would keep for two years or longer (E.C. Deloria 1967a:2).

A hunting tool mentioned among the Sioux only for the Yanktonai was the rabbit stick, used to kill small game; it resembled those of the tribes of the Southwest (Hurt 1950:1–2).

In contrast to the Teton, fishing was an important economic activity for many of the Yankton and Yanktonai groups. In addition to the weir at Drifting Goose's village, a Mandan-style fish trap on the Missouri River was used by the Upper Yanktonai at Cannon Ball, on Standing Rock Reservation. Seines made of interlaced willows weighted with rocks were described for the Lower Yanktonai, as well as a technique called "fish crowding" (*hopásipi*), in which men and boys waded along the edge of the water, driving the fish into narrow inlets where they could be caught by hand; this method was used in the shallow lakes of eastern South Dakota. Other fishing techniques documented include the use of leisters, made with bone points, hooks and lines, and bows and arrows (J.H. Howard 1972c:301, 1976:6).

Horticulture was practiced by the Yankton and some of the Yanktonai groups. They raised at least three distinct types of corn, two types of squash, and at least three types of beans. A Yanktonai tradition, similar to a story recorded for the Arikara and Omaha, relates the origin of corn from the milk of a buffalo cow (J.H. Howard 1976:6; Parks 1991, 3:187; Fletcher and La Flesche 1911:76–78).

Ceremonies

The Sun Dance was the most important ceremony. The Yankton form closely resembled that of the Teton (Olden 1918:146–152), while one description of a Yanktonai Sun Dance involved a sacred bundle and was said to have resembled in some respects that of the Plains Ojibwa and Plains Cree (Milligan 1969).

The Medicine Dance (*wakʰą́ wačʰípi* 'sacred dance'), a secret shamanistic organization, existed among the Yanktonai and probably the Yankton as well. The accounts (Gilette 1906; P. Beckwith 1886) relate to the Yanktonai at Standing Rock and Devils Lake and reveal close similarities to the Santee, Arikara, and Omaha equivalents (Dorsey 1894:438–440). The origin of the society was attributed to *ųktéxi*, the underwater being. Initiates were instructed to join as a result of visions; the society included a number of different groups, each comprising men and women who had dreamed of the same spirit. Each member had a medicine bag, usually made of the whole skin of an otter or other aquatic mammal, and a carved wooden food bowl. Secret knowledge of the society was transmitted during ritual sweatbaths. Candidates were initiated into the use of shells, eagle claws, or other similar objects, which they ritually swallowed and then brought up as signs of their power for war or curing. Society dances were held in lodges constructed of two facing tepees, pitched several hundred feet apart, which were connected by low walls of interlaced willows to form an outdoor performance space accessible to spectators (fig. 9). In the dance, the highest-ranking members demonstrated their powers by exhibitions and contests of magical feats. Gourd rattles and tall water drums were used only by the Medicine Lodge (J.H. Howard 1976:9).

Associated with the Medicine Dance was the Sacred Feast (wakʰą́ wóhąpi) whose purpose was to strengthen the members' powers. Their bowls were incensed over a central fire and huge quantities of food were served, which each member was required to consume on the spot; then the bowls were again purified over the fire. Unlike the "eat-all" feasts documented for the Santee (Landes 1968:122–128), the Yanktonai allowed members to pass food outside the lodge, to be consumed by relatives. Shell swallowing and dancing concluded the feast (Gilette 1906:468–471).

Like the Santee, one of the types of spirits invoked by the Yankton and Yanktonai were Tree Dwellers (čąʔótʰina), who appeared as elflike beings associated with wooded areas. Tree-Dweller dreamers kept wooden effigies of the spirit and probably constituted one group within the Medicine Lodge. The only description of a ritual performance is from the Yanktonai at Cannon Ball, which was held for the purpose of curing (J.H. Howard 1955b:172–173). The shaman removed the effigy from a bundle and

covered it with a red cloth. As he sang and drummed, the figure danced under the cloth.

Conjuring ceremonies, held to foretell the future or to find lost objects, are well documented for the Yankton and are clearly forms of yuwípi ceremonies as practiced by the Teton (E.C. Deloria 1967a:10–11; Vine Deloria, Sr., in DeMallie and Parks 1987:97–99). The Blue-Bead ceremony, practiced by both the Yankton and Yanktonai, honored and protected a child. A huge giveaway validated the privilege of decorating the child's forelock with a blue glass "bead." Beads of this type were made by melting trade beads and forming them into larger pendants, a technique attributed to the Arikara (J.H. Howard 1976:10). Ritualized eagle trapping involving sweatbaths and sacred songs, like that found among the Arikara, Mandan, and Hidatsa, is documented for both Lower and Upper Yanktonai (J.H. Howard 1954a).

Clothing and Adornment

Men's dress and clothing style reflected the influence of the Village tribes. Men wore their hair cut in bangs at the front (fig. 5), frequently with a longer lock left hanging over the brow and nose; the rest of the hair was braided on either side of the head and into a scalp lock at the crown. At both sides of the forehead men frequently wore small, distinctive hourglass-shaped ornaments covered with dentalia, with dentalia pendants hanging to the shoulders. Turbans of fur or finger-woven sashes were also frequently worn. The roach of porcupine- and deer-tail hair was introduced as part of the Grass Dance ritual, probably by the Omaha or Ponca, in the mid-nineteenth century. Fort Berthold influence was reflected in multistrand necklaces of cut bone beads and in the style of wearing the breechcloth longer in front, with a short flap in back, and a V-shaped ribbon work design on the seat. Leggings frequently had a beaded rosette near the bottom edge or were decorated with a box design in contrasting material. Similar influences in women's dress include high-top moccasins (in place of the Teton women's leggings) and oval-shaped belt pouches (J.H. Howard 1966:14; Wissler 1916:866).

Art styles in quill- and beadwork included both floral designs, most probably reflecting Métis influence, and geometric patterns like those of the Teton, but usually in bolder, less busy designs. Style was reported to be a matter of family specialization (J.H. Howard 1966:15).

History, 1880–1935

Reservations and Land Loss

Reservation economies failed to develop as their agents planned and the Yankton and Yanktonai remained dependent on the government. Quantities of rations were decreased at the same time that game was diminishing in numbers, creating hardship and sometimes starvation. Droughts, grasshoppers, and early frosts continued to

Smithsonian, Dept. of Anthr.: 23,553 (neg. 99-20264).

Fig. 9. Medicine Dance. Participants in horned headdresses dance in an enclosure connecting 2 tepees. Onlookers line the sides of the enclosure. Drawing on muslin, made by Walking in Light, Yanktonai, using commercial watercolor paints applied with a sharpened stick. Collected by Paul Beckwith at Devils Lake Agency, Dak. Terr., 1875.

top left, Douglas Co. Histl. Soc., Armour, S. Dak.; U. of Vt., Robert Hull Fleming Mus., Burlington: top right, 1881.3.95; bottom, 1881.3.130.

Fig. 10. Women's clothing. top left, Edward Oakiye and family, Yankton. The women, probably his wife and daughter, wear cloth blouse and skirt or dresses; the older wears a commercial blanket as a shawl. Oakiye wears a buckskin shirt, cloth leggings with sequins, and leg bands with quill-wrapped fringes. The boy wears a cloth shirt, leggings, and vest. The eagle plume in his hair indicates that the Hunka ceremony had been performed for him. Photograph by Herbert A. Perry, about 1900. top right, Dentalium shell earrings with sheet metal pendants; length 36 cm. bottom, Woman's belt of heavy leather adorned with brass tacks; the beaded pouch could have held flint and steel, or later, matches or ration tickets; length of belt 157 cm. Collected from the Yanktonai by Ogden B. Read at Camp Poplar River, Mont. Terr., 1881 (Markoe 1986).

devastate crops. By an 1886 agreement, ratified in 1888, the Fort Peck tribes accepted boundaries for their reservation, ceding their claims to other lands in Montana; Medicine Bear headed the list of Yanktonai signers (Kappler 1904–1941, 1:264–265). In 1889 the Great Sioux Reservation was reduced to six separate reservations (including Crow Creek, east of the Missouri), with a loss of half the reservation land (Kappler 1904–1941, 1:328–339). The northern portion of Standing Rock Reservation where most of the Yanktonai lived—the area south of the Cannonball River to the boundary between the new states of North and South Dakota—had been added by executive order in 1875 to the reservation as established by the 1868 treaty (Kappler 1904–1941, 1:884); the portion east of the new reservation border became a permanent part of Standing Rock Reservation. A small area east of the Missouri, where Two Bears's band farmed, was set aside for their use by executive order in 1876, but the agents continually pressured them to move to the west side of the river. The Yanktonai protested the legality of the loss of their lands east of the Missouri and refused to move, but in 1884 the executive order was rescinded and the land restored to the public domain, forcing the last of the Lower Yanktonais across the river to Standing Rock (Kappler 1904–1941, 1:884). Soon all the Sioux reservations were surrounded by White settlement.

Reservation lands for all the Yankton and Yanktonai communities were allotted to individuals, and much of the surplus land was opened for White settlement (vol. 4:227). The experience of the Yankton is representative. Allotment was completed in 1890; 1,484 individuals took land on the reservation. In the words of their agent, "they have nearly all adopted the habits of white people"; a farm was plowed on each adult's allotment (ARCIA 1890:xlv, 70). In 1893, according to the agent's report, nearly all families lived on their allotments and planted their farms (ARCIA 1893:307), but in the next year the agent explained that most of the Yanktons went out to their allotments in the spring, living in tepees while they farmed during the summer, then left their allotments and came together in villages of tepees and log cabins located in the river bottoms, where they passed the winter in "idleness," dancing and recounting past deeds in war (ARCIA 1894:303–304). In 1894 the Yankton signed an agreement by which they surrrendered the unallotted land, about half of the reservation, receiving in return $600,000 (Kappler 1904–1941, 1:523–528). During the next few years, two-room frame houses were built by the agency farmers on each allotment (ARCIA 1895:305, 1887:64; Hoover 1988:39).

Reservation institutions took over the functions of the old chiefs. In 1882 the new Yankton agent reorganized the Indian police, numbering 15 men, and praised its "efficiency and faithfulness." In 1885 the agent created a board of advisors, comprised of two men he selected from each of the eight bands, to report infractions of agency rules and to advise on cases of need; the board was headed by White Swan, one of the band chiefs. A Court of Indian Offenses, composed of three full-blood Yankton judges, established in 1884, passed sentences on Indians arrested by the police for infractions of agency rules; offenders might be incarcerated in the agency jail. In 1886 the agent reported using the police to prevent giveaways of property after a death. Both the judges and police suffered abuse and threats from offenders and their families (ARCIA 1882:49, 1884:61, 1885:59–60, 1886:94; 1887:54, 62–63; 1888:65).

The Yankton and Yanktonai suffered the ill effects of government paternalism that resulted in land leasing, inheritance of fractionalized allotments, and land sales. *791*

Around 1900, when leasing of reservation lands to non-Indians became government policy, business councils were established to approve leases, but on the Yankton Reservation, even this small measure of control ceased to function after 1912 (Hoover 1988:53). Tribal councils, lacking any political power, were gradually taken over by young men educated in boarding schools. Returned students frequently found themselves at odds both with the old chiefs and with the Indian agents. Veterans of World War I returned highly honored, but found few economic opportunities on the reservations.

Religion

The Yankton and most of the Yanktonai did not accept the Ghost Dance of 1889–1890. One of the Teton Ghost Dance leaders, who went to the Yankton Reservation and preached about his visit to Wovoka, was arrested by the agency police and put to work sawing wood until he was sent back to his home reservation (ARCIA 1891:427). Only the Yanktonai at Fort Peck and Standing Rock participated in the Ghost Dance (Mooney 1896:816–817). While the dances ended abruptly among the Teton, soon after the Wounded Knee massacre on December 29, 1890, the Yanktonai at Cannon Ball were said not to have taken up the

Ghost Dance until 1891, and practiced it for a few years thereafter (J.H. Howard 1984:174).

Christian churches, including Roman Catholic (fig. 11), Episcopal, Presbyterian, and Congregational, flourished in the Yankton and Yanktonai communities. Native Sioux clergy and catechists were effective proselytizers. For example, Philip Deloria, son of the chief of the Yankton mixed-blood band, became an Episcopal deacon in 1883 and was ordained a priest in 1892. He and other Yanktons and Santees active in the Protestant churches formed a mutual aid society called the Brotherhood of Christian Unity (Hurt 1960a:279–281). In 1892 he took charge of Saint Elizabeth's mission and boarding school on Standing Rock Reservation and remained there until his retirement in 1925 (V. Deloria 1999:48–77). Boarding schools established by Roman Catholic Benedictines at Marty, on the Yankton Reservation, and at Stephan, on Crow Creek Reservation, were successful in educating generations of children.

The Native American Church was introduced on the Yankton Reservation in 1910. The first church leaders were imprisoned by the Indian agent in 1912 until the commissioner of Indian affairs ordered their release. Meetings were held secretly until 1922, when the Native American Church of Charles Mix County was chartered by the state of South Dakota (Hoover 1988:76–77). Church members, while only a minority of Yanktons, were in each community; the church remained active throughout the twentieth century (Hurt 1960). The church did not spread to any of the Yanktonai communities.

The Yankton claimed guardianship of the Pipestone Quarry ("Environment and Subsistence," fig. 3, this vol.), a sacred place that by tradition belonged to the Sioux but was a neutral ground where Indians of many tribes went to obtain the soft red stone called catlinite from which pipe bowls were manufactured (Catlin 1926, 2:190; Nicollet in E.C. Bray and M.C. Bray 1976:75–76). The quarry was established as a one-mile square reserve after the 1858 treaty and the Yankton were given the right to quarry stone there. When Whites encroached on the area in the 1870s,

State Histl. Soc. of N. Dak., Bismarck:615.

Fig. 11. Henry Poor Dog and Rosa Cat, Yanktonai, after their wedding at the Roman Catholic Church of St. Peter, Ft. Yates, N. Dak. Photograph by Frank Bennett Fiske, Feb. 7, 1915.

Minn. Histl. Soc., St. Paul:E92/r1 (neg. no. 14867).

Fig. 12. Giveaway. Yanktonai woman displaying a star quilt. Photograph at Poplar, Mont., 1934.

DeMALLIE

the Yankton demanded their removal. In 1884 the Supreme Court decided in favor of their petition, but not until 1887 was a military detachment sent to evict the intruders. In 1892, Pipestone Indian School was built on the reserve and that same year, by agreement with the United States, the Yankton claim of ownership of the reserve was affirmed, although legal challenges remained until a Supreme Court decision in 1926 (vol. 4:212). In 1929 Congress appropriated some $300,000 for the value of the land, which was distributed per capita—about $152 each—to tribal members. The Yankton retained the right to quarry pipestone, which they continued to exercise throughout the twentieth century (Hoover 1976; Corbett 1978; V. Deloria 1999:72–75).

Sources

A.R. Woolworth (1974) is a history of the Yankton to 1860 and Champe (1974) is a historical chronology of the Yankton to 1845, both prepared for the Indian Claims Commission. Hoover (1988) is a brief historical and cultural introduction to the Yankton. Sansom-Flood (1986) is an account of events surrounding the establishment of the Yankton Reservation. J.H. Howard (1966) presents an overview of Yankton and Yanktonai history and culture. DeMallie (1986) traces the history of the Yanktonai in Montana from 1869–1884. Mission work on the Yankton reservation is well characterized in biographies of John P. Williamson, Presbyterian (Barton 1919), and Sylvester Eisenman, Roman Catholic (M.E. Carson 1989). Hurt (1960a) discusses the Yankton Dakota Church as a nationalistic movement that fostered success in mainstream American society.

The earliest ethnographic description of the Yanktonai is Beckwith (1886), based on observations at Devils Lake; this account does not differentiate between the Yanktonai and Santee. Gilette (1906) described Midewiwin among the Yanktonai at Devils Lake and Standing Rock reservations. The fullest account of Yankton culture is given in material dictated by Philip Deloria (Olden 1918; V. Deloria 1999); these books include biographical material on Deloria and information on the Sioux Episcopal missions. Ella C. Deloria (1967a) presents material recorded from Antelope, an aged Yankton, about 1937. J.H. Howard (1972c) is a detailed study of Yankton ethnogeography. Yankton claims against the United States government are summarized in Hoover (1976), which, together with Corbett (1978), gives a history of the Yanktons and their legal relations to the Pipestone Quarry. Biographical sketches of Yankton leaders appear in Sansom-Flood and Bernie (1985) and Larkin (1964). Zitkala Ša (Getrude Bonnin), a Yankton, published a collection of legends (1901) and a volume of stories (1921) that includes evocative reminiscences of her boarding school experiences. Hurt (1960) discusses the Native American Church among the Yankton.

Accounts of Yanktonai history and culture are given in Curtis (1907–1930, 3:119–123) and J.H. Howard (1976), which includes a Yanktonai winter count; Howard also published an account of Yanktonai eagle-trapping (1954a) and the only account of a Yanktonai Tree-Dweller ceremony (1955b). J.H. Howard (1971a) and Brokenleg and Hoover (1993) present a collection of watercolors by John Saul, a Lower Yanktonai, representing traditional culture. Milligan (1969) includes a brief account of the Yanktonai Sun Dance on Standing Rock Reservation in 1937.

J.P. Williamson (1902) includes many Yankton forms in his English-Dakota dictionary. J.W. Cook (1880–1882) is an unpublished compilation of data on the Yankton dialect. Parks (1999d) is an unpublished dictionary of Yanktonai based on material from Standing Rock Reservation.

Teton

RAYMOND J. DeMALLIE

Territory

When the Teton ('tē̱tän) moved west of the Missouri River in the late eighteenth century they were divided into three groups. In the vanguard were the Oglala, whose territory by the mid-nineteenth century extended from the forks of the Platte River to the forks of the Cheyenne River, an area that included the Black Hills (fig. 1). East of the Oglala were the Brule, whose territory included the upper portions of the Niobrara, White, and Bad rivers. North of the Oglala and Brule were the Saone, who lived along the tributaries of the Missouri from Cheyenne River north to Heart River; by mid-century the Saone had divided into 5 tribes: Minneconjou, Hunkpapa, Sans Arc, Blackfeet, and Two Kettles. On the northwest, the Teton range extended as far as the Yellowstone River (Lewis and Clark in Moulton 1983–, 3:415–420; Denig 1961:16–28; Nicollet in DeMallie 1976:259–262; G.K. Warren 1856:16; J.A. Hanson 1996:114).

In published sources the Oglala and Brule are usually designated the southern Teton tribes and the others the northern Teton. In contrast, the Teton themselves oriented their territory on an east-west axis, in relation to the tributaries of the Missouri River. By mid-nineteenth century, the Oglala, Brule, and Minneconjou lived in the 'uplands' (*xeyáta*), upriver, away from the Missouri, while the others lived 'below' (*kʰútahaⁿ*), downstream, and along the Missouri itself (DeMallie 1999). As buffalo became scarce near the Missouri, the Teton were drawn westward by the abundant herds beyond the Black Hills in the Powder and Yellowstone river country, while at the same time the presence of White traders, and later of military posts and Indian agencies along the Missouri, continued to pull them back.

Teton bands were free to hunt wherever game was found throughout the whole of their common territory, and bands of more than one tribe frequently came together for communal hunts and religious ceremonies. Each tribe usually occupied a separate area of land, although the boundaries between them were overlapping and were not exclusive. In the mid-nineteenth century the Teton considered the Black Hills to be the center of their world, a sacred place that was home to powerful spirits (Denig 1961:5, 15). The geological formation known to the Teton as the Race Track, which surrounds the Black Hills, was believed to be the site of the primordial race between the birds (two-leggeds), representing humankind, and the animals (four-leggeds); the birds won, establishing the natural order by which humans killed buffalo and other game for food. Stories were also told identifying the Black Hills as the site of creation of humankind, further testament to the enduring belief in the sacredness of the Black Hills (Black Elk in DeMallie 1984:309–310).

History, 1851–1879

Treaty of 1851 and First Warfare with the United States

In 1851 government commissioners met with bands representing most of the Teton and Yankton, as well as delegations representing the Arapaho, Cheyenne, Eastern Shoshone, Crow, Assiniboine, Arikara, Mandan, and

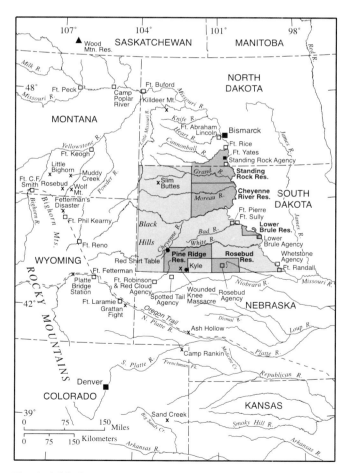

Fig. 1. Mid-19th century Teton territory, with modern reservations, and the former Great Sioux Reservation in light gray.

Hidatsa at Horse Creek, near Fort Laramie, to sign a treaty with the United States (Kappler 1904–1941, 2:594–596). This unprecedented intertribal gathering attracted some 10,000 people and lasted two weeks. Six leaders of Oglala, Brule, and Yankton signed the treaty. Then 27 wagon loads of presents were given to the Indians; in the Sioux winter counts that year is represented by a pictograph showing a bale of blankets and the designation "big distribution" (DeMallie 1980; Prucha 1994:237–240; J.R. Walker 1982:141).

The treaty was a turning point for the western Sioux. Despite the protest of the chiefs, the treaty for the first time specified boundaries among the tribes attending the council. While the signers of the treaty did not surrender their right to claim lands assigned to other tribes, nonetheless the treaty set in motion the process of limiting tribal lands. The Sioux chiefs also protested the commissioners' insistence that they elect a single head chief through whom they would enact "all national business," pointing out that they could not agree on a single leader. The commissioners themselves then appointed a Brule, Frightening Bear (*matʰó wayúhi* 'bear frightens away'), as head chief, and had all the other Sioux leaders present ratify the selection. The office of head chief proved to be ineffectual; nevertheless, during the next half-century government officials continued to rely on chiefs whom they recognized as authorized intermediaries.

In exchange for annuities over a 50-year period the Sioux agreed to allow the United States to build roads and military posts in their country, thereby providing a legal basis for the Oregon Trail, which followed the Platte River, and the military post of Fort Laramie, Missouri Territory (vol. 4:372–373), both of which were on land reserved by the treaty for the Sioux. It was the trail itself that instigated hostilities between the Sioux and Whites as throngs of emigrants passed, spreading diseases and driving the buffalo herds away from the Platte. Altercations between Indians and wagon trains were a constant source of trouble during the summer months. Crisis came in 1854, when an emigrant complained at Fort Laramie that the Sioux of Frightening Bear's camp, who were waiting for their treaty annuities, had killed his cow. The commanding officer at the fort chose to make this a test of the head chief's authority and sent Lt. John L. Grattan and a detachment of 29 men to demand the surrender of the guilty party. But the man who killed the cow was a Minneconjou visitor in the Brule camp; Frightening Bear was powerless to compel him to surrender. Grattan opened fire with a howitzer, mortally wounding the chief; within minutes he and all the soldiers of his command had been killed by the Sioux. To avenge the chief's death, the Brules began to attack travelers on the Oregon Trail. In November 1854, a Brule war party including Spotted Tail, later the leading chief of the tribe, attacked a mail wagon, killing the drivers and a passenger and taking the mail pouches (Hyde 1937:72–76; Olson 1965:8).

In response to the hostilities, the next year Gen. William S. Harney established another military post on the Missouri, Fort Pierre, formerly a fur trade post ("Sioux Until 1850," fig. 7, this vol.). Setting out from there, Harney and his troops marched along the Oregon Trail to punish the Sioux. On September 3, 1855, Harney attacked the Brule village of Little Thunder, camped near the trail at Ash Hollow. Although this was not the village involved in the Grattan affair, 86 Sioux were killed and 70 women and children were taken as prisoners to Fort Pierre (Hyde 1937:79–82). Following the Ash Hollow fight, Harney demanded the surrender of the Indians who had attacked the mail wagon. Spotted Tail and four others went to Fort Laramie and were sent as prisoners to Fort Leavenworth, Kansas, returning to their people the following year. The experience impressed Spotted Tail (fig. 2), who thereafter was a leading proponent of peace with the Whites (Hyde 1961:63–70).

In April 1856, Harney convened a council at Fort Pierre with representatives of all the Teton, Yankton, and Yanktonai tribes. As a gesture of reconciliation, One Horn, the Minneconjou chief, surrendered the killer of the cow. One purpose of the council was to recognize a head chief and eight subordinate chiefs for each tribe. Harney appointed the Hunkpapa head chief Bear Ribs as overall chief to succeed

Smithsonian, NAA: 3684-d.

Fig. 2. Part of the Sioux delegation of 1875. seated left to right, Sitting Bull, Oglala (b. 1841, d. 1876), nephew of Chief Little Wound, not the Hunkpapa chief of the same name; Swift Bear, Brule; and Spotted Tail (Brule, b. 1823, d. 1881). standing, Julius Meyer, merchant; Red Cloud, Oglala (b. 1822, d. 1909). The delegation included 13 Sioux from Red Cloud Agency and 6 from Spotted Tail Agency. The government brought the Sioux leaders to Washington in an unsuccessful attempt to persuade them to surrender the Black Hills (Olson 1965:171–191). Photograph by Frank F. Currier, Omaha, Neb., 1875.

Frightening Bear and devised an elaborate system of uniformed "chief soldiers" and "soldiers" designed to prevent the Sioux from making war on other tribes and disturbing Whites traveling through their country (F. Pierce 1856). The Sioux were deeply impressed by the council. If the treaty had been ratified, it might have had a positive effect, but Harney's authority to make a treaty came from the War Department and was contested by the Office of Indian Affairs; in the end, the Senate rejected it (Hyde 1937:81). Throughout the nineteenth century the Sioux were repeatedly caught between the opposing policies of the military and civilian arms of the federal government.

The annuity goods promised under the 1851 treaty proved to be a source of contention among the Sioux. The first shipment arrived in 1852, but to obtain their goods in 1853 the Sioux were required to sign an amendment to the treaty that reduced the number of years annuities would be provided from 50 to 10, with a 5-year extension possible at the discretion of the president. The document was signed by four of the original six signers, together with 13 other chiefs of the Brule, Oglala, Minneconjou, and Sans Arc. No representative of the Hunkpapa or Blackfeet signed either the treaty or the amendment, and the young men of the northern Sioux were opposed to accepting the treaty goods. In 1862, when Bear Ribs defied the young men by accepting the annuity goods, he was murdered by a Sans Arc. After his death, the government appointed no more "head chiefs" for the Sioux (H.H. Anderson 1956; Prucha 1994:440–442; Utley 1993:48–49).

Military and Civilian Forces in the 1860s

Following the 1862 Sioux Conflict in Minnesota, Santee refugees fled westward, pursued by military expeditions commanded by Gen. Henry H. Sibley and Gen. Alfred Sully. New military posts were built on the Missouri in Sioux country, Fort Sully in 1863 and Fort Rice in 1864. Sully's forces skirmished with Tetons and other Sioux, and at the Battle of Killdeer Mountain, July 28, 1864, attacked a large encampment of northern Tetons, Yanktonais, and Santees. The Sioux were driven off and Sully had the village destroyed (Utley 1967:276–278; Vestal 1957:52–57).

To the south of Sioux country, 137 Cheyennes were killed on November 29, 1864, when the Colorado Volunteer Militia attacked Black Kettle's village at Sand Creek, Colorado. The southern Brule and Oglala then joined the Cheyenne and Arapaho in seeking revenge. On January 5, 1865, a war party more than 1,000 strong attacked Camp Rankin, on the South Platte, and ransacked nearby Julesburg. They continued to skirmish with the army, culminating in the raid on Platte Bridge Station, on the North Platte in Wyoming, July 26, 1865, as they moved northward to the Black Hills and Powder River (Hyde 1937:109–113; Utley 1967:301–302, 319–322).

George Sword, an Oglala (vol. 17:252), related how, in 1864, a messenger went around to all the Sioux winter camps to forge an agreement to fight the Whites. Among the Oglala, Red Cloud argued for fighting to stop the Whites from taking their land and destroying them as a people. The council agreed and instructed the camp crier to announce the news: whoever counts coup on a White man counts coup on an enemy, and anyone who is wounded by White men or who takes their horses will be honored for performing a brave deed (Sword 1998:text 4). In this way, Whites were symbolically merged into the category of enemy (*thóka*), giving the same prestige value to coups counted against Whites as to those earned in intertribal warfare.

After a presidential commission investigated the massacre at Sand Creek, government policy shifted, taking control away from the War Department and adopting the more humane—and cheaper—alternative of settling the Indians on reservations. From 1865 to 1868, treaty commissions, representing both civilian and military interests, traveled along the Missouri River signing treaties with the Sioux and other tribes that formed the basis for a reservation system designed to remove Indians from the main routes of transcontinental travel (Prucha 1984, 1:479–500).

Even while the peace commissions were signing treaties with the Sioux, Whites were intruding into Indian country. The Bozeman Trail, a shortcut from the Oregon Trail in Wyoming to the gold fields of Montana, was opened in 1862, passing through the Teton hunting grounds on the Powder River. To protect citizens traveling the road, the army established Fort Conner in 1865 (renamed Fort Reno the next year), Forts Philip Kearny and C.F. Smith in 1866, and Fort Fetterman in 1867. Sioux and Cheyenne war parties kept Col. Henry B. Carrington's forces under continual siege as they built Fort Philip Kearny, and on December 21, 1866, the Indians lured Lt. Col. William J. Fetterman and a detachment of 80 men into an ambush in which they all were killed (Utley 1973:98–106; Olson 1965:41–57; Hyde 1937:140–149).

While the army clamored to punish the Sioux, Indian attacks on the Bozeman Trail forts continued in 1867. To the south, Gen. Winfield S. Hancock carried on a campaign against the Cheyenne and southern Teton. Nonetheless, the treaty commissions continued to negotiate for peace. By terms of the 1868 treaty the government agreed to abandon the Bozeman Trail posts and the Sioux agreed not to oppose the building of the Northern Pacific Railroad (DeMallie 1986:25; Utley 1973:111–137).

The Treaty of 1868

The 1868 treaty (fig. 3) shaped all future relations between the government and the Teton (Kappler 1904–1941, 2:998–1007). It set aside an area that became known as the Great Sioux Reservation, encompassing all of present South Dakota west of the Missouri and acknowledging the area in Nebraska north of the North Platte and the eastern portions of Wyoming and Montana from the reservation boundary to the summit of the Big Horn Mountains as "unceded Indian territory." It also recognized the right of the Sioux to hunt on the North Platte and Republican rivers as long as sufficient buffalo remained.

The treaty stipulated the construction of an agency, specified annuities to be distributed for 30 years, provided for education, and laid out a plan for the eventual allotment of reservation lands in severalty. The first agency was established on the Missouri River at Whetstone Creek, above Fort Randall, at the southeast corner of the reservation. Although the location was favorable for cheap transportation of goods, it was too far from Teton hunting grounds on the Powder River to be practical for any but the southern Oglala and Brule. In 1869 additional agencies were established at Cheyenne River and Grand River; in 1871 Red Cloud Agency was established on the North Platte, near Fort Laramie, for the northern Oglala; and in 1875 Lower Brule agency was established across the river from Crow Creek, the Lower Yanktonai agency, which until then had also administered the Lower Brule. Whetstone Agency was renamed Spotted Tail in 1874 and Rosebud in 1878; Red Cloud Agency was renamed Pine Ridge in 1878. Both these agencies were relocated several times before settling permanently on the White River (E.E. Hill 1974; Hyde 1956:3–25; Olson 1965:247–263).

While the new agencies were being built on the Missouri, many—perhaps most—of the Teton were living in the unceded Indian territory west of the reservation. In 1864, no Sioux were reported to live in the newly organized Montana Territory, but by 1868 large numbers of Teton were reported on the Yellowstone River; in 1869–1870 the Hunkpapa wintered there. Military observers reported that the Teton, together with large numbers of Yanktonai, were drawn to the area from the Yellowstone to the Missouri as far west as Milk River by the presence of the last abundant buffalo herds in the west. Competition over buffalo involved the Sioux in warfare with all the tribes of the region, including the Crow, Assiniboine, Gros Ventre, and Blackfeet (DeMallie 1986:28–30).

Warfare in the 1870s

In 1871 the Indian agent at Milk River, the Upper Assiniboine and Gros Ventre agency, reported that there were 6,800 Sioux in Montana. Game was being rapidly depleted and the Indians required food to survive the coming winter. Under the Hunkpapa chief Sitting Bull, the Teton were a formidable force, and the government decided to send supplies for them to Milk River. During the summer of 1871, surveying parties for the Northern Pacific Railroad worked both in Montana and Dakota territories and that November, in council with Agent A.J. Simmons, the Teton declared that they would fight the Whites if the railroad surveys continued.

While the Bureau of Indian Affairs continued to seek a peaceful solution, the army prepared for a defensive war. During the summer of 1872, military escorts accompanying the surveying parties fought off repeated Sioux attacks. In August 1872, at the trading post of Fort Peck, a government commission met with some 200 Sioux chiefs and warriors, representing an estimated 11,200 people camped in the vicinity. The commissioners then escorted a large delegation of Teton and Yanktonai leaders to Washington and sent for representatives from the other Sioux agencies. Neither Sitting Bull nor any of the chiefs who had voiced opposition to the railroad were included in the delegations. In Washington, basing the decision on the 1868 treaty, the government acknowledged the right of the Sioux to live in Montana and authorized an agency for them. The Milk River Agency was moved to Fort Peck, consolidating the Lower Assiniboine with the Sioux (DeMallie 1986:31–35).

By 1873 the Northern Pacific Railroad had been completed as far west as Bismarck. In summer 1874, Lt. Col. George A. Custer led a military expedition of some 1,000 men to explore the Black Hills and locate an appropriate site for a military post. When they returned to Fort Abraham Lincoln, across the river from Bismarck, and reported the discovery of "gold in paying quantities," the news prompted a flood of gold seekers into the Black Hills. A scientific expedition the next summer confirmed Custer's discovery, and newspaper accounts rapidly publicized the Black Hills as the latest destination for fortune seekers. The miners were trespassers on the Great Sioux Reservation, but the army was powerless to stop them, and the government had no choice but to attempt to negotiate with the Sioux for the sale of the Black Hills (Utley 1973:242–245; DeMallie 1986:36).

In fall 1875, a commission held one meeting with representatives of all the reservation Sioux, but the Sioux were unwilling to sell or even lease the Black Hills. The commission's failure left the Bureau of Indian Affairs vulnerable to pressure from the War Department and on December 6, 1875, the commissioner of Indian affairs telegraphed an order to the Sioux agents requiring all the Sioux belonging on the Great Sioux Reservation to return within the reservation boundaries by January 31, 1876—virtually impossible at that time of year—or be considered hostile (Utley 1973:245–248; Olson 1965:201:216; DeMallie 1986:36–37).

In April, Col. John Gibbon headed east from Forts Shaw and Ellis, Montana, with more than 400 men and 25 Crow scouts; in May, Gen. Alfred H. Terry led a column of more than 900 men and 39 Arikara scouts west from Fort Abraham Lincoln, and Gen. George Crook came north from Fort Fetterman, Wyoming, with over 1,000 men and some 200 Crow and Eastern Shoshone scouts. Crook's forces engaged the Sioux and Cheyenne on the Rosebud River on June 17, shortly after Sitting Bull's Sun Dance vision revealed soldiers falling upside down into the Sioux camp. The battle was not a clear victory for either side, and Crook withdrew to wait for reinforcements. Meanwhile, on June 25, Lt. Col. Custer, leading a portion of Terry's forces, attacked the Sioux and Cheyenne village on the Little Bighorn River, ending in defeat for the army and the death of Custer and 215 men under his immediate command (vol. 4:177) (Utley 1973:249–261; J.S. Gray 1976; J.A. Greene 1994; DeMallie 1986:37–38, 1993:518–523.)

Following Custer's defeat, the Indian camp broke up. The Cheyennes moved into the Bighorn Mountains; some of

797

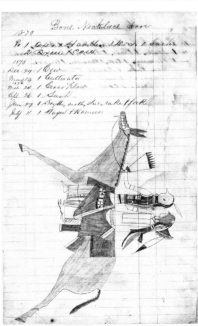

the Sioux headed back to their agencies, while the rest scattered out in the Yellowstone country. Meanwhile, the agencies on the Great Sioux Reservation were put under temporary military control, and the army confiscated the agency Indians' horses and guns to prevent them from carrying supplies and ammunition to the hold-outs. An additional 800 troops under Lt. Col. Wesley Merritt were positioned west of the Black Hills to block the route from Montana to the agencies. Throughout the fall and winter of 1876–1877 troops continued to harass the Sioux. On September 9, Crook's forces under Capt. Anson Mills attacked a Minneconjou village at Slim Buttes, south of the Grand River in present western South Dakota, killing the chief, American Horse. On December 16, when a delegation of Sioux chiefs went to Col. Nelson A. Miles's winter quarters on the Yellowstone to ask for peace, they were fired on by the army's Crow scouts and five of the chiefs were killed. On January 8, 1877, Miles's forces used artillery against Crazy Horse's Sioux and Cheyenne at the Battle of Wolf Mountain, and at the Battle of Muddy Creek, May 7, the Minneconjou chief Lame Deer was killed (Utley 1973:267–281; J.A. Greene 1991; DeMallie 1986:37–39).

In spring 1877, Sitting Bull escaped from the army by leading his followers into Canada, while in April, Crazy Horse and his followers surrendered at Camp Robinson and settled at Red Cloud Agency. The agency chiefs were jealous and suspicious of Crazy Horse, keeping alive rumors of his imminent escape from the agency and resumption of war against the army. On September 5, 1877, Crazy Horse was killed in a scuffle with a soldier at Camp Robinson and most of his followers fled north to join Sitting Bull or to settle at other agencies. His death effectively marked the end of Sioux armed resistance to White encroachment on their lands (Olson 1965:237–246; McCrady 1998:132–152; DeMallie 1986:40–42).

Culture in the Mid-Nineteenth Century

Social Organization

The Teton recognized themselves as a 'people' (*oyáte*), a term that carried a meaning of ethnic identity as Lakota (*lakȟóta*) as well as a general sense of political unity based on common relationship. Each of the seven constituent groups recognized itself as a tribe, a level of social organization that was also called *oyáte*. The seven tribes were allied with one another, as reflected in the translation of the word *lakȟóta* 'friends, allies'. They quarreled with one another and sometimes men of one tribe stole women or horses from another tribe, but they were never at war with one another. The relationship among the seven tribes was termed *ólakȟota* 'friendship, alliance, peace', and it was expressed in terms of kinship. All who were *lakȟóta* were potential relatives, people who could be trusted. All who were not *lakȟóta* were 'enemies' (*tȟóka*) unless 'peace' (*wólakȟota*) was made with them. Such was the case with the Cheyenne and Arapaho, who were part of the *lakȟólkičȟiyapi* 'alliance'. All other Indians (*ikčéwičȟaša* 'common men') were *tȟókakičȟiyapi* 'related as enemies'. White people were not 'enemies' but were called *wašíču*, a word that referred to a particular type of spirit associated with war, first bestowed on Whites because of their incomprehensible power (*wakȟą́*), most dramatically represented by guns (J.R. Walker 1914:97, 1980:73–74; DeMallie 1971:104–108).

The origin of the Sioux as a people is related in the story of the gift of the sacred pipe, which provided the foundation for society. According to the story, in the distant past at a time of famine, a spirit being in the form of a beautiful woman carrying a bundle appeared to two young men who were out hunting. One young man failed to understand that the woman was a spirit and when he made a sexual advance, he was enveloped in a cloud and reduced to a skeleton. The other young man understood that this was a spirit coming to help the people and took word back to camp. The next morning she arrived with her bundle and placed it before the chief in the council lodge. It held the first pipe, sent to the Sioux by the spirits as a means of prayer. The bringing of the pipe established kinship between the buffalo and the people; when it was smoked, the spirits would hear the prayer and send buffalo. She taught the people the fundamentals of their way of life, including the sacred rituals. Then she left, in most versions of the story transforming into a white buffalo cow before disappearing over the horizon. She is therefore known as the White Buffalo Cow Woman and the pipe she brought is the Buffalo Calf Pipe. Before that time, "the people ran around the prairies like so many wild animals" (Left Heron in DeMallie 1994:127). The pipe itself, cared for generation after generation by a keeper in the Sans Arc tribe (fig. 4), is the tangible symbol of the

top left, Newberry Lib., Chicago: E.E. Ayer Coll., AP2956; top right, Denver Public Lib., Western Hist. Dept., Colo.: B741; State Histl. Soc. of N. Dak., Bismarck, center: Fiske 189; bottom left, Fiske 584; bottom right, Smithsonian, NAA: Ms. 39D1 (11001300).

Fig. 3. Treaties and reservations. top left, Old Man Afraid of His Horse, chief of the Oglala, smoking a long-stemmed catlinite pipe in a ceremonial manner, during the Ft. Laramie treaty negotiations. To his left may be Louis Richard, who spoke in the interests of the mixed bloods during the council (DeMallie 1981:47, 58). Photograph by Alexander Gardner, May 1868. top right, 1888 Sioux Commission council at Standing Rock Agency. The Great Sioux Reservation is shown on the map. In front of the map around the table are Rev. William Cleveland; Maj. James McLaughlin, agent at Standing Rock; and Judge John V. Wright, commissioner. Photograph by David F. Barry, Ft. Yates, Dak. Terr., July 1888. center, View of Ft. Yates, Standing Rock Res., N. Dak. Photograph by Frank B. Fiske, about 1905. bottom left, Indian dance in front of the store at Ft. Yates, N. Dak. Drummers are in the center. A man on horseback holds an American flag, suggesting this may be a July 4th celebration. Photograph by Frank B. Fiske, Standing Rock Res., N. Dak., about 1900–1910. bottom right, Page from an agency account book for 1873–1875 documenting the issue of agricultural equipment and livestock to Bone Necklace Son. An unknown artist added a drawing of 2 men dressed in finery, including cloth garments and a hairpipe breastplate, riding on a mule.

799

top, Amer. Mus. of Nat. Hist., New York: 326848; Smithsonian, NAA:center left, 55900-B; bottom left, 3711-a-I; center right, Denver Public Lib., Western Hist. Dept., Colo.: X-31666; bottom right. Denver Art Mus., Colo.: 1971.562.

Fig. 4. Ritual. top, *The Third Day of the Sun Dance*, by Short Bull, watercolor on canvas, 1912, 174 cm wide (Wildhage 1990; J.R. Walker 1980:183–191). center left, Martha Bad Warrior, Sans Arc Sioux, holding the sacred Buffalo Calf Pipe. Photograph by Wilbur A. Riegert, Cheyenne River Res., Green Grass, S. Dak., 1936. center right, Singeing a dog before making dog soup, a ritual food. Photographed 1902–1907. bottom left, Sweatlodge used for purification during the Ghost Dance. Next to it is a sacrificial pole hung with cloths and bundles of tobacco (Mooney 1896:822–823). Unidentified Indian policeman is on the far right. Photograph by James Mooney, Pine Ridge Res., S. Dak., 1892. bottom right, Ghost Dance dress painted with a bird flanked by 4 stylized dragonflies, all invoking spiritual protection. Sioux Ghost Dance clothing was usually made of muslin with red-painted cloth fringes along the seams. Length 124 cm.

unity of the Sioux as a people (Finger and Tyon in J.R. Walker 1980:109–112, 148–150; Black Elk in DeMallie 1984:283–285).

Each of the Teton tribes comprised a series of *tʰiyóšpaye* 'lodge groups', each identified by a name, which varied from an extended family to a group of extended families. The *tʰiyóšpaye* are designated "bands" or "subbands" in English. The number of bands in each tribe was commonly said to be seven, reflecting a Sioux predilection for using the number seven as an organizing device. The actual number of named bands varied through time and from tribe to tribe ("Sioux Until 1850," table 5 this vol.).

The band was a group, probably averaging 10–20 nuclear families (50–100 people), who were related to one another. Frequently the core of a band was a group of 'brothers' (in the Sioux classification, that is, biological and adopted brothers and parallel cousins) with their wives and children; such a kin group was the minimal form of *tʰiyóšpaye*, and ordinarily such a group stayed together throughout the year. Sometimes two or more small lodge groups joined together in the spring, after having been separated for the winter. The usual identification of the combined group would be the name of the largest or leading *tʰiyóšpaye*. This practice may have been motivated by the fact that a band's prestige was in part determined by its size. Some bands were very large, a reflection on a leader whose success attracted individual families or small lodge groups to join his band.

Membership in a *tʰiyóšpaye* was a matter of choice, not descent. Individuals were considered to belong to the lodge group in which they were born, but they were free to leave and join another lodge group at any time. Women, for example, usually married outside the lodge group into which they were born. Membership was usually based on residence, but individuals might consider themselves to be members of more than one lodge group (J.R. Walker 1914:97–98; Mirsky 1937:390; E.C. Deloria 1995:chap. 2; DeMallie 1971:110–118).

Camps were called *wičʰótʰi* 'place where humans dwell'. A camp represented one or more lodge groups, not necessarily of the same Teton tribe, who customarily lived together. The camp included other residents as well: temporary visitors from other bands or other Sioux tribes, perhaps relatives of women married into one of the *tʰiyóšpaye*, or travelers (*íčʰimani*) seeking temporary refuge. Formal camps were always circular; informal camps were linear, the tepees strung out along a stream bank. Formal camps were used most frequently in the summer and were usually larger in size than winter camps, which were generally informal and of smaller size, located along river or creek bottoms where there was wood, protection from wind and drifting snow, and the possibility of finding game.

The camp circle (*hóčʰoka* 'circular enclosure') was arranged so that the lodges of each *tʰiyóšpaye* were contiguous along a portion of the circle. An opening (*tʰiyópa*) left at the east served as the formal entryway to the camp. The tepee doorways faced the center of the circle,

except for those at either side of the entryway (*húkpa*), which faced east. The lodge of the leading chief was located on the west, at the place of honor, directly opposite the entryway. A large lodge, sometimes made up of two lodge covers over two sets of poles adjoining one another, was erected in the center and served as the council lodge (*tʰípi íyokʰiheya* 'tepees joined together' or *tʰiyótʰipi* 'lodge of lodges', called "soldiers' lodge" in English). There a council fire burned, symbolizing the autonomy of the camp. Elsewhere on the enclosed area of the camp circle, men's societies erected tepees for their ceremonies and public dances. Temporary brush shelters in which young men stayed, sweatlodges, and menstrual lodges were placed outside the circle. A tepee on the prairie some distance away from a camp circle would belong to someone in disgrace, such as a murderer (J.R. Walker 1917:73–74; Mirsky 1937:391–393; E.C. Deloria 1995:chap. 1 and 3; DeMallie 1971:121–122).

Each tepee housed a man with his wife and children and sometimes a widowed grandmother or grandfather. If a man were married to two or more sisters, they lived together in one large lodge. If the women were not sisters, sometimes one would set up a separate tepee, outside the camp circle, behind the first wife's lodge.

The tepee was a microcosm of the camp circle. Across from the doorway was the place of honor (*čʰatkú*), where the husband sat. In front of him might be an altar cut into the earth; his sacred bundles and war equipment were hung from the tepee poles behind him. In the center was a circular fireplace, paralleling the fireplace in the council lodge. Each individual had a specific place in the lodge, defined and separated from one another by willow-rod backrests hung from tripods. The lodge was laterally divided; from the husband's point of view at the back, the right side of the lodge was the male side and the left the female side (E.C. Deloria 1995:chap. 4).

Political Organization

Each band had a leader (*itáčʰą*), usually called "chief" in English, who spoke for his people. The council, comprised of respected adult men, represented the people of the camp. As men came of age and achieved status in the community they were invited to sit in the council. Their discussions concerned everything related to the common welfare: camp moves, relations with other camps and with Whites, and when and where hunting parties should be sent. They also approved war parties before they set out and arbitrated disputes between camp members. All decisions had to be by consensus. The chief articulated the will of the council, which the crier announced publicly. Camp police, called *akíčʰita*, and referred to as "soldiers" or "marshals" in English, were appointed to carry out the chief's directives.

The chief held his position by common consent. The cultural ideal of a chief was a man who always put the welfare of the people ahead of his own, was generous, 801 spoke and did no evil, and was self-controlled. A long-stemmed pipe was the symbol of chieftainship. In the case of a dispute between members of his camp, a chief was enjoined to thrust his pipe between them and persuade them to smoke amicably with one another, giving them presents to smooth over their differences (J.R. Walker 1917:74–75; 1980:22–23, 29–30; DeMallie 1971:125–128).

The chief appointed the *akíčʰita*, in consultation with the council, to oversee specific tasks, most importantly during the large summer gatherings and the communal buffalo hunts. The council might appoint four head police (*akíčʰita itáčʰa* 'police leaders'), who were painted with four black stripes down the right side of the face, from eyebrow to mouth, to identify their office. They in turn appointed other *akíčʰita*, sometimes choosing a particular men's society. These men wore a single stripe of black paint. The *akíčʰita* were enforcers; they carried whips of ash wood, tough but bending. They were said to receive their power from the Thunderbeings, and, like them, their punishment was swift and severe. For example, if a man went to war or to hunt at a time when the council had forbidden it for possible danger to the camp, the *akíčʰita* would whip the offender and destroy some of his property, slashing his wife's tepee cover, breaking the tepee poles, or killing his horses or dogs. Such punishment was called *akíčʰita ktépi* 'soldier killing' and no one, not even a chief, was immune from it. If an offender resisted, he might even be killed. The council was the final resort: if they found that an *akíčʰita* had punished someone unjustly, he received the same punishment in return, administered twice as severely by his fellow *akíčʰita*.

There was a generational difference between the older men of the council and the younger men who were appointed *akíčʰita*. From time to time the *akíčʰita* might go against the wishes of the council. The tension between them apparently resolved itself over time as men reached the age—probably about 40—when they were incorporated into the council, a shift in an individual's life from the status of warrior to that of councilor (J.R. Walker 1917:76–77, 1980:25–34; E.C. Deloria 1995:chap. 2; DeMallie 1971:128–131).

The council appointed officials who mediated between the chief, the police, and the people. Called *wakíčʰuza* 'deciders' and referred to as "magistrates" in the anthropological literature and "subchiefs" in the historical literature, they were older men whose primary task was to guide camp movements. While the camp was moving the *wakíčʰuza* had complete control. They appointed their own *akíčʰita* or used those already appointed; they decided the route, how long to travel each day, and divided each day's journey into four equal parts, with a stop at the end of each during which tobacco was smoked as an offering to the spirits. Scouts were sent far ahead and along the sides of the moving column for protection from enemy attack. When the camp was settled again, the *wakíčʰuza* watched over the food supply, directing hunting and the sharing of meat and hides. Acting as a representative of the council, they also arbitrated disputes. The *wakíčʰuza* were heads of prominent extended families in the camp. They were considered *huká* to the people, a term that relates to a ceremony of ritual adoption and implies an intensification of kin relationship between the *wakíčʰuza* and the people of the camp. The Oglala were said to have appointed four *wakíčʰuza* (Wissler 1912a:11; J.R. Walker 1917:75; E.C. Deloria 1995:chap. 1; DeMallie 1971:131–132).

During most of the year the *tʰiyóšpaye*-based camps traveled independently, but they joined in tribal camps during the summer for the Sun Dance and communal buffalo hunts. At this time the tribes functioned as political units; sometimes more than one tribe came together. On such occasions each camped in a great circle, symbolizing tribal unity. The most famous of such camps was that at the Little Bighorn in 1876, which consisted of four Sioux and one Cheyenne-Arapaho camp circles adjoining one another along the river (Vestal 1957:map facing p. 171).

The tribal camp replicated the form of smaller camps, with each band having its defined place in the camp circle. The council lodge in the center of camp accommodated the councilors from each of the bands. The oldest, most prestigious of the band chiefs oversaw the council. The tribal council appointed yet another type of leader, the *wičʰáša yatápika* 'praiseworthy men', called "shirt wearers" in English. They were active, younger men, who had achieved exceptional success in warfare and proved their concern for the people by conspicuous acts of generosity. As symbols of their office they were given hair-decorated shirts (fig. 5), spoken of as "owned by the tribe," and pipes. Their lives were supposed to be models for the rest of society; if they showed anger or let their emotions overcome their dedication to the people, they were deposed, as in the celebrated case of Crazy Horse, who took a fellow tribesman's wife and was shot and wounded by him in return (He Dog in Hinman 1976:13, 16–18). The number of shirt wearers doubtless varied from tribe to tribe; the Oglala, for example, were said to have had four, the Minneconjou seven. These men had no more authority than other leaders, but because of their popularity and their influence with the *akíčʰita* and men's societies, they in fact exercised a considerable amount of power. At the same time, they were under constant scrutiny and held to nearly impossibly high standards of conduct.

The political organization of the Teton reflected a complex interplay of kin relationships and individual leaders' personal qualities. There was no simple hierarchy of leadership. The basic term, *itáčʰa*, designated a leadership role in any context. The term *načá* (probably borrowed from Arapaho *né·če·* 'chief') seems to have designated a leader in the context of the tribal council. Together with the *wakíčʰuza* and the *wičʰáša yatápika*, all could be designated *wičʰáša itáčʰa* 'leader men', whose power and authority rested less on their position in the political system than on their personal abilities and ambition (Black Elk in DeMallie 1984:321–322; Vestal 1934a:231–232; DeMallie 1971:132–136).

802

Fig. 5. Buckskin shirt of the type used by "shirt wearers" as badges of office. The upper portion is painted dark blue, the lower, yellow. The shirt lacks the usual strips of quillwork or beadwork but is decorated with locks of human hair and eagle feathers; a scalp in a hoop is at the front. Length at center 55 cm; collection information is unknown (Conn 1982:146).

Men's societies ($ok^hólakič^hiye$) played an important role in political organization. The societies were primarily social and fraternal organizations. Membership was by invitation and was based on success in war and on generosity. After the return of a successful war party those men who had been conspicuously brave would be invited to join various societies. They were not age-graded, but some were called on to perform $akíč^hita$ duty and so primarily attracted younger men. Others consisted of more experienced warriors and leading men and focused on the discussion of public matters rather than on rituals and dancing. Societies competed with one another for members, and some men belonged to more than one society at the same time, sometimes in different Sioux tribes (Wissler 1912a:65–67; Vestal 1934a:26, 106).

The societies provided a forum for discussion of brave deeds, for dances and feasts, and for the planning of war expeditions. They conceptualized their duty as protecting the camp and helping the elderly and those in need. Societies were organized at the band level. Most were common to all the Teton tribes but some seem to have been local organizations. The societies were most active during the summer when large camp circles formed. At such times men of a particular society in various bands might erect a tepee within the camp circle to hold their ceremonies and public dances and to initiate new members. The Chiefs' society mentioned in several sources may have constituted the tribal council. The White Owners society was said to have been organized by Red Cloud among the Oglala in opposition to the tribal council. Similarly, the White Horse Owners society organized by Sitting Bull among the Hunkpapa had an overtly political purpose (Wissler 1912a:41; Vestal 1934:183–184, 1934a:26n; DeMallie 1971:143–144, 149–150).

The Oglala societies are the best documented (table 1). According to Thunder Bear, the men's societies originated when a war party had an encounter with a spirit being who appeared alternately in the form of a man and a wolf and gave them the regalia and instructions out of which the four original societies were created: Fox, Hard Hearts, Crow Owners, and Mandans (Wissler 1912a:71–73). The other societies were created later, as the result of visions. Most societies had distinctive regalia as well as other ritual objects that were used in ceremonies or were carried to war. Those included distinctive headdresses, pipes, rattles, whips, swords, and sashes. Some societies had decorated lances that were given to the bravest members before going to war. Lance bearers were expected to be at the head of the war party when attacking the enemy and not to turn back, no matter the odds. In the midst of battle they were expected to thrust their lance into the ground through a slit in the long sash that they wore over the shoulder, pinning themselves in position to fight to the death or until freed by another society member. Societies did not organize exclusive war parties, but they did compete with one another for the record of their members' brave deeds in war. In camp, rivalry between societies was expressed by wife stealing and competition in games.

Besides promoting fraternity among the members, celebrating the virtues of bravery and generosity, and performing $akíč^hita$ duty, men's societies had other important functions. By bringing together members from different bands into common activities during the summer encampments, they helped to integrate the bands of each tribe and countered forces that might have led bands to go their separate ways. To some extent, this was probably true across the Teton tribes as well. Bonds of kinship, not exclusively based on genealogical relationship, united fellow society members and contributed to a sense of tribal unity. Also, by enlisting some of the societies as $akíč^hita$, young men were diverted from their quest for personal prestige and coopted into working for the benefit of the camp (Wissler 1912a:7–75; J.R. Walker 1917:76–77, 1980:259–270, 1982:28–36; DeMallie 1971:141–150).

Subsistence

The Teton depended on hunting for subsistence. Buffalo was the primary game, and every part of the animal was used for some purpose. From October through February, when the hair was thickest, buffalo hides were tanned with the hair on and used for robes or traded to Whites. During the rest of the year the hair was removed and the hides were used as rawhide or tanned to be used as buckskin. The meat was cut into thin strips, sun dried, and packed in rawhide containers for future use. Elk, black-tailed deer, white-tailed deer, pronghorn, and big horn sheep were also hunted, both for food and for their skins. Pronghorn, for example, was valued for shirts and big horn sheep for sleeping robes. Grizzly bears were hunted primarily for their skins and *803*

Table 1. Oglala Men's Societies

Wissler 1912a	W.P. Clark 1885:356	Sword 1995
Soldier Societies[a]		
tʰokʰála 'kit fox'		*tʰokʰála* 'kit fox'
kʰaɣí yuhá 'crow owner'	Crow	*kʰaɣí yuhá* 'crow owner'
čʰaté ḱíza 'brave heart'	Strong Heart	*čʰaté ḱíza* 'brave heart'
ikʰú sápa 'black chin'[b]		
napʰéšni 'does not flee'[b]		
Big Braves[b]	Tall Brave	
	Night Brave	
ixóka 'badger mouth'	Badger-mouth Prairie-Dog	*ixóka* 'badger mouth'
sotká yuhá '*sotká* owners'[c]		*sotká*
wíčiska 'white pack strap'[d]	White Breast Strap	*wíčiska* 'white pack strap'
Headmen's Societies		
tʰatʰáka wapʰáha ú 'buffalo-bull		
headdress wearer'; also called		
háskaska 'tall ones'; *wičʰaša*		
yatápika 'praiseworthy men';		
Big Bellies; and *načá* 'chiefs'		*načá* 'chief'
ská yuhá 'white [horse] owners'		
miwátani 'Mandan'; also called		*íyuptala*[h]
hihá šú wapʰáha 'owl feather headdress'[e]	Night-Owl Headdress	
omáha kaʔíyotag[f] 'Omaha sitting'		*pʰéží mignáka* 'grass worn under belt'[i]
War Societies		
Dog/Wolves		
blotáhuka[g] 'war leaders'		
sotká tʰáka 'big *sotká*'		
zuyá 'war'	Warrior	
Other Societies		
áʔinila wótapi 'silent eaters'		*áʔinila* 'silent ones'
		áʔinila kʰoškálaka 'young men silent ones'
	Prairie-Dog	
	Shield	
	Orphan	
		tʰačʰóla wačʰípi 'naked dance'[j]

[a]Wissler (1912a) is the fullest study of Oglala men's societies. His classification of societies is based on material recorded at Pine Ridge. All Sioux words are retranscribed by DeMallie.

  [b]Societies reported as subsidiary to the Brave Heart Society.

  [c]Wissler translates *sotká* 'bare', meaning undecorated; Buechel (1970:458) defines it "As one tall thin tree standing among smaller ones," apparently a reference to the lances carried into battle.

  [d]Wissler translates as 'white marked' and characterizes it as a branch of the *sotká yuhá* society.

  [e]Said to be the former name of the *miwátani* society (Curtis 1907–1930, 3:139).

  [f]A reference to a ceremony of the Omaha society (Dorsey 1894:463–464).

  [g]Rather than an organized society, the term denotes men chosen to be leaders of a war party.

  [h]Reported as another name for the *miwátani* society.

  [i]Grass Dance was another name for the Omaha society (Dorsey 1894:463).

  [j]The society was named after its characteristic dance.

claws. Smaller animals, including wolves, red fox, kit fox, mountain lions, beaver, otter, muskrats, badgers, skunk, rabbit, and hares, were hunted for fur or for food. Porcupines were eaten, their quills were dyed to use for embroidery, and their tails served as hairbrushes. Domestic dog was eaten ritually (fig. 4).

The Teton diet included vegetables and fruit. In the spring, prairie turnips were gathered, peeled, braided by the tap roots, and preserved by drying. They were later soaked in water, sliced, and added to soup. Wild artichokes were eaten and the stores of ground beans (*Falcata comosa*) gathered by field mice were raided and highly prized. Corn, as well as squash and melons, was obtained in trade with the Arikara. In the summer and fall, fruits including wild plums, chokecherries, and buffalo berries, were gathered in quantity and dried. Chokecherries were pounded with their pits, formed into small round cakes, and dried in the sun. The fur trader Edwin Denig reported that "immense quantities of cherries and berries" were eaten fresh. Pemmican, called *wasná*, was a great delicacy, made by mixing grease with pounded dried meat and pounded dried cherries, and adding sugar when available. In winter, during times of necessity, wild rose hips and red haws (*Crataegus chrysocarpa*) were also eaten (Denig 1961:12–13; G.K. Warren 1856:78–79; Ewers 1937:14–19; Hassrick 1964:164–180).

Hunting was an important focus of men's lives. They brought game back to camp where women processed and cooked it. Although individuals stalked game throughout the year, collaborative hunting provided potentially greater returns. On the White River, for example, the Brule hunted pronghorn by surrounding a herd and driving it through a gap in the hills and over a precipice, below which an enclosure of logs and brush had been built (Denig 1961:18).

The communal buffalo hunts (*wanásapi*), held in the late summer, were essential to the survival of the people during the coming winter. A shaman might seek a vision to foretell the success of the hunt, reporting the results to the council. Then the council would notify the men's societies to select scouts to locate the herds. Scouting was a serious responsibility, and the returned scouts reported their findings with much ritual and metaphorical language. When buffalo had been located, the *wakíčʰuza* directed the camp's movement toward the herd. The crier would announce the upcoming hunt and repeat the council's injunction that no one was to leave the camp for war or hunting, for fear of scaring away the herd. The council appointed *akíčʰita* leaders, who in turn selected other *akíčʰita* to police the hunt. They were responsible for keeping the moving camp as compact as possible.

When the camp was close to the herd, the men left at daybreak under the supervision of the hunt police. They approached from the downwind side, then separated into two parties to surround the herd. As the police gave the signal, the hunters charged the herd simultaneously, trying to keep it milling as long as possible to maximize the kill. After the hunt the animals were butchered, some women, children, and old men coming from the camp to help. Two horses were required to transport the meat from one buffalo. A man identified the animals he killed by the marks on his arrows, but anyone who helped in the butchering received a share of the meat. Sometimes the council appointed *akíčʰita* to hunt for widows and old people who had no one else to provide them with meat.

After the meat was dried and packed away the camp moved again, staying together until sufficient meat had been amassed to last the winter. After this, individuals were free to hunt by themselves and to organize war parties. Soon the bands or lodge groups separated, announcing their plans for the winter and setting a location to come together during the next spring (Densmore 1918:436–444; J.R. Walker 1982:74–94; DeMallie 1971:139–141).

Warfare

Warfare with enemy tribes was an integral part of Teton life. Success in war was, for a man, the essential foundation for achieving status in society, a status that was shared by his female relatives. Fighting the enemy was the most honorable duty in a man's life (Sword 1998:text 13). Warfare was not a temporary interruption of the normal state of affairs but was a permanent relationship between the Sioux and their enemies. George Sword, writing about 1909, incorporated the moral justification for warfare into the most sacred story of the Teton, the gift of the sacred pipe to the Sioux by White Buffalo Cow Woman. According to Sword, she instructed the Sioux that they should fight their enemies and that anything done in war was to be considered a good deed (Sword 1998:text 5).

War honors, called "coups" in English, represented a highly differentiated system of manifestations of bravery. The Lakota word *kté* 'to kill' was used metaphorically to mean "count coup on the enemy," and in its primary sense referred to touching the body of a fallen enemy; the first four individuals to do so counted first, second, third, and fourth "kills." Warriors also accrued honor from scalping the enemy dead; Sword noted that any number of men could scalp a single enemy until the hair was entirely gone. In addition, he listed as the highest war honors four ways of killing the enemy in face-to-face combat, graded from one to four (thus killing an enemy in hand-to-hand combat was more highly honored than killing an enemy by shooting from a distance); next most honorable was to be wounded in battle, which Sword also divided into four grades (thus it was more honorable to be wounded in the midst of battle than at a distance); these were followed by: wounding an enemy and bringing him down; having a horse shot out from under you in battle; rescuing the body of a fallen comrade; charging the enemy while being pursued to save a comrade from harm; and serving as scout against the enemy camp. Other honors accrued to those who captured the enemy's horses: highest honor went to those who took horses from a party of the enemy under fire; second honor went to those who took horses staked out in the enemy camp under cover of darkness. Stealing the enemy's property or capturing an enemy's pipe was honorable, and taking enemy children captive was a lesser honor (Sword 1998:text 3).

Understanding the system of war honors explicates the Sioux concept of warfare. Honorable actions in war spotlighted the individual, and battlefield tactics were primarily displays of individual bravery. Only the tactic of using decoys to lure the enemy into ambush—practiced in the eighteenth century against the Village tribes of the Missouri River and used to good advantage against the army at Fort Philip Kearny in 1866—represented a kind of battlefield strategy (Truteau in Parks 1993; Utley 1973:104–106; DeMallie 1999).

The war party (*ozúye*) provided the organization for warfare. A war party was initiated by the man who proposed to lead it. He invited one or more friends to his tepee and declared his purpose. Then the planned expedition was presented to the council for approval. After it was approved, anyone could join. War parties were usually no smaller than 8 or 10, and the ideal number was between 30 and 60; on special occasions much larger parties were formed.

The war party was surrounded with ritual. First the leader took a pipe to a shaman, who consecrated it, ritually filling it and sealing it with buffalo fat. If the party was successful, it was smoked when they returned. The pipe stem, wrapped in a wolfskin, was carried on the expedition by the leader. Sword (1998:text 4) described a ritual feast before the party set off in which food was served in a large bowl. Two spoons were placed in the bowl and as it went around the tepee men ate from it two by two. This bound each pair of men as special comrades (*kʰolá*) for the expedition, each being responsible for the welfare of the other. To return alive and abandon one's partner to the enemy was a disgrace. Singing and dancing followed.

The war party left in the morning, sometimes publicly parading around the camp circle. Sometimes a shaman accompanied the party. Sword (1998:text 4) described a practice in which the warriors offered a pipe to a holy man, asking him to perform a ceremony for the success of the party. Wearing a black veil, the shaman 'sang to the fire' and foretold the outcome of their expedition. The holy man related what he had seen in his vision, and the party planned accordingly, abandoning it if the outcome seemed to foretell disaster. A more common ritual of divination was performed by killing and gutting a badger, and allowing the blood to coagulate in the body cavity. Each man then peered into the mirror-like surface to divine the future; if he saw himself with white hair, he knew he would survive and be successful on the expedition. If his face appeared bloody and distorted he would be killed; in this case he would not lose face if he left the party and returned home (Vestal 1934:141–142).

The party was highly structured. The leader (*blotáhųka itáčʰą*) of a larger party would appoint as many as eight experienced warriors as war leaders (*blotáhųka*). They appointed two soldier leaders (*akíčʰita itáčʰą*) who in turn appointed other soldiers. Their job was to keep the war party together and to serve as scouts (*tʰųwéya*). Finally, two youths, on their first war party, were appointed as water carriers. They were given long forked lances from each of which was suspended a buffalo pericardium. When the party camped, their job was to fetch water from the nearby stream. This was a test of their bravery, requiring many trips in the dark, in unfamiliar territory, to provide enough water (Wissler 1912a:54–61; Hassrick 1964:72–94; DeMallie 1971:152–153).

If a war party was successful, the men returned home with blackened faces, symbolic of victory. They held aloft scalps stretched on willow hoops and other trophies, and the man who had first counted coup led a charge of the returning warriors on the village, singing "I bring a human scalp!" The people rushed out and grabbed weapons, clothing, or ornaments from the successful warriors, which they were allowed to keep. Captured horses were distributed along kin lines. Captured women and children were adopted by families and considered to be tribal members once they learned to speak Lakota. Men gave the scalps to their sisters or other female relatives, who carried them in the victory dances (*iwákčipi*) that followed. A tepee for the celebration of the victory (*waktégli tʰiyótʰipi*) might be erected within the camp circle, where the warriors danced and sang, accompanied by young women as singers (Sword 1998:text 4; Densmore 1918:375–381; J.R. Walker 1982:54–55; DeMallie 1971:154–156).

Religion and Ceremony

For the Sioux, all forms of being were related; the universe was characterized by its unity. Both humans and the buffalo on which they lived were believed to have been created within mother earth before they emerged on the surface and populated the plains. For this reason, in ritual, humans were called *wičʰáša akátula* 'people on top'. Of all forms of life, humans were the least powerful, and so for the Sioux the important distinction was between that which was human and everything else. The universe was fundamentally incomprehensible; it could not be fully known or controlled, but humans venerated it and dared to manipulate it to the best of their limited capacity. This incomprehensible power was called wakan (*wakʰą* 'holy') (Dorsey 1894:365, 433–434).

Wakan was "anything that was hard to understand" (Good Seat in J.R. Walker 1980:70). It was the animating force of the universe and the common denominator of its oneness. The totality of this power was called Wakan Tanka (*wakʰą tʰąka* 'big holy'). "The *Wakan Tanka* are those which made everything. . . . *Wakan Tanka* are many, but they are all the same as one" (Little Wound in J.R. Walker 1980:69–70). Like Taku Wakan (*táku wakʰą* 'holy things'), said to refer to the visible manifestations of wakan, Wakan Tanka was defined by its incomprehensibility (J.R. Walker 1917:152–156; Densmore 1918:85; DeMallie 1987:27–28).

Shamans (*wičʰáša wakʰą* 'holy man') were those who specialized in the wakan. Perhaps because it was forever beyond the grasp of humankind, the quest for understanding the wakan was the driving force of Sioux culture. Through personal experiences, shamans came to some understanding of Wakan Tanka and learned how to manipulate their power. Some shamans classified Wakan Tanka as *tobtób kį* 'the four times four', which included *tákuškąšką* 'energy', sun, moon, wind, Four Winds, whirlwind, Thunderbeings (*wakíyą*), rock, earth, White Buffalo Cow Woman (*wóxpe*), buffalo bull, two-leggeds, and a number of invisible spirit beings. All these powers could be enlisted in the aid of human beings. Outside of Wakan Tanka were other wakan beings that were evilly disposed toward humans (J.R. Walker 1917:79–92, 1980:94, 98–99). In stories all the wakan beings were personified with human characteristics (J.R. Walker 1917:164–182, 1983).

Humans could relate to Wakan Tanka through prayer (*wačʰékiye*), a word that meant both 'to call on someone for aid' and 'to address someone using a kin term'. Thus the act of prayer was an invocation of relationship, begging the spirit beings—often with cries and tears—to live up to the kindness and generosity expected of a good relative. Sacrifice, of objects or of physical suffering, frequently accompanied prayer (Dorsey 1894:435–436; E.C. Deloria 1944:28–29; DeMallie 1987:30–31).

The pipe (*čʰąnúpa*) was the preeminent means of prayer, the direct link between Wakan Tanka and the people. White Buffalo Cow Woman herself was said to be present in the smoke as it rose upward, carrying the people's prayers. The pipe was usually filled with native or trade tobacco, mixed with the inner bark of red willow. As the pipe was filled, pinches of the smoking mixture were offered to each of the four directions, and to the above and below, thereby symbolically encompassing the whole of the universe in the bowl. Prayers and songs might accompany the ritual filling of the pipe. Offering the pipe, a ritual in itself, was also the prelude and an integral part of all other rituals. Ordinarily, only men smoked the pipe in ritual (J.R. Walker 1980:82–83, 87–90, 148–150).

The ceremonies of Teton religion were based on the teachings of the White Buffalo Cow Woman as well as on visions received by religious leaders. Each consisted of sacred actions, songs, and words (J.R. Walker 1980:136). The most basic of these ceremonies is the sweatlodge (*iníkaɣapi*, freely translated as "life renewal"). A low, dome-shaped lodge was constructed of willows and covered with hides (fig. 4). Nearby a firepit was dug to heat rocks, which were ritually transported to a pit excavated in the center of the lodge. Participants sat around the periphery. The door was closed, and incense was sprinkled on the rocks, followed by douses of cold water. Steam rose up thickly; the shaman sang and prayed aloud, and participants also prayed aloud in turn. The ritual strengthened an individual's life force (*ní*) and purified the body (Sword in J.R. Walker 1980:100). Purification in the sweatlodge was the prelude and conclusion to all other ceremonies (J.R. Walker 1917:67–68, 156, 1980:83–84, 100; J.E. Brown 1953:31–43; Bucko 1998:24–58).

The ceremony of vision seeking (*hąbléčʰeyapi* 'dream cry') was essential for a man who wished success in any endeavor. Shortly after puberty, young men sought a vision, the ceremony marking their change in life status. After a sweatbath, the vision seeker went to a hilltop where he would fast as long as four days. He made himself pitiable before the wakan beings: his hair was unbraided, he was dressed only in a breechcloth and a buffalo robe, and he

cried for the vision, tears streaming down his face. Spirits might come to him in human or animal form, offering him powers for war and for curing. Afterward, the vision seeker returned to camp and performed another sweatbath ceremony, in the course of which he usually revealed his vision to the shaman who had prepared him and now helped him to understand what he had experienced. Some, like the famous Oglala, Black Elk, had visions of the Thunderbeings, after which they were required to perform the *heyókʰa* ceremony, in which they acted and talked backwards, clowning to the delight of onlookers, and ritually cooking a dog, plucking the meat from the boiling kettle with their bare hands (DeMallie 1984:111–142, 227–235). The punishment for failing to perform this ceremony was to be struck by lightning. The vision gave the seeker sacred knowledge, vesting him with wakan that set him apart from others. The power originated with the vision but must be activated by the visionary following its commands, and the meaning of the vision was developed over time through contemplation (J.R. Walker 1917:68–69, 1980:83–86, 132–135, 150–153; Densmore 1918:157–194; Curtis 1907–1930, 3:65–70; J.E. Brown 1953:44–666; DeMallie 1987:34–42).

The Sun Dance (*wiwáyąg wačʰípi* 'sun-gazing dance') was the most important public religious ceremony. Held each summer when the bands came together, it celebrated tribal unity and was a prayer for increase of the people and of the buffalo. It provided a public forum during which many lesser ceremonies, involving family groups or religious societies, were performed (Dorsey 1894:450–467; Sword in E.C. Deloria 1929; J.R. Walker 1917:94–121, 1980:176–180, 1982:96–99; E.C. Deloria 1944:55–57; Curtis 1907–1930, 3:87–99; J.E. Brown 1953:67–100).

The Hunka (*huŋká*) was a ceremony of adoption. Wands (probably pipe stems in an earlier period) decorated with fans of eagle feathers were danced and swung over the heads of participants who became ritually related to one another as hunka. Originally an intertribal adoption ceremony, the Hunka was also used among the Sioux bands as a way of forging relationships; one man honored another by adopting his child, and thereafter all the relatives of the participants were considered to be related to one another. The participants in the Hunka had a red stripe painted down the right side of the face, which they might wear on future ritual occasions as a symbol of being hunka (J.R. Walker 1917:122–140, 1980:208–240; Densmore 1918:68–77; Curtis 1907–1930, 3:71–87; J.E. Brown 1953:101–115).

The Buffalo Sing (*tʰatʰą́ka lowápi*) was the girl's puberty ceremony, performed by a buffalo shaman. In it, the girl was taught the virtues of womanhood, including modesty and generosity. Her hair was braided like an adult woman's, the part painted with vermilion, and an eagle plume was attached; thereafter she had the right to wear it as a symbol of having been honored in the ceremony (J.R. Walker 1917:141–151, 1980:241–253; J.E. Brown 1953:116–126).

The Spirit-Keeping ceremony was performed as a means of delaying the departure of the spirit of a deceased relative, *807* particularly a child. A shaman attached a lock of the deceased's hair to a painted wooden post, dressed in appropriate clothing, wrapped in a bundle, and treated as though it were alive. The individual who vowed to keep the spirit fed and ritually cared for it daily. After a year had passed, a great giveaway was held to honor the deceased and the shaman unwrapped the bundle, setting the spirit free (Fletcher 1884:296–307; Densmore 1918:77–84; Curtis 1907–1930, 3:99–110; J.E. Brown 1953:10–30).

Throwing the Ball is a lesser-known ceremony that Black Elk considered the seventh major ceremony of the Sioux, the number seven likely reflecting the influence of Roman Catholicism. It apparently originated as a puberty ceremony in which a girl tossed a ball to the four directions; those catching it received blessings (J.E. Brown 1953:127–138; M.W. Beckwith 1930:414).

There were other ceremonies integral to Sioux religious life. Many of them related to the ritual enactment of visions, because vision powers were dormant until they were publicly performed. An individual who had a vision of a particular animal sought out someone known to have had a vision of the same animal for instruction and aid; the novice sponsored a ceremony in which other dreamers participated. In this way informal societies of buffalo, elk, black-tailed deer, white-tailed deer, and other animal visionaries were formed. Bear visionaries had special powers to heal those wounded in war; when an individual was healed by a bear visionary, he became a member of the Bear Society, which made it one of the largest and most important of the religious societies (Wissler 1912a:81–99; J.R. Walker 1980:153–168; Densmore 1918:285–305; DeMallie 1987:38–42).

Division of Labor

Culturally, the most important distinction in social life was gender. Male and female roles were defined by behavior. Men were warriors, hunters, and religious and ceremonial practitioners; women took charge of the tepees, cared for their children, processed meat and hides, and cooked the food. Women also filled minor roles in religious ceremonies and some were specialists in herbal medicines. Tension between male and female roles was expressed in sexual terms. Young men attempted to seduce young women, later humiliating them publicly when their seductions succeeded. After marriage, adultery might result in severe physical punishments.

In a ceremony known as the Virgins' Fire, young women attested to their virginity, swearing an oath by biting a knife, and young men did the same by biting an arrow. Any participant who was not a virgin risked public humiliation. A similar ceremony was performed by the Owns Alone, an informal society of women who had married only once and been faithful to their husbands (Wissler 1912a:76–77; Mirsky 1937:410–411).

Other women's societies existed, although they were apparently less formally organized than men's societies.

The Tanners and the Porcupine Quill Workers specialized in their respective skills; other societies, such as *kaȟéla* (later called Shield Bearers), Praiseworthy Women, and Prairie Chicken Dance, performed public dances and ceremonies (Wissler 1912a:75–76, 78).

Following a dream experience around the age of puberty, some males opted for female roles, dressed in women's clothing, and became wives to other men in polygynous unions. Called *wįkte*, they were renowned for the artistic quality of their quillwork and beadwork. Very occasionally a woman opted for male roles, but they had no accepted place in society and were said to have wandered off to live by themselves (DeMallie 1971:195–199, 1983:243–245; Mirsky 1937:417).

Kinship

Kinship (*wótakuye*) presented the most important obligations in social life: "one must obey kinship rules; one must be a good relative" (E.C. Deloria 1944:25). The kin terms were nonunilineal and followed the Dakota type (see "Kinship and Social Organization," this vol.). Potentially, the network of kinship was coextensive with Sioux society; everyone was a potential relative. Etiquette required that everyone be addressed by kin term, rather than by personal name. This might be accomplished by figuring out a genealogical connection between two individuals or by a spontaneous decision to take someone as a sibling, child, or other relative. Such relationships became real in practice; all the relatives of these two were subsequently related to one another just as though the adoptive relationship was a genealogical one. In this way Sioux kinship transcended biological relatedness and provided a mechanism for incorporating everyone, even real outsiders, into the network of relatives (E.C. Deloria 1995:chap. 11; DeMallie 1994:130–133).

Life Cycle

• BIRTH As soon as a baby was born he was washed by an old woman. Then a relative of the same sex as the child, a "good person" chosen for his or her outstanding character, breathed into the baby's mouth. This ritual was believed to have a formative influence on the child's character. The baby was given a name shortly after birth. The child was nursed for at least a year, ideally as long as three years. From the time a woman realized she was pregnant until the child was weaned, the couple were supposed to abstain from sexual intercourse.

While the child was still an infant a shaman was engaged to pierce his ears, and small rawhide thongs were inserted to keep the holes open for earrings. Ear piercing was a public ceremony that frequently took place during a Sun Dance and was essential for proper upbringing. Symbolically, it "opened" a child's ears, making him capable of understanding and establishing him as a member of society (E.C. Deloria 1995:chap. 12–13; DeMallie 1971:199).

• CHILDHOOD From the time they could understand, children were taught the kinship terms and the attitudes and behaviors they implied. Small children were enjoined to call others by kin terms. Children were not babied, nor were they spoken to in baby talk, but were treated respectfully, like adults. Children's games and play mimicked adult roles and prepared them with skills needed later in life (Dorsey 1891).

At the time of their first menstruation, girls were secluded in small huts placed outside the camp circle. A girl might have the Buffalo Sing performed for her, if her family could afford it. After puberty, a young woman was closely supervised by her female relatives, since virginity was highly valued. Instructed in domestic arts, she practiced by making moccasins and other gifts to honor her brother. During subsequent menstrual periods a woman returned to the seclusion of the menstrual lodge (E.C. Deloria 1995:chap. 14; DeMallie 1993:257–259).

Grandparents frequently cared for young children. They counseled the young (vol. 17:223) and provided indulgent support. The relationship of parents to children, particularly of the same sex, was somewhat more formal, requiring respect. A father was his sons' principal instructor; he taught them practical skills and exhorted them to be respectful and brave. Both parents inculcated the value of bravery, admonishing them that if they were killed in battle, their names would always be honored and remembered. A mother taught her daughters the virtues of generosity and productivity. Uncles (mothers' brothers) took a protective attitude toward their nephews. The relationship was marked by reserve and respect. Uncles gave gifts to their nephews and taught them skills for war and hunting. Aunts (fathers' sisters) showed respect for their brothers by presenting their newborn nephews and nieces with elaborately beaded or quilled cradles.

The relationship between brothers (including siblings and parallel cousins) was the strongest social bond in Sioux society. Brothers were supposed to deny nothing to one another. Older brothers had the duty of disciplining their younger brothers and putting them through rigorous physical training. They helped instill bravery in their younger brothers and taught them about sex. The relationship between sisters was somewhat less strong, and they could refuse one another without giving offense. The relationship between opposite-sex siblings and cousins (hakáta) was one of great respect and partial avoidance. Around the age of seven they stopping looking directly at one another and communicated only through a third person (Mirsky 1937:394–400; DeMallie 1971:182–187).

As children grew to adulthood they sometimes established a bond of friendship with a person of the same sex that was equivalent to, and even more binding than, that with a sibling. Two males called one another kʰolá 'friend', exchanging horses and other gifts and agreeing that each would look after the other in war or any other trouble they should meet. This relationship might be entered into while the two were still children. They exchanged possessions freely, and commonly exchanged wives as well. Betrayal by a friend was a theme in tales, underscoring the importance of the relationship. Similarly, two females might enter a friend relationship, calling one another mitʰáwaše (DeMallie 1971:193–194).

• MARRIAGE A long period of patient courtship (wiʔóyušpa 'to catch a woman') was supposed to precede marriage. Before marrying, a young man must have proved himself by going to war, ideally bringing back horses with which to initiate the elaborate gift exchange that validated a marriage. Young women, always virgins, who were married in this way were said to be "purchased," and this was the most honorable form of marriage, something for a woman to boast about her entire life. Marriage by common consent was the more usual form, both families approving the union. Elopement was also acceptable, but risky, since a woman might find herself abandoned, but assuming the couple returned, the marriage was validated by the exchange of gifts between the families. When a man married a woman by purchase he gained the right to marry her sisters as well. Polygynous marriages were common; cowives who were sisters lived together harmoniously and provided support to one another throughout their lives. Jealousy between cowives who were not sisters was a theme in Teton life (E.C. Deloria 1995:chap. 5; DeMallie 1971:189).

Marriage between related individuals was prohibited, and therefore most marriages took place outside the tʰiyóšpaye. There was no formal residence rule, but a woman usually went to live with her husband's family. A girl's brothers and cousins had the most say in approving a marriage. The relationship between opposite-sex siblings-in-law was a joking one, with sexual overtones, reflecting the practice of the levirate and sororate. There was tension between same-sex siblings-in-law; if they got along well they dropped the use of sibling-in-law terms and used instead special 'friend' terms (mašé, used by a man, and wašé, used by a woman).

A man and his mother-in-law and a woman and her father-in-law did not speak to each other and were prohibited from looking into one another's faces. A man's relationship with his father-in-law required only partial avoidance; a woman's relationship with her mother-in-law was one of respect, but they cooperated and talked freely with one another. A marriage also initiated a relationship between the couples' parents, who called one another 'co-parent-in-law' (omáwahitʰu). This was an open relationship that did not require conspicuous respect behavior (E.C. Deloria 1995:chap. 8; Mirsky 1937:400–403; DeMallie 1971:190–192).

Divorce was very common, particularly among younger men, who felt a tension between family life and going to war. At a men's society dance, for example, swept up in the excitement of the moment, a man might throw a stick into the air, declaring that it represented his wife and whoever caught it could have her. To go back on this promise brought ridicule. The tepee was owned by the woman and in the case of divorce, a man had only to remove his belongings to his mother's lodge (J.R. Walker 1980:41–44, 55–57; DeMallie 1971:201–203).

• DEATH   The corpse was dressed in finery and wrapped in a buffalo hide. Burial was usually above ground, in the limbs of an old cottonwood tree or on a specially constructed scaffold. A horse or dog might be killed at the burial site and food, weapons, and tools left there in the belief that the deceased's spirit took their spiritual essence with it as it traveled south along the Milky Way (wanáγi tʰačʰáku 'ghost's road') to the land of the dead. When the body had disintegrated, the bones were gathered and buried in the earth.

Relatives mourned the deceased and gave away their own possessions as well as those of the deceased. Close relatives mortified themselves in mourning. Women gashed their legs and walked around the camp circle streaming with blood, while men stabbed their legs in various places and rode around the camp circle on a horse covered with mud and shorn of mane and tail. Both men and women cut their hair, wore ragged clothing, and left their faces unpainted. Eventually others would decide that the mourning had gone on long enough; they would take the mourners to a dance where their faces were painted and they were dressed in good clothes, thereby ending the period of mourning (E.C. Deloria 1995:chap. 7; Brackett 1877:470; DeMallie 1971:203–204; J.R. Walker 1980:163–164).

Clothing

Throughout the nineteenth century men wore breechcloths of soft hide or cloth. Moccasins were two-piece, with rawhide soles, and decorated with quill or beadwork. Leggings were close fitting, made of hide, frequently antelope, reaching from the ankles to the belt. They were often ornamented with fringe and a long quilled or beaded strip. A robe made of a complete buffalo cow hide, dressed with the hair on, was an indispensable part of male attire. The inside might be painted in a sunburst design or with pictographic representations of the wearer's brave deeds. Poncho-type shirts were made of two whole mountain sheep or antelope hides, decorated down the sleeves and across the shoulders on the chest and back with strips of quill or beadwork and fringes of hide and hair. A triangular or rectangle flap decorated the collar at front and back. Earlier in the century the body of the shirt was painted with designs indicating war exploits; later, shirts were painted blue on the top half and yellow on the bottom. Shirts were only worn on special occasions and often symbolized leadership roles.

Men wore their hair as long as possible, braiding it on either side of the head. A scalplock, formed of a circular area around the crown of the head, braided separately, was distinctive of men's hairstyle. Ear ornaments of brass wire or dentalium shell were popular. Feathers and feather bonnets were worn, each signifying particular war honors. Strips attached to the scalplock and decorated with metal disks of graduated sizes were popular in the 1860s–1870s. Red face paint was worn on a daily basis, and more elaborate face and body paints were used on ritual occasions.

A woman's dress extended to below the knees and was sleeveless, made of two skins of antelope, deer, or elk. The bottom was fringed and the yoke had an attached cape. On dresses for special occasions the yoke was covered with dentalia or tubular glass beads, or was decorated with seed beads (fig. 6). A rawhide belt, frequently decorated with metal studs, had suspended from it a rawhide case containing a butcher knife, as well as an awl case and other small bags. Women's leggings reached only to the knee and were held in place by garters tied at the top of the calf. The hair was grown long, parted in the middle, and braided on either side of the head. On ritual occasions adult women painted the part with vermilion. Elaborate dentalium shell earrings were worn on special occasions, reaching as far as the waist. Moccasins and robes were like those of men, but robes were painted in distinctive geometric designs.

Throughout the nineteenth century, hide clothing was increasingly replaced by cloth clothing and buffalo robes by wool blankets. By 1900 men had adopted western-style pants, shirts, and jackets, and women were making flowing cloth dresses using printed fabrics (Bracket 1877:468–470; Ewers 1937:20–22; Hassrick 1964:192–196).

Tepees

Tepee poles, whenever possible, were made of lodgepole pine (*Pinus contorta*) obtained in the Black Hills. An average tepee required 19–21 poles, including two to control the wind flaps, which directed smoke out of the tepee and could be closed against the weather. The Sioux used a three-pole foundation over which a cover was spread usually made from 12–18 buffalo bull hides. The doorway was covered by a skin door formed on a U-shaped willow frame (fig. 7). Wooden pegs fastened the edge of the tepee to the ground. A tepee liner or dew curtain (*ozą́*), about three and one-half feet high, was tied around the lower portion of the poles to provide insulation. The liner was frequently decorated with beaded strips or painted with geometric designs or pictographic drawings of the man's war exploits. The fire in the center was used for cooking; meat was cooked in buffalo paunches using the stone-boiling method or in metal trade kettles. The tepee was furnished with willow beds and backrests (Bracket 1977:468; Ewers 1937:24–26; Hassrick 1964:182–185; E.C. Deloria 1995:chap. 4).

Horses and Transportation

Horses were frequently obtained by raiding other tribes, and the Teton also captured wild horses on the Plains near the Rocky Mountains, in the area of the Platte and

Smithsonian, Dept. of Anthr.: top left, 210,968 (neg. 80-3671); bottom right, T-10555 (neg. MNH1956); top right, Denver Mus. of Nat. Hist., Colo.: 82-005; bottom left, Ind. U., William Hammond Mathers Mus., Bloomington: W1176.

Fig. 6. Dress clothing. top left, Woman's dress, the yoke covered with light blue beads applied in lane stitch; length 147 cm. Sioux dresses were traditionally made of 2 deerskins, with the hind section folded over at the top to create a yoke. By the reservation period, when this dress was made, large enough skins were often not available and the yoke was made from a third skin, shaped to emulate the earlier form. top right, Woman doing beadwork. Photographed at Rosebud Res., S. Dak., about 1940s. bottom left, Woman pulling quills from a porcupine. Photograph by Joseph K. Dixon, 1908. bottom right, Old Man Afraid of His Horse's painted and beaded shirt; length 81.3 cm. Symbolic wounds, representing war honors, are painted in red on a dark blue background. This poncho-style shirt is made from two skins, the hind quarters forming the body of the shirt and the forequarters sewn on to form cape-like sleeves.

Arkansas rivers. The horse travois was used for moving camp. It consisted of tepee poles that crossed at the horse's withers; a netted hoop, fastened to the ends of the poles dragging behind the horse served as a platform for transporting goods and sometimes children, the aged, and the sick. For riding, men generally used pad saddles while women used frame saddles, with high pommel and cantle. Stirrups were made of bent wood, covered with rawhide ("Sioux Until 1850," fig. 4, this vol.). The saddle was held in place by a single cinch made of buffalo hide or woven hair. Saddle blankets were of buffalo hide; later in the nineteenth century an elaborately beaded style developed, used primarily by women for parades. Women used martingales and cruppers decorated with paint or bead-work. A braided hide cord looped around the horse's lower jaw was used in place of a bridle or halter. Rawhide quirts

with decorated wood or antler handles were also used. Ropes and lassos were of braided buffalo hair or braided rawhide (G.K. Warren 1856:17; Denig 1961:16; Ewers 1937:29–31).

For winter travel and hunting, wooden snowshoes with rawhide netting were used. During the summer, bull boats, made by stretching a buffalo hide over a bowl-shaped framework of willow, were constructed to cross deep rivers or were made by war parties for fast transportation downstream (Ewers 1937:31–32).

Weapons

The bow and arrow remained the primary weapon for hunting from horseback throughout the nineteenth century. Self (one-piece) bows were generally made of ash; they were

Fig. 7. Oglala village, North Fork of the Platte River, Neb. This is believed to be the earliest photograph of Sioux tepees. A quiver hangs over the doorway, and a webbed travois platform leans against the base of the tepee. The man is wrapped in a buffalo robe. Stereograph by Albert Bierstadt, 1859.

short (three and one-half feet), for use on horseback, and usually double-curved. Compound bows were made of mountain sheep or buffalo horn. Both kinds of bows were backed with sinew, for strength, and the strings were made of twisted sinew. Arrows were of ash or other hard wood, about 25 inches long, fletched with three eagle feathers and with a fishtail nock. Grooved lightning marks were generally incised along the shafts, and the arrows were painted distinctly so that the owner could recognize them. The points were attached with glue and sinew. Although bone and stone points were used aboriginally, in the nineteenth century they were manufactured from iron, using frying pans or hoop iron. Bows and arrows were carried in separate hide cases, attached to one another, frequently decorated with beadwork or fur, and slung over the left shoulder.

Shields were made of fire-hardened buffalo bull hide, about 17 inches in diameter, painted with sacred designs based on a man's vision, and decorated with feathers or other objects relating to the vision. When not in use the shield was protected by a cover of tanned hide (fig. 8).

Long lances were used for buffalo hunting or war, and specially feathered lances, some bow-shaped, were important regalia of men's societies.

One type of war club had a stone wrapped in rawhide attached by a short cord to a wooden handle; others had the stone attached directly to the handle. Gunstock-shaped clubs, fitted with metal knife blades, and trade pipe-tomahawks were carried on ritual occasions but were probably not practical for use in fighting.

Men carried knives in quilled or beaded cases suspended from the belt.

The Sioux had muzzle-loading guns throughout the century and began to acquire breech-loading rifles by 1867 ("Sioux Until 1850," fig. 2, this vol.) (Brackett 1877:468–469; Ewers 1937:33–36).

History, 1879–1891

Reservation Life, 1879–1888

Band by band, the Teton surrendered to the army and returned to the agencies. The Sioux were not welcome in Canada, and as buffalo became increasingly scarce they had no choice but to return to the United States. Many went to Camp Poplar River, the military post at Fort Peck Agency, or to General Miles's new post, Fort Keogh, on the Yellowstone River; in 1881 they were sent downriver to their agencies. That summer, with the buffalo herds completely gone from the Canadian plains, Sitting Bull and his band of 187 people surrendered at Fort Buford. They were sent to Fort Randall as prisoners of war before being returned to Standing Rock Agency in 1883 (Vestal 1957:214–238, 1934:238–297; DeMallie 1986:45–54; Utley 1993:211–247). A few Teton families stayed in Canada at Wood Mountain, Saskatchewan, where they were eventually granted a small reserve (J.H. Howard 1984:33–35; Laviolette 1991:264–268).

At the agencies the Sioux reunited social groups that had for two decades or longer been separated over the issue of how to deal with the Whites. The *tʰiyóšpaye* groups and the all-encompassing kinship system began to knit the agency populations back together, though deep rifts remained. Men's roles as warriors and hunters abruptly ceased, leaving religion and politics as the two specifically male domains of reservation life. The equivalent of prestige gained in war was now sought by enlisting as Indian scouts for the army or joining the Indian police force. Women's roles continued as before, focused on the daily needs of family life.

Large encampments formed around the agency headquarters, and food and annuity goods (vol. 4:57) were issued to the chiefs who in turn used the *akíčʰita* to distribute them to the members of their band. Agents fomented jealousy and competition among chiefs in order to reduce their influence. For example, in 1879 there were 11 chiefs at Pine Ridge, each the leader of a band; a year later there were 30 chiefs. Agent Valentine T. McGillycuddy introduced the slogan "every man his own chief," and soon bypassed the chiefs altogether, distributing goods directly to each household. His intention was to break up the bands, preparing for the allotment of land in severalty by encouraging families to disperse and settle along the creek beds, where they would have access to arable land for farming and to pasturage for cattle (DeMallie 1978a:253).

As dispersed communities formed in the 1880s, sub-agency headquarters were established to serve as issue stations so that the people would not have to journey to the

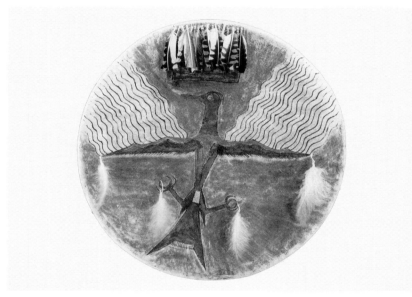

Fig. 8. Warriors and veterans. top, Presentation of a service flag at memorial ceremony for World War I veterans. Such flags originated in World War I and continued through World War II for use in the veterans' home town. They had a red border, white field, and blue stars representing members in service from that town; a gold star indicated that the member had died in service. Photograph by Joseph K. Dixon, Pine Ridge Res., S. Dak., July 4, 1920. bottom left, Buckskin shield cover stretched over a hoop, painted by Joseph No Two Horns, Hunkpapa Sioux, about 1890; diameter 45 cm. Warriors sought to acquire shield designs to offer them spiritual protection in war. After mounted warfare ended, designs were painted on light buckskin or muslin covers and carried in dances commemorating war honors. Such dance shields were often sold and at least 7 versions of this shield have been identified (Maurer 1992:113; Wooley and Horse Capture 1993:37–38). bottom right, Memorial for Ambrose White Lance, Brule, World War II or Korean War veteran. The quilts on display were part of the giveaway, which was followed by a feast. Photograph by Harvey Markowitz, Two Strike, Rosebud Res., S. Dak., 1982.

agency for rations (vol. 4:63). District or "boss" farmers served as role models and provided assistance in plowing, planting, and harvesting. Agency reports were filled with encouraging statistics concerning acres planted and the number of cattle owned; however, drought and insects frequently destroyed the crops, and with inadequate government rations and game virtually nonexistent, the Sioux were forced to slaughter and eat their cattle (vol. 4:262). Some men were able to earn money or rations by hauling freight or chopping wood.

Tepees soon gave way to log houses, though they proved to be less sanitary than tepees. Tuberculosis reached epidemic proportions. Traditional dress was replaced by "citizens' dress," clothing that was part of the treaty annuities. Mixed-blood families, a growing segment of reservation population, prospered better economically and in many communities rifts developed between mixed bloods and full bloods.

Indian police forces, reporting to the agent, were established at each agency (vol. 4:58). In 1883, agents were directed by the secretary of the interior to establish Courts of Indian Offenses and appoint judges to hear cases involving infractions of government policy. Many cases dealt with domestic matters, such as contracting a plural marriage or deserting a wife. Under government regulations, Sun Dances, healing ceremonies, and traditional dances were outlawed and punishable by fine or jail time (Prucha 1975:160–162). The Indian police and court system functioned much like the *akíčʰita* in prereservation times, and their success may be attributable to at least a nominal sharing of authority between the agent and the Indians themselves (DeMallie 1986:61). Occasionally, a chief managed to take control of the Indian police as though it were the *akíčʰita* in a traditional camp. When the police force was established at Pine Ridge in 1879, Young Man Afraid of His Horse selected the men who would become police and in the early years their loyalty was clearly to him, not the agent. In 1880, the Indian agent at Rosebud reported that Spotted Tail had taken control of the Indian police force and ordered them to picket the agency traders' stores. The incident also revealed publicly the conflict between Spotted Tail, as chief, and Thunder Hawk, one of the policemen who helped the agent regain control of the police (ARCIA 1880:47). The killing of Spotted Tail in 1881 by Crow Dog, captain of the Indian police, although triggered by a domestic dispute, suggests the depth of conflict between the old chiefs and those who built leadership positions in the context of reservation life (Hyde 1956:60–66, 1961:296–301).

In the 1880s, tribal councils were established at most of the agencies. At Pine Ridge, for example, younger Sioux leaders, acting on their own initiative, formed a council in 1884 and elected Young Man Afraid of His Horse as president (DeMallie 1978a:254). The primary purpose of these early councils was to seek payment from the government for loss of land and for horses and guns confiscated by the army.

Schools were built near the agencies, including government boarding schools and industrial farm schools, as well as Roman Catholic boarding schools (fig. 9). Churches were built, primarily Episcopal and Roman Catholic, which became the sites for marriages and funerals.

Some Sioux began to become familiar with the world beyond the reservation. Beginning in 1879, Sioux students were sent to Carlisle Indian School in Pennsylvania and to Hampton Institute in Virginia (vol. 4:292–293). There they

814

top, Smithsonian, NAA: 53,374; center, Marquette U. Arch., Bureau of Catholic Ind. Mission Records, Milwaukee, Wis: 0762; bottom, Nelson-Atkins Mus. of Art, Conception Abbey Coll., Kansas City, Mo.: 36-1987/31.

Fig. 9. School activities. top, Cutting ice, Lower Cut Meat Creek Indian Day School, Rosebud Agency, S. Dak. The school, founded in 1891, taught carpentry, blacksmithing, and farming. The students built a small dam for irrigating a garden in 1895. Dairy products were kept in a small ice house. Photograph by Jesse H. Bratley, 1898. center, Dining room at St. Francis Mission Boarding School, Rosebud Res., S. Dak. The school, run by the Roman Catholic church, opened in 1886. It was turned over by the Jesuits and Franciscan sisters to a Teton parent board in 1972. About 300 students attended during the 1908–1911 period; they were taught vocational skills as well as academics. Photographed 1908–1911. bottom, Indian School band from the Agricultural Boarding School, Ft. Yates, Standing Rock Res., N. Dak., established in 1879, the first boarding school on the reservation. Photograph by Fuller and S.T. Fansler, 1889–1900.

received basic educations, learned specific trades and domestic skills, and participated in White American life. When they returned to the reservation, many of their new skills were of no practical use, but their ability to speak and write English and their understanding of the United States government made them valuable to the chiefs, and in time, many of them assumed positions of leadership. Travel with Wild West shows (vol. 4:631), both throughout the eastern United States as well as abroad, likewise proved valuable in introducing the Sioux to the modern world (Prucha 1984, 2:687–715).

Breakup of the Great Sioux Reservation, 1888–1889

In 1888 the Great Sioux Reservation was, from the perspective of the United States, a great barrier to progress. The Northern Pacific Railroad was stalled at Bismarck, unable to build across reservation lands, and the rich farm and grazing land throughout the reservation had the potential to support homesteaders who would provide an economic boost to the region. Commissioners visited the Sioux to ask for the surrender of 9,000,000 acres, breaking up the reservation and establishing five smaller ones centered around the agencies of Standing Rock (vol. 4:664), Cheyenne River, Pine Ridge, Rosebud, and Lower Brule. Adhering to the terms of the Treaty of 1868, the commissioners sought to obtain the signatures of three-quarters of the adult male population, but the Sioux were not willing to part with the land, their only remaining asset, and the commissioners left without success.

The next year they tried again, applying more pressure. Headed by Gen. George Crook, a military officer whom the Sioux knew and respected from the war period of the 1870s, the commissioners feasted the Indians, cajoled them, and even threatened them. When they returned to Washington, the Agreement of 1889 had more than the required signatures. Although the commission's own record documents misrepresentation and fraud, this was the year of statehood for North and South Dakota, Montana, and Washington, and boosterism focused on the future, which had no place for reservation Indians (Hyde 1956:184–228; DeMallie 1986:62–63).

The Ghost Dance and Wounded Knee, 1890–1891

The winter of 1889–1890 was a hard one for the Sioux. Although they had done their best to adapt to the reservation, had tried to make a living by farming and wage work, and had joined the Christian churches, they still faced hunger and disease. Then word spread of a messiah, an Indian Christ come to earth to save the Indians from the wrongs suffered at the hands of the Whites. The spirits of the dead would return, the Whites would be buried under a new earth that would form over the old one, and on the new earth, rich with buffalo, the Sioux would live forever. Performing the Ghost Dance, a simple circle dance, would

hasten the coming of the new earth. Delegates traveled west to meet Wovoka, the Northern Paiute Indian messiah, at his home in Nevada, and on their return many Sioux embraced the ritual.

The Ghost Dance shared many features with traditional religion. Performed around a center pole (fig. 4), like the Sun Dance, participants fell into trances in which they interacted with the spirits of their dead relatives. Since giveaways and Spirit-Keeping ceremonies had been outlawed in 1883, the Sioux had no traditional means of sending the spirits of the dead to the afterworld. For this, more than anything, the Ghost Dance filled a cultural need.

For the local Whites, Indians dancing raised the specter of warfare. In response to public pressure, the commissioner of Indian affairs ordered the arrest of the Ghost Dance leaders. At Standing Rock, the attempt to arrest Sitting Bull resulted in an altercation with the Indian police in which the chief was killed. Panic spread among the Ghost Dancers. Big Foot's band of Minneconjous fled from Cheyenne River to Pine Ridge but was intercepted by the Seventh Cavalry at Wounded Knee Creek. There, on December 29, while the Sioux were being forcibly disarmed, a shot rang out and the soldiers fired on the Indians. Machine guns stationed on a nearby hill raked the fleeing men, women, and children, and soldiers chased them, shooting all indiscriminately. The army reported 146 Indian dead, though the actual number killed was certainly higher. The Ghost Dancers from Pine Ridge fled to the Badlands, along the way destroying the homes of mixed-blood farmers and stealing their stock. The army occupied Pine Ridge but aside from minor skirmishes, ending with the return of the Ghost Dancers in January 1891, the Sioux had no intention of fighting the Whites. The Wounded Knee Massacre (vol. 4:182) was the final chapter in the hostilities with the army that had begun in 1854 (Mooney 1896; J.R. Walker 1980:141–143; DeMallie 1982).

Reservation Life, 1891–1935

Economy

The Oglala on Pine Ridge are representative of the Teton reservations in general. A major change in the method of issuing beef had real symbolic and well as practical significance. During early reservation days the cattle to be issued were turned loose to be killed by men on horseback in a kind of surrogate buffalo hunt. By 1901 the distribution method had changed; cattle were butchered and the meat issued biweekly. The hides, previously a valuable source of raw material for the Sioux, were sold by the agent and the money distributed at the end of the year, averaging $2 per person (ARCIA 1901:363). The reservation economy continued as before, with men being required more and more to work for rations. A new policy began in 1902 in which 400 young men were hired for summer work and paid in cash instead of rations (ARCIA 1902:337). Other forms of   *815* modernization impinged as well. Indians were forbidden from carrying six-shooters; men were required to cut their hair; telegraph connections were replaced by telephones; roads were developed (DeMallie 1978a:256–257).

At Pine Ridge, allotment of land began in 1905 and was largely completed by 1911 (vol. 4:68). Each individual received 160 acres, and families chose contiguous allotments oriented to the various creeks flowing into White River, where they had already built houses. Mixed-blood families congregated on the best agricultural lands, separating themselves from their full-blood relatives. In 1911 this area was removed from the reservation and organized as Bennett County, and unallotted land was opened for homesteading. The county was at first governed by mixed bloods, but as White homesteaders moved in, the mixed bloods were largely pushed out of political office (Wagoner 1997).

After 1900, in recognition of the realities of the reservation land and climate, the government's emphasis switched from farming to stock raising. Cattle herds roamed the open range and the spring and fall roundups became important social events. The Sioux developed both the skills and an orientation toward cowboy life. The early years of the twentieth century were relatively prosperous, and by 1914 the government was able to reduce rations at Pine Ridge to token amounts (Macgregor 1946:38–39).

World War I brought about economic crisis. Livestock prices soared and the Sioux sold their cattle and horses, using the money to buy cars and other luxury items. The land was leased to non-Indian cattlemen; whereas in 1914 there was only one non-Indian rancher leasing land at Pine Ridge, by 1917 all the reservation lands were leased to non-Indians, and remained so until 1921. The Sioux lived on money received from stock sales and land leases (Macgregor 1946:39).

When the cattle market crashed in the postwar depression of 1921, most of cattlemen defaulted on their leases. At the same time the Sioux became eligible to sell their lands. Under provisions of the 1906 Burke Act, tribal members who were one-half or less Indian "blood" were declared competent to handle their own affairs and became citizens (vol. 4:233). They received fee patents to their allotments and were thereafter eligible to sell their land. The government advertised the availability of reservation lands (vol. 4:227), which were eagerly purchased by speculators to be resold to homesteaders. Dry farming of wheat, flax, and other grains proved successful on Pine Ridge, stimulating more land sales (Prucha 1975:207; DeMallie 1978a:258).

The government once again began to encourage the Sioux to farm, although a drought had begun in 1924 and the Indians lacked the capital and mechanized equipment to compete with their White neighbors. Farm chapters were established at each of the day schools. Five-year programs were instituted in some communities, such as Red Shirt Table and Kyle, to provide each family with milk cows, some livestock, gardens, and at least minimal farm production. The financial crash of 1929 ended the agricultural prosperity of the plains, and the Dust Bowl in the 1930s ruined the economy of the reservations. Gardens were destroyed, livestock died, and to survive, the Sioux sold everything they had—even their dishes (W.O. Roberts 1943:39; Macgregor 1946:40; DeMallie 1978a:258–259).

By 1930 the economic picture was grim. Small amounts of money came from land leases and Indian scout pensions. In the fall, families traveled to Nebraska to dig potatoes for wages, and when they left they were allowed to fill their wagons with potatoes to sustain them over the winter. Some earned money from selling hay and from salaries as agency employees, policemen, or catechists. In 1930, the annual income per family in the White Clay district was $158.80. The government provided some rations, and to survive the Sioux gathered chokecherries and other wild foods and ate horsemeat. Traditional patterns of sharing reduced everyone to the same level of poverty. Relief came in 1932 when the Red Cross and the government supplied food and other necessities. In 1933, with the founding of the Civilian Conservation Corps, nearly all the able-bodied men were put on the government payroll constructing roads, dams, and public buildings. The monies earned revitalized the reservation economy until the CCC came to an end in 1942 (Mekeel 1936:9–10; Macgregor 1946:40–41; DeMallie 1978a:259).

Politics

On each reservation, the tribal council, controlled by the old chiefs, met to discuss matters of common interest and served as the liason between government representatives and the people. During the winter of 1917–1918 the superintendent at Pine Ridge, in a dispute with the tribal council, officially dissolved it. The chiefs then established a Treaty Council, whose explicit purpose was to pursue treaty claims against the government. The superintendent used the council as a forum for explaining government programs and policies (Feraca 1964:24–25; DeMallie 1986:257–258).

Younger Sioux began to see the Treaty Council as a tool of the reservation superintendent and in 1927 they organized the Council of Twenty-One, comprised of elected representatives from each of the reservation's seven districts (which later increased to eight). Their constitution was approved by the secretary of the interior in 1928. The new council was immediately at odds with the Treaty Council, which began to call itself the Council of One Hundred, to symbolize its opposition and superiority (Feraca 1964:31–32).

The mixed bloods tended to be uninvolved in the councils and even established their own organization. It was not until the elections in the 1930s under the Indian Reorganization Act that mixed bloods began to participate with full bloods in reservation politics (DeMallie 1978a:260–261).

816

Religion

Government prohibitions prevented traditional religious beliefs from being expressed in practice, and, in any case, those beliefs and ceremonies had been founded on a lifeway based on buffalo hunting and intertribal warfare. The traditional religious leaders did not renounce the old religion, even though they joined Christian churches. But neither did most of them pass traditional religious knowledge on to their children, believing that the future lay with Christianity (DeMallie 1982:402–403).

Christian churches flourished during the early decades of the twentieth century. The old religious concepts merged with Christian ones; Wakaŋtaŋka, written as a single word using the orthography introduced by missionaries, became identified with the Christian God, and older forms of prayer assimilated to Christian ones. Membership in churches was to a large extent determined by community. Small communities had only one church, mostly Roman Catholic, Episcopal, or Congregational, and members of that community tended to join it. Community cemeteries were associated with churches, and the holding of funerals was a vitally important church function. Church services, as well as the activities of men's and women's church societies (vol. 4:497), continued tp provide opportunities to socialize and arenas in which individuals could develop leadership roles. Communities took turns hosting denominational summer convocations that attracted hundreds of participants from all over Sioux country. The week-long campouts featured religious services, the singing of hymns, and sermons and speeches by distinguished visitors. The convocations were important mechanisms for maintaining common interests among the various reservations; and like the Sun Dances of old, they offered opportunities for courtship, socializing, and politicking (Macgregor 1946:91–96).

Despite the success of Christianity, the Sioux continued to practice aspects of traditional religion. Pine Ridge and Rosebud emerged as the two reservations most committed to the perpetuation of traditional religious and healing practices. Conjuring ceremonies adapted to the reservation setting developed from older ritual forms. Called *yuwípi* 'wrapped up', in which the shaman was wrapped in a quilt and bound head to foot, to be released in the course of the ceremony by his spirit helpers, and *lowápi* 'sings', a similar form in which the shaman was not bound, they were held in darkened rooms, in a way that did not attract government attention, and brought people together for practical purposes—healing the sick, finding lost objects, or foretelling the future (Macgregor 1946:98–99; J.R. Walker 1980:153–155; Densmore 1918:204–238).

In the 1920s, the Native American Church was introduced to the Sioux, where it found a permanent constituency in some communities at Pine Ridge and Rosebud but did not spread to the other Teton reservations. There was widespread belief that Peyote and the pipe were antithetical powers, and there was real prejudice against those families who joined the church (E.C. Deloria 1944:83; Spider 1987). Native American Church members, on the other hand, perceived them as complementary. Two "ways" developed: the Half-Moon way, always held in a tepee, and consciously Indian in focus, and the Cross Fire way, which developed church buildings for services and incorporated the Bible and Christianity into its services (Macgregor 1946:100–102; Ruby 1955:53–60; Feraca 1998:59–70).

The Buffalo Calf Pipe bundle was taken to Cheyenne River Reservation by Elk Head, its keeper. Even though no public rituals were performed with it, the bundle remained a tangible link to the past and a symbol of unity for the Sioux. In 1898, at the agent's orders, the bundle was confiscated and brought to Cheyenne Agency, for reasons apparently unrecorded. The incident caused such unrest that the agent quickly had it returned. The only recorded public unwrapping of the pipe occurred in July 1936. Martha Bad Warrior, Elk Head's daughter and the first woman keeper of the bundle, in an attempt to end the drought that was devastating the plains, sat in the sun throughout an entire day, praying and holding the pipe on her lap (fig. 4). The rains eventually came, but Bad Warrior died three months later, at the age of 82 (J.L. Smith 1967:8–10; S.J. Thomas 1941).

Social Life

The reorganization of Teton society in the early reservation period brought about major changes. The *tʰiyóšpaye,* whose membership had always been fluid, were scattered, and as they disintegrated, their leaders became less important. At Rosebud, 20 communities developed out of the *tʰiyóšpaye* (Grobsmith 1981:20), and at Lower Brule, a much smaller reservation, six districts formed, each centered around a community (Estes and Loder 1971:31). A 1935 study at Pine Ridge reported 41 such communities (Macgregor 1946:77). In addition, mixed-blood communities developed, focused on ranching. The seven original district headquarters on Pine Ridge developed into villages with the building of churches, dance halls for traditional dances, and day schools. The Pine Ridge districts were organized by watershed boundaries in order to maximize efficiency in transporting rations to the district headquarters, but they cut across community boundaries and were not natural social units for the Oglala, making them ineffective as voting districts in the government (Macgregor 1946:66–77).

The reservation was a total social institution, controlling all aspects of life. The Indian police zealously guarded the borders and no tribal member could leave without a pass from the reservation superintendent. Important economic and political decisions, including land sales and leasing, were made by government agents, whose actions were automatically approved by tribal business committees. The paternalism of the reservation system produced generations who had little control over their own affairs and were dependent on the Bureau of Indian Affairs in all aspects of life. The male role as family head was undermined by a lack of economic opportunity and by a lack of relevant skills to teach the younger generations. In contrast, women became the economic mainstays of the family. Their domestic roles continued as before, but men had little to do, which over time developed into a deadening apathy that, coupled with poverty, was debilitating to reservation life.

The kinship system began to change as the nuclear family became more independent and younger people spoke English and adopted the patterns of English kin term use. Both kinship systems continued to be used throughout the twentieth century, but the use of kin terms for address lessened over time, largely replaced by nicknames, often originating in childhood and carrying through to old age. Marriages became more a private matter between couples, frequently without consulting their families in advance. As young males spent more time at home than in the former days of camp-circle life, brother-sister avoidance relaxed until it was no longer practiced. The formalities of all kin relationships lessened, although some degree of avoidance between men and their mothers-in-law continued to be practiced (Macgregor 1946:55–63; E.C. Deloria 1944:90–95).

Countering the negative social forces of reservation life were opportunities for interaction and the organization of group activities. At specified times of the year, such as holidays, traditional dances were held in arbors or in the district dance halls (fig. 10). During the reservation period the Omaha Dance (*omáha wačhípi*) developed out of the old war dance, and the Omaha society developed as a forum for fostering fraternity among members and for helping the community by providing aid to mourners (Tyon in J.R. Walker 1980:266–267; Wissler 1912a:48–52). The Rabbit Dance, said to have been introduced at Pine Ridge in 1906 by the Ute, was the first Sioux couples' dance ("Celebrations and Giveaways," fig. 3, this vol.). It was performed to songs whose lyrics parodied reservation problems and encouraged morality by publicly, but obliquely, referring to sexual misbehavior (Mekeel 1932a:172–173; W.K. Powers 1962). The summer gatherings for the Sun Dance transformed into reservation fairs that celebrated agriculture and domestic arts but also included games and horse racing. Another popular social activity involved travel to fairs, rodeos (fig. 11), and other celebrations on reservations and in nearby White communities, where parades,

top, Nebr. State Histl. Soc., Lincoln: bottom, State Histl. Soc. of N. Dak., Bismarck: Fiske 448.

Fig. 10. Dance houses. top, Log dance house with sod-covered roof, Rosebud Res., S. Dak. Women and children are viewing the activity inside. Photograph by John A. Anderson, © 1911. bottom, Omaha Dancers enacting war exploits, posing for the photographer. Photograph by Frank B. Fiske, Ft. Yates, Standing Rock Res., N. Dak., 1900–1905.

818

Fig. 11. Saddle bronc competition at Soldier Creek rodeo, Rosebud Res., S. Dak. Butch Felix, Brule, leader of the band Butch Felix and the Country Skins, is announcing the rodeo from the observation stand. Photograph by Harvey Markowitz, 1981.

dances, and other Indian activities were put on as part of the festivities. In this context, the Sioux continued to use their old political structure, including the appointing of *akíčhita,* to organize the events (Mekeel 1932:278–282).

Sources

The fullest nineteenth-century description of the Teton is that of the fur trader Edwin Denig (1961), written in 1855 but representing his experiences with the Teton beginning in 1833. Writings by United States military officers who served during the Sioux wars of the 1870s, including those of Col. Albert G. Brackett (1877), Capt. W.P. Clark (1885), and Capt. John G. Bourke (1891, and an account of the Oglala Sun Dance in Dorsey 1894:464–467), provide valuable ethnographic observations. The reminiscences of army scouts Frank Grouad (DeBarthe 1894) and James H. Cook (1923) include insightful detail, as does scout E.H. Allison's (1891) narrative of events surrounding the return of Sitting Bull from Canada. The writings of John F. Finerty (1890), a newspaper reporter who accompanied military expeditions in the 1870s, is similarly useful. The history of American Indian relations with the United States by former Commissioner of Indian Affairs George W. Manypenny (1880) is an informative counterbalance to the military perspective, and provides considerable detail on the Sioux.

Indian agents' memoirs of their experiences are helpful in understanding early reservation life; among the most ethnographically detailed are those of DeWitt Clinton Poole (1881) at Whetstone Agency, James McLaughlin (1910) at Standing Rock, Cicero Newell (1912) at Rosebud, and Valentine T. McGillycuddy at Pine Ridge (J.B. McGillycuddy 1941).

Newspaper reporters' coverage of the Ghost Dance and hostilities in 1890–1891 produced a number of ethnographi-cally and historically valuable accounts. W.F. Johnson (1891) includes a biography of Sitting Bull, accounts of the Sioux war and early reservation experiences, and a detailed account of the Ghost Dance period; James P. Boyd (1891) includes some valuable descriptions of the Ghost Dance; William Fitch Kelley (1971) presents daily dispatches from Pine Ridge from November 24, 1890 to January 16, 1891. Jensen, Paul, and Carter (1991) published a large number of the photographs taken during the newspaper coverage of the aftermath of Wounded Knee. Mooney (1896) includes a history of the military action as well as descriptions of the ceremony and texts of Ghost Dance songs collected during fieldwork to document the spread of the Ghost Dance.

Sioux perspectives are best represented in the verbatim transcripts of councils with United States commissioners. Among them are Talks and Councils (1910) and V. Deloria and DeMallie (1975), which deal with the peace commissions of 1866–1869, and United States Secretary of the Interior (1888) and President of the United States (1890), relating to the 1888 and 1889 commissions that negotiated the opening of the Great Sioux Reservation.

Doane Robinson (1904) is an overall history of the Teton to 1891. Hurt (1974) is a chronology of the Teton to 1869 prepared for the Indian Claims Commission. A short, useful historical summary is Mekeel (1943). The history of the Oglala to 1877 and from 1877–1891, focused on the life of Red Cloud, is presented in Hyde (1937, 1956). Olson (1965) presents a similar account of Oglala history from 1845 to 1909, oriented to the details of government policy and relations with the U.S. army. Mari Sandoz (1942) presents an interpretation of Oglala history from 1855 to 1877, written as a biography of Crazy Horse and based in part on unpublished interviews with Oglalas. C. Price (1996) is a history, 1841–1879, that attempts to use the Oglala social and political systems as a framework for interpreting events. Hyde (1961) is a history of the Brule to 1881, focused on the life of Spotted Tail. Schusky (1975) is an ethnohistory of the Lower Brule Reservation. Vestal (1957) and Utley (1993), both biographies of Sitting Bull, provide histories of the Hunkpapa and other northern Teton. The history of the Teton in Montana is summarized in DeMallie (1986).

Sioux perspectives on the Battle of the Little Bighorn are collected in J.A. Greene (1994). Utley (1967, 1973) are very useful histories of the Indian wars, written from the military perspective. Utley (1963) is a thorough history of the military actions surrounding the Ghost Dance and Wounded Knee.

Hassrick (1964), the only book-length ethnography of the Teton, combines data from fieldwork at Rosebud Reservation with material taken from published sources; unfortunately, it is cast in psychological terms that intrude on the cultural description. Ewers (1937) provides a useful cultural summary. Other general accounts of Teton culture and society include Mirsky (1937), based on unpublished manuscripts by Ella C. Deloria, and Sandoz (1961).

Wissler (1912a) and J.R. Walker (1917, 1982) are the basic sources on political and social organization. Kin terms are *819* most thoroughly documented in Lesser (1958); also see J.R. Walker (1914) and Hassrick (1944). Ella Deloria (1944, 1988, 1995) provides the most evocative descriptions of kinship and social life. DeMallie (1971) is a study of kinship and social organization based on published and archival material. For gender, see M.N. Powers (1986) and DeMallie (1983).

The basic documentary sources on traditional religion are J.R. Walker (1917, 1980), Densmore (1918), Curtis (1907–1930, 3), and Black Elk (in J.E. Brown 1953 and DeMallie 1984). Syntheses of Teton belief include W.K. Powers (1977), DeMallie (1987), and Steinmetz (1990). Major works on the corpus of material recorded from Black Elk include Rice (1991), Steltenkamp (1993), and Holler (1995).

Duratschek (1947) is a history of Roman Catholic missionization of the Sioux; Sneve (1977) and O. Anderson (1997) document Episcopal missionization.

Daily life on the Teton reservations in the late-nineteenth century is vividly represented in the photographs by John A. Anderson, taken on Rosebud Reservation (P, Dyck 1971; H.W. Hamilton and J.T. Hamilton 1971). Macgregor (1946) and E. H. Lewis (1980), are complementary accounts of Pine Ridge Reservation in the first decades of the twentieth century. E.C. Deloria (1944:75–135) is an evocative portrayal of reservation life, oriented to the experiences of Christian Sioux.

Blish (1967) is an invaluable pictorial record of Teton culture and history by Bad Heart Bull, an Oglala, that incorporates captions and other text in the Sioux language. White Bull, a Minneconjou, kept a personal drawing ledger (J.H. Howard 1968a) that is similar in conception, but more narrowly focused on his personal accomplishments. His autobiography (Vestal 1934a) is an important cultural and historical source. Standing Bear (1928, 1931), an Oglala, published two autobiographical volumes that are rich in ethnographic detail and include early reservation and boarding school experiences. The autobioigraphy of Black Elk, an Oglala (Neihardt 1932), has become a classic of American literature; DeMallie (1984) presents the interview transcripts on which the original book was based, which offer a wealth of additional cultural detail. W.J. Bordeaux (1929, 1952), a Brule, published two volumes, the first an historical and ethnographic account, the second a history focused on the life of Crazy Horse.

Boas and Deloria (1941) and Buechel (1939) are the standard grammatical studies of Sioux. Buechel (1970) is the fullest published dictionary. Ella Deloria's collections of oral literature, transcribed in the Sioux language with English translation, are presented in E.C. Deloria (1932) and Rice (1992, 1993, 1994). Buechel (1998), presents texts written early in the twentieth century, mostly by literate Tetons (vol. 17:451); the translations, made at the end of the century by Paul Manhart, are very literal and sometimes idiosyncratic, reflecting the difficulty of understanding the texts.

J.R. Walker (1917, 1983) presents myths recorded at Pine Ridge Reservation in the first decade of the twentieth century. The fullest and most diverse collection of oral traditions collected in English translation is M.W. Beckwith (1930); other significant collections are Zitkala-Ša (1901), Wissler (1907b), M.L. McLaughlin (1916), Standing Bear (1934), and South Dakota Writers' Project (1941).

Teton music and dance are documented in Densmore (1918), N. Curtis (1907), H.W. Paige (1970), Black Bear and Theisz (1976), and W.K. Powers (1968a, 1980a, 1990).

Wissler (1904, 1905, 1907) published the first studies of Teton art. Ewers (1937) presents a valuable overview of Teton material culture. Lyford (1940) is the basic study of Teton beadwork and quillwork. J.A. Hanson (1996) describes the Teton collection made by G.K. Warren in 1855–1856, unusual for its precise documentation. The most comprehensive study of Teton art and material culture, based on museum collections, is Hail (1980). Significant publications of men's pictographic art include H.B. Alexander (1938), Stirling (1938), Blish (1967), J.H. Howard (1968a), Wildhage (1988), and Berlo (1996).

The best-documented nineteenth-century collections are in the National Museum of Natural History, Smithsonian Institution. Other museums hold significant Teton collections, including the American Museum of Natural History, New York; the Field Museum of Natural History, Chicago; the National Museum of the American Indian, Smithsonian Institution, Washington; The Journey (formerly, Sioux Indian Museum), Rapid City, South Dakota; the Denver Art Museum, Colorado; the State Historical Society of North Dakota, Bismarck; and the South Dakota State Historical Society, Pierre.

Sioux, 1930–2000

DENNIS M. CHRISTAFFERSON

The Indian Reorganization Act (IRA) (48 U.S. Stat. 984), passed by Congress on June 18, 1934, was the centerpiece of Commissioner of Indian Affairs John Collier's New Deal reform policy. It reflected his commitment to strengthening tribal identities and reservation communities (V. Deloria and C.M. Lytle 1984:140–153, 266–270). Sioux reception of the IRA was mixed, with some reservations rejecting it altogether and others adopting it in whole or in part (Cash and Hoover 1971:121–134, 142–150; Biolsi 1992:68–84).

World War II

America's entry into World War II marked a watershed for the Sioux and other Indians. Thousands left the reservations for the first time to join the military or work in the war effort. When they returned, they were profoundly changed.

Military Service

During World War I American Indians had not been drafted because they were not American citizens, yet thousands volunteered anyway. In recognition of their distinguished service, Congress granted citizenship to all American Indians in 1924 (Bernstein 1991:22) (vol. 4:233). When the draft was revived in 1940, Indians for the most part enthusiastically complied with the registration requirement and many chose to enlist immediately (fig. 1). Fort Peck set the record for volunteers, where 113 Sioux and Assiniboine enlisted out of the 252 who registered (Bernstein 1991:35; T. Holm 1996:104).

Sioux men saw action in all branches of the service, including on submarines in the Pacific and destroyers in the Atlantic, while many Sioux women served as nurses or in the auxiliary services (Bernstein 1991:40, 51). In the South Pacific there was a unit of Sioux code talkers who, like the better-known Navajo code talkers, communicated vital information using a native language code worked out among themselves (*Indian Country Today*, June 8, 1999). For the most part, the Sioux distinguished themselves in the infantry, often in hazardous reconnaissance missions. Of the 1,250 Indian casualties in the war, 300 were Sioux (T. Holm 1996:105), and of the 550 who died, 100 were Sioux (Bernstein 1991:61).

Homefront

Sioux on the reservations supported the war effort by conserving resources, staging giveaways, performing ceremonies for those entering the service, and supporting and consoling those who lost family members (E.C. Deloria 1944:139–141; T. Holm 1996:105). On Rosebud Reservation, 30 tribal members were designated as official civil defense air-raid wardens by the South Dakota National Defense Council (Bernstein 1991:67). Newsletters, like the *Victory News* published by the Sioux at Carleton College in Minnesota, served as conduits for news between home and those serving (E.C. Deloria 1944:141). As men left the reservations, women took over much of the workload, driving tractors, repairing equipment, and herding cattle (Bernstein 1991:73; T. Holm 1996:106).

In early 1942, the army acquired 340,000 acres on Pine Ridge Reservation for use as an aerial gunnery range. The Oglala Sioux Tribe agreed to lease most of the land for a minimal payment, but individual landowners were forced to sell: 128 families were abruptly displaced, some under protest. In 1956, many of them finally received some financial compensation for their losses (Bernstein 1991:81–82). The Army promised to return the land at the end of the war, but it was not until 1975 that 248,000 acres were returned to the Oglala Sioux Tribe. A 5,000-acre area was retained by the military for cleanup, and the balance of the land was incorporated into the Badlands National Park to be jointly managed by the tribe and the U.S. National Park Service (Gonzalez and Cook-Lynn 1999:127). The returned land contained considerable unexploded ordnance, and in 1993 the tribe established the Badlands Bombing Range Project to discover and deal with these hazards (*Denver Post*, Feb. 9, 1997).

In early 1942 over 2,000 Sioux left to work on building depots and air training centers. Some residents of Pine Ridge and Cheyenne River reservations found permanent employment on nearby military facilities, allowing them to return home for visits. Off-reservation jobs provided real economic opportunities and even windfalls for Indian people, and encouraged others to seek similar employment (Bernstein 1991:68–73; G. Macgregor 1946:46).

Effect of the War

When Selective Service was reinstituted, John Collier argued for the establishment of an all-Indian division (Bernstein 1991:22–23); however, the army integrated Indians throughout the ranks. As a consequence, Indian servicemen became immersed in American culture, with steady

DAKOTA OJIBWAY POLICE SERVICE

"A Commitment to First Nations"

top, Hampton U. Mus., Va.:998.7; bottom left, Acme Newspictures Inc., San Francisco Bureau.

Fig. 1. Military tradition. top, *Horse Soldiers*, by Martin Red Bear, Oglala. A veteran of the Vietnam War, Red Bear juxtaposes images of 19th- and 20th-century Sioux militarism, merging past and present war honors. Painted 1998. bottom left, Oglala recruits in the Army Air Corps who became soldiers in World War II. left to right, Theodore Twiss, Vandall Fast Horse, Acorn A. Adams, Jerome Brown Bull, Moses Ladeaux, Patrick Fast Horse, Bert Bergen, Leonard White Bull, and Leo Red Hair. All were from Pine Ridge Res., S. Dak., except Bergen, from Rosebud Res., S. Dak. Photographed at Hamilton Field, San Rafael, Calif., Nov. 13, 1940. bottom right, Cover of recruitment brochure for the Dakota Ojibway Police Department (Santee Sioux). A community-based police agency established in 1977, it provides service to the communities of Birdtail Sioux, Sioux Village–Long Plain, Oak Lake Sioux, Roseau River, and Sioux Valley, Man.

jobs, an increased standard of living, enhanced status in both Indian and non-Indian circles, access to labor-saving devices and luxury goods, and exposure to urban society. Many of those working off-reservation had the same experiences (Bernstein 1991:58–73).

The Pick-Sloan Project

In the early 1940s, the Army Corps of Engineers and the Bureau of Reclamation separately developed major water projects for the Missouri River basin. The Corps' project, the

Pick Plan, called for the construction of five flood-control dams along the Missouri itself, while the Bureau's Sloan Plan focused on developing reservoirs and irrigation projects along its tributaries. The two projects were combined and approved by Congress as part of the 1944 Flood Control Act. From the outset, the Pick-Sloan Project as planned directly impacted five Sioux reservations—Yankton, Crow Creek, Lower Brule, Cheyenne River, and Standing Rock—as well as Fort Berthold, yet these tribes were not informed of the plan until 1947. This delay denied the Indians any meaningful input or effective opposition to the project's implementation (Lawson 1982a:24, 27, 1982:18–21, 45–47).

The construction of the dams had a devastating affect on reservation land holdings. The Fort Randall dam flooded 3,300 acres of the Yankton reservation and, in conjunction with the Big Bend dam, 38,000 acres of Crow Creek and Lower Brule. The Oahe dam produced the greatest loss: 104,000 acres on Cheyenne River; 56,000 on Standing Rock. The areas lost were primarily fertile bottomlands that constituted, according to one analysis, "90 percent of the reservations' timber land and 75 percent of the wild game and plant supply" (Lawson 1982a:25, 1982:47–52).

The impact of these losses in human terms was severe. The resources of the bottomlands had sustained a social and cultural way of life impossible on the drier uplands. Entire communities had to be relocated, including Cheyenne Agency, the largest town on Cheyenne River Reservation, as well as the agency headquarters on Lower Brule and Crow Creek. In all, some 600 families were forced to move, more than one-third of the aggregate population of the reservations; on Lower Brule the figure was nearly 70 percent. Several Lower Brule and Crow Creek families displaced by Fort Randall dam were relocated into the future flood area of the Big Bend Dam and thus were forced to endure a second relocation (Lawson 1982a:25–30, 1982:146–155). Further, because Pick-Sloan coincided with the Voluntary Relocation Program, there was little government support for reorganizing community life for those displaced.

Negotiations with the government for benefits and compensation were equally difficult, dragging on for 14 years. Each tribe had to negotiate independently, and therefore settlement amounts were not uniform. Cheyenne River lost the most land and received the least compensation. Lower Brule and Crow Creek obtained the most generous reconstruction benefits, only to see them eaten up by relocation costs (Lawson 1982a:29, 1982:134; Schusky 1975a:230). Standing Rock hired its own Washington attorney and challenged the Corps of Engineers' 1958 attempt to condemn and seize a portion of their land. In an important decision, the court affirmed that because reservation land was established by treaty, the Corps' action in taking it by eminent domain was illegal; only Congress had the right to abrogate treaties. The decision came too late to help the other tribes, but Standing Rock received $12 million, the largest compensation award of the five (Lawson 1982:116–119; L. Hinchman and S. Hinchman 1994:269).

Pick-Sloan had been represented as a balanced project: the arable land lost to the dams would be replaced with newly irrigated uplands. However, few of the planned irrigation projects were ever completed, none on Indian land, and Congress, citing high costs and poor returns, began to cut back on their funding. Rehabilitation money to develop new sources of income, such as livestock, tourism, and recreation, was included in the settlements, but such ventures had very limited success (L. Hinchman and S. Hinchman 1994:270, 292).

In the 1990s, Congress enacted legislation to adjust the original settlements to fair and just amounts according to the findings of the Joint Tribal Advisory Committee (JTAC) (PL 102-575, PL 104-223, PL 105-132). In addition, the tribes began efforts to regain the land within the borders of their reservations taken by the army but left unflooded (see PL 102-575 and PL 105-277).

Termination and Withdrawal

"Termination" signified the revocation by Congress of an Indian tribe's status as a federally recognized tribe and therefore its access and that of its members to the programs and privileges accorded such tribes. The Bureau of Indian Affairs (BIA) proposed a gradual process of withdrawal in which existing programs were to be transferred to other government departments, BIA supervision phased out, the BIA itself abolished, and individual tribes terminated. In 1953, however, Congress decided to implement some terminations immediately using as a guide the 1947 plan prepared by Assistant Commissioner of Indian Affairs William Zimmerman (Cowger 1996:122–128; Philp 1999:68–78; Schusky 1975:206).

The Sioux tribes were never in danger of immediate termination. The report categorized Cheyenne River and Fort Peck as "Semi-Acculturated" and the other reservations as "Predominantly Indian," that is, still adhering to traditional Sioux cultural values and practices (Philp 1999:75). However, termination policy also included the withdrawal of services from the BIA and other cost-cutting measures that did impact the Sioux and were vigorously opposed by them. For example, in 1951 the BIA announced plans to consolidate its operations on Cheyenne River and Standing Rock and move them off-reservation to the predominantly White town of Mobridge, South Dakota. Both tribes protested and the proposal was dropped (Lawson 1982:72–73).

Several Indian programs were transferred to other federal departments or to the states. When the BIA extension service was closed, Sioux farmers and ranchers had to rely on state systems oriented toward large-scale agriculture (Ducheneaux 1956:29; R.H. Useem and C.K. Eicher 1970:15–21). Indians were required to seek loans from the same financial markets as non-Indians, for which few Sioux could qualify (Eicher 1962:193; Grobsmith 1981:33).

823

Most serious was the movement to give the states jurisdiction over Indian reservations. In the late 1940s Congress stopped funding the salaries of Indian judges (vol. 4:234) and police, forcing the tribes to absorb the cost themselves or drop those services. Following these cutbacks, Sioux reservations were characterized as lawless, and their tribal councils accused of fostering that lawlessness by opposing state jurisdiction (Ducheneaux 1956:20–21). In 1953 Public Law 280 granted states the authority to assume jurisdiction over Indian reservations with or without tribal concurrence. Although never invoked it remained on the books for 15 years (Philp 1999:143).

Lower Brule was the only tribe in the nation to request termination. In a negotiation ploy related to the Missouri River dams construction, the tribe offered to accept termination in exchange for double its projected compensation, calculating that with the money invested properly they could achieve economic independence. The offer was heavily criticized by other Indians and eventually withdrawn; its only effect was to delay disbursement of the dam compensation funds for years (Schusky 1975:226; Lawson 1982:126).

Relocation and Urbanization

During the 1930s a number of Sioux ventured off the reservations to find work in urban areas, but one out of three returned within six months and two out of three by the end of one year (J. Useem, G. Macgregor, and R.H. Useem 1943:3). For those who remained, urban life was generally better economically than that on the reservations (Shoemaker 1988:433).

World War II instigated a substantial Indian migration to urban areas. The Sioux population of Rapid City, South Dakota, swelled to an estimated 2,000 in 1948. Significant numbers of Sioux also moved to Yankton, South Dakota, and Scottsbluff, Nebraska (Bernstein 1991:148–149; Eicher 1962:192–193; Hurt 1962:227–228). The success that these voluntary migrants enjoyed in urban wartime work and the military convinced the government that the future for Indians lay beyond the reservations.

Relocation Policy

In 1952 the BIA instituted the Voluntary Relocation Program to encourage Indians to move to urban areas. Conditions were dire for the Sioux at this time. In 1950 the annual income on the Yankton and Standing Rock reservations was under $800, while one-third of the families on the Crow Creek Reservation earned less than $500. Thousands faced losing their homes because of the Pick-Sloan dams with no guarantee of government assistance (Cash and Hoover 1971:203–204; Philp 1985:182; Burt 1986:89).

Every reservation had a relocation officer, and BIA tactics were high-pressure (Cash and Hoover 1971:138–139; Burt 1986:89). Once in the city, new arrivals received a few counseling sessions on budgeting, writing checks, using the telephone, and keeping time schedules. Since few Indians had marketable skills, they generally ended up with unskilled, low-paying jobs and housing in low-income neighborhoods. Once housing and a job were secured, assistance ended (Ducheneaux 1956:26; Fixico 1986:186; Philp 1985:183–185; Burt 1986:90–91). The problems were so widespread that the United Sioux Tribes South Dakota, a coalition formed in 1952 to promote economic and social development, established employment offices in major cities to help find jobs and provide assistance to those who relocated (One Feather in Philp 1995:171).

The return rate to the reservations was high. By the mid-1950s, 75 percent had gone back to Cheyenne River (Ducheneaux 1956:26), and by 1959, 58 percent of those from Rosebud and 45 percent of those from Standing Rock had returned to their reservations (Useem and Eicher 1970:27, 31–32). Relocation participants were critical of the lack of adequate help in adjusting to urban life and the low quality of jobs available to them (Philp 1985:189).

Urban Life

Aside from the metropolitan areas near the Sioux reservations, Sioux also represented a significant portion of the Indian populations in Chicago, Los Angeles, and San Francisco (J.A. Price 1968:169; Ablon 1964:297; Philp 1985:184). Those living in cities faced many of the same problems they had on the reservation—discrimination, unemployment, poverty, inadequate housing and health care—along with new ones like crowded living conditions, noise, pollution, and social isolation. The Sioux relied upon support networks of relatives and other Sioux to share money, goods, and housing (Ablon 1964:298).

Sioux settled into the lower and lower-middle class strata of urban society, adapting these subcultures into "their own communities with their own norms" (R.J. White 1970:187), distinct from those of the reservation. Life in the city offered more opportunities than the reservation, and some found steady work and a new home (R.J. White 1970:195–196; Hurt 1962:230–231; Cash and Hoover 1971:214; J.A. Price 1968:169). Many developed a new awareness of being Indian, and pan-Indianism blossomed in the cities. Similarly, Indian nationalism and political activism were urban phenomena (Ablon 1964:302–304; Philp 1985:189).

The growth in urban population created disputes about the role of off-reservation Sioux in tribal and reservation politics (Shoemaker 1988:434). In the 1950s, there was considerable debate on Lower Brule about the disposition of the Pick-Sloan dam project compensation award, with many arguing for per capita payments even though that would divert funds from development projects on the reservation (Schusky 1975:205). The success in the 1990s of some Sioux casino operations raised similar questions about enrollment and distributions, forcing the tribes to rethink this relationship (*USA Today*, May 13, 1994).

Economic Development

Agriculture

Government efforts in economic development focused on ranching and farming. Prior to World War II, Sioux agriculture was concentrated in small family operations, but many of them—one out of two on Rosebud—failed during the drought of the 1930s (R.H. Useem and C.K. Eicher 1970:13). Many tribes attempted to buy back parcels of land under provisions of the IRA and start their own tribal ranching ventures (Schusky 1975a:229). In one project in 1937, the BIA organized an agricultural cooperative at Red Shirt Table on Pine Ridge focusing on livestock and poultry breeding and subsistence gardening. Although generally a success, the cooperative fell apart after BIA involvement ended in 1944 (G. Macgregor 1946:212–213; DeMallie 1978a:280–283).

After World War II ranching and farming became increasingly mechanized, and the need for capital, coupled with changes in lending policy, forced many small individual and tribal operations out of business (Burt 1992:477). Some family groups formed cattle associations, pooled their lands for a joint range, and were able to continue in business for a time (G. Macgregor 1946:67; P.M. Robertson 1995:218). However, from 1940 to 1959 the number of Rosebud farmers decreased by more than half (R.H. Useem and C.K. Eicher 1970:13). On the reservations affected by the Pick-Sloan Project, the second-largest rehabilitation expenditure went for the establishment of farming and ranching programs, but their emphasis on developing small family operations met with only limited success (Schusky 1975a:229; Lawson 1982:163–173). More successful were efforts to consolidate tribal land holdings; in 1972 Cheyenne River tribal members were able to claim use of 87 percent of their own land, up from just 41 percent in 1954 (Lawson 1982:169).

Wage Labor

The decline of small-scale agriculture made the availability of wage-labor employment even more critical. During the Depression, the Indian Division of the Civilian Conservation Corps (CCC-ID) was the major employer on the reservations. The CCC-ID, unlike the regular CCC, employed married men as well as single, and concentrated its efforts on reservation development close to home (G. Macgregor 1946:40; DeMallie 1978a:259–260; R.H. Useem and C.K. Eicher 1970:13).

After the CCC-ID ended in 1942, seasonal agricultural work, primarily harvesting potatoes and sugar beets, became the principal source of employment on the reservations. In 1956 such seasonal wage work employed the greatest number of workers at Rosebud (R.H. Useem and C.K. Eicher 1970:23–24; G. Macgregor 1946:45–46; Ducheneaux 1956:26).

The IRA established a Revolving Credit Fund to be used for economic development, but in its first three decades only a small fraction was dedicated to industry and commerce. Instead, the government's approach to job development focused on attracting outside-owned enterprises by improving reservation infrastructure. In the late 1950s, BIA undertook a campaign to lure manufacturing jobs to reservations, but it was unsuccessful (Burt 1992:477–479; R.H. Useem and C.K. Eicher 1970:21).

1960s–1980s

In the 1960s Congress changed Indian policy in two important ways. First, it extended to the Sioux and other Indians eligibility for a number of existing social programs that originally had excluded them. Thus, they gained direct access to programs such as those of the Public Works Administration and Public Housing Authority, rather than funneling special grants through the BIA. Second, the Office of Economic Opportunity (OEO), established in 1964, also decided to bypass the BIA and fund tribes directly. For the first time, the Sioux had discretionary authority over much of the federal spending on their reservations (P.J. Deloria 1995:194–197). Opportunities to administer these programs drew many educated tribal members back to the reservation (Stein 1992:5) and spurred the growth of tribal government. Tribal and federal governments became the most stable employers on the reservations (Grobsmith 1981:33; R.H. Useem and C.K. Eicher 1970:14).

One of the first actions of the OEO was to organize the Three-University Consortium (TUC) consisting of the University of Utah, University of South Dakota, and Arizona State University. Advisors from the University of South Dakota trained Sioux reservation leaders in technical and managerial skills, including grant-writing, to access and administer the new government programs (Burt 1992:484; Ortiz in Philp 1995:221). Under the OEO, Sioux tribes constructed industrial parks and made other improvements, continuing the old policy of trying to make the reservation attractive to outside employers. In the 1960s the Wright and McGill fishhook factories on Pine Ridge (fig. 2) and Greenwood Electronics Industry on Yankton were established, but most closed within a few years, casualties of economic forces, foreign competition, and cultural differences (DeMallie 1978a: 285–286; Grobsmith 1981:33; Steiner 1968:124–126).

At the same time, tribal enterprises, many with Indian managers, were growing more popular. Fort Peck Tribal Industries (FPTI) incorporated in 1968, obtained a Small Business Administration loan in partnership with Dynalecton Corporation, and began reconditioning carbines for the Air Force. Initially, FPTI paid Dynalecton to manage the enterprise, but Indians were trained and phased into management roles and FPTI continued to thrive (Burt 1992:490, 495). However, the government funneled most new tribal enterprises toward tourism with only limited success (Burt 1992:484; R.H. Useem and C.K. Eicher 1970:15; Grobsmith 1981:110–111).

bottom left, Motor Vehicle Dept., Ft. Totten, N. Dak.

Fig. 2. Economy. top left, Wright and McGill Fishing Tackle Company, which had 3 factories that employed about 150 Sioux. Photograph by Don Morrow, Pine Ridge Res., S. Dak., 1964. top right, Bingo in the St. Bridget Catholic Youth organization building, Rosebud Res., S. Dak. Photograph by Skip Schiel, 1984. bottom left, License plate from Devils Lake, Ft. Totten, N. Dak., 1990. Issuing license plates asserted sovereignty, and the registration fee brought money to the tribe. Length 30.48 cm. bottom right, Bob St. John, Sisseton-Wahpeton Sioux Vietnam veteran, carrying an eagle staff at a powwow at Ft. Yates, N. Dak., on Standing Rock Res. The powwow is an annual event the first weekend in August that brings in significant revenue for the tribe. Photograph by Deborah Wallwork, 1985.

1990s

In the 1990s American Indians capitalized on their sovereign status to create new economic opportunities, most notably in gaming. Most Sioux reservations established casinos. The small Santee communities in Minnesota enjoyed unusual success, with the Mystic Lake Casino of the Shakopee Mdewakanton Sioux Community near Minneapolis reportedly ranked second in profits among all Indian casinos (*USA Today*, May 13, 1994). Along with Mystic Lake, Treasure Island Casino of the Prairie Island Sioux Community and Jackpot Junction Casino of the Lower Sioux Community in southwest Minnesota became major economic resources and employers for non-Indians as well as for their own people (C.R. Anderson 1999; *Minneapolis Star-Tribune*, July 14, 1996). Similarly, the Santee Sioux and the town of Flandreau, South Dakota, cooperated in development projects anchored by the Royal River Casino (*Indian Country Today*, January 31, 2000). The Shakopee Mdewakanton Sioux financed a $10.8 million casino expansion and hotel

construction project for the Sisseton-Wahpeton Sioux Tribe (*Omaha World-Herald*, April 8, 1999).

In the less-populous West, more modest plans for tourist hotels and recreation facilities tied to casinos were undertaken. The Santee in Nebraska, frustrated by the governor's refusal to negotiate the required gaming compact, defied the state and federal governments and opened a tiny casino in 1996. The legal battle that ensued cost the Santee $1.6 million in fines and pointed out one of the dangers of relying on casinos for development: states cannot be forced to negotiate—or renegotiate—the required compact (*Omaha World-Herald*, February 9, 2000).

Education

Primary Education

The goal of Indian education policy, except for a brief period in the 1930s, was the assimilation of Indian children into American society (M. Wax, R. Wax, and R.V. Dumont

1964:4–6; Szasz 1975:3). Those New Deal reforms included closing boarding schools and constructing community day schools as multipurpose centers. Sioux schools often had community gardens and became centers of canning and preserving projects in late summer and fall. Vocational training was reoriented toward reservation life, with Sioux students managing herds of beef cattle. Bilingual curriculum materials were produced and workshops in Sioux culture were organized for teachers. Yet, like previous policy, these reforms were imposed by the government with no provision for Indian participation, consultation, or control (Szasz 1974:60–88, 1975:4–9). Although some Sioux schools continued student community projects (Orata 1953), when World War II ended, Indian education reverted to its assimilationist goals.

The failure of education for Sioux and other Indian children was evident in "the crossover phenomenon": Indian children scored slightly above the norm in the fourth and fifth grades, then declined steadily from the norm each successive school year (Bryde 1966:127; M. Wax, R. Wax, and R.V. Dumont 1964:8). Several studies of Sioux education (Erikson 1939; M. Wax, R. Wax, and R.V. Dumont 1964; Bryde 1966) identified the problem as inherent in the conflicting goals and attitudes of cross-cultural education. Bryde (1971:2) developed a course implemented in some Sioux reservation schools that taught techniques for minimizing these conflicts by using "Indian values in adjusting to and getting along with the Non-Indian world."

The Indian Education Act of 1972 and its successor, the Indian Self-Determination and Educational Assistance Act of 1975, required Indian direction and responsibility for the design of education programs (vol. 4:298). Sioux schools began cultural and language programs, and efforts were made for similar programs in public schools. Indians lobbied to repeal the South Dakota Board of Education statute restricting the teaching of any "foreign, ancient language" except Latin, and to require all public school teachers to receive training in Sioux culture. Sioux also began to participate in and influence local boards of education (Cash and Hoover 1971:190–191, 221–223; Medicine 1975). In the 1990s, a number of tribal councils—including Cheyenne River and Standing Rock—mandated the teaching of Sioux language in all reservation schools.

Tribal Colleges

The idea of establishing a tribal college began in the 1950s on Rosebud, and by the mid-1960s interest in this idea was widespread on all the Sioux reservations. In the 1960s a number of neighboring colleges and universities began offering extension courses at education centers in many reservation communities. The Sioux tribal colleges emerged from these early centers (Stein 1992:41–43, 57–58).

Passage in 1965 of Title III of the Strengthening and Developing Higher Education Amendment of the Federal Higher Education Act provided the funds to convert the education centers into tribal colleges by means of bilateral agreements with local institutions willing to both accept credits and provide administrative support. The Sioux tribal colleges are listed in table 1. During the late 1970s and 1980s the colleges moved toward full accreditation and greater autonomy. Sinte Gleska, which was unique in focusing on humanities rather than vocational training, in 1992 became an accredited university. In 1998, it and Oglala Lakota College (vol. 4:299) were the only tribal colleges in the United States offering master's-level programs (Oppelt 1984:31; NAES 1998:7–13; Stein 1992:41, 61, 119–141).

Sioux tribal colleges were administered by local boards of trustees, fostering the conviction that the colleges were "community property, not more temporary federal programs," and that they existed to serve their communities (Stein 1992:102; Medicine 1975:17; NAES 1998:7-5). A synopsis of the founding goals of Oglala Lakota College illustrates this attitude: to provide a place for Oglala tribal members to obtain credentials; to develop teaching methods and courses to fit the needs and lifestyles of tribal members; and to plan and implement community development programs (Stein 1992:46).

In keeping with their community orientation, Sinte Gleska and Oglala Lakota colleges created a "dispersed educational system." While each had an administrative center, their educational focus was on satellite sites, or "learning centers" on their reservations. In this way, the colleges tried to tailor their programs to accommodate family responsibilities and transportation difficulties. This approach also reduced the costs associated with residential colleges (Stein 1992:62; Grobsmith 1981:103; Oppelt 1984:31; Medicine 1975:17).

In 1972 the American Indian Higher Education Consortium (AIHEC) was established to promote unity in the development of tribal colleges and to lobby for supporting legislation. The six founders of AIHEC included Oglala Lakota, Sinte Gleska, and Standing Rock colleges, and these three also supplied much of its early leadership. AIHEC was instrumental in the passage of the Tribally Controlled Community College Act of 1978, which achieved a secure federal funding base and stabilized the tribal college movement (NAES 1998:7-5, 7-7; Stein 1992:109–117).

Reservation Life

Land

For many Indians, reservation land had a symbolic worth over and above its purely economic value, a worth embodied in the belief that Sioux culture and identity could only be preserved as long as there were reservations (Schusky 1965:50). This attitude was reflected in the hopes of those who relocated to cities eventually to retire to the reservation, and in the continued resistance to BIA attempts to appropriate the tiny land parcels created by inheritance. While such parcels were a headache for the BIA, they were intensely meaningful for their owners (P.M. Robertson 1995:230–231). *827*

Table 1. Sioux Colleges

Founded	Current Name	Original Name	Original Affiliate Institution
1971	Oglala Lakota College Kyle, S. Dak.	Oglala Sioux Community College	Black Hills State College
1971	Sinte Gleska University Rosebud, S. Dak.	Sinte Gleska College	Black Hills State College
1972	Sitting Bull College Ft. Yates, N. Dak.	Standing Rock College	Bismarck Junior College
1973	Nebraska Indian Community College Niobrara	American Indian Satellite Community College	Northeast Nebraska Technical Commuity College
1973	Si Tanka College Eagle Butte, S. Dak.	Cheyenne River Community College	Northern State College and Presentation College
1974	Cankdeska Cikana Community College Ft. Totten, N. Dak.	Little Hoop Community College	Lake Region Junior College
1974	Sisseton-Wahpeton Community College Sisseton, S. Dak.	Sisseton-Wahpeton Community College	University of Minnesota-Morris
1978	Fort Peck Community College Poplar, Mont.	Fort Peck Community College	Miles Community College

Source: NAES 1998:7–21, 29, 35, 38, 40, 42, 43, 45.

The Rosebud Tribal Land Enterprise (TLE), established in 1943 to protect and expand the reservation land base, attempted to overcome the problem of inherited fragments by issuing for such parcels prorated shares in TLE called Certificates of Interest. Using these certificates, tribal members could exchange scattered small holdings for a consolidated, functional tract of land with which to support their families. Corruption in this program victimized many Indians (Burnette 1971:35–37, 120–121; Biolsi 1992:118–119). A similar exchange program on Cheyenne River was much more successful, substantially increasing the tribal land base (Lawson 1982:142).

The economics of farming and ranching forced most Sioux to lease their land. At the end of the 1960s on Pine Ridge, 83 percent of those owning land leased all or part of it; among full bloods, 95 percent leased their land (Maynard and Twiss 1969:70). While income from leasing was not taxable, it was usually too small to support an individual or family. The BIA supervised the leasing process, reviewing and enforcing the terms, and collecting and distributing the fees. For grazing land, the BIA had the power to put together "grazing units" for lease without requiring permission of the landowners, with Sioux ranchers given first chance and a reduced rate for such units. While a convenient, efficient system for the BIA, it did not always benefit the Sioux. In one instance in the 1950s, a family cattle operation involving eight nuclear families was notified that their land had been incorporated into a grazing unit. They could not raise the money to lease the unit themselves, and since they were no longer able to graze their cattle on their own land, they were forced out of business (P.M. Robertson 1995:218). In addition, this system created tension between Sioux ranchers and landowners, since landowners received significantly less from an Indian lessee than from a non-Indian lessee (Grobsmith 1981:30–33; Maynard and Twiss 1969:70–74).

Indians complained that the BIA consistently appraised the value of the land for lease purposes significantly below market value, and as a consequence, leases for Indian land were seldom comparable to those for non-Indian land (Burnette 1971:37, 55–57). Even after the tribes themselves began setting grazing regulations, the perception remained that those regulations favored the ranchers (P.M. Robertson 1995:221).

Community

At the end of World War II, most reservation Sioux lived in small cabins or frame houses dispersed along stream beds. Although as much as a mile apart, the homes along a particular stream were part of the same *tʰiyóšpaye*, the traditional Sioux extended-family community and "the only social unit . . . of the former [Sioux] social structure which has remained important in the reservation society" (G. Macgregor 1946:53). Living in such proximity to one's relatives facilitated the interaction and cooperation essential to proper kinship behavior, and those social relationships, though under strain, remained central to Sioux culture (G. Macgregor 1946:52–73).

This rural residence pattern remained essentially intact on most reservations into the 1960s, but the social strength of the *t^hiyóšpaye* was severely weakened as members moved away to find work and White cultural influences became more prevalent. The increasing isolation of those families that remained made it more difficult to maintain the traditional system of reciprocal sharing and support. Still, at the end of the 1960s on Pine Ridge, nearly half of full bloods lived in an extended-family household (Malan 1958:34–59; Maynard and Twiss 1969:114, 129–132). On the reservations affected by Pick-Sloan the communities of a substantial portion of the population were completely destroyed. While some effort was made to relocate residents onto individual homesites, it was impossible to reconstitute *t^hiyóšpaye* communities, and most of those relocated were moved into newly built tract housing in towns (Lawson 1982:145–159).

During the 1960s the Department of Housing and Urban Development constructed cluster housing projects on reservations. In the early 1970s the Porcupine District Council on Pine Ridge voted 13 times against cluster housing, and a special district meeting in 1973 resolved unanimously in favor of homes built on an individual's land, but their wishes were ignored (P.M. Robertson 1995:219–220). The housing projects were plagued by cheap materials and shoddy construction, and often houses were left unfinished (Grobsmith 1981:23–26; Burnette 1971:145). Residents found themselves living close together with strangers and conflicts became commonplace (Kurkiala 1997:93–96). With relatives scattered, kinship obligations became burdensome and were often neglected. Women in particular struggled to define new roles and responsibilities for themselves in this changing social environment (Medicine 1978:93–96; Vazeilles 1977:103–120).

In the 1990s, a movement developed among landowners on Pine Ridge to move back to their land, but they encountered numerous obstacles; those with prospective homesites on grazing land had to ask the rancher holding the permit for a waiver, which was seldom granted. Members of the Lakota Landowners Association expressed concern that access to individually owned lands and to tribal land was being progressively curtailed. They considered a 1994 proposal by two tribal council members (both ranchers) to set aside tracts of land in each district for homesites as a ploy to contain those who wished to move back to the land (P.M. Robertson 1995:221). These conflicting positions represented different visions of the reservation, as valuable property and as homeland. The landowners saw rural life as an opportunity to restore the traditional social relationships of the *t^hiyóšpaye*.

A number of works chronicled on a personal level the changes that transformed Sioux reservation life and the continuities that sustained it (Young Bear and Theisz 1994; Crow Dog and Erdoes 1995; Starita 1995; Mohatt and Eagle Elk 2000). I. Frazier (2000) presents an anecdotal portrait of life on Pine Ridge Reservation. Conventional ethnographies described contemporary life in Bennett County, South Dakota (Wagoner 1997)—once part of Pine Ridge Reservation and still considered so by many Sioux—and the renaissance of the Prairie Island Sioux Community in Minnesota (C. R. Anderson 1997).

Population figures for the United States and Canada are given in tables 2–3.

Veterans

The remarkable military contribution of Sioux men and women in World War II was duplicated in Korea, Vietnam, and Desert Storm. Serving in the military was a matter of duty and family tradition for many Sioux, and those returning from duty or home on leave were recognized and honored at powwows and with giveaways ("Teton," fig. 8, this vol.). The Flag Song became the "Sioux National Anthem," and, with the flag it honored, an essential part of all community events. The American Legion and Veterans of Foreign Wars were among the most prestigious organizations on the reservation, whose presence and conduct lent dignity and honor to the funeral of a veteran. The intense patriotism common among the Sioux, and especially among full bloods, reflected a direct, personal relationship with the federal government and the kind of reciprocal obligation usually associated with kinship (R.E. Daniels 1970:235–242; Maynard and Twiss 1969:36).

Tribal Government

Following the Indian Reorganization Act of 1934, most Sioux tribes adopted constitutions that called for an elected, representative government, a concept alien to Sioux cultural understandings of leadership and bitterly opposed by a significant portion of the tribes. These mostly traditionalist "Old Dealers" maintained that the Sioux relationship with the federal government had been established by treaties, and their hostility to the "illegal" IRA governments continued into the twenty-first century. The IRA governments were essentially powerless, since none of their decisions could be put into action without the approval of the BIA, and knowing this, most people had little respect for them (Biolsi 1992:151–181; Burnette 1971:18; Young Bear and Theisz 1994:142–145; DeMallie 1978a:260–261, 274–276; Schusky 1965:70–75). One critic suggested that this lack of power and responsibility created a climate for corruption (Burnette 1971:18, 86–87).

Throughout the 1960s and 1970s, tribal governments acquired more flexibility and authority in administering a variety of federal programs, but the creation and planning of those programs remained in Washington. Similarly, the self-determination movement in education led to three authorities on most reservations—tribe, BIA, and public school system—with no one of them ultimately responsible (V. Deloria and C.M. Lytle 1984:197, 222).

Table 2. Sioux Population in the United States, 1880–1990

Community	1880 (ARCIA 1880:240–242, 246)	1890 (ARCIA 1890:450–451)	1910 (ARCIA 1910:63–65)	1930 (ARCIA 1930:40–46)	1962 (Nurge 1970:304)	1990 (Bureau of the Census 1993:56–60)
Santee						
Devils Lake, N. Dak.[a]	839[d]	613[g]	986	917	1,476	2,139
Flandreau, S. Dak.	304	292	275	328	283	159
Santee, Nebr.	764	869	1,155	1,266	300	
Sisseton, S. Dak.	1,500	1,509	1,994	2,620	2,271	4,210[j]
Minnesota			929	560		
Lower Sioux					192	106
Prairie Island					86	58
Prior Lake					22	54
Upper Sioux					97	8
Yankton and Yanktonai						
Yankton, S. Dak.	2,019	1,725	1,753	2,029	1,533	3,703
Crow Creek, S. Dak.	969	1,058	997	936	1,058	2,123
Devils Lake, N. Dak.[a]	250	420[h]				
Fort Peck, Mont.[b]	4,713	1,121	1,102	1,079	3,071	704
Standing Rock, N. Dak.[c]	1,370[e]	1,791				
Teton						
Cheyenne River, S. Dak.		2,823	2,590	3,143	3,734	7,566
Blackfeet	239					
Minneconjou	523					
Sans Arc	322					
Two Kettle	680					
Lower Brule, S. Dak.	1,300	1,026	469	605	509	1,272
Pine Ridge, S. Dak.			6,758	7,995	8,780	18,459[k]
Oglala	7,200	5,014[i]				
Rosebud, S. Dak.			5,096	6,069	7,201	11,296
Brule	3,566	1,961				
Loafer	1,564	1,052				
Wahzahzah	1,164	1,184				
Two Kettle	228					
Northern Sioux	500	167				
Mixed Bloods	520	762				
Standing Rock, S. Dak.			3,454	3,645	2,300	6,083
Blackfeet	720	571				
Hunkpapa	521	1,734				
Other	1,116[f]					45,305[l]
Total	39,342	25,920	27,558	31,192	32,913	103,255

[a]After 1890 the Cuthead Yanktonai are included with the Santee.

[b]The Yanktonai figures include Santees and Tetons at Fort Peck.

[c]After 1890 the Yanktonai are included with the Teton.

[d]Sisseton 428, Wahpeton 411.

[e]Lower Yanktonai 882, Upper Yanktonai 488.

[f]Sioux, mostly Teton, returned from Canada.

[g]Santee 51, Sisseton 420, Wahpeton 142.

[h]Cuthead 296, Yanktonai 124.

[i]Oglala 4,486, Mixed Blood 528.

[j]Sisseton 652, Sisseton-Wahpeton 3,499, Lake Traverse 59.

[k]Oglala 17,801, Pine Ridge 668.

[l]Other identifications, not assignable to any specific reservation: Blackfeet Sioux, 474; Brule, 61; Dakota, 595; Mdewakanton, 276; Minneconjou, 24; Sans Arc, 10; Santee, 2,020; Sioux, 40,592; Teton Sioux, 1,111; Two Kettle, 1; Wahpekute, 26; Wahpeton, 98; Wazhaza, 3; Yanktonai, 14.

The Indian Self-Determination and Educational Assistance Act of 1975 gave Indian tribes the ability to contract and administer programs previously run by the BIA, and by the end of the 1990s, Sioux tribal governments wielded considerable authority over the day-to-day management of their reservations (table 4), while the BIA's role stabilized into cooperative collaboration (Kurkiala 1997:104–108). Still, the fundamental structural dilemma remained: responsibility for the most plentiful and valuable asset on the reservation—the land—rested with the federal government, not the tribe, and anything affecting the land was subject to review.

Table 3. Population of Canadian Sioux Reserves, 1970–1999

	1970	1999
Saskatchewan		
Moose Woods (White Cap)	148	375
Standing Buffalo	514	979
Sioux Wahpeton (Round Plain)	84	349
Wood Mountain	70	189
Manitoba		
Birdtail	187	582
Oak Lake	272	532
Sioux Valley (Oak River)	899	1,921
Sioux Village-Long Plain	224	493
Total	2,398	5,420

SOURCE: Canada. Department of Indian Affairs and Northern Development (1970:19, 23–24, 2000:43–44, 50, 58, 64).

Religion

Revival of Native Religion

Traditional Sioux religious ceremonies had been banned by the government from the 1880s, and although the Sun Dance had been held beginning in the late 1920s on Pine Ridge and Rosebud, its resumption was tentative. As late as 1958 there was still "great hostility" from many communities on Rosebud toward the annual Sun Dance (Feraca 1998:11, 22).

During the 1950s and 1960s the Oglala Sioux Tribe sponsored an annual Sun Dance as part of their summer celebration (fig. 3). Most of the preliminary rituals were dispensed with, the ceremony shortened to two or three days, and its religious character downplayed. Dancing ended by noon to make way for the powwow (fig. 4) that lasted far into the night, and only the last day's piercing drew a crowd (Feraca 1998:11–22; T.H. Lewis 1990:22–23, 53–65).

In the 1970s the attitude of young Sioux toward traditional religion and the Sun Dance began to change. Men and women grew their hair long, and Sun Dancing and being pierced became important components of being Indian and symbols of political commitment (Medicine 1981:281, 1987; Young Bear and Theisz 1994:157). The number of Sun Dances exploded from eight in all of South Dakota in 1978 (Medicine 1981:283) to 43 on Pine Ridge alone in 1997 (*Indian Country Today*, July 28, 1997).

Other aspects of traditional religion became more prominent. Sweatlodge ceremonies became commonplace, both as ceremonies in their own right and as purification for the vision quest, *yuwípi* (fig. 5), *lowápi*, naming, and other rituals (Bucko 1998:15). These ceremonies embodied a sense of continuity with the past, as religious specialists passed on the ritual knowledge they had preserved (T.H. Lewis 1990:71–105; Mails and Chief Eagle 1979; Crow Dog and Erdoes 1995). The central symbol of that continuity, the sacred Calf Pipe, resumed its honored role in Sioux ritual life, and individual pipe carriers, sharing in the Calf Pipe's power,

Table 4. Sioux Reservations and Reserves

Reservation or Reserve	Social Groups
Minnesota	
Lower Sioux	Santee (Mdewakanton)
Prairie Island	Santee (Mdewakanton)
Prior Lake	Santee (Mdewakanton)
Upper Sioux	Santee (Mdewakanton, Sisseton)
Montana	
Fort Peck	Santee (Sisseton, Wahpeton Wahpekute); Yanktonai; Teton (mostly Hunkpapa)
Nebraska	
Santee	Santee (Mdewakanton, Wahpekute)
North Dakota	
Spirit Lake (formerly Devils Lake)	Santee (Sisseton, Wahpeton); Yanktonai (*pʰábaksa*)
North and South Dakota	
Standing Rock	Teton (Blackfeet, Hunkpapa); Yanktonai
South Dakota	
Cheyenne River	Teton (Blackfeet, Minneconjou, Sans Arc, Two Kettle)
Lower Brule	Teton (Lower Brule)
Flandreau	Santee (Mdewakanton, Wahpeton)
Crow Creek	Yanktonai (*húkpatʰi*)
Pine Ridge	Teton (Oglala)
Rosebud	Teton (Brule)
Sisseton	Santee (Sisseton, Wahpeton)
Yankton	Yankton
Manitoba	
Birdtail (Reserve No. 57)	Santee (Wahpeton, Mdewakanton); Yanktonai
Oak Lake (Reserve No. 59)	Santee (Wahpekute, Wahpeton); Yanktonai
Sioux Valley (Oak River) (Reserve No. 58)	Santee (Sisseton, Mdewakanton, Wahpekute, Wahpeton)
Sioux Village–Long Plain (Portage La Prairie) (Reserve No. 89)	Santee (Wahpeton)
Saskatchewan	
Moose Woods (White Cap) (Reserve No. 94)	Santee (Sisseton); Yanktonai
Standing Buffalo (Reserve No. 78)	Santee (Sisseton, Wahpeton)
Sioux Wahpeton (Round Plain) (Reserve No. 94a)	Santee (Wahpeton, Mdewakanton, Sisseton, Wahpekute)
Wood Mountain (Reserve No. 160)	Teton (Hunkpapa)

SOURCE: Feraca and Howard (1963); Parks and DeMallie (1992).

once again occupied important positions in their communities (Looking Horse 1987; DeMallie and Parks 1987:4–5)

American Indian Religious Freedom Act

The resurgence of traditional religion prompted Congress to address the issue by passing the American Indian

1ˢᵀ **Annual Hollow Horn Bear**

Sundance

Location

½ mile N.W. of Joe Eagle Elk residence above the Grass Mountain Valley on the Rosebud Sioux Indian Reservation 5 miles west of St. Francis, South Dakota.

Spiritual Leaders

Joe Eagle Elk

Mato Hehlogeca-Hollow Horn Bear

Purification Days
July 23 24 25 26
1989
Sundance Days
July 27 28 29 30
1989
Information
Albert White Hat
747-2711
Duane Hollow Horn Bear
747-2718

Come pray with us. Pray with us for all that we as Indian people put our beliefs in. This gathering is not an honoring or a memorial nor is it to make a Chief. When Hollow Horn Bear walked this earth, he carried this pipe to pray for his people and to help his people.

We know that we can never be the kind of man that he was. But . . . we can do one thing as he would have done. Pray for his people..

Come pray with us.

832

Fig. 3. Sun Dance. top left, Oglala Sun Dancers coming out of the preparation tepee. Frank Fools Crow is on the left. top center, Dancers facing the center pole where prayer clothes flutter. top left and center, Photographs by Thomas Lewis, Pine Ridge Res., S. Dak., 1967. top right, Peter Catches blowing eagle-bone whistle as he prays facing the center pole. center left, Fools Crow pierces dancer on the ground (cropped). top right and center left, Photographs by Thomas Lewis, Pine Ridge Res., S. Dak. 1968. center right, Dancer blowing eagle-bone whistle pulling away from the center pole. Photograph by Richard Erdoes, Rosebud Res., S. Dak., 1971. bottom left, William Schweigman (Eagle Feather), facing front with arm raised. To the left is the pipe altar and buffalo skull. Photograph by Stephen E. Feraca, Pine Ridge Res., S. Dak., 1961. bottom right, Poster advertising the first Annual Hollow Horn Bear Sun Dance, Rosebud Res., S. Dak., July 27–30, 1989.

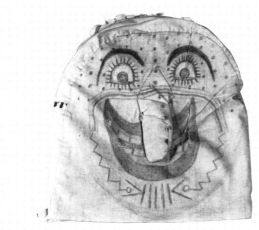

Fig. 4. Heyokas at a powwow. Heyokas were traditionally Thunder dreamers, who possessed sacred powers for war and healing. They dressed in rags, wore masks, and engaged in comic, backward behavior. Their contrary antics served to enforce social conformity (T.H. Lewis 1990:140–152). Photograph by Bates Littlehales, Pine Ridge Res., S. Dak., 1955. bottom, Mask made by Frank White-buffalo-man, Teton, painted with symbols of thunder, lightning, and hail. Collected in 1953 by James Howard near LaPlant, S. Dak., height 38.7 cm including fringe.

Religious Freedom Act (AIRFA) of 1978: "It shall be the policy of the United States to protect and preserve for American Indians their inherent right to believe, express, and exercise [their] traditional religion" (Prucha 1990:288–289). AIRFA was invoked primarily in sacred site cases, some of which involved the Sioux.

In *Fools Crow* v. *Gullett* the Sioux and Cheyenne sued the State of South Dakota to halt construction of tourist facilities at Bear Butte State Park. The Indians charged that tourists interfered with their right to carry out vision quests as guaranteed by AIRFA. In its 1982 decision the court made a distinction between religious belief and religious practice. Improvements at Bear Butte did not force Indian practitioners to relinquish their religious *beliefs*, even if their practices were disrupted on occasion by tourist activities; the plaintiffs had not proved that the site was inaccessible to them. In the court's view, AIRFA was not an enforceable statute, but merely a statement of federal policy (Forbes-Boyt 1999:307–12; S. O'Brien 1991:37–38).

United States v. *Means* grew out of a symbolic occupation of the Black Hills by the American Indian Movement (AIM) in 1988. When the Forest Service refused to issue a special use permit for the Yellow Thunder camp, AIM sued citing AIRFA. The initial ruling upheld their position, but the appeals court reversed that decision, declaring that Indians could not impose a "religious servitude" upon public lands (S. O'Brien 1991:38–39).

In another case AIRFA succeeded. Section 2 of the act required federal departments to review their policies and procedures affecting Indian religion. In 1995 the U.S. National Park Service implemented a policy strongly discouraging rock climbing on Devil's Tower, Wyoming, during the month of June, in deference to the numerous ceremonies performed there at that time. Although this voluntary ban was quickly honored by most visitors and the number of climbers fell sharply (*Denver Rocky Mountain News*, July 7, 1998), it was challenged by some commercial rock climbers. However, their suit was dismissed and upheld by an appeals court (*Denver Rocky Mountain News*, April 30, 1999).

Christianity

Christianity remained a vital force on the Sioux reservations (fig. 6). After World War II virtually all Sioux professed belief in Christianity and at least nominal membership in some church. Most *tʰiyóšpaye* communities had a church that was the center of social as well as religious activity (G. Macgregor 1946:93). In one Pine Ridge community an astonishing 98 percent claimed to attend church, with 76 percent attending

833

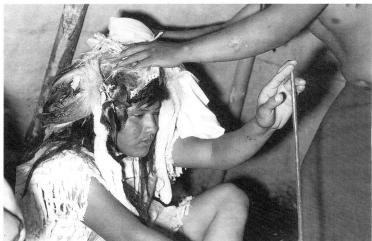

Fig. 5. Ritual. top left and right, *yuwípi* ceremony. top left, Willie Wounded, medicine man officiating at a *yuwípi* service at the home of James Red Cloud, Pine Ridge Res., S. Dak. Wounded holds a catlinite pipe and eagle feathers. The altar includes a tin can filled with earth, sticks with tied cloth offerings containing bits of tobacco, small tied pouches containing tobacco radiating out from the can, rawhide rattles, braided sweet grass and one longer staff to which 2 spotted tail feathers of the mature golden eagle are attached (Feraca 1998:30–44). Photograph by Robert Ruby, 1954. top right, Altar and participants at Crow Dog's house, Rosebud Res., Mission, S. Dak., 1969. An eagle's head is a prominent part of the altar, as are kettles of dog meat. Photograph by Richard Erdoes. bottom left, Left Hand Bull, Teton Sioux, participating in a healing ceremony. Photograph by Richard Erdoes, Rosebud Res., 1960s. bottom right, Peyote ceremony at Crow Dog's house, Rosebud Res. Loose feather fan, gourd rattles, ritual staff, and drum are pictured (Swan 1999). Photograph by Richard Erdoes, 1968.

whenever possible or whenever held (Malan and Jesser 1959:53). The reservations were relatively open to evangelism, and many Sioux enjoyed attending tent revivals and other worship services without changing their church affiliation (Feraca 1998:7).

As traditional religion grew in popularity, some clergy tried to incorporate elements of it, such as the pipe, into their worship services, but this proved controversial and was angrily resisted by many older church members (Grobsmith 1981:84; Feraca 1998:86). Still, Christian churches remained the customary site for funerals, even for traditionalists. By the 1990s evangelical denominations, such as the Baptist and Assembly of God denominations, had

established themselves among the Sioux, expanding the base of Christianity on the reservation (Poor Man 1987; DeMallie and Parks 1987:13).

Pan-Indianism

"Pan-Indianism" is an anthropological term coined to describe the development of an "Indian" consciousness, a feeling of commonality or "peoplehood," in effect, a new ethnic identity (Hertzberg 1971:viii; R.K. Thomas 1968:77; Sanford 1971a:222). Many Indians resented the term, since it was based on the premise that this new identity would replace tribal identities. Still, pan-Indianism as a state-of-

St. Joseph's Indian School

Where Wishes Come True!

Chamberlain, S.D.　57326

Marquette U. Arch., Bureau of Catholic Ind. Mission Records, Milwaukee, Wis.: top left, neg. 0532, right, neg. 0657; bottom: Smithsonian, NAA: 99-10369.

Fig. 6. Roman Catholicism on Pine Ridge Res., S. Dak. left, Corpus Christi procession under the direction of the Jesuit priest Rev. Placidus F. Sialm. Photograph possibly by Father Eugene Buechel, S.J., at St. Agnes Church, Manderson, June 1927. right, Mass at St. Elizabeth's Church, Oglala. Nicholas Black Elk, a catechist, sits in the front row second from right next to John Lone Goose. Behind Black Elk next to the wall is Jake Cow Killer and next to him is Martin Red Bear. Photograph by Rev. Joseph Zimmerman, S.J., Sept. 1936. bottom, St. Joseph's Indian School, Chamberlain, S. Dak., bumper sticker. The school was started in 1927 as a boarding school by the Priests of the Sacred Heart. In the mid-1960s nearly 350 children from Crow Creek, Lower Brule, Cheyenne River, Rosebud, and Pine Ridge reservations attended the school. In 1998–1999 the enrollment was about 200 students ages 6 to 18.

mind or situational identity was widespread, and for many Indians the traits, activities, and institutions of the Plains, particularly those of the Sioux, came to symbolize this general Indian identity (W.K. Powers 1970; R.K. Thomas 1968:79–81; Cornell 1988:126). In contrast, pan-Indianism as a political goal evolved into a strategy for protecting and strengthening tribalism (Cornell 1988:107).

The most successful pan-Indian organization was the National Congress of American Indians, established in 1944 (vol. 4:312). Many Sioux were active in the organization including Helen Peterson, Robert Burnette, and Vine Deloria, Jr., each of whom served terms as executive director. The NCAI's campaign against the termination policy was its most notable accomplishment (vol. 4:314) (Hertzberg 1971:289–292; Cornell 1988:119–125; Cowger 1999).

Deloria's career as an author had a substantial influence on political pan-Indianism. His writings detailed the common experiences of all tribes in their dealings with the government and asserted a system of shared attitudes and beliefs toward the land and nature. Deloria's fostering of an Indian consciousness in the service of maintaining and expanding tribal lands and sovereignty coincided with the rise of Indian activism and provided the ideological basis for it (V. Deloria 1969, 1973, 1974).

The American Indian Movement, the most visible pan-Indian activist organization, was founded in Minneapolis in 1968 to monitor police treatment of Indians. One of its early leaders, Russell Means (Oglala) was a master at staging highly symbolic, publicity-generating protests, and the organization grew nationwide. It was Means who urged that AIM expand from its pan-Indian urban base to involvement in reservation issues, where it became indelibly linked with Pine Ridge (Sherman 1980; Means 1995).

Wounded Knee

On March 8, 1972, an Oglala named Raymond Yellow Thunder was beaten to death in Gordon, Nebraska. Distrustful of border town justice and denied assistance by the tribe and the BIA, Yellow Thunder's family asked AIM for help in insuring that those responsible were prosecuted. AIM had not been active on the Sioux reservations, but over the next several months it acquired a reputation on the reservations as the Indians' protector, gaining recruits and support from full-blood communities (Sherman 1980:4; Burnette 1974:193; Means 1995:213–221).

At that time the full bloods on Pine Ridge were engaged in a bitter dispute with the mixed-blood tribal president

Richard Wilson. The federal government had targeted AIM as a subversive organization, and when AIM became active on the reservation, it secretly offered Wilson encouragement and support (Churchill and Vander Wall 1988). The crisis came in February 1973, when the Oglala Sioux Civil Rights Organization (OSCRO) gathered a petition to impeach Wilson. The government sent 80 federal agents to fortify the Pine Ridge BIA compound, and Wilson began deputizing supporters as tribal police. On February 21, he presided over his own highly irregular impeachment trial and acquittal. In response, OSCRO, along with the old treaty council and the landowners' association, appealed to AIM for help, and on February 28, 1973, some 200 armed men and women occupied the community of Wounded Knee (fig. 7) (Means 1995:249–253; Burnette 1974:220–225; DeMallie 1978a:306–307).

The popularity of Dee Brown's (1970) *Bury My Heart at Wounded Knee* meant that the history of Wounded Knee was fresh in the public's mind, and the government's massive response of men and modern military equipment made the symbolic parallel unmistakable. In late April, two Indians, Frank Clearwater and Buddy Lamont, were killed by government fire within days of each other, and shortly afterward, Frank Fools Crow, a respected traditional religious leader, mediated an end to the confrontation. Along with the two killed, 12 Indians and two non-Indians were injured, and the trading post, museum, and Roman Catholic church destroyed (Burnette 1974:226–250; Means 1995:258–287; Matthiessen 1980:59–83).

The Wounded Knee occupation grew out of a political dispute, and opinions about its significance were equally divided. For many Sioux, Wounded Knee became a symbol of the divisiveness that continued to plague them, and of the violence and lawlessness of AIM which generated hostility toward all Indians. To others, Wounded Knee represented a rebirth of pride and cultural discovery, a willingness to stand up for Indian rights and justice. The intensity of these contrasting positions confirmed the symbolic power of Wounded Knee.

Black Hills Claim Case

In the eyes of the western Sioux, the Black Hills were special. Beautiful and inviting, they were abundant in natural resources. Spiritually, the Black Hills were the center of the universe, believed by many to be the site of creation. Newspaper accounts in 1874 reported that "the Black Hills are holy ground of the holiest sort" to the Sioux, "the most sacred spot on earth" (Sundstrom 1997a:207). The appropriation of the Black Hills in 1877 was a catastrophic blow to the Sioux, and the effort to right this wrong became a unifying symbol of government mistreatment and Sioux resistance to acculturation (Clow 1983:315–316; Lazarus 1991:78–95; Sundstrom 1997a).

Organization for the Black Hills claim began informally in the 1880s; then, in 1891, a group of some 300 men calling

Fig. 7. Political activism. top, Josephine Gates Kelly (Yanktonai, b. 1888, d. 1976), from Ft. Yates, Standing Rock Res., N. Dak., and Ben American Horse (Teton, b. 1876, d. 1960) from Kyle, Pine Ridge Res., S. Dak. at the opening ceremony of the Republican national convention, Chicago, 1944. Kelly, the granddaughter of Yanktonai chief Two Bears, was the first woman to be a tribal chairman at Standing Rock. bottom, Bobby Onco, Kiowa, a member of the American Indian Movement (AIM), after a ceasefire agreement between AIM forces and federal marshals at Wounded Knee, Pine Ridge Res., in 1973 (vol. 4:322–323). Native Americans other than Sioux participated. Photographed March 9, 1973.

themselves the Oglala Council formally organized for monthly meetings, and similar groups soon organized on all the Sioux reservations (Lazarus 1991:119). The issue for these old warriors was simple: the Treaty of 1868 acknowledged the Black Hills as part of Sioux territory and stipulated that all subsequent agreements had to be approved by three-fourths of the adult, male Sioux; the Agreement of 1876 relinquishing the Black Hills had not met this requirement; therefore, the agreement and the transfer of the Black Hills were invalid.

The Sioux faced formidable obstacles in making this claim. Before an Indian tribe could sue the United States, Congress had to pass a special jurisdictional act that granted permission for the suit and defined the specific question to be resolved and the basis for determining relevant evidence. The Sioux also had to contend with government opposition. Reservation superintendents tried to discourage their meetings. The BIA denied them tribal funds for expenses and refused to hire an attorney to work on the claim or to provide any assistance or advice (Clow 1983:316–19; Lazarus 1991:119–130).

All the early effort for the claim had come from traditionalists. In June 1915, at the urging of Commissioner of Indian Affairs Cato Sells, the educated, more acculturated Sioux formed the Great Council of the Sioux Nation and effec-

tively wrested control of the claim process away from the traditionalists (Lazarus 1991:130–138). It was not until the 1970s that traditionalists were again able to influence the Black Hills claim.

Congress passed the Sioux Jurisdictional Act on June 3, 1920, authorizing the U.S. Court of Claims to examine the Sioux case. The act stipulated that should the court find that the Sioux had a claim, its value would be equal to its value in 1877, the time of taking (precluding consideration of the enormous mineral wealth discovered and extracted after that date) and the government could offset against it

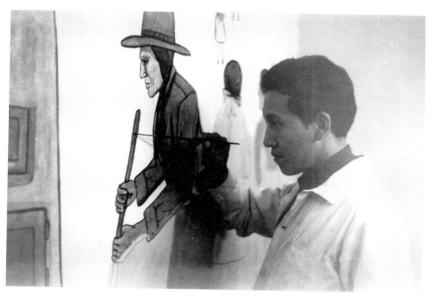

Fig. 8. Continuation of expressive culture. top left, Andrew Standing Soldier (Teton, b. 1917, d. 1967) painting a mural in the Oglala Community School auditorium, Pine Ridge, S. Dak. Photograph by Russell Lee, 1940. top right, Amos Owen (b. 1917, d. 1990), Mdewakanton Santee carver and spiritual leader from Prairie Island, Minn., finishing a catlinite buffalo-head pipe. Owen was teaching at a cultural camp for Indian youth. Photograph by Randy Croce, Pipestone National Monument, Minn., 1978. bottom left, Quilt in star design, resembling the feathered circle design of hide paintings ("Art Until 1900," fig. 2, this vol.). Star quilt ceremonies have become an integral part of high school basketball tournaments on the Ft. Peck Res., where the figure of a ball is often added to quilts (MacDowell and Dewhurst 1997). Hand-pieced quilt of satin made in 1996 by Rae Jean Walking Eagle, Assiniboine-Sioux of Brockton, Mont. Size 97 by 121 cm. bottom right, Edna Little Elk Leighton giveaway at a memorial feast. Displayed are quilts and a blue blanket with beaded strip. Photograph by Dennis Lessard, Rosebud Res., S. Dak., July 1977.

all payments made to the Sioux under the Act of 1877, as well as any other payments Congress had authorized since then. On May 7, 1923, Ralph Case, the principal attorney for the Sioux, filed the Black Hills claim. (For a concise chronology of the claim case, see Gonzalez and Cook-Lynn 1999:331–357). Although in 1923 representatives from all of the reservations voted unanimously to seek the "best price" for the land they had lost, most traditionalist Sioux continued to hope for return of the Black Hills (Lazarus 1991:148).

In 1970, the government established an important precedent by returning the sacred Blue Lake area to Taos Pueblo (V. Deloria 1993). The return of the Black Hills no longer seemed unattainable, and demands for their return by traditionalists and activists alike began to gather support. "The sacred Black Hills are not for sale" became the rallying cry (Lazarus 1991:326).

These changes in attitude were significant because by this time the momentum of the Black Hills claim had turned in the Sioux's favor. In 1957, after nothing but adverse rulings, the Sioux replaced Ralph Case with Marvin Sonosky, Arthur Lazarus, Jr., and William Howard Payne. Sonosky and Lazarus were Washington insiders who set out to win for their clients the largest cash settlement possible, and through astute legal maneuvering were close to that goal. The Sioux, however, now had a different goal.

The court case ended on June 30, 1980 when an 8–1 majority of the Supreme Court affirmed that the United States had taken the Black Hills in violation of the 5th Amendment "just compensation" clause. In other words, Congress had the power to take the Black Hills, it simply had not paid enough for them. The Sioux were awarded $17,553,484 (the calculated value in 1877) with interest at 5% from February 28, 1877, approximately $105 million. Shortly thereafter, the Oglala Sioux Tribal Council unanimously adopted a resolution disavowing any participation in the Black Hills "just compensation" settlement, an action soon duplicated by the other Sioux tribal councils. For the Sioux, the Black Hills had been seized illegally in violation of the 1868 Treaty; accepting the cash award meant accepting the government's position and ending any hope of regaining the Black Hills. In the early 1980s congressional legislation was introduced, but never considered, to return the federal land in the Black Hills to the Sioux (Lazarus 1991:419, 422). Meanwhile, the cash award remained in the United States Treasury earning interest; in 1998 the total was nearly $500 million.

Sources

Nurge's (1970) volume presents papers on diverse topics. Studies of individual communities on Pine Ridge Reservation (Mekeel 1932; Macgregor 1946; Malan and Schusky 1962), together with formerly-Pine Ridge Bennett County (Wagoner 1997) provide insight into the changes and consistencies of reservation life. Maynard and Twiss (1969) offer a snapshot of conditions on Pine Ridge in the mid-1960s. Although the preponderance of published material on the twentieth-century Sioux focuses on Pine Ridge, there are also ethnographies of Rosebud (Grobsmith 1981), Lower Brule (Schusky 1975:181–236), Cheyenne River (Vazeilles 1977; L.J. Davis 1944), and the Prairie Island Sioux (C. Anderson 1997:377–496).

Bromert (1980) provides an overview of the New Deal programs implemented on the Sioux reservations. The effort by the government to sell the IRA is documented in the minutes of the 1934 Rapid City conference (U.S. Dept. of Interior 1934). Feraca (1964) critiques contemporary arguments made against adoption of the IRA, while Biolsi (1985, 1992) and Clow (1987) are critical of the IRA's aims and effects. Personal recollections of the IRA campaign and its aftermath are presented in Cash and Hoover (1971).

Taken together, the analyses of Useem, Macgregor, and Useem (1944), Eicher (1962), Useem and Eicher (1970), and Grobsmith (1981:30–37) give a dynamic picture of economic conditions on Rosebud. DeMallie (1978) provides a historical overview of the Pine Ridge economy, while Mekeel (1936), Malan (1963), and Maynard and Twiss (1969:54–75) analyze economic conditions and prospects. Schusky (1975a, 1979) outlines the changes and challenges following the Great Society programs of the 1960s.

Mekeel (1936a) and Szaszy (1975) describe the short-lived Indian education reforms of the New Deal. The psychologically oriented studies of education by Erikson (1939), Macgregor (1946:132–148), and Bryde (1971) provide information on child-rearing practices and child development. Wax, Wax, and Dumont (1964) and Bryde (1966) seek to explain the failure of Indian education. Orato (1953) documents the programs and approaches of one Pine Ridge day school, while Vazeilles (1977:63–85) describes high school activities on Cheyenne River. Changing patterns of kinship practices and social relations in postwar Sioux society are analyzed in Macgregor (1946:52–65, 105–122), Malan (1958), Malan and Powers (1960), and Maynard and Twiss (1969:111–121).

Albers (1983), Albers and Medicine (1983), Medicine (1978:93–96), and Vazeilles (1977:103–120) analyze the changing role of women in Sioux society. Medicine (1997) has written about gender identity and Two-Spirit people.

yuwípi and related rituals in the twentieth century are documented by Macgregor (1946:98–99), Hurt and Howard (1952), Ruby (1955:62–66), Feraca (1998:30–44), Fugle (1966), Grobsmith (1974), Kemnitzer (1976), Powers (1982), and T.H. Lewis (1990:71–105). The revival of the Sun Dance is described in Feraca (1998:8–22), Nurge (1964), T.H. Lewis (1972, 1990:52–70), Mails (1978, which includes detailed photo documentaries), and Medicine (1981). The life of Frank Fools Crow, the best-known leader in the resurgence of traditional religion, is documented in Mails and Chief Eagle (1979), while Crow Dog and Erdoes (1995) and Mohatt and Eagle Elk (2000) provide accounts of other religious practitioners.

The Native American Church among the Sioux is documented in Macgregor (1946:100–102), Ruby (1955:53–60, 66–71), Feraca (1998:59–70), Steltenkamp (1982:55–76), Spider (1987), and Steinmetz (1990:87–151).

Personal experiences of Tetons with Christianity are described in DeMallie and Parks (1987:91–155), Steinmetz (1990:153–162), and Steltenkamp (1993).

Lawson (1982a) comprehensively documents the Pick-Sloan Project and its aftermath. Lazarus's (1991) detailed account of the Black Hills claim court case is marred by a lack of documentation. Gonzalez and Cook-Lynn (1999) discuss the Black Hills case and a number of other contemporary issues in the context of lobbying for a national memorial at Wounded Knee. On the 1973 occupation of Wounded Knee, accounts of participants are recorded in *Akwesasne Notes* (1974), while Dewing (1985) furnishes a scholarly account. The activities of AIM and its leaders on the reservation are sympathetically portrayed in Matthiessen (1980).

Arapaho

LORETTA FOWLER

The direction from which the Algonquian-speaking Arapaho (uˈrăpu̦hō) entered the Northern Plains is unknown, but they probably arrived at least by the early eighteenth century. At this period or perhaps earlier, their northernmost division, the Gros Ventre, broke away to form a separate tribe. During the mid-nineteenth century, the Arapaho separated into the Northern Arapahoe, who settled on the Wind River Reservation in Wyoming, and the Southern Arapaho, who settled in Canadian and Blaine counties in Oklahoma. Their division led to significant social and cultural differences between the two groups.

Language and Component Groups

According to Arapaho tradition, there were five major divisions of the tribe, each with its own dialect* (Kroeber 1902–1907:5–7, 1916:73–74; see also Mooney 1896:954–956; vol. 17:46). From north to south they were: Gros Ventre (*hitóu·nénnoˀ* 'begging people'), Besawunena (*bê·sô·wû·nennóˀ* 'big lodge people'), Hinanaeina (*hinonoˀéínoˀ*), Ha'anahawunena, and Nawathinehena 'south people,' whose dialect was the most divergent.

The first three were said to have been closely related in dialect, Ha'anahawunena to have resembled Blackfoot, and Nawathinehena to have had some phonetic similarity to Cheyenne. The Hinanaeina who stayed in the north were the Nakhaseinena (*no·khô·seinénnóˀ* 'sage people'), Ba'achinena (*boˀó·či·nénnóˀ* 'red willow people'), and Ba'akunena (*beˀé·kuunénnoˀ* 'blood pudding people'). The four divisions south of the Gros Ventre consolidated into the Arapaho and their descendants adopted the language of the Hinanaeina. The Ha'anahawunena lost their separate identity first, and the Nawathinehena merged with the Hinanaeina to become the Southern Arapaho ("The Algonquian Languages of the Plains," this vol.).

*The phonemes of Arapaho are: (voiceless unaspirated stops and affricate) *t*, *č*, *k*, *ˀ*; (voiceless spirants) *s*, *θ*, *x*, *h*; (voiced stop and resonant) *b*, *n*; (semivowels) *w*, *y*; (short vowels) *i*, *e* ([ɛ]), *o* ([ɔ]), *u* ([ɨ]); (long vowels) *i·*, *e·* ([ɛ·]), *o·* ([ɔ·]), *u·* ([ɨ·]); (tautosyllabic balanced diphthong) *ei*; (low pitch) v, v·; (high pitch) v́, v́·; (falling pitch) v̂·. There are also two- and perhaps three-syllable vowel sequences; these have contrasting pitches on each syllable.

The analysis and transcription of Arapaho follows Goddard (1998:184; Salzmann 1983:29–30). Some pitches and contrasts between two- and three-mora vowel sequences remain uncertain.

Not all these groups can be identified historically, but during the late eighteenth and early nineteenth centuries both intense warfare and epidemics may have precipitated the merging of some divisions. In 1800, the fur trader Peter Fidler obtained a map from the Gros Ventre that locates four Arapaho groups (Fidler 1789–1804, 1800; J.M. Cooper 1939); Naw cotch is seen in nin nin (perhaps the Nakhaseinena); Nun ni en (Hinanaeina), numbering 100 tepees, who were classified as "Fall Indians" and shown southeast of the Mountain Crows; Beth thow in in (Besawanena), 20 tepees, shown farther south; and Now watch e ni in (Nawathinehena), 20 tepees, also to the south.

Territory and History

Trade and contacts with Spaniards in New Mexico preceded the first mention of the Arapaho in 1795 under the name Caminanbiches. They were reported to live on the headwaters of the Cheyenne River in western South Dakota and eastern Wyoming near their friends, the Kiowa (Truteau 1912:31). Apparently they had previously traded horses with the Missouri River villagers, but since the Sioux had come to the Missouri they had stayed away and traded through Cheyenne middlemen. About 1800, according to the fur trader Pierre-Antoine Tabeau, Arikaras attending a trade fair at the Black Hills met the Arapaho, who lived between the Yellowstone and Platte (fig. 1), were wealthy in horses, and traded prairie turnip flour to the Arikaras for corn at great profit. The "Squihitanes," presumably either a southern group of Gros Ventre (Fowler 1987:45–47, 265) or the Besawunena; and the Nimoussines (the Nawathinehena, reported by Tabeau to speak a different language). The Kiowa and Plains Apache were also present, the groups communicating by sign language (Tabeau 1939:153–155; Lewis and Clark in Thwaites 1904–1905, 6:101; Fowler 1987:45–47).

By 1806 the Cheyenne and Arapaho had formed an alliance, in large measure to counter the Sioux pushing west from the Missouri. Fur trader Alexander Henry observed that the two groups wintered together in Arapaho territory (probably at the foot of the Rockies in Wyoming and Colorado) then separated in the spring when the Cheyenne moved toward the villages on the Missouri to trade beaver and other skins (Coues 1897, 1:384).

By 1811 the Arapaho ranged primarily along the North Platte and south as far as the Arkansas River. The Cheyenne

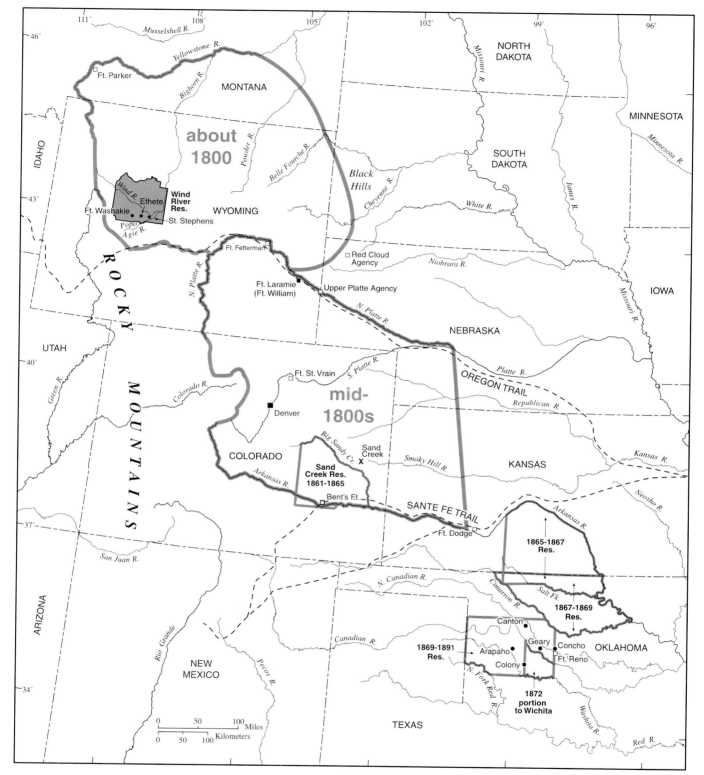

Fig. 1. Arapaho territory, about 1800, mid-19th century Arapaho and Cheyenne territory, and reservations.

generally remained farther north. A group of 250 Arapahos resided with Comanches and Plains Apaches in Texas. Although there were occasional conflicts with American trappers, there were also trade fairs where the Arapaho exchanged horses for manufactured goods. Making an uneasy alliance with the Sioux, some of the Cheyenne joined with the Arapaho and about 1826 began driving the Kiowa and Comanche south in an effort to secure the region between the Platte and Arkansas. A group of 350 Gros Ventres and 50 Blackfoots joined this alliance in the 1820s, some of whom returned north in the 1830s (Fowler 1982:40, 1987:48; H. Dodge 1836:140–141). War intensified with the Ute to the west, the Crow to the north, and the Pawnee to the east. In 1840 the allied tribes restored peace with the Kiowa and Comanche, who by this time were south of the Arkansas.

Trading posts (Bent's Fort on the Arkansas, Fort William on the North Platte, and Fort St. Vrain on the South Platte) were established between 1834 and 1839, which attracted the remainder of the Cheyenne into Arapaho territory in southeastern Wyoming and Colorado (Berthrong 1963:20–26). By the 1840s, the Sioux were established on the North Platte, competing with Arapaho and Cheyenne for game, and were making incursions on the South Platte. By 1850 the Arapaho were able to hold for themselves only the parks area at the foot of the Rockies and had no choice but to maintain an uneasy alliance with Sioux as well as Cheyenne (Fowler 1982:21–23).

These intertribal conflicts were precipitated by American expansion west. In the 1840s emigrants and travelers on the Oregon and Santa Fe trails disturbed the migratory patterns and contributed to the decline of the buffalo in Arapaho territory. Arapahos had to travel farther to find buffalo and therefore needed larger numbers of horses. Raids along the Santa Fe Trail and into New Mexico were an important source of stock, but the United States began to curb this raiding after 1848. Arapahos increasingly depended on trade goods—especially guns to facilitate the hunt for small game and to defend themselves against other tribes moving into their territory in pursuit of ever decreasing game. Sugar and coffee were also eagerly sought, and Arapahos, as well as Cheyennes, began to exact "tolls" from the emigrants, whom they blamed for the decline of the buffalo, in return for safe passage (Fowler 1982:22–26, 34).

The United States, seeking to protect settlers and emigrants, signed a peace treaty near Fort Laramie in 1851 with the tribes of the Northern and Central plains, who agreed to curtail warfare, refrain from attacks on United States citizens, and permit military posts in their country. The treaty assigned the Arapaho and Cheyenne jointly most of Colorado west to the foothills of the Rockies, the northwest part of Kansas, the southwest corner of Nebraska, and the southeast corner of Wyoming. The two tribes ranged between the Platte and Arkansas rivers east to the headwaters of the Republican River; the Arapaho generally stayed in the western limits of this region (Fowler 1982:28–32).

Despite the 1851 treaty, Americans began settling in Arapaho territory; in turn, some Arapaho bands began to move north and others south, drawing farther apart and embarking on separate political courses. In the 1850s settlers infiltrated the Smoky Hill River Valley, one of the best buffalo ranges, and in 1858 settlers and miners flooded the Pikes Peak area in Colorado in the heart of Arapaho hunting territory. Game was disturbed and the probability of violence

between Arapahos and Whites increased. As a result, the Northern Arapahoe (nenebî·nennóʔ 'northern men') began to withdraw north of the Platte into Wyoming and Montana to the Bighorn country, allying themselves with Sioux and Northern Cheyenne. The Southern Arapaho (nó·wunennóʔ 'southern men') were in greater jeopardy since their country bore the brunt of the immigration. They withdrew down the Arkansas and began a desperate effort to accommodate to the settlers. Their political history became linked to that of the Southern Cheyenne. Both Northern and Southern Arapaho tried to avoid war with Whites until 1864 (Fowler 1982:34–35, 42–44; ARCIA 1855:115–117; 1859:21, 113, 129–130; LR-NA 1858). Although small groups of Arapahos traveled back and forth between the two divisions during the 1860s and 1870s, the Southern Arapaho were assigned to the Upper Arkansas Agency; about this time they "adopted" a band of 415 Plains Apache (LR-NA 1861). The Northern division was assigned to the Upper Platte Agency.

The Southern Arapaho and Cheyenne were pressured into signing a treaty in 1861 by which they ceded rights to the territory assigned them in 1851 (ARCIA 1860:24, 228–230, 1861:17). In return they were given a small reservation on Sand Creek, which they never occupied because it was far from the buffalo range (LR 1862, 1878; ARCIA 1863:134). They supplemented meager hunts by stealing stock from settlers, while avoiding confrontations with them. In retaliation, Colorado volunteer troops began attacking Indians (ARCIA 1863:16, 127). The Sand Creek Massacre in September 1864, in which a small group of Arapaho and a much larger group of Cheyenne were attacked, provoked war between the tribes of the Southern and Central Plains and the United States army and local militias (ARCIA 1864:216–251, 1865:23–51). A peace treaty was signed with the Southern Arapaho in 1865 but Arapahos continued to be at risk, for the soldiers and settlers alike rarely bothered to distinguish between "friendly" and "hostile" Indians. By and large Arapahos tried to remain south of the Arkansas away from the fighting (ARCIA 1866:2). In 1867 another treaty was signed at Medicine Lodge Creek in which Arapahos and Cheyennes agreed to settle on a reservation in Kansas between the Arkansas and Cimmaron rivers (ARCIA 1868). Subsequently, Arapahos claimed that there was a misunderstanding about the boundaries of this reservation and pressed the government to settle them on a reservation on the Canadian River in Indian Territory (vol. 4:54). In 1869 an executive order established the Cheyenne-Arapaho Agency and reservation on the Canadian (ARCIA 1869:35, 51–59).

The Northern Arapahoe were also confronted with the trespass of settlers in Wyoming and Montana. Gold was discovered in Montana in 1862, and military posts and settlers soon followed. The threat to hunting territory led to a war between Indians and Whites, 1865–1868. During these years, presidential peace commissions negotiated with the Northern Arapahoe, Cheyenne, and Sioux, who agreed to cede much of the 1851 territory and to settle on a reservation as long as they could hunt undisturbed north of the Platte and east of the Bighorn Mountains. The Northern Arapahoe, who had refused to acknowledge the legitimacy of the 1861 cession, were determined to remain in Wyoming, politically independent from the Sioux and Cheyenne. They attempted to develop friendly relations with army officers at Fort Fetterman and to arrange a peace with their former enemies, the Eastern Shoshone, who obtained a reservation in Wyoming in 1868, with the intent of settling on that reservation, or to arrange for settlement on the Gros Ventre reservation in Montana. For a time they lived on the Eastern Shoshone reservation, but conflict with trespassing Whites led to their relocation east at the Red Cloud Agency for the Oglala Sioux.

During 1870–1876, the Northern Arapahoe predicament worsened; they suffered significant casualties in clashes with both Whites and Eastern Shoshones. In the fall of 1876 peace commissioners pressured the Arapahoe, Cheyenne and Sioux into ceding their claim to the Black Hills and to all land outside the Great Sioux Reservation. Although Northern Arapahoe agreed to settle with the Sioux or with the Southern Arapaho, they continued to negotiate for a separate reservation. In 1876–1877 most of the Northern Arapahoe warriors enlisted in the army in a campaign against the Northern Cheyenne and Sioux; subsequently, they obtained the army's backing for their settlement in Wyoming. By executive order they were permitted to settle on Wind River Reservation, where they moved from Red Cloud, arriving in March 1878 (Fowler 1982:46–67; LR-NA 1862).

Culture in the Nineteenth Century

Religion

In Arapaho belief, cosmic, natural, and social forces in the world operated harmoniously in return for supplication to the Great Mystery, whose symbol was the Flat Pipe bundle. This supplication was aided by harmonious relations among Arapahos, especially during religious ceremonies. In Arapaho belief, thoughts and their expression (for example, in words or in quillwork designs) caused things to happen; this belief underlied prayer and ritual as well as the entire value system.

The origin of the Arapaho and their way of life is explained in the Flat Pipe myth, only fragments of which were recorded. Before the Flat Pipe existed there were four successive worlds or lives (Kroeber 1902–1907:22, 35, 337). In the Flat Pipe story, the earth is covered with water, on which floats a Pipe Person, "the Creator," "thinking and planning" and praying "to get an idea" for the good. The Pipe Person received 'power' (béétee) and was able by prayer to call for and send waterfowl and other animals below the surface of the water to look for the land (Fowler 1982:68). The redheaded duck failed, but the turtle succeeded in bringing up sufficient dirt on his feet. In "deep thought," Pipe Person sang four songs and spread the mud out on the pipe, dried it, and blew it in four directions,

thereby creating the earth. The Sun and Moon and a man and a woman were made from the clay, and animal and plant life and the seasons were generated. At this time. Pipe Person instructed the first Arapahos how to live (G.A. Dorsey 1903:191–212; G.A. Dorsey and Kroeber 1903:1–2; Kroeber 1902–1907:360; Fowler 1982:68). The instructions were given through the culture hero–trickster Nih'atha (nih?ó·θo·) in some accounts, or by Buffalo, in others.

Pipe Person presumably drew on a general power or life force conceived of as Above (also referred to as Grandfather or Father) (Kroeber 1902–1907:313; Curtis 1907–1930, 6:144), though W.P. Clark (1885:400) was told that in an earlier time the life force was Below. Pipe Person was also referred to as Father. By the start of the twentieth century some elderly Arapahos hesitatingly identified both Above and Pipe Person with Nih'atha and referred to the "god of the missionaries" as hixcébe? nih?ó·θo· 'Nih'atha Above' (G.A. Dorsey and Krober 1903:6–7; Kroeber 1902–1907:313). Apparently, though, Above and Nih'atha were originally not one and the same; the "younger generation" confused them (Curtis 1907–1930, 6:144; see also G.A. Dorsey 1903:200). In any case, Pipe Person gave the Arapaho a Pipe bundle (se?î·čóo· 'flat pipe') to care for and to use as a medium for conveying prayers to Pipe Person, the creator (Mooney 1896:959).

The Flat Pipe reportedly was in the care of a particular family of the Big Lodge People (Mooney 1896:959). Tribally-owned, the pipe was tubular and made of stone; it was kept with its stem in a deerskin bundle together with a turtle and an ear of corn, both of stone (in one version of the creation story, duck and turtle gave corn to the Arapaho) (Mooney 1896:959–960; Kroeber 1902–1907:21, 308–309; Curtis 1907–1930, 6:140–141). The bundle's priest or "keeper" had his tepee in the inside of the camp circle; this tepee was the first to be taken down when the camp moved. The priest performed rites throughout the year and presided when individuals vowed to sponsor a Pipe ceremony in return for supernatural aid.

Next in importance to the Flat Pipe were seven men's and seven women's medicine bags, which were also tribally owned and in the keeping of priests. The men's bags were in the charge of the či·nécei-beh?í·hohó? 'water pouring old men'. Of buffalo skin, the bags contained objects used in these priests' sweatlodge, which occupied the center of the camp circle to the east of the tepee of the Keeper of the Flat Pipe. Their sweatlodge ceremony was conducted on behalf of all Arapahos (Curtis 1907–1930:142; Mooney 1896:986, 989; Kroeber 1902–1907:207–208). The seven women's bags contained implements for painting and quill-embroidering tepee covers, cradles, and robes. These activities could only be done under the supervision of these women priests (Kroeber 1902–1907:30, 70, 209–210; Curtis 1907–1930, 6:142).

Both Southern and Northern Arapaho had Sacred Wheels (feathered hoops) in the keeping of a priest, but when they originated as tribally owned medicine is not clear. The Wheel may have assumed greater religious significance among the Southern Arapaho after the two divisions separated, the Flat Pipe accompanying the Northern division. Individuals could vow to make a prayer-sacrifice to the Wheel, and it played a prominent role in the Offerings Lodge (Kroeber 1902–1907:309–310; Curtis 1907–1930, 6:141–142; see also G.A. Dorsey 1903).

During the mid-nineteenth century, individuals also had custody of painted buckskin pictographic records whose designs detailed myths and ceremonies. One such custodian was one of the Water Pouring Old Men (Kroeber 1902–1907:311–313; Hilger 1952:86).

The concept of prayer-sacrifice was central. The sincerity of a petitioner's prayer was validated by sacrifices of property or of the body by flesh offerings and fasting. In return for good health or other forms of supernatural aid, individuals vowed to complete sacrifices, such as sponsorship or participation in a ceremony and feasting or donating to others, especially elderly people. Individuals sometimes were instructed by supernatural beings in dreams to make these sacrifices. The major ritual of prayer-sacrifice was the *hóseihóowú?'* 'Offerings Lodge', the Arapaho counterpart of the Sun Dance.

The Offerings Lodge lasted seven days and had two phases. First was the three-day Rabbit Lodge, a secret rite involving the Lodgemaker and his wife and several elderly men and women who owned the rights to perform certain ceremonies and prepare regalia that symbolized events in the creation story.

The second phase, the Offerings Lodge itself, was a four-day public ceremony, during which the dancers or votaries—all men—were painted several times by their ceremonial grandfathers, the colors and designs symbolizing prayer-sacrifice as well as mythological themes. Throughout the ceremony the families of each grandfather and grandson exchanged food, which was subsequently distributed throughout the camp. Other themes of the Offerings Lodge included enactment of successful war exploits (also representing victory over adversity and ill health) and successful hunts (representing prosperity).

Arapahos also acquired individual supernatural helpers by dreaming or fasting for a vision; during the early nineteenth century they particularly chose to fast on various peaks in Estes Park. Power to cure and to succeed in war were the most frequently bestowed gifts, but also power to prophesy, divine, or manipulate weather. Women rarely fasted, but received unsolicited power in a dream or waking vision or received power transferred from a husband or parent. These powers generally had to do with curing (Kroeber 1902–1907:418–421, 434, 436–437, 450–451, 454; Mooney 1896:775–776, 898; Curtis 1907–1930, 6:142–143; Hilger 1952:124–130; Fowler 1982:27; Toll 1962:12, 19).

At least by the late nineteenth century, powerful curers among the Southern Arapaho were organized into societies according to the spirit-helper: Bears, Beavers, Buffalos, Foxes, Horses, Lizards. These societies accepted apprentices and a doctor could belong to more than one. Each spring the doctors met to renew the medicines (Kroeber 1902–1907:17, 317, 437–438, 444, 452; Hilger 1952:124–130, 134–141, 161; Curtis 1907–1930, 6:143).

Ceremonial and Political Organization

Men's societies (*béyóowuú* 'all the lodges') comprised a ceremonial organization with religious and political duties that were of such central importance that they colored all other Arapaho institutions (Mooney 1896:986–990; Curtis 1907–1930, 6:144–145, 159; Kroeber 1902–1907:151–209; see also Hayden 1862:325; W.P. Clark 1885:41, 355). Excluding the Offerings Lodge, in which any adult participated, the men's Lodge organization constituted an age-graded series headed by a tribal priesthood. These Lodges comprised bodies of knowledge as well as special regalia, ritual, songs, and dances. At the time of adolescence, a group of males entered the first of these Lodges and progressed through the entire series throughout their lives. If an individual failed to participate, he would be excluded from public ceremonies and war parties, but if he were unable to participate he could obtain a substitute.

Initiation into each Lodge was precipitated by a vow on the part of an individual to sponsor the ceremony. Agemates of the votary would join him and go through the ceremony as an age-group. The Lodge ceremonies were rituals of prayer-sacrifice, for the participants gave away food and property throughout the seven-day rite. Regalia used in each Lodge (fig. 2) were at once symbolic of

Smithsonian, Dept. of Anthr. a, 165,768 (neg. 80-20869-6A); b, 233,095 (neg. 80-17187-15A); c, 200,788 (neg. 80-16622-4); d, 200,906 (neg. 80-16621-14A); e, 165,800 (neg. 99-20273); f, 200,538 (neg. 81-3319-14); g, 153,056 (neg. 80-16622-31); h, 165,760 (neg. 80-16624-15); i, 153,054 (neg. 99-20266); j, 200,537 (neg. 99-20268).

Fig. 2. Society regalia. Each of the 4 societies for mature men and the one women's society had distinctive regalia worn in their dances. The two societies for young men, the Kit Fox Lodge and the Star Lodge, had no prescribed insignia. New regalia was made for members as they joined each society, and items were not usually passed down from retiring members. Tomahawk Lodge members wore no special clothing but had different staffs to designate their degree. a, Board or club of second degree member. b, Buffalo effigy staff of regular members. Spear Lodge members all wore waist pieces, head pieces, fur leg bands, and arm bands. Members of higher degrees carried lances. c, d, Arm band and head piece of regular members. Crazy Lodge members wore capes, head bands, leg bands, and bone whistles. e, Cape of regular members, made of buffalo hide with 4 lines of slashes radiating from a central hole with flap below. Dog Lodge members wore striped leggings and eagle bone whistles on straps and carried dew claw rattles. A single member of the first degree wore a feathered shirt and members of the second and third degrees wore long sashes over one shoulder. f, Yellow sash of third degree member. g, h, Whistle and rattle used by all members. Members of the women's Buffalo Lodge wore waist pieces and headdresses that varied according to their degree. i, j, Headdress and yellow hide waist piece of regular members. b, Collected by James Mooney, Arapaho reservation, Indian Terr., 1904; a, e, h, collected by Heinrich Voth, Arapaho reservation, Indian Terr., 1882–1893; c, d, f, g, i, j, collected by Emile Granier, Wyo., prior to 1891. a, length 101 cm; b, length 101 cm; c, length 30.5 cm; d, length 17.1 cm; e, width 103 cm; f, length 205 cm; g, length of whistle 19.7 cm; h, length 63.5 cm; i, height 58 cm; j, width 57 cm.

844

ARAPAHO

Arapaho values and served to reinforce bravery in battle, respect for elders, religious devotion, and the desire for an upright and prosperous life. Participation was a prayer for success in life and, at the same time, in the Lodges whose members were middle-aged or older, a means of obtaining supernatural aid. The Lodges also had important social functions, at least during the times of the year when Arapahos were in large camps. In addition, strong bonds were forged between Lodge members and between men of different Lodges, as well. At the time of the Offerings Lodge, each of these Lodges was assigned specific duties.

As an adolescent, a boy and his age-group joined the Kit Fox Lodge and after a few years one of the members would vow to sponsor the hóθoʔúhuyóowuʔ 'star lodge', the next in the series. These were secular organizations, but when the Kit Foxes were organizing to have the ceremony they selected "elder brothers" from the Tomahawk Lodge, older men who would train and assist them in all successive Lodges as well as in everyday life.

The first men's Lodge was the hiˑčeʔêˑxoówuʔ 'tomahawk lodge'. After the vow to hold the Lodge was made by a member of the Star Lodge, the elder brothers of the Stars would select four of the bravest men to receive special honors or "degrees" (including distinctive regalia) during the ceremony. Each Star member would also appeal to an older man who had already completed the Tomahawk Lodge ceremony to serve as his ceremonial "grandfather." The food and property transfers between grandfather and grandson were reciprocal and the two men gave only what they could afford. The grandfather retained his ceremonial knowledge; it could not be bought with property (see F.H. Stewart 1977:327–328 on this point, which was unique to the Arapaho and Gros Ventre). The grandfathers were supervised by the Water Pouring Old Men. Men's Lodges lasted seven days: three for instruction and preparation of regalia and four for a public dance supervised by the elder brothers. Members of the Tomahawk Lodge were divided into the Shorts and Stouts, who competed in races during the ceremony.

The second men's Lodge, reportedly borrowed in part from the Cheyenne, was the Spear or Drum Lodge (bîˑtohóowuʔ). After a Tomahawk man vowed to sponsor the ceremony, grandfathers were selected. This Lodge had nine men's honorary degrees and was also divided into Shorts and Stouts. The Lodge had primary responsibility for police duty, supervising the communal hunts, keeping order in camp, compelling attendance at ceremonies, and enforcing leaders' council decisions generally.

The hohóˑkoówuʔ 'crazy lodge' was the next in the series. Comprised of older men it had more religious content. The wives of the Crazy Men played a key role in the ceremony, receiving supernatural power from the grandfather and transferring it to their husbands. There was one honorary degree.

Next, was the héθowóowúʔ 'dog lodge'. Wives participated in this, as well, transferring power from grandfather to husband, and it was viewed as more sacred than the Crazy Lodge. Dog men served as directors of very large war parties but primarily acted to inspire the warriors. There were five honorary degrees.

In battle, the degree holders of the men's Lodges were the war chiefs or leaders. There were several exploits that counted as coups, often more important than killing an enemy: touching an enemy, alive or dead; riding a particular horse or inside breastworks; stealing a horse, especially from an enemy camp; taking away an enemy's gun or bow. Up to four men could count coup on a single enemy. Bodies of enemies might be stripped and mutilated for trophies. Many fights occurred in Estes Park with Utes, Eastern Shoshones, and Apaches; Arapahos left stone monuments to mark the sites, especially if Arapahos died there (Beals 1935:10; Grinnell 1923, 1:232, 2:32, 163; Toll 1962:17).

Upon reaching old age, men of the Dog Lodge could enter the hinénniˑnóowuʔ when one of their members so vowed. This Lodge is portrayed in mythology as the oldest of the Lodges. There were no honorary degrees, and the group's ceremonies were so sacred that they were held in secret, when the members sang and fasted for four days, praying for the people (for example, for the success of a war party). The members of this Lodge did not go to war. They were instructed by the Water Pouring Old Men, who are presented in the literature as the highest of the Lodges, but who in fact constituted a tribal priesthood comprised of seven men, the keepers of the seven tribally owned men's medicine bags. Very little is known about the old men's organizations.

There was one women's society, called beníhtóowúʔ 'buffalo lodge' (Kroeber 1902–1907:210–219; Eggan 1955a:52). A woman vowed to sponsor the ceremony, then tried to persuade other women to join her. They would appeal to women who had already participated to serve as "grandmothers" or instructors. The women fasted and prayed, representing buffalo. During the ceremony they were symbolically hunted and killed. Women also were understood to progress through the men's Lodges with their husbands; their status was linked to that of their husbands and their participation was essential to the men's Lodges.

Chieftainship

According to Sage, a Northern Arapahoe born in the early 1840s, the combined Northern and Southern Arapahos had a governing council comprising four chiefs representing the four tribal divisions (Quick to Angers, Antelopes or Long Legs, Greasy Faces, and Beavers), the Water Pouring Old Men, the members of the old men's Lodge, and the leaders (presumably the degree holders) of the other men's Lodges (Hilger 1952:188–189). Kroeber (1902–1907:8–9) and Curtis (1907–1930, 6:159) reported that the Arapaho had four chiefs, selected from the Dog Lodge. W.P. Clark (1885:43) was told that Arapahos had both a war and a peace chief (or possibly chiefs). Sweezy (b. about 1881), in

846

speaking of prereservation days, said there were four chiefs who headed four divisions of Southern Arapaho; under these were subchiefs of each band or residential group (Bass 1966:18–19).

The existence of a governing council is not entirely inconsistent with documentary accounts of Northern Arapahoe in the 1850s–1870s (Fowler 1982), although Sage's statement concerning four divisions is difficult to evaluate. He said that before the Northern and Southern Arapaho separated, there were four "bands" (divisions); people from each of the four went with both the Northern and Southern Arapaho upon separation. The date of the separation is unclear, for a differentiation into northern and southern divisions goes back to at least 1800. According to Sage, the Beavers became extinct, and in any case, after Arapaho began to have regular contact with Whites, these formal, named divisions no longer functioned. The decreasing size of buffalo herds and their dispersal beginning in the 1840s and escalating thereafter would have made large bands impractical.

Documentary sources are not consistent concerning the number of divisions or chiefs. Of the four "bands" (actually named divisions each comprising multiple bands that were the usual residential groups) reported by Kroeber (1902–1907:7–8), two were named groups among the Southern Arapaho, the Waxu'eithi and Haxaathinena (wó·xuʔéíθiʔ 'ugly people' and haxāaⁿçineʼnaⁿ 'ridiculous men'), one was the Northern division as named by the Southerners (boʔó·či·nénnoʔ) and the fourth was not remembered. Mooney (1896:954–955) recorded names for three divisions of Northern Arapahoe that clearly date to the reservation period, and five divisions of Southern Arapaho (two of which also were given by Kroeber).

Beginning in the 1840s, chieftainship essentially involved serving as intermediary between the tribe and federal officials. Dog Lodge membership and an outstanding war record probably were requirements, but the ability to reassure and deal with Whites also became a criterion. Although war chiefs rose in status during the Indian wars of the 1860s and 1870s (in the case of Northern Arapahoe), by the time of reservation settlement, war chiefs were recognized by federal officials as "peace" or "friendly" chiefs (Fowler 1982:21–66).

In 1843 the Northern Arapahoe reportedly had two principal chiefs. In 1851, at the Fort Laramie treaty council, three Arapahos were selected as chiefs, two Southern and one Northern. In 1859, five chiefs represented their people. In 1860 there reportedly were three "bands" (divisions) and three chiefs; in the later 1860s there were four chiefs. By 1873, two bands—Quick to Angers and Antelopes—were recognized by the federal government; each had a chief who continued to represent his band when the Northern Arapahoe settled on Wind River Reservation in 1878 (Fowler 1982:1–66; LR-UA 1873).

Among the Southern Arapaho, one principal chief, Little Raven, was recognized in the late 1850s and early 1860s, but

in 1863 he refused to enter important talks unless the "war" chief was present. In 1864, three chiefs were recognized and in 1866, two main bands. In 1867 and 1868 there were four chiefs; in 1869 there were three main bands and at least one additional small one, each with its own chief (LR-UA 1867–1869).

Subsistence and Technology

The chief source of food, clothing, and many other necessities was the buffalo. In the 1830s and 1840s hunting seems to have focused on the Rocky Mountain and Estes Parks areas and the adjacent plains to the east. In the summer they followed the game into the mountains and in the winter to lower elevations, although there also were summer camps in the Parks. The buffalo ranged in the Parks throughout the year. Arapahos regarded this area as their territory and tried to keep others out. There they drove game through "buffalo traps," gaps where hunters waited to kill them. Small groups of men used snowshoes to hunt buffalo in deep snow. Game was speared or shot with bow and arrow. Bows were backed with sinew, those of cedar backed on both sides. The bowstring was sinew.

Before a young man could hunt with bow and arrow he had to feast elderly men and receive advice and prayers from them while they made and painted his arrows with identifying marks. Metal knives and arrowheads were in use, although some Arapahos still used knives of stone or bone, particularly the boss rib or dorsal spines of the buffalo. Spear points often were of stone. They hunted elk as well, frequently driving them over a cliff or into an enclosure—an old method of hunting that preceded the acquisition of the horse (Toll 1962:11, 18, 20, 34; Kroeber 1902–1907:23–25; Beals 1935:4, 9–10; Grinnell 1923, 1:276).

After 1857 the Parks began to be invaded by settlers and miners and the buffalo were no longer to be found there in large numbers. The Northern Arapahoe went north, hunting year round on more open plains. The Southern Arapaho went southeast, down the Arkansas River. In the late summer and early fall, during the buffalo mating season, large herds congregated; then the residential bands all came together to hunt communally. Before the hunt began, religious ceremonies were performed. Hunters on well-trained horses surrounded a large number of animals, held them close in, and shot or speared them while they were corralled. Men with hunting power might also entice a herd near the large camp to facilitate the hunt. In the winter the herd dispersed and small groups of hunters pursued the game. In the spring, after the calves were several weeks old, bands congregated again and moved to the open prairie for the buffalo chase. As the game continued to decline during the 1860s and 1870s, more reliance was placed on smaller game, and guns began to be used instead of the bow and arrow (Fowler 1982:23; Toll 1962:34; Kroeber 1902–1907:436–437; Mooney 1896:988; Hilger 1952:169–175; Oliver 1962:15–17).

Individual hunters brought meat to their wives or mothers-in-law, but meat seems to have been shared extensively, for inviting people to eat (especially the elderly and disadvantaged) was expected of respected individuals and was a means to enhance one's reputation.

Arapahos had large numbers of horses until the wars of the 1860s and 1870s began to take their toll. In 1855 the agent estimated that 300 households of Southern Arapaho (2,400 population) owned 15,000 horses (LR-UA 1855). In 1861, 244 Southern Arapaho households reportedly owned 2,600 horses (ARCIA). This was far above the 8–12 horses per household that Ewers (1955:138–139) calculated were necessary for subsistence.

While women sometimes accompanied their husbands on the hunt, generally they stayed in camp to process the meat, drying or curing and storing it. They also dressed the hides, making tepee covers (fig. 3), clothing, containers, and other essentials. Women collected roots, berries, and other plant foods that they preserved and stored. A woman's hide scraper also served as a digging tool; on this implement she kept a record of the ages of her children. Women raised puppies that were eaten primarily on ceremonial occasions. Food was cooked in a rawhide or buffalo paunch placed in a hole and filled with water, into which hot stones were dropped. After trade goods became more commonplace, metal pots were used (Kroeber 1902:25–27; Hilger 1952:169–186).

Hides were dressed by women and, to a far greater degree than other Plains peoples, prayers in symbolic form were worked into the quilled, beaded, or painted designs. On deer or elkskin moccasins, leggings, navel cord pouches, work or storage bags, knife cases, clothing worn on gala occasions (arm bands, headdresses), certain designs, thought to have originated with mythological beings (such as Whirlwind Woman), were somewhat standardized. One of the most frequent symbols, expressed in alternative forms, was the life symbol (hiiteni) (Kroeber 1902–1907:40, 46, 70–77, 110, 120–122, 149; Hilger 1952:180–186; J.D. Anderson 2000a).

The designs on tepee covers, buffalo robes and blankets, and cradles could only be applied during the course of a ritual under the supervision of the seven old women who were the keepers of the women's tribal medicine bags. In prestige, quilling a buffalo robe was almost equivalent to a warrior's counting coup. These robes were always given away, bringing great honor to the maker.

In the winter, tepees were erected in a hollow and banked; in the summer they were fastened at the sides by rocks (later in the nineteenth century, by tepee pins). Tepees were erected on a three-pole foundation (Kroeber 1902–1907:16, 29–35, 65–66; Hilger 1952:180–186; Grinnell 1923, 1:226, 232; Toll 1962:14–15, 35).

Life Cycle

A man, his wife or wives, their children, and possibly another unmarried relative or two occupied a tepee. Several

848

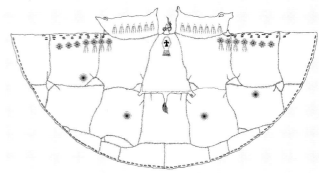

top, Smithsonian, NAA: 215-H; bottom, National Arch., Bureau of Ind. Affairs Coll.: 75-SE-6.

Fig. 3. Southern Arapaho residences. top, Cut Hair's camp of hide tepees. Girls are sitting on the skirt of the tepee, which has been affixed to the ground with tepee pins. Photograph by William S. Soule, near Ft. Dodge, Okla. Terr., 1867–1874. center, Drawing showing how the irregular hides were fitted for an Arapaho tepee collected from Little Raven in 1869 ("History of Ethnological and Ethnohistorical Research," fig. 4, this vol.). Women specialists oversaw the cutting and fitting of hides, while many women worked on the stitching. Drawn by Roger Thor Roop. bottom, Camp of Creeping Bear, a farmer, who sent his children to the government school. His residence includes a house and shed of milled lumber, tepee poles, and a windbreak. The wagon and plows were supplied by government annuities. Photographed in Seger district, 1886–1913.

such families comprised an extended family household, which worked together and shared food resources. A senior male was the head of such a household and usually the man's daughters with their husbands and children made up the other families. The cooking for all these families was done by the senior man's wife. Child care was shared by the entire group (Eggan 1955a:82–83).

Children were born with the assistance of a midwife and other older women, as well as a man or woman with knowledge of herbs that facilitated birth. Arapahos had treatments to improve fertility and to prevent pregnancy and followed food taboos and conduct prescriptions during pregnancy; they did not practice infanticide or abortion. Often children were spaced every four years or so by prolonged nursing and abstinence.

There was no puberty ceremony for either boys or girls, but a girl, in the company of an old woman, avoided activities that might be endangered by contact with the power inherent in menstrual blood. Few remained unmarried, but there were berdaches (*hoxúx*, sg.) who were viewed as having supernatural power; no women lived as men (Kroeber 1902–1907:15, 18–19; Hilger 1952:6–7, 12, 16, 40, 45, 47, 50, 70–78; Eggan 1955a:54).

Marriages were usually arranged by parents, or sometimes a man would request his female relatives to propose his marriage to a girl's family. In these cases, the two families exchanged gifts, including horses, in equal amounts. This reciprocity between in-laws was central to kinship organization; the father's family was responsible for participating in important rites of passage, including birth and mortuary rituals. Elopment was a less socially acceptable type of marriage. The groom would return with the bride after a few days, give gifts to her family, and his family would receive gifts in turn. A third, less frequent, type of marriage (perhaps only among Southern Arapaho) was one in which a family arranged for a girl to marry a high-ranking chief; they brought horses to the chief but received none in return (Eggan 1933).

Polygyny was practiced, preferably of the sororal type. In such cases, young girls were occasionally married to their sister's husband before puberty. If co-wives were not sisters, each wife would have her own tepee. The levirate was encouraged, and so were marriages between brothers from one family and sisters from another. Residence was ambilocal, although matrilocality was preferred at least in cases in which the groom was young or not very prosperous or prominent. Divorce was not infrequent; it could be initiated by either party. If the wife remarried soon after divorce, the new husband might make a payment to the first husband. In cases of adultery, a husband should accept the situation with good grace, but he might retrieve and abuse his wife, or exact damages from the paramour, who could attempt to prevent retaliation by requesting the husband's ceremonial grandfather to intervene (Kroeber 1902–1907:12–14; Hilger 1952:35, 193–194, 196–208, 211; Eggan 1955a:59–65).

Kinship

A group of related extended family households comprised a residential band; this group wintered together and moved together when large camps, such as the summer camp, were formed or disbanded. They varied in size, and were probably, at least in earlier times, affiliated with one of the named divisions. Individuals and residential bands could change their affiliation. Members of a residential band were generally consanguines and affines. These bands were not exogamous, and membership was flexible.

Arapaho kinship was based on bilateral descent, with collateral and lineal relatives classed together. Kin terminology was organized on the basis of generations (with the range of relationship wide but indefinite), sex of relatives, and relative age (in ego's generation only). Marriage was outside this group of kindred. Bonds between classificatory brothers were particularly strong. When a man died, his brothers usually took most of his valuable property (that which was not buried with him, destroyed, or given away) to prevent his ghost from troubling his family.

Behavior toward kin and affines was based on principles of either respect/avoidance or familiarity/joking. A man acknowledged authority of his parents (including father's brothers and mother's sisters), avoided contact yet was solicitious toward his sisters (including parallel and cross-cousins), was reserved toward his father-in-law, cultivated good relations and reciprocity with parents of children's spouses, and avoided his mother-in-law. By the gift of a horse or a war trophy to the mother-in-law, the avoidance relationship between them could be relaxed. A woman followed the same rules except she could be familiar with her mother-in-law. Both sexes joked "mildly" and behaved in a familiar manner with the father's sisters, mother's brothers, grandparents, and siblings of the same sex. "Rough" or obscene joking was expected between an individual and his or her brothers-in-law or sisters-in-law (Kroeber 1902–1907:10–11, 16–17; Curtis 1907–1930, 6:150; Eggan 1955a:49–58, 67, 75–79, 90, 94; Hilger 1952:187–188, 194–195, 209).

History of the Southern Arapaho

1870–1890

There were two main bands of the Southern Arapaho, the Waxu'eithi and the Haxaathinena (Mooney 1896:957; H.L. Scott 1907:559; Kroeber 1902–1907:7–8). Mooney also identified three other bands: *koúnehé·noɂ* 'Blackfoot'; *hô·xéihíinénnoɂ* 'wolf men'; and Sesabeithi 'those looking up' or 'lookouts'. During the summer, in large part to avoid being embroiled in the fighting between the Cheyenne and the army, the Southern Arapaho camped along the North Canadian River, near the agency, and from late summer through early spring they separated into several smaller bands, each of about 25–70 lodges (about six persons per lodge) to hunt along Beaver Creek, Buffalo Creek, and the Cimmaron River, occasionally coming together in one or two large camps (ARCIA 1871:469, 471, 1872:249, 1873:221, 1874:233, 1875:209, 1876:46; J.D. Miles 1873). The tribe's last buffalo hunt was in 1878, but deer and pronghorn and other small game still were available.

After buffalo hunting was no longer possible, Arapaho headmen settled in a more dispersed pattern and expanded their farms and herds. Little Raven, for example, farmed 40 acres, although the average farm was less than ten acres (ARCIA 1884:73). The four main camps or "villages" were on the South Canadian; on the North Canadian near Red Hills and near Camp Cantonment; and Seger Colony on the Washita (established in 1886). There was also a small village of Arapaho descended from John Poisal east of the agency.

Some Arapaho children attended boarding school on the reservation (vol. 4:94), either the government school or one of the two run by the Mennonites; after 1879 others attended off-reservation boarding schools. Gradually a bilingual cohort developed, although the children remained subject to parental and band authorities. By the late 1880s most Arapaho children attended school (ARCIA 1887:77).

Headmen controlled the distribution of beef and annuities and beginning in 1877 also supervised Arapaho teamsters who hauled agency supplies from Kansas. When the agent organized an Indian police force in 1878, men were selected from each of the camps but the agent apparently was unable to induce them to act against the band authorities (ARCIA 1884:76, 1885:78).

Arapahos relied on the sale of their robes for cash to supplement the issues of rations and annuities (ARCIA 1877:82, 1878:55). By the late 1870s robes were scarce, but the trader hired Arapaho women to tan hides he obtained elsewhere. Most agency employees were Arapaho.

In dealings with the government the chiefs represented the tribe as a whole. They reassured the agents that they were peaceable, could be counted on to help the government against the more hostile Cheyenne, and would farm and raise stock and send their children to school (ARCIA 1872:133–5, 144, 1874:211, 233, 1875:211, 1876:47, 1884:75). Their goal was a reservation separate from the Cheyenne. The chiefs built or were given houses (fig. 3) (although they continued to live in tepees), had corn fields and vegetable gardens, and began accummulating cattle (Hoag 1872; J.D. Miles 1872; ARCIA 1873:221–222, 1883:60, 1885:76). They exacted tolls from trespassing cattlemen and helped support their followers who, in return, remained loyal to them. In 1883–1886 the chiefs agreed to lease about three and one-half million acres of range to cattlemen, providing each Arapaho with a five-dollar cash payment twice each year, which helped purchase supplies in lieu of robe sales. In the 1870s and 1880s Left Hand and Powderface, both of whom had high rank in the men's Lodges, were the leading chiefs (Darlington 1871; ARCIA 1873:221). Little Raven, the highest-ranking ritual leader, continued to figure in Arapaho-federal relations due to his reputation among Whites.

The system of men's Lodges was integral to reservation social organization. Arapaho Lodge men policed the camps year round and protected the agency from attack by hostile Indians (ARCIA 1871:470–471, 1874:211, 233; J.D. Miles 1874).

Until the 1880s the Offerings Lodge was held in the spring after the hunt, but subsequently it was postponed until early fall to accommodate farming (Potter 1885; *The Mennonite* 1887). Mennonite missionaries arrived in 1877 but made little impact on Arapaho religious beliefs. Curing societies were active, although Arapahos consulted government physicians as well. Southern Arapahos frequently made trips by rail and stage to their relatives in Wyoming in order to participate in Flat Pipe ceremonies (Mooney 1896:961).

Gambling and horse racing were favorite entertainments at Fourth of July celebrations at Fort Reno and at annuity distributions. There also were occasions when men gained recognition for war exploits by publically piercing children's ears, or cutting their hair before they entered school; men or women honored relations by giving away property, often to members of visiting tribes, such as Kiowas.

1891–1940s

With the cession of the reservation in 1891 and the allotment of land to individuals in 1892, non-Indians outnumbered Indians nine to one, and gradually Arapahos were defrauded of their land and property (Berthrong 1976; vol. 4:225). The increasing number of landless Arapaho became dependent on elderly landowners for support (Fowler 1990).

Extended families camped in several clusters or villages that took allotments together and became named districts, replacing band names. Government farmers were located in these communities, which lent them permanence. The Cantonment district (where Little Raven settled), the Red Hills district (Left Hand's people, later the Geary community), the South Canadian district (Powderface's group), and the Seger district (ARCIA 1892; *The Mennonite* 1891, 1896; Seger 1934). Arapahos resided in these "villages" but went out to their allotments, sometimes in large work groups (ARCIA 1901). In 1903 the government established three separate agencies for the Arapaho and Cheyenne: Cantonment on the North Canadian, which served 239 Arapahos and 558 Cheyennes; Cheyenne-Arapaho, near Concho below Cantonment on the North Canadian, which served 557 Arapahos and 794 Cheyennes; and Seger on the Washita, which served 139 Arapahos and 607 Cheyennes (ARCIA 1903:244).

Polygyny did not survive reservation settlement but marriages continued to be arranged or at the very least sanctioned by the family. Marriage by "Indian ceremony" (exchange of gifts between groom's and bride's familes) was preferred, but by 1913 it was often followed by a legal ceremony to meet federal dictates (SA-C 1913, 1915, 1922). By 1933 most marriages were elopements (Eggan 1955a:59). Respect and joking relationships persisted with some modification (Eggan 1955a:41). Although children were in boarding schools most of the year, ear piercing and hair cutting ceremonies were held for them, which helped to extend the older generations' influence over them (Kroeber 1902–1907:365).

As economic conditions worsened, Arapahos continued to rely on their chiefs. It was still possible to earn money by freighting, growing hay and grain, selling wood, or working at the agency or military posts. Families kept gardens and tried to raise stock. Rations were gradually reduced until 1902, when they were cut off from all but the incapacitated. Arapahos depended in large part on leasing their allotments and, after 1903, when it became legally possible, selling allotments of deceased relatives. The houses they built on their allotments were usually rented to non-Indian tenants (ARCIA 1903). In 1898, 20 percent of the land was leased; in 1901, 50 percent (ARCIA 1898, 1901). The chiefs negotiated with officials for the sale of unalloted land in 1891, which provided per capita payments in 1891 and 1892 and thereafter a smaller payment from the interest on the balance of the land sale money.

After 1903 the attempt to stem erosion of the resource base was the preoccupation of the chiefs. They sought to meet personally with the commissioner of Indian affairs, secretary of the interior, and president, making frequent trips to Washington (vol. 4:243), usually at their own expense (*Canadian Record* 1906, 1909, 1914, 1917, 1918, 1920, 1921, 1924, 1926). Chiefs sought with little success to obtain agricultural assistance, religious freedom, separation of Arapaho assets from those of the Cheyenne, greater access to money in trust accounts, protection from exploitation by non-Indians, and schools located in the Arapaho community. At home the chiefs visited the agents and successfully persuaded them to permit gatherings and ceremonies, although they had very limited success in increasing Indian control over resources. By 1928, 63 percent of allotted Indian lands had been sold. Their efforts did help obtain an extension of the trust status of allotments in 1917 and again in 1927.

The chiefs of the early twentieth century were former scouts, police, and in a few cases, men who had some battle experience. Gradually the roles of chief and ritual leader merged, so that at Canton, Little Raven Jr. not only was "head chief" but also director of the Offerings Lodge. He was succeeded in this by Ute, from Geary.

In 1928, an elected "tribal council" was organized, primarily to pursue a claim against the United States government. It was comprised of 48 Arapaho and Cheyenne "chiefs" and young men (most of whom were educated in off-reservation boarding schools).

The Arapahos and Cheyennes accepted reorganization under the provisions of the Oklahoma Indian Welfare Act and in 1937 an elected 28-member business committee and constitutional government went into effect with Arapahos and Cheyennes having equal representation, even though the Cheyenne population was twice that of the Arapaho. The constitution provided for half the Cheyenne positions to be filled by chiefs, but the Arapaho made selection of chiefs optional (Fowler 1988).

For about 15 years after the opening of the reservation there was intense religiosity among Arapahos, with new religions or modifications of older ceremonies occuring often. This was a period when the mortality rate rose sharply, due to malaria, typhoid, and other health problems associated with reservation life. Population declined and infant mortality rose, raising anxiety.

The Southern Arapaho began to hold Ghost Dance rituals in 1890 (fig. 4), although the leaders modified the ritual from time to time and had revelations about when the "new world" would appear (ARCIA 1891, 1896, 1898, 1899, 1902). They attempted to hide the ceremonies from the federal officials, and Arapaho chiefs tried to present the Ghost Dance as an aid to civilization. In the ritual some elements of Christianity were combined with symbols from the men's Lodge organization and other traditional sources. Women played a major role in the Ghost Dance, particularly in composing songs; and they participated in even greater numbers than the men (Mooney 1896:909). The Arapaho Ghost Dance prophet Sitting Bull formally designated seven leaders, so that leadership was diffused more widely through the tribe (Kroeber 1902-1907:328). Curing rites became a predominant part of the ritual. Games such as the hand game assumed a religious aspect (Kroeber 1902–1907:319).

Grant Left Hand, son of the chief, originated the Crow Dance (ARCIA 1892; Mooney 1896:1039), which combined elements of the Omaha Dance and the Ghost Dance (Kroeber 1902–1907:368). Vows to sponsor the ceremony were generally made for health reasons. The Crow Dance was permeated with symbolism from the Offerings Lodge and men's Lodges (Kroeber 1902–1907:427).

Middle-aged men continued to fast for doctoring power during this period (Kroeber 1902–1907:419). Apparently, doctoring societies still met. Medicine men and midwives were relied on despite the construction of a small hospital for the Arapaho and Cheyenne (SA-CA 1916, 1918, 1921, 1922, 1924).

The Peyote ceremony was introduced from a small group of Plains Apache who had briefly settled with the Arapaho at the agency and a few of whom had married Arapahos. Young people became involved in the Peyote ritual (ARCIA 1895, 1896, 1899, 1902) and formed an organization to fight their superintendent's efforts to make the use of peyote illegal (SA-CA 1916, 1919; see also O.C. Stewart 1987:106–108, 138, 240). Peyote rituals varied, some men apprenticing themselves to Peyote leaders and others receiving instructions in dreams (Kroeber 1902–1907:398). Curing was an important part of the ritual, which combined native and, in some forms of the ceremony, Christian symbolism. Peyote rituals were important in the twentieth century, and a distinctive Arapaho form of the Peyote ritual emerged.

Despite these new religious movements, the Arapahos' faith in the Sacred Pipe remained strong and individuals regularly went to Wyoming to make prayer-sacrifices (Mooney 1896:961). Even Left Hand, when he converted to Christianity in 1905, insisted that he would continue his reverence for and faith in the Pipe (as well as continue to doctor) (Jayne 1907).

During the reservation period, only a minority of young men were part of the age-graded Lodge organization, and these groups functioned largely at the time of the Offerings

top, U. of Okla. Lib., Western Hist. Coll., Norman: J.A. Shuck no. 44; bottom left, Smithsonian, NAA: 91.20273; bottom right, Eiteljorg Mus. of Amer. Ind. and Western Art, Indianapolis, Ind.:1989.9.29.

Fig. 4. Southern Arapaho-Cheyenne Ghost Dance. top, Circle of dancers beyond the camp, along the North Canadian River. Photograph by Christophe C. Stotz, near Ft. Reno, Okla., 1889. bottom left, Crow Dance participants and spectators. The woman on the right wears a dress painted with Ghost Dance symbols—birds, stars, and crosses. Photograph by James Mooney, Southern Arapaho and Cheyenne Agency, Okla., 1891–1894. bottom right, Buckskin dress with white stars covering the blue painted bodice and red skirt. The figure of a woman holds a pipe and sprig of sage flanked by birds and crosses in red and yellow. Length 1.47 m.

Lodge. New initiations of the Tomahawk Lodge, Spear Lodge, and Crazy Lodge were held in the first two decades of the century (Hilger 1952:120; Warden 1903–1906). The Offerings Lodge was held fairly regularly. At this ceremony people made vows to cover the Sacred Wheel bundle with offerings, as well as to feast elderly ritual leaders.

Although the chiefs were at first hospitable to Christian missionaries, Arapahos showed little interest in joining churches. In 1897 the Arapaho Mennonite Church was organized at Canton, with a small membership. In 1901 the Arapaho Baptist Mission was opened at Geary with 22 members, including a few prominent men. In 1907 the Baptist missionaries reported Arapahos attending camp meetings. Christian converts increased, and Arapahos began to take leadership roles in the Mennonite and Baptist churches (for example, see *Canton Record* 1924).

Four large seasonal gatherings, held despite federal officials' opposition and reprisals, drew the Arapaho together. The old men who had been initiated into the Lodges

reportedly authorized younger men, particularly World War I veterans, to perform "war dances" (Fowler 1984–1995; SA-CA 1919, 1923).

1940s–1960s

By the beginning of World War II, the large blocks of allotments that had formed the basis for the communities at Geary, Canton, and Colony were fragmented due to land sales, and Arapahos depended on wage work in the rural communities. They found jobs in the war industry and in the 1940s and 1950s at least half moved away from the Canadian River communities. By 1951 two-thirds were landless, and the rest owned only small shares in inherited allotments.

Attendance at tribal gatherings, including the Offerings Lodge, declined; for many, Peyote meetings and intertribal powwows were more practical, since these could also be attended outside the Canadian River area. The last Offerings

852

Lodge was held in 1939. The Sacred Wheel was not transferred to a new keeper.

1960s–1990s

About half the Arapahos lived within the original reservation boundaries (an area roughly 80 by 50 miles), almost all in the Canton or the Geary community. About 300 lived in the Canton area and about 500 lived in the Geary vicinity, in both places on inherited allotments or in the towns. At least 1,500 lived outside the boundaries of the original reservation.

The extended family was important; its members shared resources and often lived together in one house or several nearby houses. Senior members were very influential and made a substantial contribution to the household in labor and resources. Networks of kin helped each other economically, politically, and socially (Fowler 1984–1995, 1990).

A major transformation of political processes began in 1960 after the business committee was successful in gaining the restoration (in fee status) of 3,900 acres of land at Concho. Several individuals, many from outside the local community, challenged the business committee's effort to retain and manage this land, and a movement gained gradual support for a division of tribal assets and more broad based participation in decision-making.

This movement gained impetus by the decision of the United States Claims Commission that the 1851 treaty had been violated by the United States and that the Arapaho and Cheyenne tribes were entitled to compensation. For the first time, women were vocal in political meetings and the business committee was criticized publicly. When the money from the successful claim was distributed, $500,000 was placed in a trust account, the interest on which was used for scholarships. The bulk of the award was distributed in per capita payments of $2,325 to enrolled Arapahos and Cheyennes. More significantly, the control of the tribal government by middle-aged and elderly Arapaho males ended.

A group of Arapahos and Cheyennes rewrote the 1937 constitution to allow for more control over tribal income, and by referendum, the new constitution went into effect in 1977. It required the business committee to get the approval of the "tribal council" (all eligible Arapaho and Cheyenne voters in a general meeting—a quorum was set at 200, later reduced to 75) for the budgeting of tribal funds, and mandated the recall election of a committeeman if 30 percent of the voters in the district so petitioned. An Election Board, elected by the tribal council, conducted business committee and recall elections.

During the early 1970s the Cheyenne-Arapaho business committee concentrated on obtaining eligibility for federal programs routinely available to reservation Indians but denied to those without reservation status. They suceeded in getting funds to build housing and a tribal office complex, job training programs, and economic development projects. They also obtained greater control over the leasing of tribal lands and other tasks formerly controlled exclusively by the Bureau of Indian Affairs, and restored the Concho lands to trust status. In 1974, with the help of the American Indian Movement, they and other tribal governments in western Oklahoma gained greater control over funds designated for Indian education by the Johnson O'Malley Act (48 U.S. Stat. 596). The business committee also began to contract programs from the Bureau of Indian Affairs and the Indian Health Service.

During the 1980s, the business committee established three tribally owned businesses—bingo ("United States Plains Since 1850," fig. 13, this vol.), cigarette sales (fig. 5), farming and ranching—and began to tax economic activity on trust lands. They developed a tribal legal code in 1988, which replaced one developed by the Bureau, and instituted a tribally controlled court system.

A major part of political activity focused on obtaining employment. According to a survey in 1988, at least 61 percent of the Arapahos and Cheyennes within the original reservation boundaries were unemployed. Arapahos were employed largely by private businesses or by the tribes, primarily in service industries and clerical work.

Land was a primary source of income but acreage was gradually being sold. In 1967 there were 111,864 acres in

Fig. 5. Santo Marques, Southern Arapaho employee of a tribally owned smoke shop. The case displays earrings, purses, gourd rattles, and fans for sale. Photograph by William Wyrick, along Interstate 81, Concho Res., Okla., 1991.

trust, 5,873 owned by the tribes. In 1986 the tribes (with the addition of the Concho acreage) owned 10,405 but the total acreage in trust had declined to 84,155 (Bureau of Indian Affairs. Cheyenne-Arapaho Agency 1986). Most of the land was leased.

Ritual life centered around frequent social dances. During the fall, winter, and spring, the benefit dance prevailed; in the summer, the powwow. Benefit dances were sponsored by extended families to aid an individual (a soldier or a graduate, for example) or another larger celebration (such as a powwow). These dances also were sponsored by voluntary associations, for example, a veterans' organization or a group such as the Starhawk dance society, founded in 1970. Powwow committees, representing both Arapaho and Cheyenne, managed the summer powwows and also held benefit dances. There were two summer powwows, attended primarily by Arapahos and Cheyennes: Barefoot Powwow in Canton and the Geary Fourth of July Powwow. The Arapahos and Cheyennes formed a joint committee to sponsor the Labor Day Powwow at Colony, which was attended by people from many tribes.

Most families in Canton and Geary participated in some way in the native religion, which centered on the annual Offerings Lodge in Wyoming. During this period the numbers of Southern Arapaho votaries increased and several acted as pledgers or sponsors of the ceremony. A few individuals participated in Flat Pipe rituals and a few were given the right and trained by Northern Arapahoe priests to use sacred paint in various ceremonies. In the 1970s a duplicate of the Sacred Wheel was placed in the custody of a Southern Arapaho to be used in prayer-sacrifices. The ceremonial grandfather-grandson relationship fundamental to Northern Arapahoe social organization did not characterize Southern Arapaho society; in fact, the grandfather or grandson of most Southern Arapaho participants in the Offerings Lodge was a Northern Arapahoe.

Participation in the Native American Church in some capacity was widespread among Southern Arapaho. The rituals became more intertribal but the core participants were Arapaho and Cheyenne. Men and women vowed to sponsor ceremonies for a variety of reasons, including aid for servicemen, children, newlyweds, and curing.

Most Arapahos who embraced Christianity were Protestant. Several Arapaho men became ministers, but held services in English. It was not uncommon for individuals to participate at various times or coterminously in the Offerings Lodge and other native rituals, the Native American Church, and Christian rites (Fowler 1984–1995).

History of the Northern Arapahoe

1878–1960s

In 1879 the Northern Arapahoes were settled in two large camps. About 700 *čeinówu·hunó*ʔ 'quick to anger people' camped at the forks of the Wind and Popo Agie rivers. The *nisčéhiinennoʔ* 'antelope people', a smaller band of 250, settled 15 miles up the Wind River. Friday's small camp was located nearer the agency headquarters at the mouth of Trout Creek (Fowler 1982:75). During the next decade the large camps dispersed along the rivers into six main clusters, each camp comprised of several extended families (Fowler 1982:75–76). By 1890 there were three main bands, probably aggregates of smaller camps, called *no·nóʔowúʔunennóʔ* 'forks of the river people', *woxû·čoo·nóʔ* 'bad pipes', and *té·ʔiʔéíθiʔ* 'greasy faces' (on Trout Creek) (Mooney 1896:956; Fowler 1982:77). After the reservation was allotted in 1901, extended families dispersed during the summer but came together again in the fall and winter.

The Arapahoe usually lived in extended family groups. Newly married couples tended to live with the bride's family, but, if the groom's family circumstances were better, residence might be patrilocal. Respect and joking relationships characterized kinship relations. Arapahoe children boarded at the agency government school and at Saint Stephen's Roman Catholic mission school at Arapahoe.

Unlike the Arapaho in Oklahoma, Northern Arapahoes retained and expanded their land base, which helped to validate the authority of political and religious leaders and maintain unity. At the time of settlement on the reservation, band headmen were influential and represented the interests of the group in councils involving the entire tribe, but in dealings with federal officials, a small group of "council chiefs" served as intermediaries and spokesmen. Chiefs in general were men with outstanding war records. Council chiefs also had to be good orators, capable of bringing people to consensus and persuading federal officials. Black Coal (d. 1893) and Sharp Nose (d. 1901) were the main council chiefs (fig. 6). Beginning in 1893, council chiefs became known as business councilmen. Lone Bear and Yellow Calf were the leading councilmen until the 1920s and 1930s (Fowler 1982:68–70, 76, 91, 98–101, 103–104, 130, 138–141, 146).

The councilmen worked to obtain supplies from federal officials, for there was not sufficient game for the Arapahoes to be self-supporting. They also worked to obtain official recognition of Arapahoe title to a reservation, at first apart from the Eastern Shoshone, but when that proved impossible they worked to secure title to lands on the Wind River Reservation. To accomplish these goals the council chiefs had to persuade federal agents that they were friendly toward the United States and their non-Indian neighbors, that they could be counted on as allies in the event of attack by hostile tribes, and that they were willing to farm. It was in this context that the Arapahoe accepted an elected business council (Fowler 1982:70–74, 79–81, 84–86, 91, 102, 104, 129–130, 136–141).

Arapahoes expected their intermediaries to express group consensus, or at least the consensus of influential Arapahoes. Arapahoes consistently resisted efforts on the part of federal officials in the 1930s to institute government by constitution and by-laws and soundly rejected the Indian Reorganization Act in 1935, seeing in these innovations the

Fig. 6. Leaders of the Northern Arapahoe. front row: unidentified man, Chief Friday (d. 1881), Six Feathers, Black Coal, and Sharp Nose; back row, third from left, White Horse; remainder are unidentified. Photographed at Ft. Robinson, Nebr., 1871–1877.

undermining of political values, a threat to religious beliefs, and a challenge to the authority of elders (Fowler 1982:103, 141–142, 167–169, 172–175, 187–189).

In 1900, after pressure by federal officials, the Arapahoes agreed to the allotment of the reservation. A major factor in the chiefs' acquiescence was the realization that, if they obtained allotments, their title to reservation lands would be secure. In this way they undermined the Shoshones' efforts to have them removed from the reservation. The allotments were made in a large block, which prevented the checkerboarding of their reservation lands, leaving mostly the large block of land north of the Big Wind River available for sale to non-Indians as "surplus" land. When the land sale failed to materialize, these lands were leased with the consent of the chiefs, and later the councilmen, which perpetuated the importance of lease money in reservation economy (Fowler 1982:91–96, 100–101, 130).

Oil was discovered on these lands, which the government officially restored to tribal ownership in 1940, so that a large income from royalties began to acummulate. In the 1940s several successes in gaining some control over reservation resources enhanced the prestige of the business council. As part of a land-buying program initially financed by Shoshone funds, the Arapahoe Ranch, a cattle-raising operation, was established in 1941 (Fowler 1982:131–135, 196–201).

In 1947 the business council also obtained most of the income from oil and gas on tribal land in the form of per capita payments; by 1959, 85 percent of this income was distributed in monthly payments and the remainder was used by the council for programs to aid the needy, hire legal assistance, and finance tribal government. The per capita payments led to major improvements in living standards in the 1940s and 1950s. In the 1950s the federal government attempted to use the per capita income as a reason to withdraw protection and services, but the council persuaded Congress not to "terminate" the Arapahoe and Eastern Shoshone (Fowler 1982:201–211).

Attaining supernatural aid for the Arapahoes was the responsibility of the elderly ritual authorities. With the deaths of the Water Pouring Old Men soon after reservation settlement, this priesthood ceased to exist. However, other elderly men with extensive knowledge of ritual procedures formed a new priesthood that came to be known as the Elders or Old People. During the early twentieth century, they selected two men as the highest ranking priests, who supervised the Offerings Lodge. Men who had individually owned powers did not apprentice younger men, so this type of power was no longer used in the twentieth century (Fowler 1982:109–110, 154–60).

In addition, elderly people in general exercised great influence. They supported the actions of intermediaries by public praise and at the same time checked any abuse of their power. Elders also were responsive to the pressures exerted by federal agents; they made changes, such as prohibiting the piercing rite in the Offerings Lodge in 1890, in return for compromises on the part of the agents. Elders supervised dance committees and clubs, which cross-cut kin divisions and helped circumscribe the business council's authority (Fowler 1982:161–162, 217–221).

During the twentieth century the Elders chose and, after balloting was introduced, installed business council members in a ceremony that employed sacred symbols both to validate the councilmen's positions and subordinate them to the elders. They monitored the councilmen's behavior just as they did the behavior of all Arapahoes. The political role of the elders was facilitated by their recognition of the need to promote unity in order to offset the potential hostility of non-Arapahoes; in that spirit, they were careful to select a member of each of the two main residential areas, Arapahoe and Ethete, for the Two Old Men positions. Responsive to the elders' priorities, the intermediaries made protecting the Arapahoes' right to hold the Offerings Lodge and other ceremonies a priority (Fowler 1982:124, 149–158, 170–172, 189–190).

The Episcopal missionaries at Ethete, who built Saint Michael's Mission and school in 1917, encouraged Arapahoe culture, unlike the Roman Catholic mission and school (fig. 7). The Ghost Dance, Peyote ritual, and Christianity all were integrated into Arapahoe ceremonialism as alternate forms of prayer or prayer-sacrifice; the new faiths were not opposed by elders as long as Arapahoes continued to fulfill their ritual duties toward the Flat Pipe and the Offerings Lodge (Fowler 1982:122–127, 156, 159, 214).

1960s–1980s

Throughout the 1960s, several generations of family members lived in extended family clusters on the allotments of senior family members. After federal housing was built during the next two decades, nuclear family households became more common; still, the family home on the allotment remained the focus of extended family activity. Small children were cared for by grandparents; older children lived much of the time with grandparents or alternated between the household of their parents and other relatives. Children attended either public school at Ethete, the contract school at Arapahoe, or Wyoming Indian High School (fig. 8), all controlled by the Arapaho community.

The keeperships of the Flat Pipe and Wheel bundles, the directorship of the Offerings Lodge (which twentieth-century Arapaho termed the "Sun Dance" in English), as well as other sacred knowledge, continued to be earned through a series of prayer-sacrifices and passed from one generation to the next, although some changes occurred in ceremonial organization. In the 1960s the highest ranking offices, the Two Old Men positions, were transformed into four offices—the "Four Old Men." Thus ritual authority

was gradually extended to a wider circle of men, and women's roles expanded as well (Fowler 1982:215).

The Offerings Lodge, usually held in July, brought together all Northern Arapahoe families, who camped to the north, east, and south of the ceremonial arbor. Earlier in the year men and women, motivated by some personal or family crisis, vowed to participate in return for supernatural aid. One or more men vowed to "put up" the Lodge, which entailed greater sacrifice but brought with it acquisition of ritual knowledge beyond that of the ordinary novice or dancer. Months before the ceremony, novices took gifts (for example, tobacco) to their ceremonial grandfathers and asked for counsel. Women did not select instructors but entered the Lodge, sat behind the male dancers, and fasted during one or more days of the ceremony.

In the 1980s many individuals from other tribes and larger numbers of Southern Arapaho than previously participated in the Offerings Lodge. Prayers in the Lodge were formerly in the Arapaho language, but English increasingly had to be used. The number of participants increased; in the 1940s and 1950s the dancers usually numbered about 20, but in the 1980s, nearly 100. Priests were permitting some modifications to accommodate the larger number of dancers. The number of Offerings Lodges in which individuals participated also increased. In the late 1980s two of the Four Old Men assumed "retired" status and were replaced by men in their late forties, an unprecedented action (Fowler 1988a).

Secular rituals were organized by several clubs that were generally age- and sex-specific. Two powwows were held in the summer. The influx of cash into the Arapahoe community, particularly since the 1960s, was expended largely in ceremonial contexts and was, in effect, redistributed through the community. In 1978 the Ethete powwow (fig. 9) offered $1,700 in prizes for dance contests; in 1988, $25,000. There was also a general increase in the amount of property distributed at giveaway ceremonies. Funerals became tribal, not merely family events. The community often held events to raise money for individuals who vowed the Offerings Lodge, whereas in earlier times completing the vow was solely a family responsibility.

In the 1960s and 1970s councilmen were generally middle-aged veterans with secondary school education. With the income from mineral production, the council was able to provide monthly per capita payments, develop programs, and represent Arapahoes against outside interests, thereby cushioning the effects of poverty and unemployment. The council bought land; 83 percent of the reservation's 2,268,000 acres was in trust status. On matters of joint interest they met with the Eastern Shoshone business council.

In the 1980s, due to a federal court ruling, the tribes collected taxes from companies producing oil and gas on the reservation. The council also established tribally owned businesses: a bingo operation, shopping mall, grocery store, and gas station. In addition it took successful legal action to preserve reservation water rights and other resources. Despite these successes of the business coun-

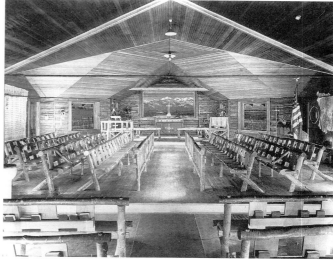

U. of Wyo., Amer. Heritage Center, Laramie: top left, IN 2-M-stm bottom left: B.H. 272a; top right, Denver Mus. Of Nat. Hist., Colo.: 83-135; bottom right, Nat. Arch., Bureau of Ind. Affairs Coll.:75-AO-461-69-177.

Fig. 7. Christianity among the Northern Arapahoe. top left, St. Michael's Mission (Episcopal), Ethete, Wyo. Symbols on the door of the church represent the morning star with rays, the sun, the earth at the beginning surrounded by water, thunderbird, and turtle (Kroeber 1900). top right, Interior of St. Michael's Mission. Behind the communion table is a window giving a view of the distant mountains. A dance bustle and lance with feathers is on the table, a tepee liner is on the left wall, and a painted hide decorates the wall on right. bottom left, Members of St. Michael's Mission. left to right, foreground, A.A. Hastings, warden; Josiah Oldman, lay reader; Anderson White Eagle; Moses Friday; Aaron Willow; and White Eagle. top left, top right, and bottom left, Photographs by Thomas G. Carrigen, 1934–1938. bottom right, St. Joseph's Roman Catholic Church at Wind River Agency, Ethete, Wyo., dedicated January 1968. The paintings on the exterior, made by the Arapaho artist Raphael Norse assisted by people from the parish, combined Christian and Indian motifs. Photographed Dec. 1969.

cils in the 1980s, the electorate remained anxious about changes in political tradition. The greatest source of tension was conflict over enrollment criteria. Many women whose children did not have Arapahoe legal fathers sought to enroll their children, while most Arapahoes, led by elders, opposed this change. In May 1987 the tribe enrolled these children as nonvoting members, ineligible for per capita payments (Fowler 1988).

Population

In 1835 Arapahos numbered at least 3,600 (H. Dodge 1836:141); they had already suffered the effects of smallpox.

They had been further decimated by smallpox and cholera in 1854, when the population was estimated at around 2,000, evenly divided between the Northern and Southern divisions of about "one hundred and thirty lodges each" (ARCIA 1854:300). In 1861 the Northern division reportedly was 650 and the Southern 1,500, which may represent a political decision on the part of many to remain in Colorado rather than to go north and ally with the Sioux and Cheyenne (ARCIA 1861:99–100, 213). After the wars of the 1860s the Southern Arapaho were estimated at 1,100 and the Arapaho population as a whole at 1,440 (ARCIA 1869:338, 462). In 1872, 1,342 (probably too high an estimate) reportedly were at Red Cloud Agency and 1,500 at the agency in

857

ARAPAHO

Fig. 8. Northern Arapahoe traditions in the 1980s–1990s. top left, Hand game at the Wyoming Indian High School, Ethete, Wyo., during Native American Heritage Day. Albert Willow is trying to guess which hand holds the game markers; Ed Soundingsides uses his guessing stick to thwart Willow's guess. seated, Susie Oldman hiding the small sticks in her fists, Michelle Jimerson, and an unidentified student. Photograph by Dianna Troyer, March 1986. top right, left to right, Paul Moss, Arnold Headly, Norman Moss, and Dale C'Hair, Gourd Clan members, performing the Gourd Dance at the Arapahoe Language and Culture Camp, Wind River Res., Wyo., 1989. bottom left, Students playing the hoop game, Native American Heritage Day, at Wyoming Indian High School, 1997. bottom right, Students at the Arapahoe Language Preschool Immersion Program, Ethete, Wyo., 1997. The Arapaho words for cold, hot, sneeze, etc. follow the Salzmann (1983) orthography. top right and bottom photographs by Sara Wiles.

Indian Territory (ARCIA 1872:267, 389). In 1874 the Northern Arapahoe totaled 1,092 and the Southern Arapaho 1,644 (ARCIA 1874:100, 102). Subsequent to reservation settlement, the population began to decline: in 1887 there were 988 Northern and 1,072 Southern Arapaho and by 1892, 829 and 1,091 respectively (ARCIA 1887:352, 364, 1892: 370,

523). Around 1900, the Northern Arapahoe population began to increase, while in the south the decline continued: in 1903 the former numbered 841 and the latter 935 (557 at Cheyenne-Arapaho, 239 at Cantonment, and 139 at Seger) (ARCIA 1903:244); in 1929, there were 979 Northern Arapahoe and 830 Southern (471 at Cheyenne-Arapaho, 216 at

Fig. 9. Powwow activities at Ethete, Wyo. top left, Ethete Eagle Drum singers participate as the host drum group. clockwise from left: Unidentified boy, John Royce Yellowplume holding the microphone, Felix Groesbeck, Alfred Willow, Ralph Hopper, and John C'Hair, all Northern Arapahoe. Photograph by Tom Stromme, 1984. top right, Marion Scott preparing the boiled beef for the community feast, 1995. bottom left, The Moss family in the Honor Dance for Ralph Hopper and Claude Moss, 1986. bottom right, Memorial giveaway by the Goggles family for Ben Goggles, Jr., Merle Goggles' father, who died in 1978. standing, Inez Oldman receiving a gift, 1979; Merle Goggles in background helping with the giveaway items, which included quilts, blankets, shawls, yard goods, and household items. Philip Warren, announcer, and Lucille Goggles Ridgely are seated. top right and bottom, Photographs by Sara Wiles.

Cantonment, and 143 at Seger) (SA-CA 1929). In the 1940s, both populations began to increase dramatically. By 1968 the number of enrolled Northern Arapahoes (requiring one-fourth Arapahoe "blood" and an enrolled Northern Arapahoe father) (Fowler 1970:9, 1982:228) reached 2,722, and by 1976 it was 3,093. The enrolled Southern Arapaho population (requiring one-fourth Arapaho or Arapaho/Cheyenne ancestry and an enrolled Southern Cheyenne-Arapaho parent) numbered about 1,750 in 1962. In 1988 the Northern Arapahoe numbered 3,774 (plus 660 members without full membership status) and in 1989 the Southern Arapaho numbered about 3,080. In 2000 there were over 6,500 enrolled Northern Arapahoe. Specific figures for the Southern Arapaho were not available as the Cheyenne-Arapaho Tribes of Oklahoma combined their membership, which in 2000 totaled about 11,800; it is estimated that about one-third of them considered themselves Arapaho.

Synonymy†

The designation Arapaho is of uncertain provenience. It is not an Arapaho term, and Arapahos, who pronounced it "N'appaho," believed it to be a Euro-American term (H.L. Scott 1907:556). Although it has been suggested that the name derives from Pawnee *rara·pihu·ru* 'one who trades' or its related form *tira·pihu·ʔu* 'he trades, barters' (John B. Dunbar in Hodge 1907–1910, 1:72), there is no evidence other than similarity of forms to support the derivation. The

†This synonymy was written by Douglas R. Parks.

name occurs as Crow *arappaho* 'many tattoo marks' (Medicine Horse 1987:15), cited also as a-rá-po-ho (Hayden 1862:402) and Adhapahó 'many tattoos' (Curtis 1907–1930, 4:180); as Hidatsa *arúpahu* (Parks 1991a), cited as Adhapí'ahú 'many tattoos' (Curtis 1907–1930, 4:185); and as Mandan Arrapahó, given as the name for the Gros Ventre, 1833 (Maximilian in Thwaites 1904–1907, 24:249) and for the Arapaho (Will and Spinden 1906:209). In both Crow and Hidatsa the twentieth-century translation 'many tattoos' is a folk etymology (Randolph Graczyk and A. Wesley Jones, personal communications 1999), probably based on the sign language designation. The same form occurs as Omaha-Ponca *aðábahu* (Dorsey 1890:652, phonemicized), Kansa *aropwahì* (Dorsey in Rankin 1987:100) or A′nipahu (Gatschet 1878), and Otoe *ara·báhu* (Parks 1988). It also appears as Shawnee *la·paho* (J.P. Dunn in C.F. Voegelin 1937–1940:345).

Arapaho first appears in American sources in the early nineteenth century as Ar-râ-pâ-hoo, 1805 (wrongly listed under "Pānis Republican" in Lewis and Clark 1832:709); Arapahoes, 1810 (John Bradbury in Thwaites 1904–1907, 5:139); Arapahays and Arapohays, 1812 (R. Stuart 1935:86, 192); Arapaos, 1812 (Manuel Lisa in Bolton 1913a:65); Arrapoho, 1821 (J. Fowler 1898:68); Rappaho (E. James 1823, 2:192); Arepahas, 1834 (Cass in Schoolcraft 1851-1857, 3:609); Aripahoes (Hildreth 1836:153); and Arapahays (A. Ross 1849:232). For other spellings, see Hodge (1907–1910, 1:73).

The Arapaho self-designation is *hinónoʔéínoʔ* (sg. *hinónoʔéí*) (Salzmann 1983:46; Loretta Fowler and Ives Goddard, personal communication 1990), cited also as Inûna-ina 'our people; people of our kind' (Mooney 1896:953). The same form, *inonoʔe·-* (A.R. Taylor 1994:31), recorded also as Inanan 'shakes his head' (Curtis 1907–1930, 5:154), is the Gros Ventre name for the Arapaho.

A common late eighteenth and early nineteenth-century designation among fur traders and explorers derives from the Arikara name *tUhkanIhná·wiš* 'gray stone village' (Parks 1999c), which occurs as Ojibwa Kaninǎ′vish or Kaninavisch (Mooney 1896:953; Curtis 1907–1930, 6:138). It appears as Caminanbiche and Tocaminanbiche, 1796 (Truteau in Parks 1993); Caneenawees, 1796 (McKay in Quaife 1916:196); Caninanbiches, 1803–1804 (Tabeau 1939:154); Tocaninambiches (Perrin du Lac 1805:260); Tokaninambich, 1796 (Collot in Nasatir 1952, 2:384); Kun-na-nar-wesh, Ca-ne-na-vich, and Kanenavich, 1804–1805 (Lewis and Clark in Moulton 1983–, 3:135, 423, 425); Kǎ ñi nā viěsch, 1810 (Biddle in D.D. Jackson 1962:535); Caneninavish, 1799–1814 (Alexander Henry the Younger in Coues 1897, 1:384); Kan-ne-na-wish, 1810 (Brackenridge 1817:147); and Kaninahoick (ARCIA 1829:100; Mooney 1896:953).

Associated with the preceding designation, and perhaps derived from the Arikara name, are Blue Beads, given by Lewis and Clark as the translation of Kun-na-nar-wesh; Blue Bead Nation (1795, Soulard in Wheat 1957–1963, 1:map 235a; 1796, Collot in Nasatir 1952, 2:384); and Big Bead Indians (Bradbury in Thwaites 1904–1907, 5:139). That name is represented by the Sioux and Assiniboine designation *maxpíyatʰo* 'blue cloud' (Curtis 1907–1930, 3:141; Buechel 1907:328; S.R. Riggs 1890:305; J.P. Williamson 1902:9; Parks and DeMallie 1996:159), which was apparently borrowed as Omaha *maxpiattu* (Fletcher and La Flesche 1911:102; Dorsey 1890:652; phonemicized) and Ponca *maxpiattą* (Parks 1988), cited also as maxpíato (J.H. Howard 1965:133). A name with the same meaning is Cheyenne *hetanevoʔeoʔo* (sg. *hetanevoʔe*) 'cloud men' (Petter 1913–1915:582; Curtis 1907–1930, 6:158; Glenmore and Leman 1985:201), cited also as I-tun-iwo, mistakenly glossed as 'shy men' (Hayden 1862:290). The Sioux and Assiniboine ethnonym is undoubtedly related to the name of a small blue bead, *maxpíyatʰola* 'little blue sky', that was tied to the forelock or around the neck or wrist of a child to safeguard against danger (Deloria 1954a). According to Sioux and Assiniboine testimony, the name *maxpíyatʰo* is a reference to the Arapaho custom of wearing blue ear pendants (Curtis 1907–1930, 3:141; 6:158). Another, unlikely, interpretation of the name is that it refers to the blue color of Arapaho men's chest tattoos (H.L. Scott 1907:557).

An alternate historical designation is 'buffalo people', cited as Gens de vash (Lewis and Clark in Moulton 1983–, 3:135) and Buffalo Indians (Alexander Henry in Coues 1897, 1:384). It is perhaps the Hidatsa name *itaʔari·* or *ita·ri·* 'its path' (Parks 1987; A. Wesley Jones, personal communication 1999), cited as E-tâh-léh or Bison Path Indians, 1819–1820 (E. James in Thwaites 1904–1907, 16:215) and Ita-Iddi (Maximilian in Thwaites 1904–1907, 24:275).

Another obscure late eighteenth and early nineteenth-century designation, recorded as an Arapaho group separate from the preceding, is Squihitanes and ski-hi-tanes, 1803–1804 (Tabeau 1939:154); Staetan, 1804–1805 (Lewis and Clark in Moulton 1983–, 3:423, 425); Sta-i-tan or Kites, 1810 (Biddle in D.D. Jackson 1962:535); Staitans or Kite Indians (J. Morse 1822:366); Stailans (ARCIA 1829a:104); Marlain or Kite Indians (ARCIA 1829:100); Marlin, 1834 (Cass in Schoolcraft 1851–1857, 3:609). Although Mooney erroneously identified this group as the Sutaio (Hodge 1907–1910, 2:632), Tabeau stated that they spoke the same language as the Arapaho, and Lewis and Clark combined them with the Arapaho.

The Eastern Shoshone name is *sati·tikkati* 'dog eater' (Wick Miller, personal communication 1991) and the Comanche equivalent is *sari·tihkati* (Casagrande 1954–1955:231; Alice Anderton, personal communication 1992), cited as Saritéka (ten Kate 1885:136), Sáditŭka (Curtis 1907–1930, 19:229), and Sarriet tuhka (H.L. Scott 1890–1900). In Southern Ute it was recorded as Saritch-ka-e (ten Kate 1884:8). That name was borrowed as Pawnee *sariʔitihka* (Parks 1999), Wichita *sá·riʔitikaʔa* (David S. Rood, personal communication 1980), and Caddo *šánitihkaʔ* (Chafe 1979). It was cited in American and Spanish sources as Seraticks, 1847 (Burnet in Schoolcraft 1851–1857, 1:239),

Seratics (Bollaert 1850, 2:265), Sarritehca (Rejón in Pimentel 1862–1865, 2:347), Charitas (Sociedad de Geografía y Estadística de la República Mexicana 1870, 2:265), and Dog-eaters (Kingsley 1885, 6:153).

The Mandan and Hidatsa generalized use of the common name for the Gros Ventre 'big belly people' to the Arapaho as well. It occurs as Mandan *é·xixte rṵwą́kaki* 'big belly people' (Hollow 1970:64; Mauricio Mixco, personal communication 2000), cited also as Axixte Numankake (Will and Spinden 1906:209), and as Hidatsa Eirichtih-Äruchpága [*e·rihtía ruxpa·ka*] (Maximilian 1839–1841, 2:213; A. Wesley Jones, personal communication 2000).

Other tribal designations for Arapaho, which have either obscure or singular references, are Kiowa *áyàttɔ*, said to refer to untying arrows in a ceremony (Laurel Watkins, personal communication 1979) or to untied shoes (La Barre 1935), cited also as Ähyä'to (unknown meaning; Mooney 1896:953); Kiowa Apache *béti'tì'é'* (no translation, Biddle 1952–1953; Mooney 1896:953); and Mandan *o·ke'hú* 'digging' (Parks 1991a). Mooney (1896:953) also recorded several names that are not reported elsewhere: Kitsai ano's-anyotskano (no translation); Wichita Niǎ'rharī's-kûrikiwǎ's-hûski (no translation); Caddo Detseka'yaa, said to mean 'dog eaters'; and Kiowa Komse'ka-K'iñahyup 'men of worn-out leggings', said to be a former name.

The sign for Arapaho was made by positioning the right hand in front of the center of the breast, with the back of the hand outward and compressed, the fingers partially curved and drawn together. The fingers were then tapped against the breast, often three times, generally in a line from right to left. The gesture signified tattooing (1819, E. James in Thwaites 1904–1907, 15:336; Ruxton 1848:220; Mallery 1881:460–461; H.L. Scott 1912–1934), which gave rise to the self-designation Tattooed People "from the custom of pricking their breasts" (Schoolcraft 1851–1857, 5:496). It was misinterpreted variously as meaning 'good hearts' (Mallery 1881:460), as representing smallpox scars after a famous chief's chest was disfigured by the disease (W.P. Clark 1885:38), and as the sign for mother, indicating that the Northern Arapahoe represent the parent division of the tribe (W.P. Clark 1885:38). After the separation of the Southern Arapaho, the sign came to designate the Northern Arapahoe.

The sign for 'tattooed' is reflected in the Blackfoot name for the Arapaho, first recorded as Nee Koo chis ak kā 'tattoo'd Inds.', 1801 (Peter Fidler in Moodie and Kaye 1977:17) and later as Ikiótsīsaka 'red tattoo' (Curtis 1907–1930, 6:155).

The sign for the Southern Arapaho is made by bringing the extended index finger of the right hand, back of the hand facing outward or to the right, alongside and touching the nose, index pointing upward and the other fingers and thumb closed. The index finger is then raised and lowered several times, rubbing against or passing along the right side of the nose (Mallery 1881:460; W.P. Clark 1885:38–39; H.L. Scott 1912–1934). The meaning of this sign is obscure,

but it has been interpreted as 'far away south', a reference to the separation of the Southern Arapaho (H.L. Scott 1912–1934).

Divisions

In the late eighteenth and early nineteenth centuries, there were five Arapaho linguistic divisions, of which one was the Gros Ventre.

The Arapaho in the narrow sense were the Hinana'eina (*hinóno'éíno'*, sg. *hinóno'éí*) (Salzmann 1983:46), cited as Inûna-ina (Mooney 1896:954) and Hinanaē'ina[n] (Kroeber 1902–1907:6).

The name Besawunena has been interpreted both as *bê·sô·wû·nénnó'* (sg. *bê·sô·wû·nén*) 'big lodge people' or *besô·wu·nénno'* 'wood lodge people' (Mooney 1896:955; Salzmann 1983:10; "The Algonquian Languages of the Plains," this vol.). An early recording of the Gros Ventre name is Beth thow in in, 1800 (Peter Fidler 1789–1804). Later spellings and glosses are Bä'sawunĕ'na 'wood lodge men' or 'big lodge men' (Mooney 1896:955), Bääsa[n]wūune'na[n] 'shelter or brush-hut men' (Kroeber 1902–1907:6), Bǎǎsawunéna 'Brush-lodge Men' (Curtis 1907–1930, 6:138), and Bawawunena 'wood-lodge men' (Hodge 1907–1910, 1:132).

The Hanahawunena were the *hó·'onohowû·nénnó'*, recorded as Aanû'hawǎ (no translation) (Mooney 1896:956), Hā[n]anaxawūune'na[n] 'rock men', a folk etymology (Kroeber 1902:6), and Hanahawunena (Hodge 1907–1910, 1:530).

The name of the Nawathinehena (*no·wóθi·néhe·nó'*, sg. *no·wóθi·néhe·*) has an uncertain meaning but refers to 'south' (cf. Proto-Algonquian *na·m-* 'downstream') (Salzmann 1983:10; Ives Goddard, personal communication 1990). Historical recordings of the name that reflect the sound *m*, which was unique to this dialect (Kroeber 1902–1907:7), are Nimoussines, 1803–1804 (Tableau 1939:154); Nemousin and Ni-mi-ou-sin, 1804–1805 (Lewis and Clark in Moulton 1983–, 3:424–425); and Ner-mon-sin-nan-see, or Southern Band (Schoolcraft 1851–1857, 5:496). That form occurs in Cheyenne as Nomsin'neo 'southerners', designating the Southern Arapaho (Mooney 1907:424). Other recordings that have w in the second syllable are Now watch e ni in, a Gros Ventre form, 1800 (Peter Fidler 1789–1804), and na-wuth'-i-ni-han (Hayden 1862:321). Later recordings include Nawathi'nĕha (Mooney 1896:955), Nā[n]waçinähä'äna[n], a Northern Arapahoe form (Kroeber 1902–1907:7), and Nawathíneha 'Southerners' (Curtis 1907–1930, 6:138).

The Nawathinehena formed the original core of the Southern Arapaho, whom the Northern Arapahoe designated *nó·wunénnó'* (sg. *nó·wunén*), anglicized as Nawunena (Hodge 1907–1910, 2:47); other spellings include Na[n]wuine'na[n] 'southern men' (Kroeber 1902–1907:7). The Southern Arapaho form of their name is *no·wû·nóno'éi·* (Loretta Fowler and Ives Goddard, personal communication 1990).

The Northern Arapahoe, who largely comprised the Arapaho proper, were known as *nenebî·nennóʔ* 'northern people' (Loretta Fowler and Ives Goddard, personal communication 1990), spelled also Nänäbine′naⁿ (Kroeber 1902–1907:7), and Mountain Band (Schoolcraft 1851–1857, 5:496). They were also called (Kroeber 1902–1907:7): *boʔó·či·nénnóʔ* (sg. *boʔó·či·nén·*) 'blood pudding people' (Salzmann 1983:46; Ives Goddard, personal communication 1990), by the Southern Arapaho, given also as Ba′achinĕna 'red willow men' or 'blood pudding men' (Mooney 1896:954–955) and Bāaⁿtcīine′naⁿ 'red willow men' and Bääkūune′naⁿ 'blood soup men' (Kroeber 1902–1907:7); and *no·khô·seinénnóʔ* (sg. *no·khô·seinén·*) 'sagebrush men' (Loretta Fowler and Ives Goddard, personal communication 1990), given also as Nāⁿk′hāaⁿsēine′naⁿ (Kroeber 1902–1907:7) and Nakasinéna (Curtis 1907–1930, 6:138). Early recordings of the name are na-ka-si′-nin 'People of the Sage' (Hayden 1862:321) and perhaps Naw cotch is seen in nin nin Blue Mud, 1800 (Fidler 1800). It was borrowed as Cheyenne *vánoʔétaneoʔo* 'sage people' (Glenmore and Leman 1985:202), cited also as Wanuǐ′tän-eo 'sage men' (Mooney 1907:424), and Kiowa Tägyä′ko [*tʰá·gyá·gɔ̀*] 'sagebrush people' (Mooney 1896:955; Laurel Watkins, personal communication 2000), both of which designate the Northern Arapahoe.

Sources

The best guide to the literature on the Arapaho is Salzmann (1988), a comprehensive indexed bibliography that includes published works, theses, dissertations, public documents, and archival and museum collections.

Working with both Northern and Southern Arapaho, Kroeber (1902–1907) studied decorative symbolism, ceremonial organization (include the men's Lodges), religion (including revitalization movements such as the Crow Dance and Peyote dating from the 1890s), and dialects (1916). G.A. Dorsey made a detailed study of the Southern Arapaho Offerings Lodge (1903), and published, with Kroeber, a collection of Northern and Southern Arapaho oral traditions recorded in English (1903). Mooney (1896) recorded some information on social organization and culture but focused on the introduction and spread of the Ghost Dance among the Arapaho in the 1890s.

Hilger (1952) recorded child rearing practices and information on culture and society in general. Michelson (1934) recorded kinship terms and Eggan studied kinship and social organization (1937a, 1966a). Densmore studied music (1936).

Studies of life among the Northern Arapahoe include J.G. Carter (1938) on the Sacred Pipe ritual; Sternberg (1946) on the Peyote religion; Nettl (1954, 1955) on music; and Salzmann (1950, 1951, 1956, 1956a, 1957) on language and oral traditions (including texts in the Arapaho language). In

the 1960s Fowler studied politics and political economy (1970, 1973, 1978a, 1985). Studies include S. Hunter (1977) on role of elders, Lah on music (1980), P.H. Welsh (1986) on economics, R. Gilmore (1990) on art, and J.D. Anderson (2000) on cultural continuity, religion, and life cycle. For the Southern Arapaho, there are several volumes of oral accounts of pre- and early reservation culture and history, as well as material from the early 1970s (Doris Duke Collection 1967–1972), and Nespor (1984) studied agriculture.

Firsthand information on the Arapahoe before their settlement on reservations is restricted to comments in travel journals and other reports from 1795 to the 1870s. F.V. Hayden (1863) recorded some information on language and history. Trenholm (1970) compiled an account of Arapahos as they appear in traders' and travelers' reports in the pre-reservation era. A history of the Arapaho during the nineteenth century was prepared for their case before the Indian Claims Commission (Gussaw, Hafen, and Ekirch 1974). Fowler (1982) studied authority relations, both secular and religious, among the Northern Arapahoe from 1851 to 1978 and compared age-group relations among Northern and Southern Arapaho from the 1870s to the 1980s (Fowler 1990). Fowler (1989, 1994) compares Northern and Southern Arapaho. Berthrong (1976, 1985) studied the Cheyenne-Arapaho Agency in Oklahoma, focusing on the affect of federal policies from 1875 to about 1920.

Native accounts from Arapaho perspectives include Michelson (1933), an authobiography of a Cheyenne woman, and the reminiscensices of Carl Sweezy, a Southern Arapaho (Bass 1966); Shakespeare (1971), presented as a native account, was actually written by a non-Indian (see Fowler 1978). Coel (1981) is a biography of Chief Left Hand, Southern Arapaho.

For linguistic analyses see Salzmann (1960, 1961, 1961a, 1965, 1965a, 1967, 1967a, 1967b) and Goddard (1974). Salzmann also published a collection of stories in Arapaho (1980) and a dictionary (1983). Picard (1981, 1994) studied historical phonology. J.D. Anderson (1998) studied Northern Arapahoe language shift.

The major collections of Arapaho material culture are at the Field Museum of Natural History, Chicago, which has the large, well-documented collection of G.A. Dorsey and Cleaver Warden; the American Museum of Natural History, New York, which has Kroeber's well-documented collection; the large but poorly documented collection at the Museum of the American Indian; the University Museum of Archeology and Anthropology at the University of Pennsylvania, which has Culin's collection; the Carnegie Museum of Natural History, Pittsburgh; and the National Museum of Natural History, Smithsonian Institution, which has items collected by Mooney. (For a summary see Smythe and Helweg 1996a). The repatriation of Arapaho human remains from the National Museum of Natural History is covered by Speaker, Killion, and Verano (1993).

Cheyenne

JOHN H. MOORE, MARGOT P. LIBERTY, AND A. TERRY STRAUS

The Cheyenne (shī'an) speak a language* of the Algonquian family. They ranged over much of the Plains, at times even sending raiding parties into south Texas and Mexico. Their westward migrations carried them more than 1,000 miles from their first remembered home in Minnesota to the Central Plains.

History

1680–1760

Before they owned horses, the Cheyenne moved among the mosaic of woodland, prairie, and plains habitats west of the Great Lakes, where they are first known by tradition in present Minnesota (fig. 1). There they lived in villages of bark-covered lodges and subsisted largely on wild rice and other local resources, although they occasionally traveled by foot to the edge of the plains to hunt buffalo. Pressured by the Chippewa and Assiniboine, who were newly armed from the expanding fur trade during the eighteenth century, the Cheyenne bands moved steadily westward, across the Missouri River to the Black Hills (Grinnell 1923, 1:4–13, 253, 1926:242–252; J.H. Moore 1987:53–87; W.R. Wood 1971a).

During this time the Cheyenne lived near bands of Sioux, many of which were also moving gradually westward and adapting a nomadic lifeway based on equestrian buffalo hunting and the acquisition of enough guns to maintain a hunting territory. Some Cheyenne bands did the same, but others adopted the horticultural practices of the Middle Missouri tribes, occupying villages between the mouths of the Heart River in North Dakota and the White River in South Dakota. It is not clear which bands went through a

settled, horticultural period, and which did not (J.H. Moore 1996:13–29; W.R. Wood 1971a:51–68).

New political forms originated during this time, and the Mandan Okipa ceremony and Hidatsa Sacred Arrow traditions, among others, no doubt helped to inspire the development of the Cheyenne ceremonial complex (Bowers 1950, 1965:31–32, 48–50, 303; Ottoway 1970:4–5; J.M. Roberts 1964:433–454). The Cheyenne began to trade and raid intensively for horses from the horse-rich tribes to their south, especially the Kiowa, Plains Apache, and Comanche. From a strategic position in the Central Plains, they became middlemen in the trade of horses from the south for guns to the north (Jablow 1951:81–82; J.H. Moore 1996:79–89; W.R. Wood 1971:67–68).

Three factors contributed to this transformation: the access provided by horses to rich game areas not securely claimed by other tribes; trade opportunities better than those on the Missouri, where the Village tribes had priority; and escape from aggression against the Village tribes by the Sioux (Jablow 1951:81–82; W.R. Wood 1971a:67–68). The Cheyenne moved into a new environment on the High Plains for which they were well equipped with horses and guns and new social organization based on fresh political and religious ideas.

1760–1850

Cheyenne bands unified in the Black Hills of South Dakota, an area rich with buffalo, where the oral literature and religion of the tribe attained its historical form. The Sweet Medicine legends explaining the origin of the Sacred Arrows place this event at their sacred mountain *nóvávóse* (Bear Butte, near present Sturgis, South Dakota). During this formative period the Sutaio (*só?taeo?o*), a closely related Algonquian group, affiliated with the Cheyenne (*tsétsEhéstAhese*), an event recounted in the legendary struggle between Sweet Medicine and Lime, an ancient leader of the Sutaio (J.H. Moore 1987:109–113). The Sutaio brought the Sacred Hat, which became the Cheyennes' second sacred tribal possession, as well as the Sun Dance (Mooney 1907:361, 1907b:256–257; Petter 1913–1915:228, 582; Stands in Timber and Liberty 1967:15).

From the Black Hills, the Cheyenne sought to extend their territory to the prime buffalo-hunting region between the forks of the Platte River, which brought on a period of continuous warfare with the Shoshone, Crow, and Pawnee.

---

*The phonemes of Cheyenne are: (voiceless unaspirated stops and affricate) p, t, ts, k, ?; (voiceless spirants) s, š, x, h; (nasals) m, n; (voiced continuant) v ([v], [w]); (voiced vowels) e ([i] to [ɛ]), a, o ([ʊ] to [o]); (voiceless vowels) E, A, O. The 4 level tones, from highest to lowest, are: (high) v́; (mid; raised low) v̄; (lowered high) v̌; (low) v. Word-final vowels are devoiced prepausally. Vowels in sequences are in separate syllables. At a more abstract level of analysis ts is a conditioned variant of t before underlying |e|.

The analysis and transcription of Cheyenne follows Leman (1981); there the lowered high tone is written v̌ and the nonphonemic variants of the high tone are distinguished as v́ (high) and v̂ (raised high). The Cheyenne practical alphabet follows the phonemic analysis closely; the glottal stop is written with an apostrophe (') and the voiceless vowels are written as dotted vowels: ė, ȧ, ȯ. The status and distribution of the lowered high tone is uncertain.

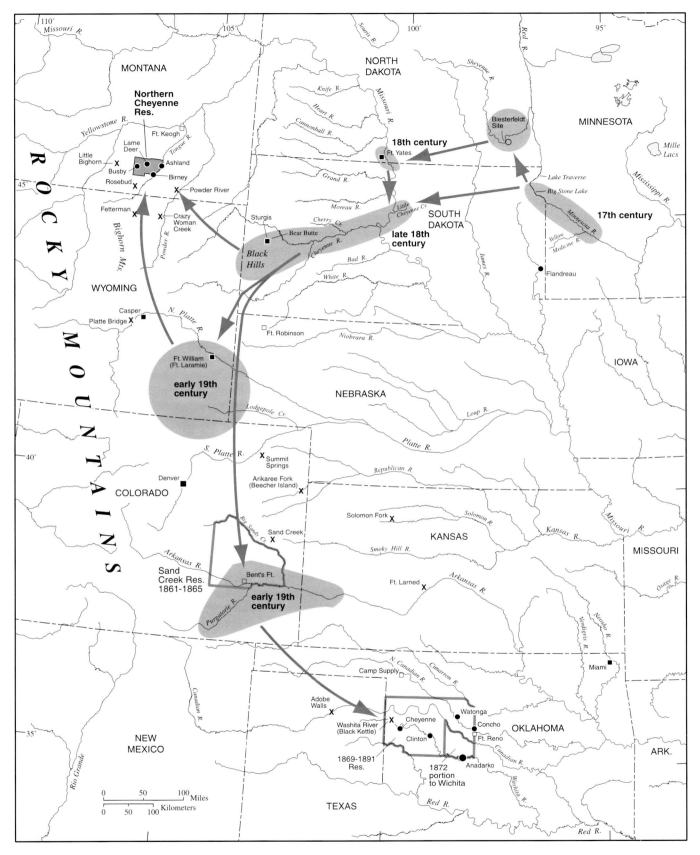

Fig. 1. Territories, migrations, and reservations of the Cheyenne, with 19th-century battle sites and 21st-century towns.

MOORE, LIBERTY, AND STRAUS

A separation of the Cheyenne into northern and southern divisions that began by the early nineteenth century was accelerated by the building of Bent's Fort on the Arkansas River in the early 1830s. The trade goods available at the fort, and the marriage of William Bent into a prominent Cheyenne family, encouraged the southern bands to live nearby (Lavender 1954:106–203; Mooney 1907:376–377). During this time the Northern Cheyenne came to depend on trade from the Missouri River and from Fort William (later called Fort Laramie) on the North Platte River beginning in 1834.

The opening of the Oregon Trail in the 1840s depleted game, grazing, firewood, and other resources along the Platte River, causing the Cheyenne bands to withdraw northward and southward from the valley. Thus the traditional summer gathering of all bands for ceremonies became difficult. The last traditional camp circle with all bands present is believed to have occurred in 1838 (Grinnell 1915:50; Hyde 1968:200; Mooney 1907:402–411). By 1849 the Cheyenne were encountering increased Anglo-American emigration, warfare, and diseases like cholera and smallpox. Cholera killed hundreds of people, eliminating two of the 10 original bands (the Poor People and Bare Shins) and forcing the survivors of a third (the Flexed Legs) into merging with the Dog Soldiers military society, among whom their identity vanished (Grinnell 1923, 1:101).

1851–1867

The Fort Laramie Treaty of 1851 set territories for all tribes in the region and officially recognized two divisions for the Cheyenne (Mooney 1907:377). Intertribal warfare continued, despite permanent peace with the Kiowa after 1840. Shoshone fights are documented for 1855, 1860 and 1865; Crow fights for 1850, 1855, and 1870 (Stands in Timber and Liberty 1967:127–160).

The Cheyennes went to war against the United States Army, engaging American forces in over 50 military actions from 1854 until 1879. The most significant are the 1856 Upper Platte Bridge Fight near present Casper, Wyoming; 1856–1857 raids along the Kansas frontier; the 1857 fight with Col. Edwin V. Sumner's troops on the fork of the Solomon River, Kansas; 1863–1864 raids along the Arkansas and Platte; the 1864 outbreak and November 29 massacre of peaceful Cheyennes at Sand Creek, Colorado; consequent raids along the Platte in a general frontier war of 1865; the August-September 1865 Gen. Patrick E. Conner campaign into the Powder River country of Wyoming; the 1865 attack upon troops by Northern Cheyennes under High Wolf at Old Platte Bridge, Wyoming; the 1866 destruction of Capt. William J. Fetterman's command at Fort Philip Kearny, Wyoming; the 1867 destruction of a Cheyenne and Sioux village near Fort Larned, Kansas; renewed raiding in 1868 followed by the battle on Arikaree Fork, eastern Colorado, where the warrior Roman Nose was killed; the November 1868 attack by Lt. Col. George A. Custer on Black

Kettle's village along the Washita River in Oklahoma; Gen. Eugene A. Carr's crushing 1869 defeat of the Dog Soldiers at Summit Springs, Colorado; the Southern Plains war of 1874–1875, including a fight at Adobe Walls, Texas; and the continued pursuit of the Southern Cheyenne resulting in their surrender March 6, 1875 (Berthrong 1963:127–405; Grinnell 1915:91–358; Mooney 1907:376–397; D.P. Schultz 1990; U.S. Army 1882).

1868–1933

While the organized military resistance of the southern bands ended with the defeat of the Dog Soldiers in 1869 (fig. 2), the resistance of Northern Cheyennes, augmented by militant groups of Southern Cheyennes, continued for several more years. In 1876 four major battles took place: the March 17 attack by Col. Joseph J. Reynolds upon Crazy Horse's village on the Powder River, Montana; the June 17 fight with Gen. George Crook at Rosebud Creek, Montana; the June 25 defeat of Custer on the Little Bighorn, Montana; and the November 25 attack of Col. Ranald S. Mackenzie upon the main Northern Cheyenne camp at Crazy Woman Creek, Wyoming. In April 1877 the Two Moons band surrendered at Fort Keogh, Montana, and the Little Wolf-Dull Knife band at Fort Robinson, Nebraska. The Fort Robinson group was transferred to the Cheyenne-Arapaho Agency in Indian Territory, but they fled north in September 1878. Little Wolf's group of 126 surrendered next spring and was allowed to join Two Moons' band at Fort Keogh. The 149 under Dull Knife imprisoned at Fort Robinson broke out January 9, 1879; more than half were killed by the army. A group under Little Chief was sent to Indian Territory in 1878 and transferred to Pine Ridge in 1881. By October 1891 all Northern Cheyennes were reunited on Tongue River in Montana (Grinnell 1915:359–427; Marquis 1931; Mooney 1907:397–400; Sandoz 1953).

The early reservation period began about 1868 in the south, after the Battle of the Washita, and about 1880 in the north. The Southern Cheyenne were administered on a reservation in west-central Oklahoma along with their Southern Arapaho allies, while the Northern Cheyenne were assigned their own reservation in eastern Montana in 1884 (Berthrong 1963, 1976; Svingen 1993; T. Weist 1977:87–212). Attempts by the Cheyenne to adopt a farming and ranching economy most often failed. Most Southern Cheyenne land was lost in 1892 under the provisions of the Dawes Severalty Act of 1887 (24 U.S. Stat. 338) and by subsequent legislative and administrative acts, many of which were later affirmed in court to be illegal. The Northern Cheyenne land was under less pressure for allotment and remained intact until 1926 (R.T. Anderson 1951; Berthrong 1976; Svingen 1993; K.M. Weist 1970).

Under authority of the 1887 Dawes Act, a three-person commission chaired by David Jerome was sent to Oklahoma Territory in 1890 to secure the approval of the Cheyennes and other tribes to a plan for allotting part of the reservation   *865*

Fig. 2. Accouterments of warfare. left, Dog Soldier society leader's sash of painted hide ornamented with porcupine quill embroidery. During battle, a sash-wearer might stake himself to the ground by driving an arrow through the slit at the bottom of the sash, pledging to die rather than retreat. center, Dragonfly effigy hair ornament of rawhide worn as war medicine. Collected by George Bird Grinnell on the Northern Cheyenne Res., Mont. right, Drawing in a ledger book showing the rescue of a comrade in battle. Pictographs above the men identify them as Wolf with Plenty of Hair and Tall Bull, the leader of the Dog Soldier band. Tall Bull carries a shield painted with protective symbols, while his rescuer wears a Dog Soldier sash. This book of drawings was captured by a member of the 5th U.S. Cavalry at the Battle of Summit Springs, Colo., July 1869, in which both men were killed (Afton, Halaas, and Masich 1997). Length of left, 196 cm; center, 5.6 cm.

land to Indian people as individual owners, and selling the "surplus" land to outsiders. Under the 1867 Treaty of Medicine Lodge (vol. 4:201) however, agreed between the Cheyenne and the federal government, "No treaty for the cession of any portion or part of the reservation herein described . . . shall be of any validity or force as against the said Indians unless executed and signed by at least three fourths of all the adult male Indians occupying or interested in the same" (Kappler 1904–1941, 2:988). Recognizing early in their visit that the Southern Cheyennes were almost unanimously opposed to the allotment plan, the Jerome Commission took steps to secure, if not the approval, at least the "appearance" of approval from the Southern Cheyennes (Berthrong 1976:150–181; J.H. Moore 1987:210–212). When the Commission could not secure the required men's signatures, they resorted to entering women's names and gave themselves powers of attorney for students at boarding school and for Cheyennes who were caught up in the Ghost Dance religion and had warned the commission not to visit them. Although the Cheyenne protested the actions of the Jerome Commission (vol. 4:225), all such complaints were dismissed after the issuance of the Supreme Court decision, *Lone Wolf v. Hitchcock*, in 1903, which stated that since Congress had ratified the allotment agreement, the actions of the commission could not be undone, no matter how fraudulent they might have been (Prucha 1975:202–203). In this way the Southern Cheyenne and Arapaho lost three million acres of land, six-sevenths

of the total reservation, nearly all of which was given over to settlement by non-Indians.

1934–2000

The Indian Reorganization Act was passed in 1934 and the Oklahoma Indian Welfare Act in 1936, addressed to the special situation of Indian tribes in Oklahoma. Under these bills, tribal governments were formed and traditional aspects of culture were formally encouraged, including native religion, a sharp reversal from previous federal policy (Officer 1971:43; Prucha 1975:222–231). Provisions of the acts enabled the Northern Cheyenne to buy back most of their reservation, and the Southern Cheyenne also purchased land.

During the early days of the New Deal, many Cheyennes in Montana and Oklahoma were involved with projects of the Civilian Conservation Corps and the Works Progress Administration. For the first time, many Cheyennes lived in villages, and in fact several of the small towns on the Northern Cheyenne reservation increased in size as the result of government programs. World War II brought many Cheyennes into military service, a development that led to a revival of traditional military societies and the formation of new groups, such as the War Mothers and local veterans' groups (R.T. Anderson 1956). Some Cheyennes who moved to Seattle, Chicago, Dallas, Denver (vol. 4:77), and Los Angeles to work in war industries or BIA relocation programs never returned to the reservation.

Culture in the Nineteenth Century

Subsistence

Economic life was based primarily upon use of the buffalo and staple plant foods including the roots of prairie turnips, Jerusalem artichokes, and groundnuts, as well as many kinds of berries, especially silver buffalo berries, and several fruits of the genus *Prunus* (Grinnell 1923, 1:67–72; 2:166–191). Gardening of corn, beans, and squash, once a major subsistence activity, was largely abandoned after the transition to a nomadic style of life. Buffalo were hunted in two ways: by small groups or individuals when the residence bands were scattered during most of the year, or tribally under strict policing by the men's societies during the early summer, and sometimes again in the fall. Hunting was men's work: shooting with arrows or lancing from horseback were the most common hunting techniques, although other methods—impounding, driving off cliffs or into deep snow—were occasionally used. Deer, elk, wild sheep, and pronghorn were also important sources of food and skins. Smaller animals were killed for food and furs: wolves, coyotes, foxes, bears, beavers, otters, and rabbits. Porcupines were hunted for quills. Birds were killed for their quills and feathers, especially eagles, which required hilltop vigils by solitary hunters in blinds baited with meat (Grinnell 1923, 1:247–311).

Horses were an important form of wealth. Raids into Mexico and among Euro-American farms and ranches in the eastern Plains, toward the middle of the nineteenth century, were sources of wealth for some bands, providing also cattle, mules, blankets, guns, clothing, household equipment, and wagons. By about 1830, after a series of shrewd military maneuvers and alliances, the Cheyenne managed to occupy the central position for trade across the Great Plains. Horses were traded north and east for guns, kettles, and other goods (Jablow 1951).

Division of Labor

Butchering was shared by men and women, but the drying and storage of meat, roots, and fruit were women's work (fig. 3), as were the preparation of clothing, lodge covers, and robes. During the early nineteenth century the buffalo robe trade became very important and enriched many Cheyenne households. Women also gathered fuel and carried water for the camp. Older women specialized in the identification and collection of more than 40 kinds of wild plant foods (J.A. Hart 1981).

The customary division of labor included also, for women, making and moving tepees, which were the property of women. Tepee covers and furnishings took much work, as did the carefully decorated garments and storage containers of rawhide provided for each household. Adult men's work, in addition to hunting, focused upon warfare and ceremonial life, while the young men herded horses. Men made weapons, horse gear, and ceremonial equipment. Robes made by women were painted by men with realistic figures of warriors and animals, often documenting personal exploits; women used geometric rather than realistic designs to decorate parfleches and tepee liners with paint or applied beads or quills to moccasins and clothing (Grinnell 1923, 1:63–72, 159–246). Some tepees were painted by men in a spectacular fashion (fig. 4), calling attention to personal medicine ways or military exploits (Fagin 1988). When ledger and other blank books were obtained by trade or

left, Smithsonian, NAA: 43118-a.

Fig. 3. Food preparation. left, Jerked beef drying on a line as well as intestines, which were used to make sausage. Filled sausage is on the ground lower right. Photographed 1895. right, Eva Elk Shoulder, Northern Cheyenne, making chokecherry patties, a mixture of chokecherry pits and fruit manually ground. Photograph by Margot Liberty, Birney, Mont., about 1957.

Fig. 4. Residences and household equipment. top left, Southern Cheyenne-Arapaho camp near Ft. Reno and Darlington Agency, Okla. Terr. The 2 largest tepees are painted with sacred symbols revealed in dreams. Photograph by Joseph Andre Shuck, about 1904–1918 (cropped). top right, Backrest. Backrests of willow rods strung together were unrolled and hung from a tripod at the end of a bed for comfortable seating. Length 144 cm. bottom, Northern Cheyenne Res., Birney, Mont. Log cabins, outhouse, canvas-covered tepee, and sweatlodge with buffalo skull on mound near it are evident. Photograph by Arthur Rothstein, 1939.

raiding, Cheyenne men filled them with colorful drawings (vol. 17:287) (Afton, Halaas, and Masich 1997; C.S. Greene 1998).

The numbers and descriptions of vocations within a Cheyenne band in 1880 have been preserved (J.H. Moore 1996:160). Generally speaking, the tasks requiring more skill were undertaken by older people. Younger people were generally hunter-warriors or housekeepers. Boys watched the horses, probably nearly 1,000 head for a band of 300 persons, and girls assisted their mothers, aunts, and grandmothers in domestic work.

Technology

Even before they had seen many White people, Cheyenne life had been much affected by Euro-American trade. Guns, ammunition, knives, arrowpoints, awls, needles, kettles, cloth, and glass beads had all become necessary items. The Cheyenne tepee, on a three-pole base, was carefully tailored from as many as 21 buffalo skins. Furnishings included decorated skin linings, rush or willow backrests (fig. 4), and mattresses, bedding, and storage containers. Men's clothing included leggings, shirts, and breechcloths. Women's clothing included dresses and leggings. Both sexes wore moccasins and buffalo robes in the winter months (figs. 5–6).

Weapons produced from native materials included bows and arrows, quivers, lances, war clubs, and several kinds of shields. Horse gear included saddles, bridles, lariats, and the travois. Pipes for smoking were made from bone and from stone (usually red catlinite). Women's tools included hooked poles and mauls for collecting firewood, as well as knives and four tanning implements: scrapers, fleshers, abraders, and softening ropes. By the 1830s, pottery had been replaced by trade goods or utensils fashioned from animal materials, including water skins of buffalo paunch or pericardium (Grinnell 1923, 1:170–246; Stands in Timber and Liberty 1967: 75–77, 80–83, 172–176).

Equipment was made for games and other amusements. The women's seed game utilized a small basket and marked

top left, Church of Jesus Christ of Latter-Day Saints, Arch., Salt Lake City: P1300/811; top center, Smithsonian, NAA: 88-2106; top right, Mont. Histl. Soc., Helena: 981-135; bottom left, U. of Okla., Sam Noble Mus. of Nat. Hist., Norman: NAM 9-6-70; Smithsonian, Dept. of Anthr.: bottom center, 152,815 (neg. 89-10279); a, 165,981 (neg. 78-12414); b, 6988 (neg. 78-12420).

Fig. 5. Women's clothing. Southern Cheyenne clothing was less heavily beaded than items made by the Northern Cheyenne. top left, Northern Cheyenne woman wearing stroud dress with elk teeth decoration. She is wearing dentalium earrings, hair decorations, and choker; multiple bead necklaces; and a belt with German silver disks. Stereograph by Charles W. Carter, 1860s–1880s. top center, Wife of Old Crow, Southern Cheyenne, wearing a buckskin dress with a Northern Plains–style heavily beaded cape and a hairpipe necklace. Photograph by Edward S. Curtis, 1926 (cropped). top right, Northern Cheyenne girl wearing a stroud dress decorated with dentalium. She holds a doll outfitted in a similar dress. Photograph by Laton A. Huffman, 1879–1890s. bottom left, Southern-style 3-skin dress of buckskin, heavily fringed, and decorated with yellow paint on the bodice and red paint around the hem. Acquired by William Munger, about 1890, from Winoma Turkey Legs. Length at center 114 cm. bottom center, Leggings with lane stitch beadwork in Cheyenne stripe style. Collected by James Mooney, 1892. Length 53 cm. a, Moccasins collected by Heinrich Voth, 1893; length 25 cm. b, Moccasins collected by Edward Palmer, 1868; same scale. All from the Southern Cheyenne-Arapaho Res., Ind. Terr.

plum stones. The hand game required marked sticks or bones. A netted wheel was used for the hoop game played by men (fig. 7). Toys included balls, dolls, sleds, and tops.

The "finger game" (ring and pin) was a device for tossing and impaling a series of deer phalangyal bones. Musical instruments, played chiefly by men, included drums, rattles,

Smithsonian, NAA: top left, 365-e; top right, T-15864; bottom left, 236; bottom right, Smithsonian, Dept. of Anthr.: 35,641 (neg. 89-10246).

Fig. 6. Men's clothing. top left, Northern Cheyenne hostages of Gen. George Custer (P.J. Powell 1981, 2:721): Curly Hair, chief of the Poor People band, wearing a buffalo robe; Fat Bear, wrapped in a blanket; and Dull Knife, wearing a buffalo robe. They also wear items of military origin, including a hat and cape. Photograph by William S. Soule, Camp Supply, Indian Terr., 1869. top right, Northern Cheyenne delegation to Washington, D.C. standing, Willis T. Rowland; Lone Elk wearing shirt and vest with warbonnet; Samuel Little Sun wearing a warbonnet and hairpipe breastplate, cloth shirt, and tie. seated, Jacob Tall-Bull in fringed buckskin shirt beaded with an American flag design, stroud leggings decorated with beaded strips, ribbon appliqued breechcloth, and warbonnet; Thaddeas Red Water; and Big Head Man wearing cloth leggings decorated with beads and cloth breechcloth, but shirt, vest and tie. Photograph by De Lancey Gill, Washington, 1914. bottom left, Poor Elk or Starving Elk of the Hill people band, Southern Cheyenne holding a banner lance of the Bowstring Society. He wears a mixture of White and Indian clothing including a cloth shirt and vest, buckskin leggings, beaded moccasins, breechcloth decorated with Prairie-style beading, hairpipe breastplate, and horned headdress. Photograph by Charles Carpenter, St. Louis World's Fair, 1904. bottom right, Hide shirt painted blue on upper body, yellow on lower body, decorated with plaited porcupine quill embroidery and fringed with human hair. Quillwork panels and tabs of red and blue trade cloth border the neck. Purchased by Frank Cushing from the Northern Cheyenne leader Little Chief in 1879, when he came to Washington as part of a tribal delegation. Length at center front 62 cm.

and wooden flageolets. Many of these items were still made and used in the twentieth century (fig. 8) (Grinnell 1923, 1:135, 202–205, 312–335).

Life Cycle

When giving birth, a Cheyenne mother was tended by other women, sometimes midwives. Men remained away.

Infants were carried on cradleboards (vol. 4:399) or in blanket slings upon their mothers' backs. The umbilicus, when it came off, was dried and preserved in a small beaded buckskin bag. There was no infant naming ceremony; nicknames for babies continued in use for several years. At some point after the first birthday, perhaps age five or six, a child's ears could be pierced ceremonially at a public gathering, and gifts distributed to honor the child. At this

Fig. 7. Games. left, Northern Cheyenne girls with toy tepees and dolls. Photograph by Julia E. Tuell, Lame Deer, Mont., 1906–1909. right, Southern Cheyenne youth, Red Moon band, playing the hoop and stick game. Played with a wheel and two pairs of throwing sticks, it was a gambling game in which high stakes were sometimes placed on the results (Culin 1907:442–446). Photograph by Elizabeth Grinnell, Spotted Horse's Camp, Okla. 1902 (cropped). inset, Game hoop. The game is played by throwing forked sticks at a wooden hoop filled with rawhide netting as it rolls along the ground, trying to pierce it near the center. Collected on the Cheyenne-Arapaho Res., Ind. Terr., by Heinrich Voth, 1881–1893. Diameter 34 cm.

time, a child might receive a formal name, selected by father's oldest sister from names on the father's side of the family. Additional names could be received at a later time, more frequently by men, in honor of some noteworthy achievement (Eggan 1955a:62–63; Grinnell 1923, 1:102–118, 2:110–111; Hilger 1946; Hoebel 1960:90–92; J.H. Moore 1984; Stands in Timber and Liberty 1967:287).

At puberty, different customs prevailed for boys and for girls. A horse was given away for a girl in honor of her first menstrual period. Isolation in a menstrual lodge was usually required each month thereafter. Girls were carefully chaperoned, since virginity was expected of all. A protective cord or chastity belt was worn from puberty until marriage, and afterward when the husband was away hunting or at war. The Cheyenne emphasis upon female chastity was unusual for the Plains (Abbott and Smith 1939:45–149; Eggan 1955a:64; Grinnell 1923, 1:129–131, 156; Hoebel 1960:94–95; Michelson 1932).

Many boys accompanied war parties by age 12 or 13. The transition to adulthood was marked more by achievement than physical change; no formal ritual marked coming of age. Adolescent boys might take part in vision quests for spiritual power, although these mostly occurred later in life (Eggan 1955a:64–65; Grinnell 1923, 1:117–126; Hoebel 1960:92–94).

Traditionally, marriage for a man was postponed until he had a respectable war record. Courtship was formal (fig. 9), often lasting several years. Marriage to a relative of any degree was forbidden, while marriage between members of

different bands seems to have predominated until warfare interrupted normal patterns (J.H. Moore 1987:251–285).

If the potential groom's family approved a match they assisted him in making a formal proposal. Horses loaded with gifts were tied outside the woman's lodge, to be returned if the proposal were refused. If the proposal was accepted, marriage took place shortly thereafter. Gifts, usually including guns and horses, were reciprocated by the bride's relatives. Residence was usually matrilocal (J.H. Moore 1980). The mother-in-law was the leader of the domestic unit; the new husband avoided his wife's mother, unless particular gift exchanges took place. Respect and avoidance in the family camp also prevailed between brother and sister, and between the bride and her father-in-law (J.H. Moore 1996:157–158). Polygyny was common in prereservation times; about one-third of Cheyenne children were born into families where the husband had more than one wife (J.H. Moore 1991).

Divorce could be instigated by either party. A woman might elope with another man; or a husband might "throw away" his wife. This could be done at a public gathering. The husband might dance to a special song, then hit the drum and throw his drumstick into the crowd, announcing that he was thereby disposing of this wife and embarrassing her publicly. If such a woman wished to marry elsewhere, her new husband was expected to make a settlement with the former husband, usually involving a gift of horses (Eggan 1955a:62; Grinnell 1923, 1:91, 153–156; Hoebel 1960:27; Stands in Timber and Liberty 1967:282–283).

Fig. 8. Life in the late 20th century. top left, Floyd Fisher and helper feeding cattle in winter. Photographed by Ken Blackbird, Northern Cheyenne Res., Mont., 1992. top right, Joe David Osage, Larry Roman Nose (partially hidden), and Freeman White Hawk, Jr., all Southern Cheyenne, placing poles for a sweatlodge near Watonga, Okla. Photograph by Darrell Rice, 1986. bottom left, Northern Cheyenne woman beading a vest. Photograph by Joseph C. Farber, 1970–1974. bottom right, Daniel Dru, Southern Cheyenne (b. 1924, d. 1998), making a drum. During the fall Veterans' Day powwow, one of his drums was raffled off as a fund-raiser. He trained 2 younger men in drum making. Photograph by Shan Goshorn, Miami, Okla., 1989.

At death, the deceased person, finely dressed, was lashed into robes or blankets and carried by travois to a place of burial. A tepee might be used for a final resting place, or a tree, scaffold, cliff face, or crevice in the rocks. Personal effects were left with the body and sometimes, for a warrior, a horse was killed at the site. Women mourners cut their clothing and gashed themselves with knives, especially if the deceased had been killed in war. Men loosened their hair and wore old clothing to show their grief. All possessions of the deceased person were given away, leaving the mourners impoverished. After a year or so the household was refurnished with gifts of necessary items from other families (Grinnell 1923, 1:150–151, 2:21–22, 91–94, 159–163; Stands in Timber and Liberty 1967:286–289; Straus 1978).

Kinship

Kinship was bilateral. There were no clans or other unilineal descent groups. Kinship terminology for the parents' generation was bifurcate merging, with the term for 'my father', *néhoʔéehe*, extended to father's brothers and the term for 'my mother', *náhkoʔéehe*, extended to mother's sisters. Special terms were used for older brothers and sisters as opposed to younger siblings. All respected older people were addressed as grandfather and grandmother (Eggan 1955a:35–95; Grinnell 1923, 1:157–158; J.H. Moore 1987:288–312, 1988).

At several times in their history, the Cheyennes experienced changes in their pattern of postmarital residence. During the height of the trade in buffalo hides and robes, trading bands tended to be matrilocal, so that sisters could

Fig. 9. Courtship. Proper Cheyenne courting couples wrapped themselves in a single blanket and stood in private conversation outside the young woman's tepee, under her family's supervision. Special courting blankets were made in double-width, half red and half black. left, Couple meeting properly. Footprints show that the man had to wait behind the woman's tepee before she came out to join him. right, Man meeting 3 women away from camp behind a screen of trees. His hat and belt are on the ground and one woman pulls on his bandolier necklace. Left drawing by Red Eagle, right by Short Horn, drawn in 1887 while both were enlisted as U.S. Army scouts at Ft. Reno, Ind. Terr. (C.S. Greene 1998:4–19).

stay with their mother after marriage, continuing their cooperative work in making robes. During the period of intensive warfare, 1830–1870, some bands became patrilocal, so that brothers, who were usually members of the same men's society, could stay together for military purposes. In reservation times, newly married couples tended to reside with whichever family lived on trust land and had space for them. In all cases, children in such arrangements called all their coresident first cousins 'brother' and 'sister', reflecting the prohibition against marrying first cousins (J.H. Moore 1988).

Religion

The Cheyenne conception of the universe consisted of the world above and the world below, separated by the earth's surface. The zenith was home of the Creator (*maʔheōʔo*; Glenmore and Leman 1984:183) while the nadir, at the center of the earth, embodied the female principle (*heʔestOtse*). At the same time, the zenith was spiritual while the nadir was material. At the horizon, where earth and sky meet, in each of the four directions a spirit lived, each associated with various sacred creatures, colors, and other phenomena. The Creator was the source of "energy" (*éxAhestOtse*), which he transmitted to the other anthropomorphic spirits, including the sun, moon, and four directions, and to birds, animals, and plants. Humans could share in this energy through prayer and fasting and by participating in sacred ceremonies. Doctors, for example, gained their powers to heal illness by establishing relationships with particular spirits, animals, and plants. This cosmic energy was understood to be finite, to become exhausted by each winter's end, requiring renewal by sacred ceremonies held during the summer (J.H. Moore 1996:203–213).

There were four major tribal ceremonies: the Sacred Arrow Renewal, the Sun Dance or Medicine Lodge, the Massaum or Animal Dance, and the Sacred Hat ceremony. Of these, the most important was the Sacred Arrow ceremony. It rested on the personal biography of the great culture hero, Sweet Medicine (*motséʔeóeve*) who came to the people when they lived near the Black Hills, bringing the major spiritual heritage of the tribe. At Bear Butte he was taken into a cave for instruction by supernatural beings, who delivered to him the four Sacred Arrows (*maahōtse*) that came to dominate Cheyenne religious life. These included two Man Arrows for warfare and two Buffalo Arrows for hunting. These arrows had old-fashioned stone points, which were renewed with fresh sinew bindings from time to time, especially when polluted by intratribal homicide. The killing of one Cheyenne by another was a criminal offense, defiling the Arrows, driving away game, and jeopardizing the life and health of everyone. Renewal of the Arrows was thus the most important of all Cheyenne ceremonies. It took place almost every summer—of necessity if there had been a homicide—or at other times if a pledger for some other reason wished to step forward (Randolph 1937; Llewellyn and Hoebel 1941:132–168; Hoebel 1960:6–10; P.J. Powell 1969, 1).

At the Arrow Renewal site, the entire camp was required to keep silent for four days of ceremony, during which the Arrow sinews and feathers were replaced, and prayers were repeated for the people. At the conclusion, men (never women) were invited to view the Arrows, after which they were returned to the Arrow tepee. If the entire tribe moved against some enemy the Sacred Arrows might be carried on the lance of a chosen warrior (Grinnell 1910:542–575, 1915:72; P.J. Powell 1958:35–40; Ottoway 1970).

873

The Sun Dance was held each summer, after the Sacred Arrow Renewal. The Cheyenne Sun Dance (*hestOsanèstOtse; hoxéheome* 'Sun Dance Lodge') had a theme of world renewal: prayers were for the welfare of the people, to increase the resources they required. The main pledger of the ceremony was instructed by a leading priest. In addition to the main pledger, other men might pledge to dance and fast for four days, each of whom taught by an instructor who himself had undergone the ordeal at least four times. During four days the participants took neither food nor water. Highlights included sunrise dances and the exhibition of sacred objects on the last day. Self-torture could occur at this time, usually piercing through the skin of the chest or back (G.A. Dorsey 1905b; Grinnell 1923, 2:211–284; Petter 1913–1915:1028–1030; Liberty 1965, 1967, 1968; P.J. Powell 1969, 2:611–856).

The Massaum (*mAsEháome* 'crazy lodge') (fig. 10) acted out the story of Yellow-Haired Girl (*heóvEstséáhé?e*), who taught the Cheyenne how to obtain the animals they needed for food, clothing, and religious purposes. During the ceremony, medicine men and women dressed themselves like various animals, emblematic of their healing powers as shamans (Grinnell 1923, 2:285–336; K.D. Petersen 1964:146–147; Schlesier 1987).

A fourth ceremony centered on the sacred object of the Northern Cheyenne, the Sacred Hat (*ésevone*) (fig. 10), which is a headdress made from buffalo hide and horns. The Sacred Hat bundle was opened on ceremonial occasions. It

top left, U. of Wyo., Amer. Heritage Center, Laramie; top right, Smithsonian, NAA: 76-15880.

Fig. 10. Sacred ceremonies and bundles. top left, Northern Cheyenne Grass Buffalo women performing a healing rite over a patient, an early photograph of the Massaum or Animal Dance (Albright 1997:29–30). Photograph by Richard Throssel, Northern Cheyenne Res., Mont., 1909. top right, Southern Cheyenne women wearing buffalo dance headdresses used in the Massaum. Photograph by Edward S. Curtis, Okla., 1926. bottom left, Fred Last Bull holding the marked leather roll of arrow mnemonics that was part of the Arrow bundle. bottom right, Fred Last Bull and John Woodenlegs at the opening of the Sacred Hat bundle, for the first time since the 1930s. It contained a bundle of sweet grass tied in red cloth; 5 scalps mounted on a willow hoop in a blue bundle; Sacred Hat in skin wrapping; a package, probably of tobacco, in blue and green print cloth; an otter or mink skin; and a bundle tied with cotton strips. bottom, Photographs by Margot Liberty, Northern Cheyenne Res., Busby and Ashland, Mont., 1957.

MOORE, LIBERTY, AND STRAUS

was respected, along with the Sacred Arrows, as a talisman to be carried into battle (Grinnell 1910:542–575; Liberty 1967; P.J. Powell 1960:36–40, 1969, 1; Stands in Timber and Liberty 1967:73–78).

Cheyenne religion also included healing and personal medicine rituals (Grinnell 1923, 2:126–165). Such rituals were used not only for curing injury and disease but also in preparation for warfare, the tanning of a white buffalo hide, the announcement of rules of conduct, the ceremonial smoking of a pipe, and the offering of individual sacrifice (Grinnell 1923, 2:192–210). Some Cheyenne traditional stories were also sacred in nature, but others were for the instruction of children or merely for entertainment (Grinnell 1926, 1923, 2:87–125, 337–381; J.H. Moore 1996:176–198).

The early reservation period was characterized by religious changes. Christianity was introduced by Mennonite and Roman Catholic missionaries in the north and Mennonites and the Society of Friends in the south. At the same time, both the Ghost Dance and Peyote religion spread to the Cheyenne, and the Sun Dance and other traditional ceremonies continued (Liberty 1965).

The Ghost Dance religion, in its Cheyenne version, prophesied that Christ was soon returning to earth to save American Indians from their hardships and to restore the continent to the way it was before Europeans came (Mooney 1896:37–40). A new, perfect earth, like a shell, would emerge in the west and cover up the old earth. All believers in the religion, as it was described by the Northern Paiute prophet Wovoka, would be able to jump up on the new earth and join Christ, his disciples, and all of their own ancestors on an earth reborn.

Both Northern and Southern Cheyennes visited Wovoka in Nevada beginning in 1889. After the massacre of Big Foot's band of Teton Sioux at Wounded Knee in 1890, a band that included several intermarried Cheyennes, the Ghost Dance was gradually abandoned by the Cheyenne, although aspects of its beliefs and rituals persisted in traditional ceremonies.

The Peyote religion appeared among the Southern Cheyenne in the early 1880s. When it was incorporated in 1918 as the Native American Church, two of the original incorporators were Southern Cheyennes.

A number of early Cheyenne Peyotists had been prisoners of war at Fort Marion, Florida, in the 1870s, including Roman Nose, William Cohoe, Little Chief, and Howling Wolf (vol. 17:210). Other early Cheyenne Peyotists had been students at the Carlisle Indian School in Pennsylvania, where knowledge of the English language, intertribal friendships, and exposure to Christian doctrine were important factors in their participation and leadership roles in the religion. Cheyenne Peyotists were important in the introduction of the religion to Taos Pueblo in New Mexico and to the Yuchi, Shawnee, and Creek in Oklahoma. The Northern Cheyenne were introduced to Peyotism in 1889–1890 by Southern Cheyennes through established patterns of visitation and ceremonial cooperation (Goggin 1938; La Barre 1990:114–115; Slotkin 1956:59; O.C. Stewart 1987:101–104).

Political Organization

The seasonal cycle profoundly affected Cheyenne social arrangements, which included, beyond the household and camp levels, chief-led residence bands, men's societies, and a council of chiefs. For most of the year, the tribe was split into 10 or more bands, each of which had a customary wintering place along a river. Each band (*manaho*, pl.) contained several hundred related persons divided into a number of extended family units (*véestOtse* 'camp'), each of which lived in from two to seven adjacent tepees.

Each band also had a usual camping place in the tribal circle, which represented a tepee with the door opening to the east. Positions changed occasionally because of historical and political circumstances. The bands were active social and economic units that frequently fused and split, and were often renamed when they did. The English names of the bands are not necessarily translations of the Cheyenne names, the analysis of which is often contested among Cheyennes and linguists (G.A. Dorsey 1905a:5, 12–13, 1905b:62–63; Grinnell 1923, 1:87–101; Hyde 1968:96ff, 197–200; Mooney 1907:402–411; J.H. Moore 1987:27–51, 205–250; see Synonymy).

• THE ARROW KEEPER   The Cheyenne polity is structured according to the instructions received by their culture hero, Sweet Medicine, and symbolized by the four Sacred Arrows he received at the sacred mountain (Bear Butte). Sweet Medicine abolished the old system of paramount chiefship and established new men's societies and a chiefs' society that were appropriate to their new situation. Uniting the bands, he defined as murder any killing of a Cheyenne by another Cheyenne, and decreed that the Sacred Arrows must be ritually renewed to atone for a killing. He made the chiefs responsible for the domestic well-being of the bands and gave responsibility for declaring war to the men's societies (G.A. Dorsey 1905a:15–16, 41–46; Grinnell 1923, 1:336–345, 2:345–381; J.H. Moore 1987:106–109).

While the Arrow Keeper has never had day-to-day political authority, he is free to step into any situation and resolve it. An oft-told story involves his instructions to the Bowstring Society in 1838 not to proceed with their plans to attack the Kiowa. The Bowstrings not only ignored his instructions, but they beat him with whips. As punishment, according to Cheyenne tradition, all 40 of the Bowstring society members were surrounded by Kiowa warriors and killed (Berthrong 1963:81–82).

• CHIEFS   The rules for election to chiefship were widely debated among Cheyennes. According to some tribal authorities, each of the 10 traditional bands was entitled to elect four tribal chiefs for 10-year terms. These, with four held over from the previous term, constituted the Council of 44, a governing body of peace chiefs kept distinct from the war chiefs, who were the leaders of the six men's societies.   *875*

An additional Sweet Medicine Chief, custodian of a sacred medicine root, also was a member of the council. Meetings of the council took place during the summer. At that time, decisions were made concerning tribal movements for hunting and warfare, the scheduling of ceremonies, and the settlement of disputes. Camp police drawn from the men's societies were appointed by the chiefs to enforce their decisions. Tribal chiefs were proven warriors, but none could retain military leadership after election to the council, whose primary function lay in assuring the integration and harmony of the entire tribe (Grinnell 1923, 1:336–358; Hoig 1980; Llewellyn and Hoebel 1941:67–98; Mooney 1907b:253; Petter 1913–1915:230–231; Stands in Timber and Liberty 1967:42–57).

• SOCIETIES   Six men's societies were important in Cheyenne politics. Most men joined one of these for life, usually that of their father. They were not secret, but open in conduct and membership. Divided for most of the year among the 10 bands, the societies functioned most actively during the summer when all members came together. They were lifelong fraternities that shared songs, dances, regalia, and comradeship. Several had honorary young women as associate members, "servants," or "princesses." The traditional men's societies are listed in table 1 (Grinnell 1915:383–397, 1923, 2:45–69; Llewellyn and Hoebel 1941; Hoebel 1954:142–170, 1960:33–36; Marquis 1931:56–69; Nagy 1994; K.D. Petersen 1964:146–169; Stands in Timber and Liberty 1967:100–103).

Women had their own associations, not necessarily based on kin relationships, and focused primarily upon successful completion of crafted articles for camp use and trade. Most important was the Quilling Society, although

other societies grew up around beadworking, making toys, and making lodge covers (Grinnell 1923, 1:156–169). These associations or guilds honored women for their production of these prized articles.

Culture in the Twentieth Century

Religion and Ceremony

All Cheyennes remained strongly bound together by aspects of traditional culture, especially religion. Two traditional ceremonies flourished during the late twentieth century: the Sacred Arrows, kept in Oklahoma; and the Sun Dance, which survived in both Oklahoma and Montana. In 1999 there were 18 Arrow Priests qualified to instruct the ceremonies, and nearly 30 Sun Dance priests. Also important to both Southern and Northern Cheyenne was the Native American Church.

Arrow ceremonies continued to involve both Southern and Northern participants, the Arrows themselves having been taken to Montana for that purpose in 1957 and 1974. The Arrow Keeper lived in Oklahoma, but the Northern Cheyenne deferred their summer ceremonies until after the Arrow Renewal ceremony in Oklahoma had been completed, out of respect for the Arrows and the Arrow Keeper.

Pilgrimages to Bear Butte were sometimes accompanied by the Sacred Arrows or Sacred Hat, and took place at least annually beginning in 1967. Although the Sacred Hat ceremony was lost, the relic itself was kept in Montana throughout the twentieth century, in a special tepee cared for by a priest of Sutaio descent. In 1998 the Sacred Hat was kept by Gilbert and Nancy WhiteDirt, in Muddy Creek (near Lame Deer), where it provided history, identity, and hope for the Northern Cheyenne people. The keeper followed a daily ritual of prayer and received all those who came to him for help or support. Rituals of protection and renewal were observed when the Sacred Hat was carried to the Sun Dance, as well.

The Sun Dance continued among the Cheyenne with remarkably little change, except for a few interludes of intense suppression in 1877–1880, 1890, 1904, and 1919–1926. Northern and Southern Cheyenne participated often in each other's ceremonies, sharing (with the Northern Arapahoe in Wyoming) a pool of ceremonial knowledge in several locations that helped the ceremony's survival (Liberty 1965; Ottoway 1970; P.J. Powell 1969). By the 1990s there were commonly two or more Sun Dances each summer both in Oklahoma and Montana.

In the late twentieth century at least four versions of the Sun Dance were maintained, each representing the practices of different priests, two in Montana and two in Oklahoma. In all cases, the cosmology of the Cheyennes was celebrated, and the spirits of the sun, moon, stars, cardinal directions, meteorological events, birds, plants, animals, stones, and earth were recognized and placed within a sacred hierarchy.

Table 1. Cheyenne Men's Societies, 19th century

English Name	Cheyenne Name
Dog Men	hotamétaneoˀo
Kit Foxes, or Flint Men	vóhkEséhetaneoˀo, mótsEsóenetaneoˀo
Elkhorn Scrapers, or Coyote Warriors	hémoˀoeoxeso, óˀOhoménotAxeoˀo
Bowstrings	hémaˀtanóohese
Crazy Dogs, Contrary Ones[a]	hotamémAsEhàòˀo, hohnókaoˀo
Red Shields, or Buffalo Bull Warriors	máˀhooheváse, hotóanótAxeoˀo
Wolf Warriors[b]	hoˀnéhenótAxeoˀo
War Dancers[c]	onéhanótAxeoˀo

SOURCES: Mooney 1907:412–414; Grinnell 1923, 2:48; Petter 1913–1915:779; Glenmore and Leman 1985:176. Transcriptions of Cheyenne names are those of Glenmore and Leman.

[a]A new organization among the Northern Cheyenne that corresponded to the Contrary Ones among the Southern Cheyenne (Petter 1913–1915:779). The Contrary Ones are not mentioned by either Mooney or Grinnell.

[b]A reformation of the former Bowstring society (Petter 1913–1915:778–779).

[c]An Omaha dance society that "started some 24 years ago and [is] made up of the younger men" (Petter 1913–1915:779).

Individual, private spiritual practice continued to include fasting in solitude on Bear Butte or elsewhere, an orientation in life defined by the Four Directions, and a general commitment to the value of prayer. The sweatlodge, once preparatory to other ceremonies, became a common, independent ritual after about 1980 (fig. 8). "Smudging" with incense and the leaving of prayer cloths also became common practices, in association with the emerging pantribalism.

Some Christian groups opposed the practice of traditional tribal ceremonies, but for the most part, the ceremonial complexes have coexisted comfortably with the several churches. This represented less a blending of traditions than a juxtaposition: an Anglican priest danced in the Northern Cheyenne Sun Dance; cedar and sage incensed the Roman Catholic Mass. Funerals openly exemplified the eclectic spirituality of the Cheyenne: they usually began in a mainstream church, followed the appropriate liturgy, but ended with the prayers and songs of traditional spiritual leaders (who may themselves have been members of the church). In fact, most tribal members participated in a variety of spiritual practices and processes, assuming that something could be gained from every one.

Powwows

Among the Cheyenne, powwows and giveaways have their roots in traditional customs of sharing and philanthropy. In modern times, a giveaway celebrates the achievements of a Cheyenne, such as retiring from military service, being elected chief, or graduating from high school or college. Guests were fed and received gifts from the family such as a blanket for a man and a shawl for a woman (J.H. Moore 1993).

Powwows constituted more elaborate celebrations extending into the night and including drum groups, singers, and traditional dancing. Among Northern Cheyennes, "tables" of gifts were distributed to guests at giveaways, each table representing a value equivalent to a horse. In the south, gifts, distributed individually, consisted of baskets of food, money, blankets, shawls, beadwork, dishes, furniture, and sometimes horses or elaborate hand-made dresses or jackets (K.M. Weist 1973).

The Northern Cheyenne

• LAND Natural resources on the reservation included coal, oil, and timber, as well as some of the best grazing land in the area. Tribal timber, mostly ponderosa pine, was selectively thinned by tribal and Bureau of Indian Affairs forestry departments since the 1960s. Approximately 2,000 acres of land were irrigated in 2000, with some 25,000 acres used for dry farming of hay, wheat, barley, and oats (Whitewolf 1991; Boggs 1984; G.R. Campbell 1987).

Most of the land within the reservation borders was communally owned tribal land. The tribal government was expressly forbidden to mortgage, sell, or cede any tribal land or to grant private ownership of tribal lands to individual tribal members. For the most part, individual homes and lands on the reservation were held by assignment or lease from the tribal government.

The Northern Cheyennes voted for allotment in 1926, which was carried out 1930–1932. The Northern Cheyenne viewed allotment as a way of securing the right of tribal members to remain in Montana (Rubie Sooktis, personal communication 1998). The Northern Cheyenne Allotment Act separated subsurface minerals from surface land ownership, granting communal ownership by the tribe of mineral rights while assigning individual allotments of surface land. A provision for allotment of mineral rights after a 50-year period was opposed by the tribe in litigation (*Northern Cheyenne Tribe* v. *Hollowbreast et al.* 1976; 425 U.S. 649–661).

In the 1990s only 2 percent of the reservation was owned by non-Indians, and the tribe purchased land outside the reservation. Acquisitions included three tracts of land at Bear Butte where they welcomed members of their own and other tribes who came to fast and pray.

Tribal headquarters, Bureau of Indian Affairs offices, and the Indian Health Service clinic were in Lame Deer, the largest town on the reservation; a tribal office building was constructed there in 1998. Other towns on the reservation were Ashland, which included Saint Labre, a Roman Catholic mission and school; Muddy Creek, where the Sacred Hat was kept; Busby, home to the tribal high school and the Chief Two Moons grave site; and Birney, the smallest and most isolated on the reservation.

• AUTHORITY The Northern Cheyenne Tribe operated under a constitution and by-laws adopted in 1935 and amended in 1960 and 1996 (Northern Cheyenne Tribe 1996).

The Council of 44 Chiefs continued in altered form with separate Chiefs Societies in the north and south. Chiefs and their families continued to occupy the highest status in Northern Cheyenne society: their traditional role was to serve and facilitate, not to direct and determine. The Kit Fox, Elk, Dog, and Bowstring societies continued among the Northern Cheyenne in 2000. Bowstring and Crazy Dog may have named the same society in the south and the north, respectively (Vernon Sooktis, personal communication 1998; P.J. Powell 1981, 1:90). The societies continued to have their own songs, stories, and traditions: they oversaw, advised, and sanctioned tribal cultural and ceremonial activities. A revitalization of men's societies occurred during the last quarter of the twentieth century, with changing roles for society members.

• EDUCATION The Indian Self-Determination and Education Assistance Act of 1975 (88 U.S. Stat. 2203) supported tribal control of education. Indian parent boards became involved in educational planning and curricula, and the cultural content of Northern Cheyenne education was given a considerable boost.

From Headstart through college, Northern Cheyenne students could receive a full education on the reservation. 877

Each community had an elementary school, and most children attended elementary school in their local community on the reservation. For high school, Northern Cheyenne youth either attended reservation schools or Colstrip high school, about 25 miles north of Lame Deer. Some Northern Cheyenne children attended Bureau boarding schools out of state.

Dull Knife Memorial College, a tribally controlled community college in Lame Deer, was chartered in 1975. The curriculum grew from a vocational training program to a broader postsecondary educational institution.

• LANGUAGE   In 1975 the majority of Northern Cheyennes were fluent in the Cheyenne language. While Cheyenne remained the language of ceremonies, even in the Native American Church, fluency in 2000 was about 40 percent.

• SOCIAL ORGANIZATION   The Northern Cheyenne lived on the reservation with other Indians and non-Indians. Southern Cheyennes living in Montana were considered members of the community but did not enjoy the full rights or responsibilities of Northern Cheyenne tribal members. The Sutaio people, once distinct, maintained a degree of differentiation from the other Cheyennes on the reservation, and some talked about seeking separate tribal recognition from the federal government.

Kinship remained the primary social organizer. The extended family, most often matrilocally extended, was the fundamental social unit; an individual's identity on the Northern Cheyenne reservation depended upon his or her relatives. Voluntary associations based on economic, intellectual, and social interests increased during the last decades of the twentieth century, but family and home were where people still spent most of their time and energy (see Sooktis 1980).

Social status was ascribed by kinship and acquired by action. Ceremonial and traditional leaders occupied the highest status, but both academic and technical expertise were recognized as well, especially when used in the service of the community. Age continued to determine social status: respectful behavior toward elders was clearly defined and violations were highly criticized.

The population center in Lame Deer became associated with the Omisis band, although the population included members of other bands, including the Sutaio. Lame Deer and the four other communities on the reservation became the new "bands" of the Northern Cheyennes. Names for these twentieth-century "bands" were Scabbies (the name of the original Oivimana band), associated with Birney; Rees with Muddy Creek; Black Lodges with Busby, and Shy with Ashland.

• ECONOMY   Native Action, an independent, community-action organization founded by tribal member Gail Small, provided the initiative behind many tribal development activities in the late twentieth century, including the building of the Lame Deer high school and the improvement of loan opportunities. Morningstar Enterprises, founded by tribal member Doreen Pond and Dr. Art McDonald of Dull Knife Memorial College, was a tribal construction company centered in Lame Deer that provided training and employment for tribal members. There were other tribally owned businesses on the reservation.

In 1999 the labor force was reported by the tribe as 1,218 with an unemployment rate of about 30 percent. Government and church programs (including the Ashland saw mill), schools, and local coal mining and electrical operations provided most long-term employment. Leasing rights to mine coal on reservation land in the 1960s and 1970s (Sooktis and Straus 1981; Ambler 1990:62–99) provided tribal income. With other energy-rich tribes, the Northern Cheyenne formed the Council of Energy Resource Tribes (CERT) in 1975. The Northern Cheyenne decided not to allow any development whatever of their coal resources, saving the coal for the benefit of future generations.

Southern Cheyenne

• LAND   Of the three and one-half million acres originally owned by the Southern Cheyenne and Arapaho in Oklahoma, all but one-half million acres were lost due to allotment in severalty in 1892. After that there was a steady attrition of the remaining land by various devices, legal and illegal, so that by the year 2000 only about 70,000 acres remained in trust under the private but nontaxable ownership of the descendants of the original allottees. In addition, the tribal government owned 10,405 acres of trust land in Oklahoma for administrative offices and tribal projects, for which they went to court and reaffirmed the legal "reservation" status of the property in 1980. In South Dakota, they shared with the Northern Cheyenne the ownership of land parcels at Bear Butte, which they used for religious purposes.

Land owned by individual Cheyennes produced income from grazing leases and mineral rights, especially oil and gas royalties. Annually, $1 million in "grass money" was distributed to about 7,000 Cheyenne and Arapaho landowners. "Oil money" was more widely distributed, because many people who did not own land retained mineral rights to land owned by their ancestors.

Heirship is a continual problem for Southern Cheyennes and Arapahos. Most trust land, and most mineral rights, are co-owned by 5 to 400 people. An individual might therefore receive small amounts of money for each of several tracts, payable at different times of the year. The federal government, in its trust role, apportioned all the payments received into tens of thousands of increments for distribution to heirs. Typically, an individual might receive 5–10 checks per year for heirship rights, a total of a few hundred dollars (Selden 1999).

• AUTHORITY   The tribal government of the Southern Cheyenne, formed jointly with the Southern Arapaho, was organized in 1937 as the "Cheyenne-Arapaho Tribes of Oklahoma" under the Oklahoma Indian Welfare Act. The area of the original reservation was divided into districts by

878

the 1937 constitution, with each district representing the location of a Cheyenne or Arapaho community, and each electing a representative to a Business Committee that was supposed to have the same number of Cheyenne and Arapaho members, originally eight and later 14 members. A new constitution was adopted in 1975.

The Business Committee oversaw an annual budget of several million dollars, mostly received for participation in different federal programs, mostly used for the benefit of children and elders. In addition to federal and state money, the Committee received income from its own enterprises, bingo halls at Concho, and Watonga. The combined tribes also received income from three smoke shops, where tobacco products were sold at bargain prices, since the tribes did not pay the same level of taxes to the state or federal governments as non-Indian establishments.

For the Southern Cheyennes, traditional authority derived from their Sacred Arrows through the agency of the Arrow Keeper, the priests, the men's societies, the chiefs' society, and participants in major ceremonies. In relations with the Business Committee, this authority was exercised through the Council of Chiefs, which was explicitly recognized in motions and by-laws enacted by the Business Committee over the years. The Cheyenne "traditional people" consisted of extended families who lived in the former reservation area.

The core traditionalists did not see the Arapaho as being so organized or traditional as themselves, and in fact the Arapaho ceremonies and sacred objects were kept on the Wind River Reservation in Wyoming, where Oklahoma Arapahos traveled to participate. Although Oklahoma Arapahos participated in Cheyenne ceremonies, this was done with the permission and under the guidance of Cheyenne traditionalists. Cheyenne traditional values were not set against Arapaho values, as was the situation on some other bitribal reservations, but against nontraditional or secular values. Especially this included drinking, inattention to one's family, and failure to participate in ceremonies, powwows and other social activities. In practice, it was difficult to enumerate and differentiate Cheyennes from Arapahos, since there has been so much intermarriage.

Southern Cheyenne traditionalists participated in Christian churches, especially the Mennonites. There was also a community of Roman Catholic nuns in Longdale.

• EDUCATION   Southern Cheyenne and Arapaho children attended regular public schools in their communities unless they had special needs, in which case they might attend a boarding school off the reservation, such as Riverside School in Anadarko (H. Mann 1997). In all the public schools, Indian children were in the minority. Headstart programs for Indian children were at Concho and Canton. High school graduates from Oklahoma often moved to the Northern Cheyenne reservation to attend Dull Knife Memorial College. Other Southern Cheyennes attended Southwestern Oklahoma State University in Weatherford, Canadian Valley Vo-Tech in El Reno, or Sayre Junior College in Sayre.

• LANGUAGE   Ability to speak Cheyenne was a large part of attaining high status among traditional people. The majority of people over 40 years of age spoke the language.

• SOCIAL ORGANIZATION   The most important activities for bringing communities together are the powwows, dinners, and dances held every weekend in community halls.

Crosscutting the Cheyenne communities are the traditional men's societies. Although nearly every community had at least some members of all the societies, the Dog Soldiers and Kit Foxes tended to live near Seiling and Canton, Oklahoma, while the Bowstrings and Elk Soldiers tended to live between Clinton and Watonga. Gourd Dance groups were ubiquitous. Some were strictly veterans' groups, while others were not.

• ECONOMY   Since the Southern Cheyennes lived in an area that was highly developed economically, they did not find it necessary to establish their own industries, except for a tribally owned cattle enterprise. Many Cheyennes worked at the tribal complex in Concho, or at the bingo halls and smoke shops. Manufacturing facilities in the area included a factory producing wallboard and other gypsum products in Watonga, a furniture manufacturing location in Clinton, and oil field facilities. Seasonal work in agriculture was also available. Many Cheyennes commuted to Oklahoma City or lived there during the week.

• SAND CREEK REPARATIONS   In 1953 three Southern Cheyenne leaders—Kish Hawkins, Sam Dicke, and Joe Antelope—organized the Sand Creek Descendants Association, Inc., and received a charter under Oklahoma law to pursue a claim for financial reparations for the Sand Creek Massacre of 1864. This had been promised in the 1865 Treaty of the Little Arkansas (Kappler 1904–1941, 2:890). By 1994 there were six different Sand Creek descendants' associations, each claiming to be the one and only legitimate representive for the thousands of people—Cheyennes, Arapahos, and other tribes—claiming descent from the people attacked at Sand Creek.

Population

From a total prereservation population of about 3,500, the Cheyenne declined to a nadir of about 2,500 in 1930, the total for both reservations (J.H. Moore 1996:145). This was largely the result of neglect, malnutrition, and poor housing (G.R. Campbell 1989, 1991; Nespor 1989). Infectious diseases such as cholera, tuberculosis, and influenza took the lives of many people.

In most respects, the Northern and Southern Cheyenne constituted two populations rather than one since about 1900. Northern Cheyenne tribal enrollment in 1996 was 6,692 (table 2); 4,254 tribal members lived on or near the reservation (Bureau of Indian Affairs 1996). In 2000 enrollment required one grandparent on the tribal roll. In 2000 in Oklahoma there were 11,800 combined Cheyennes and Arapahos, where the requirement was one-quarter blood. Approximately two-thirds of the combined Oklahoma tribes considered themselves Cheyenne.

Table 2. Population, 1780–2000

Year	S. Cheyenne	N. Cheyenne	Total	Sources
1780			3,500	Mooney 1928:12–13
1837			3,200	ARCIA 1837:594
1850			3,000	Schoolcraft 1851–1857, 3:630
1863	1,800	150 lodges	about 3,000	Mooney 1907:402; ARCIA 1863:129, 503
1875	2,055	1,727	3,782	Mooney 1907:402
1880	3,767	120, Pine Ridge Agency	3,887	ARCIA 1880:39, 242
1890	2,272	865	3,137	ARCIA 1890:454, 456
1900	2,037	1,379	3,416	ARCIA 1900:644, 648
1910	1,522	1,346	2,868	U.S. Bureau of the Census 1915:17
1920	1,858	1,412	3,270	ARCIA 1920:68–70
1939	2,911[a]	1,601 on reservation	3,600	Bureau of Indian Affairs 1939:9, 11
1950	3,102[a]	1,928 on reservation	4,000	U.S. Congress. House. Committee on Interior and Insular Affairs 1953:751–752
1960	3,500[a]	2,026	4,500	Bureau of Indian Affairs 1961:21, 27
1970	2,914	2,383	6,872[b]	Bureau of Indian Affairs 1972:12
1994	9,152[a]	5,621	11,500	Bureau of Indian Affairs 1994:2
2000	11,800[a]	7,980	15,500	Cheyenne-Arapaho Tribes; N. Cheyenne Tribe, communications to editors 2000

[a] Includes S. Arapahos.
[b] Includes 1,575 Cheyennes living elsewhere.

Synonymy†

The name Cheyenne has been used by Europeans and Americans to refer to the tribe since the late eighteenth century. It was borrowed through French from the Sioux designation, which is Santee-Sisseton, Yankton-Yanktonai, and Assiniboine *šahíyena* (S.R. Riggs 1890:440; J.P. Williamson 1902:31; Parks 1999d; Parks and DeMallie 1999), recorded also as Yanktonai and Assiniboine *šahíyana* (Curtis 1907–1930, 3:141), and Teton *šahíyela* (Buechel 1970:460). The stem of that name, *šahíya*, occurs in Assiniboine as the designation for 'Plains Cree' (Parks and DeMallie 1999) and is reported in Teton as the name for an unidentified western tribe, "but not the Cheyenne" (Buechel 1970:460), very likely the Plains Cree. It is a widespread ethnonym on the Northern Plains (see "Plains Cree" synonymy, this vol.) and was most likely borrowed into Sioux and Assiniboine, where the diminutive suffix *-la* or *-na* was added to form the designation for Cheyenne. The Sioux name is frequently folk-etymologized as 'red talkers' (*ša* 'red' + *iʔa* 'to talk' + *-na* or *-la* 'diminutive'), said to be a metaphor for 'speakers of an alien language' (S.R. Riggs 1890:440; J.P. Williamson 1902:244; Grinnell 1923, 1:2–3), but that explanation derives solely from close resemblance of forms. The Sioux form was borrowed as Omaha-Ponca *šahíeða* (Fletcher and La Flesche 1911:102; Dorsey 1890:652; J.H. Howard 1965:133; Parks 1988).

In other Siouan languages the name was borrowed as Osage *šaðáni* (Dorsey 1883, phonemicized) and Kansa

šayáni (Dorsey 1882; Rankin 1987:129), recorded also as Sháyenna (Gatschet 1878). In Algonquian languages the name occurs as Shawnee *ša·ye·ni* (C.F. Voegelin 1938–1940, 8:318) and Sáyen (pl. Sayenagi) (Gatschet 1879a), and as Fox *ša·ye·na* (Gatschet 1882–1889, phonemicized). It was borrowed as Wichita *se·yé·rih* (Parks 1988), spelled also as Sáyădĭ (Curtis 1907–1930, 19:224), and as Tonkawa Shéyen (Gatschet 1884c).

The name first appears on maps by Jean-Baptiste Louis Franquelin as the designation of a Sioux village: Chaiena, 1678–1679 (Winsor 1884–1889, 4:218; Delanglez 1941:139–140), Chaienaton, 1697 (M.M. Wedel 1974:166–167). Its earliest appearance in printed sources is as Schians and Schianese, identified as Sioux bands, 1766 (Carver 1781:80); however, Carver's original journals give Shyanawh as a Sioux band and Shyans as an independent tribe living west of the Omaha (J. Parker 1976:100, 137). (The identification as a Sioux band suggests that a portion of the Cheyenne lived with the Sioux in the seventeenth and eighteenth centuries.) Other spellings of the name include Chaquiennes and Chaguiennes, 1795–1796 (Truteau in Parks 1993); Chayennes and Chaguyennes, 1803–1804 (Tabeau 1939:68, 152); Chayon, Cheaun, Cheeons, 1804–1805 (before meeting the tribe, Lewis and Clark in Moulton 1983– , 2:195, 438); Chien, Chyenne, Shyenne, 1804 (after meeting the tribe, Lewis and Clark in Moulton 1983– , 3:133, 136,175); Chyenns, 1809 (Meriwether Lewis in D.D. Jackson 1962:461); Chienne, 1815 (Brackenridge in Thwaites 1904–1907, 6:119); Shiennes, 1819–1820 (E. James in Thwaites 1904–1907, 16:211); Shian (J.T. Irving 1835, 2:146); Shyennes and Cheyennes (Gallatin 1836:124); Sheyennes

†This synonymy was written by Douglas R. Parks.

(de Smet 1843:13); Shiann, 1851 (Ramsey 1872:46); Chaienne, Shiens, and Shienne, 1856 (T.S. Williamson 1872:299–300); and Scheyenne (Domenech 1860, 2:355). For other variant spellings, see Hodge (1907–1910, 1:256–257).

Clark spelled French *les Chayennes* as "la Chien," 1805 (Lewis and Clark 1832:715), and the name was often misinterpreted as derived from French *chien* 'dog'; hence references like Chien or Dog Indians, and Chyanne or Dog River, 1804–1805 (Lewis and Clark in Moulton 1983– , 3:136, 176, 417; Biddle in D.D. Jackson 1962:552); and Chien or Dog nation, 1807 (Gass in Moulton 1983– , 10:64).

The name Chaa, 1680 (La Salle in Margry 1876–1886, 2:54), which has been interpreted as a reference to the Cheyenne (Mooney 1907:361; Hodge 1907–1910, 1:251; Grinnell 1923, 1:3, 15), is the Illinois name for the Sioux.

The name was borrowed as Arikara *ša·hé*ʾ and South Band Pawnee *sahe*ʾ, Skiri Pawnee *sahi*ʾ (Parks 1999c, 1999a, 1999). The Arikara form occurs as Shár-há or Shar-ha, given as the "Indian name" of the tribe (Lewis and Clark in Moulton 1983– , 3:176, 420; 1810, Biddle in D.D. Jackson 1962:518); Shawhays (Brackenridge 1814:299; E. James in Thwaites 1904–1907, 16:211); Shaways (de Smet 1843:33); Sharas and Sharshas (Hayden 1862:274); and Showays (Domenech 1860, 2:60). According to Maximilian (1843, in Thwaites 1904–1907, 24:249), French traders called the Cheyenne Chats, apparently using the first syllable of Arikara *ša·hé*ʾ.

The Cheyenne self-designation is *tsétsEhéstAhese*, generally anglicized as Tsistsistas, following Grinnell (1923). Although no longer readily translatable, the name originally meant 'those who are from this (group)' (Ives Goddard, personal communication 2000; Glenmore and Leman 1985:201–202; Grinnell 1923, 1:3–4); it does not mean 'cut or gashed people' (Petter 1913–1915:2l8). Variant spellings of the name include Tse-tis-tas′ (ten Kate 1884:8), Sa-Sis-e-tas (W.P. Clark 1885:99), Dzĭtsi′stäs (Mooney 1896:1023), Dzi′tsistä′s (Mooney 1907:361), zezestas (Petter 1913–1915:582), and tsitsístas (Curtis 1907–1930, 6:158).

Among various Plains tribes a common designation for the Cheyenne is 'striped, spotted, painted, or multicolored feather or arrow'. Terms with this meaning are Crow *isa·u·špu·sé* 'striped (feathers at the) base of arrows' (G. Hubert Matthews, personal communication 1987; Randolph Graczyk, personal communication 1999), spelled also i-sōnsh′-pu-she (Hayden 1862:402); Hidatsa *ita·išupu·ši* (allegro *ita·šupu·ši*), cited also as i tá šu pu zi 'spotted arrow quills' (W. Matthews 1877:160); and Mandan *tawą́hu ruškápe* 'marks his arrow shaft' (Hollow 1970:267) or *tawą́·he óruškap(e)* [tamá·he óruškap] 'striped arrow' (Parks 1987; Mauricio Mixco, personal communication 2000), cited also as Tamáh-ónruschkahpe (Maximilian in Thwaites 1904–1907, 24:249), Tamahoⁿruckape (Will and Spinden 1906:210), and Tamáhidhushkŭp 'his arrow point adheres' (Curtis 1907–1930, 5:147).

The translation 'marked or striped arrow' occurs in Shoshone and Comanche *pakan napo·* (pl. *pakan napo·ni·*) (ten Kate l884:9, 1885:136; Demitri Shimkin and Wick Miller,

personal communications 1991), cited also as Pá ka na no (ten Kate 1884:9) and Pägănävo (Mooney 1896:1023), and for Shoshone as Pak′ an navo (Ballou 1880–1881), Pah kah nah-vo (Gebow 1868:9), and Pag-a now (G.W. Hill 1877). It appears as Paikanavos (Burton 1861:151), Pácarabó (Pimentel 1862–1865, 2:347), and Paikandoos (Blackmore 1869:307). In Ute the form was recorded as Pá-ka-na-wa (ten Kate 1884:8).

Another Comanche designation is *sianavo·* (pl.) 'painted or striped feather' (Casagrande 1954–1955 231; Demitri Shimkin, personal communication 1991; Alice Anderton, personal communication 1992), cited variously as Sianábone (Rejón in Pimentel 1862–1865, 2:347), Si′-a-na-vo and sianavo (ten Kate 1884:9, 1885:136), Shiä′navo (Mooney 1896:1023), and Siennavo, where noted as a borrowing (Curtis 1907–1930, 19:229). The Comanche form was borrowed as Caddo *siyánabu*ʾ (Chafe 1979).

The translation 'painted arrow' occurs in Nez Perce *cé·ptití·ṁeniṅ* (Aoki 1994:16; Curtis 1907–1930, 8:163). On the Southern Plains the same meaning occurs in loan translations as Caddo *ba*ʾ*hakú·sin* 'striped arrow' (Mooney 1896:1023, phonemicized), Wichita *niye·re·rikwa·ckannikih* 'the one whose arrows are striped' (Mooney 1896:1023; David S. Rood, personal communication 1999), and Kitsai ninoniks-skarĕñīki (Mooney 1896:1023).

In Crow and Hidatsa a closely related form meaning 'striped robe or blanket' was often confused with the preceding name and was also used as a designation for Cheyenne. It occurs as Crow *isa·špu·sé* (Randolph Graczyk, personal communication 1999), cited as Isashbushĕ̌ (Curtis 1907–1930, 4:180), and as Hidatsa *ita·šipo·ši* (Parks 1987; A. Wesley Jones, personal communication 1999), cited also as Elangé bugji wrach baga (*ita·šipo·ši ruxpa·ka*) 'spotted robes nation', 1805 (McKenzie in Wood and Thiessen 1985:249), a·was-she-tan-qua and it-anse-po-ǂje, 1823 (Say in Thwaites 1904–1907, 17:304), Itháh-ischipáhji (Maximilian in Thwaites 1904–1907, 24:274), and Iṭáshi-pushi (Curtis 1907–1930, 4:186).

In Blackfoot the name became *ki·xtsipimi·tapi·wa* 'spotted horse person' (Allan R. Taylor, personal communication 1987; Russell and Frantz 1989:132), also cited as Piegan and Blood kistsípimetapiwᵃ 'striped people' and Piegan kiḫtsípimitapi (Curtis 1907–1930, 6:155, 18:186). In Flathead it became Chîkîkaíyú 'spotted eyes' (Curtis 1907–1930, 7:165), apparently a truncated form of either *čq̇iq̇éyú*ʾ*s* 'spotted eyes; spotted faces' or *čq̇iq̇éyú*ʾ*se*ʾ*el* 'spotted arrow point' (Sarah G. Thomason, personal communications 1998, 2000). Six variant forms of the name were recorded, including WEtckaiu′, etckai′u′, Tskakai′u′, all interpreted as 'blue (or black) arrows (people)' (Teit 1930:302). None of those forms is any longer recognizable, and the translation is probably incorrect (Sarah G. Thomason, personal communication 2000).

The Arapaho and Gros Ventre names designate the Cheyenne as 'scarred people', said to be a reference to the Cheyenne custom of gashing themselves in religious ceremonies (Mooney 1896:1023), but more likely derived from a misinterpretation of the sign language designation for the

Cheyenne. The Arapaho form is *hítesí·noɂ* (sg. *hítesí·*) (Salzmann 1983:65; Ives Goddard, personal communication 1990), cited as It-us-shi'-na (Hayden 1862:326) and Hïtäsi'na (sg. Hi'täsi) (Mooney 1896:1023); the Gros Ventre form is *ítisí·noh* (sg. *ítisɂi*) (Allan R. Taylor, personal communication 1987), cited also as Itisĕn 'scars' (Curtis 1907–1930, 5:154).

Miscellaneous designations include Plains Cree *ka·-ne·hiyawe·sicik* 'people with a language like Cree' (Grinnell in Mooney 1896:1023; H. Christoph Wolfart, personal communication 1987) and Kiowa *tɔ́-sép* 'pierced ear' (La Barre 1935, phonemicized). Plains Apache *kʼatʼsàghí* (Bittle 1952–1953) has no known translation.

Bands

In the late eighteenth and early nineteenth centuries there were 10 or more Cheyenne bands, the names of which which were imperfectly remembered in the late nineteenth and early twentieth centuries (tables 3–4). In the late twentieth century several of those band names survived as designations for the Northern and Southern Cheyenne divisions and for reservation communities.

Jean-Baptiste Truteau, 1795–1796 (in Parks 1993), refers to three Cheyenne divisions, the Chaguiennes, the Ouisy or Wuisy, and the Chouta. The Ouisy (Omisis) are the We hee Shaw of Lewis and Clark (in Moulton 1983–, 3:136), and the Chouta are the Sutaio, whose name was borrowed as Mandan *šóta* 'Cheyenne', the name of a boys' society and a women's society ("Mandan," table 3, this vol.).

Geographical Divisions

The designation for the Northern Cheyenne was *notaméohmésEhese* (sg. *notaméohméseestse*) 'northern eat-

Table 3. Major Cheyenne Bands

	Mooney (1907b:254–255)[a]	Grinnell (1923, 1:93–96)[b]	G.A. Dorsey (1905a:62)
Hevisksnipahis	Hevïqs'-nï' 'pahïs 'closed aortas'	Ĭ vïsts' tsï nih''pah 'closed gullet or aorta'	Aorta
Moiseo	Móïséyu 'flint people'		Arrow-men
Wotapio	Wŭ'tapiu 'eaters'	Wū' tă piu 'eaters'	Eaters
Hevhaitaneo	Hévhaitä'nio 'hair men, fur men'	Hēv' ă tăn iu 'hair rope men'	
Oivimana	Oï'vimána 'scabby people'	Ŏ ïv' ĭ mă năh' 'scabby'	Hive
Hisiometaneo	Hisíometä'nio 'ridge men'	Ĭ ssïo mē' tăn iu 'hill or ridge people'	Ridge-men
Sutaio	Sūtáio	Sūh'tai	Sutayo
Oktogona	Oqtógŭnă 'bare shins' (?)	Ōhk tŏ ŭnna 'lower jaws protruding'	Prominent Jaws
Howowna	Hó'nowă 'poor people'	Hōf' nō wa 'poor people'	Poor People
Masikota	Măsï''kotă 'drawn up' (?)	Māh sïh' kŏ ta 'flexed legs'	
Omisis	O'mï'sïs 'eaters'	Ŏ mïs' sis 'eaters'	Eaters

NOTE: The order given follows one traditional arrangement in the camp circle, proceeding clockwise from the east; the location of the Sutaio was disputed (Mooney 1907b).

[a] Earlier lists appear in Mooney (1896:1025–1026, 1907:404–408).

[b] An earlier list appears in Grinnell (1905).

Abbreviations: (N) = Northern Cheyenne, (S) = Southern Cheyenne.

ers', sometimes shortened to *OhmésEhese* (sg. *Ohméseestse*) 'eaters' (Glenmore and Leman 1985:201), cited also as mi′sis (Hayden 1862:290), Hmĭ′sĭs (Mooney 1896:1026), and O′mĭ′sĭs, so-called because that band was the most numerous one in this division (Mooney 1907:377). Based on that name are the Teton Sioux designation for the Northern Cheyenne *tókč*ʰ*įka wóta* 'eats as he pleases' (Buechel 1970:496) and the Kiowa name *sá·-kɔ́t-tɔ̀* 'north biters' (Laurel Watkins, personal communication 1979). Historical citations include Upper Cheyennes (G.A. Custer 1874:88).

The designation for the Southern Cheyenne was the division name *heévAhetaneoʔo* 'roped people', the band most numerous among them (Glenmore and Leman 1985:201). Based on that name is the Teton Sioux designation *t*ʰ*ahį wič*ʰ*áša* 'buffalo hair people' (Buechel 1970:474). The Northern Cheyenne also designated them Sówoníă 'southerners' (Mooney 1907b:257), spelled also So′wănĭ̆ă

(Mooney 1896:1025) and Po-no-í-ta-ní-o, apparently a misprint for Sowonítanío 'southern men' (Hayden 1862:290; Mooney 1907b:257).

Sign Language

The sign for Cheyenne is made by extending the left forefinger horizontally to the right and front of the body, and then drawing the outer side of the little finger of the right hand across the extended forefinger from left to right three or four times. A frequent variant sign is made by drawing the right index finger across the extended left hand, sometimes as high as the forearm. These variant signs represent the characteristic Cheyenne 'striped feather', sometimes said to be a turkey feather, the left forefinger or lower arm signifying the feather and the motions of the right hand its stripes (W.P. Clark 1885:98; H.L. Scott 1912–1934)

Petter (1913–1915:777)	Curtis (1907–1930, 6:108–109, 19:225)	Hoebel (1960:37–38)	Glenmore and Leman (1985:45, 201); Wayne Leman (communication to editors, 2000)
Hevešksenxpâess, Burned Gullets	(N) Hevĭsts-uni′pahis, shriveled buffalo aorta; (S) Hĭvíĭ̆hnĭ̆ĭ̆pôĭ̆ĭ̆	heviqsnipahis, Burnt Aorta	
Môseo			
Votapeo, Eaters [from the Sioux]	(S) Wótapi, Eating band	wutapiu, Sioux-Eaters	
Hēvataneo, Rope Men, Furmen	(N) Hévhaitaneo, Hair Men; (S) Hefatáⁿyŭ, Hairy band	hevatanui, Hair Rope Men	heévAhetaneoʔo, Southern Cheyenne, lit. 'roped people'
ōevemanha, Scabby	(S) Óvimana	oivimana, Scabby	oévemana, Birney person, 'scabby person'
Heseometaneo 'Ridge Men, Men of the Divide'	(S) Ísiométaⁿyĕ, Ridge Hill band	isiometannui, 'Ridge Men'	heséʔomeétaneoʔo 'ridge person'
Sotaeo	(N) Sótaia	Sutai	sóʔtaeoʔo (sg. sóʔtaaʔe)
Oxtokoona, JawBoned	(S) Óhtoonyŭ	oktouna, Prognathous Jaws	
Hovnova, Penurious		haunowa, Poor People	
Masèkotao, Reclining Ones, or Hotamhetaneo, Dog Men	(N) Masí′kota from Hótamitáneo, Dog Men; (S) Masískuta or Hotámítaⁿyĕ, Dog band	masikota, Gray Hair	
OxmesessO, Eaters	(N) Ohmísis, (S) Omishish, Eaters	omisis, Eaters	OhmésEhese, Northern Cheyenne, lit. 'eaters' (sg. Ohméseestse); also notaméohmésEhese 'northern eaters' (sg. notaméohméseestse)

883

Table 4. Minor or Doubtful Cheyenne Bands

	Mooney 1907b:255; Hoebel 1960:38	G.A. Dorsey 1905a:62	Petter 1913–1915:777	Glenmore and Leman 1985:144
Moktavhitaneo	Moqtávhaitä′niu, 'black men; Utes'	Ute	Moxtavahetaneo, Black Men, Utes	
Woopotsit	Wóopotsi′t, 'white wolf' (?)	Young-White-Wolf		
Nakoemana	Ná'kuimana, 'bear people'		Nàkoemanha, Bear band	
Totoimana	Totoimana, 'backward, shy'		Totoemanha, Bashful band	*totoemana*, Ashland person
Anskowinis	Anskówinĭs, 'narrow nose-bridge'		Anskovenes, Narrow Nosed	
Pinatka	Pi′nûtgû′, Penatika (Comanche)		Penet'ka	
Maoom	Máhoyum, 'red tepee'		Maôom, Red Lodge	
Black Lodges	Black Lodges			
Cheyenne Sioux		Cheyenne Sioux		
Grasshoppers		Grasshoppers		
Outlaw		Outlaw		

A more common, but apparently mistaken, interpretation of the sign is that it represents cutting the fingers or gashing the arms, a supposed reference to Cheyenne self-mutilation (Mallery 1881:464–465; W.P. Clark 1885:98; Hadley 1893:36; Petter 1913–1915:228). The Cheyenne, however, did not practice self-mutilation to any greater extent than other Plains tribes, and the sign for them does not comprise the sign for 'to cut', which is made with the side of the little finger moving back and forth with a sawing motion and not, as in the Cheyenne sign, with the finger drawn across the left finger or hand from left to right using a motion that represents striping with paint (H.L. Scott 1912–1934). The reinterpretation of the sign as a reference to self-mutilation is reflected in several historical references: Cut or burned arms, 1819 (E. James in Thwaites 1904–1907, 15:338); Cut wrists (Burton 1861:151); and Scarred Arms (Sage 1846:92).

The sign for 'dog eater', the standard sign for the Arapaho, was sometimes used for the Cheyenne as well (Mallery 1881:465). That leveling of the distinction between Cheyenne and Arapaho is also represented by contemporary Ute *sarí-tṵká-ci* 'dog eater', which designates the Cheyenne specifically and Plains Indians generally (Givon 1979:174).

Sources

P.J. Powell (1980) presents an annotated bibliography of more than 200 works on Cheyenne history and culture. Hoebel (1960) and J.H. Moore (1996) are historical and ethnographic summaries.

The fundamental ethnographic sources are the works of Grinnell (1910, 1920, 1923, 1926); Petter (1913–1915), an English-Cheyenne dictionary, that provides much ethnographic detail; Mooney (1907) as well as a summary article in Hodge (1907–1910, 1:250–257); and G.A. Dorsey (1905a, 1905b), which includes a photographic record of the 1903 Southern Cheyenne Sun Dance. Curtis (1907–1930, 6:86–135, 155–158, 167–193, 19:105–148, 224–226, 230–270) provides ethnographic and linguistic data and photographs. Mooney's (1896) study of the Ghost Dance includes important material on the Cheyenne.

Collections of Cheyenne traditions and oral literature include Kroeber (1900), G.A. Dorsey (1905a), and Grinnell (1926).

Documentary and archival materials include the letters of George Bent (Coe Collection, Yale University Library), many of which were used by Grinnell in his various publications, and some of which were transformed into a narrative by Hyde (1968). Annual Reports of the Commissioner of Indian Affairs to the Secretary of the Interior (ARCIA), especially 1851–1906, contain essential data on Cheyenne history. Census rolls and agency records and correspondence, many on microfilm, are preserved at the U.S. National Archives and Records Administration, Washington, D.C. (NARA 1998).

The U.S. military view of Cheyenne history exists in firsthand accounts (G.A. Custer 1874; Finerty 1890; Bourke 1891; N.A. Miles 1897). The 1876 Battle of the Little Bighorn is analyzed in many works (Graham 1953; E.I. Stewart 1955; R.G. Jackson 1987; Hardorff 1998). A Cheyenne woman's eyewitness narrative of the battle is Marquis (1933). Other battles are described, including the 1857 Battle of Solomon Fork (Chalfant 1989), the 1864 Sand Creek Massacre (Hoig 1961; Harnish 1980; Svaldi 1989; Cutler 1995), the 1866

Fetterman Fight (D. Brown 1962; R. Tallbull 1988), the 1868 Battle of the Washita (Hoig 1976), and the 1876 Battle of the Rosebud (Vaughn 1956; Mangum 1987).

Histories of the Cheyenne are presented by Grinnell (1915), Berthrong (1963, 1976), P.J. Powell (1969, 1, 1981), T. Weist (1977), and Hoig (1980). Seger (1934) is an early account of Southern Cheyenne reservation life. M.H. Brown and W.R. Felton (1955, 1966) and D. Brown (1962) give accounts of the early Northern Cheyenne reservation, the first two with photographs by L.A. Huffman. Stands In Timber dictated a tribal history (Stands in Timber and Liberty 1967). H. Mann (1997) is a history of education. Svingen (1993) is an administrative history of Northern Cheyenne Reservation.

Cheyenne ethnohistory and prehistory are summarized by W.R. Wood (1971a); see also Gussow, Hafen, and Ekirch (1974) for the Cheyenne-Arapaho reports to the Indian Claims Commission. Trade relations, 1795–1840, are discussed by Jablow (1951). Child rearing is described by Hilger (1946). Cheyenne law is analyzed by Llewellyn and Hoebel (1941). The Cheyenne-Arapaho kinship system is discussed by Eggan (1955a, 1966a), J.H. Moore (1988, 1991, 1991a), and Straus (1994). K.D. Petersen (1964) summarizes knowledge concerning the military societies. Straus (1976, 1977, 1978) presents ethnography of the contemporary Northern Cheyenne from an ethnopsychological perspective.

Modern ceremonies are reported by R.T. Anderson (1956), Liberty (1965, 1967, 1968), Ottoway (1970), and P.J. Powell (1969). Materials on the reservation period include works by Dusenberry (1955), Pringle (1958), Liberty (1965), K.M. Weist (1970), and Marquis (1978). K.M. Weist (1973) and J.H. Moore (1993) describe Cheyenne giveaway patterns. Modern data are found for the Northern Cheyenne in

J.W. Bailey (1974) and for the Southern Cheyenne in Schlesier (1974) and J.H. Moore (1996).

Cheyenne autobiographies have been published, including those of Wooden Leg (Marquis 1931), a woman (Michelson 1932), Rubie Sooktis (1976), Wesley Whiteman (Schwartz 1989), Belle Highwalking (Highwalking and K.M. Weist 1991), Red Hat (Schukies 1993), and Bertha Little Coyote (Little Coyote and Giglio 1997).

There is a large literature on Cheyenne ledger art. Hoebel and Petersen (1964) report on the work of William Cohoe, a Southern Cheyenne artist. A Cheyenne Dog Soldier ledger is published in Afton, Halaas, and Masich (1997). Other publications include K.D. Petersen (1968, 1971), D. Dunn (1969), Supree and Ross (1971), Szabo (1994), C.S. Greene (1998), P.J. Powell (1976, 1981).

Cheyenne music was studied by Densmore (1936). Several collections of Cheyenne powwow songs have been recorded and sold commerically, as well as a book on Cheyenne women's songs (Giglio 1994).

Dictionaries of the Cheyenne language are Petter (1913–1915) and Glenmore and Leman (1985). Grammars are Petter (1907, 1952) and Leman (1980). Leman (1987) presents a collection of native-language texts.

Museum collections of Cheyenne material are plentiful. Major religious relics remain in the tribe. Other collections are at the Smithsonian Institution's National Museum of Natural History (see a summary in Smythe and Helweg 1996b) and the National Museum of the American Indian, Washington; the Field Museum of Natural History, Chicago; and the American Museum of Natural History, New York. The repatriation of Cheyenne human remains from the National Museum of Natural History is covered by Killion, Brown, and Speaker (1992).

Comanche

THOMAS W. KAVANAGH

Language and Territory

The Comanche (kə'mănchē) speak a Central Numic language moderately differentiated from Eastern (Wind River) Shoshone* (vol. 10:114, 118–119, 11:99).

Shoshonean-speaking peoples, including the ancestors of the Comanche, have lived on the Northern Plains since the 1500s; they were among the first Plains peoples to obtain horses and adopt a mounted lifeway (Shimkin 1941; Hultkrantz 1968; G.A. Wright 1978). In the eighteenth century, the Comanche dominated the Southern Plains, holding the foothills of the Rockies, from Eastern Shoshone territory in the Wind River area of Wyoming, southward to the Staked Plains of Texas and New Mexico (fig. 1).

By the 1820s, due to pressure from northern enemies and the influx of Euro-Americans on the Santa Fe Trail, the Arkansas River became the effective northern boundary of Comanche territory. The Pecos River and the eastern foothills of the Sangre de Cristo Mountains of New Mexico formed a western border, although contested by the Jicarilla and Mescalero Apache. On the east, Comanche territory overlapped the village tribes of the Arkansas and Red rivers. In the 1830s, the expansion of the Osage, combined with the presence of Indian groups removed from the Southeast, defined the Cross Timbers as the effective eastern border. With the establishment of the Republic of Texas in 1836, settlement began to expand northward. The Comanche made considerable efforts to control this encroachment, and the creation of a line separating them from the Texans was a

*The phonemes of Comanche are: (voiceless unaspirated stops and affricate) p, t, c, k, k^w, ʔ; (voiceless spirants) s, h; (voiced spirant) β; (voiced alveolar flap) r; (nasals) m, n; (semivowels) w, y; (short oral vowels) i, e, a, o, u, ɨ; (long oral vowels) i·, e·, a·, o·, u·, ɨ·; (short voiceless vowels) I, E, A, O, U, ɨ; (stress) v̆ (not marked if on the initial syllable). Before a voiceless vowel or after h, β and r are voiceless ([φ] and [r̥]).

The transcription of Comanche used indicates surface-phonemic contrasts following the analysis of Canonge (1958:xiii) and John E. McLaughlin (communications to editors 1999). Canonge (1958) writes these phonemes: p, t, ts, k, kw, ʔ; s, h; v; r; m, n; w, y; i, e, a, o, u, ʌ; ii, ee, aa, oo, uu, ʌʌ; i̠, e̠, a̠, o̠, u̠, ʌ̠. This differs from the abstract transcription of Charney (1993), who writes β as p, non-initial p as ᵖp, r as t, and non-initial t as ᵗt. Comanche words in italics were phonemicized by John E. McLaughlin (communication to editors 1999) and Jean Ormsbee Charney (communication to editors 1999). The editors are responsible for selecting between the differing transcriptions of some words.

subject of continuing diplomatic discussions in the 1830s and 1840s (Kavanagh 1996:253).

In 1865 the Treaty of the Little Arkansas reserved the Texas Panhandle for the Comanche and Kiowa. Two years later, the Treaty of Medicine Lodge reduced this area by over 94 percent. In 1901, the reservation was allotted to individual tribal members, and "surplus" lands were opened to White settlement. By 1979 the Comanche Tribe of Oklahoma held only 189 acres (Comanche Tribe. Business Committee 1979:2), and jointly with the Kiowa and Plains Apache, another 5,648 acres (Karen Edmonds, personal communication 1989). The Comanche continued to be centered in southwestern Oklahoma, although tribal members lived in most major population areas throughout the United States. Comanche tribal headquarters were in Lawton, Oklahoma.

History Until 1875

The earliest European mentions of the Comanche date from 1706 (A.B. Thomas 1935:61; C.W. Hackett 1923–1937, 3:382). Contacts with the Spaniards of New Mexico increased during the first two decades of the eighteenth century alternating between peace and hostility. By the 1730s, the Comanche had displaced the Plains Apacheans and gained control of the trade between New Mexico and the Plains. Although mutually beneficial, the trade generated frictions and often led to violence.

Meanwhile, other Comanches had established relations with French traders from Illinois and Louisiana (A.B. Thomas 1935:257, 1940:15; John 1975:316). By the late 1740s, wary of French intentions, the Spaniards decided to utilize the Comanche as a buffer against other Europeans, and they reopened contacts and trade (A.B. Thomas 1940:111). Good relations lasted until the late 1760s, when they again collapsed into hostility.

In the mid-1780s, a peace was established through treaties in San Antonio in 1785 (Faulk 1964:64) and Santa Fe in 1786 (A.B. Thomas 1932:305). In New Mexico, the formal Peace of 1786 was renewed in 1826 (B. Baca 1826), in 1828 (Arocha, Ruíz, and Cavallero 1828), and again in 1829 (Chaves, Arocha, and Ruíz 1829). Comanche-Spanish relations in Texas were less stable. In 1802, New Mexico Comanche leaders lectured their Texas kinsmen, saying that renewed war would result in the loss of benefits to all (Elguezabal 1802). With the establishment of Mexican independence, relations appeared to improve; in 1822, a delegation of

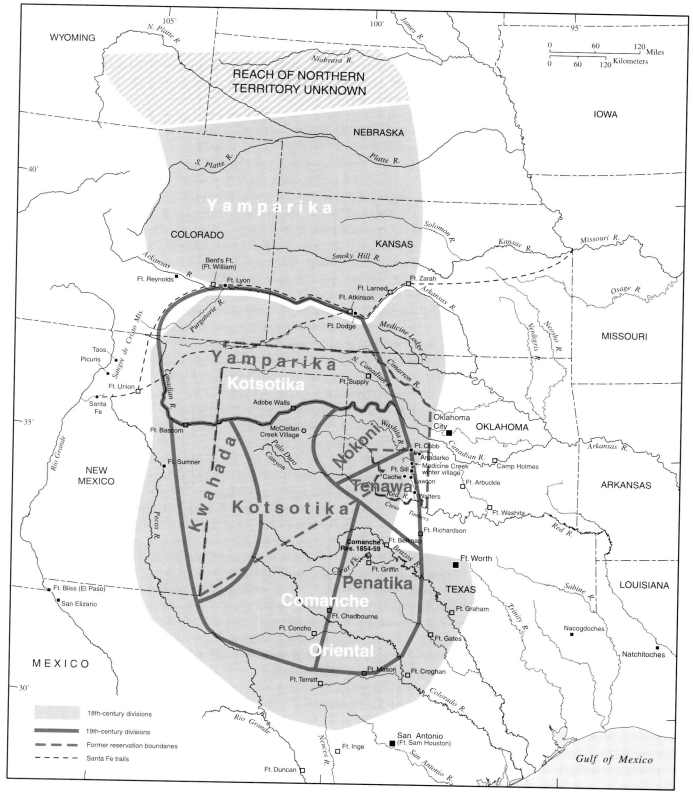

Fig. 1. Comancheria in the late 1700s and mid-1800s, with historical forts and reservations. The Comanche and Kiowa Reservation in the Texas panhandle and western Indian Territory was created in 1865 and reduced in 1867. A small reservation was on the Clear Fork of the Brazos, 1854–1859.

Texas Comanches visited Mexico City, where they signed a treaty (Mexico 1878). Peaceful conditions did not last. One

cause for the unrest was the continued presence of Anglo-American horse traders. As early as 1791, Anglo-Americans were in Texas, trading for Comanche horses (Loomis and Nasatir 1967:205). The demand for horses far outstripped the Comanche abilities to breed or capture them, and they turned to the Spanish ranches in Texas and the provinces farther south for their supply. At the same time, American diplomatic contacts were aimed at persuading the Comanche to terminate their Spanish alliances. In 1807 and 1817, Comanche leaders visited Natchitoches, Lousiana, where they were given prestige gifts of clothing, guns, and American flags (J. Sibley 1922; C.E. Carter 1934–1962, 20:352–353; Jamison 1817).

After the opening of the Santa Fe Trail in 1821, American policy became an effort to keep them away from the new route. In 1835, a group of Tenawa Comanche leaders met United States treaty commissioners at Camp Holmes on the South Canadian River and signed a treaty guaranteeing the right of United States citizens to pass through their territory to trade with the provinces of the Republic of Mexico (Kappler 1904–1941, 2:435).

There was a second covert purpose for the Treaty of Camp Holmes although it was not explicit. The Indian removal policy had assigned the area of the Wichita Mountains and Washita River, longstanding Comanche campgrounds, to the Chickasaw, and the treaty was intended to validate the rights of the migrant Indians to this area. The Comanches reportedly burned their copy of the document when they learned that it permitted the eastern Indians the right to hunt in their country (Foreman 1926:226).

Relations with Other Tribes, 1800–1850s

In the late eighteenth and early nineteenth centuries, Kiowa, Cheyenne, Pawnee, and other unidentified Plains groups (e.g., Orejones, Cuampes) attempted to gain access to Spanish goods on terms similar to those given to the Comanche (Chacón 1802). The Comanches vigorously resisted these efforts; several major battles with these "Nations of the North," particularly the Kiowa, were reported between 1801 and 1806 (Chacón 1801; John 1985). Peace with the Kiowa was arranged in 1806. The Kiowa chief El Ronco married the daughter of the Yamparika Principal Chief Somiquaso and went to live with his wife's people (Alencaster 1806; Loomis and Nasatir 1967:450; John 1985).

By the late 1820s, the Cheyenne and Arapaho had forced the Comanche from the upper Arkansas River region and were aggressively moving south, attracted to Charles Bent's trading post on the Arkansas River (G. Bent 1968). The Comanche and Kiowa, supported by guns from the Chouteau family of traders of eastern Oklahoma (Foreman 1926:238), resisted their advance in a series of battles on the Canadian River. At the Cheyennes' request, in 1840, a lasting peace was arranged. Subsequently, Bent established a post on the Canadian River near modern Amarillo for the Comanche and Kiowa trade (Grinnell 1915:60, 1923).

Relations with the Republic of Texas and Mexico

During the Texas Revolution of 1835, both Comanches and Texans attempted to establish peaceful relations (Kavanagh 1996:249–264). However, Texas refused to recognize aboriginal Indian rights. A truce with the Comanche bands closest to the settlements was arranged in 1838, and some trade took place (Winfrey and Day 1959–1966, 1:52).

Raiding by other groups of Comanche continued, and the Texas authorities blamed all Comanches. On March 19, 1840, 66 Hois Comanche men, women, and children entered the San Antonio courthouse for what they thought were to be peace talks and trade. The Texans, however, intending to take the Comanches hostage to exchange for White captives held by other Comanche bands, marched in a squad of soldiers. In the ensuing melee, 35 Comanches were killed and 27 captured (R.N. Richardson 1933:111). In summer 1843 an armistice was arranged (Winfrey and Day 1959–1966, 1:228), and in autumn 1844 a treaty was concluded (Winfrey and Day 1959–1966, 2:114). Relative peace existed between Comanches and Texans for the next decade.

Although some Comanches had been south of the Rio Grande before 1800, it was not until the late 1820s that Comanches began to cross into Mexico in large numbers (Arce 1826). Raiding increased through the 1840s and into the 1850s, peaking in 1852, when no month passed without some report of conflicts (R.A. Smith 1970:62). These raids coincided with the height of the California gold rush, which created increased demand for horses (Foreman 1939:163).

Relations with the United States

In 1846, even before the annexation of Texas, commissioners met with Penatika Comanche chiefs and concluded a treaty acknowledging the authority of the United States over Texas (Kappler 1904–1941, 2:554). In 1853, at Fort Atkinson on the Santa Fe Trail, Yamparika Comanches acknowledged a right of way along the Arkansas River and agreed to the establishment of military posts (Kappler 1904–1941, 2:600). They were to receive in return an annuity of $18,000. Although there were some incidents, Comanches generally permitted travelers on the Santa Fe Trail to pass through their country.

In 1854, the Texas state legislature established a reservation for the Penatika Comanches on the Clear Fork of the Brazos in modern Throckmorton County (R.N. Richardson 1929). However, this failed to stop northern Comanche raids into Texas. Furthermore, speculators were agitating for the opening of these lands to settlement. In August 1859 the federal government moved some 1,500 Texas Indians, including 384 Penatika Comanches, north to the newly established Wichita Agency in the Washita valley at Fort Cobb, Indian Territory.

At the onset of the Civil War, the Confederate government moved to formalize relations with the tribes of Indian Territory. After making treaties with the eastern tribes,

Confederate Commissioner Albert Pike concluded treaties with the Penatika and with the Yamparika, Nokoni and "other Comanche bands" at Fort Cobb (J. Davis 1861; A. Pike 1861, 1861a, 1861b).

In 1861 when the Yamparika brought their copy of the Confederate treaty to the Upper Arkansas Agency, Indian agent Albert G. Boone reported them to be "much astonished" to find they had made a treaty with the "enemies of our government." Boone made a temporary agreement with the Yamparika (Boone in ARCIA 1861:104–106), and in 1863, several Comanche, Kiowa, Plains Apache, Cheyenne, and Arapaho leaders went to Washington, where they reaffirmed their treaties and agreed to accept annuities of $25,000 to stay away from the Santa Fe Trail (R.N. Richardson 1933:280).

During the Civil War, the Kwahada Comanches developed a lucrative trade with New Mexico ranchers in cattle stolen in Confederate Texas. Many New Mexicans, including army officers and sutlers at Forts Bascom and Union used Comanche cattle to supply their own businesses (McCusker 1866; Kenner 1969:155; Haley 1935; Kavanagh 1996:404–405, 468–469).

In 1864, the U.S. Army, blaming the Comanche for attacks on the Santa Fe Trail, declared both the Comanche and Kiowa to be "hostile" (Kavanagh 1996:399). On November 10, 1864, Kiowa and Comanche villages near Bent's abandoned post on the Canadian River, known as Adobe Walls, were attacked by forces under Col. Christopher (Kit) Carson (Pettis 1908).

In October 1865 a presidentially appointed peace commission assembled the chiefs for a council on the Little Arkansas River, where a group of Comanches, mostly Yamparika, and Kiowa chiefs signed a treaty establishing a reservation encompassing much of the Texas Panhandle (Kappler 1904–1941, 2:894). In October 1867 another commission met with the Southern Plains tribes on Medicine Lodge Creek in southern Kansas and proposed a revision to the Treaty of the Little Arkansas. The Comanche delegation, again mostly Yamparika, agreed to a smaller reservation, schools, houses, instruction in farming, and annuities for 25 years. In a second treaty, the Plains Apache confederated with the Comanche and Kiowa (Kappler 1904–1941, 2:982).

While some Comanches moved to the reservation, others did not. The Kwahada continued their trade in Texas cattle; in a campaign designed to end this commerce, on September 29, 1872, Col. Ranald Mackenzie attacked a Kwahada village on McClellan Creek in the Texas Panhandle. Although most of the men escaped, 124 women and children were captured and taken to Fort Concho, Texas. Thereafter, many Comanches moved to the vicinity of Fort Sill, where they exchanged White captives for their relatives held at Fort Concho (Tatum 1872).

Other Comanches, particularly the Yamparika, were still involved in the robe trade along the Arkansas. The local buffalo herds were plentiful and the robes brought high prices from traders. But although both the Little Arkansas and Medicine Lodge treaties guaranteed hunting rights in these lands and excluded Whites, potential profits lured White hunters to the herds below the Arkansas.

In spring 1874 a group of hunters established a base at the old Bent post on the Canadian River. To meet this threat to their economy, the Yamparika, Kwahada, and other Comanches convened on Elk Creek in western Oklahoma. While there, a Kwahada shaman announced that he had received supernatural power that made him bulletproof and could provide unlimited supplies of ammunition. On June 27, 1874, several hundred Comanche, Cheyenne, and Kiowa attacked the hunters, but after the loss of several, the attack was called off, and the Indian forces scattered.

By summer 1875, those Comanches found life off the reservation precarious at best. Although there were still buffalo to be found, the herds were diminishing. Furthermore, U.S. Army patrols and scouts were pursuing them. In June, 400 Kwahadas surrendered at Fort Sill (Sturm 1875).

Culture in the Mid-Nineteenth Century

Subsistence

The buffalo was the foundation of Comanche domestic economy; but as the Comanche moved south they encountered a gradient of decreasing abundance of buffalo from the northern to the southern parts of their territory, influenced by both annual migration and by long-term climatic variation (Turpin 1987). While buffalo were still numerous in the northern areas as late as 1875 (Sturm 1875), by the 1850s, they were already scarce in the southern areas (J.A. Allen 1877).

Comanches used both individual stalking and group hunting methods. Group hunts usually occurred in late summer and fall when the animals were fat, robes good, and there were few flies (W.R. Wedel 1933). Group hunts began with scouts locating a herd. After reporting its location to the chiefs, the hunters were admonished to stay together (Lowie 1912a). The actual hunt was under the direction of the chief or a noted warrior (E. Wallace and E.A. Hoebel 1952:57). However, once the chase began, each hunter acted separately; hunters identified their kills by arrow marks (E. Wallace and E.A. Hoebel 1952:59). Other men could claim a portion of the meat by counting coup on it, while the hide remained the property of the killer (W.R. Wedel 1933). In addition, a variety of plant foods were utilized by the Comanche (G.G. Carlson and V.H. Jones 1940).

Trade

There were different trade contexts: trade fairs and bartering in European settlements, trading posts in Indian county and itinerant traders such as *viageros* 'travelers', later called Comancheros (M. Baca 1813; F. Levine and M. Freeman 1982:207; F. Levine 1991). In the early eighteenth century, *889*

Fig. 2. Rawhide containers painted in red, blue or green, and black. top, Flat case with fringe of tanned hide; collected in southern Tex. by Jean Louis Berlandier, 1828–1851; height 29 cm. bottom, Cylindrical case. Collected by Edward Palmer on the Kiowa and Comanche Res. in 1868 (McVaugh 1956:35–37); length 43 cm.

annual trade fairs, called *rescate* 'ransoming' by the Spaniards, were held at Taos and Picuris Pueblos, later in the Pecos valley (fig. 3). To maintain order the New Mexico colonial administration periodically published regulations governing their operations (F. Dominguez 1956:52; Gálvez 1951:51; A.B. Thomas 1932:306; Worcester 1949:246). Trade undoubtedly also occurred during visits to the settlements by Comanches, although such incidents were rarely recorded (Cháves 1831).

There is no record of permanent Spanish or French trading posts in Comanche territory (vol. 4:354, 366; F. Levine and J. Winter 1987). The earliest American trading post was Thomas James's 1823 "fort" on the North Canadian (T. James 1984:127).

The primary mode of Comanche trade was through Comancheros and other itinerant traders, both Indian and White. While some traders relied on chance meetings with Comanches, others went to specific rendezvous. There were several recognized trading sites: Basque Redondo on

Fig. 3. Deerskin robe painted white, red, and black. The border-and-hourglass design is the predominant motif on Comanche robes (Ewers 1939:15, 59–60). Collected from Pueblo Indians near Santa Fe by W.F.M. Arny, 1862–1872; length 2.11 m.

the Pecos River, Cañon del Rescate near Lubbock, Texas, and the Palo Duro Canyon on the Prairie Dog Town Fork of the Red River.

Comanches traded the products of the Plains with neighboring peoples for agricultural and European manufactured products. At a trade fair with Spaniards and Pueblos in 1786, Comanches traded "more than six hundred hides, many loads of meat and tallow, fifteen riding beasts" (A.B. Thomas 1932:306). In return, they received "sugar loaves, maize, tobacco, brandy, guns, ammunition, knives, clothing or coarse cloth, vermillion, mirrors, glass beads, and other trifles" (Gálvez 1951:46). In the 1840s, "their stock in trade was furs of all kinds, dressed buffalo robes, dressed and raw deer skins, dried buffalo tongues, beeswax" (Clift 1924:139).

The horse trade was the primary context for early Anglo-American presence in Comanche territory, supplying the Saint Louis, Natchez, and New Orleans markets (Flores 1985:10). While some of these horses were bred by the Comanche, or captured wild mustangs, most were stolen from Spanish, Mexican, and later, Anglo-American settlements in Texas and farther south.

Comanche trade in captives was probably aboriginal (Magnaghi 1970). Captives were one way the population could be restored after an epidemic, although it is not known whether expeditions were made with the specific purpose of taking captives for the trade.

Besides trade, Comanches obtained Euro-American goods as political gifts. These items included prestige items, including silver-headed canes, flags, medals, and uniforms (Kavanagh 1996:177–189, 278–291, 376–383, 453–471).

Clothing and Adornment

Children remained naked until about five years of age. For adult men, summertime and daily dress was minimal; a shirt, breechcloth, leggings, moccasins, and *savari*—a hide, cloth or piece of sheeting worn about the waist (fig. 4). Late prereservation and reservation period shirts reached mid-thigh and were decorated with twisted fringe at the shoulder and elbow. Some side-seam leggings are in museum collections, although late nineteenth-century photographs also show front-seam style, attached by thongs to the belt at the waist and tied with garters below the knee. From knee to ankle, leggings were decorated with long twisted fringe. Moccasins were of the two-piece, hard-sole variety.

Several types of women's dress were in use. The older style was a buckskin skirt suspended by shoulder straps, worn with a poncholike top (Berlandier 1969). In the 1870s women wore cloth skirts and blouses, and a cloth cape clasped with broaches. By the end of the nineteenth century, one-piece calico dresses were common (Soule 1868–1874; Gerdner 1872). Women wore an apron (*pikUsikwiʔíˑʔniˑ*), comparable to the men's *savari*, also belted at the waist (fig. 5). From the belt hung the women's tools, awl and needle cases. A shawl, sometimes fastened at the neck with a pair of silver broaches, was worn over the shoulders. Women's moccasins were hard-soled and were often attached to knee-length leggings. In the winter, painted buffalo hide robes were used.

Beads were available by 1795 (Kavanagh 1996:183), and there is a report of quillwork (Pino 1812, 1995:45). By the late nineteenth century, beadwork was restrained, often merely outlining the edges of a man's shirt or leggings, or accenting the shoulders of a woman's dress.

As early as 1786, women were reported to cut their hair short (Moorhead 1968:157); in the late 1860s and early 1870s both men and women wore short hair, parted in the middle and worn loose (Soule 1868–1874; Gardner 1872), although some women wore bangs (Gardner 1872a). Some men cut the left side at ear level to show off earrings (Gardner 1872b), others shaved the left side entirely (Grinnell 1923a:42). Some men wore their hair long, bundled, braided, or wrapped with trade cloth or otterskin (Soule 1868–1874; Gardner 1872c). Other men wore the hair of the crown in a scalp lock, decorated with German silver ornaments or a string of German silver conchos of graduated size. By the 1890s, long hair was the most common style for both men and women, the women's worn loose, the men's braided (W. Irwin 1890–1900).

Both men and women plucked the eyebrows (Berlandier 1844:178), a practice that continued into the twentieth century (Lowie 1912a). Some men, especially captives, allowed their beards to grow (Berlandier 1844:178).

bottom, Smithsonian, Dept. of Anthr.: 1471.

Fig. 4. Men's clothing. top, Frank Chikovi wearing buckskin shirt, leggings, and moccasins. His otter-fur doctor's headdress and hair wraps are decorated with beadwork and ribbons. His breechcloth, neckerchief, and *savari* are cloth, and he wears a mescal-bean and silver bead bandolier over his left shoulder. Photograph by Waldo Wedel, Walters, Okla., 1933. bottom, Moccasins with rawhide soles and uppers of soft tanned skin, the earliest documented example of Plains hard-soled moccasins (Ewers 1969:184). This type of construction replaced soft-soled moccasins in most tribes in the mid-19th century. Collected in southern Tex. by Jean Louis Berlandier, 1828–1851; length 27 cm.

Mythology

Oral traditions included semihistorical war-hero histories, stories of the origins of power, and ghost encounters (Curtis 1907–1930, 19:189–196; Wedel 1933–1935; Kardiner 1945:68; Attocknie 1969; Kavanagh 1979–1987). Animal protagonist tales often featured Coyote or Fox (Canonge

891

Fig. 5. Women's clothing. Yannytatschi (left) and Taddahki wearing Southern Plains–style 3-skin dresses decorated with beadwork and ribbons. Both wear fringed shawls as aprons, held at the waist with leather belts whose trailers are decorated with German silver plates or studs. Both hold hawk-feather fans with beaded handles. Photograph by Waldo Wedel, Walters, Okla., 1933.

1958); in several a "white man" served as antagonist (St. Clair 1909:276–277).

Only a few origin or creation myths have been recorded. R.S. Neighbors (1852:127) alluded to a culture hero who created the Comanche and taught them how to live. St. Clair (1909:280) recorded a version of the widespread "liberation of the buffalo" myth. The mythic origins of Comanche peyote were recorded in E. Wallace and E.A. Hoebel (1952:344).

Religion

Comanche religion was an individual concern, and while there was a range of variation in belief and practice, fundamental beliefs were held in common. The Creator, called niatpo 'my father' (probably ni'ahpi') according to Pino (1812, 1995:45), was sometimes identified with the sun (Ruíz [1840] in Gulick and Allen 1921–1927, 4:221), although the two are sometimes held to be distinct (R.S. Neighbors 1852). The earth, ne'pia (probably niβia 'my mother'), shared with the sun the ability to judge the validity of oaths (Ruíz [1840] in Gulick and Allen 1921–1927, 4:221; R.S. Neighbors 1852:132; E. Wallace and E.A. Hoebel 1952:195). Other aspects of nature and of particular species were personified,

and it was from them that humans could derive assistance and power (E. Wallace and E.A. Hoebel 1952:204). In smoking, the first smoke was offered to the Sun, the second to the Earth (Ruíz [1840] in Gulick and Allen 1921–1927, 4:222).

Comanche religious practice centered on the personal acquisition of puha 'power' obtained from the supernatural. Power was available to men and women, and both could become puhakatł 'possessor of power'. In this, as in other aspects of Comanche life, there was individual variation. On the one hand were those who claimed personal power, and on the other were skeptics who ridiculed the actions of the puhakatł (Pino 1812, 1995:45); in the middle were those who claimed no power for themselves but recognized it in others.

Power could be obtained in two general ways, by the vision quest, puhahaβitł 'lying down for power', and by transfer, inheritance, purchase, or training. Young people might begin to seek power in late adolescence, visiting certain places known to be powerful. There spirits might visit the seeker, offering choices of powers (Kavanagh 1979–1987), sometimes contesting with the seeker or frightening him away (D.E. Jones 1972:36). A special form of vision quest involved visiting the grave of a specific puhakatł to seek his personal power (W.R. Wedel 1933). Visions might also be sought by Sun Dance leaders, particularly when seeking information on lost relatives or foretelling the future (W.R. Wedel 1933; Attocknie 1969). They might also come through unsought dreams (W.R. Wedel 1933; E. Wallace and E.A. Hoebel 1952:156; D.E. Jones 1972:38).

Along with power, the successful seeker received rituals and prohibitions. The rituals included specific ways of contacting the supernatural, designs for shields, and other insignia (fig. 6).

Through the sharing of power with a number of people, a puhakatł might establish a medicine society (W.R. Wedel 1933; Kardiner 1945:64; E. Wallace and E.A. Hoebel 1952:165). Medicine societies were usually comprised of multiples of four up to a maximum of 12 members. They might meet periodically to renew their power (W.R. Wedel 1933).

The services of a curer were contracted for with an offer of tobacco and an agreed-upon payment; if the cure failed, payment was sometimes withheld or, if prepaid, demanded back (E. Wallace and E.A. Hoebel 1952:167). Black silk (later synthetic fiber) handkerchiefs were frequently used in curing (Slotkin 1974). Cures might also involve use of "sucking horns" and other techniques designed to locate and remove intrusive objects, as well as the prescription of specific botanical medicines (D.E. Jones 1972:49).

Ceremonies

Besides individual treatments and small medicine groups, there were larger religious events. The pianahuwaitł 'big doctoring', sometimes called in English the Beaver ceremony (E. Wallace and E.A. Hoebel 1952:175), was for curing "wasting away" (tuberculosis), but it also conferred benefits

892

Smithsonian, Dept. of Anthr.: 8443B.

Fig. 6. Buckskin shield cover. The thickened rawhide bases of shields were often fitted with buckskin covers painted with spiritual designs evocative of the owner's war medicine. This cover is unusual in being painted on both sides. top, Outer side of cover painted with a stylized face above lines radiating from a central circle. A horsehair pendant hangs from the rawhide base, indicating that the owner was an accomplished raider (E. Wallace and E.A. Hoebel 1952:107). bottom, Inner side of cover painted with representations of grizzly bears with exaggerated claws and snouts, a buffalo head, and a whirling design symbolic of a peyote button. The center design may also represent a peyote button. Peyote was used as a war medicine on the Plains long before the Peyote religion was established (La Barre 1989:25). Collected from the Comanche by Adna R. Chaffee near Ft. Griffin, Tex. in 1868 (W.K. Jones 1968:31–35). Diameter of cover, 42 cm.

on others who attended (W.R. Wedel 1933; Linton 1935; Attocknie 1969).

The Comanche Sun Dance, called *piakahni nihka* 'big house dance' or *nihkado* 'our sun dance' (borrowed from Kiowa) (ten Kate 1885:127), combined several ritual actions, animal-calling ceremonies, masked ritual clowns, mock battles and buffalo hunts, curing and foretelling the future, as well as the public announcement, demonstration and transfer of medicine power (Hoebel 1933; W.R. Wedel 1933; Linton 1935).

The antiquity of the Sun Dance among the Comanche has been the subject of debate. Although it has been asserted that the Comanche held only one Sun Dance, that of 1874

before the Adobe Walls campaign (E. Wallace and E.A. Hoebel 1952:175), evidence suggests differently. The Eastern Shoshone claimed to have learned their original Sun Dance ceremony from Yellow Hand, son of the Comanche principal chief Ecueracapa, at the beginning of the nineteenth century (Shimkin 1953:409; Hultkrantz 1968). Attocknie (1969) listed the leaders and locations of six remembered Comanche Sun Dances, including at least one led by a woman. According to Linton (1935:420), the Comanche Sun Dances were held at "irregular intervals," the last in 1878; and ten Kate (1885a:394) reported preparations for a dance in 1883 which were aborted because of the failure of the ritual hunt to obtain a buffalo bull, whose hide was required for the center pole. According to Comanches in 1933, "soon after the buffalo disappeared, the dance was given up" (W.R. Wedel 1933).

There were various ceremonies and dances connected with warfare. The nawaps pinar 'stirring up' (Lowie 1912a; Kavanagh 1979–1986) was held at an encampment a short distance from the main village. The prospective warriors periodically rode through the main camp, singing, and boasting of their prowess; at night they danced in the warriors' camp. The night before departure, the warriors danced with their wives or girl friends.

If a war party happened to catch a badger, the animal might be killed, eviscerated, and its blood allowed to collect in the body cavity. After sprinkling with dust, it was allowed to coagulate. The men of the party would then peer into the mirror to catch a view of what they would look like in the future (Wedel 1933).

There were no ceremonies for a war party that lost a man; its members merely came into camp and quietly took up their normal activities (W.R. Wedel 1933). However, on the return of a successful war party, scalps and other trophies were displayed in the Scalp Dance (*wohO taβe nihka* 'victory dance') (ten Kate 1885:128; E. Wallace and E.A. Hoebel 1952:270). In the Shakedown Dance, women praised the returning party in exchange for gifts from the spoils (E. Wallace and E.A. Hoebel 1952).

The men's societies held dances as part of their ceremonies. In most dances, the possessor of a *pia ni·pa²i* 'big club', acted as whip man (W.R. Wedel 1933).

Several other dances have been noted, including the Gourd Dance, Round Dance, Two-step, and Buffalo Dance (ten Kate 1885:128; W.R. Wedel 1933).

Men's Societies

Comanche men's societies had semimilitary functions: *piviapukuni·* 'big horse people'; *tiipukuni* 'little horse people' or 'Little Ponies'; *tu·wihikani* 'black knife people', also called the "Crow" from their crow-feather emblems (W.P. Clark 1885:341; ten Kate 1885:128; H.L. Scott 1890–1900; Lowie 1912a, 1915a). Several other society names have been reported, for example, Crow Tassel (Hoebel 1940:31) and Lobo (Ruíz 1972:11; Berlandier 1969:117).

Information on the men's societies is scanty and confused. It is sometimes suggested (Lowie 1915a) that specific societies were associated with particular Comanche political divisions, but other investigators report that, with the exception of the association of the Black Knives with the Yamparika, a society might "include men from every band" (H.L. Scott 1890–1900:11). Lowie (1912a) noted that the societies' primary function was to organize ceremonies at which volunteers for revenge war expeditions were recruited; however, their role in war is unclear. The Lobo society was reported as having the "no-flight" warrior rule (Berlandier 1969; Ruíz 1972); later the no-flight rule and pegged sash were associated with the *puhkuhci* 'contraries', but it is not clear whether they formed a society (W.R. Wedel 1933).

Besides regulating travel and patrolling the line of march, the Big Horses made peace with other tribes (Lowie 1915a:812). In the twentieth century, Comanches attributed camp and route guard functions during the Adobe Walls campaign of 1874 to the Little Ponies, who used physical force to maintain order (Attocknie 1969).

Social Organization

Each nuclear family lived in a separate lodge. In polygynous households, the chief wife lived in the main tepee with the husband, the other wives in adjacent lodges (Gladwin 1948:86). Adolescent males had separate tepees or wickiups within the family cluster. The outdoor domestic work area included meat-drying and other storage racks (fig. 7) (Soule 1873).

Extended families sometimes camped alone. Several eighteenth century travelers reported camps with as few as four lodges (Loomis and Nasatir 1967:320), but camps of 50 lodges or more were more common (Kavanagh 1996:Table 1.1). There were also large nucleated camps, often with explicit political purpose.

The kinship system was characterized by bilateral descent and bilocal residence. Polygyny tended to be of the sororal type. No form of cousin marriage was reported, and none was sanctioned by twentieth-century Comanches (W.R. Wedel 1933; Kavanagh 1979–1987).

Linguistically, the kinship terms were similar to those of other Shoshoneans, but there were variations in usage (J.H. Steward 1938; Hoebel 1939; Shimkin 1941; Gladwin 1948; Eggan 1980). In one's own generation, cousins were classified with siblings. In the parental generation, father and his brothers were identified, as were mother and her sisters, while father's sisters and mother's brothers were called by separate terms. In the first descending generation, a man's brother's children were identified with his own, as were a woman's sister's children; a man's sister's children were called by the same term used to refer to his mother's brother, and woman's brother's children were called by the same

top, Smithsonian, NAA: 1782-p.; bottom, Sam E. DeVenney, Lawton, Okla.

Fig. 7. Habitations. top, Skin tepees in the Medicine Creek winter village. Among the tepees are a number of tripods and poles where shields and other medicine objects are displayed (Kavanagh 1990, 1991). Photograph by William S. Soule, winter 1872–1873. bottom, Pahdawy (left) and Tahwahahwicki in a summer arbor used for cooking and sleeping. A high storage rack is in the rear; a table and 2 permanent sleeping platforms are under the arbor. Photographed near Walters, Okla., about 1913.

term used to refer to her father's sister. Four terms were used for grandparents. These same four terms were used to refer to grandchildren, although the distinguishing feature was sex of speaker rather than of intervening relative.

Life Cycle

At the commencement of labor, the expectant mother entered a separate lodge, assisted by a midwife or female relatives. At the birth of a first child, especially of a boy, the mother's parents gave presents to the father. (Data on the life cycle are taken from Hoebel 1933 and W.R. Wedel 1933.)

For the first several months, children were kept during the day in slat-back style cradles (fig. 8) and during the night in oval cradles made of buffalo rawhide with the hair left on. The child slept with the mother for the first three to five years, then with other children.

There were no puberty ceremonies. By early adolescence boys and girls had begun to play active roles in the family. For boys, these consisted of herding, watering, and other care for the horses, as well as some hunting. When a boy killed his first game, often a bird or other small animal, he was praised and gifts were given in his honor.

At adolescence, boys slept in a separate lodge within the family group. At the onset of menstruation, girls were sequestered to avoid contaminating the medicines of their male relatives; they also avoided red meat as "bad for the blood."

By adolescence, a boy had gone on his first war party with his father's permission and had begun to consider the need for supernatural power. However, it was not until about 20 years of age that a young man began an active search for power. Some men never obtained power, but no great deeds were ever accomplished in its absence.

Suitors might make gifts of meat, bows and arrows, or horses to a girl's male relatives. While some couples arranged matters themselves, go-betweens were often used, particularly by parents who wished to establish links with important families. Some Comanches said that girls married at 15 or 16, and boys as soon as they could, whether or not they had earned a reputation. Others said that girls did not marry before 17, possibly waiting as late as 20, and that boys first had to establish themselves as warriors and hunters.

In cases of contemplated divorce, the fathers of a young couple might be called in to arbitrate the disagreement. If they were unable to decide, the chief might be called upon, but he was unable to compel reconciliation. In divorce, men and women took their own property; children usually stayed with the father's family.

The dead were usually interred in rock crevices. In mourning, both men and women might cut their hair, gash their arms or legs, or even cut off an ear. Mourners were excused from dances, but usually some member of a family in mourning danced for a short time and was then excused. Mourning continued anywhere from a single day to several years, with a renewal of mourning upon approaching a relative's grave.

Ideally, all of a deceased person's property, including stock, was destroyed. An individual could informally bequeath a certain piece of property, but various relatives might make claims, with brothers and sisters having a greater claim than sons and daughters.

Political Organization

• LAW Comanche law distinguished between private and public spheres of action based on the scale of the social unit involved (Hoebel 1940:47). Within an extended family, and between related extended families of the same local band, relations were phrased in kinship terms, "brothers" being the strongest relationship (Gladwin 1948:81). Within these groups, domestic affairs, marriage arrangments, divorce, adultery, even murder, were primarily family matters (Hoebel 1940:49ff.), although chiefs could attempt to prevent feuds in the name of community peace (W.R. Wedel 1933). On the other hand, village movements, cooperative

Sam E. DeVenney, Lawton, Okla.
Fig. 8. Nahme Poewekuma (left) and her daughter Bertha, and an unidentified mother and her son. Boys' cradles are distinguished by the leather flap. Comanche lattice-back baby carriers are often decorated with elaborate patterns of tacks, paint, beaded amulets, and mescal beans. Photographed in Walters, Okla., about 1913.

hunts, and matters of war, peace, and international relations were public issues over which chiefs had authority to make decisions and to impose sanctions, including corporal punishment, property confiscation, and in extreme cases, capital punishment.

Comanche legal and political processes often included both the invocation of cultural "propositions," normative statements about proper behavior (Hoebel 1954:131), as well as pragmatic analyses of relative power (Hoebel 1940:60). If brave or powerful enough, plaintiffs might confront a defendant themselves to demand *nanawoki* 'damages'. Otherwise, they might gather a party of supporters who acted as spokesmen for the aggrieved (Hoebel 1940:52, 61). The extreme case was for the aggrieved to enlist the services of a single war leader to confront the accused, not as arbitrator, but as enforcer (Hoebel 1940:65).

• POLITICAL STATUSES   For the Comanche male, the route to social standing was through a war record; the *tek*ʷ*IniwapI* 'warrior' or 'hero' was the ideal Comanche man (Kavanagh 1979–1987). A brave man was one who, even though dismounted, challenged an enemy (Lowie 1912a:8).

A *paraivo* 'chief' or 'leader' had to be a warrior but there was no institutional separation between civil and military spheres of public activity (W.R. Wedel 1933). Role distinctions were expressed through modifiers: *iriri paraivo* 'good' or 'peaceful chief', *woho paraivo* 'mean' or 'dangerous chief', *mahimiana paraivo* 'war chief' (Kavanagh 1979–1987).

The term *paraivo* may imply an authoritative, directive role but it also encompasses a passive, representative, role. However, the indeterminacy between *paraivo* as chief and as representative was not random; rather, political relations varied with the social distance between the participants. Within social groups, political relations were phrased in kinship terms, while relations with nonkin were based on pragmatic considerations of relative power. The choice of role at a particular time depended on situational evaluation of the power differential. This range of behavioral variation was also expressed negatively in political contests: a common charge hurled at opponents was that they acted for personal benefit, rather than for the good of the people.

• LEVELS   Understanding the levels of sociopolitical integration has been a continuing problem in Comanche ethnography (Thurman 1980, 1982, 1987; Kavanagh 1980, 1985, 1996; Gelo 1987; Hoebel 1939, 1940; Tefft 1965). In prereservation times, there were four levels of organization: simple family, extended family, local band, and division. The basic social unit was the bilaterally extended family, *niminahkani·* 'people who live together in a house(-hold)' (Kavanagh 1979–1987).

No Comanche terms have been recorded for the higher level residential or political units. Local bands (Kavanagh 1980:57), composed of one or more extended families plus attached but unrelated simple families and individuals, were called rancherías by the Spaniards; Thurman (1980:6) calls them "subsistence bands." In the early reservation period, their size ranged from 45 to 200 individuals (Kavanagh 1979–1987). Because many of its members were related, and since marriage was prohibited with any recognized relative, marriage was normally outside the local band.

Local bands formed around a core extended family, whose leader was the local band headman. Through hunting skill, military prowess, and political acumen, he attracted and maintained peripheral families and individuals to the band. He could impose physical sanctions on troublemakers (A.B. Thomas 1940:116; T. James 1984:143; Winfrey and Day 1966, 1:266; Froebel 1859:266; Leeper in ARCIA 1858:175; R.N. Richardson 1929:56; Kavanagh 1996:36–39). Succession went to the most able (J. Gregg 1844:308), and there is no evidence that sons of chiefs were more favored than were others (Kavanagh 1979–1987).

The maximal level of Comanche political organization was the division, called in Spanish *tribu* (tribe), *parcialidad* (division or faction), *rama* (branch), and less often *nacíon* (nation). Divisions were tribally organized groups of local bands linked by ties of kinship and men's societies (Thurman 1980, 1982, 1987; Kavanagh 1980, 1985, 1996).

Divisional principal chiefs were elected from among the component local band chiefs (Nava 1793; Chacón 1797, 1801; R.S. Neighbors 1849; W. Steele 1849), but the processes of selection are unknown. While Spanish, Mexican, and American authorities recognized principal chiefs with prestige symbols, there is nothing to suggest that this recognition implied that the positions were imposed on an unwilling population.

Warfare

Horse and cattle raids were important components in the domestic and political economies, providing both direct input as well as trade items (Kavanagh 1996). Further, the redistribution of war booty was the basis for political power, "a reputation for fairness in dividing the spoils enhanced the prestige of a war leader and gained him followers" (Hoebel 1940:25).

In the eighteenth century, Comanche tactics ranged from small raids (Loomis and Nasatir 1967:363) to coordinated attacks by leather-armored horsemen deployed as shock formations (Secoy 1953). The use of full body shields was reported as late as 1751 (A.B. Thomas 1940:26). The introduction of firearms mitigated against these tactics, and with the increasing availability of horses, tactics shifted to lighter, quicker movements (Secoy 1953). Comanches allowed two men to count coups on each fallen enemy. Scalping was not particularly prized (Lowie 1912a:8; Kavanagh 1979–1987).

History Since 1875

The Reservation Period, 1867–1901

With the establishment of the reservation, Comanche leaders had difficulty maintaining their political power. The

896

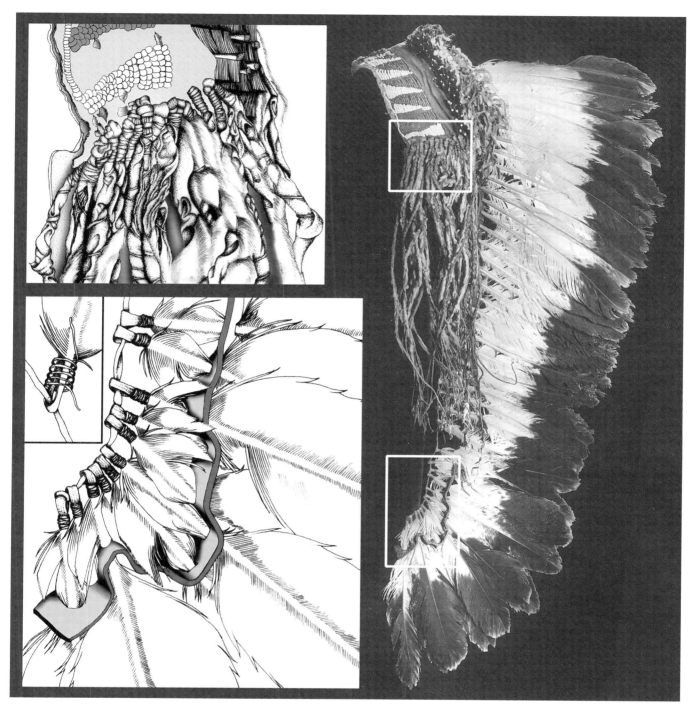

Fig. 9. Warrior headdress. The eagle feather war bonnet is commonly associated with the Sioux and other tribes of the Central Plains, but this object demonstrates that headdresses were used on the Southern Plains as well. Feathers, symbolic of brave deeds, were crafted into a variety of head gear (Hoebel 1940:29; Kavanagh 1992). The cap is soft tanned skin with a facing of red stroud cloth decorated with blue and white pony beads. Across the top is a band of clipped turkey vulture feathers. Strips of rabbit skin wrapped around twisted grass fiber are attached to the crown and along the back of the cap. The trailer consists of 43 immature golden eagle feathers. top left, Cap construction. Strips of rabbit fur are folded and bound together with sinew, giving the appearance of braiding. The head of the rabbit fur strip is folded to create an eye and wrapped with sinew then stitched through both the cloth and tanned skin backing. bottom left, Headdress trailer construction. Each quill is split, shaved, folded back to form an eye, and wrapped with sinew. It is then passed through a spacing strip and threaded on a strip of buckskin. Two other sinew cords through the upper quills also serve to keep the feathers in place. Collected by Jean Louis Berlandier, 1828–1851; length 94 cm. Drawings by Roger Thor Roop. Length 94 cm.

available resources were often scanty and difficult to control. While the Treaty of Medicine Lodge provided for annuity goods, these did not include food rations, which had to be specifically provided by annual congressional appropriations. In the early 1880s, in an attempt to force the Comanche to take up farming, Congress reduced rations. Faced with imminent starvation or outbreak of violence, Agent Philemon B. Hunt arranged with Texas cattlemen, whose stock were already trespassing on the reservation, to provide the Indians with cattle in return for permission to graze on the reservation (Hagan 1971). These leases provided not only food but also small per capita cash payments and employment for a growing number of Comanche cowboys (LaD. Harris 1956). The lease payments, referred to as "grass money," although small, were nonetheless a significant addition to the reservation economy, allowing the purchase of luxury items. Grass money distribution time was often the occasion for socializing, giveaways, and gambling. The grass money itself became a political issue as various leaders attempted either to claim credit for obtaining it or to argue against its propriety.

This dispute had repercussions for Comanche political organization. The lack of consensus among leaders was perceived as resulting from the absence of a political system that encompassed all Comanches, rather than as the operation of separate political entities with distinct strategies and goals. Indeed, by the 1880s, the fact that there were no principal chiefs was due more to insufficient political resources than to the operation of cultural propositions against political organization.

Meanwhile, local band chiefs lost what minimal support was left to them. Rations, which had been issued to them for distribution to households, were issued directly to the heads of families. By 1881, Indian Agent Hunt reported that "the band system is so changed that 'the band' is hardly more than a nominal distinction in the distribution of beef" (Hunt in ARCIA 1881:78).

But while the political power of band and divisional chiefs declined, that of "tribal" chiefs emerged. One outcome of the "grass money" dispute was the emergence of Quanah Parker as the Comanche principal chief. Recognition of this status, became the focus of political jealousy, and various individuals attempted to obtain credentials proclaiming themselves principal chiefs (Hagan 1976).

On a larger scale, by the 1890s, combined meetings of the Kiowa, Comanche, and Plains Apache tribes (KCA) were being held (fig. 10). General councils of the three tribes were held to discuss matters of concern to the reservation population as a whole. By the late 1890s, a KCA Business Committee composed of the principal chiefs of the three tribes had been established, though its functions were vaguely defined; beyond a nominal say in the dispersal of joint resources, the committee had no defined authority.

Another focus of political activity was the Court of Indian Offenses, established about 1888 (Anonymous 1900), with judges from each of the three tribes. Although

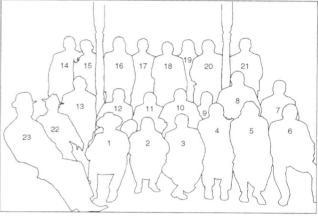

Smithsonian, NAA: 92-14646.

Fig. 10. Representatives of the Kiowa, Comanche, and Apache tribes, Nov. 26, 1907. 1, Quanah Parker, Comanche; 2, Ah-pe-ah-tone, Kiowa; 3, Lone Wolf, Kiowa; 4, Koon-kah-gah-chy, Plains Apache; 5, Cavayo, Comanche; 6, Pah-ko-to-quoddle, Kiowa; 7, George Hunt, Kiowa; 8, Mi-ziz-zoon-dy, Plains Apache; 9, Soontay, Plains Apache; 10, Arrushe, Comanche; 11, Eschiti, Comanche; 12, San-Ka-do-ta, Kiowa; 13, Otto Wells, Comanche; 14, Delos K. Lone Wolf, Kiowa; 15, Tennyson Berry, Plains Apache; 16, Peahcoose, Comanche; 17, Eustace Merrick, Comanche; 18, Kline-ko-le, Plains Apache; 19, Max Frizzlehead, Kiowa; 20, Ko-mah-ty, Kiowa; 21, Henry Tsee-lee, Plains Apache; 22, Agent Ernest Stecker; 23, Attorney John Hendricks. Photographed at the Kiowa Agency, Anadarko, Okla.

the court had little authority, the agent-appointed judgeships were a source of prestige, and thus of much jealousy.

The change in political power relations had an immediate impact on the size and composition of social groups. The 1879 census listed 42 "bands," ranging from a single extended family composed of three nuclear families to multiple extended families of more than 100 people, averaging 47 people each. By 1892, the last year in which the census implicitly recognized bands, 75 were listed, with an average of 25 persons each (Kavanagh 1989).

This new social pattern was solidified in the construction of permanent houses. In the 1870s stone houses were built for selected chiefs. In the 1880s, several dozen frame and picket (vertical log) houses were constructed for the general populace. By 1897, there were 195 houses and 98 other "permanent residences" (M.F. Long 1897).

The dispersal of the population in nuclear or small extended family groups was further effected by the allotment of the reservation in 1901. Under the provisions of the Jerome Agreement of 1892–1900, each Indian resident on the reservation could chose a quarter section of land (160 acres). A total of 1,450 such parcels were selected by Comanches. Although some Comanche allotments were certainly selected on the basis of existing social and political affiliations, the majority were not; neither prereservation divisions nor local bands were localized in the allotment pattern (Kavanagh 1989). Rather, nuclear families chose their allotments around the primary parameters of wood and water; both banks of East and West Cache, Beaver, and Medicine creeks remained in Indian hands. Another consideration in the choice of allotments was the activity of the various Christian missions, which provided food rations and schools (McBurney 1948:75).

• CHRISTIANITY AND PEYOTISM   Although the first agents to the Kiowa-Comanche-Apache Reservation were Quakers, in 1881 the first missionary assigned to the Comanche was an Episcopalian, J.B. Wicks, who left after only a few years (E. Wallace 1953). Thereafter, between 1889 and 1901, seven other churches and missions were established in Comanche communities—Deyo Mission at Cache, Baptist; Post Oak Mission at Cache, Mennonite; Cache Creek Mission at Apache, Presbyterian; Brown Church at Walters, Baptist; Yellow Mission at Lawton, Methodist; Little Washita Mission, Methodist; and Saint Patrick's Church at Anadarko, Roman Catholic. Christianity became a major force in Comanche life. Hymns were composed in the Comanche language (Canonge 1960), and many families went to summer camp meetings (Kavanagh 1979–1987).

Another response to the changed conditions emerged in the form of the Peyote ritual, which was probably brought by Lipan Apaches who moved from the Mescalero Reservation in New Mexico between 1888 and 1892 (O.C. Stewart 1987; Kavanagh 1979–1987). By the twentieth century, the basics of the ritual had been formalized. Comanches, notably Quanah Parker, had begun proselytizing among other tribal communities (O.C. Stewart 1987).

Some Comanches may have participated in the Ghost Dance of 1890 (Mooney 1896:159).

The Postreservation Period, 1901–1980

The Bureau of Indian Affairs banned or discouraged traditional social and religious activities. In the early 1900s, social gatherings called "picnics" were permitted with the proviso that no "Ghost Dances," "Give-Away Dances," or "any of the other old customs" (Meritt 1916) were to take place. These sanctions against traditional activities were relaxed in the 1920s. The army at Fort Sill played an active role in sponsoring victory dances (fig. 11), memorials, and other activities. The Craterville Park Fair was an annual

Ft. Sill Mus., Okla.: 60.11.116.

Fig. 11. Victory Dance, performed by women, sometimes wearing their husband's headdresses and carrying spears with recently taken scalps, to celebrate the successful return of a war party. Photograph by Morris Swett, Ft. Sill, Okla., 1932.

event held in the Wichita Mountains under Indian sponsorship. Later, the Caddo County Fair in Anadarko became known as the Indian Fair. These events encouraged the development and transmission of new styles of dancing and singing between tribes. In the early twentieth century, the Comanche adopted the southern Plains version of the Grass Dance, which they called *noyo nihka* 'testicle dance'.

• KCA BUSINESS COMMITTEE 1911–1966   After Quanah Parker's death in 1911, although several Comanches vied for recognition as principal chief, the agent refused to recognize a successor, arguing that with allotment there were no longer any tribal resources, and thus no need for tribal organization (Stecker 1910:846). In 1917, the agent refused to recognize the KCA Business Committee (Stinchecum 1917). But in 1922, as the result of Indian agitation, it was revived as an advisory body (Burke 1922).

Much of the activity of the revived business committee revolved around claims against the government, including a successful suit in 1926 for royalty money from oil wells in the bed of the Red River (Billington 1967:129ff.). Between 1927 and 1932, some $1.5 million was generated from these royalties, most of which was distributed in per capita payments to the tribes (Anonymous 1932).

The early KCA Business Committee operated without a written constitution. One was adopted in 1932, but the KCA rejected the provisions of the Oklahoma Indian Welfare Act of 1936, which provided the same opportunities as the Indian Reorganization Act of 1934. Throughout the 1930s, a variety of constitutions—both tribal and joint KCA—were presented to the voters, but none was mutually acceptable to the Indians and the BIA. In 1940 a KCA constitution was accepted by the voters, and although it did not abide by the provisions of the Oklahoma Indian Welfare Act, it was accepted by the BIA (fig. 12).

The constitution placed all political power in a general council of the adult population of the three tribes. A business

Fig. 12. Superintendent William McCown addressing a general council of the KCA at Riverside Indian School, Anadarko, Okla., regarding ratification of amendments to the tribal constitution. front row, left to right, Comanches Fred Ticeakie, Timbo, and Albert Attocknie. Photograph probably by Peter Sekaer, Oct. 1940.

committee composed of five Comanches, five Kiowas, and two Plains Apaches, elected by the individual tribes, managed daily affairs, consisting mainly of prosecuting claims.

Politically, there was a general linkage of the Kiowa and Plains Apache, which allowed the dominant Kiowa faction to control the KCA business committee. In 1963 Comanche "separationists" managed to gain control of a general council meeting and abolished the KCA organization. Although the BIA at first refused to acknowledge the split, in 1966 it recognized the Comanche Tribe of Oklahoma as the political representative of the Comanche people. Since some resources remain undivided among the three tribes, they are managed by the KCA Land Use Committee.

The 1980s–1990s

The Comanche lived in a relatively populated area, and were active, although partial, participants in the larger American economy. Fort Sill in Lawton, Tinker Air Force Base in Oklahoma City, and Altus Air Force Base in Altus, as well as several other federal installations provided employment for Comanches.

As a tribe, Comanches had few independent resources. In 1984, a bingo operation was begun; in 1987 it contributed $200,000 to the tribal budget (Comanche Tribe. Business Committee 1987). The tribe also acted as agent for a number of federal Indian programs; in 1984, the budget was over $5 million (Comanche Tribe. Business Committee 1984).

Although over half the 1901–1906 Comanche allotments were in Indian hands in 1987, few Comanches actively farmed their allotments. Allotments held as undivided joint property by multiple heirs of the original allottee were leased to non-Indian farmers or stockmen. Oil wells were drilled on allottments, and several Comanches became wealthy through

such revenues. Allotments also had an important symbolic value as tangible evidence of Indianness.

From the 1890s, when Comanches volunteered to join the scouting company at Fort Sill (LaD. Harris 1956), they continued to have military involvement with a distinctly Comanche flavor. During World War I, Comanche army recruits were sent off and welcomed home to men's society songs (Kavanagh 1979–1987). In World War II, many Comanches, along with other Oklahoma Indians, enlisted in the 45th, "Thunderbird" Division. Even before the war, a squad of Comanches was specifically recruited into the 4th Signal Company, 4th Infantry Regiment, 45th Division, to use the Comanche language as the basis of a signal code (Comanche Tribe. Business Committee 1986; Anonymous 1940). Veterans from both World War II and the Korean War were welcomed home with Victory Dance celebrations. The celebration in 1952 for the returning Korean veterans continued in the form of the annual "Comanche Homecoming" powwow. The Little Pony Society was revived in 1972 to honor returning Vietnam veterans (Comanche Little Ponies 1972; Kavanagh 1980). In 1976, the Black Knives were revived as part of Comanche participation in the Smithsonian Institution's Festival of American Folklife and continued as a specifically Yamparika organization. Other modern societies included the Comanche Indian Veterans Association and the Comanche War Dance Society, which was given the rights to perform the dance of the Osage Heluska society.

The Gourd Dance ritual, used by the Little Ponies, Comanche Gourd Clan, and Comanche Indian Veterans Association, was a way to interact with other tribes and to communicate a Comanche identity. In this sense, the Gourd Dance was as much a tribal as a pan-Indian ritual (Kavanagh 1980, 1982).

Comanche society and culture retained distinctiveness. The extended family continued to be an important social group, sponsoring powwows and other events (Kavanagh 1980). An innovation in social organization was the so-called descendant groups, cognatic kin groups formed, Comanches said, to "honor our grandfathers" (Kavanagh 1980:99). Hand games were a popular winter activity (fig. 14).

Population

There are no reliable population estimates. In spring 1786, eight Kotsotika rancherías, totaling 700 lodges, were reported in an area 40 leagues square; at 12 residents each, there were 8,400 persons in this dispersed population (A.B. Thomas 1932:321). In winter 1785–1786, some "600 camps" (probably meaning extended families) were on the Arkansas River near modern Pueblo, Colorado (A.B. Thomas 1932:295); in July 1788, a village on the upper Red River contained 372 lodges (Loomis and Nasatir 1967:321). David Burnet (1851), who dealt mostly with the Tenawa, estimated Comanche numbers at about 3,000 warriors out of a total population of 10,000–12,000 (Burnet 1851). In the late 1820s and early 1830s, Ruíz (1972) reported the Texas Comanche as 1,000–1,500 families,

Fig. 13. Economy in the 1990s. left, Business Committee members at the Comanche Tribal Center near Lawton, Okla. left to right, Wayne Pahcoddy, Edward Clark, Kenneth Saupitty (Chair), Mary Jo Wardeski (Vice Chair), Rolan Mason. The committee is elected at-large with terms staggered every 2 years. right, Morgan Tossee helping Shane Grant Schartzer prepare to clear smoldering fires near Tampa, Fla. Photographs by Lynn Ivory, left, 1990; right, 1998.

Fig. 14. Hand game. Members of one team hide a pair of marked bones, and accompanied by singing and hand-clapping, attempt to distract members of the other team from guessing their location. The hiders win a tally stick for each unsuccessful guess. One team wins the game when it has all the tallies. Teams come from as far as Crow Agency, Mont., to play Okla. teams. left, Sitting "hider," at right, presenting his hands with the bones, while the "guesser," standing, prepares to signal his guess. Comanche team are sitting, left to right: Carl Autivach, Donnell Autivach, Del Wermy, Dale Cable, and Kent Chasenah. right, Tally sticks. Photographs by Lynn Ivory, Comanche Cultural Center, Cache, Okla., Feb. 1990.

and Berlandier (1969), 10,000–12,000 for the same. In 1846, a total of 14,300 Comanches among the several divisions was estimated (P.M. Butler and M.G. Lewis 1846:6).

In 1870, Agent Lawrie Tatum estimated 3,742 Comanches, including some 1,000 off-reservation Kwahadas (Tatum 1870); the Kwahada figure is probably an exageration. In 1875, 1,556 Comanches were reported on the reservation south of the Washita, and another 165 Penatikas north of

the river with the Wichitas. In 1900, there were 1,499 Comanches, but measles in 1901 took 98 lives. The low point of 1,399 was reached in 1904. It was not until the 1930s that the population again surpassed 2,000. In 1979, the tribal population was approximately 7,200 (Comanche Tribe. Business Committee 1979:81). In 1984, the total enrollment for the tribe was reported at 8,131, with a local resident Indian population of 3,642; by 1989, the latter figure had grown to

4,718 (The Confederation of American Indians 1986:221; Bureau of Indian Affairs 1989:5). In 1999, total tribal enrollment was approximately 10,000 (Comanche Tribe, communication to editors 1999).

Details of the effects of European epidemic diseases on the Comanche are scanty. In 1817 the Comanche chief Chihuahua stated that smallpox had made a "dreadful havoc" during the previous winter, killing some 4,000 Comanches including four chiefs and principal men. This figure is apparently the basis of a widely cited report (J. Morse 1822:259), but there is no evidence to corroborate such a major loss (cf. Ewers 1973). L.H. Williams (1849) and R.S. Neighbors (1849) reported that the 1848–1849 smallpox-cholera epidemic killed 300.

Synonymy†

The name Comanche is used as an ethnonym by many tribes, particularly those living west of Comanche territory. It was used in Spanish in New Mexico as early as 1706. Spanish spellings attest that the name was borrowed from an early Ute form *kimanči, which is continued as Southern Ute kimá·čI 'enemy; foreigner; Comanche' (Givón 1979:125; M.K. Opler 1943:156; John E. McLaughlin, communication to editors 2000). The Western Shoshone designation was Caw-mainsh (Gebow 1868:8), but the Southern Paiute form kimmancimi 'strangers; Shoshones' (Sapir 1930–1931:637) has a different ethnic reference.

The name Comanche occurs in various Southwest languages; for example, Jemez gimà·čiš, sg. gimà·či (Ives Goddard, personal communication 1978); Zuni kúmanchiqĕ (Curtis 1907–1930, 17:194); Tewa kumántsi (Curtis 1907–1930, 17:190); and Hopi Kománchi (Curtis 1907–1930, 12:222). In the Southeast it is documented in Biloxi as Kąmá′ntci (Dorsey and Swanton 1912:204) and in Koasati as komancí (Geoffrey Kimball, personal communication 1992).

The first Spanish uses in 1706 are: Comanche (Ulibarri in A.B. Thomas 1935:61, 76), Comanches (Cuervo in C.W. Hackett 1923–1937, 3:381); the earliest occurrences in French documents are Caumuches and Caunouche, 1719 (La Harpe and Beaurain, respectively, in Margry 1876–1886, 6:289) and Cumanche, 1720 (Bandelier 1890, 5:183). Throughout the eighteenth and nineteenth centuries the name was used by Texan Spaniards, Mexicans, Anglo-Texans, and later Anglo-Americans for both the larger cultural entity and for local Comanches, in contrast to those more distant. New Mexican Spaniards used it as a generic name for the larger cultural entity and added, when necessary, a more specific native ethnonym. Examples of spelling variants are Comanché and Comanchéz, 1770–1772 (De Mézières in Bolton 1914, 1:218, 297); Camanche (Z.M. Pike 1811:214; P.L. Chouteau in ARCIA 1837:558); Cumeehes (Schermerhorn 1814:29); Comauch (Trimble in J. Morse

1822:374); Cumancias (E. James 1823, 1:478); Comancha (Barreiro 1832:9); Comandus (Alegre 1841–1842, 1:336); Kimanchies (Houston in A.W. Williams and E.C. Barker 1938–1943, 1:268); and Komantsu (ARCIA 1877:248).

Sometimes a geographical modifier precedes the name Comanche. To the Spaniards of Texas and New Mexico, the Comanches of Texas were Oriental (Vial and Chaves 1785) and Orientals or Eastern Comanches, 1840 (Ruíz in Gulick and Allen 1921–1927, 4:221). Less frequently the Texas Spaniards referred to the western Comanche of New Mexico as Occidental, 1836 (Cameron in Gulick and Allen 1921–1927, 1:475). Anglo-Americans and Anglo-Texans often used the opposite set of cardinal direction modifiers, speaking of northern or upper, middle, and southern or lower Comanches (Jamison 1817, 1717a; E. Wallace 1954; A. Pike 1833). Other examples with a geographical modifier include Comanches of the Woods and Comanches of the Prairies, 1837 (Bonneville in J.T. Irving 1837; LeGrand in Anonymous 1838), and Comanches of the Prairies and the Staked Plain (A. Pike 1861a:548). Except for 'Comanches of the Woods' (see hu·hpi and hois below), none of these geographical names corresponds to native political units.

The Comanche self-designation, like that of the related Shoshone, is pl. nimini·, sg. nimi 'person' (Jean Charney, personal communication 1987). The name has been cited variously in singular and plural form as nɨmɨ (L.W. Robinson and J. Armagost 1990:188); Näünë and Na-ü-ni (R.S. Neighbors in Schoolcraft 1851–1857, 1:518, 2:125); Neum (ARCIA 1859:166); Niménim (ten Kate 1885:123); Ni′ⁿam (W.J. Hoffman 1886:300); and Nüma (Mooney 1896:1043).

At least three tribes designated the Comanche by the name of one of their subdivisions. The Tonkawa called them penetixka? (Hoijer 1949:11) after the Penatika division. The Shoshone also generalized the division name yapa tihka 'yampa root eater' or yapani· 'yampas' to the larger cultural entity (retranscribed from Mooney 1896:1045), rendered also as Yam bah′ n ya (Ballou 1880–1881) and Yamp′ pah (G. Stuart 1865). Like the Shoshone, the Crow called them bikka·sahtakdu·še 'one who eats wild carrots' (Medicine Horse 1987:15), an apparent translation of the name 'root eaters'.

Some tribes designated the Comanche as "Snakes," the common name for the Shoshone. Thus Cheyenne sé?senovotsétaneo?o 'snake people' (Glenmore and Leman 1985:201), rendered also as Sishinoatsítaneo (Curtis 1907–1930, 6:158) and šišinovozhetaneo 'rattlesnake people' (Petter 1913–1915:582). The Sioux employ the same name: Teton sįtéxla wičⁿaša 'snake man' (retranscribed from Buechel 1970:733); Santee and Yankton sįtéxda wičⁿaša (retranscribed from S.R. Riggs 1890:434; J.P. Williamson 1902:35). One Kiowa designation, Bo′dălk′′iñago 'reptile people, snake people' has the same meaning; another obsolete name, Sänko, was thought to be related to the term for snake (Mooney 1896:1043).

Several tribal designations for the Comanche signify 'enemy'. Examples are: Kiowa kyâygù (Laurel Watkins,

†This synonymy was written by Douglas R. Parks, based in part on data provided by Thomas W. Kavanagh.

personal communication 1979); Plains Apache *ídá·hé* (Bittle 1952–1956); and Navajo *naałání*, literally 'many enemies', which also is a general designation for Plains tribes (R.W. Young and W. Morgan 1992:370; Mooney 1896:1043). Other names with the same apparent meaning are Wichita *ná·ta²áh* (David S. Rood, personal communication 1987), translated as 'snakes' and 'enemies' (Gatschet in Hodge 1907–1910, 1:328; Mooney 1896:1043); and Arapaho *čo·θó²*, sg. *čó·x*, which has been rendered 'enemies' (cf. Ojibway *pwa·n* 'Sioux', both from Proto-Algonquian **pwa·θa*; Ives Goddard, personal communication 1990, Mooney 1896:1043).

A Caddoan name with no known etymology is Pawnee *rá·rihta* (Parks 1965–1990) and Kitsai Na′nita (Mooney 1896:1043). The Caddo designation, which has no known etymology, is *sáw²łuh* (Chafe 1979), cited variously as Sau′hto (Mooney 1896:1043), Sow-a-to (R.S. Neighbors in Schoolcraft 1851–1857, 2:126), and Sotoes (Houston in A.W. Williams and E.C. Barker 1938–1943, 2:268). Another name with no known etymology is Lipan *²ina·ca·²i·hí·* (Hoijer 1975:14).

Two unrelated descriptive designations are Isleta Turţaínin, literally 'sun people' (Curtis 1907–1930, 16:253), and Yanktonai Sioux *tahí wič^haša*, literally 'hair man', the reference being to buffalo or deer hair perhaps used as clothing (Curtis 1907–1930, 3:141, phonemicized).

Padouca

The common Dhegiha and Chiwere Siouan name Padouca that until the mid-eighteenth century, and sometimes later, designated the Plains Apacheans came to be applied by these tribes to the Comanche in the late eighteenth century and subsequently. It is a generic reference that meant 'enemy'. It occurs as Quapaw *ppattokka* (Dorsey 1883b; phonemicized); as Osage *ppátǫkka* (Robert L. Rankin, personal communication 1990); as Kansa *ppádokka* (Robert L. Rankin, personal communication 1987); as Ponca *ppátakka* (Parks 1988) and Pádǫkà (J.H. Howard 1965:133); as Omaha Páda^nka (Dorsey 1890:652) and Pádu^nka (Fletcher and La Flesche 1911:102), phonemicized as *ppáddǫkka* (John E. Koontz, personal communication 1987); as Otoe *p^hadúk^ha* (Parks 1988), and as Winnebago Pa-too′-a or Pa-too′-ă-jă (David St. Cyr in Hodge 1907-1910, 1:329). This designation was borrowed into Algonquian languages as Fox *pa·to·hka* and *pa·to·hka·ha* (Ives Goddard, personal communication 2000); Shawnee *pa·to²ka*, pl. *pa·to²ka·ki*; Miami Patoka (J.P. Dunn in C.F. Voegelin 1937–1940, 1:68), the last phonemicized as *pa·to·hka* (David Costa, personal communication 1991). It also occurs in Creek as Pa-tŭ-kû (Grayson in Hodge 1907–1910, 1:329).

In seventeenth and eighteenth-century French sources, and extending into the first decade of the nineteenth century (Lewis and Clark in Moulton 1983–, 3:136, 438–439), Padouca occurs as a designation for the Plains Apacheans. In the nineteenth century it was occasionally, but never

commonly, used for Comanche. The assertion that after 1750 the name Padouca referred to the Comanche (Grinnell 1920a; Secoy 1951) is based on the incorrect identification of historical references to Padouca as Comanches, when in fact they are properly Plains Apacheans (for examples, see references in Mooney in Hodge 1907–1910, 1:328–329; Strong 1935:25–26; see "Plains Apache," synonymy, this vol.). The few examples of the name actually designating Comanche are Patokas, 1829 (Wharton in Perrine 1927:274–275); Patocahs (P.M. Butler 1846); and Pahtocahs (P.M. Butler and M.G. Lewis 1846). Some writers have erroneously suggested that Padouca derives from the Comanche band name Penatika (Mooney 1896:1043; Swanton 1952:313).

Laytane, Naytane, Ietan

An eighteenth-century French designation sometimes used as a generic reference to all Comanche but that is often restricted to only one subdivision is of unknown origin and occurs in several variant forms. Many examples have either an initial consonant l or n: for example, Laitanes and La Litanes, 1739 (Mallet brothers in Margry 1876–1886, 6:457); Laytanes, 1785 (Miró in Nasatir 1952, 1:125, misidentified by Nasatir as Apache); Laytanne, 1804 (Chouteau in Nasatir 1952, 2:760); Liahtan band (J. Morse 1822:map); and Naitanes, 1772 (De Mézières in Bolton 1914, 1:297) and Naytane, 1774 (Gaignard in Bolton 1914, 2:83).

Other examples have an initial vowel a or i, sometimes preceded by h: Heitans, 1720 (Pénicaut in B.F. French 1869:155); Halitannes, 1795 (Truteau in Parks 1993); Hietans (J. Sibley 1832); Alitanes, 1803–1804 (Tabeau 1939:160); Alitan and Aliatans, 1806 (Lewis and Clark in Moulton 1983–, 3:395, 435–436); Aytanes, 1806 (Chouteau in Nasatir 1952, 2:770); Ayetan, 1769 (Ríu in Houck 1909, 1:64; misidentified by Houck as Otoe); Ayutan (Brackenridge 1814:80); Iatan, 1844 (Gregg in Moorhead 1954:13); Ietans (Z.M. Pike 1810:3d map; E. James in Thwaites 1904–1907, 1:233); Iotans (Bradford 1819); and Ya-i-tans (J. Wilkinson 1805).

Têtes Pelées

Another French designation that also referred to the Comanche, and perhaps one division, translates as 'Bald Heads'. Examples of it are Têtes Pelées, 1795 (Truteau in Parks 1993); Pelés, 1803–1804 (Tabeau 1939:160); La Playes and La-plays, 1806 (Lewis and Clark in Moulton 1983–, 3:395, 438); and La Plais or Bald Heads, 1819–1820 (Long in E. James in Thwaites 1904–1907, 1:233).

Sign Language

In the Plains sign language the Comanche are signified by a crawling snake, the same sign that designates the Shoshone. One variant is to move the hand or forefinger forward, imitating the motion of a snake; another variant is *903* to extend the forearm and hand near the right side and then draw it back, at the same time turning it alternately to the right and left, until the points of the fingers are behind the body, thereby imitating a snake drawing itself back into the grass (W.P. Clark 1885:118: Mallery 1881:466; Hadley 1893:40).

According to Mallery (1881:466), a sign used by the Comanche themselves is to hold both hands and arms upward, both palms inward, and pass the hands upward along the lower end of the hair to indicate 'long hair', since the Comanche reportedly never cut their hair.

Subdivisions

The following list of Comanche division and band names correlates spellings of these names in sources from the mid-eighteenth to the early twentieth centuries. By the late nineteenth and early twentieth centuries, these ethnonyms had ceased to have political significance (Kavanagh 1991).

Yamparika (*yaparihka* 'yampa root eater'). This division name occurs from the mid-eighteenth century into the twentieth century. Examples are: Yamparica (Marín 1758); Manbaricas, 1773 (Gaignard in Bolton 1914, 2:88); Llamparicas (Pino 1812:36); Yamparacks, 1818 (Burnet in E. Wallace 1954); Yambaricas, 1820 (Padilla in Hatcher 1919:55); Yamparicus, 1840 (Ruíz in Gulick and Allen 1921–1927, 4:221); Samparicka (Maximilian 1843:510); Yampeucos (P.M. Butler and M.G. Lewis 1846); Yampatickara (Fitzpatrick 1847); Yaparehca (Garcia Rejon 1866:5); Yampankas (Anonymous 1865:1103); Yäp-pā-reth-kās (W.P. Clark 1885:118); Yampatéka (ten Kate 1885:123); Yapareka (Lowie 1912); and Amparacs, 1832 (Houston in A.W. Williams and E.C. Barker 1938–1943:268).

A variant is *yapaini·* 'root people' (sg. *yapai*), written Yapainé (Garcia Rejón 1866:5), Yep pe (Moulton 1983–, 1:pl. 126), a Yapai (Lowie 1912a) and Yápa (Curtis 1907–1930, 19:229).

Kotsotika (*kuhcutihka* 'buffalo eater'). This division name occurs from the late-eighteenth century into the twentieth century. Examples are: Cuchan Marica, 1778 (Miera in Bolton 1950); Come Civalos, 1778 (Mendinueta in A.B. Thomas 1940:201); Cuchanec or Cuchantica (Anza-Duran in A.B. Thomas 1932:294); Cuchunticas (Pino 1812:36); CuschuTexca, 1840 (Ruíz in Gulick and Allen 1921–1927, 4:221); Cootsentickara (Fitzpatrick 1847); Koo-che-ta-kers (R.S. Neighbors in Schoolcraft 1851–1857, 2:128); Co-cho-tih-ca (A. Pike 1861a:548); Co-Cho-te-kas (Anonymous 1865:1103); Cuhtzuteca (García Rejón 1866:5); Kōchohtēhka (A. Pike 1866); Gushodojka (Butcher, Singer, and Leyendecker 1867); Cooch-che-teth-kas (Tatum 1870); Coch-cho-theth-e-cas (Kimball 1872); Caschotethka (W.P. Clark 1885:118); Ko'stshote'ka (W.J. Hoffman 1886:299); Kohstchotéka (ten Kate 1885:123); and Ketsetéka (Curtis 1907–1930, 19:229).

Hupe (*hu·pi* 'wood, timber'). This division name occurs in the late eighteenth century. Examples, which are clearly the word *hu·pi* 'wood, timber', are: Jupes (Ugarte 1787; A.B. Thomas 1932:348, n. 105); Jupinis, 1778 (Miera in Bolton 1950); and Gente de Palo, 1778 (Mendinueta in A.B. Thomas 1940:201).

Hois. This name is sometimes identified with the preceding, but it is unlikely that Hois is based on the Comanche word for 'wood'. Examples are: Hoishe Comanche (Wheelock 1835:87); júes, 1836 (Cameron in Gulick and Allen 1921–1927, 1:475); Juez, 1840 (Ruíz in Gulick and Allen 1921–1927, 4:221); Hooish and Hoish (P.M. Butler 1846; P.M. Butler and M.G. Lewis 1846); Jui (Butcher, Singer, and Leyendecker 1867); and Ho-is (R.S. Neighbors in Schoolcraft 1851–1857, 2:127).

Tenawa (*tinahwa* '[those who stay] downstream'). This division name occurs throughout the nineteenth century. Examples are: Tenaway, 1818 (Burnet in E. Wallace 1954); Tenaywoosh (P.M. Butler and M.G. Lewis 1846; misprinted as Lenaywoosh); Teu-a-wish (R.S. Neighbors in Schoolcraft 1851–1857, 2:127); Le-na-weets (Anonymous 1865:1103); Ta-ne-i-weh and Taneiwēh (A. Pike 1861a:548, 1866); Tenéwa (ten Kate 1885:123); and Tĕna'wa or Te'nähwĭt (Mooney 1896:1045).

Tanima (*ta nimi* 'liver [eaters]'). This name, which first appears in the mid-nineteenth century and continues into the twentieth century, is frequently identified with the preceding one; they probably reflect a single division. Examples are: Tanémaez, 1840 (Ruíz in Gulick and Allen 1921–1927, 4:221); Tanimma (W.P. Clark 1885:119); Danemme (Butcher, Singer, and Leyendecker 1867); Di-na-mahs (Tatum 1870); Ta-men-e-rinds (Kimball 1872); Tini'ema (W.J. Hoffman 1886:300); Tänĭ'ma (Mooney 1896:1045); and Tanúmē (Curtis 1907–1930, 19:229).

Penatika (*penatihka* 'honey eater'). This divisional name first appears in the mid-nineteenth century and continues into the twentieth. Examples are: Penatecas (P.M. Butler 1846); Penoe-en-tickara (Fitzpatrick 1847); Peneteka and Pine-takers (R.S. Neighbors 1849; R.S. Neighbors in Schoolcraft 1851–1857, 2:127); Pen-e-tegh-ca (A. Pike 1861:546); Penadojka (Butcher, Singer, and Leyendecker 1867); Pena-teth-kas (Tatum 1870); Penetethka (W.P. Clark 1885:119); Penetéka (ten Kate 1885:123); Pe'nete'ka (W.J. Hoffman 1886:299); and Pe'nätĕka (Mooney 1896:1045).

An alternate name for this division is Penande, cited as Penandé (García Rejón 1866:5); Penä'nde (Mooney 1896:1045); and Penánde (Curtis 1907–1930, 19:229).

Nokoni (*no·koni* 'wanderer'). This divisional name first appears in the mid-nineteenth century. Examples are: Noconee (P.M. Butler and M.G. Lewis 1846); No-ko-nies (R.S. Neighbors in Schoolcraft 1851–1857, 2:127); No-co-ni (A. Pike 1861a:548); Nōk ko nē (A. Pike 1866); Nocomies (Anonymous 1865:1103); No-co-nees (Tatum 1870); and No'koni (W.J. Hoffman 1886:300).

Kwahada (*kwahari* 'antelope', *kwaharini·* 'antelopes', *kwahari ticahkina* 'antelope sewer'). This division name first occurs in the mid-nineteenth century. Examples of the form 'antelope sewer' are: Kua-hara-tet-sa-cono, 1862 (Mathew

Leeper in Abel 1915–1925, 1:354); Kwaharetetchakanænä (Gatschet 1884a:124); Kwadatitchasko (ten Kate 1885:123); and Quaradachokos 'antelope skinner' (Bogy and Irwin 1866).

The shorter form meaning 'antelope' or 'antelopes' is exemplified by Qua-ha-das (Tatum 1870); Kua'hadi (W.J. Hoffman 1886:300); Quah-ah-dahs (Kimball 1872); Quahadas (W.P. Clark 1885:119); Hwahadanä (Gatschet 1884a); Kwa'hări and Kwa'hădi (Mooney 1896:1045); Qáhadi (Curtis 1907–1930, 19:229); and kwɛháɹɛnə (Hoebel 1940:13).

Tutsakana (*ticahkina* 'sewer'). This is one of the few local band names recorded in the historical literature. It first occurs in the mid-nineteenth century and continues into the twentieth. Examples are: Tich-aih-ken-e (A. Pike 1861b:22); Tetch-a-Ken-as (Tatum 1870); Titch-ath-kin-nas (Kimball 1872); Ti'tsakanai (W.J. Hoffman 1886:300); Kitsä'kăna (Mooney 1896:1044); and tɛ'sakɛnanɛ (Hoebel 1940:12).

The names Tutsanoyeku (*tici no·yihka* 'bad camper'), and a shorter form, Noyeka, refer to the people also called Nokoni. Examples are: Tist'shinoi'ka (W.J. Hoffman 1886:299); Detsăna'yuka (Mooney 1896:1044); Dĕtsanąyúka (Curtis 1907–1930, 19:229); and dɛ'tsanɔ'yɛka (Hoebel 1940:13).

Motsai, possibly *motsa* 'mustache', referring to Moustache Hill. This apparent local band name occurs from the mid-nineteenth century into the twentieth century. Examples are: Mo-cha (A. Pike 1861b:22); Mootchas (Anonymous 1865:1103); Mōōche 'Bluff on the Staked Plains' (A. Pike 1866); Mutsha (Butcher, Singer, and Leyendecker 1867); Motsai' (Mooney 1896:1045); and Métsai (Curtis 1907–1930, 19:229); mu'tsanɛ (Hoebel 1940:13).

The following list enumerates alphabetically other known names applied to Comanche groups, mostly local bands. Their specific referents are not always clear.

Ancavistis (perhaps *ekavitɬ* 'red people'), (Pino 1812:36).

Hai-ne-na-une 'corn eaters' (perhaps *hani nimini·* 'corn people') (R.W. Neighbors in Schoolcraft 1851–1857, 2:128).

It-chin-a-bud-ah Cold Weather people (cf. *itsiʔiti* 'be cold') (R.S. Neighbors in Schoolcraft 1851–1857, 2:128); ontsontiwia 'cold territory' (Lowie 1912a).

ke tahto·ni· 'never wear moccasins' or *napɬwa·htɬ* 'lacking moccasins.' Examples are: Quetahtore (García Rejón 1866:5); Ketahtone 'never wear moccasin' (Gatschet 1884a); Ketáte (Curtis 1907–1930, 19:229); Napuat No Shoes (García Rejon 1866:5).

Ke wih che mah 'who never get enough to eat' (A. Pike 1866); Kewa'tsăna 'no ribs' (Mooney 1896:1045).

Kotsa'i (Mooney 1896:1045); Qásiner (Curtis 1907–1930, 19:229).

Ku'baratpat 'steep climbers', a group of Penatihka (Mooney 1896:1045).

ku'tsuɛka 'red buffalo' (Hoebel 1940:13).

kʷahi hiki 'back shade'. Examples are: Guageyoke 'shade of the back' (Butcher, Singer, and Leyendecker 1867); Quă-he-huk-e 'back shade' (W.P. Clark 1885:119); and kwáhihɛkɛnə (Hoebel 1940:13).

Muvinábore (García Rejón 1866:5); Muvínavore (Curtis 1907–1930, 19:229) (probably *muvinavori* 'painted nose').

námasɜne 'something together' (Hoebel 1940:13).

nimikaiwa 'Comanche Kiowa'. Example: Nemekaiwane 'part Kiowa and part Comanche" (Gatschet 1884a).

No-na-um (R.S. Neighbors in Schoolcraft 1851–1857, 2:128); Nonĕm (A. Pike 1866); and Nau'niĕm (W.J. Hoffman 1886:299).

oti taʔó·ʔ 'pounded meat'. Otetaone 'musty meat' (Gatschet 1884a); ɔtéta'o 'burnt meat' (Hoebel 1940:13).

Pa-a-bo (A. Pike 1861b:22); Pa-a-bo 'Who stays with the White People' (A. Pike 1866).

Pä'gatsû 'Head of Stream' (Mooney 1896:1045); Págatsu (Curtis 1907–1930, 19:229).

páhuɹaix 'Water Horse' (Hoebel 1940:13; R.N. Richardson 1933).

pánaixtɜ 'Those Who Live Higher' (Hoebel 1940:13).

Par-kee-na-um 'Water people' (R.S. Neighbors in Schoolcraft 1851–1857, 2:128).

Pibian (Marín 1758); and Piviones, 1778 (Miera in Bolton 1950).

poho·nimi 'sage person'. Pohonim 'people of the hills' (ten Kate 1885:123); Po'hoi 'Wild Sage People,' a group of Shoshones who reputed came to live with the Comanche (Mooney 1896:1045).

siʔanavori 'painted feather'. Example: Sianábore 'Painted Arrows', the Cheyenne (García Rejón 1866:5).

ṭásipɛnanɜ, an Apache band that joined the Comanche (Hoebel 1940:13).

Te'yuwĭt 'Hospitable' (Mooney 1896:1045).

tihkapiwaitɬ 'lacking meat'. Te''kăpwai 'no meat' (Mooney 1896:1045); Tekapwait 'without any meat to eat' (Lowie 1912a).

Wa-ai'h 'Maggot' (Mooney 1896:1045); wɔ'ai (Hoebel 1940:13); cf. *woʔa* 'maggot'.

wi'anɜ 'Hill Wearing Away' (Hoebel 1940:13).

wihyunimi 'awl person'. Examples: Wiuini'em 'Awl People'; Wĭ'dyu (Mooney 1896:1044).

Yucanticas (Padilla in Hatcher 1919:55), 1830 (Berlandier 1969:151).

Sources

Despite their historically important position, the Comanche have not attracted the intensity of ethnographic and historical attention that characterizes some other Plains peoples. The cultural context of Comanche institutions has been obscured by comparisons with the areal complexes of the Plains and the Great Basin, and by reliance on secondary sources. The major published sources are derived from fieldwork in 1933 and 1945 (Hoebel 1939, 1940; E. Wallace and E.A. Hoebel 1952; Linton 1935; Kardiner 1945). Other field studies have resulted only in brief contributions (Lowie 1915a; G.C. Carlson and V.H. Jones 1940; Gladwin 1948; J.B. Casagrande 1954–1955; D.E. Jones 1972; McAllester 1949; Tefft 1960, 1960a, 1961, 1965). For critical comments on these standard sources, see Thurman (1982, 1987); Kavanagh (1985, 1996), and Gelo (1987). Pedro Bautista Pino (1812, 1995) gave a brief early description.

There is relatively little published linguistic material on the Comanche language. García Rejón's Comanche-Spanish lexicon (1866, 1995) is generally accurate. St. Clair (1909) published some texts in translation; more of his unpublished texts are in the National Anthropological Archives, which also houses several vocabularies collected in the nineteenth century (MacGowan 1865, 1865a; Detrich 1894, 1895; Gatschet 1879, 1884a, 1893; Butcher, Singer, and Leyendecker 1867). Canonge has published some texts and translations (1958, 1958a) and Comanche language church songs (1960).

Historical coverage of the Comanche is uneven. There are numerous references to the Comanche in the literature on the Spanish borderlands (Bolton 1914; A.B. Thomas 1929, 1932, 1935, 1940), but focus is not on the Comanche themselves, and synthesis is not attempted. Hyde's (1959) reconstruction of tribal movements on the Plains is highly speculative. John (1975) discusses eighteenth-century White-Comanche relations in New Mexico and Texas in the context of general European-Indian relations in the Southwest. R.N. Richardson (1933) discusses post-Mexican Texas relations with the Comanche, but his treatment of relations in New Mexico and elsewhere is minimal. Conversely, Kenner (1969, 1994) treats Comanche relations in New Mexico but not elsewhere. F. Levine and M. Freeman (1982; F. Levine 1991) summarize available information on the New Mexico Comanchero trade. While Nye's histories of the southern Plains wars (Nye 1937, 1969) are based on extensive interviews with the aged Indian survivors, they are limited to the military perspective. Kavanagh (1996) synthesizes European political relations with the Comanche 1706–1875. Hagan (1976) discusses reservation politics. Tate (1986) provides a comprehensive bibliography of materials bearing on Comanche relations with Texas.

There are extensive archival resources on the Comanche, both in English and Spanish. The Spanish and Mexican period archives of New Mexico (Twitchell 1914) are available on microfilm (New Mexico Province 1968, 1969) as are the Texan Béxar Archives, at the University of Texas (Kielman 1967–1971). The Archivo General de la Nación in Mexico City holds much material on the Spanish and Mexican periods of northern New Spain; Bolton (1913) notes several references to Comanches in other Mexican archives. The National Archives and Record Service has holdings covering the American period, both from the Indian Bureau (Record Group 75) and the military branch (Record Group 393). The Fort Worth regional center of the National Archives has records of the Kiowa, Comanche, and Apache Agency, 1900–1960. The Oklahoma Historical Society in Oklahoma City has the surviving agency records from the 1860s through the early 1900s.

Kiowa

JERROLD E. LEVY

Territory and Language

Kiowa (ˈkīəwu) tradition locates their earliest remembered homeland in western Montana near the headwaters of the Yellowstone River. Subsequently they moved east, established friendly relations with the Crow, and lived in the vicinity of the Black Hills. In 1805, Meriwether Lewis and William Clark were told that the Kiowa lived near the North Platte River; but by the mid-nineteenth century, they had been driven south by the Cheyenne and Sioux. In 1870, older Kiowas could remember having lived on the south fork of the Platte River. From there they moved south across the Republican, Smoky Hill, and Arkansas rivers, where they lived north of the Wichita Mountains and the headwaters of the Red River (fig. 1) (Mooney 1898:153–156).

Kiowa is a member of the Kiowa-Tanoan language family,* whose other branches are spoken in the Pueblo Southwest. This linguistic relationship suggests a southern origin for the Kiowa, although many scholars believe that the Tanoans separated from the ancestors of the Kiowa in the north before they entered the Plains (K.L. Hale 1967; J.P. Harrington 1910; Kroeber 1939:33, 48, 79–80, 86; G.L. Trager and E.C. Trager 1959; Vestal and Schultes 1939; Whorf and Trager 1937). This raises the possibility that the Kiowa may once have been sedentary horticulturalists who entered the Plains from the southwest rather than hunter-gatherers who came from the north.

Spanish sources take note of the Kiowa on the plains as early as 1732, and they may have acquired enough horses to become a mounted buffalo hunting tribe by 1725 (Haines 1938). They were able to mount at least some of their

warriors as early as 1748 (Mooney 1898:148, 161). J.H. Gunnerson and D.A. Gunnerson (1971:16–19) believe that the Plains Apache joined with the Kiowa around 1700, and that the two tribes obtained horses from the Wichita and Caddo. The acquisition of the horse reshaped the entire culture. Differences in wealth and status developed; a leadership hierarchy was formed that united the bands in one political entity with shared tribal ceremonies and men's societies whose membership cut across band divisions.

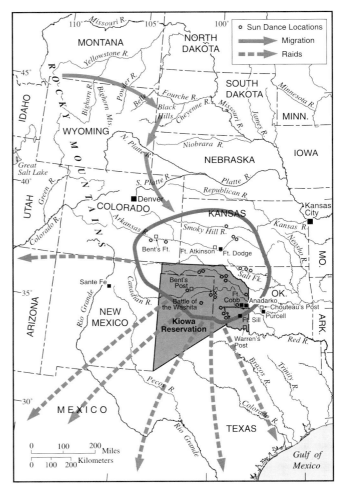

Fig. 1. Kiowa migration in the 18th century to their 19th-century territory, with annual Sun Dance locations. Reservation boundaries date from 1865, reduced to southwestern Ind. Terr. in 1867, and allotted in 1901 and 1906.

*The phonemes of Kiowa are: (voiceless unaspirated stops and affricate) p, t, c, k, $ʔ$; (voiced stops) b, d, g; (aspirated stops) p^h, t^h, k^h; (glottalized stops and affricate) $\dot{p}$, $\dot{t}$, $\dot{c}$, $\dot{k}$; (voiceless spirants) s, h; (voiced spirant) z; (nasals) m, n; (resonants) l, y; (short plain vowels) i, e, a, $ɔ$, o, u; (long plain vowels) $i\cdot$, $e\cdot$, $a\cdot$, $ɔ\cdot$, $o\cdot$, $u\cdot$; (short nasalized vowels) $į$, $ę$, $ą$, $ǫ$, $ǫ$, $ų$; (long nasalized vowels) $į\cdot$, $ę\cdot$, $ą\cdot$, $ɔ̨\cdot$, $ǫ\cdot$, $ų\cdot$; (tones) high ($\acute{v}$); low ($\grave{v}$); falling ($\hat{v}$). Long and short vowels contrast only in open syllables; falling tone is found only on a long vowel or a vowel that is followed by a nasal or resonant. Glottal stop ($ʔ$) is not written; it occurs predictably before all syllable-initial vowels in careful speech.

This phonemic analysis of Kiowa follows Watkins (1984:6–30), whose transcription matches the Handbook Technical Alphabet. Phonemic transcriptions of Kiowa words were supplied by Laurel J. Watkins (communications to editors 1979, 2000), with the assistance of Parker McKenzie.

After the Kiowa and Comanche alliance in 1806 (Mooney 1898:163–165), the two tribes shared common territory. The Kiowa camped more to the northwest along and south of the Arkansas River, while the Comanche tended to keep near the Staked Plains and the Texas frontier. The alliance made it possible for the Kiowa to pass through the southern extent of Comanche territory and to join the Comanche in raiding the Mexican settlements. After 1830, Kiowa raiding into Mexico became persistent and destructive (Mooney 1898:164–165). By 1840, peace was made with the Osage, Cheyenne, Arapaho, and Sioux, which served to protect the northern and eastern borders of the Kiowa range (Mooney 1898:169–172).

Environment

The Kiowa were close enough to Mexico to obtain a plentiful supply of horses and captives. They were able to trade with the Rio Grande Pueblos and the New Mexicans as well as with the Arikara and Mandan to the northeast. Moreover, the country around the Washita and Arkansas rivers was rich in buffalo and had mild winters. South of the Arkansas River, the country became progressively more drought prone, which meant that graze for both horses and buffalo was scarce during dry years. Unlike the buffalo herds of the central and northern Plains, Texas buffalo herds made seasonal migrations in large numbers (Roe 1951; Sandoz 1954). With the drying of the water courses, these herds moved northward in spring to the Arkansas River country (J.A. Allen 1876:137–141, 1876a).

A comparison of tree ring growth records with pictographic calendars kept by the Kiowa reveals that during dry periods the tribe was often unable to come together for the annual Sun Dance or to mount large-scale raids into Mexico (Levy 1961). The last mention of "many buffalo" in the Kiowa calendars was made in 1840. During the relatively dry years between 1846 and 1874 the Kiowa failed five times to hold the Sun Dance, and presumably the communal hunt. For three of these years the calendars note drought or dust during the summer. In contrast, prior to 1845 the Sun Dance was foregone only in 1841, a very wet year, when conditions were so good that the tribe scattered out in the Staked Plains to make horse raids into Mexico.

Culture, 1800–1870

Subsistence

Subsistence activities centered around the hunt, primarily for buffalo, and raiding for horses, both of which varied with the seasons. Fairly large winter camps were located along water courses where there was firewood and shelter. In late winter or early spring, when food supplies were low, small bands scattered over the countryside in search of game. By late spring, the buffalo began moving north out of Texas in increasing numbers. Related bands would then

Mus. für Völkerkunde, Berlin.

Fig. 2. Camp showing 7 tepees. According to the artist's journal the Kiowa camp "in sight of a small river shaded by cottonwood trees and shrubs . . . was of eighteen large tents" (Möllhausen 1858, 1:212). A war bonnet, lance, and shield are on a rack in front of the painted tepee. A woman on the left is scraping a hide, and behind the tepee is another hide being stretched. Drawing by Baldwin Möllhausen, on A.W. Whipple Expedition, 1853.

come together to hunt. In years when hunting was good, a number of bands moved together. In June and early July, the whole tribe gathered to conduct the Sun Dance. At this time, communal hunts were undertaken and raids were planned. Drought years often caused the buffalo to scatter, necessitating early dispersal of the bands for hunting. Hunting activity intensified during the fall in an effort to gather a supply of dried meat for the coming winter.

Technology

Kiowa material culture relied on the hides of buffalo, antelope, and elk for clothing, tepees, and equipment. Horns and antlers were used to make ladles, awls and knife handles. Carved stone pipes, feather bonnets, some metal work, and undecorated coiled gambling baskets were also made.

The pictographic calendars collected by Mooney (1898) documented historical events from Kiowa points of view during the period 1833–1893. Each calendar recorded an outstanding event for each winter and summer.

Clothing and Adornment

Men's dress consisted of two-piece moccasins with rawhide soles and uppers of tanned buffalo calfskin. Buffalo calfskin was also used to make shirts, leggings, breechcloths, and belts. Men wore buffalo robes over the upper half of the body, the tanned side often painted in a sunburst design of concentric circles composed of featherlike elements. Women wore high moccasin leggings (fig. 3), the tops of which were tied with hide strips. They also wore a

Smithsonian, Dept. of Anthr.: top left, 152,879, neg. 91-19243; bottom (dress), 385,892, neg. 38709-J; bottom (leggings), 152,836, neg. 79-5066. top center, Smithsonian, NAA:42997-A; top right, U.S. Dept. of Interior, Ind. Arts and Crafts Board, Southern Plains Ind. Mus., Anadarko, Okla.: A-79.7.1.

Fig. 3. Women's clothing and accessories. The Southern Plains style of woman's dress was made with 3 pronghorn or deer skins, 2 for the front and back of the skirt and one for the attached poncho-style top. Fringe and paint were used extensively for ornamentation, with elk teeth, prized throughout the Plains, added on the finest garments. top left, Cases for a knife and an awl made from commercial leather fitted with German silver. Collected by James Mooney in 1891; length of left 27 cm. top center, seated: woman wearing a velveteen dress; Maude Rowell (Mahbonee) wearing a fringed shawl; Amy Bear wearing fringed buckskin dress decorated with elk teeth, beaded legging-moccasins, dentalium choker and ball-and-cone earrings; Daisy Waterman wearing fringed buckskin dress decorated with elk teeth and leather belt with metal studs; Pau-tay, Tahbone's daughter, wearing fringed buckskin dress with beaded strip at neck; standing, girl wearing buckskin dress with cowrie shell decoration and flowered cloth shawl held in place with leather belt. Photograph by George Addison, Ft. Sill, Okla. Terr., 1890s. top right, Beaded buckskin bag made by Alice Littleman (b. 1910). The circular medallion is characteristic of 20th-century Kiowa beadwork. The use of pictorial designs in hanging bead fringe was Littleman's innovation, an elaboration of the simple bead fringe introduced by the Chiricahua Apaches imprisoned at Ft. Sill, adjacent to the Kiowa Res. Made in Anadarko, Okla., in 1979; length 38 cm. bottom, Buckskin dress painted yellow with bands of red and green, adorned with elk teeth, beadwork, fringe, and tin cones. Collected by James Glennan from the wife of Odlepah, 1892–1897; length 107 cm. Moccasin leggings of buckskin painted green and decorated with beadwork and metal sequins. They were worn tied just below the knee with the long upper flaps folded over. Collected by James Mooney in 1891; height 85 cm. All collected on the Kiowa Res., Okla. Terr.

blouse that hung over a skirt, and a wide rawhide belt from which were suspended a knife in its scabbard, an awl in a case (fig. 3), and a number of small bags containing sewing material and face paint. Women's robes were often painted in the border-and-box design.

Kiowa, Comanche, and Plains Apache clothing was distinctive among Plains tribes. There is no evidence that they ever used porcupine quillwork decoration, and, although the Kiowa sometimes made fully beaded moccasins and cradleboards (fig. 4), they preferred a delicate, light beaded trim around the edges of clothing. Women's dresses generally had only a simple beaded band across the shoulders. Men's garments normally employed simple

Fig. 4. Cradles. top, Family posed before canvas tepees, tent, and brush arbor. The girls wear fringed buckskin dresses with tin tinklers, necklaces of beads, moccasin leggings; one wears a finger-woven sash atypical of Kiowa, while the other wears a more typical belt of leather and metal studs. The girl on the right holds a doll cradle with a china-headed doll in it. The woman wears a cloth dress and shawl around her waist. The man wears Euro-American suit and shoes with watch chain and lapel pin. His braids and earrings are his only traditional adornment. Photograph by William Edward Irwin, 1893–1903. bottom, Lattice frame cradle with beaded cover made about 1900. It was used for Dorothy Rowell (b. 1903), daughter of Maude Rowell, a Kiowa, and her White husband, Dr. James Rowell. Representative of much of Kiowa beadwork, the design is asymmetrical, with a geometric pattern worked in netted stitch on one side and an abstract floral design in overlay stitch on the other side. Cradle covers are the only items that the Kiowa decorate with large areas of solid beadwork. Length 106 cm.

geometric elements done with a single row of lane stitch. Rather than using beadwork, they often filled large areas on buckskin clothing by painting them yellow, blue, or green and decorated them with fine, long, and sometimes twisted fringes.

The Kiowa are noted for two distinct forms of bead decoration, an overlay bead sewing technique used for abstract

floral designs and a technique of bead netting formerly used to decorate moccasins, baby carriers, and beaded pouches. Known as the "gourd" or "peyote" stitch, it came to be used throughout the Plains to decorate the fans, staffs, and rattles used in Native American Church ceremonies. Both styles may have been introduced to the Southern Plains by Delawares and Shawnees (Feder 1969:67–68).

Social Organization

The basic and most stable economic and social group was the extended family, which consisted of the families of several brothers and, under certain conditions, sisters. Classificatory siblings (cousins) and even adopted brothers might also be permanent members. Normally, the oldest brother was the recognized leader. Such a group was suited for the tasks of hunting and raiding because it was organized around active adult males whose primary allegiance was to one another (D. Collier 1938).

Descent was bilateral, permitting individuals to establish close ties with both the mother's and father's side of the family. Kinship terminology was generational: all children of parents' siblings were called brothers and sisters. In the parents' generation the terminology was bifurcate merging; mother and mother's sister were addressed by one term, while father and father's brother were addressed by another term. Separate terms were used for the father's sister and mother's brother. A man's brothers' children were called sons and daughters; his sisters' children were addressed by the term that was used for the mother's brother. Similarly, a woman's sisters' children were called sons and daughters; those of her brothers were addressed by a separate term. Men addressed maternal and paternal grandfathers and all grandchildren by the same term. Women used this term only for grandfathers and referred to grandchildren by separate terms. Men and women used separate terms for their paternal and maternal grandmothers. All great grandparents and great-grandchildren were addressed as brothers and sisters.

• FAMILY Consisting of parents and their unmarried children, the family was the smallest recognized unit of Kiowa society. Brothers exercised a degree of control over their sisters' choice of mates to guarantee compatibility with brothers-in-law who might join in their hunting activities. Men were also responsible for their sisters' well-being and were expected to take their part in marital conflicts. This responsibility was also extended to sisters' children, who often regarded their maternal uncles as second fathers. Most often polygyny was sororal, whereby a man married two or more women related to one another as "sisters." A man was responsible for his brother's wife and, in the event his brother died, the levirate obligated him to marry the widow and provide for her children. A man addressed his wife, his wife's sister, and his brother's wife by the same term, indicating the equating of these relatives and the possibility of marriage to them.

It was not uncommon for two or more brothers and sisters to marry siblings from another family. This practice enlarged the hunting group of the same generation. Residence after marriage was bilocal. Sometimes band leaders gave their daughters or sisters to men of lesser rank who would then join the wife's band.

• BANDS The basic political unit was the band (tò·pɔ̀tó·gɔ̀) headed by a band leader (tò·pɔ̀tó·k̓ì·). Band size varied considerably according to the wealth and prestige of the leader and to the season. Wealthy band leaders would attract sons-in-law, poor relatives, and individuals who had no kin.

There may have been as many as 40 bands averaging about 35 people but ranging in size from the smallest viable extended family of about 20 persons to bands three to four times that size. In late spring, as the food supply became more plentiful, small bands would combine to form groups large enough to hunt the buffalo herds coming north from Texas. During this period there may have been as few as 20 bands.

The band leader was usually the oldest brother of the core extended family. When two or more bands combined, the senior band leader was recognized as headman so that there was only one leader regardless of the size or composition of the group. The band leader was responsible for maintaining law and order without the use of force, directing the movements of the band, and planning for defense against enemy attack (J.H. Richardson 1940:77).

• TRIBE When the Kiowa developed a tribal identity is unknown, but it may have occurred when they adopted the Sun Dance. All the bands came together to perform the ceremony, and leaders came to be recognized at the tribal level. According to Kiowa tradition, there were seven autonomous, named divisions, each comprising a number of bands: Biters, or Arikara, so called because they had an intimate trading relationship with the Arikara; Elks; Kiowa proper, who were perhaps the original nucleus of the Kiowa tribe; Big Shields; Thieves, the Plains Apache, who spoke an Athapaskan language and who were an integral part of the tribal circle for as long as the Kiowa could remember; Black Boys, or Sendeh's children, the smallest division; and Pulling Up, who were said to have been exterminated by the Sioux about 1780, and to have spoken a peculiar dialect of Kiowa (Mooney 1898:228–229).

The bands were organized into local groups called by geographical designations. The Cold People (t'ó·k̓yą́·hyòp) lived along the Arkansas River in southwestern Kansas, while the Hot People (sálk̓yą́·hyóp) lived farther south; during the 1860s the latter group became associated with the Kwahada Comanche on the Staked Plains of the Texas Panhandle and became known as Guhale (gúhàlè·gɔ̀), the Kiowa form of the name Kwahada. Some Comanches recognized an unnamed middle group as well (Mooney 1898:227; Kracht 1989:371–374). These groups were strictly geographical and ceased to exist after the Kiowa moved to their reservation.

During the annual encampment the named divisions occupied set places forming a large circle; the Sun Dance was performed; one or more communal hunts were organized and policed by one of the men's societies; and the principal chiefs discussed affairs important to the entire tribe. Decisions to wage war or to make peace with other tribes or with the Anglo-Americans were made at this time.

Leadership roles accrued to those with demonstrated ability and were not inherited. Besides the band leaders there was also a ranking chief of each division and a nominal head chief of the whole tribe. Tribal affairs were conducted by the head chief, the chiefs of the divisions, and a group of war chiefs comprised of the most respected and powerful of the band leaders.

• RANK AND STATUS Status ranking was central to Kiowa social organization. The development of status differentiation was probably a direct consequence of the horse economy. As hunting and raiding on horseback permitted the skilled individual to accrue more wealth and consumable goods than was possible for the hunters of the prehorse period, horses became the principal form of wealth. Some families owned no horses, many owned 6–10, and well-to-do families owned herds numbering 20–50 animals or more. An average family of five adults required 10 pack horses, 5 riding horses, and 2–5 buffalo runners (Mishkin 1940:19–20). With a herd larger than 20 head, a wealthy man could loan a few horses to enable a promising youth to go on a raid. If he were successful, the loan would be repaid with interest in the form of a share in the bounty, whether horses or captives (Mishkin 1940:45).

The Kiowa formalized status differences by creating a system of named ranks (J.H. Richardson 1940:15; Mishkin 1940:35):

1. ɔ̂·dèk̓ì· ɔ̂·gòp 'rich, of high society', composed of the greatest warriors, the most important band leaders, most owners of the 10 medicine bundles, and men of great wealth if also distinguished with good war records.

2. ɔ̂·dègù·pày 'followers of the elite', composed of lesser band leaders (often men of wealth but possessing fewer war honors), most medicine men, and some successful younger warriors.

3. kʰɔ́·ɔ̀n 'mediocre, pitiable, humble', meaning commoners, who owned few horses and so could not join raiding parties frequently enough to accumulate war honors.

4. dɔ̀pôm 'nobodies', the tribe's bad characters and misfits, who did not share the major Kiowa values.

The basic distinction was between the rich and the poor, the two higher ranks versus the two lower. Enterprising men could rise from the commoner rank. Because rank depended on a war record and exemplary behavior as well as on horse wealth, it is difficult to estimate the number of men in each rank. In 1871 the Kiowa, with a population of about 1,330, owned approximately 3,750 of the 5,000 horses owned by the combined Kiowa and Plains Apache tribes, and it is possible that they owned as many as 4,500 head in 1868 (Ewers 1955:23). Mishkin's (1940:37) more conservative estimate of highest rank, 10 percent; second rank, 40 percent; commoners, 40 percent; lowest rank, 10 percent agrees with these data if the first rank averaged a herd of 50 horses per active male; second rank, 30; third rank, 5; and fourth rank, 0. By this count the horses owned by 240 active males come to 4,080. According to J.H. Richardson (1940:24), half of the "great" band leaders were also owners of the 10 medicine bundles, suggesting that there were about 20 great band leaders of the highest rank.

Women had the rank of the family they were born into; a commoner woman could become a member of one of the higher ranks through marriage. Mexican captives were most often adopted into a family in the two higher ranks. The adoptee was a commoner, but could aspire to become a member of the second rank.

The system allowed for social mobility, but if it was possible to gain wealth, it was quite as easy to lose it. A horse herd could be wiped out by a single raid or by a severe blizzard or drought. There was, in consequence, a need for some means to preserve a man's social status and to reestablish his herd. The first was accomplished by dissociating status rank from actual wealth and linking it to achieved war honors. The second was accomplished by the men's societies whose membership cut across kin lines, providing a network of brothers in other bands who were obliged to help fellow society members. In this way, an extensive support system based on the social prestige reflected in society membership was brought into being.

All Kiowa men, but especially the two higher ranks, were supposed to be dignified, peaceful, generous, hospitable, and gentle toward women. In theory, the high-ranking individual who did not live up to the ideal would lose status. Yet disputes were almost always settled in favor of higher-ranking individuals and many high-ranking warriors flagrantly breached behavioral norms without suffering any consequences of note.

Men's Societies

According to Lowie (1916a:841–842) and D. Collier (1938) all Kiowa men's societies (*yàppàhê·*) were of equal rank. Other investigators reported that with the exception of two age-graded societies—the *pʰòlą̀·hyòp* 'rabbits' for young boys and the *áltóyòy* 'herders' (also called Sheep) for youths—the societies for adult males were ranked by social status (Mooney 1898:230; Marriott 1936–1956; Mishkin 1940). It is not certain whether these societies had a formal ranking or could increase their prestige by attracting more successful members.

The *cè·tʰánmɔ̀* 'horses' headdresses' was the lowest in rank; its members were young and included some commoners as well as higher-ranked men.

The *tʰò·kʰǫ́·gɔ́* 'black legs' was the only society other than the Principal Dogs for which the achievement of war honors was a prerequisite for membership. The Black Legs ranked slightly beneath the Gourd Dancers; its members

were said to have been younger on average, although most of them were of the second rank, and many went on to become members of the Gourd Dance society.

The *táypègɔ̀* 'skunkberry people' was known in the twentieth century as the Gourd Dance society, and Marriott (1936–1956) was told that it was considered to have been the oldest of the men's societies. In its organization and functions it resembled the Cheyenne Bowstring society. While it demanded brave conduct in warfare, war honors were not a prerequisite for membership. Its members were from the higher ranks.

The *kóycégɔ̀* 'principal dogs' was founded after the Gourd Dancers but came to outrank it. It was the most exclusive of the societies and was open to only the highest-ranking war chiefs. There were only 10 full members, each having a younger partner (Mooney 1898:285). According to Marriott's informants, these neophytes were not relatives of the members but were chosen by them and were called brothers. They were all from the higher ranks and had achieved at least four war honors. When a full member died, the younger partner became a member in his place.

The relative social ranking was a consequence of the expansion of the system of men's societies. All the societies demanded some wealth of their members at the time of initiation and in order to dance and validate war honors. But as time passed, young men started new societies that may well have attained status as their members matured. The exception, of course, was the Principal Dogs, which appears to have been founded specifically for the purpose of setting the great and wealthy warriors apart. The social ideal was egalitarian, and it is often said that all Kiowa males were members of one society or another. But, as each society only had 50 members on average, it seems that over one-third of the adult male population was unable to accumulate the wealth necessary for membership.

The *čálì·cò·hyòp* 'calf old women' society was the women's counterpart of the men's societies and was equal in rank to the Gourd Dancers. The society had war power. Men presented the members with gifts before setting out on a war party and feasted them on their return from a successful raid. There was a large initiation fee, which served to restrict membership to higher-ranking women (Lowie 1916a:849–850).

Each society had two leaders and two whip bearers who watched over the behavior of their members. These societies functioned only during the four weeks of the Sun Dance encampment (J.H. Richardson 1940:9). During this time, they sponsored feasts and entertainments and accepted new members. They kept order in the camp and participated in the sham battles and bringing of the pole in preparation for the Sun Dance. Except for policing the communal hunt, their functions were social and economic.

Men's societies validated members' war honors and their social status by hosting feasts and presenting gifts to guests. By so doing, wealth was redistributed; generosity and hospitality were qualities demanded of all members of the higher ranks. Another means for the display and redistribution of wealth by families of the highest rank was through the selection of a child to be honored as ɔ́·dé· 'favored child' who would be given a separate tepee in which to live and to entertain friends. The youth's friends and fellow society members would be entertained lavishly for several nights in a row (Marriott 1945:101–111).

Religion

The foundation of Kiowa religion was a belief in dɔ́y 'sacred power', a pervasive force that could be localized in specific spirits, objects, or places. Animals like the eagle, hawk, or buffalo, as well as the sun, moon, and winds were recognized as important personifications, or loci, of supernatural power. This force was neither good nor bad but could help or harm depending on the user's intent and qualifications. In a dream or trance state human beings could receive specific powers from spirits, together with instructions for their proper use. An individual who controlled power was called a dɔ́yɔ́mk̓í· 'medicine man' or shaman.

A man sought power at an isolated spot in the hills, where he fasted, smoked and prayed. If successful, a vision was induced in which a spirit appeared who became a guardian and helper. It was thought unlikely that a man could succeed in life without a spirit helper, and it was therefore common for men to repeat the quest, to attain power through inheritance or purchase (E.C. Parsons 1929:xix; Marriott 1945:44–49), or to dance for power in the Sun Dance.

It was not considered appropriate for an individual to announce publicly the results of his vision quest, but rather to do so through demonstrations of his power. However, many men went through life without ever attaining power, and the chances for success appear to have favored those of the higher ranks. It was very difficult for commoner youths, without horses, to attain war honors, and only those who could get higher-ranking backers were likely to be successful and, in consequence, become known as possessors of supernatural power.

• SACRED BUNDLES   Ten tribal "medicines" belonged to the Kiowa for as long as they could remember. They are referred to as t̓à·lî·dɔ́y 'boy medicines' (Mooney 1898:239; J.P. Harrington 1928:184), sometimes called in English the Ten Grandmothers (Marriott 1945). (Some Kiowas identify the first element of this term with t̓à·lî· 'paternal grandmother (vocative)' rather than t̓àlí· 'young boy, two young boys'.) The sacred myth of the Split Boys explained the origin of these medicine bundles. In this story, a variant of the Star Husband narrative, a woman married Sun Boy and bore his son. Following the mother's death, the boy was raised by Spider Old Woman. After being split in two, the resulting twins experienced a series of adventures in which they rid the world of monsters. Finally, one brother disappeared into the water and the survivor transformed himself into a "medicine" that, divided into 10 portions, was preserved in the Boy Medicine bundles (Mooney 1898:238–239; E.C. Parsons 1929:1–8).

The Boy Medicine bundles were the most revered powers the tribe possessed and were used to settle disputes and cure the sick. Anyone could offer gifts to a bundle and pray to it. The keeper of a bundle had to care for it and observe its taboos, among which was the stipulation that no violence could occur in its presence. In consequence, the 10 tepees in which the bundles were kept served as sanctuaries where individuals might take refuge. The keeper of a Boy Medicine bundle presented the peace pipe to disputants and helped them agree to settle their quarrel (J.H. Richardson 1940:10–12). Because the Boy Medicines represented the supernatural sanctions underlying tribal mores, their very presence helped maintain social harmony.

The Sun Dance, called k̓ɔ́·tó, was the major religious ceremony. The symbolic center of the ceremony was the Taime (t̓áymé), a small image representing a human figure, which assured a plentiful supply of buffalo and general well-being for the entire tribe. Individuals participated in the ceremony to obtain supernatural power or to add to the power they already possessed. The Kiowa Sun Dance did not include self-torture, and it was believed that any blood shed accidently during the ceremony would negate its power and bring misfortune to the entire tribe (Mooney 1898:242–243).

According to tradition, two Taime bundles, one male, the other female, were obtained from an Arapaho man who had received them as a gift from the Crow and brought them with him when he married a Kiowa woman. According to Mooney (1898:241), this occurred around 1770, although apparently the Kiowa had been performing the ceremony for some years previously (see also H.L. Scott 1911; Spier 1921a). In addition to its use in the Sun Dance, the male Taime bundle might also be carried to war. The Kiowa later captured another male Taime bundle from the Blackfoot. However, in a battle in 1868, both male Taime were lost to the Ute and were never returned (Mooney 1898:242).

The Big Shield division of bands once owned a small image known as "Old Woman Under the Ground," which was exposed in front of the Taime during the Sun Dance. This image was stolen some time before 1890. There was also a woman's ritual dedicated to the "star girls" (Pleiades) that was obsolete by 1890 (Mooney 1898:239).

• SHIELD SOCIETIES   Keepers of the Boy Medicines passed them on to their heirs along with the attendant powers that belonged to the tribe rather than to the keeper. Shamans passed their powers on to chosen apprentices who paid for their instruction. However, it was preferred that a man acquire power on a vision quest before obtaining it by purchase or inheritance. Individuals often made war shields with designs that depicted the nature of their power (fig. 5). A man could bequeath his shield to a son or sell it to a friend. The Kiowa developed several associations, known as shield societies, which enabled a man to share supernatural power with his relatives and closest friends, thus

913

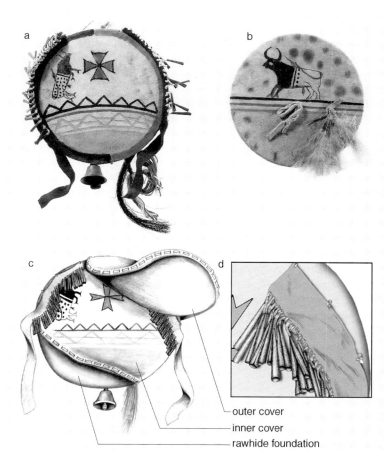

Fig. 5. Shields. left, Tsentainte (*cê·tàỳdè*; White Horse) (d. 1892) holding a war shield and Winchester carbine. He wears a horn head ornament with feathers attached. Photograph by W. Lenny, Purcell, Okla. Terr., 1892. right, Models copied from the Cow Shield carried by Tsentainte. The designs originated in a vision that Guikati (*kûyk̀ɔ·dè*; Wolf Lying Down) had while on a cattle raid into Mexico in the 1820s. The cross on the inner cover (a) represents the Morning Star, while a longhorn bull, a source of spiritual power, is depicted on both the inner and outer cover (b) (Merrill et al. 1997:24-25). James Mooney hired the artist Silverhorn (*hɔ́·gὺ·*) to paint these models on buckskin in 1902–1904. Kiowa shields typically consisted of 3 layers (c), an unpainted rawhide foundation, a painted inner buckskin cover exposed only when the shield was carried into battle, and an outer buckskin cover, usually also painted. This shield was trimmed with metal cones hanging from red wool streamers (d), and a large cowbell, which rang when the outer cover was thrown back and the shield shaken at the enemy. Tsentainte's horn head ornament was attached to the inner cover of the shield when not in use. Base of each model, 17 cm in diameter. Drawings by Roger Thor Roop.

enhancing the power and prestige of a group of brothers and their allies. The most detailed accounts of the shield societies were recorded by Marriott (1936–1956).

The Taime Shields were the oldest of the men's shield societies and represented the power of the Taime. Members had to be rich, present many gifts to the Taime keeper, and guard the Taime and its keeper during tribal encampments. One Taime keeper, while still a young man, had a vision during which he was instructed to make seven shields "for the Taime" to protect it. The shields, covered with elk hides, were hung behind the Taime in the Sun Dance lodge. Over time the membership was expanded until there were about 20 members in the 1870s. Because additional shields were never made, by 1889 there were only four left.

The Eagle Shields society started after the Taime Shields and had comparable prestige. Sitting Bear (*sétą́·gyày*, known to the Whites as Satank), the greatest war chief of

the tribe and the last chief of the Principal Dogs (Mooney 1898:284), was the leader of this society from about 1850 to 1870, having received his shield from the society's founder. The originator of the society made 23 shields, suggesting that one of the important motivations was the desire to establish a network of alliances. The eagle power was for war, and those who owned eagle shields were particularly courageous and believed to be invulnerable in battle.

In addition, the society's founder had other sacred powers that instructed him to make two tepees, one decorated with birds, the other with fishes. These sacred powers also gave him a magic knife that could be swallowed and hidden until needed. The founder offered an eagle shield to Sitting Bear when he was still a young man. According to family tradition, Sitting Bear initially refused the offer because of the number of taboos surrounding the power. After his father dreamed he should take the shield, he accepted but also asked for the magic knife, which many Kiowa believe he used on the occasion of his death at Fort Sill (Mooney 1898:332–333; Nye 1937:144–147). The shields were decorated with gun designs, but, according to one of Marriott's informants, seven shields were painted like the Taime shields with an eagle, wings spread, in the center.

The Buffalo Shields society members had healing power. They cured wounds and broken bones and accompanied war parties as doctors. The society was founded by a woman sometime after the Eagle Shields. There were at first only 12 buffalo shields, but by 1870 there were 20 and as many as 30 members who were the elite of the curers. No woman could belong to the society. The leaders were all descendants of the woman who first had the vision and, if a patient being doctored by a society member was going to get well, her voice, coming from the top of the tepee, would join those of the singers.

During the years immediately preceding the Treaty of Medicine Lodge of 1867, the Five Shields and Owl Shield societies were founded. Like the Eagle Shields, the Five Shields were based on war power; however, they were not accepted until the founder demonstrated that his shield had saved his life in battle. The society never had more than five members.

Members of the Owl Shields had the power to prophesy and to enlist the spirits of the dead to find lost articles. The society was started by Mamanti (*mâmą̀·tè* 'sky walker'), whose owl power could foretell the outcome of a raiding party. He and his three apprentices painted themselves white with blue owl designs on their chests and backs when going into battle (Nye 1937:194). Shields were passed from father to son, nephew, or occasionally, a son-in-law. The transfer had to be made before the owner's death. The core of the society comprised several related extended families.

The Bear Old Women Society was considered by some Kiowas to have been related to the shield societies in general and to the Taime Shields in particular. It was a greatly feared women's secret society that controlled bear power. The members were women of various ages who selected their daughters or close kin to succeed them (Lowie 1916:849–850). The society members acted like bears (Marriott 1968:151), wore bear claw necklaces as medicine, and some of them dressed like men (E.C. Parsons 1929:xv). Parents of a sick child might promise a feast to these women at the Sun Dance so that the child might get well (E.C. Parsons 1929:96). On their meeting days, children and young people were sent out of the camp. Bear power was stronger even than the power of the Boy Medicines; even the Taime was said to have been afraid of Bear, and the animal was taboo to all Kiowa. It is possible that this society was one of the oldest Kiowa societies.

Mythology

The myth of the Split Boys was part of a sacred cycle of myths about Spider Old Woman and her grandsons. These could only be told during the summer months and, in theory, only by keepers of the Boy Medicines. The keepers convened each year at the time of the Sun Dance when each bundle was opened in turn and its part of the myth cycle told (Marriott and Rachlin 1975:39–40). A second cycle of myths concerning Sendeh (*séndé*)—creator, culture hero, and trickster—was told during the winter (vol. 17:271). For example, one origin narrative recorded by Mooney (1898:152) tells how the trickster led the people out of a dark world into the present one by climbing up a hollow cottonwood log; when a pregnant woman became stuck in the log, the way was blocked for the remainder of the people. This accounted for the small size of the Kiowa tribe.

History

Trade and Treaties, 1802–1867

Contacts between itinerant American traders and the Kiowa began about 1802. By the late 1820s trading posts were established for the Kiowa, Comanche, and Wichita. William Bent built a substantial adobe trading post on the Arkansas River in 1834; in 1835 Auguste Chouteau built a post on the Canadian River and in 1837 another on Cache Creek, three miles south of later Fort Sill. These were followed in the early 1840s by Bent's Post on the South Canadian River, in the Texas Panhandle, near the principal Kiowa trails (fig. 1).

In 1833, Tohausen (*tòhɔ̀sàn*; Little Bluff [I]) became principal chief of the Kiowa, retaining the position until his death in 1866 (Mooney 1898:164). Under his leadership the Kiowa prospered. In 1834 friendly relations were established between the allied Kiowa and Comanche, the United States government, and the Creek and Osage with whom the Kiowa had been at war. The peace with the Osage and Creek was never broken. The federal government signed formal treaties with the Comanche in 1835 and the Kiowa in 1837 (Kappler 1904–1941, 2:435–439,489–491; see also DeMallie 1986a). The two tribes agreed to peace with the United States and Mexico and recognized the government's right to build roads and military posts in their territory when they signed the Treaty of Fort Atkinson in 1853 (Kappler 1904–1941, 2:600–602). Although relatively good relations were maintained with the United States government, the tribes continued to raid into Texas, Mexico, and New Mexico until after the Civil War. In 1864, Tohausen's village near Adobe Walls, the ruins of Bent's trading post on the Canadian River, was attacked and burned by federal troops under command of Lt. Col. Christopher Carson (Pettis 1908). The Little Arkansas Treaty of 1865 attempted to restore peaceful conditions, and—over the objection of Tohausen—the Kiowa agreed to accept a reservation in western Oklahoma and Texas jointly with the Comanche (Kappler 1904–1941, 2:892–895). By the Treaty of Medicine Lodge with the Kiowa, Plains Apache, Comanche, Cheyenne, and Arapaho, the United States government prohibited White hunters from invading reser-

Fig. 6. War shirt acquired from the Kiowa Tohausen (Little Bluff III, d. 1894). His father, Chief Little Bluff (I), was an ally of the Crow, and the shirt is of Crow origin, as evident in the poncho cut and the flat panels of beadwork (C.S. Greene 1996:237–239). left, Tohausen and his wife Ankima. Photograph by James Mooney, Anadarko, Okla. Terr., 1893. right, Shirt made of soft tanned hide streaked with blue paint and trimmed with pendants of ermine skin, horsehair, and human hair (reported to be from Navajos killed by the Kiowa) and painted rawhide case in which the shirt was kept. Width of shirt, 127 cm, length of case, 52 cm. Both collected by James Mooney on the Kiowa Res., Okla. Terr.

vation lands and granted annuities (including rifles and ammunition), schools, churches, and farming implements. In return the Indians ended hostilities, granted railroad rights of way, and agreed to settle on a smaller reservation (Kappler 1904–1941, 2:177–184).

The Reservation Period, 1868–1900

Early in 1868, when the government rations promised by treaty failed to arrive, the Kiowa and Comanche began raiding the Wichita, Caddo, and Chickasaw for food and horses. They made raids into Texas during the summer and fall while the Cheyenne and Arapaho made similar raids in Colorado and Kansas. As the army planned a winter campaign against the Cheyenne, efforts were made to get the Kiowa and Comanche to settle on their reservation to avoid embroiling them in the conflict (Nye 1937:54). By November, many Kiowas were camped along the Washita River, presumably out of harm's way; others, including the Comanche, were farther to the south and west hunting buffalo. Kiowa chiefs Big Tree and Woman's Heart were with the Cheyenne. On November 26, 1868, Lt. Col. George A. Custer attacked the Cheyenne under Black Kettle, who had moved his people south and camped downstream from the large winter camps of the Kiowa, Plains Apache,

Comanche, and Arapaho. As a consequence of Black Kettle's defeat, known as the Battle of the Washita, all these tribes complied with government demands and settled within the confines of their reservations. Within a year, Fort Sill was built in the center of the Kiowa, Plains Apache, and Comanche reservation.

The Kiowa and Comanche continued to raid into Texas throughout the early 1870s, on one occasion even attacking the agency at Fort Sill. The Indians' grievances included violations of the Medicine Lodge treaty, most importantly the illegal slaughtering of buffalo by the thousands by White hunters on lands designated as Indian hunting territory. It was alleged that these hunters sold liquor, arms, and ammunition to the Indians in return for stolen livestock. The winter of 1873–1874 was a time of hardship; rations were so scanty that the Indians living close to the agency were forced to kill their horses and mules for food at the same time they were being robbed of their stock by bands of horse thieves (Mooney 1898:199–201; Nye 1937:188).

Hostilities that erupted during 1874 clearly defined the peaceful and hostile factions. Prior to this time, the majority of chiefs sided with the one side or the other depending on their estimation of each situation as it arose. Sitting Bear (Satank, *sétá·gyày*) (fig. 7), who frequently refrained from joining raiding parties after the Medicine Lodge treaty,

916

Fig. 7. Chiefs—3 of 9—who signed the Treaty of Medicine Lodge in 1867. left, Lone Wolf (d. 1879) holding pipe tomahawk. He was imprisoned at Ft. Marion, Fla., 1875–1878. center, Sitting Bear (b. 1810, d. 1871) in a buffalo robe, leader of the Principal Dogs Society, the highest-ranking men's society. He was killed at Ft. Sill while trying to escape arrest. right, Kicking Bird (d. 1875) wearing a hairpipe breastplate and holding what appears to be a quiver of arrows. Although a warrior of high standing he realized early the unequal struggle against the U.S. Army and became a persistent advocate for peace. His death may have been due to poison (Nye 1937:234; Mayhall 1962:254). Photographs by William Soule, left and center, Ft. Sill., Okla., 1869–1872; right, Ft. Dodge, Kan., 1868.

ultimately joined the hostiles again when his son was killed in Texas. During the outbreak the only chiefs who clearly identified themselves as peacefuls were Kicking Bird (tè·néɔgópté) (fig. 7) and his cousins Stumbling Bear (sétèmkí·ą· 'bear comes throwing himself forward') and Goon-saudl-te (gų·sɔ́ldè 'the horned'), who remained at Fort Sill. The rest of the important chiefs and virtually all the younger warriors sided with Lone Wolf (kûypá·gɔ̀y) (fig. 7), leader of the hostiles and the principal chief. About half the tribe remained with Kicking Bird at Fort Sill.

In December, after a series of defeats, most of the hostiles were returned to the reservation. The army jailed the principal hostile chiefs and confiscated their weapons, horse herds, and most of their material goods. Women and children were placed in detention camps on East Cache Creek (Nye 1937:229). The government recognized Kicking Bird as principal chief and instructed him to select 26 of the hostiles for imprisonment at Fort Marion in Florida. Kicking Bird, desiring to protect his friends, chose only a few of the prominent leaders, making up the rest of the quota with Mexican captives and young men of no great reputation (Mooney 1898:215–216). This created a division between the peacefuls' bands and the rest of the tribe that lasted for many years.

• RELIGION   After the military defeat in 1874, many Kiowa realized that the powers of individual warriors were ineffective against the army. The greater number of Kiowa and Comanche warriors "threw their powers away," and a search for new sources of power began.

The Sun Dance was outlawed by the federal government, and the last one was performed in 1887. Episcopalians began missionizing in 1882, followed by Methodists in 1887, and later by Presbyterians, Baptists, and Roman Catholics. A number of nativistic religions came into being shortly after the reservation was established. Prophets, foretelling the return of the buffalo and the old way of life, and the destruction of White civilization, began their activities in 1882 (Mooney 1898:350). Many Kiowas became involved in the Ghost Dance movement in 1890. Peyote, said to have been introduced to the Kiowa and Comanche around 1870 by the Mescalero Apache and other tribes to the south, developed into a religion by the 1880s (La Barre 1938:111–112).

The choice to follow one of the nativistic leaders or Christianity was left to the individual and did not require the rejection of tribal religion. Kiowas became involved in the prophetic movements at the same time they were active Peyotists or churchgoers; few abandoned their belief in the Boy Medicines or the Taime. However, there was a brief period in the late 1880s when the followers of the prophet Pau-in-kie (pɔ́ygyày), calling themselves the Sons of the Sun, objected to Peyotism on the ground that it conflicted with traditional Kiowa religion (La Barre 1938:112).

Ultimately, the Ghost Dance and the local prophetic movements died out while the Peyote ritual survived and spread, providing an accommodation to reservation conditions through the establishment of the Native American

Church (fig. 8) (Slotkin 1956:17–21). In addition to the rapid spread of the Peyote religion, the final years of the nineteenth century witnessed the proliferation of celebrations—which came to be called powwows—during which Indians from several tribes gathered, sharing songs, dances, and news. In short, a pan-Indian identity began to form that served as the foundation for cultural revival in the twentieth century. In this process, the Kiowa were prominent as disseminators of Peyotism and participants in powwows.

• ECONOMY   In the economic sphere, two programs for rehabilitation fought for supremacy on the reservation. On the one hand, Texas cattle interests sought to preserve the reservation as cheap grazing land, blocking westward expansion of White farmers. Lease payments provided cash income, and some individual Indians built up herds of their own. On the other hand, Eastern reformers sought to have reservation lands allotted in the attempt to transform the Indians into farmers.

Although the Indians preferred ranching to farming and several chiefs had built up sizable herds, the Bureau of Indian Affairs discouraged the development of a ranching economy and pushed instead for the adoption of agriculture. Agents leased tribal pastures to Texas cattlemen in return for beef to supplement inadequate government rations in 1881, and in 1885 for cash distributed on a per capita basis. From 1892 to 1897 a number of Kiowa men gained employment in the Indian cavalry troop at Fort Sill; however, by the end of the century the role of farmer came to offer greater economic rewards.

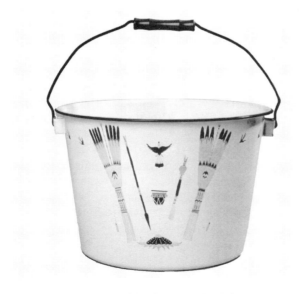

U. of Okla., Sam Noble Okla. Mus. of Nat. Hist., Norman: NAM 9-13-110.
Fig. 8. Peyote bucket, enameled metal, painted by Lee Monette Tsatoke with images from the Native American Church—fans, staff, rattle, drum, birds, and a peyote button resting on a bed of sage. Such buckets are used to bring water into the ceremonial tepee at midnight and at dawn. Purchased in 1967 in Anadarko, Okla.; height 20 cm.

Allotment, 1901–1932

In 1892 the Cherokee Commission held meetings with the Kiowa, Comanche, and Plains Apache to persuade them to sign the Jerome Agreement, which stipulated that all tribal members, young or old, were to receive 160 acres of land of their own selection. Excess land was to be sold by the government for $1.25 per acre. Allotments were to be held in trust for 25 years, after which they were to be given to the owner as fee simple titles. The government agreed to pay $2,000,000 to draw 5 percent interest annually in the United States Treasury. By late October 1892 the Commission was satisfied that enough signatures had been obtained, but before it could be implemented, Congress had to give its approval (U.S. Senate 1893; Hagan 1976:205–215; Nye 1937:388–389).

The Indians claimed they were misled and that the agreement was obtained by fraud; they were aided in their opposition by Capt. Hugh L. Scott and the cattlemen who benefited from the leasing of Indian range land. Although article 12 of the Medicine Lodge treaty stipulated that future land cessions would require the consent of at least three-fourths of the adult male Indians, the Jerome Agreement was signed by only 456 members of the three tribes, and when it was presented to the Senate in 1899, the secretary of the interior noted that the required percentage of signatures had not been obtained. Nonetheless, the agreement was ratified in June 1900.

Lone Wolf, the adopted son of the principal chief of the same name, filed a bill in equity on the grounds that the Medicine Lodge treaty had been violated and that the signatures had been obtained by fraud and misrepresentation. In what has come to be known as the "Lone Wolf doctrine," the Supreme Court, in 1903, decided the case (*Lone Wolf* v. *Hitchcock*) in favor of the government. The opinion of the Court was that (1) the Indians had only the right of occupancy but that the fee was in the United States; (2) Indian occupancy could be interfered with or determined by the government; (3) the propriety of such action toward the Indians was not open to inquiry in the courts (M.E. Price 1973:425–427).

The immediate effect of the Jerome Agreement was the destruction of the political and geographic integrity of the Kiowa, Comanche, and Plains Apache reservation. In 1901, two-thirds of the original 2,968,893 acre reservation was opened to non-Indian settlement; 551,680 acres were reserved as pasture for common use; 443,338 acres were allotted to 2,759 members of the three tribes. In 1906, 480,000 acres of the tribal pasture were sold by the secretary of the interior leaving the tribes in possession of only 17 percent of their original reservation.

Despite their subordinate position under the reservation system, Indian leadership and community organization had not been entirely subverted. Law and order were maintained for the most part by Indian police; civil cases were decided in Indian court, and the only Whites with sustained contact with Indian people were federal employees and missionaries. Between 1901 and 1906, the last vestiges of political autonomy and legal corporateness were destroyed as the Indians were surrounded by non-Indian settlers. In 1907, immediately after the dissolution of the reservations, what had been Indian and Oklahoma territories were united in the new state of Oklahoma.

The three tribes' affairs were handled by an agent in Anadarko, Oklahoma, who also had jurisdiction over the Caddo and Wichita. A business council was established whose members were at first appointed by the agent, and subsequent to 1908 were elected. The money the government paid for the land was kept in trust and dispensed at intervals on a per capita basis. In addition, the three tribes received small oil royalties on land along the Red River, which formed the southern boundary of the former reservation. Few Kiowas became farmers; most leased their land to White tenants. The vast majority of the tribe was exceedingly poor even before the collapse of the agricultural economy in 1920 and the great drought of 1934, which turned the southern Plains into a "dust bowl." The tenants, themselves on relief, were often unable to pay for their leases either in cash or crops, and it was not until the New Deal policies of President Franklin D. Roosevelt that conditions began to improve.

The New Deal and Beyond, 1933–1980s

The Oklahoma Indian Welfare Act of 1936 provided for the establishment of tribal governments incorporated under state law with limited powers of self-government, the cessation of Indian land sales, and the establishment of a revolving credit fund. Although the Kiowa, Comanche, and Plains Apache never drew up a charter of incorporation under the act, the government dealt with their intertribal business committee as if it were a corporate body. In the late 1960s, the Comanche withdrew from the committee, and subsequently each tribe was governed by its own Tribal Business Committee according to a constitution and bylaws accepted by the Bureau of Indian Affairs for the Comanche in 1966, the Kiowa in 1970, and the Plains Apache in 1972.

The subdivision of land among descendants of each original allottee deprived successive generations of commercially viable acreage until by 1972 only 3.5 percent of all Kiowa lived on working farms despite the fact that the total of their allotted land—229,926 acres—had not declined appreciably since the 1930s.

During the New Deal years, Indians were given preference in government employment; the Bureau of Indian Affairs was expanded, and civilian employment on military reservations increased markedly after 1960. Thus, it is not surprising that 39 percent of all employed Kiowa over age 15 were in the employ of federal, tribal, or local government in 1970. In 1970, the median Kiowa family income was $5,285 while that of the nation was $14,465, and unemployment stood at about 16 percent. At the same time, 52 percent of all

Natl. Arch.: 75-N-K10-80.

Fig. 9. Service station on the Kiowa Indian Agency, Anadarko, Okla. It was partly owned and operated by the students of the vocational training school at Ft. Sill, who shared in the profits. Photograph by Peter Sekaer, 1940.

Kiowas 25 and older were high school graduates (U.S. Bureau of the Census 1973:165).

The descendants of Kicking Bird and his brothers, the "peace chiefs," lived near Fort Sill while those of the "hostiles" lived to the north along the Washita River. The former were said to be predominantly Christian (Methodist), the latter Peyotist. The Taime and Boy Medicines were still cared for. The preservation of Kiowa identity was made difficult by the migration of younger families to cities and by the increased level of educational attainment in the public schools. Kiowa was not spoken by many children and those younger Kiowa who did speak it used a simplified vocabulary mixed with many English words. There were only a small number of older Kiowa who could speak the old language of oratory or knew the proper forms of address for relatives. Pantribal activities such as powwows and Indian veterans' clubs became popular in urban as well as rural areas.

During the reservation period and throughout the years of the Depression, local and intertribal powwows became popular social events. With the exception of the Principal Dogs, which had been disbanded, the men's societies continued as organizers of social dances as did the Ohumu (*óhò·mò·*) society, which was borrowed from the Cheyenne before 1900. These societies all ceased to function by the 1940s.

The participation of Indians in World War II (fig. 10) and the Korean and Vietnam conflicts enhanced the pride of a large proportion of younger Indians. Prior to the Second World War, there were few opportunities for young men to gain war honors although there were stories of scalp dances held in secret after both world wars. Veteran's status was always important, and after the Korean conflict, 919

Fig. 10. Horace Poolaw (b. 1906, d. 1984), right, an aerial photographer, and Gus Palmer, a gunner, in World War II. Poolaw trained Army Air Corps servicemen in aerial photography. His photograph collection spans the 1920s to 1978 (Poolaw 1990). Photograph by Horace Poolaw, MacDill Air Base, Tampa, Fla., about 1944.

an interest in Indian veterans' associations began to be noticeable in Oklahoma City as well as in the Kiowa area. Military service and a degree of economic success conferred status on those individuals who participated in the powwows, where accomplishments were publicly recognized. The old ranking system became moribund, although families were often referred to as high ranking or commoner on the basis of descent alone, and the term for the lowest class was still used as a derogatory epithet.

The powwow provided the occasion for sponsoring public giveaways to honor friends from other tribes as well as family members. In earlier years, at the Sun Dance, families gave away horses and other goods to honor favored children or young men returned from war. Not realizing that the giveaway was a form of social security as well as a display of wealth and a validation of family status, Indian agents and missionaries opposed it vociferously; but because it expressed the central Kiowa values of hospitality and generosity it retained its meaning and popularity.

The powwow and the giveaway became the vehicles for the revival of the Gourd Dance society (fig. 11), which was organized in 1956 by descendants of White Bear, its last

chief, and which the next year sponsored its first Fourth of July powwow at Carnegie, Oklahoma. To many Kiowas, it came to take the place of the Sun Dance (Marriott 1968:125–135). In 1958, families of society members pledged beef to support the next year's event and money to the Native American Church. The two elderly surviving Ohumu society members were honored and invited to revive that society, and the Black Legs society announced its resuscitation (fig. 12). The revival of the men's societies, especially the Gourd Dance society, heralded a cultural revival throughout the Plains (Levy 1959; J.H. Howard 1976a). The Kiowa Historical and Research Society published *Kiowa Voices* (Boyd 1981–1983), which described ceremonies and oral literature.

Individual Kiowas were successful in Euro-American society. N. Scott Momaday won the Pulitzer prize for literature in 1961 for his novel *House Made of Dawn*, and Kiowa physician Everett Rhoades served as assistant surgeon general in the U.S. Public Health Service, 1982–1993.

Art

Kiowa artists are considered to have played a part, even if indirectly, in creating the symbols of Indian nationalism. Sometime between 1917 and 1926, a Bureau of Indian Affairs employee, Susan Peters, organized a group of Kiowas into a fine arts club (Brody 1971:120–126) and gave them some formal instruction. She then arranged for some of the best students to attend classes at the University of Oklahoma. There, Spencer Asah, James Auchiah, Jack Hokeah, Stephen Mopope, and Monroe Tsa Toke, later known as the Kiowa Five, were placed in segregated art classes under Oscar B. Jacobson (fig. 13). Their more stylized paintings depicted powwow costumes, while others were nostalgic recreations of the old Plains Indian way of life. The style was decorative, with a stencil-like quality derived from the art moderne style of the 1920s and 1930s. It was thought of as uniquely Indian and persisted among Oklahoma Indian artists through the late twentieth century.

The work of the Kiowa painters had a great influence on the style of art taught at other schools, notably the Santa Fe Indian School and Bacone College, Muskogee, Oklahoma (Brody 1971:132–134). After the Second World War, Indian painting combined a number of styles and can usually be identified with either a Santa Fe or an Oklahoma pan-Indian tradition. These distinctive Indian styles not only were commercially successful but also provided many of the nostalgic, nationalistic symbols of the postwar cultural revitalization of the Plains and other tribes. Kiowa artists, notably Lee Tsa Toke, Dennis Belindo, Blackbear Bosin, and Herman Toppah worked in the Indian tradition.

Population

Kiowa population, according to Mooney (1898:235–237), was never much more than 1,200 or, at most, 1,350. No really

Fig. 11. Gourd Dance clan. left to right in line: John or Horace Gouladdle, Vernon Burr Ahtone, and Clyde Daingkau. Others in the dance group have been identified as: George Tsoodle, Henry Kaulaity, Jack Quetone, John Oliver Tenedooah (Tenadoah or Tanedoah), Ralph Kauley, Henry Tointigh, Kenneth Moore, and Leo Tsoodle. Photograph by Fred Huston, Carnegie, Okla., July 1969.

accurate count was made until the whole tribe settled on their reservation in 1875, at which time the Kiowa and Plains Apache combined totaled 1,414, the Kiowa accounting for about 1,000. Smallpox and cholera epidemics hit the Kiowa in 1801, 1816, 1839, and 1849 (Mooney 1898:168, 172, 173). The cholera epidemic of 1849 was remembered by the Kiowa as the most terrible experience in their history: "Hundreds died and many committed suicide in their desperation" (Mooney 1898:173). If as many as 200 or 300 died, the losses would have between 13 and 20 percent of the total population. In 1896, 15 percent of the population died in a measles epidemic (Mooney 1898:235). The earlier losses appear to have been recouped by assimilating captives, the majority of whom were Mexicans, into the tribe.

The Kiowa population was a young one, some 40 to 50 percent under 18 years of age (Salzano 1972). Mortality was probably high among infants and young children, and again between the ages of 25 and 45, especially among males who risked death in warfare and hunting. Perhaps less than 20 percent of the total population was over 65 years of age (Laughlin 1972). This means that there may have been from 600 to 675 adults of both sexes. It is also probable that there were more adult females than males so that a total of from 240 to 270 active adult males would be a generous estimate.

In 1970 approximately 48 percent of all Kiowa identified by the census lived in the area of the old reservation and 29 percent lived in other states (U.S. Bureau of the Census 1973). Sixty-four percent of the population lived in urban areas, more than the 49 percent average reported for all the Indians of Oklahoma. In the 1990 census some 9,421 individuals identified themselves as Kiowa (U.S. Bureau of the

Fig. 12. The Black Legs Society, a veterans' association that was a revival of an earlier men's society, restricted to veterans who have seen active duty. Members meet on Memorial Day and Veterans' Day and serve as flag bearers at other events. left, Procession of members wearing red capes and black leggings. The man carrying the lance is George Tahbone, Sr.; to his left is Rudy Bantista, carrying a feather fan. They have just emerged from the tepee, in which prayers were offered. Around the tepee are poles flying the American flag, regimental flags, and a crooked lance, which is an insigne of the society. right, Section of the striped tepee cover with names of Kiowa soldiers killed in World War II, Korea, and Vietnam. Photographs by Candace Greene, Memorial Day, Anadarko, Okla., 1993.

Census 1992:31). By January 2000, the total enrollment for the Kiowa Tribe was reported at about 12,500 members (Lisa Koomsa Lucero, communication to editors 2000).

Synonymy†

The most common Kiowa designation for themselves is *kɔ́ygú*, the name of one of the bands and the source of the contemporary name Kiowa. It is also the form on which most names for the tribe among Plains groups are based. All the Caddoan tribes use variants of it: Caddo *káhiwaʔ* (Chafe 1979), Wichita *káhiwaʔa* (Parks 1988; David Rood, personal communication 1989), Kitsai Gahewa (*kahíwa*) (Mooney 1893), Pawnee *káʔiwa* (Parks 1965–1990), and Arikara *kaʔíwA* (Parks 1970–1990). It is the most common Comanche designation: *kaiwa* or *kaiwi* (James Armagost, personal communication 1989; Jean O. Charney, personal communication 1990), sometimes given in its plural form *kaiwini·* (kaiwúna, as in Curtis 1907–1930, 19:229). Dhegiha Siouan forms are similar: Osage *kkáðowa* (Robert Rankin, personal communication 1990), Kansa *kkáyowa* (Robert Rankin, personal communication 1987), Ponca *kkáʔiwa* (Parks 1988) or Gaíwa (Fletcher and La Flesche in Mooney 1898:148), Omaha Gaíwa (Fletcher and La Flesche in Mooney 1898:148). So also is the Otoe name *kaíwa* (Parks 1988). The same name is used by tribes to the west, for example, Shoshone *kaiwah* (David Shaul, personal commu-

nication 1989), Jemez *gáiwa* (Ives Goddard, personal communication 1989), Sandia Kaiowan (Hodge 1895), Picuris Kai-wané (Hodge 1895), and Tewa kaiwa, which is said to be an adopted word (Curtis 1907–1930, 17:190).

The name most commonly cited for the Kiowa in early European sources is based on this same form, presumably taken from intermediary Indian languages. Following Spanish orthographic usage, renditions of the name in that language have c for the initial consonant *k* and gu where English has *w*. Examples are Cargua (misprinted) and Caigua, 1732 and 1735 (Columbian Historical Exposition 1895:323), Cayguas (Villaseñor y Sánchez 1746–1748, 2:413), and Cahiguas and Cahiaguas (Escudero 1849:83, 87). Presumably based on the Spanish forms are other citations like Cayohuas (Bandelier 1892:43), Cayugas (C. Bent 1850:185), and Kayuguas (C. Bent in Schoolcraft 1851–1857, 1:244).

Examples of French renditions are Quiouaha, 1687 (Joutel in Margry 1876–1886, 3:409), Quíohohouans (Baudry des Lozières 1802:244), and Quiouahan, 1700 (Iberville in Margry 1876–1886, 4:464). Quichuan, (La Harpe in Margry 1876–1886, 6:278) is apparently a mistranscription of c for o.

American renditions are variants of the contemporary spelling. Most citations have an initial *k*, as in Kiawas and Kie-wah (Lewis and Clark in Moulton 1983–, 3:136, 403), Kaiawas and Kiaways (Gallatin 1848:cvii, 20), Kaí-ó-wás (Whipple 1856:31), Kayaways (Z.M. Pike 1810, 3:iii), Keaways (1843:29), Kiowahs (W.H.H. Davis 1857:17),

†This synonymy was written by Douglas R. Parks.

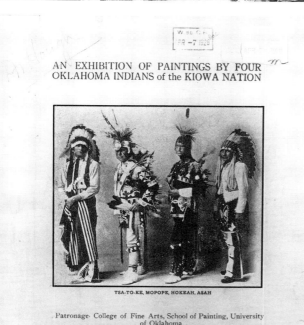

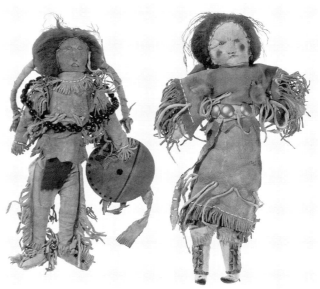

AN EXHIBITION OF PAINTINGS BY FOUR
OKLAHOMA INDIANS of the KIOWA NATION

TSA-TO-KE, MOPOPE, HOKEAH, ASAH

Patronage· College of Fine Arts, School of Painting, University
of Oklahoma
Address, Oscar B· Jacobson, Director, Norman, Oklahoma

top, U. of Okla. Lib., Western Hist. Coll., Norman:1170; bottom, Smithsonian, NAA: 91-8604.

Fig. 13. Kiowa Five. top, Monroe Tsatoke, Jack Hokeah, Stephen Mopope, Spencer Asah, and James Auchiah with their mentor Oscar B. Jacobson, professor in the Art Department of the U. of Okla. The paintings, drawings, and murals by these artists, often of dancers, inspired many younger artists. Photographed at Jacobson's house, Norman, Okla., 1929. bottom, Advertisement poster for an exhibition of paintings by 4 of the artists, 1928.

Smithsonian, Dept. of Anthr.: bottom, 152,918 and 152,920.

Fig. 14. Buckskin dolls. top, Vanessa Paukeigope Morgan (right) wearing beaded moccasin leggings and a cloth wing dress. In addition to dolls, she made cradleboards, saddles, bowcases, and quivers. Her daughter, Summer Red-Paint-Girl, is wearing a beaded buckskin dress and leather concho belt. Photograph by Lynn Ivory, Santa Fe Indian Market, August 1988. bottom, Dolls, with carefully detailed clothing and minimal attention to facial features, made for play. This pair, with hide faces, buffalo wool hair, and buckskin clothing, was collected by James Mooney in 1892 for display at the World's Columbian Exposition in Chicago. Male doll is dressed in fringed clothing with a mescal bean bandolier, holding a painted shield. Female doll has a German silver concho belt. Length of left 36 cm; right same scale.

Kioways (Brackenridge 1814:80), Kiwaa, given as the pronunciation of Caygüa (G.W. Kendall 1844, 1:198), and Kuyaways (Sage 1846:167). Others have an initial *c*: Cayowa, 1803–1804 (Tabeau 1939:154), Cayanwa (Lewis and Clark 1809:15), Cai-a-was (U.S. Congress. House Committee on Indian Affairs 1876:1). Some citations have confused r with k: Ryuwas (Brackenridge 1814:85) and Riana (W. Kennedy 1841, 1:189).

Mooney (1898:149) gives three other names that Kiowas used for themselves, apparently representing former divisions. Ko′mpabi′ănta (*kʰòmpɔbî·dɔ̀*) 'people of large tepee

flaps' was remembered in the mid-twentieth century but no longer used. The Comanche name Peveatetsiparane 'big tepee flaps' is an apparent calque (H.L. Scott 1912–1934; Thomas Kavanagh, personal communication 1990). The other two names, Kwŭ′′dă′ (*kʰúttɔ̀*) 'pull out, pop out' and Te′pdă′ (*tʰépdɔ·*), 'be issuing forth' were not recognized by Kiowas in the twentieth century.

923

A late eighteenth-century name for a Kiowa division is Witapahatu or Pitapahatu, 1795–1796 (Truteau in Parks 1993), which is always cited subsequently with an initial w, as Wetepahatoes (Lewis and Clark in Moulton 1983–, 3:403), Wettaphato and Wetapahato (J. Morse 1822:253, 366), Wate-panatoes (Brackenridge 1814:85), and Wetapahata, Wetopahata, and Watahpahata (Mallery 1886:109). It survives in the twentieth century as the Sioux and Cheyenne names for the Kiowa. The Sioux form is variously cited as *wítapahatu* (Curtis 1907–1930, 3:141; Buechel 1983:590) and *wítapaha* (S.R. Riggs 1890:579; J.P. Williamson 1902:95), said to mean 'island hill (people)', which is probably a folk etymology. Similar in form is the Cheyenne name, *vétapAhaetóʔeoʔo* (Glenmore and Leman 1985:202), cited in earlier sources as Vitapāto (Petter 1913–1915:582), Wi'tăpähät and Wităp'ätu (Cheyenne) and Vi'täpä'tu'i (Sutaio) (Mooney 1898:149–150), and Wítapáto (Curtis 1907–1930, 6:158). Hayden (1862:290) mistakenly transposed this form, wi-tup-a'-tu, with the one designating the Comanche. Petter (1913–1915:582) and Curtis (1907–1930, 6:158) attribute the Cheyenne name to the Sioux, but Mooney (1898:150) says that either tribe could have been the source. The name, like many for more westerly Plains tribes from the same period, may in fact have been taken over by fur traders on the Missouri from Pawnee *pi·tapaha·tuʔ* and Arikara *wi·tapaha·tuʔ* 'red man', which are unattested usages in those languages (see Parks 1993).

Other tribal designations for the Kiowa are Arapaho *ni·či·héhi·nén* 'river person' (Ives Goddard, personal communication 1990; cf. Hayden 1862:326 cited as 'water men'); Crow *rû·swače·* 'rib men' (Medicine Horse 1987:15); Plains Apache *béšílčą·h* (no meaning, Bittle 1952–1956; see also Mooney 1898:148). A Hidatsa name, Datŭmpa'ta, that was recorded from a Kiowa informant (Mooney 1898:148) may be related to the Crow word or to the Kiowa name *tʰépdɔ·*. An apparent confusion in the literature is Omaha *mąxpíattu*, said to designate Kiowa as well as Arapaho (Fletcher and La Flesche 1911:102; Swetland 1977:108).

Clark's gloss of the name of the Kiowa as "Tideing Indians" (Moulton 1983–, 3:136) is obscure.

Descriptions of the sign language designation for the Kiowa are in general agreement: the right hand, held at the height of the lower part of the ear and near the chin, with palm upward, is rotated in a circular manner. Some descriptions specify the rotary movement as upward and downward, while others stipulate it to be free from side to side. Specification of finger position varies. Interpretations of the meaning of the sign also vary: one is reputed to be a reference to a former practice of clipping the hair above the right ear (Hadley 1893:103; Mallery 1881:470); another is to 'prairie people constantly rising up' (W.P. Clark 1885:229); and a third is to some form of craziness, either 'crazy headed' (Mallery 1881:470) or 'Crazy Knife people' (W.P. Clark 1885:229).

Bands

Mooney (1898:228–229, 412) recorded seven band names: K'at'a, modern form *kɔ́ttɔ́*, meaning Arikara ('biters'); Ko'gúi, modern form *kʼógûy*, meaning Elks; Gâ'-igwû, *kɔ̀ygú*, meaning Kiowa proper; Kiñep, modern form *kʰį·èp*, *kʰį·èt*, meaning Big Shield; Koñtä'lyui, modern form *kʰɔ̀·tʰàlyôy*, meaning Black Boys; K'úato, modern form *kʰúttɔ́*, meaning Pulling Up; and Semät, modern form *sémhát*, meaning Apaches ('thieves'). W.P. Clark (1885:230) mentions four of these—Cut-Off (Arikara), Elk, Shield, and Black—as well as the "Apache Kiowa," which some claim to be a fifth band.

Sources

The earliest and most comprehensive study of Kiowa culture and history is Mooney's (1898) study of the calendar histories; it remains the single most important source concerning the pre-reservation period. Marriott (1945) is the closest to a tribal ethnography; although it is a fictional history of one Kiowa family from the pre-reservation years to the outbreak of the Second World War, the work is based on several years of ethnographic fieldwork and is an invaluable source. Marriott's field notes (1936–1956) are a major unpublished source of Kiowa ethnography.

Nye's (1937) history of Fort Sill tells of the Indian wars and the early years of the reservation period. The military history is quite accurate, although the interpretation of Kiowa lifeways is often insensitive and biased. Mooney's (1896) study of the Ghost Dance gives a general account of Kiowa participation in the movement and includes a number of Kiowa Ghost Dance songs in the original and in translation. Kracht (1992) writes on the Ghost Dance and on religion (1989).

Mayhall (1971) attempts a comprehensive review of Kiowa culture and history to 1960 but is an unreliable synthesis of previously published materials. Levy (1959a) discusses political and social organization from the reservation period to the 1950s.

Specialized studies on rank and warfare by Mishkin (1940) and on law and status by J.H. Richardson (1940) are based on field research conducted in 1935 by the Santa Fe Laboratory of Anthropology field party directed by Alexander Lesser. Copies of their voluminous unpublished notes are in the National Anthropological Archives, Smithsonian Institution. La Barre (1938) includes material on Peyotism from the 1935 field party as well as from later fieldwork.

The kinship system has been described by Lowie (1923), and lists of kin terms appear in E.C. Parsons (1929) and Watkins (1984). Lowie (1916a) reports on the men's societies, incorrectly concluding that the societies were not ranked, probably because the information was provided by only one individual, a low-status Mexican captive. Meadows (1999) studied men's societies. A brief description of Kiowa conjuring is provided by D. Collier (1944). Gamble

(1952) looked at changes in Kiowa dances. Kiowa singing is described in Lassiter (1998).

Kiowa myths and tales have been collected by E.C. Parsons (1929), the most comprehensive collection, Marriott (1947, 1963), and Boyd (1981–1983). E.W. Voegelin (1933) examines stories dealing with early Kiowa-Crow contacts.

Harrington's (1928) vocabulary and Watkins's (1984) grammar are the most comprehensive works on the language.

Kiowa artist Monroe Tsa Toke (1957) has written about Peyotism from the viewpoint of a participant, and N. Scott Momaday (1967, 1968, 1969, 1976) has written sensitive accounts of his own discovery of Kiowa identity, traditions, and world view. The work of Kiowa photographer Horace Poolaw is discussed by his daughter (Poolaw 1990, 1990a).

The best-documented collection of Kiowa artifacts is that of Mooney in the National Museum of Natural History, Smithsonian Institution (Merrill et al. 1997). Other large collections are in the Panhandle-Plains Historical Museum, Canyon, Texas, and the Museum of the Great Plains, Lawton, Oklahoma.

Plains Apache

MORRIS W. FOSTER AND MARTHA McCOLLOUGH

Language and Origins

The Plains Apache language,* often called Kiowa Apache, is one of the six that make up the Apachean branch of Athapaskan (the others are Lipan, also spoken by a Plains people; and Navajo, Western Apache, Chiricahua-Mescalero, and Jicarilla, all spoken by groups in the Southwest) (Hoijer 1971; vol. 10:393–400). As a tribal designation Plains Apache and Kiowa Apache refer to a people identified in the historical literature by a number of often unrelated terms that obscure their distinctness and continuity as a people (Mooney 1898, 1907e). Since 1972 the group has been officially called the Apache Tribe of Oklahoma and, informally, the Plains Apache (fig. 1). The term Plains Apachean is used in a broader sense to refer to any Apache-speaking groups on the Plains in early historic times (called Plains Apache in vols. 9:162, 10:380–392).

Scholars have disagreed on the origins of the Plains Apache. According to Mooney (1907e) they originated on the Northern Plains, where they allied with the Kiowa in the Black Hills of western South Dakota and eastern Wyoming sometime in the early eighteenth century, and then accompanied the Kiowa onto the Southern Plains around 1780 (fig. 1). J.H. Gunnerson and D.A. Gunnerson (1971, 1988) argued that the Plains Apache were part of the older migration of Athapaskan peoples from western Canada to the Southwest, and that they were subsequently driven back north by the movement of Comanche bands onto the southern Plains in the early 1700s. They identify the archeological remains of the late seventeenth- to early eighteenth-century ceramic-

---

*The phonemes of Plains Apache are: (lenis voiceless stops and affricates) b, d, λ, ʒ, ǯ, g, ʔ; (voiced prenasalized stop) ⁿd; (voiceless aspirated stop and affricates) λ, c, č, k; (glottalized stops and affricates) t́, λ́, c̓, č̓, k̓; (voiced spirants) z, ž, γ; (voiceless spirants) ł, s, š, x, h; (nasals) m, n; (lateral) l; (semivowel) y; (short oral vowels) i, e, a, o; (long oral vowels) i·, e·, a·, o·; (short nasal vowels) į, ę, ą, ǫ; (long nasal vowels) į·, ę·, ą·, ǫ·; (low tone) unmarked, (high tone) v́, (falling tone) v̂, (rising tone) v̌. Rising and falling tones occur only on long vowels.

Information on Plains Apache is from Bittle (1963) and Willem J. de Reuse (communication to editors 1998). In Bittle's (1963) orthography the phonemes are written: b, d, dl, dz, dž, g, ʔ; ⁿd; tł, ts, tš, k; t', tł', ts' tš', k'; z, ž, γ; ł, s, š, x, h; m, n; l; y; i, e, a, o; ii, ee, aa, oo; į, ę, ą, ǫ; įį, ęę, ąą, ǫǫ; (low tone) v̀, v̀v̀, (high tone) v́, v́v́, (falling tone) v̀v̀, (rising tone) v̀v̀.

The phonemicization of Plains Apache words from Bittle's (1952–1975) notes has been done by the editors and must be considered uncertain in many cases.

---

using, horticultural peoples of the Dismal River aspect in western Kansas and Nebraska and eastern Colorado and Wyoming with the ancestral Plains Apache (see "Plains Village Tradition: Western Periphery," this vol.).

Mooney assumed that the Plains Apache functioned more or less exclusively as a band of the Kiowa from the early eighteenth century to reservation settlement in 1875. However, even though throughout their history the Plains Apache as a small tribe often found it politically and economically necessary to associate for extended periods with the Arapaho, Cheyenne, Comanche, Kiowa, and Mescalero, the maintenance of the Plains Apache language into the twentieth century indicates their persistence as a distinct sociocultural community in the midst of numerous contacts and alliances with other Plains tribes.

History Until 1875

The Apaches mentioned by Francisco Vásquez de Coronado, Juan de Oñate, Alonso de Benavides, Alonso de Posada, and other Spaniards on the Southern Plains beginning in 1541 apparently lived in bands (rancherias) that were relatively small and politically autonomous, with headmen who attained prominence through individual achievement and who led by example rather than by formal authority (Posada 1982:41–42; Schroeder 1974; V.F. Ray 1974).

All the Apacheans living on the eastern margin of the Rocky Mountains were bison hunters, but unlike the others, the ancestors of the Plains Apache were nomads who did not practice horticulture, lived in hide tepees, and used dogs as pack animals (Schroeder 1974:235, 253). Those other Apacheans included the Jicarilla, Cuartelejo, Faraon, Sierra Blanca, Carlanas, Natagé, Llanero, and Palomas, whose communities, primarily located in northeastern New Mexico, eastern Colorado, and western Kansas, had developed the role of intermediary traders between the Spaniards in New Mexico and Plains communities to the west and north. To the south, the Lipan Apache were also horticulturalists who hunted bison and engaged in trade with the Spaniards.

Some hostility existed between those Apacheans who pursued a mixed horticultural and bison hunting strategy and those who specialized exclusively in bison hunting, perhaps based on competition for the trade with Puebloan and Spanish settlements (R.A. Smith 1959; Brant 1951). This trade was mainly in bison products from the Plains and

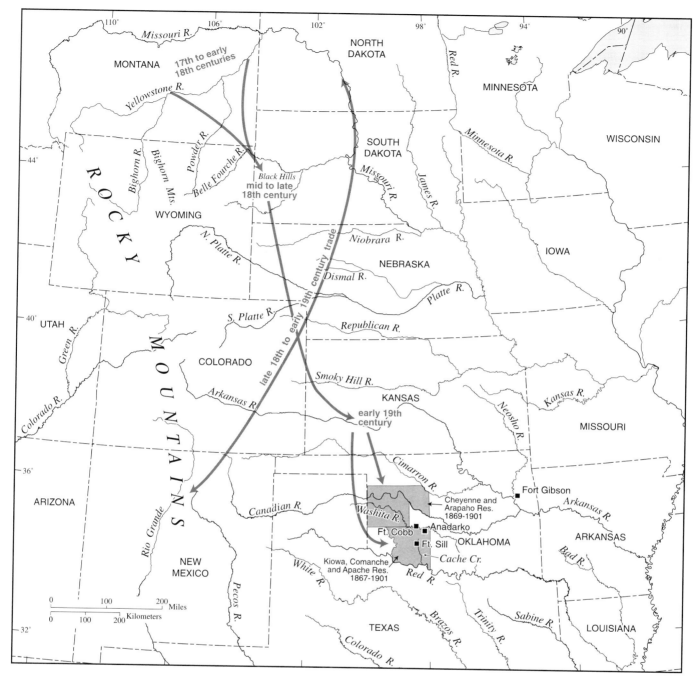

Fig. 1. Plains Apache approximate areas of residence and movements in the 17th to 19th centuries (following Mooney 1907e), with trade route between the Pueblo region of New Mexico and Mandan-Arikara territory in North Dakota.

agricultural products along with obsidian and turquoise from the Pueblos (T.G. Baugh 1991:125). Having adopted a fully nomadic lifeway, the ancestral Plains Apache would have had both a larger surplus of bison products to trade and a greater motivation to enter Puebloan markets.

That motivation no doubt increased with the introduction, by the Spaniards, of horses, which by 1660 had become available on the southern Plains in some numbers (Schroeder 1974:113). In 1682 René-Robert Cavelier de La Salle, visiting the Wichita villages, learned that they obtained horses from

the Gattacka (some or all of whom were ancestors of the Plains Apache) and Manrhout (an unidentified group), who lived to the south and traded with Spaniards in New Mexico (Margry 1876–1886, 2:201). In 1719, when Jean-Baptiste Bénard de La Harpe visited the Wichita peoples, he learned that the Cancy and Padouca groups of Plains Apacheans had plentiful horses obtained from Spaniards and traded both to other Southern Plains peoples and to Arikara villages on the Northern Plains (R.A. Smith 1959:379). La Harpe noted that the Cancy and Padouca were at war with   927 one another, perhaps a continuation of the hostilities between the semisedentary and nomadic Plains Apaches competing for control of the Southern Plains–Puebloan horse trade (R.A. Smith 1959:529–530).

That growing trade attracted other peoples to the Southern Plains. By 1720, Comanches had displaced Apaches as intermediaries between the New Mexican sources for horses and southern and central Plains village markets (A.B. Thomas 1932:57–58, 1940:20). At the same time, French traders were establishing relationships with Caddo, Wichita, and Pawnee villages, both adding to the demand for horses and providing an alternative source for European goods. With the exception of the Lipan in southern Texas, most of the semisedentary Apacheans moved into New Mexico, closer to the Pueblos, where they could take advantage of Spanish protection from the Comanche.

While some of the Plains Apacheans probably responded to the pressure of the Comanche intrusion by moving east into New Mexico or south to join the Lipan, the balance of them moved north to South Dakota, closer to the villages of the Arikara, with whom they traded. The Vermale map of 1717 shows what are identified as 10 Padouca villages north of the Pawnee villages, where previous maps had located the Plains Apacheans (Gattacka or Padouca) south of the Pawnee (Wheat 1957–1963, 1:map 98). By moving north, these Plains Apacheans, who may now be referred to as the historical Plains Apache, were able to continue their bison hunting and trading activities, although they were farther removed from the Spanish sources of horses.

A 1785 Spanish report located the "Pados or Toguibacós" in "small forts" near the Little Missouri (Bad) River; the term Pados is the first unambiguous historical reference to the Plains Apache. (For Toguibacó see "Enigmatic Groups," this vol.). According to the report: "The Pados were in former times the most numerous nation on the continent, but the wars which other nations have made against them have destroyed them to such an extent that at present they form only four small groups [*parcerías*] who go wandering from one side to the other continually, which saves them from the fury of the other nations. They number about three hundred and fifty men, very skillful with the arrow and in running" (Gov.-Gen. Esteban Rodriguez Miró in Nasatir 1952, 1:124, 127). In 1796 the Pados were reported to live on the southwest branch of the Platte River (Jean-Baptiste Truteau in Nasatir 1952, 2:379, 384).

In 1800 and 1801, under the designation of Apaches del Norte, the Plains Apache were said to be associated with the Kiowa and other "Nations of the North" that had moved onto the Southern Plains (John 1985:382–383). These peoples made several indirect attempts at establishing a trade relationship with Spaniards in Texas and New Mexico but were deterred by the Comanche.

Such historical references suggest a pattern in which the Plains Apache bands were associated, for political and economic reasons, with the larger Arapaho, Cheyenne, and Kiowa tribes. Most documented associations were for purposes of trading with Euro-Americans or for protection from hostile Plains peoples such as the Pawnee. In general, the Plains Apache allied with nomadic peoples who enjoyed amicable relations with Euro-American authorities and tended to avoid associations with peoples who were engaged in hostilities with Euro-Americans.

In 1835 the Plains Apache frequented the same area of the west-central Plains as the Kiowa (H. Dodge 1836:25). In 1837, at Fort Gibson, Indian Territory, the Plains Apache were signatories with the Kiowa and Wichita to a treaty of peace and friendship with the United States (Kappler 1904–1941, 2:489–491). In 1846 the Plains Apache were reported as allying with the Mescalero Apache (V.F. Ray 1974:79). In 1848 they were described as associating with the Arapaho and Cheyenne, and between 1850 and 1855 they associated primarily with the Comanche and Kiowa, signing the Treaty of Fort Atkinson, Kansas, along with those two tribes and the United States in 1853 (ARCIA 1848:472, 1850:21–22, 1855:255; Kappler 1904–1941, 2:600–602). This treaty promised annuities and protection to the tribes. Between 1858 and 1867 they were primarily associated with the Arapaho and Cheyenne, though in 1863 they were party to an unratified treaty involving the Kiowa and Comanche (ARCIA 1858:97–99; 1867:18–19; DeMallie 1977a). Another treaty signed in 1865 would have placed them on a reservation with the Arapaho and Cheyenne (Kappler 1904–1941, 2:891–892).

In 1867, after careful evaluation of the comparative advantages, the Plains Apache, in signing the Treaty of Medicine Lodge, chose to take a reservation with the Comanche and Kiowa (Kappler 1904–1941, 2:982–984). However, Plains Apache bands once again were associated with the Arapaho and Cheyenne from 1868 to 1875, the beginning of the reservation period.

Culture in the Nineteenth Century

Subsistence

The Plains Apache utilized a wide variety of wild game and plant resources (Brant 1951:10–13). The most important of the wild game were bison and deer, hunted both individually and communally. Communal hunts were policed by the Manatidie society, whose members could whip offenders or shoot their mounts (McAllister 1955:153). The Plains Apache, though, given their small size, did not emphasize large-scale seasonal communal bison hunts as did other nomadic Plains communities. Rabbit, turtle, beaver, badger, oppossum, bear, otter, geese, and a variety of other fowl were also hunted on a regular basis. Dogs and horses may have been used for subsistence in times of hardship.

While men were the hunters, women were responsible for butchering and preparing the meat. The women used strips of hide to string together slabs of bison meat and stack them on pack horses. At the camp, the meat was sliced thin

928

and hung on drying racks. Little, if any, of the bison was wasted. Hides, used for tepee covers, blankets, robes, parfleches, shields, and rope, were important trade items. The paunch and large intestine were used for storing and transporting water. Bison horns were carved into spoons and ladles. They were also worn as headdresses by warriors, who believed that the horns protected them from being hit by arrows or bullets. Because of the perceived healing power associated with the whiskers and tail hairs of the bison, these items were mixed with herbs and used to treat wounds, hemorrhages, or other medical conditions in which blood was involved (Brant 1951:15).

Numerous varieties of fruits, vegetables, and tubers were gathered including chokecherries, plums, grapes, blackberries, wild onions, and prairie turnips. These were used not only for food, but also for medicines, decorative coloring, and other purposes (Jordan 1965). The trade in horses, hides, and, later, cattle, provided considerable economic support, some of which was in the form of foodstuffs. The Plains Apache obtained agricultural products from Plains and Southwest villagers as well as from Euro-American traders through trade and raiding. After 1853, the Plains Apache received federal government annuities at irregular intervals under the provisions of their various treaties.

Social Organization

At least four levels of social organization may be identified: the extended family, which tended to be matrilocal and was based primarily upon kin relationships; the local or residence band, made up of clusters of extended families held together by the reputation of a leader or leaders; the division, made up of local bands that were loosely allied to one another and symbolized by the four sacred tribal bundles; and the Plains Apache tribe as a whole, which was a single sociolinguistic community that shared a common identity but was not organized as a centralized polity.

• EXTENDED FAMILIES   The Plains Apache kin term system merged same-sex consanguineal kin at each generational level with the following exceptions: in the parental generation, separate terms were used for mother's brother (extended also to father's sister's husband) and for father's sister (extended also to mother's brother's wife); in one's own generation, same-sex and opposite-sex sibling terms were extended to parallel and cross-cousins respectively; and in one's children's generation, the children of same-sex siblings, biological and classificatory, were distinguished from the children of opposite-sex siblings, biological and classificatory. Older siblings were distinguished from younger siblings. No generational merging occured. In contrast to the Lipan kin term system, which it otherwise resembled, the Plains Apache system used self-reciprocal terms for persons in the grandparental and grandchild generations.

A system of avoidance was practiced between affinal kin of the opposite sexes. The strictest avoidance occurred between the mother-in-law and the son-in-law and between the father-in-law and the daughter-in-law. These relatives were not permitted to speak one another's name, make eye contact, or be alone together. Joking behavior was expected between brothers-in-law, grandparents and grandchildren, and mother's brother and sister's children. The last relationships were most important in that brothers-in-law tended to dominate the pool of younger males present in the matrilocal band, grandparents often were responsible for child rearing, and a mother's brother had greater responsibility for his sister's children than did the sister's husband, their father, including advice, economic provision, and sponsorship in public gatherings (Brant 1951:24–37; McAllister 1955:114–136).

Marriage, whether through arrangement or elopement, was legitimized by the exchange of gifts between the two families. Unlike the more populous Comanche, the Plains Apache defined the incest prohibition narrowly to allow for marriages between some consanguineal kin (McAllister 1955:145–146). The levirate and the sororate were the preferred patterns of remarriage after the death of a spouse. If a woman died, her unmarried sister was expected to take care of her children and marry their father. An unmarried brother of a deceased man was also expected to care for his sister-in-law and rear her children. At the death of her husband, a widow wore a smoke-blackened dress manufactured from the flaps of an old tepee. She was required to continue mourning until released by her husband's sisters. A widower was also expected to mourn the death of his wife. He would ask close relatives of his wife to gash his forehead or cut off his hair (M.E. Opler and W.E. Bittle 1961:383–384). When remarriage followed the levirate or sororate, the period of mourning was greatly reduced. Even if this preferred second marriage did not transpire, affinal kin terms continued to be used between the families.

Institutionalized friendships between pairs of individuals of the same sex were formed within the men's and women's societies. Two members of a society would choose to use sibling terms for one another and to extend other appropriate kin terms to members of their families (McAllister 1955:123–125). Such friendships may also have occurred outside the context of the societies. In either case, they often marked alliances between extended families who resided and worked together. Fictive kinship was used elsewhere to facilitate long-term relationships and to fill vacancies in significant social roles defined by kinship criteria.

• LOCAL OR RESIDENCE BANDS   While a single extended family could constitute a local or residence band, the more usual practice was for several extended families to camp together. Residence bands developed around the reputation of a leader or leaders for knowledge, skill in hunting and raiding, and power. These headmen held no formal positions, and they led by example and consensus building. Owners of the four tribal bundles were more effective leaders than headmen who were not bundle owners because the

Fig. 2. Gambling. top, Women gambling. Photograph by James Mooney, Okla. Terr., 1890s. bottom, Gambling set. Both men and women played gambling games using specially marked sticks as dice. These dice are for the women's awl game. A set of four sticks was thrown down on a stone in the center of a board marked on cloth or rawhide. Using her awl as a marker, the player advanced around the board through various hazards based on the markings displayed on the fallen sticks (Culin 1907:124–130). Collected by Pliny E. Goddard in Okla. in 1911. Length of longest stick 20 cm.

families, despite their matrilocal foci, were sufficiently flexible to allow for the movement of personnel from one residence band to another. Such movements were fairly frequent during the early reservation period, but it is unclear whether those can be taken as typical of the prereservation period.

Residence band size is known best from the early reservation period, when it ranged between 20 and 80 members. Some residence bands camped together for communal hunts, the renewal ceremonies of the tribal bundles, and, increasingly in the nineteenth century, as a function of Plains Apache relations with Euro-Americans. Headmen with especially strong reputations, such as Pacer (fig. 3), led relatively large clusters of residence bands in which other leaders functioned as their lieutenants, but these larger groups were supported by specific economic or military circumstances and did not remain at full strength when those circumstances changed. In some cases, these larger aggregations may have constituted Plains Apache divisions.

• DIVISIONS Prior to 1848, the use of a variety of names for the peoples ancestral to the Plains Apache and the reference to the existence of four Pado groups in 1785 (Miró in Nasatir 1952, 1:124), reinforced by the history of the sacred tribal bundles, suggests that divisional identities may have been used as a means for organizing residence bands and their leaders.

It is unclear, though, how formal or informal such divisional organization might have been and how the relations among the divisions were organized, if at all. Divisional affiliation probably fluctuated with proximity to one of the four tribal bundles and was more likely a basis for irregular cooperation among residence bands and their leaders than for more structured and enduring relations. After 1848, divisional organization is not evidenced. Population losses due to epidemics and volatile Indian–Anglo-American relations on the Plains may explain the disappearance of divisions. In place of divisional alliances, Plains Apaches relied upon their alliances with the Kiowa, Cheyenne, Arapaho, and Comanche.

• TRIBE As a means for regulating social interaction and claims to a common identity, the Plains Apache tribe was a crucial social unit from at least 1720. That function, though, did not require tribal-level political organization—for which no evidence exists—nor did it require tribal-wide gatherings, though such may have occurred.

Although the Plains Apache have been described as constituting a band in the Kiowa tribal circle (Mooney 1898, 1907e), this is based on a place marked for their participation at the Kiowa Sun Dance in a manner that made the Plains Apache the equivalent of a Kiowa band. However, the leap from ceremonial participation to political organization is not well supported. While the Plains Apache were numerically smaller than the other Plains peoples with whom they were allied, they were never politically or organizationally subsumed by another tribe. Nor does it seem that all Plains Apache residence bands were party to each prereservation alliance.

bundles could be used to force the resolution of interpersonal conflicts (McAllister 1965:214–215). The extended

 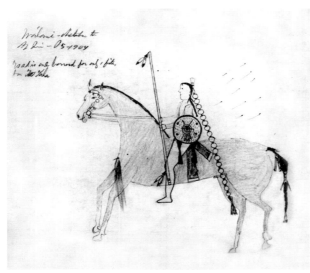 

Fig. 3. Headmen and warriors. left, Koon-kah-zah-chy, also known as Chief Apache John, wearing fringed buckskin leggings, shirt, moccasins, and cloth breechcloth. He wears a horned eagle feather headdress and his braids are wrapped in fur. He also wears a peace medal and bead or seed necklace. The flicker feather on his shoulder indicates his association with the Peyote ritual. He holds the Manatidie society whip. Photograph by Joseph K. Dixon, Crow Res., Mont., 1909. center, Drawing of the warrior Walami, dressed for battle wearing only a breechcloth and a long set of hairplates, his wounded horse's tail braided and decorated. He carries a coup stick and shield. An inscription by James Mooney explains that he borrowed the shield from Taha for this battle. Drawing by Apache Jim from dictation by Walami, Dec. 5, 1904. right, Pacer, while a delegate to Washington, D.C., 1872. Photograph by Alexander Gardner.

Societies

The Plains Apache had children's, men's, and women's societies (Brant 1951:51–56; McAllister 1955:139–142, 150–157; Bittle 1962). The Rabbit (*gáłcoé·h*) society included all children and was an important locus for their socialization. The society, led by an owner of one of the sacred bundles, sponsored rabbit dances at which young children publicly were given names. The Manatidie (*má·natí²de²é* 'black foot') and Klintidie (*łi·tí²de²é* 'horsemen') societies were military organizations of adult men who had distinguished themselves in warfare. The Manatidie was responsible for policing communal hunts and camp movements. Four ceremonial staffs and a whip were the focus of this organization's dances and were passed down through specific families (Bittle 1952–1956, 1962). The Klintidie society was similar to other Plains Dog Soldier organizations, with greater emphasis on bravery in warfare manifested in other contexts through contrary speech and actions. Members of the Klintidie society were older than members of the Manatidie society and may also have had some duties in religious ceremonies.

It is unclear whether men's society membership cut across residence band and divisional lines, whether there was more than one chapter of each organization, or whether different residence bands and divisions had different military societies. However, because the Plains Apache had no regular occasions for large communal gatherings, it is likely that men's societies functioned more through the personal relations among those members who were able to regularly interact with one another than as corporate groups. As among the Kiowa and Comanche, raiding and revenge parties were organized through individual initiative and personal networks rather than by residence band, divisional affiliation, or men's society organizations.

One shield society was reported, the Red Shields, and there may have been others (McAllister 1935:18–22). Shield societies were looser in organization than men's societies, usually consisting of seven men who painted their shields with the same emblem (fig. 3), each drawing his power from the same source. It is likely that the personal relationships among these seven men were more significant than any corporate charter or organization. One women's society, called the Izuwe, was reported (McAllister 1935:111–115, 1955:156–157). This society was made up of 20 older women and one older man who served as the drummer. Members met in secret and would, when specifically requested, pray for men going to war and for those in the community who were sick. The society owned its songs and dances, which also were performed in secret.

Religion

Although the Plains Apache recognized a creator, referred to as Nuakolahe 'maker of the earth', the principal figures in their mythology were Coyote and the twin culture heros, Water Boy and Fire Boy. Coyote was a trickster who exhibited characteristics of greed, irresponsibility, and cunning (McAllister 1949; Brant 1953:196). Water Boy and Fire Boy, on the other hand, epitomized heroic behavior through their

931

destruction of dangerous entities in the Plains Apaches' mythic past (McAllister 1949; Brant 1951:90–104). The defeat of these forces, associated with the power of the natural world and the four directions of the physical landscape, represents the triumph of human cleverness; Coyote, in contrast, illustrates the dangers of depending too much on clever strategies alone.

The Plains Apache believed that power could exist in any natural object, including animals, plants, water, and geographic features (Brant 1951:38–42). Power continuously resided in natural forces such as lightning, thunder, and whirlwinds. Usually, humans received such power passively, through a dream or illness. During these visitations the supernatural entity instructed the individual about the paraphernalia required to use its power for doctoring, luck in gambling or hunting, or success in warfare. Power could be sought through a vision quest, but its active pursuit was not the preferred method of acquisition. In these instances, though, a person would travel to an isolated hillside and fast for four days and nights. The individual would pray, think good thoughts, and attempt to gain pity from the surrounding spirits. If successful, a spirit would give power to the supplicant. Power could also be inherited from a close relative. Songs, shield designs, herbal medicines, amulets, and personal medicine bundles were generally passed on to a close male relative.

Critical to the well-being of the Plains Apache people was the presence of their sacred bundles. According to tradition, when the Plains Apache were living in the Black Hills, a young man named Running toward the Enemy traveled to a sacred lake called Medicine Water where, after numerous ordeals, he acquired the first of the original three bundles (McAllister 1965:215–220). Later, one of the three bundles was divided into two to accommodate residence bands that ranged too far to have regular access to the benefits that the bundles provided. The bundles protected the Plains Apache from all kinds of communal and personal disaster and were addressed as šíšó·yą́ 'my grandfather'. Bundles were inherited in the male line by those who were judged to be worthy of ownership. Because of the importance and intracommunity authority of the bundles, their keepers or owners were expected to exhibit honesty, kindness, dependability, thoughtfulness, generosity, and humility (McAllister 1965:213). Not coincidentally, these qualities also were expected of successful headmen. Bundle owners tended to be leaders of residence bands. The ritual knowledge that allowed the keepers to renew or feed the bundles and to maintain them properly was passed along with ownership. Once a year after the first thunder of spring, a bundle was opened for renewal by its keeper in a ceremony attended by men from his and other nearby bands. During the rest of the year, the bundle was kept in the owner's residence suspended over his bed. In times of personal misfortune, supplicants would visit one or more of the bundles with gifts. These offerings, usually including a cloth that would be wrapped around the bundle, were left in proximity to the bundle for four days and then became the property of the owner.

Disease and death were believed to be caused by breaches of taboo, contact with powerful spirits including ghosts, or witchcraft. Families had an extensive knowledge of practical herbal medicines for illness (Jordan 1965). When these failed, the intervention of a shaman was required. Relatives of the patient offered tobacco to a shaman who was thought to have the power necessary to cure the suspected cause of the illness. If the shaman, who was invariably male, accepted the tobacco, he was obligated to take the case. A separate tepee was erected for the curing ceremony, wherein the shaman and one or two assistants would give medicine, recite or sing curative formulas, and, in the case of witchcraft, remove objects from the patient's body through sucking horns (Bross 1962).

Patients exhibiting any form of paralysis were believed to be suffering from ghost sickness. In these cases, a shaman with owl or ghost power was necessary to effect a cure. Shamans with power from these sources were thought to be extremely dangerous, as they could easily subvert their power to evil purposes. The best-known Plains Apache shaman, Daveko (b. about 1818, d.1898) (fig. 4), was such a figure. Daveko was both sought after as a curer and feared as a possible agent of witchcraft (McAllister 1970). Like the owners of the sacred bundles, Daveko used his personal power to form and lead his own reservation-era band and, later, residential cluster.

Death, except in the case of the very young or the very old, was thought to result from supernatural causes (Brant 1951:70–72). The hooting of an owl or the constant howling of a dog were interpreted as portents of the end. At death, the life principle or animating spirit of the deceased was led by the ghosts of relatives to the sky world, a place of abundance and happiness. Malevolent tendencies, such as jealousy or meanspiritness, were believed to accumulate throughout one's life and remained on the earth after one's death. These antisocial tendencies, released by death, emanated from the skull and motivated ghosts to do harm to the living. Such ghosts would often linger near their former body, possessions, favorite haunts, or closest relatives. Because ghosts had the ability to transform themselves into owls, these birds were viewed as dangerous, capable of committing witchcraft. Children were thought to be particularly susceptible to ghost sickness. Due to the potential presence of a spiteful ghost, burial occurred as soon as possible after death, and relatives avoided speaking the name of the deceased (M.E. Opler and W.E. Bittle 1961; Sanford 1971).

Plains Apache extended families and residence bands participated in the Sun Dances of the Kiowa, Cheyenne, and Arapaho. Their participation was not annual nor was it connected to their sacred bundles. Instead, the Plains Apache attended Sun Dance gatherings during those periods in which they were allied with a tribe holding one. Thus, they may have valued these as occasions for social

top left, Smithsonian, Dept. of Anthr.: 245,039; top right, Frontier Originals, Topeka, Kan.

Fig. 4. Moon tepee of Daveko. The design on this tepee was received in a vision by Daveko, who passed it to his son of the same name in 1867. The design came with such stringent prohibitions that the son considered its power too dangerous to live with, and he destroyed the tepee after his father's death in 1873 (Ewers 1978:44). top left, Model of the Daveko tepee produced as a part of the anthropologist James Mooney's 1892–1904 studies of Kiowa and Apache shield and tepee designs. The buckskin cover is black with light blue crescents on broad bands of red; width 135 cm. bottom, Full scale version made in 1973 for an exhibition organized by the Indian Arts and Crafts Board of the Dept. of the Interior. The canvas cover was made by Gertrude Chalepah and Irene Poolaw and was painted by Elton Stumblingbear in the same colors as the earlier model (Libhart and Ellison 1973:26). Photograph by Candace Greene on the grounds of the Southern Plains Indian Museum, Anadarko, Okla., 1992. top right, Dorconealhla (Chief White Man) and Daveko. Chief White Man wears a hairpipe breastplate and fringed shirt. Daveko wears a breechcloth, vest, and moccasins. Photograph by W. Lenny and Sawyers, Ft. Sill, Indian Terr., 1890.

interaction as well as religious experience. There is no record that they held their own Sun Dances.

History, 1875–1901

By 1875, most nomadic peoples in Indian Territory had begun to reside full-time on their respective reservations. In that year, 120 Plains Apaches were resident on the Cheyenne and Arapaho Reservation while 444 were resident on the Kiowa, Comanche, and Apache Reservation (fig. 1). Some remained on the Cheyenne and Arapaho Reservation

throughout the reservation period, and, over time, an unspecified number, most of whom had married Cheyennes and Arapahos, were transferred to the Cheyenne and Arapaho rolls.

After an initial period during which the nomadic bands moved about the reservation area between annuity and ration days, a semisedentary lifeway developed, fragmenting the nomadic bands into smaller domestic units, usually extended families. In 1875, the Kiowa Agency recognized 12 Plains Apache bands for ration distribution. This number had grown to 15 bands by 1885. During the 1890s, when rations were distributed to family units rather than bands, those units tended to cluster in five geographic areas of the reservation.

In 1890, the Plains Apache held their own version of the Ghost Dance. Like the Kiowa, though, most of the Plains Apache community soon abandoned the Ghost Dance, though some continued intermittent participation in it until 1910 (Brant 1951:145).

The more pervasive religious innovation of the reservation period was the Peyote ritual (T.G. Baugh 1970). The first recorded evidence of Kiowa, Comanche, and Apache Peyote meetings was in 1883, but each of the three communities had been acquainted with peyote as a medicinal herb used by shamans prior to the reservation era. There is some dispute as to which of the three communities first developed the specific rituals associated with the more communal Peyote gatherings, but it is clear that, by 1890, most of the adult men of all three communities were participants. The Plains Apache Peyote (fig. 5) ceremony is somewhat distinct from those of the Kiowa and Comanche, reflecting the boundary maintenance among the three communities. Women, for instance, were not allowed as regular participants in Plains Apache meetings, as they could be in Comanche and Kiowa meetings, and the etiquette of appropriate behavior within the tepee differed in some details (Brant 1950; Bittle 1954, 1960; T. Hill and K.L. Beals 1966; K.L. Beals 1967).

Prominent Plains Apache shamans of the prereservation period were leaders in the reservation-era Peyote meetings. This resulted in a degree of factionalization between the older shamans, who were using the gatherings as an arena in which to maintain traditional beliefs and rituals, and a group of younger Plains Apache Peyote leaders, who incorporated Christian symbols and beliefs into the Peyote ceremony. Not surprisingly, the younger group charged the older with using Peyote meetings as a means for continuing the practice of witchcraft. The innovations of the younger Peyote leaders prevailed (K.L. Beals 1967:20–21).

During the reservation era, Plains Apache leaders functioned primarily as intermediaries between their people and agency officials, but they appear to have been less influential than Comanche and Kiowa leaders, who represented larger populations. The representation of significant numbers of reservation Indians was an important political factor in the negotiations surrounding the Jerome Agreement of 1892, which mandated the eventual allotment of reservation lands (U.S. Senate 1893; Hagan 1976).

Culture and History in the Twentieth Century

Social Organization

Reservation and allotment experiences brought extensive changes in the internal tribal organization. When lands were allotted to individual tribal members in 1901, Plains Apaches tended to choose acreages in the north of the reservation area, nearer Kiowa than Comanche clusters of allotments. Two clusters of Plains Apache residences developed, one in the Cache Creek area and the other in the Washita River area. The first was dominated by the Chalepah family, while the second was dominated by the Tselee or Redbone family. They came to be known, respectively, as the South and North sides or bands of the Plains Apache. These residential clusters were the basis for the two primary social identities that characterized political and other forms of social participation in the Plains Apache community throughout the twentieth century.

The immediate postallotment period also saw an increase in summer and winter encampments (fig. 6), focused either around Christian church participation or traditional dancing. Christian missionization of the Plains Apache had begun during the reservation period, but conversions increased significantly after allotment. The revival of traditional dancing occurred on the allotments of older Plains Apache men's society members. In contrast to the Comanche practice, for example, before World War II Plains Apaches tended to move easily between Christian church participation and traditional dance and Peyote gatherings. This was probably a function of the smaller size of their community. Exclusionary rules or boundaries around public gatherings may have been impractical given the networks of private relationships that linked all 200 or so Plains Apaches.

World War II brought a number of changes. Most younger men enlisted in the military, and others were able to enter the workforce for the first time. War-related civilian jobs and, later, veterans' benefits enabled Plains Apaches to obtain jobs and educational opportunities that previously had been reserved exclusively for non-Indians. Nonetheless, Plains Apache unemployment remained more than twice as high as non-Indian unemployment in the reservation area. One consequence of this was the relocation of a significant number of Plains Apaches outside the reservation area for the first time since 1875.

During and after World War II, dance gatherings were used to send off and welcome home servicemen. These gatherings were the forerunners of the postwar powwow, which became the primary form for public gatherings of the Plains Apache. As such, powwows developed both secular and religious aspects, and they were the principal occasions

Fig. 5. The morning after a Peyote ceremony. The Big Moon altar and ceremonial objects are still visible. left to right, Joe Blackbear, Jim White, Apache Ben, and Noble Starr. Photograph by J. Gilbert McAllister, near Ft. Cobb and Apache, Okla., 1934.

Fig. 6. Structures during postreservation period. left, Rush windbreak with canvas tents and tepees. A group of men and women appear to be engrossed in a gambling game in the center. Photograph by Ed Irwin, Okla., late 1890s. right, Summer brush shelter where cooking, eating, and everyday living took place. Photograph by J. Gilbert McAllister, near Ft. Cobb and Apache, Okla., 1933–1934.

through which Plains Apaches were able to associate with one another outside private networks of family and friends. Consequently, social business of various sorts was transacted in the context of powwows. Powwows took on a religious aspect through the revival of traditional dances by the Manatidie men's society (fig. 7) in 1960 (Bittle 1962). These revivals used traditional symbols to express the continuity of a distinctively "Plains Apache" identity.

The Plains Apache language was largely replaced by English during the twentieth century. By 1956, only one in four Plains Apaches were fluent speakers of their traditional language (Bittle 1956:6–7), and by 1992 the language was spoken by only a handful of elders who used it primarily in ritual contexts. While periodic efforts were made to revive the language (Liebe-Harkort 1980), the few remaining speakers evidenced phonological, morphological, and syntactic reductions indicative of the final stage of language obsolescence (M.R. Collins 1983). Several of those speakers claimed that there were two dialects of Plains Apache, mirroring the two geographically separated residential clusters that developed after allotment. However, the differences cited between the two speech communities were phonological and lexical, not morphological or syntactic.

The Rabbit society dances were held into the 1970s, though the society itself ceased functioning in a formal way in the early postallotment period. The two postallotment bands at various times revived separate versions of the Manatidie society and held separate dances (Beals 1967). The underlying network of family and friendship ties within the relatively small community has mitigated most of the more overt manifestations of political factionalism. Peyote gatherings decreased in frequency, and by the 1990s were held only intermittently, primarily on holiday weekends such as Labor Day, Easter, Thanksgiving, Memorial Day, and Father's Day. Peyote gatherings lost most of their community-maintenance functions to powwows and became primarily occasions for seeking personal help or power.

The other significant postwar public manifestation of the Plains Apache community was the establishment of a tribal government separate from the Kiowa-Comanche-Apache (KCA) Business Committee, which was the advisory administrative unit set up after allotment. Prior to 1936, the KCA Business Committee had little power. The Plains Apache members, who were in a minority due to the smaller population they represented, were elected at tribal councils and functioned primarily as intermediaries between individual Plains Apaches and agency officials. After 1936, the business committee gained limited control over economic resources as a result of the Oklahoma Indian Welfare Act. Beginning in 1938, attempts were made to set up separate tribal governments for each of the three native communities. These efforts did not achieve the approval of a majority of tribal members until 1966. Subsequently, Plains Apaches established their own business committee with a complex in Anadarko. Since 1966, the Apache Tribe of Oklahoma Business Committee provided some formal political organization, but the authority of the Business Committee was limited mainly to the area of relations with the federal government.

With the Indian Self-Determination and Education Assistance Act of 1975 and a federal land claims settlement over the disputed Jerome Agreement of 1892 in 1974, the Plains Apache Business Committee was able to provide its membership with social services and initiated some economic development projects. After 1987, the Plains Apaches required that enrolled members demonstrate only Plains Apache ancestry and one-eighth blood quantum. This allowed the much smaller Plains Apache tribal unit to successfully compete with the larger Comanche and Kiowa tribal units for enrolled members, many of whom have their choice of membership among the three tribes.

Economy

By 1875, when many Plains Apaches moved onto the Kiowa-Comanche-Apache Reservation full-time, they were

936

dependent on federal rations and annuities. These were supplemented by agricultural and stock-raising efforts during the reservation period (Hagan 1976). Those efforts, though, were blunted by the economics of the postallotment period, in which Indian farmers and stockmen were at a financial disadvantage vis-à-vis other farmers. Consequently, after 1901 most Kiowa Apaches leased their allotments and relied upon those rents in addition to annuity and other forms of per capita payments for economic support. Small gardens and a few stock animals for household consumption were maintained by some extended families, but lease money was the single most important source of income in the period after allotment. However, the alienation of allotment land has reduced original Plains Apache holdings by more than half while individual holdings have been reduced in each generation through multiple inheritance.

The Apache Tribe of Oklahoma Business Committee engaged in several small-scale economic development projects, funded in part by the proceeds of the 1974 federal land claims settlement. Federal social service programs, such as housing, commodity foods, and health care assistance, were administered through the tribal government, providing both assistance to those in need and employment for others.

Religion

Peyote gatherings continued to be important intracommunity occasions from allotment to World War II, though Peyote participation was increasingly in competition with the growing number of Plains Apache converts to Christianity. However, the opposition between Peyote people and church people was not mutually exclusive in respect to public social identities, as it was in the Comanche and Kiowa communities. Perhaps as a result of the early, successful incorporation of elements of Christianity into the Plains Apache version of the ceremony, a number of Plains Apaches were able to participate in both religious gatherings (Brant 1951:172–173). A split did develop, though, among Plains Apache Peyote circles or chapters in the 1940s. As with the revival of the Manatidie society in the 1960s, disagreements developed between Peyote participants who were members of the two bands or sides of the postallotment community (K.L. Beals 1967:21). Peyote participation declined after World War II, as powwows and, later, Manatidie society dances became more popular forms

of public gathering. By the 1990s, Peyote meetings were used mostly as occasions at which people could find physical or spiritual healing and, as such, they complemented rather than competed with dance gatherings and church meetings.

All four Plains Apache bundles survived into the 1960s, but they were increasingly left in the care of older women or in the abandoned houses of deceased owners. In one case, a bundle was left for some years with an anthropologist who had long worked with the Plains Apache community. While belief in the power of the bundles had not decreased, the rituals for the proper maintenance and renewal of the bundles had been lost in part or in whole. One of the bundles was buried with its last owner. The three remaining bundles were held by members of the two bands or sides of the community and served more as symbols of a traditional Plains Apache identity than as medicines, though they were sometimes used as such.

As a result of Christian missionization, Methodist, Baptist, and Dutch Reformed congregations with primarily Plains Apache memberships were established in five locations (Brant 1951:169–75). Three of these churches remained active in the 1990s. The Plains Apache Christian churches, which sponsored Christmas and summer encampments, were important features of the rural communities that developed after allotment, constituting social gathering places for both the devout and the nonconverted.

In the 1990s, Plains Apache religious participation was divided among Christian churches, Peyote meetings, the surviving sacred bundles, and Manatidie society dances. None of these represented an exclusive strategy and each was, to some extent, influenced by the others.

Population

The population of Plains Apachean bands was likely larger than that of the Plains Apaches (Kiowa Apaches) who moved north to escape Comanche raids in the early 1700s. However, there is no basis upon which to estimate that population. In 1804, Meriwether Lewis and William Clark estimated that the Cataka (Plains Apache) numbered 300 to 400 (Moulton 1983–, 3:423). In 1820, J. Morse (1822:366) put the Cataka at 375. Neither estimate was based on firsthand observation. Ruiz (1972:8) noted 80 to 100 families of what he called the "Lipans of the Plains" in association with the Arapaho in 1828, but this was likely only one of several

Plains Apache bands. H. Dodge (1836:25) estimated 1,200 "Appachees of the Plains" in 1835.

In 1850, the Upper Arkansas agent counted 50 lodges of Plains Apaches (ARCIA 1850:21–22). In 1861, 60 lodges were recorded with a total population of 415 (A.G. Boone 1861). At the negotiation of the 1867 Medicine Lodge treaty 86 lodges of Plains Apaches were counted for a total population of 516 (T. Murphy 1867). Of the prereservation population estimates, this is probably the most accurate and likely included more than one band with some Plains Apaches absent from the gathering.

In 1869, 288 Plains Apaches were reported camped on the Kiowa-Comanche-Apache Reservation, with 200 camped there in 1871 (ARCIA 1869:385; Townsend 1871). Twelve bands of Plains Apache were enumerated in 1874 with a total population of 602, but most of these bands were absent from the reservation and the numbers may have included those living with the Cheyenne and Arapaho. In 1875 the count was 344 Plains Apaches living on the Kiowa-Comanche-Apache reservation with 180 estimated as absent, a number that probably included those living with the Cheyenne and Arapaho. By 1880, the count was 332. In 1892, the population was 241. In 1900, on the eve of allotment only 173 Plains Apaches remained (Bureau of Indian Affairs. Kiowa Agency 1990).

While the exact numbers sometimes may be in doubt, it is clear that the Plains Apache experienced a consistent population decline from the eighteenth century to allotment. In part, that decline is the result of disease: smallpox epidemics occurred in 1816, 1839–1840, and 1861–1862; a cholera epidemic occurred in 1849; measles and fever struck in 1877; whooping cough and malarial fever in 1882; and measles, influenza, and whooping cough in 1892. Each of these epidemics resulted in significant loss of life (Ewers 1973:108–109). Malnutrition, particularly during the reservation period, also played a role. Transfers to the Cheyenne and Arapaho rolls and intermarriage with, and subsequent identification as, Kiowas and Comanches may also have contributed to population loss.

In 1910, the population was 139, and in 1930 it was 184 (Swanton 1952:296). In 1951, the enrolled Plains Apache population was approximately 400 (Brant 1951:148); in 1981, it was 833 (vol. 10:400). In 1992, after reducing the blood-quantum requirement to one-eighth in 1987, the enrolled population was 1,342.

Synonymy†

Historically, the name Plains Apache designated various Apachean groups formerly residing in the Plains area. Throughout the nineteenth and twentieth centuries, including officially by the United States government, these people were more commonly known simply as Apaches (Kappler 1904–1941, 2:600, 891, 982; ARCIA 1850:52). The name was modified as, for example, Appachees of the Plains (H. Dodge 1836:25), Apaches of Arkansas River (ARCIA 1855:255), and Prairie Apache (ARCIA 1854:297), to differentiate them from the Lipan and Apache groups in the Southwest. One form, Pacer band of Apaches, is a reference to its chief (B.R. Cowen 1872:3). In the late twentieth century the descendants of those groups, and particularly those who had been closely associated with the Kiowa, referred to themselves as Plains Apache, and in 1972 they officially designated themselves the Apache Tribe of Oklahoma (Morris Foster, personal communication 1992).

Among the earliest references to the Plains Apache in which their name is combined with the qualifier Kiowa are Hapache Caigua (Casados and Quintana 1746:4) and Kiawa Padduce, 1821 (Jacob Fowler in Coues 1898a:55), Padouca in the name being an eighteenth-century designation for Plains Apacheans. Modern use of the name Kiowa Apache (or Kiowa-Apache) dates to at least the late nineteenth century, when it was common locally because of the tribe's close association with the Kiowa (W.P. Clark 1885:33; Mooney 1898:246). It has continued to be used throughout the twentieth century, especially by anthropologists and historians (as in vols. 4, 9, 10, 17) but has never been used by the people whom it designates.

The Plains Apache name for themselves has been recorded in various forms and with conflicting etymologies. Late nineteenth century recordings of one variant are Na'isha (Mooney 1896:1081), Na-i-shan-dina, in which the tribal name modifies de·ná· 'people' (Mooney 1907e:702), and Na-ishi Apache (Gatschet quoted in J.W. Powell 1888:xxxv). In the mid-twentieth century this variant was recorded as na-e-ca 'thieves' (McAllister 1949:1), nạ²iśą́ 'steal here and there', and as ná²i·ša or ná²ęsa (Bittle 1952–1975), the last two given with conflicting meanings. The name is apparently etymologically obscure. Another variant is represented by two late seventeenth-century recordings, Nadeicha and Nardichia, 1687 (Joutel in Margry 1876–1886, 3:409); a late nineteenth-century recording of it is Nadíisha-déna, translated as 'our people' (Mooney 1898:245). Bittle (1952–1975) also recorded na²dí²įšą² and nạdí²į·šạ·, said to mean 'steal here and there', hence 'thieves', and gives dadíš²išą́· (Bittle 1963:89). In the 1990s the tribe used the spelling Na-I-Sha.

Most Plains tribes used a generic name 'Apache' for the Plains Apache, generally not differentiating them from other, particularly Plains, Apachean groups. One example is Comanche ta·si² (Thomas Kavanagh, personal communication 1992), which designates all Plains Apacheans and has been rendered variously as Tachi and Tazi 'eastern Apache' (ten Kate 1885a:136) and Tah-see 'whetstone men' (H.L. Scott 1890–1900). A variant recording of this Comanche form is ta·si²ni· 'spotted people', apparently a twentieth-century reinterpretation based on tasi²A 'smallpox' (J.B. Casagrande 1954–1955, [2]:231, 236). Almost identical in form to the Comanche designation is Shawnee ta·ši 'Apache' (C.F. Voegelin 1937–1940, [2]:140). A common

†This synonymy was written by Douglas R. Parks.

Kiowa name for the tribe is *tʰɔ́gûy* 'Apache' (Laurel Watkins, personal communication 1979), reputed to mean 'lazy people' (Gatschet 1884f:184) or 'poor outside' (J.P. Harrington 1939–1945). The Wichita designation for Plains Apache is the generic *kinne·sʔa* 'Apache, enemy', although some modern speakers use the compounded form *ka·hi·wáʔaskinne·sʔa*, literally 'Kiowa Apache', to distinguish them (David S. Rood, personal communication 1987; Parks 1988). Kitsai *kĭriʹnăhĭs* also designates other Apachean groups as well as the Plains Apache (Mooney 1896:1081); either it is cognate with the Wichita name or one tribe has borrowed the name from the other.

Another generic term formerly designating the Plains Apacheans generally and only later the Plains Apache specifically is Pawnee *kátahka* and its Arikara cognate *katAhká* 'Apache; alien tribe, enemy', both of which forms also mean 'inside out' (Parks 1965–1990). The Wichita were said to use sometimes the same designation, Gataqkä, although in the late nineteenth century they more commonly called the Plains Apache *kinne·sʔa* (Mooney 1896:1081). A borrowing of the Pawnee or Arikara forms is Omaha and Ponca name Gûʹtaʻk (La Flesche, quoted in Mooney 1898:245). The Pawnee and Arikara forms also frequently occur in various European and American sources, the earliest of which are Gataea and Gattacka, 1682, the former a misprint (La Salle in Margry 1876–1886, 2:168, 201). Eighteenth- and nineteenth-century examples are: Quataquois and Quataquon, 1719 (La Harpe and Beaurain, respectively, in Margry 1876–1886, 6:289); Catarkas, 1803–1804 (Tabeau 1939:154); Gataka (J. Harris 1705, 1:map, 685); Cat-tar-kah, Cataka, Katteka, 1804–1805 (Moulton 1983–, 3:136, 403, 439); Catakâ (Lewis 1832:716); Cataha, 1810 (Biddle in D.D. Jackson 1962:535); Cuttako (Lewis and Clark 1832:710); Cah-tah-kahs or a band of Apaches, 1836 (Chouteau in L. Barry 1972:305), and Ka-ta-ka (Kappler 1904–1941, 2:489); and Ca-ta-ka tribe of Pado (Clark map in Tucker 1942:plate xxxi), with Pado for Padouca (vol. 10:391; Synonymy in "Comanche," this vol.).

In early French sources the Plains Apacheans are designated Padouca, a Dhegiha and Chiwere Siouan name applied to the Plains Apacheans until the Comanche displaced them on the High Plains in the mid-eighteenth century. After that time the meaning of the term in Siouan languages shifted to designate the Comanche (Secoy 1951). Variants include Parouke, as in Rivière des Parouke, 1684 (Franquelin 1684:map); Apaches ou Padoucas Orientaux, 1717 (Vermale map cited in Champe 1949:291); Padouca, 1719 (Dutisné in Margry 1876–1886, 6:312); Padouka, as in Padouka blanc and Padouka Noirs, 1720 (Beauvillier map in Wheat 1953, 1:facing p. 70); Padokas, 1739–1740 (Mallet brothers in Margry 1876–1886, 6:461); Paducar, Paducies, Padoucas, Paducas, 1804–1805 (Moulton 1983–, 3:136, 395, 438–439); Peducas (Perrin du Lac 1805:225–226); and Padduca, 1821 (Jacob Fowler in Coues 1898a:58).

A shortened variant of Padouca is Pado, which was said to be the French Canadian nickname for the Plains Apacheans

(Moulton 1983–, 3:438). The form appears as Padós, 1785 (Miró in Nasatir 1952, 1:127), Pado, 1795–1796 (Truteau in Parks 1993; erroneously identified as Comanche in Nasatir 1952, 1:301); padoo (Moulton 1983–, 3:438); and Padaws (Perrin du Lac 1807:63).

The Caddo name, formerly a designation for Plains Apacheans, also appears in early European sources. Occurrences of it in Spanish and French documents are Cantey, apparently a misprint for Cantcy, 1687 (Joutel in Margry 1876–1886, 3:409); Canchy and Connessi, 1700 (Bienville in Margry 1876–1886, 4:442); Cannecy, 1717 (Bienville in Swanton 1942:55); Cancy, 1719 (La Harpe in Margry 1876–1886, 6:277); Cannecy, Canzes, Cannecis, Cancis, Cansis, 1768–1780 (De Mézières et al. in Bolton 1914, 1:26, 74, 162, 2:20, 23); Cancer, Canceres, Canzeres, Kanses, Canseres, 1719–1724 (Valverde et al. in A.B. Thomas 1935:143, 169, 196, 211); and Cances (Alcedo in G.A. Thompson 1812–1815, 1:285). Although formerly this Caddo name was more commonly used to designate the Lipan, in the twentieth century it came to be used for the Plains Apache specifically. In the late nineteenth century it was recorded as Kāntsi (Gatschet 1882:65) and Kántsi 'liars' (Mooney 1898:245). In the mid-twentieth century it was recorded as *kʼánʔciʔ* 'little duck' (Wallace L. Chafe, personal communication 1992), a reinterpretation of *kanʔciʔ* 'little thief', a meaning that would accord with their own name and the Kiowa designation, *sémhát* 'thieves' (Mooney 1898:245; La Barre 1935; Laurel Watkins, personal communication 1992).

The sign language designation for the Plains Apache, which was also used for other Apachean groups, was made by extending outward from the body the forefinger of the left hand, other fingers closed, and then extending the forefinger of the right hand outward, other fingers closed. The right forefinger was placed on the left one and moved backward and forward repeatedly by wrist action. There are two interpretations for this gesture: one is that it imitates the playing of a musical instrument made from elk horn; the other is a reference to a particularly good whetstone made and used by the Apache, hence 'whetstone people' (W.P. Clark 1885:33; H.L. Scott 1912–1934).

These alternate interpretations of the sign language gesture are reflected in the designations of several Plains tribes for the Plains Apache. An obsolete Kiowa name is *kʼɔ́·pa·tòp*, literally 'knife whetter' (Mooney 1898:245; Laurel Watkins, personal communication 1992). Related to it semantically is another Plains Apache self-designation *bekʼáʔde·kʼasé* 'scrapers' (Bittle 1952–1956). Contrasting with them are the forms in three Sioux dialects: Assiniboine Chíⁿchakiⁿze (Curtis 1907–1930, 3:141), Santee Sioux *čʰíčákįze* (S.R. Riggs 1890:101), and Teton Sioux *čʰíčakize* (Buechel 1970:733) or *čʰíčakįze* (H.L. Scott 1912–1934; Boas and Deloria 1941:8), literally 'squeak by striking against wood', a reference to playing a musical instrument. The Sioux forms designate the Apache in general, including the Plains Apache. Boas and Deloria give the apparently mistaken identification of the Teton form as 'Arapaho'.

The Cheyenne and Arapaho names, which designate other Apache groups as well, have been recorded with both sign language interpretations. Cheyenne *mOhtséheonetaneo?O*, cited also as Mòzeheonetan and Mútsíănă-täníu, has been translated, respectively, as 'occupied-camp people' (Glenmore and Leman 1985:201), 'people of the rasp fiddle' (Petter 1913–1915:582), and 'whetstone people' (Mooney 1898:245). The Arapaho name, *θohkóheinénno?*, has been recorded as thaĥ-a-i-nin' 'people who play on bone instruments' (F.V. Hayden 1862:236) and as Tha·ká-hinĕ'na or Tha·ká-itän, which have 'people' and 'tribe,' respectively, as their second elements and have been translated as 'whetstone people' (Mooney 1896:1081). Neither translation is linguistically demonstrable (Ives Goddard, personal communication 1992).

In two Southwest languages the Plains Apache are also designated as Apaches: Jemez Tâ'gugala and Pecos Tágukerésh (Hodge 1895).

An anomalous Kiowa name designating the Plains Apache is Sádalsómte-k'íägo 'weasel people' (Mooney 1898:245).

The Caddo name for the Comanche, *sáw?íuh*, recorded by Robert S. Neighbors, has been erroneously cited as a designation for the Plains Apache and Lipan (Swanton 1942:7).

Early historical names that have been suggested as references to the Plains Apache are Cuampe, Orejones, Tuhkiwaku, Tuhpahkas, Dotame, Witapahato, and Kaskaia. See "Enigmatic Groups," this volume, for a discussion of these names.

Sources

A synthetic study of Plains Apache history and culture remains to be written. A.B. Thomas (1932, 1940) and Nasatir (1952) are among the most informative sources for seventeenth- and eighteenth-century Southern Plains history.

The Spanish Archives of New Mexico and Texas are important sources for primary documents in which Plains Apacheans and Plains Apaches are mentioned. Anglo-American military and travel journals provide glimpses of the Plains Apache during the early nineteenth century, though often hidden in the midst of the more populous Arapaho, Cheyenne, Kiowa, and Comanche with whom they associated. Closer account of the Plains Apache is taken in United States military and Bureau of Indian Affairs records beginning in 1865 and continuing into the reservation period. The Kiowa, Comanche, and Apache Agency records are at the Oklahoma Historical Society in Oklahoma City and at the National Archives Center in Fort Worth, Texas. Mooney (1898, 1907e) collected some information on the Plains Apache, but this is colored by a Kiowa-centric perspective. The first sustained ethnographic effort with the Plains Apache was by McAllister in 1933–1934. McAllister's (1935, 1949, 1955, 1965, 1970) publications are focused primarily on social organization and religion. Brant (1949, 1950, 1951, 1953, 1969) worked in the Plains Apache community in 1948–1949. Bittle (1954, 1956, 1962, 1963, 1971; M.E. Opler and W.E. Bittle 1961) pursued linguistic and ethnographic fieldwork beginning in 1951 and continuing into the 1970s. Bittle's linguistic notes (1952–1956) and ethnographic notes (1952–1975) are archived at the University of Oklahoma. Bittle's students at the University of Oklahoma and Indiana University studied Plains Apache topics (Bross 1962; P.A. Freeman 1965; Jordan 1965; T. Hill and K.L. Beals 1966; K.L. Beals 1967; T.G. Baugh 1970; Sanford 1971; M.R. Collins 1983). Meadows (1999:177–250) describes men's societies. Plains Apache oral histories are recorded in both the Indian-Pioneer Papers, housed at the Oklahoma Historical Society and the Western History Collection of the University of Oklahoma, and the Doris Duke Oral History Collection.

Lipan Apache

MORRIS E. OPLER

The Lipan (lĭ'pän) are one of the seven Apachean-speaking* tribes of the Southwest and Southern Plains, the others being the Chiricahua, Jicarilla, Mescalero, Navajo, and Western Apache (see vol. 10), and the Plains Apache (this vol.). Lexicostatistical study, which may provide rough estimates for the length of time speakers of related languages have been separate from one another, suggests a time divergence of 227 years between Lipan and Jicarilla (Hoijer 1956), and 429 years between Lipan and Plains Apache (Bittle 1961; cf. Hymes 1957).

About 1830, Berlandier (1969:130) recorded a Bidai tradition that the Lipan had come from the north to Texas before either the Wichita or Comanche, that is, before the beginning of the eighteenth century. The cause of the migration was said to have been a quarrel that split the tribe. The first mention of the Lipan in Spanish documents occurred in 1718, when they attacked the newly founded town of San Antonio. Historians have suggested that the Lipan had only shortly before then arrived in Texas, having been driven south by the expansion of the Comanche (Bolton 1914, 1915; Dunn 1911, 1912, 1914). However, the southward trek of the Apacheans was in progress long before the Comanche became a factor, and it occurred west as well as east of the Rio Grande. Furthermore, Lipan history is not one of unrelieved defeat at the hands of the Comanche. Bolton chronicled Lipan triumphs over the Comanche in 1771 (1911:83–84) and 1789 (1915:127).

Other scholars favor the theory of a late entrance into Texas by the Lipan because of the identification of the Dismal River archeological aspect of Kansas, Nebraska, and Colorado, which flourished from 1675 to 1725, with Apacheans. To accommodate the theory that the Lipan were responsible for the Dismal River remains it is necessary not only to assume an extremely speedy tribal relocation, but also to accept, because of sharp differences in Lipan and Dismal River house forms, economy, food habits, and technology, that Lipan culture was virtually transformed in a remarkably short time in its new setting (vol. 10:382–384).

Both linguistic evidence and the existence of various unique features of Lipan culture that must have taken considerable time to develop support the conclusion of Secoy (1953:22) and Worcester (1944:227) that the Lipan were firmly entrenched in central and south Texas by the second half of the seventeenth century (fig. 1). Throughout the eighteenth century they moved progressively south, their territory extending from the Rio Grande on the west to the Colorado River on the east. By the mid-nineteenth century they had moved north again, to the Colorado River north of Austin, and hunted east from the Colorado to the Brazos with the Tonkawa (M.E. Opler 1974a:166).

In the third quarter of the nineteenth century a portion of the Lipan were driven westward across the Rio Grande, and the remainder fled north. The survivors were so dispersed and reduced in numbers that they found difficulty in maintaining a distinct tribal cultural tradition, intermarriage further blurring their cultural identity. They settled predominantly on the Mescalero Reservation in southeastern New Mexico with the Mescalero and Chiricahua Apache. Consequently, by mid-twentieth century their culture tended to become assimilated to that of their hosts and neighbors, and the reservation language became an amalgam of Apachean dialects, with Mescalero perhaps dominating (vol. 10:409).

History

Once colonization began in earnest in the province of Texas, clashes between the Lipan and the Spanish intruders became frequent. There were constant raids for slaves by which Spanish officials enriched themselves, and the horse herds of the presidios and missions were a tempting target for Apache raiders. Various strategies were tried to curb

*The phonemes of Lipan are: (lenis voiceless stops and affricates) b, d, λ, ʒ, ǯ, g, ʔ; (voiced prenasalized stop) ⁿd; (voiceless aspirated stops and affricates) t, λ, c, č, k; (glottalized stops and affricates) t̓, λ̓, c̓, č̓, k̓; (voiced spirants) z, ž, γ; (voiceless spirants) ł, s, š, x, h; (nasals) m, n; (lateral) l; (semivowel) y; (short oral vowels) i, e, a, o; (long oral vowels) i·, e·, a·, o·; (short nasal vowels) į, ę, ą, ǫ; (long nasal vowels) į·, ę·, ą·, ǫ·; (low tone) unmarked, (high tone) v́, (falling tone) v̂, (rising tone) v̌. Rising and falling tones occur only on long vowels. In his earlier writings Hoijer (1938, 1956:225–226) distinguished Lipan ⁿd ([ⁿd]~[n]) from d ([t]) and n (consistent [n]); later he phonemicized his earlier ⁿd as n and mentioned reanalyzing as b an earlier ⁿb, which he seems not to have used in print (Hoijer 1975:5–6).

Information on Lipan comes from Hoijer (1938, 1956:225–226, 1975) and Hoijer's unpublished field notes and typed texts (Scott Rushforth, communication to editors 1992, 1999; Willem J. de Reuse, communication to editors 1999). In Hoijer's (1975) orthography the phonemes are written: b, d, L, j, ǰ, g, ʔ; n; t, Ł, c, č, k; t̓, Ł̓, c̓, č̓, k̓; z, ž, γ; ł, s, š, x, h; m, n; l; y; i, e, a, o; ii, ee, aa, oo; į, ę, ą, ǫ; įį, ęę, ąą, ǫǫ; (low tone) v̀, v̀v̀, (high tone) v́, v́v́, (falling tone) v̂v̂, (rising tone) v̌v̌.

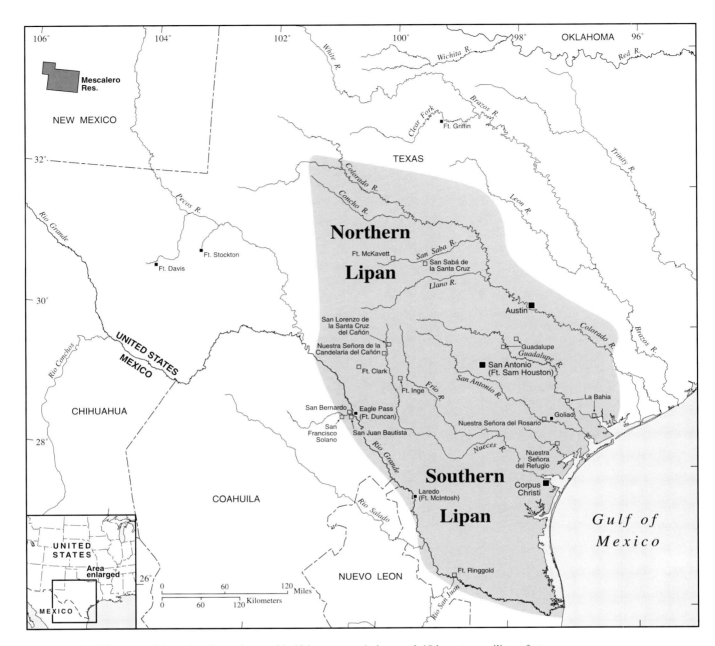

Fig. 1. Early 19th-century Lipan Apache territory with 18th-century missions and 19th-century military forts.

Lipan forays, such as inciting strife between the Lipan and Mescalero, plying them with liquor, and supplying them with trade goods to make them dependent on Spanish favors. Efforts to missionize the Lipan were also attempted, stimulated in part by the conviction that Lipan territory contained mineral wealth that could not be exploited until the Indians were concentrated.

In 1754 a mission for the Lipan was established west of the Rio Grande in Coahuila. In 1755 its occupants burned the buildings and departed (Dunn 1912:199–200). Another mission was founded on the San Sabá River in 1757. The Lipan came occasionally for presents but refused to live there. In March 1758 this mission, too, was sacked and burned, this

time by a combined force of Comanches, Bidais, Tonkawas, Hasinais, and others (Weddle 1964:73). In January 1762 the mission of San Lorenzo de la Santa Cruz del Cañón was founded on the upper Nueces River for the followers of a Lipan local group leader (Tunnell and Newcomb 1969). A month later a second mission, Nuestra Señora de la Candelaria del Cañón, was established about 10 miles south at the behest of another Lipan leader. These two Lipan local group leaders had a combined following of 700 people. The Spaniards hoped to induce 10 other known local groups to settle down eventually. This suggests that there were between 3,000 and 4,000 Lipans living in central Texas during this period (Tunnell and Newcomb 1969:166–169). Whether the Lipan ever really lived in the missions or merely camped near them is not clear. Certainly the population was in constant flux, and there was a steady stream of Indian visitors who arrived to solicit provisions and left immediately afterward. Father Diego Jiménez, the priest in charge, who was desperately seeking increased government support and was striving to show that progress was being made in conversions and pacification, had to admit in 1763 that the Spaniards exercised very little control over the Indians (Tunnell and Newcomb 1969:170). In 1764 an outbreak of smallpox devastated the mission area.

By 1767 all the Lipan had deserted the missions. When the Marqués de Rubí came to inspect the frontier and visited San Lorenzo and Candelaria missions in the summer of 1767, he and Nicolás de Lafora, his cartographer and chronicler, scoffed at the notion that the Lipan had ever been induced to live in these places (Tunnell and Newcomb 1969:163–176). Instead of missions Rubí counseled a war of extermination against the Apache and removal of the survivors to Mexico, believing that this would end Spanish troubles with the Comanche (Webb 1931:130).

During the last quarter of the eighteenth century the Lipan received some respite from Spanish arms and were even sought as allies at times, mainly because the Spaniards were campaigning vigorously against the Mescalero (Reeve 1946:197–200). Yet the truce was often interrupted by hostilities. As internal political problems in the Spanish provinces steadily increased, Spanish control over the northern and eastern frontiers became more precarious, and Lipan hostility increased.

According to Berlandier, early in the nineteenth century the Lipan joined forces with the Comanche, proving a formidable enemy to the Spaniards. During an interlude of peace, the Lipan planted gardens of corn and other vegetables on the Llano River, while maintaining their nomadic lifeway. However, by 1822 their alliance with the Comanche failed, the Lipan putting to death a number of Comanche men married to Lipan women. They fled farther south, beyond the line of Spanish settlement, for protection from the Comanche (Berlandier 1969:131–134). According to Lipan tradition, in the early nineteenth century the tribe claimed as their homeland the area of the Texas gulf region around Houston and Galveston (M.E. Opler 1938a:271).

The hostility of the Lipan toward the Spaniards was well appreciated by Americans as they edged toward Texas, and in 1807 John Sibley (1922:93–94) reported that the Lipan were "warmly attached to the Americans." In the revolt against Spanish rule led by the forces of Augustus William Magee and José Bernardo Maximiliano Gutiérrez de Lara forces in 1812–1813, the Lipan not only took part in the fighting but also supplied the rebels with provisions (H. McC. Henderson 1951:50; Thrall 1879:449; H.P. Walker 1963:577; Wooten 1898, 1:79–81). The letters of the last Spanish governor of Texas attest to his difficulties with the Lipan (Martínez 1957:144, 331). After achieving independence in 1821, the Mexican government tried to restore

peace with the Lipan by negotiating a treaty and conferring the rank of lieutenant colonel on one of their leaders, Cuelgas de Castro (Reeve 1946:201).

The growing body of persons of American origin in Texas was also eager to court Lipan good will. In 1825 Stephen Austin, acting as "Commandant of the Colony on the Brazos and Colorado Rivers in the province of Texas," presented a "passport" to a Lipan chief, Huan Novale, which identified him as "a principal chief of the Lipan Nation of Indians who are friends and brothers of the american settlers in this province" and urged "all americans who may meet with said Capt. Huan Novale to receive him in friendship and treat him with kindness and attention" (E.C. Barker 1925:162–163).

The initial cordiality between the Lipan and Americans was genuine as far as the Lipan were concerned. The Americans in Texas were still too few to pose a threat to hunting territories and offered a good opportunity for trade relations (Sowell 1964a, 2:424–425, 1964:183–184; G.W. Tyler 1966:21). In 1833, when sentiment for separation from Mexico was gaining ground, the Lipan traveled to Houston to seek treaty negotiations with the dissidents (Holt 1966:230).

Lipan friendship with Texans of American origin flourished in the years immediately following the declaration of Texan independence in 1836. Lipan warriors began to act as scouts and guides for the Texas Rangers and distinguished themselves in this role until 1843, when disenchantment set in (Reading 1960:29, 39, 42, 72–74, 242). The Lipan leaders were on excellent terms with Sam Houston and often went to Houston to visit him and to trade (Dresel 1954:33; Winfrey and Day 1959–1966, 1:44). During 1838 the Lipan received presents and payments from the Republic of Texas (Winfrey and Day 1959–1966, 1:32–42, 163–164, 225–226), and in 1839 the Lipan and Texas signed a treaty of friendship (Oberste 1953:233). One of the policies that solidified Lipan-Texan amity was the new republic's hostility toward the Comanche and its determination to keep them to the north. The Lipan joined assaults on the Comanche enthusiastically and earned high praise for their services (Hyde 1952:39–41; Jenkins 1958:184–187; Nance 1963:54, 103, 544; Winfrey and Day 1959–1966, 1:57; Wooten 1898, 1:732–737). They also lent their military support to the Texans when Mexico attempted a reconquest of its lost province (Hendricks 1919:122, 137; Nance 1964:41, 66–67; Smithwick 1900:220–224). During this period the Lipan were being assured that a permanent line would be drawn between the White settlements and the main Indian hunting grounds that would guarantee abundant lands for perpetual Indian use.

In 1843 Lipan-Texan relations took an abrupt change for the worse. It was apparent by this time that Texas would be annexed to the United States. In anticipation of the event, new waves of immigrants reached Texas, bringing many land-hungry adventurers who knew nothing about past Indian relations and made no distinctions among Indian groups. A symptom of the times was the murder in 1843 of *943* young Flacco, on his return from scouting for the Texas Rangers. The son of a prominent chief of the same name, young Flacco had been killed by Americans, although the Texas government tried to blame the murder on Mexican bandits. Sam Houston wrote an emotional letter of condolence to the older Flacco, but the crime went unpunished, and the Lipan were thoroughly angered, Flacco leading his band into Mexico (Winfrey and Day 1959–1966, 1:165).

The annexation of Texas in 1846 precipitated war between the United States and Mexico, at the close of which, in 1848, thousands of soldiers were mustered out of service in Texas; many chose to stay there, and they clamored for land. With resources still undeveloped, Texas was admitted to the Union directly as a state, with title to all "unoccupied" lands and full responsibility for past debts incurred during the struggle for independence and the Indian wars. As Texans saw it, the only means of satisfying their debts, raising capital, attracting desirable immigrants, and rewarding the militia was by the disposal of parts of the public domain. The presence of Indians on the land, the argument ran, made it impossible for the state to utilize its one valuable resource. The Indians, Texas contended, were a federal problem. It was the responsibility of the national government to control them and to move them out of Texas to federal lands, meanwhile defending its citizens in Texas (Webb 1965:127–128).

For nearly a decade the federal government tried to induce the state of Texas to appropriate or cede some of its public lands for the creation of Indian reservations. In 1854, two small reserves were established in the north central part of the state. By 1859 an organized campaign of slander and violence had so endangered the resident Indians that they had to be moved to Indian Territory in present-day Oklahoma (Neighbours 1955, 1957, 1958, 1960).

The two tribes that refused to enter the reserves in 1855 were the Lipan and the Mescalero. Robert S. Neighbors, the Indian agent, mentioned a vague plan, never implemented, to create a reserve for them farther west. Instead, the full might of the American army and state forces was turned against them. Military action against the Lipan had begun in 1846, when the Texas Rangers attacked a Lipan village, and continued intermittently throughout the next four decades. Army posts were established in Lipan territory, and surveyors and settlers followed. Any Lipan resistance or attempt to regain lands was labeled a "depredation" and evoked instant reprisal. By 1873 many of the surviving Lipan had been driven across the Rio Grande into Mexico. On the grounds that they raided into the United States from their Mexican sanctuaries, Col. Ranald S. Mackenzie, acting under orders from Lt. Gen. Philip H. Sheridan, resolved to strike at them. Using an American consul in Mexico as a spy, Mackenzie learned the location of the Indian camps. Then on May 17, 1873, the soldiers violated the international border and on the next day destroyed a Lipan encampment and a Mescalero and Kickapoo village as well. These incursions into Mexico

continued until late 1877 in spite of strong protests by Mexican authorities. It was 1881 before the army decided that the Lipan were destroyed as an effective force (R.G. Carter 1961; Mexican Border Commission 1875; Cecil B. Smith 1928; ARCIA 1872; Edward S. Wallace 1951, 1953; Ernest Wallace 1964, 1967, 1968).

During the war of extermination waged against them some Lipan found refuge in widely separated places. A few escaped to Indian Territory and eventually joined the Plains Apache (Sjoberg 1953a:80). Some combined with the Tonkawa, who were being protected at Fort Griffin in north Texas. In 1883 there were 19 Lipans camping there with 79 Tonkawas (ARCIA 1883:136, 278, 1884:153–154). In 1884 they were all removed to Indian Territory and eventually were settled near Tonkawa in Kay County, Oklahoma (ARCIA 1885:LVII–LVIII). An estimated 30 Lipans were living in Oklahoma in 1951 (M.H. Wright 1951:180) . A number of Lipans made their way to New Mexico and were found on the Mescalero Reservation in 1879 (Reeve 1946:208; Sjoberg 1953:80). At first their relations with the Mescalero were not always smooth (ARCIA 1886:202). In 1904, 37 more Lipans reached Mescalero, the remnants of a band that had been living in Coahuila, Mexico (ARCIA 1905:251).

Sociocultural Situation in the 1990s†

Lipan people living on the Mescalero Apache Reservation have shared most features of their lives with Mescalero and Chiricahua Apaches who live there. While the Apache peoples who settled on the reservation experienced tremendous changes in their language, culture, social organization, and economy, there also has been important sociocultural persistence (vol. 10:424). Despite intermarriage, synthesis, and amalgamation, reservation people continued to distinguish among members of the three Apachean groups. At Mescalero in the 1990s, at least 34 families (50 adults) considered themselves to have Lipan ancestry.

As a distinct Athapaskan language, Lipan was no longer used by people in everyday situations. It was possibly known only by 2 to 10 elderly people and was rarely spoken (Hoijer 1975:5).

Most Lipan people participated with other Apaches of the reservation in traditional cultural activities. The most important of such events is probably the Girls' Puberty ceremony, held at least once each summer.

Lipans are represented by the Mescalero Apache tribal government, which also represented Mescalero and Chiricahua Apaches. Many people of Lipan descent have served on the tribal council or held other positions in the tribal government.

---

†This section was written by Scott Rushforth with the assistance of Evelyn Breuninger and Elbys Hugar.

Population estimates are often much too low because, though the tribal name is used, it is obvious from context that the reference is to Lipans of a certain region or those associated with a certain leader. Moreover, many estimates were made before all parts of Lipan territory were penetrated. A judicious estimate of all Lipan Apache in 1700, including those living in Mexico, would be about 6,000. M.H. Wright (1951:180) estimated the Lipan population in 1736 to have been about 8,000. John Sibley (1922:93) reported that the number of Lipans between the Llano and the San Sabá rivers in 1807 was 1,200 to 1,300 with 200 to 250 warriors. J. Morse (1822:374) put the number of Lipans between the Rio Grande and the sources of the Nueces in 1820 at 3,500.

The Lipans led by Cuelgas de Castro who continually traveled between Goliad and Laredo in 1828 were put at 150 families or approximately 750 people by Sánchez (1926:252). About 1830, Berlandier estimated the Lipan at 400 families (400 men). In 1836 "part of the Lipan Apache tribe numbering some 500 members headed by chief Castro" was near the Rio Grande (Santos 1968:51).

The number of Lipans "principally above the Colorado and San Antonio" in 1836 was placed at 250 warriors or 900 souls (Muckleroy 1922:241–242). In the 1840s the population of Lipans in the northwest part of Starr County was quoted at 900 (J.C. Rayburn and V.K. Rayburn 1966:12, 18). The Lipans who ranged between the Guadalupe and the Rio Grande in 1840 numbered about 200 warriors or 1,000 individuals (Nance 1964:447). Lipans between the Rio Grande and the Colorado were given as 250 warriors in 1840; this would suggest a minimum of 1,000 individuals (F. Moore 1965:31).

In 1847 it was said that the Lipan could "raise about 200 warriors of their own band" (Winfrey and Day 1959–1966, 3:96–97); from this could be inferred a total population of 800–1,000. Figures supplied by Neighbors in 1849 listed Lipan numerical strength at 100 warriors and 500 people (Winfrey and Day 1959–1966, 3:108–109). In the middle of the nineteenth century "the friendly Lipan in Texas" were estimated at 300–500 (Reebe 1946:203).

Culture in the Mid-Nineteenth Century

The Lipans at Mescalero were a group sufficiently large to preserve their language and traditions for some time, at least until a core of information concerning them was obtained through anthropological work (M.E. Opler 1931–1935), which provides the source for most of the following material.

Subsistence

• HUNTING The mainstay of the food economy was the buffalo hunt. Annual migration brought the buffalo herds south into Lipan territory in the fall "when the geese were flying," and the Lipan considered the animals to be fattest and their hides to be at their best then. The Lipan knew the approximate time of their arrival and the watering places where they congregated. Local groups gathered near the hunting grounds in a large camp, and the necessary horses, tools, and weapons (primarily the bow and the lance—fig. 2—though the Lipan also possessed a few guns) were made ready. Local group leaders supervised the preparations of their followers. Shamans with ceremonial power associated with the buffalo prayed that the hunt would be successful and accident-free. Scouts were sent ahead to find the first arrivals, for invariably some animals traveled in advance of the main herd. When they were sighted, the hunters began to move toward the hunting grounds, and some of the women, leading horses equipped with packsaddles, followed behind to assist in butchering and transporting the meat to the main camp. One of the first buffalo to appear was killed, and a shaman with requisite sacred power welcomed the buffalo and blessed the food. A bit of this first kill was distributed to each participating family.

When the main herd arrived, the hunters, mounted on fast, well-trained horses, remained to the sides and faced away from the buffalo to reduce the chance of startling them. After the herd had passed, they wheeled their mounts around and closed in. The animals were skinned and butchered where they had fallen, and the meat and hides were transported to the large encampment as quickly as possible. There drying racks had been set up, and the meat was jerked, sun-dried, and stored in parfleches. Certain ritual precautions were heeded: the meat was not thrown about carelessly during butchering but was neatly stacked on the hide; when the brain was removed, it was replaced by sacred grama grass; the offal was left with a prayer for Crow, who could withhold game animals if aggrieved. Once the hunt had begun, the hunters and women worked together in family units. Hunters had family requirements in mind and selected game of appropriate age, size, and sex.

The fall buffalo hunt lasted about three weeks; the associated labor continued for some time beyond this. When an ample supply of hides and meat had been obtained, the people moved to smaller, more dispersed encampments within local group territories for the winter. The buffalo remained in the area until spring; consequently, buffalo hunting on a smaller scale during this period was possible if the need arose. Ordinarily, however, the main effort supplied the annual requirements for buffalo meat and skins.

All parts of the buffalo were utilized. The tongue, entrails, heart, stomach, kidney, udders of the buffalo cow, and the fetal buffalo were eaten. So was the brain, when it was not needed for tanning. The stomach was consumed or used as a water container. From the hide came blankets, robes, tepee covers, parfleches (fig. 3), bullboats, shields, quivers, feather containers, moccasin soles, and carriers shaped like burden baskets. The sinew made excellent bowstrings. From the horn were fashioned spoons, dippers, *945*

Fig. 2. Detail of map of Sonora and Nueva Vizcaya showing 2 Indian figures in the area labeled "Apaches Lipanes" (full map in Fireman 1977:10). They wear feathers in their hair and have bows, arrows, quivers, and a lance. By Juan de Pagazaurtundúa, in Mexico, 1803.

drinking cups, and ornaments for the ends of the bow. The war leader's headdress was sometimes adorned with buffalo horns. A horn rattle occasionally substituted for a gourd rattle in the Peyote ceremony. Other rattles were made from the tail or hooves of a young buffalo. The hair was used to ornament shields, was braided for rope, became a component of medicines, and, combined with hair from the tail of a colt, provided material for saddle cinches. Buffalo chips served as fuel, and even the scrotum of the bull was utilized as a bag.

The Lipan range included mountain and foothill areas where other game animals were found. As a source of meat deer was second only to the buffalo. Deer were stalked by solitary hunters or by men in pairs or small parties. Wives and female relatives aided the enterprise by ceremoniously bringing out the implements with which they hoped to prepare the hides, and by praying for the man's success. Tanned deerskin was the favorite material for the upper part of moccasins, men's leggings and shirts, and women's blouses and skirts. Products from the deer supplemented what could be obtained from the buffalo; for instance, deer horn was used for the saddle frame and for chipping flint for arrowheads and knives. Deer blood was often drunk fresh and warm as a health measure. Deer were considered to be under the protection of Mountain Spirits, who could withhold them if angered. These supernaturals were impersonated by masked dancers in rituals.

Lipan canons of generosity were much in evidence during the deer hunt, since someone seeking game was likely to come upon a fellow tribesman who had just made a kill. It was expected that the successful hunter would step aside and offer to share his spoils; the new arrival was free to take the skin and some of the meat. Deer hunting prevailingly took place within local group territory, and sharing and exchanges were characteristic of local group socioeconomic relations.

Antelope were plentiful in lowlands adjoining the hilly regions. A lone hunter might try to steal up on them, sometimes using a head mask, but the discovery of a large number was usually the signal for an antelope surround. Since an antelope drive was a rather informal affair, an initiator would sketch a picture of an antelope on a thin piece of rawhide to invite participation. Because the antelope was not considered a dangerous quarry, the event was treated as a festive occasion and as an opportunity for women to demonstrate their riding and roping skills. Etiquette required that a man should not overtake and pass a woman who was chasing an antelope. The only weapon a woman carried was a lasso, and if she roped an antelope or merely struck it, the nearest man was obligated to shoot it for her.

Another event in which women participated as equals was the rabbit surround, conducted on foot. Other animals that served as sources of food and also contributed materials for

946

The British Mus., Mus. of Mankind, London: 1954.W.AM5.951.

Fig. 3. Parfleche taken at the Battle of Remolino, Coahuila, during the 4th Cavalry raid under Gen. Ranald S. Mackenzie, May 19, 1873. It is painted red, green, yellow, and black on a natural background and has tassels of tanned hide. Collected by Capt. John A. Wilcox; 25 cm square, excluding fringe.

• GATHERING The most important wild vegetal food of the Lipan was the agave or mescal. Although gathering plant foods was mainly the responsibility of women, obtaining mescal was a group enterprise in which men also participated. In late spring a party would travel to a locality where the mescal was plentiful. The women would pry up the large crowns with a sharpened wooden wedge and trim them with a broad-bladed cutting tool. The men, who had come to guard the women and assist in the heavy work, helped carry the crowns to a central place. When enough of them were accumulated, a circular pit about four feet deep was dug. Wood was stacked in it, and flat, heavy rocks were placed on top of the wood. The wood was fired, and by the time it burned to ashes the rocks were extremely hot. Then a man or woman born in the summer stood to the east of the pit, traced a cross of charcoal on top of one of the crowns, prayed, and, after four ritual feints, threw the crown into the pit. The other crowns followed, and wet grass and finally earth sealed the underground oven. The mescal crowns were allowed to steam for two days. During this period water could not be spilled and the hands could not be washed, precautions against a heavy rain shower. When the crowns had been cooked and removed, those that were not going to be eaten fresh were pounded and sun-dried at the site. This meant several days' work by both men and women before the return journey could begin.

Sotol was another Lipan food staple. Its crowns were prepared much as those of mescal and were sometimes steamed with mescal. The inner portion of the young stalk was roasted, and sotol was the plant that yielded wood for the fire drill. The fruit of the yucca was eaten fresh and was also sun-dried. The tender inner portion of the stalk was roasted. Yucca flowers were mixed with wild onion to make a flavoring for soup, the juice of the leaves was mixed with coloring material to fix paint, and the mashed roots provided an excellent soap.

Other important food plants were prickly pear, mesquite, juniper, agarita, piñon, oak, walnut, pecan, screwbean, sumac, palmetto, locust, elderberry, Texas persimmon, hackberry, mulberry, wild plum, sunflower, cattail, western yellow pine, wild potatoes, lamb's-quarters, seed grasses, devil's claw, strawberry, raspberry, gooseberry, blackberry, wild cherry, wild rose, hawthorn, wild grape, and wild onion. These were also a source of paints, poultices, medicines, firewood, bow wood, and wood for windbreaks, frameworks for lodges, saddle frames, fire pokers, tepee pegs, stakes with which to peg out hides, food bowls, buckets, and arrows. They also contributed boughs and leaves for bedding, pollen for ritual, leaves for shingling wickiups, and the outer cover of cigarettes. Many other plants, though they had no food value, were gathered for artifacts, medicine, and ritual.

Salt, found in layers of rock in caves, was sought. One of the prime sweeteners was wild honey. Piloncillo (brown sugar loaf), obtained through trade with Mexicans, was greatly prized.

artifacts and medicines were the black bear, beaver, bighorn, burro, elk, horse, mountain lion, mule, prairie dog, squirrel, wood rat, and even the skunk in times of scarcity. It is surprising to find the bear described as an article of Lipan diet, since so many Apachean groups, including the closely related Jicarilla, considered it evil. Fish and turtles, though not too greatly savored, were consumed on occasion, and turkeys, ducks, quail, and mourning doves were eaten.

947

• HORTICULTURE   A little corn and squash were raised at level places along streams. A digging stick was used in planting the seeds, and men and women shared agricultural work. Irrigation ditches might be run to the small plots if the field was close to water. There was no attempt to irrigate on higher ground. Dependence on the agricultural crop was minimal, and it was not unusual for the Lipan to depart for the hunt with the intention of harvesting what survived after their return. If they came back before the corn was ripe, they might pull weeds, pile up earth around the plants, or even carry water in buckets to the field. Most of the corn was eaten fresh, boiled or roasted. Some was roasted, sun-dried, and stored. A few ears were braided together and saved for seed. Though corn was highly esteemed, the Lipan depended on trade and raid rather than cultivation for the major part of their supply. Many of their corn dishes, such as tortillas, tamales, piñole, and hominy, reflected Mexican or Southeast influence. Corn pollen, prized by more agriculturally minded Apacheans, was not used ritually. The Lipan claim that though they knew that certain Indian tribes of Mexico manufactured it, they themselves did not brew tiswin or corn beer until they were settled at Mescalero. No tobacco was cultivated; wild tobacco was gathered when smoking material was needed.

Structures

The Lipan lived in two types of lodges. In the high, wooded country they built a melon-shaped wickiup, made of a circular framework of saplings fixed at intervals in the ground and lashed together at the top. The floor was at ground level. This dwelling was about seven feet high at the center and had a diameter of approximately eight feet. Layers of large leaves or boughs were lashed to the sides as a covering, and in wet weather hides might be thrown on top. A nuclear family would inhabit such a dwelling. This type of home was easily and quickly constructed and could be abandoned without serious economic loss. In good weather, rectangular shades were built adjoining the wickiups.

   The second type of lodge was the tepee, made for use on the plains. A good-sized tepee required 12 to 14 buffalo skins. A woman skilled in the procedure was asked to cut and fit the skins. The sewing of the cover was a cooperative venture of all the women of the extended family and perhaps even some friends from neighboring camp clusters. When the poles, pegs, and stakes had been gathered, an elderly woman shaman blessed them. Early the next morning, when the tepee was erected for the first time, the same shaman presided in a ceremony to bless the home and its occupants. The construction and maintenance of the lodge was the responsibility of the women. According to Berlandier (1969:134), the tepee always faced east, away from the prevailing winds.

   The tepee poles were carefully selected and were very valuable on the treeless plains. They were dragged along on either side of a pack animal when the group was traveling.

Smithsonian, NAA:84-4696.

Fig. 4. Man, woman, and children in front of house. The man has cloth-wrapped braids, otter-fur turban, and trade silver gorget around his neck. He holds an 1873 Winchester carbine gun. The house is wattle and daub with a chimney (right) and grass-covered roof. Stereograph by Henry A. Doerr, San Antonio, Tex., 1880–1885.

The Lipan had no real travois: since there were no cross-pieces to link together the poles being dragged on either side of the horse, no baggage or passengers could be transported on the poles. The folded tepee cover was carried on top of the pack animal. In the 1930s the Lipan had no tradition of using dogs as pack animals nor of raising them for food; the very thought was repugnant to them. In fact, the Lipan had few dogs and had mixed feelings concerning them. To a degree, the dog was classified with the wolf and coyote, which were considered unclean and dangerous.

Technology

Because of the mobile life, little pottery was made. A few women, working the clay up from the mass, fashioned unpainted utility ware of a squat, broad shape. The only other Lipan venture in ceramics was the manufacture of small pipe bowls into which a reed stem was fixed.

   Hide was a favorite material in the construction of Lipan artifacts. For instance, the baby carrier was made entirely of hide instead of having a wooden frame and canopy. During her food-gathering activities the Lipan woman carried a hide container on her back, supported by a tumpline across her chest. This fulfilled the function of the woven burden basket common to most other Apacheans. Such extensive use of hide suggests Plains orientation, yet this was balanced by a tendency to employ wooden containers to a greater extent than was possible for most Plains tribes.

Clothing and Adornment

In 1828 Lipan men wore cloth breechcloths and deerskin leggings secured by a belt, from which a knife was often suspended. They covered themselves with painted buffalo robes (fig. 5), many with pictographic designs, probably representing war deeds. Men wore sandals, borrowed from Indians in Mexico, or moccasins. The hair was never cut, and was worn loose or tied at the back of the neck and braided. A man might add hair from his wife or from buffalo or horse tails to lengthen his own, the braid reaching to his knees. Women wore two piece dresses of deerskin, consisting of an upper garment "with intricate decorations of glass beads" and a knee-length skirt, as well as leggings attached to moccasins (Berlandier 1969:128–129).

Political and Social Organization

Because of the nature of the economy, the scattered condition of the tribe, and the virtual independence of the bands and local groups, there was little tribal cohesion and no centralized authority. Yet the people involved did recognize the existence of a Lipan tribe based on unity of language, dress, and customs. In aboriginal times there was probably no occasion when the whole tribe congregated at one time, acted as a unit, or recognized one leader. Yet there was sufficient solidarity and interchange among segments of the tribe to preserve internal peace and a collective identity.

Lipanes.

Lipans Du Texas inferieur et les rives du Rio Grande.

Thomas Gilcrease Inst. of Amer. Hist. and Art, Tulsa, Okla.

Fig. 5. Clothing. The man wears red face paint, a red cloth breechcloth, buckskin leggings tied with garters below the knee, moccasins, painted buffalo robe, bandolier, necklace, and metal arm bands. He holds a rifle covered by a fringed case; a powder horn and bullet pouch are attached to his bandolier. His hair is worn in a single long braid. The woman wears a fringed buckskin poncho and skirt and buckskin moccasins with attached leggings (Ewers 1969:136). Watercolor by Lino Sánchez y Tapia, 1834–1838, after a sketch by Lt. José María Sánchez y Tapia.

Mainly on geographical grounds the tribe was divided into two bands, a northern group and a southern group. The northern band was closer geographically to the Mescalero, had considerable contact with them, and, at least in the late period of tribal history, intermarried to some extent with them. The band had more cohesion than the tribe. The local groups of a band participated together in the annual buffalo hunt. Quite often there was intermarriage between members of neighboring local groups of the same band, as well as various ritual, economic, and social exchanges. Yet there was no central band leadership.

The unit in which face-to-face relationships were constant and in which leadership was manifest was the go·kah 'local group', a body of people who identified themselves with a given territory and with a specific leader (na·iáh) who had risen to prominence in that locality as a result of his wisdom, courage, persuasiveness, wealth, and generosity. His position was not hereditary and was not even guaranteed for his lifetime. It depended on the approval of the members and had to be constantly validated in action. If a leader's abilities deteriorated or his failures multiplied, he would be replaced. The authority of the leader was limited; he seldom acted in any grave matter without conferring with the family heads. He could advise and urge but could not coerce. Primarily, he summed up the consensus reached by the council of family representatives. The Lipan had criers whose duty it was to announce to the camp the chief's orders (Berlandier 1969:134).

The composition of a local group was not rigidly fixed. A family could leave and become attached to some other local group if it became dissatisfied; however, this was not lightly done, for local group economic and social ties were strong. There was a tendency for marriages to be arranged between persons of the same local group, but local group endogamy was not required.

The local group was comprised of a number of extended families, varying from 10 to 30. Some were related by blood or marriage; some were not. The extended family had a recognized headman, usually the oldest active male, who supervised its internal affairs and acted as its spokesman. The elementary families that composed the extended family had their individual dwellings (go·γạh) and together constituted a camp cluster. The members of the extended family formed the primary work unit and cooperated in all economic and social undertakings. Because residence after marriage was matrilocal, the extended family would ideally consist of an older man and woman, their unmarried sons and daughters, their married daughters, and the husbands and children of these women.

Life Cycle

Although the feelings of the young principals were not ignored, marriage was essentially an arrangement between families. The family of the boy took the initiative and offered presents to the girl's kin. Once arrangements were   949 concluded, the young couple started to live together without further formalities, the man moving to his wife's encampment. He was expected to contribute generously to the economy and defense of his wife's extended family. If his wife died, he was still bound to her family, who could exercise their sororate privilege and require him to wed an unmarried sister or cousin of his deceased spouse. The Lipan observed the levirate. Divorce was permitted for infidelity, incompatibility, or cruelty. The Lipan did not practice polygyny, even sororal polygyny.

The Lipan performed a number of life cycle ceremonies to protect a growing child from one precarious stage of life to the next. Among these were a first moccasins ceremony, a spring haircutting ceremony, and the girl's puberty rite. The last was an especially important occasion, for the fecundity and longevity of the girl depended on it. It was of great significance socially, also, for the girl's family played host to friends and neighbors to announce that they had successfully brought a daughter to maturity. There was no exactly equivalent rite for a young male, but when a boy underwent his first raid or warpath experience, he was considered holy and was in some respects treated much like the pubescent girl.

The Lipan death practices, while they involved much purification and ritual behavior, emphasized the speedy disposal of the body, the destruction of the personal property of the dead, and the suppression of his memory. So strong was the close kin's fear of the ghost of the departed that they tried to find outsiders who would bury the corpse. The anxiety was much less if the deceased was a very young child or a very old person who had lived out his life fully. The dead were thought to travel, guided by relatives who had died earlier, to an underworld where those who had been wicked in life lived in a separate section under miserable conditions and those who had been kind and good enjoyed an underground paradise.

Kinship

The Lipan kinship system was bilateral, but because of matrilocality children had more opportunity to interact with their maternal grandparents than with their paternal grandparents. Grandparents were expected to train, advise, and help discipline the young. They were the ones to discuss intimate matters with the grandchild, and they could tease a grandchild about sex and mating. A rivalry and teasing relationship existed between the mother's brother and his sister's children. Siblings and cousins of the same sex were supposed to be boon companions and to cooperate in all ventures. Great restraint existed between siblings and cousins of the opposite sex; in the case of cousins there could even be an avoidance relationship, the only one that the Lipan observed. Kinship terms of ego's generation indicated relative age, and an older sibling did exercise considerable authority over his younger relatives.

San Antonio Conservation Soc., Tex.: 75-1101.
Fig. 6. Man and 2 girls in front of a canvas tent. The man wears a cloth shirt, breechcloth, and has a wool blanket over his shoulders. The girls wear cloth blouses and skirts and have shell and bead necklaces. Photographer and date not recorded on this stereograph.

Raiding and Warfare

About 1830, the Lipan were described as "skilled at warfare, excellent horsemen, and with great talent for breaking and training wild horses." They were skilled with the bow and arrow and used guns "only in special circumstances." They also used a distinctive lance, more than eight feet long, "usually tipped with the straight blade of a Spanish sabre," and decorated with feathers and other ornaments. It was used for fighting on horseback, and was grasped in both hands. Like other tribes of the region, the Lipan occasionally ate the flesh of enemies killed in battle "to satisfy their vengeance." Male prisoners were tortured and killed, but women and children might be spared. Captive boys, in particular, might be raised as tribal members (Berlandier 1969:75–78, 129–130).

A raid for booty was distinguished from a war party, though raiders had to be prepared to fight if they were pursued. Warfare was initiated when an enemy killed a Lipan and his relatives clamored for revenge. A war dance and protective ceremony preceded an expedition against the enemy. To fight with a lance, which required engagement at close quarters, was considered a mark of great courage. The bravest deed was to strike a fallen enemy, for his companions could be expected to rush to his aid. The Lipan took scalps, but without much enthusiasm, in retaliation for scalping they had suffered at the hands of others. The scalp was carried home on a long pole, and, for fear of harming the "tender" children, it was kept at some distance from the camps until the victory dance. It was disposed of soon afterward, for scalps were not used to adorn shields or clothing. After a successful war party a victory dance was held at which booty was distributed and warriors told of their own deeds and verified those of others. If a war party failed, its members did not enter the encampment singing but quietly dispersed to their homes. If a Lipan warrior was killed in fighting, the other men did not cut their hair, gash their limbs, or engage in conspicuous mourning as the Comanche did (Berlandier 1969:134).

Religion

The Lipan believed that mankind was created in an underworld from which they ascended to the present world. Monsters threatened the people, who were in danger of extinction until the divine heroine Changing Woman (isʒánáλi·dí) gave birth to the culture hero Killer of Enemies (naɣíni·syání) who grew rapidly and soon was able to vanquish a number of the monsters. Though much evil was destroyed, some persisted, and the people still had to look to supernatural aid for survival. Individuals could appeal to deities such as Changing Woman and Killer of Enemies or seek to obtain some supernatural power (diɣih) of their own. This power reached humans through the media of familiar animals, plants, and natural forces; it could grant songs, prayers, and ceremonial procedures that would help individuals to cure and protect themselves and others. Such power was supposed to be used for beneficial ends, but in the hands of malicious persons it might be used to harm and then became witchcraft (ʔíniłi).

Sickness arose not only from witchcraft but also from contact with inherently evil animals or birds such as the snake, coyote, and owl. Also, powerful forces such as the Mountain Spirits (ha·šči·) or Lightning could become angered and cause sickness or misfortune. Such calamities could be countered by shamans, who might be either men or women, and who, through their ceremonies and contact with the supernaturals, learned the cause of the disaster and the way to remedy it. If witchcraft was involved, a shaman powerful enough to nullify the evil was sought. Most shamanistic rites had the curing of sickness as their aim, although control of the enemy, finding lost items, and foretelling the future were other objectives.

Besides these shamanistic rites, the Lipan practiced the Peyote ceremony, which was reported to have been introduced to them in pre-European times by their neighbors, the Carrizo, living to the east in the Texas gulf region (M.E. Opler 1938). Subsequently, the Lipan introduced the Peyote religion to the Mescalero. First limited to men seeking visions, the Peyote ceremony later became used for healing and admitted women for that purpose.

Writing in about 1830, Berlandier (1969:130) was able to record almost nothing about Lipan religion, although he mentioned the existence of medicine bundles comparable to those of the Comanche, apparently individually owned.

Synonymy‡

The name Lipan as a tribal designation appears in Spanish documents as early as the mid-eighteenth century, cited as Ypandis, 1732 (Bustillo y Zevallos in Dunn 1911:232, 235); Ypandes, 1743 (Santa Ana in Dunn 1911:267); and Ipandes and Ipandi, 1745 (Arricivita in Bandelier 1890–1892, 1:181). In historical documents throughout the second half of the eighteenth and all of the nineteenth centuries the modern form of the name occurs most commonly; for example, Lipan, 1772 (Morfi 1935:51); Lipans, 1783 (Cabello in Kinnaird 1946–1949, 2:70); and Lipanes, 1849 (Pino, Barreiro, and Escudero in Carroll and Haggard 1942:128). Notable spelling variants are Lipanos (Escudero 1834:244); Lipaines (Alegre 1841–1842, 1:336); Lapane, Lapanne, and Lipanis (Drake 1845:vi, viii, ix); and Lapanas (Bollaert 1850:276). Misprints include Lipau (ARCIA 1875:176) and Lipaw (W.J. Hoffman 1883:206); and occasionally the name is confused with the French designation for the Pawnee, as Le Panis and Les Pawnees (Z.M. Pike 1810, app. 3:9, 29). Occasionally the name Lipan is also preceded or followed by Apache or a similar modifier, as, for example, Lipan Apaches, 1786 (Galvez 1951:39); Apaches Lipanes, 1791–1792 (anonymous manuscript cited in Hodge 1907–1910, 1:769); and Apacheria Lipana, 1791 (Pedro de Nava in Twitchell 1914, 2:332); Lipanes Llaneros, 1828 (Payno 1870:264). The source of the name Lipan is not known, although it has been suggested that it is an adaptation of ipa-nde, composed of an initial syllable ipa that may be a personal name and (Mescalero) ⁿdé 'person, Indian' (Bandelier 1890–1892, 1:181; Hoijer 1938:77, 1938a:189).

The northern band of the Lipan has been cited as Lipanes de Arriba (Orozco y Berra 1864:59), Apaches Lipanes de Arriva (De Mézières in Bolton 1914, 2:150), and Lipanes del Norte, 1828 (Payno 1869:504); while the southern band has been referred to as Lipanes de Abajo (Orozco y Berra 1864:59), Apaches Lipanes de Abajo (de Mézières in Bolton 1914, 2:150), and Lipanes del Sur, 1828 (Payno 1869:504).

Several names have been given as the Lipan designation for themselves. Na'-izhǎ'ñ 'ours' (Mooney 1897) was first recorded in 1743 as Azain (Santa Ana in Dunn 1911:264) and is cognate with the Plains Apache self-designation. Lipan speakers in the mid-twentieth century accepted this name only as a circumlocution and preferred the partially analyzable form gołdiⁿdiʔi̜·lí, putatively compounded of the elements for 'people' and 'to be' (Morris Opler, personal communication 1975); it is apparently related to gołgahi̜ 'Plains Lipan' (Hoijer 1975:8, 25).

The accepted tribal name was čiši̜·hi̜· 'Forest Lipan' (Morris Opler, personal communication 1974; Hoijer 1975:8, 25), perhaps better translated 'forest Apache', an appellation said to derive from their frequenting the Cross Timbers of Texas (H.L. Scott 1912–1934). This name is partially cognate with Navajo Chíshí 'Chiricahua Apache' (R.W.

‡This synonymy was written by Douglas R. Parks.

Young and W. Morgan 1980:272), formerly designating the southern Apache and Mescalero (Gatschet 1885:786; J.P. Harrington 1936–1941; see vol. 10:417). It seems to have been borrowed into several Keresan languages, for example, Santa Ana *cʰišé* (Irvine Davis, personal communication 1977) and Acoma *cʰíšé* (W.R. Miller 1965:210; see also vol. 10:386). The meaning attributed to this Lipan self-designation is reflected in two apparently related names for the tribe in other languages: Comanche Hu-taʹ-ci or Houtachi, literally 'forest Apache' (ten Kate 1884:9, 1885:136); and Kiowa *á·tʰɔ̀gùy*, literally 'wood Apache' (Laurel Watkins, personal communication 1979). The Kiowa name was said to refer to the Mescalero as well as the Lipan (Mooney 1897).

The Lipan names for the northern and southern bands of the tribe were *kóʔídįhí·* 'no water people' and *kónicạ·hí·* 'big water people', respectively, the latter sometimes glossed simply as 'Lipan' in the twentieth century (Morris Opler, personal communication 1974; Hoijer 1975:7, 25). The latter band name is reflected in two other tribal designations for the Lipan: Mescalero Tu-tsan-nde 'great water people' (Mooney 1897); and Plains Apache *kódicahé* 'big water' (Bittle 1952–1975).

The Big Water People band name is also reflected in the sign language gesture for the Lipan, which was made by holding the hand at arm's length on the left side, with the index and second fingers extended, and drawing it back in five or six distinct jerks. At the end of each jerk the extended fingers come to rest against the inside of the thumb, and then the fingers are snapped to full length for repetition of the movement. This gesture was said to represent a reptile found along the shores of large lakes or ponds where the Lipan formerly lived (Mallery 1881:471).

The Tonkawa designation for the Lipan was *hoxol, hoxolatak* (Hoijer 1949:59), said to be derived from the term for a spiral shell that the Lipan hairstyle resembled (Gatschet 1884c:184).

A common designation for the Lipan in French and Spanish documents from the seventeenth to the nineteenth centuries is a variant of the Caddo name, which also referred to the Plains Apacheans.

The Wichita, Kitsai, Cheyenne, and Arapaho similarly referred to the Lipan as 'Apache', not distinguishing between them and other Plains Apachean groups.

An Apache group apparently related to, but distinct from, the Lipan was the Sipan. The earliest references to them are in the mid-eighteenth century, the latest in the nineteenth century. Renditions of the name include Sinapans, 1699 (Iberville in Margry 1876–1886, 4:316); Ysandis, 1732 (Bustillo y Zevallos in Dunn 1911:232); Yxandi, 1732 (Almazán in Dunn 1911:236); Sypanes (Robin 1807, 3:15); Seepans (Lane in Schoolcraft 1851–1857, 5:689); and Siapanes (Uhde 1861:121).

Sources

Writing between 1828 and 1834, Berlandier (1969) provides a contemporary sketch of some details of Lipan culture and history. Schilz (1987) gives a historial overview of the Lipan, and M.E. Opler (1974a) chronicles Lipan relations with Texas and the United States.

Relatively little attention has been paid to the Lipan by anthropologists. Gatschet (1884d) and Mooney (1897, 1897a) collected word lists and some miscellaneous information from them before the turn of the century. P.E. Goddard (1909) recorded the Lipan texts of a few trickster cycle episodes. None of this material has been published. Hoijer (1934) gathered texts and linguistic material from Lipan living at Mescalero, New Mexico, but while the data have been utilized in his general and comparative Apachean writings, no separate treatise on the language has resulted. One long text on Lipan history and customs has been published in the original language with a literal translation (Hoijer 1975). M.E. Opler (1931–1935) carried on intensive fieldwork among the Lipan at Mescalero, which resulted in a volume of myths and tales (M.E. Opler 1940), articles on special topics (M.E. Opler 1938, 1945, 1946, 1959), and a book-length ethnography (M.E. Opler 1974).

A summary article on Lipan culture (Dennis and Dennis 1925) may not be based on facts (Sjoberg 1953). A documentary and archeological study of San Lorenzo de la Santa Cruz del Cañon (Tunnell and Newcomb 1969) attempts to throw light on the Lipan.

Tonkawa

WILLIAM W. NEWCOMB, JR., AND THOMAS N. CAMPBELL

Territory

The Tonkawa ('täŋkəwu; earlier 'täŋkəwā) have lived near the town of Tonkawa in northern Oklahoma since 1885. In the preceding year the fewer than 100 surviving Tonkawa had been moved to Indian Territory from Fort Griffin in northern Texas. Although they have long been regarded as native to Texas, where they lived during most of the eighteenth and nineteenth centuries, when first recorded by name in 1601 the Tonkawa were living in Oklahoma in an area not very far west of where their descendants lived in the twentieth century. Historical documents indicate a slow movement of the Tonkawa south-southeastward into north and east-central Texas (fig. 1). In the early eighteenth century the eastern part of central Texas became a refuge area for Indian populations displaced by the eastward and southeastward expansion of mounted Apache groups from the Southern plains, and also by the northward advance of the Spanish frontier in northeastern Mexico. The Tonkawa were one of many immigrant groups who occupied this refuge area alongside declining Indian populations native to it. The various groups, both immigrant and native, further declined later in the eighteenth century, and most of them lost their separate identities through absorption by a few groups, such as the Tonkawa, or through amalgamation and acculturation in Spanish missions.

Language

Historical documentary sources suggest that the Tonkawa language* was spoken only by people recorded by the name Tonkawa, and they show that a sign language was used as the means of communication among the various linguistic groups in the central Texas refuge area. For

*The phonemes of Tonkawa are: (voiceless stops and affricate) p, t, c, k, k^w, $ʔ$; (voiceless spirants) s, x, x^w, h; (nasals) m, n; (resonants) w, l, y; (short vowels) a, e, a, o, u; (long vowels) $i·$, $e·$, $a·$, $o·$, $u·$. The oral stops are lenis; t, n, and l are dental; s and c vary from dental to alveolar; the nasals and resonants are syllabic word-finally. Consonants followed by a glottal release are analyzed as clusters with $ʔ$. Vowels do not occur word-initially; initial $ʔ$ is phonemic.

The phonemic analysis follows Hoijer (1946a:290), who gives further details. In an earlier analysis Hoijer (1933:2–4) analyzed the clusters with $ʔ$ as unitary glottalized consonants, which included ⟨t'⟩ and ⟨k'⟩. These 2 phonemes (or clusters) were eliminated from the later transcription because "glottalized stops occur only in abnormally slow speech" (Hoijer 1946a:290).

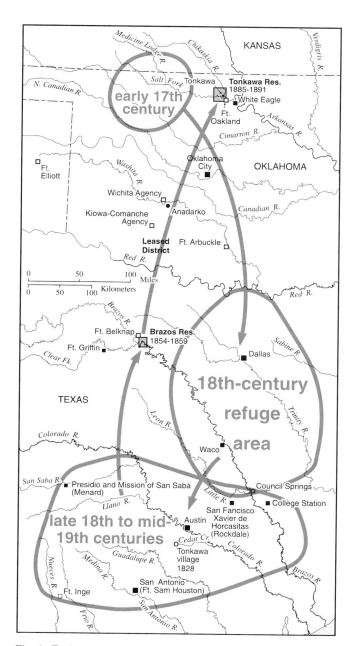

Fig. 1. Tonkawa territories from the early 17th through mid-19th centuries, with migration routes, and 19th-century reservations.

example, in 1768 a Spanish missionary, Gaspar José de Solís, visited encampments of Coco (Karankawa), Mayeye, Tonkawa, Yojuane, and other groups on the Brazos River northwest of modern College Station. He noted that "all the nations have one thing that is common, that is the sign-language with which they talk, not only for hours but entire days" (Kress and Hatcher 1932:58). In the refuge area in 1768 there clearly was still considerable linguistic diversity, and with availability of a sign language there was no need for wide use of a single spoken language. Gatschet (1884c) found that some of the Fort Griffin Tonkawa remembered a few sign language gestures.

The belief that the Tonkawa were native to Texas led linguists to compare the Tonkawa language with languages recorded for other hunting and gathering populations of lower Texas and adjacent northeastern Mexico, particularly Coahuilteco, Comecrudo, Cotoname, and Karankawa (vol. 10). Certain similarities were noted, and the five languages were assigned to a family of languages designated as Coahuiltecan, which was thought to be remotely related to the Hokan languages of California (Swanton 1915, 1940; Sapir 1920, 1925, 1929). This assessment was accepted until it was realized that the language samples used varied in size and representativeness and that for some of the languages there was little or no information on internal changes and borrowing from other languages. Modern linguists seem to be more cautious and regard the five languages as isolates (Goddard 1979a).

Component Groups

Eight Indian groups have been generally accepted as Tonkawa subdivisions: Cava, Emet, Ervipiame, Mayeye, Sana, Tohaha, Toho, and Yojuane (Bolton 1910b). Although small remnants of some of these groups, and perhaps others, at one time or another were absorbed by the Tonkawa, there is no clear evidence indicating that they were originally Tonkawa in speech and culture, and considerable evidence suggesting they were not (L. Johnson and T.N. Campbell 1992). The key to this misidentification is the statement made about groups said to have been assigned to Mission San Francisco Xavier de Horcasitas (one of the missions founded on the San Gabriel River near present Rockdale, Texas) because they all spoke the Tonkawa language. Four groups are specified: Ervipiame, Mayeye, Tonkawa, and Yojuane. But the mission registers (Dolores 1750) actually record 80 individuals from six Indian groups: Apache (1), Bidai (9), Ervipiame (35), Mayeye (22), Tonkawa (1), and Yojuane (12). The single Tonkawa listed is a three-year-old girl. There is no justification for considering the other names from this list as Tonkawa speakers. The remaining groups classified as Tonkawa subdivisions—Cava, Emet, Sana, Tohaha, and Toho—were identified as Tonkawa only because they were associated with Ervpiame and Mayeye (but not with Tonkawa) at San Antonio missions (Hodge 1907–1910, 2:424–426).

It is now known that the name Ervipiame itself was used in referring to an assemblage of over 20 displaced remnant Indian groups from northeastern Coahuila and vicinity who had migrated to the refuge area in Texas, where they were collectively called Indians of Rancheria Grande. Some of these groups spoke the Coahuilteco language (T.N. Campbell 1979; vol. 10:346; Foik 1933; Wheat 1957–1963, 1:map 115). The Yojuane are identifiable as an immigrant Wichita-speaking group from what is now Oklahoma (Newcomb and Campbell 1982). The remaining six groups, whose languages were never recorded, were native to an inland area north of Matagorda Bay on the Texas coast, and they were recorded in late seventeenth-century documents before the Tonkawa had arrived in the refuge area (Canedo 1968).

History Until 1891

The earliest recognizable rendition of the name Tonkawa appears in documents of the Juan de Oñate expedition from New Mexico to the Plains in 1601. During a battle with Aguacane, believed to be a Wichita-speaking people, the Spaniards captured an Indian they called Miguel. Taken to Mexico City, he was interrogated along with some of the expedition's soldiers. He related that while a boy he had been captured by Aguacane and that his own people lived at a place called Tancoa (Hammond and Rey 1953:874). A map prepared under Miguel's direction indicates that Tancoa was west of Aguacane territory, and apparently somewhere between the Salt Fork and the Medicine Lodge rivers in north-central Oklahoma (Newcomb and Campbell 1982).

The Tancoa of the Oñate documents, as well as some of the Aguacane subdivisions, particularly the Yojuane (Yuhuanica on Miguel's map), were evidently displaced during the seventeenth century by the rapid expansion of mounted Apache. Both groups were recorded in 1691 by a Spanish missionary, Casañas de Jesus Maria, who listed "Tanquaay" and "Diujuan," and also Apache, among 18 Indian groups said to be enemies of the Hasinai of eastern Texas (Swanton 1942). Specific locations are not given, but most groups are referred to as living north, northwest, and west of the Hasinai. It thus appears likely that, by 1691, the Tonkawa, Yojuane, and other peoples had moved southward at least as far as the Red River. In 1719 a party of French explorers traveled up the Red River some 200 miles and reported meeting warriors from five groups, including Tonkawa and Yojuane, who were returning from a successful attack on Apaches farther west (M.M. Wedel 1971). In 1723, another French expedition recorded Tonkawas on the Red River (Bridges and De Ville 1967). These are the earliest definite references to Tonkawa in Texas, although they indicate a peripheral location.

The Tonkawa seem to have entered Texas at the northern end of a grassland belt, known as the Blackland Prairie, that extends from the Red River southward, mainly east of a line drawn through the cities of Dallas, Waco, Austin, and San Antonio. The eastern margin of the Blackland Prairie marks the beginning of the extensive woodlands of eastern Texas. The southward movement of the Tonkawa was probably

954

along the grassland-woodland boundary. It provided access to two environmental zones, thus increasing their subsistence resources, and the woodlands provided cover from attacks by Apache groups who were in control of the central Texas highlands to the west.

The Spaniards were never able to missionize the Tonkawa effectively or to exercise much control over them, although the Tonkawa were not overtly hostile toward Europeans until the second half of the eighteenth century. By that time Apaches had become more amenable to friendly relations with the Spaniards and reversing their policy, in 1757 the Spaniards established a mission for the Lipan Apache and a presidio near modern Menard on the San Sabá River. Although virtually no Lipan Apaches could be persuaded to settle at the mission, former mission Indians, other ancient enemies of Apaches including Tonkawas, and recent foes such as Comanches, joined forces in 1758 to sack and destroy the San Sabá mission (Nathan and Simpson 1959; Weddle 1964). In the following year a retaliatory expedition attacked an encampment of Yojuane. So few Yojuane survived the massacre that they apparently could no longer maintain their independence as a people. Some, and likely the bulk of them, joined the Tonkawa, and within a generation one of them had become the Tonkawa chief (Cabello 1786).

Until late in the eighteenth century the Tonkawa did not range much farther to the south than the junction of the Brazos and Little rivers. Population decline and disruptions resulting from Comanche displacement of Apaches from the central Texas highlands led at least some of the Tonkawa to move southward to an area along the Brazos and Colorado rivers. In 1828 the Mexican boundary survey party visited a Tonkawa village about halfway between the Guadalupe and Colorado rivers, where they were allied with the Lipan Apache. They were described as living in poverty, rarely hunting buffalo for fear of the Comanche and their allies (Berlandier 1969:8–9, 146).

The Tonkawa became well known to the earliest Anglo-American colonists, who regarded them as native to that area. After the Texas Revolution of 1836, increasing Anglo-American settlements forced the Tonkawa to move westward (J. Sibley 1922; Gatschet 1891; Sjoberg 1953). In 1837 and 1838, Tonkawa chiefs signed treaties with Texas that established peace, regulated trade, and permitted Texans to travel through Tonkawa territory (Winfrey and Day 1959–1966, 1:28–29, 46–48). In 1844 the Tonkawa were reported to be camped on Cedar Creek, hunting buffalo with the Lipan, and the two tribes were accused of making occasional raids against the cattle of Texas settlers (Winfrey and Day 1959–1966, 2:150–151, 167). Both the Tonkawa and the Lipan were at war with the Wichita, resulting in deaths on both sides and considerable loss of horses (Winfrey and Day 1959–1966, 1:253, 261, 2:341). In 1846 the Tonkawa, along with the Comanche and other tribes, signed a peace treaty with the United States at Council Springs, Texas, promising to surrender prisoners and cease horse stealing in return for trade goods and protection (Kappler 1904–1941, 2:554–557; Winfrey and Day 1959–1966, 3:53–57).

Settlers in Texas continued to complain of raids on their livestock by Tonkawa, Lipan, and other Indians. In 1854, at the request of their Indian agent, the Tonkawa surrendered nine men who had participated in a raid on Bosque County, who were imprisoned at Fort Inge. To curtail hostilities, in 1854 Texas established a reservation on the Brazos River at the junction of the Clear Fork for the small remnant tribes, and the Tonkawa were moved there. During its brief existence, Tonkawas, together with other reservation Indians, served as scouts (fig. 2) and guides with both the Texas Rangers and federal troops in campaigns against Comanches and other tribes. Hostility of the local settlers, who continued to blame the Tonkawa and Lipan for depredations, forced the abandonment of the Brazos Reservation in 1859. The Indians resident there, including about 245 Tonkawas, were escorted by the army northward across the Red River to the Leased District in Indian Territory, and placed under supervision of the Wichita Agency (Winfrey and Day 1959–1966, 5:68, 170, 179–181, 232–236, 3:184, 268; Neighbours 1975).

Unlike other Indians removed from Texas, the Tonkawa remained loyal to the South during the Civil War, and in autumn 1862 a joint force of Union Indians attacked and burned the Wichita Agency. The next day a Tonkawa encampment near present Anadarko was attacked. Some 137 men, women, and children were killed (Bolton 1910b:782; W.K. Jones 1969). The survivors, many of whom had been absent on a hunt during the massacre, fled to Fort Arbuckle.

Most of the impoverished survivors found their way back to Texas, some serving as scouts for Confederate forces; others survived by begging and raiding settlements (Gatschet 1884c). The governor of Texas wrote of the destitution of the Tonkawa in 1866, requesting the Commissioner of Indian Affairs to provide relief (Winfrey and Day 1959–1966, 4:110–112). In 1867 Texas persuaded the United States Army to assume responsibility for the Tonkawa, who had gathered around newly established Fort Griffin on the Clear Fork of the Brazos (Winfrey and Day 1959–1966, 4:214). The state of Texas was unwilling to provide land for a reservation, and the Tonkawa were fearful and unwilling to move to Indian Territory where their enemies might exterminate them (Dunlay 1982:117–118). Tonkawa scouts provided valuable service in the various campaigns against Kiowas and Comanches, and in return the army supplied rations for the dwindling tribe. But after 1875 and the conclusion of these conflicts even this occupation vanished. The army, despite orders to the contrary, continued to supply rations to the destitute Tonkawa, and finally in 1884, 92 survivors, including some Lipan Apaches, consented to be moved to Indian Territory.

The Tonkawa were first settled on the Iowa Reservation, where they were not welcome; and in spring 1885 they were moved to the recently abandoned 90,760-acre reservation of the Nez Perce, located on the west side of the Chikaskia

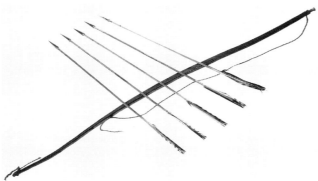

top, Panhandle-Plains Histl. Mus., Canyon, Tex.; bottom, Smithsonian, Dept. of Anthr.: 8,461.

Fig. 2. Scouts and their equipment. top, Scouts at Ft. Elliott, Tex. The fort was established in 1875 and closed in 1890. Photographed in the 1880s. bottom, Bow and arrows from Tonkawa scouts serving out of Ft. Griffin, Tex. The recurved bow is of Osage orange wood with string of twisted sinew. The arrows have iron points. The shafts are incised with grooves and painted with bands of blue, red, and yellow; the arrows are fletched with wild turkey and turkey vulture feathers. Collected by D. Henry McElderry in 1868. Length of bow, 134 cm.

River in northern Oklahoma. They were utterly destitute and dependent upon the government, and their condition and prospects were hardly improved when the Cherokee Commission in 1891 forced them to agree to allotment in severalty. By this action almost 80,000 acres of the reservation were acquired by the government for $30,000. The 73 surviving Tonkawa were each allotted approximately 160 acres (Foreman 1946).

Population

It was not until the second half of the eighteenth century that estimates of Tonkawa numbers were made, by which time the tribe had already absorbed other ethnic groups. The initial estimate in 1772 of something more than 150 warriors, which included Mayeyes and Yojuanes (Bolton 1914, 1:289–290), provides a good example of why the Tonkawa continued to embrace alien groups: they were a small tribe, and epidemics, warfare, and other forces

continued to exact a heavy toll on them. To survive as an independent body they had to welcome if not recruit outsiders.

Apparently Tonkawa population was fairly stable from the late eighteenth century into the third decade of the following century, hovering around 1,000 persons, after which their population began its decline. The half-century of stability, also apparently marking their maximum population, coincided with the lessening of Spanish presence in Texas and the weakening of the Apaches. Their population decline was precipitated by American settlement on lands Tonkawas had utilized and was accompanied by or caused an increasing incidence of epidemics, alcoholism, and destitution. In 1849 they were estimated at 650 (including 130 "warriors") (Winfrey and Day 1959–1966, 3:108), while by 1863 the population had fallen to about 165 (including about 50 "warriors") (Winfrey and Day 1959–1966, 4:78). In 1884, when they were moved to Oklahoma, the Tonkawa—including a number of Lipan, apparently intermarried with them—

numbered 92, and by 1910 they were reduced to 42 (Bolton 1910b:782; U.S. Bureau of the Census 1915:106). In 1962 the population was 62 (Hasskarl 1962:228), about 250 in 1985, and the enrolled membership of the tribe was 383 in 2000 (Dawena Pappan, communication to editors 2000).

Culture

Subsistence

The earliest known Tonkawa subsisted by hunting, fishing, and food-gathering. There is no evidence that horticulture was practiced until shortly before they were placed on the Brazos Reservation in the nineteenth century. When early Anglo-American colonists tried to persuade them to settle down and become farmers, the Tonkawa claimed that a supernatural figure, Wolf, had long ago instructed them to avoid building permanent houses and cultivating the soil (W.B. Parker 1856; Marcy 1866; Gatschet 1884c).

The principal large game animals were bison, deer, and bear. Apparently, wild horses were sometimes killed for food (Bollaert 1956). Of the smaller game animals hunted or collected, specific mention is made of rabbits, field rats, turtles, and snakes, especially the rattlesnake. Dogs were also occasionally eaten. Numerous birds were probably taken, but only the turkey is recorded. Indirect evidence suggests that one insect, the grasshopper, was eaten. Fish were taken by hook and line and by a fish spear, and oysters were eaten (Gatschet 1884c; Sjoberg 1953; Newcomb 1961:139).

Edible products of numerous wild plants, many not clearly identified, were collected for use as food. These probably bulked larger in the Tonkawa diet than is indicated by some documents, which merely refer to food provided by large game animals. In general, Tonkawa plant foods included roots, tubers, and bulbs; a variety of fruits—berries, haws, plums, grapes, cactus fruits, and the persimmon; nuts, particularly acorns and pecans; and various seeds and seed pods (Marcy 1866; Gatschet 1884c; Smithwick 1900; Bollaert 1956; Sjoberg 1953).

Horses

The Tonkawa probably first acquired horses in the seventeenth century before they had moved southward across the Red River. In the eighteenth, and particularly in the nineteenth century, observers noted that the Tonkawa had good horses and were excellent horsemen (J.O. Dyer 1920; Kuykendall 1903; Sánchez 1926; J. Sibley 1922). Although they must have done a certain amount of horse breeding, most documents refer to the Tonkawa as obtaining horses through combat, theft, and trade, and there is one eyewitness account of wild horses being captured (J. Pike 1932). Rope was made from horse hair, and horse ribs were used as fleshing tools in processing animal hides. Gelded horses were preferred for use in warfare (Gatschet 1884c).

Structures

There seems to have been a special structure for council meetings (Gatschet 1884c), and another for ceremonies, which was said to have been long, low, and made of poles covered by grass (W.B. Parker 1856). There were isolation huts for use by women during menstruation and childbirth (Gatschet 1884c). At least three kinds of lodges, apparently all round in floor plan, are recorded: skin-covered, brush-covered (fig. 3), and grass-covered. The brush-covered lodge, seen in two Tonkawa encampments in 1828, was 5 or 6 feet high and 10 to 12 feet in diameter; it had a low door, a central hearth, and beds of Spanish moss covered by animal skins. It accommodated 12 to 15 individuals. Some of these houses had a few animal skins on the roof (Gatschet 1884c, 1891; Sánchez 1926; Berlandier 1969:147, 1980).

The few documents that describe Tonkawa lodges in at least some detail date from the nineteenth century and indicate considerable variety in construction materials. This variety may be explained as being a consequence of decline in availability of bison hides for tepee construction, but early, exclusive use of the tepee has not been documented. Some of the variety may reflect Tonkawa absorption of remnant Indian groups whose house styles differed.

Smithsonian, Natl. Mus. of the Amer. Ind., top, 15205; bottom, 15202.
Fig. 3. Structures. top, Summer brush-covered shelter, with wooden frame house behind. bottom, Tepee belonging to George Miles, Tonkawa Res., Okla. Open-sided brush-covered sunshade and drying rack are in the background. Photographs by Thomas F. Croft, 1893–1894.

Clothing and Adornment

Descriptions of early Tonkawa clothing indicate that the basic garments were a very long breechcloth for men and a knee-length skirt for women, both usually made of deer skin. A robe of bison hide, sometimes with painted designs, was worn by both sexes in cold weather. Both men and women wore moccasins and leggings. Garments and footgear were commonly fringed (fig. 4), the fringe elements often terminating in small, sound-producing ornaments. In battle men wore leather vests as armor, and their leaders wore headdresses ornamented with bison horns and feathers. In the early nineteenth century factory-woven cloth slowly replaced animal skin as material for clothing, and by the end of the century Tonkawa clothing had become essentially Euro-American (Berlandier 1969:147; Gatschet 1884c; Bollaert 1956; W.K. Jones 1969; Sánchez 1926).

Pl. IX

Sáncahues.

Sáncahues: peuplade misérable des côtes du Texas.

The Thomas Gilcrease Inst. of Amer. Hist. and Art, Tulsa, Okla.

Fig. 4. Clothing and adornment. The man on left wears a beechcloth and a bandolier. The center man wears fringed buckskin leggings, moccasins, a decorated hide shirt, a robe over his shoulder, and a bandolier. He holds a long-barreled flintlock. The woman wears a buckskin skirt. The men have facial decorations, and the woman has paint or tattooing on her breasts and stomach. A bow is leaning against the tree. Watercolor by Lino Sánchez y Tapia, 1834–1838, after a sketch by José María Sánchez y Tapia.

958

Both sexes parted their hair in the middle. Men wore their hair quite long, sometimes hanging loose but more commonly braided or wrapped with strips of fur and cloth. The hair of women, worn either long or short, was allowed to hang loose (Duval 1871; W.K. Jones 1969; Red 1913; Sánchez 1926).

Tonkawas decorated unclothed parts of their bodies by tattooing and painting. Some confusion results from the fact that early documents do not distinguish between the two techniques. Both sexes tattooed, but it appears that painting was done mainly by males. Men had one or more vertical lines tatooed on both forehead and chin. Women had similar tattooed lines that extended from the forehead down the nose to the chin; they also tattooed vertical lines on the back and abdomen, and each breast was covered with concentric circles (Berlandier 1969:147; Gatschet 1884c; Sánchez 1926). Body painting by males is known to have been done prior to certain occasions: departure of a war party, ceremonial dancing, and formal signing of treaties with Whites. It consisted of linear designs in several colors (red, green, yellow, black) on face and torso. A man who had a notable war record was entitled to private use of a special design (Gatschet 1884c; Red 1913).

The principal ornaments of the Tonkawa were earrings, necklaces, bracelets, breastplates, and items attached to head hair (fig. 5) and clothing. The materials used for ornamentation were varied: shell and river pearls; bone, including beaks and claws; feathers; fur, horsehair, and bits of colored cloth; metal (copper, brass, iron, and German silver); and glass trade beads. Men seem to have been more ornamented than women (Berlandier 1969; Duval 1871; Gatschet 1884c; Bollaert 1956; W.K. Jones 1969; Red 1913).

Technology

The little that is known about the smaller items of Tonkawa material culture comes from the nineteenth century, prior to removal to Indian Territory. A museum collection obtained from Tonkawas at Fort Griffin in 1868 includes bows, arrows (with metal points) (fig. 2), a trade tomahawk, a drum, a rattle, a wooden scraping tool, a few waist and head ornaments, and two male dolls dressed in mid-nineteenth-century Tonkawa style (fig. 6) (W.K. Jones 1969). (The tinder pouch and metal striker also described by Jones are of Comanche origin; Candace Greene, communication to editors 1999). Of some interest, particularly to archeologists, is lack of evidence that Tonkawas ever made pottery vessels, and indications that artifacts made of stone slowly dropped out of Tonkawa culture during the nineteenth century (Gatschet 1884c).

Social Organization

The basic social group was an extended matrilineal family, composed of a senior woman, her husband, unmarried sons, daughters and their spouses and small children. Such

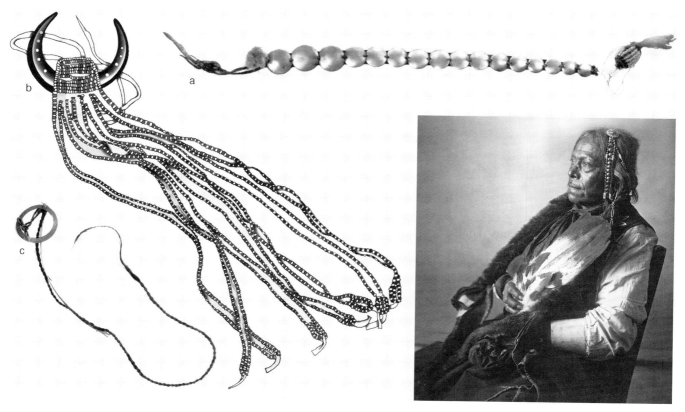

Smithsonian, Dept. of Anthr.: a, 8,447; c, 8,446; b, Field Mus., Dept. of Anthr., Chicago: 92,171; right, Smithsonian, NAA: 1199-B.

Fig. 5. Hair ornaments. a, German silver buttons ranging in size from 1 to 2 cm in diameter stitched to a leather backing with a tuft of blue feathers. b, 2 eagle claws mounted in a buckskin base, above a fringe of edge-beaded thongs painted red, blue, green, and yellow. Collected by Fred W. Starr at White Eagle, Okla. Terr., 1905. Drawn by Roger Thor Roop. c, Braided strands of hair on metal hoop. a and c, Collected by D. Henry McElderry in 1868 at Ft. Griffin, Tex. Length of a, 30 cm; c to same scale; length of b, 20 cm. right, John Williams wearing a hair ornament of German silver and beads; his braids are wrapped with long strips of fur. He also wears a long metal loop earring and holds an eagle feather fan. Photographed in Washington, D.C., 1898.

families apparently counted 12–15 people, all of whom lived together in a single dwelling. Presumably such family units camped and moved with other similar units. In 1828 Berlandier (1980) counted 21 such "cabins" in the camp he visited.

Many practices followed from figuring descent in the maternal line. Property not destroyed after a man's death descended to his sister's children; children remained with their mother in the case of divorce, and in the event of her death the children were cared for by maternal relatives. The sororate, in which a man married his deceased wife's sister, was practiced, but the data on sororal and other forms of polygyny are not clearcut (Gatschet 1884c; Hoijer 1933). Polygyny was apparently uncommon. Data about kinship terminology and behavior is fragmentary and somewhat conflicting, but it is apparent that the Tonkawa had a Crow-type system (Sjoberg 1953; Newcomb 1961:143; L. Johnson 1994a). Reciprocal avoidance characterized relationships between men and their mothers-in-law; avoidance regulations were less extreme between women and their fathers-in-law (Hoijer 1933; Padilla 1919; Gatschet 1884c; Mooney 1901).

Smithsonian, Dept. of Anthr.: left, 8,445; right, 8,444.

Fig. 6. Buckskin dolls that represent the type of clothing worn by Tonkawa men in the 1860s. Both are dressed in cloth shirts, cloth breechcloths, and beaded leggings, with bead necklaces and earrings, and have human hair attached. left, Leggings of red flannel. right, Buckskin leggings. Collected by D. Henry McElderry in 1868 at Ft. Griffin, Tex. Height of left, 10 cm; right to same scale.

Extended families were grouped into exogamous clans, in this instance named groups of kin descended through women of the decimated or refugee groups or of the original Tonkawa, each of which had a recognized leader. According to Gatschet (1891:36) there were 13 clans, although his 1884 field notes list names for only 10 clans, four of which then had no living members (table 1). The clan with the largest membership was *tickanwa·tic*, also the general term for Tonkawa (Hoijer 1949:19), implying that the other clans were descendants of Indian groups that had been absorbed by the Tonkawa in Texas. At least four clan names resemble names of Indian groups associated with the inner coastal plain east and southeast of San Antonio: Meyei (Mayeye), Paxalatch (Pajalat), Sanux (Sana), and Tchoyopan (Chayopin). According to Kenney (1897:30) the clans were grouped into two complementary but not exogamous moieties, which may also represent the coalescence of composite groups. The structure of Tonkawa society has seemed anomalous since similar nonhorticultural societies are not characterized by clan organizations. However, the historic genesis of the Tonkawa tribe solves this seeming anomaly.

In the nineteenth century the Tonkawa apparently had a simple but well-ordered system of government. An observer (Kenney 1897) of a council held in Austin in 1841 to select a new chief noted that the men gathered around a council fire in two distinct groups (perhaps representing the moieties). Speeches were made by the clan leaders, and after a long and earnest discussion all the men participated in the selection of the new chief (Newcomb 1961:141–142).

Life Cycle

Tonkawa ritual and social activities connected with birth, puberty, and marriage were either minimal or unrecorded. They had isolated parturition and menstruation lodges, and there are a few recorded taboos on parental behavior before and after birth of a child and during a girl's first menstruation. The mother of a girl to be married received gifts from the prospective husband, usually horses, which were returned in case of divorce. The tip of an adulterous wife's nose was cut off by her husband (Gatschet 1884c).

Accounts of Tonkawa behavior relating to death and burial vary in descriptive detail, but these seem to indicate a single pattern. Prior to death a supportive ceremony was sometimes performed around individuals thought to be dying (Kenney 1897; Nance 1952). On the day that death occurred the corpse was wrapped in a skin robe or blanket and placed in an east-west oriented grave shaft six or seven feet deep, the head pointing westward. Clothing and ornaments were buried with both sexes, but with adult males other things were included—weapons, saddles, and scalps of slain enemies. A man's horse or dog was sometimes killed at or near the grave site.

Four days of ceremonial activity followed burial. This was controlled by belief that the spirit of a dead person remained in the vicinity for four days, departing on the fourth day for the land of the dead to the west. For three days there was grave-side mourning twice a day, at dawn and at sunset. A critical point was reached on the fourth day, when adults of both sexes smoked a ceremonial pipe near the grave to send the spirit westward. This phase of the ceremony was supervised by a specialist who knew how to satisfy spirits, for displeased spirits could cause additional deaths. At this time relatives brought presents that were destroyed. Ceremonial smoking lasted less than an hour, and thereafter all connections with the departed spirit were severed. Ashes from the pipe were buried. The name of the dead person was no longer spoken by anyone, nor was it later used in naming children. Survivors who had the same name, or a similar one, changed their names (Gatschet 1884c; Smithwick 1900).

Religion and Ceremonies

Undoubtedly the belief system of the Tonkawa was varied, considering their heterogeneous origins and their lack of religious specialists who might have codified and integrated their beliefs. Notably lacking in the records is clear indication that the Tonkawa were influenced by Christian ideology, which seems to reflect their consistent refusal to live in Spanish missions.

Few supernaturals are recorded for the Tonkawa. Among these was a creator who made the earth and the first Tonkawa, after which he retired to a distant place in the sky. Apparently this creator was not approached ceremonially. The Sun, who did figure in ceremonies, seems to have originally been a powerful and destructive male god. A myth, briefly recorded, tells of a boy who shot an arrow into the arrogant sun, splitting it into two parts, one part becoming the present sun, the other the moon. Although the moon seems to have been regarded as a supernatural, no details are known. During solar eclipses the Tonkawa

Table 1. Tonkawa Clans Recorded in 1884

Clan Name	Surviving Members
Haiwal 'acorn, acorn tree' (*haywal* 'blackjack tree')	1 or 2
Kwesh	none
Meyei, Maye 'dizziness'	none
Nelawe, Nilawe, Nilhawai 'long penis'	6
Nintropan, Nintchopan 'bear' (*nencopan*)	7 to 9
Paxalatch 'mouth open'	8
Sanux	none
Talpkweyu 'a short snake'	4 or 5
Tchoyopan 'moving the eyebrows or eyelids'	none
Titskanwatikchatak 'the real Tonkawa' (*tickanwa·ticatak*)	20 to 25

Source: Gatschet (1884c); phonemic forms from Hoijer (1949).
Note: Hodge (1907-1910, 1:119, 536, 2:191) identifies 3 additional Tonkawa clan names: Awash 'bison', Hátchukuni 'wolf', and Pákani. Gatschet recorded the first 2 as names of specific "dances;" Pákani does not appear in his field notes.

became excited, shot guns, and whipped their dogs. Several constellations seem to have been regarded as "star gods" (Gatschet 1884c).

The principal terrestrial supernatural was an animal, Wolf, a cultural benefactor who stole fire and gave it to the Tonkawa. He taught them the art of flint knapping, and he seems to have been in control of game animals, particularly deer. The killing of wolves and coyotes was tabooed (Gatschet 1884c).

At Fort Griffin Gatschet (1884c) recorded at least 17 special ceremonies that the Tonkawa referred to as "dances." Brief descriptive notes link about half of these with hunting, warfare, and curing. There are occasional references to deities (Sun, Wolf), and two ceremonies involved the use of intoxicating plants, apparently the mescal bean and peyote. Some ceremonies were performed at night, others in day time. All participants were adults, certain ceremonies being performed by men only, others by women only, and still others by both sexes. Descriptive details make it clear that Tonkawa ceremonies involved dramatic action, dancing in circular or linear formations, singing, limited costuming, and use of musical instruments—rattles, drums, and musical rasps (fig. 7).

The Wolf Dance was a ceremony that probably had special importance to Tonkawas because it re-enacted their origin and justified their mode of existence. It was performed

Fig. 7. Dances and musical instruments. top, Preparing for the Scalp Dance. left to right, Women dancers: Brenda Warrior, Lisa Norman, Toni Norman, Mitzi Cornell, Marilyn Cornell, Joyce Gonzalez, Barbara All, Madaline Norman, Vivian Cornell, Rosemary Haymond, and Mildred Warrior. Men with drum: Don Patterson, Jack Norman, and Charles Norman. Photograph by Don Patterson, 1990. bottom left, Gourd rattle decorated with incised dots mounted on a bead-wrapped wooden handle. Gourd rattles were essential ritual equipment for the Peyote religion. This one is unusual in having feathers rather than horsehair at the tip of the beaded rod projecting from the head. Collected by Fred W. Starr at White Eagle, Okla. Terr., 1905; length about 31 cm. bottom right, Dance in 1901. Drummers are on the right, and male dancers are on the left. Photograph by Annette Ross Hume, Kiowa-Comanche Agency, Okla.

secretively in a large dance lodge by some 50 men draped in wolf skins who entered the lodge in single file, imitating the actions of wolves. They sniffed the ground and after a time one of them stopped suddenly, yelped, and began to scratch the ground. The other wolves gathered around him, and in a few moments they uncovered a live Tonkawa. Excitedly, the wolves sniffed and examined this person, and after he had expressed a desire to be reburied, since he had no knowledge of how to exist in their world, the older wolves held a council to decide his fate. After deliberation the council refused to return the Tonkawa to his underground home, but supplied him with a bow and arrows to secure his food and clothing and instructed him to live as the wolves did. He was further enjoined on pain of death from building a permanent dwelling or cultivating the soil (W.B. Parker 1856; Winfrey and Day 1959–1966, 3:211–212; Marcy 1866; Gatschet 1876a; J. Pike 1932).

Tonkawa shamans, usually male, possessed supernatural powers that enabled them to cure illness and control weather (bring rain). It is not clear just how shamans functioned in major curing ceremonies. Apparently these specialists were called upon to treat illness that did not respond to folk medicines. Occasionally shamans misused their powers and were regarded as malevolent wizards or witches (Gatschet 1884c).

Cannibalism

The Tonkawa have been portrayed as inveterate cannibals, and as a consequence they are said to have become pariahs to other Indians. That they ate portions of enemy bodies is well established, although eyewitness accounts of the practice are few (Smithwick 1900; Mooney 1901; J. Pike 1932; Jenkins 1958). Motivation for their anthropophagy seems to have been acquisition of an enemy's courage, revenge, and prevention of rebirth of an enemy's soul in another body. One source states that the Tonkawa ate only the hands and feet of enemies slain in battle in order to gain their "fleetness of foot and extra strength of hand" (J.O. Dyer 1920). Virtually all accounts of Tonkawa cannibalism date to the nineteenth century, unlike those of neighboring peoples such as Wichita and Caddo, who had abandoned the custom well before 1800.

The Twentieth Century

In 2000 most of the enrolled Tonkawa tribe lived in Fort Oakland village (the old agency headquarters) a few miles southeast of Tonkawa, Oklahoma. In 1985, through a program of the federal Department of Housing and Urban Development, over 90 modern houses had been constructed in the village. A ceremonial dance ground, site of the annual tribal "powwow," is located in Fort Oakland, as is the tribal headquarters complex. It consists of an administration building (housing a hall for the tribal bingo operation), a tribal museum, and offices (fig. 8).

Fig. 8. Tonkawa tribal administrative building and bingo hall, Tonkawa, Okla. Photograph by Don Patterson, 1991.

Tribal affairs were conducted by a three-member business committee elected biannually. Community programs, workshops, and informal classes were held to foster knowledge of the tribe's heritage. Although a few older persons had some comprehension of the native language, in 1990 no native speakers remained.

Intermarriage, perpetuating a Tonkawa custom, has resulted in the disappearance of all persons who might claim purity of descent. Participation in the pan-Indian social milieu was evident by the popularity of the Native American Church (Peyotism). Despite economic and political integration into the larger society the survival of the Tonkawa as a community and a corporate entity seems assured.

Synonymy†

The name Tonkawa is not a native Tonkawa term. Although its origin is unknown, it has been suggested that it derives from Waco Tonkawéya, said to mean 'they all stay together' (Gatschet 1891:37), a questionable translation. Variants of the name occur in various Indian languages. Among Caddoans it appears as Caddo tankaway (Chafe 1979), Pawnee taríkawa (Parks 1999), and Wichita táriko·ra (Parks 1980, 1988). It was also borrowed as Comanche Caricoë, 1830 (Berlandier 1969:100), Quapaw ttákkawa (Dorsey 1891b, phonemicized), Miami to·nkawia (Gatschet 1895b, phonemicized), Koasati tonkawí (G.D. Kimball 1994:227), and Karankawa Tchankáya (Gatschet in Hodge 1907–1910, 2:783).

Throughout the historical period the name Tonkawa appears in Euro-American documents in easily recognizable spellings. Early French forms include Tancaoye, 1719 (Bénard de La Harpe in Margry 1876–1886, 6:277); Tankaway, 1719 (Pénigaut in French 1869:155); Tancaoüeys, Tancaoueys, and Tancaüeys, 1770 (De Mézières in Bolton 1914, 1:149, 201, 217); and Tancaües and

†This synonymy was written by Douglas R. Parks.

Tancaoues, 1772–1774 (Baron de Ripperdá in Bolton 1914, 1:344; 2:59). Spanish spellings are Tanquaay, 1691 (Francisco de Jesus María in Hodge 1907–1910, 2:779); Tancaguies, 1752 (De Soto Vermudez in Hodge 1907–1910, 2:780); Tancagues (1748, Ortiz in Bolton 1915:154; 1756–1766, Morfí 1935, 1:56); Tanchagues and Tancahue, 1749 (Santa Ana in Bolton 1915:190, 198); Tancahue and Tancahueses, 1830 (Berlandier 1969:42, 146); Tancagués, 1771–1772 (De Mézières in Bolton 1914, 1:289); Thancahues, 1774 (Menchaca in Bolton 1914, 2:38); and Tancagua, 1774 (Miguel Santa María y Silva in Bolton 1914, 2:72). Those spellings are reflected in American renditions that include Tenkahuas (Neighbors in ARCIA 1829:80), Tancahuas (Whiting 1850:242), Ton-ka-hues (ARCIA 1853:257), and Tonkhuas (Coombs in ARCIA 1859:233).

Most American spellings of Tonkawa are largely minor variants of the contemporary spelling: Tancards (Z.M. Pike 1811:319), Tonkewas, 1843 (Eldredge 1928:118), Tonkahans, 1848 (Drake 1880:15), Tonquoways (Webber 1849:191), Tonkaways (Latham 1856:103), Tancoways (Whipple 1856:76), Tonkahaws (Domenech 1860, 1:441), Ton-ka-ways, 1851 (Marcy in R.C. Crane 1938:134), Tonkowas (Marcy 1859:197), and Ton-ca-wes and Toncawes, 1861 (V. Deloria and DeMallie 1999, 1:630, 643). The French shortened the name to Tanks, 1805 (J. Sibley 1832:723), and Texans used Tonks (Hodge 1907–1910, 2:783). For other spellings, including numerous misprints, see Hodge (1907–1910, 2:782–783).

The Tonkawa self-designation is *tickanwa·tic*, also *tickanwa·c*, 'those like people' (Hoijer 1949:19), also cited as Titska watitch 'indigenous people' (Gatschet 1884c).

Among most tribes the Tonkawa were designated 'cannibals; man or people eaters', 1851 (Marcy in R.C. Crane 1938:134–135). Names with that meaning are Cheyenne *mévavEheoʔo* (Glenmore and Leman 1985:201), cited also as Mevaveo (sg. Mevave) (Petter 1913–1915:583) and Mivafw'éo (Mooney 1907:426); Comanche nimirika (Alice Anderton, personal communication 1992), cited also as Néméréxka (Gatschet 1884a), Nimĕtéka (ten Kate 1885:383), and Nimmetuhka (H.L. Scott 1890–1900); Kiowa *kʼyáhį-pì·-gɔ́* (Laurel Watkins, personal communication 1979), cited also as Kádiko (Gatschet 1884e) and K'iñähi-píäko (Mooney 1898:411); Osage *waðáni* 'eaters' (Carolyn Quintero, personal communication 1999); Omaha *níkkaðatʰe* (J.H. Howard 1965:133, phonemicized) and Ponca *níkkawaðatʰe* (Parks 1988); and Plains Apache dìndégòyijáni (Bittle 1952–1956), cited also as Tineyizháne (Gatschet 1884b). The Lipan name, recorded with no translation as Yané (Berlandier 1969:100) and Yánehe (Gatschet 1884d), was also said to mean 'man eaters' (Bollaert 1850:275).

A name with no known underlying meaning is Kitsai kĭwahǎ (Mooney 1893). Another Cheyenne designation was recorded, perhaps incorrectly, as Miúχsĕn (Gatschet 1884c).

Although the Tonkawa were reported to have used the Plains sign language extensively (Z.M. Pike 1811:333), no sign for the tribe was recorded.

Divisions

In addition to the Tonkawa proper, there were several divisions or remnants of other tribes, some speaking the same or a related language, others speaking an unrelated language, who were associated with them and became extinct in the early historical period.

Yerbipiame or Ervipiame. Recordings of the name include Yrbipias and Yrbipimas, 1675 (Bosque 1903:340, 343); Enepiahe, 1719 (Joutel 1962:114) and Exepiahohé, 1719 (Joutel in Margry 1876–1886, 3:288); Enepiahoes (Barcia 1723:271); and Ervipiames, 1736 (Rivera); Yorbipianos, 1762; Hierbipiames, 1771 (Barrios); and Yerbipiame (Ramón) (all in Hodge 1907–1910, 1:432).

Mayeye. The Tonkawa name for this group was recorded as Méye and Miyi (Gatschet 1891:36). Euro-American spellings of it are Meghey (Joutel in Margry 1876–1886, 3:288), Maghai and Meghty, 1687 (Joutel in B.F. French 1846–1853, 1:137, 152); Meihites (Barcía 1723:271); Macheyes and Maheyes, 1772 (De Mézières in Bonilla 1905:66); Mayeyes, 1779 (Morfí in Casteñeda 1935:81; Census of 1790 in Gatschet 1891:35); Mayes, 1805 (J. Sibley 1832:722); Mayees (Brackenridge 1814:87). Spanish renderings in manuscripts include Maieyes, 1768, and Mayeces, 1771 (in Hodge 1907–1910,1:825).

Yojuane. Variant renderings of this name are Diujuan, 1691 (Francisco de Jesus María in Hodge 1907–1910, 2:779); Ayennis, 1698 (Talon in Margry 1876–1886, 3:616); Joyvan, 1719 (La Harpe in Margry 1776–1786, 6:255); Yacavanes, 1772 (Bonilla 1905:66); Yocouanés and Yocuanas, 1772 (De Mézières in Bolton 1914, 1:289, 308). Other variants occurring in Spanish manuscripts are Yojuanes, 1716 (Ramón); Yujuanes, 1748 (Gabzabla); and Iohuan, 1782 (Morfí) (all in Hodge 1907–1910, 2:999) .

Sana. References to this group occur in late seventeenth- and eighteenth-century documents, in which the name is most frequently spelled Zanas, but occurs also as Canas, Chanas, Chanes, and Sanas (Hodge 1907–1910, 2:423).

Tohaha. Variants of this name include Tohaha, 1687 (Joutel in Margry 1876–1886, 3:288); Toaa, 1689 (Manzanet 1899:286); Toao, 1689 (Manzanet in E.H. West 1905:213); Tuxaxa, 1683 (Sabeata in Hodge 1907–1910, 2:771); Tohahe (Shea in Charlevoix 1866–1872, 4:78); and possibly Toyals, 1719–1721 (Belleisle in Margry 1876–1886, 6:339).

Toho. This group, closely associated with but distinct from the Tohaha, appears in the historical record through the mid-eighteenth century. Variant spellings include Atayos and Tayos, 1534 (Cabeza de Vaca 1871:121; Barcía 1723:13); Too and Toxo, 1689 (Manzanet 1899:309); Thoo, 1690 (Massanet in Hodge 1907–1910, 2:771); and Tohau, 1719 (Joutel in Margry 1876–1886, 3:288).

Sources

An exhaustive study of recorded information on the Tonkawa during the entire historic period has not been published, and the modern Tonkawa tribe of northern Oklahoma has not been systematically studied. The Tonkawa language was recorded by linguists in the late-nineteenth to the mid-twentieth century (Gatschet 1884c; Hoijer 1933, 1946a, 1949, 1972; see also Hymes 1987; L. Johnson and T.N. Campbell 1992; L. Johnson 1994a), and by the 1980s there were apparently no speakers still living. What is otherwise known about the Tonkawa is derived mainly from limited observations recorded by European observers between the years 1601 and 1884, during which changes must have occurred that are not discernible in the record. The Tonkawa do not figure very prominently in documents of the Spanish-French colonial period. They are best known from nineteenth-century documents because the Tonkawa were one of the few surviving Indian groups who ranged over the area occupied by the earliest White settlements. *The Indian Papers of Texas and the Southwest* (Winfrey and Day 1959–1966, 1–5) chronicle their last displacements and expulsion from the Texas area. Himmel (1999) focuses on Tonkawa (and Karankawa) history during 1821–1859.

The first informative attempt to view the Tonkawa in historical perspective and summarize their culture was a short essay by Bolton (1910b), who regarded the Tonkawa as native to the Texas area and claimed to have conclusive evidence that certain other Texas Indian populations were subdivisions of the Tonkawa. Sjoberg (1953) presented a lengthy article that accepted most of Bolton's interpretations but also contained more detailed information on Tonkawa culture. Sjoberg was the first to make extensive use of ethnographic materials in Gatschet's (1884c) field notes. Her lengthy bibliography identifies many of the primary documents that refer to the Tonkawa. Newcomb (1961) relied heavily on Sjoberg's summary. Other studies have added considerably to the record of Tonkawa interaction with Whites (Hasskarl 1962; Newlin 1982). Information on Indian groups that Bolton mistakenly classified as Tonkawa may be found in publications by Newcomb and Campbell (1982) and T.N. Campbell (1988). W.K. Jones (1969) presents an ethnohistorical account of the Tonkawa and describes the only substantive collection of Tonkawa artifacts.

Enigmatic Groups

DOUGLAS R. PARKS

In the historical literature from the period of first exploration until the early nineteenth century, a number of names of Plains tribes or social groups are not easily identified with any historical group known later in the nineteenth century. The origin of many of the names is obscure. Some were self-designations, while others were names given by another tribe. Undoubtedly some are the names of groups that became extinct or merged with other, larger groups. A few names appear to be applied during a brief encounter by a sole explorer or his party and never mentioned again.

The tribal synonymies throughout this volume identify many formerly unidentified, or incorrectly identified, tribal ethnonyms. The most problematic names that still cannot be confidently associated with later known social entities, together with previous attempts at establishing their identity, are reviewed here.

Seventeenth Century

Escanjaque or Aguacane

During his expedition into the southern Plains in 1601, Juan de Oñate visited a village consisting of skin-covered tents placed in a circle, estimated at 5,000 inhabitants, whom the Spaniards called Escanjaque (Bolton 1908:257–261; Hammond and Rey 1953, 2:752–755). A Tonkawa captive in the village, taken by Spaniards to Mexico City, later drew a map that depicted eight villages of the Escanjaque, who lived scattered along both sides of a river. He called them Aguacane, apparently the native name for this people (Hammond and Rey 1953, 2:871–873; W.W. Newcomb and T.N. Campbell 1982:31). The Escanjaque depended on buffalo hunting for their subsistence and were enemies of the Wichita, whose "great settlement" was 15 days' march away.

The Escanjaque have been identified with numerous tribes: Kansa (Hodge 1907–1910, 1:655) and Kansa or Osage (Hammond and Rey 1953, 2:752); Apache (Secoy 1953:12; Hyde 1959:11–12; W.R. Wedel 1959:51; W.W. Newcomb 1961:106); Tonkawa (J.D. Forbes 1960:103); and Wichita bands, either Iscani (Schroeder 1962:18; J.T. Hughes 1968:319) or a group ancestral to the Iscani (W.W. Newcomb and T.N. Campbell 1982:29–38). A review of the documentary references to the Escanjaque indicates that their village was in the North Canadian valley near present Watonga, Oklahoma, either on the Elm Fork of the Red River or near the Red River in southwestern Oklahoma. By examining those sources it is also possible to eliminate most of the possible identifications that have been made. They were not Apache, since Oñate had a Mexican Indian with him who spoke Apache but was unable to communicate with the Escanjaque, and since the Apache were culturally different from Oñate's description of the Escanjaque. They were not Tonkawa, since Oñate derived information from a Tonkawa taken captive by the Escanjaque; and they were not the Kansa or Osage, who lived farther to the east. The Escanjaque were distinct from the Tawakoni, but based on similarity of the names Aguacane and Iscani, it is possible that they were either the same people, or a separate group who merged with the Iscani (W.W. Newcomb and T.N. Campbell 1982:35–38).

Variant spellings of Escanjaque include Escansaques, 1629 (Zárate-Salmerón in Lummis 1899:45), Extcanjaque (Zárate-Salmerón in Bancroft 1882–1890, 1:599), and Escanxaques and Estanxaques, 1662 (Peñalosa in Freytas 1882:29, 83).

The name Aguacane appears to be reflected in aucanis, 1720 (La Harpe in M.M. Wedel 1981a:30, where identified as Yscanis) and Aquajuani, 1754 (Anonymous in W.W. Newcomb and T.N. Campbell 1982:37).

Ahijados

The designation Ahijados (Spanish 'adopted ones') occurs in various documents that refer to a people in a land of gold south of Quivira, east of the Jumano of west-central Texas, and west of the Hasinai Caddo, a region little known to Spaniards in the seventeenth century. Although modern writers have assumed that the name referred to a specific tribe or group, examination of the primary documents shows that no Spaniard ever encountered a people who identified themselves as Ahijado. Oñate used the term only to refer to two captives taken by Escanjaques; but a royal fiscal in Mexico City mentioned "the kingdom of Aijaoz," which was said to contain much wealth (de Leoz in Hammond and Rey 1953, 6:1070). Subsequently, three missionaries in New Mexico used the term but undermined the existence of any such group. Zárate-Salmerón (1856:27–28) first used it to refer to captives taken by the Escanjaque but later wrote of the Ahijado as an ethnic unit. Benavides, in the first version of his *Memorial* of 1630, mentions the kingdom of Aixaos, placing it near the kingdom of Quivira, but his 1634 revision deletes references to both kingdoms

(Ayer 1916:63; Forrestal 1954:62–63). Posada, reporting in 1686 on Oñate's expedition of 1601, substituted the name Ahijado for Escanjaque (Tyler and Taylor 1958:296–297). Later, Posada wrote of the Escanjaque and Ahijado as separate and distinct groups living east of the Jumano in western Texas (Tyler and Taylor 1958:294–295). These Spanish sources, all secondary, make clear that Ahijado represented a fictional "kingdom" designed to stimulate Spanish expeditions into the plains (W.W. Newcomb and T.N. Campbell 1982:38–39).

Despite the spurious existence of Ahijado as a social group, several writers have identified it with the names of known historical peoples: the Haxa of the Francisco de Vásquez Coronado documents (Ayer 1916:278; Hodge, Hammond, and Rey 1945:319); the Eyeish of eastern Texas (Forrestal 1954:xi); the Taovaya or Tawehash division of the Wichita (Hodge 1907–1910, 2:706, 1023; Schroeder 1959:55, 1962:18); and the Tonkawa (J.D. Forbes 1960:145).

Other spellings of Ahijados include Aixas, 1630 (Benavides in Ayer 1916:63–64); Aijados, Aijaos, Ayjados, Ayjaos, and Ayxaos (W.W. Newcomb and T.N. Campbell 1982:38).

Cuitoas

The only reference to a tribe named Cuitoa is in a secondary source, Posada's report of 1686 (Tyler and Taylor 1958:293–296, 301, 313), which includes brief accounts of two expeditions, one in 1650 and the other in 1654, sent from Santa Fe to explore the Jumano country and the lands adjoining it to the east in present western Texas. The first expedition, led by Hernando Martín and Diego del Castillo, reached the Concho River (Bolton 1911, 1912), then traveled downstream in a southeasterly direction, where they encountered "the Indian nations called Cuytoas, the Escanjaques, and Ahijados" (Tyler and Taylor 1958:294). The second expedition, under Diego de Guadalajara, followed the same route and met the Cuitoa, Escanjaque, and Ahijado in battle, winning a decisive victory over them (Tyler and Taylor 1958:295–296).

No copies of the primary records of the two expeditions have been found. The names Escanjaques and Ahijados, apparently drawn from the records of the Oñate expedition a half-century earlier, derive from people encountered in present Oklahoma and southern Kansas but were not self-designations or ethnonyms used by other tribes. Hence it seems most probable that Posada, or someone from whom he obtained his information, assumed that the tribes of western Texas included those met by Oñate farther north. Moreover, Domíngues de Mendoza, a member of Guadalajara's expedition of 1654, led another expedition to the same general area in 1683–1684; none of the Indian groups he mentions between present El Paso and San Angelo corresponds to Escanjaque, Ahijado, or Cuitoa (Bolton 1908:339–340). There is no evidence to lend credence to the existence of a tribe named Cuitoa (W.W. Newcomb and T.N. Campbell 1982:39–41).

Despite the implausibility of Cuitoa as the name of a distinct people, it has been identified as a Tonkawa subdivision (J.D. Forbes 1960) and as Bénard de La Harpe's Quisitas (Wichita) of 1719 (Schroeder 1962:18). It has also been cited as a tribe with an unknown habitat and identity (Duro 1882:57; Hodge 1907–1910, 1:371).

Manrhout

In 1683, when Réné-Robert Cavelier, sieur de La Salle, was at Fort Saint Louis on the upper Illinois River in present La Salle County, Illinois, he wrote that horses would be a practical means of transporting furs from the Illinois country to Lake Michigan and that they could be obtained from tribes to the west by either ascending the Missouri or walking across the prairies. Among those western tribes—which included the South Band and Skiri Pawnee, Wichita, and Osage—were the Manrhout and the Gattacka ("Gataea"; Plains Apache), both of whom engaged in horse trading (Margry 1876–1886, 2:168; M.M. Wedel 1988:68). In another document La Salle wrote that the Manrhout and Gattacka lived south of the Pawnee, whom they provided with horses obtained in New Mexico (Margry 1876–1886, 2:201; M.M. Wedel 1988:68).

Since there are no other historical references to the Manrhout and since the name is not recognizable as any known Plains ethnonym, these people cannot be confidently identified with any known historical group. Several writers have suggested, probably correctly, that the name designated the Kiowa because it was mentioned in association with the Plains Apache and because both the Kiowa and Plains Apache specialized in horse trading and had many horses (Mooney in Hodge 1907–1910, 1:701; J.H. Gunnerson and D.A. Gunnerson 1971:16). Another suggested but unlikely identification, based solely on approximate similarity in forms of the name, is Mentons, a Wichitan group (M.M. Wedel 1988:68).

Variant spellings of the name include Marhout and Manrhoat, the latter a transcriptional error (Margry 1876–1886, 2:168, 201; M.M. Wedel 1988:68); Manihaut or Mamhaut, 1684 (Franquelin 1684); Manruth, 1688 (Franquelin map in Tucker 1942:pl. 11A); and perhaps Mayoahc (Coxe 1722, Carolana map).

Early Eighteenth Century

For more than a decade beginning in 1731, the French-Canadian trader Pierre Gaultier de Varennes de La Vérendrye opened a route west of Lake Winnipeg in his search for the Western Sea. He visited the Mandan on the Missouri River in 1738–1739, and in 1742–1743 he sent his two sons Louis-Joseph and François on another expedition west-southwest beyond the Mandan villages in search of a tribe that could guide them to the inland sea. The exact route that the brothers followed is not clear. The farthest point west that they reached was a high range of mountains, probably the

Big Horns in present Wyoming, but possibly only the Black Hills of South Dakota. The party then traveled east-south-east, reaching the Missouri River at present Fort Pierre, South Dakota, visiting nine different tribes along the way.

Most of the tribal designations given by the La Vérendryes, like those given by Louis-Antoine de Bougainville, who wrote an account of the tribes visited by the La Vérendryes, do not correspond to documented ethnonyms. Since the La Vérendrye family spoke Ojibwa, and one son learned to speak Cree, most likely the Plains dialect, the names given by the La Vérendryes are probably French translations of Ojibwa or Cree designations, as are those cited by Bougainville. Whether Bougainville obtained those names personally from the La Vérendryes, or whether they came from other sources, is uncertain. Some of the names, however, do not occur in the La Vérendryes' own accounts. In a nearly contemporary document, Claude Godefroy Coquart, a Jesuit priest who had accompanied the elder La Vérendrye in his western explorations, gives another list of tribes encountered along the Missouri River (Burpee 1927:19; E.D. Neill 1876:309–311). The identity of most of the names has been the object of speculation, much of it simple guesswork.

Beaux Hommes

After they proceeded west-southwest from the Mandan villages for 20 days, taking them through places with different colored earth—undoubtedly the badlands of present western North Dakota—the La Vérendrye party reached a landmark they called Mountain of the Gens des Chevaux (Horse People), named for a tribe they were seeking. They then met the Beaux Hommes (Handsome Men), enemies of the Mandan; the party's Mandan guides had to use sign language to communicate with them (Burpee 1927:409–410). Bougainville (in Thwaites 1908:189), who stated that the Beaux Hommes were 40 leagues from the Mahantas (probably a Hidatsa village), gave their name as Owilinioek, which may represent an otherwise unattested Old Ojibwa *owe·liliniwak* 'well arranged people' (David Pentland, personal communication 2000), the source of the French name Beaux Hommes (see "Crow," synonymy, this vol.).

Several writers, beginning with Francis Parkman, have suggested that the Beaux Hommes were probably Crow, assuming that the party was west of the Little Missouri River (Parkman 1897, 2:2; Thwaites 1908:190; Hyde 1959:129). Others have speculated that they might be Gros Ventre (Morton 1973:16), Blackfoot, or even Arapaho (G.H. Smith 1980:119–120). Their identification as Gros Ventre was inferred from the statement of the voyageur Joseph La France that the Beaux Hommes were located south of the Assiniboine, between them and the Sioux (Dobbs 1744:35; La France 1749:245). However, that statement more accurately describes the location of the Crow. Similarly, their identification as Blackfoot is based on the same information from La France. The suggestion that they were Arapaho is derived solely from the similarity in meaning between Beaux

Hommes and the translation of the name of a local Arapaho band, Aqáthiněʼena 'pleasant men' (Mooney in Hodge 1907–1910, 1:73; G.H. Smith 1980:119). The evidence reasonably allows the conclusion that the Beaux Hommes were Crow.

Petits Renards

After proceeding south-southwest for two days the party met a village of the Petits Renards (Little Foxes) and subsequently came to another, large village of the same tribe (Burpee 1927:410–411). Bougainville (in Thwaites 1908:189) gives their name as Makesch or Petits Renards, the first form their Cree name *mahke·si·s* 'fox' (Lacombe 1874:430; Wolfart and Ahenakew 1998a:77).

Although no modern writer has suggested an identification of these people, they are most likely the Tuhkiwaku mentioned in the late-eighteenth and early nineteenth centuries.

Pioya

Two days after leaving the second Petits Renards village, the party came to a Pioya village and, after traveling two more days in a southwesterly direction, they came to a larger Pioya village (Burpee 1927:411). Bougainville (in Thwaites 1908:189) later cited the name as Piwassa together with the French rendition Grands-Parleurs (Great Talkers).

Most writers have assumed that Pioya is a mistranscription of the name Kiowa, with whom they identified the group (Thwaites 1908:190; G.H. Smith 1980:120; Hyde 1959:130), but the name may very likely designate some other tribe, especially if Bougainville's spelling is closer to the actual form of the name.

Gens des Chevaux

Continuing southward for two days, the party reached the Gens des Chevaux (Horse People), whose villages had just been destroyed by the Gens du Serpent (Snake People, that is, Eastern Shoshone) and only a few people had survived (Burpee 1927:411–413).

Most writers have not attempted to identify this tribe, but Parkman (Burpee 1927:407) proposed they were Cheyenne because the Cheyenne had a tradition that they were the first people in this region to have horses. However, his interpretation is implausible since the Cheyenne were living east of, or perhaps along, the Missouri River in the early eighteenth century, while the La Vérendrye party was apparently farther west (Grinnell 1923, 1:22–31).

Gens de la Belle Rivière

From the village of the Gens des Chevaux, the La Vérendrye party traveled in a southwestern direction and came to "a very populous village" of Gens de la Belle Rivière (People of the Beautiful River), where they were told that the Gens de l'Arc lived nearby (Burpee 1927:414).

Based on that minimal information, the Gens de la Belle Rivière have been identified as Arikara who were on the upper Cheyenne River, since the Sioux name for that river is *wakpá wašte* 'beautiful river', presumably borrowed from the designation of other tribes formerly in the region (D. Robinson 1913–1914:149). Reflecting that name is the northern fork of the Cheyenne, now known as Belle Fourche 'beautiful fork'. If these people were Arikara, they were at the beginning of their winter buffalo hunt (G. H. Smith 1980:120).

Gens de l'Arc

The Gens de l'Arc (Bow People), reputed to be the only tribe to cause fear among the Gens du Serpent, lived in a very large village southwest of the Gens des Chevaux and, like other tribes of the region, had many horses, mules, and donkeys used for transport and for hunting. After the party arrived there, the head chief ushered them into his large lodge. When asked if he knew the Whites on the coast, the chief responded that he had learned of them from the Gens du Serpent. He spoke a few words of their language, which was Spanish, and then described what must have been the massacre in 1721 of a Spanish expeditionary force from New Mexico under Pedro de Villasur that had come to attack the French traders residing among the Pawnee. Subsequently, the La Vérendrye party accompanied the Gens de l'Arc and members of other tribes on an aborted expedition against the Gens du Serpent. Upon returning to the Gens de l'Arc village, the party learned that the Gens de la Petite Cerise were close by and had invited the Frenchmen to join them. Before leaving, the La Vérendryes promised the Gens de l'Arc chief that they would come again if the chief would "establish himself near a little river that I indicated, and build a fort and raise grain there" (Burpee 1927:414–425).

The Gens de l'Arc, who were said to live in four villages opposite the Arikara, were known to the Plains Cree as Atchapcivinioques (probably for Atchapirinioek, unattested dialectal Cree *ahca·piyiriniwak* 'bow men') and to the Assiniboine as Utasibaoutchactas (*itázipa-wič*ʰ*ašta* 'bow man') (Bougainville in Thwaites 1908:189; David Pentland, personal communication 2000; Parks and DeMallie 1999).

Speculation on Gens de l'Arc identity has ranged widely: a Teton Sioux band (Parkman 1897, 2:26), and specifically the Sans Arcs or No Bows band (Burpee 1927:15); the Bow Indians of the Bow River, an affluent of the upper South Saskatchewan (Prud'homme 1905:50–51); Cheyenne or Arapaho, who "were expert in the use of bow and arrow" (Thwaites 1908:190); and Pawnee or Arikara (D. Robinson 1913–1914:146; Burpee 1927:22), Arikara specifically (E.D. Neill 1876:308), or Pawnee specifically because of the chief's account of the Villasur incident (G.H. Smith 1980:120). There is no reason, other than similarity of name, to assume the Bow People were either Sans Arcs Sioux or Bow Indians of Saskatchewan, and the argument for identifying them as Cheyenne or Arapaho is not compelling.

Based on the fragments of information from the La Vérendryes' journal, including the implication that the Gens de l'Arc built "forts" (that is, palisaded earthlodge villages) and planted corn, the most likely identification is an Arikara or Pawnee band.

Gens de la Flèche Collée

After leaving the village of the Gens de l'Arc, the La Vérendrye party met the Gens de la Petite Cerise (Little Cherry People), an Arikara band that had just returned from its winter quarters to take up residence in their earthlodge village on the Missouri River at present Fort Pierre. After leaving them the party traveled north to the Mandan villages, and eight days later encountered a village of 25 lodges of the Gens de la Flèche Collée (Glued Arrow People), known otherwise as Prairie Sioux, whom they did not visit, and then continued on their return journey to Fort La Reine, on the Assiniboine River in present Manitoba (Burpee 1927:429).

Although there is no reason to doubt the Glued Arrow People's identification as western Sioux, it is impossible to determine the specific subdivision or band. It has been suggested that because these people were not overtly unfriendly, they were perhaps Yanktonai (G.H. Smith 1980:121). Equally facile is their identification as Cheyenne based apparently on the partial resemblance of the name 'glued arrow' to the common designation for the Cheyenne 'marked or striped arrow' (Will 1917:297).

Brochet

In 1736, the elder La Vérendrye reported to the governor-general of New France that the country through which the Saskatchewan River passed in the area of Cumberland and Cedar lakes was inhabited by the Brochet tribe (Burpee 1927:246–247). That location suggests that the Brochet were probably Woods Cree. However, Bougainville (in Thwaites 1908:188), in his account of the tribes visited by the La Vérendryes, portrayed the Brochet, whom he also called Kinongewiniris, as living in three villages north of the Mandan on the Missouri River. North of them, on the upper part of the same river, were the Mahantas (probably a Hidatsa group), also living in three villages. Coquart (E.D. Neill 1876:309–311), too, portrays the Brochet as living just north of the Mandan. Kinongewiniris is Old Ojibwa *kino·še·wirini* or the Missinipi Cree dialect form *kinoše·wiriniw* 'pike person' (David Pentland, personal communication 2000).

It is difficult to reconcile the accounts that place the Brochet in two entirely separate areas. While the elder La Vérendrye's description of them clearly suggests the Woods Cree, the location and number of their villages on the Missouri River equally clearly indicate the Hidatsa. Thwaites (1908:188) notes that some writers have identified the Brochet as Assiniboine, based on an erroneous assumption that the Sioux name for the Assiniboine, *hóhe*, means 'fish catchers' (E.D. Neill 1876:310; Granville Stuart in E.D. Neill 1876:312); Thwaites concludes that, based on their location, they were Hidatsa. It is unclear whether there were two tribes named Brochet or whether Bougainville's and Coquart's statements of their location are confused, especially since the La Vérendrye sons did not mention the Brochet in their journal.

Other names cited by Bougainville

In 1757 Louis-Antoine de Bougainville, a military and naval officer who served in New France, wrote a description of the posts in Upper Canada, drawing his information from others since he himself had never visited the western posts. Included in his memoir is a description of the tribes visited by the La Vérendryes, some of which do not appear in the La Vérendrye documents and may have been learned from La Vérendrye's sons or other traders who had been in the west (Thwaites 1908:188–190).

Along the Missouri River above the Mandan villages, Bougainville (in Thwaites 1908:188) located three villages of the Mahantas above the Brochet villages. Coquart stated that the "Gros Ventre" (presumably the Hidatsa) were north of the Brochet (E.D. Neill 1876:309–310). Mahanta appears to be a plausible rendition of the Mandan name *wiʔtixata* that designated the Awaxawi division of Hidatsa.

Opposite—that is, west of—the Brochet were 300 lodges of Macateoualasites or Pieds-Noirs (Blackfoot). Macateoualasites is Old Ojibwa *mahkate·walahsit* (later *makkate·wanassit* 'Blackfoot'). However, assuming that the Brochet were Hidatsa, Thwaites (1908:190) identified these Pieds-Noirs, not as Blackfoot, but as a group of Hidatsa known to French traders as Souliers Noirs 'black moccasins'. Although his interpretation cannot be dismissed, it is less compelling than the Blackfoot identification.

Opposite the Mandan were four villages of the Ospekakaerenousques or gens du plat côté 'people of the side, set of ribs' (Bougainville in Thwaites 1908:189). The Old Cree form is *ospike·kan-iriniwak* 'rib people' or *ospikay-iriniwak* 'side people', referring to the rib cage (David Pentland and Ives Goddard, personal communications 2000). It may be a reference to the Flathead, whose sign language name indicates a flattening of the sides of the head, if French *plat côté* has its literal meaning 'flat side'. That interpretation is bolstered by a translation of the Cree name as Flathead (E.D. Neill 1876:314), as well as Coquart's statement (E.D. Neill 1876:309–311) that, after meeting the Crow and Gros Ventre, the La Vérendryes encountered the Flathead and then the Blackfoot, living along the Missouri River in present Montana.

Listed also, but with no location given, are five villages of the Kakakoschena or gens de la Pie (Magpie People) (Bougainville in Thwaites 1908:189). The Cree form, which is *ka·hka·kiwace·n*, is that tribe's designation for the Crow. Bougainville's French equivalent, 'magpie people',

is consonant with occasional historical references to birds other than the crow when explaining that tribe's name (see "Crow," synonymy, this vol.). If both the Beaux Hommes and Gens de la Pie are correctly identified as Crow, the separate listings of them would indicate two divisions of the Crow in the eighteenth century.

The final name on Bougainville's list is Kiskipisounouinini or gens de la Jarretière (Garter People), who occupied seven villages. The native form is Swampy Cree *ki·ske·pison-ininiw* 'garter person' (Faries 1938:273). Their identity is not known.

Late Eighteenth and Early Nineteenth Century

Dotame

The few references to the Dotame come from the first decade of the nineteenth century, first by Pierre-Antoine Tabeau (1939:154). A nomadic tribe, whose population was given as 30 men, they inhabited the area between the headwaters of the Platte, Cheyenne, and Yellowstone rivers, shared also by Cheyenne, Arapaho, Kiowa, Plains Apache, and other nomadic groups (Clark in Moulton 1983–, 1:map 32a). They traded with the Arikara and were at peace with all neighboring tribes except the Sioux. Statements about their tribal and linguistic affiliation are vague: William Clark (Moulton 1983–, 3:425–426, 439; D.D. Jackson 1962:535) said that they had formerly been a tribe of the Padoucas and spoke Padouca (at that time Plains Apachean), but he applied this label to a diverse set of tribes.

Two identifications of the Dotame with known tribes have been suggested. Hodge (1907–1910, 1:399) proposed they were Kiowa, because of their affiliation with the Katahka (Plains Apache) and Nemousin (whom he identified, probably incorrectly, as Comanche). The original sources list the Dotame as separate from the Kiowa and Plains Apache (Tabeau 1939:154; Lewis and Clark in Moulton 1983–, 3:439; D.D. Jackson 1962:535), contradicting that identification. More likely is the suggestion that they were a Plains Apachean group separate from the Plains Apache (Clark in Moulton 1983–, 3:439; also 448).

The name Dotame, which has an unknown source, was spelled variously: Datamis or Datamixes, 1803–1804 (Tabeau 1939:154); Do-ta-ne, Dotome, Dotame, and Do-ta-na, 1804–1805 (Clark in Moulton 1983–, 3:425); Detain and Do-ta-mi (D.D. Jackson 1962:229, 535); and Detame (W. Fisher 1812:26).

Tuhkiwaku

The earliest mentions of Tuhkiwaku are from the early eighteenth century, in which they were called Petits Renards (Little Foxes) and Makesch in Cree. Later, in Esteban Rodríguez Miró's 1785 description of Louisiana, the name appears as "Pados or Toguibacós" (Nasatir 1952, 1:124), identified as Plains Apache. (The same document is 969 printed in Kinnaird 1946:163, in which the designations are "Comanches, or Toquibacos", with Pado misidentified as Comanche.) Truteau (Parks 1993) cites the name as Tokiwako, spelled also as Torkirwaco and Tokiouco, which, like Toquibacos, reflect Pawnee *tuhkiwaku?* 'fox village', that is, Fox tribe (Parks 1999, 1999a). Tabeau (1939:154) spelled the name Tchiwak and tchiwâk, which is the cognate Arikara form *tUhčiwáku?* (note that Tabeau omitted the initial syllable, in which the vowel is whispered in Arikara; Parks 1999). Other sources also cite the Arikara form: To-che-wah-Coo, translated as 'Fox Indians', and Wah too che work koo (Clark in Moulton 1983–, 3:136); and Toot. che.wâ ku (J. Wilkinson 1805).

La Vérendrye wrote that there were two villages of the tribe, one very populous (Burpee 1927:410–411). Miró's 1785 report describes them as once having been the most numerous nation on the continent but because of devastating wars with other tribes (notably Comanche), they were reduced to four small wandering groups whose villages were in the vicinity of the White (then designated Little Missouri) River (Kinnaird 1946–1949, 2:163, 166; Nasatir 1952, 1:124, 127); Truteau placed them on a tributary of the Cheyenne River in 1796. Tabeau (1939:154) noted that although constant visiting helped the nomadic tribes living west and southwest of the Arikara to understand one another, members of those tribes were unable to understand a word of Tuhkiwaku. Clark (Moulton 1983–, 3:136) listed them as one of the nomadic tribes who went to the Arikara villages to trade horses and hides for horticultural produce.

Because of paucity of data, most writers have not attempted to identify the Fox tribe, which is clearly not the Algonquian Fox. Abel (Tabeau 1939:154–155), following Hodge, suggested that the Tuhkiwaku may have been Chawi Pawnee, but that proposal is not supported by any evidence. Hyde (1959:130), who recognized that the Petits Renards were the Tuhkiwaku, identified them as a group of Kiowa; however, there is no known basis for that conclusion either. The only historical documents that give an identification are Miró's 1785 description of Louisiana and Lewis and Clark's journal, which clearly portray the Tuhkiwaku as Plains Apacheans. However, without further corroboration, that identification cannot be accepted as conclusive.

Witapahatu or Pitapahatu

This name appears in a pair of spellings, one apparently reflecting a Pawnee and the other an Arikara form. Truteau (Parks 1993) provided the earliest recording of it as Pitapahato (Pawnee *pi·tapaha·tu?* 'red man'), the designation of a nomadic tribe located on branches of the Cheyenne River southwest of the Arikara villages, which were then at the mouth of the Cheyenne. He gave the same location for the Kiowa and Arapaho and distinguished the Pitapahato from the "Pados" (Plains Apacheans), whom he

placed on the Platte and one of its tributaries farther south and southwest.

In his list of the tribes on the Missouri River and west of the Mississippi, William Clark (Moulton 1983–, 3:421–423) grouped the We ta pa ha to, spelled also Wetepahatoe and Wetephatoe, into a set with the Cay-au-wa (Kiowa), treating them as separate groups but a single "nation"; on his map he cited them as the "We ta pa ha to & Kiowas tribes" (Moulton 1983–, 1:map 32a); and in his population figures he gave a combined number for the Kiowa and Witapahato (D.D. Jackson 1962:229). The two groups bartered with the Arikara, Mandan, and Hidatsa for articles of European manufacture, much of which they then traded to the Dotame and Castahana. In his notes from an interview with Clark, Nicholas Biddle (D.D. Jackson 1962:535) wrote that west of the Arapaho are "the *Wĕ tă pă hā tŏ & Kiăwàs* on heads of the Platte who amount to 200 men living together for mutual protection. They are conjectured to have been a tribe formerly of the Padukas." Brackenridge (1814:85) listed the Witapahato and Kiowa together, with a population of 900, and living on Padouca Fork.

Although never reported as a Pawnee or Arikara ethnonym, the forms Pitapahatu and Witapahatu are transparent Pawnee and Arikara words that are typical of ethnonyms in these languages. That they may represent obsolete names in Pawnee and Arikara is further supported by the fact that the first traders and explorers in the middle and upper Missouri River regions frequently borrowed Pawnee-Arikara names (for example, Pawnee *kátahka* and Arikara *katAhká* 'Plains Apache' and *tUhkanIhna·wíš* 'Arapaho') for nomadic groups farther west. The name occurs in both Sioux and Cheyenne, in which it designates the Kiowa. However, in neither language does it have a satisfactory etymology, suggesting that the Sioux and Cheyenne borrowed the name.

The Witapahatu are commonly identified as Kiowa (Mooney in Hodge 1907–1910, 1:701; Moulton 1983–, 3:448), both because the name is the Sioux and Cheyenne designation for the Kiowa and because references to the Witapahatu always associate them with the Kiowa. The original sources, however, depict the Witapahatu and Kiowa as separate but allied groups and consequently suggest at least two equally likely identifications: the Witapahatu and the Kiowa were cognate tribes or bands that merged, and in the early nineteenth century the Witapahatu lost their identity, with the name preserved in the Sioux and Cheyenne ethnonyms for the Kiowa; or the Witapahatu were Plains Apache, who were associated with the Kiowa since the eighteenth century and lived with them for protection. Both interpretations are contradicted by one or more statements or readings of data in the historical sources, so that at present it is not possible to resolve the identification.

Other spellings of this name include Wetabato (Clark in D.D. Jackson 1962:229), Wate-pana-toes (Brackenridge 1814:85), and Oue-ta-pa-ha-to, 1821 (R. Stuart 1935:map).

Castahana

Castahana as the name of an independent group occurs almost exclusively in the Lewis and Clark expedition records. A nomadic group living between the headwaters of the Platte and Yellowstone rivers and along the Big Horn River, they were characterized as like the Dotame except that they traded with the Crow as well as with the Mandan and Hidatsa (Moulton 1983–, 3:426–427). Clark later placed them, together with the Cheyenne, Arapaho, Kiowa, and others, in the area of the headwaters of the Teton (Bad) and Platte rivers. In his map they are located immediately west of two Arapahoan groups (Staetan and Kan ne na viech) (Moulton 1983–, 1:map 32a). They were the most populous of those groups (D.D. Jackson 1962:229). Clark told Biddle (D.D. Jackson 1962:535) that most of those tribes were remnant subdivisions of the Padoukas (Plains Apacheans); but that statement is partly incorrect, since he included in that group, among others, the Kiowa and an Arapahoan group. The only other reference to the Castahana is Breckenridge's (1814:86) inclusion of them in his list of tribes, where the name is misspelled Pasta-now-nas.

Clark recorded the "nickname" of the Castahana as Gens des Vache (People of the Cows), a designation for the Arapaho, and as speaking Minitari, which in this context refers to Gros Ventre, a northern Arapahoan dialect. Later he grouped the Castahana, here spelled Castihania, with the Can nar vesh (Arapaho) and Cheyenne (Moulton 1983–, 3:426, 487). That evidence strongly suggests they were an Arapahoan group, an identification noted previously by D.D. Jackson (1962:535) and Moulton (1983–, 3:448).

Tuwasa

The ethnonym Tuwasa (Arikara *tuwá·sA*) was recorded twice in the first decade of the nineteenth century. Clark (Moulton 1983–, 3:136–138) listed the name, spelled Too war Sar, after the Kiowa, as one of 10 nomadic tribes that went to the Arikara villages to trade. He translated the name as 'skin pricks', a meaning that suggests the word came from another language since it has no literal meaning in Arikara. James Wilkinson (1805) recorded the name as Too. wâ sâ, from an Arikara chief in Saint Louis, who enumerated some of the tribes living southwest of the Missouri River. No information on the tribe is provided other than a population figure of 250 warriors. The name does not appear on Clark's map of tribal distributions (Moulton 1983–, 1:32a).

In the twentieth century Tuwasa survived in Arikara as the name of a doctors' society, which was also named *neksá·nu?* 'Ghost (Society)'. Inside that society's medicine bundle is a little image of a man called *ka?íwA* 'Kiowa' (Parks 1999c). The association of the name Tuwasa with Kiowa suggests that the Tuwasa were either a cognate band of the Kiowa or another tribe associated with them. They were not Wichita (Moulton 1983–, 3:138).

Tuhpahkas

The Arikara name of another nomadic tribe cited by Clark (Moulton 1983–, 3:136, 217) and J. Wilkinson (1805) is *tUhpAxkás* 'white-haired village', that is, White Haired tribe (Parks 1999). Clark spelled the name To-pah-cass, translated as 'White hair's' and later as Te pah cus, while Wilkinson listed the name as Too pâ cas and noted that they "are white Haired from youths" and counted 200 warriors. Both Clark and Wilkinson listed the name either before or after the ethnonym *katAhká* (or Pawnee *kátahka*) 'Plains Apachean', suggesting that it designated a Plains Apachean group. Clark did not include it on his map (Moulton 1983–, 1:map 32a). The suggestion that it was an old name for the Great Osage, under their chief White Hair, incorrectly associates two names that fortuitously have the same meaning (Moulton 1983–, 3:138, n. 13).

Other Arikara Names

Clark (Moulton 1983–, 3:136, 217) and J. Wilkinson (1805) gave the names of two other nomadic tribes whose identity is unknown and who also do not appear on the Clark map. Clark spelled one as Noo-tar-wau, translated 'Hill Climbers' and later as Wa na tar wer; J. Wilkinson recorded it as Û. tâ. wâ and gave the number of warriors as 400. Although the name appears to be an Arikara word, its form is obscure.

Clark cited the name of the other tribe as Au ner-hoo 'the people who pen Buffalow to Catch them' and again as An nah hose, while J. Wilkinson rendered it lA. t̂a. ĥe. and as having 250 warriors. This name is also an obscure Arikara form.

A or Aa

A tribal designation that occurs from 1740 to 1840 in New Mexican church records and administrative reports, is A or Aa. Many of the references to the Aa are baptismal and burial records of women and children whom the Comanche had taken as captives and sold as slaves in New Mexico, where they were widely dispersed as servants throughout the Spanish settlements and Rio Grande Pueblos (Brugge 1965:181–189). Their territory on the western Plains was east and northeast of Santa Fe and extended as far north as the Yellowstone River. They warred with the Comanche and generally had friendly relations with most other tribes, including the Kiowa, Pawnee, and Wichita.

The Aa were most closely associated with the Cheyenne and Cuampe, the latter the Plains Apache. Berlandier (Ewers 1969:102) wrote that they "closely resemble the Pacanabos," that is, the Cheyenne. In 1805 two Cuampe chiefs went to Taos to request peace and trade for themselves and their allies, the Cheyenne and Aa (Loomis and Nasatir 1967:423–426). In the following year the governor wrote that these three allied tribes had been coming to Santa Fe regularly in recent years, and in 1819 a party of Aas from the Yellowstone River region visited the Spanish governor (Simmons 1973:75–80).

Writers have suggested many identifications of the Aa, most of which are clearly untenable. Schroeder (1959:67) inferred that they were Plains Apache, who were allied with the Kiowa during the eighteenth century but are rarely mentioned in Spanish documents of the period; however, there is no direct evidence to support that identification. Other proposals—that they were Caddo or Eyeish (Loomis and Nasatir 1967:423–426), Skiri Pawnee (Simmons 1973; John 1994:51), or Crow (J.H. Gunnerson and D.A. Gunnerson 1988:49–50)—do not fit the historical facts, since, with the exception of the Crow, the location of those tribes was too far east and their relations with tribes on the western Plains do not fit what is recorded about the Aa.

Several salient facts stand out to assist in identifying the Aa. There were apparently at least two divisions of the Aa, one on the Southern Plains (west Texas, Oklahoma, Kansas) and another on the Northern Plains (southern Montana, Wyoming, and probably Colorado). They were closely associated with the Cheyenne and Plains Apache, were culturally closer to the Cheyenne, and were distinct from Kiowa, Comanche, Pawnee, and Wichita. Since the name Arapaho does not appear in Spanish or Mexican records prior to 1840, and the Arapaho would certainly have been known in New Mexico, it may be reasonably inferred that the Aa were Arapaho, an identification first suggested by Thomas (1940:109; see also Ewers 1969:102).

Variant spellings of the name Aa include A, Aaa, AA, ÂÂ, Aâ, ââ, À, Àa, Aà, Haâ (Brugge 1965:181), and Aé (A.B. Thomas 1940:21).

Cuampe

Cuampe, another ethnonym that appears in Spanish and Mexican documents of the eighteenth and early nineteenth centuries, is frequently mentioned as a tribe closely allied with the Kiowa, Cheyenne, and Aa, all of whom occupied the same general area of the western Plains. The Cuampe were, for example, reported as living on the headwaters of the Platte in 1805, and two years later were located from the headwaters of Fountain River (in central Colorado) to as far east as the Arkansas River (Loomis and Nasatir 1967:176, 459; Simmons 1973:78–79). In 1806 they were said to reside between the Pecos and Rio Grande rivers (Bloom 1927:372).

There have been several proposed identifications of the Cuampe. Their identification as Comanche is mistaken (Loomis and Nasatir 1967:440). Unlikely, too, is the suggestion that the name Cuampe is a Spanish borrowing of Kiowa $k^h\grave{o}mp\grave{o}b\hat{\imath}\cdot d\grave{o}$ 'large tepee flap people' (J.H. Gunnerson and D.A. Gunnerson 1988:12–13), an old name sometimes used by the Kiowa for themselves (Mooney 1898:412). The Cuampe were most frequently mentioned together with the Kiowa, but they are clearly a separate tribe. Their identity as Arapaho (Simmons 1973:78–79) is likewise unlikely since what is recorded about the Aa more closely resembles what

is known of the Arapaho. Because the Cuampe are so frequently associated with the Kiowa, they were presumably Plains Apache (Ewers 1969:103, n.118). The name was also mentioned as one of the divisions of the Faraon Apache (Orozco y Berra 1864:59; Hodge 1907–1910, 1:369), but that citation may be a reference to another Apachean group or simply a mistake.

Variant spellings include Cuampis (Villaseñor y Sánchez, 1746–1748, 2:413), Cuampes (Orozco y Berra 1864:59), and Cuampas, 1805 (Alencaster in Loomis and Nasatir 1967:176–177).

Orejones

The name Orejones (Spanish 'big ears') occurs infrequently in New Mexico documents. In 1806 13 lodges of Orejones were living in a Kiowa village, and the tribe was said to inhabit the country near the Missouri in an area also frequented by the Kiowa (Alencaster in Loomis and Nasatir 1967:450–451). An 1812 enumeration of the tribes surrounding New Mexico includes Cuampes, Cahiguas (Kiowa), and Aas-orejones together; an 1820 report by Father Juan Guevara lists Orejones and Aas in the same context (Simmons 1973:79).

The Orejones have been identified as one of the divisions of the Faraón Apache (Orozco y Berra 1864:59; Hodge 1907–1910, 2:147), but that association is probably a confusion of Apachean groups or a mistake, since there is no other corroborating evidence. Their identification as a tribe on the Texas coast (Loomis and Nasatir 1967:450–451) is a confusion with a Coahuiltecan tribe that went by the same designation (Bolton in Hodge 1907–1910, 2:147). The Orejón here seem most likely to have been a Plains Apachean group, perhaps another name for the Plains Apache, since in the few references to them they are associated with the Kiowa, Cheyenne, and Arapaho. However, based on their reported association with the Aa, they may also have been an Arapahoan group. The evidence is too scanty to resolve their identification.

Kaskaia

A nomadic group whose name appears rarely in the early nineteenth century is Kaskaia. The single first-hand account of them appears in James's account of the Stephen H. Long expedition (Thwaites 1904–1907, 15:211–212, 282; 16:105–119; 17:156–157). He associates them with the Kiowa, Arapaho, Comanche, and a small band of Cheyenne who had seceded from their kindred on the Cheyenne River, all living on the plains from the sources of the Platte and Arkansas to the Red and Rio Grande rivers. The Kaskaia, Kiowa, and Arapaho were noted for their large herds of horses, which they traded to the Cheyenne and others for European trade goods obtained from British traders in the Mandan village on the Missouri.

The source of the name Kaskaia is obscure, but French traders called them Bad Hearts. James (Thwaites 1904–1907,

972

17:157) noted that the Kaskaia and Kiowa languages were exceptionally difficult to learn and that the party's interpreter, who had lived with the two tribes for several years, could only make himself understood by use of the sign language and some words of Crow that the Kaskaia and Kiowa understood.

Thwaites (1904–1907, 15:211) wrote that the Kaskaia were closely akin to the Comanche, if not identical with them, but his observation is not borne out by any evidence; moreover, James grouped the Comanche (Ietan) as one of the nomadic tribes that included the Arapaho, Kaskaia, Kiowa, and Cheyenne. Mooney (Hodge 1907–1910, 1:701) suggested that they were Plains Apache; Hyde (1959:204) similarly identified them as "probably Gatakas or Prairie Apaches." Four observations—their association with the Kiowa and Arapaho, their renown as horse traders, their reputation for speaking a difficult language distinct from those of the Kiowa and other nomadic tribes, and their knowing some Crow words—together suggest that they were most likely Plains Apache, or some other Plains Apachean group, who, like the Kiowa, had formerly lived farther north.

Variant spellings of Kaskaia include Kaskaya, 1843 (*American Pioneer* 1842–1843, 2:189) and Kaskia (Drake 1848:viii).

Archithinue, Slave, and Plains Indians

During the eighteenth century the Cree used a generic term *ayahciyiniwak* 'alien people, strangers; enemies' to designate various tribes living to the west and southwest of them, and Hudson's Bay Company traders in turn used the term, anglicized by them as Archithinue, for those distant tribes with whom direct trade had not yet been established. The traders, following Cree usage, most commonly used the name for the Blackfoot tribes (Blackfoot, Blood, Piegan) as well as their allies, the Gros Ventre and Sarcee, but the term was applied to other tribes as well.

The earliest references to the Archithinue are in the letters and journals of Hudson's Bay traders before actually meeting them: the Atchue-thinnies are described as a people "bordering near the Western Ocean," 1738 (Norton in Davies 1965:249); the Atch-thin-nies attacked Hudson's Bay Company "trading Indians" while beaver hunting (Knight in Davies 1965:292, 318); and the Earchethinues were said to live "westward of the Churchhill River, where

the Spaniards frequents those seas," 1743 (Isham in Rich 1949:113). Those references are so general as to suggest many possible identifications, including, in addition to tribes in the Blackfoot confederacy, Athapaskan and Shoshonean tribes. In the 1756–1757 York Factory post journal (HBCA B.239/a/42, 25 June 1757, microfilm roll 1M157, fol. 46), the Crow are identified as Earchithinues, while in 1772 Andrew Graham (HBCA E.2/9, microfilm roll 4M101, p. 138) describes the Archithinue as being village Indians with permanent residences. The first actual enumeration of tribes designated as Archithinue appears in the published, abridged edition of Matthew Cocking's 1772–1773 journal (Burpee 1908:337), in which the name is said to refer to the five tribes of the Blackfoot confederacy; but in the unpublished, official version Cocking actually listed nine Yeachithinneethe—the five preceding tribes, as well as their enemies, the Eastern Shoshone, Flathead, Kootenai, and another unidentified tribe cited as Wahtee or vault Indians (Russell 1991:190). Although many references to the Archithinue are to the Blackfoot and their confederates specifically, others are clearly to different tribes, and some are too vague to identify with certainty (Russell 1991:187–199).

Other citations of Archithinue include: earsheadeneys (Joseph Smith in HBCA B.239/a//52 13, 18 Nov. 1763); Ye,arch,a,thin,a,wocke and Ye,artch,a,thyne,a Wock (William Pink in HBCA B.239/a/56, 28 January 1767, HBCA B.239/a/58 26 Sept. 1767); and archethynnawock (Pink in HBCA 239/a/63 13 Dec. 1769).

From the late eighteenth to the early nineteenth century, another generic Cree term *awahka·n* 'slave' was used by that tribe to designate their enemies, including the Blackfoot tribes, the Gros Ventre, and the Sarcee, as well as Athapaskan groups to the north, 1809 (Henry in Gough 1988–1992, 2:376), 1841 (George Simpson in Dempsey 1990:3). Among British traders on the upper North Saskatchewan River, Slave Indians and Plains Indians became common designations for the tribes of the Blackfoot confederacy as a group in the 1780s, when Archithinue ceased to be used. When speaking about any one of the constituent tribes, they used the name of that tribe. Farther downriver at Carlton House, Slave was also used to designate two or more members of the Blackfoot confederacy, but Plains Indians (or Plains tribes) was a designation there for the Assiniboine and Plains Cree (David Smyth, personal communication 2000).

973

Kinship and Social Organization

FRED EGGAN AND JOSEPH A. MAXWELL*

Overview

The Plains culture area is usually divided into the eastern, or Prairie Plains and the western, or High Plains regions. Each has a distinctive subsistence pattern and type of social structure, although the two have interacted over a long period of time.

The historic Indian populations in the Prairie Plains lived mainly in sedentary villages composed of earthlodges, cultivated bottomlands along the Missouri River and its tributaries, and periodically hunted bison, whose main habitat was the plains to the west. Most of these Village tribes spoke languages of the Siouan family and had traditions of coming from the east, which was inhabited by tribes having a similar social organization, but mostly speaking languages of the Algonquian family. The social organization of the Prairie Plains tribes was much more elaborate and specialized than that of the High Plains tribes, and tribal integration was more complex and rigid.

To the south and west of these groups were a number of semisedentary tribes, living in villages of grass lodges in the south and earthlodges in the north, who spoke languages of the Caddoan family. These tribes shared many features of social organization with the Siouan village tribes but were economically intermediate between these two regions, and some tribes resembled the High Plains nomads in particular aspects of their social organization. Traditionally they came from the Southeast, but the diversity of social structures in this region (Urban 1994) provides little basis for inference about their prior forms of social organization. Various Caddoan groups had moved into the Plains area in early prehistoric times (Schlesier 1994a:346–361), eventually becoming the historic Wichita, Kitsai, Pawnee, and Arikara.

In the High Plains, the historic tribes were nomadic within claimed hunting areas. Each tribe (or, in the case of the larger tribes, subtribe) came together in the early summer for the Sun Dance and other ceremonies, and for tribal bison hunts. In the fall the bands dispersed and wintered in camps along the streams, where wood and water were available. The historic High Plains tribes belonged to a variety of linguistic families, and many had moved into the Plains relatively recently from surrounding areas, including the horticultural areas to the east, the northern forests, and the Great Basin.

The pioneering field studies of Lewis Henry Morgan (1871, 1959) (fig. 1) revealed that the Prairie Plains and High Plains were distinctive with regard to almost all aspects of their social structures. The Siouan tribes, for example, represented three systems of kinship organization, called the Dakota, the Omaha, and the Crow (Lesser 1928:563) (fig. 2). These correlated with three distinct types of social organization: the bilateral local bands of the Sioux and Assiniboine, the patrilineal exogamous moieties composed of clans of the Central Siouans, and the matrilineal exogamous clans grouped into phratries of the Crow, Hidatsa, and Mandan. Bilateral band organization was thus strongly correlated with the High Plains and unilineal clan organization with the Prairie Plains. Kin terminologies of the Dakota type were nonunilineal, emphasizing the unity of groups of siblings and parallel cousins, while the Omaha and Crow terminologies were lineal, classing clan relatives together across generations.

The Plains Caddoan tribes present a significant contrast to the Siouan. Despite their position among the Prairie tribes, all lacked clan organization. Lesser (1979) found two distinct kinship systems. The Wichita and Kitsai classified both cross-cousins and parallel cousins with siblings, much like the High Plains Siouans, while the Pawnee and Arikara used a modified Crow-type system.

Differences between the Prairie and High Plains tribes in terms of kinship and social organization undoubtedly relate to historical and ecological factors. The clan-based systems and unilineal descent patterns characteristic of the Prairies were more elaborate and specialized and as a result, tribal integration was more complex and rigid. The social structures and kinship systems of the Prairie Plains tribes were developed in connection with a sedentary or semisedentary life, based to a substantial degree on horticulture. It was a pattern that was well suited to a stable mode of existence. The clan or lineage structures were highly functional in perpetuating property rights, social distinctions, and ceremonial activities, and the Crow-type and Omaha-type kin terminologies expressed a complex set of distinctions that sustained this pattern. Such a pattern was not well suited to the full-time nomadic bison-hunting life of the High Plains tribes. Tribal organization among those tribes centered on the band and camp circle, with a seasonal variation related to ecological factors—climate and the habits of the buffalo. The High Plains bands were bilateral and composite, with fixed positions in the camp circle, but otherwise little differentiated

*The Overview and Prairie Plains sections were composed by Eggan; Maxwell completed the chapter.

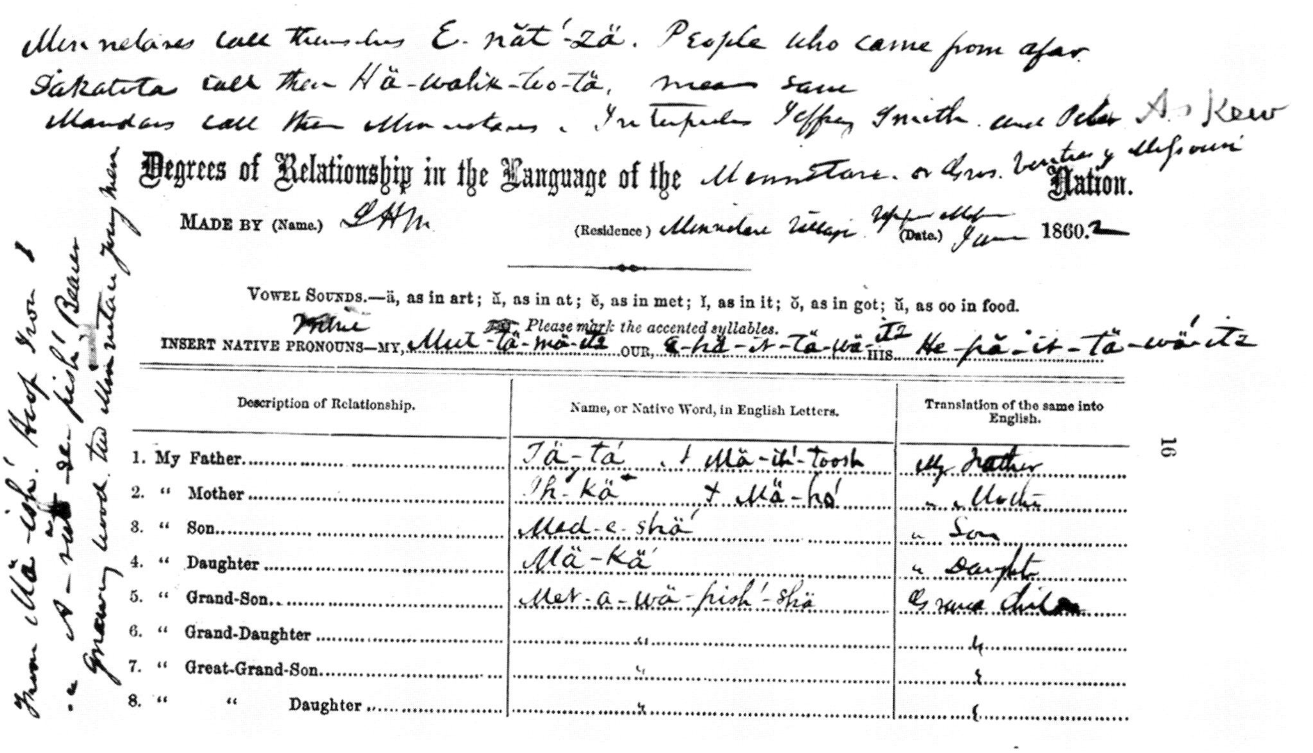

Minnetares call themselves E-nät'-zä. People who came from afar.
Dakotas call them Hä-wahk-to-tä, mean same
Mandans call them Minnetares. Interpreters Jeffrey Smith and Peter Askew

Degrees of Relationship in the Language of the *Minnetare, or Gros Ventre of Missouri* Nation.

MADE BY (Name.) *L H M*   (Residence) *Minnetare Village Upper Missouri*   (Date.) *June* 1860.*

VOWEL SOUNDS.—ä, as in art; ă, as in at; ĕ, as in met; I, as in it; ŏ, as in got; ŭ, as oo in food.
Please mark the accented syllables.
INSERT NATIVE PRONOUNS—MY, *Mä-tä-mä-dä* OUR, *Ē-hä-it-tä-wä* HIS *He-pä-it-tä-wä-itä*

Description of Relationship.	Name, or Native Word, in English Letters.	Translation of the same into English.
1. My Father...............	*Tä-tä' + Mä-it'-toosh*	*My Father*
2. " Mother...............	*Ih-kä + Mä-ho'*	*" Mother*
3. " Son...............	*Med-e-shä*	*" Son*
4. " Daughter...............	*Mä-Kä'*	*" Daughter*
5. " Grand-Son..............	*Met-a-wä-hish'-shä*	*Grand Child*
6. " Grand-Daughter...............	"	"
7. " Great-Grand-Son...............	"	"
8. " " Daughter...............	"	"

16

From Mä-ih'-ish' Half Son
A-nit-se-hish' Beaver
Grown Wood, two Minnetare boys here

U. of Rochester Lib., Dept. of Rare Books and Special Coll., N.Y.

Fig. 1. Part of the form designed by Lewis Henry Morgan to record kinship terms. This questionnaire was filled out by Morgan at the Hidatsa village on the Upper Missouri in June 1862 with the aid of interpreters Jeffrey Smith and Peter Askew.

from one another. Kin terminologies tended to be organized according to generation.

Prairie Plains

The Prairie Plains includes areas both east and west of the Mississippi River. The eastern part of this region is covered in volume 15 of the *Handbook, Northeast*, which contains accounts of the Central Algonquian–speaking tribes and the Siouan-speaking Winnebago, as well as a survey of sociopolitical organization (vol. 15:610–621). West of the Mississippi, in the Missouri region, were the Siouan-speaking Mandan and Hidatsa and the Caddoan-speaking Arikara; the Santee and Yankton-Yanktonai Sioux, who are classed in this volume with the High Plains tribes; the Central Siouans—Ponca, Omaha, Osage, Kansa, and Quapaw, speaking Dhegiha languages; and the Iowa, Otoe, and Missouria, speaking Chiwere. The Central Siouans can be classified on a continuum from east to west, with the easternmost tribes being the most horticultural in orientation, and the westernmost tribes, the Ponca and Omaha, being the most influenced by mounted bison hunting. Somewhat to the southwest of these were the Caddoan-speaking Pawnee, Wichita, and Kitsai, whose economy was less tied to horticulture and more dependent on bison hunting than that of the Central Siouans.

In the nineteenth century the social systems of these groups, with the exception of the Sioux and the Caddoan tribes, were organized in terms of unilineal descent. The Mandan and Hidatsa were divided into matrilineal clans, which were grouped into dual divisions, or moieties, and it is probable that at an earlier time the neighboring Pawnee and Arikara were also so organized. The Central Siouans farther south were organized in patrilineal clans, usually grouped into moieties. Clans regulated marriage, but had a number of other functions as well. They usually owned a stock of personal names, they frequently controlled political or ritual positions, they had symbolic relationships to some aspect of nature, and they often had ritual duties to perform throughout the ceremonial calendar. In addition there were various associations centered on war and curing, some of which were age-graded and all of which were involved in the great tribal ceremonies.

Marital residence in the earthlodges was generally with the wife's family (a pattern termed uxorilocal), regardless of the formal pattern of descent; the husband came to live with his wife and her relatives in a multifamily structure, which facilitated female cooperation in cultivation of the family's fields. After the fields were planted the able-bodied men and their wives went on the summer communal hunt, where they traveled with tepees and camped in a camp circle like their High Plains nomadic neighbors. For the Omaha and

975

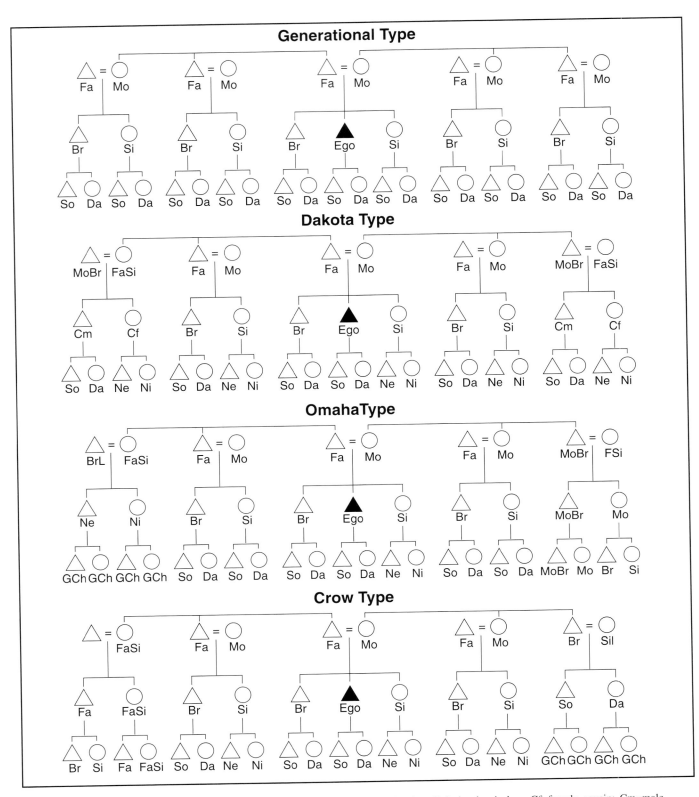

Fig. 2. Four types of Plains kinship terminological systems. Abbreviations: Br=brother; BrL=brother-in-law; Cf=female cousin; Cm=male cousin; Da=daughter; Fa=father; FaSi=father's sister; GCh=grandchild; GFa=grandfather; Mo=mother; MoBr=mother's brother; Ne=nephew; Ni=niece; Si=sister; SiL=sister-in-law; So=son. Bracketed terms vary; Omaha-type terms as shown represent the Omaha tribe; Crow-type terms as shown represent the Hidatsa. (Eggan 1968).

some of their relatives having patrilineal descent, the camp circle directly reflected the social structure of the tribe, the clans of one moiety having fixed positions in the northern half and being symbolically associated with the sky, and the clans of the other moiety being arranged in the southern half and symbolically associated with the earth. This was accomplished by virilocal residence, a man and his wife, or wives, camping with his clan mates. This structure facilitated male cooperation in both hunting and defense against enemy attacks.

In Omaha tradition the patrilineal moieties associated with the sky and earth were exogamous, but smallpox epidemics destroyed their demographic balance, so that control of marriage had devolved to the clans and subclans by the time the kinship terminology was recorded. In some Omaha-type systems the affected moieties were restructured by alternately allocating children to different moieties, destroying their exogamous character in favor of maintaining ceremonial structure in demographic balance.

The Wichita, Kitsai, and Pawnee were also basically uxorilocal in residence after marriage, and the grass houses and earthlodges accommodated large extended families based on matrilineal kin groups. The Pawnee villages in historic times had consolidated in larger units for defensive purposes, and each unit had become independent and endogamous; earlier they may have had exogamous matrilineal clans. Each village had its own myth that told of its founder having been created by a star or constellation, who subsequently gave the founder a sacred bundle that was the source of his power. When the founder of the village died his bundle and his chieftaincy passed to his son. The village was thought of as a large extended family, centered on the bundle ceremonies, and owning its own fields for horticulture (Parks 1989:7). Weltfish (1965) describes the practice of avunculocal residence, in which a boy was sent for instruction and training to live with a maternal uncle or older brother and shared that man's wife or wives, a special form of marriage known as fraternal polyandry (Lesser 1930).

The Arikara, who had moved farther up the Missouri River, were apparently undergoing a similar change. Deetz (1960:101) concluded that "the Arikara began to change their social structure in a direction away from the earlier Crow type to a more generationally based system, better suited to meet the effects of rapidly changing conditions."

The Wichita and Kitsai were the only historic Prairie Plains village tribes for whom a significant part of the tribe had at one time completely abandoned horticulture for nomadic bison hunting, during the early eighteenth century (Hyde 1959:45; Secoy 1953:27–32). Marital residence was strongly uxorilocal, similar to the other Caddoan tribes, but other aspects of their social system resembled the High Plains system more than that of the Prairie Plains tribes.

With the exception of the Wichita and Kitsai, the kin terminologies of the Prairie Plains tribes were organized in terms of the lineage principle, the Mandan, Hidatsa, Pawnee, and (probably) the Arikara having variants of a Crow-type system, and the Omaha, Ponca, Kansa, Iowa, Otoe, and related groups having an Omaha-type system (Barnes 1984). In these systems, the kinship terminology was organized vertically in terms of the descent pattern, rather than

horizontally in terms of generation. In a Crow-type terminology, a person's mother's brother, who is a member of his or her matrilineal clan, is called 'brother'; in an Omaha-type terminology, a person's father's sister (a member of his or her patrilineal clan) is called 'sister'. These types of terminology are thus consonant with unilateral descent, although many tribes outside the Plains with unilineal descent do not have Crow or Omaha terminologies.

The Pawnee and Arikara had a Crow-type terminology characterized by additional features of lineage-based generational skewing. For the Pawnee, the speaker's father's sister's children (who belonged to the father's matrilineage) were called 'mother' and 'father', and these terms descended to subsequent generations in the father's matrilineage. Conversely, the speaker's mother's brother's children were called 'children', as were all children of males in the speaker's own matrilineage.

The Wichita and Kitsai, in contrast, lacked the Crow-type terminological features of the Pawnee and Arikara. All cousins were called by the same terms as siblings, a pattern labeled generational (fig. 2), and there was no skewing of terms across generations that would correspond to a matrilineal descent system. However, K. Schmitt and I. Schmitt (1952) found evidence for a shift from a prior matrilineal type of social structure, with Crow-type kin terms, to a bilateral type of social system.

High Plains

The fundamental problem in the social organization of the High Plains tribes was succinctly stated by Eggan (1937:93): "Tribes coming into the Plains with *different* backgrounds and social systems ended up with *similar* kinship systems" (Eggan 1937:93). Later he added: "They achieved a common pattern of social structure as well" (Eggan 1966:72). The historic High Plains tribes exhibited considerable diversity in their former subsistence patterns, social structures, and kin terminologies, as these can be inferred from historical records, comparison with related tribes, archeological evidence, and linguistic reconstruction. However, virtually all these tribes possessed a common pattern of subsistence, social structure, and terminology when these features were first recorded by Europeans. These tribes united in the summer and separated into bands in winter; the tribe formed a camp circle of tepees, with the various bands of the tribe each having its own place, and with lodges for chiefs and other officials in the central area; men's societies were responsible for protection and keeping order during the summer hunt; band membership and marital residence were flexible; there was a lack of descent groups or their terminological correlates; and the kin terminology exhibited a wide extension of sibling terms to other relatives of the same generation (including a generational-type pattern of cousin terms) and a bifurcate merging pattern of terms in adjacent generations (fig. 3). Bifurcate merging terms for uncles and aunts group father's brother with father, and mother's sister 977

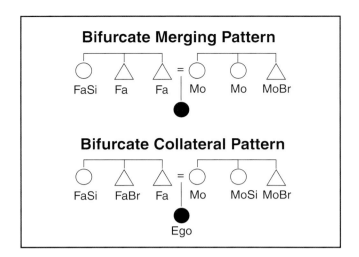

Bifurcate Merging Pattern

FaSi Fa Fa = Mo Mo MoBr

Bifurcate Collateral Pattern

FaSi FaBr Fa = Mo MoSi MoBr

Ego

Fig. 3. Bifurcate merging and bifurcate collateral patterns of kin terminology (Eggan 1968).

with mother but separate terms are used for father's sister and mother's brother; reciprocally, a woman's sister's children are grouped with her own, and her brother's children are called by separate terms, while a man's brother's children are grouped with his own children, and his sister's children are called by separate terms. This larger pattern, embracing three generations, will be referred to as "generational/bifurcate merging."

Although the particular pattern varied somewhat from tribe to tribe, all Plains Indians united in large groups (as many as several thousand people) during part of the year and separated into smaller groups at other times, mainly during the winter. This annual cycle has been attributed primarily to the migration pattern of the bison, but the need to gather in large groups for defense during the summer, when most warfare took place, was probably an important factor as well. The winter dispersal was an economic necessity, due to the absence of large herds of bison at this time except in the southernmost Plains. In one year, around 1837, the Cheyenne tribe attempted to stay together for the winter and nearly perished as a result (Lowie 1954:92).

There seem to have been both upper and lower limits on viable tribal size. The two High Plains tribes with populations under 1,000, the Plains Apache and Sarcee, were closely associated with the Kiowa and Blackfoot, respectively, and the Plains Apache functioned as a band of the Kiowa in the summer camp circle. On the other hand, the three groups with populations over 5,000, the Blackfoot, Teton Sioux, and Comanche, were divided into subgroups, comparable to tribes, that combined only irregularly if at all.

The Plains Cree, Plains Ojibwa, and Assiniboine bands also failed to unite consistently in tribal groups for the summer hunt, and here an ecological explanation is plausible. All three tribes inhabited primarily prairie and parkland rather than true plains and could get bison during most of the year. All were short of horses and used the pound as a major hunting method, often in winter; in 1853 the Plains

Cree and Assiniboine were the only tribes using this method (Rodnick 1938:24). All depended more on food sources other than bison than did other High Plains tribes, and at least some bands of each tribe did considerable trapping. All had more guns than their enemies to the south and west, giving them a substantial military advantage in wooded country, although their lack of horses put them at a disadvantage on the plains (Secoy 1953). These factors clearly lessened the value of gathering in large groups, for either hunting or defense, and contributed to band independence.

Most High Plains tribes had men's societies that were involved in warfare and in keeping internal order. Normally they were active only during the summer camp circle, when they initiated new members and served as police, both in camp and on the tribal hunt. For the most part the men's societies were not hierarchically ranked, and initiates usually joined the societies of their father, but in a few Plains tribes they were age-graded: the Mandan and Hidatsa in the Prairie Plains and the Blackfoot, Arapaho, and Gros Ventre in the High Plains (Lowie 1916; Bowers 1950, 1965; Fowler 1982, 1987).

Marital residence was flexible in all Plains tribes, although some tribes tended toward a unilocal rule. There was a greater incidence of virilocality among Northern Plains tribes than in the Central or Southern Plains, and this can be plausibly ascribed to the greater amount of nonsororal polygyny in these tribes, stemming from the effects of the fur trade. Preferred marriage with a close or classificatory cross-cousin (a man's father's sister's daughter or mother's brother's daughter), although found in many tribes to the north of the Plains, was prohibited in all High Plains tribes, even those tribes that had previously practiced such a marriage pattern.

An institutionalized "friend" or "comrade" relationship is reported for every High Plains tribe for which data on behavior exists. Generally the relationship was similar to that between brothers, although for the Cheyenne and Wichita it involved more respect and formality. The terms for 'brother' and 'friend' could be used quite widely in many tribes, in some cases including virtually all men of ego's age or generation.

The systems of kin terminology found in High Plains tribes show some striking similarities. Eight of the High Plains tribes—Lipan Apache, Comanche, Plains Apache, Kiowa, Cheyenne, Arapaho, Gros Ventre, and Blackfoot—had a pattern of generational-type cousin terms and bifurcate merging terms in the speaker's parents' and children's generations; a ninth, the Sarcee, may well have had this pattern, but data are not adequate to determine this. The two clear exceptions to this pattern are the Sioux, with separate terms for cross-cousins (known as Dakota-type cousin terms), and the Crow, with a Crow-type terminology. The Tonkawa also apparently had Crow-type kinship terms (L. Johnson 1994).

Among the other High Plains tribes, the Hawaiian/bifurcate merging pattern is reported for the Lipan Apache. The

Wichita and Kitsai had most of this pattern but equated father's sister with mother (a generational pattern for aunts). All these tribes had engaged to a major extent in mounted bison hunting on the plains. In native North America, primary terminological usages conforming to this generational/bifurcate merging pattern were limited to the tribes mentioned; most tribes to the east of the High Plains had Dakota-, Crow-, or Omaha-type cousin terms, while those to the north and west usually had either Dakota-type cousin terms or bifurcate collateral terms in the speaker's parents' and children's generations.

Causes of Terminology Patterns

There have been several attempts to explain the presence of this pattern of kin terminology. Murdock (1949) and Dole (1969) interpreted the kin terminologies of this area as, respectively, the result of particular features of kinship structure (primarily residence patterns, descent groups, and forms of marriage), or the consequences of the social disorganization produced by depopulation, war, and forced migration. However, these theories fail to fit the evidence for the High Plains tribes; differences between this pattern and others in the High Plains region do not correlate strongly with either differences in these features of kinship structure or with the amount of depopulation or social disruption (Maxwell 1971, 1978).

A third explanation was proposed by Eggan (1937, 1955, 1966), who saw the fluidity, bilaterality, and absence of distinctions between cross- and parallel cousins in High Plains tribes as creative and adaptive responses to this environment, rather than as the reflection of particular features of social structure or the results of demographic change. These characteristics of High Plains kinship systems supplied the required flexibility while maintaining the integration of the tribe and its component units. The clan and lineage systems of the village horticulturalists were well suited to the transmission of land, property, and social status, but were relatively rigid. In contrast, as Eggan (1966:56) noted, the amorphous bands of the High Plains were flexible: "A successful leader attracted new members, while those of a poor leader were lost or melted away." Holder (1970) also contrasted the adaptive potential of the two types of social organization.

In warfare and hunting, the cooperation and solidarity of the men of the tribe were essential to survival, and Eggan felt that this was responsible for the wide extension of the behavior and kin terms used between brothers. Similarly, the abandonment of cross-cousin marriage by several tribes in moving onto the plains was not a symptom of social disorganization, but a response to the need for a wider range of social integration due to the increased importance of large-scale cooperation in hunting and warfare (Eggan 1966:102).

Maxwell (1971, 1978) developed Eggan's theory, incorporating work in kinship theory (D.M. Schneider 1968, 1972, 1976; Cottrell 1965; Tambiah 1965; Murphy 1967; Bloch 1971; McKinley 1971, 1971a). He viewed kin terminology not as a reflection of social groupings and relationships but as a cultural phenomenon, one that is grounded in social life but that may "contradict" the social order as manifested behaviorally. Kin terminology has a dialectical relationship with social structure; it can have important ideological and symbolic functions separate from the representation of social relationships and may independently contribute to group adaptation (Maxwell 1986, 1994).

For example, the generational-type cousin terminology of most High Plains tribes was not necessarily a reflection of a lack of social distinctions between siblings and cousins, but, by equating all male cousins with brothers, ideologically emphasized the importance of male solidarity and contributed to wide-ranging cooperation and aid. In this view, it is plausible that, instead of the extension of sibling terms to cousins mirroring a prior shift in social behavior, the change in cousin terminology may have preceded and facilitated the social changes, through a metaphorical or tactical use of the sibling terms to address other relatives who later became incorporated in the referential terminology (Maxwell 1978).

Typical Terminology

Obviously, the value of this theory depends on its ability to account for the exceptions to the generational/bifurcate merging kinship pattern among High Plains tribes. There are two kinds of exceptions to this pattern. First, there are tribes where wide-ranging male solidarity was not so important as it was for most High Plains tribes, for ecological reasons. Second, some tribes developed alternative ways of meeting the need for increased solidarity. In addition, the Blackfoot and Sarcee carried the process emphasized by this theory to an extreme, which in combination with unique historical circumstances led to an unusual pattern of terminology.

The Assiniboine, Stoney, Plains Cree, and Plains Ojibwa, who retained Dakota-type cousin terms, are examples of the first type of exception. These tribes were late arrivals on, and somewhat marginal to, the true short-grass plains. At least until 1812, these tribes had more guns than their enemies to the south and west, giving them a military advantage in wooded country, but were short of horses, putting them at a disadvantage on the plains. For this reason, they used the pound as a major bison-hunting technique. In contrast to the other High Plains tribes, in which a bison was exclusively the property of the man who killed it and the meat shared on an informal basis along kin and friendship lines, the pound hunts of the Assiniboine and Plains Cree were formally organized and directed and the meat divided equally among the participating families. All these tribes were less dependent on wide-ranging male solidarity than other High Plains tribes.

The two exceptions among the High Plains tribes, the Sioux and Crow, are not so amenable to an ecological explanation. The Sioux were among the last tribes to enter the High Plains, and although they still had Dakota-type cousin terms, their behavior pattern had changed to equate all cousins with siblings. Eggan (1966:103) suggested that this lack of terminological change was due to the short time the Teton had been on the plains. However, the Cheyenne were a full Plains tribe for an even shorter period, yet developed generational-type cousin terms. The Cheyenne were closely associated with their linguistic relatives the Arapaho, who had entered the Plains considerably earlier, and there was some intermarriage between the two tribes (Eggan 1937:74). It seems likely, therefore, that this difference between the Sioux and the Cheyenne was an important factor in their different rates of terminological change.

For the Crow, continued close contact with the Hidatsa may have played a role in the retention of a Crow-type terminology by the former, in part by helping to maintain the Crow clan system. The Crow acquired a number of societies and ceremonies from the Hidatsa and were otherwise influenced by

Fig. 4. Paul Moss (center), Northern Arapahoe, naming his newborn great-grandson, Raphael. The name he chose is the one his own deceased son held: Hiinooko3onit or Golden Eagle. left to right: Ava Moss Glenmore, mother of the infant; Mylan, Jr., brother; and Mylan Glenmore, Sr., father. At Moss's feet are blankets, towels, socks, and cash, which were common gifts for the name giver. Photograph by Sara Wiles, Ethete, Wyo., 1994.

Hidatsa customs (Lowie 1935:194–206), while after the epidemic of 1837 many Hidatsas joined the River Crow for a time (Bowers 1965:24). However, a closer examination of Crow social structure and kin terminology suggests that other factors were involved as well.

Crow kin terminology exhibits some important differences from that of the Hidatsa (Cottrell 1965). For relatives outside the "core" range of the speaker's own clan and his father's and sons' clans, in his own generation and his parents' and children's generation, all changes constitute a reclassification of relatives by "natural" generation at the expense of the clan-based Crow-type skewing of generation, as Eggan's theory would predict. However, within the core range, the only change in referential usage involves a strengthening of the Crow skewing rule, and vocative uses for males preserve the terminological uniqueness of the clan. This suggests that the Crow clans must have retained an important solidarity function in adapting to the High Plains situation. Cottrell argued that the Crow clan lost its economic corporateness and authority but retained its solidarity significance, coming to resemble the kindred in other High Plains tribes. However, in denying the corporateness of the clan, Cottrell misjudged the nature of Crow residence. Despite Lowie's (1935:57–58) claim that Crow households were "independent," and his denial that members of the same clan camped and hunted together (1935:12), there is evidence, both in Lowie's own work (1912:186) and in D. Collier's (1938–1939), that Crow winter camps were often led by a clan chief and contained many of his clansmen, and that clansmen tended to hunt and camp together when the entire division was united. Collier's data also show that a man's ties to his clan "brothers" were an important determinant of marital residence. The Crow residence pattern was based on common clan membership rather than residence with a particular relative.

In this situation, the Crow-type terminology would have retained a substantial solidarity value, since it classed as "brothers" those men on whose cooperation and aid the speaker most often depended. However, the clan structure would not have been so flexible as the bilateral bands of other High Plains tribes, and Collier noted a shift toward bilateral camps during the period from 1860 to 1885. If this shift had not been cut short by the destruction of the bison and the confinement of the Crow on reservations, the Crow would presumably have eventually acquired a generational-type pattern of cousin terms; both Collier (1938–1939) and Eggan (1966:65) interpreted the reclassification of father's sister's children as siblings as the beginning of such a change.

The kin terminologies of the three Blackfoot tribes and the closely associated Sarcee also constitute a special case, one that illuminates some of the factors at work in High Plains kinship systems in general. This system is complex and unusual; not until Hanks and Hanks's (1945) analysis of North Blackfoot terminology was a clear understanding of this system achieved. Briefly, Blackfoot terminology largely conforms to the generational/bifurcate merging pattern of most other High Plains tribes, but with a pervasive substitution of relative age for generation in terms used for older male relatives and by male speakers for younger relatives, and the presence of some Crow-type features. Men used the 'older brother' and 'younger brother' terms for all other relatives of about the same age, there being no separate 'cousin' term; older men in one's father's family were classed with one's father or grandfather if significantly older than the speaker, while men in one's mother's family were classed with one's brothers except for one's mother's father and mother's father's brother, who were called grandparents. The Blood, Piegan, and Sarcee terminologies seem similar, with some overriding of generation by the 'brother' terms, but are less well documented, so apparent differences may be due only to the absence of detailed data comparable to what is known for the Blackfoot.

A major factor in this emphasis on relative age was the fur trade, called "the mainspring of Blackfoot cultural change" (O. Lewis 1942:61). The trade in bison hides created a highly unequal distribution of wealth, greater individualism, and a massive increase in polygyny (O. Lewis 1942:22–59). It also fueled the age-graded men's societies of the Blackfoot, which intensified and provided an outlet for the status differences resulting from the increased wealth. Age thus became the major determinant of men's activities and associations (Hanks and Hanks 1945:15–16). At the same time, the widespread polygyny and the disparity in age of marriage between brothers and sisters weakened the connection between relative age and generation. As a consequence, because of the overriding importance of male solidarity in High Plains tribes, brother terms were extended to male relatives in other generations whose age was close to the speaker's, while terms for women show much less overriding of generation by relative age.

However, the widespread extension of the brother terms included many relatives whose relationship was inherently unequal, and conflict even between full brothers was not uncommon, despite the norm of cooperation (O. Lewis 1942:55–57; Hanks and Hanks 1945:25–26). In addition, the 'older brother' and 'younger brother' terms themselves carried connotations of hierarchy and inequality. These factors lessened the solidarity value of the brother terms, and one response to this was the widespread use of the 'comrade' term, not only between those in a formal comrade relationship but also between twin brothers, stepbrothers, cousins, men who married sisters, and indeed between any two men of about the same age. In effect, the 'comrade' term became a third 'brother' term, connoting equality rather than inequality and authority; it was the only kin term for someone in the speaker's generation that could be used reciprocally. Hanks and Hanks (1945:15) note that "the only security in a system of rank is in the group of those with identical rank."

In contrast, the Sarcee, less involved in the fur trade and lacking the age-grading of their men's societies, also had a comrade relationship, but lacked a separate kin term for this;

comrades used the 'older brother' term reciprocally, as did adult brothers (Honigmann 1956a). This usage avoided the connotations of authority present in the Blackfoot terms.

Conclusion

It is clear that there was more than one way of adapting to the plains environment; this case supports J.H. Steward's (1955) idea of "multilineal evolution," and the broader evolutionary arguments for the centrality of variation presented by Gould (1989, 1996), rather than a single pattern of development or an environmental determinism. Analysis also suggests that an increased importance of male solidarity was a key part of the adaptation process in all tribes, and it led to some typical features of social organization in most High Plains tribes, even though particular ecological or historical circumstances altered this pattern in some tribes.

The argument presented above for the extension of sibling terms to cousins (and others of about the same age) says nothing about the development or persistence of bifurcate merging terminology for aunts and uncles in virtually all Plains tribes, despite its absence in many tribes to the north, west, and southwest of the Plains. This pattern is not a relic of a prior form of social structure; there is clear comparative evidence that the Plains Cree, Plains Ojibwa, Sarcee, Comanche, and Eastern Shoshone, and possibly the eastern Apachean tribes shifted from a bifurcate collateral to a bifurcate merging pattern in moving onto the Plains. It is also clear that this pattern was not transitional to a generational terminology that eliminated the distinction between cross- and parallel relatives, although such a generational pattern would be consistent with the generational-type cousin terms of most High Plains tribes. Only a few matrilineal or formerly matrilineal tribes (Crow, Pawnee, Wichita) show any evidence of such a shift toward a generational pattern prior to White acculturative influence, and this only for aunts; furthermore, two of these tribes lacked generational-type cousin terms.

No satisfactory explanation has been proposed for the presence of the bifurcate merging pattern in Plains tribes. The shift is not correlated with any systematic changes in marital residence, marriage practices, or kin group structure. Opler (1936:632) and Shimkin (1941:234) attributed the shift in some Apache and Shoshone groups, respectively, to an unspecified "Plains influence." Callender (1962:57), dealing with the emergence of a bifurcate merging pattern in the Central Algonquian tribes, argued that this terminological shift resulted from moving out of a forested environment onto the plains: "Ecological adaptations requiring large-scale cooperation in communal agriculture or the buffalo hunt and taking emphasis from the nuclear family may be involved in an explanation." While the mechanism for this change is unclear, the approach presented here implies that there is no requirement that stable terminological systems exhibit a logical consistency across generations. The assumption of logical consistency has led many students of

Plains terminology to argue, in the face of most of the evidence, that the High Plains tribes were in the process of shifting to a "consistent" generational system in all generations. In contrast, the approach presented here emphasizes that different parts of the terminological system may have been responding to different societal or adaptive needs. The primary cause of the development of a generational-type terminology, for example, was not the loss of social distinctions between cross- and parallel relatives generally, but the specific value of such a terminology in creating solidarity among same-generation relatives, particularly males. The value of bifurcate merging terms may well have been different.

Such an approach may have significance beyond the Plains. There are four predominant patterns of kin terminology in native North America. Of them, only one—that which incorporates Dakota-, Crow-, or Omaha-type cousin terms and bifurcate merging terms for adjacent generations, which is found in much of eastern North America south of the Great Lakes and among the Pueblos and Navajo of the Southwest—is "consistent" in its distinctions across these three generations. The other three patterns—the generational/bifurcate merging pattern of the High Plains; the Dakota/bifurcate collateral pattern of the Eastern Subarctic and some Western Apache, Northern Athapaskan, and Shoshone tribes; and the generational/bifurcate collateral pattern of many Great Basin, Plateau, Western Subarctic, and some Southwest tribes—are all "inconsistent" by traditional theories of kin terminology. An adequate understanding of these patterns requires re-examination of some of the traditional assumptions of kinship theory.

Sun Dance

JoALLYN ARCHAMBAULT

The Sun Dance was a complex, beautiful, and powerful ceremony that during the nineteenth century was the highlight of the annual summer encampments of almost all the Plains buffalo hunters. While it may not have been the most important religious ritual of a particular tribe, it was among the most public and dramatic. It was a communal ceremony that for many tribes required the participation of the entire group, or, in the case of larger groups such as the Teton Sioux, at least as many bands as could camp together. During most of the year bands camped by themselves but during the summer, when the bison gathered in large numbers and other food resources were abundant, tribes converged in large encampments for a festive period of intense social activity. Leaders gathered in council to discuss matters of common interest; religious and men's societies met and held private and public rites; camp discipline was maintained by the men's societies with enlarged responsibilities; friends and kin living apart during most of the year renewed their ties; tribal hunts and war parties were organized; ceremonies, both large and small, private and public, were held; young people courted and marriages were arranged; and gift-giving and trading were everywhere. The Sun Dance was a focus of religious and social activity that confirmed tribal membership and helped to secure a healthy, peaceful, and bountiful future for a tribe and its individual members. Dramatic and lavish, it evoked the values central to a tribe's ethos and gave them full expression for all to see (Wissler 1918; J.R. Walker 1917; Lowie 1915b; Liberty 1980:164–165).

The Sun Dance in the late twentieth century retained its opulent qualities and became the most important public ritual on all the reservations where it survived or was revived. Many tribal members who resided off reservation returned home to attend. The large encampments diminished in size as many families chose to sleep at home and drive in every day, but strict etiquette was maintained in the camp. All who attended must refrain from negative thoughts and deeds, dress in an appropriate manner, and pray for the success of the ceremony. The modern Sun Dance integrated tribal members for a short period regardless of diverse political or sectarian beliefs. All the people acted as one, engaged in the most sacred event of the year, praying for health and well-being for all (A. Fire/Lame Deer and Erdoes 1972:198–213; Amiotte 1987:75–89; Yellowtail as told to Fitzgerald 1991; Fools Crow in Mails 1979:114–138; P.J. Powell 1969, 2:481–855, 1981, 1:247–249; Grobsmith 1981:69–76).

The Name of the Ceremony

The name "Sun Dance" as found in the anthropological and popular literature is a misnomer (Spier 1921:459; Dusenberry 1962:186; Stallcop 1968:149; Liberty 1980:164; R.L. Hall 1997:19–20). There are various native names for this rite, sometimes more than one within the same group: Ute, Shoshone, Plains Cree, and Plains Ojibwa 'thirsting dance' (Spier 1921:464); Sioux (J.R. Walker 1917) and Ponca (G.A. Dorsey 1905) 'sun-gazing dance'; Assiniboine 'lodge-making dance' (Parks and DeMallie 1996); Cheyenne 'new life lodge' (G.A. Dorsey 1905b:57) or 'medicine tepee ceremony' (J.H. Moore 1987:38, both explanations rather than translations); Gros Ventre 'sacrifice lodge' (Kroeber 1908:229) or 'prayer lodge' (Stallcop 1968:149); Arapaho 'sacrifice lodge' or 'offerings lodge' (Kroeber 1902–1907:152); Crow 'miniature lodge' (Lowie 1915b:8) or 'imitation lodge' (Frey 1987:182); Arikara 'house of whistling' (Curtis 1907–1930, 5:150). Among some groups the sun had little or no place in the ceremony (Stallcop 1968:149; M.C. Wilson 1981:355; J.M. Cooper 1957:182; Lowie 1915b:8), and only among the Sioux and Ponca was the sun referenced in the name of the ceremony.

The designation Sun Dance was first used by the fur trader Jean-Baptiste Truteau, in a memoir concerning his experiences on the Upper Missouri River in 1794–1796 (Parks 1993; Perrin du Lac 1805, 1807:75). Truteau wrote that the ceremony was found among the Sioux, Cheyenne, Arapaho, and several neighboring tribes. In 1832 George Catlin witnessed a Sioux Sun Dance ("Sioux Until 1850" fig. 5, this vol.); his painting of a dancer, a part of his Indian Gallery, was the first European depiction of the ceremony (Catlin 1844, 1:232–233). In 1849 Mary Eastman called the Santee version of the ritual a "sun dance," and misinterpreted it to mean that the Sioux worshiped the sun (M. Eastman 1849:xxii). Her book contributed to the popularization of the term Sun Dance, which eventually became the standard English designation for the ceremony, used both by non-Indians and by Indians when speaking in English.

The Identity of the Sun Dance

The diversity of names for the Sun Dance reflected similar diversity in the ceremony. Despite great variation in symbolism and meaning, there were some features of the Sun Dance shared by all the tribes who practiced it. These included the communal nature of the ritual; a tribally specific body of songs, rituals, and sacred knowledge unique to the Sun Dance; a circular, enclosed arbor open to the sky, newly built for the ceremony; the ritual discovery of a tree, treated symbolically as an enemy, that was cut down, carried to the camp, and placed upright at the center of the arbor as the focus for prayer and ceremony; a buffalo skull or hide placed on the center pole or at its base as part of an altar; and a predominance of male singers and dancers, although among some tribes women might participate in both activities.

The ceremony was held annually or less frequently; individuals vowed to sponsor it as the result of a vision or a promise made in a time of personal need; dancers pledged to participate as a result of a vow taken in time of personal need or in search of supernatural power; one or more tepees were pitched adjacent to the dance arbor where private rituals were held; religious bundles associated with the Sun Dance or related rituals were brought out and used by their owners; dancers sought the assistance of experienced ritualists who aided them both before and during the ceremony; spectators tied offerings to the center pole and sought healing and supernatural assistance through prayer; the ceremony was associated with tribal buffalo hunts; and military symbolism was expressed at specific times during the ceremony.

In the Sun Dance as performed by tribes such as the Sioux, Cheyenne, Arapaho, and Blackfoot (fig. 1), dancers and even some spectators made flesh sacrifices by cutting tiny pieces from the arms. Dancers might also pierce the flesh with small pegs that were attached to buffalo skulls or to the center pole by tethers; pulling against the anchor eventually pulled the peg from the flesh. Sometimes dancers' bodies were painted during the ritual; tribes such as the Arapaho and Cheyenne had elaborate body paints worn at various stages of the ceremony (fig. 2). Male dancers wore a wraparound kilt, a sage wreath around the head, and one or more eagle feathers and sage sprigs. They danced in a line, keeping time to the music with a wingbone whistle and bobbing up and down in place. The ritual started at first light of day. All dancers went through a purifying sweatlodge beforehand and fasted until the end of the ceremony, which was generally three to four days.

The Sun Dance was held around midsummer at the height of the growing season. A knowledgeable religious leader directed the ceremony, usually with a number of assistants. Experienced singers chanted the appropriate songs at each stage of the ritual. The arbor was surrounded by a camp of tribal members who participated as spectators, singers, dancers, or assistants. Ideally the entire tribal community participated in some way, as the prayers of everyone were needed for the success of the ceremony. Other than those core elements there was a wide range of ritual elements and rationale for the ceremony.

Among most tribes, the Sun Dance was a celebration of fertility, a prayer for increase of both the people and the buffalo. The welfare of the entire tribe was the explicit motivation for the ceremony. The Sioux Sun Dance, for example, was initiated by one or more men who vowed to sponsor it, usually as a prayer for personal success in war, for curing illness, or for gaining spiritual power, but it was carried out "for the benefit of both the dancer and the people" (J.R. Walker 1917:58). It has been characterized as "the great corporate prayer" (E.C. Deloria 1944:55). Similarly, the Blackfoot Sun Dance was characterized as a "true tribal festival," but in this case the ceremony was held in response to a vow made by a woman, often as a prayer for health. She herself did not dance but fasted and was involved in other ritual activities throughout the duration of the Sun Dance (Wissler 1918:229, 232). Both the Cheyenne and Arapaho ceremonies were pledged by a man; if a woman vowed to sponsor the ceremony the vow was carried out by her husband or brother (G.A. Dorsey 1903:5–9, 1905b:57–58). Again, the vow was a prayer for health or spiritual aid. The Cheyenne ceremony was a drama of rebirth: in the words of a Cheyenne religious leader, "the object of the ceremony is to make the whole world over again" (G.A. Dorsey 1905b:186).

For some tribes, the Sun Dance was a more focused ritual in which the outward forms and self-sacrifice of the dancers were comparable to those tribes whose ceremonies were held as tribal festivals of fertility and renewal, but that had a more restricted purpose. The Crow and Kiowa ceremonies, for example, were pledged by a man seeking revenge for the death of a relative killed by enemies. Central to the ceremony was a small sacred effigy or doll (fig. 3) that was the medium through which a vision of a vanquished enemy would appear, ending the ceremony. Thus the Crow and Kiowa Sun Dances were intimately connected to patterns of

top right, after Etnografiska Museet, Stockholm, Sweden: 1854.2.27; Glenbow-Alberta Inst., Calgary: top left, NA-668-22; center left, NB-3-6; center right, NA-667-1039; bottom left, McGill U., McCord Mus., Montreal: MP 1358(7).

Fig. 1. Blackfoot Sun Dance. top left: Members of the Blood *máóto?kiiksi* 'buffalo women's society' (Frantz and Russell 1989:141), erecting the framework for the annual lodge, made from travois poles, in the center of the Sun Dance camp. Photograph by Robert Nathaniel Wilson, Blood Res., Alta., 1891–1893. top right, Elkskin robe worn by the Holy Woman in the Sun Dance. The maltese crosses painted in red represent the Morning Star and similar figures in green represent butterflies, both spiritual intermediaries. Robe collected by Armand Fouche d'Otrante at Ft. McKenzie, 1843–1844, in present-day Mont. Length 196 cm. Drawn by Roger Thor Roop. center left, Pipe Woman, wife of Bull Shield, and Always Calling, wife of Weasel Fat, wearing the buffalo bull headdress of the *máóto?kiiksi* society (J.C. Stewart 1989:126). Photograph possibly by John F. Atterton, Blood Res., Alta., about 1916. center right, Blood Indians putting prayer cloths onto the center pole. Photograph by Arnold Lupson, about 1940. bottom left, Ritual preparations before the self-sacrifice, including smoking, prayers, and painting the participants (Scherer 1999). Photograph by William Hanson Boorne, Blood Indian Res., Alta., 1887. bottom right, Charlie Iron Breast (center standing wearing beaded buckskin vest and tie) at a Sun Dance food giveaway. Photograph by Susan Dietrich, Blackfoot Indian Res., Mont., 1939.

ARCHAMBAULT

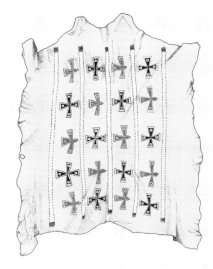

THE SUN DANCE

Field Mus., Chicago: top left, 1432; top right, 10084; center right, 1528.

Fig. 2. Arapaho and Cheyenne Sun Dances. After attending the 1901 Arapaho ceremony, G.A. Dorsey (1903) studied the ceremony with Háwkan (Crazy), a priest and director of the Sun Dance, and his interpreter Cleaver Warden. top left, Building the altar, 1902. Wátānāh (Black Horse), a ceremonial grandfather, and his assistant Nakaásh (Sage), insert rabbit bushes into the sods of the Sun Dance altar (G.A. Dorsey 1903:110, pl. 53). The buffalo skull is in the background, just behind the sod excavation. top right, Dancer being painted by a grandfather, 1901 (G.A. Dorsey 1903:131, pl. 66). center left, S. Cheyenne bison skull. The skull is painted red to symbolize the earth; black and white lines represent night and day; the circle represents the sun and the crescent the moon. The swamp grass in the nasal cavity and eyes stands for the earth's vegetation (G.A. Dorsey 1905b:96–97). Skull collected by James Mooney, near Dillon, Okla. Terr., 1903. Drawn by Roger Thor Roop. center right, Arapaho dancers Tepeish (Cut Hair) and Hiséhaseh (Sun Ray or George Hócheni), 1902. They wear varieties of the Yellow Earth paint with sage inserted under their waistbands (G.A. Dorsey 1903:164, 167, pl. 118). top and center right, Photographs by George Dorsey, Darlington, Okla., 1901–1902. bottom, N. Cheyenne Sun Dance. bottom left, Sponsor carrying dry buffalo hide used as a drum. bottom center, Dancers getting coals for their grandfathers. bottom right, Last offering of food. The sponsor, Abraham Spotted Elk (not shown), is delivering a speech and prayer. bottom, Photographs by Margot Liberty, Cheyenne Res., Mont., 1959.

ARCHAMBAULT

left, Smithsonian, NAA: 92-11368; right, after Amer. Mus. of Nat. Hist., New York: 50.1/4011a.

Fig. 3. Sun Dance effigies, an essential part of the Crow and Kiowa Sun Dance rituals. Among the Crow only the owner of a doll could sponsor the ceremony. The Kiowa effigy, known as Taime, was kept by a priest for the benefit of the entire tribe. left, Drawing by Silverhorn of a ritual participant with the Taime supported on a post behind him, about 1892. Collected on the Kiowa Res., 1897 (cropped). right, Crow doll purchased by Robert Lowie on the Crow Res., 1910. Drawing by Roger Thor Roop.

warfare (Lowie 1915b:7; Spier 1921a:437). Similarly, among the Arikara, the Sun Dance was a minor ceremony, also symbolically associated with war (Curtis 1907–1930, 5:76–80). For the Hidatsa, pledging a Sun Dance was an inherited right, during which the pledger's father transferred to him the powers of the sacred bundle associated with the ceremony. The ceremony was a ritual enactment of the myth of the Twin Boys; the young men who participated sought success in war as well as general well-being for the people (Lowie 1919:415–431).

A number of major ceremonies among other tribes shared characteristics of the Sun Dance. For example, the Omaha Hédewachi, held in midsummer, celebrated abundance and involved a sacred pole ritually treated as a symbolic enemy, erected in the center of the tribal camp circle (Dorsey 1894:391). The dance around the pole was a ceremony of thanksgiving for victories in war, a celebration of tribal unity, and "a festival of joy" (Fletcher and La Flesche 1911:260). The Skiri Pawnee Four Pole Ceremony, which enacted the founding myth of the Skiri as a political confederacy, was held before the autumn buffalo hunts and invoked success in war and hunting. The central act was the ritual scouting of four trees of different types, each treated as an enemy and brought back to camp to be raised in a ceremonial circular enclosure (Murie 1981, 1:107–111). The Okipa ceremony of the Mandan, pledged by a man who dreamed four times that he should sponsor the ceremony, also enacted a tribal origin myth, invoked tribal unity and fertility of both buffalo and the people, and involved suffering and the offering of flesh by young male participants (Curtis 1907–1930, 5:25–37). Despite the similarities of such ceremonies to the central themes and ritual actions of the Sun Dance, none of them has ever been considered as such.

In short, a number of ritual elements involving tribal unity, midsummer celebration, fertility, warfare, and individuals' suffering and sacrifices of their bodies coalesced in various patterns among the Plains tribes. Some anthropologists argue that the name Sun Dance "is a convenience that historians, travelers, and ethnologists have fallen back upon to refer to a range of midsummer tribal ceremonies" (R.L. Hall 1997:20); some have dismissed it as "an anthropological invention" (Schlesier 1990:13), pointing out the wide variation among tribes in the purpose, motivation, and ritual details of the ceremony (Liberty 1980:164; R.L. Hall 1997:20–21). Schlesier (1990) makes distinctions among tribal Sun Dances and relates them to other ceremonial complexes as well as suggesting historical sequences for the adoption of different ceremonies, all of which came to be called Sun Dances. R.L. Hall (1997) builds a series of cultural relationships between the Cheyenne and Arapaho Sun Dances and older Woodland and Hopewell cultural features from the East. Despite anthropologists' arguments concerning the origins of the ceremony and its relationships to ancient ceremonial complexes, twentieth-century American Indians considered all rituals called Sun Dances in English to belong to a single category. The assumption of common identity facilitated intertribal participation by dancers and religious specialists.

Suppression

The Sun Dance was performed continuously on the Plains throughout the nineteenth and twentieth centuries despite predictions of its demise (Lowie 1935:297; Dorsey 1894:461; G.A. Dorsey 1910:649–652) and official attempts to stop it. Once tribes were interned on reservations the federal government began systematic efforts to civilize its charges, which included eradication of Indian cultural practices, especially religious customs that were considered detrimental and offensive. In 1883 Secretary of the Interior H.M. Teller wrote Commissioner of Indian Affairs Hiram Price, condemning the Sun Dance, medicine men, and the traditionalists who supported them. He was concerned that the ritual would inflame the warlike passions of young men, possibly leading to the renewal of hostilities between Indians and Whites. Price assured Teller that Sun Dance rituals would be declared Indian offenses and a Court of Indian Offenses would be established to hear cases and decide on penalties for those found guilty (Commissioner of Indian Affairs 1883; ARCIA 1883:xiv–xv, 1892:28–31). These courts, located on reservations, were intended to assist in the elimination of such practices under the guidance of the Indian agent (Prucha 1984, 2:646–648, 953–954).

The Sun Dance, particularly when piercing and flesh offerings were part of the ritual, was a favorite target for suppression. These efforts continued through the remainder of the nineteenth century and into the twentieth. Commissioner of Indian Affairs Charles Burke in April 1921 called for the abolition of "the sundance and all other similar dances and so-called religious ceremonies" (Burke 1921).

Enforcement of the directives to suppress the Sun Dance was left to the discretion of agency superintendents, some of whom were more energetic than others. One of the reasons for the survival of the ceremony may have been the pattern of erratic suppression by the local agent, who either ignored or neglected to report to Washington the continuation of Indian religious ceremonies. In central and western Oklahoma, Indian religious dances, after a short cessation, "went underground and reemerged when excitement had died down" (Rachlin [1965:93] in Kracht 1994:327).

At times repression of the Sun Dance was harsh. Some agency superintendents used the U.S. Army or the threat of it. In 1890 the Kiowa Sun Dance was disrupted by the rumor of army patrols and the dance was abandoned, never to be observed again (Kracht 1994:327). Other agency superintendents stopped the dance in person with the assistance of Indian policemen, as did James McLaughlin about 1880–1881 on Devils Lake Reservation in North Dakota. By his own account "in the midst of this barbarous ceremony we broke through their ring and stopped the affair" (J. McLaughlin 1926:32). In 1914 even a planned reenactment was not allowed on the Crow Reservation (Hoxie 1995:209).

Similar policies were enforced in Canada. In 1922 an Indian agent caused a Royal Canadian Mounted Police constable to stop a Sun Dance at the Red Pheasant Reserve, Saskatchewan, where he cut down the center pole in a camp of 500 people (Hasse 1969).

The effect of this repression was the disappearance of the Sun Dance in some tribes—Kiowa (Spier 1921a), Ponca (G.A. Dorsey 1905), Crow (Lowie 1915b), and Montana Blackfeet (Wissler 1918)—and resistance in other tribes that took the form of subterfuge, holding Sun Dances in secret.

The policy of suppressing native rituals remained in effect until Commissioner John Collier, during the Franklin Roosevelt administration, issued a circular called "Indian Religious Freedom and Indian Culture" in 1934, which guaranteed Indians the right to practice their religions and observe their cultural traditions (Prucha 1984, 2:951–952). However, many federal employees and Christian missionaries on reservations resisted the policy and discouraged sweatbaths, the Sun Dance, and other religious practices (Roubideaux in Cash and Hoover 1971:165–166). In the 1970s missionaries on the Rosebud Reservation made lists of families they observed attending sweatbaths and other ceremonies and refused them admission to church services and social assistance until they recanted (Archambault 1975).

Twentieth Century

By 1900 there were 19 groups that were still practicing the Sun Dance, or had until recently: Blackfoot, Northern and Southern Cheyenne, Northern Arapahoe, Gros Ventre, Plains Cree ("Plains Cree," fig. 7, this vol.), Plains Ojibwa, Arikara, Sarcee, Kiowa, Hidatsa, Crow, Ponca ("Ponca," fig. 5, this vol.), Assiniboine, Santee (Sisseton and Canadian Sioux), and Teton in the Plains; and Eastern Shoshone and Ute in the Great Basin. Sun Dances among 12 of these groups were reported to be extinct in 1965 (Liberty 1965:135). However, by the end of the twentieth century all but two performed their traditional ritual or had adopted a modified form from another tribe in those cases where the original ceremony was lost. The two exceptions were the Ponca, who last held a Sun Dance about 1908 (Anonymous 1908), and the Sarcee, whose last dance was about 1890 (Jenness 1938).

There were two pulses of Sun Dance revitalization, one around 1900 and the second beginning about 1960 and building momentum throughout the rest of the twentieth century. The survival and renewal of the Sun Dance sprang from a tradition of intertribal religious movements on the Plains and can be discussed with some precision in the nineteenth century and earlier ("Intertribal Religious Movements," this vol.). In all cases the contemporary Sun Dance was a potent signal of renewed Indian identity and cultural nationalism that attracted scores of Indians and non-Indians to its celebration.

The Arapahoe and Cheyenne Sun Dances were held with some regularity throughout the twentieth century. The Arapahoe Sun Dance was held only on the Wind River Reservation, Wyoming, although Southern Arapahos participated in large numbers, as did Sioux from North and South Dakota. The communal aspect of the Sun Dance was evident from the large encampment, participation by all generations, and the fact that the tribe held only one Sun Dance each summer (Starkloff 1974). Some Sioux from Pine Ridge Reservation attended and danced at the Arapahoe Sun Dance since at least 1946 because they considered it a more rigorous ceremony than their own (Feraca 1998:11; Archambault 1972).

The Cheyenne held Sun Dances in both Oklahoma and Montana (Liberty 1965:128–129; Stands In Timber and Liberty 1967:94–95; P.J. Powell 1969, 2:338–355). The encampments of both Northern and Southern Cheyenne were large, and participation was drawn from both divisions as well as visitors from other tribes: Arapahoes and Sioux in the north, and Kiowas in the south.

The Crow stopped holding their Sun Dance about 1875 (Lowie 1915b:5). In 1941 John Truhujo, an Eastern Shoshone religious leader, was invited by the Crow to perform a Sun Dance on the Crow Reservation. That summer the revived Sun Dance was performed in two communities under two different sponsors, and multiple dances have been performed nearly every summer since (Voget 1984). The twentieth-century Crow Sun Dance (fig. 4) was never a single, tribal ritual although it was held with more regularity than was the nineteenth-century ceremony. The contemporary Sun Dance was organized on a district level, and its communal aspects were based more on kin and friendships than on tribal-wide membership (Jorgensen 1972: 282–285). It attracted some non-Crow participants, particularly Eastern Shoshones and Kiowas. Some Crow ritualists assisted at other Sun Dances held away from the reservation, although only one person held a Sun Dance in the Crow manner off the reservation. In 1997 an attempt by a Kiowa woman to sponsor a Crow Sun Dance on private land near Anadarko, Oklahoma, was stopped by some Kiowa tribal members who opposed any reintroduction of the Sun Dance there (Jones 1997; Brinkman 1997). The next year, a young Kiowa man put on his own Sun Dance, which he established as an annual tribal event.

The Sun Dance continued throughout the twentieth century on the Northern Plains among the Blackfoot tribes, the Plains Cree, and the Plains Ojibwa (fig. 5). Beginning in the 1980s Sun Dances were revived among the Assiniboine at Fort Peck and Fort Belknap reservations, combining local traditions with the assistance of Canadian Assiniboine and Stoney Sun Dance leaders, and an Assiniboine Sun Dance was transferred to the Blackfeet at Browning, Montana.

The Sioux

In the late nineteenth century the Sioux Sun Dance ceased among the Santee, Yankton, and most of the Teton and was assumed to have become extinct (J.R. Walker 1917; Liberty 1980). However, on the Pine Ridge and Rosebud reservations private, semipublic, and public Sun Dances were held regularly throughout the twentieth century (Feraca 1998:11; Paige 1970:102; Mails 1978:197, 1979:31, 118–119; Steinmetz 1990:28; Archambault 1972–1990; A. Fire/Lame Deer and Erdoes 1992:230–231; L. Crow Dog and Erdoes 1995:241). At Pine Ridge, Fools Crow claimed to have led public Sun Dances, without piercing, since 1929 (Mails 1979:117–120), and a public Sun Dance at Rosebud without piercing was held in 1928 (Mails 1979:118; Feraca 1998:11). By the 1960s a public Sun Dance was held annually in late July on the tribal fairgrounds east of Pine Ridge Village. This Sun Dance was held in a carnival atmosphere with the ritual in the morning and a powwow and carnival in the afternoon and evening. The tribal council promoted it as part of an effort to bring in tourist dollars. There was substantial criticism by some tribal members about the laxness with which the celebrants performed the ritual; they compared it unfavorably to the Arapahoe Sun Dance (Feraca 1963:12, 18; T.H. Lewis 1990:52–70; Mails 1978:223–225, 228, 232; W.K. Powers 1975:139–142; Zimmerly 1969:62–63).

Piercing, an essential part of the Sioux ritual, was part of the hidden Sun Dances on Pine Ridge Reservation until sometime between 1952 and 1960 (Mails 1979:119, 1978:46; W.K. Powers 1970:287, 1977:141), when it was performed in the public Sun Dances led by Fools Crow (Steinmetz 1990:29). Piercing became a part of all subsequent public and private Sun Dances.

The revitalization of the Pine Ridge ritual continued through the 1960s (Nurge 1966; R. Lessard 1970; T.H. Lewis 1972; J.A. Hanson 1965; Zimmerly 1968; Zelitch 1970), and by 1970 substantial numbers of urban Indians began to attend and participate, many of whom were associated with the American Indian Movement (AIM), a political movement that sought to redress the wrongs done to Indian people by American colonization and by racism and poverty. In 1970 an Oglala Vietnam veteran, speaking for some younger Sioux and AIM participants, convinced Frank Fools Crow to stop the practice of Jesuit priests saying Mass in the dance arbor, which had begun in 1965 at the request of tribal elder Jake Herman, and with the participation of other older Oglala ritualists. In 1972 increased AIM participation and political chaos on the reservation led tribal chairman Richard Wilson to prohibit the Sun Dance for two years, after which it was held in Porcupine, a conservative community on Pine Ridge Reservation, South Dakota, that had become an AIM enclave (Steinmetz 1990:31–32). The Porcupine Sun Dance came to be known as an AIM dance, and some older Sioux refused to go in disapproval of what they thought was the politicization of the ritual; its urban, intertribal nature; and the ignorance of many of the dancers and participants that might bring misfortune on anyone present.

Private Sun Dances began to appear again after a period of attrition as some Sioux, disapproving of the large, public dances sponsored either by the tribal council or AIM and yet desirous of praying in the traditional way, began to sponsor rituals that were open only to family and guests

bottom left, Dennis Sanders, Hardin Photo Service, Hardin, Mont.; bottom right, after Voget 1984:opp. p. 237.

Fig. 4. Crow Sun Dance, Crow Agency, Mont. In 1941 the Eastern Shoshone Sun Dance was transferred to the Crow, who had given up their own Sun Dance in the early reservation period. William Big Day, Crow, pledged to sacrifice himself in the Sun Dance so that his brother's infant, Raymond Big Day, would recover from illness (Voget 1984:195). top left, Raising the center pole using interlocking rafter poles; willow bundle and a buffalo head are attached to the center pole. top right, Encampment, with Peter Chivers Left Hand, Voget's interpreter. Photographs by Fred Voget, Pryor, Mont., 1941. bottom left, Dancers with eagle-bone whistles around the center pole. Photograph by Lyle Tintinger, 1954. bottom right, Plan of the Shoshone-Crow Sun Dance Lodge of 1946; a, women's chorus; b, drum chief; c, drummer-singers; d, renowned old men; e, fasters; f, dancers; g, medicine man; h, sponsor; i, assistant to sponsor. Drawn by Roger Thor Roop.

(W.K. Powers 1987:172; Testerman 1998; Lurie 1998). Similar developments occurred on the Rosebud Reservation where Henry and Leonard Crow Dog, father and son, aligned themselves with AIM and began hosting Sun Dances on their own land in 1971 (L. Crow Dog and Erdoes 1995:241). These large, well-advertised events drew participants from all over the country and even internationally. At

times there were over 200 dancers, male and female, and over 1,000 onlookers. In contrast, other Rosebud Sun Dances were, by design, much smaller and served the local population (Grobsmith 1981:74–76).

The number of Sun Dances held on the Pine Ridge and Rosebud reservations increased dramatically, and the ritual become more of a family than a tribal event (Young Bear and

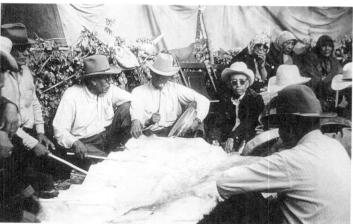

top left, Glenbow-Alberta Inst., Calgary: NA 667-950; top right, Mont. State U., Mus. of the Rockies, Bozeman; center left and right, Smithsonian, Handbook of North Amer. Indians Photo. Coll.; bottom left, Natl. Arch. of Canada, Ottawa: PA 28834.

Fig. 5. Northern Plains Sun Dances. top left, Prayers before cutting the center pole for the Stoney lodge. left to right (left of the tree): Hansen Bearspaw; Joe Kootenay, Sr., leading the prayer; John Peacemaker; Paul Francis; David Simeon, holding the eagle feather fan to bless the tree; and Jonas Rider. Photograph by Arnold Lupson, Morley, Alta., about 1937. top right, *Medicine Lodge of the Assiniboines*. Dancers are behind a brush partition, singers are on the right, and man at the center pole is dragging buffalo skulls. Painting by Assiniboine William Standing (Fire Bear), 1929. center left, Assiniboine singers seated around a rawhide used as a drum. The men sang for 2- or 3-hour shifts and the women, in the background, added their voices when appropriate. Photograph by J.W. Wellington, Ft. Belknap Res., Mont., 1952. center right, Plains Ojibwa singers around a bass drum. The dancers, Mr. and Mrs. Howard Kinawa, holding cloth banners as offerings, are behind the brush barrier at the rear of the lodge. Photograph by James Howard, Turtle Mountain Res., N. Dak., 1952. bottom left, Plains Cree drummers using rawhide and hand drums at the Sun Dance near Battleford, Sask. Chief Thunderchild is standing wearing a medal. Photograph by Geraldine Moodie, 1895 (cropped). bottom right, Plains Cree center pole and lodges amid tall grass. Photograph by Michael Crummett, Rocky Boy's Res., Mont., 1994.

Theisz 1994:xxiii; A. Fire/Lame Deer and Erdoes 1992:240; Steinmetz 1990:32–33; Hamilton 1995; W.K. Powers 1987). Its ability to strengthen solidarity among all assembled remained intact, but the participants were fewer in number. Some were sponsored by a medicine man who was also the intercessor (organizer), others by an individual and his extended family who asked a holy man (*wičháša wakhą́*) to serve as the intercessor. All of them shared the basic ritual with some individual variation (Feraca 1963:14; W.K. Powers 1975:139; Nurge 1962:113), but there were major differences in their principal constituency, that is, dancers and supporters. Before 1970 all Sun Dances were meant to sustain the well-being of all the Sioux and the natural world, but they were intended primarily for a Sioux audience. Beginning in 1970 some Sun Dances and the men who sponsored them developed particular constituencies, and some of them were not Sioux and not even Indian. While not entirely new, there was increasing emphasis placed on the universality of the ritual, extending to all of humankind (DeMallie 1984:89–90, 93) and open to all people with good intentions.

The renewed Teton ritual was different in some ways from that of the nineteenth century ("Sioux, 1930–2000," this vol.), but the core of the Sun Dance remained intact (T.H. Lewis 1972). The length of the entire ceremony was shorter, generally scheduled around a weekend, making it easier for participants to attend (Holler 1995:194–203). There were far more dancers at some of the large, public ones than was considered common in the past (E.C. Deloria 1929; Mails 1978:228; Rice 1989:59). Certainly the dancers were younger on average than was common before 1960 (J.E. Brown 1984:31; Feraca 1963:15), and there were many more women and children dancing. Women began to be pierced at the collarbone in the AIM dances in the late 1970s (A. Fire/Lame Deer and Erdoes 1992:246), and the piercing for men appeared more severe than was common in the past, with some piercing multiple times at several dances in one summer (Mails 1978:223, 228; Holler 1995:198; Thunder 1995).

All the intercessors of these ceremonies were Sioux men who obtained their ritual expertise by participating in Sun Dances and sometimes by a period of instruction by older, skilled ritual specialists. It is difficult to judge the amount of formal training. Fools Crow was reported to have been teaching only six men to undertake some of the responsibilities necessary during a dance (Mails 1979:137–138), yet after his death far more men claimed to have received their authority to run a Sun Dance from him. The demand for intercessors encouraged men with little or no formal training to offer themselves as ritual leaders. Many of these men obtained students of their own by running dances on and off Sioux reservations.

Participation of non-Indians, particularly Whites, as dancers was widely debated. The AIM Sun Dances and some intercessors restricted Whites to supporting roles, except in rare cases (A. Fire/Lame Deer and Erdoes

1992:238–240). Other intercessors allowed Whites to dance so long as they displayed humility and good intentions, a strategy in keeping with the nonracist attitudes held generally by earlier generations (J.R. Walker 1980:181; Mails 1979:45, 51; Zimmerly 1969:63; Steinmetz 1990:34–35). Participants in these dances sometimes objected, particularly when Whites were allowed to dance or occupy important ritual positions (B. Lincoln 1994).

During the 1980s the Sun Dance was reestablished on most Sioux reservations, including Sioux Valley Reserve, Manitoba. Sun Dance intercessors from Pine Ridge and Rosebud established Sun Dances at the request of reservation residents and taught them how to conduct the ritual. Generally there were two or more Sun Dances on each Sioux reservation, each ceremony supported by a different community or set of families. Except for those held at Green Grass on Cheyenne River Reservation, South Dakota, the home of the sacred Calf Pipe, none of them attracted large numbers of intertribal or international visitors. Their constituency was the local Sioux (Amiotte 1987; Först 1994; Medicine 1981:281). Some tribes whose own Sun Dance was moribund adopted a Sioux-style Sun Dance and modified it with their own traditions. For example, for a time the Three Affiliated Tribes of Fort Berthold held two Sun Dances, both of which were Sioux in origin.

Popularizing the Sun Dance

Of all the twentieth-century tribal Sun Dances that either survived or were renewed, the Sioux traditions, particularly those originating on the Pine Ridge and Rosebud reservations, played the most significant role in the diffusion of an intertribal, interracial Sun Dance that became international in scope. Popularization of the Sun Dance in the late twentieth century was linked to the development of AIM. Seeking a religious base early in its history, AIM leaders, many of whom were Sioux, focused on the religious leaders and traditions of Pine Ridge and Rosebud. Fools Crow and Leonard Crow Dog became the spiritual guides for the organization (L. Crow Dog and Erdoes 1995:159–176). Many disaffected young Indians, largely ignorant of their tribal traditions, had their first taste of Indian religion on Sioux reservations in the sweatlodge and Sun Dance arbor. Leonard Crow Dog and some associated with him disseminated the Sun Dance to tribes and communities outside the Plains as part of an intertribal political movement. Many individuals who participated in Crow Dog's dance as helper, singer, or dancer went on to teach others.

About 1982 a Pine Ridge Sioux started a Sun Dance on the campus of D-Q University, an alternative college near Davis, California, dedicated to enhancing educational opportunities for Indians and Hispanics who identified with their Indian ancestry. In 1988 Crow Dog initiated a Sun Dance on the Tohono O'odham (Papago) reservation and scheduled it for April instead of the typical summer season (Swa Sa:ak 1989). Both dances were tied to larger political struggles within these groups at the time. By 1982 a Sun Dance in Mexico was led by a man who had participated in AIM dances (Thunder 1995:154–158). In 1985 Fools Crow established a Sun Dance for the Piscataway of Port Tobacco, Maryland (*Piscataway News* 1989; Oppenheim 1989). In 1988 a Sun Dance held in Micmac territory on Cape Breton Island, Canada, after some young Micmacs had attended Sun Dances on the Rosebud Reservation, elicited opposition from Micmac cultural leaders.

In 1990 AIM established a Gathering of the Sacred Pipes Sun Dance at the pipestone quarry in Minnesota; in 1998 it was described as an international youth and elder spiritual gathering and purification. The pipestone quarries were the subject of controversy since Arvol Looking Horse, Keeper of the Calf Pipe, declared his opposition to the continued sale of pipestone objects, even by Sioux carvers (Little Eagle 1993). In 1994 and 1995 Sun Dances were held at Gustafsen Lake, British Columbia, by participants in a land dispute with the Canadian government (Switlo 1997).

There was another type of Sioux Sun Dance that evoked an interracial sentiment of reconciliation. The intercessors for these dances received spiritual directions in a vision quest or other religious experience to help all people, no matter their race. In 1982 Fools Crow authorized Devere Eastman of Rosebud to initiate a Sun Dance on Mount Hood, Oregon, with the approval of elders from the Siletz and Warm Springs reservations. Martin High Bear was the intercessor until 1989, when he established the Four Nations Sun Dance outside Medford, Oregon. High Bear believed that all races must learn to accept and forgive one another, an ethic that was prominent in all the Sun Dances that he led, for example, at the Alkali Lake Shuswap Reserve in British Columbia (Blue Mountain's Sun Dance Society 1999). He did not encourage Whites to dance but they were welcome to participate as helpers, workers, and as general supporters.

There were Sun Dances led by Sioux intercessors off reservations in which most or all of the participants were non-Indian. These garnered the most criticism from the Sioux, who perceived this as an unwelcome intrusion and appropriation of traditional religion in which self-interested tribal members were said to "sell" the religion. The Sioux attempted to stem this behavior by organizing a medicine men's society on the Rosebud Reservation in the 1970s, releasing a list of Sioux men and women engaged in this illicit selling in the 1980s, and picketing an all-White Sun Dance in Ohio in 1993 (Little Eagle 1993; Sangiacomo 1993; Giago 1994). None of these strategies was effective, and New Age Sun Dances continued in the United States and in Europe. There were Sun Dances in England (Ziegler 1998), Germany, and France (A. Fire/Lame Deer and Erdoes 1992:240–241; Pazola 1994:21–22). The ecumenicism of some Sioux religious leaders was easily taken advantage of by others, and some intercessors were seduced by the fawning attention they received from non-Indian spiritual seekers (W.K. Powers 1987:153–161). For the most part the Sun Dances of tribes other than the Sioux have escaped the attentions of New Agers seeking Indian spirituality and writing about their experiences.

Native Accounts

It was not until the twentieth century that a substantial body of Sun Dance accounts by Natives began to be published. Most of them relate to the Sioux. It was George Bushotter, a Teton, who first wrote an account of the Sun Dance in his native language, which was published in translation (Dorsey 1894:450). George Sword, an Oglala, provided native language texts on the Sun Dance to Walker (J.R. 1917, 1980), but they were not available in Lakota until Ella C. Deloria (1929), herself a Yankton Sioux, presented a translation in an article that is the first scholarly account of the Sun Dance published by a native person. J.R. Walker's (1980:176–191, 1982:96–99) studies at Pine Ridge Reservation from 1896 to 1914 preserved other native accounts of the Sun Dance.

Densmore (1918:87–151) recorded detailed descriptions and songs of the Sun Dance and collected drawings from a group of Teton and Yanktonai men on Standing Rock Reservation, all of whom had participated in the ceremony. An account by Charles A. Eastman (1911:55–63), a Santee, is unique in presenting the ceremony as having degenerated from a genuine religious expression to mere display of physical endurance. A more compassionate description of the Yankton Sun Dance was narrated by Philip Deloria (Olden 1918:146–152; V. Deloria 1999:195–200); his daughter, Ella C. Deloria (1944:55–58) wrote an evocative account based on her work with Sword's text. She also published a brief account of the Santee Sun Dance from material she recorded in the 1930s (E.C. Deloria 1967).

The best-known of all of the native descriptions is that by the Oglala religious leader Nicholas Black Elk (J.E. Brown 1953). Other Oglala accounts include those of Luther Standing Bear (1928:113–122, 1933:222–225) and Jake Herman (1963).

Reflecting the tremendous religious revitalization among the Sioux from the 1960s on, much of which was expressed in large public Sun Dances, several religious leaders dictated accounts of their experiences for publication. Of these leaders, by far the best known and most widely accepted by reservation people was Frank Fools Crow, from Pine Ridge (Mails 1979). Pete Catches, also a respected Oglala Sun Dance leader, gave interviews on the significance of the Sun Dance (Zimmerly 1969; Rice 1989). John Fire (Lame Deer), a controversial ritualist from the Rosebud Reservation, narrated a colorful story of his life and religious philosophy that is often at variance with the accepted norms of other Sioux people (J. Fire/Lame Deer and Erdoes 1972). Bill Schweigman (Eagle Feather), who returned to Rosebud after living in California, embarked on a career as a ritualist (Mails 1978).

Together these books provide an elaborate multidimensional account of the rapidly evolving Sun Dance movement   993 that characterized the 1970s and 1980s. While their publication gained these ritual leaders recognition among non-Indians and some off-reservation Indians, it compromised their standing in their own communities given the general disapproval by traditionally oriented Sioux of behavior perceived by others as self-aggrandizement and publicity seeking. The publication of these books and the effect of media celebrity obscured the presence of many other Sioux ritualists who served their communities in quiet dedication and eschewed the rewards that accompany fame in the non-Indian world. In addition, Sioux religion was represented in print from the perspectives of a small number of ritualists who were not necessarily representative of all religious practitioners.

Other Sioux also published about the Sun Dance. A participant in a 1972 Rosebud Sun Dance elucidates the individual experience of one who is not a ritual leader (Millard 1973). Two other books that discuss the Sun Dance, particularly in relation to AIM, were coauthored by Mary Crow Dog, wife of Leonard Crow Dog, a ritual leader from Rosebud (Brave Bird and Erdoes 1993; M. Crow Dog and Erdoes 1995). John Around Him and Albert White Hat, from Rosebud, transcribed a few of the numerous Sun Dance songs in a booklet intended to assist younger Sioux, many of whom do not speak the language, to learn and understand them (Around Him 1980). Arthur Amiotte, from Pine Ridge, provided an excellent description of the modern Sun Dance along with a discussion of some basic concepts central to Sioux belief and practice gained from his own career as a ritualist (DeMallie and Parks 1987:75–89).

Controversy swirled around some Sun Dances and it was one such event that prompted Sam DeCory (1989), from Pine Ridge, to publish an article discussing his version of the events that prompted the public debate. Beatrice Medicine (1981, 1987), from Standing Rock, published two articles that are the first analytical studies published by a native on the subject of the Sun Dance. In both, Medicine argued persuasively that the Sioux Sun Dance had become a ritual of religious revitalization, initially for the Sioux and eventually for AIM and far-flung non-Sioux communities, both reservation and urban.

Ed McGaa (1990), from Pine Ridge, wrote an account of the Sun Dance as part of his personal endeavor to bring Sioux spirituality and rituals to a broader, principally non-Indian audience, an effort that was very controversial among many Sioux. Gary Holy Bull (Keeney 1999) presented his Sun Dance as a redemptive ritual, but made statements contradicted by the vast majority of native accounts of the ceremony.

Several native accounts of the contemporary Crow Sun Dance were published. John Cummins gave an in-depth interview about the Crow Sun Dance tradition (Cash and Hoover 1971:39–44) while Joe Medicine Crow wrote about the Sun Dance for use in reservation schools (Medicine Crow and Bradley 1976) as well as an account of the Sun Dance leader, Thomas Yellowtail (Medicine Crow 1992:54–

57). Yellowtail himself dictated a thoughtful and detailed account of Sun Dance history and modern practice on his reservation (Yellowtail as told to Fitzgerald 1991). Heywood Big Day arranged to have the fiftieth anniversary of the first Crow Sun Dance photographed (Crummett 1993).

Shoshone accounts include Dick Washakie's appeal in 1930 for the value and integrity of the Shoshone Sun Dance (cited in Moquin and Van Doren 1995:74) and a brief introduction to the Sun Dance published for tribal members (St. Clair et al. 1977). Emily Hill, Angelina Wagon, Helene Furlong, and Lenore Shoyo described their participation in the Sun Dance, particularly with regard to music and song (Vander 1988).

George Hunt, a Kiowa who witnessed one of the last Kiowa Sun Dances in 1887, narrated an account of it (Nye 1934). The Kiowa Sun Dance was described in a book authorized by the Kiowa Historical and Research Society (Boyd 1981–1982, 1). A largely secondary account by another tribal member (Mikkanen 1987) owes much to Boyd (1981–1982, 1) and Mooney (1898) but also includes contemporary Kiowa sentiments about the continuing importance of the Sun Dance.

Plains Cree accounts include those of Thunderchild, who in 1923 narrated long texts, including some information about the Sun Dance, to the missionary Edward Ahenakew, himself a Plains Cree. The material on the Sun Dance, although brief, includes an elegant plea for religious tolerance at a time when little support was available for native religions in either Canada or the United States (E. Ahenakew 1973). Raining Bird, Pete Favel, and Pete Gardipee, also Plains Crees, narrated personal accounts of their reasons for Sun Dancing (Dusenberry 1962:223–224). Accounts by members of other tribes include those of Carl Sweezy, Arapaho (A. Bass 1966), and John Stands In Timber, Cheyenne (Stands In Timber and Liberty 1967).

Robert L. Hall (1997), a Stockbridge Mohican, analyzed the Sun Dance within a larger framework of intertribal influences and great historical time-depth to establish complex and divergent relationships among tribes, rituals, and beliefs.

Indian accounts of the Sun Dance vary in length, content, and stated purpose. The majority of authors indicated that their reason for writing or dictating their material was to educate readers about the ceremony, correcting common misunderstandings, particularly with regard to the practice of piercing. Most descriptions are cursory and provide a level of general information without betraying strong contemporary Indian precepts against scholarly or popular study of the Sun Dance, including photographic documentation.

Anthropological Study

Anthropological consensus, based on the analysis of culture traits associated with the Sun Dance, suggests that the ceremony originated among the Algonquian-speaking tribes, specifically the Cheyenne and Arapaho (Spier 1921).

Discussion and critique of Spier's data and conclusions are found in Dixon (1928), Kroeber (1929), Clements (1931), Driver and Kroeber (1932), Kroeber (1939), and Steward (1943). J.W. Bennett (1944) examined the contribution of research about the Sun Dance to the development of anthropological theory. Spier first raised the issue of the integration of the Sun Dance into tribal societies, which Linton and others followed up with studies of the Comanche (Linton 1935), Ute (Opler 1941a), Shoshone-Bannock (Gerritsen 1961), and Crow (Voget 1964). Jorgensen's (1972) analysis of the Ute and Shoshone ritual employed a political and economic framework placing the dance within a neocolonial context. Some scholars have examined psychological factors in connection with the Sun Dance (Voget 1948, 1950, 1953; Shimkin 1953; Hassrick 1964:268–269; Hammerschlag 1988; Jilek 1982, 1992; G. Macgregor 1946:88–91; Erikson 1950:147–149). The best comprehensive guides to the literature on the Sun Dance are J.W. Bennett (1944), Liberty (1980:164–178), DeMallie and Parks (1987:221–222), Melody (1976), Hultkrantz (1980), P.J. Powell (1969), Jorgensen (1972), Shimkin (1953), Spier (1921), and P.M. White (1998).

Intertribal Religious Movements

GLORIA A. YOUNG

In the 1890s two well-known intertribal religious movements—the Ghost Dance and the Peyote religion—swept across the Plains. These were not isolated movements. They developed from tribal religious beliefs and ceremonies, individual visions, and the custom of transfering dances and rituals from tribe to tribe. To understand the Ghost Dance and Peyote religion, their relation to earlier intertribal movements on the Plains must be considered. These movements were the Sun Dance, the Midewiwin (or Medicine Dance) of the Prairies, the Grass (or Omaha) Dance, and the Dream Dance that came from the Great Lakes area (Hyde 1956; W.K. Powers 1975; Fowler 1982; Thornton 1986; R. Wilson 1983). Liljeblad (1972) and Snyder (1969) have analyzed the Peyote religion.

Before 1885: Sun Dance, Midewiwin, and Grass Dance

Sun Dance

Sometime after 1800, the Sun Dance spread from tribe to tribe across the High Plains. It was an annual religious ceremony held when each tribe congregated as a whole in the summer to hunt buffalo. Danced in a circle around a large pole in a specially built enclosure, it featured prolonged dancing (including bodily sacrifice in some tribes) by young men guided by experienced instructors. Involving both men and women in about a week of intense activity, it consisted of carefully enacted sequences that moved to a dramatic close. Special body painting and paraphernalia were employed as well as Sun Dance songs performed by singers who provided their own accompaniment on a drum (see Liberty 1980).

For most tribes the Sun Dance was an earth-renewal ceremony and a prayer for fertility; however, the ideology of the ceremony varied widely from tribe to tribe. Each group accepted the external features but adapted the motive for holding the ceremony to its own tribal needs and philosophy. Among all tribes, participants strove to attain personal power. Healing was often attempted. The dance was sometimes pledged by an individual who was prompted by a vision, and the quest for a personal vision was often the aim of dancers who anticipated falling unconscious after fasting, self-torture, and denying themselves water (Liberty 1980:167).

The center of development of the Sun Dance was among the Mandan and Hidatsa tribes, and the center of elaboration and diffusion of the ceremony was among the Cheyenne and Arapaho tribes, joined later by the Teton Sioux (Spier 1921). Other tribes adopting the Sun Dance were the Sarcee, Blackfoot, Gros Ventre, Plains Cree, Plains Ojibwa, Crow, Assiniboine, Sisseton and Santee Sioux on the northern High Plains, the Kiowa and Comanche on the Southern Plains, and the Arikara and Ponca on the Prairies (Liberty 1980:165–167; Linton 1935).

Midewiwin

The Midewiwin entered the prairies of Minnesota, Iowa, Kansas, and Nebraska in the mid-1800s when the Sauk, Fox, Potawatomi, Kickapoo, Miami, and Winnebago tribes had been removed from the Great Lakes area by the United States government and resettled among the Siouan-speaking Sioux, Omaha, Iowa, Otoe, and Ponca. In each place they settled, the Great Lakes tribes founded the Midewiwin (Midé societies) among the Prairie tribes (fig. 1).

The Santee Sioux had a single Medicine Dance society (Lowie 1913:137–139; Densmore 1913) and the Omaha had two, one for shamans and one "for the prestigious class of high chiefs" (Landes 1968a:178). Fortune (1932:85–102) presented a theory for the existence of two Omaha societies. He equated the society for shamans, the Pebble society (Lowie 1963:190), which practiced curing, with the Water Monster society, which had a large membership recruited from members of the "medicine" or "doctoring" societies of the tribe (see Dorsey 1884). Membership was gained by individuals who had personal visions. These shamans altered the Midewiwin somewhat to more closely resemble their tribal medicine societies. The other Midé society, the Shell society, had a completely different membership. It was made up of chiefs who had adopted the Midewiwin from the Sauk and Fox and continued it in its original form. Membership in the Shell society was hereditary (see Radin 1911).

The Midewiwin had begun as an intertribal religious movement spreading through the Great Lakes region in the late 1700s. It was a curing ceremony led by tribal shamans ("Plains Ojibwa," fig. 3, this vol.), who performed magical feats of healing on its membership of men, women, and children (Hickerson 1970). As a shamanistic ceremony, its underlying principle was the ability of shamans to communicate with the spirit world. Its inception, as with all shamanistic ceremonies, was credited to an individual's dream or vision, that of a young man named Cutfoot (Landes 1968a:96–111).

Some of the shamanistic elements of the Great Lakes Midewiwin were modified in the move west. The Iowa, for

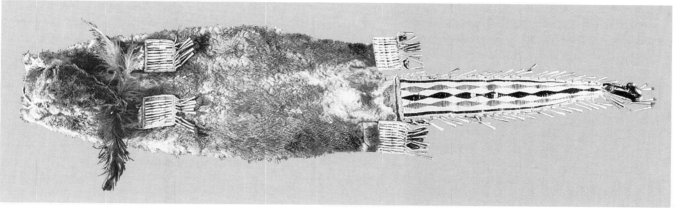

Fig. 1. Midewiwin or Medicine Dance ceremony and paraphernalia. top, Plains Ojibwa ceremony. top left, Lodge, oriented east and west, made of poles with a ridgepole at the top and lined with boughs and brush to a height of about 4 ft. This style is typical of the western Plains Ojibwa groups. top right, Part of the "shooting" rite. The candidate is seated (foreground) on a pillow of grass, covered with calico; she is supported by an official who is bracing her shoulders. The man in the center is magically "shooting" her with a bear claw, while the man behind him waits for his turn (J.H. Howard 1965a:118–125). A man with a drum sits in the shade on the right. Photographs by James Howard, near Angusville, Lizzard Point Res., Man., Aug. 1958. bottom, Otterskin Medicine Dance bag from the Wahpeton Sioux, with the paws and tail adorned with porcupine quill embroidery. The bag was used to magically shoot small objects into initiates (Skinner 1920:262–267). The dance had not been performed in 50 years when this bag was collected by Alanson Skinner near Sisseton, S. Dak., in 1914. Length 1.13 m.

example, called the shooting of "medicine arrows" (shells, in the original ceremony, the shooting of which was one of the most serious parts and included curing and resurrection from the dead), "going on the warpath," and regarded it rather lightly (Skinner 1920:239), more like the battle pantomimes in war dances. The Wahpeton society, called *wakʰá wačʰípi* 'sacred dance', had apparently come from the Sauk and used Algonquian songs; but a small Plains tepee was attached to the end of a rectangular Algonquian wigwam for the ceremony, and *akíčʰita* guarded the entrance as they did in other Sioux ceremonies. Changes like these did not affect the efficacy of the Midé, since the ceremony was amenable to innovation and any member could introduce elements from dreams or visions.

The Midewiwin, in turn, introduced change to Wahpeton traditionalism: both men and women received eagle feathers to wear when they were initiated into the society. At no other time might a woman wear an eagle feather, for although women had the right to receive eagle feathers, custom demanded that they give them to their male relatives to wear. The Wahpeton society ceased to function at Sisseton in the 1860s, after the Sioux Conflict in Minnesota (Skinner 1920: 273–290), as the Midé also waned among the other Prairie tribes, perhaps in response to the spread of the Grass Dance.

Grass Dance

The Grass Dance, which was not in itself a curing ceremony or religious movement, probably developed out of the Pawnee Iruska and the Omaha Water Monster society. Like the Water Monster society, the Pawnee Iruska was a society made up of the head shamans of each animal curing society of the Pawnee tribe. Its major ritual was an annual ceremony called Big Sleight of Hand (last held in 1878 or 1879) in which feats of legerdemain were accompanied by the songs and dances of the societies (Murie 1914:600–608, Lesser 1933a). Once again, its origin was attributed to a vision, that of a young man named Crowfeather (Murie 1914:609–616).

Another society spread from the Omaha to the Sioux and across the Plains sometime before 1860, coming to be called the Grass Dance or Omaha Dance (fig. 2). (Wissler 1916:865). Its origins were attributed to a society made up of several kinds of shamans like the Pawnee Iruska and Omaha Water Monster societies. As it spread, some of the shamanistic features were discarded and it was transformed into a men's society. By 1880, it had been adopted by most of the Plains and Prairie tribes from Oklahoma Territory to Canada.

Having lost the healing focus, the Grass Dance apparently did not conflict with, nor amalgamate with, the Sun Dance or tribal healing ("medicine" or "bundle") rituals. Although its membership was limited to warriors and the dress and paraphernalia of the society was much like that of the earlier *akíčʰita* and warrior societies, the Grass Dance by the 1880s had become a benevolent association among many tribes (for the Iowa, see Skinner 1915). It provided the organizational principles for the next intertribal religious movement on the prairies: the Dream Dance.

Dream Dance

From an amalgamation of elements of both the Prairie Plains Midé societies and the Grass Dance societies came the religious movement called variously the Dream Dance, Drum Dance, Society of Dreamers, Drum Lodge or cult, or Pow-wow (among the Menominee). It arose in Minnesota in the late 1870s out of a background of not only the Midé societies and Grass Dance but also warnings by prophets of the loss of power of old sacred objects and devastation in the wake of the crushing of the Sioux Conflict.

The inception of this movement was credited to the vision of a young Sioux woman, probably a Santee. The woman, whose Ojibwa name was Wananikwe, told of a vision in which, as she lay under water, a spirit said to her: "Go at once to your people and tell them to stop their war and become friends with the white man....Do you see the sky, how it is round?...Go, then and tell your people to make a circle on the ground just like the round sky. Call that holy ground. Go there, and with a big drum in the center, sing and dance and pray to me" (W.J. Hoffman 1896:61). The Sioux woman traveled east, perhaps as early as 1876 (Michelson 1911) taking the ceremony to the Winnebago, "Forest" Potawatomi, Ojibwa, and Menominee (see W.J. Hoffman 1896). These tribes then passed the dance southwest from the Menominee through the Fox in Iowa, back onto the Plains (see Densmore 1932). This clockwise movement paralleled the movement of the dance around a large central drum in a specially prepared circular dance ground (Vennum 1982:71).

The means of transfer of the Dream Dance was much like that of the Grass Dance. One Dream Dance society manufactured an elaborately decorated drum, drumsticks, and the four legs to support the drum above the ground (fig. 3), and took them, with songs and other presents, to a receiving host tribe. The hosts responded by giving gifts to the visitors, thereby "paying" for the knowledge of the ceremony

Smithsonian, NAA: 56,130.

Fig. 2. Omaha Dance, Northern Cheyenne. The dancers wear feather bristles and bells around their knees and ankles. Spectators sit in wagons and stand in the background. Photograph by Christian Barthelmess, Ft. Keogh, Mont., 1888–1897.

(Barrett 1911:280). Some adherents saw the purpose of the Dream Dance as replacing shamanistic rites. As one man said: "We have no medicine dance. We hope by and by to break up the old medicine dance, and all such things" (W.J. Hoffman 1896:160–161).

The Dream Dance reached the Potowatomi Agency in Kansas about 1883. The agent reported that "They seem to have adopted the religion as a means of expressing their belief in the justice and mercy of the Great Spirit and of their devotion to him, and are so earnest in their convictions as to its affording them eternal happiness that I have thought it impolitic so far to interfere with it any further than to advise as few meetings as possible" (Mooney 1896:706).

In 1880 or 1881, the Dream Dance arrived among the Great Lakes Algonquian tribes that had been moved to Indian and Oklahoma territories: the Registered Delaware who received a drum from the Ojibwas in 1800 or 1881 (J.H. Howard 1978), and the Potawatomi, Kickapoo, and the Sauk, who received their drum from the Prairie Potawatomi of Kansas (Landes 1970:243). Involvement in the Dream Dance by the Plains tribes there is uncertain, but Wissler (1916:867) wrote that a Potawatomi from Kansas "began to introduce this dance and made a strong effort to plant it among all the Oklahoma tribes. Little progress was made, but the Oto, Ponca, and possibly the Shawnee took it up." The Ponca apparently amalgamated the Dream Dance with their already existing Grass Dance society. About 1880 the Ponca *heðúška* society moved from emphasis on warfare pursuits to interest in prayers for the benefit of the group and gift giving as the basis of admission. J.H. Howard (1965:107) equated this dance with the "Dream Dance or Drum Religion."

The Ponca gave this dance to the Kansa and then the two tribes passed it on to the Osage in 1885, the Kansa giving

State Histl. Soc. of N. Dak., Bismarck:463.

Fig. 3. Robert Grass and Two Shields, Teton Sioux, drumming on a Dream Dance drum with 4 legs to hold it above the ground. Photograph by Frank B. Fiske, Ft. Yates, Standing Rock Res., N. Dak., 1900–1905.

the dance to the Hominy and Fairfax bands of the Osage and the Ponca taking it to the Grayhorse band. It was adopted by the Osage bands as their major annual tribal ceremony, the Iloshka, which continued through the twentieth century (G.A. Young 1981:169).

After 1890, when the Ghost Dance and Peyote religion brought a wave of revitalization of old traditions to the Southern Plains, the Dream Dance also experienced a resurgence. Among the Pawnee and Otoe, these later dances exhibited a return to one of the original shamanistic characteristics of the Pawnee Iruska, the vision. Dream Dance innovations were passed around the circle of tribes, given each time with a new drum made especially for the occasion. For example, in 1898, the Iowa received a drum and new version of the Dream Dance from the Kickapoo who lived in Kansas (Skinner 1915:721).

A Transition Period on the High Plains

Perhaps because of its Christian elements and perhaps because the dancers did not wear the dress of warriors, the Dream Dance was never considered by government agents or the military to be "demoralizing" to the Indians, and it was never banned. In contrast, the Sun Dance faced strong opposition in some quarters, and attempts by the government to suppress it began in the early 1880s. Some tribes such as the Crow and Teton Sioux were forced to abandon it at that time, while the Cheyenne, Arapaho, Piegan Blackfeet, Assiniboine, Plains Cree, and Plains Ojibwa went more or less underground, performing their ceremonies in secret (Liberty 1980:164, 169).

Government suppression in the 1880s was sparked, in part, by the fact that the Sun Dance activity of some tribes became more intense as the bison hunters witnessed the disappearance of bison herds from the Plains. Also, in the 1870s, the Sun Dances of some tribes began to include elements characteristic of the Ghost Dance of the 1870s. This early Ghost Dance movement was begun by a Northern Paiute Indian in Nevada who went into trances and preached that the deceased were about to return to earth and that the ancient life was to be restored along with the game animals then growing scarce (vol.11:660–662; Spier 1935). It did not reach eastward to the Plains, but it apparently did influence certain individuals.

The Demise of the Sun Dance on the Southern Plains

From at least 1860 the Comanche Sun Dance was held, the last in 1878 (Linton 1935:420). A tribal "medicine dance," it was introduced in 1874 by Isatai, a man who was credited with being invulnerable to bullets and had been "raised from the dead." He gained followers when, based on a vision, he had successfully predicted that a comet, the sighting of which was causing much apprehension, would disappear in five days and be followed by a drought. All the bands of the Comanches participated as well as some Cheyennes and Arapahos (Hoebel 1941:302–303; Kavanaugh 1996:446). 999

From about the same time, among the Kiowa, the ceremonies of regeneration at the Sun Dance which were aimed at replenishing the bison (and, thus, the well-being of the tribe), performed by the buffalo shamans, apparently took on much the same character. By 1878, all the bison were exterminated from the Kiowa Reservation and at the 1879 Sun Dance gathering, the Kiowa had to kill and eat their horses to keep from starving. In 1881, a bison bull and cow were killed on the Staked Plains of Texas for a large Kiowa Sun Dance held on the North Fork of the Red River. It was visited by about 200 Cheyenne, Arapaho, and Sioux, and, as had been the case for several years, accompanied by a detachment of U.S. cavalry. The Kiowa Buffalo shaman, Datekan (*tɔ́·dèkʰɔ̀·* 'keeps his name a long time'), made a special effort to regenerate the bison through a shamanistic feat (fig. 4) (E.L. Clark 1881; Nye 1937:264), and the troops feared that failure might lead to an uprising by the Indians. According to Kiowa calendars, Datekan (who renamed himself Pau-tape-ty [*phɔ́·tʰèptè* 'buffalo bull coming out']) attempted to restore the bison again in 1882, even though no Sun Dance was held (Mooney 1898:350). Sometime thereafter, another shaman, Botalye, made an attempt, and at the 1887 or 1888 Kiowa Sun Dance, a shaman named Paingya (*pɔ́ygyày* 'in the middle') attempted to resurrect the vanished bison herds. Paingya promised not only the return of the bison but also a revival of traditional lifeways and that all Whites and unbelieving Indians would be destroyed in tornadoes and a great prairie fire. He also claimed the power to resurrect the dead and to destroy enemies at a glance by lightning. Paingya set up a medicine tepee and kindled a sacred fire. Those who set up camp around his tepee started their fires from his fire rather than

Fig. 4. *Tau-ta-kah (Kiowa) Making Medicine in Accordance with Old Custom*, by Silverhorn, Kiowa. This rare depiction of the Buffalo Calling ceremony shows Datekan making medicine behind a red blanket stretched between forked poles. He is attempting to animate a buffalo effigy made of a feather-decorated hide stretched over a wooden armature. From a book of 75 drawings collected in 1883 by Dudley P. Brown, on the Kiowa-Comanche Reservation, Ind. Terr., and extensively captioned by him with information provided by the artist.

using White men's matches and were encouraged to throw away White men's dress and weapons (Mooney 1898:220; Nye 1937; E.L. Clark 1881).

Paingya's tornado and prairie fire failed to materialize in 1887 or 1888 and there were some skeptics among the Kiowa. A further damper was the outright prohibition of the Sun Dance by the new agent. An attempt to hold a Sun Dance in the summer of 1890 was terminated when word was received that army troops had been dispatched to stop the dance (Mayhall 1971:205–206; R.H. Lowie Museum 1968:12). However, that same summer the first large gathering of the 1890 Ghost Dance was held when the Kiowa received their payments from leased grazing lands. Paingya hailed the Ghost Dance as fulfillment of his prophecy.

A Militaristic Movement on the Northern Plains

On the Northern Plains, the story was much the same. Among the Crow as early as 1882, tribal religion was suppressed, and agency rules forbade participation in the "sundance, scalp dance, war dance, and even feasts" (Voget 1984:274–275). The last Sun Dance took place about 1875. But, in 1887, a man named Wraps Up His Tail (Sword Bearer) fasted in the mountains and from a dream began to believe he could exterminate the White soldiers by cutting them down with a sword painted red. Then, his people would be "free...[to] move around like in the olden times." He was confident that he would not be brought down by bullets and that lightning would strike down the soldiers, probably when he pointed his sword and sang his medicine song. Painting himself, the sword, and all his clothing red, he staged an "uprising" but was killed at the hands of a Crow policeman (Voget 1984:274–275).

Thus, it is clear that the prophecy of world renewal, including the destruction of White people, had spread across the Plains in the 1870s and 1880s, foreshadowing and then shaping the character of the 1890 Ghost Dance. It was in the vacuum created by the loss of the Sun Dance that the Ghost Dance of 1890 took root first and best on the Plains. There was, for example, no real break in intent between the Kiowa Sun Dance and the 1890 Ghost Dance among the Kiowa; and the Kiowa Ghost dance, like the Sun Dance, was performed around a cedar pole (Mooney 1896:921).

The Ghost Dance of the 1890s

The Ghost Dance of the 1890s was named by some tribes for the spirits of the dead: for example, *wanáɣi wačʰípi* among the Sioux, Thigûʼnawat in Arapaho (Mooney 1896:791, 1022; perhaps *θi·kónohwô·t*). Fueled by reports from frightened White settlers on the Plains and the government's experience with the "uprisings" of the 1870s and 1880s, a prominent characteristic of the Ghost Dance was said to be the promise of the destruction of the White men. Armed rebellion by the Indians was said to be imminent. This interpretation was predominant among many contemporary observers as well as subsequent historians (Mooney 1896; Lowie

1954). In fact, the original tenets of this particular movement promised that it was peaceful adjustment with the Whites that would hasten the restoration of days of Indian prosperity. Faithful dancing, clean living, hard work, and following God's chosen leaders were other attributes that would bring about the resurrection of dead relatives. There is no evidence to substantiate that the Ghost Dance among any tribe, even among the Sioux where violence eventually erupted, had any warlike connotations. The Sioux Ghost Dance leaders, like those of other tribes, preached peace and faith in the dance as the means to salvation in an approaching millennium (Fletcher 1891; DeMallie 1991:xxi).

The 1890 Ghost Dance movement began in Nevada, at Walker River Reservation, when a Northern Paiute shaman, Wovoka (also known as Jack Wilson), reported that Jesus appeared to him in a vision. The original dance for the 1890 Ghost Dance was a Northern Paiute world-renewal Round Dance in which dancers held hands as they circled by stepping sideways (O.C. Stewart 1980:180; Mooney 1896:798). However, new songs were composed especially for the Ghost Dance. As in most vision-based ceremonies, people who received instructions from supernaturals in visions were encouraged to compose new songs and to modify the ceremonies to conform to their visions.

Arrival on the Plains

Shortly after its inception, the Ghost Dance spread to the northern Plains tribes. Its center of development was among those tribes that had just lost their Sun Dance as a public annual ceremony: the Cheyenne, Arapaho (fig. 5), and Teton Sioux. Among the Sioux, as among the Kiowa, the Ghost Dance was held around a pole as had been the Sun Dance (DeMallie 1991:xxiii).

Word of the new religious movement reached as far east as the Oglala in South Dakota in 1889. By June 1890, at the Tongue River Agency in Montana, six-day and night dances "every new moon" were being held by Porcupine, a Northern Cheyenne shaman who declared himself to be the new messiah after visiting Wovoka in Nevada (T.J. Morgan 1890:37–40). Porcupine promised his Cheyenne and Arapaho followers that the depleted bison, elk, and other game animal herds would be restored and their dead relatives would be resurrected. He also promised that his believers would be endowed with perpetual youth (Mooney 1896:793–196, Fletcher 1891).

The Ghost Dance spread eastward, and by the summer of 1890 a considerable portion of the Sioux population on Pine Ridge, Rosebud, Cheyenne River, and Standing Rock reservations were dancing the Ghost Dance, temporarily setting aside older rituals in favor of the new. On August 22, some 2,000 dancers gathered on White Clay Creek, 18 miles from Pine Ridge Agency, for the first large Ghost Dance of the Sioux; and by October, dances were being held on Cheyenne River, Rosebud, and Standing Rock reservations. Yankton Sioux Ghost Dancers took the message of the messiah to the

Lower Brule, although no Ghost Dances were reported at Yankton. A number of Lower Brule dancers—17 (Schusky 1975:132) or 23 (T.J. Morgan 1890)—were arrested and confined at Fort Snelling.

Fearing that Ghost Dances among the Sioux would initiate hostilities toward Whites, the U.S. Army dispatched a military force consisting of five companies of infantry, three troops of cavalry, and one Hotchkiss and one Gatlin gun to Pine Ridge in November. Two troops of cavalry and six companies of infantry were stationed at Rosebud. Troops were ordered to other agencies until finally nearly half the infantry and cavalry of the U.S. Army were concentrated on the Sioux reservations (T.J. Morgan 1890). Confrontations were inevitable, climaxing in December 1890 with the Wounded Knee Massacre at Pine Ridge. Ghost Dances were thereafter forbidden on the Sioux reservations in South Dakota.

Spread Across the Northern Plains

A few ceremonial leaders continued to proselytize for the Ghost Dance, and some groups on the Northern Plains accepted the dance while others, apparently, did not. Ghost Dances were not reported at Crow Creek or Sisseton (T.J. Morgan 1890; Schusky 1975).

In 1891 the Ghost Dance spread to the Yanktonai Sioux at Cannon Ball, North Dakota, on Standing Rock Reservation (DeMallie and Parks 1987:8, J.H. Howard 1984:174). From there, it spread to the Sioux in Saskatchewan but did not reach Manitoba. In Saskatchewan, it was performed among the Teton Sioux by 1895 at Wood Mountain. However, it was among the Santee at White Cap and Round Plain that the dancers were most active and the dance persisted longest.

At least some Ghost Dance activity is said to have been reported also among the Mandan, Arikara, Assiniboine, Bannock, and Gros Ventre (P.M. Thomas 1972:198). It was not reported among the Hidatsa, Plains Cree, Omaha, Stoney, Blackfoot, Sarcee, or Plains Ojibwa.

The Classic Plains Ghost Dance

The classic form of the Plains Ghost dance was a four-day Round Dance with dancers holding hands (fig. 6) and sidestepping in a clockwise direction for several hours at a time. As the dance continued, the leaders, often called prophets, would wave eagle-wing fans before the faces of the dancers or shine mirrors in their eyes. Together with the hypnotic effect of the singing and dancing this would induce trance in a dancer. In trance, the dancer would be transported to the afterworld where departed relatives would be seen living the life of the prereservation era, where bison and other game were abundant (Mooney 1896; J.H. Howard 1984:174).

For the dances, special shirts and dresses began to be made of buckskin or white muslin cloth, decorated with symbols referring to the visions of the dancers—usually stars, suns, moons, eagles and other birds associated with the heavens. Ghost Dance adherents, especially among the Sioux, began to *1001*

Smithsonian, NAA: top left, 91-20160; center left, 55298; bottom left, 91-20182; top right, 55-296; bottom right, after Amer. Mus. of Nat. Hist., New York: cat. 50/301.

Fig. 5. Southern Arapaho–Cheyenne Ghost Dance. top left, Small circle. Leaders are in the center, and participants join the circle until it includes 50–500 men, women, and children (Mooney 1896:920). center left, Women dancing. Young women were usually first affected, then older women, and then men. bottom left, Dancer in a trance: "rigid." top right, Praying, accompanied by the laying on of hands and stroking of face and body (Mooney 1896:921). The individual with back to the camera wears a dance bustle. Photographs by James Mooney, Southern Arapaho and Cheyenne Agency, Ind. Terr., 1891–1894. bottom right, Bustle, known as a Crow belt, the type used by male dancers in the Crow Dance, which was closely associated with the Ghost Dance among the Southern Arapaho, often danced in the afternoon before the Ghost Dance performance. Two strips of hide, painted yellow and red and hung with hawk and owl feathers and small bells, are suspended from a rawhide cutout of an eagle, pierced with many holes representing the metallic sheen of its body. When the belt was secured around a dancer's waist, the eagle feathers and two beaded spikes attached to the body of the bird fanned outward. The bustle represents the thunderbird, the spikes lightning, and the bells both thunder and hail. A headdress of crow feathers, shown tied to the eye of the bird, would have been worn by the dancer (Kroeber 1902–1907:340–342, pl. LXXIV). Collected by Alfred Kroeber in Okla. Terr., 1899; length 111 cm. Drawing by Roger Thor Roop, based on research and preliminary sketch by Karen Ackoff.

believe that Ghost Dance raiment could deflect the bullets of White men's weapons. Short Bull, a Brule Sioux from Rosebud Reservation, said of the Ghost Dance among his people:

First: purification by sweat bath. Clasp hands and circle to left. Hold hands and sing until a trance is induced, looking up all the time. Brought to pitch of excitement by singing songs prescribed by the Messiah. Dress as prescribed. Froth at mouth when in trance. They must keep step with the cadence of the song. The[y] go into trance in from ten minutes to three quarters of an hour. Each one described his vision. Each vision is different from others. Men, women, children have visions.

The ghost shirt is *wakan* [*wakʰą́* 'spiritually powerful']. It is impervious to missiles (J.R. Walker 1980:143).

Smithsonian, Dept. of Anthr.: 165,127, neg. 76-4941.

Fig. 6. Painting of the Ghost Dance on buckskin by Yellow Nose, Cheyenne, 1891. The Southern Cheyenne learned of the Ghost Dance from the Arapaho in 1890, and this painting shows members of both tribes. The dancers around the periphery of the circle hold hands, while those in the center are in an ecstatic trance, some fallen to the ground, others standing rigid (Mooney 1896:pl. CIX). Collected in Okla. Terr. by James Mooney, 1891. Width 1.27 m.

INTERTRIBAL RELIGIOUS MOVEMENTS

For discussions of the Ghost Dance among the Sioux see D.M. Johnson (1969), Hyde (1956), and E.G. Eastman (1978); among the Northern Cheyenne and Arapaho see Mooney (1896), Stands in Timber and Liberty (1967), Fowler (1982), Kroeber (1902–1907), and Grinnell (1962).

Canada

As with all vision-inspired dances, the Ghost Dance in Canada underwent successive alterations in form. Some features of Ghost Dance belief and ritual became routinized and incorporated into the traditional religious structure. According to Sam Buffalo, a Wahpeton Santee from Round Plain, the Ghost Dance developed into the *wačʰékiye dowápi* 'prayer singing', which did not involve dancing. Around 1900, an Assiniboine from Fort Peck Reservation brought a new version of the Ghost Dance called *wóyaka tʰéča* 'new tidings'. Ghost Dance shirts continued to be worn in both these rituals, but rather than bullet proof they were considered "sin proof" (J.H. Howard 1984:175–177). These later Canadian ceremonies were forged from a combination of the Ghost Dance and the earlier tribal Medicine Dance, Medicine Feast, and old Santee "eat-all" feast.

Arrival on the Southern Plains

Rumors of the Ghost Dance had also reached the Southern Plains in 1889, perhaps through Porcupine. The first Ghost Dance on the Southern Plains was held in April 1890 at Watonga, Oklahoma Territory. Because of the emphasis of the Ghost Dance on old-time ways, many earlier dances were revived at that time. The Cheyenne and Arapaho usually danced together, singing Arapaho songs. Black Coyote, an Arapaho, became the major Ghost Dance shaman for the two tribes (Mooney 1896:895). The Ghost Dance reached a fervor state in September 1890 when Sitting Bull, a Southern Arapaho who had lived among the Northern Arapaho since youth (Fowler 1982:23), but had failed to attract a following there, returned to the Southern Plains to impart the proper observance of the ceremony. A great gathering was held on the South Canadian River two miles from the Darlington Cheyenne and Arapaho Agency, Indian Territory. Some 3,000 Indians, virtually all of the Cheyenne, Arapaho, Kiowa, Wichita, Caddo, and Plains Apache tribes, danced every night for two weeks. The first trances by Oklahoma dancers were achieved at this gathering. Throughout the autumn of 1890, Sitting Bull visited individual tribes, presenting feathers to them as authorization to dance.

After the Wounded Knee massacre of Ghost Dancers on Pine Ridge Reservation in December 1890, Commissioner of Indian Affairs T.J. Morgan visited Oklahoma Territory to assess the situation. Seeing no signs of an armed uprising there as a result of the Ghost Dance, he made no attempt to prohibit the dance on the Southern Plains but commissioned Army Lt. Hugh Lenox Scott to investigate it. Scott persuaded the Indian Office that the Ghost Dance was actually a step toward christianization, and a policy of non-interference among the Plains tribes of Oklahoma Territory was adopted (Mooney 1896:897–900) ("Wichita," fig. 7, this vol.).

Throughout 1891, large dances were held about every six weeks, each lasting about five days. Several tribes sent delegations to Wovoka in Nevada and the delegates brought back red paint and magpie feathers for the rituals of the Ghost Dance. Sitting Bull used a feather to hypnotize dancers, just as shamans had in the earlier Feather Dances of the Kiowa Sun Dance. Kiowa men and women Ghost Dancers were given feathers in 1891 and, for the first time, Kiowa women were authorized to wear feathers. The feathers were usually eagle or crow feathers painted in several colors, each tipped with a small down feather of another color. As in the Sun Dance, only certain persons were allowed to paint and prepare feathers (Mooney 1896:908–919).

In 1893, at a Ghost Dance led by Paingya, the Kiowa shaman who had attempted to restore the vanished bison, one Ghost Dance shaman, Red Buffalo, the son of a former buffalo shaman, attempted to raise Paingya's son from the dead after receiving a special song while in a trance (Mooney 1896:1083).

Some Kiowas, followers of Apeatone (*á·pì·tʰɔ̀·* 'wooden lance'), ceased to participate in Ghost Dances in 1891, after Apeatone visited Wovoka in Nevada and discredited him as a fraud. But by 1894, most Kiowas were once again attending most Ghost Dances in their area (Mooney 1896:914). The Kiowa and Comanche Ghost Dancers, along with nearby Cheyenne and Arapaho, carried Ghost Dance enthusiasm into the twentieth century. The dance changed over time with each vision-inspired innovation to such an extent that the twentieth-century version in Oklahoma little resembled the ceremony as it had originally entered the Plains. Thus, most authorities reported that it died out in Oklahoma Territory in the 1890s. In fact, the Kiowa Ghost Dance continued uninterrupted until at least 1916 (Kracht 1992).

The Prairie Tribes

During 1891 and 1892, the Ghost Dance spread to many of the southern tribes, including the Pawnee (Murie 1914:630–635), Otoe (Mooney 1896:902), Iowa (Skinner 1915:719), Osage (Messer 1937), Ponca (Fletcher 1891), and Quapaw (Valliere and Valliere 1937). As different tribes adopted it, they composed their own songs and adapted the dance in accordance with their own visions. Individuals from tribes other than those that had been settled on reservations on the Southern Plains also attended Ghost Dances. For example, in 1892, the commissioner of Indian affairs sent a telegram to Anadarko, Oklahoma Territory, ordering "visiting Cherokee engaged in Messiah dance to leave Kiowa reservation immediately. Tell them if they refuse troops will be sent to compel obedience" (Belt 1892).

1004

The subsequent history of the Ghost Dance differed from tribe to tribe. The Otoe gave up the dance after the arrest of their leader, Buffalo Black, in 1892 (Mooney 1896:902). The Pawnee Ghost Dance leader, Frank White, was also arrested for sponsoring dances. However, when he was released, he began to amalgamate the Ghost Dance among the Pawnees with the Peyote ritual into a religion magnifying the Christian symbols (Murie 1914:635; Lesser 1933). After White's death, visiting Wichitas brought their version of the Ghost Dance to the Pawnee. In 1904, three Pawnees traveled to Walker Lake, Nevada, for instruction. Murie (1914:636) reported: "This religion now flourishes, but has evolved into a Christian ethical belief demonstrated by ritual. The trance and its intensity have passed out, but dreams and ordinary visions are still valued."

There were other outgrowths from the Ghost Dance among the Pawnee. One was the Ghost Dance hand game (see Lesser 1933). Murie (1914:635) reported that "all the old Pawnee medicine men took the trances as forms of powers formerly expressed by the animal lodges and began a vigorous revival, each setting himself up as a prophet and seeking to outdo others." After White's death in 1893, the religion quickly disappeared. The Ghost Dance among the Pawnee led to the revival of the hand game because it was played as an accompaniment to the dances. Likewise, there was a revival of the old Iruska society dances because these old dances had been witnessed in trances during Ghost Dances. About 1894 Sitting Bear dreamed of the Iruska. He organized his own ceremony and led it until his death in 1903 (Murie 1914:628).

Ghost Dances and hand games occurred as often as anyone authorized to give them desired to do so. "All classes" participated although the "great body" of the dancers were "uneducated full bloods." The dances that Pawnee Agent George Nellis called Ghost Dances were called "modern Iruska" by Murie (1914) and Lesser (1933a) and were the revived Iruska society dances accompanied by the trances and visions of the Ghost Dance. Controversy erupted in 1912, when some tribe members complained of the dances. Agent Nellis (1913) responded that "we have no legal authority to stop [the dances] as long as they are conducted decently and are not attended by immoral practices." By 1914, still other Pawnees, along with James Murie (who was himself Pawnee), and an attorney had entered the dispute, with the Indian Office still attempting to stop the dancing through "moral suasion" and the attorney stating that his search of the statutes revealed no law declaring any kind of Indian dance a crime. In 1918, at the close of World War I, Densmore (1919) attended "Grass Dances" based on visions concerning the Pawnee servicemen who were fighting in Europe. They were danced in the servicemen's honor upon their return from war. These Ghost Dance–influenced Iruska dances and the hand game long outlived the original Ghost Dance among the Pawnee.

Arapaho Innovations

Among the Arapaho, Ghost Dance visions led to the revival, by Grant Left Hand in the south (Mooney 1896:[158,186 reprint 1965]) and Yellow Calf in the north (Fowler 1982:123–124), of the Crow Dance, a version of the Grass Dance, as an afternoon activity before nighttime Ghost Dances. Mooney (1896:901) described this dance as really only a modification of the Omaha or Grass Dance, with religious features borrowed from the new doctrine. An immense drum was an important feature. Men and women took part, and the songs referred to the crow and the messiah but were set to a variety of dance steps.

Peyote Religion and the Native American Church

At the same time as the Ghost Dance, and a part of its movement on the Southern Plains in the 1890s, a ritual involving the ingestion of peyote also spread from tribe to tribe. The center of development and diffusion of the Peyote religion was among the Plains tribes of Oklahoma Territory. Originally coming from the Apache in the Southwest, it spread across the Southern Plains, then northward. It has been suggested that the preoccupation of Plains Indians with the ability of adults to obtain visions aided in the rapid movement of the ritual between tribes. Peyote facilitated visions, offering communicants the opportunity of contacting the supernatural through use of a hallucinogen without recourse to long periods of fasting or dancing (Shonle 1925:58–59; Hultkrantz 1960).

Peyote (*Lophophora williamsii*) grows wild in the Rio Grand River valley and southwestward. It is a small, spineless, carrot-shaped cactus the top of which is harvested to become the "peyote button" that will be ingested (fig. 7b). Chemically, the button is complex and contains a variety of alkaloids, some with effects like strychnine and others with effects like mescaline. Those who eat the button or drink a tea steeped from it experience a variety of effects following ingestion. Excitement and exhilaration are sometimes followed by alterations in the sense of time and by auditory hallucinations and optical visions such as brilliance of colors. The toxic effects seem minor, and some say the plant is not addictive (Wax and Wax 1978; La Barre 1938).

The Peyote ritual that entered the Southern Plains was credited by the Plains Apache to the vision of a Lipan Apache woman and, later, to that of a young man. In his vision, the young man related, he saw long-haired Indians sitting in a tepee and was told by their leader: "This is our way from a long time ago. The Lord made this way just for the Indians, and I want you to learn to use it, and take it back to your people" (Bittle 1954:72).

The Lipan Apache near Laredo, Texas, may have begun using peyote by 1770 to 1830, perhaps obtaining it from the Carrizo or Apache groups living in Mexico (O.C. Stewart 1987:50–53). From the Lipan, the Peyote ritual was introduced to the Comanche, Kiowa, and Plains Apache in Oklahoma Territory, perhaps as early as 1870, but became well known in the 1890s (because of attention given it by Mooney 1892, 1892a, 1892b, 1896, 1898). The Plains Indians began to perform individual pilgrimages to the regions where peyote *1005*

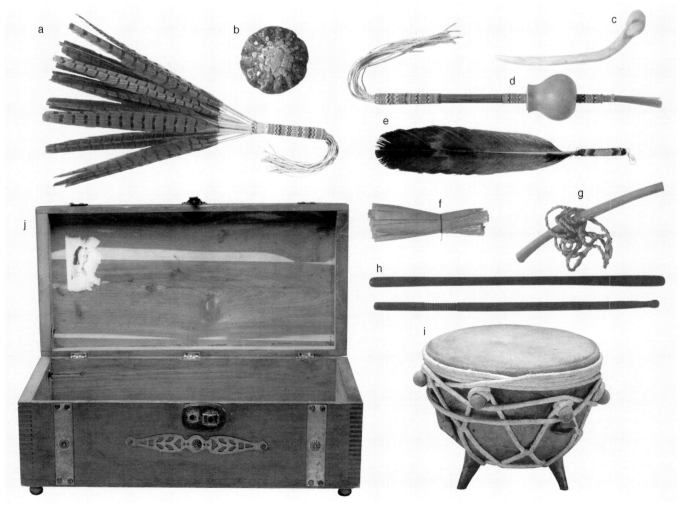

a

b

c

d

e

f

g

h

i

j

Smithsonian, NAA: top left, 265-F; top center, 1747-A-1; top right, The Thomas Gilcrease Inst. of Amer. Hist. and Art, Tulsa, Okla.; bottom, Peabody Mus. of Salem, Mass.: a, E31,618; b, E31,626; c, E31,623; d, E31,617; e, E31,619; f, E31,625; g, E31,616; h, E31,621 and E31,622; i, E31,628; j, E31,614.

Fig. 7. Peyote religious leaders and paraphernalia. top left, Bob-Tailed Wolf, Southern Cheyenne. He holds a peyote fan, wears a bandolier made of mescal beans, and has a Christian cross on his breechcloth. Photograph by J.A. Shuck, El Reno, Okla., 1938. top center, Quanah Parker, Comanche. He introduced peyote to the Cheyenne, Arapaho, Otoe, Pawnee, Delaware, and Caddo (Swan 1999:6). He sits in his modern home next to a portrait of his mother, Cynthia Ann Parker, holding her daughter Prairie Flower, and paintings of the crucifixion of Jesus and portrait of Christ. He holds Peyote paraphernalia. Photograph by Hutchins and Lanney, near Ft. Sill, Okla. Terr., 1892. top right, Preston Morrell, an Osage Roadman, holding the staff used in the Big Moon peyote ceremony (Swan 1999:37–39). Photograph by Shane Culpepper, Tulsa, Okla., 1998. bottom, Osage Roadman's ritual objects. The smaller items are kept in a wooden box, often made of cedar (j). The Roadman, or leader of the ceremony, provides the Chief Peyote (b), a large, perfectly formed button placed on the altar during the ceremony and not consumed. A rattle (d), staff, and fan (a) are passed around the circle of participants as each member sings and prays, accompanied by a drum (i), traditionally made of a three-legged iron kettle partially filled with water. A buckskin head is laced over the drum in an elaborate pattern with the assistance of a drum tightener made of antler (c). Drumsticks may be either plain or incised with designs (h). Anyone who leaves during the ceremony to carry out ritual tasks may carry an eagle feather (e) to signify his authorization to go. The Roadman goes out once during the all-night ritual and blows an eagle bone whistle (g) to the 4 directions. Participants smoke ritual cigarettes of tobacco rolled in corn husks (f) as well as consume peyote. Collected in Okla. before 1954. a, Length 55 cm including fringe; b, diameter 4.5 cm; e, length 33.5 cm, c and d to same scale. h, Lengths 34 cm and 20 cm, f and g to same scale. i, Height 16.2 cm; j, length 48 cm.

was found, reciting prayers on encountering the first specimen (for the history of Peyotism see Mooney 1910a; O.C. Stewart 1987; Tunnell and Newcomb 1969; M.E. Opler 1936a, 1938; Wax and Wax 1978; J.H. Howard 1957; Slotkin 1955).

For its communicants, Peyote was a beneficent and potent deity, capable of healing and of conferring a variety of blessings and advantages. For this reason, among some tribes the practice of the Peyote ritual deterred acceptance of the Ghost Dance. Many Comanches, for example, encouraged by their chief, Quanah Parker (fig. 7), did not adopt the Ghost Dance, nor did some Kiowas, including the influential Apeatone. These Peyotists may have felt that they already had sufficient means of communicating with the spirits of their ancestors through the Peyote ritual. The Comanche version of the Peyote ritual became known as the Half-Moon ritual because of the use of a half moon-shaped altar made of clay (fig. 8).

Other Peyotists practiced both the Ghost Dance and the Peyote ritual, and several leaders were tribal shamans as well. Among the Plains Apache, one Peyote leader was the well-known shaman, Daveko, who had helped revive ancient customs by challenging the Kiowa shaman Datekan to a hand game in 1881 to see who had the most power to resurrect the vanished bison (Mooney 1898:348–349). But at the same time that Daveko was including peyote in his shamanistic rituals, other Plains Apache Peyote leaders were eliminating shamanism from the ritual while incorporating God and Jesus (O.C. Stewart 1987:84).

The Pawnee Peyote ritual was learned from the Quapaw, "during the Ghost Dance excitement" (Murie 1914:638). Soon the Pawnee founder (perhaps Frank White) added old Pawnee characteristics from bundle and society ceremonies. He claimed that this lore, previously unknown to him, was revealed when under the influence of peyote.

The best-known religious leader on the Southern Plains was the Caddo tribal shaman niš kániuh (Moon Head or John Wilson). He reported that he was transported to the moon in a peyote-induced trance in 1880. He then introduced his own version of the Peyote ritual in accordance with his vision, the Big Moon (later identified with the Cross Fireplace ritual). He became a Ghost Dance leader and

underwent remarkable trances in the Ghost Dance. Nishkuntu was the most active leader in spreading the Peyote ritual and the Ghost Dance throughout Oklahoma and Indian Territories (Mooney 1896:903–905; O.C. Stewart 1980:184–185, 1987:84–93; Slotkin 1956; vol. 15:234). As he visited each tribe, such as the Osage and Quapaw, he apparently introduced both ceremonies at the same time. For this reason, although the Osage and Quapaw are reported to have accepted the Ghost Dance, in actuality it was the Peyote ritual that they performed (see "Quapaw," and "Osage," fig. 12, this vol.). Thus, Peyotism spread from tribe to tribe across Oklahoma and Indian Territories until, by 1900, there were Peyote congregations among all the Southern Plains and Prairie tribes.

Southern Plains

As with the other religious movements, Plains religious characteristics were instilled into the Peyote ritual. Among the Mexicans, the main objective of the ritual (a seasonal ceremony) was curing and success in war, corn growing, and deer hunting, and there was considerable dancing but no society of peyote eaters. In contrast, in the versions that developed on the Plains, curing, though important, was not essential; dancing was generally lacking; the ceremony could be held at any time; and the Peyote ritualists belonged to a society. Plains Peyotism did incorporate the earlier custom of holding sessions at night, followed by a ritual breakfast in which parched corn, sweetened water, and boneless meat were prominent. The Kiowa added characteristics unique to the Plains such as holding meetings in a tepee (fig. 8 top left), calling meetings in accordance with a vow (on the pattern of a Sun Dance), the ritual number four, the desire for a vision through peyote ingestion, and a preparatory sweatbath (Lowie 1954; O.C. Stewart 1980:188–189). In accordance with individual visions, more Christian elements such as Bible reading were added. The three Osage officials were said to represent the trinity; a bird image of ashes made by the Otoe was interpreted as the spirit descending at Jesus's baptism; the Wichita leader's staff was called the "staff of life" and that of the Iowa, the "savior's staff" (Lowie 1954:203). *1007*

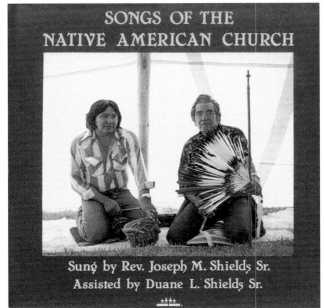

SONGS OF THE
NATIVE AMERICAN CHURCH

Sung by Rev. Joseph M. Shields Sr.
Assisted by Duane L. Shields Sr.

INDIAN HOUSE ®

top left, The Thomas Gilcrease Inst. of Amer. Hist. and Art, Tulsa, Okla.: 0127.2002; top right, U.S. Dept. of Interior, Indian Arts and Crafts Board, Southern Plains Ind. Mus., Anadarko, Okla.: 72.36.3.

Fig. 8. Native American Church. top left, *Indians in Worship-Native American Church* by Tennyson Echiwaudah, Comanche. Some branches of the Native American Church emphasize the union of Native religion, symbolized here by worshipers within the tepee, with Christianity, represented by the figure of Christ above the smokehole. Unlike most other Plains artists of his generation, Echiwaudah (b. 1912, d. 1988) worked primarily in oil on canvas. top right, *Native American Church (Peyote)*, by Stephen Mopope, Kiowa, showing the Roadman, or leader of the ceremony, holding the fan, staff, and rattle. He sings to the accompaniment of a water drum, played by the man seated to his right. In front of them, the Chief Peyote rests on the rim of the crescent altar within which burns a fire, its ashes sculpted in the shape of the peyote bird. The 4-pointed figure represents the Morning Star, especially revered by Peyotists. Watercolor on matboard, acquired 1972. bottom left, Headstone of Rev. Oliver Paul Spider, Oglala Sioux, Cross Fire Cemetery, Porcupine, S. Dak., depicting Peyote paraphernalia. Photograph by Omer Stewart, 1971. bottom right, *Songs of the Native American Church* tape cover. Sung by Rev. Joseph M. Shields, Sr., with accompaniment by Duane L. Shields, Sr. © 1983, both Yankton Sioux. Recorded at Lake Andes, S. Dak., 1979, and published by Indian House, Taos, N. Mex. Photograph by Tony Isaacs.

Also, special songs were composed (fig. 8), this time in a unique musical style (see McAllester 1949; Nettl 1954). Many different tribal and intertribal versions of Peyote meetings developed. Some were held in tepees, others in specially made buildings, some in homes. All incorporated a fire and crescent-shaped altar of clay or concrete ("Plains Apache," fig. 5, this vol.). Paraphernalia included feathers, feather fans, gourd rattles, staffs, cedar smoke incense, and a drum partially filled with water (fig. 7). Macaw feathers from Mexico were especially prized for use during ceremonies. They replaced the painted feathers of the Sun Dance and Ghost Dance.

Discussions of Peyotism and descriptions of meetings are extant for the following Southern Plains tribes: Kiowa (Mooney 1896), Quapaw (C.V. Wilson 1978), Plains Apache (Brant 1950), Iowa (Skinner 1915:725–), Arapaho (Kroeber 1902–1907:398–410; Rachlin 1964), Pawnee (Murie 1914:636–638), Cheyenne (Goggin 1938; Stands in Timber and Liberty 1967), Otoe (J.H. Howard 1956), and the Osage, Ponca, Comanche, and Wichita (Stewart 1980a, 1987; La Barre 1935, 1938).

Northern Plains

By 1905, the Peyote ritual had spread northward, possibly from the Southern Arapaho to their northern kinsmen (along the Ghost Dance path but in the opposite direction). From the Arapaho, it was transmitted to the Omaha and to the southernmost Sioux reservations (Yankton, Rosebud, and Pine Ridge). The Northern Cheyenne passed it to the Crow. It eventually spread to all the tribes of the Northern Plains. Rapid transmission of the movement was spurred by friendly relations between tribes and the ease of communication and transportation of the early twentieth century (Shonle 1925:57–59). For discussions of Peyotism among northern tribes of the United States see O.C. Stewart (1987); for the Omaha, Arth (1956) and J.H. Howard (1956); and for the Blackfoot, Wissler (1913). In Canada, by the 1980s Peyotism had been introduced to the Sioux but was still not practiced by the Sioux in Saskatchewan, although it had a large and enthusiastic following among the Plains Cree (J.H. Howard 1984:179–180) ("Plains Cree," fig. 9, this vol.).

Native American Church

Peyotism became the subject of governmental and religious attacks, and legislation against peyote was introduced in both the Congress and some state legislatures. Numerous lawsuits and countersuits ensued (for detailed discussion see Slotkin 1975, O.C. Stewart 1987). Partly in an effort to accommodate the sacramental usage of peyote to Christian religious traditions, and to provide themselves with the religious protection of the federal constitution, some Indians began a process of formal organization. In 1914, the Firstborn Church of Christ was organized under the laws of Oklahoma (La Barre 1938:186; Slotkin 1956:53; O.C. Stewart 1987:123–124). Since strong Christian elements pervaded the Plains ritual (fig. 8 top left), the title was not a misnomer;

nevertheless, many peyotists were uncomfortable about it, and, in 1918, a group of representatives from Oklahoma tribes incorporated themselves as the Native American Church (Slotkin 1957:58–54; O.C. Stewart 1987:224–226). That title, which symbolizes the intertribal and aboriginal nature of the religion, has proved more popular and durable. The church was established and incorporated in a number of states, but the general organizational structure was congregational and federal; to be more exact, the structure was loose and uncentralized in the fashion characteristic of the earlier religious movements and tribal and intertribal societies of the Plains (Wax and Wax 1978).

Typically, the religious service of a Native American Church group began on Saturday night and continued until Sunday morning. The location may be a tepee, but in practice, the service can be held anywhere so long as there is space for a central altar, including a fire (or coals), about which the participants will be seated. In Canada, when meetings were held in a home, the fire was kept burning outside the house to provide the coals needed for burning cedar incense (J.H. Howard 1984:180). At midnight and dawn there were ceremonies involving water, and, in the morning, there was a ritual breakfast including corn, fruit, and boneless meat. The service was conducted by a leader called a Roadman ("following the Peyote Road"). During the service, peyote was passed among the communicants. In the ritual of some Plains tribes, each person usually consumed four buttons. Others, like the Quapaw, drank an infusion ("tea") instead of eating the buttons. A water drum and other ritual paraphernalia were passed about the circle, and each person sang four peyote songs, while accompanied on the drum by the person on his right. Some meetings included a sermon or reading from the Bible; some included prayers for curing. Meetings were held on holidays, called for at times of stress or illness, or convened to express gratitude or thanksgiving for a special event like the birth of a healthy child.

Among Plains Indians, services are sponsored for the purposes of securing a vision that will confer blessings and power upon the supplicant. O.C. Stewart (1987) provides a comprehensive summary of the history and the ritual of the Peyote religion; see also La Barre (1975) and Wax and Wax (1978).

The Twentieth Century

One important aspect of the intertribal movements of the nineteenth century was the emphasis on continuing and reviving old customs, games, and dances. On the other hand, some tribal ceremonies were discarded in favor of the new movements. The express goal of the Dream Dance was to replace old curing ceremonies such as bundle ceremonies and the Medicine Dance. The Osage opted to keep only their version of the Dream Dance, the Iloshka, as their major annual tribal ceremony, abandoning all others. Likewise, the Ghost Dance, whether or not purposefully, replaced and caused the revision of earlier dances. The Peyote religion replaced earlier tribal ceremonies among several tribes. *1009*

Among the Quapaw, for example, Peyotism probably caused the Quapaw Green Corn ceremony to be abandoned in the 1890s. While the intertribal movements caused whole complexes of music and dance to disappear, at the same time, they introduced new music. Soon, many tribes had their own repertoire of new songs resulting from the inspiration of visions, trances, and peyote-induced hallucinations. This occurred during the period from the 1880s until World War I, the very time when the disruptive move to reservation life could have caused a stultification in Native American ceremonialism and the demise of tribal ritual and music.

The Native American Church flourished. In 1958, the Native American Church of Canada was incorporated (O.C. Stewart 1987:256–264). On Pine Ridge Reservation in the 1960s, less than one percent of the population listed the Native American Church as their primary religious affiliation; nevertheless, 11 percent of full-bloods and 6 percent of mixed-bloods acknowledged attending meetings (Wax and Wax 1978:34). The Native American Church is visible and important for the Sioux; many Sioux people, both members and nonmembers of the Native American Church, sense an antagonism between the use of peyote and the traditional tribal use of the pipe as a means of prayer. Others find them compatible. Among the Sioux, one Cross Fire (Big Moon) group of Native American Church members more fully integrates the Bible and adds a greater number of Christian teachings to their services; under the name of the Native American Church of Jesus Christ, they sought to make the Peyote religion a Christian sect. The more traditionally oriented Cross Fire groups, as well as the Half-Moon groups, identified themselves as members of a traditional Native American religion and rejected formal connections with Christianity. The Peyote religion did not become integrated into the fabric of Sioux traditionalism, but it had an undoubted effect in relating Sioux individuals through the Native American Church to groups in Oklahoma and throughout the country (DeMallie and Parks 1987:8–9).

The Peyote ritual has not changed fundamentally over the years. Each weekend, both tribal and intertribal meetings were held on reservations, in homes and backyards, and in open-air settings close to urban areas across the Plains.

Vestiges of most of the other movements survived throughout the 1990s. Dream Dance, Grass Dance, and Ghost Dance songs were sung in many settings across the Plains. There were vestiges of the Ghost Dance among the Sioux in Canada (J.H. Howard 1984), and the Sioux in the United States made occasional attempts to revive the dance portion of the Ghost Dance, such as that in conjunction with the 1973 American Indian Movement takeover of the village of Wounded Knee (DeMallie and Parks 1987:8).

Celebrations and Giveaways

GLORIA A. YOUNG AND ERIK D. GOODING

Nineteenth- and twentieth-century Native American life on the Plains was replete with celebrations, defined as "demonstrations of respect or rejoicing." World-renewal rites, bundle and curing rituals, age-grade and warrior ceremonials, seasonal hunting and planting observances, adoptions, giveaways, society ceremonies, and social dances filled the calendar. Celebrations changed over time. Some ceremonies, like the Teton Sioux girl's puberty rite and Throwing the Ball, became nearly extinct (Grobsmith 1981a); others, like the Quapaw Green Corn and Osage Scalp Dance, were deliberately put aside (G.A. Young 1972–1979). Warrior societies changed character as warfare ceased (Skinner 1915; J.H. Howard 1965; G.A. Young 1981; Kavanagh 1992). Elements of larger events were separated out to become the celebration themselves, like the Pawnee Hand Game from the Ghost Dance (Lesser 1933). Or elements from many events were amalgamated into one large celebration, like the powwow.

Gatherings to celebrate tribal and pantribal culture continued from prereservation times to the end of the twentieth century. After Commissioner of Indian Affairs John Collier (1934) stated that "no interference with Indian religious life or ceremonial expression will be tolerated," old ceremonials that had continued covertly in the face of United States government and missionary opposition were made public once more. Others were revived at an astonishing rate, sometimes being adapted for new uses (G.A. Young 1981; C. Ellis 1999). Some rituals, like the Cheyenne Sacred Arrow Renewal, remained tribal. Some, like men's societies and the Sun Dance, extended across many tribes, although each tribe adhered to its own style. Others, like the powwow, while spread across the Plains, were regional in character, conforming to Northern, Southern, and sometimes Central Plains (or Prairie) styles.

Although Plains celebrations ranged from the ritually sacred to the purely social, most fell somewhere in between. Adequate characterization of these events has proved problematic for those wishing to describe them in print, but the terms "honor" and "respect," as well as "spirit" and "power," have been used to define the type of sentiment attached to Plains Indian gatherings. Academics have also used the terms "identity" and "communitas" to suggest the emotional sentiment attached to even the most secular event. Key to the presence of this feeling was the use of music, in the form of Plains Indian songs, for all dances and hand games, and for many giveaways and other events.

Within a well-marked "ceremonial space" in which the event was held, songs charged the air with excitement or remembrance or devotion.

By the end of the twentieth century perhaps the most widespread public assembly was the powwow, an intertribal event of music, dance, and ceremonies. Powwows were held after World War II to honor returned servicemen. In urban areas, they brought together Native Americans of many tribes. The music, dances, and ceremonies of powwows grew out of early intertribal movements and men's societies. Native Americans of the 1950s and 1960s created a national powwow movement spanning regional boundaries, reminiscent of intertribal movements of the nineteenth century that had spread across the Plains (J.H. Howard 1955; G.A. Young 1981; Corrigan 1970).

The primary components of the powwow developed out of those historical ceremonial dances that were most widely shared among Indian groups—notably, the men's society dances, the Ghost Dance, gift-giving dances, and the Drum or Dream Dance (G.A. Young 1989; Kavanagh 1992; C. Ellis 1999). The styles of all these intertribal dances were greatly influenced by the tribal music, dances, customs, and religion of the participants. Part of the unique flavor of the powwow, however, came from the blending of Native American ceremonialism with a more raucous historical celebration: the commercial Indian dance.

Early Historical Gatherings

Early European chroniclers on the Plains reported large gatherings for ceremonials and celebrations as a regular feature of Native American culture (E. James 1823; Catlin 1841; Maximilian 1843; Battey 1875). A people recognized as a cultural group because of commonality of language, but who were usually dispersed in small bands, came together for large summer tribal gatherings, such as buffalo hunts and the Sun Dance.

People from very different groups often visited each other. One reason for intertribal visits in the 1600s and 1700s was to hold a ceremony called the Calumet by the French. This ceremony may have originated among the Pawnee and then was "communicated from village to village" (Perrot in E.H. Blair 1911–1912, 1:186; Fenton 1953:171). It was an adoption ceremony that included warriors' dances and might be used to form an alliance for war, such as that between the Ottawa and Santee Sioux after the

Sioux "sang the calumet" for a visiting Ottawa chief (Perrot in E.H. Blair 1911–1912, 1:182). Giftgiving was an important part of the Calumet ceremony.

Large numbers of people also met at European- (and later American-) sponsored events, such as councils or trading fairs. One council sponsored by the French was called by Étienne de Venyard, sieur de Bourgmont, in 1724. Their allies, the Kansa, Otoe, Iowa, Osage, Missouria, and Pawnee, were invited to make peace with the Padouca (Plains Apache). This council, held at the Kansa Grand Village on the Missouri River, included dancing. First, the allies danced; then, "After an entertainment prepared for them, the Padoucas sang the songs, and danced the dances of peace; a kind of pantomimes" (Le Page du Pratz 1975[1774]:67).

In 1819, the American expedition led by Stephen H. Long was treated to dancing by Otoe and Iowa warriors. The musical instruments used were a drum made of a large keg over one end of which a skin was stretched and "a stick of firm wood, notched like a saw, over the teeth of which a smaller stick was rubbed" (E. James in Thwaites 1904–1907, 14:230–231). An Iowa dancer wore "a handsome robe of white wolf skin, with an appendage behind him called a *crow* . . . a large cushion made of the skin of a crow . . . stuffed with any light material, and variously ornamented; it has two decorated sticks projecting from it upward, and a pendant one beneath; this apparatus is secured upon the buttocks by a girdle passing round the body" (E. James in Thwaites 1904–1907, 14:235).

During the 1860s and 1870s a men's society became widespread, known by names including Iruska, Hethuska, Inloshka, Grass Dance, Omaha Dance, and Ohoma Society. The characteristic paraphernalia of the society were a large drum and dance bustles. Men taking the society to another tribe would make headdresses, bustles, and a drum and take them on a visit to a receiving group. At first, in the receiving tribe, only men who had distinguished themselves in war and boys who were the sons of chiefs were taught the songs and dances and given the paraphernalia (Dorsey 1884:330). The hosts responded with gifts of horses and goods. The society passed to the Omaha, perhaps from the Pawnee, and then to the Teton Sioux in 1860, according to a Sioux winter count (J.H. Howard 1965:106). The Arikara received the society about 1864 when "Pawnee Tom visited the Arikara and assisted Enemy-heart to inaugurate the ceremony. Later, Enemy-heart sold the dance to the Crow Indians and then to other tribes" (Murie 1914:629). It quickly spread to the Assiniboine, Gros Ventre, Blackfoot, Sarcee, Plains Cree, and Flathead.

Later, three Skiri Pawnee men who visited the Oglala Sioux in South Dakota attended a society dance, called there an Omaha Dance, which was like their own Iruska. However, they noted that the Sioux songs were different from theirs and the Sioux wore "ornamental clothes," a different sort of feather bustle, and "sleigh bells upon their bodies." Returning home, the Pawnee men began to teach other young men the songs and organized a new dance society incorporating the Sioux elements (Murie 1914:624).

At gatherings and visits such as these, people from diverse groups learned or purchased new songs and dances from one another. Or they would pick up new elements to add to preexisting ceremonies or adapt old forms to newer styles (Blakeslee 1975; W.R. Wood 1980; G.A. Young 1981). The numerous interactions and exchanges among the people of the Plains brought about a commonality of style in widespread intertribal dances and ceremonies.

Celebrations on the Southern Plains

World-renewal rites, like the Sun Dance and the Quapaw Green Corn ceremony, were summer tribal ceremonials of the Southern Plains. During reservation times, the federal government assembled tribes for the disbursement of rations and annuities, and this assembly was an especially popular time for tribal dances and celebrations. Also, a regular pattern of visits between groups continued, such as the 1873 visit of the Pawnee to the Kiowa (Battey 1875) and the annual visits between the Pawnee and Wichita (M.R. Blaine 1982), which continued throughout the twentieth century. In Indian Territory, later Oklahoma, the close proximity of over 30 tribes and bands brought people together more often.

At the beginning of the twentieth century, large tribal and intertribal gatherings on the Southern Plains were often called homecomings, picnics, or celebrations. More specific events were called Ghost Dances (based on the 1890 Ghost Dance) and Gift Dances. Some Gift Dances were probably men's society dances, like the Kiowa Ohoma Society dances (M. Boyd 1981–1983, 1:65) at which gifts were given.

The first use of the term "powwow" to refer to Southern Plains Indian dances and gatherings may have been by the popular press. A 1902 Elk City, Oklahoma, newspaper article reported that "Cheyennes from the Hammond Agency held a big pow wow here last week." The Cheyenne and Arapaho agent (Whitewell 1902) discounted the report by writing to the commissioner of Indian affairs: "They went on request of the merchants and there was no pow wow about it. . . .They simply danced enough times in a circle to satisfy the populace that they had seen an Indian dance."

Powwow was originally a Southern New England Algonquian term for 'shaman' (R. Williams 1643:119). English speakers applied the word *powwowing* to Indian curative ceremonies and later to any Indian meeting that involved declamations. Despite the fact that the agent did not consider the Cheyenne dance a powwow, the description in the newspaper article was of an event later powwow-goers would recognize. Music was provided by "nine musicians, each having a small stick about two feet long with a rag wound around the end after the fashion of a swab. They sat in a circle around the big drum and sang and pounded that instrument. An old timer led the music and began his tune very faintly, gradually increasing in volume, the others joining in and [the women] helping out with the chorus. About twenty [men] were gaily dressed with feather and headgear and having strings of sleighbells around their ankles and about the knees" (Whitewell 1902).

By 1920, Indian agents, too, began regularly using powwow to refer to dances, as in an annual report for the Kansa: "The Indians of this tribe are taking less interest each year in the old Indian dances . . . Indian pow wows do not appeal very strongly to any of the younger people" (Pawnee Agency 1920:2). Commissioner of Indian Affairs Charles Henry Burke (1922a) used the single word "powwow" in his open letter to all agents: "unprogressive conditions among the Indians due chiefly to Fourth of July celebrations, dances, ceremonials and powwows for various purposes . . . involve a great waste of time and property."

The Haskell Celebration of 1926

The era of the modern powwow on the Southern Plains may have begun in 1926 at a large gathering (not called a powwow) at Haskell Indian School in Lawrence, Kansas, to dedicate the football stadium. Thousands of people from dozens of different tribes filled the stadium for the ceremony, which featured Secretary of the Interior Hubert Work, Indian Affairs Commissioner Burke, and Sen. Charles Curtis, a member of the Kansa tribe. A four-year-old Otoe boy, Sugar Brown, was the featured dancer of the ceremony. The climax was the Haskell-Bucknell football game. Many guests camped in the "Indian village," made more spectacular by the tepees of visiting Blackfeet. Several wealthy Osages and Quapaws served, through their gifts of money, as unofficial patrons of the event (*American Indian* 2:8–12).

Dancing formed a large part of the Haskell celebration. Daytime was devoted to tribal dances, and at night intertribal championship dancing contests were held (*American Indian* 2:8–12; G.A. Young 1972–1989).

Northeastern Oklahoma Powwows in the 1920s

Four annual events formed the basis for the post-World War II powwow in northeastern Oklahoma: the Ponca, Pawnee, and Quapaw powwows and the Osage tribal dances (Inloshka). Because Gus MacDonald (Ponca) had won the Haskell Fancy Dance contest, the Ponca were charged with sponsoring future Fancy Dance championship contests (Turley 1961:180). The championship dance contests became part of the Ponca powwow, which in 1928 was held on the Fourth of July and included the dedication of a dance hall. The Indian agent reported: "At night, about one and one-half hours was [sic] taken up in a program contesting Indian dancing. Prizes of $5.00 for first, $3.00 for second, and $1.00 for third were offered . . . a Ponca boy was awarded first place, a[n] Otoe boy second prize, and a Kaw [Kansa] boy third prize" (A.R. Snyder 1928).

Gus MacDonald has been credited with the introduction of the Fancy Dance outfit, featuring brightly colored feather bustles. He may have introduced the bright regalia as a joke when he filled the role of clown (G.A. Young 1972–1989), but the style caught on quickly. An eighteen-year-old Creek Fancy Dancer was reported to have spent one year and 500 dollars making his dance outfit (*American Indian* 3[2]:13) .

Besides the Ponca powwow, the Pawnee and Quapaw powwows and the Osage tribal dances were large annual events attended in the 1920s by people from many tribes. At the June Quapaw powwow, a continuation of the earlier tribal annuity distribution and picnic, visitors were provided food and everything they needed except bedding and cutlery by the zinc-mining rich Quapaw (*American Indian* 1[9]:13). The Osage, wealthy once again after a prolonged period of privation after the Civil War, were able to offer monetary incentives for members of many tribes to attend their annual Inlonshka, such as payment to Kansa and Ponca singers and the purchase of beadwork and other finery from Cheyenne craftspeople (G.A. Young 1981).

The 1928 Pawnee powwow, sponsored by the Pawnee Indian Junior Council, was attended by around 3,000 people and, like other powwows of its day, featured afternoon dances, a terrapin derby, and a baseball game. At night there were said to be Fancy Dances, women's dances, Gourd Dances, and "stomp dances by Eastern Indians" (*American Indian* 2[1]:13).

Western Oklahoma Indian Fairs

The term "powwow" was not used in the 1920s in western Oklahoma for dance events. There, the government sought to replace Gift Dances and Ghost Dances with "picnics" and "fairs." The forerunner of the American Indian Exposition at Anadarko, Oklahoma, was called a fair and by 1923 was a commercial attraction held at a resort, Medicine Park. Dancing formed a large part of the event. In 1927, cash premiums were awarded to winners of horse races, bow and arrow contests, the wheel game, kickball (probably Indian football), and women's shinny. By 1929, the booklet for the fair announced that "Special contest war dances and ghost dances will be given each night in front of the grandstand." That year the Oklahoma State Legislature appropriated 1,000 dollars for cash premiums for the fair at Craterville Park (fig. 1) (Rush Fair 1927, 1929), perhaps in order to compete favorably with New Mexico's two new fairs, the Gallup Ceremonial and the Southwest Indian Fair at Santa Fe.

Another popular tribal fair during the 1920s was that of the Cheyenne and Arapaho at Watonga, Oklahoma. By 1929, the Cheyenne and Arapaho Fair included an "Indian maiden contest." Four years earlier, the Pendleton, Oregon, Roundup had featured an Indian princess or queen, Esther Lee Montanic (Cayuse), and the Tulsa, Oklahoma, periodical, *American Indian* (1[1]:11), had encouraged nominations from "Oklahoma's forty tribes." Also in 1926, the International Petroleum Congress and Exposition in Tulsa had featured a princess representing the Osage tribe. This *1013*

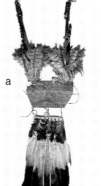

a

b

c

YOUNG AND GOODING

top left, Philbrook Mus. of Art, Okla.: 1967.16.21; top right, Ft. Sill Mus., Ft. Sill, Okla.:60.11.90; center left, Smithsonian, NAA: 3567-b; center center, Smithsonian, NAA: James Howard Papers; bottom left, Kansas State Histl. Soc., Topeka: 57.154; bottom right, Milwaukee Public Mus. 64083.

Fig. 1. Men's Dance. top left, *Modern Dancer*, an early Fancy Dance outfit. Watercolor on paper by Allan Bushyhead, Southern Cheyenne, 1937. top right, Southern Cheyenne young men ready for performance at Craterville Park, Okla. They wear early Fancy Dance outfits including beaded breechcloths, bells on their ankles and legs, and 1920s-style feather headpieces. The man on the far left has decorated a leather biker's cap with a roach, feather, and sequins. His breechcloth is decorated with the Cheyenne Morning Star design (Gordon Yellow Man, communication to editors 2000). The other men have feather rosettes on foreheads and feather bustles on arms. Photograph probably by Horace Poolaw, 1928. center left, Long Foot, Yankton, wearing a Grass Dance bustle and beaded leggings. He holds a painted buffalo robe and a pipe tomahawk. He was a member of the Yankton delegation that visited Washington along with Santee and Teton. Photograph by Alexander Gardner, Washington, D.C., Feb. 1867. center center, Joseph Greatwalker, Plains Ojibwa, champion Grass Dancer. His shirt, breechcloth, and leggings are decorated with fringes, sequins, and beads. He wears beaded arm bands and tie as well as a headband with roach and plumes. Photograph by James Howard, Turtle Mountain Res., N. Dak., 1959. center right, Don Rush, Jr., Three Affiliated Tribes, in a traditional outfit with eagle-feather bustle, beaded and fringed yoke, beaded arm bands, and dance apron. He wears a number for the dance competition. Photograph by Ilka Hartmann, Little Shell Celebration, North Dakota Powwow, Ft. Berthold, N. Dak., 1989. bottom left, Wooden dance mirror in the form of a horse head. Mirrors were carried in dances by young men to attract women's attention. Collected among the Kansa in Okla. in the 1920s. Length 28.5 cm. bottom right, Grass Dance bustle, or "crow belt," about 1900–1925. This is part of a complete Grass Dance outfit that belonged to and was probably made by Fire Cloud, a dancer and craftsman on the Lower Brule Res., S. Dak. It combines eagle, owl, and hawk feathers with dyed plumage from domestic chickens, geese, and turkeys. The foundation of the bustle (a) consists of 2 spikes and an eagle feather "tail," the basic elements of 19th-century bustles. A rosette (b) and feathered cloth trailers (c) complete this early 20th-century example. Collected by Albert Williamson from Mrs. Fire Cloud about 1925 (J.H. Howard 1972b). Length about 160 cm.

may have been the beginning of the selection of Oklahoma tribal and powwow princesses (G.A. Young 1981).

Regionalism in the 1930s and 1940s

Oklahoma powwows continued throughout the 1930s. Commissioner of Indian Affairs John Collier's Circular 2970, which removed from official policy any governmental interference with Indian religious life and declared Indian cultural liberty "in all respects to be considered equal to that of any non-Indian group" (Collier 1934), left the way open for the spread of the Oklahoma-style powwow to any Indian group.

Such expansion did not occur until after World War II. In the United States in the 1930s, regional culture and pride remained strong. The Northern and Southern Plains were two distinct stylistic areas. This was reflected in the music, dress and regalia, giveaway and dance styles of Indian gatherings.

On the Southern Plains during the 1930s, hard economic times forced the closure of journals such as the *American Indian*, which had brought news to the Southern Plains about events among the Northern tribes. However, intertribal interaction between the two regions during the 1930s was strengthened through travels to exhibitions such as the National Folk Festival in Washington, D.C., the Anadarko Fair, and the Gallup Ceremonial.

World War II provided the opportunity for singers and dancers from 50 Plains, Southwest, and Oklahoma tribes to continue, in the military, the camaraderie begun at dances such as the Anadarko Fair. In the Army's famous all-Indian 45th Division, soldiers from the Arapaho, Cheyenne, Pawnee, Ponca, Otoe, Sioux, Kiowa, Quapaw, and other tribes were said to have used "home-made drums—some of them fashioned from oilcans or beer kegs—and the feathers they carried with them from the West" to accompany, "outside the barracks . . . their traditional songs" and danced "the dances of their fathers" (*Indians at Work* 1942:17). Pyle (1945:12–13) described "ceremonies" held in the South

Pacific by Sioux, Comanche, Apache, Kiowa, and Crow servicemen in the First Marine Division. Even more important was the fact that military service in time of war provided an impetus for the recognition of veterans after the war in a florescence of nationwide ceremonies, many of them held at powwows (D.B. Lee 1995:57; C. Ellis 1999:147–151).

Pan-Indian Movement

When World War II was over, many veterans and their families moved to urban areas, where they missed the support of their families. The situation in Tulsa, Oklahoma, was typical: "In the 1940s, there weren't many Indian families in Tulsa and there was a great need to identify. . . they were absorbed in this urban setting, even in the 1940s, so they got together to begin something" (G.A. Young 1981). Some families began to hold dances in their own back yards. The Tulsa Indian population included accomplished singers and dancers, who began to sponsor dances at an amusement park where the owner provided rations for the participants. This coalesced, in 1952, into the Tulsa Indian Club. The club secured the city park, Mohawk Park, as a powwow site, arranged for generators to be donated by businesses for light, began a publicity campaign to draw an audience, and won an appropriation from the state legislature (G.A. Young 1981). The Tulsa powwow was held annually in Mohawk Park throughout the twentieth century.

Similar stories were told from other cities in the South and Southwest where Native American veterans, especially those from the Southern Plains, resided from the 1950s through the 1970s (Ablon 1964; Hirabayashi, Willard, and Kemnitzer 1972; Krutz 1973; Margolies 1973; J.A. Price 1975). It was the Southern Plains style of dance that became the show dance at most of these public events. Part entertainment for the public, part serious memorials to veterans and those who lost their lives in war, the powwows were sponsored in Los Angeles and Kansas City by urban Indian clubs, by schools and colleges, by veterans' organizations *1015* like the VFW and American Legion, and, in some cases, by individual families. These were intertribal events, in cities where many tribes were represented by too few members to hold tribal ceremonials. In powwows, people of many tribes could participate as "Indian" and yet feel some of the aura of their own unique tribal heritages.

Two factors probably contributed most to the rapid expansion of powwows in the 1950s and 1960s. One was the relocation of many families to urban areas, augmented by the federal government's policy of relocation, which fostered a Native American exodus from reservations and rural areas to Los Angeles, Denver, Dallas, and other cities (Ablon 1964; S. Stanley and R.K. Thomas 1968; Tax 1978).

The other factor was the movement named by anthropologists "pan-Indianism" (J.H. Howard 1955; Newcomb 1955; R.K. Thomas 1968; Sanford 1971; Hirabayashi, Willard, and Kemnitzer 1972). The movement sought to forge a national (and then hemispheric) identity as "Native American" or "Indian." This pan-tribal identity existed alongside various regional identities. Pan-Indianism paralleled the post-World War II movements toward establishing national identities for other segments of the population of the United States such as Blacks, Hispanics, and women. These movements grew in part out of the United States government's call to national unity in the face of war in the 1940s. After the war, regional cultures began to blend more cohesively into national cultures by social class and ethnic group, whose leaders operationalized the call to national unity that they had heard as children during the war years of the 1940s into the social movements of the 1960s and 1970s. Pan-Indianism was one of these social movements.

Powwows

From the 1950s through the 1970s, powwows based on a format of Southern Plains styles, held in urban areas as well as in the traditional tribal arenas, included most of the characteristics of earlier fairs, homecomings, and powwows: a campground, rations for dancers, Indian arts and crafts displays and sales, Indian food sales, and, sometimes, rodeos, baseball games, and other events. The focal point of the powwow was an evening program of dancing (fig. 2).

In a circular arena flanked by some sort of seating for an audience, a large drum, the "Southern drum," was set up in the center. The singers, always men, formed a circle closely around the drum, each man beating it with a single stick as they sang. Women sat in a circle behind the men facing the drum and sang a women's part. Most evening powwows began with a grand entry of all persons attired in dance dress and then a Round Dance led by the Head Lady Dancer, although a few merely began with the women dancing the opening Round Dance. The opening was followed by intertribal dancing, dance competitions, exhibition ceremonial or tribal dances, special dances honoring individuals (which usually included giveaways), and, sometimes, a powwow

princess pageant. One or more master of ceremonies directed the flow of events from a speaker's stand. Actions and etiquette within the arena were controlled by arena directors. A head staff had been chosen to lead the dances. One or two Head Man dancers and Head Lady dancers were mandatory. Sometimes Head Little Boy and Head Little Girl dancers were added (G.A. Young 1981).

Powwow dancing has been called "solo dancing en masse" (J.H. Howard 1955:216) because each person danced his or her own interpretation of a basic style. Many dances were open to all dancers, some to the audience as well. Over the years the term for open dances changed from War Dances to Intertribals at some powwows, although warriors' songs continued to provide the music for these dances.

Powwows almost always included dance contests categorized by gender, dress, music, and dance style. Men's Straight and Fancy Dance, Boys' Straight and Fancy Dance, Women's Cloth Dress and Buckskin Dress, Girls' Cloth Dress and Buckskin Dress, and often boys' and/or girls' Tiny Tot categories were the staple contests through the 1970s. Four categories of dress categorized the Southern powwow: two for women (cloth or buckskin dresses) and two for men (Fancy Dance or Straight Dance outfits). Women's cloth dresses followed tribal styles. Dresses of Plains and Prairie tribes were usually two piece, some embroidered or appliquéd, some decorated with cowrie shells, worn with leggings and moccasins. All women in cloth dresses wore or carried a fringed shawl. The two-piece buckskin dresses were fringed on the skirt, sleeves, and bodice, and decorated with beadwork or shells. Tribal and powwow princesses wore a princess crown, most with an eagle feather erect at the back.

Despite the difference in dress, all women and girls danced in the same style through the 1970s: a slow, graceful step forward and a flexing of the knee as the back foot was brought forward, the torso always held erect. For the Round Dance, the step was to the side with the other foot brought adjacent to the stepping foot as the stepping knee was flexed (G.A. Young 1981).

The men's and boy's Fancy and Straight dance styles both were derived from dances of the nineteenth-century warrior societies. The basic movement consisted of two steps with each foot, using a "toe-flat" or "flat-flat" step (J.H. Howard and G. Kurath 1959) at the same tempo as the drum beat. One step was often taken in place, the other causing forward movement. Fancy dancers transformed the basic two-step into a whirling, leaping, acrobatic genre: the dancer twisting or turning, crouching or standing upright, shaking the feathers in the porcupine- and deer-hair roach worn on his head. The Fancy Dance outfit of the 1970s consisted of at least an apron, feather bustles attached to the upper and lower back (and sometimes the upper arms), garters of goat skin with the hair attached worn below the dancer's knee, and a roach, with one or more feathers, worn on the head. Additions to the outfit might include gauntlets, a breastplate, a choker around the

1016

Fig. 2. Powwows. top left, Setting up camp at the powwow grounds. Containers include food boxes and parfleches. top right, Couples doing a two-step dance. Man leading is Neil Benaley, Omaha. Maxine and Rufus White, Omaha, are also participants. top, Photographs by Ilka Hartman, Omaha powwow, Macy, Nebr., 1989. center left, Allan Morin, Plains Cree from Hobbema, Alta., getting a touch-up before the Enoch Cree Nation powwow. Photograph by Rob McKinley, outside Edmonton, Alta., 1998. center center, Man's dance breastplate made of rawhide slats wrapped with dyed porcupine quills and trimmed with dyed chicken plumes. It was made by Sophie New Holy, Oglala Sioux, Pine Ridge Res., S. Dak., 1978. Length 63 cm. center right, Young dancers being instructed by Howard Wolfe, Omaha. Photograph by Ilka Hartman, Omaha powwow, Macy, Nebr., 1989. bottom left, Tai Piah singers at Omaha powwow, Macy, Nebr. left to right: Clyde Ago Sheridan III, Lawrence Gilpin, unidentified boy, Andrew Thundercloud, Marline Mitchell, Frank Cayou, Jr., and Dewey Sheridan. Photograph by Carl Fleischhauser, 1983. bottom right, Cigarettes given to spectators. It was believed that the smoke provided transport for prayers. Photograph by Michael Crummett, Crow Fair, Mont., 1979.

1017

CELEBRATIONS AND GIVEAWAYS

neck, sleigh or jingle bells at the knee, and various belts or sashes. Footwear was moccasins or sport shoes. From the 1950s until the 1980s, dancers wearing either the brightly colored Oklahoma-style bustles made of dyed feathers or the more traditional feather bustles (fig. 1) of the 1920s and 1930s made of natural feathers of eagles, hawks, or other birds competed in the Fancy Dance category (G.A. Young 1981).

In the mid-1980s, male dancers wearing the "traditional" undyed natural colored feathers (most often dancers from the Kiowa, Cheyenne, Comanche, Arapaho or other western Oklahoma tribes) began to enter the Straight Dance contests. Until then, the Straight Dance had almost invariably reflected the dress of the Prairie tribes (Ponca, Osage, Pawnee, Omaha, Kansa, Quapaw, Iowa, Otoe, and Missouria) and was always danced to songs honoring warriors of the Prairie tribes. This traditional attire of the Prairie tribes consisted of a cloth shirt and leggings decorated with beadwork or appliqué overlaid by a wide belt, crossed beaded bandoliers, ornaments, and jewelry. Rather than a feather bustle, a beaver or otter fur trailer hung down the back from the dancer's neck to the ground. A roach, with a single eagle feather attached, was worn on the head. The Straight Dance style of weaving, gliding body movements simulated a hunter stalking prey or, sometimes, a strutting turkey (G.A. Young 1981).

Although Native American veterans led the way toward establishing a national Indian identity, the pan-Indian movement of the 1950s through the 1970s did not establish political or cultural unity. Instead, some national ideals and styles emerged and continued into the 1990s, but, on the whole, the national character of "Indianism" remained fluid, encompassing many regional and local variations. This can be seen clearly in the Southern Plains powwows of the 1990s. Throughout the 1980s, several components from the Northern Plains were added to the Southern powwow. Northern Plains music, higher in pitch and faster in tempo, gained a place. The central Southern drum began to alternate songs with one or more Northern drums placed at the periphery of the arena. On occasion, the singers around the Northern drums would even sing songs of the Southern tribes in the strident, falsetto style of the Northern Plains (G.A. Young 1972–1989).

Four dance styles that incorporated faster, more expansive dance movements to the accompaniment of the Northern Plains songs were added to the southern Plains powwow. A men's Northern Traditional dress style incorporated bustles and headgear of the natural-colored feathers of eagles, hawks, crows, turkeys, owls, and pheasants. The dance style was a dignified yet energetic version of the Fancy Dance pattern. Another new style was called the Grass Dance style (but should not be confused with the nineteenth-century warrior society called the Grass or Omaha Dance). Wearing outfits decorated with brightly colored long yarn or ribbon fringes rather than feather bustles, Grass dancers kicked their feet higher and farther out to the sides, rolling their bodies in such a way as to swing their fringes in time to the music.

Two women's categories were added to the contests. They both incorporated rapid footwork, leaps and twirls, more like the earlier men's dances than like the Southern Plains women's dance. One was called the Women's Shawl Dance in the south and the Women's Fancy Dance in the north. The other was the Jingle Dance or Jingle Dress Dance. Shawl dancers in cloth dresses wore their fringed women's shawl rather than carrying it over the arm. Holding their elbows away from the body made the fringe "dance" to the music. Jingle Dress dancers wore cloth dresses on which were sewn conical metal jingles. When the style was first introduced, most dresses were adorned with 365 jingles, one for each day of the year. By the 1990s, some dresses had as many as 500 jingles sewn onto them. The jingles created the same type of accompaniment to the music as did the sleigh bells of the men's Fancy Dance (Kavanagh 1992).

After the florescence of change brought about by the addition of the 1980s Northern Plains music and the new dances, events built on this new basic powwow could be found virtually every weekend somewhere on the Southern Plains. The reasons for holding powwows were myriad—annual tribal celebrations; annual events sponsored by family descendent groups, service organizations, urban powwow clubs, churches, or student associations of universities and other schools; private powwows to honor individuals at birthdays, graduation, retirement, return from military service, or the award of some distinction; money-raising affairs; Veterans' Day, New Year, and Fourth of July celebrations; or powwows just for fun sponsored by a drum group.

The Gourd Dance

The Gourd Dance, an event specifically honoring veterans, became widespread in the late twentieth century, both as an afternoon or evening adjunct to the powwow and as an event in its own right. The source of the Gourd Dance was the Kiowa Taimpego (*táypègɔ*) warrior society's Rattle Dance (J.H. Howard 1976a; Kracht 1994a; Lassiter 1997). During the early twentieth century, the Taimpego Society had met only sporadically, but did not die out. A "Gourd Dance of the Tia-pe-ga Society" was one of the demonstration dances performed in the 1930s at the National Folk Festival in Washington, D.C. (Anadarko Agency 1938).

In 1957, a group of men formally revived the dance by founding a new organization, the Kiowa Gourd Clan, to carry on the dance (Levy 1959a). During the 1960s and 1970s, more Gourd Clan societies were formed, both among the Kiowa and in other tribes, principally in Oklahoma. By the end of the twentieth century it was possible to attend a Gourd Dance every weekend in southwestern Oklahoma.

As at other Southern warrior society dances, a drum, surrounded by male singers (who beat the drum with long handled sticks), was set up in the center of a circular dance space. Men, at first only veterans, faced the drum as they danced. As with other dances deriving from warrior societies, there were actually two types of Gourd dances. One type comprised the more ceremonial dances held to honor specific Gourd Clan organizations: for example, the Fourth of July or Labor Day dances of several Kiowa Gourd Clans. These paralleled similar events held by societies like the Ponca Hethushka societies. Attire was more reminiscent of historical Indian dress, and specific songs were sung because of their historical significance. Participants were mostly members of the society.

The other type of Gourd Dance was a more public event, held as part of a powwow or as a weekend dance with a somewhat more social objective. Attire consisted of street clothes (jeans or slacks) with boots, athletic shoes, or moccasins as footwear. Sometimes a ribbon shirt was worn and, if outdoors, a Western hat or baseball cap, perhaps decorated with a feather or beadwork. Paraphernalia for the dance included several articles of special attire—bandoliers of German silver beads or mescal beans with a small silk scarf containing medicine tied over the left scapula, a cloth fringed sash, and, sometimes, a half red-half blue blanket draped over one or both shoulders and decorated with the veteran's service ribbons. Each dancer held a rattle in his right hand and a feather fan in his left. The rattle was made of a gourd or a large metal salt shaker (also known as a sugar shaker), or was a German silver replica of either, usually having decorations attached and a beaded handle. These types of rattles and fans were also paraphernalia of the Native American Church, and often other Peyote symbols such as water birds were also incorporated into Gourd Dance outfits.

The dances incorporated two movements. Men began by dancing in place, shaking their rattles to the beat of the drum. At certain breaks in the song, they moved forward and clockwise around the circle for a few steps. Their forward progress necessitated moving back several steps if they wished to begin the next dance at their original starting place, but, overall, there was very little dance movement in contrast to other Plains dances. The step in place was a restrained version of the Plains double step. Dancers stood lightly on the ground or floor, knees slightly bent with weight forward, in a stance suggesting that they could spring forward at any moment. Instead, they flexed their knees with the weight on their toes synchronously with the beat of drum and rattle, transferring the weight to their heels as they straightened their knees. The moment the knees were straight, they crouched again to be ready for the next flexing of the knees. This quick movement created a small "jump" upward between each beat, adding vitality to the dance. When moving forward with a double step much like that of the Straight Dance, they crouched slightly. One dance consisted of a song sung four times, tension building throughout, rising in a crescendo to the final beat. As dancers relaxed after each dance, the tension with which they had danced, imbuing the Gourd Dance with an excitement belied by the lack of expansive movements, became apparent.

The heart of a Gourd dance was the songs that were sung. The innumerable Gourd Dance songs commemorated events and families, communicated to participants and audience on several different levels of meaning, and evoked an appreciation of the inherent power of song which is central to the Native Americans' own theory of music. In whatever context they were held, Gourd Dances created a feeling of community (Lassiter 1997; Kracht 1994, 1994a).

Celebrations on the Northern Plains

The Northern Plains powwow, like its Southern counterpart, developed from the historic dances of the various tribal groups. Some of these dances were widespread on the Northern Plains: warrior society dances, dream societies, religious dances like the Ghost Dance, and social dances such as the Owl Dance. The dance forms, traditions, regalia, and music of these dances were the foundation of the contemporary powwow.

Northern Plains dance forms were varied in style. Some incorporated dance movement through space; some consisted of dancing in place. Styles varied by gender. Two dance forms for males were based on movement through space. One of these was a pantomime form in which dancers re-enacted war deeds or the stalking of prey. The other, a form often referred to as "Chief's style," was similar to the modern Southern Plains Straight Dance style. Other dance styles for men were danced without forward movement, incorporating steps similar to the modern Gourd Dance. Many of these were the dances of men's societies held within special ceremonial lodges such as those made by the Teton Sioux, created by combining two or more tepees, which limited the amount of space for dancing. Among the Plains Cree two types of structures were used for ceremonial dances, the *sa·pohtawa·n*, a lodge some 25 feet long with a ridgepole supported by a tripod of poles at either end and forked poles in the center, and covered with brush and tepee covers; and the *wi·watahoka·n*, a double-sized tepee requiring two teepee covers (Mandelbaum 1979:90).

Dance styles for females also varied by movement. Women participated in dances such as the Sun Dance by executing a simple in-place bobbing step on the outside edges of the dance areas (M.N. Powers 1988). In other dances, such as Victory Dances, women moved around the dance area in a stylized walk based on the basic double step (Black Bear, Sr. and Theisz 1976).

Historical Dances

During the early reservation era the content and form of Northern Plains dances changed. Many government officials in both the United States and Canada believed that the practice of traditional culture, including dance, deterred the transition to a Euro-American way of life. As a result, controls, restrictions, and prohibitions were placed on traditional dances (Prucha 1975:160, 187). Nevertheless, dancing *1019* continued on and off the reservations and reserves on the Northern Plains.

Dances that had militaristic overtones, either through regalia, movement, or meaning, drew quick attention from Indian agents. These dance types were typical of the men's societies found among all Northern Plains groups. Some forms that were either semireligious or semimilitaristic or combinations of the two were modified into secular social forms. For the Teton Sioux this occurred with the Omaha Dance, an amalgamation of several forms that were semireligious and militaristic in nature. Once established as a new "social" form, the Omaha Dance became a repository of elements from other organizations and dances. Men's society songs were incorporated into the corpus of songs used in the Omaha Dance. In addition to songs, regalia, dance movements, and traditions from other forms were also incorporated.

In the context of life on reservations and reserves social dances, both new and old, replaced war-related dances as the main type of Northern Plains dance. Two of the more popular were the Round Dance (known variously as the Circle Dance, Crow Dance, or Dragging-Feet Dance) and the Rabbit or Owl Dance (fig. 3). These dances allowed the

Fig. 3. Rabbit Dance. Although usually danced by men and women together, these elderly ladies, wearing fringed dance shawls, lead the line of couples at the home of Red Cloud, Oglala Sioux. front pair: Jessie Running Horse and Laura Horn Cloud; second pair: Liz Iron Heart and unidentified individual. Photograph by John Vachon, Pine Ridge Res., S. Dak., 1941.

participation of both men and women and could be performed with no special regalia. Dances were held on special occasions such as national holidays or ration-distribution days. In some tribes, such as the Sioux of Devils Lake and Standing Rock reservations, clubs or societies similar to service organizations began hosting weekly or monthly get-togethers where members danced and feasted. The names of groups were from traditional organizations, such as the Omaha Club, or from new sources, such as the Star Club. The main social dances, the Round Dance and Rabbit Dance, varied in their dance steps. Round Dances were based on a side-step. Rabbit Dances were male-female partner dances with steps varying from group to group. Women continued to play supporting roles in men's performances, as well as participating in the popular social dances.

With involvement in World War I came a resurgence of the warrior ethos among Northern Plains peoples. Dances were held, often with the permission of government officials, to send soldiers off to duty, to raise money for the war effort, and to welcome veterans returning home. The last decades of the 1800s and the first decade of the 1900s saw the emergence of Indian cultural exhibitions sponsored by non-Indians. These fairs, exhibitions, stampedes, or powwows, were held off the reserves and reservations, often in nearby non-Indian communities, in conjunction with other activities or as separate events. Events in Canada were the Winnipeg Stampede, Calgary Stampede, Regina Fair, and Banff Indian Days; similar events took place in the United States (fig. 4).

In the late 1800s, another form of cultural exhibition appeared, the Wild West Show. The Chief's Dance and men's pantomime dances, while giving way to social dances on the reservations and reserves, thrived in the touring shows, where dancers were often encouraged to "fancy up" their dancing. These "fancy" modifications inevitably found their way back to the reservations and reserves.

Between the World Wars, many of the controls, restrictions, and prohibitions on traditional dances were lifted. A reinvigoration of the warrior ethos with the onset of World War II led to a resurgence of Northern Plains dancing.

Powwows

As soldiers returned from World War II, they were greeted with victory dances, homecomings, and celebrations. The popularity of these early powwows grew, and they became major aspects of local fairs and holidays. Occasionally, singing and dancing clubs, such as the Many Trails Club in Los Angeles, were organized in the cities to sponsor events for both Southern and Northern Plains peoples.

The northern and southern powwows began influencing and contributing to each other. On the Northern Plains, several of the male dance styles of the late twentieth century began to standardize into the Traditional Dance

Smithsonian, NAA: top left, 89-11672, top right, 89-11671; bottom right, Natl. Cowboy Hall of Fame, Okla. City: insert, Milwaukee Public Mus. Wis.: 222 (neg. A-677-H).

Fig. 4. Activities at Indian Days. top left, Kiowa Indians of Okla. float during parade at the All-American Indian Days in Sheridan, Wyo., an event held annually 1953–1984. top right, Boy wearing beaded headband, moccasins, and cloth breechcloth and holding a salt shaker can rattle and girl wearing a Kiowa-style buckskin dress. Photographs probably by Ziemer Studio, 1954. bottom left, Tyrone Whitegrass, Blackfeet Traditional Dancer at the North American Indian Days, Browning, Mont. Photograph by Joe Fisher, Blackfeet Res., 1994. bottom right, Assiniboine and Sioux dancing at the Wolf Point Stampede. Photograph by Ralph Russell Doubleday, Ft. Peck Res., Mont., about 1935. inset, Sioux rattle with shaker made from a metal can, probably a baking powder container, covered with beadwork and mounted on a handle with horsehair and ribbon. Collected before 1900 by H.W. Shaw on the Rosebud Res., S. Dak., and reported to have been used in the Omaha Dance. Length of stick 45 cm.

and the Grass Dance (fig. 1) (J.H. Howard 1960b; Hatton 1986). As these two dance styles spread from the Northern Plains to the Southern Plains, along with the higher-pitched Northern style of singing, the Southern Plains men's Fancy Dance style headed north (T. Stewart and J. Smith 1973).

By the 1960s, the dance possibilities for women had increased throughout the Plains. In addition to the older forms of dance consisting of dancing in place or with little movement, which came to be called Women's Traditional, new forms began to emerge: Women's Fancy Dance (from the Southern Plains and other sources) and Jingle Dance (from the Ojibwa of the eastern Plains) (fig. 5). These women's dances became accepted forms throughout the Plains.

By the end of the twentieth century, the Northern Plains powwow existed in a variety of forms. Some were called celebrations or fairs and some were known by indigenous terms, such as the Sioux and Assiniboine *wačhípi*. They 1021

Red Cloud Ind. School Heritage Center, Pine Ridge, S. Dak.: top left, 708, top right, 704.

Fig. 5. Women's modern dance outfits. top left, Jingle dress made by Caroline Titus, Oglala Sioux, in 1987. Machine sewn of cotton cloth with appliqué, commercial braid trim, and a fringe of hand-made metal cones that jingle with movement. Length 117 cm. top center, Entry procession with women wearing Jingle dresses. Dancers include: Barbara Smith and Stacy Fox, Three Affiliated Tribes; Virginia Spotted Bird, Ft. Peck Sioux; Sandra Ironroad and Tracy Ironroad, Standing Rock Sioux. Photographs by Ilka Hartmann, Ft. Berthold, N. Dak. Powwow, 1989. top right, "Princess set" of matching beaded dance accessories, consisting of a headband, leggings, and moccasins. Made by Caroline Titus, Oglala Sioux, for a Powwow princess at Pine Ridge Res., S. Dak., in 1978. Length of headband 43 cm, leggings and moccasins to scale. bottom left, Thomasine Moore, Osage, dressed in buckskin-fringed dress used in Traditional Dance at the Sandy Creek Powwow, Athens, Ga. bottom center, Fancy Shawl dancers, Red Earth powwow, Oklahoma City, Okla. bottom right, Elizabeth Olney, Plains Cree, Chippewa, and Yakima descent, holding a fringed shawl and fan used by women in modern dancing at competition for Miss National Congress of the American Indian, Albuquerque, N. Mex. She wears moccasin leggings with beaded floral design and beaded hair ties on her braids. She was Miss Plains Indian in 1988 and Miss Indian Montana in 1989. bottom, Photographs by Lynn Ivory, left, 1989, center, 1994; right, 1990.

were held in small community centers or in large outdoor dance arbors, or in basketball arenas or football stadiums (Corrigan 1970; Grobsmith 1981b; W.K. Powers 1980, 1990). Powwows ranged in size from several dozen participants to several thousand. Some were held for socialization and enjoyment to commemorate holidays and special occasions. Others were contest-based with thousands of dollars offered in prize money. The larger powwows were intertribal and offered combinations of Northern and Southern Plains traditions.

Dance categories were characterized by dance style, gender, and age. For contest purposes, participants were divided into age-based groups: tiny tots, teens, juniors, adult, and golden age. For the men of the Northern Plains, there were three main dance styles: Fancy, Grass, and Traditional.

The Grass and Traditional styles were remnants of the prereservation dance forms, while the Fancy style was an innovation from the Southern Plains. Each of these styles had its own footwork and body movements, from the movements of warriors and hunters of the Traditional dancers to the graceful full-body flowing dance style of the Grass dancer, to the athletic, spinning, intricate footwork of the Fancy dancer.

The women also had three dance styles: Traditional, Jingle, and Fancy. The Traditional and Jingle styles had connections to prereservation and reserve forms while the Fancy Dance had more modern roots. The women's Traditional style retained the stylized walk and the bobbing in place movements of its historical antecedents. The women's Jingle Dance style was characterized by the unique "slide step." This dance step began with the feet side-by-side, slightly separated. The movement was accomplished by the shifting of weight from the balls of the feet to the toes, while sliding both feet along (J. Johnston and M. Johnston 1991). Women's Fancy Dance style, like its male counterpart, was energetic and athletic, marked by spinning and intricate footwork.

Other kinds of dance contests were held at some powwows. Team competitions were danced by groups of similar style dancers in unison against other similar style groups—usually in groups of four. In Switch Dances, dancers dressed and danced in the style of the opposite gender: men dancing a Jingle Dance or women dancing a Grass Dance.

Singing competitions were also held. These might be at the "traditional" large skin-headed drum or bass drum or they might be accompanied by small hand drums.

Many Northern Plains peoples participated in powwows in capacities other than dancing and singing. They served as masters of ceremonies, arena directors, host drums, head dancers, and judges for dancing and singing contests. Or they participated as craftspeople and vendors.

Activities other than dances were held in conjunction with Northern Plains powwows. These included golf and softball tournaments, rodeos, running events, art shows, hand games (recreational and competitive) (fig. 6), as well as feasts, parades, and giveaways.

Giveaways

The late-twentieth-century giveaway on the Plains had its roots in indigenous social and religious rituals based on the public redistribution of goods. The role of the giveaway in Plains life, like so many other forms of traditional culture, changed to meet the needs of the people. Giveaways might be used as the public announcement and validation of a new status within an Indian group (A.B. Kehoe 1980), a social institution often referred to as "Indian insurance" (Grobsmith 1981a), or a forum to display one's love for a child or relative (K.M. Weist 1973).

Giveaways were held for a variety of reasons: birth; death or memorial; a child's first participation in a powwow; graduation; marriage (fig. 7); retirement; leaving for or returning from military service; and in recognition of an honor, award, or public service (A.B. Kehoe 1980; Grobsmith 1981a). They were held as separate events or in conjunction with other events such as powwows, naming ceremonies, funerals, graduation ceremonies, Sun Dances, and other religious or public rituals.

Southern Plains

Most Southern Plains celebrations included some type of giveaway, a formal period of gift-giving by persons honored in some way in connection with the event. Sometimes an adoption was associated with the giveaway. A person adopted by another gained privileges related to the family, society, or tribe of the adopter. For example, two Otoe men were formally adopted into the Kiowa Gourd Clan in the 1950s and could thereafter wear the attire of the society and participate in Gourd Clan ceremonies (Kracht 1994:264). Women belonging to tribes whose tribal dresses were made of cloth were adopted into families of the Kiowa, Comanche, or other tribes who wore buckskin dresses (fig. 8). This gave them the appropriate approval to wear buckskin dresses and compete in the Buckskin category of dance contest (G.A. Young 1972–1989).

Ceremonies of gift-giving have been reported since the first European contact along the Mississippi and Missouri rivers. The French described Calumet ceremonies and the attendant adoption and gift-giving ceremonies. Dances that came to be called smoke dances were held by the Osage as early as the second decade of the eighteenth century (La

Philbrook Mus. of Art, Tulsa, Okla.: 1956.10.

Fig. 6. *The Hand Game*, by Victor Pepion, Blackfoot, watercolor, about 1956. Opposing teams face each other across a display of the goods they have wagered. Members of the hider's team sing and beat time with sticks, while one man tosses the markers into the air.

Fig. 7. Heywood Big Day, Jr., and his wife Veronica, Crows, inside tepee displaying their wedding presents: a dresser, blankets, fringed shawls, pieces of cloth, and a buckskin dress. Photograph by Michael Crummett, Crow Indian Res., Mont., 1977.

Flesche 1939:205). In 1819, Thomas Nuttall (in Thwaites 1904–1907, 13:248) reported: "a general council of the natives, friendly disposed toward the Osages, took place at their village; amongst them were Shawnees, Delawares, Creeks, Quapaws, Kanzas, Ouitigamis, &c. Their ostensible object was not known; it would appear, however, that they had been invited by the Osages, who on this occasion gave away more than 300 horses."

By the late twentieth century, most large giveaways on the Southern Plains were part of public celebrations such as powwows. Within the schedule of a powwow, giving away by the head staff was common. Giveaways were held for celebrating a child's first entry into the powwow as a dancer. Giveaways often were held in the afternoon of a large two or three-day powwow. Sometimes giveaways were held as a part of Gourd Dances. Giving away was especially important at powwows or Gourd Dances that were held specifically to honor an individual, such as a powwow honoring a retiree or a Gourd Dance held to honor a returning veteran. Items given away included fringed shawls, Pendleton blankets, other kinds of blankets; any item with "Indian" designs; sheets, towels and other household items; and special items such as antiques or items personally associated with the honored individual or family (G.A. Young 1972–1989).

Northern Plains

The format and content of Northern Plains giveaways was fairly uniform. The giveaway typically began with the singing of a traditional national anthem by a singing group. During this song, the honoree and the family paraded around the arena while the spectators stood or joined in the dance. Following the acknowledgment of the spectators through a receiving line and the announcement or speech by the master of ceremonies, the distribution of gifts began. As their names were called, individuals, families, or groups approached the honoree and the family and received their gifts. Also at this time, as well as after the completion of the formal giveaway, family members might move through the spectators handing out gifts. If the giveaway was a part of a larger event such as a powwow, the larger event would continue after the giveaway. Many giveaways concluded with a feast (A.B. Kehoe 1980; M.J. Schneider 1981; K.M. Weist 1973; Voget 1987).

An example of giving away among the Teton Sioux was the one-year anniversary memorial of a deceased relative (Grobsmith 1981a; Trimble 1934–1935; Hurt 1952a). In the nineteenth century, a four-day period of mourning was followed by the creation of a "ghost bundle," cared for by the family while they prepared for the anniversary giveaway to celebrate the ritual releasing of the soul and an end to formal mourning. Items such as moccasins, robes, dresses, and leggings made by the family were given away at the anniversary ceremony along with whatever belongings the family had, including food, clothing, and shelter. After

1024

Fig. 8. Adoption. Dressing a Kiowa woman in an Otoe dress as a bond of friendship. left to right, E.O. Hudson; Mabel Tsoodle Cozad, Kiowa; Marjorie Hudson and her brother Jim Cleghorn, Otoe. Photograph by Marjorie Schweitzer, at the annual powow, Otoe-Missouria dance ground, near Red Rock, Okla., July 1983.

providing an enormous feast, the family was destitute, as the visitors carried away their belongings. The family was highly regarded for their generosity and were provided for by the community—to a certain extent by other families' giveaways.

Throughout the twentieth century, at least the deceased's belongings continued to be given away, although sometimes, larger giveaways were held immediately after the death or one year later. This developed into the custom of holding a specific kind of giveaway each year after a relative's death, beginning with the first-year anniversary. Items given away, in order of their prestige, were star quilts and patchwork quilts (the best ones fully quilted, the next best only tied, and the lowest only quilt tops), shawls, blankets, bedding, and miscellaneous items such as trunks, dishes, kitchen paraphernalia, assorted cloth, knick-knacks, and jewelry. The family began preparing by making, or ordering from a maker, the quilts and shawls soon after the relative's death. During the year, the site was selected for the giveaway, outdoors in an area shaded by arbors or indoors in a hall or gymnasium. A man was selected to officiate as master of ceremonies.

On the day of the giveaway, honoring songs and dances opened the ceremony, the master of ceremonies spoke on behalf of the family, announcing the purpose of the giveaway. Eulogies followed, during which women wept openly for the deceased. The master of ceremonies called forward individuals to receive gifts. Gifts were distributed almost always to nonrelatives. Following the distribution, a feast was served to all present, sometimes several hundred people.

Hand Games and Ball Games

Songs were central to the hand game, another event that brought people together on the Plains (Culin 1907; Mooney

1896:348, 1008; Grinnell 1898:27; G.A. Dorsey 1901a; R.I. Dodge 1882; Nettl 1989; Lesser 1933). Also called bone games, stick games, or moccasin games, hand games consisted of teams hiding an object in the hand to a rhythmic accompaniment. Songs were usually sung, accompanied by a drum, often a hand drum, or by beating sticks. The songs not only provided the rhythm for the actions of the game but also brought special meaning to the game by introducing humor (Nettl 1989:145) or paying tribute to people and events (W. Smyth 1989:64).

In historic times, men played against men, women against women. The hiding team sang the songs. The score of this gambling game was kept with counters, especially decorated sticks, and the winning team might take home all manner of objects wagered by the losing team.

In the late nineteenth century, the hand game was among the old games revived as part of the Ghost Dance, but by the twentieth century, hand games were held as separate events. Among some tribes, such as the Pawnee and Arapaho (who transmitted it to the Gros Ventre and Assiniboine), the hand game became a sacred ritual, not a gambling game, and was played by men against women. In most tribes, however, two teams consisting of any number of both men and women sat facing each other. Two players from one side were each given short sticks or bone markers, which they placed behind their backs hidden from the person on the opposing team who would try to guess which hands held the markers. The hiders brought their closed fists in view of the guesser and moved them around to the beat of the song and drum. When the guesser believed he or she knew the location of the markers, he cried out a word such as "that" and pointed to the hiders' hands. If the guesser was correct, points were scored for the guessing team. If not, the hiders' team was awarded points (W. Smyth 1989:64; Lesser 1933). Hand games were played throughout the Plains (Culin 1907; Maximilian 1843:196, 254; Grinnell 1892:184, 1898:28).

In historic times, ball games were community events in their own right. In the eighteenth and nineteenth centuries, Plains Indians came together in large numbers to participate in or be spectators at racketball (stickball or lacrosse) and shinny games. Racketball was played using two rackets, each a long handle of wood curving at one end into a loop crossed by a buckskin netting. Shinny was played with one stick curved slightly at the end. Balls carved from wood or made of stuffed buckskin were used in both games. Goals were set up at both ends of a level playing area. Two teams comprised of people from particular men's societies, clans, villages, or tribes, or who might be divided into sides just for the game, tried to hit the goals with the ball or throw the

ball across the goal line (Culin 1907). European observers noted men playing against men (Yankton, Assiniboine, Gros Ventre, Omaha, Santee Sioux), men and women on the same team (Assiniboine), men against women (Santee Sioux, Crow), and women against women (Santee Sioux, Hidatsa, Omaha). Arapaho women were observed playing against women in Indian Territory, but as part of the Ghost Dance, not as a competition (Mooney 1898). Cheyenne, Pawnee, Wichita, and Kiowa ball games of the same era also may have been Ghost Dance activities. However, in 1882, well before the arrival of the Ghost Dance in Indian Territory, the Quapaw agent had received a request that Quapaws be allowed to join a traveling show to play "exhibition lacrosse games" (Basye 1882). Wagering was a part of the activities surrounding ball games, as were, in some instances, singing, dancing, and sorcery (Culin 1907).

In the late twentieth century, ball games remained only as parts of larger events, such as the game of Indian football, men against women, played at the Quapaw powwow (G.A. Young 1983).

Negotiating Celebratory Events

At the end of the twentieth century, celebrations following the powwow format were the most visible Plains events. Giveaways, Gourd Dances, Rabbit Dances, and hand games were also organized and carried out as events with spectators. Although there was some commonality of form, each event was unique. Forces such as the styles, beliefs, traditions, and histories of the organizing group, tribe, reservation and reserve, or individual sponsoring the celebration molded the activities and the manner in which they were presented.

The postwar Plains powwow grew naturally out of centuries of dynamic events affecting Plains music and dance. Continual change was brought about by Native Americans themselves, who were active players in the history of their celebrations, not passive reactors to experiences thrust upon them, such as the nineteenth-century government bans on dances or the recruitment of Indians for Wild West shows. Because the players in this historical drama came from so many different backgrounds—tribes, clans, societies, reservations, reserves, regions, cities, rural areas, schools, and churches—they brought their own ideas, their own songs, dances, and dress, their own history, to be a part of Plains celebrations. In even the most organized events there was room for innovation and active negotiation, by groups and by individual participants (G.A. Young 1978, 1994; Mattern 1996).

Music

GLORIA A. YOUNG

Virtually all Plains music was song. There were songs to greet the new day, and for curing, prayer, initiation, hunting, influencing nature, putting children to sleep, storytelling, performing magic, playing games, courting, public ceremonies, dances, and performing private affective magic (Heth 1989). Twentieth-century Plains Indians recalled: "For as long as I remember, my dad had a hand drum and at daylight every morning he was thanking the Lord for giving us another day" (Dorothy White Horse De Laune, Kiowa, in D.B. Lee 1995:68); "My grandma used to sing in our house. She would sing when something good would happen, and she would sing when something sad happened. She had a song for everything" (Annabelle Medicine Chips, Cheyenne, in D.B. Lee 1995:64).

Plains music was monophonic, with rhythmic pulsation throughout. Rather than using harmony, a thick texture was produced by the layering of voices and instruments. Abrupt layering created dynamic change (Heth 1994:34, 1999:2). Nettl (1954a:28–29, 1968:15) characterized Plains songs as strophic (containing sections or phrases which become longer toward the end of the strophe), having an average range of a tenth, and frequently using tetratonic and pentatonic scales. The melodic movement of Plains songs tended to be descending, usually in a contour of the terrace type. The most frequent "trends" in melodic movement in Teton Sioux songs at the beginning of the twentieth century were: (1) descending movement with no ascending tones but with repetition of some tones creating "terraces" and (2) "horizontal progression, followed by a descent to the final tone". Three additional "trends" were variations of melodies that descended to a "keynote," returned to various higher tones or terraces, and then descended again to the keynote, usually closing with a repetition of that tone

(Densmore 1918:52–54). Tones were distributed evenly in Blackfoot songs, with the principal scalar intervals being major and minor thirds, major seconds, and, rarely, semitones (Nettl 1989:43).

Plains vocal style has been described as having the following traits: vocal tension, harshness of sound, pulsation (a quavering quality that affects both pitch and dynamics), loudness, high pitch, and some ornamentation. Pulsation often resulted when words or vocables were lengthened. Of course, not all singing demonstrated all of the characteristic traits. Blackfoot women's vocal style was distinguished from men's by the lower quantity and intensity of pulsations and the greater amount of ornamentation.

In the north, songs might be sung falsetto at the beginning, dropping into raspy throaty registers, a "head voice." In classic Southern Plains style, there was an absence of falsetto, but an abundance of nasal and quavering tones. The development of these characteristics into a Plains singing style with regional variations may have been a twentieth-century development (Nettl 1968:206–207, 1989:43; W.K. Powers 1990:25, 32; Heth 1992:2; Hatton 1974, 1986).

Some Plains songs were sung in English and some in tribal languages, but a large percentage were sung in vocables or a mixture of words and vocables. Vocables (untranslatable syllables) formed identifiable texts. Some songs used vocables in conjunction with language, acting as introductory or closing parts, or added to phrases of language text to fill out a melodic line. It has been postulated that vocables were made up of the primary vowels of various Plains languages; thus songs from different language groups employed different vowels in the vocables (Ruggles 1995:28; Heth 1976).

Glenbow-Alberta Inst., Calgary: top left, ND-24-45, center right, NA-667-774; center left, Field Mus., Chicago: 79,365 (neg. A111,788); bottom left, State Histl. Soc. of N. Dak., Bismarck: 39-70.

Fig. 1. Drummers and singers. top left, Black Feather Society, Sun Dance singer-drummers with rawhide drum beaten with sticks. left to right: Black Eagle, Peace Maker, The Fox, Little Person, Wolf Carrier, Northern Axe, and Not Good. Photograph by Sidney Richard Reeves, Blackfoot Res., Gleichen, Alta., June 1913. top right, Blackfoot Rough Rider Society singers around a drum. clockwise from lower left, Fred Horn (light colored cap), Lloyd Little Plume, Windy Old Chief, Kenny Old Person, Archie St. Goddard, and Clarence Whitegrass. The drum head is elk hide, painted with an eagle. Photograph by Joe Fisher, summer ceremony dance, Mont., July 1996. center left, Pawnee drum painted with celestial motif. The old, wooden water drums were put away when ceremonies were suspended during the winter and were not brought out again until certain constellations appeared in the sky (Murie 1981:167). This hand drum with a single rawhide head stretched over a wooden hoop is the type that came into use among the Pawnee in the 1890s for the new Ghost Dance hand game (Lesser 1933:321). Collected by James Murie in Okla., 1906. Diameter 36 cm. center right, Sarcee drummers at a medicine pipe ceremony. The drum heads are fastened to hoops by thongs stretched and tied together. Photograph by Arnold Lupson, Sarcee Indian Res., Alta., about 1926. bottom left, Three Affiliated Tribes drummers at powwow at Elbowoods, N. Dak. Photograph by Monroe Killy, Ft. Berthold Res., N. Dak., June 1942. bottom right, Three Affiliated Tribes singer-drummer. Photograph by Edward Bruner, N. Dak., 1951–1953.

Instruments

While some songs, such as lullabies, were usually sung unaccompanied, most Plains songs were accompanied by rhythm instruments. These included single- or double-headed frame drums (with and without water), kettle drums, struck logs or rawhide, hand-held rattles, strung rattles or bells worn on various parts of the body, striking sticks, and rasps (Heth 1989:13; Nettl 1967:150). Melodic instruments on which songs were played were vertical (end-blown), tubular flutes and stringed instruments known as Apache violins or fiddles (W.R. Brown 1989). Whistles were used for rhythm and for various signals.

Drums

Frame drums were one-sided or two-sided, large or small, and usually were beaten with sticks. Kettle drums were small and water-filled.

Large drums were used in public ceremonies and dances (fig. 1 top right). In the nineteenth-century Blackfoot Sun Dance, a large wash tub with a single head was used or a hollowed out portion of a tree trunk covered with two drum heads tied together with thongs (Nettl 1967:151) The Omaha used a large flat one-sided frame drum, constructed by stretching a calfskin over a hoop of withes. When played by men sitting around it in a circle, it was supported by four sticks driven into the ground ("Omaha," fig. 12, this vol.) and beaten by sticks muffled by buckskin. Ordinary commercial bass drums supplanted this type in the twentieth century (Fletcher and La Flesche 1893:54). The Oglala Kit Fox Society used a drum made of a large hollow tree trunk and black-tailed deer skin, decorated with porcupine quillwork, bells, scalps, and eagle plumes. The drum was supported by quill-wrapped forked sticks with feathers. A Badger Society drum was made from a cottonwood trunk (Wissler 1912a:21, 31). For the Assiniboine Grass Dance, women were said to have their own drum, slightly smaller than the men's, and their own drumkeeper (M.S. Kennedy 1961:135).

Large, deep frame water drums were used historically for many religious ceremonies ("Intertribal Religious Movements," fig. 7, this vol.). Omaha drums were formerly made from the trunks of trees, hollowed out, over the open ends of which stretched were skins. They were tuned by partly filling them with water kept sweet by charcoal, the skins being moistened, strained, and dried to the desired tone. Kegs were later substituted for logs (Fletcher and La Flesche 1893:54). Among the Ponca, only the wáwą adoption dance used a hollow-log water drum. This type of drum was used by the Central Algonquians in their Midewiwin rites, but the Ponca Medicine Lodge used a large dry drum instead (J.H. Howard 1965:106, 121).

Kettle drums were water drums like those made from number 8 brass kettles used in the Native American Church (W.R. Brown 1989:33). A Southern Arapaho Peyote drum

was made of a three-legged iron kettle, half-filled with water, into which a dozen live coals were thrown before a well-soaked buckskin was stretched into place (Trenholm 1970:298–299)

Small drums similar in size and shape to tambourines were beaten in tremolo by the fingers or a small reed, among the Omaha, for Mystery and Dream songs (Fletcher and La Flesche 1893:72). The Blackfoot used one-sided drums 12 to 24 inches in diameter and two to three inches deep, beaten with wooden drumsticks covered with rawhide. In the 1950s and 1960s, Blackfoot used two-headed drums 18 to 30 inches in diameter (Nettl 1967:151). Hand-held two-sided drums were used for Crow hand games (Lowie 1935:210). For the twentieth-century Shoshone-Crow Sun Dance, a commercial bass drum replaced the individual hand-carried circular drums (Voget 1984:310–311).

Struck logs or rawhides might be used instead of drums in certain situations. An early practice documented for the Blackfoot, Arapaho, Cheyenne, Sioux, and other tribes was beating with sticks on a large piece of rawhide (fig. 1 top left) stretched, without a resonator, along several vertical poles or simply lying on the ground. Sometimes, rattles were used instead of sticks for beaters (Nettl 1967:151). Omaha women stood in front of their lodges and sang songs to send power to family members away at war, accompanying their songs by beating on rawhide. At the Teton Sioux Sun Dance, a similar song was sung by women, who held a rawhide as they beat it (Fletcher and La Flesche 1893:46).

Rattles, Bells, Striking Sticks, and Rasps

Hand-held rattles made of gourds filled with fine or coarse gravel or pebbles, according to the tone required, were played by the Omaha, either shaking the gourd in a tremolo or a strong stroke with a rebound. Gourd rattles ("Arikara," figs. 9–10 and "Quapaw," fig. 6, this vol.) were associated with an appeal to the supernatural and used with mystery songs and in the wáwą ceremony (Fletcher and La Flesche 1893:55). The Ponca used rattles of gourd, rawhide or deer hoof, especially in sacred rituals (J.H. Howard 1965:80). Rattles were the most varied instruments of the Blackfoot. Container rattles were made of rawhide (fig. 2), sometimes covered with brownish-red pigment, in a variety of sizes, external ornaments, and painted designs ("Assiniboine," fig. 4, this vol). Different types of rattles were used by men's societies ("Gros Ventre," fig. 6, this vol.) and medicine societies, and they were frequently part of sacred bundles. They functioned, like drums, to provide percussive accompaniment, but were used at smaller, more intimate, sometimes indoor gatherings. Different types of rattles were not used for different kinds of music (Nettl 1967:151). Late twentieth-century rattles were made of coconuts, milk cans, metal baking powder cans, and metal salt shakers. Artists made rattles of German silver or brass in the shape of a gourd or shaker (W.R. Brown 1989:41). Rattles were important accoutrements in the Gourd Dance and the Native

Fig. 2. Rawhide rattle. Most Plains rawhide rattles had globular-shaped heads. This Hidatsa cone-shaped rattle with a handle of willow twigs was probably made as a model of the sacred rattle used by that tribe in the Sun Dance and other ceremonies (Gilman and Schneider 1987:151). Collected from Wolf Chief by G. Wilson at Ft. Berthold, N. Dak., 1913–1915. Length, 26.3 cm.

American Church ("Intertribal Religious Movements," fig. 7, this vol).

Bells were used to accompany Thunder songs, which Fletcher and La Flesche (1893:50) recorded as a type of mystery song among the Omaha. Pawnee, Cheyenne and Sioux Grass Dance society dancers wore bells attached to their legs (La Barre et al. 1935:1212; Murie 1914:624–625). Twentieth-century powwow dancers often wore small jingle bells, sheep bells, or large sleigh bells. The bells added a thickening to the texture of the music.

In 1819, Stephen Long's expedition was entertained by dances ("Kansa," fig. 7, this vol.) accompanied by Otoe singers who played a drum and a rasp. The drum was made of a keg. The rasp was "another instrument, consisting of a stick of firm wood, notched like a saw, over the teeth of which a smaller stick was rubbed forcibly backward and forward" (E. James in Thwaites 1904–1907, 14:230–231).

Flutes and Whistles

Vertical flutes, sometimes called "courting" flutes and used by men, were the only traditional Plains musical instruments used alone. An Omaha "flageolet" which was 24½ inches long and made of red cedar ornamented with lead run into grooves (Fletcher and La Flesche 1893:72). Twentieth-century flutes were made from a round and hollowed-out piece of wood that contained a plug dividing it into two chambers. Two rectangular openings were placed on both sides of the plug, and a carved ornament or bird was attached to the flute over the opening near the mouth hole and plug. As the player blew, the air stream was directed through a narrow duct formed by the plug and the bird. Since the bird was movable, it could be used to tune the instrument (fig. 3). Older red cedar flutes were crafted according to the maker's dimensions: length corresponded to the distance from arm-pit to fingertips, and the bore was made the diameter of the index finger. Tone holes fit the fall of the maker's fingers. Some flute makers worked to improve the instrument's acoustical qualities, while others made flutes as a form of

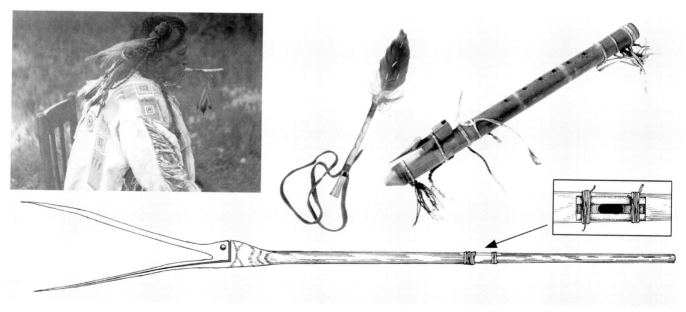

Fig. 3. Wind instruments. top left, Curly Head, Gros Ventre, demonstrating blowing a bone whistle. He wears a war charm in his hair made of a red squirrel skin, which was inherited from his father Bull Lodge. Curly Head was Feathered Pipe Keeper 1910–1938. Photograph by Richard Pohrt, Hays, Ft. Belknap Res., Mont., 1937. center, Eagle-bone whistle with feather, Southern Cheyenne. Collected from A. Bushyhead by Heinrich Voth in Ind. Terr., 1882–1891. right, Cedar flute with bird effigy for adjusting the tone, Kiowa. Collected by James Glennan, Ind. Terr., 1890–1892. bottom, Snipe whistle made by the grandfather of Spotted Elk, Hunkpapa Sioux. Detail shows mouthpiece construction: bone strips fastened with sinew. Collected by A. McG. Beede in Sioux County, N. Dak., before 1915. Drawn by Roger Thor Roop.

artistic expression (Wapp 1984:52; W.R. Brown 1989:34). Almost any song might have been played on a flute, including Christian hymns utilizing a pentatonic scale, such as "Amazing Grace," but flutes were traditionally used for playing love songs.

Whistles of eagle bone (fig. 3) were used in the Sun Dance (Densmore 1918:125, 150) and in rites of the Native American Church. Cedar whistles were used in the Ponca Hethuska. A Grass Dance official, known as a whistle man, carried a whistle, the head of which was carved to look like a crane. By approaching the drum and blowing his whistle he could prolong the dance by as many as 20 songs (J.H. Howard 1965:80, 1960b). Twentieth-century war dancers at powwows blew eagle bone or metal whistles.

Continuity and Change

The hallmark of Plains music has been its receptiveness to change. This was due, in part, to the Plains ideal of individualism, which afforded the makers (composers) and users of songs a great deal of creative latitude within the boundaries of style, religion, ceremonialism, and society. The concept of vision or dream was integral to the creation and use of songs. Early in the nineteenth century, all songs were seen as coming to individuals in dreams or visions. Usually, the person learned the song from animals or other natural phenomena in his or her dream.

Change occurred easily when songs spread from tribe to tribe. Even within a tribe, a song may be modified for a different dance. "Religious songs become social dance songs, round dances become war dances, love songs become two-steps, and so on in an unending cycle of borrowing and trading, changing and adapting" (W.K. Powers 1961:97).

New settings for music were developed in the twentieth century (fig. 4), such as the powwow ("Blackfoot," fig. 9 and "Wichita," fig. 10, this vol.) or the recording studio (fig. 5), and scores of new songs were composed each year. However, Plains music remained constant, and songs were based on a similar foundation. Thus, Plains songs could not be categorized chronologically. Any song heard at the dawn of the twenty-first century might trace its origin to the week before, the nineteenth century, or time immemorial. Thus, Plains songs were usually categorized by musical style or by use. The following discussion of songs by use refers to the entire nineteenth and twentieth centuries.

Types of Songs

Individual

Songs accompanied most activities of a Plains Indian's life. Many individual songs ("Gros Ventre," fig. 7, this vol.), such as prayers, story songs, and songs for success in an endeavor might be sung by anyone. Some categories of "songs not connected with war" that were sung by men

included hunting songs, ballad-like songs, and love songs. Lullabies were usually, but not always, sung by women. They and flute songs consisted of unaccompanied melodic lines.

Lullabies had a more horizontal melodic line than more vigorous Plains songs (W.K. Powers 1961b:164; Lowie 1935:34–35; J.H. Howard 1965:81; W. Smyth 1989:64, Giglio 1994:43–65). N. Curtis (1907:128, 160, 181, 211, 238–239) collected Pawnee, Kiowa, Arapaho, and Cheyenne lullabies. A Sioux lullaby with the words "Be still. Sleep" had a compass of only four notes (Densmore 1918:493). An Arapaho lullaby is translated "That's the way he quiets us down, Our Father. Sweet little one, go to sleep" (D.B. Lee 1995:62).

Nineteenth-century Blackfoot sang riding songs to the rhythm of the movements of the horse and sang songs for a prosperous and safe journey (Nettl 1967:149; D.B. Lee 1995:67). N. Curtis (1907:153) transcribed a Cheyenne song for greeting the morning.

Several types of individual songs were heard by Fletcher and La Flesche (1893:42–54) among the Omaha. Songs of thanks were sung as the acknowledgement of a gift. At the beginning of the second part of the song, the giver's name was mentioned, followed by ðaʔéq̓ðaðe, wįðakʰe 'you pity me, you tell the truth' (1893:51). Anyone might sing these songs, but especially a poor man who had been remembered. Pawnee songs of thanks were collected by N. Curtis (1907:113, 133, 135).

Omaha waʔú waą́ 'woman songs' told a story somewhat like a ballad. Often humorous and sometimes vulgar, these were sung by young men in each other's company and seldom heard by women. J.H. Howard (1965:81) mentioned "mock love songs," in which young men imitated love-sick young women, among the Ponca. Hunting and trapping songs, seldom elaborate in melody or rhythm, were sung after setting a trap or before tracking an animal. These esoteric songs (W.K. Powers 1961b:164) or "Mystery songs" (Fletcher and La Flesche 1893:49) were sung to insure success in a particular undertaking by an individual. Fletcher's Mystery category included songs for times of danger and to secure general benefits. One with the text "walk this way" (toward the singer) was an invitation that indicated the singer's willingness to yield to the magic of the song. Among the Omaha, these songs could be purchased, but the sale did not preclude the use of the song by the seller. Thus, several men might use the same song. Fletcher and La Flesche (1893:49) recorded an Omaha tribal song called the Tribal Prayer. It was taught to every Omaha child by its parents and used throughout life at solemn experiences and important events by the whole tribe.

Funeral and mourning songs might be individual, although Fletcher and La Flesche (1893:42) reported that the Omaha funeral song was sung by a group of mourning men beating two willow sticks together for rhythm. A Pawnee song of mourning was sung by his father to a small boy at the time of his mother's death. The father said, "We can do

Fig. 4. Indian women performing with modern instruments. top left, Crying Woman Singers, the first women's drumming-singing group. left to right, back row: Kim Geer (Gros Ventre), Toni Rae Blueshield (Gros Ventre), Marcella Bird (Plains Cree), Wallisa Doney (Chippewa-Cree), Iris Main (Gros Ventre); front row: Celina Bird-Jones (Plains Cree) the lead singer-drummer, Garrett Snell (Gros Ventre), Christina Jones (Gros Ventre), Ramona Cochran (Yakima). Bird-Jones and her sister Marcella were taught drumming and singing by their uncles Fred Sangrey and Victor Thunderchild, and their grandfather Ed Thunderchild, who reared them near the Thunderchild Res. in Sask. The sisters moved to Ft. Belknap Res., Mont., where the group was formed in 1993, with the help of Ron (Super) Doney, a Ft. Belknap singer. Photograph by Ted Whitecalf, Saskatoon, Sask., for Sweetgrass Records, Feb. 1994. top right and bottom left, Performing at the Smithsonian Institution Festival of American Folklife. top right, Georgia Wettlin-Larsen, Assiniboine; bottom left, Anita Anquoe George and her sister Mary Ann Anquoe, Kiowa. Photographs by Rick Vargas, Washington, D.C., 1995. bottom right, Omnichord, an electronic instrument resembling a chorded zither, demonstrated by Virginia Giglio. This instrument was used to accompany Christian songs at gospel revivals (Giglio 1994:178–181). Photograph by Mary Jo Ruggles, Okla., 1991.

nothing when a person dies; we can only pray. Perhaps some day you will be a man and have children around you." When the boy grew up, he made the song into a War Dance song and it was known as his song (Densmore 1929:112).

Love songs (Fletcher and La Flesche 1893:53–54; Parks 1991, 2:759–760; W.K. Powers 1962a:166; N. Curtis 1907:82–86) were sung by men. Among the Omaha they were sung around daybreak. The style was "*ad libitum* as feeling may sway the singer," in a flowing style and the singer's hand was sometimes "waved before the mouth to enhance the effect by vibrations" (Fletcher and La Flesche 1893:53). Densmore (1918:370–371) characterized the style of "old" love songs, connected with war among the Sioux, as "wavering." Old love songs were "associated with a man's *1031*

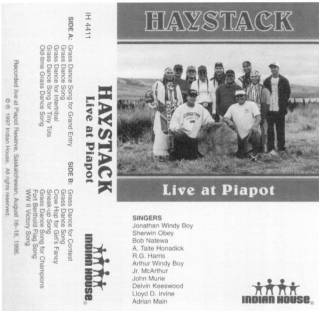

Fig. 5. Native American recordings. top, *War Dance Songs of the Ponca*. Record album No. 2002 published by Indian House, Taos, N. Mex., 1967. Ponca men seated around drum are, left to right, Lamont Brown, Albert Waters, Russell Rush, Louis Yellow Horse, Harry Buffalohead, Joe H. Rush, and Sylvester Warrior. The women seated behind are, left to right, Alice Cook, Stella Yellowhorse, and Lucy C.F. Ribs. Standing is James Waters, the Camp Crier for the Poncas. Photographed by a reporter from *The Ponca City News*, under the dance arbor of Albert Waters, White Eagle, Okla., 1967. bottom, *Haystack: Live at Piapot*, tape cover. Tape includes Grass Dance songs and others sung by Jonathan Windy Boy (Chippewa-Cree), Sherwin Obey (Cree-Sioux), Bob Natewa (Chippewa), A. Taite Honaclick (Dine-Paiute), R.G. Harris (Sauk and Fox-Ponca), Arthur Windy Boy (Chippewa-Cree), Junior McArthur (Cree-Assiniboine), John Murie (Chippewa-Cree), Delvin Keeswood (Dine), Lloyd D. Irvine (Assiniboine-Salish-Kootenai), and Adrian Main (Assiniboine-Gros Ventre). Recorded at Piapot Res., Sask., 1996, and published in 1997 by Indian House, Taos, N. Mex.

qualification to wed, this being determined by his success in war or in the buffalo hunt." She analyzed love songs recorded in 1911 among the Santee Sioux and found a wider range of tones than that of five-note older songs; "the progressions show a greater variety than in the majority of the Sioux songs. This appears to be a characteristic of the more modern songs" (Densmore 1918:509–512).

In 1988, Ponca singer Maynard Hinman recorded three Ponca love songs. One portrayed a man saying to a woman "You are looking, come over this way. Maybe you are looking for me." Another indicated what people were saying of a woman who did not keep her word and lost her lover: "Sister, it is your own fault. You tore your vow and commitment." The third was the lament of a woman who regretted leaving Oklahoma and becoming involved with an Omaha man in Nebraska (W. Smythe 1989:63).

Cheyenne women sang courting and flirting songs (Giglio 1994:162). One was recalled when a similar song reported by Densmore (1929:104) was discussed.

Myth and Story

Story songs, used as a part of storytelling, might be sung by individuals or groups and were typically unaccompanied. Sioux story songs included narratives, travel songs, and songs learned in dreams from legendary characters (W.K. Powers 1961b:164).

Myths and stories told by storytellers sometimes had sections in which songs, often attributed to the animal heroes of the story, were sung (Nettl 1967:158). Fletcher and La Flesche (1893:51, 142) recorded a song from "How the Rabbit Lost its Tail" sung by Omaha women and the children of the audience. Cheyenne women recalled three songs from "Why the Mud Hen Has Red Eyes" (Giglio 1994:75–84).

Medicine Songs

Individual medicine songs were used for curing and as a prophylactic (Lowie 1935:64–66; J.H. Howard 1965:81; W.K. Powers 1962a:166; Densmore 1918:244–283). These songs could be sung only by certain people, such as the initiated or the individuals who had received them in dreams. N. Curtis (1907:152–153, 159–160, 254–257) collected Sioux and Cheyenne medicine songs. The songs were often used to cure specific patients (Nettl 1961:146). Examples include an Arikara Midwife's song "in the prayer style of doctors in a Medicine Lodge" (Parks 1991, 2:757–759) and a Crow "Rock Medicine Song" (P.J. Powell 1988:14). A song of the Omaha Buffalo Doctors sung for preparing and administering an herbal remedy, while attending to a wounded man, indicated that the mode of treatment was learned in a vision: "From here do I send it (the medicine to the wound) thus,— in this manner am I bidden to send it" (Fletcher and La Flesche 1893:50, song 78).

Individual medicine songs often formed part of the ceremony of a medicine society. Among the Pawnee Buffalo

Doctors, songs were sung as drums were passed around to each seated participant in a clockwise motion, completing four circuits around the interior of a Pawnee earthlodge. Each song was owned by an individual and commemorated the original experience on which his healing power was based. A song had four, six, or eight stanzas, with each stanza having two lines alluding to his original vision. After the first line was a one-line refrain, and after the second was a chorus (Murie 1914:605, 1981:12–13, 17–18).

Blackfoot songs were sung during the use and transfer of medicine bundles (fig. 6). The seven-hour Horse Medicine ceremony, as recorded (Ewers 1955:262–271) in the 1940s, included about five hours of singing. Each man sang three songs accompanied by three drums, his own and two played by men on his left. Then the drums passed to the left. The songs were personal property and could be purchased or borrowed. The singer's wife might sing softly with him although she did not sit in the circle of men.

Although the Blackfoot of the time found Horse Medicine songs "particularly attractive" and would have liked to sing them outside the ritual context, they were forbidden to do so. Nettl (1967a:147–149) found that among the many recordings of ceremonial Blackfoot songs throughout the twentieth century there were very few Horse Medicine songs. For the Medicine Pipe Bundle ceremony, Nettl and Blum found more variation in the grouping and repetition of phrases and in the melodic contours and motifs than was found in Sun Dance or hand game songs (Nettl 1968:19–48, 1989:34). In older recordings, many of these songs were sung softly, without the high tension and high pitch level of Sun Dance songs. Thus, Nettl (1967a:143,146) postulated that Blackfoot medicine songs were probably performed privately, not at public ceremonies. However, he believed that some, especially the Beaver Medicine Bundle songs (fig. 6), may have become Sun Dance songs in the nineteenth century, since both were intensely religious ceremonies.

top, Glenbow-Alberta Inst., Calgary: NA-667-230; Prov. Mus. of Alta., Edmonton: bottom left, 780-453-9161-58; bottom right, 780-453-9161-15.

Fig. 6. Transfer of Blackfoot bundles. top, Transfer of the medicine pipe bundles during the Sun Dance ceremony. Men are carrying portions of one or more medicine bundles, while drummers are part of the procession. Photograph by Arnold Lupson, Blackfoot Res., Alta., probably 1924. bottom, Ritual during the Beaver bundle transfer ceremony. bottom left, Women dance on their knees, imitating the beaver, as the men sing. left to right: unidentified woman; Mrs. Mistaken Chief or Mrs. White-Man-Left; Mrs. Rides-at-the-Door, a holy woman, and a former caretaker of the Beaver bundle; Porcupine Woman, wife of Bob Black Plume; and Bob Black Plume, also known as Skunk Man, singing to the accompaniment of rawhide rattles. bottom right, Women dancing. left to right: 2 unidentified women, Porcupine Woman, Rosie Cutter, Mrs. Rides-at-the-Door, and an unidentified woman. Photographs by Karl Kaescamp, Blood Res., Alta., Sept. 1965.

Sacred Songs not for Curing

Historic tribal sacred songs were sung by individuals or groups and usually were accompanied by rhythm instruments. Fletcher and La Flesche (1893:18–22) described songs that could be sung only by the males of clans or subclans who had charge of Omaha sacred or tribal possessions. One clan was entrusted with the preservation of the songs and rituals of the Sacred Pole and the Buffalo Hide used in rites performed after the annual summer buffalo hunt. On the third day of the ceremony, men of a subclan belonging to a different clan were charged with providing singing and drumming for a "tribal dance" danced by men and women. Other clans and groups were authorized to sing songs of the Tent of War and the ritual of the filling of the tribal pipes.

Crow religious songs were Tobacco songs and vision songs, and a Sacred Pipe ceremony that had come from the Hidatsa (Lowie 1935:73–74, 261, 305). Densmore (1918:63–77, 152) described Sioux songs sung only by persons qualified to sing them and used in connection with ceremonies, two of which were Buffalo Calf Pipe ceremony and the ceremony of Spirit-Keeping. The twentieth-century *yuwípi* rituals of the Sioux used individual and ritualistic songs, as did the Sweatlodge and the Pipe ceremony when it was not part of another ceremony (W.K. Powers 1961b:161–163). Sacred songs were "still received by the older adherents of the Sioux way of life" in dreams.

Sun Dance

Like the Sioux Spirit-Keeping and Buffalo Calf ceremonies, the Sun Dance employed a series of sacred songs sung in a specific order (W.K. Powers 1961b:164; Trenholm 1970; Lowie 1935:305, 321; Densmore 1918:84–156). Among the Blackfoot, they numbered 413 (Wissler 1918:268). There were "songs essentially for listening, i.e., songs which did not accompany any other activity, and also songs sung by ceremonial personnel while performing delicate and strenuous tasks such as raising the sun pole, riding, or putting the sacred buffalo tongues in the kettles" (Nettl 1967:143–144). There was great contrast between the uses of songs, but a high degree of homogeneity in the musical style, even though the nonritual songs were associated with groups and activities separate from the Sun Dance proper, such as social dance songs and songs of men's societies.

The leader of the Sioux Sun Dance was required to either compose the ceremonial songs he sang or purchase them from someone who had previously held the office (Densmore 1918:101–102).

Singing was vital to the attainment of a vision. In the Shoshone-Crow Sun Dance, "Good drum-singers stimulate dancers and keep them going. When a dancer appears on the point of being 'run over' by Buffalo, they step up the tempo to bring him into the mystic state of communication with the divine" (Voget 1984:310). There were never fewer than four singers, preferably seven, and "women have always been a part of the singing team."

Ghost Dance

As the Ghost Dance movement spread in the late nineteenth century, songs were passed from tribe to tribe. N. Curtis (1907:47–48, 63–65, 114–116, 139–143, 200–201, 208–210) collected Sioux, Pawnee, and Arapaho Ghost Dance songs.

In Oklahoma, the Ghost Dance replaced the Sun Dance and continued, as a curing ceremony, well into the twentieth century. Many songs used by the Caddo came from the neighboring Plains tribes. An Arapaho Ghost Dance song adopted by the Caddo sung by Randlett Edmonds had the words "In the end the Caddos will all go to the land above" (W. Smythe 1989:67). Another said "The raven is standing on the hill. When you get to the top of the hill, Down below, the buffalo are there" (D.B. Lee 1995:55)

Peyote

Songs sung in Peyote meetings (later, Native American Church meetings) ("Intertribal Religious Movements," fig. 8, this vol.) resembled medicine rituals in that the participants sat in a circle in a sacred space, usually a tepee or a round house, and passed a drum clockwise to each person whose turn it was to sing (McAllester 1949; W.K. Powers 1961b:164; J.H. Howard 1965:81, 125; La Barre 1938). The ritual spread from tribe to tribe with, and following, the Ghost Dance.

McAllester (1949) analyzed Peyote songs from the Comanche, Sioux, Kiowa, Pawnee, Tonkawa, Arapaho, and Cheyenne ceremonies. He found melodic contours to be, generally, in the Plains tradition of descending movement from high to low tones, but within a restricted range. He suggested that a relatively "mild" vocal technique contrasted to the Plains tense vocal style of songs other than lullabies, children's songs, and love songs. Since other ethnomusicologists had noted a more relaxed style for indoor, private rites such as medicine bundle ceremonies and even hand games, this style of vocal delivery was expected. The tempo of analyzed Peyote songs was faster than most Plains songs with a quick duple rattle beat adding to the impression of speed. There was a consistency of note length "in the use of only eighth and quarter note values in the vocal melody," that is, the songs incorporated neither long notes nor rapid embellishments. The songs consisted of the usual Plains phrase patterns but also showed a marked incidence of paired patterns, a Great Basin trait. The final phases showed a cumulative use of the tonic for phrase endings and at the end of a typical song the phrase "He ne ne yo wa" was invariably sung. Some characteristics could be attributed to the influence of Ghost Dance songs and some, perhaps, to the influence of Indian music of the Southwest, especially Yaqui (McAllester 1949:84–85). In Pawnee songs, some characteristics may have come from songs of the Iloshka, the Grass Dance-type societies that were being revived as a result of the Ghost Dance in the 1890s when the Peyote rite was adopted.

The all-night Peyote ritual incorporated periods of singing before and after midnight ceremonies. Among the Ponca, each individual participant sang four songs, using a gourd rattle for accompaniment, while a water drum was played by the person to the right. Individual Peyotists had their own personal songs, but anyone who learned them might use them. The songs were always referred to by the name of the composer (J.H. Howard 1965:97). Song selection was up to the individuals, who were also allowed to sing the songs outside of the ceremony. Arapaho Peyote songs were sung subdued during the early part of the night, but became spirited, increasing in tempo and volume after midnight (Trenholm 1970:298–299) N. Curtis (1907:188–192) transcribed early Mescal songs.

Christian

Songs with words pertaining to Christianity ("Algonquian Languages," fig. 3, this vol.) were composed in the cascading and terraced melodic style of Plains song, as well as in a more horizontal style melodically influenced by Christian hymn music but distinctively Plains. Kiowa twentieth-century Christian-influenced tribal style was strong and melodious. A prayer song translated "Let us pray to our heavenly father. When he opens the heavenly gates for us, we will be glad. When he gives us everlasting life, we will live happily ever after" (Ralph Kotay in W. Smythe 1989:66–67).

A song composed by an older woman at baptism that translated "Lord I give my life to you, show me the way, lead me, bless me and don't ever leave me; and as I am praying, I am crying, Lord bless me and don't ever leave me," was sung by Comanche church members (Laverna Hoahwah in W. Smyth 1989:65–66). Doc Tate Nevaquaya explained that they "are religious songs, and like all songs, are inspired by God. They are giving praises to God so, whether they are old or new, they're still pointed in the same direction" (D.B. Lee 1995:67).

Civil Ceremonial

The Cheyennes had more than 15 chief's songs for the Council of Forty Four (Stands in Timber and Liberty 1967:59). Council songs, sung when chiefs met in the council tent to decide important matters, and two kinds of chief's songs were found among the Sioux: those that voiced the thought of the chiefs and those sung in honor of the chiefs (Densmore 1918:448, 452, 455). Honor dance songs and divorce songs were used in civil ceremonies among the Sioux and Crow (W.K. Powers 1961b:164; Lowie 1935:59; Densmore 1918:453–460).

An adoption ceremony called the Calumet ceremony or pipe dance (Omaha *wáwą*, Pawnee Hako, Teton Sioux *alówąpi* or *hųká*) cemented relationships between families,

clans, or tribes (Densmore 1918:68–77; Fletcher and La Flesche 1893:35–42; La Flesche 1939:205). When a child was adopted, a bond was forged between the child's father, who accepted the calumet(s) and to whom the songs were sung, and the man who presented the calumet(s) and "sang" the ceremony. A small group of men accompanied by a drum sang most of the songs ("Arikara," fig. 8, this vol.), occasionally joined by all men and women present at the ceremony. Dances were a part of this ceremony, if it was continued over several days.

Songs Pertaining to War

There were songs for every stage of nineteenth-century fighting and warfare—some sung unaccompanied by individuals, and some sung by individuals or groups of singers with drums (Densmore 1918:332–435, 1929:50–53, 60–64; N. Curtis 1907; J.H. Moore 1996:108; Giglio 1994:110–129). Some songs belonged to military societies and were sung at dances ("Ponca," fig. 8, this vol.) as well as in war. Some songs were sung by anyone, others only by those taking a vow (Stands in Timber and Liberty 1967:64). Baker (1882) transcribed war songs.

Wolf songs were sung by warriors leaving for battle (Fletcher 1900:90–91; Densmore 1918:333–348; N. Curtis 1907:78, 206). Omaha Wolf songs were sung by men when they decided to go out as a war party, as they were leaving the village, and when the party was traveling and in no immediate danger (Fletcher and La Flesche 1893:46). Before going to war, each young Cheyenne man chose a Wolf song, one at a time going around the circle all night. They danced in the morning, then the war party left (Stands in Timber and Liberty 1967:143).

Some types of songs sung on the way to battle were individual power songs, songs sung while horses were being painted, and scout songs. When a Crow man succeeded in battle, praises were sung by his father's clan (Lowie 1935:220–229, 16). Cheyenne warriors would sit on their horses taunting the enemy with soldier songs. "Suicide boys" would trot their horses toward the enemy and sing their Death songs, indicating that they were brave and ready to die. When fighting began, everyone sang their Death songs. Passed down through families, Death songs were simple songs with words such as "Tell the girl in white buckskin that I love her," or "Today is a good day to die; only the stones live forever" (J.H. Moore 1996:106; Stands in Timber and Liberty 1967:146). Captive songs were much like death songs. W.K. Powers (1961b:164) mentions Sioux Horse Stealing songs and Victory songs.

Women sang as the war party moved out of camp. Brave Heart songs were sung by the women of the tribe in their relatives' absence (J.H. Howard 1965:81; Fletcher and La Flesche 1893:46–47; Stands in Timber and Liberty 1967:63). One Omaha Brave Heart song translated "Exert yourselves that the tribes may hear of your bravery" (Fletcher and La Flesche 1893:47).

Riding homeward, men began to sing as they approached camp with their war trophies. A Scalp Dance was held. Parts of Scalp Dance songs were sung by women alone (Fletcher and La Flesche 1893:47). Of a Tonkawa Scalp Dance, singer Don Patterson said, "Today the dance itself runs in segments and phases. Different kinds of songs go with each phase. The songs themselves have messages in them that suggest the attitudes that prevailed in the early days. About midway through the first set of songs is the Water Song. The women will bring water to everybody with the water bucket and dipper. 'Come up, women. Carry the water for dancing.'" The third phase of the Tonkawa Scalp Dance depicted men leaving on a war expedition. "Don't cry for me. The enemy is calling me. I've got to answer the call" (D.B. Lee 1995:56).

In the twentieth century, songs pertaining to war continued to be sung to aid and honor members of the armed forces (W.K. Powers 1961b:163, 1968:68; D.B. Lee 1995:65; Giglio 1994:118–126; Densmore 1929:64–69). Among the Kiowa "There were songs for tour of duty, songs for when they returned—they called those homecoming songs." One composed for a specific soldier at the request of his family had the words "We are glad to have our son home from the Army. We are happy to have him with us here for awhile. He will be going back, But we are glad that he has come home to us safe" (Ralph Kotay in D.B. Lee 1995:57). Another Kiowa song was named "Empty Saddle Song." Before singing it, Billy Evans Horse said "There is more to a song than just listening to the song. It has a kind of history behind it. This is a symbolic song that was done late in the 1940s and was in tribute to the service men that didn't come back . . . . 'And he died in the time of battle. I want you to remember and feel good when you hear this song'" (D.B. Lee 1995:59).

Men's Society

Many songs about war comprised part of the ceremonies of men's societies called warrior or military societies. One of the most widespread was the Fox society, whose members while at war were as active and wily as foxes, and there were also many Wolf or Dog societies. The Arikara Fox society was mentioned as early as 1833 (Densmore 1918:315), and there were Fox societies among the Cheyenne, Hidatsa, Mandan, and Crow (N. Curtis 1907:73, 129–131, 169). A Sioux Fox society song recorded by Densmore (1918:414–415) said "The fox I am. Something difficult I seek." Crow Big Dog and Fox war chant words are in Lowie (1935:113); Cheyenne Fox songs are in Stands in Timber and Liberty (1967).

Not all men's societies were strictly military, and not all their songs pertained to war. Some Crow songs were derisive and meant to "take away" other societies' songs (Lowie 1935:191–200). Songs received in visions (Dream songs) might be society songs, such as those that were part of instructions for forming a new society (W.K. Powers 1961b:164). When an Omaha Hethuska society member performed a brave deed, "the society decided whether it

should be celebrated and without this dictate no man would dare permit a song to be composed in his honor" (Fletcher and La Flesche 1893:25).

For Play and Games

Children sang unaccompanied songs while at play. Sioux girls sang "The deer follow each other" when moving in a weaving line, one behind the other (Densmore 1918:492) and Omaha children had songs for "Follow my leader" (Fletcher and La Flesche 1893:102). A Sioux song "I catch but I cannot hold you," sung when playing a game sitting in a circle (Densmore 1918:493), was like songs sung by Cheyenne and Arapaho women for children's pinching games late in the twentieth century (Giglio 1994:67–74, 217).

Songs sung with words or, more often, vocables, accompanied the many guessing and betting games and sports of Plains tribes (Fletcher and La Flesche 1893:34; W.K. Powers 1962a:166; Nettl 1967:150; Lesser 1933; Densmore 1918:485–491, 1929:71–78; Giglio 1994:86–109). Hand games could not be played without music, the side hiding the object providing the song. Drums, sticks, or other rhythm instruments kept an urgent tempo ("Crow," fig. 4, this vol.). Women sometimes shook rattles to add to the sound of the game but they were "not considered to be musical instruments, but to function more like a cheerleader's pompon at a football game" (Giglio 1994:92). The songs were narrow in range with short repeated phrases and a "choppy effect" provided by staccatos and rests. The players hid the object, keeping rhythm with the song (Nettl 1968:16; Heth 1999:12). Ponca Moccasin and hand game songs were sung not only to distract players on the opposing team (J.H. Howard 1965:81) but also to bring special social meaning by paying tribute to people or events (Tony Arkeketa in W. Smyth 1989:64). In the 1960s, about 50 hand game or stick game songs were used among the Blackfoot. Nettl (1968:15–19) found more variety in the song structure and composition techniques in game songs than in dance songs and regarded them as the most sophisticated musical products of the Blackfoot.

Songs accompanied ball games, which, like horse races, were frequently held between members of different men's societies. Society songs were sung and victory songs accompanied a win. The person entrusted with the care of a winning horse among the Crow "sang to it softly" (Nettl 1967:149–150; W.K. Powers 1961b:164).

To Accompany Dances

Nearly every public gathering of Plains Indians included dancing, whether sacred, ceremonial, or social. One could not dance unless an appropriate song was being sung. At a twentieth-century powwow, one could not dance a war dance if singers were singing round dance songs (W.K. Powers 1960:5, 1961a:97). Sacred dances were the tribal dances centered around sacred objects or bundles ("Sarcee," fig. 6, this vol.), and the Sun Dance and Ghost

Dance. The dances of curing, of men's and women's societies, of hand games, and of adoption (Calumet) were somewhat religious in character but not sacerdotal. Besides these ceremonial dances, there were numerous social dances, some tribal and some widespread, which were danced in connection with the ceremonies. And sometimes social dances were held separately just for entertainment.

Many twentieth-century social dances had been more ceremonial in the nineteenth century, such as the Scalp Dance for women ("Tonkawa," fig. 7, this vol.) and old victory and society dances for men. Most social dances were shared by several tribes or spread across the entire Plains. Some mixed social dances were the Rabbit Dance, Crow Dance, Fox Dance, Owl Dance, Shuffling-feet Dance, and Night Dance, Two-step, Stomp Dance, and Squaw Dance. Some dances had traditionally been women's dances: the Scalp Dance, Round Dance, the Goose society ("Mandan," fig. 6, this vol.), and the Assiniboine Women's Circle Dance, which included a Bonnet song (Densmore 1918:479–480; W.K. Powers 1961; Nettl 1967:151; M.S. Kennedy 1961:135).

Grass Dance

One men's society dance that spread across the Plains in the nineteenth century was the Grass Dance or Omaha Dance (Kiowa *óhò·mó·*). One version, the Southern Arapaho Crow Dance, which featured an "immense drum" and incorporated songs referring to the crow and the Messiah, was an integral part of the Ghost Dance. Both men and women participated (Mooney 1896:901). In the twentieth century, versions called the Omaha Dance or Grass Dance (not to be confused with the late twentieth-century Grass Dance of the powwows) continued as a social dance of the Northern Plains.

Assiniboine Grass Dance songs from the traditional ceremony included the Spoon song, Forked Spit song, Belt song, Spoon Keepers song, Servers song, and Big Spit Keepers song. The last was sung without words once, then with the words "Arise, arise, 'they say' it means you, Big Spit Keeper" (M.S. Kennedy:1961:143). Also sung by at least one singer and an assistant were War Dance songs, and a closing song.

Sioux Omaha Dance

W.K. Powers (1961c) characterized mid-twentieth-century Sioux Omaha Dance songs as being of three classes: with words, with vocables, and with both words and vocables. Those with words were social songs and war songs (victory songs, flag songs, honor songs). The structure of these war songs differed from the structure of War Dance songs in that they consisted of eight parts rather than six. Several renditions of a song formed a complete dance. Powers considered the songs with words as older: "most of the songs were made on the reservation by Sioux songmakers and were about the Sioux. Fifty per cent of the songs had words, and many of them spoke the language of the old-timers, the 'ehank' wicasa' [ehák wičháša]. The remaining percentage had no words but they were still very definitely Sioux in melody, vocables, and voice quality" (W.K. Powers 1961c:31). Many Omaha Dance songs sung only with vocables came in from other tribes.

A characteristic style of drumming accompanied Omaha Dance songs. Although the tempo of a song might be slow, medium, or fast, the tempo always increased after the second rendition of the song with the volume becoming louder at the beginning of each new rendition, softer at the beginning of every repeat chorus, and louder again as the ending approached (W.K. Powers 1961c).

War Dance

Perhaps the songs considered most quintessentially Plains in the twentieth century were those called War Dance songs. War dances incorporated a type of dancing where men used their own individualistic steps and body movement and women danced in one of several group-style steps, moving or in place. Sometimes old society songs, family songs, Ghost Dance songs, or community songs were sung, usually for special events. Those in honor of war heroes, such as Sioux Omaha Dance, Arapaho Wolf Dance, and Assiniboine Grass Dance songs were sung with words. But many songs were composed specifically for the twentieth-century intertribal war dance and used vocables or a combination of vocables and words. Music most often consisted of descending melodies using pentatonic scales. In the north, pitch was higher, at some points falsetto; in the south, there were "nasal, quavering tones" (W.K. Powers 1968:68–69).

War Dance songs were accompanied by drumbeats. Usually, a group of men sat around a big drum, beating it with sticks long enough to accommodate a large circle of chairs around a single drum. Women singers sat in a circle behind the men. Songs were sung in unison with women singing an octave above men, voices trailing off after each chorus.

There were songs of slow, medium and fast tempo. The rhythm was pulsating, increasing and decreasing in volume intermittently. Accented duple drumbeats and secondary accented drumbeats occurred at specific junctures. There was a coordination of voice and drum. In some songs, the drum beat coincided precisely with the utterance of the vocable, but more often the beat occurred "between" the vocables. When tempo accelerated or retarded, there was a constant relationship between voice and drum. Word songs, vocable songs, and songs with both words and vocables were used (W.K. Powers 1961a:128–129, 1968:71). The overall feeling was 6/8 time.

War Dance songs were probably the most homogenous in style of all Plains songs. The repertoire was enormous, and singers were often obliged to learn a song quickly and remember it for many years.

The structure of War Dance songs has been characterized as "incomplete repetition." There were two basic sections, the second a diminished version of the first. Each song had six parts. (1) The introduction was sung by the leader "to identify the song for the other singers, to establish the pitch in the first rendition." (2) The second was a repeat of the lead by the rest of the group. (3) The chorus was sung by the entire group in vocables. (4) The first ending, sung by the entire group, signaled the halfway point of the song. Here women singers would join in. On the Southern Plains, the first ending might be sung to the accompaniment of seven beats of the drum called "honor beats." These were duple accents beginning with the last beat of the first ending and continuing, to introduce the repeat chorus. Here the women's voices trailed off behind the men's. This was called a five-count ending because the drum accented the last five beats of the song. (5) The repeat chorus, repeating the chorus only, was sung by the entire group in words or vocables. On the Northern Plains, the honor beats occurred in the middle of the repeat chorus. In Oklahoma, the repeat chorus began with a three-beat accent, then sometimes softened so that the words could be heard. (6) The final ending, corresponding to the first ending, except for a slight change in vocables, signaled the end of one complete song.

For a War Dance, the complete song was repeated as many as 20 times in the north and usually three or four times in the south. At the end of a dance, a "tail" might be sung. In the south, this usually consisted of one rendition of the repeat chorus and the final ending, separated from the last song by a short pause. In the north this might be the repeat chorus plus another complete song. Whether or not a song was repeated was governed by the lead singer, who would begin the lead again while the rest were still singing the final ending. The lead singer might start the pitch higher or increase tempo (with a series of accented duple beats picking up tempo) before he began his lead line (W.K. Powers 1961a:128–133, 1968:71–72).

Composing and Learning Songs

Historically, musical composition was probably not a recognized activity among Plains tribes. Songs were not considered to be products of individual creation. Nettl (1967:299) wrote of the Blackfoot: "Songs were given to one in dreams by guardian spirits, they could be learned from other tribes, or they might be so old that no one was willing to speculate on their origin." Songs from visions or dreams were heard only once—sung in the vision by animals or natural phenomena. Eagle Chief, a Pawnee, told Natalie Curtis (1907:96) that the sacred songs and ceremonial dances of his people were given through the animals. Writing of the Cheyenne, Stands in Timber and Liberty (1967:64) stated: "There were hundreds of songs, and they came to the people in many ways. Sometimes a man made one up or heard it in a dream or vision. Sometimes he heard it from an animal out in the hills." Songs, like names, were incorporeal property (Llewellyn and Hoebel 1941:237).

In the twentieth century, the sense of "working out" a song to oneself permeated the process of composition although the terms "make" or "compose" were rarely used in reference to songs. Songs, including both music and words or vocables, were usually composed by individuals established as singers or composers (D.B. Lee 1995:59, 65).

Learning songs was the most important aspect of nineteenth- and twentieth-century Plains music. Because songs were not written down, only by memorizing them could people keep their music alive. Some individuals used "whisper whistling" to learn a song. They whistled or aspirated to themselves while they listened to the song, enabling them to hear both the singers and their own renditions (Powers 1960:7). By the late twentieth century, cassette tape recorders were ubiquitous at powwows and became an important medium for the spread of songs. Songs were learned as wholes. Nettl (1989:103) found that Blackfoot singers felt that songs should not be taken apart, analyzed, or learned by components because songs had integrity and continuity and, "in certain respects, an existence outside the realm of everyday life."

At the close of the twentieth century, Plains singers and composers were concerned that their songs be carried into the new millennium by the next generation. Songs and dances were considered to be fundamental elements of tribal cultures. In the words of Ponca singer Maynard Hinman (D.B. Lee 1995:73), "We have to do this to remain who we are."

Art Until 1900

CANDACE S. GREENE

Art was an integral part of life, not a separate domain in Plains society. No objects were created purely for visual reflection, and there was no word that was used inclusively to refer to items of esthetic appeal. Art production was closely integrated into other aspects of life, rather than set apart as a distinct type of activity. However, the elaboration and decoration of functional objects were major opportunities for creative expression in Plains culture. Although these societies did not support full-time artists, individuals with particular skill were recognized and honored. Judgments of quality were based on fine craftsmanship and technical virtuosity in production, as well as on visual creativity within established formal boundaries. The distinction between art and craft is not meaningful in traditional Plains Indian art. The categories of objects described here have been chosen because they met modern criteria as art, many have been preserved in museums, and a discussion of their history and cultural context should be useful.

Plains art is inherently linked to the material goods that served the Plains lifeway. In historic times, the area was inhabited by nomadic, bison-hunting tribes, as well as by horticulturalists who maintained permanent villages but also regularly went on lengthy hunting expeditions. Portable goods were important under such conditions, and tribes such as the Pawnee abandoned the production of breakable ceramic vessels as they became increasingly nomadic (Weltfish 1965:363). A large percentage of material goods—clothing, domestic furnishings, and tepee covers—were made of animal skins, with bison hide the most important.

The Plains was a dynamic region experiencing enormous cultural and economic change during historic times. New peoples moved into the area, each bringing their own artistic traditions. The introduction of the horse opened new economic opportunities, as well as providing the means to transport a much richer suite of material culture than could have been assembled in prehorse times. As the mercantile networks and expanding populations of the United States and Canada spread around and across the Plains, the art of the area changed continually in response to new materials, influences, and social circumstances.

Knowledge of Plains art from before the nineteenth century is quite limited. Most art was made of perishable materials that are poorly preserved in archeological sites, and there were few non-Native visitors to the region to record their observations of customs or acquire and preserve examples of local crafts. The completeness of the material record increases through the century, and the majority of artifacts preserved in collections are from the late nineteenth and early twentieth century, documenting patterns of the reservation era. The names of only a few artists are known, and the work of most individuals has become submerged within broader tribal or regional traditions.

Forms and Techniques

Quillwork and Beadwork

Quillwork was a major decorative art form on the Plains over a long period of time (fig. 1). The hollow quills of the porcupine (*Erethizon dorsatum*) were dyed, flattened, and sewn with sinew to many objects, particularly clothing and personal accessories ("Omaha," fig. 5 and "Santee," fig. 2, this vol.). Quillwork was widespread throughout northern North America where porcupines were abundant. It was produced on the Northern and Central Plains, but not among southern tribes such as the Kiowa and Comanche. Although occasionally found along wooded river courses, porcupines were not common throughout the Plains, and quills must have been a regular item of intertribal trade. Split bird quills were sometimes used in place of porcupine quills ("Blackfoot," fig. 6f, this vol.) (Feder 1987). Prepared plant fibers were also incorporated into quillwork, particularly by the Southern Cheyenne and Arapaho after their removal to present-day Oklahoma (Grinnell 1923, 1:164; Kroeber 1902–1907:60). Originally produced entirely of indigenous materials (quills, sinew, and vegetal dyes), quillworking is believed to be an ancient art. Archeologists have discovered quillworking tools in a Plains site dated to the 6th century A.D. (Wormington and Forbis 1965:149). Once European trade materials became available, native vegetal dyes were supplemented with colors obtained from boiling quills with strips of brightly dyed blankets, and by the 1880s brilliant aniline dyes were widely used (Bebbington 1982:13, 50; Lyford 1940; Orchard 1916). A rich variety of quilling techniques was used on the Plains. Some, such as two-thread sewing, were practiced throughout the region, while loom weaving (fig. 1) was produced only on the eastern margin of the Plains by the Santee (Feder 1964). Early nineteenth-century travelers on the Plains commented upon the abundance and beauty of elaborately quilled garments (Catlin 1844; Kurz 1937; Coues 1897; Maximilian 1843, 1976), but quillworking declined during the second *1039*

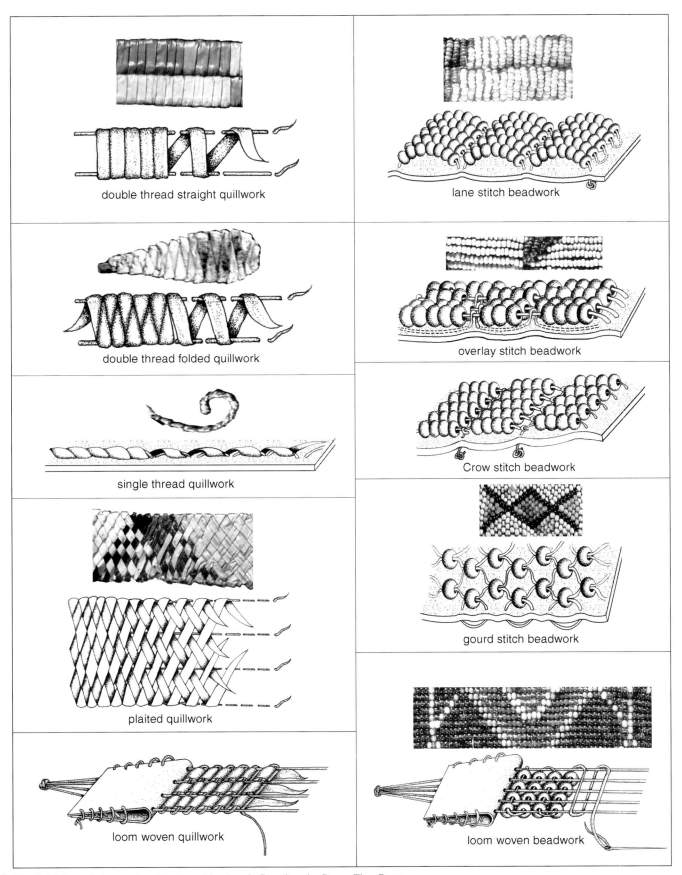

double thread straight quillwork

lane stitch beadwork

double thread folded quillwork

overlay stitch beadwork

single thread quillwork

Crow stitch beadwork

plaited quillwork

gourd stitch beadwork

loom woven quillwork

loom woven beadwork

Fig. 1. Major techniques of quillwork and beadwork. Drawings by Roger Thor Roop.

half of the century as small glass beads suitable for producing similar decoration became widely available. Most tribes had abandoned quillwork by the 1870s except for the Teton Sioux and the tribes of Fort Berthold ("Mandan," fig. 4, this vol.) (Pohrt 1989:77). By the start of the twentieth century, only the Teton produced quillwork in quantity (Bebbington 1982:30), and they were the primary Plains quillworkers about 2000.

Beadwork was a direct outgrowth of quillwork, and beadworkers adapted many of their techniques, forms, and designs from the earlier craft. Virtually all the Native people of North America produced beadwork, but the craft was developed to its highest level by the Indians of the Plains region. Glass trade beads of Italian manufacture were a staple item of the European traders from earliest contact, but it was not until around 1800 that small beads suitable for sewing together to create designs began to appear on the Plains. By 1840 beadwork was widely produced throughout the region. The early embroidery beads, known as pony beads, were three to four millimeters in diameter and offered a limited range of colors, primarily white, black, and blue ("History of the United States Plains Until 1850," fig. 5, this vol.). Early designs consisted of broad bands with simple blocks of color. Smaller beads, with diameters of one and one-half to two millimeters or smaller, known as seed beads, began to enter the Plains in quantity around 1850. They offered a much wider range of colors and the potential to create more finely detailed designs. Within two decades the majority of beadwork was done in seed beads, with only a few beadworkers on the northwestern Plains continuing to prefer pony beads (Hail 1980:15; Lyford 1940; Orchard 1929; C.F. Taylor 1994:139–140; Wildschut and Ewers 1959:2). Various techniques were developed, most based on quillwork prototypes (Barth 1993). Lane stitch (lazy stitch) and overlay were always the most common forms. Crow stitch was confined almost exclusively to the northwestern Plains and adjacent Plateau regions, while gourd stitch was a technique of the Southern Plains. Loom-woven beadwork was produced primarily by the tribes along the eastern margin of the Plains, particularly the Santee (Lyford 1940:64). Another shift in materials occurred after World War I when inexpensive beads from Czechoslovakia became widely available, largely displacing the similarly sized Italian seed beads (Conn 1986:26). Seed beadwork was usually applied in bands or patterns placed against an unmodified background, but it could be used to cover large surfaces such as cradleboards or dress yokes. Beadworking continued as a vigorous art tradition on the Plains into the twenty-first century.

Hide Painting

Hide painting was a highly developed art form on the Plains. Once widely practiced in many areas of North America, few examples of painted hides from outside the Plains have survived. The art is undoubtedly ancient, and it is mentioned in one of the earliest written records regarding Plains customs, the reports of Francisco Vásquez de Coronado's expedition of 1540 (Winship 1896:404). Native paints were primarily earth pigments, occasionally supplemented with vegetal substances. The collecting and processing of paints required special skills, and paints of various colors were widely traded. Commercial pigments obtained from traders entered the Plains in the eighteenth century and had replaced native earth pigments by the last quarter of the nineteenth century. Paints were stored dry and prepared for use by grinding a piece to powder and mixing in a liquid, either plain water or water in which hide scrapings had been boiled to create a thin glue. Paint was applied with a porous piece of bone or wood. A flat spongy piece from the interior of a buffalo leg bone was a favored paint applicator ("Introduction," fig. 3g–h, this vol.). One edge was sharply beveled for drawing fine lines while the others were rounded for applying paint to larger surfaces. Designs on both tanned and raw hides were first carefully outlined, then filled in with solid, unshaded blocks of color (Ewers 1939:4; Torrence 1994:45).

Rawhide containers made from bison hide were extensively used during the nomadic bison hunting era. They were often painted with geometric designs created by dividing a decorative field into smaller and smaller elements, often outlined with fine black lines ("Comanche," fig. 2, and "Iowa," fig. 5, this vol.). Some rawhide containers from the northwestern Plains and adjacent Plateau region have designs created by incising the surface rather than painting. After bison hide was no longer available, containers made of rawhide from domestic cattle continued to be painted in traditional techniques, but the art declined as Plains people came to rely upon manufactured containers for daily use. Folded rawhide containers known as parfleches ("Introduction," fig. 3, this vol.) continued to be produced for gift giving into the early decades of the twentieth century among the Northern Arapahoe, Teton Sioux, Blackfoot, and Crow. Many parfleches in museum collections were not produced by the tribe from which they were acquired due to this extensive intertribal exchange (Morrow 1975; Torrence 1994).

Geometric designs were also painted on tanned hides, most often buffalo robes and tepee liners (figs. 2–3). Ewers (1939:8) defined five basic geometric designs used on wearing robes during the nineteenth century, several of which were used by a number of tribes. Early European collections, although often poorly documented, suggest that a greater variety of designs existed at an earlier time (Horse Capture 1993). Geometric hide painting declined as trade blankets replaced buffalo robes.

Hides were also painted with pictorial representations, usually scenes of war and other male accomplishments ("History of the United States Plains Until 1850," fig. 5, and "Quapaw," fig. 3, this vol.). Such pictures were placed not only on buffalo robes and tepee liners, but also on buckskin shirts and occasionally on tepee covers. Figures were drawn *1041*

a

b

in strong outline, sometimes filled in with color. Elements necessary to convey the action of the story and identify individuals were included, but background was omitted and there was no concern with creating the illusion of three dimensionality. Large surfaces were covered with a scattering

of independent scenes rather than a connected narrative (Maurer 1992). Rock art is the earliest representational art known from the Plains. A broad variety of figures were produced over time, but the "biographic" style that emerged in the late eighteenth century is similar in form and content

a, Harvard U., Peabody Mus., Cambridge, Mass.: 99-12-10/53121 (neg. 27515); b, Deutsches Ledermuseum, Offenbach, Federal Republic of Germany: 4.44.09; bottom left, Smithsonian, Natl. Mus. of the Amer. Ind.: 19/630; bottom right, Denver Art Mus.: 1980.35.

Fig. 2. Painted robes. Pictorial hides were produced throughout the Plains, painted primarily with scenes of warfare. a, Earliest firmly dated pictorial robe, Mandan, collected by Lewis and Clark in 1805. The figures are drawn in outline, some filled in with color. The pictures represent battles of the Mandan and their Hidatsa allies against the Sioux and Arikara. Geometric designs were more regionally restricted in production but were often widely distributed through trade. b, Horizontal stripe robe, Blackfeet. Stripes were beaded or quilled on robes throughout the Plains, but they were also painted on robes on the Northern Plains. bottom left, Feathered Circle design robe, Mandan. A man's design, it has been interpreted as representing a war bonnet (Horse Capture 1993:65). bottom right, Border and Box design robe, Yankton Sioux. The design, most common among the Sioux, was considered a women's design, which would not be worn by men. Compare the Border and Hourglass design of the Southern Plains ("Comanche," fig. 3, this vol.). The Bilaterally Symmetrical design was characterized by horizontal upper and lower borders with inward pointing geometric designs (Ewers 1939: pl. 13). a, Width 2.43 m; b, collected by Maximilian, Price of Wied, 1833, width 2.25 m; bottom left, collected at Ft. Berthold Res., Dak. Terr., 1878–1885, width 2.54 m; bottom right, collected about 1870, width 1.96 m.

to pictorial hide painting, which may have taken on its present form around the same time (Keyser 1977:52).

Even before hides became scarce, artists began placing pictures on convenient trade materials, such as the bound pages of account ledgers ("Cheyenne," figs. 2, 9, this vol.). Nineteenth-century drawings on paper of many types are often called "ledger art." Pictures on paper and on muslin, which replaced hides for tepee liners and some clothing, were drawn with commercial pens, pencils, crayon, and occasionally watercolor paints. Throughout the last half of the nineteenth century, pictures became increasingly detailed and naturalistic. After tribes were confined to reservations, drawings continued to focus on scenes of action; but the subject range expanded to include hunting, courting, and public religious gatherings in addition to warfare. Many drawings on paper, muslin, and various types of hides were made for outside sale (Berlo 1996; P.J. Powell 1976). A group of Southern Plains men who were held as prisoners at Fort Marion, Florida, from 1875–1878, developed a major market for their artwork and sold hundreds of their drawings (fig. 4). Working in isolation from their home communities, they developed a distinctive approach to style and content, introducing environmental elements into a rich variety of subjects set both in Florida and at home (K.D. Petersen 1971; C.S. Greene 1992). Plains pictorial art continued among many tribes as an active tradition until

about 1900. Very little pictorial art was produced over the following two to three decades, until the academically based Plains painting revival began in the late 1920s.

In addition to recording scenes of action, pictorial art was used in ways more akin to picture writing—to record and communicate specific information. The best-preserved records of this type are the pictorial calendars maintained by several tribes, but best known among the Sioux, Kiowa, and Blackfoot. They are often called "winter counts" as the Teton Sioux, among whom they were first reported, counted their years by winters (J.R. Walker 1982:123); however, the Kiowa calendars recorded both a summer and a winter event for each year (Mooney 1898). A tribal historian gave each year a name based on a memorable occurrence of the season, and other events could be placed in time by reference to that year name. As an aid to keep the years in sequence, pictures evocative of the year names were painted in a linear sequence, originally on buffalo hides. These images were much cruder than other forms of pictorial art, but served adequately as a mnemonic device. Like other pictorial art, calendars were transferred from hide to paper and muslin when these materials became commonly available. Most of the surviving calendars on hide are late nineteenth or early twentieth-century copies made for sale, some by noted tribal historians. Picture writing was also used to leave messages for the scattered members of camps, and, during the reservation era, to send messages through the mail (Mallery 1893:336, 359, 363).

Geometric and representational forms were combined in paintings that reproduced in symbolic form encounters with the spiritual world. Such images were usually received during a vision quest, in which a man sought supernatural assistance. Visionary designs were painted on war shields ("Arikara," fig. 5, and "Crow," fig. 6, this vol.), tepee covers, and clothing as a form of protection. Individual animal or spirit figures ("Assiniboine," fig. 4, "Plains Apache," fig. 4, this vol.) were drawn in the flat, outlined style of the pictorial tradition, but the intent was not to convey a clear story but rather to allude to a private spiritual encounter. Other elements were represented in abstract form by geometric shapes, placed on the object in accordance with their meaning rather than for decorative effect. Abstract images appearing in ancient rock art throughout North America are assumed to be early examples of visionary art. The tradition was well developed on hide by the early historic period and *1043*

Canadian Mus. of Civilization, Hull, Que.: 52840.

Fig. 3. Men painting a hide with war deeds as dictated by Old Sarcee or White Antelope (center). The completed hide is in the Canadian Mus. of Civilization (Jenness 1938:33–35). A decorated tepee liner is in the background as are two backrests on tripods. Photograph by Diamond Jenness, Sarcee Res., Calgary, Alta., 1921.

Smithsonian, NAA: left, Ms. 39C (08547601); right, Ms. 154,064C (08511200).

Fig. 4. Drawings made at Ft. Marion, Fla. Early works by the men imprisoned at Ft. Marion 1875–1878 were similar to those produced by artists who remained at home, while later works included new subjects and forms of composition. left, Drawing of warfare by the Kiowa artist Koba on a ruled page from a composition book, similar to ledger books produced on the Southern Plains. right, Camp scene in a landscape of hills and trees, a more complex composition, by a Cheyenne artist.

continued with vigor throughout the period of Plains warfare. It was a conservative art experiencing little change, thanks to its religious associations as well as the practice of passing powerful designs down through the generations (Ewers 1978; Nagy 1994; Penney 1992:279–281). With the end of Plains warfare, the production of visionary art atrophied. However, some old designs were reproduced on muslin dance shields, and the Blackfoot and Sarcee continued to paint traditional designs upon their canvas tepee covers ("Blackfoot," fig. 4, and "Sarcee," fig. 3, this vol.) (Libhart and Ellison 1973:45). A rich body of visionary art was produced during the Ghost Dance movement ("Arapaho," fig. 4, this vol.) (H.L. Peterson 1976; Josephy, Thomas, and Eder 1990; Wissler 1907:31–40), and the Peyote religion has been a major inspiration for art in several media, although Peyote painting did not develop until well into the twentieth century ("Intertribal Religious Movements," fig. 8, this vol.) (Wiedman and Greene 1988).

Carving

Both stone and wood were carved to produce a variety of practical items that were sometimes further elaborated into sculptural forms. Wood sculpture was probably the older form, but evidence of its early history is poorly preserved. Stone was also carved to create pipe bowls and animal effigies in prehistoric times, but the introduction of metal tools greatly increased productivity in both media.

Pipe bowls continued to be the primary item of stone sculpture, carved and polished with decorative shaping or figural forms. The material most extensively used was catlinite, an easily worked red stone primarily derived from a quarry in southeastern Minnesota, now the site of Pip-

estone National Monument. It was widely traded throughout the Plains, and many tribes traveled to the area to quarry it themselves. A fine-grained black shale was also used for carving. Both were at times decorated with a lead inlay poured into shallowly incised areas, then polished smooth with the surface. Beautifully shaped and crafted T-shaped, elbow, tubular, and simple effigy pipes were produced throughout a long period of time. Elaborate effigy pipes appeared in the early decades of the nineteenth century, principally made for sale by Santees and Pawnees, once steamboat service on the Mississippi and Missouri rivers brought increased numbers of travelers ("Santee," fig. 10, this vol.). A large number of catlinite pipes and other sale items were produced in the last three decades of the nineteenth century by a community of Santee Sioux carvers, who relocated to Flandreau, South Dakota, near the quarry in 1869 (Ewers 1986; Penney 1992:267–272).

In contrast to stonework, wood carving was almost entirely for Native consumption until the final decades of the nineteenth century. Bowls, spoons, war clubs, pipe stems, flutes, and effigies for victory dances and hunting magic were produced by many Plains groups, but carving was most developed among the eastern tribes. Both styles and forms were closely related to the carving traditions of the woodlands (Ewers 1986:11; Penney 1992:273–278).

Other Media

The production of metal ornaments was an important minor craft, and supplemented the many trade items in use. Decorations for horse gear and personal adornment were made from sheets of brass, copper, tin, silver, and German silver. Unwrought metals were sometimes obtained through traders, but were often reworked from manufactured items. Brass and copper trade kettles were cut apart to obtain sheet goods, and silver coins were hammered into thin disks. Metalworking techniques were simple. The base material was hammered, rough cut with a chisel, and filed into final shape. Common methods of decoration included stamping with repeating patterns, scratch engraving, and rocker engraving, which created figures with a zigzag outline. Metalworking was dependent upon access to suitable trade materials. As refined metals became available in various areas of North America, Native people were quick to adopt them as well as to fashion their own tools, such as arrowheads and hide scrapers, from scrap iron. The same methods were applied to the creation of ornaments when decorative materials such as silver and brass became available on the Plains around 1800. The horticultural tribes of the eastern Plains favored forms common throughout eastern North America, such as a proliferation of pierced brooches applied to cloth garments. These followed forms manufactured by French and British smiths for the Indian trade. Other Plains people developed distinctive forms influenced more by Hispanic sources, via the Southwest and Mexico, including silver-mounted bridles, conchos, crescents, and large crosses (Ellison 1976:14). Hairplates were one of the most highly developed ornaments on the Plains. They consisted of a set of metal disks of graduated size attached to a strap of hide, braided buffalo hair, or trade cloth, which was worn trailing from the back of the head ("Sioux Until 1850," fig. 4, bottom right, this vol.). Another distinctive form was a broad, scalloped pendant, which was worn on the chest. For decades decorative metals were scarce, and items made of silver or brass were highly valued symbols of wealth and status. Around 1865 German silver, an inexpensive, easily worked, white-metal alloy of copper, nickel, and zinc, became widely available in sheet form, and sparked a florescence in metalworking and widespread use of such ornamentation. By 1880 these abundant ornaments had passed out of fashion, and metalworking was largely limited to the production of jewelry associated with the Peyote religion, which continued to be the mainstay of the craft, as well as dance accessories (Ellison 1976; Feder 1962).

Textile production may once have been widespread among the horticultural people of the Plains, to judge from the twined containers that have survived only for ceremonial objects ("Osage," fig. 4, this vol.), but little is known about it. By the last half of the nineteenth century, the only textiles being produced in quantity were sashes, garters, and other strip textiles worked in a technique commonly called finger-weaving. Without the use of a loom, commercial yarns in often brilliant colors were braided together to create complex patterns, often outlined with glass beads woven into the fabric. This technique is ancient in North America, originally using fibers spun of native plants, with the Prairie people of the eastern Plains representing its westernmost extent. Their practice of this craft was reinforced when Eastern tribes who also practiced it were relocated among them in the 1830s and 1840s (F.H. Douglas 1938; Fletcher and LaFlesche 1911:348; J.H. Howard 1965:52; Penney 1992:26; Skinner 1919c:166, 1926:285). Finger-weaving continued into the 1990s on a small scale as essential for the production of clothing for ceremonies and other traditional dress occasions.

Some eastern Plains tribes decorated their best trade cloth garments with appliqué made from silk ribbons or other bright colored cloth ("Otoe and Missouria," fig. 10, and "Iowa," fig. 8, this vol.). Bands of different colors were cut into decorative shapes and sewn along the borders of blankets, skirts, breechcloths, leggings, and on moccasin cuffs. In one technique, overlapping layers of ribbons were cut and folded to create complex, banded, saw-toothed patterns. An alternate technique was to cut large, often curvilinear designs out of the surface layer to expose a contrasting color of fabric below. As with finger-weaving, ribbonwork appliqué was primarily a Northeast art form, which Prairie tribes shared with the woodlands people displaced to their area (Abbass 1980; Marriott 1959). Nomadic Plains tribes placed on reservations in Indian Territory adopted the concept of appliqué from their eastern neighbors to a limited extent, adorning wool breechcloths and saddle blankets with simple edgings of cotton cloth appliquéd in serrated designs created by folding (M.J. Schneider 1980:201).

Two crafts, pottery and basketry, were practiced by only a few of the horticultural tribes during the nineteenth century, although they were once much more widespread ("Arikara," fig. 2, and "Plains Village Tradition: Postcontact," fig. 3, this vol.). Earthenware vessels in a variety of bowl and jar shapes were produced to hold liquids and for cooking. They were hand-built and unpainted. A variety of surface treatments provided decoration, including cord marking, incising, stamped and punctate designs. Ceramic production is well documented archeologically. It appears in the Early Woodland period, circa 400 B.C., probably introduced from the east (Gregg et al. 1996:84; W.R. Wedel 1961:90–96). It was produced by all the Plains Village groups and persisted into the historic era among the horticultural tribes. Groups such as the Cheyenne and Crow, who adopted a nomadic hunting economy, discarded their pottery-making traditions (Grinnell 1923, 1:49; W.R. Wood 1962:27). Once metal trade vessels became available, they largely replaced the native earthenware forms. Pottery making persisted longest among the Mandan (Bowers 1950:91), Hidatsa ("Hidatsa," fig. 5, this vol.) (Gilman and Schneider 1987:118–119), and Arikara (Gilmore 1925a).

Basketry was another craft practiced primarily by a few horticultural tribes. Large baskets plaited of wood splints made from willow and box elder were made by the Hidatsa, Mandan, and Arikara. Geometric patterns were created by using splints of different colors, either naturally occuring or dyed (F.H. Douglas 1941; Gilmore 1925; M.J. Schneider 1984). While the particular forms of Upper Missouri River basketry are distinctive, the basic craft technique of plaited *1045* wood splint basketry is widely practiced throughout the woodlands to the east of the Plains. Small, coiled baskets worked on a bundle foundation were made by a number of tribes ("Mandan," fig. 7, and "Pawnee," fig. 7, this vol.). They were a part of the equipment of a gambling game in which plum pit dice were tossed in the basket (Weltfish 1930). Coiled basketry was a craft practiced to the west of the Plains region.

Beautiful items were crafted in a rich variety of other media. For many garments, the fine processing of the hide itself was a major esthetic component. On the Southern Plains, garments were sparingly decorated with beadwork, but hides were often stained in a solid color and lavishly adorned with long fringe ("Kiowa," fig. 3, and "Cheyenne," fig. 5, this vol.). Featherworking was highly developed for fans, headdresses, and dance accessories. Feathers were mounted into elaborate constructs and the shafts decorated with beading or quillwork ("History of Ethnological and Ethnohistorical Research," fig. 2, and "Comanche," fig. 9, this vol.). Drawings and descriptions record that the body was another site for esthetic embellishment. Tattooing was practiced among some groups, and face and body paint was widely used for warfare and ceremony.

Regional and Tribal Styles

Many forms of art were practiced throughout the Plains, but there was regional and tribal variation in preferences for certain techniques and designs. There are not enough well-documented materials from the years before the 1850s to define clear stylistic boundaries, but certain forms appear to have been shared over wide geographical areas. A generalized Upper Missouri River style has been described, which was shared among the Mandan, Hidatsa, and Arikara as well as the more nomadic Blackfoot and Assiniboine, who came to their villages for trading ("Blackfoot," fig. 6, this vol.) (Penney 1992:149–150; Pohrt 1989:73). Most of the collections from the first half of the nineteenth century are from this northern area, leaving considerable uncertainty about activities in other parts of the region. Scattered material from the Central Plains suggests widely shared styles there as well, with simple striped and banded patterns developing with the newly introduced pony beads (Conn 1986:99). The only collection of any size from the far Southern Plains, that assembled by Louis Berlandier between 1828–1851, indicates that the art of that area was quite different (Ewers 1969).

Stylistic diversity increased dramatically after 1860 when seed beads became generally available, and there are sufficient materials with clear provenience to allow the identification of regional and often tribally specific style traditions (fig. 5). Five regional styles have been identified for geometric beadwork, which correspond generally with regional traditions defined in other media such as quillwork and geometric hide painting (Bebbington 1982:19; Torrence 1994:83). There are also floral and pictoral styles.

On the Northern Plains during this period, there was general similarity among the beadwork of the Blackfoot, Sarcee, Stoney, Plains Cree, Assiniboine, Hidatsa, and Mandan (Conn 1986:100; Ewers 1945). All richly decorated their clothing, containers, and household goods with beadwork produced in the overlay technique. Lane stitch was used sparingly for edging. Large, solid geometric figures bordered in one or two contrasting colors were spaced over a background that was usually white or light blue ("Assiniboine," fig. 8, and "Sarcee," fig. 4, this vol.). Distinctions within this style developed among reservation communities as well as along tribal lines, so that a Fort Berthold (Mandan, Hidatsa, Arikara) style and a Fort Belknap (Gros Ventre, Assiniboine) style can be identified (Penney 1992:204–206; Pohrt 1989:77). Floral styles of beadwork were introduced by contact with eastern tribes being shifted west in response to the fur trade ("Plains Métis," fig. 8, this vol.). Floral work was produced by the Santee Sioux in the late eighteenth century and by more westerly Plains tribes as early as the 1860s (Conn 1986:22). It gained in popularity throughout the century but never displaced the geometric tradition (Ewers 1945:36).

South and west of these groups, a style of beadwork known as Transmontane was produced by a single Plains tribe, the Crow, together with several Plateau groups, principally the Nez Perce, Northern Shoshone, and Flathead (Conn 1986:128; Dyck 1988; Lessard 1984a; Wildschut and Ewers 1959). The primary technique used was the Crow stitch, with overlay used only for producing curved lines and outlining of figures. As on the Northern Plains, lane stitch was used only for edging. Geometric designs consisted primarily of defined panels or bands divided by transverse stripes, containing smooth hourglass or triangular forms. Within these, complex interlocking geometric forms were created in contrasting colors. Designs in a rich mix of pastel colors were placed against a ground of light blue or lavender pink, often demarcated by a line of white beads laid in separately. Sections of red trade cloth might be set into unbeaded areas as an accent. This complex beadwork style, the only one on the Plains that appears more closely related to geometric painting on rawhide than to quillwork designs, was displaced in the early twentieth century by floral beadwork produced in overlay stitch ("Crow," fig. 8, this vol.) (Conn 1986:129), and reemerged at the end of the twentieth century.

The beadwork of the Central Plains tribes—Teton and Yankton and Yanktonai Sioux, Gros Ventre, Cheyenne, and Arapaho—was worked almost exclusively in lane stitch, with designs built up across several lanes. A white background was most common, although the Yankton and Yanktonai also frequently used a blue ground. All these tribes produced work with simple striped designs, as well as more complex geometric patterns with triangles, squares, and other basic shapes internally elaborated in a variety of colors. Initially, these forms were placed separately to stand out individually against the background, but over

1046

a   b   c   d   e   f   g

Smithsonian, Dept. of Anthr.: a, 425,910 (neg. 99-20272); c, 21,671 (neg. 99-20270); d, 151,926 (neg. 78-15898); e, 397,809 (neg. 89-10291); f, 152,889 (neg. 92-10733); Smithsonian, Natl. Mus. of the Amer. Ind.: b, 2/9637 (neg. N29344); g, Denver Art Mus. Colo.: 1970.423.

Fig. 5. Bags showing regional beadwork styles. a, Northern-style beadwork with block geometric designs worked in overlay stitch. b, Transmontane-style beadwork worked in Crow stitch with elongate hourglass figures outlined with a double line of beads against a solid background. The Crow stitch produces a smooth surface much like the overlay stitch. c, Floral-style beadwork worked in overlay stitch, with curving lines following the plant forms. This style, often using European motifs, was adopted by many tribes, particularly on the Northern Plains. d, Central-style beadwork with complex geometric designs built up over several rows of lane stitch. Pictorial beadwork required the creative application of a variety of stitches to produce tiny, detailed figures. There are subtle tribal differences within the Central style in the treatment of geometric figures. e, Stepped triangles with internal rectangles, more elongated in Cheyenne beadwork than in Sioux. f, Southern-style beadwork with abstract design worked in overlay stitch and outlines with a double row of dark and light beads set against a plain hide background. Such overlay designs were restricted almost exclusively to bags and cradles. g, Prairie-style beadwork with abstract designs worked in bright colors and outlined with a double line of white beads. a, Blackfeet, collected by Donald and Alice Dutcher on the Blackfeet Res., Mont., 1892–1898, length 39.7 cm; b, Crow, length 35.2 cm; c, Yankton Sioux, collected by J. Frazer Boughter in Dak. Terr., before 1875, length 53 cm; d, Sioux, collected by John G. Bourke before 1891, length 53 cm; e, Cheyenne, collected by B.W. Butler from George Bent, about 1915, length 45.7 cm; f, Kiowa, collected by James Mooney in Ind. Terr., 1891, length 25 cm; g, Otoe, length 28 cm; all measurements without fringe.

time they became connected into increasingly complex patterns. Teton work in particular became elaborated into a style known as "many points," as well as covering increasingly large areas, by the beginning of the twentieth century even entire garments (Conn 1986:29; Kroeber 1908; Lessard 1990a). Another late development was pictorial beadwork, which appeared in the 1890s (Lessard 1990, 1991; Penney 1992:187). Images based on the hide painting and ledger art traditions were first drawn, then beaded in overlay stitch on bags and occasionally garments. Many changes in tribal art traditions on the Central Plains were the result of contacts generated by the reservation system. Gros Ventre work, for example, became more closely tied to northern styles after they were settled at Fort Belknap with the Assiniboine (Penney 1992:206). Similarly Southern Cheyenne and Arapaho work took on new characteristics after they were settled in Indian Territory in close association with Southern Plains tribes (Conn 1961, 1976).

On the Southern Plains, the Kiowa, Comanche, and Plains Apache had no previous tradition of quillwork, and their decorative esthetic was designed to draw attention to the finely processed hide of the garment itself, often adorned with broad areas of paint and long fringes. Beadwork was used sparingly on garments, primarily as narrow borders worked in lane stitch and single figures placed against a buckskin background. Complex geometric designs were created, often within a single lane. Larger abstract designs were placed on bags and cradleboards, particularly by the Kiowa ("Kiowa," fig. 4, this vol.), with the central figure worked in overlay surrounded by a solid lane-stitch background, usually in a dark color. Gourd stitch was another technique distinctive of Southern Plains beadwork. Used extensively on equipment made for the Peyote ritual, it spread northward as other tribes accepted the religion. Among the Kiowa and Comanche, it was used on secular objects as well and can be found both in narrow lanes on moccasins and covering the large surfaces of cradleboards (Conn 1976; Merrill et al. 1997).

Along the eastern border of the Plains, a number of Plains horticultural tribes, together with eastern Indians who had been relocated to reservations with them, developed the Prairie style of beadwork. Emerging in the 1850s and 1860s, *1047* it was produced by the Pawnee, Osage, Omaha, Ponca, Otoe, Missouria, and Kansa ("Iowa," fig. 7, and "Otoe and Missouria," fig. 11, this vol.). Worked in overlay stitch, it was based upon curvilinear, abstract designs filled with closely nested strands of beads running in different directions within each design. Early work was often on hide bags and moccasins, while later designs, often more floral in character, were spread out against the dark wool background of skirts, breechcloths, and blankets. Hot colors contributed to the energy of the style, with white outlines emphasizing the complex shapes (Penney 1992:114–119).

Regional styles developed along lines of tribal interaction, following both prereservation alliances and reservation-era residence. Extensive trade in finished items as well as raw materials was noted by early travelers on the Plains (Jablow 1951:39–50; "Kiowa," fig. 6, and "Comanche," fig. 3, this vol.). Such exchange continued through the reservation period. The Crow, for example, were rich in horses during this time, and many tribes received horses from them in exchange for craftwork (Wildschut and Ewers 1959:50), while the Blackfoot received all their quillwork in trade from the Assiniboine and Teton (Ewers 1945:30). In 2000, gift exchange remained an important part of intertribal visiting. In addition to trade, ethnic boundaries were fairly fluid and many men and women married into allied tribes, bringing their skills and designs with them. Designs as well as completed items were given as gifts, giving the recipient the right to reproduce them. The design for the Kiowa Tepee with Battle Pictures was a gift from a Cheyenne ally (C.S. Greene 1993; C.S. Greene and T.D. Drescher 1994). At times, designs were captured from enemy tribes.

While many factors promoted similiarity in the arts among tribes, tribal differences were also well developed in most groups and were undoubtedly very clear to members of these communities. Differences in tribal beadwork styles escalated with the introduction of seed beads around 1860. These beads offered both a much wider palette of colors

and the opportunity to craft more intricate and varied patterns. During the same era other forms of trade materials, such as dyes for quills, pigments for hide painting, and steel tools used in craftwork, such as knives, awls, and needles became more widely available. Materials provided the opportunity for diversification in the arts, but social factors provided the motivation.

Art offered a highly visible marker of ethnic identity, perhaps of increasing importance during this period of intensified resource competition on the Plains as more tribes were pushed into the area from the East and bison herds began to diminish. These are also the arts that continued to fluorish during the reservation period. Stripped of political autonomy and pressured to conform to new cultural models, people responded by lavishing attention upon highly visible personal markers of ethnic identity (Logan and Schmittou 1995, 1995a; Penney 1992:28–54). Other arts that were based upon military achievements or spiritual access declined during these years.

The Production of Art

Art was produced by many members of society in Plains communities. However, social rules guided what an individual might produce and how the act of artistic production was viewed.

Personal Factors

Gender was the most pervasive factor controlling the production of art. Men generally made and decorated the primary weapons, utensils, and religious items that they used themselves and produced representational forms of art, both drawings and carvings. Women produced objects for their own use as well as making the clothing, housing, and furnishings that were used by the entire family. Beadwork and quillwork were exclusively women's arts, as

Fig. 6. Teton woman painting geometric designs on rawhide for parfleches. The skin is fixed to the ground with wooden stakes while another skin, not yet staked, is lying on the ground a short distance away. Photograph by John A. Anderson, Rosebud Res., S. Dak., © Jan. 1897.

were hide processing, pottery making, and basketry. Both men and women did wood carving, while stone carving, like metal smithing, appears to have been practiced only by men (Ewers 1945:58; M.J. Schneider 1983:103). Both men and women engaged in hide painting, men producing representational as well as visionary images, while women applied geometric designs to both tanned skins and rawhide surfaces (fig. 6) (Ewers 1939:7).

Girls' instruction in craft production was early, rigorous, and universal. All women were expected to be competent in the production of decorative art, although the particular craft specialities varied somewhat among tribes. Such skill was an attribute that enhanced a girl's desirablity as a marriage partner. Boys on the other hand took up art production at a later age and with greater reference to individual inclination. Such talents did not affect their standing as potential husbands (Grinnell 1923, 1:121; M.J. Schneider 1983). The statement made by Bol (1989:454) for the Teton that the production of art was an essential aspect of a woman's role but an incidental one for men applies well throughout the Plains region.

The linkage of craft production with female virtue was widespread on the Plains. Productivity was taken as an indicator not only of industry and hard work but also of high moral character, particularly sexual chastity (fig. 7). Prestigious craft associations accepted as members only women of acknowledged virtue. Young girls were exhorted to stay home and do beadwork as the alternative to running

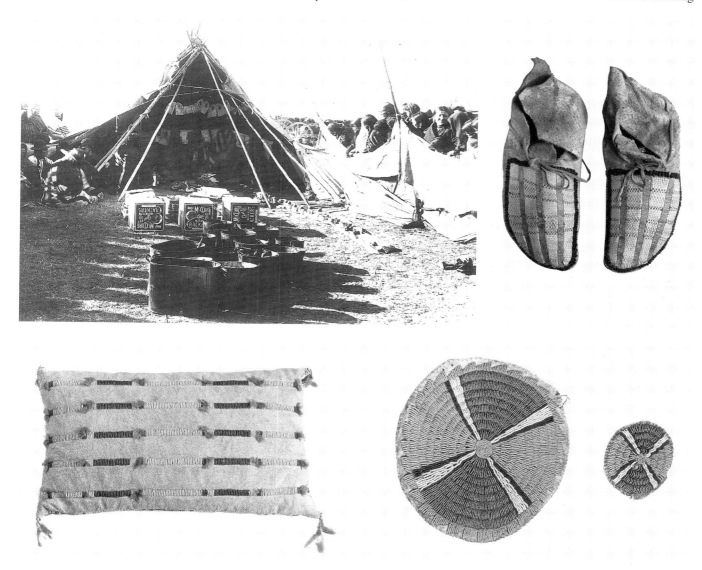

Fig. 7. Craft work. Women could achieve personal status through the production of fine work and manage social relationships by producing special items as gifts. top left, Lodge for Teton Sioux girls' puberty ceremony, with the moccasin tops displayed inside. Photograph by John A. Anderson, Rosebud Res., S. Dak., about 1892 (cropped). top right, Sioux moccasins elaborately decorated with bands of quillwork in a basket-weave technique. Collected by L.A. Schoch, 1837. bottom, Cheyenne sacred beadwork designs on a pillow and part of a set of tepee ornaments. Collected by Heinrich Voth in Ind. Terr., 1890s. top right, Length 25 cm; bottom, pillow 37 cm wide, others to same scale.

around with young men (DeMallie 1983). Among the Teton, a girl spent the time of seclusion during her first menses in doing quillwork (Hassrick 1964:41). She was thus guided in her choice between two opposing courses of life, one of modesty and the other of lewdness (Bol 1989:178). Double Woman, the Teton spiritual patron of quilling, is a figure of some ambiguity (Theisz 1988), associated with both creativity and powers of sexual seduction. Women who dreamed of Double Woman were chosen to become noted artists (M. Morrow 1975:43; W.K. Powers 1975:58; Theisz 1988:13; Wissler 1904:247).

Male involvement in the production of art differed from that of women. The emphasis for men was on the acquisition of social honors and spiritual distinctions suitable to form the content of artistic images. The visual representation was secondary, an advertisement of the primary accomplishment. Men sought spiritual assistance in the form of visions, which were represented on shields and tepees. They achieved war honors, which could be painted upon their robes or the pages of ledger books. Even some geometric beadwork designs among the Teton were schematic representations of men's war honors, which they directed women in producing (Wissler 1904:259–271) . Images might be produced by a commissioned artist, but the art was credited to the owner of the achievement represented rather than to the man who drew it.

In reviewing these differences, it becomes evident that for women greater emphasis was placed upon the processes involved in the production of art than it was for men. There was great emphasis upon gaining technical skill, with virtuosity recognized and esteemed. Associations existed to provide training and monitor the quality of work produced. A woman's frame of mind was perceived to shape the quality of her work, and quarrelsome thoughts had to be put away while doing certain forms of work. While a woman might acquire a design through a vision, the most powerful vision was the mandate to become an artist.

In contrast, how men were trained in the visual arts is little known. The training for a shield maker was evidently rigorous but focused primarily on spiritual rather than visual aspects (Grinnell 1923, 1:192). Training in secular representational arts appears to have been informal, men learning by observing others at work. Information about men's involvement in the arts stresses instead the acquisition of the content of the image itself, the sacred design or secular event to be depicted. The creation or ownership of the image itself appears to have been of more importance than the process of its replication (DeMallie 1983:248–249).

These gender differences affected the age at which individuals began to produce art. Girls entered into art production at an early age, as part of general preparation for womanhood. Men's arts, however, were associated with accomplishments in war and with the possession of spiritual power. Their active involvement in art was deferred until they had achieved some success in these areas, which generally came with greater maturity. The most prestigious art-producing positions, such as the Cheyenne quilling society or Sioux shield makers, were held by older persons who had knowledge as well as skill.

Family had a major influence on the artist, as it did on all aspects of life in Plains society. Most skills were learned from kin, and a person who was skilled was expected to share that knowledge with family members. Designs were often given to relatives, and the rights to tightly controlled crafts were normally inherited within a family (Bowers 1950:62; M.J. Schneider 1982).

The names of few artists working prior to the reservation era have been preserved; all were men who painted pictorial hides. Most are from chiefly families (Ewers 1981:61). While such men would have had more contact with early collectors, as they hosted visitors to their camps, they also were more likely to have had deeds to record in this medium.

Social Factors

Individuals with specialized abilities were recognized in many media. The nature of Plains economy was sufficiently generalized that individuals could not pursue art to the exclusion of other subsistence activities. However, individuals might be part-time specialists. Their services were sought out by members of their community, and they were paid for their work.

Specialization might be based on either ownership of rights to that position or purely on acquired skill. The rights to carry out a creative role could be acquired through purchase, which would include both transmission of knowledge and the authority to use that knowledge, including both technical and spiritual components. Among the Mandan and Hidatsa, many skills were connected to the ownership of specific bundles. The rights to pottery making were owned, and there were only a few potters per village from whom others had to purchase all the vessels they needed (Bowers 1950:91, 1965:373). Among the Blackfoot, the right to produce quillwork was likewise restricted to a few individuals (Dempsey 1963; Ewers 1945:29).

Other specialized artistic roles were based on personal knowledge in addition to artistic skills. The role of shield maker, for example, combined that of a visual artist with that of a ritual specialist in order to create an object of power. Only holy men who had acquired spiritual power could make shields. Among tribes that maintained pictographic calendars, a select individual was designated as the tribal historian (Mooney 1898:144; Blish 1967:xx–xxi). This role became more widely shared over time as many calendar keepers arose among the Kiowa and the Sioux. Other specialists were noted for their skill alone, although the acquisition of that skill may have involved payment for training. Pipe-making was a specialized craft among the Blackfoot, practiced by only a few men (Ewers 1945:58).

Many arts were widely practiced and not restricted to a few producers, but individuals of particular skill were nevertheless recognized. Among the Mandan, particularly skilled painters were noted and received a considerable amount of goods for their services. Each village sought to have at least two such painters from different moieties, as work commissioned from a member of the opposite moiety brought his prayers with it (Bowers 1950:92). Many Plains communities still remember and revere master beadworkers or metalworkers of previous generations.

At times the role of specialized artist was thrust upon a person through supernatural selection. A Teton woman who dreamed of Double Woman was recognized as having been selected to become particularly skilled in quilling (Lyford 1940). Although rare, similar spiritual callings to take up women's crafts and other aspects of the woman's role are reported to have been received by men as well. Those receiving such a calling were often noted to have been skilled artists, as well as fulfilling other ritual roles (Callender and Kochems 1983:447; DeMallie 1983:244).

Like many other forms of work, artistic production was often undertaken as a communal activity in which a social group was involved. Women gathered together to do craft work, passing the time in conversation while busy with their work (Flannery 1953:71; Wallace and Hoebel 1952:81). While each woman might produce objects individually, the work was subject to constant review and comment by others, thus influencing the nature of the final product. Other craft forms required more active collaboration. Paint had to be applied to rawhide while the hide was moist enough to absorb it, and women often worked together to paint parfleches, one laying out the design while another filled in the color (M. Morrow 1975:40).

The factor of time may have been important in encouraging communal production in many large projects, which often involved laying work out on the ground under minimal shelter. The designs on tepee covers might be sketched out by one person, but others participated in the painting, ranging from only the immediate family (Fletcher and LaFlesche 1911:354) to a substantial segment of the community (C.S. Greene 1993:75). Men worked together on pictorial hides, some dictating their deeds while others painted them (Ewers 1939:6). While the work of separate hands cannot readily be identified in geometric painting, an examination of pictographic hides often reveals the work of multiple artists (Maurer 1992).

This tradition of communal production of pictographic images is evident in the smaller medium of ledger books as well. The presence of work by multiple artists is characteristic of books of drawings that were produced for use within the Native community, although single authorship became more common in works produced for sale (C.S. Greene 1992a; Szabo 1994:39).

Skill in the arts brought prestige in Plains societies. Among men, painters in particular were highly regarded and ability in this field was viewed as equal to success in other valued fields of endeavor (Bowers 1950:92; Wissler 1904:271). For women, skill in the arts was the primary way to achieve high status (La Barre et al. 1935:562; Mishkin

1940:55; M.N. Powers 1986:137; Penney 1992:34). Among the Hidatsa, particular marks of honor were given to women for their craft accomplishments (C. Gilman and M.J. Schneider 1987: 53). Women's ability was measured by how many items they had produced as well as how skillfully they were made (Grinnell 1923, 1:166; Wissler 1904:275).

While technical skill was essential in all arts, an artist's success might also require spiritual assistance to varying degrees. Some art forms were themselves of spiritual origin, gifts to the tribe from a mythical instructor, so that a measure of sacredness surrounded the craft as a whole. For example, Whirlwind Woman taught the Arapaho to make parfleches and gave them certain designs (Kroeber 1902–1907:109; Torrence 1994:247), as Buffalo Wife taught the Cheyenne the art of quilling (Grinnell 1923, 2:385–391). In producing art, as in other endeavors, an individual might pray for skill or success, and designs might be received in dreams or visions (Kroeber 1902–1907:107; Wissler 1904:247). The most powerful of such designs were related to men's war medicine. The painting of such designs on the shield often required the services of an artist who was also a ritual specialist, himself possessed of spiritual power (P.J. Powell 1977:51; J.R. Walker 1982:100–101).

Plains artistic products were not signed in the way that works of art often are in literate societies, but their authorship was well known within the communities of their makers. It was only when those works left their communities that their makers became anonymous and they were viewed as the products of a culture rather than of an individual.

Craft Associations

Craft associations of varying levels of formality are reported from a number of Plains groups. All of these are concerned exclusively with women's decorative arts, most often quilling. The most highly structured craft associations were those of the Cheyenne, the Arapaho, and the Gros Ventre, which have been described as societies or guilds. The ones about which information was recorded were devoted to the production of quillwork and, later, beadwork (Coleman 1980; Grinnell 1923, 1:159–164; Kroeber 1902–1907:29–35; Marriott 1956).

The Cheyenne craft society remained active for the longest period. Membership was formalized, with new members joining at the invitation of those who already belonged. Women who were members had the right to produce items using the special designs of the society, which were applied to tepee ornaments and furnishings, robes, cradles, and moccasins (fig. 7). They learned how to make the designs as well as the ritual procedures that had to be followed in their production. Although only members could produce these designs, the objects on which they were placed could be freely given to non-members and no particular restrictions applied to their use. The women who belonged to craft societies were expected to be virtuous and chaste and to have skill in the craft. Their work was *1051* considered sacred and was usually produced in fulfillment of a vow. Attention was devoted to technical perfection in the precise reproduction of the society designs rather than to the creation of new forms, and a special ritual was required to correct any errors in the work. Women gained prestige from the number and type of society items they produced. The society was evidently at one time graded, with eligibility for various levels determined by the work members had done. Women's "quilling counts" were considered comparable to men's coup counts and might be formally recited on public occasions (Coleman 1980; Grinnell 1923,1; Marriott 1959). P.J. Powell (1977:36) has suggested that similar formal associations existed among the Cheyenne for other craft media.

Somewhat less formalized sodalities of craft workers existed among other tribes. Teton women who had been selected to become quillers through dreams of Double Woman were linked by their common dream. They met periodically to exhibit and discuss their work, but there were no common designs shared by the group (Lyford 1940:55; M.N. Powers 1986:73; Wissler 1912a:79). A similar association of women specialized in the cutting and sewing of tepee covers (Wissler 1912a:79).

Among the Blackfoot, quillworking was restricted to a small set of women, but the nature of their association is not well known. There was an initiation process, and members followed ritual restrictions while they were engaged in quilling. According to Dempsey (1963), rights to the craft itself were owned by the members rather than specific designs. Quillwork was regarded as sacred work (Ewers 1945:29). It could be given away or made on commission, but it could not be made purely for sale.

Craft workers were sometimes grouped together through recognition of a shared status rather than through formal association. For example, the Kiowa had a distinct term of honor for women who were skilled in craftwork and who were expected to instruct young women in such skills, but they did not form an association (La Barre et al. 1935:561–562, 582).

One source (Merritt 1988:47) reports that the Crow formerly had a beading and quilling guild. Murie (1914:598) was unable to find any evidence of such a type of association among the Pawnee.

Information about the religious restrictions that surround the work of the more formalized craft associations has caused confusion in the literature, as these rules have sometimes been misunderstood as applying to all female craftwork. It was only the work using the society designs that was considered "sacred work." Other craftwork was also produced by women of these tribes, even by members of the societies, which did not use the same designs and was not governed by the same restrictions.

Ownership of Designs

Designs originated in various ways. Individual creativity and imagination were the primary source for designs, but some were supernatural in origin. Elements ranging in size and importance from beadwork borders to tepee covers were attributed to revelations in visions or dreams. Once created, a design might be used over a long period of time, reproduced on many different items.

Many designs used in Plains art were considered a form of property and were conceived of as independent from the objects on which they were placed. Art production was governed by social rules regarding design ownership. Designs were viewed as a form of intangible property governed by complex systems of ownership and rights over production and display. The owner of a design had the exclusive right to reproduce it, and the acquisition of an object bearing a design did not confer upon the new owner the right to copy it. Some designs belonged to individuals, while others were owned by larger groups, such as clans or societies. Some designs were the prerogative of a class of individuals who had earned the right to use them, principally through achievements in war (Bowers 1950:91, 1963:120; Dorsey 1894:394–394; Blish 1967:xx).

Regardless of their origin, designs that were owned circulated as a form of valued property and could be sold, loaned, given as gifts, inherited, captured in war, or received as a right of initiation. Decorative designs used in beadwork, quillwork, or rawhide painting usually originated with the maker and did not circulate, although an older woman might give a design as a gift to a younger woman she was instructing in the craft. Respect for individual ownership protected these designs from being copied (Lyford 1940:55). This system created conflict in the early twentieth century when trading establishments such as the Mohonk Lodge in Oklahoma created mail order catalogs featuring various designs and expected their craft providers to replicate those that proved popular (Marriott and Rachlin 1977:59).

Shield and tepee designs were highly valued images received in visions. They were only a part of a larger spiritual complex, which might include songs, prayers, behavioral proscriptions, and other material symbols such as face paint. Not all men were successful in obtaining visions, but those who did were able to replicate or divide the power that they received. A series of similar shields could be made based on one vision and sold to others. The transfer of such a design was one aspect of a transfer of the full power and involved instructing the recipient in the complex of associated elements. Some shields were replicated many times over and passed through a series of owners who obtained the right to make and use the design. Many tepee designs originated in the same way, and also passed through a series of owners, often within the same family. Tepees wore out and had to be replaced every year or two. The designs endured, however, and would be painted on a new cover when it was made. Tepee designs sometimes went unused for a period of years, but even when not in use they remained the property of the owner (Ewers 1978; Flannery 1953:68; Grinnell 1901:655). When a tepee design was to be renewed, the owner often called upon one or more skilled artists to do the painting upon the cover under his or her direction (Ewers 1945:25). Tepee designs were also acquired by capture, when a man entered an enemy camp and cut off a piece of a cover, thereby claiming the right to reproduce it (Ewers 1978:41).

The rights to represent personal achievements were owned, much like other designs. Representations might be broadly symbolic and would be owned by a class of individuals. Among the Blackfoot, a man who had killed enemies had the right to paint stripes on his leggings and shirt (Ewers 1945:48). Many representations were pictorial and were painted on robes or the pages of ledger books. A man might paint his own image or call upon the services of a skilled artist who worked to his dictation (fig. 3). A man's deeds were never represented without his permission (C.S. Greene 1993; C.S. Greene and T.D. Drescher 1994). When the reservation system made it no longer possible to gain recognition through new achievements in war, the right to represent a man's deeds became a transferrable form of property that could be passed on to a new owner through purchase or inheritance (E. Wallace and E.A. Hoebel 1952:242, 250).

Consumption of Art

The social factors that guided the production of art were paralleled by concepts regarding its use. Objects signaled information about their owners with regard to gender, wealth, personal achievement, and identity. Gender determined not only the general form of dress, but also what types of painted designs might be used. Pictorial images were painted only on men's robes, while geometric designs were worn by women. An exception to this was the feathered circle design, which was used only by men (Ewers 1939:7). Personal wealth was demonstrated through the possession and display of highly decorated objects that combined costly materials and substantial labor. Wealth in intangible goods depended entirely upon artistic representations for its display. Spiritual powers were represented by paintings on shields, tepee covers, or clothing. Military deeds and other valued achievements were recounted visually through pictorial representations as well as symbolic marks (Bowers 1965:279).

In many societies, clothing is used as a primary marker of personal identity. On the Plains, much art was focused on personal apparel, including gear for horses ("Sioux Until 1850," fig. 4, this vol.), which were virtually an extension of the individual in Plains society. In addition to making a personal statement, art served as a social marker of membership within a wider component of society. Shield designs were associated with particular families to such an extent that James Mooney (1902:13) considered them incipient heraldic markers. Among tribes that maintained a clan system, certain designs were used only by clan members (Dorsey 1896:274; J.H. Howard 1965:57). Tribal distinc-

tions in styles marking ethnic affiliations grew increasingly pronounced during the last half of the nineteenth century. During the reservation period while visionary and pictorial hide painting declined, the arts of personal adornment flourished.

Art objects were used to negotiate social relationships through exchange. Certain formalized exchanges solidified kinship relations. A Teton marriage was not considered finalized until the bride beaded a pair of moccasins and presented them to her mother-in-law (Standing Bear 1933:110). A Cheyenne woman wishing to put aside the mother-in-law restrictions that prevented her from speaking with her daughter's husband could be released from that custom by making certain items of sacred bead or quillwork and presenting them to him (Grinnell 1923, 1:147; Marriott and Rachlin 1977:70). Among the Arapaho, the cradle for a new child was made as a gift from the father's sister as a statement of respect for the mother and an affirmation of kinship with the child (C.S. Greene 1992:95; Hilger 1952:141; Kroeber 1902–1907:16). A demonstration of kin solidarity that has continued to the present is the contribution of craft items needed for distribution in "giveaways," which honor family members on various occasions.

All important transfers of property were marked with return gifts, which included craft items. It was not possible for an individual to rise in status through the acquisition of important property, such as bundles, designs, or memberships, or through the display of generosity at giveaways, without having access to fine craft items for distribution (Bol 1985:37). Intertribal trade that centered upon economic commodities such as guns, horses, and foodstuffs, also regularly included the exchange of decorated objects as

Deutsches Ledermuseum, Offenbach, Federal Republic of Germany: 4.43.01.

Fig. 8. Bag with protective designs. This Sioux saddlebag is quilled with narrow red stripes, symbolic of long life, which women placed on many types of items. The 4-pointed figure in the center represents a spider web. The design can also be interpreted as representing the heavens, with the thunder powers at the 4 directions (Wissler 1907:48–52). Length 60 cm.

gifts, which forged links of mutual generosity between trading partners (Jablow 1994:44–45).

Relationships with the supernatural were also mediated through art. Women's craft societies sought to invoke blessings for their members through the production of work in fulfillment of spiritual vows. In other instances, the designs themselves conveyed blessings (fig. 8). Protective designs were placed on children's cradles to keep them safe (C.S. Greene 1992:95; Hilger 1952:30), and on rawhide cases to keep the food stored in them from spoiling (Wissler 1904:256). Other images were used more actively to invoke spiritual assistance. Images and carvings might be manipulated by men to assist them in attracting women (Wildschut 1925; Wissler 1905:266). Prior to going into battle, men's war medicine powers were invoked through ritual, including exposing the inner designs painted on shields (Wissler 1907:22–31).

Artwork was an important economic commodity within Plains society. It could be a significant source of income for those who were particularly recognized for their skills, or in some tribes for those who held the exclusive rights to produce desired goods. While there were no full-time artists, skilled individuals who were commissioned to produce items were fed while they worked as well as rewarded with gifts (M.J. Schneider 1983:113–115). Commissioned production and intertribal trade in craft items laid the foundation for sale to non-Natives. A flourishing trade to Whites was established at frontier posts as early as the 1830s when "tourism" was introduced with the earliest steamboat service (Ewers 1986:12). Such sales grew with the increasing presence of non-Natives at trading posts, military forts, and Indian agencies, most of whom wished to acquire Indian art as a souvenir of their frontier experience. As Plains people were increasingly forced into participation in a cash economy over the course of the nineteenth century, the production of craftwork became one of the few means of earning some income through traditional pursuits. The quantity of Plains Indian material preserved in museum collections attests to the scope of this trade.

The visual arts were a major medium for creative expression in Plains society. The high social value placed on art as well as the sheer volume of material produced attest to the keen esthetic enjoyment of both producers and consumers of art.

Art Since 1900

JoALLYN ARCHAMBAULT

To most non-Indians the material items created by members of American Indian societies were not considered art in the western European sense until well into the twentieth century. Collected as examples of primitive material culture and stored in museums, they became data to be studied by scholars reconstructing the history of civilization (G. Wright 1996; Hinsley 1981; Krech and Hall 1999). With the development of anthropology as an academic discipline during the late nineteenth century, systematic collections of American Indian material culture were made and deposited in museums around the world. These collections documented cultures that were widely believed by both Indians and non-Indians to be on the verge of extinction. The collection of objects continued to be a focus of American anthropology into the 1930s.

History of Research

Scholars such as Robert H. Lowie, Alfred L. Kroeber, and Clark Wissler were interested in establishing the origin and course of material culture development over long periods of time. They were less interested in discovering a tightly ordered historical sequence, which, given the nature of the data and absence of a deep, recorded history, was impossible anyway. They shared three reasonable but wrong assumptions that had significant implications for their findings. They assumed that the developmental history of Plains material culture could be reconstructed through the comparison of museum specimens without questioning the validity of collection records. They thought the evolutionary development of material culture was independent of Euro-American influence except for the introduction of trade items, like glass beads and trade cloth. Last, they used criteria borrowed from natural history to gauge relative change such as typological similarities and geographical distribution (Ewers 1983). During this period anthropologists focused most of their fieldwork on other aspects of Indian culture such as kinship and religion and relatively little on material culture. They were aware of the importance of direct information gathered from native experts but emphasized theoretical questions while in the field. The overreliance on museum collections, the ahistorical nature of the research, and the lack of substantial fieldwork with native people severely undercut the ability of early researchers to produce findings that might have stimulated others to follow.

Some early studies addressed theoretical positions posed by others. Kroeber's (1900, 1901) study of Arapaho design and Wissler's (1904) study of Sioux decorative art addressed A.C. Haddon's (1895) hypothesis about the nature of decorative art and the derivation of geometric designs from realistic forms. Their findings did not support Haddon's position. Wissler's (1927) analysis of moccasin distribution did not support the ahistorical typological analysis of G. Hatt (1916; Ewers 1983). The best example of corrective research is the Wildschut and Ewers (1959) monograph on Crow beadwork that superseded Lowie's (1922a) study.

Generally descriptions of material culture were part of comprehensive accounts of a single group and were contextualized as part of a living society (Kroeber 1902–1907, Pt.2, 1908; Fletcher and La Flesche 1911; Lowie 1909, 1909a; Densmore 1918; G.A. Dorsey 1905a, 1905b; Wissler 1911, 1913; Will and Spinden 1906). Sometimes tribally specific material culture was described in separate accounts, as for Blackfeet (Wissler 1910, 1912), Crow (Lowie 1922, 1922a), and Sioux (Wissler 1905a). Some articles focused on specific aspects of a tribe's material culture, such as clothing (Wissler 1916a; Wildschut 1926b), basketry (Gilmore 1925; Weltfish 1930, 1930a), painted tepees (Barrett 1921; Grinnell 1901; W.S. Campbell 1915, 1927), bead and quillwork (Gilmore 1924b; Wissler 1910; Lyford 1933), and feather work (Speck 1928). Other research examined topics from a regional perspective looking for shared characteristics that would help to establish diffusion of people and techniques over time, for example, bead and quillwork (Wintemberg 1928; Orchard 1916; Roth 1908, 1923), clothing (Farabee 1921; Wissler 1915, 1916, 1927), and riding gear (Wissler 1915a). Religious art and symbolism were thoroughly described (G.A. Dorsey 1903, 1905a, 1905b; Kroeber 1900, 1901; Wildschut 1925a, 1925b, 1926, 1926a, 1926b, 1926c, 1927, 1928; Wissler 1904, 1905a, 1907, 1912, 1913; Lowie 1913a, 1915b, 1922b; Skinner 1920, 1925b; H.L. Scott 1911).

None of the above examined the role of the individual artist, gender roles in the production of art, the creation of objects for sale to non-Indians and the significance of that income for native families, the tendency to value men's art over women's, or the imposition of European-derived notions of art and beauty onto Plains objects. These were questions that would be raised later in the century.

Continuity of Production

While industrial American material culture replaced most native manufactures, there was always some production of traditional forms for domestic use as well as for sale to outsiders, continuing an ancient tradition of commerce. Trading-post owners on or near reservations played major roles in the sale of Indian-made items to non-Indians (W.Y. Adams 1963), as did railroad tourism, which started with the completion of transcontinental railroads in the 1880s. By 1902 the Santa Fe Railroad was regularly selling Indian-made items in its Harvey House hotels and gift shops as part of the attractions designed for its passengers (Myrick 1970:34; K.L. Howard and D.F. Pardue 1996). Organized excursions from the hotels provided opportunities for buying objects directly from the artists during visits to reservation villages (D. Thomas 1978; K.L. Howard and D.F. Pardue 1996). In the Northern Plains the Great Northern Railway played a similar role in the merchandizing of Indian objects, primarily Blackfeet (Walton, Ewers, and Hassrick 1985).

On Plains reservations, traditional social life required the creation of items for use in ceremony, celebration, dance, and gift giving, even if done in the face of official disapproval. Clothing, dance, and ceremonial regalia, even horse trappings, were made routinely as the occasion required. Some items may have been sold; others remained in family ownership indefinitely.

Around 1900 some missionary and Indian reform groups decided that the production of native crafts would assist Indians in their economic assimilation into mainstream society (Schrader 1983:4–5). Interest in Indian arts was stimulated by railway tourism, museum exhibitions, and the Arts and Crafts movement. In 1900 Commissioner of Indian Affairs William A. Jones offered Indian Office support for training in traditional art forms. In 1901 the Lake Mohonk Conference of the Friends of the American Indian, one of the important reform groups of the era, accepted the importance of traditional arts as a means of economic, artistic, and social occupation and progress (Schrader 1983:5). Beginning in 1900 there was a historic confluence of economic, social, and cultural forces that ultimately led to the creation in 1935 of the Indian Arts and Crafts Board in the Department of the Interior. As part of the New Deal, the Board was created to advance the "development of Indian arts and crafts...and promote the economic welfare of the Indian tribes...through...the expansion of the market for the products of Indian art and craftsmanship" (Schrader 1983:299). In an effort to encourage craftsmanship for silver jewelry and Navajo weaving the Board immediately established standards that were backed by a government seal of approval. The organization created marketing plans, established workshops and craft cooperatives, and promoted new and existing markets (fig. 1) (Schrader 1983:132–138). One of the earliest and most visible activities was an exhibition at the 1939 San Francisco Golden Gate International Exposition that highlighted the value of Indian cultures and their arts to native people and to the nation. Sales rooms exhibited fine native arts and placed them in contemporary settings, illustrating their suitability for modern home decoration. The exhibit was regarded as a resounding success and evidence of the shift in federal attitudes toward Indian peoples and their products (Schrader 1983:163–198; Vaillant 1939). René d'Harnoncourt, general manager of the Board, planned another exhibition with similar goals at the

Fig. 1. Arts and Crafts Board. left, Art class in the Okreek Day School, Rosebud Res., S. Dak. right, Woman making pottery at the Oglala Boarding School on the Pine Ridge Res., S. Dak. Using clay found on the reservation, students were taught pottery making by the Indian Service instructor. A cooperative sold their pottery. Photographs by John Vachon, 1940.

Museum of Modern Art in New York City. Like the first it educated the American public about the contributions of Indian culture and arts to American culture at large and the "uses of Indian art in the modern world, as in a home, in personal adornment, and as fine art" (Schrader 1983:225). At the New York City exhibition for the first time modern Indian art was presented as a fine art, worthy of consideration on a par with that produced by other civilizations and an integral part of national culture. Contemporary Indian artists, like all artists everywhere, were constantly creating new expressions of native life in a seamless connection between the old and the new. The acceptance of Indian arts and the development of a larger market for their work would benefit and enrich everyone (d'Harnoncourt and Douglas 1941; Rushing 1992). The Indian Arts and Crafts Board continued to promote Indian arts through marketing; artist lists available to the public; and the establishment of museums dedicated to Indian arts in Montana, South Dakota, and Oklahoma with active exhibit programs (Ewers 1943,1952). Efforts focused on specific topics such as porcupine quillwork, modern painters, and tepee covers (Libhart 1970, 1972; Libhart and Ellison 1973; D.J. Ray 1972).

Formal Education

Federal education policy in Indian schools mandated that Indians be trained to support themselves in the national economy and to assimilate into the Euro-American population. The preservation of traditional art forms was not encouraged unless their sale could provide a cash income, thus promoting self-sufficiency, and in no case would formal instruction be given. However, some schools had different perspectives. In 1878, 17 Arapaho, Cheyenne, and Kiowa men, former prisoners of war at Fort Marion, Florida, enrolled at the Hampton Institute in Virginia to "learn more of the white man's road" (Hultgren and Fairbanks Molin 1989:17). From the beginning, instruction in some Indian arts (drawing, basketry) was provided and the sale of handicrafts to visitors was encouraged. This continued until the closure of the Hampton Indian program in 1923 (Hultgren and Fairbanks Molin 1989:47). Carlisle Indian School, Pennsylvania, maintained formal art classes in the European tradition, which were run by Angel De Cora-Dietz (Winnebago) ("Santee," fig. 9, this vol.) and her husband William Dietz (Sioux). A campus store sold traditional items by mail order (Garmhausen 1988:18), but there were no classes in native culture or arts. The federal Indian boarding schools run by the Bureau of Indian Affairs banned classes in traditional arts and music until 1930, at which point Indian Commissioners Charles Rhoads and then John Collier mandated that classes in Indian history, art, and culture be added to the curriculum. The new policy reversed the longstanding position that cultural assimilation was the only desirable goal for Indian people and instead insisted that native arts and cultures offered a rich, desirable heritage to students. The Santa Fe Indian School became a force in the maintenance,

revival, and marketing of Indian arts and contributed to the development of Santa Fe as a major art center for Indian artists in the last quarter of the twentieth century (S. Hyer 1990:29–32; Garmhausen 1988:30). A group of Kiowa artists (five men and one woman) were trained at the University of Oklahoma, Norman, around 1926 under the supervision of Edith Mahier and with the support of Professor Oscar B. Jacobson. Lois Smoky dropped out but the five men— Spencer Asah, Jack Hokeah, Stephen Mopope ("Intertribal Religious Movements," fig. 8, this vol.), James Auchiah, Monroe Tsatoke (fig. 2)—went on to become well known, professional artists (Jacobson 1929; Snodgrass 1968:56–57; D. Dunn 1968; J.J. Brody 1971; Ewers 1971:50). At Bacone College near Muskogee, Oklahoma, the art department was directed by three of the most important Indian artists of the time, and hundreds of aspiring Indian students took courses under the direction of Acee Blue Eagle (Creek-Pawnee), Woody Crumbo (Potawatomi), and Richard West (Cheyenne) (fig. 3) over a 40-year period.

It was the intersection of people and talent between the Santa Fe Indian School, Bacone College, and the University of Oklahoma that forged the Studio Style of Indian painting. Dorothy Dunn, art teacher 1932–1937 in Santa Fe, is generally considered a pivotal figure in developing a format that dominated native fine arts until the 1960s. Viewed as the culmination of Indian easel painting, many Indian artists painted in this style characterized as flat, two-dimensional, usually without background, with traditional subject matter

Smithsonian, NAA: 92-11010.

Fig. 2. *First Dance of Sun Dance* by Monroe Tsatoke, watercolor, 1929. Tsatoke was one of the artists working at the University of Oklahoma who came to be known as the Kiowa Five. They produced many paintings of dancers and of the Native American Church, important avenues for contemporary cultural expression, as well as imagined scenes of the past such as this.

top, U.S. Dept. of Interior, Ind. Arts and Crafts Board, Southern Plains Ind. Mus., Anadarko, Okla.: A70.7; bottom left, Smithsonian, Dibner Lib.: 92-6117; bottom right, The Thomas Gilcrease Inst. of Amer. Hist. and Art, Tulsa, Okla.: GM69.142.
Fig. 3. Spiritual expressions. Religious images have remained a source of inspiration for Plains artists in work made for sale as well as for ceremonial use. top, *Cheyenne Sun Dance*, by Richard West, Cheyenne, 1970, one of a series on the Southern Cheyenne ceremony. West studied at Bacone College and the University of Oklahoma (B.F.A. 1941, M.F.A. 1950) and was the director of the Art Department at Bacone, 1947–1970 (Libhart 1972:78). bottom left, *The Vision*, by Calvin Larvie, Teton (Jacobson and d'Ucel 1950). Raised on the Rosebud Res., Larvie studied art at Bacone College, graduating in 1940. Many of his works depict a spiritual past, such as this image of a young man's successful vision quest. bottom right, Native American Church blanket pin in German silver by Julius Caesar, Pawnee, who was trained through apprenticeships with metalsmiths Hiram Jake, Pawnee, and Bill Leaf, Sac and Fox (Ellison 1976:67). The pin combines elements of Peyote ceremonialism: fan, staff, water drum, drum stick, and gourd rattle arranged beneath the crescent altar with a stylized peyote button at center. Width 12 cm.

of feasts, hunts, dances, pastoral, and family scenes from a nostalgic and sanitized native world that no longer existed (D. Dunn 1968; Strickland 1992; J.J. Brody 1971; Bernstein and Rushing 1995; Silberman 1978). The Studio Style was well received by the public and was considered "real" Indian painting by many contemporary native people. After Dunn's departure Geronima Cruz Montoya directed the art department at the Santa Fe Indian School, where students continued to use the visual vocabulary of the Studio Style (Strickland 1992). Artists who worked in this style include Lorenzo Beard (Cheyenne-Arapaho), Carl Sweezy (Arapaho), the Kiowa Five, Paul Goodbear (Cheyenne), Oscar Howe (Sioux), Acee Blue Eagle, Archie Blackowl (Cheyenne), Lee Tsatoke (Kiowa), Richard West, Blackbear Bosin (Kiowa-Comanche), Herman Red Elk (Sioux), George Keahbone (Kiowa), Carl Woodring (Osage), and Calvin Larvie (Sioux), among others (Snodgrass 1968; Matuz 1998; Lester 1995). Some of these artists' work moved beyond the Studio Style in their later years, and many younger artists experimented with it as they developed their own expression.

The Studio Style fell into disfavor with artists and art critics, although not necessarily with the buying public. It was dismissed as purely decorative and artificial in its presentation and patronizing in its development (J.J. Brody 1971). Indian artists, particularly those trained at mainstream art schools, were energetic in discrediting its basic tenets and attempting to gain acceptance for other interpretive modalities. Oscar Howe (Sioux) (vol. 17:223) was one of the best-known graduates of the Studio School and was acknowledged as the leading Sioux artist of his generation. After World War II he earned a B.A., M.F.A., and several prestigious awards and commissions; by 1957 he was a professor of fine art at the University of South Dakota, Vermillion (Pennington 1961). In 1958 he protested the rejection of one of his paintings by the Philbrook Museum, Tulsa, Oklahoma, saying "There is much more to Indian art than pretty, stylized pictures..." (Dockstader 1982). The Philbrook revised its standards, admitting more contemporary art into competition (Berlo and Phillips 1998:221), and began collecting and sponsoring exhibits of contemporary Indian art. Indian artists from other areas were creating individual syntheses using their specific heritage with mainstream contemporary art, for example, George Morrison (Chippewa) and Allan Houser (Apache).

In 1962 the Institute of American Indian Arts, a federally supported school for native students located in Santa Fe under the aegis of the Bureau of Indian Affairs, opened with a curriculum originally intended to provide both humanities and artistic training (Garmhausen 1988:62–126). Students were exposed to a wide range of artistic styles and techniques and encouraged to develop their creative impulses using their own cultural heritage and to be open to other artistic traditions. The Studio Style began to fade. Many students attended mainstream art schools such as the San Francisco Art Institute, Chicago Art Institute, and California College of Arts and Crafts, Oakland, where they were exposed to the entire range of contemporary art, theories, and art history. Indian artists began to think of themselves as artists who happened to be Indian and tried to break out of the arcane modes that had stifled them.

Among the teachers at the new Institute of American Indian Arts, Fritz Scholder (Luiseño) and Allan Houser helped to create an atmosphere in the studios that encouraged Indian students to explore, invent, and confront the dilemmas of modern Indian life. No longer should they avoid uncomfortable realities, or create only marketable paintings. Indian students in mainstream art schools internalized the same attitudes and by 1965 art created by Indian artists exploded in every direction. Exhibits at important galleries, catalogs, major publications, competitions, artist associations, scholarly organizations, grants, prestigious awards, teaching appointments, museum curatorial positions—all indicators of a healthy art scene in both the United States and Canada—were present.

Artistic Efflorescence

Indian artists began to control the interpretation and representation of their art and cultures. Some Indian organizations mounted art shows dedicated to contemporary art and artists, the most successful of which has been the Northern Plains Tribal Arts in Sioux Falls, South Dakota. These competitive exhibits have media specific categories and two best of show awards, one for fine arts and the other for tribal (traditional) arts. The preeminence normally given to fine arts in the mainstream art world is not honored in the Indian-operated shows, and equal prestige is given to both. As a result, artists working in traditional media created spectacular items that can only be considered fine art.

Indian communities experienced a resurgence of ethnic pride that began in the 1960s and has not abated. More people were participating in powwows and other activities *1059*

Mont. Histl. Soc., Helena.

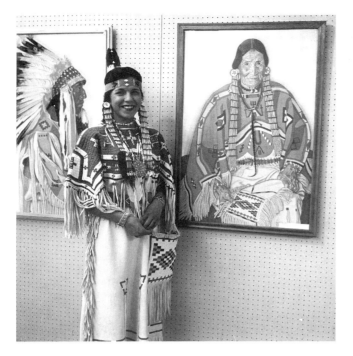

Fig. 4. Clothing as art. The continuation of the artistry of bead working is exemplified in the beaded dress and bag worn by Delores Racine, Blackfeet, named Miss Indian America in 1959. The portrait is of her great-grandmother, Julia Wades-in-the-Water (Blackfeet, b. 1870, d. 1954), painted by Winold Reiss in 1943. Reiss was hired by the Great Northern Railway to paint Blackfeet portraits that would be used to promote tourism in Montana. Both Julia Wades-in-the-Water and her husband were employed by the railroad to dress in their traditional finery, greet tourists at the Glacier National Park station, and present a program demonstrating Plains Indian sign language, story telling, singing, and dancing (J.C. Stewart 1989:114–116, 140). Photographed at an exhibit of Reiss's Blackfeet Indian portraits at the Montana Historical Society, Helena, 1960.

that required the creation of traditional objects, like beaded clothing (fig. 4), shawls, fans, dance regalia, horse gear, and quilts. Innovation and style changes were typical, and artists delighted in keeping ahead of the curve. Thousands of women and some men created these items for family and friends and a few became professional artists, creating objects that transcended their utilitarian quality to become fine art, even through they might be used in daily life. Donald B. Tenoso (Sioux) created dolls and toys and Vanessa Jennings (Kiowa) made beaded dresses and cradles that were unique and exquisite.

In 1972 the National Museum of American Art in Washington, D.C., exhibited the work of Fritz Scholder and T.C. Cannon (fig. 5 top left) (Caddo, Kiowa), which effectively placed it within the mainstream of contemporary American art. The ironic critique of the Indian in modern society by both artists opened new avenues of access and expression for others (Berlo and Phillips 1998:225).

In 1982 President Ronald Reagan sponsored the Night of the First Americans at the Kennedy Center in Washington. The benefit allowed the work of more than 150 native artists to be seen by thousands of Washingtonians (Anonymous 1982).

There are two centers of Plains Indian artistic activity. One is the Santa Fe–Scottsdale area in the Southwest, which comprised the largest concentration of galleries, dealers, and resident artists dedicated to Indian art in the country. The second is more diffuse and includes the larger cities of Oklahoma, South Dakota, and Montana, which have galleries for Indian art. Arthur Amiotte (Sioux) (fig. 5) was the most influential artist on the Northern Plains. Amiotte's work incorporated elements of Lakota culture in new directions, and he melded his art into traditional cultural life such as ceremony and feasts (Amiotte 1989, 1989a, 1994).

Ledger art (vol. 17:387) stimulated both scholarship and inspiration to modern Indian artists. A number of artists incorporated ledger art into their work, using it to create a new synthesis of work. Amiotte created a series using the form of ledgerbooks to tell modern stories of family. Early scholarship focused on ledgerbooks as history, documentation of actual events, and their potential for understanding events from an Indian perspective. Later work asked new questions of the material, looking within images to reveal internal social structure, resistance, ambiguity. What was earlier understood to be simple visual histories became more sophisticated works testifying to kin, friend, and enemy.

top left, Heard Mus. Lib., Phoenix, Ariz.: N-353c; top center, McMichael Canadian Art Coll., Kleinburg, Ont.: 1990.1; top right, Ernie Pepion, Bozeman, Mont.; center, Ind. Art Centre, Dept. of Ind. and Northern Affairs, Ottawa, Ont.: 407202; bottom left, Buffalo Bill Histl. Center, Cody, Wyo.: 17.95; bottom right, Fonseca Gallery, Santa Fe, N. Mex.

Fig. 5. Art as social commentary. top left, *Collector #5, or Osage with Van Gogh*, by T.C. Cannon, Kiowa-Caddo, woodcut, about 1980. In this image the Indian, whose cultural heritage is so often collected, is presented as the collector of European painting. top center, *Bases Stolen from the Cleveland Indians and a Captured Yankee*, by Gerald McMaster, Plains Cree, mixed media, 1989. McMaster has reappropriated symbols of Indianness and displayed them as war trophies. top right, *Buffalo Jump*, by Ernie Pepion, Blackfeet, oil on canvas, 1990. Pepion's wheelchair-bound figure riding a stick horse breaks free of his physical limitations. center, *Wounded Knee #2*, by Rick Rivet, Subarctic Métis. Figures of a conquistador, a Nazi, and a member of the Ku Klux Klan are incorporated into the painting, based on a photograph of the burial of Wounded Knee victims. bottom left, *The Visit*, by Arthur Amiotte, Sioux, collage, 1995. Here some relatives, borrowed from ledger art, visit Amiotte's great-grandparents, the artist Standing Bear and his Austrian wife, photographed in front of their house. A new automobile is parked in front, while figures in Ghost Dance clothing appear on the roof, surrounded by symbols of celestial powers. bottom right, *Coyote's Wild and Woolly West*, by Harry Fonseca, Maidu. Plains Indian feather bonnets and painted tepees are the essence of the stereotyped Indian, and artists from many regions have seized upon them to provide their own humorous commentary on stereotypes.

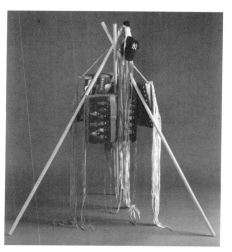

Tribal Traditions and Records

RAYMOND J. DeMALLIE AND DOUGLAS R. PARKS

Stories and Storytellers

The historical traditions of Plains Indians were fundamentally a form of oral literature, handed down from generation to generation as memorized myths and stories. For Plains peoples, the good storyteller was not an innovator, but rather a narrator who manipulated the traditional form well, who had a good sense for interesting detail and dramatic structure, and who elaborated the plot to the extreme, rather than merely sketching in the outline (Lowie 1935:110). This underscores the role of oral traditions both as entertainment, which might stretch out night after night through a long winter, and as instruction, particularly for the young (fig. 1) (vol. 17:223).

Over time, additions, borrowings, and blendings of parts of various stories affected the nature of the body of tradition. Clark Wissler, after studying Blackfoot oral traditions, concluded that the differing versions of myth reflected the contributions of different storytellers, and that these different details might be considered the narrator's "ownership marks." He wrote (Wissler and Duvall 1908:5): "Once when discussing this matter with a Blood Indian, the venerable old man pulled up a common ragweed, saying, 'The parts of this weed all branch off from the stem. They go different ways, but all come from the same root. So it is with the different versions of a myth'." It is therefore pointless to search for "correct" or "pure" versions of oral tradition. Each teller stood by his or her own version as the truth. As an Assiniboine narrator commented, beginning a storytelling session with a well-known tale, "All over, people tell it differently, so I myself will tell it as I remember it" (Leo Wing in DeMallie 2000). Remembering was the key; traditions were memorized and passed down in social groups—families, religious societies, communities—and became distinctive representations of group identity.

Although oral traditions fulfilled a variety of functions, including artistic and recreational, their basic purpose was to answer the human quest for knowledge about the world: how the physical environment took its present shape, how the cultural world came to its present form, where the social group came from, and who were eventful players in its past. Oral traditions contextualized the individual's existence in the world, giving it meaning and temporal as well as spatial orientation (Parks 1991, 3:121). While written Euro-American history requires objective evaluation of source material, Plains Indian history, as oral tradition, was more localized and personalized, and focused largely on the intervention of supernatural forces in human life. Tribal traditions frequently violate credibility from a Western point of view, yet they were fundamental to Plains cultures. Understanding the historicity of oral traditions, rather than treating them as outside history by relegating them to the category of myth, is essential for insightful interpretation of the history of interactions between Euro-Americans and Plains peoples from the sixteenth century to the twenty-first (Nabokov 1997).

Classification of Oral Traditions

Among most Plains tribes oral traditions were classified into two fundamental categories: true stories that conceptually were history, and fictional stories that were told for entertainment or amusement. The narratives that fit within this binary classification differed slightly from tribe to tribe, and within each category varying types can be distinguished, only some of which were denoted by native-language terms.

The Arikara classification of oral traditions exemplifies the categorization of many tribes, especially those of the prairie plains. Fictional stories were termed *na·ʔi·káwIš* 'tale', which twentieth-century Arikaras generally translated into English as "fairy tales." True stories, in contrast, had no special denotation. If narrators had to specify a story as true, they said *tira·ná·nIš* 'it is true'. True stories, which from the Arikara perspective comprised their history, were again subdivided into two groups, sacred stories that told about "holy" or mysterious events in the remote past, and the secular stories that were not so remote in time and lacked the supernatural element. From a Western perspective, the secular stories are historical narratives, whereas the sacred stories are categorized as myths and legends.

The most specialized type of sacred stories among the Arikara included the genesis tradition and the traditions associated with tribal sacred bundles. Before the Arikara were decimated by smallpox epidemics in the late eighteenth and early nineteenth centuries, they lived in separate villages, each with its own sacred bundle that symbolized the history of the group and its covenant with the deities. The origin of each village was traced to a supernatural experience in which a deity instructed a dreamer to make a bundle of objects, some to recall what happened in the dream and some to be used in subsequent

Fig. 1. Storytelling and oral tradition. top left, Running Rabbit (Blood Blackfoot, Chief of Biters band, b. 1833, d. 1911), making a hide painting depicting his war deeds. He is pointing with a piece of porous bone, his tool for applying paint to the hide. The young man to his left is his son, Houghton, who with paper and pencil is writing down the explanation of the painting. This painted hide was commissioned by the artist/photographer, Edmund Morris, who provided the buffalo hide for the pictographic record, collected the translations, and donated them to the Royal Ontario Museum (Brownstone 1993:46-49). Photograph by Edmund Morris, Man., Aug. 1909. top right, a Teton grandmother telling stories to her granddaughter while cooking. Photograph by John A. Anderson, Rosebud Res., S. Dak. about 1900. bottom left, John Fire Lame Deer explaining a Teton ceremony. Photograph by Richard Erdoes, Rosebud Res., S. Dak., 1970. bottom right, White Bull, Northern Cheyenne, describing the Battle of the Little Bighorn to Olin D. Wheeler. William Rowland, the interpreter, is in the center. Photograph by Laton A. Huffman, Northern Cheyenne Res., Mont., 1901.

rituals. The stories of those origins were ritually recited whenever bundles were ceremonially opened. By the nineteenth century, after the former villages had coalesced into one village, many of the traditions were lost, but what did survive into the twentieth century was a single genesis story that accounted for the origins and migration of the Arikara as a people (C.L. Hall 1891:32; Grinnell 1893a:122–128; G.A. Dorsey 1904:12–35).

Myths formed a second type of sacred story. They recounted incidents and events during a period before the earth had fully taken its present form and human institutions had developed. It was a time when animals were the actors in dramas and deities came down to earth from the heavens, when animals killed humans and buffalo ate people. In that period a dangerous natural world was evolving into the present one in which humans hunted animals and rode horses and lived much as they did before the arrival of Euro-Americans. The Arikara referred to it as the holy period, and stories of that time were termed holy stories.

1063

A third type of sacred story was the legendary event, of which there were several varieties. One was the etiological narrative, a dream or vision story that related a supernatural encounter between a human and some animal spirit or other agency who taught an Arikara a ritual for the benefit of the tribe. Related to this variety was the dream story, in which a poor boy or some other hapless young man happened upon an animal or other supernatural power whom he was able to help or please and who then pitied him by endowing him with powers to insure success in hunting, warfare, or healing and became his life-long spiritual helper. Another variety of sacred story included accounts of supernatural occurrences, as when an offended person pouted or a young woman was shamed, left the village, and subsequently turned into stone.

Among nonsacred true stories, war stories that recounted incidents during the period of intertribal warfare in the nineteenth century constituted a prominent type, while narratives of nineteenth-century historical events in which the Arikara participated—their tribal migration to Pawnee country and their participation in the 1851 Fort Laramie Treaty council and the campaigns of Lt. Col. George A. Custer—formed another. Personal anecdotes that told about a supernatural encounter but lacked the element of power bestowal comprised a third group. In recounting humanly inexplicable experiences or phenomena, this type served as testimonial to the existence of supernatural beings or events and assured Arikaras that the world about them was imbued with mysterious power.

Arikara tales can similarly be grouped into types, although none of those types is distinguished by a native-language term. One of the most common was the Coyote story ("Caddoan Languages," fig. 5, this vol.), in which the trickster Coyote or some other animal was the protagonist. Unlike many Plains tribes, the Arikara did not put Coyote into the role of a divine being or transformer. Although he was endowed with mysterious power, he was always portrayed as tricky and deceitful, trying to outwit others but invariably bungling and generally dying as a result of his own folly. Frequently these were etiological tales that ended with an explanation of some feature of the natural world, but Arikaras attached little significance to Coyote stories since they were told primarily to evoke laughter.

Another type consisted of tales that were more novelistic, similar to European Mother Goose stories. They were told on winter nights for diversion, and frequently to lull children to sleep. In contrast to Coyote stories, they had a serious, often frightening, tone and a primarily human cast of characters. The actors in these tales were sometimes the same as those that appear in myths, illustrating the secularization of mythic figures and also placing some stories as transitional between myth and tale (G.A. Dorsey 1904:6–9; Parks 1991, 4:44–49).

The Hidatsa and Mandan also classified stories into two general categories: secular (Hidatsa *ma·ši·* 'a story', Mandan *hok*) and sacred (*ma·ši· aruxupa·* 'a sacred story', Mandan *xoxopri(n)*). Many sacred stories of these two groups were shared with the Arikara, but among the Mandan and Hidatsa most of those shared myths became associated with the origin of bundles and rituals. These tribes attempted to interrelate myths; among the Hidatsa, for example, certain myths followed from the Sacred Arrow account of the Awatixa division origin, forming a sacred myth complex. The bundles, each with their associated myths, were likened to knots in a string (Bowers 1950:105–110, 1965:303–304). Among the Arikara, in contrast, most of those stories were not interrelated, nor did they serve as explanations of origins or rituals, but rather were accounts of events in a remote, mysterious, unstructured past. The Arikara elaborated a different set of narratives—accounts of doctors' powers and the Medicine Lodge—rather than linking ritual with myth. Among the Hidatsa and Mandan the events in myths were also localized to a region in which they had lived longer, while among the Arikara, who came into that region more recently, the association of myths with landmarks was less developed; among the nomadic Sioux it was even less apparent (M.W. Beckwith 1937:xvii).

Nonsacred Hidatsa and Mandan stories, which included comic, hunting, and war narratives, were generally distinguished by a secularization of characters and actions that in holy stories were regarded as sacred (M.W. Beckwith 1937:xvi–xvii).

The Sioux also categorized stories into two types. One, the *ohúkaką*, were fictional stories, myths and tales set in a time remote from the present world, told for amusement or entertainment and lacking the sacredness found in comparable Arikara, Mandan, and Hidatsa narratives. Such stories could be narrated only in the winter, after sunset, and among the Teton had the formulaic ending *hehályela owíhąke lo* 'that is all; that is the end.' One of two types of *ohúkaką* comprised those stories farthest removed from the present; these were the ones most widely known among the general population. They were cast with mythological characters, such as the trickster Iktomi (literally, 'spider', the equivalent of Coyote among other tribes), Iya, Crazy Bull, Witch, or Cold, or by animals endowed with supernatural powers. Iktomi stories, because of their widespread familiarity, provided the Sioux with literary allusions and character traits that served to criticize or comment upon individual behavior. The second type of *ohúkaką* were novelistic in nature and were not as widely known as the preceding group. These stories generally lacked a cast of supernatural characters, and, although they told of miraculous events, the characters and their activities were not radically different from those of the contemporary world, and the stories were thought to have been at least possible.

The second major category of Sioux narratives, the *wičhówayake* 'stories', were those believed to be true. One subgroup comprised stories said to have taken place in relatively recent times, perhaps two or three generations ago. Most were legendary and often told of miraculous, but believable, events in which someone was aided by a supernatural power. The other subgroup comprised accounts of events that took place within the band or residential group and were told as history and entertainment (M.W. Beckwith 1930:339–341; E.C. Deloria 1932:ix–x).

Tribal Origin Stories

Plains tribes generally lacked a sacred canon that provided an account of the origin of the world and humankind. Most tribes, particularly the nomadic ones, either lacked cosmological accounts altogether or had a variety of traditions, each generally known only to specific individuals or families. The Comanche and Kiowa, for example, had no genesis stories, while the Cheyenne, Crow, and Hidatsa had multiple accounts of the origin of the world, illustrating the fluid nature of cosmological explanations. Among the nomadic groups, in fact, it appears that many tribal members had little or no familiarity with such traditions, which were known only by specific shamans and raconteurs. For most individuals, origin stories were told like other myths, and were subject to constant reshaping and borrowing. Sometimes a cosmological explanation was incorporated into a widespread myth that, among other tribes who told it, was not an origin story. In contrast, some Prairie tribes, like the Pawnee and Arikara, had priests who recited memorized liturgies recounting tribal origins. These elaborate narratives were usually known only in part to the general populace and were taught, ostensibly verbatim, to apprentices in younger generations. Such accounts approached a cosmological canon, but the significant differences, for example, between the genesis tradition of the Arikara and that of the Skiri Pawnee make it clear that cosmologies changed over time, even among closely related peoples.

World origin myths on the Plains fall into four general categories, most of which are found elsewhere in North America and beyond.

The most common category is the earth-diver motif in which an animal, bird, or human dove to the bottom of the water covering a primordial world to retrieve a small amount of mud from which land was fashioned (Hultkrantz 1979:31). Typical of this cosmology is a Crow account in which Old Man Coyote, the tribal trickster, was on the primal water together with some ducks. He decided to send the ducks to the bottom of the water to fetch mud out of which he could create the world. Three ducks dove down and failed in their attempts, but the fourth one, a hell-diver, succeeded in bringing up a small bit of soil. Old Man Coyote then became Sun and created the earth. At the same time voices of beings, who by their own mysterious powers became animate, were heard; from the east came a wolf and from the west a coyote, both of which animals have symbolic significance in Crow culture. From there the story tells of a star that came to earth and transformed itself into Tobacco, the plant that was so integral to Crow religious life; and then Sun created grass, mountains, trees, and people (Lowie 1918:14–15).

Other tribes with similar earth-diver origin stories include the Arapaho (G.A. Dorsey 1903:191–212; G.A. Dorsey and A.L. Kroeber 1903:1–6), Gros Ventre (J.M. Cooper 1957:22–23), Blackfoot (Wissler and Duvall 1908:19), Hidatsa (M.W. Beckwith 1937; Bowers 1965), and Mandan (M.W. Beckwith 1937; Bowers 1950). In some, the culture hero or trickster was the transformer—Old Man, or Napi, of the Blackfoot; First Creator, identified with Coyote, of the Mandan and Hidatsa—while in other traditions, like the Cheyenne, the creator was unnamed. Among the Arapaho the creator was also a nameless manlike being who, before diving underwater, merged his body with the Flat Pipe, the primary religious shrine of the tribe. Flat Pipe Man and Turtle then dove down and remained underwater for seven days, after which they surfaced with mud that enabled them to create the world. The Gros Ventre had two traditions: in one the trickster Nih'atah created the earth and taught the tribe its rituals, while in a parallel account, Earthmaker, a human being who possessed the Flat Pipe, was the creator and giver of rituals who disappeared after giving the Gros Ventre the pipe.

A variant of the earth-diver motif is an account of the Wahpeton Sioux, in which Wakan Tanka, the Great Spirit, came down to earth in the form of a rainbow when the world was completely covered with water. He threw two of his ribs into the water and they surfaced as male and female water spirits (ųkt^héxi) who were instructed to be the leaders of the Medicine Dance. The water spirits then sent two birds and two mammals to the bottom of the water to obtain soil. Three failed, but the fourth one, a muskrat, was successful, and the water spirits threw the mud he obtained to the west, where land was created. A lodge happened to be there, and the two water spirits entered and called into it different groups of animals, all of whom sang their medicine songs, thereby establishing the Wahpeton society. Afterward the animals appeared to individuals in dreams to instruct them in both songs and rituals (Skinner 1920:273–278).

Another common origin motif was emergence from an underground world. It was most developed among the Arikara, whose priests chanted the account when opening sacred bundles and in other religious rituals. Here, as in the accounts of other tribes who had this story type, human beings were already in existence. Some Arikara versions begin by telling of a primordial race of giants who displeased the supreme being, the Chief Above. He instructed the animals to take the smaller people of the earth—the Arikara specifically—into an underground cave and then flooded the earth, killing the giants. Other versions commenced with the people already living in the underworld. Afterward the Chief Above sent Mother Corn to lead the people out of their subterranean home. Four animals—mole, badger, shrew, and gopher—burrowed a passage to the earth's surface, and then Mother Corn led them on a journey beset with obstacles that different birds helped them overcome. Finally, Mother Corn placed the Arikara in their historical territory, where she gave them corn plants, their staple of life, as well as their social institutions and rituals (G.A. Dorsey 1904:12–35). *1065*

The Mandan and Hidatsa also had emergence traditions that built upon the earth-diver accounts. The origin myth of one Mandan sacred bundle, perhaps representing a former village, tells that the Corn People formerly lived beside a lake below the surface of the earth before they were brought up into this world by a chief named Good Furred Robe. After climbing to the earth's surface on a grapevine, they began a long migration northward until they reached the Heart River region, their early historic home, where they eventually united with other peoples having bundles and became the Mandan of historic times (Bowers 1950:117, 156–153, 183). One of the two major Hidatsa origin stories—probably borrowed from the Mandan—relates that after First Creator and Lone Man created the earth, First Creator caused people, who were living underground, to emerge by climbing up a vine (Bowers 1965:290, 298).

A less widespread cosmological motif on the Plains was a celestial origin. This type was most fully developed by the Skiri Pawnee, who had the most intricate cosmology of all Plains tribes. Their account begins with the supreme deity, Tirawahat (The Heavens), calling the celestial powers together in council and giving them their names, stations in the heavens, and powers. After giving structure to the celestial world, Tirawahat told Sun, a male power, that he would mate with Moon, a female, in order to create the first human male child. Similarly, Morning Star was to mate with Evening Star to beget the first female. Then Tirawahat called together the four world-quarter stars, who sang ritual songs to the accompaniment of gourd rattles while Tirawahat created a sphere of water from a pebble dropped into rain clouds. The four world-quarter deities then struck the waters with their war clubs, separating the waters and creating land. While those deities sang other ritual songs, Wind, Cloud, Lightning, and Thunder created the various physical features of the earth, including plant and animal life. After the earth had been given its full form, the first boy and girl were placed on it and given the necessities of life. The children began to multiply and eventually divided into villages, while the heavenly beings in a step-by-step manner gave them their rituals (G.A. Dorsey 1904b:3–14). Later, in the annual Thunder, or bundle renewal, ritual, Skiri priests sang the corpus of songs sung by the four world-quarter gods describing in minute detail the acts of creation, the songs forming the core of the ceremony (Murie 1981, 1:43–52).

The Osage had a number of celestial origin stories, each known to the religious leaders. The account of the Wazhazhe moiety began with children in the sky—sometimes identified as stars—whose parents were Sun and Moon. Moon instructed her children to go down to earth to live. Arriving below, they found the earth covered with water and began crying. An elk pitied them and, dropping into the water, called to the winds for assistance. The winds blew the waters upward into a mist, first exposing only rocks and later land. The elk then rolled on the earth and all types of vegetation grew from his hairs. The people then

discovered members of the other Osage social groups and united with them into a single people (Fletcher and La Flesche 1911:62–64).

Another Osage origin story, told by a member of the Tsizhu moiety, made reference to a sacred chart that depicted four upper worlds, the lowest of which was held up by a red oak tree. The story began with people journeying from the lowest part of the upper world to the highest part, where they were given human souls in the bodies of birds. Then they descended to the lowest upper world, alighted on the red oak tree, and dropped to earth, where they divided into two groups, one that subsisted on roots and the other on animal flesh, and that eventually began to exchange food with one another. A female red bird gave human bodies to the people, and then buffalo bulls gave corn and squash to the Tsizhu. The remainder of the account described how the Osage social groups came together and searched for a country in which to live together. Portions of the sacred chart were reproduced by tattooing on the necks and chests of religious leaders (Dorsey 1888b:377–381) ("Osage," fig. 4, this vol.).

The Omaha origin story, like that of one of the Osage social groups, begins with emergence from under the waters of a lake (Fletcher and La Flesche 1911:64, 70). Unlike the Osage, in which each moiety or clan had its own origin story, the Omaha had a single tribal account.

Among the Hidatsa, the Awatixa division had a sky origin account that represents the fourth type of origin tradition: a creation episode attached to a geographically widespread myth that among other tribes did not have cosmological significance. The Awatixa myth of the Sacred Arrows was a composite of mythic themes, primarily the Star Husband and Twins motifs. The story began with Charred Body living in a village in the sky and coming down to earth in the form of an arrow. After establishing a village, he returned to the sky and brought other people down to earth. The narrative continued with a series of episodes, among which was the story of the Twins, represented by Lodge Boy and Spring Boy, who, possessing the supernatural powers of arrows, embarked on adventures in which they overcame various fearsome antagonists and in the process acquired Awatixa ceremonies (Bowers 1965:126, 303–308).

The preceding story illustrates how explanatory elements are often incorporated into older myths to account for the origins of rituals. Among the Kiowa, for example, the Twins story occurs as the origin tradition of the 10 tribal Boy Medicine bundles (E.C. Parsons 1929:1–8), but among other tribes, like the Arikara, the cognate myth is no more than a popular story from the holy period or mythic times that does not account for any origins. Similarly, the Star Husband and other episodes comprising the Awatixa myth of the Sacred Arrows lack explanatory functions or ritual associations in those same stories that were told by the Arikara and Pawnee (G.A. Dorsey 1904b:60–65; Parks 1991, 4:575–590).

Migration Stories

For many Plains tribes, migration stories played a larger role in tribal history and cosmology than did creation stories. Non-Indian scholars have always more readily accepted migration traditions, in opposition to creation stories, as genuinely historical. J.O. Dorsey (1886) compiled the migration traditions of Plains Siouan tribes, bringing fragmentary material from written sources beginning in the seventeenth century together with contemporary stories told by reservation Indians recorded by himself and others. Dorsey reconstructed Siouan history from these stories, beginning east of the Mississippi along the Ohio River where the Dhegiha and Chiwere Siouans lived in loose alliance with the Skiri Pawnee and Arikara. As they moved down the Ohio and reached the Mississippi, a portion of the Dhegiha went downstream and became the Quapaw ('downstream people') while the remainder went upstream and became the Omaha ('against the wind or current'). The Omaha group (including also the Ponca, Kansa, and Osage) continued up the Mississippi, then ascended the Missouri. At the mouth of the Osage River the Osage broke off and followed that river upstream. Then the Kansa broke off, settling at the mouth of the Kansas River. About this time the Iowa joined the Omaha and Ponca, and the three tribes moved up the eastern tributaries of the Missouri, reaching the headwaters of the Des Moines River. The Omaha and Ponca then moved to the Pipestone Quarry in southwest Minnesota and later to the Big Sioux River. There they fought with the Yankton Sioux living to the northeast on the Minnesota River, who forced the Omaha and Ponca to flee southwestward where, at Lake Andes, South Dakota, they received the Sacred Pole, symbol of Omaha tribal unity. They continued up the Missouri, the Omaha stopping at the mouth of the White Earth River and the Ponca continuing up that river to the area of the Black Hills and the Little Missouri River. The Ponca later rejoined the Omaha and together the two tribes backtracked down the Missouri, the Ponca eventually settling at the mouth of the Niobrara and the Omaha continuing downriver to their historical village sites in Nebraska.

Such a reconstruction is plausible and fulfills a Western sense of history. Archeologists have used Dorsey's reconstruction as a guide to the possible identification of prehistoric sites, with a hypothetical connection being drawn between the mound-building Mississippian cultures of the Ohio Valley and the ancestral Siouan groups (Kroeber 1939:91; Eggan 1952:41), and linguists have identified the Dhegiha and Chiwere linguistic subgroupings of Siouan as Mississippi Valley Siouan (C.F. Voegelin 1941:249).

Similar migration stories told as oral traditions, bolstered by evidence from historical documents and archeology, are recorded for the Kiowa and Cheyenne. In the Kiowa case, the tribe traced its earliest-remembered homeland to the Yellowstone valley of Montana, then to the Black Hills of South Dakota. They were driven from that area around 1800 by the Sioux and Cheyenne, who arrived at the Black Hills from the east. Subsequently the Kiowa migrated southward to their historic homeland in Oklahoma (Mooney 1898:153–156). In the Cheyenne origin story the tribe first emerged from underground in a rocky area where they subsisted on rabbits, then moved on to a great water where they subsisted on waterfowl. Grinnell (1923, 1:4–8) interpreted these traditions as reflecting an origin in the Northeast, presumably along Lake Superior. The Cheyenne subsequently moved to Minnesota, where they lived in the vicinity of the Sioux until gradually migrating westward to the area of the Black Hills. Historical documentation and archeological excavation of a presumed prehistoric Cheyenne village (the Biesterfeldt site) on the Sheyenne River in North Dakota provide plausible evidence of the Cheyenne migration from Minnesota (W.R. Wood 1971a:52–60).

During the twentieth century a distinctive genre of tribal migration stories developed in English renditions whose intentions were to establish cultural antiquity and articulate group solidarity. Such stories involved movements over long distances and through considerable periods of time. Based on tribal traditions, these epics took on the quality of origin myths. While some of these migration stories have historical validity, others do not. These epics require interpretation as sacred texts and are valuable for understanding twentieth-century cultures.

Two published examples present the interrelated migration stories of the Crow (Medicine Crow 1992:16–24) and Hidatsa (Ahler, Trimble, and Thiessen 1991), but stories told by members of other Plains tribes circulated orally. The Crow migration story begins with the people living near the western Great Lakes, then moving to northern Minnesota and southern Manitoba. As told in 1932 to Joseph Medicine Crow, a native Crow anthropologist, by an elder named Cold Wind, the ancestral people then moved southwest to Devils Lake, North Dakota. There a chief named No Vitals received the gift of sacred tobacco seeds in a vision and was instructed to go west to the high mountains to plant them. At the same time another chief, Red Scout, was given corn in a vision and instructed to remain there and plant it. No Vitals led his people westward to the Mandan villages on the Missouri River, then north to the mouth of the Knife River. No Vitals, now at middle age, led a part of the people farther up the Missouri, then up the Milk River to Alberta. Finding the winters too harsh, they migrated south through the Rocky Mountains, passing the Great Salt Lake, and going perhaps as far south as Texas. Turning north, they arrived at their promised homeland in the Yellowstone valley in southeastern Montana a century after separating from their relatives on the Missouri River. Those who stayed behind at Devils Lake ultimately joined their relatives on the Missouri, forming the Hidatsa. The story of Hidatsa migrations is based on a reading of Hidatsa myths as history, bolstered by an interpretation of the archeological record as supporting evidence. It represents a blending of native and anthropo- *1067* logical perspectives characteristic of the cooperation between archeologists and American Indian tribes in the late twentieth century.

Winter Counts

Some of the Plains tribes kept calendars, called winter counts in English (a literal translation of their Sioux name, *waníyetu yawápi*), that are unique in North America. Extant winter counts were recorded by the Blackfoot, Kiowa, Teton and Yanktonai Sioux, Mandan, and Hidatsa. Originally they were oral documents, which is documented for the Blackfoot (Wissler 1911:45), but they are best known in conjunction with painted and written charts that served both as calendars and as true histories. It seems likely that such memorized oral documents existed among other Plains tribes as well, and it is known that other tribes used particular events (most famously, "the year the stars fell," referring to the Lenoid meteorite shower of 1833) as names to mark time.

The Sioux winter counts typically consisted of series of pictographs drawn in rows or in a spiral on hide, cloth, or paper, that represented memorable events of each "winter," meaning a year (starting at the first snowfall; therefore the Sioux "winter" spanned parts of two years of the western calendar). Most winter count pictographs were relatively crude, with minimal detail, although some dating from the late nineteenth and twentieth centuries were highly elaborated works of art. The pictographs were secondary to the winter count, which was most importantly preserved as oral tradition; they were mnemonic devices, each representing a short, memorized phrase that served as the name of the winter. The series of names served as a calendar. Individuals, for example, knew the name of the winter in which they were born, and would refer to the winter count, counting backwards, to determine their age. For example, in the early years of the twentieth century, James R. Walker (1982:87), physician on the Pine Ridge Reservation, kept a winter count in his office for his patients' use when he asked them their ages. More than 100 winter counts are preserved, but many are copies or partial copies of one another. The earliest of the Sioux winter counts is the John K. Bear count, kept by Drifting Goose's band of Lower Yanktonai, which begins in 1682 and continues for 200 winters (J.H. Howard 1976).

Blackfoot winter counts differ from those of the Sioux in that the unit of time used to record years was from one summer to the next. Only one example was known to have been drawn in pictographic form on hide; the others were written from dictation. Like the Sioux counts, each year was designated by a short phrase that served as the name of the year. The earliest of them, kept by the Blood leader Bad Hand, began in 1810 and ended in 1883. Six counts are preserved in archives, representing all three Blackfoot tribes (Dempsey 1965).

The Kiowa winter counts included two pictographs for each year, one showing a Sun Dance lodge or tree, indicating summer, the other a black bar (signifying lack of vegetation), indicating winter. Most of the surviving counts were drawn on hide or paper and the names associated with each pictograph were dictated by a keeper and written down, either in Kiowa or English. The name of each pictograph, like those of the Sioux and Blackfoot, was a short phrase. The earliest Kiowa count began in 1833 and continued to 1892. A unique Kiowa calendar, kept by Anko, who also kept a winter count, consists of monthly pictographs, each indicated by a crescent moon, that spans 37 months from 1889 to 1892 (fig. 2) (Mooney 1898; Lowie Museum 1968).

Mandan and Hidatsa winter counts also used winters as the measure of the year. Only one example, the count by Butterfly, a Mandan, is preserved in pictographic form, using very minimal figures to recall the year names. Each winter camp was represented by a circle with an interior cross. Some years had additional pictographs recalling summer events (J.H. Howard 1960c). A similar Mandan winter count was kept by Foolish Woman; both counts began in 1833 and ended in 1876. A winter count by Hair Necklace, a Hidatsa, covers the years 1844–1863 (M.W. Beckwith 1937:308–320; J.H. Howard 1960a; M.W. Smith 1960; Tannenbaum 1992).

Winter counts are rich sources of historical data, limited only by interpretation. No full explication of the stories behind each year name was ever recorded for any winter. Most winter counts lack any explication beyond the year names themselves, which are usually cryptic and difficult, sometimes impossible, to translate with certainty. With these limitations understood, the winter counts document locations, individuals, and events that can corroborate or explicate written historical accounts.

Smithsonian, NA: 2538 (top left, neg. 92-11151, top right, neg. 92-11132); bottom right, Smithsonian, Dept. of Anthr.: 6931 (neg. 99-20263); center, Brown U., Haffenreffer Mus. of Anthr., Bristol, R.I.: 96.38.1.

Fig. 2. Record keeping. Pictorial calendars were regularly copied over as old versions wore out or space was needed to add new entries. Each recopying offered an opportunity for slight revisions. In the 20th century, calendar keepers sometimes based their copies on published versions as well as on calendars passed down within a community. Anko, a Kiowa, kept both his annual calendar (top left) and a monthly calendar (top right) in a pocket memorandum book, which James Mooney acquired in Ind. Terr. in 1892. Mooney (1898:pl. LXXX) had a Smithsonian illustrator combine the 2 calendars on a drawing of a buffalo hide, and several Kiowa artists have produced similar calendars on hide, using the published version as a model. center, Pictorial calendar by Kiowa artist Charles E. Rowell, about 1934. Width 86 cm. bottom left, Doris Old Person (Blackfeet, b. 1938), wife of Chief Earl Old Person, who taught school children about traditional Blackfeet winter counts. This winter count was made by Percy Bull Child (Blackfeet, b. 1916). Photograph by Joe Fisher, K.W. Bergan Elementary School, Browning, Mont., 1998. bottom right, Census sticks recording the number of women in the Nokoni Comanche in 1868, still tied together with government-issued red cloth tape. Collected by Edward Palmer on the Kiowa-Comanche reservation, Okla.

TRIBAL TRADITIONS AND RECORDS

Sioux Calendars and Histories

Pictographs

The native record of the past preserved by the Sioux is remarkable for its diversity and richness. Sioux chronologies were first noted by outsiders in 1876, when a copy of a winter count kept by Lone Dog, a Yanktonai, was made by Lt. H.T. Reed (vol. 17:286). Explications of the symbols were obtained from Sioux living near Forts Sully and Rice; and the winter count, covering the years 1800–1801 to 1870–1871, was first published the next year (Mallery 1877, 1886; C.E. Burke 2000). The pictographs spiraled from the center outward; Reed's copy was made on a square of muslin, but Lone Dog's original was said to be on a buffalo hide. Also in 1877, Lt. James Bradley, a military officer serving at the post near Red Cloud Indian Agency, was present when the Tetons under Crazy Horse came in to surrender, less than a year after the Battle of the Little Bighorn. One 84-year-old man, Bradley wrote, "carried a stick about six feet long, covered with notches, thousands of them. I asked him what it was, and he said it was the history of the world from the beginning, handed down by his fathers." It is apparent that this carved archive also represented a winter count (DeMallie 1992).

The form of the document was inconsequential. Whether carved on a pole or painted on hide, cloth, or paper, the winter count was fundamentally an oral document, memorized and passed down using the carved or pictured representations as mnemonic devices. Taking the Lone Dog count as an example, the names of the winters include catastrophic events—1800–1801, "Thirty Sioux were killed by Crow Indians"; 1801–1802, "Many died of smallpox"; natural events—1833–1834, "The stars fell"; or other memorable events—1867–1868, "Many flags were given" (the 1868 treaty). The winter counts did not consist of year names alone; each year name was in itself a mnemonic device that served to bring to the keeper's mind the detailed story of that particular event. These stories, related at various times as independent tales, formed a native history; because many of the events chosen for winter counts were of local interest, a winter count served as a history of a particular band (Meya 1999). However, since winter counts were shared by sale or gift, many cannot be directly correlated with the history of a single social group. Moreover, as time passed, and the counts were circulated from band to band, the knowledge of those stories behind the year names was frequently lost.

Among the dozens of winter counts that have been preserved, one stands out as most closely approximating the unnamed old man's "history of the world" mentioned by Bradley in 1877. This is the winter count of Brown Hat, a member of Spotted Tail's Brule Teton, whose English name was Battiste Good (or Good Chief). In fact, it may represent a pictographic version of that very one; it is not unlikely that Good was the son of the old man who carried the carved pole. Multiple copies of this winter count are deposited in archives and museums from Washington, D.C., to Los Angeles, most of which were made in turn by Good's son, High Hawk, who sold copies to collectors.

The first of these copies to come to the attention of scholars was drawn by Good himself in 1880 for William Corbusier, an army physician stationed near the Red Cloud Agency (Mallery 1893:287–328). The count comprises pictographs representing each winter from 1700–1701 to 1879–1880; in addition, there are 12 composite pictographs, each comprising a generation—culturally defined as a period of 70 years—that take the count back to the origin of the Sioux as a people (fig. 3).

Although Good apparently did not learn to write the Sioux language, he did learn to write some English words and numbers. During Good's lifetime, an aura of sacredness surrounded writing, as it did art; for the Sioux during the prereservation period, writing was conceived of as an important source, or vehicle, of the power of Whites. Written documents, particularly from government officials, were highly valued and kept like sacred bundles. Significantly enough, Good's decision to draw a winter count documenting the history of his people originated in a vision experienced in the Black Hills, a sacred place.

In the Sioux language the word meaning 'to draw' (owá) referred to anything depicted in two dimensions, including flags, body paint, drawings, and writing. Just as the Whites' flags, coins and medals, and books and papers, were expressions of their power, so, too, Good's painted winter count was an expression of Teton power. Good's inscription of the winter count on paper was a means of meeting the Whites on their own ground. In this count, both Good and High Hawk were at pains to relate the Sioux past to that of the Whites.

When Good made the copy for Corbusier, the last pictograph represented the year 1879–1880; it represents children attending school for the first time (fig. 3). Counting backward, pictograph by pictograph, to the first of these annual depictions reveals that the count began in 1700–1701, the winter two men were killed going to hunt. Then, continuing through time, begins the twelfth generational pictograph. Knowing that each of the generational pictographs represents 70 years—symbolized by the seven sticks held in the pipekeeper's hand in most of the pictographs—and again counting backward, Good dated the second of these composite pictographs at A.D. 931–1000. The first pictograph, representing the origin of the Teton as a people, covered only 30 years, dated 901–930 (fig. 3).

By contextualizing his people's past in the White people's numerical calendar, Good was in a position to assert the antiquity of the Sioux way of life, as well as to lay the basis for cross-referencing events of White history with those of the Sioux. Good's count is not only a cultural chronicle but also a political statement.

Each of the pictographs centers around an event, chosen as the memorable event of that generation. Unfortunately,

 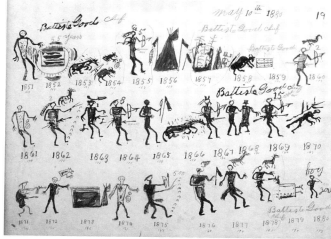

Fig. 3. First and last entries in the Battiste Good calendar. left, The first generational pictograph, with White Buffalo Woman in the center of a circle of tepees. right, Individual pictographs representing years 1851–1880. Several figures are accompanied by glyphs representing their names.

Corbusier did not record much information about these generational pictographs, probably because, to him, most of them seemed so similar as to be repetitive. High Hawk, interviewed in old age, apparently knew little about them. Knowledge of most of the stories behind these complex pictographs apparently died with Good. Yet the fragmentary records that do exist, combined with the testimony of the generational pictographs themselves, provide a good deal of information.

The first generational pictograph in Corbusier's copy depicted the coming of White Buffalo Woman, a sacred being, who brought the sacred pipe to the Sioux and taught them to use it as a mediator between humankind and Wakan Tanka, the Great Spirit (fig. 3). She also brought corn, symbolically depicted as dripping from her udders. The dotted line connecting the pipe to a blue cloud in the east (at the top of the page) represents, according to Good, the direct link to the heavens; the smoke from the pipe rises to carry the people's prayers to Wakan Tanka. The sacred woman first appeared to a man who was 30 or 40 years old, shown seated inside the circle of tepees. He is depicted outside the circle in his role as custodian of the pipe until his death 30 years later, when it passed to succeeding keepers, each fulfilling that role for 70 years.

For his publication of Good's winter count, Mallery had the pictographs redrawn to omit the English words and most of the numbers that Good had added. Mallery characterized these as "unnecessary additions and presumptuous emendations on the pictographs . . . To prevent the confusion to the reader which might result from Battiste's meddlesome vanity, these interpolated marks are in general omitted from the plates and figures." And lest anyone have any doubt about Mallery's evaluation of Good, he added: "He is simply the bad editor of a good work" (Mallery 1893:288).

The original Good drawing from which Mallery's illustration was made in fact provides considerably more information. He bracketed the pictograph with dates, and the image of the white buffalo was clearly labeled "woman." Understanding that White history required historical events to take place on a particular date, Good chose July 4 as the date of the White Buffalo Woman's arrival, doubtlessly appreciating the importance of that particular day to Americans. On the right side the list of animals serves as an inventory of important Plains fauna, and here Good has the pipekeeper speaking in the first person, as a chief, for the people as a whole: "my buffalo, my beaver," etc. The result of the White Buffalo Woman's coming was to formalize the compact between animals and humankind by which animals allowed themselves to be killed for food and also provided sacred and healing powers to people.

The pictograph also depicted some of the oldest features of the Sioux way of life, those that Good seems to have understood to predate the arrival of the White Buffalo Woman and the foundation of their society and religion. The yucca plant represented the use of its dried stalk, twirled in the hand on a piece of wood, to make fire. The elm was the wood from which bows were made, and the bow and arrow on the right symbolized its use in hunting.

The High Hawk copies of the count add another pictograph preceding this one to depict how the people lived before the White Buffalo Woman. They are shown living in makeshift shelters rather than tepees; the fundamental features of the Teton way of life are not yet fully known. The people use crude bows and arrows, shells for knives, and stone clubs; they boil water in rawhide basins, using rocks heated in the fire. Men are shown packing their belongings on their backs, but the use of tamed wolves to haul travois is also shown. High Hawk said that the number 6,000, repeated three times on the drawing, was the number *1071* of years from the beginning during which the people lived in this manner. Other numbers along the side seem to represent a chronology of fundamental cultural features (Curtis 1907–1930, 3:facing p. 158).

The cumulative effect of the generational pictographs was to show the development of Sioux society and culture, with particular emphasis on their adaptation to the environment. The first horses were seen interspersed in a buffalo herd in the generation from 1141–1210, and the first use of horses for hunting buffalo was recorded in the generation from 1631–1700. Here Good again ran into trouble with White scholars. Curtis (1907–1930, 3:31), for example, dismissed High Hawk's interpretation of these pictographs as representing 70 years, substituting seven in its place. This brought the coming of the White Buffalo Woman to 1540 and the first horse to 1624, dates more acceptable to Western history.

Although White scholars have been led to deny the validity of this native history, Good and High Hawk were more charitable toward Whites, whose history they did not fully understand, yet accommodated. The High Hawk version, for example, recorded the arrival of the first White men in the New World, shown with their boat and the date 1492; Columbus remained outside the tepee circle of Sioux history, yet firmly connected to it by High Hawk's chronology (High Hawk 1907).

The generational pictographs were in the most fundamental way a record of change, presenting a history of the development of Sioux culture. The yearly pictographs, in contrast, were a record of equilibrium, providing chronology in a culture that did not embrace time as a relentless, forward-moving force impinging on human life. As expressed by the Sioux scholar Ella C. Deloria, "You see, we Indians lived in eternity!" (quoted in Malan and McCone 1960:13).

Taken as a whole, the Good–High Hawk winter count on the one hand is a native document that preserves a record of the winters (in increasing detail) from the beginning to the present, and validates by its ever-increasing size the integrity of the Sioux as a people. On the other hand, by appropriating the numerical chronology of the White people, it serves as a bridge from the traditional way of life to the present.

Writing

The Sioux were unique among Plains tribes for the development of widespread native-language literacy. After the introduction of a writing system designed for the Sioux by Christian missionaries in the mid-nineteenth century, native-language literacy spread rapidly. Most winter counts were converted from pictographic to written form. Although writing was faster than drawing, it required the keeper to remember the meaning of the year name without the aid of a mnemonic pictograph. As a result, many year names came to be passed down without real comprehension of their significance.

In addition to winter counts, some Sioux men produced ledger books of traditional pictographic art depicting war exploits and other deeds explicated in the margins by written inscriptions. The best-known example is the record created by Bad Heart Bull, an Oglala, that parallels Good's winter count in that it was undertaken as a result of a dream. In the end the volume became a record of traditional culture, intertribal fights, battles and treaties with the Whites, and selected aspects of reservation culture (Blish 1967). Even though Bad Heart Bull's record related almost entirely to public aspects of Sioux culture and included very little relating to religious ceremonies, after his death the book itself was considered a sacred object. Eventually it was buried with his daughter.

Others kept pictographic autobiographies, memorializing their brave deeds. That of the Hunkpapa chief Sitting Bull is the most famous (fig. 4) (Stirling 1938). Sitting Bull's nephew, White Bull, a Minneconjou, kept a similar autobiography. He made at least two copies for White collectors, and perhaps this led him to add additional drawings depicting important aspects of Sioux culture; he even added an unprecedented self-portrait with his wife (J.H. Howard 1968a). The margins of most pages are liberally covered with inscriptions in Sioux that explicate details of the drawings and provide context.

Some records of tradition consisted entirely of written text, with only occasional drawings. The earliest of such efforts was undertaken in 1887 by George Bushotter, a young Sioux educated at Hampton Institute, Virginia. While employed by the Bureau of American Ethnology at the Smithsonian Institution, he worked under the supervision of ethnologist James Owen Dorsey and wrote more than 3,000 pages of texts that include autobiographical material, myths, descriptions of a wide variety of customs and ceremonies, and a long catalog of games (Dorsey 1894; DeMallie 1978).

In the first years of the twentieth century, George Sword, an Oglala, wrote a similar series of texts for Dr. James R. Walker, who worked at Pine Ridge as an amateur ethnologist (Sword 1998). Unlike Bushotter, Sword was an elder whose life experiences included participation in intertribal warfare, fights with the United States Army, and service as an army Indian scout, reservation policeman, judge, and Episcopal deacon. Many of his writings dealt with religious ceremonies and belief and as such are an invaluable historical record of Sioux tradition.

The writings of Ivan Stars and other Pine Ridge Sioux, also composed during the early twentieth century, represent an effort to record traditional stories and historical accounts from elders, in the Sioux language (Buechel 1998). The project was initiated by the Jesuit missionary Eugene Buechel, in part to provide lexical material for his dictionary.

During the early twentieth century several Sioux writers chose to preserve historical traditions in English. The books of Santee author Charles A. Eastman (1902, 1907, 1911), Yankton author Gertrude Bonnin (Zitkala-Ša 1901, 1921), and Tetons Luther Standing Bear (1928, 1931, 1933,

Fig. 4. Transition from pictures to text. top left, Watercolor by Titian Peale of a Pawnee buffalo hide painted with battle scenes that he copied while traveling with Maj. Stephen H. Long's expedition of 1819-1820. top right, Autobiographical drawing of Sitting Bull (Hunkpapa Teton) overcoming an Assiniboine enemy (computer enhanced). It was produced in 1882, by which time he had learned to sign his name (Stirling 1938). bottom left, Extensive text in the Sioux language added by White Bull (Minneconjou Teton) to the drawings of his life history, which he drew in 1931 for North Dakota Congressman Usher L. Burdick (J.H. Howard 1968a). bottom right, Dust jacket from the first edition of *Black Elk Speaks* (Neihardt 1932), text by John G. Neihardt with illustrations by Standing Bear (Oglala Teton). It depicts an episode in Black Elk's vision.

1934) and William Bordeaux (1929, 1952) documented the Sioux past and situated it in relation to White history and civilization. Nicholas Black Elk, an Oglala, dictated his life story; the resulting book (Neihardt 1932) became one of the most widely read books on American Indians of the twentieth century (fig. 4). In 1944 Black Elk dictated a history of his people, conceptualized as a series of visions and not precisely ordered chronologically, that closely paralleled the iconography of Good's pictorial account (Neihardt 1951; DeMallie 1984).

Contributors

This list gives the academic affiliations of authors at the time this volume went to press. The dates following the entries indicate when each manuscript was (1) first received in the General Editor's office; (2) accepted by the General Editor's office; and (3) sent to the author (or, if deceased, a substitute) for final approval after revisions and editorial work.

ALBERS, PATRICIA C., Department of American Indian Studies, University of Minnesota, Minneapolis. Plains Ojibwa: 4/28/95; 5/21/98; 12/18/98. Santee: 10/2/89; 12/6/99; 8/1/00.

ARCHAMBAULT, JOALLYN (Standing Rock Sioux), Department of Anthropology, Smithsonian Institution, Washington, D.C. Sun Dance: 10/22/99; 2/17/00; 8/1/00. Art Since 1900: 8/4/00; 8/7/00; 9/13/00.

BAILEY, GARRICK A., Department of Anthropology, University of Tulsa, Oklahoma. Kansa: 7/15/91; 4/7/98; 6/11/98. Osage: 7/17/89; 6/1/98; 6/30/98.

BELL, ROBERT E. (emeritus), Department of Anthropology, University of Oklahoma, Norman. Plains Village Tradition: Southern: 7/24/87; 10/7/98; 7/23/99.

BROOKS, ROBERT L., Oklahoma Archeological Survey, University of Oklahoma, Norman. Plains Village Tradition: Southern: 7/24/87; 10/7/98; 7/23/99.

BROWN, DONALD N., Department of Sociology, Oklahoma State University, Stillwater. Ponca: 9/25/89; 6/30/98; 7/16/98.

BROWN, JENNIFER S.H., Department of History, University of Winnipeg, Manitoba. History of the Canadian Plains Until 1870: 8/12/98; 9/15/98; 9/14/99.

CAMPBELL, THOMAS N. (emeritus), Department of Anthropology, University of Texas, Austin. Tonkawa: 2/10/88; 5/24/99; 2/10/00.

CHRISTAFFERSON, DENNIS M., American Indian Studies Research Institute, Indiana University. Sioux, 1930-2000: 7/19/00; 8/7/00; 8/31/00.

DARNELL, REGNA, Department of Anthropology, University of Western Ontario, London. Plains Cree: 7/21/89; 4/21/98; 1/27/99.

DeMALLIE, RAYMOND J., American Indian Studies Research Institute, Indiana University, Bloomington. Introduction: 10/12/99; 10/29/99; 12/20/99. History of Ethnological and Ethnohistorical Research: 8/10/99; 8/12/99; 11/23/99. Assiniboine: 9/15/98; 9/15/98; 1/25/99. Sioux Until 1850: 6/19/00; 7/13/00; 8/21/00. Yankton and Yanktonai: 8/29/00; 9/1/00; 10/4/00. Teton: 8/8/00; 8/30/00; 9/27/00. Tribal Traditions and Records: 11/8/00; 11/14/00; 12/7/00.

DEMPSEY, HUGH A. (emeritus), Glenbow Museum, Calgary, Alberta. Sarcee: 11/9/87; 3/17/98; 11/25/98. Blackfoot: 11/9/87; 3/19/98; 12/17/98.

DYCK, IAN, Archaeological Survey of Canada, Canadian Museum of Civilization, Hull, Quebec. Hunting and Gathering Tradition: Canadian Plains: 4/21/93; 11/17/98; 8/10/99.

EGGAN, FRED (deceased), Department of Anthropology, University of Chicago, Illinois. Kinship and Social Organization: 11/4/98; 12/14/98; 4/17/00.

EWERS, JOHN C. (deceased), Department of Anthropology, Smithsonian Institution, Washington, D.C. History of Ethnological and Ethnohistorical Research: 8/10/99; 8/12/99; 11/23/99.

FLANNERY, REGINA (emerita), Department of Anthropology, Catholic University, Washington, D.C. Gros Ventre: 7/11/88; 9/30/98; 10/5/98.

FOSTER, MORRIS W., Department of Anthropology, University of Oklahoma, Norman. Plains Apache: 10/29/92; 11/23/98; 1/24/00.

FOWLER, LORETTA, Department of Anthropology, University of Oklahoma, Norman. History of the United States Plains Since 1850: 7/23/99; 7/29/99; 11/23/99. Gros Ventre: 7/11/88; 9/30/98; 10/5/98. Arapaho: 6/8/90; 6/25/99; 4/12/00.

FRISON, GEORGE C. (emeritus), Department of Anthropology, University of Wyoming, Laramie. Environment and Subsistence: 7/21/89; 4/7/99; 9/14/99. Hunting and Gathering Tradition: Northwestern and Central Plains: 3/25/88; 1/16/92; 8/13/99.

GETTY, IAN A.L., Nakoda Institute, Stoney Tribal Administration, Morley, Alberta. Stoney: 7/9/98; 7/28/98; 1/5/99.

GODDARD, IVES, Department of Anthropology, Smithsonian Institution, Washington, D.C. The Languages of the Plains: Introduction: 8/6/99; 8/12/99; 9/3/99. Algonquian Languages of the Plains: 4/24/90; 12/14/98; 7/28/99.

GOODING, ERIK D., American Indian Studies Research Institute, Indiana University, Bloomington. Stoney: 7/9/98; 7/28/98; 1/5/99. Celebrations and Giveaways: 6/21/99; 4/10/00; 8/1/00.

GREENE, CANDACE S., Department of Anthropology, Smithsonian Institution, Washington, D.C. Art Until 1900: 7/1/98; 7/9/98; 8/24/00.

GUNNERSON, JAMES H. (emeritus), Department of Anthropology, University of Nebraska State Museum, Lincoln. Plains Village Tradition: Western Periphery: 7/23/87; 10/30/98; 5/24/99.

HENNING, DALE R., Department of Anthropology, Illinois State Museum, Springfield. Plains Village Tradition: Eastern Periphery and Oneota Tradition: 12/21/87; 10/2/98; 5/21/99.

HOFFMAN, MICHAEL P., Department of Anthropology, University of Arkansas, Fayetteville. Quapaw: 9/13/88; 8/13/98; 9/10/98.

IRWIN, LEE, Deparment of Religious Studies, College of Charleston, South Carolina. Mandan: 11/30/87; 6/5/98; 6/29/98. Omaha: 3/20/92; 7/20/98; 6/29/98. Ponca: 9/25/89; 6/30/98; 7/16/98.

JOHNSON, ALFRED E., Museum of Anthropology, University of Kansas, Lawrence. Plains Woodland Tradition: 9/4/87; 11/24/98; 5/11/99.

KAVANAGH, THOMAS W., William Hammond Mathers Museum, Indiana University, Bloomington. Comanche: 9/8/87; 7/28/99; 1/20/00.

KRAUSE, RICHARD A., Department of Anthropology, University of Alabama, Tuscaloosa. History of Archeological Research: 4/28/95; 11/5/98; 6/4/99. Plains Village Tradition: Coalescent: 7/21/87; 9/2/98; 7/6/99.

LEHMER, DONALD J. (deceased), Department of Anthropology, Dana College, Blair, Nebraska. Plains Village Tradition: Postcontact: 6/11/73; 10/8/98; 6/10/99.

LEVY, JERROLD E. (emeritus), Department of Anthropology, University of Arizona, Tucson. Kiowa: 8/24/87; 6/9/99; 2/4/00.

LIBERTY, MARGOT P., Trail's End Historical Center, Sheridan, Wyoming. Omaha: 3/20/92; 7/20/98; 6/29/98. Cheyenne: 1/3/00; 3/10/00; 8/1/00.

MCCOLLOUGH, MARTHA, Department of Anthropology and Ethnic Studies, University of Nebraska, Lincoln. Plains Apache: 10/29/92; 11/23/98; 1/24/00.

MCCRADY, DAVID, Department of History, University of Winnipeg, Manitoba. History of the Canadian Plains Since 1870: 7/27/99; 7/29/99; 9/10/99.

MAXWELL, JOSEPH A., Graduate School of Education, George Mason University, Fairfax, Virginia. Kinship and Social Organization: 11/4/98; 12/14/98; 4/17/00.

MILLER, DAVID REED, Department of Indian Studies, Saskatchewan Indian Federated College, University of Regina, Saskatchewan. Assiniboine: 9/15/98; 9/15/98; 1/25/99.

MOORE, JOHN H., Department of Anthropology, University of Florida, Gainesville. Cheyenne: 1/3/00; 3/10/00; 8/1/00.

MORLAN, RICHARD E., Archaeological Survey of Canada, Canadian Museum of Civilization, Hull, Quebec. Hunting and Gathering Tradition: Canadian Plains: 4/21/93; 11/17/98; 8/10/99.

NEWCOMB, WILLIAM W., JR., (emeritus), Department of Anthropology, University of Texas, Austin. Wichita: 11/13/87; 8/5/98; 8/26/98. Tonkawa: 2/10/88; 5/24/99; 2/10/00.

OPLER, MORRIS E. (deceased), Department of Anthropology, University of Oklahoma, Norman. Lipan: 2/15/74; 5/24/99; 12/15/99.

PARKS, DOUGLAS R., American Indian Studies Research Institute, Indiana University, Bloomington. Siouan Languages: 10/19/99; 10/29/99; 1/10/00. Caddoan Languages: 5/14/99; 7/26/99; 8/11/99. Arikara: 9/26/77; 7/1/98; 7/2/98. Pawnee: 10/30/98; 11/6/98; 1/29/99. Kitsai: 6/17/98; 6/22/98; 8/31/98. Enigmatic Groups: 8/11/00; 8/15/00; 10/4/00. Tribal Traditions and Records: 11/8/00; 11/14/00; 12/7/00.

PAYMENT, DIANE PAULETTE, Parks Canada, Western Canada Service Centre, Winnipeg, Manitoba. Plains Métis: 7/26/93; 5/4/98; 12/11/98.

RANKIN, ROBERT L., Department of Linguistics, University of Kansas, Lawrence. Siouan Languages: 10/19/99; 10/29/99; 1/10/00.

SCHNEIDER, MARY JANE, Department of Indian Studies, University of North Dakota, Grand Forks. Three Affiliated Tribes: 6/22/98; 7/22/98; 9/9/98.

SCHWEITZER, MARJORIE M. (emerita), Department of Sociology, Oklahoma State University, Stillwater. Otoe and Missouria: 7/21/89; 4/6/98; 5/8/98.

STEWART, FRANK HENDERSON, Department of Islamic and Middle Eastern Studies, Hebrew University, Mt. Scopus, Jerusalem. Hidatsa: 11/4/74; 7/8/98; 7/9/98.

STRAUS, A. TERRY, Master of Arts Program in Social Sciences, University of Chicago, Illinois. Cheyenne: 1/3/00; 3/10/00; 8/1/00.

SWAGERTY, WILLIAM R., Department of History, University of Idaho, Moscow. History of the United States Plains Until 1850: 3/11/99; 6/10/99; 9/15/99.

VEHIK, SUSAN C., Department of Anthropology, University of Oklahoma, Norman. Hunting and Gathering Tradition: Southern Plains: 10/29/98; 12/15/98; 6/2/99.

VOGET, FRED W. (deceased), Department of Anthropology, Southern Illinois University, Edwardsville. Crow: 6/29/87; 5/21/98; 10/30/98.

WEDEL, MILDRED MOTT (deceased), Department of Anthropology, Smithsonian Institution, Washington, D.C. Iowa: 4/22/88; 10/22/91; 5/20/98.

WEDEL, WALDO R. (deceased), Department of Anthropology, Smithsonian Institution, Washington, D.C. History of Archeological Research: 4/28/95; 11/5/98; 6/4/99. Environment and Subsistence: 7/21/89; 4/7/99; 9/14/99. Plains Village Tradition: Central: 6/4/73; 12/15/98; 7/6/99.

WOOD, W. RAYMOND, Department of Anthropology, University of Missouri, Columbia. Plains Village Tradition: Middle Missouri: 8/11/87; 11/23/98; 7/6/99. Mandan: 11/30/87; 6/5/98; 6/29/98. Omaha: 3/20/92; 7/20/98; 7/30/98.

YOUNG, GLORIA A., University Museum, University of Arkansas, Fayetteville. Kansa: 7/15/91; 4/7/98; 6/11/98. Quapaw: 9/13/88; 8/13/98; 9/10/98. Intertribal Religious Movements: 4/28/95; 5/21/98; 3/14/00. Celebrations and Giveaways: 6/21/99; 4/10/00; 8/1/00. Music: 7/14/99; 7/15/99; 3/14/00.

List of Illustrations

This list identifies the subjects of all illustrations, organized by chapter. All artists, photographers, and some individuals depicted (but not collectors) are included. Every identified individual depicted is found in the index, but not the photographers.

Southern Arapaho-Cheyenne Ghost Dance. Small circle. Women dancing. Dancer in trance. Dancers praying. Photographs by James Mooney, 1891–1894. Crow belt. Drawing by Roger Thor Roop. *1002–1003*

Ghost Dance. Painting by Yellow Nose, Cheyenne, 1891. *1003*

Peyote religious leaders. Bob-Tailed Wolf, Southern Cheyenne. By J.A. Shuck, 1938. Quanah Parker, Comanche. By Hutchins and Lanney, 1892. Preston Morrell, Osage Roadman. By Shane Culpepper, 1998. Osage Roadman's ritual objects. *1006–1007*

Indians in Worship-Native American Church. Painting by Tennyson Echiwaudah, Comanche, about 1960. *Native American Church (Peyote)*. Watercolor by Stephen Mopope, Kiowa, before 1972. *Songs of the Native American Church*, tape cover with photograph by Tony Isaacs. Recorded 1979, © 1983. Headstone of Oglala Sioux peyotist. By Omer Stewart, 1971. *1008*

Celebrations and Giveaways

Modern Dancer, fancy dance outfit. Watercolor by Allan Bushyhead, Southern Cheyenne, 1937. Southern Cheyenne men in fancy dance clothes. Probably by Horace Poolaw, 1928. Yankton man with Grass Dance bustle. By Alexander Gardner, 1867. Plains Ojibwa Grass Dancer. By James Howard, 1959. Three Affiliated Tribes man wearing eagle-feather bustle. By Ilka Hartmann, 1989. Dance mirror, Kansa. Grass Dance bustle or "crow belt," Brule Sioux. *1014–1015*

Camp at powwow. Couples in a two-step dance. Instructing young Omaha dancers. Photographs by Ilka Hartmann, Omaha Powwow, 1989. Plains Cree man being made up. By Rob McKinley, 1998. Dance breastplate. Tai Piah singers at Omaha powwow. By Carl Fleischhauser, 1983. Cigarette gifts. By Michael Crummett, 1979. *1017*

Elders at a Rabbit Dance. By John Vachon, 1941. *1020*

Kiowa float and young costumed participants at All-American Indian Days. Photographs probably by Ziemer Studio, 1954. Blackfeet Traditional Dancer at North American Indian Days. By Joe Fisher, 1994. Assiniboine and Sioux dancing at the Wolf Point Stampede. By Ralph Russell Doubleday, about 1935. Sioux rattle. *1021*

Jingle dress, Oglala Sioux. Entry procession at Ft. Berthold powwow with women wearing Jingle dresses. By Ilka Hartmann, 1989. "Princess set" beaded dance accessories. Osage woman in buckskin-fringed dress used in Traditional Dance. Fancy Shawl dancers. Woman dressed for modern dancing competition. Photographs by Lynn Ivory, 1989–1994. *1022*

The Hand Game. Watercolor by Victor Pepion, Blackfoot, about 1956. *1023*

Crow couple with wedding gifts. By Michael Crummett, 1977. *1023*

Otoe adoption of Kiowa woman. By Marjorie Schweitzer, 1983. *1024*

Music

Blackfoot Sun Dance singer-drummers with rawhide drum. By Sidney Richard Reeves, 1913. Blackfoot Rough Rider Society singers. By Joe Fisher, 1996. Pawnee drum. Sarcee drummers at medicine pipe ceremony. By Arnold Lupson, about 1926. Three Affiliated Tribes drummers at powwow. By Monroe Killy, 1942. Three Affiliated Tribes drummer. By Edward Bruner, 1951–1953. *1026–1027*

Rawhide rattle, Hidatsa. *1029*

Gros Ventre man blowing a bone whistle. By Richard Pohrt, 1937. Eagle bone whistle, Southern Cheyenne. Kiowa cedar flute. Snipe whistle, Hunkpapa Sioux. Detail shows mouthpiece construction. Drawing by Roger Thor Roop. *1029*

Crying Woman Singers, Gros Ventre, Plains Cree and Yakima. By Ted Whitecalf, 1994. Assiniboine woman performing with hand drum. Kiowa women in performance. Photographs by Rick Vargas, 1995. Omnichord. By Mary Jo Ruggles, 1991. *1031*

War Dance Songs of the Ponca. Record album, 1967. *Haystack:Live*

at Piapot. Tape cover, published 1997. *1032*

Transfer of the Blackfoot medicine pipe bundles during the Sun Dance. By Arnold Lupson, probably 1924. Beaver bundle transfer ceremony. Photographs by Karl Kaescamp, 1965. *1033*

Art Until 1900

Major techniques of quillwork and beadwork. Drawings by Roger Thor Roop. *1040*

Earliest Mandan pictorial robe, collected 1805. Blackfeet horizontal striped robe. Mandan feathered Circle robe. Yankton Sioux border and box design robe used by women. *1042–1043*

Sarcee men painting a hide with war deeds. By Diamond Jenness, 1921. *1043*

Drawing of warfare by Koba, Kiowa, 1875–1887. Camp scene of painted tepees by a Cheyenne artist, 1875–1887. *1044*

Bags showing regional beadwork styles: Northern (Blackfeet); Transmontane (Crow); Floral (Yankton Sioux); Central (Sioux, Cheyenne); Southern (Kiowa); Prairie (Otoe). *1047*

Teton Sioux woman painting rawhide for parfleches. By John A. Anderson, © 1897. *1048*

Teton Sioux girls' puberty ceremony. By John A. Anderson, about 1892. Sioux moccasins. Cheyenne sacred beadwork designs on a pillow and part of tepee ornaments. *1049*

Saddlebag with quilled protective designs, Sioux. *1054*

Art Since 1900

Art class, Rosebud Sioux Res. Sioux woman making pottery. Photographs by John Vachon, 1940. *1056*

First Dance of Sun Dance. Watercolor by Monroe Tsatoke, Kiowa, 1929. *1057*

Cheyenne Sun Dance. Casein painting by Richard West, Cheyenne, 1970. *The Vision*. Print by Calvin Larvie, Teton Sioux, 1950. Native American Church blanket pin by Julius Caesar, Pawnee. *1058–1059*

Clothing as art. Delores Racine, Blackfeet, wearing beaded dress standing beside painting of Julia Wades-in-the-Water by Winold Reiss, 1943. Photographed 1960. *1060*

Collector #5, or Osage with Van Gogh by T. C. Cannon, Kiowa-Caddo, about 1980. *Bases Stolen from the Cleveland Indians and a Captured Yankee* by Gerald McMaster, Plains Cree, 1989. *Buffalo Jump* by Ernie Pepion, Blackfeet, 1990. *Wounded Knee #2* by Rick Rivet, Subarctic Metis. The Visit by Arthur Amiotte, Sioux, 1995. *Coyote's Wild and Woolly West* by Harry Fonseca, Maidu, about 1980. *1060–1061*

Tribal Traditions

Running Rabbit, Blood Blackfoot, making a hide painting depicting his war deeds. By Edmund Morris, 1909. Teton Sioux woman telling stories. By John A. Anderson, about 1900. John Fire Lame Deer explaining a Teton ceremony. By Richard Erdoes, 1970. Northern Cheyenne man describing the Battle of the Little Bighorn. By Laton A. Huffman, 1901. *1063*

Record keeping. Anko's, Kiowa, annual calendar and monthly calendar, before 1892. Pictorial calendar by Charles E. Rowell, Kiowa, about 1934. Blackfeet woman teaching using a winter count made by Percy Bull Child. By Joe Fisher, 1998. Census sticks, Comanche. *1068–1069*

First and last entries in the Battiste Good calendar. Drawn in 1880. *1071*

Transition from pictures to text. Watercolor by Titian Peale of Pawnee hide with battle scenes, 1819–1820. Autobiographical drawing of Sitting Bull, Hunkpapa Teton Sioux, overcoming an Assiniboine, 1882. Autobiographical drawing by White Bull, Minneconjou Teton Sioux, with text in Sioux language, 1931. *Black Elk Speaks*, dust jacket, 1932. *1073*

Bibliography

This list includes all references cited in the volume, arranged in alphabetical order according to the names of the authors as they appear in the citations in the text. It also includes works submitted by the contributors or consulted by the Handbook research staff but not cited in the chapters. Multiple works by the same author are arranged chronologically; second and subsequent titles by the same author in the same year are differentiated by letters added to the dates. Where more than one author with the same surname is cited, one has been arbitrarily selected for text citation by surname alone throughout the volume, while the others are cited with added initials; the combination of surname with date in text citations should avoid confusion. Where a publication date is different from the series date (as in some annual reports and the like), the former is used. Dates, authors, and titles that do not appear on the original works are enclosed by brackets. For manuscripts, dates refer to time of composition. For publications reprinted or first published many years after original composition, a bracketed date after the title refers to the time of composition or the date of original publication.

ARCIA = Commissioner of Indian Affairs
1824–1848 Annual Report of the Commissioner of Indian Affairs to the Secretary of War. [Issued both as *House* and *Senate Documents.*] Washington: Government Printing Office. (See also ARCIA 1849–.)

1849– Annual Report of the Commissioner of Indian Affairs to the Secretary of the Interior. Washington, D.C.: U.S. Government Printing Office. (Reprinted: AMS Press, New York, 1976–1977; originally issued both as *House* and *Senate Documents*, and as Department of the Interior separate publications; *see* Key to the Annual Reports of the United States Commissioner of Indian Affairs, by J.A. Jones. *Ethnohistory* 2(1):58–64, 1955.)

ARDIA *see* Canada. Department of Indian Affairs

Abbass, D. Kathleen
1980 American Indian Ribbonwork: The Visual Characteristics. Pp. 31–43 in Fourth Annual Plains Indian Seminar: Ribbonwork and Cloth Applique. [Cover title:] Native American Ribbonwork: A Rainbow Tradition. George P. Horse Capture, ed. Cody, Wyo.: Buffalo Bill Historical Center.

Abbott, Edward Charles, and Helena Huntington Smith
1939 We Pointed Them North: Recollections of a Cowpuncher. New York: Farrar and Rinehart. (Reprinted: Lakeside Press, Chicago, 1991.)

Abbott, Lawrence
1994 I Stand in the Center of the Good: Interviews with Contemporary Native American Artists. Lincoln and London: University of Nebraska Press.

1994a Contemporary Native Art: A Bibliography. *The American Indian Quarterly* 18(3):383–403. Los Angeles.

Abel, Annie Heloise
1915–1925 The American Indian as Slaveholder and Secessionist. 3 vols. Cleveland, Ohio: Arthur H. Clark.

_____, ed. 1932 *see* Chardon, Francis A. 1932

_____, ed. 1939 *see* Tabeau, Pierre-Antoine 1939

Abel, Kerry, and Jean Friesen, eds.
1991 Aboriginal Resource Use in Canada: Historical and Legal Aspects. *Manitoba Studies in Native History* 6. Winnipeg: The University of Manitoba Press.

Aberle, David F.
1973 The Sun Dance and Reservation Underdevelopment: A Review Essay. *Journal of Ethnic Studies* 1(2):66–73. Bellingham, Wash.: Western Washington State College.

Abert, James W.
1846 Reconnaissance by Lt. James W. Abert, Topographical Engineers, 1845: Bents Fort to St. Louis via Canadian River. *29th Congress. 1st Session. Senate Document* 438. Washington.

1848 Report of the Secretary of War, Communicating, in Answer to a Resolution of the Senate, a Report and Map of the Examination of New Mexico, Made by Lieutenant J.W. Abert of the Topographical Corps [1846–1847]. *30th Congress. 1st Session. Senate Executive Document* 23. (Serial No. 506.) Washington: Government Printing Office. (Reprinted under title: Abert's New Mexico Report, 1846–'47; Horn and Wallace, Albuquerque, 1962; also under title: The Original Travel Diary of Lieutenant J.W. Abert, Who Mapped New Mexico for the United States Army. John Galvin, ed., John Howell Books, San Francisco, 1966.)

Abler, Thomas S., and Sally M. Weaver
1974 A Canadian Indian Bibliography, 1960–1970. Toronto: University of Toronto Press.

Ablon, Joan
1964 Relocated American Indians in the San Francisco Bay Area. *Human Organization* 23(4):296–304. (Reprinted: Pp. 422–438 in Urban Place and Process: Readings in the Anthropology of Cities. M. Estellie Smith, ed. Macmillan, New York, 1980.)

Absaraka 1968 *see* Whitebear, Pease, ed. 1968

Ace, Barry, and July Papatsie
1977 Transitions: Contemporary Canadian Indian and Inuit Art. Ottawa: Minister of Public Works and Government Services Canada.

Adair, James
1775 The History of the American Indians. Particularly Those Nations Adjoining the Mississippi, East and West Florida, Georgia, South and North Carolina, and Virginia... London: Printed for Edward and Charles Dilly. (Reprinted as: Adair's History of the American Indians. Samuel C. Williams, ed. Watanga Press, Johnson City, Tenn., 1930; also, Argonaut Press, New York, 1966.)

Adair, Mary J.
1977 Subsistence Exploitation at the Young Site: A Predictive Model for Kansas City Hopewell. (M.A. Thesis in Anthropology, University of Kansas, Lawrence.)

1982 Spatial Patterning at the Two Deer Site (14BU55): A Preliminary Report. Pp. 305–355 in Archaeological Investigation at El Dorado Lake, Butler County, Kansas (Phase III). Alfred E. Johnson, principal investigator; assembled by Paul E. Brockington, Jr. *University of Kansas. Museum of Anthropology. Project Report Series* 51. Lawrence.

1984 Prehistoric Cultivation in the Central Plains: Its Development and Importance. (Ph.D. Dissertation in Anthropology, University of Kansas, Lawrence.)

1988 Prehistoric Agriculture in the Central Plains. *University of Kansas Publications in Anthropology* 16. Lawrence.

1996 Woodland Complexes in the Central Great Plains. Pp. 101–122 in Archeology and Paleoecology of the Central Great

Plains. With Contributions by Mary J. Adair, [et al.]. Jack L. Hofman, ed. *Arkansas Archeological Survey Research Series* 48. Fayetteville.

1999   Great Plains Ethnobotany. (Manuscript in M.J. Adair's possession; Museum of Anthropology, University of Kansas, Lawrence.)

Adair, Mary J., and Marie E. Brown
1981   The Two Deer Site (14BU55): A Plains Woodland-Plains Village Transition. Pp. 237–356 in Prehistory and History of the El Dorado Lake Area. Kansas. (Phase II). Mary J. Adair, ed. *University of Kansas. Museum of Anthropology. Project Report Series* 47. Lawrence.

Adams, Alexander B.
1977   Sunlight and Storm: The Great American Plains. New York: G.P. Putnam's Sons.

Adams, Franklin G.
1904   Reminiscences of Frederick Chouteau. *Transactions of the Kansas State Historical Society* 8:423–434. Topeka.

Adams, Gary F.
1977   The Estuary Bison Pound Site in Southwestern Saskatchewan. *Canada. National Museum of Man. Mercury Series. Archaeological Survey Paper* 68. Ottawa.

Adams, Howard
1975   Prison of Grass: Canada from the Native Point of View. Toronto: New Press. (Reprinted, rev. ed.: Fifth House Publishers, Saskatoon, Sask., 1989.)

1995   A Tortured People: The Politics of Colonization. Penticton, B.C.: Theytus Books.

Adams, William Y.
1963   Shonto: A Study of the Role of the Trader in a Modern Navaho Community. *Bureau of American Ethnology* 188. Washington: Smithsonian Institution; U.S. Government Printing Office.

Adelung, Johann Christoph, and Johann Severin Vater
1806–1817 Mithridates oder allgemeine Sprachenkunde: mit dem Vater Unser als Sprachprobe in bey nahe fünf hundert Sprachen und Mundarten. 4 vols. (vol. 3 in 3 pts.) Berlin: Vossischen Buchhandlung.

Afton, Jean, David F. Halaas, and Andrew E. Masich
1997   Cheyenne Dog Soldiers: A Ledgerbook History of Coups and Combat. Niwot, Colo.: Colorado Historical Society and the University Press of Colorado.

Agnew, Allen F.
1965   A Guide to the Stratigraphy of South Dakota. *[South Dakota] State Geological Survey Bulletin* 14. Vermillion, S.Dak.: University of South Dakota, Science Center.

Agogino, George A., and Weldon D. Frankforter
1960   A Paleo-Indian Bison-Kill in Northwestern Iowa. *American Antiquity* 25(3):414–415.

Agonito, Joseph
1998   Young Man Afraid of His Horses: The Reservation Years. *Nebraska History* 79(3):116–132. Lincoln.

Ahenakew, Edward
1973   Voices of the Plains Cree. Edited with an Introduction by Ruth M. Buck. Toronto: McClelland and Stewart.

Ahenakew, Freda
1987   Cree Language Structures: A Cree Approach. Winnipeg, Man.: Pemmican Publications.

1987a   Stories of the House People. *Publications of the Algonquian Text Society.* Winnipeg, Man.: University of Manitoba Press.

_____, ed.
1987b   A Preliminary Check-list of Plains Cree Medical Terms; by Rose Atimoyoo ... [et al.], elders; Lorna A. MacDonald and Barbara MacLeod, organisers; Freda Ahenakew, ed. Saskatoon, Sask.: Saskatchewan Indian Languages Institute.

Ahlbrandt, Thomas S., James B. Swinehart, and David G. Maroney
1983   The Dynamic Holocene Dune Fields of the Great Plains and Rocky Mountain Basins, U.S.A. Pp. 379–406 in Eolian Sediments and Processes. M.E. Brookfield and Thomas S. Ahlbrandt, eds. *Developments in Sedimentology* 38. Amsterdam, The Netherlands: Elsevier Science Publishers.

Ahler, Janet G.
1974   A Cross-cultural Comparison of Meaning Ascribed to Social Studies Concepts. (Ph.D. Dissertation in Education, The University of Missouri, Columbia.)

1985   A Proposed Use of the Semantic Differential Technique in Studies Involving Acculturation. *Plains Anthropologist* 30(107):1–8.

Ahler, Stanley A.
1986   The Knife River Flint Quarries: Excavations at Site 32DU508. Bismarck, S.Dak.: State Historical Society of South Dakota.

Ahler, Stanley A., and Dennis L. Toom
1995   Reflections on the Archeology of the Medicine Crow Site Complex. Pp. 375–378 in Archeology of the Medicine Crow Site Complex (39BF2), Buffalo County, South Dakota. Stanley A. Ahler and Dennis L. Toom, eds. *Illinois State Museum. Report of Investigations* 52. Springfield. (Originally submitted by Illinois State Museum Society to Branch of Interagency Archeological Services, U.S. National Park Service, Rocky Mountains Regional Office, Denver, 1986.)

_____, eds.
1995a   Archeology of the Medicine Crow Site Complex (39BF2), Buffalo County, South Dakota. *Illinois State Museum. Report of Investigations* 52. Springfield. (Originally submitted by Illinois State Museum Society to Branch of Interagency Archeological Services, U.S. National Park Service, Rocky Mountains Regional Office, Denver, 1986.)

Ahler, Stanley A., Thomas D. Thiessen, and Michael K. Trimble
1991   People of the Willows: The Prehistory and Early History of the Hidatsa Indians. Grand Forks, N.Dak.: University of North Dakota Press.

Ahler, Stanley A., Craig M. Johnson, H. Haas, and G. Bonani
1994   Radiocarbon Dating Results. Pp. 97–173 in A Chronology of Middle Missouri Plains Village Sites, by Craig M. Johnson. Washington: Smithsonian Institution, National Museum of Natural History, Department of Anthropology.

Aikens, C. Melvin
1966   Fremont-Promontory-Plains Relationships: Including a Report of Excavations at the Injun Creek and Bear River Number 1 Sites, Northern Utah. *University of Utah Anthropological Papers* 82. Salt Lake City.

1967   Plains Relationships of the Fremont Culture: A Hypothesis. *American Antiquity* 32(2):198–209.

Akewsasne Notes
1979   Voices from Wounded Knee, 1973: In the Words of the Participants. Rooseveltown, N.Y.: Akewsasne Notes.

Akridge, Scott
1986   De Soto's Route in North Central Arkansas. *Field Notes: Newsletter of the Arkansas Archeological Society* 211 (July/August):3–7. Fayetteville.

Albers, Patricia C.
1968–1976 [Santee Sioux Fieldnotes.] (Manuscripts in P.C. Albers's possession.)

1969   The Vision Experience: A Neo-evolutionary Study. (M.A. Thesis in Anthropology, Michigan State University, East Lansing.)

1974   The Regional System of the Devil's Lake Sioux: Its Structure, Composition, Development, and Functions. (Ph.D. Dissertation in Anthropology, The University of Wisconsin, Madison.)

1982   Sioux Kinship in a Colonial Setting. *Dialectical Anthropology* 6(3):253–269. Amsterdam.

1983   Sioux Women in Transition: A Study of Their Changing Status in Domestic and Capitalist Sectors of Production. Pp. 175–234 in The Hidden Half: Studies of Plains Indian Women. Patricia C. Albers and Beatrice Medicine, eds. Washington: University Press of America.

1985   Autonomy and Dependency in the Lives of Dakota Women: A Study in Historical Change. *Review of Radical Political Economics* 17(3):109–134. Cambridge.

1993   Symbiosis, Merger, and War: Contrasting Forms of Intertribal Relationship among Historic Plains Indians. Pp. 94–132 in Political Economy of North American Indians. John H. Moore, ed. Norman: University of Oklahoma Press.

1994   Thoughts Have Power, Words Have Privilege: Some Reflections on Social Scientific Observations and Understandings of the Ojibwe People. Pp. 116–161 in Essays from "Teaching and Writing Local History, Lac Courte Oreilles", May, 1993. (Papers presented at a Seminar organized by the D'Arcy McNickle Center for the History of the American Indian, The Newberry Library.) *The Newberry Library, Occasional Papers in Curriculum Series* 16. Chicago.

1996   Changing Patterns of Ethnicity on the Northeastern Plains, 1780–1870. Pp. 90–118 in History, Power and Identity: Ethnogenesis in the Americas, 1492–1992. Jonathan D. Hill, ed. Iowa City: University of Iowa Press.

Albers, Patricia C., and William R. James
1986   On the Dialectics of Ethnicity: The Case of the Santee Sioux. *Journal of Ethnic Studies* 14(1):1–27. Bellingham, Wash.

Albers, Patricia C., and Jeanne Kay
1987   Sharing the Land: A Study in American Indian Territoriality. Pp. 47–92 in A Cultural Geography of North American Indians. T.E. Ross and T.G. Moore, eds. Boulder, Colo.: Westview Press.

Albers, Patricia C., and Beatrice Medicine, eds.
1983   The Hidden Half: Studies of Plains Indian Women. Washington: University Press of America.

1983a   The Role of Sioux Women in the Production of Ceremonial Objects: The Case of the Star Quilt. Pp. 123–140 in The Hidden Half: Studies of Plains Indian Women. Patricia C. Albers and Beatrice Medicine, eds. Washington: University Press of America.

Albers, Patricia C., and Seymour Parker
1971   The Plains Vision Experience: A Study of Power and Privilege. *South-western Journal of Anthropology* 27(3):203–233. Albuquerque.

Alberta Federation of Métis Settlement Associations
1982   Metisism: A Canadian Identity. (Alberta Federation of Métis Settlement Associations: Statement on Aboriginal Rights in the Constitution of Canada.) Edmonton, Alta.: Alberta Federation of Métis Settlement Associations.

Albright, Peggy
1997   Crow Indian Photographer: The Work of Richard Throssel. With Commentaries on the Photographs by Crow Tribal Members Barney Old Coyote, Jr., Mardell Hogan Plainfeather, and Dean Curtis Bear Claw. Foreword by Joanna Cohan Scherer. Albuquerque: University of New Mexico Press.

Alcedo, Antonio de
1786–1789 Diccionario geográfico-histórico de las Indias occidentales ó América... 5 vols. Madrid: B. Cano [etc.]. (Reprinted in English under title: The Geographical and Historical Dictionary of America and the West Indies; Containing an Entire Translation of the Spanish Work of Colonel Don Antonio de Alcedo ... by George Alexander Thompson, 5 vols. J. Carpenter, London, 1812–1815.)

1812–1815 The Geographical and Historical Dictionary of America and the West Indies; Containing an Entire Translation of the Spanish Work of Colonel Don Antonio de Alcedo ... with Large Additions and Compilations from Modern Voyages and Travels, and from Original and Authentic Information, by George Alexander Thompson. 5 vols. London: J. Carpenter. (Reprinted: Burt Franklin, New York, 1970.)

Alegre, Francisco Javier
1841–1842 Historia de la Compañía de Jesús en Nueva España. 3 vols. México: Impr. de J.M. Lara.

Alencaster, Joaquin Real
1806   [Letter to Comandante-General Nemesio Salcedo, dated Santa Fe, August 30, 1806.] (Manuscript, Twitchell No. II: 2006 Spanish Archives of New Mexico, State Records Center and Archives, Santa Fe. [Reprinted: AMS Press, New York, 1973.])

Alex, Lynn Marie
1979   The Ceramics from Ludlow Cave, Harding County, South Dakota. Pp. 49–62 in Symposium on the Crow-Hidatsa Separations. Leslie B. Davis, ed. *Archaeology in Montana* 20(3). Billings, [etc.].

1980   A Fortified Late Prehistoric Site in Western South Dakota. Abstracts: p. 12 in *Proceedings of the 38th Plains Conference.* Iowa City.

1994   Oneota and the Olivet Phase, South Dakota. *Newsletter of the South Dakota Archaeological Society* 24:1–4. Vermillion, S.Dak.

Alex, Robert A.
1973   Architectural Features of Houses at the Mitchell Site (39DV2), Eastern South Dakota. *Plains Anthropologist* 18(60):149–159.

1981   The Village Cultures of the Lower James River Valley, South Dakota. (Ph.D. Dissertation in Anthropology, University of Wisconsin, Madison.)

Alexander, Hartley Burr
1916   North American Mythology. Vol. 10 of *Mythology of All Races*. Louis Herbert Gray, ed. Boston: Marshall Jones Company.

1938   Sioux Indian Painting. 2 portfolios. Nice, France: C. Szwedzicki.

1953   The World's Rim: Great Mysteries of the North American Indians. Lincoln: University of Nebraska Press. (Reprinted in 1967; also, Dover Publications, Mineola, N.Y., 1999.)

1953a   The Sun Dance. Pp. 136–169 in The World's Rim: Great

Mysteries of the North American Indians, by Hartley Burr Alexander. Lincoln: University of Nebraska Press.

Alford, Dan K., and Wayne E. Leman, comps. and eds.
1976 English-Cheyenne Student Dictionary. Lame Deer, Mont.: Language Research Department of the Northern Cheyenne Title VII ESEA Bilingual Education Program.

Algier, Keith W.
1993 The Crow and the Eagle: A Tribal History from Lewis and Clark to Custer. Caldwell, Id.: Caxton Printers.

Allan, Robert S.
1983 A Witness to Murder: The Cypress Hills Massacre and the Conflict of Attitudes towards the Native People of the Canadian-American West during the 1870s. Pp. 229–246 in As Long as the Sun Shines and Water Flows: A Reader in Canadian Native Studies. Ian A.L. Getty and Antoine S. Lussier, eds. Vancouver: University of British Columbia Press.

Allen, Charles W.
1997 From Fort Laramie to Wounded Knee. In: The West That Was. Edited and with an Introduction by Richard E. Jensen. Lincoln: University of Nebraska Press, in association with the Nebraska State Historical Society.

Allen, Clifford, et al.
1971 History of the Flandreau Santee Sioux Tribe. Flandreau, S.Dak.: Flandreau Santee Sioux Tribe, Tribal History Program.

Allen, Joel A.
1876 The American Bisons, Living and Extinct. Cambridge, Mass.: Harvard University Press.

1876a Geographical Variation among North American Mammals; Especially in Respect to Size. Bulletin of the U.S. Geological and Geographical Survey of the Territories 2(4):309–344. Washington.

1877 History of the American Bison, Bison americanus. Pp. 443–587 in 9th Annual Report of the U.S. Geological and Geographical Survey of the Territories, Embracing Colorado and Parts of Adjacent Territories: Being a Report of Progress of the Exploration for the Year 1875. By F.V. Hayden, U.S. Geologist. Washington: Government Printing Office.

Allen, Louis
1931 Siouan and Iroquoian. International Journal of American Linguistics 6(3–4):185–193. Chicago.

Allen, Mark
1994 Native American Control of Tribal Natural Resource Development in the Context of the Federal Trust and Tribal Self-Determination. Pp. 151–204 in Native American Resurgence and Renewal: A Reader and Bibliography. Robert N. Wells, Jr., ed. Native American Resources Series 3. Metuchen, N.J.: Scarecrow Press.

Allen, Paul
1915 Meriwether Lewis and William Clark. 2 vols. Chicago: Elliott-Madison Company.

Allen, R.S.
1977 Big Bear. Saskatchewan History 25:1–17. Saskatoon, Sask.

Allis, Samuel
1887 Forty Years among the Indians and on the Eastern Borders of Nebraska. Transactions and Reports of the Nebraska State Historical Society, 1st ser., 2:133–166. Lincoln.

1918 Letters Concerning the Presbyterian Mission in the Pawnee Country, Near Bellevue, Nebr., 1831–1849. Collections of the Nebraska State Historical Society for 1915–1918, Vol. 14:690–741. Lincoln.

Allison, Edwin H.
1891 The Surrender of Sitting Bull, Being a Full and Complete History of the Negotiations Conducted by Scout Allison, which Resulted in the Surrender of Sitting Bull and His Entire Band of Hostile Sioux in 1881. A Vivid Description of Indian Life and Thrilling Adventure, Written by Scout Allison in His Own Graphic Style. Dayton, Ohio: The Walker Litho. and Printing Company.

1897 [Lakota Vocabulary from Standing Rock Reservation; entered into a copy of Introduction to the Study of Indian Languages by John Wesley Powell (1880).] (Manuscript No. 874, National Anthropological Archives, Smithsonian Institution, Washington.)

1899 [Two Lakota Texts with Interlinear Translations.] (Manuscripts No. 945 and No. 3738, National Anthropological Archives, Smithsonian Institution, Washington.)

Alwin, John A.
1979 Pelts, Provisions and Perceptions: The Hudson's Bay Company Mandan Indian Trade, 1795–1812. Montana: The Magazine of Western History 29(3):16–27. Helena.

Amérique Septentrionale [map] 1827 see Maelen, Philippe Marie Guillaume van der 1827

Amadeus, Mary
1895 [Letter to J. Kelley, dated March 16, 1895.] (Manuscript, in Box 49, Fort Belknap Records, Records of the Bureau of Indian Affairs, Record Group 75, National Archives-Pacific Northwest Region, Seattle, Wash.)

Ambler, Marjane
1990 Breaking the Iron Bonds: Indian Control of Energy Development. Lawrence, Kans.: University Press of Kansas.

Amenta, Rosalyn Marie
1987 The Earth Mysticism of the Native American Tribal Peoples with Special Reference to the Circle Symbol and the Sioux Sun Dance Rite. (Ph.D. Dissertation in Mythology and Religion, Fordham University, New York.)

American Indian
1926–1928 The American Indian. Tulsa, Okla.

American Pioneer
1842–1843 American Pioneer: A Monthly Periodical, devoted to the Objects of the Logan Historical Society; or, to Collecting and Publishing Sketches Relative to the Early Settlement and Successive Improvement of the Country. Vols. 1–3. Cincinnati, Ohio: John S. Williams.

Amiotte, Arthur
1987 The Lakota Sun Dance: Historical and Contemporary Perspectives. Pp. 75–89 in Sioux Indian Religion. Raymond J. DeMallie and Douglas R. Parks, ed. Norman: University of Oklahoma Press.

1989 An Appraisal of Sioux Arts. Section II in: An Illustrated History of the Arts in South Dakota, by Arthur R. Huseboe. Sioux Falls, S.Dak.: The The Center for Western Studies, Augustana College.

1989a Eagles Fly Over. I Become Part of It. New York: Parabola Books.

1989b Our Other Selves. I Become Part of It. New York: Parabola Books.

1989c The Road to the Center. I Become Part of It. New York: Parabola Books.

1994 Interview. In: Vision Quest: Men, Women, and Sacred Sites of the Sioux Nation. Don Doll, ed. New York: Crown Publishers.

Amundson, Leslie J.
1986   The Amisk Site: A Multi-Component Campsite in South-Central Saskatchewan. (M.A. Thesis in Anthropology, University of Saskatchewan, Saskatoon, Sask.)

Anadarko Agency 1938 see Bureau of Indian Affairs. Anadarko Agency 1938

Anctil, Pierre
1979   Recit d'une Danse du Soleil chez les Crows. *Recherces amérindiennes au Québec* 8(3):223–233. Québec.

Andersen, Raoul R.
1968   An Inquiry into the Political and Economic Structures of the Alexis Band of Wood Stoney Indians, 1880–1964. (Ph.D. Dissertation in Anthropology, University of Missouri, Columbia.)

1970   Alberta Stoney (Assiniboin) Origins and Adaptations: A Case for Reappraisal. *Ethnohistory* 17(1–2):49–61.

Anderson, Adrian D.
1961   The Glenwood Sequence: A Local Sequence for a Series of Archeological Manifestations in Mills County, Iowa. *Journal of the Iowa Archeological Society* 10(3). Iowa City.

Anderson, Anne
1975   Plains Cree Dictionary in the "y" Dialect. Rev. ed. Edmonton, Alta.: A. Anderson.

Anderson, Carolyn R.
1997   Dakota Identity in Minnesota, 1820–1995. (Ph.D. Dissertation in Anthropology, Indiana University, Bloomington.)

1999   High Stakes Modernity: Cockfighting vs. Casinos. In: Interpreting Cultures: A Symposium. Paula L. Wagoner and Mindy J. Morgan, eds. Bloomington: Indiana University Department of Anthropology.

Anderson, Duane C.
1969   Mill Creek Culture: A Review. *Plains Anthropologist* 14(44):137–143.

1972   The Ceramic Complex at the Brewster Site (13CK15): A Mill Creek Component in Northwestern Iowa. (Ph.D. Dissertation in Anthropology, The University of Colorado, Boulder.)

1973   Ioway Ethnohistory: A Review. *Annals of Iowa* 41(8):1228–1241, 42(1):41–59. Des Moines.

1973a   Brewster Site (13CK15): Lithic Analysis. *Journal of the Iowa Archeological Society* 20. Iowa City.

1975   Western Iowa Prehistory. Ames, Iowa: Iowa State University Press.

1977   The Crim Site (13ET403). *University of Iowa. Office of the State Archaeologist. Research Papers* 2(9). Iowa City.

1981   Mill Creek Ceramics: The Complex from the Brewster Site. *University of Iowa. Office of the State Archaeologist. Research Papers* 14. Iowa City.

1985   Models of Mill Creek Midden Formation: Implications for Future Research. *Proceedings of the Iowa Academy of Science* 92(2):53–57. Iowa City.

1987   Toward a Processual Understanding of the Initial Variant of the Middle Missouri Tradition: The Case of the Mill Creek Culture of Iowa. *American Antiquity* 52(3):522–537.

1994   Stone, Glass, and Metal Artifacts of the Milford Site (13KD1): An Early 18th Century Oneota Component in Northwest Iowa. *University of Iowa. Office of the State Archaeologist. Report* 19. Iowa City.

Anderson, Duane C., and Holmes A. Semken, eds.
1980   The Cherokee Excavations: Holocene Ecology and Human Adaptations in Northwestern Iowa. New York: Academic Press.

Anderson, Edward F.
1980   Peyote, The Divine Cactus. Tucson: The University of Arizona Press. (Reprinted, 2d ed., 1996.)

Anderson, Gary Clayton
1980   Early Dakota Migration and Intertribal War: A Revision. *Western Historical Quarterly* 11(1):17–36. Logan, Utah.

_____ 1984 *see* 1997 (reprint info.)

_____
1986   Little Crow: Spokesman for the Sioux. St. Paul: Minnesota Historical Society Press.

1996   Sitting Bull and the Paradox of Lakota Nationhood. New York: Harper Collins.

1997   Kinsmen of Another Kind: Dakota-White Relations in the Upper Mississippi Valley, 1650–1862. With a New Introduction by the Author. St. Paul: Minnesota Historical Society Press. (Originally publ.: University of Nebraska Press, Lincoln, 1984.)

1999   The Indian Southwest, 1580–1830: Ethnogenesis and Reinvention. Norman: University of Oklahoma Press.

Anderson, Harry H.
1956   An Investigation of the Early Bands of the Saone Group of Teton Sioux. *Journal of the Washington Academy of Sciences* 46:87–94. Washington.

1956a   The Controversial Sioux Amendment to the Fort Laramie Treaty of 1851. *Nebraska History* 37(3):201–220. Lincoln.

1960   [Report of Harry H. Anderson, Before the Indian Claims Commission; Docket No. 74, Sioux Nation et al. *v.* United States of America.] Washington: Indian Claims Commission.

1961   The Letters of Peter Wilson, First Resident Agent among the Teton Sioux. *Nebraska History* 42(4):237–264. Lincoln.

1973   Fur Traders as Fathers: The Origins of the Mixed-blooded Community among the Rosebud Sioux. *South Dakota History* 3(3):233–270. Pierre.

Anderson, Jeffrey D.
1994   Northern Arapaho Knowledge and Life Movement. 2 vols. (Ph.D. Dissertation in Anthropology, University of Chicago, Chicago.)

1998   Ethnolinguistic Dimensions of Northern Arapaho Language Shift. *Anthropological Linguistics* 40(1):43–108. Bloomington, Ind.

2000   The Four Hills of Life: Northern Arapaho Knowledge and Life Movement. (Pre-publication draft: University of Nebraska Press, Lincoln.)

2000a   The Motion-Shape of Whirlwind Woman in Arapaho Women's Quillwork Art. *European Review of Native American Studies* 14(1):11–21. Vienna, Austria [etc.].

Anderson, John A. 1971 *see* Hamilton, Henry W., and Jean Tyree Hamilton 1971

Anderson, Joseph
1872   The Newly Discovered Relationship of the Tuteloes to the Dakotan Stock. *Transactions of the American Philological Society for 1871,* Vol. 2:15–16. Philadelphia.

Anderson, Mrs. E.
1919   At Bellevue in the Thirties. *Publications of the Nebraska State Historical Society* 19:72–77. Lincoln.

Anderson, Owanah
1997   400 Years: Anglican/Episcopal Mission Among American Indians. Cincinnati: Forward Movement Publications.

Anderson, Robert T.
1951   A Study of Cheyenne Cultural History, with Special Reference to the Northern Cheyenne. (Ph.D. Dissertation in Anthropology, University of Michigan, Ann Arbor.)

1956   The Northern Cheyenne War Mothers. *Anthropological Quarterly* 29(3):82–90. Washington.

Anderson, William B.
1984   Hondale, New Mexico: An Agricultural Transition Community, 1907–1930. (M.A. Thesis in History, New Mexico State University, Las Cruces.)

Anderson, William M.
1967   The Rocky Mountain Journals of William Marshall Anderson: The West in 1834. Dale L. Morgan and Eleanor Towels Harris, eds. San Marino, Calif.: The Huntington Library. (Reprinted: University of Nebraska Press, Lincoln, 1987.)

Andrews, Isabel
1975   Indian Protest Against Starvation: The Yellow Calf Incident of 1884. *Saskatchewan History* 28:41–51. Saskatoon, Sask.

Andros, Francis
1883   The Medicine and Surgery of the Winnebago and Dakota Indians. *Journal of the American Medical Association* 1:116–118. Chicago.

Andruschuk, Sue
1978   Blood Sun Dance. *Mod-Nu Set* 1(1):37–38.

Anfinson, John O.
1987   Transitions in the Fur Trade: Transformations in Mandan Culture. Pp. 31–334 in Le Castor Fait Tout: Selected Papers of the Fifth North American Fur Trade Conference, 1985. Bruce Trigger, Toby Morantz, and Louise Dechêne, eds. Montreal: Lake St. Louis Historical Society.

Anfinson, Scott F.
1979   A Handbook of Minnesota Prehistoric Ceramics. *Occasional Publications in Minnesota Anthropology* 5. Fort Snelling: Minnesota Historical Society.

1982   The Prehistoric Archaeology of the Prairie Lake Region: A Summary from a Minnesota Perspective. *Journal of the North Dakota Archaeological Association* 1:66–90. Grand Forks, N.Dak.

1997   Southwestern Minnesota Archaeology: 12,000 Years in the Prairie Lake Region. St. Paul: Minnesota Historical Society Press.

Anfinson, Scott F., and H.E. Wright, Jr.
1990   Climatic Change and Culture in Prehistoric Minnesota. Pp. 213–232 in The Woodland Tradition in the Western Great Lakes: Papers Presented to Elden Johnson. Guy E. Gibbon, ed. *University of Minnesota. Department of Anthropology. Publications in Anthropology* 4. Minneapolis.

Anonymous
1794   Extract from a Manuscript Journal of a Gentleman Belonging to the Army, while under the Command of Major-General St. Clair. Pp. 21–26 in *Collections of the Massachusetts Historical Society for the Year 1794*, Vol. 3. Boston. (Reprinted in 1810.)

1824   [Indian speech.] *The Arkansas Gazette*, November 30:3. Little Rock.

1838   [Article.] *Telegraph and Texas Register*, May 30. San Felipe, Tex.

1865   Compact Made and Entered into Between the Confederate Indian Tribes and the Prairie Tribes of Indians, Made at Camp Napoleon, on Washita River, May 26, 1865. Pp. 1102–1103 in The War of Rebellion: A Compilation of the Official Records of the Union and Confederate Armies, 1861–1865, Series 1, Vol. 48, Pt. 2. Washington: Government Printing Office. (Available also on Microfilm No. 262, Roll 102, Pt. 2:1102–1103, Official Records of the Union and Confederate Armies, 1861–1865, National Archives, Washington.)

1883   [Reports of Inspection of the Federal Jurisdiction of the Office of Indian Affairs, 1873–1900.] (Osage Agency, Microfilm 1070, Roll 33, No. 0833, Records of the Bureau of Indian Affairs, Record Group 75, National Archives, Washington.)

1883a   [Quapaw Green Corn Ceremony.] *Indian Journal,* August 16:1. Muskogee, Okla.

1884   Tunkans'ina Waowicakiye. *Iapi Oaye* 13(9):33. Greenwood, Dak.Terr. [S.Dak.]: Dakota Mission.

1890   Torture Ordeal at the Blackfeet Sun Dance. *Harper's Weekly* 34(Dec. 13):975–976. New York.

1900   [Documents Relating to the History of the Court of Indian Offenses, 1888–1901.] (Manuscript, Microfilm Publication KA, Roll 48, Frames 873–961, Kiowa Agency Records, Oklahoma Historical Society, Indian Archives Division, Oklahoma City.)

1908   Sun Dance of the Ponca Indians. *American Antiquarian* 25(5):372–374.

1911   Indians Hold Annual Sun Dance to Cure Plague. *The Denver Republican,* July 3. Denver.

1919   Titles of the Sioux Tribes. *The Indian Sentinel* 1(12):23.

1928   Quapaw Powwow. *The American Indian* 1(18):13. Tulsa, Okla.

1932   [Red River Fund, as of September 1, 1932.] (File 067 in Kiowa Agency Records, National Archives, Fort Worth Federal Records Center, Fort Worth, Tex.)

1939   The Sun Dance of the Plains Tribes. *Indians at Work* 7(2):24–25. [Washington: Bureau of Indian Affairs.]

1940   Comanches Again Called for Army Code Service. *The New York Times,* Dec. 13:16; Dec. 16:22. New York.

1941   Indian Sun Dance Is Unusual Religious Ceremony. *Wyoming State Tribune,* July 23. Cheyenne, Wyo.

1941a   Shoshone Sun Dance. *The Denver Post,* August 10. Denver.

1941b   The Sun Dance. *Scarlet and Gold* 23:63. Vancouver, B.C.

1942   Indian Sun Dances. (Manuscript, Wyoming Department of Commerce, Cheyenne.)

1959   The Sun Dance. *Scarlet and Gold* 42:101–103. Vancouver, B.C.

1971   Oglala Sioux Tribe Sun Dance Souvenir Book, Pine Ridge, South Dakota, August 5–6–7–8. [Pine Ridge, S.Dak.: Oglala Sioux Tribe.]

1972   (Ehanna Woyakapi) *see* Black Thunder, et al. 1975

1972a   Photo Feature: Southern Arapaho Sun Dance. *American Indian Crafts and Culture Magazine* 6(1):10–11.

1972b   New Horizons in American Indian Art. Los Angeles: Southwest Museum.

1977   W. Hanson Boone, Photographic Artist. *Alberta History* 25(2):12–22. Calgary.

1979   T.C. Cannon Memorial Exhibit, December 1979. New York: Aberbach Fine Art.

1981   Confluences of Tradition and Change / 24 American Indian Artists. Davis, Calif.: Regents of the University of California.

1982   Night of the First Americans. Washington: John F. Kennedy Center for the Performing Arts.

1982a   New Work by a New Generation. Regina, Sask.: Norman Mackenzie Art Gallery.

1985a   Two Worlds. Regina, Sask.: Norman Mackenzie Art Gallery.

1985   Summary of the Archaeology of the Bozner Site - Artifacts. *Journal of Intermountain Archeology* 4(2); *Western Prehistoric Research. Intermountain Archeology Memoir* 1. Rock Springs, Wyo.

1987   New Directions Northwest: Contemporary Native American Art. Olympia, Wash.: Evergreen State College.

1987a   Honorariums Given for Arapahoe Sundance. *Wind River News* 10(27):4. Lander, Wyo.

1987b   Sun Dance News: Right To Pierce (Sioux Sun Dance) Presented to Crow Tribe. *Absaloka News* 4 (July 11):2.

1989   Swa Sa:ak Sun Dance: Gu Achi Cuksan. [Pamphlet in J.A. Archambault's possession.]

1994   This Path We Travel. Washington: Smithsonian Institution.

1996   Movements. Meadville, Pa.: Penelec Gallery, Allegheny College.

1996a   Native Streams: Contemporary Native American Art. Chicago: Jan Cicero Gallery.

1997   Crows Hold Two Meetings: Opposition Wants Nomee Out. *Big Horn County News*, October 15:1. Hardin, Mont.

1999   Blue Mountain's Sun Dance Society. [Pamphlet.] Benton City, Wash.: [Privately printed.]

Anpao Kin
1878–1937   *Anpao Kin/The Day Break.* Forest City, S.Dak.; Santee, Nebr., [etc.]: Protestant Episcopal Church among the Sioux Indians of South Dakota.

Antevs, Ernst
1948   Climatic Changes and Pre-White Man. *Bulletin of the University of Utah* 38(20):168–191. Salt Lake City.

1955   Geologic-climatic Dating in the West. *American Antiquity* 20(4):317–335.

Aoki, Haruo
1994   Nez Perce Dictionary. *University of California Publications in Linguistics* 122. Berkeley and Los Angeles.

Arce, José Antonio
1826   [Message to Chihuahua State Legislature, dated July 1, 1826.] (Microfilm MANM, Roll 5, Frames 451–454 in Mexican Archives of New Mexico, State Records Center and Archives, Santa Fe, N.Mex.)

Archambault, JoAllyn
1972–1990 [Sioux Fieldnotes.] (Manuscripts in J. Archambault's possession.)

Archer, John H.
1980   Saskatchewan: A History. Saskatoon, Sask.: Western Prairie Books.

Archuleta, Margaret, and Rennard Strickland
1991   Shared Visions: Native American Painters and Sculptors in the Twentieth Century. Phoenix: The Heard Museum.

Arden, Harvey, ed.
1994   Noble Red Man, Lakota Wisdom Keeper Mathew King. Hillsboro, Oreg.: Beyond Words Publishing.

Arese, Francesco
1934   A Trip to the Prairies and in the Interior of North America, 1837–1838. Travel notes, now first translated from the original French by Andrew Evans. New York: Harbor Press. (Reprinted: Cooper Square Publishers, New York, 1975.)

Arken, William
1903   A New Story of Custer's Last Battle Told by the Messenger Boy Who Survived. *Contributions of the Historical Society of Montana* 14:277–279. Helena.

Armitage, C. Lawrence, Steven D. Creasman, and J.C. Mackey
1982   The Deadman Wash Site: a Multi-Component (Paleo-Indian, Archaic, Late Prehistoric) Site in Southwestern Wyoming. *Journal of Intermountain Archeology* 1(1):1–10. Rock Springs, Wyo.

Armstrong, Alex
1857   Personal Narrative of the Discovery of the North West Passage. London: Hurst and Blackett.

Armstrong, William 1839 *see* ARCIA 1824–1848

Arnold, Morris S.
1991   Colonial Arkansas: A Social and Cultural History. Fayetteville: University of Arkansas Press.

1991a   The Myth of John Law's German Colony on the Arkansas. Pp. 69–73 in Arkansas Before the Americans. Hester A. Davis, ed. *Arkansas Archeological Survey Research Series* 40. Fayetteville.

1994   Eighteenth-Century Arkansas Illustrated. *Arkansas Historical Quarterly* 53(2):119–136. Fayetteville.

Arnold, Morris S.
1998   Eighteenth-Century Arkansas Illustrated: A Map Within an Indian Painting? Pp. 187–204 in Cartographic Encounters: Perspectives on Native American Mapmaking and Map Use. G. Malcom Lewis, ed. Chicago and London: University of Chicago Press.

Arocha, Juan José, José Francisco Ruiz, and José Francisco Cavallero
1828   [Ratification by the Cuchunticas (Comanche) of the Treaty of Peace celebrated in Chihuahua in 1826.] (Microfilm, Roll 7, Frames 155–157 in Mexican Archives of New Mexico, State Records Center and Archives, Santa Fe, N.Mex.)

Around Him, John
1980   Lakota Ceremonial Songs; Translated by Albert White Hat, Sr. Rosebud, S.Dak.: Sinte Gleska College.

Arrowsmith, Aaron
1814   A Map Exhibiting All the New Discoveries in the Interior Parts of North America. Inscribed by Permission to the Honourable Governor and Company of Adventurers of England Trading into Hudson's Bay... January 1st, 1795 [with] additions to June 1814. London.

Arth, Malcolm J.
1956   A Functional View of Peyotism in Omaha Culture. *Plains Anthropologist* 7:25–29.

Arthur, George W.
1962   The Emigrant Bison Drives of Paradise Valley, Montana.

Pp. 16–27 (Arthur et al., pp. 40–56: Panel Discussion on Buffalo Jumps) in Symposium on Buffalo Jumps. Carling Malouf and Stuart Conner, eds. *Montana Archaeological Society. Memoir* 1. Missoula and Helena.

1966   An Archaeological Survey of the Upper Yellowstone River Drainage, Montana. *Montana State University. Agricultural Economics Research. Report* 26. Bozeman.

1975   An Introduction to the Ecology of Early Historic Communal Bison Hunting among the Northern Plains Indians. *Canada. National Museum of Man. Mercury Series. Archaeological Survey Paper* 37. Ottawa.

Arthurs, David
1978   Sandy Lake Ware in Northwestern Ontario: A Distribution Study. *Manitoba Archaeological Quarterly* 2(1–2):57–64. Winnipeg.

Artz, Joe
1981   Test Excavations at El Dorado Lake, 1978. Pp. 54–168 in Prehistory and History of the El Dorado Lake Area, Kansas, (Phase II). Mary J. Adair, ed. *University of Kansas. Museum of Anthropology. Project Report Series* 47. Lawrence.

Ashe, Thomas
1808   Travels in America: Performed in 1806, for the Purpose of Exploring the Rivers Alleghany, Monongahela, Ohio, and Mississippi and Ascertaining the Produce and Condition of Their Backs and Vicinity. London: E.M. Blunt for W. Sawyer.

Atimoyoo, Rose, et al., elders 1987 *see* Ahenakew, Freda, ed. 1987b

Atkinson, Henry
1826   Letter from the Secretary of War [...] Respecting the Movements of the Expedition Which Lately Ascended the Missouri River, &c. *19th Congress. 1st Session. House Document* 117. (Serial No. 136.) Washington.

Atkinson, Mary Jourdan
1935   The Texas Indians. San Antonio, Tex.: The Naylor company.

Attocknie, Joseph
1969   [Interview with Joe Attocknie, by Peggy Dycus, dated June 9, 1969.] (Manuscript T-508, Doris Duke Oral History Project, Western History Collection, University of Oklahoma, Norman.)

Atwater, Caleb
1831   Remarks Made on a Tour to Prairie du Chien; Thence to Washington City, in 1829, by Caleb Atwater, Later Commissioner Employed by the United States To Negotiate with the Indians of the Upper Mississippi, for the Purchase of Mineral Country, [etc.]. [Pp. 149–172: Rudiments of the Grammar and Vocabulary of the Sioux Language, by John Marsh.] Columbus, Ohio: Jenkins and Grover; also, Isaac N. Whiting. (Reprinted: Arno Press, New York, 1975.)

Audubon, John James 1900 *see* Audubon, Maria R. 1900

Audubon, Maria R.
1900   Audubon and His Journals; by Maria R. Audubon. With Zoological and Other Notes by Elliott Coues. 2 vols. New York: Charles Scribner's Sons. (Originally publ. in 1897. Reprinted: Dover Publications, New York, 1960.)

Aughey, Samuel
1876   Report of Samuel Aughey: The Superficial Deposits of Nebraska. Pp. 241–249 in [*8th Annual*] Report of the U.S. Geological and Geographical Survey of the Territories, Embracing Colorado and Parts of Adjacent Territories: Being a Report of the Progress of the Explorations for the Year 1874. Washington: Government Printing Office.

Aurbach, Herbert A., ed.
1967   Proceedings of the National Research Conference on American Indian Education, Pennsylvania State University, University Park, May 24–27, 1967. An Interim Report to the Office of Education. Kalamazoo, Mich: Society for the Study of Social Problems.

Austin, Stephen J.
1829   Mapa original de Texas por el Cuidadano. Estevan F. Austin presentato al Exmo Sor Presidente por su autor, 1829. (Manuscript in Archivo General y Publico de la Nation, Mexico City.)

Ayer, Mrs. Edward E., trans. 1916 *see* Benavides, Fray Alonso de 1916

BIC = Board of Indian Commissioners
1870–1933 Annual Reports of the Board of Indian Commissioners to the Secretary of the Interior. Washington: U.S. Government Printing Office.

Babbitt, Charles H.
1916   Early Days at Council Bluffs. Washington: Press of Byron S. Adams.

Baca, Bartolomé
1826   [Treaty with the Comanche, Dated October 6–8, 1826.] (Manuscript, Roll 5, Frames 425–431 in Mexican Archives of New Mexico, State Records Center and Archives, Santa Fe, N.Mex.)

Baca, Manuel
1813   [Letter to Governor José Manrique, dated San Miguel del Bado, June 1, 1813.] (Manuscript, Twitchell No. II:2492 in Spanish Archives of New Mexico, State Records Center and Archives, Santa Fe, N.Mex.)

Bacqueville de la Potherie, Claude C. LeRoy
1722   Historie de l'Amérique septentrionale. 4 vols. Paris: J.L. Nion and F. Didot. (Reprinted in 1753.)

Bad Heart Bull, Amos
1967   A Pictographic History of the Oglala Sioux. Drawings by Amos Bad Heart Bull; Text by Helen H. Blish; Introduction by Mari Sandoz. Lincoln: University of Nebraska Press.

Baerreis, David A.
1950   Woodland Pottery of Northeastern Oklahoma. In: Prehistoric Pottery of the Eastern United States. James B. Griffin, ed. Ann Arbor: University of Michigan, Museum of Archaeology.

_____, ed.
1970   Environmental Archaeology in Western Iowa. *Newsletter of the Iowa Archaeological Society* 58. Iowa City.

Baerreis, David A., and Reid A. Bryson
1965   Historical Climatology and the Southern Plains: A Preliminary Statement. *Bulletin of the Oklahoma Anthropological Society* 13:69–75. Norman.

1965a   Climatic Episodes and the Dating of the Mississippian Cultures. *The Wisconsin Archeologist*, n.s. 46(4):203–220. Milwaukee.

1966   Dating the Panhandle Aspect Cultures. *Bulletin of the Oklahoma Anthropological Society* 14:105–116.

_____, eds.
1967   Climatic Change and the Mill Creek Culture of Iowa. *Archives of Archaeology* 29. Salt Lake City: Society for American Archaeology. (Reprinted: Dale R. Henning, ed. 2 vols. *Journal of the Iowa Archeological Society* 15–16, 1968–1969.)

_____, eds. 1968–1969 *see* 1967 (reprint info.), *and* Henning, Dale R., ed. 1968–1969

Bahr, Howard M.
1972   An End to Invisibility. Pp. 404–412 in Native Americans Today. Howard M. Bahr, Bruce A. Chadwick, and Robert C. Day, eds. New York: Harper and Row.

Bailey, Garrick A.
1968–1989 [Osage Fieldnotes.] (Manuscripts in G.A. Bailey's possession.)

1972   The Osage Roll: An Analysis. *The Indian Historian* 5(1):26–29. San Francisco.

1973   Changes in Osage Social Organization, 1673–1906. *University of Oregon. Anthropological Papers* 5. Eugene.

1978   John Joseph Mathews, Osage, 1894–[1979]. Pp. [204] 205–214 in American Indian Intellectuals. Margot Liberty, ed. *1976 Proceedings of the American Ethnological Society.* Robert F. Spencer, gen. ed. St. Paul, Minn.: West Publishing Co.

_____, ed. 1995 *see* La Flesche, Francis 1995

1999   The Osage and the Valley of the Middle Arkansas. *Bulletin of the Oklahoma Anthropological Society* 47 (for 1998):119–131. Norman.

Bailey, John W.
1974   General Terry and the Decline of the Sioux, 1866–1890. (Ph.D. Dissertation in History, Marquette University, Milwaukee, Wis.)

Baillargeon, Morgan, and Leslie Tepper
1998   Legends of Our Times: Native Cowboy Life. Vancouver: UBC Press; Seattle: University of Washington Press.

Baird, Elizabeth Thérèse (*née* Fisher)
1998   O-de-jit-wa-win-ning; or, Contes du temps passé: The Memoirs of Elizabeth T. Baird. Green Bay, Wis.: Heritage Hill Foundation. (Originally publ. as a serial article in: *Green Bay State Gazette*, Dec. 4, 1886 – Nov. 16, 1887.)

Baird, W. David
1972   The Osage People. Phoenix: Indian Tribal Series.

1980   The Quapaw Indians: History of the Downstream People. Norman: University of Oklahoma Press.

1989   The Quapaws. New York: Chelsea House Publishers.

1994   Quapaw. P. 523 in Native America in the Twentieth Century: An Encyclopedia. Mary B. Davis, ed. *Garland Reference Library of Social Science* 452. New York: Garland Publishing.

Baker, Theodore
1882   Über die Musik der nordamerikanischen Wilden. Leipzig: Breitkopf & Härtel. (Reprinted under title: On the Music of the North American Indians. Ann Buckley, trans.; F. Knuf, Buren, The Netherlands, 1976; also, Da Capo Press, New York, 1977.)

Bakker, Peter
1990   The Genesis of Michif: A First Hypothesis. Pp. 12–35 in Papers of the Twenty-First Algonquian Conference. William Cowan, ed. Ottawa: Carleton University.

1991   The Ojibwa Element in Michif. Pp. 11–20 in Papers of the Twenty-second Algonquian Conference. William Cowan, ed. Ottawa: Carleton University.

1992   "A Language of Our Own": The Genesis of Michif, the Mixed Cree-French Language of the Canadian Métis. (Ph.D. Dissertation in Linguistics, University of Amsterdam, The Netherlands. Published in rev. form: Oxford University Press, New York and Oxford, 1997.)

1997   A Language of Our Own: The Genesis of Michif, the Mixed Cree-French Language of the Canadian Métis. *Oxford Studies in Anthropological Linguistics* 10. New York [and] Oxford: Oxford University Press. (Originally issued as the

Author's Ph.D. Dissertation in Linguistics, University of Amsterdam, 1992.)

Balbi, Adrien (i.e. Adriano)
1826   Atlas ethnographique du globe, ou classification des peuples anciens et modernes d'apres leurs langues, [etc.]. 2 vols. Paris: Rey et Gravier.

Balgooyen, Theodore John
1968   The Plains Indian As a Public Speaker. *University of Wyoming Publications* 34(2). Laramie, Wyo.

Ballou, E.
1880–1881 [Shoshone Vocabulary; Shoshone and Bannock Agency, Wyoming Territory.] (Manuscript No. 790, National Anthropological Archives, Smithsonian Institution, Washington.)

Bamforth, Douglas B.
1988   Ecology and Human Organization on the Great Plains. New York: Plenum Press.

1991   Population Dispersion and Paleoindian Technology at the Allen Site. Pp. 357–374 in Raw Material Economies among Prehistoric Hunter-Gatherers. Anta Montet-White and Steven Holen, eds. *University of Kansas. Publications in Anthropology* 19. Lawrence, Kans.

Bancroft, George
1834–1875 History of the United States from the Discovery of the American Continent to the Declaration of Independence. 10 vols. Vols. 1–3: History of the Colonization of the United States. Vols. 4–10: The American Revolution. Boston: C.C. Little, J. Brown, and Company; and, London: R.J. Kennett.

Bancroft, Hubert Howe
1874–1876 The Native Races of the Pacific States of North America. 5 vols. Vol. 1: Wild Tribes; Vol. 2: Civilized Nations; Vol. 3: Myths and Languages; Vol. 4: Antiquities; Vol. 5: Primitive History. New York: D. Appleton and Company. (Vol. 3 publ. as Vol. 3 of "The Works of Hubert Howe Bancroft", San Francisco, 1882.)

1882–1890 The Works of Hubert Howe Bancroft. 39 vols. San Francisco: A.L. Bancroft and Company, Publishers. (Another edition: The History Company, Publishers, San Francisco, 1886–1890.)

Bandelier, Adolph F.A.
1890   Contributions to the History of the South-Western Portion of the United States. *Papers of the Archaeological Institute of America. American Series* 5. Cambridge, Mass.

1890–1892 Final Report of Investigations among the Indians of the Southwestern United States, Carried on Mainly in the Years from 1880 to 1885. 2 vols. *Papers of the Archaeological Institute of America. American Series* 3–4. Cambridge, Mass.: University Press; and, J. Wilson and Son. (Reprinted: Kraus Reprint Company, Millwood, N.Y., 1976; also, AMS Press, New York, 1976.)

1892   An Outline of the Documentary History of the Zuñi Tribe. *Journal of American Ethnology and Archaeology* 3(1):1–115. Boston.

_____, ed. 1905, 1922, 1964, 1973 *see* Núñez Cabeza de Vaca, Alvar 1905 (and reprint info.)

Banks, Larry D.
1984   Lithic Resources and Quarries. Pp. 65–95 in Prehistory of Oklahoma. Robert E. Bell, ed. Orlando, Fla.: Academic Press.

1990   From Mountain Peaks to Alligator Stomachs: A Review of Lithic Sources in the Trans-Mississippi South, the Southern Plains, and Adjacent Southwest. *Oklahoma Anthropologi-*

cal Society. Memoir 4. Norman: University of Oklahoma Printing Services.

Bannon, John F., ed.
1964   Bolton and the Spanish Borderlands. Norman: University of Oklahoma Press.

———, ed.
1970   The Spanish Borderland Frontier, 1531–1821. New York: Holt, Rinehart and Winston.

Baraga, Friedrich (i.e. Fridrik)
1878   A Theoretical and Practical Grammar of the Otchipwe Language; for the Use of Missionaries and Other Persons Living among the Indians. Montreal: Beauchemin et Valois.

1878–1880 A Dictionary of the Otchipwe Language, Explained in English. 2 Pts. Pt. I: English-Otchipwe. Pt. II: Otchipwe-English. Montreal: Beauchemin et Valois. (Vol. 2 cover page has 1881 imprint date. Reprinted: Ross and Haines, Minneapolis, 1966, 1973; also, Minnesota Historical Society Press, St. Paul, 1992.)

Barbeau, C. Marius
[1939]   Assomption Sash. National Museum of Canada. Bulletin 93; Anthropological Series 24. Ottawa. (Reprinted in 1972.)

1960   Indian Days on the Western Prairies. Portraits by W. Langdon Kihn. Design and Illus. by Arthur Price. National Museum of Canada. Bulletin 163; Anthropological Series 46. Ottawa. (Reprinted 1965, 1970.)

Barcía Carballido y Zúñiga, Andrés González de
1723   Ensayo cronológico, para la história general de la Florida ... desde el año de 1512 ... hasta el de 1722. Madrid: En la Officina real, y à costa de N. Rodriguez Franco.

1951   Barcia's Chronological History of the Continent of Florida ... from the Year 1512 ... until the Year 1722. Translated with an Introduction by Anthony Kerrigan; Foreword by Herbert E. Bolton. Gainesville: University of Florida Press.

Barker, Anne E.
1886   [English Equivalents of Words, Phrases, &c., in the Mountain Stoney Dialect.] (Manuscript No. 83-3859, Library of Congress, Manuscript Division, Washington; also, Manuscript No. 419 in the Library of the American Philosophical Society, Philadelphia; and pp. 165–180 in Indian Days on the Western Prairies. C. Marius Barbeau, ed. National Museum of Canada Bulletin 163, Anthropological Series 46. Ottawa, 1960.)

Barker, Eugene C.
1925   The Life of Stephen F. Austin, Founder of Texas, 1793–1836: A Chapter in the Westward Movement of the Anglo-American People. Nashville, Tenn., and Dallas, Tex.: Cokesbury Press.

Barnes, Lela, ed.
1967   Letters of Allen T. Ward, 1842–1851, from the Shawnee and Kaw (Methodist) Missions. Kansas Historical Quarterly 33(3):321–376.

Barnes, R.H.
1980   Hidatsa Personal Names: An Interpretation. Plains Anthropologist 25(90):311–331.

1984   Two Crows Denies It: A History of Controversy in Omaha Sociology. Lincoln: University of Nebraska Press.

1996   Lounsbury's Analysis of Republican Pawnee Terminology: Comparison with Lushbaugh's Original Data. Plains Anthropologist, n.s. 41(156):117–133.

Barnosky, Cathy W., Eric C. Grimm, and H.E. Wright, Jr.
1987   Towards a Postglacial History of the Northern Great Plains: A Review of the Paleoecologic Problems. Annals of

Carnegie Museum 56(16):259–273. Pittsburgh.

Barnouw, Victor
1950   Acculturation and Personality among the Wisconsin Chippewa. Memoirs of the American Anthropological Association 72; American Anthropologist, n.s. 52(4, Pt.2). Menasha, Wis. (Originally presented as the Author's Thesis in Anthropology, Columbia University, New York City, 1950. Reprinted: AMS Press, New York, 1980.)

Barr, M.R.
1884   [Inspection Report 4200, Fort Belknap Agency, Montana, September 5, 1884.] (Manuscript M1070, Roll 12, Records of the Bureau of Indian Affairs, Record Group 75, National Archives, Washington.)

Barr, Tom
1971   K.A.A. Fall Dig, 1971. Newsletter of the Kansas Anthropological Association 17(3):1–2. Topeka.

Barreiro, Antonio
1832   Ojeada sobre Nuevo-México. Puebla: J.M. Campos.

Barrett, Samuel A.
1911   The Dream Dance of the Chippewa and Menominee Indians of Northern Wisconsin. Bulletin of the Public Museum of the City of Milwaukee 1(4):251–406. Milwaukee, Wis. (Reprinted: AMS Press, New York, 1971, 1979; and Garland Press, New York, 1979.)

1921   The Painted Lodge or Ceremonial Tipi of the Blackfoot. Public Museum of the City of Milwaukee. Yearbook 1:85–88. Milwaukee, Wis.

Barron, F. Laurie
1984   A Summary of Federal Indian Policy in the Canadian West, 1867–1984. Native Studies Review 1(1):28–39. Saskatoon, Sask.

1988   The Indian Pass System in the Canadian West, 1882–1935. Prairie Forum 21(1):25–42. Regina, Sask.: Canadian Plains Research Center, University of Regina.

1990   The CCF and the Development of Métis Colonies in Southern Sasketchewan during the Premiership of T.C. Douglas, 1944–1961. The Canadian Journal of Native Studies 10(2):243–271. Brandon, Man.

1997   Walking in Indian Moccasins: The Native Policies of Tommy Douglas and the CCF. Vancouver: University of British Columbia Press.

Barron, F. Laurie, and James B. Waldram, eds.
1986   1885 and After: Native Society in Transition. Regina, Sask.: Canadian Plains Research Center, University of Regina.

Barry, Edward E.
1974   The Fort Belknap Indian Reservation: The First Hundred Years, 1855–1955. Bozeman, Mont.: Big Sky Books, Montana State University.

Barry, Louise
1972   The Beginning of the West: Annals of the Kansas Gateway to the American West, 1540–1854. Topeka: Kansas State Historical Society

Barsh, Russel Lawrence, and Katherine Diaz-Knauf
1984   The Structure of Federal Aid for Indian Programs in the Decade of Prosperity, 1970–1980. American Indian Quarterly 8(1):1–35. Hurst, Tex.

Barth, Georg J.
1993   Native American Beadwork: Traditional Beading Techniques from the Modern-Day Beadworker. Foreword by Bill Holm. Stevens Point, Wis.: R. Schneider.   1095

Bartlett, Richard A.
1962   Great Surveys of the American West. Norman: University of Oklahoma Press. (Reprinted in 1980).

Bartlett, Robert B.
1994   Middle Archaic Mobility on the Southern Plains: Frisco Chert Use in Calf Creek Biface Production. (M.A. Thesis in Anthropology, University of Oklahoma, Norman.)

Bartlett, Robert B., Leland C. Bement, and Robert L. Brooks
1993   A Cultural Resource Assessment of Promontories in Western Oklahoma. *Archeological Resource Survey Report* 38. Norman: Oklahoma Archeological Survey.

Barton, Winifred W.
1919   John P. Williamson: A Brother to the Sioux. Drawings by John Redowl. New York: Fleming H. Revell Company. (Reprinted: Sunnycrest Publishing, Clements, Minn., 1980.)

Basehart, Harry Wetherold, and Willard Williams Hill
1965   Leslie Spier 1893–1961. *American Anthropologist,* n.s. 67(5):1258–1277.

Bass, Althea
1966   The Arapaho Way: A Memoir of an Indian Boyhood. Illustrated by Carl Sweezy. New York: Clarkson N. Potter, Inc.

Bass, William M.
1964   The Variation in Physical Types of the Prehistoric Plains Indians. *Plains Anthropologist. Memoir* 1.

Bass, William M., and Walter H. Birkby
1962   The First Human Skeletal Material from the Huff Site, 32M011, and a Summary of Putative Mandan Skeletal Material. *Plains Anthropologist* 7(17):164–177.

Bass, William M., and Patricia A. Grubbs
1966   Human Skeletal Material from a Keith Focus Plains Woodland Site, 14PH10, Kirwin Reservoir, Phillips County, Kansas. *Plains Anthropologist* 11(32):135–143.

Bass, William M., David R. Evans, and Richard L. Jantz
1971   The Leavenworth Site Cemetery: Archaeology and Physical Anthropology. *University of Kansas. Publications in Anthropology* 2. Lawrence.

Bass, William M., Dick McWilliams, and Bruce A. Jones
1967   Archeological Investigations at Five Sites in Lyon, Jefferson, and Phillips County, Kansas. *Transactions of the Kansas Academy of Science* 70(4):471–489. Lawrence.

Basso, Keith H.
1971   Western Apache Raiding and Warfare: From the Notes of Grenville Goodwin. Tucson: University of Arizona Press.

Basso, Keith H., and Morris E. Opler, eds.
1971   Apachean Culture, History, and Ethnology. *Anthropological Papers of the University of Arizona* 21. Tucson.

Bastian, Tyler
1964   Radiocarbon Date from an Archaic Site in Southwest Oklahoma. *Oklahoma Anthropological Society Newsletter* 12(9):1–4. Norman.

1969   Hudsonpillar and Freeman Sites, North-Central Oklahoma. *University of Oklahoma. River Basin Survey. Archaeological Site Reports* 14. Norman.

Basye, Ed T.
1882   [Letter to Quapaw Agency, dated February 4, 1882, re: Indians for Exhibitions. (Manuscript in Indian Archives Division, Oklahoma Historical Society, Oklahoma City.)

Bates, Frederick
1926   The Life and Papers of Frederick Bates. Thomas M. Marshall, ed. 2 vols. *Missouri Historical Society* 1–2. St. Louis. (Reprinted: Arno Press, New York, 1975.)

Batkin, Jonathan, comp. and ed.
1995   Splendid Heritage: Masterpeices of Native American Art from the Masco Collection. Commentary by Arthur Amiotte, John C. Ewers, Richard A. Pohrt, and Others. Santa Fe: Wheelwright Museum of the American Indian.

Battey, Thomas C.
1875   The Life and Adventures of a Quaker among the Indians. Boston: Lee and Shepard, Publishers. (Reprinted: University of Oklahoma Press, Norman, 1968.)

Baudry des Lozières, Louis Narcisse
1802   Voyage à la Louisiane; et sur le continent de l'Amérique septentrionale, fait dans les années 1794 à 1798; contenant un tableau historique de la Louisiane; des observations sur son climat, ses riches productions, le caractère et le nom des sauvages; [etc.]. Paris: Dentu. (Reprinted: *Travels in the Old South* 2, T.D. Clark, ed.: Lost Cause Press, Louisville, Ky., 1960.)

Bauer, Geoge W.
1979   Symbolism of the Plains Indians' Sun Dance. *Canadian Geographic* 98(3):58–65. Ottawa.

Baugh, Susan T.
1986   Late Prehistoric Bison Distribution in Oklahoma. Pp. 83–96 in Current Trends in Southern Plains Archaeology. Timothy G. Baugh, ed. *Plains Anthropologist* 31(114, Pt. 2); *Memoir* 21. Lincoln.

Baugh, Timothy G.
1970   Revitalization Movement among the Kiowa and Kiowa-Apache. *University of Oklahoma, Papers in Anthropology* 11(1):66–83. Norman.

——, ed.
1982   Edwards I (34BK2): Southern Plains Adaptations in the Protohistoric Period. *Oklahoma Archaeological Survey, Studies in Oklahoma's Past* 8. Norman.

——, ed.
1984   Archaeology of the Mixed Grass Prairie. Phase I: Quartermaster Creek. Contributions by Susan M. Berta, Peggy Flynn, John A. Harrington, Jr., Michael C. Moore. *Oklahoma Archaeological Survey. Archeological Resource Survey Report* 20. Norman.

——
1986   Culture History and Protohistoric Societies in the Southern Plains. Pp. 167–187 in Current Trends in Southern Plains Archaeology. Timothy G. Baugh, ed. *Plains Anthropologist* 31(114, Pt. 2); *Memoir* 21. Lincoln.

——
1991   Ecology and Exchange: The Dynamics of Plains-Pueblo Interaction. Pp. 107–127 in Farmers, Hunters, and Colonists: Interaction between the Southwest and the Southern Plains. Katherine A. Spielmann, ed. Tucson: University of Arizona Press.

——
1994   Holocene Adaptations in the Southern High Plains. Pp. 264–289 in Plains Indians, A.D. 500–1500: The Archaeological Past of Historic Groups. Karl H. Schlesier, ed. Norman and London: University of Oklahoma Press.

Baugh, Timothy G., and Frank W. Eddy
1987   Rethinking Apachean Ceramics: The 1985 Athapaskan Ceramics Conference. *American Antiquity* 52(4):793–799.

Baugh, Timothy G., and Jonathon E. Ericson
1994   Prehistoric Exchange Systems in North America. *Interdisciplinary Contributions to Archaeology.* New York and London: Plenum Press.

Baugh, Timothy G., and Charles W. Terrell
1982   An Analysis of Obsidian Debitage and Protohistoric Exchange Systems in the Southern Plains as Viewed from the Edwards I Site (34BK2). *Plains Anthropologist* 27(95):1–17.

Baugh, Timothy G., Stephanie A. Makseyn-Kelley, and John W. Verano
1993   "With a Lock of Hair for Remembrance": Nakota and

Central Dakota Legacy at the Smithsonian Institution. Washington: Smithsonian Institution, National Museum of Natural History, Repatriation Office.

Baughman, Robert W.
1961   Kansas in Maps. Topeka: The Kansas Historical Society.

Beach, William Wallace, ed.
1877   The Indian Miscellany: Containing Papers on the History, Antiquities, Arts, Languages, Religions, Traditions and Superstitions of the American Aborigines; with Descriptions of Their Domestic Life, Manners, Customs, Traits, Amusements and Exploits; Travels and Adventures in the Indian Country; Incidents of Border Warfare; Missionary Relations, etc. Albany, N.Y.: J. Munsell.

Beal, Carl
1994   Money, Markets and Economic Development in Saskatchewan Indian Reserve Communities, 1870–1930s. (Ph.D. Dissertation in Economics, University of Manitoba, Winnipeg.)

Beal, Robert F., and Rod C. Macleod
1984   Prairie Fire: The 1885 North-West Rebellion. Edmonton, Alta.: Hurtig, Publishers. (Reprinted: McClelland and Stewart, Toronto, 1994.)

Beal, Robert F., John E. Foster, and Louise Zuk
1987   The Métis Hivernement Settlement at Buffalo Lake 1872–1877. (Unpublished Report by Alberta Culture, Historic Sites and Provincial Museum, Edmonton, Alta.)

Beals, Kenneth L.
1971   The Dynamics of Kiowa Apache Peyotism. University of Oklahoma. Papers in Anthropology 12(1). Norman. (Originally presented as the Author's M.A. Thesis in Anthropology, University of Oklahoma, Norman, 1967.)

Beals, Ralph L.
1935   Ethnology of Rocky Mountain Park: The Ute and Arapaho. [Berkeley, Calif.]: U.S. Department of the Interior, National Park Service.

Bean, Janathan L.
1839   [Letter to Joshua Pilcher, dated October 24, 1839.] (Microfilm No. M234, Roll 3017, Frames 0253–0256, National Archives, Washington.)

Bearss, Edwin C.
1969   Fort Smith: Little Gibraltar on the Arkansas. Norman: University of Oklahoma Press.

———
1970   Bighorn Canyon National Recreation Area, Montana-Wyoming: History, Basic Data. Washington: U.S. Office of History and Historic Architecture, Eastern Service Center.

Beaudoin, Alwynne B.
1991   Alberta Radiocarbon Dates 1988–1989. Pp. 239–253 in Archaeology in Alberta 1988 and 1989. Martin Magne, ed. Archaeological Survey. Provincial Museum of Alberta. Occasional Paper 33. Edmonton.

Bebbington, Julia Marie
1982   Quillwork of the Plains. Photography by John Dean. Calgary, Alta.: Glenbow Museum.

Beckwith, Martha Warren
1930   Mythology of the Oglala Dakota. Journal of American Folk-lore 43(170):339–442.

———
1937   Mandan-Hidatsa Myths and Ceremonies. Memoirs of the American Folk-lore Society 32. New York: J.J. Augustin. (Reprinted: Kraus Reprint, New York, 1969.)

Beckwith, Paul
1889   Notes on Customs of the Dakotahs. Pp. 245–257 in

Smithsonian Institution Annual Report for the Year 1886. Washington: U.S. Government Printing Office.

Beckwourth, James P.
1856   The Life and Adventures of James P. Beckwourth, Mountaineer, Scout, and Pioneer, and Chief of the Crow Nation of Indians. Thomas D. Bonner, ed. New York: Harper and Brothers. (Reprinted: Harcourt, Brace and World, New York, 1968; also, University of Nebraska Press, Lincoln, 1972.)

Beede, Aaron McGaffey
1912–1920 [Journals and Letters.] (Manuscripts in Orin G. Libby Manuscript Collection, University of North Dakota, Grand Forks.)

———
1942   The Dakota Indian Victory Dance. North Dakota Historical Quarterly 9(3):167–178. Grand Forks and Bismarck.

Begg, Alexander
1871   The Creation of Manitoba; or, A History of the Red River Troubles. Toronto: Hunter, Rose and Company.

Belcourt/Bellecours, George Antoine see Bellecourt, George-Antoine

Belden, George P.
1870   Belden, the White Chief; or, Twelve Years among the Wild Indians of the Plains: From the Diaries and Manuscripts of George P. Belden. General James S. Brisbin, ed. Cincinnati: C.F. Vent. (Reprinted: Ohio University Press, Athens, 1974.)

Bell, Catherine E.
1994   Alberta Métis Settlements Legislation: An Overview of Ownership and Management of Settlement Lands. Regina, Sask.: Canadian Plains Research Center, University of Regina.

Bell, Earl H., and Robert E. Cape
1936   The Rock Shelters of Western Nebraska in the Vicinity of Dalton, Nebraska. Pp. 357–399 in Chapters in Nebraska Archaeology, by Earl H. Bell, et. al. Lincoln: The University of Nebraska.

Bell, Earl H., and G.H. Gilmore
1936   The Nehawka and Table Rock Foci of the Nebraska Aspect. Pp. 301–355 in Chapters in Nebraska Archaeology, by Earl H. Bell, et al. Lincoln: The University of Nebraska.

Bell, Earl H., et al.
1936   Chapters in Nebraska Archaeology. Lincoln: The University of Nebraska.

Bell, John R.
1957   The Journal of Captain John R. Bell, Offical Journalist for the Stephen H. Long Expedition to the Rocky Mountains, 1820. Edited and with Introductions by Harlin M. Fuller and LeRoy R. Hafen. The Far West and the Rockies Historical Series, 1820–1875, Vol. 6. Glendale, Calif.: Arthur H. Clark.

Bell, Michael
1993   Of Public Concern, the Pensioning of the Visual Arts in Canada Since 1945. Pp. 197–212 in In the Shadow of the Sun: Perspectives on Contemporary Native Art. Hull, Que.: Canadian Museum of Civilization.

Bell, Patricia
1976   Spatial and Temporal Variability with the Troubridge Site, A Kansas City Hopewell Village. Pp. 16–58 in Hopewellian River Archaeology in the Lower Missouri Valley. Alfred E. Johnson, ed. University of Kansas. Publications in Anthropology 8. Lawrence.

Bell, Robert E.
1957   Pedernales Point. Oklahoma Anthropological Society. Newsletter 6(6):2–4. Norman.

———
1958   Guide to the Identification of Certain American Indian Projectile Points. Oklahoma Anthropological Society Special. Bulletin 1. Norman.

1971   Bison Scapula Skin-Dressing Tools? *Plains Anthropologist* 16(52):125–127.

_____, ed.
1984   Prehistory of Oklahoma. Orlando, San Diego, San Francisco, [etc.]: Academic Press.

_____
1984a   The Plains Villagers: The Washita River. Pp. 307–324 in Prehistory of Oklahoma. Robert E. Bell, ed. Orlando, San Diego, San Francisco, [etc.]: Academic Press.

_____
1984b   Protohistoric Wichita. Pp. 363–378 in Prehistory of Oklahoma. Robert E. Bell, ed. Orlando, San Diego, San Francisco, [etc.]: Academic Press.

Bell, Robert E., and David A. Baerreis
1951   A Survey of Oklahoma Archaeology. *Bulletin of the Texas Archeological and Paleontological Society* 22:7–100. Lubbock, Tex.

Bell, Robert E., and Tyler Bastian
1974   Survey of Potential Wichita Archeological Remains in Oklahoma. Pp. 119–127 in Wichita Indian Archaeology and Ethnohistory: A Pilot Study. Robert E. Bell, Edward B. Jelks, and W.W. Newcomb, comps. *American Indian Ethnohistory: Plains Indians.* David Agee Horr, comp. and ed. New York and London: Garland Publishing. (Originally issued as: Final report of the National Science Foundation Grant, G.S.-964, Washington, 1967.)

Bell, Robert E., Edward B. Jelks, and W.W. Newcomb
1974   Wichita Indian Archaeology and Ethnohistory: A Pilot Study. *American Indian Ethnohistory: Plains Indians.* David Agee Horr, comp. and ed. New York and London: Garland Publishing. (Originally issued as: Final Report for National Science Foundation Grant GS-964, Washington, 1967.)

Bellam, Ernest Jay
1975   Studies in Stoney Morphology and Phonology. (M.A. Thesis in Linguistics, University of Calgary, Calgary, Alta.; Microfiche: *Canadian Theses on Microfiche* 24970, National Library of Canada, Ottawa, 1976.)

Bellecourt, George-Antoine
1839   Principes de la langue des sauvages appelés Sauteux. Québec: Fréchette.

_____
1872   Department of Hudson's Bay [1853]. Translated from the French by Mrs. Letitia May. *Collections of the Minnesota Historical Society* 1:207–244. St. Paul. (Previously publ. under title: Prince Rupert's Land - The Hudson's Bay and Northwest Company, in Minnesota and Its Resources, by J.W. Bond, New York, 1853.)

Belous, Russell E., and Robert A. Weinstein
1969   Will Soule: Indian Photographer at Fort Sill, Oklahoma 1869–74. Los Angeles: Ward Ritchie Press.

Belt, R.V.
1892   [Letter to Kiowa Agent, Ordering Cherokees Home; written in Washington, D.C., n.d.] (Manuscript *Messiah Craze*, Newspaper/Archives and Manuscript Division, Oklahoma Historical Society, Oklahoma City.)

Beltrami, J.C. (i.e. Giacomo Costantino)
1824   La découverte des sources du Mississipi et de la Riviere Sanglante. Description du cours entíer du Mississipi, [etc.]. Nouvelle-Orleans [New Orleans, La.]: Benj. Levy.

_____
1828   A Pilgrimage in Europe and America, Leading to the Discovery of the Sources of the Mississippi and Bloody River. 2 vols. London: Printed for Hunt and Clarke. (Reprinted, Vol. 2 only, under title: A Pilgrimage in America; Quadrangle Books, Chicago, 1962.)

_____, collect.
1995   The Sioux Vocabulary 1823 in the Archivio Beltrami of Count G. Luchetti, Filottrano, Italy. Cesare Marino and Leonardo Vigorelli, transcribers and eds. Kendall Park, N.J.: Lakota Books.

Belue, Clarence Thomas
1991   White Oppression and Enduring Red Tears: Indian Law and the Real Rules of White Control of Crow Lands. (L.L.D. Thesis, University of Wisconsin, Madison.)

Bement, Leland C.
1994   Hunter-Gatherer Mortuary Practices during the Central Texas Archaic. Austin: University of Texas Press.

Bement, Leland C., and Kent J. Buehler
1994   Preliminary Results from the Certain Site: A Late Archaic Bison Kill in Western Oklahoma. *Plains Anthropologist* 39(148):173–183.

_____, eds.
1997   Southern Plains Bison Procurement and Utilization from Paleoindian to Historic: Proceedings of a Symposium from the 52nd Plains Anthropological Conference, Lubbock, Texas. *Plains Anthropologist* 42(159); *Memoir* 29. Lincoln.

Benavides, Fray Alonso de
1916   The Memorial of Fray Alonso de Benavides, 1630. Mrs. Edward E. Ayer, trans.; Annotated by Frederick Webb Hodge and Charles Fletcher Lummis. Chicago: Privately Printed. (Reprinted: Horn and Wallace, Albuquerque, 1965. Orginially publ. in Spanish under title: Memorial que fray Iuan de Santander de la orden de San Francisco, comissario general de Indias, presenta a la Magestad catolica del rey Don Felipe Quarto nuestro señor. Hecho por el padre fray Alonso de Benavides, Madrid, Imprenta real, M.DC.XXX.)

_____
1945   Fray Alonso de Benavides' Revised Memorial of 1634. With Numerous Supplementary Documents Elaborately Annotated. Frederick Webb Hodge, George P. Hammond, and Agapito Rey, eds. and trans. *Coronado Cuarto Centennial Publications, 1540–1940,* Vol. IV. Albuquerque: University of New Mexico Press.

Benedict, James B.
1975   The Albion Boardinghouse Site: Archaic Occupation of a High Mountain Valley. *Southwestern Lore* 41(3):1–12. Boulder, Colo.

_____
1979   Getting Away from It All: A Study of Man, Mountains, and the Two-Drought Altithermal. *Southwestern Lore* 45(3):1–12. Boulder, Colo.

Benedict, James B., and Byron L. Olson
1973   Origin of the McKean Complex: Evidence from Timberline. *Plains Anthropologist* 18(62, Pts.1–2):323–327.

_____
1978   The Mount Albion Complex: A Study of Prehistoric Man and the Altithermal. *Center for Mountain Archaeology. Research Report* 1. Ward, Colo.

Benedict, Ruth F.
1922   The Vision in Plains Culture. *American Anthropologist,* n.s. 24(1):1–23.

_____
1938   Religion. Pp. 627–665 in General Anthropology. Franz Boas, ed. Boston and New York: D.C. Heath & Co. (Reprinted: Johnson Reprint, New York, 1965.)

Benn, David W.
1980   [MAD: Ceramics.] (Manuscript at Luther College Archaeological Research Center, Decorah, Iowa.)

_____
1981   [Archaeological Investigations at the Rainbow Site, Plymouth County, Iowa.] (Manuscript at Luther College Archaeological Research Center, Decorah, Iowa.)

_____
1984   Excavations at the Christenson Oneota Site (13PK407), Central Des Moines River Valley, Iowa. Springfield, Mo.:

Southwest Missouri State University, Center for Archaeo-logical Research.

1988   Mound Salvage Excavations at Blood Run; 1985. *Newsletter of the Iowa Archeological Society* 38(2):1–3. Iowa City.

1989   Hawks, Serpents, and Bird-Men: Emergence of the Oneota Mode of Production. *Plains Anthropologist* 34(125):233–260.

1990   Woodland Ceramics and Historical Context on the Western Prairies. Pp. 50–70 in Woodland Cultures on the Western Prairies: The Rainbow Site Investigations. David W. Benn, ed. *University of Iowa. Office of the State Archaeologist Report* 18. Iowa City.

1992   Ceramics from the Lake Oscar Sites. Pp. 80–95 in Vol. 1 of Archeological Investigations in the Vicinity of Lake Oscar, Douglas County, Minnesota, S.P. 2101–18 (T.H.27). Jonathan R. Sellars, ed. Decorah, Iowa: Bear Creek Archeology, Inc.

Bennett, Gwen Patrice
1984   A Bibliography of Illinois Archaeology. *Illinois State Museum. Scientific Papers* 21. Springfield, Ill.

Bennett, John W.
1944   The Development of Ethnological Theory as Illustrated by Studies of the Plains Sun Dance. *American Anthropologist,* n.s. 46(2, Pt.1):162–181.

1969   Northern Plainsmen: Adaptive Strategy and Agrarian Life. Chicago: Aldine Press.

Benoist, Marius
1975   Louison Sansredret, Métis. St. Boniface, Man.: Les Éditions du Blé.

Bent, Charles
1850   [Letter to the Commissioner of Indian Affairs, dated Santa Fe, New Mexico, November 10, 1846.] Pp. 183–186 in Message from the President of the United States, [etc.]. *31st Congress. 1st Session. Senate Executive Document* 18. (Serial No. 557.) Washington.

Bent, George 1968 *see* Hyde, George E. 1968

Bent, William 1860 *see* ARCIA 1849–

Bentzen, Raymond C.
1962   The Powers-Yonkee Bison Trap, 24PR5. *Plains Anthropologist* 7(16):113–118.

1966   The Powers-Yonkee Bison Trap, by Sheridan Chapter, 1961. *The Wyoming Archaeologist* 9(1):7–20. Cheyenne, [etc.,] Wyo.

1966a   The Mavrakis-Bentzen-Roberts Bison Trap [48SH311], by Sheridan Chapter, 1962. *The Wyoming Archaeologist* 9(1):27–39. Cheyenne, [etc.,] Wyo.

Berghaus, Heinrich Karl Wilhelm
1845–1848 Berghaus Physikal atlas. 3 vols. Vol. 1: Berghaus Physikal atlas; Vols. 2–3: Dr. Heinrich Berghaus Physikalischer Atlas oder Sammlung von Karten, auf denen die hauptsächlichsten erscheinungen der anorganischen und organischen Natur nach ihrer geographischen Verbreitung und Vertheilung bildlich dargestellt sind. Gotha, Germany: Justus Perthes.

1887   Physikalischer Atlas oder Sammlung von Karten, auf denen die hauptsächlichsten erscheinungen der anorganischen und organischen Natur nach ihrer geographischen Verbreitung und Vertheilung bildlich dargestellt sind. Gotha.

Berkhofer, Robert F., Jr.
1965   Salvation and the Savage: An Analysis of Protestant Mis-sions and American Indian Responses, 1787–1862. Lexington: University of Kentucky Press. (Reprinted: Greenwood Press, Westport, Conn., 1977.)

Berlandier, Jean Louis
1844   Caza del Oso y Cíbola, en el Nordeste de Tejas. *El Museo Mexicano* 3(8):177–187. [Mexico City.]

1960   America. Mexico-Journal of Louis Berlandier During 1846–7 Including the Time He was Driven from Matamoros by the Americans. 2 vols. (Photocopy of Journal in the Library of The University of Texas at Brownsville and the Texas Southmost College.)

1969   The Indians of Texas in 1830. John C. Ewers, ed.; Patricia Reading Leclercq, trans. Washington: Smithsonian Institution Press.

1980   Journey to Mexico; During the Years 1826 to 1834. Sheila M. Ohlendorf, Josette M. Bigelow, and Mary M. Standifer, trans. Introduction by C.H. Muller. Botanical Notes by C.H. Muller and Katherine K. Muller. 2 vols. Austin: The Texas State Historical Association in Cooperation with the Center for Studies in Texas History, The University of Texas at Austin.

Berlandier, Jean Louis, and Rafael Chowell
1828–1829 [Vocabularies of the Languages of South Texas and the Lower Rio Grande.] (Manuscript, Additional Manuscripts No. 38720, British Library, London.)

Berlo, Janet Catherine, ed.
1992   The Early Years of Native American Art History: The Politics of Scholarship and Collecting. Seattle: University of Washington Press; Vancouver: UBC Press.

——, ed.
1996   Plains Indian Drawings, 1865–1945: Pages from a Visual History. New York: Harry N. Abrams in association with the American Federation of Arts and the Drawing Center.

2000   Spirit Beings and Sun Dancers: Black Hawk's Vision of the Lakota World. Forewords by Arthur Amiotte and Eugene V. Thaw. New York: George Braziller.

Berlo, Janet Catherine, and Ruth B. Phillips
1998   Native North American Art. Oxford, England: Oxford University Press.

Berman, Tressa L.
1996   Mandan. Pp. 353–354 in Encyclopedia of North American Indians. Frederick E. Hoxie, ed. Boston: Houghton Mifflin.

1996a   Bringing It to the Center: Artistic Production and Economic Development among Indian Women at Fort Berthold, North Dakota. *Research in Human Capital and Development* 10.

1998   The Community as Worksite: American Indian Women's Artistic Production. In: More Than Class: Studying Power in U.S. Workplaces. Albany: State University of New York.

Bernardis, Tim
1986   Crow Social Studies: Baleeisbaalichiwee History. 2 vols. Crow Agency, Mont.: Bilingual Materials Development Center.

Bernstein, Alison R.
1991   American Indians and World War II: Toward a New Era in Indian Affairs. Norman: University of Oklahoma Press.

Bernstein, Bruce, and W. Jackson Rushing
1995   Modern By Tradition: American Indian Painting in the Studio Style. Santa Fe: Museum of New Mexico Press.

Berry, Brewton, and Carl H. Chapman
1942   An Oneota Site in Missouri. *American Antiquity* 7(3):290–305, 311–318.

Berry, Brewton, Carl H.Chapman, and John Mack
1944   Archaeological Remains of the Osage. *American Antiquity* 10(1):1–11.

Berryman, Florence
1941   Indian Art of the United States. *Magazine of Art* 34:216, 218.

Berta, Susan M., and John A. Harrington, Jr.
1984   Quartermaster Creek Watershed Land Cover Types: An Analysis of Current Conditions and Recent Change(s). Pp. 33–49 in Archaeology of the Mixed Grass Prairie. Phase I: Quartermaster Creek. Timothy G. Baugh, ed. *Oklahoma Archeological Survey. Archeological Resource Survey Report* 20. Norman.

Berthrong, Donald J.
1963   The Southern Cheyennes. Norman: University of Oklahoma Press. (Reprinted in 1972, 1979, 1986.)

_____
1976   The Cheyenne and Arapahoe Ordeal: Reservation and Agency Life in the Indian Territory, 1875–1907. Norman: University of Oklahoma Press.

_____   1979 *see* 1963 (reprint info.)

_____   1979a *see* 1985

_____
1985   Legacies of the Dawes Act: Bureaucrats and Land Thieves at the Cheyenne-Arapaho Agencies of Oklahoma. Pp. 31–53 in The Plains Indians of the Twentieth Century. Edited and with an Introduction by Peter Iverson. Norman and London: University of Oklahoma Press. (Reprinted from: *Arizona and the West* (Winter 1979):335–354.)

Bettis, Elmer A., III, and D.M. Thompson
1982   Interrelations of Cultural and Fluvial Deposits in Northwest Iowa. Vermillion, S.Dak.: University of south Dakota Archaeology Laboratory.

Biddle, Thomas
1820   [Letter to H. Atkinson regarding Indian Trade, dated Camp Missouri, Missouri River, October 29, 1819.] *16th Congress. 1st Session. Senate Document* 47A (Serial No. 26). Washington.

Bierstadt, Alfred
1863   [Lakota Vocabulary.] (Manuscript No. 916, National Anthropological Archives, Smithsonian Institution, Washington.)

Big Horn County (Montana). Assessment Appraisal Office
1998   Crow Tribe of Indians [Land Held by Crow Tribe in Fee Status Within Exterior Boundaries of Reservation in Big Horn County]. (Handwritten compilation, as of 6/10/98, Big Horn County, Hardin, Mont.)

Big Man, Max
1979   The Beaver Dance and Adoption Ceremony of the Crow Indians. (With an Introduction by Jesse Schultz and Notes by C. Adrian Heindenreich.) Pp. 43–56 in Lifeways of Intermontane and Plains Montana Indians. Leslie B. Davis, ed. *Occasional Papers of the Museum of the Rockies* 1. Bozeman, Mont.: Montana State University.

Billard, Jules B.
1974   The World of the American Indian. Washington: National Geographic Society.

Billeck, William T.
1993   Time and Space in the Glenwood Locality: The Nebraska Phase in Western Iowa. (Ph.D. Dissertation in Anthropology, University of Missouri, Columbia.)

_____
1995   Comments on the Cultural Affiliation of the Steed-Kisker Phase. Washington, D.C.: Smithsonian Institution, National Museum of Natural History, Repatriation Office.

Billeck, William T., and Javier Urcid
1995   Assessment of the Cultural Affiliation of the Steed-Kisker Phase for Evaluation by the National Museum of Natural History Native American Repatriation Review Committee. Washington, D.C.: Smithsonian Institution, National Museum of Natural History, Repatriation Office.

Billington, Monroe L.
1967   Thomas P. Gore, the Blind Senator from Oklahoma. Lawrence: University of Kansas Press.

Binford, Lewis R.
1962   Archaeology as Anthropology. *American Antiquity* 28(2):217–225.

_____
1980   Willow Smoke and Dogs' Tails: Hunter-gatherer Settlement Systems and Archaeological Site Formation. *American Antiquity* 45(1):4–20.

Bingaman, Sandra E.
1975   The Trials of Poundmaker and Big Bear, 1885. *Saskatchewan History* 28:81–94. Saskatoon, Sask.

Biolsi, Thomas
1985   The IRA and the Politics of Acculturation: The Sioux Case. *American Anthropologist* 87(3):656–659.

_____
1992   Organizing the Lakota: The Political Economy of the New Deal on the Pine Ridge and Rosebud Reservations. Tucson: University of Arizona Press.

_____
1997   The Anthropological Construction of Indians: Haviland Scudder Mekeel and the Search for the Primitive in Lakota Country. Pp. 133–159 in Indians and Anthropologists: Vine Deloria, Jr., and the Critique of Anthropology. Thomas Biolsi and Larry J. Zimmerman, eds. Tucson: University of Arizona Press.

Bird, James
1793   [Letter to William Tomison, dated November 8, 1793.] (Manuscript, South Branch Journal, B205a/b, Hudson's Bay Company Archives, Provincial Archives of Manitoba, Winnipeg.)

Birk, Douglas A., and Elden Johnson
1988   The Mdewakanton Dakota and Initial French Contacts: The Archaeological and Historical Evidence. *The Institute for Minnesota Archaeology. Report of Investigations* 32. Minneapolis.

Birk, Douglas A., and Judy Poseley
1978   The French at Lake Pepin: An Archaeological Survey for Fort Beauharnois, Goodhue County, Minnesota. Final Report of Minnesota Historical Society Project No. 4094. St Paul: Minnesota Historical Society.

Birrell, Andrew J.
1996   The North American Boundary Commission: Three Photographic Expeditions, 1872–74. *History of Photography* 20(2):113–121. London and Washington, D.C.: Taylor & Francis.

Bishop, Charles A.
1975   The Origin of the Speakers of the Severn Dialect. Pp. 196–208 in Papers of the Sixth Algonquian Conference, 1974. William Cowan, ed. *Canada. National Museum of Man. Mercury Series. Ethnology Service Paper* 23. Ottawa.

Bishop, Charles A., and M. Estellie Smith
1975   Early Historic Populations in Northwestern Ontario: Archaeological and Ethnological Interpretations. *American Antiquity* 40(1):54–63.

Bittle, William E.
[1952–   [Kiowa Apache Linguistic Fieldnotes.] (Manuscripts on file
1956]   in the American Indian Studies Research Institute, Indiana University, Bloomington.)

[1952–1975]   [Kiowa Apache Ethnographic Fieldnotes.] (Manuscripts in Morris Foster's possession.)

1954   The Peyote Ritual: Kiowa-Apache. *Bulletin of the Oklahoma Anthropological Society* 2:69–78. Oklahoma City.

1956   The Position of Kiowa-Apache in the Apachean Group. (Ph.D. Dissertation in Anthropology, University of California, Los Angeles.)

1960   The Curative Aspects of Peyotism. *Bios* 31(3):140–148. Madison, N.J.: Beta Beta Beta National Biological Society.

1961   [Letter to Morris E. Opler, dated November 10, 1961.] (Manuscript formerly in M.E. Opler's possession.)

1962   The Manatidie: A Focus for Kiowa Apache Tribal Identity. *Plains Anthropologist* 7(17):152–163.

1963   Kiowa-Apache. Pp. 76–101 in Studies in the Athapaskan Languages, by Harry Hoijer and others. *University of California Publications in Linguistics* 29. Berkeley.

1971   A Brief History of the Kiowa Apache. *University of Oklahoma Papers in Anthropology* 12(1):1–34. Norman.

Bizzell, David W.
1981   A Report on the Quapaw: The Letters of Governor George Izard to the American Philosophical Society, 1825–1827. *Pulaski County Historical Review* 29:66–79. Little Rock, Ark.

Black Bear, Ben, Sr., and R.D. Theisz
1976   Songs and Dances of the Lakota. Song Texts and Introductions in Lakota, with English Translations by Howard P. Bad Hand. Aberdeen, S.Dak.: Northern Plains Press, Rosebud, S.Dak. (Reprinted in 1984.)

Black Bear, Floyd
1997   Arrow Keepers. [Pamphelt prepared for Cheyenne religionists.]

Black Elk 1984 *see* DeMallie, Raymond J., ed. 1984

Black Plume, Reggie
1964   The Sun Dance. *Sun Dance Echo* 1(2):10.

Black Thunder, Elijah, Norma Johnson, Larry O'Connor, and Muriel Pronovost
1975   Ehanna Woyakapi: History and Culture of the Sisseton-Wahpeton Sioux Tribe of South Dakota. Sisseton, S.Dak.: Sisseton-Wahpeton Sioux Tribe. (Earlier ed., 1972.)

Black, Stephen L.
1986   The Clemente and Herminia Hinojosa Site, 41 JW 8: A Toyah Horizon Campsite in Southern Texas. With Contributions by R.G. Holloway ... [et al.]. Report Prepared under the Supervision of Thomas R. Hester, Principal Investigator. *University of Texas at San Antonio. Center for Archaeological Research. Special Report* 18. San Antonio, Tex.

1989   Central Texas Plateau Prairie. Pp. 17–38 in From the Gulf to the Rio Grande: Human Adaptation in Central, South, and Lower Pecos Texas; by Thomas R. Hester ... [et al.]. Prepared by the Center for Archaeological Research at the University of Texas at San Antonio, Texas A&M University, and the Arkansas Archeological Survey. *Arkansas Archeological Survey Research Series* 33. Fayetteville.

Blackman, Elmer E.
1903   Report of Department of Archaeology. Pp. 294–326 in *Nebraska State Board of Agriculture, Annual Report for 1902.* Omaha.

1907   Prehistoric Man in Nebraska. *Records of the Past* 6(3):76–79. Washington, D.C.

1930   Archaeological Work in 1929. *American Anthropologist,* n.s. 32(2):357.

Blackmore, William
1869   The North American Indians: A Sketch of Some of the Hostile Tribes, Together with a Brief Account of General Sheridan's Campaign of 1868 against the Sioux, Cheyenne, Arapahoe, Kiowa, and Comanche Indians. *Journal of the Ethnological Society of London,* n.s. 1:287–320. London.

Blaine, Garland, and Martha R. Blaine
1964–1974 [Fieldnotes, Pawnee, Oklahoma.] (Manuscripts in G. and M.R. Blaine's possession.)

Blaine, Martha Royce
1979   The Ioway Indians. Norman: University of Oklahoma Press.

1980   The Pawnees: A Critical Bibliography. *The Newberry Library Center for the History of the American Indian Bibliographical Series.* Bloomington: Indiana University Press.

1982   The Pawnee-Wichita Visitation Cycle: Historic Manifestations of an Ancient Friendship. Pp. 113–134 in Pathways to Plains Prehistory: Anthropological Perspectives of Plains Natives and Their Pasts. Papers in Honor of Robert E. Bell. Don G. Wyckoff and Jack L. Hofman, eds. *Oklahoma Anthropological Society Memoir* 3, *The Cross Timbers Heritage Association Contributions* 1. Duncan, Okla.: The Cross Timbers Press.

1990   Pawnee Passage: 1870–1875. Norman: University of Oklahoma Press.

1997   Some Things Are Not Forgotten: A Pawnee Family Remembers. Lincoln: University of Nebraska Press.

Blair, Emma Helen, trans. and ed.
1911–1912 The Indian Tribes of The Upper Mississippi Valley and Region of the Great Lakes, as Described by Nicolas Perrot, French Commandant in the Northwest; Bacqueville de la Potherie, French Royal Commissioner to Canada; Morrell Marston, American Army Officer; and Thomas Forsyth, United States Indian Agent at Fort Armstrong. 2 vols. Cleveland, Ohio: Arthur H. Clark. (Reprinted: Kraus Reprint, New York, 1969; also, 2 vols. in 1, with an Introduction by Richard White: University of Nebraska Press, Lincoln, 1996.)

Blair, Thomas A.
1941   Climate of Nebraska. Pp. 967–978 in Climate and Man: 1941 Yearbook of Agriculture. Washington: U.S. Government Printing Office.

Blair, W.F.
1939   Faunal Relationships and Geographic Distribution of Mammals in Oklahoma. *The American Midland Naturalist* 22(1):85–133. Notre Dame, Ind.

Blakeslee, Donald J.
1975   The Plains Interband Trade System: An Ethnohistoric and Archaeological Investigation. (Ph.D. Dissertation in Anthropology, University of Wisconsin, Milwaukee.)

_____, ed.
1978   The Central Plains Tradition: Internal Development and External Relationships. *University of Iowa. Office of the State Archaeologist. Report* 11. Iowa City.

1978a   Assessing the Central Plains Tradition in Eastern Nebraska: Content and Outcome. Pp. 134–143 in The Central Plains Tradition: Internal Development and External Relationships. Donald J. Blakeslee, ed. *University of Iowa. Office of the State Archaeologist. Report* 11. Iowa City.

1981   The Origin and Spread of the Calumet Ceremony. *American Antiquity* 46(4):759–769.

Blakeslee, Donald J., and Warren W. Caldwell
1979   The Nebraska Phase: An Appraisal. *Reprints in Anthropology* 18. Lincoln: J&L Reprint Company.

Blakeslee, Donald J., and Arthur H. Rohn
1982–1986 Man and Environment in Northeastern Kansas: The Hillsdale Lake Project, Final Report. 6 vols. Kansas City, Mo.: U.S. Army Corps of Engineers, Kansas City District.

Blish, Helen H.
1926   Ethical Conceptions of the Oglala Dakota. *University Studies* 26(3/4):79–123. Lincoln: University of Nebraska.

1933   The Drama of the Sioux Sun Dance. *Theatre Arts Monthly* 17(8):629–634. New York.

_____, ed. 1967 *see* Bad Heart Bull, Amos 1967

Bliss, Wesley L.
1950   Birdshead Cave, a Stratified Site in the Wind River Basin, Wyoming. *American Antiquity* 15(3):187–196.

Bloch, Maurice
1971   The Moral and Tactical Meaning of Kinship Terms. *Man* 6(1):79–87. London.

Bloom, Lansing B.
1927   The Death of Jacques D'Eglise. *New Mexico Historical Review* 2(4):369–379. Albuquerque.

Bloomfield, Leonard
1928   The Plains Cree Language. Pp. 427–431 in Vol. 2 of *Atti del XXII Congreso Internazionale degli Americanisti. Roma, settembre 1926. [Proceedings of the 22d International Congress of Americanists].* 2 vols. Roma, [Italy].

1930   Sacred Stories of the Sweet Grass Cree. *National Museum of Canada. Bulletin* 60; *Anthropological Series* 11. Ottawa: Department of Northern Affairs and National Resources. (Reprinted: AMS Press, New York, 1976; also, Fifth House, Saskatoon, Sask., 1993.)

1934   Plains Cree Texts. *Publications of the American Ethnological Society* 16. New York: G.E. Stechert & Co. (Reprinted: AMS Press, New York, 1974.)

1946   Algonquian. Pp. 85–129 in Linguistic Structures of Native America. Harry Hoijer, ed. *Viking Fund Publications in Anthropology* 6. New York: Wenner Gren. (Reprinted: Johnson Reprint, New York, 1971.)

1962   The Menomini Language. New Haven, Conn.: Yale University Press.

1975   Menomini Lexicon. Charles F. Hockett, ed. *Milwaukee Public Museum Publications in Anthropology and History* 3. Milwaukee. (The spelling 'Menominee' appears on the cover.)

1984   Cree-English Lexicon. 2 vols. *HRAFlex Books* NG4-001. *Language and Literature Series: Native American Linguistics* 2. New Haven, Conn.: Human Relations Area Files.

Blumensohn, Jules Henry
1933   The Fast among North American Indians. *American Anthropologist,* n.s. 35(3):451–469.

Board of Commissioners
1865   Proceedings of a Board of Commissioners to Negotiate a Treaty or Treaties with the Hostile Indians of the Upper Missouri. Newton Edmunds, President of Commission. [Washington: Government Printing Office.]

Board of Indian Commissioners 1870–1933 *see* BIC = Board of Indian Commissioners 1870–1933

Boas, Franz
1896   The Limitations of the Comparative Method of Anthropology. *Science,* n.s. 4(103):901–908. (Reprinted: Bobbs-Merrill, Indianapolis, 1967.)

1907   Notes on the Ponka Grammar. Pp. 317–337 in *Extrait des Mémoires et d élibérations du XVe Congrès des Américanistes tenu à Québec, du 10 au 15 Septembre 1906.* Québec: Dussault et Proulx.

1937   Some Traits of the Dakota Language. *Language: Journal of the Linguistic Society of America* 13(2):137–141. Baltimore.

Boas, Franz, and Ella C. Deloria
1933   Notes on the Dakota, Teton Dialect. *International Journal of American Linguistics* 7(3–4):97–121. Chicago.

1941   Dakota Grammar. *Memoirs of the National Academy of Sciences* 23(Pt. 2). Washington: U.S. Government Printing Office. (Reprinted: AMS Press, New York, 1976; also, Dakota Press, Sioux Falls, S.Dak., 1979.)

Boas, Franz, and John R. Swanton
1911   Siouan: Dakota (Teton and Santee Dialects), with Remarks on the Ponca and Winnebago. Pp. 879–965 in Handbook of American Indian Languages. Franz Boas, ed. *Bureau of American Ethnology Bulletin* 40(Pt. 1). [Pp. 959–965 is: Winnebago Text, by Paul Radin.] Washington: Smithsonian Institution; U.S. Government Printing Office.

Bobrowsky, Peter T., et al.
1990   Archaeological Geology of Sites in Western and Northwestern Canada. Pp. 87–122 in Archaeological Geology of North America. N.P. Lasca and J. Donahue, eds. *Geological Society of America. Centennial Special Volume* 4. Boulder, Colo.

Bodmer, Karl
1984   Karl Bodmer's America. Introduction by William H. Goetzmann; Annotations by David C. Hunt and Marsha V. Gallagher; Artist's Biography by William J. Orr. Lincoln: Joslyn Art Museum and University of Nebraska Press.

Boggs, James P.
1984   Challenge of Reservation Resource Development: A Northern Cheyenne Instance. Pp. 205–236 in Native Americans and Energy Development. Joseph G. Jorgensen, ed. Boston: Anthropology Resource Center.

Bogy, Charles, and W.R. Irwin
1866   [Letter to Louis Bogy, dated 26 November 1866.] (Manuscript No. M234, Roll 375, Frame 55, Letters Received, Kiowa Agency 1864–1868, Records of the Bureau of Indian Affairs, Record Group 75, National Archives, Washington.)

Bohannon, Charles F.
1973   Excavations at Mineral Springs Site, Howard County, Arkansas. *Arkansas Archeological Survey Research Series* 5. Fayetteville.

Boheme, Sarah, Christian F. Feest, and Patricia Condon Johnston
1995   Seth Eastman: A Portfolio of North American Indians. Afton, Minn.: Afton Historical Society Press.

Boilvin, Nicolas
1811   [Letter to the Secretary of War (William Eustis), dated Georgetown, March 5, 1811, Containing a Description of "Prairie des Chiens," etc.] (Manuscript No. 221, Roll 34B, Letters Received, the Secretary of War, Registered Series 1801–1860, National Archives, Washington.)

Boimare, A.-L., ed.
1831   Journal historique de l'établissement des Francais à la Louisiane. J.-B. Bénard de La Harpe, comp. New Orleans and Paris: Hector Bossange.

Boise Cascade Center for Community Development
1972   Indian Economic Development: An Evaluation of EDA's Selected Indian Reservation Program. (EDA-72-59847.)

Washington: U.S. Department of Commerce, Economic Development Administration.

Bol, Marsha C.
1985   Lakota Women's Artistic Strategies in Support of the Social System. *American Indian Culture and Research Journal* 9(1):33–51. Los Angeles.

1989   Gender in Art: A Comparison of Lakota Women's and Men's Art, 1820–1920. 2 vols. (Ph.D. Dissertation in Art History, University of New Mexico, Albuquerque.)

1992   "All Around Rise Hundreds of Habitations of Buffalo Skin, Some Covered with Fantastic and Primitive Paintings": The Painted Tepee and the Lakota People. In: Archaeology, Art, and Anthropology: Papers in Honor of J.J. Brody. Albuquerque: Archaeological Society of New Mexico.

Bol, Marsha C., and Nellie Z. Star Boy Menard
2000   "I Saw All That": A Lakota Girl's Puberty Ceremony. *American Indian Culture and Research Journal* 24(1):25–42. Los Angeles.

Bollaert, William
1850   Observations on the Indian Tribes of Texas. *Journal of the Ethnological Society of London* 2:262–283. London.

1956   William Bollaert's Texas. W. Eugene Hollon and Ruth Lapham Butler, eds. Norman: University of Oklahoma Press. (Reprinted in 1989.)

Boller, Henry A.
1868   Among the Indians: Eight Years in the Far West, 1858–66; Embracing Sketches of Montana and Salt Lake. Philadelphia: T.E. Zell. (Reprinted, Milo M. Quaife, ed.: The Lakeside Press, Chicago, 1959; also, Books for Libraries Press, Freeport, N.Y., 1973.)

_____   1959, 1973 *see* 1868 (reprint info.)

Bolton, Herbert E.
1905   The Spanish Abandonment and Re-Occupation of East Texas, 1773–1779. *Texas State Historical Association Quarterly* 9(2):67–137. Austin.

1908   Spanish Exploration in the Southwest, 1542–1706. *Original Narratives of Early American History.* New York: Charles Scribner's Sons. (Reprinted in 1916, 1925; also, Barnes & Noble, New York, 1946, 1952, 1963, 1967, 1976.)

1908a   The Native Tribes About the East Texas Missions. *Texas State Historical Association Quarterly* 11(4):249–276. Austin.

1910   Tawakoni. Pp. 701–706 in Vol. 2 of Handbook of American Indians North of Mexico. Frederick W. Hodge, ed. 2 Pts./vols. *Bureau of American Ethnology Bulletin* 30. Washington: Smithsonian Institution; U.S. Government Printing Office. (Reprinted: Rowman and Littlefield, New York, 1971.)

1910a   Yscanis. P. 1002 in Vol. 2 of Handbook of American Indians North of Mexico. Frederick W. Hodge, ed. 2 Pts./vols. *Bureau of American Ethnology Bulletin* 30. Washington: Smithsonian Institution; U.S. Government Printing Office. (Reprinted: Rowman and Littlefield, New York, 1971.)

1910b   Tonkawa. Pp. 778–783 in Vol. 2 of Handbook of American Indians North of Mexico. Frederick W. Hodge, ed. 2 Pts./vols. *Bureau of American Ethnology Bulletin* 30. Washington: Smithsonian Institution; U.S. Government Printing Office. (Reprinted: Rowman and Littlefield, New York, 1971.)

1911   The Jumano Indians in Texas, 1650–1771. *Texas State Historical Association Quarterly* 15(1):66–84. Austin.

1912   The Spanish Occupation of Texas, 1519–1690. *Southwestern Historical Society Quarterly* 16(1):1–26. Austin, Tex.

1913   Guide to Materials for the History of the United States in the Principal Archives of Mexico. *Carnegie Institute Publications* 163. Washington.

1913a   New Light on Manuel Lisa and the Spanish Fur Trade. With an Unpublished Letter from Manuel Lisa, dated 8 September 1812. *Southwestern Historical Quarterly* 17(1):61–66. Austin, Tex. (Bound vol., July 1913 to April 1914, has 1914 imprint date.)

_____, trans. and ed.
1914   Athanase de Mézières and the Louisiana-Texas Frontier, 1768–1780: Documents Published for the First Time, from the Original Spanish and French Manuscripts, Chiefly in the Archives of Mexico and Spain. 2 vols. Cleveland, Ohio: Arthur H. Clark. (Reprinted, 2 vols. in 1: AMS Press and Kraus Reprint, New York, 1970.)

1915   Texas in the Middle Eighteenth Century. (Studies in Spanish Colonial History and Administration.) *University of California Publications in History* 3. Berkeley. (Reprinted: Kraus Reprint, Millwood, N.Y., 1974.)

_____, trans. and ed.
1916   Spanish Exploration in the Southwest, 1542–1706. *Original Narratives of Early American History.* New York: C. Scribner's Sons. (Reprinted in 1925.)

1916a   The Beginnings of Mission Nuestra Señora del Refugio. *Southwestern Historical Quarterly* 19(4). Austin, Tex.

1917   French Intrusion into Mexico, 1749–1752. Pp. 389–407 in The Pacific Ocean in History: Papers and Addresses Presented at the Panama-Pacific Historical Congress ... July 19–23, 1915. H. Morse Stephens and Herbert E. Bolton, eds. New York: Macmillan. (Reprinted: Pp. 150–171 in Bolton and the Spanish Borderlands. John F. Bannon, ed. University of Oklahoma Press, Norman, 1964.)

1949   Coronado: Knight of Pueblos and Plains. New York: Whittlesey House. (Reprinted: University of New Mexico Press, Albuquerque, 1964, 1990.)

1950   Pageant in the Wilderness: The Story of the Escalante Expedition to the Interior Basin, 1776; Including the Diary and Itinerary of Father Escalante. *Utah Historical Quarterly* 18(1–4):1–265. Salt Lake City.

_____   1964 *see* Bannon, John F., ed. 1964

Bonaparte, Roland
1992   "Peaux-Rouges": Author de la collection anthropologique du prince Roland Bonaparte. Sous la direction de Benoit Coutancier. Paris: Photothèque du Musée de l'Homme.

Bonilla, Antonio
1905   Brief Compendium of the Events Which Have Occurred in the Province of Texas from Its Conquest, or Reduction, to the Present Date [1772]. Elizabeth Howard West, trans. *Texas State Historical Association Quarterly* 8(1):9–22.

Bonine, Michael E., et al.
1970   Atlas of Mexico. Austin: Bureau of Business, The University of Texas at Austin.

Bonner, Thomas D., ed. 1856 *see* Beckwourth, James P. 1856

Bonneville, Benjamin Louis Eulalie de
1837   [Letter to Roger Jones, dated 24 January 1837.] (Manuscript No. M234, Roll 922, Frame 13, Letters Received, Western Superintendency, Records of the Bureau of Indian Affairs, Record Group 75, National Archives, Washington.) *1103*

Bonney, Rachel A.
1970   Early Woodland in Minnesota. *Plains Anthropologist* 15(50):302–304.

Boone, A.G.
1861   [Report to the Commissioner of Indian Affairs, dated Upper Arkansas Agency, November 2, 1861.] (Manuscript No. M234, Roll 878, Letters Received, Upper Arkansas Agency, Records of the Bureau of Indian Affairs, Record Group 75, National Archives, Washington.)

Borchert, John R.
1950   The Climate of the Central North American Grassland. *Annals of the Association of American Geographers* 40(1):1–39. Minneapolis.

Bordeaux, William J.
1929   Conquering the Mighty Sioux. Sioux Falls, S.Dak.: [privately printed.]

————
1952   Custer's Conqueror. Rapid City, S.Dak.: Smith and Company.

Bosque, Fernando del
1903   Expedition into Texas of Fernando del Bosque, Standard-bearer of the King, Don Carlos II, in the Year 1675. Translated from an Old Unpublished Spanish Manuscript by Betty B. Brewster. *National Geographic Magazine* XIV(9/September):339–348. Washington. (Reprinted, ed. by George C. Martin: N. Brock, San Antonio, Tex., 1947.)

Bossu, Jean-Bernard
1771   Travels Through That Part of North America Formerly Called Louisiana. Translated from the French by John Reinhold Forster; Illustrated with Notes Relative Chiefly to Natural History. To Which Is Added by the Translator a Systematic Catalogue of All Known Plants of English North-America, or, A *Flora Americae Septentrionalis*. Together with an Abstract of the Most Useful and Necessary Articles Contained in Peter Loefling's Travels Through Spain and Cumana in South America. 2 vols. London: T. Davies.

————
1777   Nouveaux voyages dans l'Amérique septentrionale, contenant une collection de lettres écrites sur les lieux, par l'auteur à son ami, M. Douin... Amsterdam: Chez Changuion, à la Bourse.

————
1962   Travels in the Interior of North America, 1751–1762. Seymour Feiler, trans. and ed. [1st American ed.] *American Exploration and Travel Series* 35. Norman: University of Oklahoma Press.

————
1982   New Travels in North America (Nouveaux voyages dans l'Amérique septentrionale.) Translated, edited, and annotated by Samuel D. Dickinson. Natchitoches, La.: Northwestern State University Press.

Boszhardt, Robert F.
1994   Oneota Group Continuity at La Crosse: The Brice Prairie, Pammel Creek, and Valley View Phases. *The Wisconsin Archeologist* 75(3–4). Milwaukee.

Botari, Victor A.
1996   A Model of Community Centered Education; the Evolution of Post-secondary Education Programming on the Stoney Indian Reserve. (Ph.D. Dissertation in Education Curriculum and Instruction, University of Calgary, Calgary, Alta.)

Bottineau, J.B.
1900   Turtle Mountain Band of Chippewa Indians. Pp. 1–178 in *56th Congress. 1st Session. Senate Document No.* 444. Washington: U.S. Government Printing Office.

Bouchard, Rémi
1975   Chansonniers Manitobains. Tome 3: Hommage à Riel. Saint-Boniface, Man.: Les Éditions du Blé.

Boudinot, Elias
1816   A Star in the West; or, A Humble Attempt to Discover the Long Lost Ten Tribes of Israel.... Trenton, N.J.: D. Fenton, S. Hutchinson and J. Dunham.

Bougainville, Louis Antoine 1757, 1908 *see* Thwaites, Reuben G., ed.
1908

Boughter, Judith A.
1998   Betraying the Omaha Nation, 1790–1916. Norman: University of Oklahoma Press.

Bourgeault, Ron G.
1984   The Indian, the Métis and the Fur Trade: Class, Sexism and Racism in the Transition from "Communism" to Capitalism. *Studies in Political Economy* 12(Fall):45–80. Ottawa.

Bourgmont, Étienne de Véniard, sieur de 1988 *see* Norall, Frank, ed.
1988

Bourke, John Gregory
1891   On the Border with Crook. New York: Charles Scribner's Sons. (2d ed., 1892. Reprinted: Westernlore Press, Los Angeles, 1969; Greenwood Press, Westport, Conn., 1971; also, Rio Grande Press, Glorieta, N.Mex., 1971.)

————
1894   Capt. Bourke on the Sun-Dance. Pp. 464–467 in A Study of Siouan Cults, by James Owen Dorsey. Pp. 351–544 [pp. 545–553, Vol. Index] in *11th Annual Report of the Bureau of [American] Ethnology [for] 1889–'90*. Washington: Smithsonian Institution; U.S. Government Printing Office.

Bovay, Émile Henri
1976   Le Canada et les Suisses, 1604–1974. Préf. de F.T. Wahlen; Introd. par R. Ruffieux. Fribourg, Switzerland: Éditions universitaires.

Bowden, Henry W.
1981   American Indians and Christian Missions: Studies in Cultural Conflict. Chicago: University of Chicago Press. (Reprinted in 1985.)

Bowers, Alfred W.
1950   Mandan Social and Ceremonial Organization. Chicago: University of Chicago Press. (Reprinted in 1957, 1973; also, University of Idaho Press, Moscow, Idaho, 1991.)

————
1965   Hidatsa Social and Ceremonial Organization. *Bureau of American Ethnology Bulletin* 194. Washington: Smithsonian Institution; U.S. Government Printing Office. (Reprinted, with an Introduction by Douglas R. Parks: University of Nebraska Press, Lincoln, 1992.)

Bowman, Peter W.
1972   Weather in the West Central Plains and Its Significance in Archeology. *Newsletter of the Kansas Anthropological Association* 18(1–2):1–32. Topeka.

Boyd, Douglas K.
1995   Rethinking the Palo Duro Complex: Jornada Mogollon Influences in the Texas Southern Plains? Pp. 27–50 in Transactions of the 30th Regional Archeological Symposium for Southeastern New Mexico and Western Texas. El Paso, Tex.: El Paso Archaeological Society.

Boyd, James P.
1891   Recent Indian Wars, under the Lead of Sitting Bull, and Other Chiefs; With a Full Account of the Messiah Craze, and Ghost Dances. Philadelphia: Publishers Union.

Boyd, Maurice
1981–1983 Kiowa Voices. 2 vols. Vol.1: Ceremonial Dance, Ritual, and Song; Vol. 2: Myths, Legends, and Folktales. Linn Pauahty, Kiowa consultant; the Kiowa Historical and Research Society, consultants. Fort Worth, Tex.: Texas Christian University Press.

Boyd, Stephen G.
1885   Indian Local Names, with Their Interpretation. York, Penn.: [The Author.]

Bozell, John R.
1988   Changes in the Role of the Dog in Protohistoric-Historic Pawnee Culture. *Plains Anthropologist* 33(119):95–111.

Brackenridge, Henry Marie
1814   Views of Louisiana. Together with a Journal of a Voyage Up the Missouri River, in 1811. Pittsburgh, Pa.: Cramer, Spear and Eichbaum, Franklin Head Office. (Facsimile reprint: Quadrangle Books, Chicago, 1962.)

1815   Journal of a Voyage Up the River Missouri: Performed in Eighteen Hundred and Eleven. [2d ed. rev. and enl.; the 1st ed. was appended to Brackenridge's *Views of Louisiana,* 1814.] Baltimore, Md.: Coale and Maxwell, Pomeroy and Troy. (Reprinted in 1816; also in Vol. 6 [1904] of Early Western Travels, 1748–1846, Reuben G. Thwaites, ed. Arthur H. Clark, Cleveland, Ohio, 1904–1907; and, Kraus Reprint, Millwoood, N.Y., 1976.)

1817   Views of Louisiana: Containing Geographical, Statistical and Historical Notices of That Vast and Important Portion of America. Baltimore: Printed by Schaeffer and Maund.

1955   Exploring the Northern Plains, 1804–1876. Lloyd McFarling, ed. and illus. Caldwell, Idaho: The Caxton Printers.

_____ 1962 *see* 1814 (reprint info.)

Brackett, Albert G.
1877   The Sioux or Dakota Indians. Pp. 466–472 in *Annual Report of the Board of Regents of the Smithsonian Institution [...] for the Year 1876.* Washington: U.S. Government Printing Office.

Bradbury, Ellen, Eileen Flory, and Moira Harris 1976 *see* Peterson, Harold L., ed. 1976

Bradbury, John
1817   Travels in the Interior of America, in the Years 1809, 1810, and 1811; Including a Description of Upper Louisiana, Together with the States of Ohio, Kentucky, [...], with the Illinois and Western Territories; and Containing Remarks and Observations Useful to Persons Emigrating to Those Countries. Liverpool: Printed for the author, by Smith and Galway; London: published by Sherwood, Neely, and Jones. (Facsimile reprint: Readex Microprint, New York, 1966.)

1819   Travels in the Interior of America, in the Years 1809, 1810, and 1811; [etc.]. 2d ed. London: Sherwood, Neely, and Jones. (Reprinted in Vol. 5 [1904] of Early Western Travels, 1748–1846, Reuben G. Thwaites, ed. Arthur H. Clark, Cleveland, Ohio, 1904–1907; also, with a Foreword by Donald D. Jackson: University of Nebraska Press, Lincoln, 1986.)

Bradford, William
1819   [Letter to John C. Calhoun, dated 28 March 1819.] (Manuscript No. M221, Roll 80, Document 1819–B287, Letters Received, the Secretary of War, Regular Series, National Archives, Washington.)

Bradley, Charles C., Jr.
1972   After the Buffalo Days: An Account of the First Years of Reservation Life for Crow Indians, Based on Official Government Documents from 1880 to 1904 A.D. Vol.1: Civilizing the Crows. Crow Agency, Mont.: Crow Central Education Commission.

Bradley, Charles C., Jr., and Susanna R. Bradley
1974   From Individualism to Bureaucracy: Documents on the Crow Indians. (Manuscript in C.C. and S.R. Bradley's possession, Lodge Grass, Mont.)

Bradley, James H.
1896–1923 Journal of James H. Bradley. 4 Pts. *Contributions to the Historical Society of Montana* II [Pt. 1]:140–228, III [Pt. 2]:201–287, VIII [Pt. 3]:105–250, IX [Pt. 4]:29–351. Helena, Mont. (Title of each part varies. Pt. 1 reprinted under title: The March of the Montana Column: A Prelude to the Custer Disaster. Edgar I. Stewart, ed. University of Oklahoma Press, Norman, 1961. See also Bradley 1927.)

1927   The Journal of Lieutenant James H. Bradley; in the Vicinity of and Within the Custer Battlefield Area, Early Summer of 1876. Edited, and Illustrations supplied by Robert Bruce. [New York: U.S. Army, Recruiting Publicity Bureau.] (Extracted from: *United States Army Recruiting News;* see Bradley 1896–1923.)

Bradley, Lawrence E.
1973   Subsistence Strategy at a Late Archaic Site in South-Central Kansas. (M.A. Thesis in Anthropology, University of Kansas, Lawrence.)

Brain, Jeffrey P.
1985   Introduction: Update of De Soto Studies Since the United States De Soto Expedition Commission Report. Pp. xi–lxxii in Final Report of the United States De Soto Expedition Commission [1935]. John R. Swanton, ed. Washington: Smithsonian Institution Press.

1988   Tunica Archaeology. *Papers of the Peabody Museum of Archaeology and Ethnology, Harvard University* 78. Cambridge, Mass.

Brant, Charles S.
1949   The Cultural Position of the Kiowa-Apache. *Southwestern Journal of Anthropology* 5(1):56–61. Albuquerque.

1950   Peyotism among the Kiowa-Apache and Neighboring Tribes. *Southwestern Journal of Anthropology* 6(2):212–222. Albuquerque.

1951   The Kiowa Apache Indians: A Study in Ethnology and Acculturation. (Ph.D. Dissertation in Anthropology, Cornell University, Ithaca, N.Y.)

1953   Kiowa Apache Culture History: Some Further Observations. *Southwestern Journal of Anthropology* 9(2):195–202. Albuquerque.

_____, ed.
1969   Jim Whitewolf: The Life of a Kiowa Apache Indian. Edited with an Introduction and Epilogue by Charles S. Brant. New York: Dover Publications. (Reprinted in 1991.)

Braroe, Neils
1975   Indian and White: Self-image and Interaction in a Canadian Plains Community. Stanford, Calif.: Stanford University Press.

Brass, Eleanor
1987   I Walk in Two Worlds. Calgary, Alta.: Glenbow Museum.

Brasser, Theodore J.
1979   The Pedigree of the Hugging Bear Tipi in the Blackfoot Camp. *American Indian Art Magazine* 5(1):32–39. Scottsdale, Ariz.

1984   Backrest Banners among the Plains Cree and Plains Ojibwa. *American Indian Art Magazine* 10(1):56–63. Scottsdale, Ariz.

1985   In Search of Métis Art. Pp. 221–229 in The New Peoples: Being and Becoming Métis in North America. Jacqueline Peterson and Jennifer S.H. Brown, eds. *Manitoba Studies in Native History* 1. Winnipeg: The University of Manitoba Press; Lincoln: University of Nebraska Press.

1987   By the Power of Their Dreams: Artsitic Traditions of the Northern Plains. Pp. 93–131 in The Spirit Sings: Artistic *1105*

Traditions of Canada's First Peoples. Toronto: McClelland and Stewart [and the Glenbow Museum, Calgary, Alta.].

Braun, David P., and Stephen Plog
1982   Evolution of "Tribal" Social Networks: Theory and Prehistoric North American Evidence. *American Antiquity* 47(3):504–525.

Brave Bird, Mary, and Richard Erdoes
1993   Ohitika Woman. New York: Grove Press.

Bray, Edmund C., and Martha C. Bray, trans. and eds. 1976 *see* Nicollet, Joseph N. 1976

Bray, Kingsley M.
1994   Teton Sioux Population History, 1655–1881. *Nebraska History* 75(2):165–188. Lincoln.

———
1998   Crazy Horse and the End of the Great Sioux War. *Nebraska History* 79(3):94–115. Lincoln.

Bray, Martha C., ed. 1970 *see* Nicollet, Joseph N. 1970

Bray, Robert T.
1963   Southern Cult Motifs from the Utz Oneota Site, Saline County, Missouri. *The Missouri Archaeologist* 25(December):1–40. Columbia.

———
1991   The Utz Site: An Oneota Village in Central Missouri. *The Missouri Archaeologist* 52(December). Columbia.

Bray's Treaty Paylist
1877   Bray's Treaty Paylist. (Manuscript, Public Archives of Canada, Ottawa.)

Breternitz, David A.
1969   Radiocarbon Dates: Eastern Colorado. *Plains Anthropologist* 14(44, Pt. 1):113–124.

———, ed. and comp.
1971   Archaeological Investigations at the Wilbur Thomas Shelter, Carr, Colorado. *Southwestern Lore* 36(4):53–99. Albuquerque.

Breton, Adela C.
1920   The Stoney Indians. *Man: Journal of the Royal Anthropological Institute of Great Britain and Ireland* 20(5):65–67. London.

Bridgeman, M.L.
1902   [Letters to Commissioner of Indian Affairs, January 4 and 6, 1902.] (Manuscripts in Box 19, Fort Belknap Records, Records of the Bureau of Indian Affairs, Record Group 75, National Archives—Pacific Northwest Region, Seattle, Wash.)

Bridges, Katherine, and Winston De Ville, eds. and trans.
1967   Natchitoches and the Trail to the Rio Grande: Two Early Eighteenth Century Accounts by the Sieur Derbanne. *Louisiana History* 8(3):236–259. Baton Rouge.

Brightman, Robert
1993   Grateful Prey: Rock Cree Human-Animal Relationships. Berkeley: University of California Press.

Brink, Jack, and Stuart J. Baldwin
1988   The Highwood River Site: A Pelican Lake Phase Burial from the Alberta Plains. *Canadian Journal of Archaeology* 12:109–136. Ottawa.

Brink, Jack, and Bob Dawe
1989   Final Report of the 1985 and 1986 Field Season at Head-Smashed-In Buffalo Jump, Alberta. *Archaeological Survey of Alberta. Manuscript Series* 16. Edmonton, Alta.

Brink, Jack, and Maureen Rollans
1990   Thoughts on the Structure and Function of Drive Lane Systems at Communal Buffalo Jumps. Pp. 152–167 in Hunters of the Recent Past. Leslie B. Davis and Brian O.K. Reeves, eds. London: Unwin Hyman.

Brinkman, Lillie-Beth
1987   Tribal Judge Delays Ritual of Sun Dance. *The Daily Oklahoman*, June 6:3. [City ed.]

Brinton, Daniel Garrison
1891   The American Race: A Linguistic Classification and Ethnographic Description of the Native Tribes of North and South America. New York: N.D.C. Hodges.

Briscoe, James, and Roger Burkhalter
1986   Preliminary Report on Archaeological and Geomorphological Investigations at the Swift Horse Site, 34RM501 AR-03-03-06-098 Roger Mills County Oklahoma. *Anadarko Basin Museum of Natural History. Natural History Research Reports* 1. Elk City, Okla.

Brito, Silvester J.
1984   American Indian Political Participation: From Melting Pot to Cultural Pluralism. *American Indian Culture and Research Journal* 7(4):51–68. Los Angeles.

Britten, Thomas A.
1997   American Indians in World War I: At War and At Home. Albuquerque: University of New Mexico Press.

Brockington, Paul E., Jr., comp.
1982   Archaeological Investigation at El Dorado Lake, Butler County, Kansas (Phase III). Alfred E. Johnson, principal investigator. *University of Kansas. Museum of Anthropology. Project Report Series* 51. Lawrence.

Brodhead, John R.
1853–1887 Documents Relative to the Colonial History of the State of New York; Procured in Holland, England, and France, by John Romeyn Brodhead. Edited by Edmund B. O'Callaghan. With a General Introduction by the Agent. 15 vols. Albany, N.Y.: Weed, Parsons, Printers. (Reprinted: AMS Press, New York, 1969.)

Brody, Hugh
1971   Indians on Skid Row. Ottawa: Northern Science Research Group, Department of Indian Affairs and Northern Development.

Brody, Jacob J.
1971   Indian Painters and White Patrons. Albuquerque: University of New Mexico Press.

Brogan, William T.
1981   The Cuesta Phase: Settlement Pattern Study. *Kansas State Historical Society. Anthropological Series* 9. Topeka.

Brokenleg, Martin, and Herbert T. Hoover
1993   Yanktonai Sioux Water Colors: Cultural Remembrances of John Saul. Sioux Falls, S.Dak.: The Center for Western Studies, Augustana College.

Bromert, Roger
1978   The Sioux and the Indian-CCC. *South Dakota History* 8(4):340–356. Pierre.

———
1980   The Sioux and the Indian New Deal, 1933–1944. (Ph.D. Dissertation in History, University of Toledo, Ohio.)

Bronson, Edgar Beecher
1911   Reminiscences of a Ranchman. Rev. ed. Chicago: A.C. McClurg. (Reprinted: University of Nebraska Press, Lincoln, 1962.)

Brooks, George P., ed.
1965   George C. Sibley's Journal of a Trip to the Salines in 1811. *Missouri Historical Society Bulletin* 21(3):167–207. St. Louis.

Brooks, Robert L.
1983   Community Structure and Settlement Distributions in the Washita River Phase. (Paper presented at the 41st Annual Plains Conference Rapid City, S.Dak.)

1985   Excavations at the Manwell Site: A Transitional Plains Woodland-Plains Village Settlement on the Southern Periphery of the Flint Hills. (Paper presented at the 7th Annual Flint Hills Conference, Norman, Okla.)

1987   The Arthur Site: Settlement and Subsistence Structure at a Washita River Phase Village. *Oklahoma Archaeological Survey. Studies in Oklahoma's Past* 15. Norman.

1994   Warfare on the Southern Plains. Pp. 317–323 in Skeletal Biology in the Great Plains: Migration, Warfare, Health, and Subsistence. Douglas W. Owsley and Richard L. Jantz, eds. Washington, D.C.: Smithsonian Institution.

Brooks, Robert L., Michael C. Moore, and Douglas W. Owsley
1992   New Smith, 34RM400: A Plains Village Mortuary Site in Western Oklahoma. *Plains Anthropologist* 37(138):59–78.

Brosowske, S.D., and L.C. Bement
1998   Plains Interaction during the Late Prehistoric: A View From Some New Sites in the Oklahoma Panhandle. (Paper presented at the 56th Annual Plains Conference, Bismarck, N.Dak.)

Bross, Michael G.
1962   The Kiowa-Apache Body Concept in Relation to Health. (M.A. Thesis in Anthropology, University of Oklahoma, Norman. Published in: *University of Oklahoma. Papers in Anthropology* 12(2):1–80. Norman, 1971.)

Brotherton, Ethel Crawfish
1937   [Interview.] (Manuscript, *Indian and Pioneer History* 66:394–395, in Newspapers/Archives and Manuscripts Division, Oklahoma Historical Society, Oklahoma City.)

Brower, Jacob V.
1897   The Missouri River and Its Utmost Source. St. Paul, Minn: Pioneer Press.

1898   Quivira. *Memoirs of Explorations in the Basin of the Mississippi* 1. St. Paul, Minn.: H. L. Collins.

1899   Harachey. *Memoirs of Explorations in the Basin of the Mississippi* 2. St. Paul, Minn.

1904   Mandan. *Memoirs of Explorations in the Basin of the Mississippi* 8. St. Paul, Minn.

Brown, David O.
1998   Late Holocene Climates of North-Central Texas. *Plains Anthropologist* 43(164):157–172.

Brown, Dee Alexander
1962   Fort Phil Kearney: An American Saga. New York: G.P. Putnam's Sons.

1970   Bury My Heart at Wounded Knee: An Indian History of the American West. New York: Holt, Rinehart and Winston. (Several reprints, incl.: 1972, 1989, 1991.)

Brown, Donald N.
1972–1988 [Ponca Fieldnotes.] (Manuscripts in D.N. Brown's possession.)

1979   The Ponca Population. (Paper presented at the Annual Meeting of the American Anthropological Association, Cincinnati, Ohio, Nov. 27–Dec. 1, 1979.)

1979–1989 [Ethnographic Fieldnotes on the Ponca of Oklahoma.] (Manuscripts in D.N. Brown's possession.)

1994   Southern Ponca. Pp. 460–461 in Native America in the Twentieth Century: An Encyclopedia. Mary B. Davis, ed. *Garland Refrence Library of Social Science* 452. New York: Garland.

Brown, Donald N., and Kenneth H. McKinley
1979   Ponca Adult Education Survey: Prepared for Ponca Tribal Business Committee. Ponca City, Okla.: The Committee.

Brown, George, and Ron Maguire, comps.
1979   Indian Treaties in Historical Perspective. Ottawa: Department of Indian and Northern Affairs.

Brown, James A.
1983   What Kind of Economy Did the Oneota Have? Pp. 107–112 in Oneota Studies. Guy E. Gibbon, ed. *University of Minnesota. Publications in Anthropology* 1. Minneapolis. (Title page has 1982 imprint date.)

1990   Ethnohistoric Connections. Pp. 155–160 in At the Edge of Prehistory: Huber Phase Archeology in the Chicago Area. James A. Brown and Patricia J. O'Brien, eds. Kampsville, Ill.: Illinois Department of Transportation, Center for American Archeology.

Brown, James A., Robert E. Bell, and Don G. Wyckoff
1978   Caddoan Settlement Patterns in the Arkansas River Drainage. Pp. 169–200 in Mississippian Settlement Patterns. Bruce D. Smith, ed. New York: Academic Press.

Brown, Jennifer S.H.
1980   Strangers in Blood: Fur Trade Company Families in Indian Country. Vancouver: University of British Columbia Press.

1980a   Linguistic Solitudes and Changing Social Categories. Pp. 147–159 in Old Trails and New Directions. C.M. Judd and A.J. Ray, eds. Toronto: University of Toronto Press.

1982   Children of the Early Fur Trades. Pp. 44–68 in Childhood and Family in Canadian History. Joy Parr, ed. Toronto: McClelland and Stewart.

1983   Women as Centre and Symbol in the Emergence of Métis Communities. Pp. 39–46 in The Métis Since 1870. Antoine S. Lussier, guest ed. *The Canadian Journal of Native Studies* 3(1)[Special issue]. Brandon, Man.

1985   Diverging Identities: The Presbyterian Métis of St. Gabriel Street, Montreal. Pp. 195–206 in The New Peoples: Being and Becoming Métis in North America. Jacqueline Peterson and Jennifer S.H. Brown, eds. *Manitoba Studies in Native History* 1. Winnipeg: University of Manitoba Press; Lincoln: University of Nebraska Press.

1987   The Métis: Genesis and Rebirth. Pp. 136–147 in Native People, Native Lands. Bruce Allen Cox, ed. *Library Series* 12. Ottawa: Carleton University Press.

1988   Métis. Pp. 1343–1346 in Canadian Encyclopedia. Mel Hurtig, ed. Edmonton, Alta.: Hurtig Publishers.

1988a   Cameron, Duncan. Pp. 137–139 in Dictionary of Canadian Biography, Vol.VII: 1836 to 1850. Toronto: University of Toronto Press.

Brown, Jennifer S.H., and Robert Brightman
1988   "The Orders of the Dreamed": George Nelson on Cree and Northern Ojibwa Religion and Myth, 1823. Winnipeg: University of Manitoba Press.

Brown, Joseph Epes
1953   The Sacred Pipe: Black Elk's Account of the Seven Sacred Rites of the Oglala Sioux. New York: Penguin Books. (Reprinted: University of Oklahoma Press, Norman, 1971.)

1978   Sun Dance: Sacrifice — Renewal — Identity. *Parabola* 3(2):12–15. Mt. Kisco, N.Y.: Tamarack Press. (Reprinted: pp. 101–105 in The Spiritual Legacy of the American Indian, by Joseph Epes Brown. Crossroad, New York, 1982.)

1984   The Persistence of Essential Values among North American Plains Indians. *Interculture* 17(4):26–33. Montréal.   *1107*

1987   Sun Dance. Pp. 143–147 in Vol. 14 of The Encyclopedia of Religion. Mircea Eliade, ed. New York: Macmillan.

Brown, Joseph R.
1867   [Letter to Chairman, March 11, 1867, Committee of Indian Affairs, United States Senate.] Washington: United State Senate, Committee of Indian Affiars. [Joseph R. Brown and Samuel J. Brown Papers, Manuscript A.B878, Minnesota Historical Society, St. Paul, Minn.]

Brown, Kenneth L.
1981   Excavations at the Sperry Site, 23JA85. Pp. 190–283 in Prehistoric Cultural Resources within the Right-of-Way of the Proposed Little Blue River Channel, Jackson County, Missouri. Kenneth L. Brown and Robert J. Ziegler, comps. Kansas City: Department of the Army, Corps of Engineers.

1985   Pomona: A Plains Village Variant in Eastern Kansas and Western Missouri. 2 vols. (Ph.D. Dissertation in Anthropology, University of Kansas, Lawrence.)

Brown, Kenneth L., and Marie E. Brown
1986   The Archaic, Ceramic and Historic Periods. Pp. 34–311 in Kansas Archaeological Preservation Plan. Kenneth L. Brown and Alan H. Simmons, eds. (Manuscript on file at Kansas State Historical Society, Topeka.)

Brown, Kenneth L., and Alan H. Simmons, eds.
1987   Kansas Prehistoric Archaeological Preservation Plan. (Report prepared for the National Park Service, Washington.) Lawrence, Kans.: Office of Archaeological Research, Museum of Anthropology and Center for Public Affairs, University of Kansas.

Brown, Lionel A.
1966   Temporal and Spatial Order in the Central Plains. *Plains Anthropologist* 11(34):294–301.

1967   Pony Creek Archeology. *Smithsonian Institution. River Basin Surveys. Publications in Salvage Archeology* 5. Washington: Government Printing Office.

1968   The Gavins Point Site (39YK203): An Analysis of Surface Artifacts. *Plains Anthropologist* 13(40):118–127.

Brown, Marie E.
1982   Site 14BU57. Pp. 259–304 in Archaeological Investigation at El Dorado Lake, Butler County, Kansas (Phase III). Paul E. Brookington, Jr., ed. *University of Kansas. Museum of Anthropology. Project Report Series* 51. Lawrence, Kanas.

Brown, Mark H.
1961   Plainsmen of the Yellowstone. Lincoln: University of Nebraska Press.

Brown, Mark H., and William R. Felton
1955   The Frontier Years: Laton A. Huffman, Photographer of the Plains. New York: Bramhall House.

1966   Before Barbed Wire: Laton A. Huffman, Photographer on Horseback. New York: Bramhall House.

Brown, Randall J.
1982   Hobbema Sun Dance of 1923. *Alberta History* 30(3):1–8. Calgary.

Brown, Samuel R., ed.
1817   The Western Gazetteer; or, Emigrant's Directory; Containing a Geographical Description of the Western States and Territories, [etc.]. Auburn, N.Y.: H.C. Southwick.

Brown, Vinson
1974   Voices of Earth and Sky: the Vision Life of the Native Americans and Their Culture Heroes. Harrisburg, Penn.: Stackpole Books.

Brown, William R., Jr.
1989   The Art of Native American Music. Pp. 32–42 in Songs of Indian Territory: Native American Music Traditions of Oklahoma. Willie Smyth, ed. Oklahoma City, Okla.: Center of the American Indian. (Book and Cassette.)

Browning, Thomas B.
1888   Chart of Elocutionary Drill. *Proceedings of the Canadian Institute* 24(6/8):40. Toronto.

Brownstone, Arni
1993   War Paint: Blackfoot and Sarcee Painted Buffalo Robes in the Royal Ontario Museum. Toronto: Royal Ontario Museum.

1996   Tradition Embroidered in Glass. *Rotunda: the Magazine of the Royal Ontario Museum* 29(1):11–21. Toronto.

Bruce, Robert J.
1932   The Fighting Norths and Pawnee Scouts: Narratives and Reminiscences of Military Service on the Old Frontier. Lincoln: Nebraska State Historical Society.

Brugge, David M.
1965   Some Plains Indians in the Church Records of New Mexico. *Plains Anthropologist* 10(29):181–189.

Brumley, John H.
1975   The Cactus Flower Sites in Southeastern Alberta: 1972–1974 Excavations. *Canada. National Museum of Man. Mercury Series. Archaeological Survey Paper* 46. Ottawa.

1976   Ramillies: A Late Prehistoric Bison Kill and Campsite in Southeastern Alberta, Canada. *Canada. National Museum of Man. Mercury Series. Archaeological Survey Paper* 55. Ottawa.

1981   Result of Salvage Excavations at the Southridge Site, EaOq-17. (Manuscript, Permit 79-151, Vol. 2, Provincial Museum of Alberta, Edmonton, Alta.)

1983   Interpretive Model for Stone Circles and Stone Circle Sites within Southeastern Alberta. Pp. 171–191 in From Microcosm to Macrocosm: Advances in Tipi Ring Investigation and Interpretation. Leslie B. Davis, ed. *Plains Anthropologist* 28(102, pt. 2) *Memoir* 19. Lincoln.

Brumley, John H., and Barry J. Dau
1988   Historical Resource Investigations with the Forty Mile Coulee Reservoir. *Archaeological Survey of Alberta. Manuscript Series* 13. Edmonton, Alta.: Alberta Environment; Alberta Culture and Multiculturalism.

Brumley, John H., and Carol A. Rushworth
1983   A Summary and Appraisal of Alberta Radiocarbon Dates. Pp. 142–160 in Archaeology in Alberta 1982. David Burley, ed. *Archaeological Survey of Alberta. Occasional Paper* 21. Edmonton, Alta.

Bruner, Edward M.
1953   Assimilation among Fort Berthold Indians. *The American Indian* 6(4):21–29. New York.

1955   Two Processes of Change in Mandan-Hidatsa Kinship Terminology. *American Anthropologist*, n.s. 57(4):840–850.

1956   Primary Group Experience and the Processes of Acculturation. *American Anthropologist*, n.s. 58(4):605–623.

1956a   Cultural Transmission and Cultural Change. *Southwestern Journal of Anthropology* 12(2):191–199. Albuquerque.

1961   Mandan. Pp. 187–277 in Perspectives in American Indian Culture Change. Edward H. Spicer, ed. Chicago. University of Chicago Press.

Bruseth, James E., Daniel E. McGregor, and William A. Martin
1987   Hunter-Gatherers of the Prairie Margin: Summary of the Prehistoric Archaeological Record. Pp. 229–256 in Hunter Gatherer Adaptation along the Prairie Margin: Site Excavations and Synthesis of Prehistoric Archaeology. Daniel E. McGregor and James E. Bruseth, eds. *Southern Methodist University. Richland Creek Technical Series* 3. Dallas, Tex.

Bryan, Alan L.
1970   An Alternative Hypothesis for the Origin of the Name Blackfoot. *Plains Anthropologist* 15(50/1):305–306.

Bryan, Kirk
1950   Flint Quarries: The Sources of Tools and, at the Same Time, the Factories of the American Indian; with a Consideration of the Theory of the "Blank" and Some of the Techniques of Flint Utilization. *Harvard University. Papers of the Peabody Museum of American Archaeology and Ethnology* 17(3). Cambridge, Mass.

Bryan, Liz
1991   The Buffalo People: Prehistoric Archaeology on the Canadian Plains. Edmonton, Alta.: University of Alberta Press.

Bryan, William L., Jr.
1985   Montana's Indians: Yesterday and Today. Photography by Michael Crummett. *Montana Geographic Series* 11. Helena, Mont.: Montana Magazine.

Bryde, John F. (S.J.)
1966   The Sioux Indian Student: A Study of Scholastic Failure and Personality Conflict. Pine Ridge, S.Dak.: Rev. John Francis Bryde, S.J.

1971   Modern Indian Psychology. Rev. ed. Vermillion, S.Dak.: Institute of Indian Studies, University of South Dakota.

Bryson, Reid A., and F. Kenneth Hare
1974   The Climates of North America. Pp. 1–47 in Climates of North America. Reid A. Bryson and F. Kenneth Hare, eds. *World Survey of Climatology* 11. Amsterdam and New York: Elsevier Scientific Publishing Company.

Bryson, Reid A., and Wayne M. Wendland
1967   Tentative Climatic Patterns for Some Late Glacial and Postglacial Episodes in Central North America. Pp. 271–298 in Life, Land and Water. *Proceedings of the 1966 Conference on Environmental Studies of the Glacial Lake Region.* William J. Mayer-Oakes, ed. Winnipeg: University of Manitoba Press.

Bryson, Reid A., David A. Baerreis, and Wayne M. Wendland
1970   The Character of Late-Glacial and Post-Glacial Climatic Changes. Pp. 53–74 in Pleistocene and Recent Environments of the Central Great Plains. Wakefield Dort, Jr., and J. Knox Jones, Jr., eds. *University of Kansas. Department of Geology. Special Publication* 3. Lawrence: University Press of Kansas.

Bucca, Salvador, and Alexander Lesser
1969   Kitsai Phonology and Morphophonemics. *International Journal of Linguistics* 35(1, Pt. 1):7–19. Chicago.

Buchanan, James
1824   Sketches of the History, Manners, and Customs of the North American Indians with a Plan for Their Melioration. London: Printed for Black, Young, and Young. (American ed., 2 vols.: Wm. Borradaile, New York, 1824.).

Buchler, Ira R.
1964   A Formal Theory of Kinship Reckoning. (Ph.D. Dissertation in Anthropology, University of Pittsburgh, Pittsburgh, Penn.)

Buchler, Ira R., and Henry A. Sibley
1968   Kinship and Social Organization: An Introduction to Theory and Method. New York: MacMillan.

Buchner, Anthony P.
1979   The 1978 Caribou Lake Project, Including a Summary of the Prehistory of East-Central Manitoba. *Manitoba Historic Resources Branch. Papers in Manitoba Archaeology. Final Report* 8. Winnipeg.

1980   Cultural Responses to Altithermal (Atlantic) Climate along the Eastern Margins of the North American Grasslands 5500 to 3000 B.C. *Canada. National Museum of Man. Mercury Series. Archaeological Survey Paper* 97. Ottawa.

Buchner, Anthony P., and L. Pujo
1977   A Preliminary Report on the Whitemouth Falls Site, Feature No. 10–76: An Archaic Burial from Southeastern Manitoba. *Archae-Facts: The Journal of the Archaeological Society of South-Western Manitoba* 4(3):26–30. Brandon, Man.

Buck, Arthur D., Jr.
1959   The Custer Focus of the Southern Plains. *Bulletin of the Oklahoma Anthropological Society* 7:41–31. Oklahoma City.

Buckles, William G.
1964   An Analysis of Primitive Rock Art at Medicine Creek Cave, Wyoming, and Its Cultural and Chronological Relationships to the Prehistory of the Plains. (M.A. Thesis in Anthropology, University of Colorado, Boulder.)

Buckley, Helen
1992   From Wooden Ploughs to Welfare: Why Indian Policy Failed in the Prairie Provinces. *McGill-Queen's Native and Northern Series* 7. Montreal and Buffalo: McGill-Queen's University Press. (Reprinted in 1993.)

Bucko, Raymond A.
1998   The Lakota Ritual of the Sweat Lodge: History and Contemporary Practice. *Studies in the Anthropology of North American Indians.* Raymond J. DeMallie and Douglas R. Parks, eds. Lincoln: University of Nebraska Press, in cooperation with the American Indian Studies Research Institute, Indiana University, Bloomington.

Buckstaff, Ralph N.
1927   Stars and Constellations of a Pawnee Sky Map. *American Anthropologist,* n.s. 29(2):279–285.

Bucsis, Wiliam
1968   Notes on Some Assiniboine Indian Religious Beliefs and Ceremonies. *Na'pāo: A Saskatchewan Anthropology Journal* 1(1):17–22. Saskatoon, Sask.

Buechel, Eugene (S.J.)
[1910–1954]   [Lakota-English Dictionary.] Pine Ridge, S.Dak.: Holy Rosary Mission.

1924   Wowapi Wakan Wicwoyake Yutecelapi kin: Bible History in the Language of the Teton Sioux Indians. New York: Benziger Brothers.

1927   [Sursum corda]. Lakota Wocekiye na 'Olowan Wowapi. Sioux Indian Prayer and Hymn Book. St. Louis, Mo.: Central Bureau of the Catholic Central Verein of America.

1939   A Grammar of Lakota. The Language of the Teton Sioux Indians. (St. Francis, S.Dak.: St. Francis Mission.) St. Louis, Mo.: John S. Swift.

1970   A Dictionary of the Teton Dakota Sioux Language: Lakota-English, English-Lakota, with Considerations Given to Yankton and Santee. Paul Manhart, S.J., ed. Pine Ridge, S.Dak.: Holy Rosary Mission, Red Cloud Indian School; Vermillion, S.Dak.: University of South Dakota.

1978   Lakota Tales and Texts. Paul Manhart, S.J., ed. Pine Ridge, S.Dak.: Red Cloud Indian School.

1983   A Dictionary — Oie Wowapi Wan — of Teton Sioux. Paul

Manhart, S.J., ed. Pine Ridge, S.Dak.: Red Cloud Indian School, Holy Rosary Mission.

1998   Lakota Tales and Texts. Collected by Eugene Buechel in Lakota; Paul Manhart, S.J., trans.; Black and White Art by Anna Manhart; Color Cover Art by Daniel Long Soldier. 2 vols. Chamberlain, S.Dak.: The Tipi Press.

Buecker, Thomas R.
1994   The Crazy Horse Surrender Ledger: A New Source for Red Cloud Agency History. *Nebraska History* 75(2):191–194. Lincoln.

Buecker, Thomas R., and R. Eli Paul, eds.
1994   The Crazy Horse Surrender Ledger. Foreword by Harry H. Anderson. Lincoln: Nebraska State Historical Society.

Buehler, Kent J.
1997   Where's the Cliff? Late Archaic Bison Kills in the Southern Plains. Pp. 135–143 in Southern Plains Bison Procurement and Utilization from Paleoindian to Historic: Proceedings of a Symposium from the 52nd Plains Anthropological Conference, Lubbock, Texas. Leland C. Bement and Kent J. Buehler, eds. *Plains Anthropologist* 42(159); *Memoir* 29. Lincoln.

Bullchild, Percy
1985   The Sun Came Down: The History of the World As My Blackfeet Elders Told It. San Francisco: Harper and Row.

Bunnell, Glenn E.
1958   No Night, No Death, No Winter: A Picture Story of What May Well Be the Last Medicine Lodge Ceremony of the Great Blackfeet Tribe. *Montana: The Magazine of Western History* 8(2):21–25. Helena.

Bureau of Indian Affairs
1883   [Report of Inspector Benedict to the Secretary of the Interior, dated Guilford, Kansas, Jan. 13th, on the Condition of the Kansa Indians and the Kaw Agency.] (Microfilm M1070, Roll 33, Frames 722–729, Records of the Bureau of Indian Affairs, Record Group 75, National Archives, Washington.)

1884   [Report of Inspector Benedict to the Secretary of the Interior, dated Osage Agency, Indian Territory, May 16th, Concerning the Osage and Kaw Agencies.] (Microfilm M1070, Roll 33, Frames 876–892, Records of the Bureau of Indian Affairs, Record Group 75, National Archives, Washington.)

1887   [Synopsis of Report of Inspector Gardner, dated Osage Agency, July 16th, 1887, relative to the Kaw Agency.] (Microfilm M1070, Roll 33, Frames 1120–1139, Records of the Bureau of Indian Affairs, Record Group 75, National Archives, Washington.)

1920   [Report for the Kaw Sub-Agency, prepared by J.W. Clendening.] (Microfilm M1011, Roll 100, Frames 0140–0152, Records of the Bureau of Indian Affairs, Record Group 75, National Archives, Washington.)

1922   [Annual Report on the Kaw Indian Agency, Prepared by J.W. Clendening.] (Microfilm M1011, Roll 100, Frames 0865–0878, Records of the Bureau of Indian Affairs, Record Group 75, National Archives, Washington.)

1934   [Statistical Report for the Kaw Tribe, submitted to the Commissioner of Indian Affairs, by P.W. Danielson, Superintendent, Pawnee Agency, Okla., dated June 22 and Sept. 27, 1934.] (Manuscript M1011, Roll 101, Frames 982–1007, Records of the Bureau of Indian Affairs, Record Group 75, National Archives, Washington.)

1934a   [Minutes of the Plains Congress. Rapid City Indian School,

Rapid City, S.Dak. March 2–5, 1934.] Lawrence, Kans.: Haskell Institute.

1939   Statistical Supplement to the Annual Report of the Commissioner of Indian Affairs, for the Fiscal Year Ended June 30, 1939. Washington: U.S. Department of the Interior, U.S. Indian Service.

1945   Statistical Supplement to the Annual Report of the Commissioner of Indian Affairs, for the Fiscal Year Ended June 30, 1945. Washington: U.S. Department of the Interior, U.S. Indian Service.

1953   The Osage People and Their Trust Property: A Field Report. Pawhuska, Okla.: Bureau of Indian Affairs, Osage Agency.

1961   United States Indian Population and Land, 1960–1961. Washington: U.S. Department of the Interior, Bureau of Indian Affairs.

1967   [Omaha Tribe: Report of the Superintendent of Winnebago Agency, Nebraska, to the Bureau of Indian Affairs Central Office, Washington.] (Typescript.)

1968   Crow Cattle Ranching Operations. *Missouri River Basin Investigation Project Reports* 187. Billings, Mont.: Bureau of Indian Affairs, Crow Agency.

1972   [American Indian Population Statistics.] Washington: U.S. Department of the Interior, Bureau of Indian Affairs.

1974   Aberdeen Area Statistical Data. Aberdeen, S.Dak.: Bureau of Indian Affairs, Aberdeen Area Office.

1977–1987 [Labor Force Participation Statistics. Mimeographs.] Washington: U.S. Department of the Interior, Bureau of Indian Affairs.

1978   American Indian Tribes of Montana and Wyoming. *Bureau of Indian Affairs. Planning Support Group. Report* 262. Billings, Mont.: Bureau of Indian Affairs.

1983   Local Estimates of Resident Indian Population and Labor Force Status: January 1983. Washington: U.S. Department of the Interior, Bureau of Indian Affairs.

1985   Local Estimates of Resident Indian Population and Labor Force Status: January 1985 [i.e.] September 1984, DOI. Washington: U.S. Department of the Interior, Bureau of Indian Affairs.

1985a   [People/Employment Report.] Billings, Mont.: Bureau of Indian Affairs.

1985b   Branch of Acknowledgment and Research: Status of Petitions for Federal Acknowledgment, 1985. Washington: U.S. Department of the Interior, Bureau of Indian Affairs, Branch of Acknowledgment and Research.

1987   Indian Service Population and Labor Force Estimates, January 1987. Washington: U.S. Department of the Interior, Bureau of Indian Affairs.

1989   Indian Service Population and Labor Force Estimates, January 1989. Washington: U.S. Department of the Interior, Bureau of Indian Affairs, Office of Financial Management.

1991   Indian Service Population and Labor Force Estimates: Local Estimates of Resident Indian Population and Labor Force Status, January 1991. Washington: U.S. Department of the Interior, Bureau of Indian Affairs.

1992   *Indian News* 16(8). Washington: U.S Department of the Interior, Bureau of Indian Affairs.

1994   [Draft: Enrollment, Reservpop., Census80, ICWANO.] (Printout of comparative population and enrollment figures, Office of Tribal Enrollment/Tribal Relations, Bureau of Indian Affairs; Lathel F. Duffield, Ph.D., Branch Chief, Washington.)

1996   Indian Service Population and Labor Force Report for 1996. Washington: U.S. Department of the Interior, Bureau of Indian Affairs.

Bureau of Indian Affairs. Anadarko Agency
1938   [Letter to M.J. Pickering, dated Kiowa Agency, Anadarko, Okla., April 22, 1938, re: National Folk Festival.] (Manuscript in Decimal File .072, Fiestas and Festivals, 1936–1939, Anadarko Area Office: General Correspondence; Records of the Bureau of Indian Affairs, Record Group 75, National Archives, Fort Worth, Tex.)

Bureau of Indian Affairs. Cheyenne-Arapaho Agency
1986   [Cheyenne-Arapaho Lands Records.] Concho, Okla.: Bureau of Indian Affairs, Cheyenne-Arapaho Agency.

Bureau of Indian Affairs. Crow Agency
1997   Natural Resource Information System - Inventory and Production Report: Trust Lands on Crow Reservation. (Report No. 55-38x, Bureau of Indian Affairs, Crow Indian Agency, Crow Agency, Mont.)

Bureau of Indian Affairs. Crow Agency. Land Services Office
1998   LST98 [Land Status] Area Report. (Computer printout concerning Surface Land Ownership on Crow Reservation [November 1997 data], Bureau of Indian Affairs, Crow Indian Agency, Crow Agency, Mont.)

Bureau of Indian Affairs. Kiowa Agency
1900   Census File: Kiowa Agency. (Manuscript [copy] in Oklahoma Historical Society, Norman.)

Bureau of the Census see U.S. Bureau of the Census

Burke, Charles H.
1922   [Letter to John A. Buntin, dated December 12, 1922.] (Manuscript, File 067 in Kiowa Agency Records, Records of the Bureau of Indian Affairs, Record Group 75, Fort Worth Records Center, National Archives, Fort Worth, Tex.)

1922a   [Letter to All Superintendents, dated Washington, D.C., June 12, 1922, re: July 4th Celebrations, Dances, and Powwows.] (Manuscript in Indian Archives Division, Pawnee Celebrations, Oklahoma Historical Society, Oklahoma City.)

Burke, Christina E.
2000   Collecting Lakota Histories: Winter Count Pictographs and Texts in the National Anthropological Archives. *American Indian Art Magazine* 26(1):82–92. Scottsdale, Ariz.

Burley, David V., Gayel A. Horsfall, and John D. Brandon
1992   Structural Considerations of Métis Ethnicity: An Archaeological, Architectural, and Historical Study. Vermillion, S.Dak.: University of South Dakota Press.

Burlin, Natalie Curtis, ed.
1907   The Indians' Book: An Offering by the American Indians of Indian Lore, Musical and Narrative, to Form a Record of the Songs and Legends of Their Race. Illustrations from Photographs and from Original Drawings by Indians. New York: Harper and Brothers. (Reprinted in 1935.)

Burnaby, Barbara
1980   Languages and Their Roles in Educating Native Children. Toronto: Ontario Institute for Studies in Education.

Burnet, David G.
1851   The Comanches and Other Tribes of Texas. Pp. 229–241 in Vol. 1 of Information Respecting the History, Condition and Prospects of the Indian Tribes of the United States. Henry Rowe Schoolcraft, comp. and ed. Seth Eastman, illus. 6 vols. Philadelphia: Lippincott, Grambo.

Burnette, Robert
1971   The Tortured Americans. Englewood Cliffs, N.J.: Prentice-Hall.

1974   The Road to Wounded Knee. New York: Bantam Books.

Burnham, Philip
2000   Indian Country, God's Country: Native Americans and the National Parks. Washington, D.C., [and] Covelo, Calif.: Island Press.

Burns, Louis F.
1984   Osage Indian Bands and Clans. Fallbrook, Calif.: Ciga Press.

Burpee, Lawrence J., ed. 1907 *see* Hendry, Anthony 1907

_____, ed. 1908 *see* Cocking, Matthew 1908

_____, ed. 1927 *see* La Vérendrye, Pierre Gaultier de Varennes, Sieur de 1927

Burt, Larry W.
1986   Roots of the Native American Urban Experience: Relocation Policy in the 1950s. *American Indian Quarterly* 10(2):85–99. Hurst, Tex.

1987   Nowhere Left to Go: Montana's Crees, Métis, and Chippewas and the Creation of the Rocky Boy Reservation. *Great Plains Quarterly* 7(3):195–209. Lincoln, Nebr.

1992   Western Tribes and Balance Sheets: Business Development Programs in the 1960's and 1970's. *Western Historical Quarterly* 23(4):475–495. Logan, Utah.

Burton, Richard F.
1861   The City of the Saints and Across the Rocky Mountains to California. London: Longman, Green, Longman, and Roberts. (American ed.: Harper and Bros., New York, 1862. Reprinted, Fawn M. Brodie, ed.: Alfred A. Knopf, New York, 1963; AMS Press, New York, 1971; also, with a Foreword, Photographs, and a Brief Bibliography by Baker H. Morrow: University Press of Colorado, Niwot, Colo., 1990.)

Buschmann, Johann C.E.
1859   Die Spuren der aztekischen Sprache im nördlichen Mexico und höheren amerikanischen Norden. *Abhanlungen der Königlichen Akademie der Wissenschaften zu Berlin, Supplemental vol.* 2. Berlin.

Bush, Alfred L., and Lee Clark Mitchell
1994   The Photograph and the American Indian. Princeton, N.J.: Princeton University Press.

Bushnell, David I., Jr.
1909   The Various Uses of Buffalo Hair by the North American Indians. *American Anthropologist*, n.s. 11(3):401–425.

1922   Villages of the Algonquian, Siouan, and Caddoan Tribes West of the Mississippi. *Bureau of American Ethnology Bulletin* 77. Washington: Smithsonian Institution; U.S. Government Printing Office. (Reprinted: Scholarly Press, St. Clair Shores, Mich., 1976.)

1927   Burials of the Algonquian, Siouan, and Caddoan Tribes West of the Mississippi. *Bureau of American Ethnology Bulletin* 83. Washington: Smithsonian Institution; U.S. Government Printing Office.

Bushotter, George
1887–1888 [Lakota Texts by George Bushotter; interlinear translations *1111*

by James Owen Dorsey, aided by George Bushotter and
John Bruyier.] (Manuscript No. 4800/103(1–3), Dorsey
Papers, National Anthropological Archives, Smithsonian
Institution, Washington.)

1894   A Dakota's Account of the Sun Dance. Pp. 450–464 in A
           Study of Siouan Cults, by James Owen Dorsey. Pp. 361–
           544 [pp. 545–553, Vol. Index] in *11th Annual Report of the
           Bureau of [American] Ethnology [for] 1889–'90.* Wash-
           ington: Smithsonian Institution; U.S. Government Printing
           Office.

Butcher, H.B., A.A. Singer, and John Z. Leyendecker
1867   [Comanche Vocabulary, dated Laredo, Texas, April 23,
           1867.] (Manuscript No. 767, National Anthropological Ar-
           chives, Smithsonian Institution, Washington.)

Butler, George 1853 *see* ARCIA 1849–

Butler, Pierce M.
1846   [Letter to William Medill, dated March 4, 1846.] (Micro-
           film Publication M234, Roll 444, Frames 48–50 in Office
           of Indian Affairs, Letter Received, National Archives,
           Washington.)

Butler, Pierce M., and M.G. Lewis
1846   [Report to the Commissioner of Indian Affairs, dated Wash-
           ington City, August 8, 1846.] (Manuscript, Microfilm T-
           494, Roll 4, Frames 260–277, Documents Relating to the
           Negotiation of Ratified and Unratified Treaties with Vari-
           ous Tribes of Indians, 1801–1869, National Archives,
           Washington.)

Butler, William B.
1980   Comments on a Research Design for the State Historic
           Preservation Plan: Eastern Colorado. (Paper presented at a
           Meeting of the Colorado Council of Professional Archae-
           ologists, March 1980.)

1986   Taxonomy in Northeastern Colorado Prehistory. (Ph.D.
           Dissertation in Anthropology, University of Missouri, Co-
           lumbia.)

1988   The Woodland Period in Northeastern Colorado. *Plains
           Anthropologist* 33(122):449–465.

Butler, William F.
1874   The Great Land. London: Sampson, Low, Martson, Low and
           Searle.

1891   The Great Lone Land: A Narrative of Travel and Adventure
           in the North-West of America. London: Sampson Low,
           Marston and Co.

Button, Van Tries, and George A. Agogino
1986   A Report on Additional Human Skeletal Material Exposed
           by Reservoir Induced Erosion at Lake Altus, Southwestern
           Oklahoma. (Report submitted to U.S. Department of the
           Interior, Bureau of Reclamation, Amarillo, Tex.)

Byington, Cyrus
1915   A Dictionary of the Choctaw Language. John R. Swanton
           and Henry S. Halbert, eds. *Bureau of American Ethnology
           Bulletin* 46. Washington: Smithsonian Institution; U.S.
           Government Printing Office.

Byrne, William J.
1973   The Archaeology and Prehistory of Southern Alberta as
           Reflected by Ceramics. 3 vols. *Canada. National Museum
           of Man. Mercury Series. Archaeological Survey Paper* 14.
           Ottawa.

1978   An Archaeological Demonstration of Migration on the
           Northern Great Plains. Pp. 247–273 in Archaeological
           Essays in Honor of Irving B. Rouse. R.C. Dunnell and
           Edwin S. Hall, Jr., eds. The Hague: Mouton.

Cabello, Domingo
1786   [Letter to Ugarte, dated July 3, 1786.] (Manuscript No. 232
           in Bexar Archives, Barker Texas History Center, University
           of Texas, Austin.)

Cabeza de Vaca, Alvar Núñez *see* Núñez Cabeza de Vaca, Alvar

Calabrese, Francis A.
1967   The Archaeology of the Upper Verdigris Watershed. *Kan-
           sas State Historical Society. Anthropological Series* 3.
           Topeka.

1972   Cross Ranch: A Study of Variability in a Stable Cultural
           Tradition. *Plains Anthropologist* 17(56, Pt. 2); *Memoir* 9.
           Lincoln.

1977   Ceramic Classification in Middle Missouri Prehistory. Pp.
           28–37 in Trends in Middle Missouri Prehistory: A
           Festschrift Honoring the Contributions of Donald J.
           Lehmer. Proceedings of a Symposium held at the 34th
           Plains Conference, Minneapolis, Minnesota, 22 October
           1976. W. Raymond Wood, ed. *Plains Anthropologist* 22
           (78, Pt. 2), *Memoir* 13. Lincoln.

Caldwell, Dorothy J.
1970   The Big Neck Affair: Tragedy and Farce on the Missouri
           Frontier. *Missouri Historical Review* 64(4):391–412.

Caldwell, Joseph R.
1964   Interaction Spheres in Prehistory in Hopewellian Studies.
           Illinois State Museum Scientific Papers 12:135–143.
           Springfield, Ill.

Caldwell, Warren W.
1964   Fortified Villages in the Northern Plains. *Plains Anthro-
           pologist* 9(23):1–7.

1966   The Black Partizan Site. *Smithsonian Institution. River
           Basin Surveys. Publications in Salvage Archaeology* 2.
           Lincoln.

1966a   Archeological Investigations at the McKensey Village
           (39AR201), Oahe Reservoir, Central South Dakota. *Plains
           Anthropologist* 11(31):4–38.

Caldwell, Warren W., and Richard E. Jensen
1969   The Grand Detour Phase. *River Basin Surveys. Publications
           in Salvage Archeology* 13. Lincoln.

Caldwell, Warren W., C. Bertrand Schultz, and T. Mylan Stout, eds.
1983   Man and the Changing Environments in the Great Plains.
           *Transactions of the Nebraska Academy of Sciences and
           Affiliated Societies* 11(Special issue). Lincoln.

Calihoo [Chalifoux née Belcourt], Victoria
1953   Early Life in Lac Ste. Anne and St. Albert in the 1870s.
           Alberta Historical Review 1(3):21–25. Calgary, Alta.

Callahan, Alice A.
1990   The Osage Ceremonial Dance I'n-Lon-Schka. Norman:
           University of Oklahoma Press.

Callender, Charles
1962   Social Organization of the Central Algonkian Indians. *Mil-
           waukee Public Museum Publications in Anthropology* 7.
           Milwaukee.

           1978 *see* Handbook Vol. 15 (1978:610–621)

Callender, Charles, and Lee M. Kochems
1983   The North American Berdache. *Current Anthropology*
           24(4):443–470. Chicago.

Cameron, William Bleasdell
1925   The War Trail of Big Bear. Toronto: Ryerson Press.

Camp, Gregory Scott
1984   The Chippewa Transition from Woodland to Prairie, 1790–

1112

BIBLIOGRAPHY

1820. *North Dakota History* 51(3):39–47. Bismarck.

1987   The Turtle Mountain Plains-Chippewa and the Métis, 1791–1935. (Ph. D. Dissertation in History, University of New Mexico, Albuquerque.)

1990   Working Out Their Own Salvation: The Allotment of Land in Severalty and the Turtle Mountain Chippewa Band, 1870–1902. *American Indian Culture and Research Journal* 14(2):19–38. Los Angeles.

1990a   The Chippewa Fur Trade in the Red River Valley of the North, 1790–1830. Pp. 33–46 in The Fur Trade in North Dakota. Virginia L. Heidenreich, ed. Bismarck, N.Dak.: State Historical Society of North Dakota.

Camp, Walter Mason
1976   Custer in '76: Walter Camp's Notes on the Custer Fight. Kenneth Hammer, ed. Provo, Utah: Bigham Young University Press. (Reprinted: University of Oklahoma Press, Norman, 1990.)

1995   Camp on Custer: Transcribing the Custer Myth. Bruce C. Liddic and Paul Harbaugh, eds. *Hidden Springs of Custeriana* 11. Spokane, Wash.: A.H. Clark. (Reprinted, with an Introduction by Jack D. McDermott: University of Nebraska Press, Lincoln, 1998.)

1999   Camp, Custer, and the Little Bighorn: A Collection of Walter Mason Camp's Research Papers on General G.A. Custer's Last Fight. Richard G. Hardorff, comp. and ed. *Montana and the West Series* 10. El Segundo, Calif.: Upton and Sons.

Campbell, Glen
1985   Dithyramb and Diatribe: The Polysemic Perception of the Métis in Louis Riel's Poetry. Pp. 31–43 in The Métis: Past and Present. Thomas Flanagan and John Foster, eds. *Canadian Ethnic Studies* 17(2)[Special issue]. Toronto.

Campbell, Gregory R.
1987   Northern Cheyenne Ethnicity, Religion, and Coal Energy Development. *Plains Anthropologist* 32(118):378–388.

1989   Plains Indian Historical Demography and Health: An Introductory Overview. Pp. v–xiii in Plains Indian Historical Demography and Health: Perspectives, Interpretations, and Critiques. Gregory R. Campbell, ed. *Plains Anthropologist* 34(124, Pt. 2); *Memoir* 23. Lincoln.

1989a   Epidemiological Consequences of Forced Removal: the Northern Cheyenne in Indian Territory. Pp. 85–97 in Plains Indian Historical Demography and Health: Perspectives, Interpretations, and Critiques. Gregory R. Campbell, ed. *Plains Anthropologist* 34(124, Pt. 2); *Memoir* 23. Lincoln.

1991   Changing Patterns of Health and Effective Fertility among the Northern Cheyenne of Montana, 1886–1903. *The American Indian Quarterly* 15(3):339–358. Hurst, Tex.

Campbell, Lyle
1997   American Indian Languages: The Historical Linguistics of Native America. Oxford: Oxford University Press.

Campbell, Maria
1973   Halfbreed. Toronto: McClelland and Stewart; New York: Saturday Review Press. (Reprinted: University of Nebraska Press, Lincoln, 1982; also, Goodread Biographies, Halifax, N.S., 1983.)

1978   Riel's People: How the Métis Lived. Vancouver, B.C.: Douglas and McIntyre. (Reprinted in 1983.)

1992   The Road Allowance People. Saskatoon, Sask.: Halfbreed Productions.

_____, trans.
1995   Stories of the Road Allowance People. Paintings by Sherry Farrell Racette. Penticton, B.C.: Theytus Books.

Campbell, Robert G.
1969   Prehistoric Panhandle Culture on the Chaquaqua Plateau, Southeastern Colorado. (Ph.D. Dissertation in Anthropology, The University of Colorado, Boulder.)

1976   The Panhandle Aspect of the Chaquaqua Plateau. *Texas Tech University Graduate Studies* 11. Lubbock, Tex.

Campbell, Thomas J.
1983   The Greenbelt Site: An Example of Variation among Prehistoric Plains Village Sites in the Texas Panhandle. (M.A. Thesis in Anthropology, Texas Tech University, Lubbock, Tex.)

Campbell, Thomas N.
1958   Origin of the Mescal Bean Cult. *American Anthropologist*, n.s. 60(1):156–160.

1979   Ethnohistoric Notes on Indian Groups Associated with Three Spanish Missions at Guerrero, Coahuila. *The University of Texas. Center for Archaeological Research. Archaeology and History of the San Juan Bautista Mission Area, Coahuila and Texas. Report* 3. San Antonio, Tex. (Reprinted: pp. 127–172 in The Indians of Southern Texas and Northeastern Mexico: Selected Writings of Thomas Nolan Campbell. The University of Texas at Austin, 1988.)

_____ 1983 *see* Handbook Vol. 10 (1983:343–358); *and* 1988a

1988   The Indians of Southern Texas and Northeastern Mexico: Selected Writings of Thomas Nolan Campbell. Austin: Texas Archeological Research Laboratory, The University of Texas at Austin.

1988a   The Coahuiltecans and Their Neighbors. Pp. 39–59 in The Indians of Southern Texas and Northeastern Mexico: Selected Writings of Thomas Nolan Campbell. Austin: The University of Texas at Austin. (Reprinted from: *Handbook of North American Indians*, Vol. 10:343–358. Smithsonian Institution, Washington, 1983.)

1988b   Names of the Indians of the Bastrop Area. Pp. 71–77 in The Indians of Southern Texas and Northeastern Mexico: Selected Writings of Thomas Nolan Campbell. Austin: The University of Texas at Austin. (Reprinted from: *Sayersville Historical Association Bulletin* 7:7–10. Sayersville, Tex., 1986.)

Campbell, Thomas N., and Tommy Jo Campbell
1988   Cabeza de Vaca among the Indians of Southern Texas. Pp. 7–38 in The Indians of Southern Texas and Notheastern Mexico: Selected Writings of Thomas Nolan Campbell. Austin: The University of Texas at Austin. (Reprinted from: *The University of Texas at San Antonio. Center for Archaeological Research. Choke Canyon Series* 13:3–40. San Antonio, 1981.)

1988a   Indian Groups Associated with Spanish Missions of the San Antonio Missions National Historical Park. Pp. 79–93 in The Indians of Southern Texas and Northeastern Mexico: Selected Writings of Thomas Nolan Campbell. Austin: The University of Texas at Austin. (Reprinted from: *The University of Texas at San Antonio. Center for Archaeological Research. Special Report* 16:1–2, 22–23, 67–78. San Antonio, 1985.)

Campbell, Walter Stanley
1915   The Cheyenne Tipi. *American Anthropologist*, n.s. 17(4): 685–694.

1927   The Tipis of the Crow Indians. *American Anthropologist*, n.s. 29(1):87–104.

_____ see also titles under_ Vestal, Stanley

Camponi, Linda, comp.
1981   Maps of Indian Reserves and Settlements in the National Map Collection. Volume II: Alberta, Saskatchewan, Manitoba, Yukon Territory. Ottawa: National Map Collection; Public Archives of Canada.

Canada
1871   Sessional Papers of the Canadian Parliament [for] 1871. Ottawa: Queen's Printer.

_____
1891   Indian Treaties and Surrenders, from 1680 to 1890. 2 vols. in 1. Ottawa: Brown Chamberlin. (Reprinted with Vol. 3 [Canada 1912]: Coles Publishing Canadiana Collection, Toronto, 1971, 1973.)

_____
1912   Indian Treaties and Surrenders from No. 201 to No. 483. Vol. 3. Ottawa: C.H. Parmelee. (Reprinted, with Vols. 1–2 [Canada 1891]: Coles Publishing Canadiana Collection, Toronto, 1971, 1973.)

_____
1973   Indian Treaties and Surrenders. 3 vols. Vol. 1: Treaty Nos. 1–138; Vol. 2: Treaty Nos. 140–280; Vol. 3: Treaty Nos. 281–483. Toronto: Canadiana House; Ottawa: C.H. Parmelee. (Originally publ.: Vols. 1–2, 1891; Vol. 3, 1912.)

Canada. Department of Indian Affairs
1877–1910 Annual Reports of the Department of Indian Affairs. [Published in Sessional Papers of the Canadian Parliament and issued also as separate publications.] Ottawa: Queen's Printer; [also,] Department of Indian Affairs.

Canada. Department of Indian Affairs and Northern Development
1967   Indians of the Prairie Provinces (An Historical Review). Ottawa: Department of Indian Affairs and Northern Development.

_____
1969   Statement of the Government of Canada on Indian Policy. Ottawa: Department of Indian Affairs and Northern Development.

_____
2000   Registered Indian Population by Sex and Residence 1999. Ottawa: Department of Indian Affairs and Northern Development.

Canada. Department of Indian Affairs and Northern Development, Indian Affairs Branch 1970 _see_ Neville, G.W., comp. and ed. 1970

Canada. Deputy Superintendent General of Indian Affairs
1881   [Letter to Edgar Dewdney, dated 24 April 1881.] (Manuscript in Vol. 3740, File 28748-1, Record Group 10, National Archives of Canada. Ottawa.)

Canada. Dominion Bureau of Statistics
1886   Census of the Three Provisional Districts of the North-West Territories, 1884–1885. Ottawa: Maclean, Roger, and Co.

Canada. Energy, Mines and Resources
1974   The National Atlas of Canada. Ottawa: Macmillan Canada.

Canada. House of Commons
1880–1882 Annual Report of the Department of the Interior [for] 1879, 1880, 1881. _Sessional Papers._ Ottawa: Queen's Printer.

Canada. Indian Affairs Branch 1970 _see_ Neville, G.W., comp. and ed. 1970

Canada. Indian and Northern Affairs
1981   Indian and Inuit Affairs Program. Reserves and Trusts, Registered Indian Population by Sex and Residence 1979. Ottawa: Indian and Northern Affairs Canada.

_____
1987   Indian Register Population by Sex and Residence for Registry Groups, Responsibility Centers and Regions, December 31, 1987. Ottawa: Department of Indian Affairs and Northern Development, Indian and Inuit Affairs Program.

_____
1997   Indian Register Population by Sex and Residence 1996. Ottawa: Department of Indian Affairs and Northern Development, Indian and Inuit Affairs Program.

_____
1998   Indian Register Population by Sex and Residence 1997. Ottawa: Department of Indian Affairs and Northern Development, Indian and Inuit Affairs Program.

Canada. National Map Collection 1981 _see_ Camponi, Linda, comp. 1981

Canada. Royal Commission on Aboriginal Peoples
1996   Métis Perspectives. Pp. 199–384 (Chapter 5) in Royal Commission on Aboriginal Peoples Report. Ottawa: Indian and Northern Affairs Canada.

Canada. Statistics _see_ Statistics Canada

Canadian Record
1906–1926 _The Canadian Record._ Canton, Okla.

Canedo, Lino Gómez
1968   Primeras exploraciones y poblamiento de Texas (1686–1694). _Publicaciones del Instituto Tecnológico y de Estudios Superiores de Monterrey. Serie Historia_ 6. Mexico. (Reprinted: Editorial Porrúa, Monterrey, Mexico, 1988.)

Cannon, Carl L., ed. 1932 _see_ Pike, James 1932

Canonge, Elliott D.
1958   Comanche Texts. Illustrated by Katherine Voigtlander; Introduction by Morris Swadesh; Edited by Benjamin Elson. _University of Oklahoma. Summer Institute of Linguistics Series_ 1. Norman.

_____
1958a   Voiceless Vowels in Comanche. _International Journal of American Linguistics_ 23(1):63–67. Chicago.

_____
1960   Nümühuviyanüü: Comanche Hymns. Norman: University of Oklahoma, Summer Institute of Linguistics, with The Wycliffe Bible Translators.

Canton Record
1924   _The Canton Record._ Canton, Okla.

Capellini, Giovanni
1867   Ricordi di un viaggio scientifico nell'America settentrionale nel MDCCCLXIII. Bologna: Tipografia di Giuseppe Vitali.

Capes, Katherin H.
1963   The W.B. Nickerson Survey and Excavations, 1912–1915, of the Southern Manitoba. Mounds Region. _National Museum of Canada. Anthropological Papers_ 4. Ottawa.

Cardinal, Harold
1969   The Unjust Society; The Tragedy of Canada's Indians. Edmonton, Alta.: M.G. Hurtig.

Carleton, Lieut. James Henry
1943   The Prairie Logbooks: Dragoon Campaigns to the Pawnee Villages in 1844, and to the Rocky Mountains in 1845. Edited with an Introduction by Louis Pelzer. Chicago: The Caxton Club. (Reprinted: University of Nebraska Press, Lincoln, 1983.)

_____ 1983 _see_ 1943 (reprint info.)

Carlson, Gayle F.
1971   A Local Sequence for Upper Republican Sites in the Glen Elder Reservoir Locality, Kansas. (M.A. Thesis in Anthropology, University of Nebraska, Lincoln.)

Carlson, Gayle F., and Curtis A. Peacock
1975   Lithic Distribution in Nebraska. In: Lithic Source Notebook.

Ronald A. Thomas, ed. Milford, Del.: State of Delaware, Division of Historical and Cultural Affairs, Section of Archaeology.

Carlson, Gayle F., et al.
1999   The Sidney Burial: A Middle Plains Archaic Mortuary Site from Western Nebraska. *Plains Anthropologist* 44(169): 105–119.

Carlson, Gustav G., and Volney H. Jones
1940   Some Notes on Uses of Plants by the Comanche Indians. *Papers of the Michigan Academy of Science, Arts and Letters* 25:(for 1939):517–542. Ann Arbor.

Carlson, Paul H.
1998   The Plains Indians. College Station: Texas A&M University Press.

Carlson, Richard George
1973   From the Sun Dance to the Ghost Dance: A Social and Intellectual History of the Lakotas, 1868 to 1890. (Ph.D. Dissertation in History, University of Virginia, Charlottesville.)

Carlson, Roy L.
1965   Eighteenth Century Navajo Fortresses of the Gobernador District. *University of Colorado Studies. Series in Anthropology* 10. Boulder.

Carnegie Foundation for the Advancement of Teaching
1989   A Special Report: Tribal Colleges: Shaping the Future of Native America. Princeton, N.J.: Carnegie Foundation for the Advancement of Teaching.

Carpenter, Jock
1977   Fifty Dollar Bride: Marie Rose Smith [née Delorme]: A Chronicle of Métis Life in the 19th Century. Sidney, B.C.: Gray's Publishing. (Reprinted: Gorman and Gorman, Hanna, Alta., 1988.)

Carriker, Eleanor, Robert C. Carriker, Clifford A. CarRoll, and W.L. Larsen
1976   Guide to the Microfilm Edition of the Oregon Province Archives of the Society of Jesus Indian Language Collection: The Pacific Northwest Tribes. [Assiniboine; Crow; Blackfeet/Piegan; Gros Ventre; etc.] Spokane, Wash.: Gonzaga University.

Carrington, Henry Beebe
1875   The Indian Question: An Address. Boston: DeWolfe & Fiske Company.

Carroll, H. Bailey, and J. Villasana Haggard, eds. and trans.
1942   Three New Mexico Chronicles: The *Exposición* of Don Pedro Bautista Pino, 1812; the *Ojeada* of Lic. Antonio Barreiro, 1832; and the Additions by Don José Agustín de Escudero, 1849. *Quivira Society Publications* 11. Albuquerque: The Quivira Society.

Carson, Mary Eiseman
1989   Blackrobe for the Yankton Sioux: Fr. Sylvester Eisenman, O.S.B. (1891–1948). Chamberlain, S.Dak.: Tipi Press.

Carter, Clarence Edwin, comp. and ed.
1934–1962 The Territorial Papers of the United States. 26 vols. Washington: U.S. Government Printing Office. (Reprinted: AMS Press, New York, 1972.)

Carter, John G.
1938   The Northern Arapaho Flat Pipe and the Ceremony of Covering the Pipe. *Bureau of American Ethnology Bulletin* 119; *Anthropological Papers* 2. Washington: Smithsonian Institution; U.S. Government Printing Office.

Carter, Richard T.
1974   Teton Dakota Phonology. *University of Manitoba. Anthropology Papers* 10. Winnipeg, Man.

_____
1983   Root-final Consonant Clusters in Mandan. Pp. 1–4 in Proceedings of the Second Siouan Languages Conference, 1982. Mary C. Marino, ed. *Na'p̄āo: A Saskatchewan Anthropology Journal* 13(October): Special Issue. Saskatoon, Sask.

_____
1991   Maximilian's Ruptare Vocabulary: Philological Evidence and Mandan Phonology. Pp. 479–489 in 1990 Mid-America Linguistics Conference Papers. Frances Ingemann, ed. Lawrence: University of Kansas Linguistics Department.

Carter, Richard T., A. Wesley Jones, and Robert L. Rankin
[1975– [Comparative Siouan Dictionary.] (Manuscript in prepara-
1989]   tion, from a database compiled at the Comparative Siouan Workshop, University of Colorado, Boulder, 1984.)

Carter, Robert Goldthwaite
1961   On the Border with Mackenzie; or, Winning West Texas from the Comanches. New York: Antiquarian Press.

Carter, Sarah
1983   Agriculture and Agitation on the Oak River Dakota Reserve, 1875–1895. *Manitoba History* 6(2):2–9. Winnipeg, Man.

_____
1985   Controlling Indian Movement: The Pass System. *Newest Review* (May 1985):8–9. Edmonton, Alta.: Newest Press.

_____
1989   Two Acres and a Cow: 'Peasant' Farming for the Indians of the Northwest, 1889–1897. *Canadian Historical Review* 70(1):27–52. Toronto.

_____
1990   Lost Harvests: Prairie Indian Reserve Farmers and Government Policy. Montreal and Buffalo: McGill-Queen's University Press.

_____
1991   Demonstrating Success: The File Hills Farm Colony. *Prairie Forum* 16(2):157–183. Regina, Sask.: Canadian Plains Research Center, University of Regina.

Cartwright, Charles Edward
1980   The Board of Indian Commissioners: Hope, Failure and Abandonment 1869–1887. (M.S. Thesis in History, University of Arizona, Tucson.)

Cartwright, George
1792   A Journal of Transactions and Events, During a Residence of Nearly Sixteen Years on the Coast of Labrador....3 vols. Newark, England: Allin and Ridge.

Carver, Jonathan
1778   Travels Through the Interior Parts of North America, in the Years 1766, 1767, and 1768. Illustrated with copper plates. [1st. ed.] London: Printed for the Author, and sold by J. Walter and S. Crowder. (Reprinted: Coles Publishing Company, Toronto, 1974.)

_____
1781   Travels Through the Interior Parts of North America, in the Years 1766, 1767, and 1768. Illustrated with copper plates, coloured. Third edition. To which is added, Some Account of the Author, and a Copious Index. London: Printed for C. Dilly, in the Poultry; H. Payne, in Pall-mall, [etc.]. (Reprinted: Ross and Haines, Minneapolis, 1956.)

Casados, Antonio, and Luis Quintana
1764   Indios Genizaros *vs.* Berrera, Diego de Torres, and Antonio Salazar. (Series I, Document No. 183, Spanish Archives of New Mexico, State Records Center and Archives, Santa Fe.)

Casagrande, Joseph B.
1954–1955 Comanche Linguistic Acculturation I, II, III. *International Journal of American Linguistics* 20(2):140–151, 20(3): 217–237; 21(1):8–25. Chicago.

1115

Casagrande, Louis B., and Phillips Bourns
1983   Side Trips: The Photography of Sumner W. Matteson, 1898–1908. Milwaukee, Wis.: Milwaukee Public Museum.

Casagrande, Louis B., and Melissa M. Ringheim
1980   Straight Tongue: Minnesota Indian Art from the Bishop Whipple Collections. An Exhibition at The Science Museum of Minnesota, St. Paul, MN. October 17, 1980, to April 30, 1981. St. Paul, Minn.: The Science Museum of Minnesota.

Casañas de Jesus María, Fray Francisco
1927   Descriptions of the Tejas or Asinai Indians, 1691–1722. Parts I–II: Fray Francisco Casañas de Jesus Maria to the Viceroy of Mexico, August 15, 1691. Translated from the Spanish [and ed.] by Mattie Austin Hatcher. *Southwestern Historical Quarterly* 30(3):206–218, (4):283–304. Austin, Tex.

Case, Harold W., and Eva Case
1977   100 Years at Ft. Berthold: The History of Fort Berthold Indian Mission, 1876–1976. Compiled by Rev. and Mrs. Harold W. Case. Bismarck, N.Dak.: Bismarck Tribune.

Cash, Joseph H., and Herbert T. Hoover, eds.
1971   To Be An Indian: An Oral History. New York: Holt, Rinehart and Winston. (Reprinted: Minnesota Historical Society Press, St. Paul, 1995.)

1971a   John Cummins, Crow. Pp. 39–44 in To Be An Indian: An Oral History. Joseph H. Cash and Herbert T. Hoover, eds. New York: Holt, Rinehart and Winston. (Reprinted: Minnesota Historical Society Press, St. Paul, 1995.)

Cash, Joseph H., and Gerald W. Wolff
1974   The Three Affiliated Tribes (Mandan, Arikara, and Hidatsa). Phoenix: Indian Tribal Series.

1975   The Ponca People. Phoenix, Ariz.: Indian Tribal Series.

Cassells, E. Steve
1983   The Archaeology of Colorado. Boulder: Johnson Books. (Rev. ed., 1997.)

Castañeda, Carlos E., comp.
1931   Manuscripts for the History of Texas and the Internal Provinces, 1673–1800. Selected and Calendered from the Archivo de San Francisco el Grande. Austin, Tex.: Mexican Photo Print Company. (Reprinted in 1990.)

_____, comp.
1936–1958 Our Catholic Heritage in Texas, 1519–1936. Paul J. Folk, ed. 7 vols. Austin, Tex.: Von Boeckmann-Jones.

Castetter, Edward F., and Morris E. Opler
1936   The Ethnobiology of the Chiricahua and Mescalero Apache. A: The Use of Plants for Food, Beverages and Narcotics. Pp. 1–63 in *Ethnobiological Studies in the American Southwest* 3; *University of New Mexico Bulletin* 297; *Biological Series* 4(5). Albuquerque.

Castile, George P.
1998   To Show Heart: Native American Self-Determination and Federal Indian Policy, 1960–1975. Tucson: University of Arizona Press.

Catches, Pete
1999   Sacred Fireplace (Oceti Wakan): Life and Teachings of a Lakota Medicine Man. Peter V. Catches, ed. Santa Fe, N.Mex.: Clear Light Publishers.

Catlin, George
1841   Letters and Notes on the Manners, Customs, and Condition of the North American Indians. 2 vols. London. Published by the Author; printed by Tosswill and Myers. (Reprinted as: Letters and Notes on the Manners, Customs, and Conditions of the North American Indians, David Bogue, London, 1844; and as: North American Indians, John Grant, Edinburgh, 1926; also, Dover Publications, New York, 1973; C.N. Potter, distributed by Crown, New York, 1975.)

1844   Letters and Notes on the Manners, Customs, and Condition of the North American Indians. Written during Eight Years' Travel amongst the Wildest Tribes of Indians in North America, in 1832, 33, 34, 35, 36, 37, 38, and 39... With Four Hundred Illustrations, Carefully Engraved from His Original Paintings. 3d ed. 2 vols. New York: Wiley and Putnam. (Also, 4th ed.: David Bogue, London, 1844. Reprinted: see Catlin 1866, 1926, 1973, 1975.)

1844a   Unparalleled Exhibition: The Fourteen Ioway Indians and Their Interpreter, Just Arrived from the Upper Missouri, Near the Rocky Mountains. [Exhibition Catalogue.] London: W.S. Johnson.

1845   Notice sur les Indiens Ioways, et sur le Nuage Blanc, 1er chef de la tribu, venus des plaines du Haut-Missouri, près des montagnes Rocheuses. [Exhibition Catalogue.] Paris: Imprimerie de Wittersheim.

1866   Illustrations of the Manners, Customs and Condition of the North American Indians: With Letters and Notes Written during Eight Years of Travel and Adventure among the Wildest and Most Remarkable Tribes Now Existing. With Three Hundred and Sixty Engravings from the Author's Original Paintings. 10th ed. 2 vols. London: Henry G. Bohn. (Reprinted in 1876.)

1867   O-Kee-Pa, A Religious Ceremony, and other Customs of the Mandans. London: Trübner and Co. (Reprinted: John C. Ewers, ed. Yale University Press, New Haven, Conn., 1967.)

1913   North American Indians. Philadephia: Leary, Stuart & Company.

1926   North American Indians; Being Letters and Notes on Their Manners, Customs, and Condition, Written during Eight Years Travel amongst the Wildest Tribes of Indians in North America, 1832–1839. With Three Hundred and Twenty Illustrations, Carefully Engraved from the Author's Original Paintings. 2 vols. Edinburgh [Scotland]: John Grant.

1973   Letters and Notes on the Manners, Customs, and Condition of the North American Indians. With an Introduction by Marjorie Halpin and over 250 photographic reproductions of paintings in the Catlin Collection of the United States National Museum. 2 vols. New York: Dover Publications. (Originally publ. in 1841.)

1975   Letters and Notes on the Manners, Customs, and Condition of the North American Indians. Edited and with an Introduction by Michael Macdonald Mooney. New York: C.N. Potter; distributed by Crown Publishers. (Originally publ. in 1844.)

Cavelier, Jean
1938   The Journal of Jean Cavelier; the Account of a Survivor of La Salle's Texas Expedition, 1684–1688. Translated and annotated by Jean Delanglez. Chicago: Institute of Jesuit History.

Chaboillez, Charles Jean Baptiste 1797–1798 see Hickerson, Harold 1959

Chabot, Frederick C., ed. and trans. 1932 see Morfi, Juan Agustín 1932

Chacón, Fernando de
1797   [Report on Election of a Comanche "General", dated Santa Fe, November 18, 1797.] (Manuscript, Twitchell No. II:1404, Spanish Archives of New Mexico, State Records Center and Archives, Santa Fe.)

1801 [Diaries, dated Santa Fe, August 6–31, 1801.] (Manuscript, Twitchell No. II:1565, Spanish Archives of New Mexico, State Records Center and Archives, Santa Fe.)

1802 [Letter to Comandante-General Pedro de Nava, dated Santa Fe, August 30, 1802.] (Manuscript, Twitchell No. II:1621, Spanish Archives of New Mexico, State Records Center and Archives, Santa Fe.)

Chafe, Wallace L.
1962 Estimates Regarding the Present Speakers of North American Indian Languages. *International Journal of American Linguistics* 28(3):162–171. Chicago.

1964 Another Look at Siouan and Iroquoian. *American Anthropologist*, n.s. 66(4, Pt. 1):852–862.

1968 Language and Linguistics. Pp 48–75 in Introduction to Cultural Anthropology. James A. Clifton, ed. Boston: Houghton Mifflin.

1973 Siouan, Iroquoian and Caddoan. Pp. 1164–1209 in *Current Trends in Linguistics*, Vol. 10: *Linguistics in North America* (Pt. 2). Thomas A. Sebeok, ed. The Hague [and] Paris: Mouton.

1976 The Caddoan, Iroquoian, and Siouan Languages. *Trends in Linguistics. State-of-the-Art Reports* 3. W. Winter, ed. The Hague-Paris: Mouton.

1979 [Caddo-English Lexicon.] (Manuscript in W.L. Chafe's possession.)

1979a Caddoan. Pp. 213–235 in The Languages of Native America: Historical and Comparative Assessment. Lyle Campbell and Marianne Mithun, eds. Austin: The University of Texas Press.

Chalfant, William Y.
1989 Cheyennes and Horse Soldiers: The 1857 Expedition and the Battle of Solomon's Fork. Norman and London: University of Oklahoma Press.

1991 Without Quarter: The Wichita Expedition and the Fight on Crooked Creek. Norman and London: University of Oklahoma Press.

1997 Cheyennes at Dark Water Creek: The Last Fight of the Red River War. Foreword by Father Peter John Powell. Norman and London: University of Oklahoma Press.

Chalmers, John W.
1972 Treaty No. Six. *Alberta History* 25(2):23–27. Calgary.

Chamberlain, Alexander F.
1892 The Language of the Mississaga Indians of Sk gog: A Contribution to the Linguistics of the Algonkian Tribes of Canada. Philadelphia: MacCalla & Co.

Chamberlain, Von Del
1982 When Stars Came Down to Earth: Cosmology of the Skidi Pawnee Indians of North America. *Ballena Press Anthropological Papers* 26. Thomas C. Blackburn, ed. (A Ballena Press/Center for Archaeoastronomy Cooperative Publication.) Los Altos, Calif.: Ballena Press; College Park, Md.: Center for Archaeoastronomy, University of Maryland.

Champagne, Duane
1983 Organizational Change and Conflict: A Case Study of the Bureau of Indian Affairs. *American Indian Culture and Research Journal* 7(3):3–28. Los Angeles.

————, ed.
1994 Native America: Portrait of the Peoples. Detroit, Mich.: Visible Ink Press [for] Gale Research, Inc.

Champagne, Juliette
1990 Lac La Biche: une communauté métisse au XIXème siècle. (M.A. Thèse, Faculté St. Jean, University of Alberta, Edmonton.)

Champe, John L.
1936 The Sweetwater Culture Complex. Field work directed by W.D. Strong. Excavations in charge of W.R. Wedel. Study under the direction of Earl H. Bell. Pp. 249–299 in Chapters in Nebraska Archaeology, by Earl H. Bell, et al. Lincoln: The University of Nebraska.

1946 Ash Hollow Cave. A Study of Stratigraphic Sequence in the Central Great Plains. *University of Nebraska Studies* 1. Lincoln.

1949 White Cat Village. *American Antiquity* 14(4, Pt. 1):285–292.

1949a A Report for the Laboratory of Anthropology, University of Nebraska, 1940–1947. Pp. 14–17 in Proceedings of the Fifth Plains Conference for Archeology. *University of Nebraska. Laboratory of Anthropology. Note Book* 1. Lincoln.

1974 Yankton Chronology. Pp. 247–274 in Sioux Indians III. *American Indian Ethnohistory: Plains Indians*. David Agee Horr, comp. and ed. New York: Garland Publishing.

Champe, John L., and Franklin Fenega
1974 Notes on the Pawnee. In: Pawnee and Kansa (Kaw) Indians. *American Indian Ethnohistory: Plains Indians*. David Agee Horr, comp. and ed. New York and London: Garland Publishing. (Originally publ.: Clearwater, New York, 1954.)

Chapman, Berlin B.
1933 Establishment of the Wichita Reservation. *Chronicles of Oklahoma* 11(4):1044–1055. Norman.

1936 Dissolution of the Iowa Reservation. *Chronicles of Oklahoma* 14(4):467–477. Norman.

1943 Establishment of the Iowa Reservation. *Chronicles of Oklahoma* 21(4):366–377. Norman.

1944 Dissolution of the Wichita Reservation. *Chronicles of Oklahoma* 22(2):192–209, (3):300–314. Norman.

1947 Charles Curtis and the Kaw Reservation. *Kansas Historical Quarterly* 15(4):337–351.

1948 The Otoe and Missouria Reservation. Pt. 1. *Chronicles of Oklahoma* 26(2):132–158. Norman.

1965 The Otoes and Missourias: A Study of Indian Removal and the Legal Aftermath. Oklahoma City: Times Journal Publishing Company.

1974 Testimony on History of the Otoe and Missouria Lands before the Indian Claims Commission [1950]. Pp. 77–226 in Oto and Missouri Indians. *American Indian Ethnohistory: Plains Indians*. David H. Horr, comp. and ed. New York and London: Garland Publishing.

Chapman, Carl H.
1946 A Preliminary Survey of Missouri Archaeology. Part 1: Historic Indian Tribes. *The Missouri Archaeologist* 10(1):1–56. Columbia.

1947 A Preliminary Survey of Missouri Archaeology. Part 2: Middle Missouri and Hopewellian Cultures. *The Missouri Archaeologist* 10(2):[57]–94. Columbia.

1948 A Preliminary Survey of Missouri Archaeology, Part 3: Woodland Cultures of the Ozark Bluff Dwellers. *The Missouri Archaeologist* 10(3):95–113. Columbia.

1952   Culture Sequence in the Lower Missouri Valley. Pp. 139–151 in Archaeology of the Eastern United States. James B. Griffin, ed. Chicago: The University of Chicago Press.

1959   The Little Osage and Missouri Indian Village Sites, ca. 1727–1777 A.D. *The Missouri Archaeologist* 21(1):1–67. Columbia.

1968   The Havana Tradition and the Hopewell Problem in the Lower Missouri River Valley. (Manuscript in Department of Anthropology, University of Missouri, Columbia.)

1974   Osage Village Locations and Hunting Territories to 1808. (The Aboriginal Use and Occupancy of Lands West of the Mississippi River by the Osage Indian Tribe ... to 1808 A.D.) Pp. 173–249 in Osage Indians IV. *American Indian Ethnohistory: Plains Indians.* David Agee Horr, comp. and ed. New York and London: Garland Publishing.

1974a   Osage Village Sites and Hunting Territory: 1808–1825. (Location of Osage Indian Village Sites and Hunting Territory West of the Osage Line, 1808 to 1825 A.D.) Pp. 251–293 in Osage Indians IV. *American Indian Ethnohistory: Plains Indians.* David Agee Horr, comp. and ed. New York and London: Garland Publishing.

1974b   The Indomitable Osage in Spanish Illinois (Upper Louisiana) 1763–1804. Pp. 287–313 in The Spanish in the Mississippi Valley, 1762–1804. John Francis McDermott, ed. Urbana and Chicago: University of Illinois Press.

1980   The Archaeology of Missouri, II. Columbia: The University of Missouri Press.

1982   Osage Indians in Missouri and Oklahoma, A.D. 1796–1825. Pp. 19–28 in Pathways To Plains Prehistory: Anthropological Perspectives of Plains Natives and Their Pasts; Papers in Honor of Robert E. Bell. Don G. Wyckoff and Jack L. Hofman, eds. *Oklahoma Anthropological Society. Memoir 3; The Cross Timbers Heritage Association Contributions 1.* Duncan, Okla.

Chapman, Carl H., and Eleanor F. Chapman
1964   Indians and Archaeology of Missouri. Columbia: The University of Missouri Press.

Chapman, Carl H., et al.
1985   Osage and Missouri Indian Life Cultural Change: 1675–1825. (Final Report on National Endowment for the Humanities Research Grant RS-20296; on file at Division of American Archaeology, University of Missouri, Columbia.)

Chardon, Francis A.
1932   Chardon's Journal at Fort Clark, 1834–1839; Descriptive of Life on the Upper Missouri; of a Fur Trader's Experiences among the Mandans, Gros Ventres and Their Neighbors; of the Ravages of the Small-pox Epidemic of 1837. Edited, with Historical Introduction and Notes by Annie Heloise Abel. Pierre, S.Dak.: South Dakota State Department of History, State of South Dakota. (Reprinted: Books for Libraries Press, Freeport, N.Y., 1970; also, William Swagerty, ed., University of Nebraska Press, Lincoln, 1997.)

Charette, Guillaume
1976   Vanishing Spaces: Memoirs of a Prairie Métis. Ray Ellenwood, trans. Winnipeg, Man.: Editions Bois-Brûlés. (Originally publ. in French under title: L'espace de Louis Goulet, Éditions Bois-Brûlés, Winnipeg, 1976. Reprinted: Pemmican Publications, Winnipeg, 1983.)

Charlevoix, Pierre François Xavier de
1761   Journal of a Voyage to North-America; Undertaken by Order of the French King. Containing the Geographical Description and Natural History of That Country, Particularly Canada; Together with an Account of the Customs, Characters, Religion, Manners and Traditions of the Original Inhabitants in a Series of Letters to the Duchess of Lesdiguiéres. Translated from the French. 2 vols. London: Printed for R. and J. Dodsley. (Reprinted: University Microfilms International, Ann Arbor, Mich., 1966.)

1763   Letters to the Duchess of Lesdiguiéres; Giving an Account of a Voyage to Canada, and Travels Through That Country, and Louisiana, to the Gulf of Mexico. London: Printed for R. Goadby [etc.].

1866–1872   History and General Description of New France. Translated, with Notes, by John Gilmary Shea. 6 vols. New York: John Gilmary Shea. (Reprinted: Loyola University Press, Chicago, 1962.)

_____ 1966 *see* 1761 (reprint info.)

Charney, Jean Ormsbee
1993   A Grammar of Comanche. *Studies in the Anthropology of North American Indians.* Lincoln: University of Nebraska Press in cooperation with the American Indian Studies Research Institute, Indiana University, Bloomington.

Chartrand, Paul L.A.H.
1991   "Terms of Division": Problems of 'Outside-Naming' for Aboriginal People in Canada. *Journal of Indigenous Studies* 2(2):1–22. Regina, Sask.

1991a   Manitoba's Métis Settlement Scheme of 1870. Saskatoon, Sask.: University of Saskatchewan Law Centre.

Chase, Haldon
1949   [Fieldnotes and Manuscript Regarding Excavation at the Snake Blakeslee Site.] (On file at the Department of Anthropology, University of Denver, Denver, Colo.)

Cháves, José Antonio
[1831]   [Report of Indian Depredations, September 1831.] (Manuscript, Microfilm publication MANM, Roll 13, Frames 559–584 in Mexican Archives of New Mexico, State Records Center and Archives, Santa Fe.)

Cháves, José Antonio, Juan José Arocha, and José Francisco Cavallero
1829   [Documents Relative to a Council with the Comanche, dated July 19–31, 1829.] (Manuscript, Vol. 89, June–September 1829/443 in New Mexico Archives, Special Collections, Zimmerman Library, University of New Mexico, Albuquerque.)

Chávez, Thomas E.
1994   The Villasur Expedition and the Segesser Hide Painting. Pp. 90–113 in Spain and the Plains: Myths and Realities of Spanish Exploration and Settlement on the Great Plains. Ralph H. Vigil, Frances W. Kaye, and John R. Wunder, eds. Niwot, Colo.: University Press of Colorado.

Cheatum, Elmer
1976   Molluscan Fauna of the Gore Pit Site in Comanche County, Oklahoma. *Plains Anthropologist* 21(74):279–282.

Cheney, Roberta Carkeek
1998   Sioux Winter Count: A 131-Year Calendar of Events. Traditional Interpretation by Kills Two; Illustrations by Ralph Shane. Happy Camp, Calif.: Naturegraph.

Cherokee Commission 1892 *see* U.S. Senate 1893

Chesterfield House [Reports/Journals]
1822–1823   (Manuscript No. B34/e/1, Hudson's Bay Company Archives, Provincial Archives of Manitoba, Winnipeg, Man.)

Chief Eagle, Dallas
1967   Winter Count. Boulder, Colo.: Johnson Publishing Company.

Chiniki Research Team
1987   Stoney Place Names: Ozade, Mmnotha Wapta Makochi. Morley, Alta.: Chiniki Band.

Chittenden, Hiram M.
1902   The American Fur Trade of the Far West: A History of the Pioneer Trading Posts and Early Fur Companies of the Missouri Valley and the Rocky Mountains and of the Overland Commerce with Santa Fe. 3 vols. New York: Francis A. Harper. (Reprinted in 2 vols.: University of Nebraska Press, Lincoln, 1986.)

——— 1903   History of Early Steamboat Navigation on the Missouri River: Life and Adventures of Joseph La Barge. 2 vols. New York: Francis P. Harper.

Chittenden, Hiram M., and Alfred T. Richardson, eds. 1905 *see* Smet, Pierre-Jean de 1905

Choquette, Wayne T.
1981   The Role of Lithic Raw Material Studies in Kootenay Archaeology. *B.C. Studies* 48:21–36. Vancouver.

Chouteau, Auguste
1816   [Notes; dated St. Louis, February 21, 1816.] (Manuscript in Ancient and Miscellaneous Surveys, Vol. 4, No. 123, National Archives, Washington.)

Christianson, Andrew L.
1986   Projectile Point Size and Projectile Aerodynamics: An Exploratory Study. *Plains Anthropologist* 31(112):109–128.

Christianson, Andrew L., and E.K. Sauer
1988   Age of the Frenchman Valley and Associated Drift South of the Cypress Hills, Saskatchewan, Canada. *Canadian Journal of Earth Sciences* 25(10):1703–1708. Ottawa: National Research Council Canada.

Christie, Robert
1951   Dance to the Sun. *The Saturday Evening Post* (Dec. 22): 30–31, 61. New York.

Chuinard, Eldon G.
1979   Only One Man Died: The Medical Aspects of the Lewis and Clark Expedition. *Western Frontiersman Series* 19. Glendale, Calif.: The Arthur H. Clark Company.

Chumak, Sebastian, ed.
1983   The Stonies of Alberta: An Illustrated Heritage of Genesis, Myths, Legends, Folklore and Wisdom of Yahey Wichastabi, the People-who-cook-with-hot-stones. Narrated by 12 Stoney Elders; translated by Alfred "Toots" Dixon, Jr.; recorded by Thomas T. Williams; written by Sebastian Chumak. Special ed. Calgary, Alta.: The Alberta Foundation.

Church, Tim
1994   Ogalalla Orthoquartzite: An Updated Description. *Plains Anthropologist* 39(147):53–62.

Churchill, Ward, and Jim Vander Wall
1988   Agents of Repression: The FBI's Secret War Against the Black Panther Party and the American Indian Movement. Boston: South End Press.

Clark, Ann Helen
1943   About the Hen of Wahpeton—Unjincala Waȟpet'un Etanhan Kin He. Illustrated by Andrew Standing Soldier. *Indian Life Readers*. Lawrence, Kans.: U.S. Office of Indian Affairs, Education Division.

——— 1944   Brave Against the Enemy. *Indian Life Readers*. Lawrence, Kans.: U.S. Office of Indian Affairs, Education Division.

——— 1947   Singing Sioux Cowboy Reader. *Indian Life Readers*. Lawrence, Kans.: U.S. Office of Indian Affairs, Education Division.

Clark, Blue
1994   Lone Wolf vs. Hitchcock: Treaty Rights and Indian Law at the End of the Nineteenth Century. Lincoln: University of Nebraska Press.

Clark, Edward L.
1881   [Letter to Col. P.B. Hunt, dated Camp on North Fork or R[ed] R[iver], July 20, 1881.] (Manuscript, Archives/Newspaper Division, Oklahoma Historical Society, Oklahoma City.)

Clark, Ella Elizabeth
1960   The Origin of the Sun Dance. Pp. 63–67 in Indian Legends of Canada, by Ella Elizabeth Clark. Toronto: McClelland and Stewart Limited.

——— 1960a   The Origin of the Sun Dance Songs. Pp. 67–78 in Indian Legends of Canada, by Ella Elizabeth Clark. Toronto: McClelland and Stewart Limited.

Clark, Gerald R., and Michael C. Wilson
1981   The Ayers-Frazier Bison Trap (24PE30): A Late Middle Bison Kill Site on the Lower Yellowstone River. *Archaeology in Montana* 22(1):23–77. Billings, [etc.].

Clark, Joseph Stanley
1940   The Ponca Indian Agency. (Ph.D. Dissertation in History, University of Wisconsin, Madison.)

——— 1942   A Pawnee Buffalo Hunt. *Chronicles of Oklahoma* 20(4): 387–395. Norman.

——— 1943   Irregularities at the Pawnee Agency. *Kansas Historical Quarterly* 12(4):366–377. Topeka.

Clark, W. Leland
1983   The Place of the Métis within the Agricultural Economy of the Red River during the 1840s and the 1850s. *The Canadian Journal of Native Studies* 3(1):69–84. Brandon, Man.

Clark, William
1828   [Letter to Thos. L. McKenney, dated February 25, 1828.] (Microfilm M234, Roll 748, Records of the Bureau of Indian Affairs, Record Group 75, National Archives, Washington.)

——— 1832   [Statement of Location of Posts for Fur Trade with the Several Indian Tribes Within the Superintendency of Indian Affairs at St. Louis.] *22d Congress. 1st Session. Senate Executive Document* 90. (Serial No. 213.) Washington.

Clark, William Philo
1885   The Indian Sign Language; With Brief Explanatory Notes on the Gestures Taught Deaf-Mutes in Our Institutions for Their Instruction, and a Description of Some of the Peculiar Laws, Customs, Myths, Superstitions, Ways of Living, Code of Peace and War Signals of Our Aborigines. Philadelphia: L.R. Hamersly and Company. (Reprinted: University of Nebraska Press, Lincoln, 1982.)

Clarke, David L.
1968   Analytical Archaeology. London: Meuthen and Co. (Reprinted, 2d ed., rev. by Bob Chapman: Meuthen and Co., London, 1978; also, Columbia University Press, New York, 1978.)

Clarke, Grant Murray
1995   The Hartley Site (FaNp-19): Interpreting a Transitional Avonlea/Old Women's Faunal Assemblage. (M.A. Thesis in Anthropology and Archaeology, University of Saskatchewan, Saskatoon.)

Clayton, Lee, W.B. Bickley, Jr., and W.J. Stone
1970   Knife River Flint. *Plains Anthropologist* 15(50, Pt.1):282–290.

Clayton, William
1921   William Clayton's Journal: A Daily Record of the Original Company of "Morman" Pioneers from Nauvoo, Illinois, to the Valley of the Great Salt Lake. Salt Lake City, Utah: The Desert News. (Reprinted: Arno Press, New York, 1973.)

Clements, Forrest Edward
1931   Plains Indian Tribal Correlations with Sun Dance Data. *American Anthropologist*, n.s. 33(2):216–227.

Clift, William H.
1924   Warren's Trading Post. *Chronicles of Oklahoma* 2(2):129–140. Norman.

Clifton, F.
[1961] [Fieldnotes.] (Manuscript, University of Colorado, Boulder.)

Clow, Richmond L.
1983   A New Look at Indian Land Suits: The Sioux Nation's Black Hills Claim as a Case for Tribal Symbolism. *Plains Anthropologist* 28(102, Pt.1):315–324.

1987   The Indian Reorganization Act and the Loss of Tribal Sovereignty: Tribal Constitutions on the Rosebud and Pine Ridge Reservations. *Great Plains Quarterly* 7(2):125–134. Lincoln, Nebr.

Coates, Kenneth, ed.
1992   Aboriginal Land Claims in Canada: A Regional Perspective. Toronto: Copp Clark Pitman.

Cobb, Daniel M.
1998   Philosophy of an Indian War: Indian Community Action in the Johnson Administration's War on Indian Poverty, 1964–1968. *American Indian Culture and Research Journal* 22(2):71–102. Los Angeles.

Cock, George B. 1894 *see* U.S. Census Office 1894

Cocking, Matthew
1908   An Adventurer from Hudson Bay: Journal of Matthew Cocking, from York Factory to the Blackfeet Country, 1772–1773. Lawrence J. Burpee, ed. Pp. 89–121 in *Proceedings and Transactions of the Royal Society of Canada*, 3d ser., Vol. 2, Sect. 2. Ottawa.

Coel, Margaret
1981   Chief Left Hand, Southern Arapaho. Norman: University of Oklahoma Press.

Cohen, Felix S.
1942   Handbook of Federal Indian Law. Washington: U.S. Government Printing Office. (Reprinted, rev. ed.: Michie Bobbs-Merrill, Charlottesville, Va., 1982.)

Cohen, Lucy Cramer
1939   Big Missouri's Winter Count: A Sioux Calendar, 1796–1926. *Indians at Work* (Febr.). Washington: U.S. Department of the Interior, Bureau of Indian Affairs.

1940   Swit Bear's Winter Count. *Indians at Work* (Jan., Febr., March). Washington: U.S. Department of the Interior, Bureau of Indian Affairs.

Colby, William M.
1977   Routes to Rainy Mountian: A Biography of James Mooney, Ethnologist. (Ph.D. Dissertation in Anthropology, University of Wisconsin, Madison.)

Coleman, Winfield W.
1980   The Cheyenne Women's Sewing Society. Pp. 50–69 in Plains Indian Design, Symbology and Decoration. Gene Ball and George P. Horse Capture, eds. Cody, Wyo.: Buffalo Bill Historical Society.

Collaer, Paul
1973   Music of the Americas: An Illustrated Music Ethnology of the Eskimo and American Indian Peoples. With Contributions by Willard Rhodes and Others. New York: Praeger.

Collier, Donald
1938   Kiowa Social Integration. (M.A. Thesis in Anthropology, University of Chicago, Chicago.)

1938–1939 [Crow Fieldnotes.] (Manuscripts formerly in F. Eggan's possession.)

1940   The Sun Dance of the Plains Indians. *Indians at Work* 7(8):46–50. Washington: U.S. Department of the Interior, Bureau of Indian Affairs.

1940a   Plains Camping Groups. (Manuscript in R.J. DeMallie's possession.)

1943   Sun Dance of the Plains Indians. *América indígena* 3:359–364. México.

1944   Conjuring among the Kiowa. *Primitive Man* 17(3–4):45–49. Washington: The Catholic University of America.

Collier, Jane Fishburne
1988   Marriage and Inequality in Classless Societies. Stanford, Calif.: Stanford University Press.

Collier, John
1934   [Circular No. 2970, Indian Religious Freedom and Indian Culture.] (Manuscript in Decimal File .073, Cheyenne River Agency, Records of the Bureau of Indian Affairs, Federal Records Center, Kansas City, Mo.)

1947   Indians of the Americas. New York: The New American Library.

Collins, Melanie R.
1983   Plains Apache: Strength Relations among the Phonological Elements in a Dying Language. (M.A. Thesis in Linguistics, University of Oklahoma, Norman.)

Collins, Michael B.
1966   The Andrews Lake Sites: Evidence of Semisedentary Prehistoric Occupation in Andrews County, Texas. Pp. 27–43 in Transactions of the Second Regional Archeological Symposium for Southeastern New Mexico and Western Texas, 1966. *Special Bulletin* 1. Midland, Tex.

1968   The Andrews Lake Locality: New Archaeological Data from the Southern Llano Estacado, Texas. (M.A. Thesis in Anthropology, University of Texas, Austin.)

1995   Forty Years of Archaeology in Central Texas. *Bulletin of the Texas Archaeological Society* 66:361–400. Austin.

Collot, Georges Henri Victor
1924   A Journey in North America: Containing a Survey of the Countries Watered by the Mississippi, Ohio, Missouri, and other Affluing Rivers with Exact Observations on the Course and Soundings of These Rivers; and on the Towns, Villages, Hamlets and Farms of That Part of the New-world; Followed by Philosophical, Political, Military and Commercial Remarks and by a Projected line of Frontiers and General Limits. With an Introduction and a Critical Index, also a Translation of the Appendix from the French Edition, by J. Christian Bay. 2 vols. and Atlas. Firenze: O. Lange. (Reprinted: AMS Press, New York, 1974.)

Columbian Historical Exposition *see* U.S. Commission to the Columbian Exposition in Madrid 1895

Comanche Teh-Da Puku Nu [Comanche Little Ponies]
1972   Constitution: Comanche Teh-Da Puku Nu. (Xerox copy of original document in Thomas W. Kavanagh's possession.)

Comanche Tribe Business Committee
1979–1986 [Annual Reports.] (Mimeo.) Lawton, Okla.: Comanche Tribe Business Committee.

1987   Comanche. *Newsletter of the Comanche Tribe of Oklahoma,* (August 1987). Lawton, Okla.

Comeau, Pauline, and Aldo Santin
1990   The First Canadians: A Profile of Canada's Native People Today. Toronto: James Lorimer and Company.

Comer, Douglas C.
1996   Ritual Ground: Bent's Old Fort, World Formation, and the Annexation of the Southwest. Berkeley: University of California Press.

Comfort, A.J.
1873   Indian Mounds Near Fort Wadsworth, Dakota Territory. Pp. 389–402 in *Smithsonian Institution Annual Report for the Year 1871*. Washington: U.S. Government Printing Office.

Commissioner of Indian Affairs
1837   Treaties Between the United States of America, and the Several Indian Tribes, from 1778 to 1837: With a Copious Table of Contents. New edition, Carefully Compared with the Originals in the Department of State. Compiled and Printed by the Direction , and under the Supervision, of the Commissioner of Indian Affairs. Washington: Langtree and O'Sullivan. (Reprinted: Kraus Reprint, Millwood, N.Y., 1975.)

1883   Rules for the Courts of Indian Offences. [Circular dated April 10, 1883.] Washington: U.S. Department of the Interior, Bureau of Indian Affairs.

_____ ; Annual Reports *see* ARCIA 1824–1848 and 1849–

Conaty, Gerald T., Margaret G. Hanna, and Lawrence Melit
1988   Patterns from the Past: Saskatchewan's Collection Registration Program. *Saskatchewan Archaeology* 9:15–42. Regina.

Confederation of American Indians
1986   Indian Reservations: A State and Federal Handbook. Jefferson, N.C.: McFarland.

Conference on Problems and Issues Concerning American Indians Today
1980   Urban Indians: Proceedings of the Third Annual Conference on Problems and Issues Concerning American Indians Today. Chicago: Center for the History of the American Indian, Newberry Library.

Conn, Richard G.
1961   Cheyenne Style Beadwork. *American Indian Hobbyist* 7(2):47–62.

1976   Southern Plains Beadwork in the Fred Harvey Fine Arts Collection. Pp. 82–110 in Fred Harvey Fine Arts Collection, Heard Museum. Phoenix: Heard Museum.

1980   Native American Cloth Applique and Ribbonwork: Their Origins and Diffusion in the Plains. Pp. 9–22 in Fourth Annual Plains Indian Seminar: Ribbonwork and Cloth Applique. [Cover title:] Native American Ribbonwork: A Rainbow Tradition. George P. Horse Capture, ed. Cody, Wyo.: Buffalo Bill Historical Center.

1982   Circles of the World: Traditional Art of the Plains Indians. Denver, Colo.: Denver Art Museum.

1986   A Persistent Vision: Art of the Reservation Days. Denver: Denver Art Museum.

Connelley, William E.
1918   Notes on the Early Indian Occupancy of the Great Plains. *Collections of the Kansas State Historical Society for the Years 1915–1918,* 14:438–470. Topeka.

Conner, Stuart W.
1970   Religious Practices among the Crow Indians: Survival and Innovation in Crow Indian Religion. (Paper presented at the Annual Meeting of the American Society for Ethnohistory.)

Conner, Stuart W., and Betty Lu Conner
1971   Rock Art of the Montana High Plains. (Exhibition Catalog for the Art Galleries, University of California, Santa Barbara.)

Connor, Melissa A.
1986   Jackson Lake Archeological Project, 1985: An Interim Report. Lincoln, Neb.: U.S. Department of the Interior, National Park Service, Midwest Archaeological Center.

Conrad, Lawrence A., and David J. Nolan
1991   Some Preliminary Observations on the Occurrence of Catlinite in West Central Illinois. (Paper presented at the 36th Annual Meeting of the Midwest Archaeological Conference, La Crosse, Wis.)

Cook, Eung-Do
1972   Stress and Related Rules in Tahltan. *International Journal of Linguistics* 38(4):231–233.

1984   A Sarcee Grammar. Vancouver: University of British Columbia Press.

1995   Is There Convergence in Language Death? Evidence from Chipewyan and Stoney. *Journal of Linguistic Anthropology* 5(2):217–231. Arlington, Va.

Cook, Eung-Do, and Camille Owens
1991   Conservative and Innovative Features of Alexis Stoney. Pp. 135–146 in Papers from the American Indian Language Conference Held at the University of California-Santa Cruz, July and August 1991. James E. Redden, ed. Carbondale, Ill.: Department of Linguistics, Southern Illinois University.

Cook, James H.
1923   Fifty Years on the Old Frontier as Cowboy, Hunter, Guide, Scout, and Ranchman. New Haven, Conn.: Yale University Press. (Reprinted: Norman, University of Oklahoma Press, 1957, 1980.)

Cook, Joseph W.
1880–1882 [A Study in the Yankton Dialect of the Dakota, by the Rev. Joseph W. Cook, Missionary, aided by Charles S. Cook, Alfred C. Smith, Battiste Defond, Frank Vassar ... begun in the Winter of 1880–1881, finished August 1882.] (Manuscript No. 1486, National Anthropological Archives, Smithsonian Institution, Washington.)

Cook, Joseph W., and Charles S. Cook
1882   Calvary wiwigawangapi kin qa wokiksuye anpetu kin koya. [Calvary Catechism in the Yankton Dialect; written by Mrs. D.C. Weston; interpreted by Rev. Joseph W. Cook and Mr. Charles S. Cook.] Santee Agency, Nebr.: Mission Press, Archdeaconry of the Niobrara.

Cooper, Barry
1985   Alexander Kennedy Isbister: A Respectable Victoria. Pp. 44–63 in The Métis: Past and Present. Thomas Flanagan and John Foster, eds. *Canadian Ethnic Studies* 17(2)[Special issue]. Toronto.

Cooper, John Montgomery
1939   [Gros Ventres Fieldnotes, Fort Belknap, N.Dak.] (Manuscript on file at Catholic University of America, Washington, D.C.)

1940   The Religion of the Gros Ventres of Montana. *Annali Lateranensi* 4:97–115. Città del Vaticano, [Italy].

1944   The Shaking Tent Rite among Plains and Forest Algonquians. *Primitve Man* 17(3–4):60–84. Washington: The Catholic University of America.

1957   The Gros Ventres of Montana. Part 2: Religion and Ritual. Regina Flannery, ed. *The Catholic University of America. Anthropological Series* 16. Washington: The Catholic University of America. (See also Flannery 1953.)

Cooper, Leland R., and Elden Johnson
1964   Sandy Lake Ware and Its Distribution. *American Antiquity* 29(4):474–479.

Cooper, Paul L.
1936   Archaeology of Certain Sites in Cedar County, Nebraska. *1121*

Field Work and Study under the Direction of Earl H. Bell. Pp. 11–145 in Chapters in Nebraska Archaeology, by Earl H. Bell, et al. Lincoln: The University of Nebraska.

1940   The Archeological Explorations of 1938. *Nebraska History* 20(2):94–151. Lincoln.

1949   Recent Investigations in Fort Randall and Oahe Reservoirs, South Dakota. *American Antiquity* 14(4):300–310.

Corbett, William P.
1977   The Red Pipestone Quarry: The Yanktons Defend a Sacred Tradition, 1859–1929. *South Dakota History* 8(1):99–116. Pierre.

Corbusier, William T.
1961   Camp Sheridan, Nebraska. *Nebraska History* 42(1):29–53. Lincoln.

Corliss, A.H.
1874   [Burle Lakota Vocabulary; White River, Dakota and Nebraska Terrs.] (Manuscript No. 1384, National Anthropological Archives, Smithsonian Institution, Washington.)

Cornell, Stephen
1988   The Return of the Native: American Indian Political Resurgence. New York: Oxford University.

Corrigan, Samuel W.
1970   The Plains Indian Powwow: Cultural Integration in Prairie Canada. *Anthropologica* 12(2):253–277. Ottawa.

Corrigan, Samuel W., and Lawrence J. Barkwell, eds.
1991   The Struggle for Recognition: Canadian Justice and the Métis Nation. Winnipeg, Man.: Pemmican Publications.

Cortés, José
1989   Views from the Apache Frontier: Report on the Northern Provinces of New Spain. Elizabeth A.H. John, ed.; John Wheat, trans. Norman: University of Oklahoma Press.

Cortambert, Louis R.
1837   Voyage au pays des Osages. Paris: A. Bertrand.

Cottrell, Calvert B.
1965   Changes in Crow Kinship. (M.A. Paper, Department of Anthropology, University of Chicago, Chicago.)

Couch, Carl J., and Joseph D. Marino, Jr.
1979   Chippewa-Cree Peyotism at Rocky Boy's. Pp. 7–15 in Lifeways of Intermontane and Plains Montana Indians: In Honor of J. Verne Dusenberry. Leslie B. Davis, ed. *Occasional Papers of the Museum of the Rockies* 1. Bozeman, Mont.: Montana State University.

Coues, Elliott, ed.
1893   History of the Expedition Under the Command of Lewis and Clark; to the Sources of the Missouri River, Thence Across the Rocky Mountains and Down the Columbia River to the Pacific Ocean, Performed during the Years 1804–5–6. New ed. 4 vols. New York: Francis P. Harper. (Reprinted in 3 vols.: Dover Publications, New York, 1965.)

_____, ed.
1895   The Expeditions of Zebulon Montgomery Pike, to the Headwaters of the Mississippi River, Through Louisiana Territory, and in New Spain, During the Years 1805, 1806, 1807. 3 vols. New York: Francis P. Harper.

_____, ed.
1897   New Light on the Early History of the Greater Northwest: The Manuscript Journals of Alexander Henry, Fur Trader of the Northwest Company, and of David Thompson, Official Geographer of the Same Company, 1799–1814. Exploration and Adventure among the Indians of the Red, Saskatchewan, Missouri, and Columbia Rivers. 3 vols. New York: Francis P. Harper. (Reprinted, in 3 vols.: Ross and Haines, Minneapolis, 1965.)

_____, ed.
1898   Forty Years a Fur Trader On the Upper Missouri: The Personal Narrative of Charles Larpenteur, 1833–1872. 2 vols. *American Explorers Series* 2. New York: Francis P. Harper. (Reprinted, Milo M. Quaife, ed.: The Lakeside Press, Chicago, 1933; also, Ross and Haines, Minneapolis, 1962; and, with an Introduction by Paul L. Hedren, University of Nebraska Press, Lincoln, 1970, 1989.)

_____, ed.
1898a   The Journal of Jacob Fowler: Narrating an Adventure from Arkansas through the Indian Territory , Oklahoma, Kansas, Colorado, and New Mexico, to the Sources of Rio Grande del Norte, 1821–22. New York: Francis P. Harper. (Reprinted in 1975.)

Coulter, Margaret
1943   The Sun Dance of the Blackfoot Indians. (Manuscript, Harvard University, Cambridge, Mass.)

Council of Texas Archaeologists
1940   Recent Field Work in Texas. *Texas Archaeological News* 2. Austin.

Coutts, Robert C.
1988   The Forks of the Red and Assiniboine: A Thematic History 1734–1850. (Manuscript Report No. 383a, Environment Canada, Parks Service, Ottawa.)

1988a   The Role of Agriculture in an English-Speaking Halfbreed Economy: The Case of St. Andrew's, Red River. *Native Studies Review* 4(1–2):67–93. Saskatoon, Sask.

1991   Anglican Missionaries as Agents of Acculturation: The Church Missionary Society at St. Andrew's, Red River, 1830–1870. Pp. 50–60 in The Anglican Church and the World of Western Canada, 1820–1870. Barry Ferguson, ed. Regina, Sask.: Canadian Plains Research Center.

1991a   St. Andrew's Church, Red River: An Historical and Architectural Survey. *Environment Canada. Parks Service. Research Bulletin* 289. Ottawa.

Couzzourt, James E.
1985   Preliminary Report: Testing at the Tascosa Creek Site, Oldham County, Texas. Pp. 65–142 in Transactions of the 20th Regional Archaeological Symposium for Southeastern New Mexico and Western Texas. El Paso, Tex.: El Paso Archaeological Society.

1988   The Tascosa Creek Site: New Developments and Dates. Pp. 44–79 in Transactions of the 23rd Regional Archaeological Symposium for Southeastern New Mexico and Western Texas. El Paso, Tex.: El Paso Archaeological Society.

Cowen, B.R.
1872   Letter from the Acting Secretary of the Interior, Relative to The Southern Cheyennes and Arapahoes, for the Release of Land Ceded to Them by Second Article of Treaty of 28th October, 1867. *42d Congress. 3d Session. House Executive Document* 43. Washington.

1873   Letter from the Secretary of the Interior Relative to the Condition, Location, &c., of the Teton-Sioux. *42d Congress. 3d Session. House Executive Document* 96. Washington.

Cowen, Ron
1991   The Sacred Turnip: Dietary Clues Gleaned from Tuber Traditions. *Science News: The Weekly Newsmagazine of Science* 139(20): 316–317. Washington.

Cowger, Thomas W.
1996   "The Crossroads of Destiny": The NCAI's Landmark Struggle to Thwart Coercive Termination. *American Indian Culture and Research Journal* 20(4):121–144. Los Angeles.

1999   The National Congress of American Indians. Lincoln: University of Nebraska Press.

Cowgill, George
1956   Social Organization, History and Mode of Subsistence among the Crow, Hidatsa and Cheyenne. (M.A. Thesis in Anthropology, University of Chicago, Chicago.)

Cowie, Issac (i.e. Isaac)
1913   The Company of Adventurers; A Narrative of Seven Years in the Service of the Hudson's Bay Company during 1867–1874, on the Great Buffalo Plains; with Historical and Biographical Notes and Comments, by Issac Cowie. Illustrated by black and white copies of water-color sketches made by a Swiss settler on his journey from Europe, via Hudson Bay, to Red River Settlement in 1821 [etc.]. Toronto: William Briggs. (Reprinted, with an Introduction to the Bison Book ed. by David Reed Miller: University of Nebraska Press, Lincoln, 1993.)

Cox, Pauline
1997   Lucy Tayiah Eads. *Wind People: Magazine of the Kanza Museum* 2:7. Okla.

Coxe, Daniel
1722   A Description of the English Province of Carolana; by the Spaniards Call'd Florida, and by the French, La Louisiane. As also of the Great and Famous River Meschacebe or Missisipi, [...]: Together with an Account of the Commodities of the Growth and Production of the Said Province, and a Preface Containing Some Considerations on the Consequences of the French Making Settlements There. London: B. Crowse. (Reprinted: University Presses of Florida, Gainesville, 1976.)

1741   A Description of the English Province of Carolana; by the Spaniards Call'd Florida, and by the French, La Louisiane...To Which Is Added a Large and Accurate Map of Carolana, and of the River Meschacebe. 3d ed. London: Printed for and sold by O. Payne.

Coyner, David H.
1847   The Lost Trappers: A Collection of Interesting Scenes and Events in the Rocky Mountains; Together with a Short Description of California. Cincinnati: J.A. and U.P. James.

Crabb, Martha L.
1968   Some Puebloan Trade Pottery from Panhandle Aspect Sites. *Bulletin of the Texas Archeological Society* 38:83–89. Dallas.

Craine, Eugene R.
1956   The Pfaff Site: A Preliminary Report. *Newsletter of the Kansas Anthropological Association* 6:1–4. Topeka.

Crane, H.R., and James B. Griffin
1962   University of Michigan Radiocarbon Dates, VII. *Radiocarbon* 4:183–203. New Haven, Conn.

Crane, R.C.
1938   Report of Captain R.B. Marcy, of the Fifth Infantry, United States Army, on His Exploration of Indian Territory and Northwest Texas. *West Texas Historical Association Year Book* 14:116–136. Abilene.

Crapo, Richley H.
1982   Wind River Sun Dance: An Ecological Interpretation. *Tebiwa: Journal of the Idaho State University Museum* 19:41–46. Pocatello, Idaho.

Crawford, Isabel
1915   Kiowa: The History of a Blanket Indian Mission. New York: Fleming H. Revell Company. (Reprinted under title: Kiowa, A Woman Missionary in Indian Territory. Introduction by Clyde Ellis: University of Nebraska Press, Lincoln, 1998.)

Crawford, John C.
1985   What Is Michif? Language in the Métis Tradition. Pp. 231–241 in The New Peoples: Being and Becoming Métis in North America. Jacqueline Peterson and Jennifer S.H. Brown, eds. Winnipeg, Man.: The University of Manitoba Press.

Creel, Darrell, Robert F. Scott, IV, and Michael B. Collins
1990   A Faunal Record from West Central Texas and Its Bearing on Late Holocene Bison Population Changes in the Southern Plains. *Plains Anthropologist,* n.s. 35(127):55–69.

Criswell, Elijah Harry
1940   Lewis and Clark: Linguistic Pioneers. *The University of Missouri Studies* 15(2). Columbia.

Croft, Kenneth, ed.
1988   Cheyenne Ribaldry: Texts by William Guerrier and Others. *Algonquian and Iroquoian Linguistics* 13(2):13–31. Winnipeg, Man.

Croghan, George
1831   The Journal of Col. Croghan. *Monthly American Journal of Geology and Natural Science* 1(6):257–272. Philadelphia: Henry H. Porter. (Reprinted, with Introduction by George W. White: Hafner Publishing Company, New York and London, 1969.)

Crosby, Alfred W., Jr.
1972   The Columbian Exchange: Biological and Cultural Consequences of 1492. Westport, Conn.: Greenwood Press.

1976   Virgin Soil Epidemics as a Factor in the Aboriginal Depopulation of America. *William and Mary Quarterly* 33(2):289–299. Williamsburg, Va.

1986   Ecological Imperialism: The Biological Expansion of Europe, 900–1900. Cambridge and New York: Cambridge University Press.

Crow Dog, Leonard, and Richard Erdoes
1995   Crow Dog: Four Generations of Sioux Medicine Men. New York: Harper Collins Publishers.

Crow Dog, Mary, and Richard Erdoes
1995   Lakota Woman. New York: Grove Weidenfeld.

Crow Tribe of Indians and United States of America
1994   Setlement Agreement between The Crow Tribe of Indians and The United States To Resolve the 107th Meridian Boundary Dispute. (Agreement signed by Secretary of the Interior Bruce Babbit and Crow Tribe Madam Chairman Clarna Nomee in Washington, D.C., November 28, 1994.)

Crow Tribe of Indians. Finance Department
1998   Schedule A: Crow Tribe of Indians Tribal Status Funds As of 4/30/98. (Computer printout relating to Crow Coal Severance Tax Account No. 7449, Crow Tribe of Indians, Crow Agency, Mont.)

Crow Tribe of Indians. Per Capita Department
1998   Statistical List by Age for All Members. (Computer printout of Crow Tribal Members, dated 7/15/98, Crow Tribe of Indians, Crow Agency, Mont.)

Crummett, Michael
1993   Sun Dance: The Fiftieth Anniversary Crow Indian Sun Dance. Helena, Mont.: Falcon Press.

Cruse, Jimmy B.
1989   Archaeological Investigations at the Kent Creek Site (41HL66): Evidence of Mogollon Influence on the Southern Plains. (M.A. Thesis in Anthropology, Texas A&M University, College Station, Tex.)

1992   Archaeological Investigations at the Kent Creek Site (41HL66): Evidence of Mogollon Influence on the Southern Plains. *Panhandle Archaeological Society Publication* 6. Amarillo, Tex.

[Cruyzat y Gongora, Gervasio]
1735   [Proceedings against Diego de Torres.] (Microfilm T-402,

Roll 7, Frame 364, Archives of New Mexico, State Records Center and Archives, Santa Fe, N.Mex.)

Culbertson, Thaddeus A.
1851   Journal of an Expedition to the Mauvaises Terres and the Upper Missouri in 1850. Pp. 84–145 in *Fifth Annual Report of the Smithsonian Institution for the Year 1850.* Washington: U.S. Government Printing Office. (Reprinted, John F. McDermott, ed.: Smithsonian Institution, Washington, 1952.)

1952   Journal of an Expedition to the Mauvaises Terres and the Upper Missouri in 1850. John F. McDermott, ed. *Bureau of American Ethnology Bulletin* 147. Washington: Smithsonian Institution; U.S. Government Printing Office.

Culin, Stewart
1907   Games of the North American Indians. Pp. 3–809 [pp. 811–846, Vol. Index.] in *24th Annual Report of the Bureau of American Ethnology [for] 1902–'03.* Washington: Smithsonian Institution; Government Printing Office. (Reprinted: Dover Publications, New York, 1975; also, University of Nebraska Press, Lincoln, 1992.)

1907a   Games. Pp. 483–486 in Pt./vol. 1 of Handbook of Americans Indians North of Mexico. Frederick W. Hodge, ed. 2 Pts./vols. *Bureau of American Ethnology Bulletin* 30. Washington: Smithsonian Institution; U.S. Government Printing Office. (Reprinted: Rowman and Littlefield, New York, 1971.)

Culleton, Beatrice
1983   In Search of April Raintree. Winnipeg, Man.: Pemmican Publications.

Cumming, Alfred
1857   [Letter to J.W. Dennis, Dated 16 May 1857.] (Manuscript, Microfilm NA-56 in National Archives, Washington.)

Cumming, Peter A., and Neil H. Mickenberg, eds.
1972   Native Rights in Canada. 2d ed. Toronto: The Indian-Eskimo Association of Canada in association with General Publishing Co.

Cummings, Linda Scott
1989   Pollen Analysis at the Cramer Site (5PE484). Appendix II in: Apishapa Canyon Archeology: Excavations at the Cramer, Snake Blakeslee and Nearby Sites, by James H. Gunnerson. *Reprints in Anthropology* 41. Lincoln: J&L Reprint Company.

Cunningham, Robert E.
1957   Indian Territory: A Frontier Photographic Record by W.S. Prettyman. Norman: University of Oklahoma Press.

Cuoq, Jean A.
1886   Lexique de la langue algonquine. Montréal: J. Chapleau.

Current, Karen
1978   Photography and the Old West. Text by Karen Current; Photographs Selected and Printed by William R. Current. New York: Harry N. Abrams, in association with the Amon Carter Museum of Western Art, Fort Worth, Tex.

Curtis, Edward S.
1907–1930   The North American Indian: Being a Series of Volumes Picturing and Describing the Indians of the United States, the Dominion of Canada, and Alaska. Frederick W. Hodge, ed. 20 vols. Norwood, Mass.: Plimpton Press. (Reprinted: Johnson Reprint, New York, 1970.)

Curtis, Natalie B. 1907 *see* Burlin, Natalie Curtis, ed. 1907

Custer, Elizabeth Bacon
1885   Boots and Saddles: or, Life in Dakota with General Custer. New York: Harper and Brothers. (Reprinted: University of Oklahoma Press, Norman, 1961.)

Custer, George Armstrong
1874   My Life on the Plains: or, Personal Experiences with Indians. New York: Sheldon and Company. (Originally publ. in *Galaxy* 13–18, 1872–1874. Reprinted in 1876; see also 1952 and 1962.)

1952   My Life on the Plains; or, Personal Experiences with Indians. Milo Milton Quaife, ed. *The Lakeside Classics* 50. Chicago: Lakeside Press. (Reprinted: Promontory Press, New York, 1995.)

1962   My Life on the Plains; or, Personal Experiences with Indians. Introduction by Edgar I. Stewart. *The Western Frontier Library* 52. Norman: University of Oklahoma Press. (Reprinted in 1976.)

Cuthand, Stan
1978   The Native Peoples of the Prairie Provinces in the 1920's and 1930's. Pp. 31–42 in One Century Later: Western Canadian Reserve Indians Since Treaty 7. Ian A.L. Getty and Donald B. Smith, eds. Vancouver: University of British Columbia Press.

Cutler, Bruce
1995   The Massacre at Sand Creek: Narrative Voices. Norman: University of Oklahoma Press.

Cutright, Paul Rusell
1968   Lewis on the Marias, 1806. *Montana: The Magazine of Western History* 18(3):30–43. Helena.

Cutschall, Colleen
1990   Voice in the Blood. [Exhibit catalog.] Brandon, Man.: Art Gallery of Southwestern Manitoba.

Dahlstrom, Amy Louise
1989   Morphological Change in Plains Cree Verb Inflexion. *Folia Historica Linguistica* IX(2):59–71.

1991   Plains Cree Morphosyntax. *Outstanding Dissertations in Linguistics.* New York: Garland. (Originally presented as the Author's Ph.D. Dissertation in Linguistics, University of California, Berkeley, 1986.)

Dale, Harrison Clifford, ed.
1941   The Ashley-Smith Explorations and the Discovery of a Central Route to the Pacific, 1822–1829. Revised ed. Glendale, Calif.: Arthur H. Clark. (Originally publ.: Arthur H. Clark and Co., Cleveland, Ohio, 1918.)

Damon, Paul E., Charles W. Ferguson, Austin Long, and Ed I. Wallick
1974   Dendrochronologic Calibration of the Radiocarbon Time Scale. *American Antiquity* 39(2):350–366.

Dancey, William S., ed.
1992   The First Discovery of America: Archaeological Evidence of the Early Inhabitants of the Ohio Area. Columbus: The Ohio Archaeological Council.

Dangberg, Grace M., ed.
1957   Letters to Jack Wilson, the Paiute Prophet, Written between 1908 and 1911. *Bureau of American Ethnology Bulletin* 164; *Anthropological Paper* 55. Washington: Smithsonian Institution; U.S. Government Printing Office.

Daniel, Forrest W.
1969   Running Antelope — Misnamed Onepapa. *Paper Money* 8(1)[Whole No. 29]:4–9. Dover, Del. [etc.]: Society of Paper Money Collectors.

Daniels, Harry W.
1979   We Are the New Nation: the Métis and National Native Policy. Ottawa: Native Council of Canada.

1992   Keystone of Confederation: A Métis Gift to Canada. *Makekun Productions and Canada* 125. Winnipeg, Man.

Daniels, Helen Sloan
1941   Sun Dancing by Moonlight. Pp. 113–116 in The Ute

Indians of Soutwestern Colorado. Helen Sloan Daniels, ed. Durango, Colo.: Durango Public Library Museum Project.

Daniels, Robert E.
1970   Cultural Identities among the Oglala Sioux. Pp. 198–245 in The Modern Sioux: Social Systems and Reservation Culture. Ethel Nurge, ed. Lincoln: University of Nebraska Press.

1958   Journal of an Indian Fighter, 1869: Diary of Frank J. North. *Nebraska History* 42(3):161–178. Lincoln.

1961   Man of the Plains: Recollections of Luther North, 1856–1882. Lincoln: University of Nebraska Press.

1961a   The North Brothers and the Pawnee Scouts. *Nebraska History* 42(3):161–178. Lincoln.

1981   The Wounded Knee Interviews of Eli S. Ricker. *Nebraska History* 62(2):151–243. Lincoln.

Danziger, Edmund J., Jr.
1984   A New Beginning of the Last Hurrah: American Indian Response to Reform Legislation of the 1970s. *American Indian Culture and Research Journal* 7(4):69–84. Los Angeles.

Darlington, Brinton
1871   [Letter to Enoch Hoag, dated January 23, 1871.] (Manuscript No. M234, Letters Received, Records of the Bureau of Indian Affairs, Record Group 75, National Archives, Washington.)

Darnell, Regna
1969   The Development of American Anthropology, 1879 to 1920: From the Bureau of American Ethnology to Franz Boas. (Ph.D. Dissertation in Anthropology, University of Pennsylvania, Philadelphia.)

1971   The Bilingual Speech Community: A Cree Example. Pp. 155–172 in Linguistic Diversity in Canadian Society. Regna Darnell, ed. Edmonton, Alta., and Champaign, Ill.: Linguistic Research, Inc.

1974   Correlates of Cree Narrative Performance. Pp. 315–336 in Explorations in the Ethnography of Speaking. Richard Bauman and Joel Scherzer, eds. Cambridge and New York: Cambridge University Press.

_____, ed.
1976   Language Use in Canada. *Current Inquiry into Language and Linguistics* 12; *Sociolinguistic Series* 4. Edmonton, Alta.: Linguistic Research.

1998   And Along Came Boas: Continuity and Revolution in Americanist Anthropology. *Amsterdam Studies in the Theory and History of Linguistic Science,* Series III; *Studies in the History of the Language Sciences* 86. Philadelphia: John Benjamin.

1999   Theorizing Americanist Anthropology: Continuities from the B.A.E. to the Boasians. Pp. 38–51 in Theorizing the Americanist Tradition. Lisa Philips Valentine and Regna Darnell, eds. Toronto: University of Toronto Press.

Darnell, Regna, and Anthony L. Vanek
1973   The Psychological Reality of Cree Syllabics. Pp. 171–191 in Canadian Languages in Their Social Context. Regna Darnell, ed. Edmonton, Alta., and Champaign, Ill.: Linguistic Research, Inc.

Darton, Nelson H., and W.S.T. Smith
1904   Description of the Edgemont Quadrangle: The Edgemont Folio. *Atlas of the United States, Folio* 108: South Dakota-Nebraska. Washington: U.S. Geological Survey.

Davies, K.G., ed.
1965   Letters from Hudson's Bay, 1703–40. London: Hudson's Bay Record Society.

Davis, Barbara A.
1985   Edward S. Curtis: The Life and Times of a Shadow Catcher. With an Appreciation by Beaumont Newhall. Foreword by Bill Holm. San Francisco: Chronicle Books.

Davis, Carl M., and James D. Keyser
1999   McKean Complex Projectile Point Typology and Function in the Pine Parklands. *Plains Anthropologist* 44(169):251–270.

Davis, Charles L.
1890   [Letter to Hon. D.J.M. Wood, U.S. Indian Agent, Ponca Agency, Oklahoma Terr., regarding Marriage Customs of the Otoe, dated Otoe Agency, Oklahoma Terr., September 29, 1890.] (Manuscript No. 3653, National Anthropological Archives, Smithsonian Institution, Washington.)

1913   [Report of July 5, 1913.] (Manuscript in Box 92, Fort Belknap Records, Records of the Bureau of Indian Affairs, Record Group 75, National Archives-Pacific Northwest Region, Seattle, Wash.)

Davis, Hester A.
1973   [Quapaw.] (Manuscript in Arkansas Archeological Survey, Fayetteville.)

_____, ed.
1991   Arkansas Before the Americans. *Arkansas Archeological Survey Research Series* 40. Fayetteville.

Davis, Irvine
1974   Keresan-Caddoan Comparisons. *International Journal of American Linguistics* 40(3):265–267. Chicago.

1979   The Kiowa-Tanoan, Keresan, and Zuni Languages. Pp. 390–443 in The Languages of Native America: Historical and Comparative Assessment. Lyle Campbell and Marianne Mithun, eds. Austin: University of Texas Press.

Davis, Jefferson
1861   Message of the President, and Report of Albert Pike, Commissioner of the Confederate States to the Indian Nations West of Arkansas, of the Result of His Mission. Richmond, Va.: Enquirer Book and Job Press. (Reprinted: Ancient and Accepted Scottish Rite, Washington, 1968.)

Davis, Lawrence J.
1944   The Socio-Cultural Changes in the Cheyenne River Sioux Indians as a Result of Contact with White Civilization. (M.A. Thesis in Sociology, University of Southern California, Los Angeles.) (Microfilm: University Microfilms, Ann Arbor, Mich., 1959.)

Davis, Leslie B.
1960   Peyotism and the Blackfeet Indian of Montana: An Historical Assessment. *Museum of the Plains Indians Studies in Plains Anthropology and History* 1. Browning, Mont.: Bureau of Indian Affairs.

1966   Avonlea Point Occurence in Northern Montana and Canada. *Plains Anthropologist* 11(32):100–116.

1973   Schmitt (24BW559): A Middle Period Mine at the Missouri River Headwaters, Montana. (Paper Presented at the 31st Plains Conference, Columbia, Mo.)

_____, ed.
1979   Symposium on the Crow-Hidatsa Separations. *Archaeology in Montana* 20(3). Billings, [etc.].

_____, ed.
1979a   Lifeways of Intermontana and Plains Montana Indians: In Honor of J. Verne Dusenberry. *Occasional Papers of the Museum of the Rockies* 1. Bozeman, Mont.: Montana State University.

1982   Montana Archaeology and Radiocarbon Chronology: 1962–1981. *Archaeology in Montana. Special Issue* 3. Billings, [etc.].

1982a   Archaeology and Geology of the Schmitt Chert Mine, Missouri Headwaters. *Guidebook for Fieldtrip, 35th Annual Meeting of the Geological Society of America.* Bozeman: Montana State University.

1983   Stone Circles in the Montana Rockies: Relict Households and Transitory Communities. Pp. 235–278 in From Microcosm to Macrcosm: Advances in Tipi Ring Investigation and Interpretation. Leslie B. Davis, ed. *Plains Anthropologist* 28(102, Pt. 2); *Memoir* 19. Lincoln.

_____, ed.
1983a   From Microcosm to Macrocosm: Advances in Tipi Ring Investigation and Interpretation. *Plains Anthropologist* 28(102, Pt. 2); *Memoir* 19. Lincoln.

1987   Quarriers of Stone. *Montana Outdoors* 18(4):27–31. Helena: Montana Department of Fish and Game.

Davis, Leslie B., and John W. Fisher, Jr.
1988   Avonlea Predation on Wintering Plains Pronghorns. Pp. 101–118 in Avonlea Yesterday and Today: Archaeology and Prehistory. Leslie B. Davis, ed. Saskatoon, Sask.: Saskatchewan Archaeological Society.

1990   A Late Prehistoric Model for Communal Utilization of Pronghorn Antelope in the Northwestern Plains Region, North America. Pp. 241–276 in Hunters of the Recent Past. Leslie B. Davis and Brian O.K. Reeves, eds. London and Boston: Unwin Hyman.

Davis, Leslie B., and Brian O.K. Reeves, eds.
1990   Hunters of the Recent Past. London and Boston: Unwin Hyman.

Davis, Leslie B., and Emmett Stallcop
1965   The Keaster Site (24PH401): A Stratified Bison Kill Occupation in the Missouri Breaks Area of North Central Montana. Keaster Geology Report by David M. Lane. *Montana Archaeological Society. Memoir* 2. Billings, [etc.].

1966   The Wahkpa Chu'gn Site (24HL101): Late Hunters in the Milk River Valley, Montana. *Montana Archaeological Society. Memoir* 3. Billings, Mont. [etc.]

Davis, Leslie B., Stephen A. Aaberg, and Sally T. Greiser
1988   Paleoindians in Transmontane Southwestern Montana: The Barton Gulch Occupations, Ruby River Drainage. *Current Research in the Pleistocene* 5:9–11. Jim I. Mead, ed. Orono, Maine: Center for the Study of Early Man, University of Maine.

Davis, Leslie B., Stephen A.Aaberg, Michael Wilson, and Robert Ottersberg
1982   Floodplain Archaeology at the Holmes Terrace Site (24FR52), Fergus County, Montana. *Montana Archaeology Society Memoir* 3. Billings, [etc.].

1982a   Stone Circles in the Montana Rockies: Systematic Recovery and Culture Ecological Inference. (Manuscript Report to the Montana Army National Guard by Montana State University Department of Sociology, Bozeman.)

Davis, Mary B., ed.
1994   Native America in the Twentieth Century: An Encyclopedia. *Garland Reference Library of Social Science* 452. New York and London: Garland.

Davis, Theodore
1868   A Summer on the Plains. *Harper's New Monthly Magazine* 36(213):292–307. New York.

Davis, W.W.H.
1857   El Gringo: New Mexico and Her People. New York: Harper & Row. (Reprinted: University of Nebraska Press, Lincoln, 1982.)

Dawson, Brian J.
1979   The Relationship of the Catholic Clergy to Métis Society in the Canadian North-West 1845–85. (Manuscript Report No. 376, Environment Canada, Parks Service, Ottawa.)

Dawson, Sheila M., and E.G. Walker
1988   The Bethune Site: An Avonlea Burial from Saskatchewan. *Sakatchewan Archaeology* 9:3–14. Regina.

Day, John A.
1990   A Critical View. Pp. 27–30 [31] in Andrew Standing Soldier: A Retrospective Exhibition. Organized by: The Heritage Center, Inc., Red Cloud Indian School, The University Art Galleries, The University of South Dakota. [Vermillion, S.Dak.]: University Art Galleries, The University of South Dakota.

Day, Robert C.
1972   The Emergence of Activism as a Social Movement. Pp. 506–532 in Native Americans Today. Howard M. Bahr, Bruce A. Chadwick, and Robert C. Day, eds. New York: Harper and Row.

Day, Sara, ed.
1997   Heart of the Circle: Photographs by Edward S. Curtis of Native American Women. Introduction by Pat Durkin; Captions by Alan Bisbort and Sara Day; Edited by Sara Day; Technical Consultant: Joanna C. Scherer. San Francisco: Pomegranate Artbooks.

Deane, William, Jr.
1977   Young Elk and Long Horned Elk: An Arikara Story. Bismarck, North Dakota: Mary College.

DeBarthe, Joe
1894   Life and Adventures of Frank Grouard. St. Joseph, Mo.: Combe Printing Company. (Abridged ed., Edgar I. Stewart, ed., University of Oklahoma Press, Norman, 1958.)

de Cessac, Leon
1973   Ethnographic Information on the Comanches Gathered from the Mouth of a Trapper Who Was Their Prisoner for Thirteen Years. Edited and annotated byThomas R. Hester. Fred H. Stross, trans. Pp. 25–53 in Two Nineteenth Century Ethnographic Documents on the Wiyot and Yurok of Northern California and the Comanches of New Mexico and Texas. Berkeley: University of California, Department of Anthropology, Archaeological Research Facility.

Decora, Marie, Rebecca Flute, and Timothy Dunnigan
1972–1973 Dakota Lessons. 2 vols. Minneapolis: University of Minnesota, Department of American Indian Studies.

DeCory, Sam
1989   Red Feather Society Member Explains Objectives of Sun Dance. *The Lakota Times,* July 4:6. Pine Ridge, S.Dak.

Deetz, James
1965   The Dynamics of Stylistic Change in Arikara Ceramics. *University of Illinois. Studies in Anthropology* 4. Urbana.

Deevy, Edward S., Jr., and Richard F. Flint
1957   Postglacial Hypsithermal Interval. *Science* 125(3240):182–184. Washington.

[Defoe, Daniel]
1720   A Full and Impartial Account of the Company of Mississippi, Otherwise Call'd the French East-India-Company, Projected and Settled by Mr. Law ... With an Account of the Establishment of the Bank of Paris, by the Said Mr. Law. To Which Is Added, A Description of the Country of Mississipi [sic], and a Relation of the First Discovery of It, in Two Letters from A Gentleman to His Friend; in French and English. London: Printed for R. Francklin, etc.

De Lahontan, Baron 1905 *see* Lahontan, Louis Armand, baron de 1703 (reprint info.)

DeLand, Charles E.
1906   The Aborigines of South Dakota. *South Dakota Historical Collections* 3:267–586. Pierre.

Delanglez, Jean, trans. and ed. 1938 *see* Cavelier, Jean 1938

————, ed.
1939   Documents: Tonti Letters. *Mid-America*, 21, n.s. 10(3):209–238. Chicago.

1941   Hennepin's *Description of Louisiana*: A Critical Essay. Chicago: Institute of Jesuit History.

1943   Franquelin, Mapmaker. *Mid-America* 25(1):29–74. Chicago

de Liette, Pierre-Charles *see* Liette, Pierre-Charles de

Delisle, Claude
[1702]   "Memoires de Mr le Sueur " [1699–1702]. (Manuscript No. 2JJ56-9 [94 folios], Archives Nationales, Archives de la Marine, Paris.)

Delisle, Guillaume *see* L'Isle, Guillaume de

Deloria, Ella Cara
1929   The Sun Dance of the Oglala Sioux. *Journal of American Folk-lore* 42(166):354–413.

1932   Dakota Texts. *Publications of the American Ethnological Society* 14. New York: Stechert. (Reprinted: AMS Press, New York, 1974; also, University of South Dakota Press, Freeman, S.Dak., 1992.)

1935   Lakota Stem Dictionary. (Manuscript No. 30(X8a.6) in the Library of the American Philosophical Society, Philadelphia.)

1936   [Notes on the Assiniboine: Belknap or *Watóphaxnathǫ* Dialect.] (Manuscript No. 30(X8d.1), Franz Boas Collection, in the Library of the American Philosophical Society, Philadelphia.)

1937   Dakota Autobiographies. (Manuscript No. 833 [Freeman No. 30(X8a.4)] in the Library of the American Philosophical Society, Philadelphia.)

1937a   Dakota Commentary on [James R.] Walker's Texts. (Manuscript No. 834 [Freeman No. 30(X8a.5)] in the Library of the American Philosophical Society, Philadelphia.)

1944   Speaking of Indians. New York: Friendship Press. (Reprinted: Dakota Press, Vermillion, S.Dak., 1979.)

1954   Short Dakota Texts, Including Conversations. *International Journal of American Linguistics* 19(1):17–22. Chicago.

1954a   The Dakota Way of Life. (Manuscript in Dakota Indian Foundation, Chamberlain, S.Dak.)

1967   Some Notes on the Santee. *University of South Dakota. W.H. Hover Museum. Museum News* 28(5–6):1–21. Vermillion, S.Dak.

1967a   Some Notes on the Yankton. *University of South Dakota. W.H. Hover Museum. Museum News* 28(3–4):1–30. Vermillion, S.Dak.

———— 1979 *see* 1944 (reprint info.)

1988   Waterlily. Lincoln: University of Nebraska Press. (See also DeMallie, Raymond J., 1988.)

1995   The Dakota Way of Life. Raymond J. DeMallie, ed. (Manuscript in R.J. DeMallie's possession.)

Deloria, Ella Cara, and Jay Brandon
1961   "The Origin of the Courting Flute," a Legend in the Santee Dakota Dialect. *University of South Dakota. Museum News* 22(6):1–7. Vermillion, S. Dak.

Deloria, Philip S.
1995   The Era of Indian Self-Determination: An Overview. Pp. 191–207 in Indian Self-Rule: First-Hand Accounts of Indian-White Relations from Roosevelt to Reagan. Kenneth R. Philp, ed. Logan, Utah: Utah State University. (Originally publ.: Howe Brothers, Salt Lake City, 1986.)

Deloria, Vine, Jr.
1969   Custer Died for Your Sins: An Indian Manifesto. New York and London: Macmillan; also, Avon Books, New York. (Several reprints, incl.: Avon Books, New York, 1970; University of Oklahoma Press, Norman, 1988. Issued also as a sound recording under title: Custer Died for Your Sins, Red Crow. Words and Music based on the Book of the Same Title by Vine Deloria, Jr., Words and Music by Jimmy Curtis and Floyd Westerman. Red Cross Production, Malibu, Calif., 1970, 1982.)

1970   We Talk, You Listen: New Tribes, New Turf. New York: Macmillan; also, Dell Publishers. (Reprinted: Dell Publishers, New York, 1972, 1974.)

1973   God Is Red. New York: Gosset & Dunlap. (Reprinted: Fulcrum Publishing, Golden, Colo., 1994.)

1974   Behind the Trail of Broken Treaties: An Indian Declaration of Independence. New York: Delacorte Press.

1993   Review of *Black Hills/White Justice* [by Edward Lazarus]. *American Historical Review* 98(1):227–228. Washington.

1999   Singing for a Spirit: A Portrait of the Dakota Sioux. Santa Fe: Clear Light Publishers.

Deloria, Vine, Jr., and Raymond J. DeMallie, eds.
1975   Proceedings of the Great Peace Commission of 1867–1868. Washington: Institute for the Development of American Indian Law.

1999   Documents of American Indian Diplomacy: Treaties, Agreements, and Conventions, 1775–1979. 2 vols. *Legal History of North America* 4. Norman: University of Oklahoma Press.

Deloria, Vine, Jr., and Clifford M. Lytle
1984   The Nations Within: The Past and Future of American Indian Sovereignty. New York: Pantheon Books.

Deloria, Vine V., Sr.
1987   The Establishment of Christianity Among the Sioux. Pp. 91–111 in Sioux Indian Religion: Tradition and Innovation. Raymond J. DeMallie and Douglas R. Parks, eds. Norman, Okla.: University of Oklahoma Press.

Delorme, David P.
1955   A Socio-Economic Study of the Turtle Mountain Band of Chippewa Indians and a Critical Evaluation of Proposals Designed to Terminate Their Federal Wardship Status. (Ph.D. Dissertation in Economics, University of Texas, Austin.)

1955a   History of the Turtle Mountain Band of Chippewa Indians. *North Dakota History* 22(3):121–134. Bismarck.

DeMallie, Raymond J.
1969   Bibliography: The Sioux. *Indian Historian* 2(2):49–50. San Francisco.

1970   A Partial Bibliography of Archival Manuscript Material Relating to the Dakota Indians. Pp. 312–343 in The Modern Sioux: Social Systems and Reservation Culture. Ethel Nurge, ed. Lincoln.: University of Nebraska Press.

1127

1971   Teton Dakota Kinship and Social Organization. (Ph.D. Dissertation in Anthropology, University of Chicago, Chicago.)

1975   Joseph Nicollet's Account of the Sioux and Assiniboine in 1839. *South Dakota History* 5(4):343–359. Pierre.

———, ed.
1976   Nicollet's Notes on the Dakota. Appendix 3, pp. 250–281 in Joseph N. Nicollet on the Plains and Prairies: The Expeditions of 1838–39 With Journals, Letters, and Notes on the Dakota Indians. Edmund C. Bray and Martha Coleman Bray, trans. and eds. St. Paul: Minnesota Historical Society Press.

———, ed.
1976a   Carver's Dakota Dictionary. Pp. 210–221 in The Journals of Jonathan Carver and Related Documents, 1766–1770. John Parker, ed. St. Paul: Minnesota Historical Society.

1976b   Teton Dakota Time Concepts: Methodological Foundations for the Writing of Ethnohistory. *Indiana University. Folklore Forum* 9:7–17. Bloomington, Ind.

1976c   (Review Essay) Sioux Ethnohistory: A Methodological Critique. *The Journal of Ethnic Studies* 4(3):77–83. Bellingham, Wash.

1977   American Indian Treaty Making: Motives and Meanings. *American Indian Journal* 3(1):2–10. Washington.

1977a   The Unratified Treaty between the Kiowa, Comanche, and Apache and the United States of 1863. Washington, D.C.: Institute for the Development of Indian Law.

1978   George Bushotter: The First Lakota Ethnographer, Teton Sioux, 1864–1892. Pp. 91–102 in American Indian Intellectuals. Margot Liberty, ed. *1976 Proceedings of the American Ethnological Society*. St. Paul, Minn.: West Publishing.

1978a   Pine Ridge Economy: Cultural and Historical Perspectives. Pp. 237–312 in American Indian Economic Development. Sam Stanley, ed. The Hague: Mouton Publishers.

1979   Change in American Indian Kinship Systems: The Dakota. Pp. 221–241 in *Current Trends in Anthropology: Essays in Honor of Sol Tax.* Robert Hinshaw, ed. The Hague: Mouton.

1980   Touching the Pen: Plains Indian Treaty Councils in Ethnohistorical Perspective. Pp. 38–53 in Ethnicity on the Great Plains. Frederick C. Luebcke, ed. Lincoln: Unversity of Nebraska Press.

1981   "Scenes in the Indian Country": A Portfolio of Alexander Gardner's Sterographic Views of the 1868 Fort Laramie Treaty Council. *Montana: The Magazine of Western History* 31(3):42–59. Helena.

1982   The Lakota Ghost Dance: An Ethnohistorical Account. *Pacific Historical Review* 51(4):385–405. Berkeley, Calif.

1983   Male and Female in Traditional Lakota Culture. Pp. 237–265 in The Hidden Half: Studies of Plains Indian Women. Patricia C. Albers and Beatrice Medicine, eds. Washington, D.C.: University Press of America.

———, ed.
1984   The Sixth Grandfather: Black Elk's Teachings Given to John G. Neihardt. Introduction by Raymond J. DeMallie; Foreword by Hilda Neihardt Petri. Lincoln: University of Nebraska Press.

1986   The Sioux in Dakota and Montana Territories: Cultural and Historical Background of the Ogden B. Read Collection. Pp. 19–69 in Vestiges of a Proud Nation: The Ogden B. Read Northern Plains Indian Collection. Glenn E. Markoe, ed. Burlington: Robert Hull Fleming Museum, University of Vermont.

1986a   Early Kiowa and Comanche Treaties: The Treaties of 1835 and 1837. *American Indian Journal* 9(2):16–22. Washington.

1987   Lakota Belief and Ritual in the Nineteenth Century. Pp. 25–43 in Sioux Indian Religion: Tradition and Innovation. Raymond J. DeMallie and Douglas R. Parks, eds. Norman: University of Oklahoma Press.

1987a   The Sioux in Dakota and Montana Territories: Cultural and Historical Background of the Ogden B. Read Collection. Pp. 19–69 in Vestiges of a Proud Nation: The Ogden B. Read Northern Plains Indian Collection. Glenn E. Markoe, ed. Burlington, Vt.: Robert Hull Fleming Museum, University of Vermont.

1988   Afterword. Pp. 233–244 in Waterlily, by Ella C. Deloria. Lincoln: University of Nebraska Press.

1991   Introduction to the Bison Book Edition. Pp. xv–xxvi in The Ghost-Dance Religion and the Sioux Outbreak of 1890, by James Mooney. Lincoln: University of Nebraska Press.

1992   Dissonant Voices: Anthropologists, Historians, and the Lakota People. (Paper presented at the Conference "Crosscurrents of Culture, 1492–1992", New York University, New York, April 4, 1992.)

1993   "These Have No Ears": Narrative and the Ethnohistorical Method. *Ethnohistory* 40(4):515–538. Lubbock, Tex.

1994   Kinship and Biology in Sioux Culture. Pp. 125–146 in North American Indian Anthropology: Essays on Society and Culture. Raymond J. DeMallie and Alfonso Ortiz, eds. Norman: University of Oklahoma Press.

1994a   Fred Eggan and American Indian Anthropology. Pp 3–22 in North American Indian Anthropology: Essays on Society and Culture. Raymond J. DeMallie and Alfonso Ortiz, eds. Norman: University of Oklahoma Press.

1999   George Sword Wrote These: Lakota Culture as Lakota Text. Pp. 245–258 in Theorizing the American Tradition. Lisa Philips Valentine and Regina Darnell, eds. Toronto: University of Toronto Press.

1999a   Northern Plains Culture and the Warrior Complex. (Paper presented at the Bozeman Trail Heritage Conference, July 28–30, 1999, Bozeman, Mont.)

———   1999[b] *see* Deloria, Vine, Jr., and Raymond J. DeMallie, eds. 1999

———, ed.
2000   Seven Nakoda Stories. Bloomington, Ind.: Indiana University and Nakoda Language Project, Fort Belknap College, Harlem, Mont.

DeMallie, Raymond J., and Elaine A. Jahner, eds. 1980, 1982 *see* Walker, James R. 1980, 1982

DeMallie, Raymond J., and Robert H. Lavenda
1977   Wakan: Plains Siouan Concepts of Power. Pp. 154–166 in The Anthropology of Power: Ethnographic Studies from Asia, Oceania and the New World. Richard Adams and Raymond D. Fogelson, eds. New York: Academic Press.

DeMallie, Raymond J., and Alfonso Ortiz, eds.
1994   North American Indian Anthropology: Essays on Society and Culture. Norman: University of Oklahoma Press.

DeMallie, Raymond J., and Douglas R. Parks, eds.
1987   Sioux Indian Religion: Tradition and Innovation. Norman: University of Oklahoma Press.

1999   George A. Dorsey and the Development of Plains Indian Anthropology. In: Anthropology, History, and the American Indian: Essays in Honor of William C. Sturtevant. William Merrill and Ives Goddard, eds. Washington: Smithsonian Institution. (In press.)

DeMarcay, Gary B.
1986   Vertebrate Fauna from Landergin Mesa: An Antelope Creek Period Village Site. (M.A. Thesis in Anthropology, Texas A&M University, College Station.)

Dempsey, Hugh A.
1955   The Band System of the Blood Indians. (Manuscript in H.A. Dempsey's possession.)

1956   Social Dances of the Blood Indians of Alberta, Canada. *Journal of American Folklore* 69(271):47–52.

1957   The Early West. Edmonton, Alta.: Historical Society of Alberta.

1957a   Sweetgrass Hills Massacre. *Montana: The Magazine of Western History* 7(2):12–18. Helena.

1961   Robertson-Ross' Diary, Fort Edmonton to Wildhorse, B.C., 1872. *Alberta Historical Review* 9(3):5–22. Calgary.

1963   Religious Significance of Blackfoot Quillwork. *Plains Anthropologist* 8(19):52–53.

1965   A Blackfoot Winter Count. *Glenbow Foundation Occasional Paper* 1:3–20. Calgary, Alta.

1966   Thompson's Journey to the Bow River [1800]. *Alberta Historical Review* 13(2):7–15. Calgary.

1972   Crowfoot, Chief of the Blackfeet. Foreword by Paul F. Sharp. Edmonton, Alta.: Hurtig Publishers; Norman: University of Oklahoma Press. (Reprinted: Hurtig, Edmonton, 1976; also, Alberta Heritage Learning Resources Project, Edmonton, 1979; Goodread Biographies, Halifax, N.S., 1988; University of Oklahoma Press, Norman, 1989.)

1976   Maskepetoon. Pp. 537–538 in Dictionary of Canadian Biography, Vol. IX: 1861 to 1870. Toronto: University of Toronto Press.

1977   A Century of Trust, 1877–1977: A Recollection of the Historic Signing of Treaty No. 7 at Blackfoot Crossing, Southern Alberta. *Kainai News* 10(13):1–3.

1977a   The Centennial of Treaty Seven, and Why the Indians Think the Whites Are Knaves. *Canadian Geographic* 95(2):10–19.

_____, ed. 1977[b] *see* Rundle, Robert Terrill 1977

1978   Charcoal's World: The True Story of a Canadian Indian's Last Stand. Saskatoon, Sask.: Western Producer Prairie Books; Lincoln: Univrsity of Nebraska Press. (Reprinted, 3d ed.: Fifth House Publishers, Calgary, Alta., 1998.)

1980   Red Crow, Warrior Chief. Saskatoon, Sask.: Western Producer Prairie Books; Lincoln, Nebr.: University of Nebraska Press. (Reprinted, 2d ed.: Fifth House, Saskatoon, Sask., 1995.)

1982   History and Identification of Blood Bands. Pp. 94–104 in Plains Indian Studies: A collection of Essays in Honor of John C. Ewers and Waldo R. Wedel. Douglas H. Ubelaker and Herman J. Viola, eds. *Smithsonian Contributions to Anthropology* 30. Washington: Smithsonian Institution.

1984   Big Bear: The End of Freedom. Vancouver, B.C.: Douglas and McIntyre [and] Lincoln, Nebr.: University of Nebraska Press.

1986   The Gentle Persuader: A Biography of James Gladstone, Indian Senator. Saskatoon, Sask.: Western Producer Prairie Books.

1986a   Indian Tribes of Alberta. Rev., expanded and updated. Calgary, Alta.: Glenbow Museum. (Originally publ. in 1978, 1979.)

1987   Indian Names for Alberta Communities. Rev. ed. *Glenbow Museum. Occasional Paper* 4. Calgary, Alta.

_____, ed.
1989   Heaven Is Near the Rocky Mountains: The Journals and Letters of Thomas Woolsey, 1855–1869. Calgary, Alta.: Glenbow Museum.

_____, ed.
1990   Simpson's Essay on the Blackfoot, 1841. *Alberta History* 38(1):1–14. Calgary.

1995   The Blackfoot Indians. Pp. 381–413 in Native Peoples: The Canadian Experience. Bruce Morrison and C. Roderick Wilson, eds. 2d ed. Toronto: McClelland & Stewart.

1998   Indians of the Rocky Mountain Parks. Calgary, Alta.: Fifth House Publishers.

Dempsey, Hugh A., and Lindsay Moir
1989   Bibliography of the Blackfoot. *Native American Bibliography Series* 13. Metuchen, N.J., and London: The Scarecrow Press.

Dempsey, L. James
1983   The Indians and World War One. *Alberta History* 31(3):1–8. Calgary.

1987   Indians of the Prairie Provinces in World War I. (M.A. Thesis in History, University of Calgary, Calgary, Alta.)

1988   Persistence of a Warrior Ethic among the Plains Indians. *Alberta History* 36(1):1–10. Calgary.

1989   Problems of Western Canadian Indian War Veterans After World War One. *Native Studies Review* 5(2):1–18. Saskatoon, Sask.

1999   Warriors of the King: Prairie Indians in World War I. Regina, Sask.: University of Regina, Canadian Plains Research Center.

de Mun, Jules 1928 *see* Mun, Jules Louis René de 1928

Denig, Edwin Thompson
1854   [Comparative Vocabularies and Numerals]: Assiniboine. Pp. 416–431 in Vol. 4 of Historical and Statistical Information Respecting the History, Condition, and Prospects of the Indian Tribes of the United States; Collected and Prepared under the Direction of the Bureau of Indian Affairs, Per Act of Congress of March 3d, 1847. Illustrated by S. Eastman. Henry Rowe Schoolcraft, comp. and ed. 6 vols. Philadelphia: Lippincott, Grambo, 1851–1857. (Reprinted: Paladin Press, New York, 1969.)

1930   Indian Tribes of the Upper Missouri. Edited with Notes and Biographical Sketch by J.N.B. Hewitt. Pp. 375–628 in *46th Annual Report of the Bureau of American Ethnology [for] 1928–1929.* Washington: Smithsonian Institution; U.S. Government Printing Office. (Reprinted: Shorey Book Store, Seattle, Wash., 1967, 1973.)

1953   Of the Crow Nation, by Edwin Thompson Denig. Edited with Biographical Sketch and Footnotes by John C. Ewers. *Bureau of American Ethnology Bulletin* 151; *Anthropological Paper* 33. Washington: Smithsonian Institution; U.S. Government Printing Office.

1961   Five Indian Tribes of the Upper Missouri: Sioux, Arickaras, Assinboines, Crees, Crows. Edited and with an Introduction by John C. Ewers. Norman: University of Oklahoma Press. (Reprinted in 1985.)

Dennis, T.S., and Mrs. T.S. Dennis
1925   Life of F.M. Buckelew, the Indian Captive, as Related by Himself; Written by T.S. Dennis and Mrs. T.S. Dennis. Bandera, Tex.: Hunter's Printing House.

Densmore, Frances
1910   Chippewa Music I. *Bureau of American Ethnology Bulletin* 45. Washington: Smithsonian Institution; U.S. Government Printing Office. (Reprinted: Da Capo Press, New York, 1972; also, Ross & Haines, Minneapolis, Minn., 1973; and, Scholarly Press, St. Clair Shores, Mich., 1976.)

1913   Chippewa Music II. *Bureau of American Ethnology Bulletin* 53. Washington: Smithsonian Institution; U.S. Government Printing Office.

1918   Teton Sioux Music. *Bureau of American Ethnology Bulletin* 61. Washington: Smithsonian Institution; U.S. Government Printing Office. (Reprinted: Da Capo Press, New York, 1972; also, University of Nebraska Press, Lincoln, 1992.)

1919   Material Culture among the Chippewa. Pp. 114–118 in *Explorations and Fieldwork of the Smithsonian Institution in 1918*. Washington: Smithsonian Institution; Government Printing Office.

1920   The Sun Dance of the Teton Sioux. *Nature* 104(2618):437–440. London, England.

1922   The Sun Dance. Pp. 79–81 in Northern Ute Music. *Bureau of American Ethnology Bulletin* 75. Washington: Smithsonian Institution; U.S. Government Printing Office.

1923   Mandan and Hidatsa Music. *Bureau of American Ethnology Bulletin* 80. Washington: Smithsonian Institution; U.S. Government Printing Office. (Reprinted: Da Capo Press, New York, 1972.)

1929   Pawnee Music. *Bureau of American Ethnology Bulletin* 93. Washington: Smithsonian Institution; U.S. Government Printing Office. (Reprinted: Da Capo Press, New York, 1972.)

1932   Menominee Music. *Bureau of American Ethnology Bulletin* 102. Washington: Smithsonian Institution; U.S. Government Printing Office.

1936   Cheyenne and Arapaho Music. *Southwest Museum Papers* 10. Los Angeles, Calif.

1948   Teton Material Culture. *Indian Notes and Monographs* 11. New York: Museum of the American Indian. Heye Foundation.

1954   The Collection of Watercolor Drawings of the North American Indian by Seth Eastman in the James Jerome Hill Reference Library. St. Paul, Minn.: James J. Hill Reference Library.

Denver Post, February 9, 1997. Denver, Colo.

Denver Rocky Mountain News, July 7, 1998; [and] April 39, 1999. Denver, Colo.

Department of the Interior, Census Office 1894 *see* U.S. Census Office 1894

de Reuse, Willem J.
1981   Grassmann's Law in Ofo. *International Journal of American Linguistics* 47(3):243–244. Chicago.

1987   One Hundred Years of Lakota Linguistics (1887–1987). *Kansas Working Papers in Linguistics* 12:13–42. Lawrence: Linguistics Graduate Student Association, University of Kansas.

1990   A Supplementary Bibliography of Lakota Language and Linguistics (1887–1990). *Kansas Working Papers in Linguistics* 15(2):146–165. Lawrence: Linguistics Graduate Student Association, University of Kansas.

1994   Noun Incorporation in Lakota (Siouan). *International Journal of American Linguistics* 60(3):199–260. Chicago.

De Shields, James T.
1912   Border Wars of Texas. Tioga, Tex.: The Herald Company. (Reprinted: Texian Press, Waco, Tex., 1976.)

De Smet/de Smet, Pierre-Jean *see* Smet, Pierre-Jean de

de Trémaudan, Auguste Henri *see* Trémaudan, Auguste Henri de

Detrich, Charles
1894   [Comanche Vocabulary.] (Manuscript No. 788, National Anthropological Archives, Smithsonian Institution, Washington.)

1895   [Comanche Dictionary and Linguistic Notes.] (Manuscript No 744a–b, National Anthropological Archives, Smithsonian Institution, Washington.)

de Trobriand, Philippe Régis
1951   Military Life in Dakota; the Journal of Philippe Régis de Trobriand [1867–1869]. Translated and edited from the French original by Lucile M. Kane. *The Clarence Walworth Alvord Memorial Commission of the Mississippi Valley Historical Society. Publications* 2. St. Paul, Minn.: Alvord Memorial Commission. (Reprinted: University of Nebraska Press, Lincoln, Nebr., 1982.)

Detwiler, Frederick E., Jr.
1983   The Sun Dance of the Oglala: A Case Study in Religion, Ritual and Ethics. (Ph.D. Dissertation in Religious Studies, Pennsylvania State University, State College, Pa.)

Devereux, George
1951   Reality and Dream: Psychotherapy of a Plains Indian. Prefaces by Karl A. Menninger and Robert H. Lowie. Psychological Tests Edited and Interpreted by Robert R. Holt. New York: International Universities Press. (Reprinted: New York University Press, New York, 1969 [2d ed.]; and, Anchor Books, Garden City, N.Y., 1969 [2d ed.]; also, Doubleday, Garden City, N.Y., 1969 [rev. ed.].)

DeVoto, Bernard A.
1947   Across the Wide Missouri; Illustrated with Paintings by Alfred Jacob Miller and Charles [i.e., Karl] Bodmer. Boston: Houghton Mifflin. (Reprinted in 1964, 1975, 1987, 1998.)
_____, ed.
1953   The Journals of Lewis and Clark. Boston: Houghton Mifflin. (Reprinted in 1963, 1981, 1997.)

Dewdney, E.
1880   [Letter to Deputy Superintendent-General of Indian Affairs, dated 2 January 1880.] (Manuscript in National Archives of Canada, Record Group 10, v. 3704, f. 17858, Ottawa.)

1880a   [Letter to Superintendent-General of Indian Affairs, dated 19 November 1880.] (Manuscript in National Archives of Canada, Record Group 10, v. 3726, f. 24800, Ottawa.)

Dewdney, Selwyn
1978   Birth of a Cree-Ojibway Style of Contemporary Art. Pp. 117–125 in One Century Later: Western Canadian Reserve Indians Since Treaty 7. Ian A.L. Getty and Donald B. Smith, eds. Vancouver: University of British Columbia Press.

Dewing, Rolland
1985 Wounded Knee: The Meaning and Significance of the Second Incident. New York: Irvington Publishers.

Dexter, Ralph W.
1966 Putnam's Problems Popularizing Anthropology. *American Scientist* 54(3):315–332. New Haven, Conn.

d'Harnoncourt, René
1941 Living Arts of the Indian. *Magazine of Art* 34:72–77. Washington.

1969 René d'Harnoncourt [Oral History]. (Transcripts of interviews conducted by Isabel Grossner in 1968.) *Columbia University Oral History* Collection, Pt. 6. New York: Columbia University, Oral History Research Office.

d'Harnoncourt, René, and Frederic H. Douglas 1941 *see* Douglas, Frederic H., and René d'Harnoncourt 1941

Dickason, Olive Patricia
1985 From "One Nation" in the Northeast to "New Nation" in the Northeast: A Look at the Emergence of the Métis. Pp. 19–36 in The New Peoples: Being and Becoming Métis in North America. *Manitoba Studies in Native History* 1. Winnipeg: The University of Manitoba Press; Lincoln: University of Nebraska Press.

1992 Canada's First Nations: A History of Founding Peoples from Earliest Times. Toronto: McClelland and Stewart. (Reprinted: Oxford University Press, Toronto, 1997.)

Dickinson, Samuel D.
1984 Quapaw Indian Dances. *Pulaski County Historical Review* 32(3):42–50. Little Rock, Ark.

1986 The River of Cayas, the Ouachita or the Arkansas River? *Field Notes: Newsletter of the Arkansas Archeological Society* 209(March/April):5–11. Fayetteville.

1991 Shamans, Priests, Preachers, and Pilgrims at Arkansas Post. Pp. 95–104 in Arkansas Before the Americans. Hester A. Davis, ed. *Arkansas Archeological Survey Research Series* 40. Fayetteville.

Dickinson, Samuel D., and Samuel C. Dellinger
1941 A Survey of the Historic Earthenware of the Lower Arkansas Valley. *The Arkansas Archeologist* 4(4):9–18. Fayetteville. (Reprinted from: *Bulletin of the Texas Archeological and Paleontological Society* 12:76–96, 1940, Abilene.)

Dickson, Albert Jerome
1929 Covered Wagon Days: A Journey Across the Plains in the Sixties and Pioneer Days in the Northwest: From the Private Journals of Albert Jerome Dickson. Cleveland: Arthur H. Clark Company.

Dickson, Robert, and Augustin Grignon
1888 Dickson and Grignon Papers, 1812–1815. *Wisconsin Historical Society Collections* 11:271–315. Madison, Wis.

Diedrich, Mark
1987 Famous Chiefs of the Eastern Sioux. Minneapolis: Coyote Books.

Diffendal, Anne P.
1994 The La Flesche Sisters: Victorian Reformers in the Omaha Tribe. *Journal of the West* 33(1):37–48.

Dill, C.L.
1990 Early Peoples of North Dakota. Illustrations by Brian R. Austin. Bismarck, N. Dak.: State Historical Society of North Dakota.

Dillehay, Tom D.
1974 Late Quaternary Bison Population Changes on the Southern Plains. *Plains Anthropologist* 19(65):180–196.

Diller, Aubrey
1949 Pawnee House: Ponca House. *Mississippi Valley Historical Review* 36(2):301–304. Urbana, Ill.

Din, Gilbert C., and Abraham P. Nasatir
1983 The Imperial Osages: Spanish-Indian Diplomacy in the Mississippi Valley. Norman: The University of Oklahoma Press.

Dion, Joseph F.
1979 My Tribe, the Crees. Edited by Hugh A. Dempsey. Calgary, Alta.: Glenbow-Alberta Institute.

Dippie, Brian W.
1982 The Vanishing American: White Attitudes and U.S. Indian Policy. Middletown, Conn.: Wesleyan University.

Dittert, Alfred E., Jr., Jim J. Hester, and Frank W. Eddy
1961 An Archaeological Survey of the Navajo Reservoir District, Northwestern New Mexico. *Monographs of the School of American Research and the Museum of New Mexico* 23. Santa Fe.

Dixon, Roland B.
1913 Some Aspects of North American Archeology. *American Anthropologist,* n.s. 15(4):549–577.

1928 The Building of Cultures. New York and London: Charles Scribner's Sons. (Reprinted: AMS Press, New York, 1982.)

Dobbin, Murray J.
1981 The One-and-A-Half Men: The Story of Jim Brady and Malcom Norris, Métis Patriots of the Twentieth Century. Vancouver, B.C.: New Star Books.

1984 The Métis in Western Canada since 1945. Pp. 183–193 in Making of the Modern West: Western Canada since 1945. A.W. Rasporich, ed. Calgary, Alta.: University of Calgary Press.

Dobbs, Arthur
1744 An Account of the Countries Adjoining to Hudson's Bay in the Northwest Part of America. Containing a Description of Their Lakes and Rivers, [...], Shewing the Benefit To Be Made by Settling Colonies, and Opening a Trade in These Parts, Whereby the French Will Be Deprived in a Great Measure of Their Traffick in Furs, and the Communication between Canada and Mississippi Will Be Cut Off. London: Printed for J. Robinson. (Reprinted: S.R. Publishers, Yorkshire, England, 1967; also, Johnson Reprint, New York, 1967.)

Dobbs, Clark A.
1983 Oneota Origins and Development: The Radiocarbon Evidence. Pp. 91–105 in Oneota Studies. Guy E. Gibbon, ed. *University of Minnesota. Publications in Anthropology* 1. Minneapolis. (Title page has 1982 imprint date.)

1984 Oneota Settlement Patterns in the Blue Earth River Valley, Minnesota. (Ph.D. Dissertation in Anthropology, The University of Minnesota, Minneapolis.)

1989 [Letter from C.A. Dobbs to D.R. Henning, dated March 1, 1989.] (Document on file, Archeology Laboratory, Luther College, Decorah, Iowa.)

Dobbs, Clark A., and Orrin C. Shane, III
1983 Oneota Settlement Patterns in the Blue Earth River Valley, Minnesota. Pp. 55–68 in Oneota Studies. Guy E. Gibbon, ed. *University of Minnesota. Publications in Anthropology* 1. Minneapolis. (Title page has 1982 imprint date.)

Dobyns, Henry F.
1983 Their Number Become Thinned: Native American Population Dynamics in Eastern North America. Knoxville: The University of Tennessee Press.

1989   Native Historic Epidemiology in the Greater Southwest. *American Anthropologist,* n.s. 91(1):171–174.

1993   Disease Transfer at Contact. *Annual Review of Anthropology* 22:273–291. Palo Alto, Calif.

Dockstader, Frederick J.
1982   Oscar Howe: A Retrospective Exhibition. Tulsa, Okla.: Thomas Gilgrease Museum Association.

Dodge, Henry
1836   Colonel Dodge's Journal: Report of the Secretary of War in Compliance with a Resolution of the Senate, Transmitting a Report of the Expedition of the Dragoons, Under the Command of Colonel Henry Dodge, to the Rocky Mountains, during the Summer of 1835. *24th Congress. 1st Session. Senate. War Department Document* 209. Washington: Blair and Rives Printers.

1861   Report on the Expedition of Dragoons, Under Colonel Henry Dodge, to the Rocky Mountains in 1835. Pp. 130–146 in *American State Papers. Class* 5; *Military Affairs* 6. Washington: Government Printing Office.

Dodge, Richard Irving
1877   The Plains of North America and Their Inhabitants. New York: G.P. Putnam's Sons. (Reprinted: University of Delaware, Newark, Del., 1989.)

1882   Our Wild Indians; Thirty Three Years Personal Experience among the Red Men of the Great West. A Popular Account of Their Social Life, Religion, Habits, Traits, Customs, Exploits, etc. With Thrilling Adventures and Experiences on the Great Plains and in the Mountains of Our Wide Frontier. With an Introduction by General Sherman. Hartford, Conn.: A.D. Worthington and Company; also, Chicago: A.G. Nettleton & Co. (Reprinted: Archer House, New York, 1959; and, Books for Libraries Press, Freeport, N.Y., 1970.)

Dole, Gertrude E.
1969   Generation Kinship Nomenclature as an Adaptation to Endogamy. *Southwestern Journal of Anthropology* 25(2): 105–123. Albuquerque.

Doll, Don, and Jim Alinder, eds.
1976   Crying for a Vision: A Rosebud Sioux Trilogy 1886–1976. Photographs by John A. Anderson, Eugene Buechel, S.J., Don Doll, S.J.; Foreword by Ben Black Bear, Jr.; Introduction by Herman Viola. Dobbs, Ferry, N.Y.: Morgan & Morgan.

Doll, Maurice F.V.
1982   The Boss Hill Site (FdPe 4) Locality 2: Pre-Archaic Manifestations in the Parkland of Central Alberta, Canada. *Provincial Museum of Alberta. Human History. Occasional Paper* 2. Edmonton.

Dollar, Clyde D.
1977   The High Plains Smallpox Epidemic of 1837–38. *Western Historical Quarterly* 8(1):15–38. Logan, Utah.

Dolores, Mariano Francisco de los
1750   Padrones de los Misioneros del Rio de San Xavier [de la Provincia de Texas] en 13 de Enero de 1750. Pp. 46–55 in Vol. 5 (1749–1754) of Manuscripts for the History of Texas and the Internal Provinces, 1673–1800. Selected and Calendered from the Archivo de San Francisco el Grande. Carlos E. Castañeda, comp. Austin: Mexican Photo Print Company, 1931. (Reprinted in 1990.)

Domenech, Emmanuel
1860   Seven Years' Residence in the Great Deserts of North America. 2 vols. London: Longman, Green, Longman, and Roberts. (Reprinted in 1870.)

Dominguez, Francisco
1956   The Missions of New Mexico, 1776: A Description by Fray Francisco Atanasio Dominguez, with Other Contemporary Documents. Eleanor B. Adams and Angelico Chavez, trans. Albuquerque: The University of New Mexico Press.

Dominguez, Susan
1995   Zitkala-Sa (Gertrude Simmons Bonnin), 1876–1938: (Re)discovering the Sun Dance. *The American Music Research Center Journal* 5:83–96. Los Angeles.

Dominion of Canada. Department of Indian Affairs *see* Canada. Department of Indian Affairs

Donaldson, Thomas
1887   The George Catlin Indian Gallery in the U.S. National Museum (Smithsonian Institution), with Memoir and Statistics. *Report of the United States National Museum for 1885.* Washington: Government Printing Office.

Dorge, Lionel
1974   The Métis and Canadiens Councillors of Assiniboia. *The Beaver* (Winter):51–58. Winnipeg, Man.

Doris Duke Collection
1967–1972 Doris Duke Indian Oral History Collection: Interviews with Members of the Apache, Arapaho, Caddo, Cayuga, Cherokee, Cheyenne, [etc.] Tribes, along with Interviews of Non-Indians and the Proceedings of Intertribal Meetings. (Transcripts on Microfiche and Cassette Tapes in Western History Archives, University of Oklahoma, Norman.)

Dorn, Edward, and LeRoy Lucas
1966   The Shoshoneans: The People of the Basin-Plateau. New York: William Morrow & Company, Inc.

Dorsey, George A.
1900   An Aboriginal Quartzite Quarry in Eastern Wyoming. *Field Columbian Museum Publication* 51; *Anthropological Series* 2(4). Chicago. (Reprinted: Kraus Reprint, New York, 1986.)

1900a   The Department of Anthropology of the Field Columbian Museum—A Review of Six Years. *American Anthropologist,* n.s. 2(2):247–265.

1901   [Letter to F.J.V. Skiff, Director, Field Columbian Museum, dated January 17, 1901.] (Manuscript in The Department of Anthropology Archives, Field Museum of Natural History, Chicago.)

1901a   Hand or Guessing Game among the Wichitas. *American Antiquarian* 23(6):363–370.

1902   The Osage Mourning-War Ceremony. *American Anthropologist,* n.s. 4(3):404–411.

1903   The Arapaho Sun Dance: The Ceremony of the Offerings Lodge. *Field Columbian Museum Publications* 75; *Anthropological Series* 4. Chicago. (Reprinted: Kraus Reprint, Millwood, N.Y., 1973.)

1903a   Traditions of the Arapaho: Collected Under the Auspicies of the Field Columbian Museum and the American Museum of Natural History. *Field Columbian Museum Publication* 81; *Anthropological Series* 5. Chicago.

1904   Traditions of the Arikara. *Carnegie Institution of Washington Publication* 17. Washington.

1904a   The Mythology of the Wichita. *Carnegie Institution of Washington Publication* 21. Washington. (Reprinted, with an Introduction by Elizabeth A.H. John, University of Oklahoma Press, Norman, 1995. The "Introduction" also reprinted separately under title: Introduction to the Mythology of the Wichita. Wichita Cultural Society, Anadarko, Okla., 1990.)

1904b   Traditions of the Skidi Pawnee. *Memoirs of the American Folk-Lore Society* 8. Boston and New York. (Reprinted: Kraus Reprint, New York, 1969.)

1904c   Traditions of the Osage. *Field Columbian Museum Publication* 88; *Anthropological Series* 7(1). Chicago. (Reprinted: Kraus Reprint, New York, 1968, 1973; also, AMS Press, New York, 1978.)

1905   The Ponca Sun Dance. *Field Columbian Museum Publication* 102; *Anthropological Series* 7(2):67–88. Chicago. (Reprinted: Kraus Reprint, Millwood, N.Y., 1973.)

1905a   The Cheyenne I: Ceremonial Organization. *Field Columbian Museum Publication* 99; *Anthropological Series* 9(1). Chicago. (Reprinted together with Cheyenne II: The Sun Dance: Kraus Reprint, New York, 1971; also, Rio Grande Press, Glorieta, N.Mex., 1971; and, Ye Galleon Press, Fairfield, Wash., 1975.)

1905b   The Cheyenne II: The Sun Dance. *Field Columbian Museum Publication* 101; *Anthropological Series* 9(2). Chicago. (Reprinted together with Cheyenne I: Ceremonial Organization: Kraus Reprint, New York, 1971; also, Rio Grande Press, Glorieta, N.Mex., 1971; and, Ye Galleon Press, Fairfield, Wash., 1975.)

1905c   Traditions of the Caddo. *Carnegie Institution of Washington Publication* 41. Washington. (Reprinted, with an Introduction by Wallace L. Chafe: University of Nebraska Press, Lincoln, 1997.)

1906   The Pawnee: Mythology. Part I. *Carnegie Institution of Washington Publication* 59. Washington. (Reprinted, with an Introduction by Douglas R. Parks: University of Nebraska Press, Lincoln, 1997.)

1906a   Pawnee War Tales. *American Anthropologist*, n.s. 8(2):337–345.

1907   The Skidi Rite of Human Sacrifice. Pp. 65–70 in Vol. 2 of *Congrès International des Américanistes, XV Session, tenue à Québec en 1906*. Québec: Dussault et Proulx.

1907a   Social Organization of the Skidi Pawnee. Pp 71–77 in Vol. 2 of *Congrès International des Américanistes, XV Session, tenue à Québec en 1906*. Québec: Dussault et Proulx.

1907b   [Pawnee Language Notebook.] (Manuscript in George A. Dorsey Papers, Department of Anthropology, Field Columbian Museum of Natural History, Chicago.)

1907c   The Anthropological Exhibits at the American Museum of Natural History. *Science*, n.s. 25(641):584–589. Washington.

1910   Sun dance. Pp. 649–652 in vol. 2 of Handbook of American Indians North of Mexico. Fredrick W. Hodge, ed. 2 Pts./vols. *Bureau of American Ethnology Bulletin* 30. Washington: Smithsonian Institution; U.S. Government Printing Office. (Reprinted: Rowman and Littlefield, New York, 1971.)

Dorsey, George A., and Alfred L. Kroeber
1903   Traditions of the Arapaho. *Field Columbian Museum Publication* 81; *Anthropological Series* 5. Chicago. (Reprinted: Kraus Reprint, Millwood, N.Y., 1976; also, with an Introduction by Jeffrey D. Anderson: University of Nebraska Press, Lincoln, 1998.)

Dorsey, George A., and James R. Murie
1907   The Pawnee: Society and Religion of the Skidi Pawnee. (Unpublished manuscript; copy in D.R. Parks's possession.)

1940   Notes on Skidi Pawnee Society. Alexander Spoehr, ed. *Field Columbian Museum of Natural History Publication* 479; *Anthropological Series* 27(2). Chicago. (Reprinted: Kraus Reprint, New York, 1968.)

Dorsey, James Owen
1872–1894   [Omaha-Ponca Linguistic and Ethnographic Notes.] (Manuscripts Nos. 4800/129, 132, 135–137, 141–158, 160–161, Dorsey Papers, National Anthropological Archives, Smithsonian Institution, Washington.)

1873   Ponka A B C wa-bá-ru. New York: Missionary Jurisdiction of Niobrara.

1877   [A Grammar and Dict(ionary; torn page) of the Ponka Language.] (Manuscript No. 4800/217, National Anthropological Archives, Smithsonian Institution, Washington.)

1878–1880   On the Gentile System of the Omahas. *Bulletin of the Philosophical Society of Washington* 3:128–139. Washington.

1878–1881   [Chiwere Dictionary, Texts, and Linguistic Notes.] (Manuscripts Nos. 4800/292–313, Dorsey Papers, National Anthropological Archives, Smithsonian Institution, Washington.)

1878–1894   [Comparative Siouan Linguistics and Ethnology.] (Manuscrips Nos. 4800/1, 5–6, 9–13, 15–20, 22–26, 31, 33–34, 36–40, 43–55, etc., Dorsey Papers, National Anthropological Archives, Smithsonian Institution, Washington.)

———— 1879 *see* 1878–1881 (inclusive)

1879a   [Extracts from Mss. by William Hamilton, 1848–1852, concerning the Iowa and Otoe.] (Manuscript No. 4800/296, Dorsey Papers, National Anthropological Archives, Smithsonian Institution, Washington.)

1879b   [Extracts from a Series of Letters Concerning the Iowa and Other Siouans Published ca. 1848 by William Hamilton.] (Manuscript No. 4800/297, Dorsey Papers, National Anthropological Archives, Smithsonian Institution, Washington.)

1879c   How the Rabbit Killed the (Male) Winter: An Omaha Fable. *American Antiquarian* 2(2):128–132.

1880   [Origin of the Iowas, Otos and Missouris.] (Manuscript No. 4800/293, Dorsey Papers, National Anthropological Archives, Smithsonian Institution, Washington.)

1880a   [Ȼegiha-English Dictionary.] (Manuscript No. 4800/188, Dorsey Papers, National Anthropological Archives, Smithsonian Institution, Washington.)

1880b   [Extracts from Manuscripts by William Hamilton concerning the Iowa and Otoe.] (Manuscript No. 4800/303, Dorsey Papers, National Anthropological Archives, Smithsonian Institution, Washington.)

1880c   [Extracts from a Series of Letters concerning the Iowas and Other Siouans published ca. 1848 by William Hamilton.] (Manuscript No. 4800/297, Dorsey Papers, National Anthropological Archives, Smithsonian Institution, Washington.)

1880d   [Otoe and Missouria Census, 1880.] (Manuscript No. 4800/298–299, Dorsey Papers, National Anthropological Archives, Smithsonian Institution, Washington.)

1880e   [Iowa, Otoe and Missouria Personal Names.] (Manuscript No. 4800/303, Dorsey Papers, National Anthropological Archives, Smithsonian Institution, Washington.)

1880f   [Chiwere Texts; Otoe Stories and Fables; Otoe Myths and Legends; Chiwere Verbs of Saying; Chiwere-English Vocabulary; German-English-Otoe Vocabulary; German-Otoe

Vocabulary.] (Manuscripts No. 4800/304, 305, 306, 307, 310, 311, Dorsey Papers, National Anthropological Archives, Smithsonian Institution, Washington.)

1880g [Otoe Myths from Betsy Dick.] (Manuscript No. 4800/313, Dorsey Papers, National Anthropological Archives, Smithsonian Institution, Washington.)

1880h [A Comparative Name List of the Iowas, Otos and Missouris.] (Manuscript No. 4800/301, Dorsey Papers, National Anthropological Archives, Smithsonian Institution, Washington.)

1880i [Otoe and Missouria Gentes.] (Manuscript No. 4800/295, Dorsey Papers, National Anthropological Archives, Smithsonian Institution, Washington.)

1880–1881 The Rabbit and the Grasshopper: An Otoe Myth. *American Antiquarian and Oriental Journal* 3(1):24–27.

1880–1883 [Osage-English Vocabulary, Personal Names, Linguistic and Ethnographic Notes.] (Manuscripts Nos. 4800/254–256, 260, 263, 268–269, Dorsey Papers, National Anthropological Archives, Smithsonian Institution, Washington.)

1881 [List of 138 Iowa Personal Names with English Translations by William Hamilton.] (Manuscript No. 4800/920, Dorsey Papers, National Anthropological Archives, Smithsonian Institution, Washington.)

1881a [Tciwere (and Winnebago) Folk-lore, Including Iowa Cults. From the Letters of the Late Rev. Wm. Hamilton.] (Manuscript No. 4800/292, Dorsey Papers, National Anthropological Archives, Smithsonian Institution, Washington.)

1881b [Iowa Grammar, Conjugations of Iowa Verbs; Miscellaneous Linguistic Notes; and Iowa Clans.] (Manuscript No. 4800/309, Dorsey Papers, National Anthropological Archives, Smithsonian Institution, Washington.)

1881c [Notes on the Verbs "To Say" in Chiwere.] (Manuscript No. 4800/306, Dorsey Papers, National Anthropological Archives, Smithsonian Institution, Washington.)

1881d How the Rabbit Caught the Sun in a Trap. Pp. 581–583 in Illustration of the Method of Recording Indian Languages; from the Manuscripts of Messrs. J.O. Dorsey, A.S. Gatschet, and S.R. Riggs. Pp. 579–589 [Vol. Index, pp. 591–603] in *1st Annual Report of the Bureau of [American] Ethnology [for] 1879–'80.* Washington: Smithsonian Institution; U.S. Government Printing Office.

1882 [Kansa-English Vocabulary.] (Manuscript No. 4800/249, Dorsey Papers, National Anthropological Archives, Smithsonian Institution, Washington.)

1882a The Siouan or Dakota Stock. Otis T. Mason, ed. *American Naturalist* 16(10):829. Philadelphia.

1882–1890 [Kansa-English Vocabulary, Personal Names, Geographical Names, Linguistic and Ethnographic Notes.] (Manuscripts Nos. 4800/226–253, Dorsey Papers, National Anthropological Archives, Smithsonian Institution, Washington.)

1882–1894 [Quapaw-English Vocabulary, Texts, Personal Names, Linguistic and Ethnographic Notes.] (Manuscripts Nos. 4800/273–291, Dorsey Papers, National Anthropological Archives, Smithsonian Institution, Washington.)

1883 [Osage-English Vocabulary.] (Manuscript No. 4800/268, Dorsey Papers, National Anthropological Archives, Smithsonian Institution, Washington.)

1883a The Religion of the Omahas and Ponkas. *American Antiquarian and Oriental Journal* 5(3):271–275.

1883b [U-ga'-qpa (Kwapa)/Quapaw Vocabulary. Osage and Quapaw Reservations, Ind. Terr.] (Manuscript No. 4800/278, Dorsey Papers, National Anthropological Archives, Smithsonian Institution, Washington.)

1883c [Kansa-English Vocabulary.] (Manuscript No. 4800/253, Dorsey Papers, National Anthropological Archives, Smithsonian Institution, Washington.)

1883–1891 [Omaha-Ponca Dictionary.] (Manuscript No. 4800/188, Dorsey Papers, National Anthropological Archives, Smithsonian Institution, Washington.)

1884 Omaha Sociology. Pp. 205–370 [Vol. Index, pp. 595–606] in *3d Annual Report of the Bureau of [American] Ethnology [for] 1881–'82.* Washington: Smithsonian Institution; U.S. Government Printing Office. (Reprinted: Johnson Reprint Company, New York, 1970.)

1884a Siouan Folk-lore and Mythologic Notes. *American Antiquarian and Oriental Journal* 6(3):174–176.

1884b An Account of the War Customs of the Osages. *American Naturalist* 18(2):113–133. Philadelphia.

1885 On the Comparative Phonology of Four Siouan Languages. Pp. 919–929 in *Annual Report of the Smithsonian Institution for the Year 1883.* Washington: Government Printing Office.

1885a Siouan Folk-lore and Mythologic Notes. *American Antiquarian and Oriental Journal* 7(1):105–108.

1885b Mourning and War Customs of the Kansas. *American Naturalist* 19(7):670–680. Philadelphia.

1886 Migrations of Siouan Tribes. *American Naturalist* 20(3):210–222. Philadelphia.

1886a Indian Personal Names. *Proceedings of the American Association for the Advancement of Science* 34:393–399. Salem, Mass. (Reprinted: *American Anthropologist*, o.s. 3(3):263–268, 1890.)

_____, [ed.] 1887–1888 *see* Bushotter, George 1887–1888

1888 Ponka Stories; Told by Tim Potter, or Big Grizzly Bear, in 1872, at Ponka Agency, Dakota Territory. *Journal of American Folk-lore* 1(4):73.

1888a [Letter to C.P. Cotesworth, dated September 22, 1888.] (Manuscript No. 4800/Box 72, General Correspondence, National Anthropological Archives, Smithsonian Institution, Washington.)

1888b Osage Traditions. Pp. 373–397 [pp. 671–675, Vol. Index] in *6th Annual Report of the Bureau of [American] Ethnology [for] 1884–'85.* Washington: Smithsonian Institution; U.S. Government Printing Office.

1889–1890 [Kansa Personal Names.] (Manuscript No. 4800/251, Dorsey Papers, National Anthropological Archives, Smithsonian Institution, Washington.)

1890 The Ȼegiha Language. *Contributions to North American Ethnology* 6. Washington: U.S. Geographical and Geological Survey of the Rocky Mountain Region.

1891 The Social Organization of the Siouan Tribes. *Journal of American Folk-lore* 4(14):257–266, (15):331–342.

1891a Omaha and Ponka Letters. *Bureau of American Ethnology Bulletin* 11. Washington: Smithsonian Institution; U.S. Government Printing Office.

1891b   [Quapaw-English Vocabulary.] (Manuscript No. 4800/289, Dorsey Papers, National Anthropological Archives, Smithsonian Institution, Washington.)

1891c   Games of Teton Dakota Children. *American Anthropologist*, o.s. 4(4):329–345. (Reprinted: Lakota Books, Kendall Park, N.J., 1996.)

1892   [Population of the Siouan Family.] (Manuscript No. 4800/17, Dorsey Papers, National Anthropological Archives, Smithsonian Institution, Washington.)

1894   A Study of Siouan Cults. Pp. 351–544 [pp. 545–553, Vol. Index] in *11th Annual Report of the Bureau of [American] Ethnology [for] 1889–'90*. Washington: Smithsonian Institution; U.S. Government Printing Office.

1894a   A Synonymy of the Siouan Family. (Manuscript No. 4800/16, Dorsey Papers, National Anthropological Archives, Smithsonian Institution, Washington.)

1894b   [Winnebago-English Vocabulary.] (Manuscript No. 4800/535, Dorsey Papers, National Anthropological Archives, Smihsonian Institution, Washington.)

1894c   The Biloxi Indians of Louisiana: Address by James Owen Dorsey, Vice-President, Section H: Anthropology. *Proceedings of the American Association for the Advancement of Science for the 42d Meeting Held at Madison, Wisconsin; August, 1893*:267–287. Salem, Mass. (Issued also an extract, with new pagination.)

1896   Omaha Dwellings, Furniture, and Implements. Pp. 263–288 [pp. 449–462, Vol. Index] in *13th Annual Report of the Bureau of American Ethnology [for] 1891–'92*. Washington: Smithsonian Institution; U.S. Government Printing Office.

1897   Siouan Sociology. A Posthumous Paper. Pp. 205–244 [pp. 351–366, Vol. Index] in *15th Annual Report of the Bureau of American Ethnology [for] 1893–'94*. Washington: Smithsonian Institution; U.S. Government Printing Office. (Reprinted: Lakota Books, Kendall Park, N.J., 1993.)

Dorsey, James Owen, and Cyrus Thomas 1907 *see* Hodge, Frederick Webb, ed. 1907–1910 (Vol. 1:612–614, Iowa)

———— 1907a *see* Hodge, Frederick W., ed. 1907–1910 (Vol. 1:796–799, Mandan)

———— 1910 *see* Hodge, Frederick W., ed. 1907–1910 (Vol. 2:119–121, Omaha)

———— 1910a *see* Hodge, Frederick W., ed. 1907–1910 (Vol. 2:278–279, Ponca)

Dorsey, James Owen, and John R. Swanton
1912   A Dictionary of the Biloxi and Ofo Languages; Accompanied with Thirty-one Biloxi Texts and Numerous Biloxi Phrases. *Bureau of American Ethnology Bulletin* 47. Washington: Smithsonian Institution; U.S. Government Printing Office. (Reprinted in 1916.)

Doty, James
1966   A Visit to the Blackfoot Camps [1855]. *Alberta Historical Review* 14(3):17–26. Calgary, Alta.

Douaud, Patrick C.
1985   Ethnolinguistic Profile of the Canadian Métis. *Canada. National Museum of Man. Mercury Series. Ethnology Service Paper* 99. Ottawa.

Doucedame, M.F.
1982   Sun Dances and Christ: RCs Take a Friendlier Look at Indian Religion. *Alberta Report*, Sept. 27:40. Edmonton.

Dougherty, John
1831   [Letter to Lewis Cass, dated Cant. Leavenworth, Nov. 19, 1831, on the Fur Trade, etc.] (Microfilm M234, Roll 883, Letters Received, Upper Missouri Agency, 1824–1835, Records of the Bureau of Indian Affairs, Records Group 75, National Archives, Washington.)

1837   Report from the Agent at Council Bluffs. Pp. 525–672 in *25th Congress. 2d Session. Senate Document* 1. (Serial No. 314.) Washington.

1838   [Letter to William Clark, dated BelleVue, Upper Mo., April 1838, regarding a Visit to Sac and Iowa Villages, and Treaty Negotiations.] (Microfilm M234, Roll 307, Frames 0133–0134, Letters Received, Great Nemaha Agency, 1837–1847, Records of the Bureau of Indian Affairs, Record Group 75, National Archives, Washington.)

1838a   Letter on the Defense of the Western Frontier. *25th Congress. 2d Session. House Document* 276. (Serial No. 328.) Washington.

Doughty, Arthur G., and Chester Martin
1929   Introduction to the Kelsey Papers. Ottawa: Public Archives of Canada.

Douglas, Frederic H.
1932   The Wichita Indians and Allied Tribes, Waco, Towakoni, and Kichai. *Denver Art Museum. Department of Indian Art. Leaflet* 40. Denver.

1932a   The Sioux or Dakota Nation: Divisions, History and Numbers. *Denver Art Museum. Department of Indian Art. Leaflet* 41. Denver.

1932b   The Grass House of the Wichita and Caddo. *Denver Art Museum. Department of Indian Art. Leaflet* 42. Denver.

1936   Plains Beads and Beadwork Designs. *Denver Art Museum. Department of Indian Art. Leaflet* 73–74. Denver.

1938   Osage Yarn Bag. *Denver Art Museum. Material Culture Notes* 7:26–30. Denver. [Reprinted, rev. ed., 1969.]

1941   An Hidatsa Burden Basket. *Denver Art Museum. Material Culture Notes* 14:60–65. Denver. [Reprinted, rev. ed., 1969.]

Douglas, Frederic H., and René d'Harnoncourt
1941   Indian Art of the United States. New York: Museum of Modern Art. (Reprinted: Arno Press, New York, 1969.)

Doyle, W.B.
1877   Indian Forts and Dwellings. Pp. 46–65 in *Smithsonian Institution Annual Report for 1876*. Washington: U.S. Government Printing Office.

Drake, Samuel G.
1833   The Book of the Indians of North America: Comprising Details on the Lives of about Five Hundred Chiefs and Others, the Most Distinguished among Them. Also, a History of Their Wars; Their Manners and Customs; Speeches of Orators, etc., From Their First Being Known to Europeans to the Present Time. Exhibiting also an Analysis of the Most Distinguished Authors who have Written upon the Great Question of the First Peopling of America. Boston: Josiah Drake; and Antiquarian Bookstore. (Reprinted, 2d ed., 1836; 8th ed., 1845; 9th ed. published as: Aboriginal Races of North America, B.B. Mussey, Boston, 1848. Originally publ. under title: Indian Biography: The Book of the Indians. J. Drake, Boston, 1832. Reprinted also: Books for Libraries Press, New York, 1973; AMS Press, New York, 1976; Heritage Books, Bowie, Md., 1995.)

1834   Biography and History of the Indians of North America; Comprising a General Account of Them, and Details in the *1135*

Lives of all the Most Distinguished Chiefs, and Others Who Have Been Noted, among the Various Indian Nations; Also a History of Their Wars, Their Customes, and the Most Celebrated Speeches of Their Orators; Likewise Exhibiting an Analysis of the Most Distinguished, as well as Absurd Authors Who Have Written upon the Great Question of the First Peopling of America. With Large Additions and Corrections and Numerous Engravings. Boston: O.L. Perkins; New York: G.&C.&N. Carvell; and, Collins, Hannay & Company. (Several reprints, incl.: 4th–6th ed., Boston: J. Drake; and, Antiquarian Institute, 1835, 1837. Originally publ. under title: Indian Biography: The Book of the Indians. J. Drake, Boston, 1832. Reprinted also: Books for Libraries Press, New York, 1973; AMS Press, New York, 1976; Heritage Books, Bowie, Md., 1995.)

———— 1845, 1848 see 1833 (reprint info.)

1859   The Aboriginal Races of North America; Comprising Biographical Sketches of Eminent Individuals, and an Historical Account of the Different Tribes, from the First Discovery of the Continent to the Present Period: With a Dissertation on Their Origin, Antiquities, Manners and Customs, Illustrative Narratives and Anecdotes, and a Copious Analytical Index. 15th ed. rev. with Valuable additions by J.W. O'Neill and Illustrated with Numerous Colored Steel-plate Engravings. Philadelphia: C. Desilver. (Reprinted in 1860; also, revised ed., Hurst & Company, New York, 1880, 1890. Originally publ. under title: Indian Biography: The Book of the Indians. J. Drake, Boston, 1832. Reprinted also: Books for Libraries Press, New York, 1973; AMS Press, New York, 1976; Heritage Books, Bowie, Md., 1995.)

1880   The Aboriginal Races of North America; Comprising Biographical Sketches [etc.]. 15th ed. Revised with Valuable additions by Professor H.L. Williams. New York: Hurst & Company, New York (Reprinted in 1890. Originally publ. under title: Indian Biography: The Book of the Indians. J. Drake, Boston, 1832.)

Draper, Lyman Copeland, ed.
1903   Lieut. James Gorrell's Journal [1855]. Pp. 24–48 in *Collections of the State Historical Society of Wisconsin* 1. Madison.

Draper, Lyman Copeland, and Reuben G. Thwaites, eds. see WHC 1855–1911

Drass, Richard R.
1979   Roulston-Rogers; A Stratified Plains Woodland and Late Archaic Site in the Cross Timbers. *Bulletin of the Oklahoma Anthropological Society* 28:1–135. Norman.

1997   Culture Change on the Eastern Margins of the Southern Plains. *Oklahoma Archaeological Survey. Studies in Oklahoma's Past* 19; *Oklahoma Anthropological Society Memoir* 7. Norman.

1998   The Southern Plains Villagers. Pp. 415–455 in Archaeology on the Great Plains. W. Raymond Wood, ed. Lawrence, Kans.: University Press of Kansas.

Drass, Richard R., and Timothy G. Baugh
1997   The Wheeler Phase and Cultural Continuity in the Southern Plains. *Plains Anthropologist* 42(160):183–204.

Drass, Richard R., and Michael C. Moore
1987   The Linville II Site (34RM492) and Plains Village Manifestations in the Mixed Grass Prairie. *Plains Anthropologist* 32(118):404–418.

Drass, Richard R., and Fern E. Swenson
1986   Variation in the Washita River Phase of Central and Western Oklahoma. *Plains Anthropologist* 31(111):35–49.

Drass, Richard R., and C.L. Turner
1136 1989   An Archeological Reconnaissance of the Wolf Creek Drain-

age Basin, Ellis County, Oklahoma. *Oklahoma Archeological Survey. Archeological Resource Survey Report* 35. Norman.

Drees, Lauri Meijer
1996   Reserve Hospitals and Medical Officers: Health Care and Indian Peoples in Southern Alberta, 1890's–1930. *Prairie Forum* 21(2):149–176. Regina, Sask.: Canadian Plains Research Center, University of Regina.

Dresel, Gustav
1954   Gustav Dresel's Houston Journal: Adventures in North America and Texas, 1837–1841. Max Freund, trans. and ed. Austin: University of Texas Press.

Driben, Paul
1985   We Are Métis: The Ethnography of a Halfbreed Community in Northern Alberta. New York: AMS Press. (Originally issued as the Author's Ph.D. Dissertation in Anthropology, University of Minnesota, Minneapolis, 1975.)

Driver, Harold E.
1961   Indians of North America. Chicago: University of Chicago Press.

1962   The Contributions of A.L. Kroeber to Culture Area Theory and Practice. *Indiana University Publications in Anthropology and Linguistics* 18. Bloomington.

Driver, Harold E., and Alfred L. Kroeber
1932   Quantitative Expression of Cultural Relationships. *University of California Publications in American Archaeology and Ethnology* 31(4):211–256. Berkeley. (Reprinted: Kraus Reprint Company, New York, 1965.)

Driver, Harold E., and William C. Massey
1957   Comparative Studies of North American Indians. *Transactions of the American Philosophical Society*, n.s. 47(2). Philadelphia.

Driver, Harold E., J.A. Kenny, H.C. Hudson, and O.M. Engle
1972   Statistical Clssification of North American Indian Ethnic Units. *Ethnology* 11(3):311–339.

Driver, Harold E., John M. Cooper, Paul Kirchoff, Dorothy Rainier Libby, William C. Massey, and Leslie Spier
1953   Indian Tribes of North America. *Indiana University. Publications in Anthropology and Linguistics.* Memoir 9. Bloomington.

Driver, Jonathan C.
1987   Hypsithermal Paleoecology and Archaeology of the Canadian Rockies. Pp. 345–360 in Man and the Mid-Holocene Climatic Optimum. Neil A. McKinnon and Glenn S.L. Stuart, eds. Calgary: The University of Calgary Archaeological Association.

1990   Meat in Due Season: The Timing of Communal Hunts. Pp. 11–33 in Hunters of the Recent Past. Leslie B. Davis and Brian O.K. Reeves, eds. London: Unwin Hyman.

Driver, Wilhemine
1969   Music and Dance. Pp. 194–207 in Indians of North America. Rev. ed. Harold E. Driver, ed. Chicago: University of Chicago Press.

Drooker, Penelope B.
1997   The View from Madisonville: Protohistoric Western Fort Ancient Interaction Patterns. *University of Michigan. Memoirs of the Museum of Anthropology* 31. Ann Arbor.

Drummond, Valerie
1976   Carry-The-Kettle Texts. (M.A. Thesis in Linguistics, University of Toronto, Toronto.)

1976a   Relative Clauses in Sioux Valley Santee and Carry-The Kettle Assiniboine. (Manuscript in V. Drummond's possession.)

Du Breuil, Jacobo
1943   Documents [Letter to Governor Miro, dated Ft. Charles III, Arkansas, August 26, 1783.] *Arkansas Historical Quarterly* 2(1):54–55.

Ducheneaux, Frank
1956   The Cheyenne River Sioux. *The American Indian* 7(3):20–29. New York.

Duffield, Lathel F., and Edward B. Jelks
1961   The Pearson Site: A Historic Indian Site at Iron Bridge Reservoir, Rains County, Texas. *The University of Texas. Department of Anthropology. Archaeology Series* 4. Austin.

Duflot de Mofras, Eugène
1844   Exploration du territoire de l'Orégon, des Californies et de la Mer Vermeille, exécutée pendant l'années 1840, 1841 et 1842. 2 vols. Paris: Arthus Bertrand.

Dugan, Kathleen Margaret
1985   The Vision Quest of the Plains Indians: Its Spiritual Significance. *Studies in American Religion* 13. Lewiston, N.Y.: The Edwin Mellen Press.

Dull Knife Memorial College
1998   1998/9 College Catalog. Lame Deer, Mont.: Dull Knife Memorial College Printing Office.

Dumont de Montigny, Jean F.B.
1753   Mémoires historiques sur la Louisiane; contenant ce qui y est arrivé de plus mémorable depuis l' anneé 1687. Jusqu'a' Présent...2vols. Paris: C.J.B. Bauche.

Dumont, Yvon
1994   Métis Nationalism: Then and Now. Pp. 82–89 in Pt. 2 of The Forks and the Battle of Seven Oaks in Manitoba History. Robert Coutts and Richard Stuart, eds. 2 Pts. Winnipeg: Man. Historical Society.

Dunbar, John
1910   The Presbyterian Mission among the Pawnee Indians in Nebraska, 1834–1836. *Collections of the Kansas State Historical Society [for] 1909–1910,* Vol. 11:323–332. Topeka.

Dunbar, John, and Samuel Allis
1918   Letters Concerning the Presbyterian Mission in the Pawnee Country, Near Bellvue, Neb., 1831–1849. [Pp. 570–741, Dunbar and Allis Letters; pp. 570–784, Dunbar et al. Letters.] *Collections of the Kansas State Historical Society [for] 1915–1918,* Vol. 14:570–784. Topeka.

Dunbar, John, et al. 1918 *see* Dunbar, John, and Samuel Allis 1918

Dunbar, John B.
1836   Lawyrawkōlârits Pany Kwta [Pawnee Spelling Book]. [Boston: American Board of Commissioners for Foreign Missions.]

1880   The Pawnee Indians: Their History and Ethnology. *Magazine of American History* 4(4):241–281. New York and Chicago.

1880a   The Pawnee Indians: Their Habits and Customs. *Magazine of American History* 5(5):321–342. New York and Chicago.

1880b   Pitalescharu—Chief of the Pawnees. *Magazine of American History* 5(5):343–345. New York and Chicago.

1882   Lone Chief and Medicine Bull. *Magazine of American History* 8(11):754–756. New York and Chicago.

1910   Massacre of the Villazur Expedition by the Pawnees on the Platte, in 1720. *Collections of the Kansas State Historical Society [for] 1909–1910,* Vol. 11:397–423. Topeka.

1911   Pawnee-English Vocabulary. (Manuscripts Nos. 1992a–b, National Anthropological Archives, Smithsonian Institution, Washington.)

Duncan, Kate C.
1980   American Indian Lace Making. *American Indian Art Magazine* 5(3):28–35–80. Scottsdale, Ariz.

Duncan, Mary Ann
1995   Calf Creek Foragers: Mobility on the Southern Plains During the Altithermal. *Bulletin of the Oklahoma Anthropological Society* 42:89–143. Norman.

Dunlay, Thomas W.
1982   Wolves for the Blue Soldiers: Indian Scouts and Auxiliaries with the United States Army, 1860–1890. Lincoln: University of Nebraska Press. (Reprinted in 1987).

Dunlevy, Marion Lucile
1936   A Comparison of the Cultural Manifestations of the Burkett (Nance County) and the Gray-Wolfe (Colfax County) Sites. Field work directed by William Duncan Strong and Waldo Wedel. Study directed by Earl H. Bell. Pp. 147–247 in Chapters in Nebraska Archaeology, by Earl H. Bell, et al. Lincoln: The University of Nebraska.

Dunn, Dorothy
1968   American Indian Painting of the Southwest and Plains Areas. Albuquerque: University of New Mexico.

1969   Introduction in 1877: Plains Indian Sketch Books of Zo-Tom and Howling Wolf. Flagstaff, Ariz.: Northland Press.

Dunn, William Edward
1911   Apache Relations in Texas, 1718–1750. *The Quarterly of the Texas State Historical Association* 14(3):198–274. Austin.

1912   Missionary Activities among the Eastern Apaches Previous to the Founding of the San Sabá Mission. *The Quarterly of the Texas State Historical Association* 15(3):186–200. Austin.

1914   The Apache Mission on the San Sabá River; Its Founding and Failure *Southwestern Historical Quarterly* 17(4):349–414. Austin, Tex.

1917   Spanish and French Rivalry in the Gulf Region of the United States, 1687–1702: The Beginnings of Texas and Pensacola. *University of Texas Bulletin* 1705. Austin.

Dunraven, Windham T. W.
1876   The Great Divide: Travels on the Upper Yellowstone in the Summer of 1874. London: Chatto and Windus. (Reprinted: University of Nebraska Press, Lincoln, 1967.)

Dunwiddie, Peter W.
1974   The Nature of the Relationship between the Blackfeet Indians and the Men of the Fur Trade. *Annals of Wyoming* 46(1):123–134. Cheyenne.

Duratschek, Sr. Mary Claudia O.S.B.
1947   Crusading Along Sioux Trails: A History of the Catholic Indian Missions of South Dakota. Yankton, S.Dak.: Benedictine Convent of the Sacred Heart.

Durham, Jimmie
1986   Ni'Go Tlunh A Doh Ka (We Are Always Turning Around on Purpose). Long Island, N.Y.: Amelie A. Wallace Gallery, State University of New York at Westbury.

Durkin, Pat, Alan Bisbort, and Sara Day *see* Day, Sara, ed. 1997

Duro, Cesáreo Fernández *see* Fernández Duro, Cesáreo

Dusenberry, Verne
1954   The Rocky Boy Indians. *Montana: The Magazine of Western History* 4(1):1–15. Helena.

1137

1955   The Northern Cheyenne: A Remarkable Account of a Group of First Americans Who Asked Only They Be Allowed to Live in a Land of Their Own Choosing. *Montana Heritage Series* 6. Helena: Montana Historical Society Press.

1958   Waiting for a Day That Never Comes. *Montana: The Magazine of Western History* 8(1):23–31. Helena. (Reprinted in 1985.)

1960   Notes on the Material Culture of the Assiniboine Indians. *Ethnos* 25(1–2):44–62. Stockholm: National Museum of Ethnography.

1961   The Significance of the Sacred Pipes to the Gros Ventre of Montana. *Ethnos* 26(1–2):12–29. Stockholm: National Museum of Ethnogaphy.

1962   The Montana Cree: A Study in Religious Persistence. *Stockholm Studies in Compartive Religion* 3. Uppsala, Sweden: Almquist and Wiksells Boktryckeri. (Reprinted: University of Oklahoma Press, Norman, 1998.)

1963   Ceremonial Sweat Lodges of the Gros Ventre Indians. *Ethnos* 28(1):46–62. Stockholm: National Museum of Ethnography.

1965   The Métis of Montana. Pp. 88–105 in The Red Man's West. Michael S. Kennedy, ed. New York: Hastings House.

1985   Waiting for a Day That Never Comes: The Dispossessed Métis of Montana. Pp. 119–136 in The New Peoples: Being and Becoming Métis in North America. Jacqueline Peterson and Jennifer S.H. Brown, eds. *Manitoba Studies in Native History* 1. Winnipeg: The University of Manitoba Press; Lincoln: University of Nebraska Press. (Article orginally publ. in 1958.)

Duval, John C.
1871   The Adventures of Big-foot Wallace; The Texas Ranger and Hunter. Philadelphia: Claxton, Remsey and Haffelfinger. (Reprinted: University of Nebraska Press, Lincoln, 1966.)

Dyck, Ian
1972   The Grandora Site: A Besant Campsite near Saskatoon, Saskatchewan. *Saskatchewan Archaeology Society Newsletter* 39:1–17. Saskatoon, Sask.

1977   The Harder Site: A Middle Period Bison Hunter's Campsite in the Northern Great Plains. *Canada. National Museum of Man. Mercury Series. Archaeological Survey Paper* 67. Ottawa.

1983   The Prehistory of Southern Saskatchewan. Pp. 63–139 in Tracking Ancient Hunters: Prehistoric Archaeology in Saskatchewan. H.T. Epp and I. Dyck, eds. Regina: Saskatchewan Archaeological Society.

Dyck, Ian, and Richard E. Morlan
1995   The Sjovold Site: A River Crossing Campsite in the Northern Plains. *Canada. Museum of Civilization. Mercury Series. Archaeological Survey Paper* 151. Ottawa.

Dyck, Noel
1986   An Opportunity Lost: The Initiative of the Reserve Agricultural Programme in the Prairie West. Pp 121–137 in 1885 and After: Native Society in Transition. F. Laurie Barron and James B. Waldram, eds. Regina, Sask.: Canadian Plains Research Center, University of Regina.

1991   What Is the Indian "Problem": Tutelage and Resistance in Canadian Indian Administration. *Social and Economic Studies* 46. St. John's, Nfld.: Institute of Social and Economic Research, Memorial University of Newfoundland.

Dyck, Paul
1971   Brulé: The Sioux People of the Rosebud. Flagstaff, Ariz.: Northland Press.

1975   The Plains Indian Shield from the Paul Dyck Research Foundation. *American Indian Art Magazine* 1(1):34–42. Scottsdale, Ariz.

1988   Elegance Mingled with Beauty. Pp. 9–11 in To Honor the Crow People. Father Peter J. Powell, ed. Chicago: Foundation for the Preservation of Indian Art and Culture.

Dyer, J.O.
1920   The History of the Tonkawai Tribe. *Galveston Daily News,* July 11. Galveston, Tex.

Dyer, Mrs. D.B.
1896   "Fort Reno": or Picturesque "Cheyenne and Arapahoe Army Life" Before the Opening of "Oklahoma." New York: G.W. Dillingham.

Eakin, Daniel H., Julie E. Francis, and Mary Lou Larson
1997   The Split Rock Ranch Site: Early Archaic Cultural Practices in Southcentral Wyoming. Pp. 395–435 in Changing Perspectives of the Archaic on the Northwestern Plains and Rocky Mountains. Mary Lou Larson and Julie E. Francis, eds. Vermillion: The University of South Dakota Press.

Earl of Southesk 1875 *see* Southesk, James Carnegie, Earl of 1870

Eastman, Charles A. (Ohiyesa)
1902   Indian Boyhood. New York: McClure, Phillips and Co. (Reprinted: Dover Press, New York, 1971.)

1907   Old Indian Days. Illustrations in color by Dan Sayre Groesbeck. New York: The McClure Company. (Reprinted: University of Nebraska Press, Lincoln, 1991.)

1911   The Soul of the Indian. Boston: Houghton Mifflin Company (Reprinted: University of Nebraska Press, Lincoln, 1980.)

1916   From the Deep Woods to Civilization: Chapters in the Autobiography of an Indian. Boston: Little, Brown, and Company. (Reprinted, with Introduction by Raymond Wilson: University of Nebraska Press, Lincoln, 1977.)

Eastman, Elaine G.
1978   Sister to the Sioux: The Memoirs of Elaine Goodale Eastman, 1881–91. Kay Graber, ed. *The Pioneer Heritage Series* 7. Lincoln: University of Nebraska Press.

Eastman, John
1970   Powwow. *Natural History* 79(9):24, 26–27.

Eastman, Mary Henderson
1849   Dahcotah: or, Life and Legends of the Sioux around Fort Snelling; with Preface by Mrs. C.M. Kirkland. Illustrated from Drawings by Captain Eastman. New York: J. Wiley. (Reprinted: Ross and Haines, Minneapolis, 1962; also, Arno Press, New York, 1975; and, with a Preface by Rena Neumann Coen: Afton Historical Society Press, Afton, Minn., 1995.)

1853   The American Aboriginal Portfolio. Illustrated by S. Eastman, U.S. Army. Philadelphia: Lippincott, Grambo. (Title on cover: Eastman's Aboriginal Portfolio.)

_____   1962, 1975, 1995 *see* 1849 (reprint info.)

Ebell, S. Biron
1988   The Dunn Site. *Plains Anthropologist* 33(122):505–530.

Eccles, William J.
1969   The Canadian Frontier, 1534–1763. New York: Holt, Rinehart and Winston. (Reprinted: University of New Mexico Press, Albuquerque, 1974; rev., ed., 1983.)

Echo-Hawk, Roger C., and Walter R. Echo-Hawk
1994   Battlefields and Burial Grounds: The Indian Struggle to Protect Ancestral Graves in the United States. Minneapolis: Lerner Publications.

Edgar, Bob, and Jack Turnell
1978   Brand of a Legend. Centennial ed. Cody, Wyo.: Stockade Publishing.

Edmonton House Journals
1799–1824   [Journals for 1822–1823 and 1823–1824]. (Hudson's Bay Company Collection, Reel 1m776, Public Archives of Canada, Ottawa.)

Edmunds, F.H., J.L. Jackson, J.W.T. Spinks, and V.A. Vigfusson
1938   Some Skeletal Remains in Saskatchewan. *American Antiquity* 3(3):244–246.

Edmunds, R. David
1976   The Otoe-Missouria People. Phoenix, Ariz.: Indian Tribal Series.

Edmunds, R. David, and Joseph L. Peyser
1993   The Fox Wars: The Mesquakie Challenge to New France. Norman: University of Oklahoma Press.

Eggan, Fred
1933   [Fieldnotes on the Cheyenne and Arapaho of Oklahoma.] (Copy of fieldnotes in L. Fowler's possession.)
_____, ed.
1937   Social Anthropology of North American Tribes. Chicago: University of Chicago Press. (Reprinted, enlarged ed., 1955.)

1937a   The Cheyenne and Arapaho Kinship System. Pp. 33–95 in Social Anthropology of North American Tribes. Fred Eggan, ed. Chicago: University of Chicago Press. (Reprinted, enlarged ed., 1955.)

1952   The Ethnological Cultures and Their Archeological Backgrounds. Pp. 35–45 in Archeology of Eastern United States. James B. Griffin, ed. Chicago: University of Chicago Press.

1954   Social Anthropology and the Method of Controlled Comparison. *American Anthropologist,* n.s. 56(5, Pt.1):307–408.
_____, ed.
1955   Social Anthropology of North American Tribes. Enlarged ed. Chicago: University of Chicago Press. (Originally publ. in 1937.)

1955a   The Cheyenne and Arapaho Kinship System. Pp. 35–95 in Social Anthropology of North American Tribes. Enlarged ed. Fred Eggan, ed. Chicago: University of Chicago Press.

1955b   Social Anthropology: Methods and Results. Pp. 485–551 in Social Anthropology of North American Tribes. Enlarged ed. Fred Eggan, ed. Chicago: University of Chicago Press.
_____, ed.
1966   The American Indian: Perspectives for the Study of Social Change. Chicago: Aldine.

1966a   The Cheyenne and Arapaho in the Perspective of the Plains: Ecology and Society. Pp. 45–77 in The American Indian: Perspectives for the Study of Social Change, by Fred Eggan. Chicago: Aldine.

1968   [Lecture notes from course: "Kinship and Social Organization", Department of Anthropology, The University of Chicago, taken by Raymond J. DeMallie.] (Manuscript in R.J. DeMallie's possession.)

1980   Shoshone Kinship Structures and Their Significance for Anthropological Theory. *Journal of the Steward Anthropological Society* 11(2):165–193. Urbana, Ill.

Ehrlich, Clara Hildermann
1937   Tribal Culture in Crow Mythology. *Journal of American Folk-lore* 50(198):307–408.

Eicher, Carl
1962   An Approach to Income Improvement on the Rosebud Sioux Indian Reservation. *Human Organization* 20(4):191–196. Washington.

Eighmy, Jeffrey L.
1994   The Central High Plains: A Cultural Historical Summary. Pp. 224–238 in Plains Indians, A.D. 500–1500: The Archaeological Past of Historic Groups. Karl H. Schleiser, ed. Norman and London: University of Oklahoma Press.

Eighmy, Jeffrey L., and Caryl Wood
1984   Dated Architecture on the Southern Colorado Plains. Pp. 273–292 in Papers of the Philmont Conference on the Archeology of Northeastern New Mexico. Carol J. Condie, ed. *Proceedings of the New Mexico Archeological Council* 6(1). [New Mexico.]

Elam, Earl H.
1971   The History of the Wichita Indian Confederacy to 1868. (Ph.D. Dissertation in History, Texas Tech University, Lubbock, Tex.)

1979   A Historical Report Concerning the Wichita Indians from 1859 to 1895 and Indian and Non-Indian Occupancy of Certain Lands in Texas, Kansas, and Indian Territory Prior to 1895. Alpine, Tex.: Sul Ross State University.

Eldredge, J. C.
1928   Eldredge's Report on His Expedition to the Comanches. *West Texas Historical Association Year Book* 4:114–139. Abilene.

Elguezabal, Juan Bautista de
1802   [Letter to Pedro de Nava, dated July 1802.] (Manuscript, Microfilm Publication BA, Roll 30, Frame 510, Bexar Archives, University of Texas Archives, Barker Texas History Center, Austin.)

Elias, Peter Douglas
1988   The Dakota of the Canadian North-West: Lessons for Survival. *Manitoba Studies in Native History* 5. Winnipeg: The University of Manitoba Press.

Elkin, Henry
1940   The Northern Arapaho of Wyoming. Pp. 207–255 in Acculturation in Seven American Indian Tribes. Ralph Linton, ed. New York: Appleton-Century Company.

Ellis, C. Douglas
1960   A Note on Okima·hka·n. *Anthropological Linguistics* 2(3):1. Bloomington.

1973   A Proposed Standard Roman Orthography for Cree. *Western Canadian Journal of Anthropology* 3(4):1–37. Edmonton, Alta.

1983   Spoken Cree: West Coast of James Bay. Rev. ed. Informants: John Wynne, Anne Scott, Xavier Sutherland. Edmonton, Alta.: Pica Pica Press. (Originally publ.: Anglican Book Centre, Toronto, 1962.)

Ellis, Clyde
1996   To Change Them Forever: Indian Education at the Rainy Mountain Boarding School, 1893–1920. Norman and London: University of Oklahoma Press.

1999   "We Don't Want Your Rations, We Want This Dance": The Changing Use of Song and Dance on the Southern Plains. *Western Historical Quarterly* 30(2):133–154. Logan, Utah.

Ellison, Rosemary
1969   Contemporary Southern Plains Indian Art. [Introduction by *1139*

Rosemary Ellison.] Anadarko: Oklahoma Indian Arts and Crafts Cooperative.

1972   Contemporary Southern Plains Indian Painting. With an Essay by Rosemary Ellison. Myles Libhart, ed. Anadarko: Oklahoma Indian Arts and Crafts Cooperative.

1976   Contemporary Southern Plains Indian Metalwork. [Introduction by Rosemary Ellison.] Anadarko: Oklahoma Indian Arts and Crafts Cooperative.

Ellwood, Priscilla B.
1987   Bayou Gulch (5DA265) Ceramics. *Plains Anthropologist* 32(116):113–139.

Elmendorf, William W.
1963   Yukin-Siouan Lexical Similarities. *International Journal of American Linguistics* 29(4):300–309. Chicago.

1964   Item and Set Comparison in Yuchi, Siouan, and Yukian. *International Journal of American Linguistics* 30(4):328–340. Chicago.

Emerson, Thomas A., and James A. Brown
1992   The Late Prehistory and Protohistory of Illinois. Pp. 77–128 in Calumet & Fleur-de-Lys: Archaeology of Indian and French Contact in the Midcontinent. John A. Walthall and Thomas E. Emerson, eds. Washington: Smithsonian Institution Press.

Energy, Mines and Resources. Canada *see* Canada. Energy Mines and Resources

Ens, Gerhard J.
1989   Dispossession or Adaptation? Migration and Persistence of the Red River Métis, 1835–1890. Pp. 120–144 in *Canadian Historical Association. Historical Papers/Communications historiques [for] 1988.* Ottawa.

1996   Homeland to Hinterland: The Changing Worlds of the Red River Métis in the Nineteenth Century. Toronto: University of Toronto Press.

Epp, Henry T., ed.
1993   Three Hundred Prairie Years. Regina, Sask.: Canadian Plains Research Center, University of Regina.

Epp, Henry T., and Ian Dyck, eds.
1983   Tracking Ancient Hunters: Prehistoric Archaeology in Saskatchewan. 2 vols. Regina, Sask.: Saskatchewan Archaeological Society.

Erdoes, Richard
1972   The Sun Dance People: the Plains Indians, Their Past and Present. New York: Alfred A. Knopf; also, Random House, New York.

Erikson, Erik H.
1939   Observations on Sioux Education. *The Journal of Psychology* 7:101–156. Provincetown, Mass.

1950   Childhood and Society. 2d ed., rev. and enl. New York: W.W. Norton & Co.

Ermatinger, Francis
1980   Fur Trade Letters of Francis Ermatinger, Written to His Brother Edward during His Service with the Hudson's Bay Company, 1818–1853. Lois Halliday McDonald, ed. Glendale, Calif.: Arthur H. Clark.

Erwin, Sarah
1998   Along the Wide Missouri: Maximilian and Bodmer in the Western Frontier, 1832–34. *Gilcrease Journal* 6(1):30–47. Tulsa: Thomas Gilcrease Museum Association.

Escudero, José A. de
1834   Noticias estadísticas del estado de Chihuahua. México: Juan Ojeda.

1849   Noticia estadísticas de Sonora y Sinaloa. Mexico: Tup. de R. Rafael.

Eslamidoust, Pouran, and M. Stephanie Reynolds
1987   The Sundance among Pre-Reservation North American Indians: A Multivariate Model. (Paper presented at the Annual Meeting of the American Society for Ethnohistory.)

Estes, George C., and Richard R. Loder
1971   Kul-Wicasa-Oyate: Lower Brule Sioux Tribe. Lower Brule, S.Dak.: Lower Brule Sioux Tribe.

Etchieson, Gerald M.
1981   Archeological Survey at Lake Meredith Recreation Area, Moore and Potter Counties, Texas. Amarillo, Tex.: U.S. Department of the Interior, Water and Power Resources Service. Southwest Region.

Evans, G. Edward
1961   Ceramic Analysis of the Blackduck Ware and Its General Cultural Relationships. *Proceedings of the Minnesota Academy of Science* 29:33–54. St. Paul.

Evarts, Mark
1967   Music of the Pawnees Sung by Mark Evarts. Documentary Recording by Gene Weltfish. Washington: Ethnic Folkways Library.

Evening Star [editorial]
1873   The Indian Council of To-Day - An Official Talk with the Crows - What They Ask of Their Great Father. *Evening Star,* October 21:1. Washington.

Everette, Willis E.
1878   [Alphabetical Vocabulary of Adjectives, Nouns, Verbs, Pronouns, etc., in the Oglälä Dialect of the Sioux Language.] (Manuscript; collected in Sitting Bull's camp on Milk River, Montana Terr., October 24, 1878; cited in Pilling 1885:941, and Pilling 1887:27.)

1881   [Vocabulary of the (Teton) Sioux, Alphabetically Arranged.] (Manuscript collected in 1881; cited in Pilling 1885:247, and Pilling 1887:27.)

Ewers, John C.
1937   Teton Dakota: Ethnology and History. Berkeley, Calif.: U.S. Department of the Interior, National Park Service.

1939   Plains Indian Painting: A Description of an Aboriginal American Art. Palo Alto, Calif.: Stanford University Press. (Reprinted: AMS Press, New York, 1979.)

1943   Primitive American Commandos. *The Masterkey* 17(4): 117–125. Los Angeles: The Southwest Museum.

1943a   Museum: The Blackfeet Indians Now Have a Word for It. *The Museum News* 20(18):12.

1944   The Story of the Blackfeet. *Indian Life and Customs Pamphlet* 6. Lawrence, Kans.: Department of the Interior, United States Indian Service, Education Division; Printed by Haskell Institute.

1944a   The Blackfoot War Lodge: Its Construction and Use. *American Anthropologist,* n.s. 46(2):182–192. (Reprinted in rev. form: pp. 117–130 in Indian Life on the Upper Missouri, by John C. Ewers, University of Oklahoma Press, Norman, 1968.)

1944b   Food Rationing Is Nothing New to the Blackfeet. *The Masterkey* 18(3):73–80. (Reprinted in rev. form under title: Food Rationing—From Buffalo to Beef, pp. 169–174 in Indian Life on the Upper Missouri, by John C. Ewers, University of Oklahoma, Norman, 1968.)

1945   Blackfeet Crafts. *Indian Handcrafts Series* 9. Lawrence,

1140

Kans.: U.S. Department of the Interior, Bureau of Indian Affairs, Branch of Education; Printed by Haskell Institute Press. (Reprinted in 1960, 1962, 1968; also, R. Schneider Publishers, Stevens Point, Wis., 1986.)

1946   Identification and History of the Small Robes Band of Piegan Indians. *Journal of the Washington Academy of Sciences* 36(12):397–401. Washington.

1948   Self-torture in the Blood Indian Sun Dance. *Journal of the Washington Academy of Sciences* 38(5):166–173. Washington. (Reprinted in rev. form: pp. 146–156 in Indian Life on the Upper Missouri, by John C. Ewers. University of Oklahoma Press, Norman, 1968.)

1948a   Gustavus Sohon's Portraits of Flathead and Pend d'Oreille Indians, 1854. *Smithsonian Miscellaneous Collections* 10(7). Washington: Smithsonian Institution; Government Printing Office.

1949   The Last Bison Drives of the Blackfoot Indians. *Journal of the Washington Academy of Sciences* 39(11):355–360. Washington. (Reprinted in rev. form: pp. 157–168 in Indian Life on the Upper Missouri, by John C. Ewers, University of Oklahoma Press, Norman, 1968.)

1952   Museums for Indians in the United States. *Fundamental Education: A Quarterly Bulletin* 4(1):3–9.

1954   The Indian Trade of the Upper Missouri before Lewis and Clark: An Interpretation. *Bulletin of the Missouri Historical Society* 10(4):429–446. St. Louis. (Reprinted in rev. form: pp. 14–33 in Indian Life on the Upper Missouri, by John C. Ewers, University of Oklahoma Press, Norman, 1968.)

1955   The Horse in Blackfoot Indian Culture: With Comparative Material from Other Western Tribes. *Bureau of American Ethnology Bulletin* 159. Washington: Smithsonian Institution; U.S. Government Printing Office. (Reprinted in 1969, 1980.)

1955a   The Bear Cult among the Assiniboins and Their Neighbors of the Northern Plains. *Southwestern Journal of Anthropology* 11(1):1–14. Albuquerque. (Reprinted in rev. form: pp. 131–145 in Indian Life on the Upper Missouri, by John C. Ewers, University of Oklahoma Press, Norman, 1968.)

1956   The Assiniboine Horse Medicine Cult. *Anthropological Quarterly* 29(3):57–68.

1956a   The North West Trade Gun. *The Alberta Historical Review* 4(2):3–9. Calgary, Alta. (Reprinted in rev. form: pp. 34–44 in Indian Life on the Upper Missouri, by John C. Ewers, University of Oklahoma Press, Norman, 1968.)

1956b   The Gun of Sitting Bull. *The Beaver* 287(Winter:20–23). (Reprinted in rev. form under title: Where Sitting Bull Surrendered His Winchester, pp. 175–181 in Indian Life on the Upper Missouri, by John C. Ewers, University of Oklahoma Press, Norman, 1968.)

1956c   Plains Indian War Medicine. *Tomorrow: Quarterly Review of Psychical Research* 4(3):85–90.

1957   Early White Influence Upon Plains Indian Painting: George Catlin and Carl Bodmer among the Mandans, 1832–1834. *Smithsonian Miscellaneous Collections* 134(7):1–11. Washington: Smithsonian Institution; Government Printing Office. (Reprinted in rev. form: pp. 98–109 in Indian Life on the Upper Missouri, by John C. Ewers, University of Oklahoma Press, Norman, 1968; also, Shorey Book Store, Seattle, 1971.)

1957a   Three Ornaments Worn by Upper Missouri Indians a Century and a Quarter Ago. *The New-York Historical Society Quarterly* 41(1):24–33. New York. (Reprinted in rev. form under title: Three Ornaments Worn by Upper Missouri Dandies in the 1830's, pp. 91–97 in Indian Life on the Upper Missouri, by John C. Ewers, University of Oklahoma Press, Norman, 1968.)

1957b   Hair Pipes in Plains Indian Adornment, a Study in Indian and White Ingenuity. *Bureau of American Ethnology Bulletin* 164; *Anthropological Paper* 50. Washington: Smithsonian Institution; U.S. Government Printing Office.

1958   The Blackfeet: Raiders on the Northwestern Plains. Norman: University of Oklahoma Press. (Several reprints, incl., 1967, 1971, 1982, 1989.)

1959   A Century of American Indian Exhibits in the Smithsonian Institution. Washington: Smithsonian Institution Press.

1960   A Blood Indian's Conception of Tribal Life in Dog Days. *The Blue Jay* 18(1):44–48. Regina, Sask.: Saskatchewan Natural History Society. (Reprinted, pp. 7–13 in: Indian Life on the Upper Missouri, by John C. Ewers, University of Oklahoma Press, Norman, 1968.)

1960a   Selected References on the Plains Indians. [Mimeograph.] *Smithsonian Anthropological Bibliographies* 1. Washington: Smithsonian Institution.

_____, ed. 1960[b], 1975 Wildschut, William 1960, 1975

_____, ed. 1961 *see* Denig, Edwin Thompson 1961

1962   Mothers of the Mixed Bloods. *El Palacio: A Quarterly Journal of the Museum of New Mexico* 69(1):20–29. (Reprinted in rev. form: pp. 57–67 in Indian Life on the Upper Missouri, by John C. Ewers, University of Oklahoma Press, Norman, 1968.)

1963   Blackfoot Indian Pipes and Pipe Making. *Bureau of American Ethnology Bulletin* 186; *Anthropological Paper* 64. Washington: Smithsonian Institution; U.S. Government Printing Office.

1965   The Emergence of the Plains Indian as the Symbol of the North American Indian. Pp. 531–544 in *Smithsonian Institution Report for 1964*. Washington. (Reprinted in rev. form: pp. 187–203 in Indian Life on the Upper Missouri, by John C. Ewers, University of Oklahoma Press, Norman, 1968.)

1966   "Chiefs from the Missouri and Mississippi" and Peale's Silhouettes of 1806. *Smithsonian Journal of History* 1(1):1–26. Washington.

1966a   Reactions of the Plains Indians to the Lewis and Clark Expedition. *Montana: The Magazine of Western History* 16(1):2–12. Helena. (Reprinted in rev. form: pp. 45–56 in Indian Life on the Upper Missouri, by John C. Ewers, University of Oklahoma Press, Norman, 1968.)

1968   Indian Life on the Upper Missouri. Norman: University of Oklahoma Press. (Reprinted in 1988.)

1969   Artifacts Collected by Jean Louis Berlandier among the Indian Tribes of Texas. Pp. 167–189 in The Indian of Texas in 1830 [by Jean Louis Berlandier]. John C. Ewers, ed. Washington: Smithsonian Institution Press.

_____, ed. 1969[a] *see* Berlandier, Jean Louis 1969

1971   Winold Reiss: His Portraits and Proteges. *Montana: The Magazine of Western History* 21(3):44–55. Helena.

1972   The Influence of the Fur Trade Upon the Indians of the Northern Plains. Pp. 1–26 in People and Pelts: Selected *1141*

Papers of the Second North American Fur Trade Conference. Malvina Bolus, ed. Winnipeg, Man.: Peguis Publishers.

1972a   Folk Art in the Fur Trade of the Upper Missouri. *Prologue: The Journal of the National Archives* 4(2):99–108. Washington, D.C.

1973   The Influence of Epidemics on the Indian Populations and Cultures of Texas. *Plains Anthropologist* 18(60):104–115.

1974   Blackfeet Indians: Ethnological Report on the Blackfeet and Gros Ventre Tribes of Indians. *American Indian Ethnohistory: Plains Indians.* David Agee Horr, ed. New York: Garland Publishing.

1974a   Ethnological Report on the Chippewa Cree Tribe of the Rocky Boy Reservation and the Little Shell Band of Indians. Pp. 9–182 in Chippewa Indians VI. *American Indian Ethnohistory: North Central and Northeastern Indians.* David Agee Horr, ed. New York: Garland Publishing.

1974b   Symbols of Chiefly Authority in Spanish Louisiana. Pp. 272–286 in The Spanish in the Mississippi Valley, 1762–1804. John Francis McDermott, ed. Urbana: University of Illinois Press. (Reprinted: Pp. 103–118 in Plains Indian History and Culture: Essays on Continuity and Change. University of Oklahoma Press, Norman, 1997.)

1975   Intertribal Warfare as the Precursor of Indian-White Warfare on the Northern Great Plains. *Western Historical Quarterly* 6(4):397–410. Logan, Utah.

1975a   Conclusions. Pp. 169–175 in Crow Indian Medicine Bundles, by William Wildschut. John C. Ewers, ed. 2d ed. *Museum of the American Indian. Heye Foundation. Contributions* 17. New York. (Originally publ. in 1960.)

1976   Blackfeet Indian Tipis: Design and Legend. [Portfolio organized by Jessie Wilber; Silk-screened Plates printed by Jessie Wilber ... et al.; Project started by Olga Ross Hannon, revived and completed by the Museum of the Rockies.] Bozeman, Mont.: Museum of the Rockies.

1976a   Indian Views of the White Man to 1850: An Interpretation. Pp. 7–24 in Red Men and Hat-Wearers: Viewpoints in Indian History. Daniel Tyler, ed. Fort Collins, Colo.: Colorado State University.

1977   Notes on the Weasel in Historic Plains Indian Culture. *Plains Anthropologist* 22(78):253–262.

1978   Murals in the Round: Painted Tipis of the Kiowa and Kiowa-Apache Indians. Washington: Smithsonian Institution Press.

1978a   Three Effigy Pipes by an Eastern Dakota Master Carver. *American Indian Art Magazine* 3(4):51–55, 74. Scottsdale, Ariz.

1979   Indian Art in Pipestone: George Catlin's Portfolio in the British Museum. London and Washington: British Museum Publications, Ltd., and Smithsonian Institution Press.

1980   Climate, Acculturation and Costume: A History of Women's Clothing among the Indians of the Southern Plains. *American Indian Art Magazine* 6(2):63–82. Scottsdale, Ariz.

1981   The Emergence of the Named Indian Artist in the American West. *American Indian Art Magazine* 6(2):52–61, 77. Scottsdale, Ariz.

1981a   Pipes for the Presidents. *American Indian Art Magazine* 6(3):62–70. Scottsdale, Ariz.

1981b   Water Monsters in Plains Indian Art. *American Indian Art Magazine* 6(4):38–45. Scottsdale, Ariz.

1982   The Awesome Bear in Plains Indian Art. *American Indian Art Magazine* 7(3):36–45. Scottsdale, Ariz.

1982a   Assiniboin Antelope-Horn Headdresses. *American Indian Art Magazine* 7(4):44–51. Scottsdale, Ariz.

1982b   Artists' Choice. *American Indian Art Magazine* 7(2):40–49. Scottsdale, Ariz.

1983   A Half Century of Change in the Study of Plains Indian Art and Material Culture. *University of Oklahoma. Department of Anthropology. Papers in Anthropology* 24(2). Norman.

1983a   Plains Indian Artists and Anthropologists: A Fruitful Collaboration. *American Indian Art Magazine* 9(1):36–49. Scottsdale, Ariz.

1985   Blackfeet: Their History. Surrey, B.C.: Hancock House.

1986   Plains Indian Sculpture: A Traditional Art from America's Heartland. Washington: Smithsonian Institution Press.

1994   Women's Roles in Plains Indian Warfare. Pp. 325–332 in Skeletal Biology in the Great Plains: Migration, Warfare, Health, and Subsistence. Douglas W. Owsley and Richard L. Jantz, eds. Washington: Smithsonian Institution Press.

1997   Plains Indian History and Culture: Essays on Continuity and Change. Norman: University of Oklahoma Press.

Ewers, John C., Helen M. Mangelsdorf, and William S. Wierzbowski
1985   Images of a Vanished Life. Philadelphia: Pennsylvania Academy of the Arts.

Ewers, John C., Marsha V. Gallagher, David C. Hunt, and Joseph C. Porter
1984   Views of a Vanishing Frontier. (Catalog of an Exhibition, Joslyn Art Museum, Omaha, Nebr., February 12 to April 8, 1984 ... The Metropolitan Museum of Art, New York, N.Y., July 17 to October 6, 1985.) Omaha: Center for Western Studies, Joslyn Art Museum; distributed by University of Nebraska Press, Lincoln.

Eyerly, T.L.
1908   The Buried City of the Panhandle. *Transactions of the Kansas Academy of Science* 21(1):219–228. Topeka.

1910   Indian Remains of the Canadian River Valley. *The Archaeological Bulletin* 1(3):77–80.

Eyman, Charles E.
1966   The Schultz Focus: A Plains Middle Woodland Burial Complex in Eastern Kansas. (M.A. Thesis in Archaeology, University of Calgary, Calgary, Alta.)

Fagin, Nancy L.
1988   James Mooney Collection of Cheyenne Tipi Models at the Field Museum of Natural History. *Plains Anthropologist* 33(120):261–278.

Falconer, Thomas
1844   On the Discovery of the Mississippi, and on the Southwestern, Oregon, and North-western Boundary of the United States; with a Translation from the Original Ms. of Memoirs, etc., Relating to the Discovery of the Mississippi, by Robert Cavelier de La Salle and the Chevalier Henry de Tonty. London: S. Clarke. (Reprinted, 2d ed., 1845; also, a facsim. reproduction of the 1844 ed. with an Introduction by Dorman H. Winfrey: Shoal Creek Publishers, Austin, Tex., 1975.)

Falk, Carl R.
1981   Vertebrate Remains. Pp. 223–259 in Archaeological Inves-

tigations at the Rainbow Site, Plymouth County, Iowa. David W. Benn, ed. (Report sponsored by the National Park Service, Interagency Archaeological Services, Denver; copy in the U.S. Department of the Interior, Natural Resource Library, Washington.)

_____, ed.
1984   Archeological Investigations within Federal Lands Located on the East Bank of Lake Sharpe Project Area, South Dakota: 1978–1979. Vol 2: Final Report. (Sponsored by the U.S. Army Corps of Engineers, Omaha District.) *University of Nebraska. Department of Anthropology. Division of Archeological Research. Technical Report* 83-04. Lincoln.

Falk, Carl R., and Francis A. Calabrese
1973   Helb: A Preliminary Statement. *Plains Anthropologist* 18(62):336–343.

Farabee, William Curtis
1921   Dress among Plains Indian Women. *Journal of the University of Pennsylvania Museum* 12:239–251. Philadelphia.

Farber, William O.
1970   Representative Government: Application to the Sioux. Pp. 123–139 in The Modern Sioux: Social Systems and Reservation Culture. Ethel Nurge, ed. Lincoln: University of Nebraska Press.

Faries, Richard, ed.
1938   A Dictionary of the Cree Language, as Spoken by the Indians in the Provinces of Quebec, Ontario, Man., Saskatchewan and Alberta. Based upon the Foundation Laid by Rev. E. A. Watkins, 1865, C.M.S. Missionary. Revised, Enriched and Brought Up To Date by The Late Ven. J. A. Mackay ... [et al.]. Toronto: Published under the Direction of the General Synod of the Church of England in Canada. (Reprinted: Anglican Book Centre, Toronto, 1986.)

Farmer, Malcolm F.
1942   Navaho Archaeology of Upper Blanco and Largo Canyons, Northern New Mexico. *American Antiquity* 8(1):65–79.

Farnell, Brenda
1995   Do You See What I Mean?: Plains Indian Sign Talk and the Embodiment of Action. Austin: University of Texas Press.

Farnham, Thomas J.
1843   Travels in the Great Western Prairies, the Anahuac and Rocky Mountains, and in the Oregon Territory. New York: Greeley and McElrath. (Reprinted in Vols. 28–29 [1906] of Early Western Travels, 1748–1846. Reuben G. Thwaites, ed. 32 vols. Arthur H. Clark, Cleveland, Ohio, 1904–1907; also, Da Capo Press, New York, 1973.)

_____ [1904–1907], 1906 *see* Thwaites, Reuben G., ed. 1904–1907 (Vols. 28–29, 1906)

Farr, William E.
1984   The Reservation Blackfeet, 1882–1945: A Photographic History of Cultural Survival. With a Foreword by James Welch. Seattle and London: University of Washington Press. (Reprinted in 1986.)

Farrokhi, Abdollah
1993   Rapid City Native American Population Needs Assessment. *American Indian Culture and Research Journal* 17(2):153–173. Los Angeles.

Faulk, Odie B.
1964   The Last Years of Spanish Texas, 1778–1821. The Hague: Mouton.

Fay, George E., ed.
1967   Charters, Constitutions and By-Laws of the Indian Tribes of North America. Part I: The Sioux Tribes of South Dakota. *Colorado State College. Museum of Anthropology. Occasional Publications in Anthropology* 1; *Ethnology Series*. Greeley, Colo.

_____, ed.
1977   Treaties between the Tribes of the Great Plains and the United States of America: Cheyenne and Arapaho, 1825–1900, [etc.]. Greeley, Colo.: Museum of Anthropology, University of Colorado.

Faye, Stanley
1943   The Arkansas Post of Louisiana: French Domination. *Louisiana Historical Quarterly* 26(3):633–721.

Featherstonhaugh, George W.
1844   Excursion Through the Slave States, from Washington on the Potomac to the Frontier of Mexico: With Sketches of Popular Manners and Geological Notices. New York: Harper and Brothers.

_____
1847   A Canoe Trip Up the Minnay Sotor, with an Account of the Lead and Copper Deposits in Wisconsin, [etc.]. 2 vols. London: Richard Bentley. (Reprinted: Minnesota Historical Society, St. Paul, 1970.)

Febre, Luis, et al.
1749   [Proceedings to Investigate the Visit of Three Frenchmen Who Arrived in Taos, New Mexico, Accompanying the Comanche Indians.] (Manuscript, Provincias Internas 37, Archivio General de Mexico; William E. Duncan Transcripts in The University of Texas Library, Austin.)

Feder, Norman
1962   Plains Indian Metal-working, with Emphasis on Hairplates. *American Indian Tradition* 8(2):55–76. Alton, Ill.

_____
1964   Art of the Eastern Plains Indians: The Nathan Sturges Jarvis Collection. Brooklyn, N.Y.: The Brooklyn Museum.

_____
1964a   Origin of the Oklahoma Forty Nine Dance. *Ethnomusicology* 8(3):290–294. Middletown, Conn. and Ann Arbor, Mich.

_____
1968   Elk Antler Roach Spreader. *Denver Art Museum. Material Culture Monographs* 1. Denver.

_____
1969   American Indian Art. New York: Harry N. Abrams.

_____
1978   Pawnee Cradleboards. *American Indian Art Magazine* 3(4):40–50. Scottsdale, Ariz.

_____
1980   Introduction: Crow Indian Art — The Problem. *American Indian Art Magazine* 6(1) [Special Crow Issue]:30–31. Scottsdale, Ariz.

_____
1980a   Crow Blanket Strip Rosettes. *American Indian Art Magazine* 6(1) [Special Crow Issue]:40–45, 88. Scottsdale, Ariz.

_____
1987   Bird Quillwork. *American Indian Art Magazine* 12(3):46–57. Scottsdale, Ariz.

Federal Writer's Project. Montana 1942, 1961, 1975 *see* Kennedy, Michael Stephen, ed. 1961

Fedje, Daryl
1984   Archaeological Investigations in Banff National Park-1983. Pp. 77–95 in Archaeology in Alberta 1983. David Burley, ed. *Archaeological Survey of Alberta. Occasional Paper* 23. Edmonton.

_____
1986   Banff Archaeology, 1983–1985. Pp. 25–62 in Eastern Slopes Prehistory: Selected Papers. Brian Ronaghan, ed. *Archaeological Survey of Alberta. Occasional Paper* 30. Edmonton.

Feest, Christian F., ed.
1999   Sitting Bull, "der letzte Indianer". "Austellung, Hessisches Landesmuseum Darmstadt, 13. Juni bis 17. Oktober 1999". Darmstadt, Germany: Hessisches Landesmuseum.

Feest, Christian F., and Sylvia S. Kasprycki
1998   Peoples of the Twilight: European Views of Native Minne-
         sota, 1823–1862; Containing Illustrations Exclusively from
         European Museum Collections. Afton, Minn.: Afton His-
         torical Society Press.

Feezor, Barbara Yvonne
1994   Mdewakanton Dakota Women: Active Participants in
         Mdewakantonwan Cultural Transformations, 1860–1900.
         (Ph.D. Dissertation in Anthropology, University of Califor-
         nia, Los Angeles.)

Feltskog, E.N., ed.
1969   Parkman: The Oregon Trail. Madison: University of Wis-
         consin Press.

Fenneman, Nevin M.
1931   Physiography of Western United States. New York:
         McGraw-Hill.

Fenton, William N.
1953   The Iroquois Eagle Dance, an Offshot of the Calumet
         Dance; with an Analysis of the Iroquois Eagle Dance and
         Songs, by Gertrude Prokosch Kurath. Bureau of American
         Ethnology Bulletin 156. Washington: Smithsonian Institu-
         tion; U.S. Government Printing Office.

Feraca, Stephen E.
1957   The Contemporary Teton Sioux Sun Dance. (M.A. Thesis in
         Anthropology, Columbia University, New York City.)

1961   The Yuwipi Cult of the Oglala and Sicangu Teton Sioux.
         Plains Anthropologist 6(13):155–163.

1963   Wakinyan: Contemporary Teton Dakota Religion. Studies
         in Plains Anthropology and History 2. Browning, Mont.:
         Museum of the Plains Indian. (Reprinted, rev. ed.: see
         Feraca 1998.)

1964   The History and Development of Oglala Sioux Tribal Gov-
         ernment. (Typescript; copy in R.J. DeMallie's possession.)
         Office of Tribal Operation, Bureau of Indian Affairs, Wash-
         ington.

1966   The Political Status of the Early Bands and Modern Com-
         munities of the Oglala Dakota. University of South Dakota.
         W.H. Over Museum. Museum News 27:1–26. Vermillion,
         S.Dak.

1990   "Why Don't They Give Them Guns?": The Great American
         Indian Myth. Lanham, Md.: University Press of America.

1994   The Wounded Bear Winter Count. Kendall Park, N.J.:
         Lakota Books.

1998   Wakinyan: Lakota Religion in the Twentieth Century. [Rev.
         ed.] Lincoln: University of Nebraska Press. (Originally
         publ. under title: Wakinyan, Contemporary Teton Dakota
         Religion, Studies in Plains Anthropology and History 2,
         Museum of the Plains Indian, Browning, Mont., 1963.)

Feraca, Stephen E., and James H. Howard
1963   The Identity and Demography of the Dakota or Sioux Tribe.
         Plains Anthropologist 8(20):80–84.

Fernández Duro, Cesáreo
1882   Don Diego de Peñalosa y su descubrimiento del reino de
         Quivira. Madrid: Imprenta y Fundición de Manuel Tello.

Ferris, Warren A.
1940   Life in the Rocky Mountains; A Diary of Wanderings on the
         Sources of the Rivers Missouri, Columbia, and Colorado
         from February, 1830, to November, 1835, by W.A. Ferris,
         Then in the Employ of the American Fur Company, and
         Supplementary writings by Ferris, with a Detailed Map of
         the Fur Country, drawn by Ferris in 1836. Edited, and with
         a Life of Ferris, and a History of Explorations and Fur

Trade, by Paul C. Phillips. Denver, Colo.: F.A. Rosenstock,
         Old West Publishing Company (reprinted in a new rev. ed.,
         1983); also, arranged by Herbert S. Auerbach, annotated by J.
         Cecil Alter. Salt Lake City, Utah: Rocky Mountian Book
         Shop. (Originally publ. in: Western Literary Messenger,
         July 13, 1842 to May 4, 1844. St. Louis, Mo.)

Feyhl, Kenneth J.
1972   The Stark-Lewis Site, 24GV401. Archaeology in Montana
         13(2):1–55. Billings, [etc.].

Fidler, Peter
1789–1804 [Untitled Indian Map.] (Manuscript E.3/2 fos. 105d, 106, in
         Hudson's Bay Company Archives, Provincial Archives of
         Manitoba, Winnipeg.)

1792–1793 [Journal of a Journey over Land from Buckingham House to
         the Rocky Mountains in 1792 & 1793.] (Manuscript A.36/6
         in Hudson's Bay Company Archives, London.)

1800   [Journal from Cumb(erland) H°ouse up the South Branch to
         the Junction of Red Deers & Bad River.] (Manuscript No.
         B.34/a/1 in Hudson's Bay Company Archives, Provincial
         Archives of Manitoba, Winnipeg.)

Fields, Ross C.
1995   The Archaeology of the Post Oak Savannah of East Central
         Texas. Bulletin of the Texas Archaeological Society 66:301–
         330. Austin.

Figgins, Jesse D.
1933   A Further Contribution to the Antiquity of Man in America.
         Proceedings of the Colorado Museum of Natural History
         12(2):4–8. Denver.

Findley, Palmer
1927   Sun Dance of the Shoshone Indians Lasts for Three Days.
         American Indian 2(1):14. Tulsa, Okla.

Finerty, John F.
1890   Warpath and Bivouac, or the Conquest of the Sioux. A
         Narrative of Stirring Personal Experiences and Adventures
         in the Big Horn and Yellowstone Expedition of 1876, and
         in the Campaign on the British Border, in 1879. Chicago:
         Donohue and Henneberry. (Reprinted: Oliver Knight, ed.,
         University of Oklahoma Press, Norman, 1961.)

Finnegan, Michael
1981   Archaic Skeletal Remains from the Central Plains: Demog-
         raphy and Burial Practices. Pp. 85–92 in Progress in
         Skeletal Biology of Plains Populations. Richard L. Jantz
         and Douglas H. Ubelaker, eds. Plains Anthropologist
         26(94, Pt.2); Memoir 17. Lincoln.

Finney, Frank F.
1957–1958 The Kaw Indians and Their Indian Territory Agency.
         Chronicles of Oklahoma 35(4):416–424. Norman.

Finnigan, J.
1981   The Elma Thompson Site: A Preliminary Report.
         Saskatchewan Archaeology Society Newsletter 2(4):72–73.
         Saskatoon, Sask.

1982   Elma Thompson Tipi Ring Site (EiOj-1) Radiocarbon Date
         Obtained. Saskatchewan Archaeology Society Newsletter
         3(4):62. Saskatoon, Sask.

Finster, David
1968   The Hardin Winter Count. University of South Dakota W.H.
         Over Museum. Museum News 27(3–4):1–59. Vermillion,
         S.Dak.

Fire/Lame Deer, Archie, and Richard Erdoes
1992   Gift of Power. Santa Fe, N.Mex.: Bear & Company, Publish-
         ing.

Fire/Lame Deer, John, and Richard Erdoes
1972   Lame Deer: Seeker of Visions, The Life of a Sioux Medi-

cine Man. New York: Simon & Schuster. (Reprinted: Washington Square Press and Pocket Books, New York, 1976, 1978, 1994.)

Fireman, Janet R.
1977   The Spanish Royal Corps of Engineers in the Western Borderlands, Instrument of Bourbon Reform 1764 to 1815. Glendale, Calif.: The Arthur H. Clark Company.

Fishel, Richard L.
1995   Excavations at the Dixon Site (13WD8): Correctionville Phase Oneota in Northwest Iowa. *University of Iowa.Office of the State Archaeologist. Report* 442. Iowa City.

_____
1996   A Reanalysis of Mill Creek Midden Formation. *Journal of the Iowa Archaeological Society* 43:119–128. Iowa City.

Fisher, Elizabeth Thérèse Baird *see* Baird, Elizabeth Thérèse (*née* Fisher)

Fisher, Marc
1995   The Voice of a People: Public Radio Is the Lakotas' Town Crier. But What Is Its Future? *The Washington Post,* Wednesday, April 12:C1, C10–C11. Washington.

Fisher, Morton C.
1869   On the Arapaho, Kiowa, and Commanche. *Journal of the Ethnological Society of London,* n.s. 1(3):274–287. London.

Fisher, William
1812   An Interesting Account of the Voyages and Travels of Captains Lewis and Clark, in the Years 1804, 1805, and 1806, [etc.]. Baltimore, Md.: Printed by Anthony Miltenberger. (A spurious account, originally publ. as: The Travels of Capts. Lewis and Clarke, Philadelphia, 1809.)

Fisk, James L.
1908   North Overland Expedition for Protection of Emigrants from Fort Abercrombie to Fort Benton, 1862. *Collections of the State Historical Society of North Dakota* 2(2):35–85. Bismarck.

Fitzgerald, Michael O.
1991   Yellowtail, Crow Medicine Man and Sun Dance Chief: An Autobiography; as told to Michael Oren Fitzgerald. Introduction by Fred Voget. Norman: University of Oklahoma Press.

Fitzpatrick, T. J.
1931   The Place-names of Van Buren County, Iowa. *Annals of Iowa,* 3d ser., vol. 18(1):12–41. Des Moines.

Fitzpatrick, Thomas 1847 *see* ARCIA 1824–1848

Fixico, Donald L.
1986   Termination and Relocation: Federal Indian Policy, 1945–1960. Albuquerque: University of New Mexico Press. (Reprinted: 1990.)

_____
1998   The Invasion of Indian Country in the Twentieth Century: American Capitalism and Tribal Natural Resources. Niwot, Colo.: University Press of Colorado.

Fladmark, Knut
1979   Routes: Alternate Migration Corridors for Early Man in North America. *American Antiquity* 44(1):55–69.

Flanagan, Thomas E.
1979   Louis 'David' Riel: 'Prophet of the New World.' Toronto: University of Toronto Press.

_____
1983   Riel and the Rebellion of 1885 Reconsidered. Saskatoon, Sask.: Western Producer Prairie Books.

_____
1985   Louis Riel and the Dispersion of the American Métis. *Minnesota History* 49(5):179–190. St. Paul.

_____
1991   Market for Métis Lands in Manitoba: An Exploratory Study. *Prairie Forum* 16(1):1–20. Regina, Sask.: Canadian Plains Research Center, University of Regina.

Flanagan, Thomas E., and John E. Foster, eds.
1985   The Métis: Past and Present. *Canadian Ethnic Studies* 17(2)[Special issue]. Toronto.

Flanders, Richard E.
1960   A Re-examination of Mill Creek Ceramics: The Robinson Technique. *Journal of the Iowa Archeological Society* 10(2):1–34. Iowa City.

Flanders, Richard E., and Rex Hansman
1961   A Woodland Mound Complex in Webster County, Iowa. *Journal of the Iowa Archeological Society* 11(1):1–12. Iowa City.

Flannery, Regina
1941   The Dearly-loved Child among the Gros Ventres of Montana. *Primitive Man* 14(3):33–37. Washington: Catholic University of America.

_____
1944   The Gros Ventre Shaking Tent. *Primitve Man* 17(3–4):54–59. Washington: Catholic University of America.

_____
1946   Men's and Women's Speech in Gros Ventre. *International Journal of American Linguistics* 12(3):133–135. Chicago.

_____
1947   The Changing Form and Functions of the Gros Ventre Grass Dance. *Primitive Man* 20(3):39–70. Washington: Catholic University of America.

_____
1953   The Gros Ventres of Montana. Part 1: Social Life. *The Catholic University of America. Anthropological Series* 15. Washington. (See also Cooper 1957.)

_____, ed. 1957 *see* Cooper, John M. 1957

_____
1960   Individual Variation in Culture. Pp. 87–92 in Men and Cultures: Selected Papers of the fifth International Congress of Anthropological and Ethnological Sciences, Philadelphia, September 1–9, 1956. Anthony F.C. Wallace et al., eds. Philadelphia: University of Pennsylvania Press.

Fleming, Paula Richardson
1998   '*A portion of the promises made to us have not been fulfilled*': Little Crow and the Sioux Revolt. Pp. [168] 169–184 in Native Nations: Journeys in American Photography. London: Barbican Art Gallery.

Fleming, Paula Richardson, and Judith Luskey
1986   The North American Indians in Early Photographs. New York, Cambridge, [etc.]: Harper and Row, Publishers.

Fletcher, Alice C.
1883   The Sun Dance of the Ogalalla Sioux. Pp. 580–584 in *Proceedings of the American Association for the Advancement of Science, 31ˢᵗ Meeting, Held at Montreal, Canada, August, 1882.* Salem, Mass.

_____
1885   Historical Sketch of the Omaha Tribe of Indians of Nebraska. Washington: Judd and Detweiler.

_____
1885a   Observations upon the Usage, Symbolism and Influence of the Sacred Pipes of Fellowship among the Omahas. [Abstract.] Pp. 615–617 in *Proceedings of the American Association for the Advancement of Science, 33d Meeting, Held at Philaldephia, Penn., September, 1884.* Salem, Mass.

_____
1885b   Lands in Severalty to Indians; Illustrated by Experiences with the Omaha Tribe. Pp. 654–665 in *Proceedings of the American Association for the Advancement of Science, 33d Meeting, Held at Philadelphia, Penn., September, 1884.* Salem, Mass.

_____
1887   [Indian Ceremonies]: The White Buffalo Festival of the Uncpapas.The Religious Ceremony of the Four Winds or

1145

Quarters, as Observed by the Santee Sioux. Pp. 260–275 in *16th Report of the Peabody Museum of American Archaeology and Ethnology, Harvard University [for] 1882*, Vol. 3 [1880–1886]. Cambridge, Mass.

1887a   [Indian Ceremonies]: The Elk Mystery Festival. Oglala Sioux. Pp. 276–288 in *16th Report of the Peabody Museum of American Archaeology and Ethnology, Harvard University [for] 1882*, Vol. 3 [1880–1886]. Cambridge, Mass.

1887b   [Indian Ceremonies]: The Religious Ceremony of the Four Winds or Quarters, as Observed by the Santee Sioux. Pp. 289–295 in *16th Report of the Peabody Museum of American Archaeology and Ethnology, Harvard University [for] 1882*, Vol. 3 [1880–1886]. Cambridge, Mass.

1887c   The Shadow or Ghost Lodge: A Ceremony of the Ogallala Sioux. Pp. 296–307 in *16th Report of the Peabody Museum of American Archaeology and Ethnology, Harvard University [for] 1882*, Vol. 3 [1880–1886]. Cambridge, Mass.

1887d   The "Wawa*n*," or Pipe Dance of the Omahas. Pp. 308–333 in *16th Report of the Peabody Museum of American Archaeology and Ethnology, Harvard University [for] 1882*, Vol. 3 [1880–1886]. Cambridge, Mass.

1888   Glimpses of Child-Life among the Omaha Tribe of Indians. *Journal of American Folk-lore* 1(2):115–123.

1891   The Indian Massiah. *Journal of American Folk-lore* 4(12):55–57.

1892   Hae-Thu-Ska Society of the Omaha Tribe. *Journal of American Folk-lore* 5(17):135–144.

1893   Personal Studies of Indian Life: Politics and "Pipe-Dancing." *Century Magazine* 45:441–455. New York.

1895   New Religion: Otoe. (Manuscript [Typescript] No. 4558/113, Fletcher and La Flesche Papers, National Anthropological Archives, Smithsonian Institution, Washington.)

1896   Tribal Life among the Omahas: Personal Studies of Indian Life. *Century Magazine* 51:450–461. New York.

1896a   The Sacred Pole of the Omaha Tribe. Pp. 270–280 in *Proceedings of the American Association for the Advancement of Science, 44th Meeting, Held at Springfield, Mass., August–September, 1895.* Salem, Mass.

1897   Home Life among the Indians. *Century Magazine* 54:252–263. New York.

1899   A Pawnee Ritual Used When Changing a Man's Name. *American Anthropologist*, n.s. 1(1):82–97.

1900   Giving Thanks: A Pawnee Ceremony. *Journal of American Folk-lore* 13(51):261–266.

1900a   Indian Story and Song from North America. Boston: Small, Maynard & Company; also, London: D. Nutt. (Reprinted in 1970; also, AMS Press, New York, 1970; and, University of Nebraska Press, Lincoln, 1995.)

1902   Star Cult among the Pawnee: A Preliminary Report. *American Anthropologist*, n.s. 4(4):730–736.

1903   Pawnee Star Lore. *Journal of American Folk-lore* 16(60):10–15.

1907   The Indian and Nature. *American Anthropologist*, n.s. 9(2):440–443.

1907a   Caddo. Pp. 179–182 in Pt./vol. 1 of Handbook of American Indians North of Mexico. Frederick W. Hodge, ed. 2 Pts./ vols. *Bureau of American Ethnology Bulletin* 30. Washington: Smithsonian Institution; U.S. Government Printing Office. (Reprinted: Rowman and Littlefield, New York, 1971.)

1910   Pawnee. Pp. 213–216 in Pt./vol. 2 of Handbook of the American Indians North of Mexico. Frederick W. Hodge, ed. 2 Pts./vols. *Bureau of American Ethnology Bulletin* 30. Washington: Smithsonian Institution; U.S. Government Printing Office. (Reprinted: Rowman and Littlefield, New York, 1971.)

1912   Wakondagi. *American Anthropologist*, n.s. 14(1):106–109.

Fletcher, Alice C., and Francis La Flesche
1893   A Study of Omaha Indian Music; by Alice C. Fletcher, aided by Francis La Fleche. With a Report on the Structural Peculiarities of the Music by John Comfort Fillmore. *Harvard University. Archaeological and Ethnological Papers of the Peabody Museum* 1(5). Cambridge, Mass. (Reprinted: Kraus Reprint, New York, 1978; also, University of Nebraska Press, Lincoln, 1994.)

1911   The Omaha Tribe. Pp. 17–672 [pp. 655–672, Vol. Index] in *27th Annual Report of the Bureau of American Ethnology [for] 1905–'06.* Washington: Smithsonian Institution; U.S. Government Printing Office. (Reprinted: Johnson Reprint, New York, 1970; also, University of Nebraska Press, Lincoln, 1992.)

Fletcher, Alice C., and James R. Murie
1904   The Hako: A Pawnee Ceremony. Assisted by James R. Murie; Music transcribed by Edwin S. Tracy. Pp. 1–368 [pp. 369–372, Vol. Index] in Pt. 2 of *22d Annual Report of the Bureau of American Ethnology [for] 1900–'01.* Washington: Smithsonian Institution; U.S. Government Printing Office. (Reprinted under title: The Hako: Song, Pipe, and Unity in a Pawnee Calumet Ceremony; with an Introduction by Helen Myers: University of Nebraska Press, Lincoln, 1996.)

Flint, James [1904–1907] 1904 *see* Thwaites, Reuben G., ed. 1904–1907 (Vol. 9, 1904)

Flood, Renée S. *see* Sansom-Flood, Renée

Flores, Dan
1985   Journal of an Indian Trader: Anthony Glass and the Texas Trading Frontier. College Station, Tex.: Texas A&M University Press.

Floyd, Charles (Lewis and Clark Expedition) *see* Thwaites, Reuben G., ed. 1904–1905

Flynn, Catherine M.
1993   The Horticultural Component at the Lockport Site (EaLf-1): An Overview of Ceramic and Cultural Affiliations. (Paper presented at the 51st Annual Meeting of the Plains Anthropological Society, Oct. 13–16, Saskatoon, Sask.)

Flynn, Peggy
1982   Distribution of Prehistoric Bison on the Southern Plains: A Test of Dillehay's Model. Pp. 7–35 in Southern Plains Archaeology. Susan C. Vehik, ed. *University of Oklahoma. Papers in Anthropology* 23(1). Norman.

1984   An Analysis of the 1973 Test Excavations at the Zimms Site (34RM72). Pp. 215–290 in Archaeology of the Mixed Grass Prairie. Phase I: Quartermaster Creek. Timothy G. Baugh, ed. *Oklahoma Archeological Survey. Archeological Resource Survey Report* 20. Norman.

1986   Analysis of Test Excavations at the Zimms Site (34RM72), Western Oklahoma. Pp. 129–140 in Current Trends in Southern Plains Archaeology. Timothy G. Baugh, ed. *Plains Anthropologist* 31(114, Pt.2); *Memoir* 21. Lincoln.

Först, Dietmar
1994   The Revival of the Santee Sioux Sun Dance, 1988–1994. *European Review of Native American Studies* 8(2):11–18. Vienna, Austria [etc.].

Foik, Paul J., trans. 1933 *see* Ramón, Domingo 1933

Foley, Michael F.
1975   An Historical Analysis of the Administration of the Fort Belknap Indian Reservation by the United States 1855–1950s. (Manuscript in Special Collections, Montana State University Library, Bozeman.)

Foley, William E., and C. David Rice
1983   The First Chouteaus: River Barons of Early St. Louis. Urbana and Chicago: University of Illinois Press.

Folmer, Henri
1939   The Mallet Expedition of 1739 through Nebraska, Kansas and Colorado to Santa Fe. *Colorado Magazine* 16(5):161–173. Denver.

1953   Franco-Spanish Rivalry in North America 1524–1763. Glendale, Calif.: Arthur H. Clark Company.

Folwell, William Watts
1921–1930 A History of Minnesota. 4 vols. [First impression.] *Publications of the Minnesota Historical Society*. S.J. Buck, ed. St. Paul: Minnesota Historical Society. (Second impression, 1922–1930.)

Fontenelle, Henry
1885   History of Omaha Indians. *Transactions and Reports of the Nebraska State Historical Society* 1:76–83. Lincoln.

Foo, Rodney
1980   Bringing Back the Indian Sun Dance. *Honolulu Star-Bulletin,* Oct. 3:c2. Honolulu, Hawaii.

Foor, Thomas Allyn
1982   Cultural Continuity on the Northwestern Great Plains-1300 B.C. to A.D. 200, the Pelican Lake Culture. (Ph.D. Dissertation in Anthropology, University of California, Santa Barbara.)

1985   Archaeological Classification in the Northwestern Plains Region. *Plains Anthropologist* 30(108):123–135.

Forbes-Boyte, Kari
1999   *Fools Crow versus Gullett*: A Critical Analysis of the American Indian Religious Freedom Act. *Antipode* 31(3):304–323. Cambridge, Mass.

Forbes, Bruce D.
1977   Evangelization and Acculturation among the Santee Dakota Indians: 1834–1864. (Ph.D. Dissertation in Religion, Princeton Theological Seminary, Princeton, N.J.)

Forbes, Donna M., and Terry Karson
1990   L.A. Huffman, Pioneer Photographer. Introduction by Donna M. Forbes; Essay by Terry Karson. Billings, Mont.: Yellowstone Art Center.

Forbes, Jack D.
1959   Unknown Athapaskans: The Identification of the Jano, Jocome, Jumano, Manso, Suma, and Other Indian Tribes of the Southwest. *Ethnohistory* 6(2):97–159.

1959a   The Appearance of the Mounted Indian in Northern Mexico and the Southwest, to 1680. *Southwestern Journal of Anthropology* 15(2):189–212. Albuquerque.

1960   Apache, Navaho, and Spaniard. Norman: University of Oklahoma Press.

1966   The Early Western Apache, 1300–1700. *Journal of the West* 5(3):336–354. Manhattan, Kans.

1981   Native Americans and Nixon: Presidential Politics and Minority Self-Determination 1969–1972. Los Angeles: American Indian Studies Center.

Forbis, Richard G.
1960   Some Late Sites in the Oldman River Region, Alberta. *National Museum of Canada Bulletin* 162:119–164. Ottawa.

1962   The Old Women's Buffalo Jump, Alberta. *National Museum of Canada. Bulletin* 180(1):56–123. Ottawa.

1962a   A Stratified Buffalo Kill in Alberta. Pp. 3–7 (et al., pp. 40–56: Panel Discussion on Buffalo Jumps) in Symposium on Buffalo Jumps. Carling Malouf and Stuart Conner, eds. *Montana Archaeological Society, Memoir* 1. Missoula and Helena.

1968   Fletcher: A Paleo-Indian Site in Alberta. *American Antiquity* 33(1):1–10.

1970   A Review of Alberta Archaeology to 1964. *National Museum of Canada. Publications in Archaeology* 1. Ottawa.

1977   Cluny: An Ancient Fortified Village in Alberta. *University of Calgary. Department of Archaeology. Occasional Papers* 4. Calgary.

1985   The McKean Complex as Seen from Signal Butte. Pp. 21–29 in McKean/Middle Plains Archaic: Current Research. Marcel Kornfeld and Lawrence C. Todd, eds. *Occasional Papers on Wyoming Archaeology* 4. Laramie: Wyoming Recreation Commission.

Forbis, Richard G., William Duncan Strong, and Maurice E. Kirkby
[1950]   Signal Butte and MacHaffie: Two Stratified Sites on the Northern Great Plains. (Unpublished report; copy in G.C. Frison's possession.)

Ford, James A.
1961   Menard Site: The Quapaw Village of Osotouy on the Arkansas River. *American Museum of Natural History Anthropological Papers* 48(2):133–191. New York.

Foreman, Grant
1926   Pioneer Days in the Early Southwest. Cleveland, Ohio: Arthur H. Clark.

1930   Indians & Pioneers: The Story of the American Southwest before 1830. New Haven, Conn.: Yale University Press; also, London: H. Milford, Oxford University Press. (Reprinted, rev. ed.: University of Oklahoma Press, Norman, 1936.)

1933   Advancing the Frontier, 1830–1860. Norman: University of Oklahoma Press.

1936   Indians & Pioneers: The Story of the American Southwest before 1830. Rev. ed. Norman: University of Oklahoma Press. (Originally publ. by Yale University Press, New Haven, Conn., and H. Milford, Oxford University Press, London, 1930.)

1936a   Fort Gibson: A Brief History. Norman: University of Oklahoma Press.

1939   Marcy and the Gold Seekers: The Journal of Captain R.B. Marcy, with an Account of the Gold Rush Over the Southern Route. Norman: University of Oklahoma Press.

1946   The Last Trek of the Indians. Chicago: University of Chicago Press.

Forrestal, Peter P., trans.
1954   Benavides' Memorial of 1630. *Publications of the Academy* **1147**

of American Franciscan History. Documentary Series 2. Washington.

Fort Belknap Education Department
1982   Recollections of Fort Belknap's Past. Harlem, Mont.: Fort Belknap Education Department, Fort Belknap Community Council.

——— 1982a   War Stories of the White Clay People. Harlem, Mont.: Fort Belknap Education Department, Fort Belknap Community Council.

Fort Benton Journal *see* McDonnell, Anne, ed. 1940

Fort Philip Kearney Commission
1867   Report of Special Indian Commission to Fort Philip Kearney. Washington: National Archives and Records Service.

Fort Sarpy Journal *see* McDonnell, Anne, ed. 1940a

Fortune, Reo F.
1932   Omaha Secret Societies. *Columbia University Contributions to Anthropology* 14. New York. (Reprinted: AMS Press, New York, 1969.)

Foster, John E.
1985   Some Questions and Perspectives on the Problem of Métis Roots. Pp. 73–91 in The New Peoples: Being and Becoming Métis in North America. Jacqueline Peterson and Jennifer S.H. Brown, eds. *Manitoba Studies in Native History* 1. Winnipeg: The University of Manitoba Press; Lincoln: University of Nebraska Press.

——— 1986   The Plains Métis. Pp. 375–404 in Native Peoples: The Canadian Experience. R. Bruce Morrison and Antoine S. Lussier, eds. Toronto: McClelland and Stewart.

——— 1987   Indian-White Relations in the Prairie West During the Fur Trade Period: A Compact? Pp 181–200 in The Spirit of the Alberta Indian Treaties. Richard Price, ed. Edmonton, Alta.: Pica Pica Press.

——— 1994   Wintering, the Outsider Male and the Ethnogenesis of the Western Plains Métis. *Prairie Forum* 19(1):1–13. Regina, Sask.: Canadian Plains Research Center, University of Regina.

Foster, Morris W.
1991   Being Comanche: A Social History of an American Indian Community. Tucson: University of Arizona Press.

Foster, Thomas, ed.
1876–1877 Foster's Indian Record and Historical Data: Vol. 1(Nos. 1–2). Washington.

Fowke, Gerard
1910   Antiquities of Central and Southeastern Missouri. (Report of Explorations Made in 1906–07 under the Auspices of the Archaeological Institute of America.) [*With* Report on Skeletal Material from Missouri Mounds, Collected in 1906–07 by Mr. Gerard Fowke, by Aleš Hrdlička, pp. 103–112.] *Bureau of American Ethnology Bulletin* 37. Washington: Smithsonian Institution; U.S. Government Printing Office.

——— 1912   Some Notes on the Aboriginal Inhabitants of Missouri. *Missouri Historical Society Collections* 4(1):82–103. St. Louis.

Fowler, Arlen L.
1971   The Black Infantry in the West, 1869–1891. With a Foreword by William H. Lekie. Westport, Conn.: Greenwood Publishing Corp. (Reprinted by University of Oklahoma Press, Norman, 1996.)

Fowler, Jacob 1898 *see* Coues, Elliott, ed. 1898a

Fowler, Loretta
1970   Political Process and Socio-Cultural Change among the Arapaho Indians. (Ph.D. Dissertation in Anthropology, University of Illinois, Urbana.)

——— 1973   The Arapahoe Ranch: An Experiment in Cultural Change and Economic Development. *Economic Development and Cultural Change* 21(3):446–464. Chicago.

——— 1978   Oral Historian or Ethnologist?: The Career of Bill Shakespeare — Northern Arapahoe, 1901–1975. Pp. 226–240 in American Indian Intellectuals. *1976 Proceedings of the American Ethnological Society.* Margot Liberty, ed. St. Paul, Minn.: West Publishing Company.

——— 1978a   Wind River Reservation Political Process: An Analysis of the Symbols of Consensus. *American Ethnologist* 5(4):748–769.

——— 1982   Arapahoe Politics, 1851–1978: Symbols in Crisis of Authority. Lincoln: University of Nebraska Press.

——— 1982a   "Look at My Hair, It is Gray": Age, Grading, Ritual Authority, and Political Change among the Northern Arapahoes and Gros Ventres. Pp. 73–93 in Plains Indians Studies: A Collection of Essays in Honor of John C. Ewers and Waldo R. Wedel. Douglas H. Ubelaker and Herman J. Viola, eds. *Smithsonian Contributions to Anthropology* 30. Washington: Smithsonian Institution.

——— 1984   Political Middlemen and the Headmen Tradition among the Twentieth-Century Gros Ventres of Fort Belknap Reservation. *Journal of the West* 23(3):54–63. Manhattan, Kans.

——— 1984–1995 [Fieldnotes, Southern Arapaho and Southern Cheyenne, Oklahoma.] (Manuscripts in L. Fowler's possession.)

——— 1985   "What They Issue You": Political Economy at Wind River. Pp. 187–217 in The Plains Indians of the Twentieth Century. Peter Iverson, ed. Norman: University of Oklahoma Press.

——— 1987   Shared Symbols, Contested Meanings: Gros Ventre Culture and History, 1778–1984. Ithaca, N.Y.: Cornell University Press.

——— 1988   Oklahoma Arapaho Chieftainship: Rethinking Cultural Perspective in Ethnohistory. (Paper presented at the American Society for Ethnohistory Meeting, Nov. 11, 1988.)

——— 1988a   [Arapaho Fieldnotes, Wind River Indian Reservation, Wyo., July 1988.] (Manuscript in L. Fowler's possession.)

——— 1989   The Arapaho. New York: Chelsea House Publishers.

——— 1990   Colonial Context and Age Group Relations among Plains Indians. *Journal of Cross-Cultural Gerontology* 5:149–168. Boston.

——— 1994   The Civilization Strategy: Gros Ventres, Northern and Southern Arapaho Compared. Pp. 220–257 in North American Indian Anthropology: Essays on Society and Culture. Raymond J. DeMallie and Alfonso Ortiz, eds. Norman: University of Oklahoma Press.

——— 1996   The Great Plains from the Arrival of the Horse to 1885. Pp. 1–55 in The Cambridge History of the Native Peoples of the Americas, Vol. 1: North America, Part II. Bruce G. Trigger and Wilcomb E. Washburn, eds. Cambridge and New York: Cambridge University Press.

——— 2000   Tribal Sovereignty and the Historical Imagination: Cheyenne-Arapaho Politics. (In press.)

Franchère, Gabriel
1854   Narrative of a Voyage to the Northwest Coast of America in

the Years 1812, 1813, and 1814. J.V. Huntington, trans. and ed. New York: Redfield.

Francis, Julie E.
1983   Procurement and Utilization of Chipped Stone Raw Materials: A Case Study from the Bighorn Mountains and Basin of Northcentral Wyoming. (Ph.D. Dissertation in Anthropology, Arizona State University, Tempe.)

1991   An Overview of Wyoming Rock Art. Pp. 397–430 in Prehistoric Hunters of the High Plains. George C. Frison, ed. San Diego, Calif.: Academic Press.

1996   Rock Art of the Northwestern Plains. Pp. 50–55 in Archeological and Bioarcheological Resources of the Northern Plains. George C. Frison and Robert C. Mainfort, eds. *Arkansas Archeological Survey Research Series* 47. Fayetteville.

Francis, Julie E., and Mark E. Miller
1992   Early Archaic Adaptations in the Upper Green River Basin, Wyoming: Preliminary Report of Investigations at Trappers' Point 48SU1066. (Paper presented at the 50th Plains Conference, Lincoln, Nebr.)

Franciscan Fathers
[1910] An Ethnologic Dictionary of the Navaho Language. St. Michaels, Ariz.: The Franciscan Fathers. (Reprinted: Max Breslauer, Liepzig, 1929.)

Frankforter, Weldon D.
1969   Faunal Study of Large Ruminants from Mill Creek Culture Sites in Northwest Iowa. Pp. 286–301 in Vol. 2 of Climatic Change and the Mill Creek Culture of Iowa. Dale R. Henning, ed. *Journal of the Iowa Archeological Society* 16. Iowa City.

Frankforter, Weldon D., and George A. Agogino
1960   The Simonsen Site: Report for the Summer of 1959. *Plains Anthropologist* 5(10):65–70.

Franklin, Sir John
1823   Narrative of a Journey to the Shores of the Polar Sea, in the Years 1819, 20, 21, and 22; With an Appendix on Various Subjects Relating to Science and Natural History. London: John Murray. (American ed.: H.C. Carey, Philadelphia, 1824; reprinted: Greenwood Press, New York, 1969.)

1824   Narrative of a Journey to the Shores of the Polar Sea, in the Years 1819, 20, 21, and 22; With an Appendix on Various Subjects Relating to Science and Natural History. Philadelphia: H.C. Carey. (Originally publ. in London by J. Murray, 1823. Reprinted: Greenwood Press, New York, 1969.)

Franks, Kenny A.
1996   La Flesche Family. Pp. 324–327 in Encyclopedia of North American Indians. Frederick E. Hoxie, ed. Boston: Houghton Mifflin.

Franks, Kenny A., and Paul F. Lambert
1994   Pawnee Pride: A History of Pawnee County. Oklahoma City, Okla.: Western Heritage Books.

Franquelin, Jean-Baptiste Louis
1684   Map of Louisiana. (Manuscript copy in Tozzer Library, Harvard University, Cambridge, Mass.; Facsimile reprod. in Glenn A. Black Laboratory of Archaeology, Indiana University, Bloomington.)

1697   Cours du grand fleuve Missisipi depuis sa source jusqu'a son embouchure avec toutes les Revières qui y tombent, ou est compris la Decouverte du Sr. le Sueur qui se rend sur les pays et nations de l'est et de l'ouest de ce fleuve à prendre depuis la Riviere Ouisconsing en montant jusqu'a la source du même fleuve. [Paris.] (Tracing in Edward E. Ayer College, The Newberry Library, Chicago.)

1699   Partie de l'Amérique septentrionale, etc. Map. Paris: Archives Nationale de la Marine, Bibliothèque du Service Hydrographique. B4040-12. (Photostat, Geography and Map Division, Lowery Collection No. 219, Library of Congress, Washington.)

Frantz, Donald G.
1991   Blackfoot Grammar. Toronto: University of Toronto Press.

Frantz, Donald G., and Norma Jean Russell
1989   Blackfoot Dictionary of Stems, Roots, and Affixes. Toronto: University of Toronto Press. (Reprinted: 2d ed., 1995.)

1995   Blackfoot Dictionary of Stems, Roots, and Affixes. 2nd [rev.] ed. Toronto, Buffalo, London: University of Toronto Press. (Originally publ., 1st ed., 1989.)

Frantz, Wendell P.
1962   The Crazy Bull site (39LM220), Big Bend Reservoir, South Dakota. *Plains Anthropologist* 7(15):36–42.

1964   1963 Excavation in the Elk City Reservoir. *Newsletter of the Kansas Anthropological Association* 9(6):104. Topeka.

Fraser, William B.
1963   Plains Cree, Assiniboine and Saulteaux (Plains) Bands, 1874–1884. (Manuscript M4379, Glenbow Museum Archives, Calgary, Alta.)

1966   Big Bear, Indian Patriot. *Alberta Historical Review* 14(2):1–13. Calgary.

Frazier, Ian
2000   On the Rez. New York: Farrar, Straus and Giroux.

Frederick, Charles D.
1998   Late Quaternary Clay Dune Sedimentation on the Llano Estacado. *Plains Anthropologist* 43(164):137–155.

Frederick, Joan
1995   T.C. Cannon: He Stood in the Sun. Flagstaff: Northland Publishing.

Fredlund, Glen G., C. Britt Bousman, and Douglas K. Boyd
1998   The Holocene Phytolith Record from Morgan Playa in the Rolling Plains of Texas. *Plains Anthropologist* 43(164):187–200.

Fredlund, Lynn B.
1979   Benson's Butte 24BH1726. *Montana Tech Alumni Foundation. Cultural Resources Division. Mineral Research Center. Report of Investigations* 8. Butte, Mont.

1988   Distribution and Characteristics of Avonlea South of the Yellowstone River in Montana. Pp. 171–182 in Avonlea Yesterday and Today: Archaeology and Prehistory. Leslie B. Davis, ed. Saskatoon: Saskatchewan Archaeological Society.

Fredlund, Lynn B., Dale P. Herbort, and Gene Munson
1985   Investigations at a Besant Stone Ring Site (32OL270) in Central North Dakota. Pp. 116–154 in Contributions to Plains Prehistory: The 1984 Victoria Symposium. David V. Burley, ed. *Archaeological Survey of Alberta. Occasional Paper* 26. Edmonton.

Freeman, John F., comp.
1966   A Guide to Manuscripts Relating to the American Indian in the Library of the American Philosophical Society. Murphy D. Smith: Editorial Consultant. *Memoirs of the American Philosophical Society* 65. Philadelphia. (Reprinted in 1980.)

Freeman, Patricia A.
1971   Kiowa-Apache Concepts and Attitudes Toward the Child. *1149*

University of Oklahoma, Papers in Anthropology 12(1):90–160. Norman. (Originally presented as the Author's M.A. Thesis in Anthropology, University of Oklahoma, Norman, 1965.)

Frémont, John Charles
1845   Report of the Exploring Expedition to the Rocky Mountains in the Year 1842, and to Oregon and California in the Years 1843–'44, 1845. 28th Congress. 2d Session. Senate Document 174. (Serial No. 461.) Washington.

———
1854   The Exploring Expedition to the Rocky Mountains, Oregon and California; To Which Is Added a Description of the Physical Geography of California; with Recent Notices of the Gold Region from the Latest and Most Authentic Sources. Auburn, N.Y.: Derby and Miller; Buffalo: Derby, Orton, and Mulligan. (Reprinted, with an Introduction by Herman J. Viola and Ralph E. Ehrenberg: Smithsonian Institution Press, Washington, 1988.).

French, Benjamin F.
1846–1853 Historical Collections of Louisiana, Embracing Many Rare and Valuable Documents Relating to the Natural, Civil and Political History of That State. Compiled with Historical and Biographical Notes, and an Introduction, By B.F. French. 5 Pts. New York: G.P. Putnam; D. Appleton; [etc.]. (Reprinted, 5 vols.: AMS Press, New York, 1976.)

———
1869   Historical Collections of Louisiana and Florida, Including Translations of the Original Manuscripts Relating to Their Discovery and Settlement, with Numerous Historical and Biographical Notes. New Series, Vol. 1. New York: J. Sabin and Sons; Albert Mason. [Some eds. bound with Vol. 2, 2d ser., 1875.]

———
1875   Historical Collections of Louisiana and Florida, Including Translations of Original Manuscripts Relating to Their Discovery and Settlement, with Numerous Historical and Biographical Notes. Vol. 2, 2d ser. New York: Albert Mason. [Some eds. bound with Vol. 1, new series, 1869.]

French, David
1942   Comparative Notes on Chiricahua Apache Mythology. Pp. 103–111 in Myths and Tales of the Chiricahua Apache Indians, by Morris E. Opler. Memoirs of the American Folklore Society 27. Menasha, Wis. (Reprinted: Kraus Reprint, New York, 1969.)

Frey, Rodney
1970   On the Concept of Medicine among the Crow Indians: A Sun Dance Perspective. (Paper presented to the Department of Anthropology, University of Colorado, Boulder.)

———
1974   To Pray and Sacrifice: Aspects of Crow Religion and Medicine. (Paper presented to the Department of Anthropology, University of Colorado, Boulder.)

———
1976   Sacred Symbols of the Apsáalooke Sun Dance Religion. (Paper presented to the Department of Anthropology, University of Colorado, Boulder.)

———
1979   To Dance Together: Ethnography in Apsáalooke (Crow) Culture. (Ph.D. Dissertation in Anthropology, University of Colorado, Boulder.)

———
1987   The World of the Crow Indians: As Driftwood Lodges. Norman: University of Oklahoma Press. (Originally publ. under title: As Driftwood Lodges: The World of the Aps'aalooke (Crow Indians), 1985; reprinted in 1993.)

Freytas, Nicholas de
1882   The Expedition of Don Diego Dionisio de Peñalosa, Governor of New Mexico, From Santa Fe to the River Mischipi and Quivira in 1662. With an Account of Peñalosa's Projects To Aid the French To Conquer the Mining Country in Northern Mexico; and His Connection with Cavelier de la Salle. John Gilmary Shea, ed. and trans. New York: John G. Shea.

Frideres, James S.
1974   Canada's Indians: Contemporary Conflicts. Scarborough, Ont.: Prentice Hall of Canada.

Fried, Morton H.
1968   Reading in Anthropology. 2d ed. 2 vols. Vol. 1: Physical Anthropology, Linguistics, and Archeology; Vol. 2: Cultural Anthropology. New York: Thomas Y. Crowell.

Friederici, Georg
1906   Der Tränengruss des Indianer. Globus: Illustrierte Zeitschrift für Länder- und Völkerkunde 89(2):30–34. Braunschweig, Germany: F. Vieweg und Sohn.

Friesen, Gerald
1979   Homeland to Hinterland: Political Transition in Manitoba, 1870 to 1879. Pp. 33–47 in Canadian Historical Association. Historical Papers/Communications historiques/ for 1979. Ottawa.

———
1996   River Road: Essays on Manitoba and Prairie History. Winnipeg: University of Manitoba Press.

Friesen, Jean
1986   Magnificent Gifts: The Treaties of Canada with the Indians of the Northwest, 1869–76. Transactions of the Royal Society of Canada, 5th ser., Vol. 1:41–51. Ottawa.

Friesen, John W., and Terry Lusty
1980   The Métis of Canada: An Annotated Bibliography. Toronto: Ontario Institute for Studies in Education.

Frink, Maurice
1958   A Little Gift for Last Bull: A Tribute to that Beloved Westerner, Stanley Vestal. Montana: The Magazine of Western History 8(2):2–7. Helena.

Frison, George C.
1962   Wedding of the Waters Cave: A Stratified Site in the Bighorn Basin of Northern Wyoming. Plains Anthropologist 7(18):246–265.

———
1965   Spring Creek Cave, Wyoming. American Antiquity 31(1): 81–94.

———
1967   Archaeological Evidence of the Crow Indians in Northern Wyoming: A Study of a Late Prehistoric Period Buffalo Economy. (Ph.D. Dissertation in Anthropology, The University of Michigan, Ann Arbor. Photocopy: University Microfilms International, Ann Arbor, Mich., 1984, 1986.)

———
1967a   The Piney Creek Sites, Wyoming. University of Wyoming Publications 33(1):1–92. Laramie.

———
1968   Daugherty Cave, Wyoming. Plains Anthropologist 13(42): 253–295.

———
1968a   Site 48SH312: An Early Middle Period Bison Kill in the Powder River Basin of Wyoming. Plains Anthropologist 13(39):31–39.

———
1970   The Kobold Site, 24BH406: A Post-Altithermal Record of Buffalo-Jumping for the Northwestern Plains. Plains Anthropologist 15(47):1–35.

———
1971   The Buffalo Pound in Northwestern Plains Prehistory: Site 48CA302, Wyoming. American Antiquity 36(1):77–91.

———
1973   Early Period Marginal Cultural Groups in Northern Wyoming. Plains Anthropologist 18(62):300–312.

———
1973a   The Wardell Buffalo Trap, 48SU301: Communal Procurement in the Upper Green River Basin, Wyoming. University of Michigan. Anthropological Papers of the Museum of Anthropology 48:1–111. Ann Arbor.

1974   The Casper Site: A Hell Gap Bison Kill on the High Plains. New York: Academic Press.

1976   Crow Pottery in Northern Wyoming. *Plains Anthropologist* 21(71):29–44.

1976a   The Chronology of Paleo-Indian and Altithermal Period Groups in the Bighorn Basin, Wyoming. Pp. 147–173 in Cultural Change and Continuity: Essays in Honor of James Bennett Griffin. Charles E. Cleland, ed. New York: Academic Press.

1978   Prehistoric Hunters of the High Plains. New York: Academic Press. (2d ed., 1991.)

1979   The Crow Indian Occupation of the High Plains: The Archeological Evidence. Pp. 3–16 in Symposium on the Crow-Hidatsa Separations. Leslie B. Davis, ed. *Archaeology in Montana* 20(3). Billings, [etc.].

1981   Linear Arrangements of Cairns in Wyoming and Montana. Pp. 133–147 in Megaliths to Medicine Wheels: Boulder Structures in Archaeology. Michael Wilson, Katie L. Road, and Kenneth J. Hardy, eds. *Proceedings of the Eleventh Annual Chacmool Conference.* Calgary: University of Calgary, Department of Archaeology, Archaeological Association.

1983   Comments on Native Subsistence Adaptations in the Great Plains. Pp. 111–113 in Man and the Changing Environments in the Great Plains: A Symposium. Warren W. Caldwell, Charles B. Schultz, and Thompson M. Stout. *Transactions of the Nebraska Academy of Science* 11. [Special issue]. Lincoln.

1983a   The Lookingbill Site, Wyoming 48FR308. *Tebiwa: Journal of the Idaho State University Museum* 20(1):1–16. Pocatello, Idaho.

1983b   Stone Circles, Stone-filled Fire Pites, Grinding Stones and High Plains Archaeology. Pp. 81–92 in From Microcosm to Macrocosm: Advances in Tipi Ring Investigation and Interpretation. Leslie B. Davis, ed. *Plains Anthropologist* 28(102, Pt.2); *Memoir* 19. Lincoln.

1988   Avonlea Contemporaries in Wyoming. Pp. 155–170 in Avonlea Yesterday and Today: Archaeology and Prehistory. Leslie B. Davis, ed. Saskatoon: Saskatchewan Archaeological Society.

1988a   Paleo-Indian Subsistence and Settlement During Post-Clovis Times on the Northwestern Plains, the Adjacent Mountain Ranges, and Intermontane Plains. Pp. 83–106 in Americans Before Columbus: Ice-Age Origins: Selected Papers from the First Columbian Quincentenary Symposium, Smithsonian Institution, September 26, 1987. Ronald C. Carlisle, comp. and ed.; Foreword by Jeremy A. Sabloff. Pittsburgh, Pa.: Department of Anthropology, University of Pittsburgh.

1991   Prehistoric Hunters of the High Plains. 2d ed. San Diego, Calif.: Academic Press.

1998   The Northwestern and Northern Plains Archaic. Pp. 140–172 in Archaeology on the Great Plains. W. Raymond Wood, ed. Lawrence, Kans.: University Press of Kansas.

Frison, George C., and Donald C. Grey
1980   Pryor Stemmed, a Specialized Late Paleo-Indian Ecological Adaptation. *Plains Anthropologist* 25(87):27–46.

Frison, George C., and Marion Huseas
1968   Leigh Cave, Wyoming, Site 48WA304. *The Wyoming Archaeologist* 11(3):20–33. Cheyenne, [etc.,] Wyo.

Frison, George C., and Robert C. Mainfort, eds.
1996   Archeological and Bioarcheological Resources of the Northern Plains. With Contributions by George C. Frison, [et al.]. *Arkansas Archeological Survey Research Series* 47. Fayetteville.

Frison, George C., and Dennis J. Stanford, eds.
1982   The Agate Basin Site: A Record of the Paleoindians Occupation of the Northwestern High Plains. New York: Academic Press.

Frison, George C., and Zola Van Norman
1985   The Wind River Canyon Burial and Cache: 48HO10. *Archaeology in Montana* 26(2):43–52. Billings, [etc.].

Frison, George C., and Danny N. Walker, eds.
1984   The Dead Indian Creek Site: An Archaic Occupation in the Absaroka Mountains of Northeastern Wyoming. *The Wyoming Archaeologist* 27(1–2):11–122. Cheyenne, [etc.,] Wyo.

Frison, George C., James M. Adovasio, and Ronald C. Carlisle
1986   Coiled Basketry from Northern Wyoming. *Plains Anthropologist* 31(112):163–167.

Frison, George C., Michael C. Wilson, and Diane J. Wilson
1976   Fossil Bison and Artifacts from an Early Altithermal Period Arroyo Trap in Wyoming. *American Antiquity* 41(1):28–57.

Frison, George C., R.L. Andrews, James M. Adovasio, Ronald C. Carlisle, and Robert Edgar
1986   A Late Paleoindian Animal Trapping Net from Northern Wyoming. *American Antiquity* 51(2):352–361.

Fritz, Henry E.
1963   The Movement for Indian Assimilation. Philadelphia: University of Pennsylvania Press.

Froebel, Julius
1859   Seven Year's Travel in Central America, Northern Mexico, and the Far West of the United States. London: R. Bentley.

Fromhold, John
1981   Inter-tribal Influences in Plains Cree Societies. Pp. 411–424 in Networks of the Past: Regional Interaction in Archaeology. *Proceedings of the Twelfth Annual Conference, The Archaeological Association of the University of Calgary [1979].* Peter D. Francis, F.J. Kense and P.G. Duke, eds. Calgary: University of Calgary Archaeological Association.

Frye, John C., and A. Byron Leonard
1952   Pleistocene Geology of Kansas. *State Geological Survey of Kansas. Bulletin* 99. Lawrence.

Frye, John C., and Ada Swineford
1946   Silicified Rock in the Ogallala Formation. *State Geological Survey of Kansas. Bulletin* 64(2):33–76. Topeka.

Fugle, Eugene
1962   Mill Creek Culture and Technology. *Journal of the Iowa Archeological Society* 11(4):1–126. Iowa City.

1966   The Nature and Function of the Lakota Night Cults. *University of South Dakota. W.H. Over Museum. Museum News* 27(3/4):1–38. Vermillion, S.Dak.

Fugle, Eugene, and James H. Howard
1962   The Nebraska Santee. *American Indian Tradition* 8(5):215–217. Alton, Ill.

Fulmer, Darrell W.
1976   Archaeological Excavations within the El Dorado Reservoir Area, Kansas (1974). *University of Kansas. Museum of Anthropology. Project Report Series* 37. Lawrence.

Fulton, Alexander R.
1882   The Red Men of Iowa: Being a History of the Various Aboriginal Tribes Whose Homes were in Iowa.... Des Moines, Iowa: Iowa Mills and Company.

Fumoleau, René
1977   As Long As This Land Shall Last: A History of Treaty 8 and
            Treaty 11, 1870–1939. Toronto: McClelland and Stewart.

Funk and Wagnalls Standard Dictionary
1963   Funk and Wagnalls Standard Dictionary of the English
            Language: Combined with Britannica World Language Dic-
            tionary. International ed. 2 vols. Chicago: Encyclopedia
            Britannica. (Cover title: Britannica World Language Edi-
            tion of Funk and Wagnalls Standard Dictionary.)

Furbee, Louanna
1990   [Fieldnotes on Chiwere: Submitted to Douglas R. Parks.]
            (National Science Foundation Grant No. BNS#8818393:
            Documenting the Chiwere Language.)

Furbee, Louanna, and Jill D. Hopkins, comps.
1990   [Plains Tribal Names and Miscellaneous Linguistic Notes
            in the Iowa and Otoe-Missouria Language.] (National Sci-
            ence Foundation Grant BNS#8818393: Documenting the
            Chiwere Language.)

Gálvez, Bernardo de
1951   Instructions for Governing the Interior Provinces of New
            Spain, 1786. Donald E. Worcester, ed. and trans. Berkeley,
            Calif.: The Quivira Society.

Gómara, Francisco López de
1587   Histoire generalle des Indes Occidentales, et terres neuves,
            qui iusques à present ont esté descouvertes [...] traduite en
            françois par Mart. Fumée. Paris: Michel Sonnius.

Gadacz, René R., and Michael I. Asch
1984   Thesis and Dissertation Titles and Abstracts on the Anthro-
            pology of Canadian Indians, Inuit, and Métis, from Cana-
            dian Universities. Report 1: 1970–1982. *Canada. National
            Museum of Man. Mercury Series. Ethnology Service Paper*
            95. Ottawa.

Gadus, Eloise F., Ross C. Fields, C. Britt Bousman, Steve A. Tomka,
and M.A. Howard
1992   Excavations at the Finley Fan Site (41HP159), Cooper Lake
            Project, Hopkins County, Texas. *Prewitt and Associates.
            Report of Investigations* 78. Austin, Tex.

Gaffen, Fred
1985   Forgotten Soldiers. Penticton, B.C.: Theytus Books.

Gagnon, François-Marc
1979   L'expérience ethnographique de Louis Nicolas. *Recherches
            amérindiennes au Québec* 8(4):281–295. Montréal.

Gairdner, Doctor
1841   Notes on the Geography of Columbia River. *Journal of the
            Royal Geographic Society* 11. London.

Galante, Gary
1980   Crow Lance Cases or Sword Scabbards. *American Indian
            Art Magazine* 6(1) [Special Crow Issue]:64–73. Scottsdale,
            Ariz.

Gale, George
1867   Upper Mississippi: Or, Historical Sketches of the Mound-
            Builders, the Indian Tribes, and the Progress of Civilization
            in the North-West; from A.D. 1600 to the Present Time.
            Chicago: Clarke. (Reprinted: Kraus Reprint, Millwood,
            N.Y., 1975.)

Gale, John
1969   The Missouri Expedition 1818–1820. The Journal of Sur-
            geon John Gale with Related Documents, edited by Roger
            L. Nichols. Norman: University of Oklahoma.

Galinat, Walton C., and James H. Gunnerson
1963   Spread of Eight-rowed Maize from the Prehistoric South-
            west. *Harvard University. Botanical Museum Leaflets*
            20(5):117–160. Cambridge, Mass.

Galindo, Frances
1984   James Mooney: Photography in Anthropology. (Typescript;
            copy in "Plains" volume photographic files, Handbook of
            North American Indians, Smithsonian Institution, Washing-
            ton.)

Gallagher, Brian
1988   A Re-examination of Race, Class, and Society in Red River.
            Native Studies Review 4(1–2):25–66. Saskatoon, Sask.

Gallatin, Albert
1836   A Synopsis of the Indian Tribes Within the United States
            East of the Rocky Mountains, and in the British and
            Russian Possessions in North America. Pp. 1–422 in
            *Archaeologia Americana: Transactions and Collections of
            the American Antiquarian Society* 2. Cambridge, Mass.
            (Reprinted: AMS Press, New York, 1973.)

———— 1848   Hale's Indians of North-West America, and Vocabularies of
            North America: With an Introduction. Pp. xxiii–clxxxviii,
            1–130 in *Transactions of the American Ethnological Soci-
            ety* 2. New York.

Galloway, E.
1962   The Leath Burial: A Preliminary Report. *The Wyoming
            Archaeologist* 5(2):3–9. Cheyenne, [etc.,] Wyo.

———— 1968   The Billy Creek Burials. *The Wyoming Archaeologist*
            11(1):16–19. Cheyenne, [etc.,] Wyo.

Galloway, Patricia
1982   Frenchmen and Indians in the Lower Mississippi Valley.
            Jackson, Miss.: University of Mississippi Press.

———— 1991   Couture, Tonti, and the English-Quapaw Connection: A
            Revision. Pp. 74–94 in Arkansas Before the Americans.
            Hester A. Davis, ed. *Arkansas Archeological Survey Re-
            search Series* 40. Fayetteville.

Galm, Jerry R.
1979   The Uncas Site: A Late Prehistoric Manifestation in the
            Southern Plains. *University of Oklahoma. Archaeological
            Research and Management Center. Research Series* 5.
            Norman.

Galpin, Charles 1868, 1930 *see* Garraghan, Gilbert J., ed. 1930

Gamble, John I.
1951   Changing Patterns in Kiowa Indian Dances. Pp. 94–104 in
            Vol. 2: Acculturation in the Americas. Sol Tax, ed. With an
            Introduction by Melville J. Herskovits. *Proceedings and
            Selected Papers of the 29th International Congress of
            Americanists. [New York 1949].* 3 vols. Chicago: Univer-
            sity of Chicago Press.

Gant, Robert D.
1967   Archeological Investigations at the Arp Site, 39BR101,
            Burle County, South Dakota, 1961. *University of South
            Dakota. W.H. Over Museum. Archeological Studies
            Circulars* 12. Vermillion, S.Dak.

Garavaglia, Louis A., and Charles G. Worman
1998   Firearms of the American West, 1803–1865. Niwot, Colo.:
            University Press of Colorado.

Garbarino, Merwyn S.
1971   Life in the City: Chicago. Pp. 168–205 in The American
            Indian in Urban Society. Jack O. Waddell and Oscar M.
            Watson, eds. Boston: Little, Brown and Company.

Garber, James F.
1987   Transitional Archaic Structure and Activity Areas at the
            Zapotec Site, San Marcos, Texas. *La Tierra* 14(2):19–30.

Garcia, Louis
1977   Sioux Songs from Sisseton. *Whispering Wind* 10(6):6–11.
            New Orleans.

1979   Women's Dance Society, Devil's Lake Sioux Reservation. *Minnesota Archaeologist* 38(4):190–198. Minneapolis.

Garcia Rejon, Manuel
1866   Vocabulario del idioma comanche. México: Impr. de Ignacio Cumplido. (Cover page has 1865 imprint date.)

_____ 1995 *see* Gelo, Daniel J., trans. and ed. 1995

Gardner, Alexander
1872   [Wife of Asa Havie, the Noted Chief.] (Photograph, negative 1727a, National Anthropological Archives, Smithsonian Institution, Washington.)

1872a   [Wife of To-sho-way.] (Photograph, negative 1731a, National Anthropological Archives, Smithsonian Institution, Washington.)

1872b   [Asa Havie, or The Milky Way.] (Photograph, negative 1727, National Anthropological Archives, Smithsonian Institution, Washington.)

1872c   [Cheevers, or He Goat, Chief of Yamparika Band.] (Photograph, negative 1732a, National Anthropological Archives, Smithsonian Institution, Washington.)

Gardner, William H.
1868   [Sisseton Dakota Vocabulary.] (Manuscript No. 940, National Anthropological Archives, Smithsonian Institution, Washington.)

Garmhausen, Winona
1988   History of Indian Arts Education in Santa Fe: The Institute of American Indian Arts with Historical Background, 1890 to 1962. Santa Fe: Sunstone Press.

Garraghan, Gilbert J. (S.J.)
1927   The Emergence of the Missouri Valley into History. *Illinois Catholic Historical Review* 9(4):306–322. Chicago.
_____, ed.
1930   Father De Smet's Sioux Peace Mission of 1868 and the Journal of Charles Galpin. *Mid-America* 13, n.s. 2:141–163. Chicago.

Garrett, Julia K.
1946   Dr. John Sibley and the Louisiana-Texas Frontier, 1803–1814. *Southwestern Historical Quarterly* 49(3):399–431. Austin, Tex.

Garrett, Kathleen
1955   Music on the Indian Territory Frontier. *Chronicles of Oklahoma* 33(3):339–348. Norman.

Garter Snake 1980 *see* Horse Capture, George P., ed. 1980a

Garvin, Paul L.
1950   Wichita I: Phonemics. *International Journal of American Linguistics* 16(4):179–184. Chicago.

Gass, Patrick
1807   Journal of the Voyages and Travels of a Corps of Discovery, Under the Command of Capt. Lewis and Capt. Clarke of the Army of the United States, from the Mouth of the River Missouri through the Interior Parts of North America to the Pacific Ocean, during the Years 1804, 1805, and 1806. Pittsburgh, Pa.: Printed by Zadok Cramer for David M'Keehan. (Reprinted: Ross and Haines, Minneapolis, 1958.)

1810   Journal of the Voyages and Travels of a Corps of Discovery, Under the Command of Capt. Lewis and Capt. Clarke of the Army of the United States from the Mouth of the River Missouri through the Interior Parts of North America to the Pacific Ocean, during the Years 1804, 1805 and 1806. 2nd ed. Philadelphia: Printed for Matthew Carey.

Gates, Charles M., ed.
1965   Five Fur Traders of the Northwest: Being the Narrative of Peter Pond and the Diaries of John Macdonell, Archibald N. McLeod, Hugh Faries, and Thomas Connor; with an Introduction by Grace Lee Nute and a Foreword by Theodore C. Blegen. St. Paul: Minnesota Historical Society.

Gatschet, Albert S.
1876   Zwölf Sprachen aus dem Südwesten Nordamerikas (Pueblos- und Apache-Mundarten; Tonto, Tonkawa, Digger, Utah). Weimar, Germany: Hermann Böhlau. (Reprinted: Humanities Press, New York, 1970.)

1876a   Remarks upon the Tonkawa Language. Pp. 318–327 in *16th Proceedings of the American Philosophical Society*. Philadelphia.

1877   Die Sprache der Tonkawas. *Zeitschrift für Ethnologie* 9:64–73. Berlin: Berliner Gesellschaft für Anthropologie, Ethnologie und Urgeschichte.

1878   [Kansas or Kaw Indian Vocabulary.] (Manuscript No. 1485, National Anthropological Archives, Smithsonian Institution, Washington.)

1879   [Comanche Vocabulary and Linguistic Notes.] (Manuscript No. 1568, National Anthropological Archives, Smithsonian Institution, Washington.)

1879a   [Sàwânô or Shawani Vocabulary.] (Manuscript No. 885, National Anthropological Archives, Smithsonian Institution, Washington.)

1879b   Linguistic Notes. *American Antiquarian: A Quarterly Journal Devoted to Early American History, Ethnology and Archaeology* 2(1):76–79. Chicago: Jameson and Morse.

1881   ["Wandot" (Wyandot) Vocabulary. Wyandot Reserve, Indian Terr., January 8, February 7, March 15, 1881.] (Manuscript No. 1549, National Anthropological Archives, Smithsonian Institution, Washington.)

1882   [Caddo; taken in Mades' Hotel, Washington, D.C. from Aimai=só-e "stout man", delegate of Caddo tribe, Ind. Terr., through Mr. Jos. Leonard, Anadarko, P.O. Indian Terr., April–May 1882.] (Manuscript No. 2017 (old No. 1563), National Anthropological Archives, Smithsonian Institution, Washington.)

_____ 1882a *see* 1883a

1882–1889 [Notes and Text on the Fox or Utagami Language; also, Earliest Examples of Kickapoo Syllabics.] (Manuscript No. 63, National Anthropological Archives, Smithsonian Institution, Washington.)

1883   [Pinal Apache; Vocabulary and Texts with Ethnographic Notes and Interlinear Translation.] (Manuscript No.1567, Apache Catalog, National Anthropological Archives, Smithsonian Institution, Washington.)

1883a   Chief Deities in American Religions [Abstract]. Pp. 573–584 in *Proceedings of the American Association for the Advancement of Science, 31st Meeting, Held at Montreal, Canada, August, 1882*. Salem, Mass.

1884   [Yatasi Notes, in Caddo Notebook, 1882–1888.] (Manuscript No. 2017, National Anthropological Archives, Smithsonian Institution, Washington.)

1884a   [Comanche Language: Collected at the Kiowa, Comanche and Apache Reservation, Indian Terr., in Oct., Nov., Dec., 1884. With one page of additions by James Mooney, 1891.] (Manuscript No. 748, National Anthropological Archives, Smithsonian Institution, Washington.)

1884b [Apache-Tinné Language. Dialect of the Ná-isha Band; collected at Kiowa, Apache, and Comanche Agency, Anadarko, Indian Terr. in Nov. and Dec. 1884.] (Manuscript No. 62, Apache Catalog, National Anthropological Archives, Smithsonian Institution, Washington.)

1884c [Tonkawe Language; Collected at Fort Griffin, Shackleford Co., Texas, Sept.–Oct. 1884.] (Manuscript No. 1008, National Anthropological Archives, Smithsonian Institution, Washington.)

1884d [Lipan, a Dialect of the Apache-Tinné Family, collected at Fort Griffin, Texas (Shackleford County), ... September and October 1884.] (Manuscripts Nos. 81-a and 81-b, Apache Catalog, National Anthropological Archives, Smithsonian Institution, Washington.)

1884e [Káyowē Language, Collected at the Kiowa, Comanche and Apache Reservation, in Fort Sill and Anadarko, Indian Territory, Oct.–Dec. 1884.] (Manuscript No. 520a, National Anthropological Archives, Smithsonian Institution, Washington.)

1884f [Káyowe. Apache, Comanche and Kiowa Reservation, Ind. Terr.] (Manuscript No. 520b [old No. 1444], National Anthropological Archives, Smithsonian Institution, Washington.)

1884–1888 A Migration Legend of the Creek Indians, with a Linguistic, Historic and Ethnographic Introduction. 2 vols. [Vol. 1 issued as *Brinton's Library of Aboriginal American Literature* 4; Vol.2 titled: A Migration Legend of the Creek Indians, Texts and Glossaries in Creek and Hitchití with a Linguistic, Historic, and Ethnographic Introduction and Commentary.] Philadelphia: D.G. Brinton; St. Louis, Mo.: Printed for the Author by R.P. Studley. (Reprinted, 2 vols. in 1: Kraus Reprint, New York, 1969.)

1885 [Navajo Words and Tribal Names, "from Interpreter", dated Nov. 28, 1885.] (Pp.78a–78b [insert], Pinal Apache Vocabulary, Manuscript No. 1567, National Anthropological Archives, Smithsonian Institution, Washington.)

1891 The Karankawa Indians: The Coast People of Texas. With Notes by Charles A. Hammond and Alice W. Oliver, and a Vocabulary Obtained from Alice W. Oliver. *Papers of the Peabody Museum of American Archaeology and Ethnology. Harvard University* 1(2):9–106. Cambridge, Mass.

1893 [Comanche Vocabulary, from Information from Phillip Bloch, Indian Scout.] (Manuscript No. 751, National Anthropological Archives, Smithsonian Institution, Washington.)

1895 [Notes on Peoria and Miami.] (Manuscript No. 236, National Anthropological Archives, Smithsonian Institution, Washington.)

1895a [Notes on Peoria and Miami.] (Manuscript No. 2481, National Anthropological Archives, Smithsonian Institution, Washington.)

1895b [Notes on Peoria and Miami.] (Manuscript No. 2483, National Anthropological Archives, Smithsonian Institution, Washington.)

Gebow, Joseph A., interpreter
1868 Vocabulary of the Snake, or, Sho-sho-nay Dialect. 2d ed., rev. and improved. Green River City, Wyo.Terr.: Freeman and Bro., Printers. (Originally printed at the "Daily Union Vedette" Book and Job Office, Camp Douglas, U.T., 1864.)

Gelo, Daniel J.
1986 Comanche Belief and Ritual. (Ph.D. Dissertation in Anthropology, Rutgers University, New Brunswick, N.J.; Re-

printed: University Microfilms International, Ann Arbor, Mich., 1987, 1989.)

_____, trans. and ed.
1995 Comanche Vocabulary / Vocabulario del idioma comanche, compiled by Manuel García Rejón. Trilingual ed., 1st ed. *Texas Archaeology and Ethnohistory Series.* Austin: University of Texas Press. (See also García Rejón 1866.)

George, Preston
1981 Unusual Chert Blades Found at Kaw Lake. *Bulletin of the Oklahoma Anthropological Society* 30:1–10. Norman.

George, Preston, and Don G. Wyckoff
1980 Clues to Archaic Occupations in North-Central Oklahoma. *Oklahoma Anthropological Society Newsletter* 28(8):6–8. Norman.

Gerard, William R.
[1900] [Iowa.] (Manuscript No. 2842-C, National Anthropological Archives, Smithsonian Institution, Washington.)

Gerber, Linda
1979 The Development of Canadian Indian Communities: A Two-Dimensional Typology Reflecting Strategies of Adaptation to the Modern World. *Canadian Review of Sociology and Anthropology* 16:404–424. Toronto and Montreal.

Gerritsen, William D.
1961 The Shoshone-Bannock Sun Dance: A Study in Integration. (M.A. Thesis in Anthropology, University of New Mexico, Albuquerque.)

Getty, Ian A.L., and John W. Larner, Jr.
1972 The Kootenay Plains and the Big Horn Wesley Stoney Band: An Oral and Documentary History Study, 1800–1970. (Unpublished Research Report to Stoney Tribal Council, Morley, Alta.)

Getty, Ian A.L., and Donald B. Smith, eds.
1978 One Century Later: Western Canadian Reserve Indians Since Treaty Seven. Vancouver: University of British Columbia Press.

Getty, Wayne Edwin Allen
1974 Perception as an Agent of Sociocultural Change for the Stoney Indians of Alberta. (M.A. Thesis in Anthropology, University of Calgary, Calgary, Alta.)

_____
1975 A Case History and Analysis of Stoney Indian—Governmental Interaction with Regard to the Bighorn Dam: The Effects of Citizen Participation — A Lesson on Government Perfidy and Indian Frustration. (M.A. Thesis in Social Work, University of Calgary, Calgary, Alta.)

Gettys, Francie
1991 Salvage Excavation in Roger Mills County. *Oklahoma Archeological Survey Newsletter* 10(3):1–2. Norman.

Gettys, Marshall
1975 Preliminary Report on Archaeological Investigations at Lukafta Reservoir, Southeastern Oklahoma. *Oklahoma River Basin Survey. Archaeological Site Report* 31.

_____
1976 Paleo-Indian and Early Archaic Occupations of Oklahoma. *University of Oklahoma, Papers in Anthropology* 17(1): 51–74. Norman.

Ghostkeeper, Elmer, ed.
1982 Métisism: A Canadian Identity. Edmonton, Alta.: Alberta Federation of Métis Settlements Association.

Giago, Tim
1994 The Rights of Passage: Indian Spirituality Must Stay Indian. *Indian Country Today* 13(29):A-4. Rapid City, S.Dak.

Gibbon, Guy E.
1974 A Model of Mississippian Development and Its Implications for the Red Wing Area. Pp. 129–137 in Aspects of Upper

Great Lakes Anthropology: Papers in Honor of Lloyd A. Wilford. Elden Johnson, ed. *Minnesota Prehistoric Archaeology Series* 11. St. Paul: Minnesota Historical Society.

1983 The Blue Earth Phase of Southern Minnesota. *Journal of the Iowa Archeological Society* 30(1):1–84. Iowa City.

   , ed.
1983a Oneota Studies. *University of Minnesota. Publications in Anthropology* 1. Minneapolis. (Title page has 1982 imprint date.)

1983b Oneota Origins Revisited. Pp. 85–89 in Oneota Studies. Guy E. Gibbon, ed. *University of Minnesota. Publications in Anthropology* 1. Minneapolis. (Title page has 1982 imprint date.)

1994 Cultures of the Upper Mississippi River Valley and Adjacent Prairies in Iowa and Minnesota. Pp. 128–148 in Plains Indians, A.D. 500–1500: The Archaeological Past of Prehistoric Groups. Karl H. Schlesier, ed. Norman and London: University of Oklahoma Press.

Gibbon, Guy E.
1995 Oneota at the Periphery: Trade, Political Power, and Ethnicity in Northern Minnesota and on the Northeastern Plains in the Late Prehistoric Period. Pp. 175–199 in Oneota Archaeology: Past, Present, and Future. William Green, ed. *University of Iowa. Office of the State Archaeologist. Report* 20. Iowa City.

Gibbon, Guy E., and Clark A. Dobbs
1991 The Mississippian Presence in the Red Wing Area, Minnesota. Pp. 281–306 in New Perspectives on Cahokia: Views from the Periphery. James B. Stoltman, ed. *Monographs in World Archaeology* 2. Madison, Wis.: Prehistory Press.

Gibbs, Peter
1982 Duke Paul Wilhelm Collection in the British Museum. *American Indian Art Magazine* 7(3):52–61. Scottsdale, Ariz.

Gibson, Arrell M.
1980 The American Indian: Prehistory to the Present. Lexington, Mass.: D.C. Heath and Company.

Gibson, Terrance H.
1981 Remnant Oxbow on the Northern Plains: The Evidence and Its Implications for Regional Prehistory. *Canadian Journal of Archaeology* 5:131–136. Ottawa.

1998 Site Structure and Caramic Behavior of a Protohistoric Cree Aggregation Campsite. (Ph.D. Dissertation in Anthropology, University of Alberta, Edmonton.)

Gidley, Mick
1998 Edward S. Curtis and the North American Indian, Incorporated. Cambridge, U.K., and New York: Cambridge University Press.

Giglio, Virginia
1994 Southern Cheyenne Women's Songs. [Book and audiocassette.] Norman: University of Oklahoma Press.

Gilbert, B. Miles
1980 The Plains Setting. Pp. 8–15 in Anthropology on the Great Plains. W. Raymond Wood and Margot Liberty, eds. Lincoln: University of Nebraska Press.

Gilder, Robert F.
1907 Archeology of the Ponca Creek District, Eastern Nebraska. *American Anthropologist*, n.s. 9(4):702–719.

1907a The Nebraska Loess Man. *Records of the Past* 6(2):35–39. Washington.

1908 Oto Village Site in Nebraska. *American Anthropologist*, n.s. 10(1):56–84.

1908a Indian Sites near Frederick, Wyoming. *Records of the Past* 7(4):179–182. Washington.

1913 A Prehistoric "Cannibal" House in Nebraska. *Records of the Past* 12(3):106–116. Washington.

1916 The Nebraska Culture Man. Omaha, Neb: H.F. Kieser. (Reprinted in 1926.)

   1926 see 1916 (reprint info.)

Gilette, J.M.
1906 Medicine Society of the Dakota Indians. Pp. 459–474 in *Collections of the State Historical Society of North Dakota* 1. Bismarck.

Gill, George W.
1974 Human Skeletons from Wyoming and Their Bearing on the Concept of Morphological Dating. Pp. 100–107 in Applied Geology and Archaeology: The Holocene History of Wyoming. Michael Wilson, ed. *Geological Survey of Wyoming. Report of Investigations* 10. Laramie.

1981 Human Skeletal Populations of the Northwestern Plains: A Preliminary Analysis. Pp. 57–70 in Progress in Skeletal Biology of Plains Populations. Richard L. Jantz and Douglas H. Ubelaker, eds. *Plains Anthropologist* 26(94, Pt. 2); *Memoir* 17. Lincoln.

1984 The Partial Skeleton of a Child from Dead Indian Creek. Pp. 97–98 in The Dead Indian Creek Site: An Archaic Occupation in the Absaroka Mountains of Northeastern Wyoming. George C. Frison and Danny N. Walker, eds. *The Wyoming Archaeologist* 27(1–2). Cheyenne, [etc.,] Wyo.

1991 Human Skeletal Remains on the Northwestern Plains. Pp. 431–447 in Prehistoric Hunters of the High Plains. 2d ed. George C. Frison, ed. San Diego, Calif.: Academic Press.

Gill, Sam D.
1982 Native American Religions: An Introduction. Belmont, Calif.: Wadsworth Publishing Company.

Gilman, Carolyn
1992 The Grand Portage Story. St. Paul: Minnesota Historical Society Press.

Gilman, Carolyn, and Mary Jane Schneider
1987 The Way to Independence: Memories of a Hidatsa Indian family, 1840–1920. With Essays by W. Raymond Wood, Gerard Baker, Jeffery R. Hanson, and Alan R. Woolworth. St. Paul: Minnesota Historical Society Press.

Gilman, Rhoda R., Carolyn Gilman, and Deborah M. Stultz
1979 The Red River Trails: Oxcart Routes between St. Paul and the Selkirk Settlement, 1820–1870. St. Paul, Minn.: Minnesota Historical Society.

Gilmore, Melvin R.
1913 Some Native Nabraska Plants with Their Uses by the Dakota. *Collections of the Nebraska State Historical Society* 17:358–370. Lincoln.

1913a A Study in the Ethnobotany of the Omaha Indians. *Collections of the Nebraska State Historical Society* 17:314–357. (Originally presented as the Author's M.A. Thesis in Anthropology, University of Nebraska, Lincoln.)

1919 Uses of Plants by the Indians of the Missouri River Region. Pp. 43–154 in *33d Annual Report of the Bureau of American Ethnology [for] 1911–1912*. Washington: Smithsonian Institution; U.S. Government Printing Office. (Originally issued as the Author's Ph.D. Dissertation in Anthropology, University of Nebraska, Lincoln. Reprinted, with a Foreword by Hugh Cutler: University of Nebraska

Press, Lincoln, 1977; also, Enlarged ed. with Illus. by Bellamy Parks Jansen, 1991.)

1919a   The Mescal Society among the Omaha Indians. *Publications of the Nebraska State Historical Society* 19:163–167. Lincoln.

1920–1930   [Arikara Agriculture.] (Manuscript in National Museum of the American Indian Archives [formerly, Museum of the American Indian, Heye Foundation], New York.)

1920–1930a   [Old Arikara Method of Butchering a Buffalo.] (Manuscript in State Historical Society of North Dakota, Bismarck.)

1924   [Account of the Sacred Bundle, obtained from Mrs. Ida Phillips, at Pawnee, Oklahoma, December 1924.] (Manuscript in the Archives of the Museum of Anthropology, University of Michigan, Ann Arbor.)

1924a   Arikara Fish-trap. *Indian Notes* 1(3):120–134. New York: Museum of the American Indian. Heye Foundation.

1924b   Glass Bead Making by the Arikara. *Indian Notes* 1(1):20–21. New York: Museum of the American Indian. Heye Foundation.

1925   Arikara Basketry. *Indian Notes* 2(2):89–95. New York: Museum of the American Indian. Heye Foundation.

1925a   Arikara Uses of Clay and Other Earth Products. *Indian Notes* 2(4):283–289. New York: Museum of the American Indian. Heye Foundation.

1926   An Hidatsa Shrine and the Beliefs Respecting It. *American Anthropologist,* n.s. 28(3):572–573.

1926a   Arikara Genesis and Its Teachings. Told by Four-Rings, an Old Man of the Arikara Tribe, and now Summarized in English. *Indian Notes* 3(3):188–193. New York: Museum of the American Indian. Heye Foundation.

1927   Notes on Arikara Tribal Organization. *Indian Notes* 4(4):332–350. New York: Museum of the American Indian. Heye Foundation.

1929   The Dakota Ceremony of Huⁿká. *Indian Notes* 6(1):75–78. New York: Museum of the American Indian. Heye Foundation.

1929a   The Old-Time Method of Rearing a Dakota Boy. *Indian Notes* 6(4):367–372. New York: Museum of the American Indian. Heye Foundation.

1929b   Prairie Smoke. Louis Schellbach, illus. New York: Columbia University Press. (Reprinted: AMS Press, New York, 1966; also, with a Bibliography of Gilmore's works Compiled by Alan Woolworth, Minnesota Historical Society, St. Paul, 1987.)

1930   The Arikara Book of Genesis. *Papers of the Michigan Academy of Science, Arts and Letters* 12(for 1929):95–120. Ann Arbor.

1931   The Arikara Tribal Temple. *Papers of the Michigan Academy of Science, Arts and Letters* 14(for 1930):47–70. Ann Arbor.

1932   The Sacred Bundles of the Arikara. *Papers of the Michigan Academy of Science, Arts, and Letters* 16(for 1931): 33–50. Ann Arbor.

1933   The Victory Dance of the Dakota Indians at Fort Yates on the Standing Rock Reservation in November, 1918. *Paper of the Michigan Academy of Science, Arts and Letters* 17(for 1932):23–30. Ann Arbor.

1934   The Arikara Method of Preparing a Dog for a Feast. *Papers of the Michigan Academy of Science, Arts, and Letters* 19(for 1933):37–38. Ann Arbor.

Gilmore, Robert
1990   The Northern Arapaho Cradle. *American Indian Art Magazine* 16(1):64–71. Scottsdale, Ariz.

Giorda, Joseph, Joseph Bandini, Joseph Guidi, Gregory Mengarini, and Leopold Van Gorp
1877–1879   A Dictionary of the Kalispel or Flat-head Indian Language. Compiled by the Missionaries of the Society of Jesus. Pt. I: Kalispel-English; Pt. II: English-Kalispel. [St. Ignatius, Mont.]: St. Ignatius Print.

Girard, Jeffrey S., and Helen S. Carr
1995   Archaeological Investigations at the Bellcow Site (34LN29), Lincoln County, Oklahoma. *Oklahoma Anthropological Society Memoir* 6. Norman.

Giraud, Marcel
1945   Le Métis canadien: son rôle dans l'histoire des provinces de l'Ouest. *Université de Paris. Institut d'ethnologie. Travaux et mémoires de l'Institut d'ethnologie* 44. Paris: Institut d'ethnologie. (Reprinted in French, with an Introduction by J.E. Foster and Louise Zuk. 2 vols.: Éditions du Blé, Saint-Boniface, Man., 1984. Publ. in English under title: The Métis in the Canadian West. George Woodcock, trans. 2 vols. University of Alberta Press, Edmonton, 1986; also, University of Nebraska Press, Lincoln, 1986.)

_____, ed.
1958   Etienne Veniard de Bourgmont's "Exact Description of Louisiana." Mrs. Max W. Myers, trans. *Bulletin of the Missouri Historical Society* 15(1):3–19. St. Louis.

1986   The Métis in the Canadian West. 2 vols. George Woodcock, trans. Edmonton: University of Alberta Press; [also] Lincoln: University of Nebraska Press. (Originally publ. in French under title: Le Métis canadien [etc.], Institute d'ethnologie, Paris, 1945.)

Givón, Talmy, comp.
1979   Ute Dictionary. Preliminary ed. Ignacio, Colo.: Ute Press, The Southern Ute Tribe.

Gladwin, Thomas
1948   Comanche Kin Behavior. *American Anthropologist,* n.s. 50(1):73–94.

Glancy, Diane
1988   Sun Dance. Pp. 117–123 in Native American Religious Identity: Unforgotten Gods. Jace Weaver, ed. Maryknoll, N.Y.: Orbis Books.

1998   The Cold-and-Hungry Dance. Lincoln: University of Nebraska Press.

Glass, Anthony, and Dan Flores, eds.
1985   Journal of an Indian Trader: Anthony Glass and the Texas Trading Frontier, 1780–1810. *Texas A&M Southwestern Studies* 4. College Station: Texas A&M Press.

Glassow, Michael A.
1980   Prehistoric Agricultural Development in the Northern Southwest: A Study in Changing Patterns of Land Use. *Ballena Press Anthropological Papers* 16. Socorro, N.Mex.

Glenmore, Josephine Stands-in-Timber, and Wayne Leman
1984   Cheyenne Topical Dictionary. Busby, Mont.: Cheyenne Translation Project.

1985   Cheyenne Topical Dictionary. Revised ed. Busby, Mont.: Cheyenne Translation Project.

Glenn, James R.
1981   The 'Curious Gallery': The Indian Photographs of the

McClees Studio in Washington, 1857–1858. *History of Photography* 5(3):249–262.

1983   De Lancey W. Gill: Photographer of the Bureau of American Ethnology. *History of Photography* 7(1):7–22.

Glover, Richard, ed. 1962 *see* Thompson, David 1962

Goddard, Ives
1965   Sketch of Arapaho Linguistic History. *Papers from the Seminar in American Indian Languages* 2. Cambridge: Harvard University, Department of Linguistics.

1967   Notes on the Genetic Classification of the Algonquian Languages. Pp. 7–12 in Contributions to Anthropology: Linguistics, I (Algonquian). *National Museum of Canada Bulletin* 214; *Anthropological Series* 78. Ottawa.

1967a   [Fieldnotes of work on Arapaho Linguistics with Bill Sutton, in Canton, Okla., July 18, 1967.] (Manuscript in I. Goddard's possession.)

1974   An Outline of the Historical Phonology of Arapaho and Atsina. *International Journal of American Linguistics* 40(2):102–116. Chicago.

1978   The Sutaio Dialect of Cheyenne: a Discussion of the Evidence. Pp. 68–80 in Papers of the Ninth Algonquian Conference. William Cowan, ed. Ottawa: Carleton University.

1978[a], 1978[b]   *see* Handbook Vol. 15 (1978:70–77, 583–587)

1979   Comparative Algonquian. Pp. 70–132 in The Languages of Native America: Historical and Comparative Assessment. Lyle Campbell and Marianne Mithun, eds. Austin: University of Texas Press.

1979a   The Languages of South Texas and the Lower Rio Grande. Pp. 355–389 in The Languages of Native America: Historical and Comparative Assessment. Lyle Campbell and Marianne Mithun, eds. Austin: University of Texas Press.

1984   The Study of Native North American Ethnonymy. Pp. 95–107 in Naming Systems: 1980 Proceedings of the American Ethnological Society. Elisabeth Tooker, ed.; Harold C. Conklin, Symposium Organizer. Washington, D.C.: American Ethnological Society.

1988   Pre-Cheyenne *ȳ. Pp. 345–360 in In Honor of Mary Haas: From the Haas Festival Conference on Native American Linguistics. William Shipley, ed. Berlin: Mouton de Gruyter.

1994   The West-to-East Cline in Algonquian Dialectology. Pp. 187–211 in Actes du Vingt-cinquième Congrès des Algonquinistes. William Cowan, ed. Ottawa: Carleton University.

1994a   Leonard Bloomfield's Fox Lexicon. Critical Edition. *Algonquian and Iroquoian Linguistics, Memoir* 12. John D. Nichols, ed. Winnepeg, Man.

1996   Native Languages and Language Families of North America. (Map, to accompany: *Handbook of North American Indians*, Vol. 17: Languages. Ives Goddard, vol. ed.; William C. Sturtevant, gen. ed.) Washington: Smithsonian Institution. (Reprinted, rev. and enl. ed., with additions and corrections, 1998.)

1998   Recovering Arapaho Etymologies by Reconstructing Forwards. Pp. 183–200 in Mír Curad: Studies in Honor of Calvert Watkins. Jay Jasanoff, H. Craig Melchert, and Lisi Oliver, eds. *Innsbrucker Beiträge zur Sprachwissenschaft*

92. Innsbruck, Austria: Institut für Sprachwissenschaft der Universität Innsbruck.

Goddard, Pliny Earle
1909   Lipan Texts. (Manuscript, interlinear texts, in the Archives of the Languages of the World at Indiana University, Bloomington.)

1914   Dancing Societies of the Sarsi Indians. *American Museum of Natural History Anthropological Papers* 11(5):461–474. New York. (Bound with other monographs in: Societies of the Plains Indians, Clark Wissler, ed., New York, 1916.)

1915   Sarsi Texts. *University of California Publications in American Archaeology and Ethnology* 11(3):189–277. Berkeley.

1917   The Beaver Indians. *American Museum of Natural History Anthropological Papers* 10(4):201–293. New York.

1919   Notes on the Sun Dance of the Sarsi. *American Museum of Natural History Anthropological Papers* 16(4):271–281. New York.

1919a   Notes on the Sun Dance of the Cree in Alberta. *American Museum of Natural History Anthropological Papers* 16(4):295–310. New York.

1919b   Plains Ojibwa Sun Dance. *American Museum of Natural History Anthropological Papers* 16(7):453–522. New York.

Godfrey, Edward Settle
1892   Custer's Last Battle: By One of His Troop Commanders. With Comments on the Battle by General James B. Fry. *Century Illustrated Monthly Magazine* 33/35. New York. (Reprinted: Seventh U.S. Cavalry Memorial Association, Omaha, Nebr., 1926; also, With an Introduction Eugene McAuliffe, Shorey Book Store, Seattle, 1964; and, Outbooks, Olympic Valley, Calif., 1976; also, under title: General George A. Custer and the Battle of the Little Big Horn, June 25, 1876; The Century Company, New York, 1908, 1921.)

Goetzmann, William H.
1959   Army Exploration in the American West, 1803–1863. New Haven, Conn.: Yale University Press. (Reprinted: University of Nebraska Press, Lincoln, 1979.)

Goggin, John M.
1938   A Note on Cheyenne Peyote. *New Mexico Anthropologist* 3(2):26–30. Albuquerque.

Goldfrank, Esther S.
1943   Historic Change and Social Character: A Study of the Teton Dakota. *American Anthropologist*, n.s. 45(1):67–83.

1945   Changing Configurations in the Social Organization of a Blackfoot Tribe During the Reserve Period (The Blood of Alberta, Canada). *American Ethnological Society Monograph* 8. Washington: American Anthropological Association; also, New York: J.J. Augustin; and, Seattle: University of Washington Press.

1978   Notes on an Undirected Life: As One Anthropologist Tells It. *Queens College Publications in Anthropology* 3. Flushing, N.Y.: Queens College Press.

Goldring, Philip
1973   The Cypress Hills Massacre—A Century's Retrospect. *Saskatchewan History* 26(3):81–102. Saskatoon, Sask.

1979   Whiskey, Horses and Death: The Cypress Hills Massacre and Its Sequel. *Canadian Historical Sites. Occasional Papers in Archaeology and History* 21:41–70. Ottawa.

Goldstein, Lynne, ed.
1987   Current Research. *American Antiquity* 52(3):631–645.

Gone, Fred P.

[1941– Works Progress Administration Interviews, Fort Belknap
1942] Reservation. (Manuscripts in Special Collections, Montana State University Library, Bozeman.)

_____, comp. 1980 *see* Horse Capture, George P., ed. 1980a

Gonzáles Lòpez-Briones, Carmen

1995 Reacciones diferentes ante una política similar: los indios Osages y los Quapaws ante la política comercial franco-española en la Luisiana durante el siglo XVIII. *Anales del Museo de América* 3:119–130. Madrid.

Gonzalez, Mario, and Elizabeth Cook-Lynn

1999 The Politics of Hallowed Ground: Wounded Knee and the Struggle for Indian Sovereignty. Urbana, Ill.: University of Illinois Press.

Good Tracks, Jim G., comp. and ed.

1992 Baxoje - Jiwere - Nyut'aji - Ma'unke / Iowa - Otoe - Missouria Language To English. Boulder, Colo.: Distributed by the Center for the Study of the Languages of the Plains and Southwest, Department of Linguistics, University of Colorado.

Goodbear, Paul Flying Eagle

1961 Cheyenne Sun Dance Pp. 259–262 in Paul "Flying Eagle" Goodbear, by Luella Thornburgh. *New Mexico Historical Review* 36(4):[256] 257–262. Albuquerque.

Goodbird, Edward

1914 Goodbird the Indian; His Story. Told by Himself to Gilbert L. Wilson. New York: Fleming H. Revell.

Goodbody, Bridget Luette

1996 George Catlin's Indian Gallery: Art, Science, and Power in the Nineteenth-Century. (Ph.D. Dissertation in Art History and Archaeology, Graduate School of Arts and Sciences, Columbia University, New York.)

Gooding, John D.

1981 The Archaeology of Vail Pass Camp: A Multi-Component Base Camp Below Treelimit in the Southern Rockies. Colorado Department of Highways. *Highway Salvage Report* 35. Boulder.

Goodrich, Thomas

1977 Scalp Dance: Indian Warfare on the High Plains, 1865–1879. Mechanicsburg, Pa.: Stackpole Books.

Goodwin, Grenville

1933 Clans of the Western Apache. *New Mexico Historical Review* 8(3):176–182. Albuquerque.

1938 White Mountain Apache Religion. *American Anthropologist,* n.s. 40(1):24–37.

1939 Myths and Tales of the White Mountain Apache. *Memoirs of the American Folklore Society* 33. New York.

1942 The Social Organization of the Western Apache. Chicago: University of Chicago Press. (Reprinted, 2d ed.: University of Arizona Press, Tucson, 1969.)

Gordon, Raymond G., Jr.

1972 Pitch Accent in Crow. *International Journal of American Linguistics* 38(3):191–200. Chicago.

Gordon, Raymond G., Jr., and Randolph Graczyk, comps.

1985 Crow Dictionary. (Manuscript in R.G. Gordon, Jr., and R.Graczyk's possession.)

Gough, Barry M., ed. 1988–1992 *see* Henry, Alexander (the Younger) 1988–1992

Gould, Charles N.

1898 The Timbered Mounds of the Kaw Reservation. *Transactions of the Kansas Academy of Science* 15:78–79. Topeka.

1899 Additional Notes on the Timbered Mounds of the Kaw Reservation. *Transactions of the Kansas Academy of Science* 16:282. Topeka.

Gould, Ronald R.

1975 An Archaeological Survey of the Bluff Creek Drainage System. (M.A. Thesis in Anthropology, Wichita State University, Wichita, Kans.)

Gould, Stephen Jay

1989 Wonderful Life: The Burgess Shale and the Nature of History. New York: WW Norton.

1996 Full House: The Spread of Excellence from Plato to Darwin. New York: Three Rivers Press.

Gourneau, Charles J.

[1989] Old Wild Rice. ("This book is intended as a commemorative marking the Centennial of the State of North Dakota, 1889–1989.") Belcourt, N.Dak.: The Author. (Reprinted, 2d ed. under new title and Author's new name: Old Wild Rice, the Great Chief, Genesis of the Pembina/Turtle Mountain Chippewa, by Charlie White Weasel, Belcourt, N.Dak., 1990, 1995.)

Gourneau, Patrick

1989 History of the Turtle Mountain Band of Chippewa Indians, by Aun nish e naubay. 8th ed. Belcourt, N.Dak.: Turtle Mountain Heritage Center. (Originally publ. in 1971.)

Gowans, Fred R.

1975 Rocky Mountain Rendezvous: A History of the Fur Trade Rendezvous, 1825–1840. Provo, Utah: Brigham Young University Press.

Graczyk, Randolph

1975 The Sweat Lodge. *Close-Up: A Supplement to Kit* (April):1–4.

1984 Crow as an Active Language. (Master's Essay in Linguistics, University of Chicago, Chicago.)

1990 Incorporation and Cliticization in Crow Morphosyntax. 2 vols. (Ph.D. Dissertation in Linguistics, University of Chicago, Chicago.)

1991 Relative Clauses in Crow. Pp. 490–504 in 1990 Linguistics Conference Papers. Francis Ingemann, ed. Lawrence, Kans.: University of Kansas Press.

1992 The Decline in Crow Language Viability: Data and Analysis. (Paper presented at the Conference on American Indian Languages, Annual Meeting of the American Anthropological Association, San Francisco, Dec. 5, 1992.)

Gradwohl, David M.

1969 Prehistoric Villages in Eastern Nebraska. *Nebraska State Historical Society. Publications in Anthropology* 4. Lincoln.

1969a Salvage Archaeology during 1967 in the Saylorville Reservoir, Iowa. *Plains Anthropologist* 14(46):298.

1969b Salvage Archaeology in Saylorville Reservoir, Iowa, 1968. *Plains Anthropologist* 14(46):311.

1974 More Site Seeking in Saylorville: An Intensive Archaeological Site Survey of Reconnaissance Units 2 and 4, Saylorville Reservoir, Iowa. (Research Report, Iowa State University Archaeological Laboratory, Ames, Iowa.)

1982 Shelling Corn in the Prairie-Plains: Archaeological Evidence and Ethnographic Parallels Beyond the Pun. Pp. 135–156 in Plains Indian Studies: Collection of Essays in Honor of John C. Ewers and Waldo R. Wedel. Douglas H. Ubelaker and

Herman J. Viola, eds. *Smithsonian Contributions to Anthropology* 30. Washington: Smithsonian Institution.

Graham, Andrew
1969 Andrew Graham's Observations on Hudson's Bay, 1767–91. Glyndwr Williams, ed. *Publications of the Hudson's Bay Record Society* 27. London.

Graham, Mary Ann, Michael C. Wilson, and Russell W. Graham
1987 Paleoenvironments and Mammalian Faunas of Montana, Southern Alberta, and Southern Saskatchewan. Pp. 410–459 in Late Quaternary Mammalian Biogeography and Environments of the Great Plains and Prairies. Russell W. Graham, Holmes A. Semken, Jr., and Mary Ann Graham, eds. *Illinois State Museum Scientific Papers* 22. Springfield.

Graham, William A.
1926 The Story of the Little Bighorn: Custer's Last Fight. New York: The Century Company.

_____
1953 The Custer Myth: A Source Book of Custeriana [...] To Which Is Added Important Items of Custeriana and A Complete and Comprehensive Bibliography by Fred Dustin. New York: Bonanza Books.

Grange, Roger T., Jr.
1968 Pawnee and Lower Loup Pottery. *Nebraska State Historical Society. Publications in Anthropology* 3. Lincoln.

_____
1979 An Archeological View of Pawnee Origins. *Nebraska History* 60(2):134–160. Lincoln.

_____
1980 Archeological Investigations in the Red Willow Reservoir, Nebraska. *Nebraska State Historical Society. Publications in Anthropology* 9. Lincoln.

Grant, Agnes
1994 James McKay: A Métis Builder of Canada. Winnipeg, Man.: Pemmican Publications.
_____, ed.
1990 Our Bit of Truth: An Anthology of Canadian Native Literature. Winnipeg, Man.: Pemmican Publications.

Grant, John Webster
1984 Moon of Wintertime: Missionaries and the Indians of Canada in Encounter Since 1534. Toronto: University of Toronto Press.

Graspointner, Andreas
1980 Archaeology and Ethno-history of the Milk River in Southern Alberta. Calgary, Alta.: Western.

Graves, William W.
1916 Life and Letters of Fathers Ponziglione, Shoenmakers and Other Early Jesuits at Osage Mission. St. Paul, Kans.: W.W. Graves.

Gravier, Jacques
[1700] Dictionary of the Illinois Language. (Manuscript in Watkinson Library, Trinity College, Hartford, Conn.; Photocopy, Manuscript No. 4871, National Anthropological Archives, Smithsonian Institution, Washington.)

Gray, John M.
1963 Lord Selkirk of Red River. Toronto: Macmillan.

Gray, John S.
1976 Centennial Campaign: The Sioux War of 1876. Fort Collins, Colo.: Old Army Press. (Reprinted: University of Oklahoma Press, Norman, 1988.)

_____
1978 Itinerant Frontier Photographers and Images Lost, Strayed or Stolen. *Montana: The Magazine of Western History* 28(2):2–15. Helena.

Gray, Judith
1989 Early Ethnographic Recordings in Today's Indian Communities. Pp. 49–55 in Songs of Indian Territory. Willie Smyth, ed. Oklahoma City, Okla.: Center for the American Indian.

Gray, Viviane
1993 Indian Artists' Statements Through Time. Pp. 137–164 in In the Shadow of the Sun: Perspectives on Contemporary Native Art. Hull, Que.: Canadian Museum of Civilization.

Grayson, G.W.
1885 [Maskoki or Creek (Vocabulary) Recorded at Eufala, Indian Terr., June–August 1885.] (Manuscript No. 568-a, National Anthropological Archives, Smithsonian Institution, Washington.)

Green, Albert L.
1930 The Otoe Indians. *Publications of the Nebraska State Historical Society* 21:175–209. Lincoln.

Green, James, Capt. E.B. Murphy, and John Gilbert
1919 Incidents of the Outbreak of 1864. *Publications of the Nebraska State Historical Society* 19:1–28. Lincoln.

Green, Jerry
1994 The Medals of Wounded Knee. *Nebraska History* 75(2):200–208. Lincoln.

Green, Norma Kidd
1967 The Presbyterian Mission to the Omaha Indian Tribe. *Nebraska History* 48(3):267–288. Lincoln.

_____
1969 Iron Eye's Family: The Children of Joseph La Flesche. Lincoln, Nebr.: Johnson Publishing Co.

Green, Thomas L., ed.
1954 Notes on a Buffalo Hunt: The Diary of Mordecai Bartram. *Nebraska History* 35(3):193–222. Lincoln.

Green, William
1997 Middle Mississippian Peoples. *The Wisconsin Archeologist* 78(1–2):202–222. Milwaukee.

Greenberg, Adolf, and James Morrison
1981 Group Identities in the Boreal Forest: The Origin of the Northern Ojibwa. *Ethnohistory* 29(2):75–102.

Greenberg, Joseph H.
1963 Some Universals of Grammar with Particular Reference to the Order of Meaningful Elements. Pp. 73–113 in Universals of Language. Joseph H. Greenberg, ed. Cambridge, Mass.: MIT Press.

_____
1987 Language in the Americans. Stanford: Stanford University Press.

Greene, Candace S.
1992 Soft Cradles of the Central Plains. *Plains Anthropologist* 37(139):95–113.

_____
1992a Artists in Blue: The Scouts of Fort Reno and Fort Supply. *American Indian Art Magazine* 18(1):50–57. Scottsdale, Ariz.

_____
1993 The Tepee with Battle Pictures. *Natural History* 102(10):68–76.

_____
1993a Saynday Was Coming Along.... Washington, D.C.: Smithsonian Institution Traveling Exhibition.

_____
1996 Exploring the Three "Little Bluffs" of the Kiowa. *Plains Anthropologist* 41(157):221–242.

_____
1998 Courting and Counting Coup: Cheyenne Ledger Art at Gilcrease. *Gilcrease Journal* 6(1):4–19. Tulsa, Okla.: Thomas Gilcrease Museum Association.

Greene, Candace S., and Thomas D. Drescher
1994 The Tipi with Battle Pictures: The Kiowa Tradition of Intangible Property Rights. *The Trademark Reporter 1159*

84(4):418–433. New York: United States Trademark Association.

Greene, D'Arcy C.
1998   A Re-evaluation of the Oxbow Dam Site (DhMn-1): Middle Holocene Cultural Continuity on the Northern Plains. (M.A. Thesis in Anthropology and Archaeology, University of Saskatchewan, Saskatoon.)

Greene, Jerome A.
1982   Slim Buttes, 1876: An Episode of the Great Sioux War. Norman: University of Oklahoma Press.

1991   Yellowstone Command: Colonel Nelson A. Miles and the Great Sioux War, 1876–1877. Lincoln: University of Nebraska Press.

1994   Lakota and Cheyenne: Indian Views of the Great Sioux War, 1876–1877. Norman: University of Oklahoma Press.

Greer, John W.
1978   Wortham Shelter: An Avonlea Site in the Bighorn Canyon, Wyoming. Archaeology in Montana 19(3):1–104. Billings, Mont. [etc.]

Gregg, John B., and Pauline S. Gregg
1987   Dry Bones: Dakota Territory Reflected. 2d ed. Grand Forks, S.Dak: University of South Dakota Press.

Gregg, John B., and Larry J. Zimmerman
1986   Malnutrition in Fourteenth Century South Dakota: Osteopathological Manifestations. North American Archaeologist 7(3):191–214.

Gregg, Josiah
1844   Commerce of the Prairies; or, The Journal of a Santa Fé Trader. 2 vols. New York: J. and H.G. Langley. (Reprinted, 2d ed. in 1845; also, in Vols. 19 and 20 of Early Western Travels, 1748–1846. Reuben G. Thwaites, ed., Arthur H. Clark, Cleveland, Ohio, 1905; and, Max L. Moorhead, ed.: University of Oklahoma Press, Norman, 1954.)

_____ 1845, 1905, 1954 see 1844 (reprint info.)

_____ [1904–1907] 1905 see Thwaites, Reuben G., ed. 1904–1907 (Vols. 19–20, 1905)

Gregg, Kate L., ed.
1937   Westward with the Dragoons; the Journal of William Clark on His Expedition to Establish Fort Osage, August 25 to September 22, 1808... Fulton, Mo.: The Ovid Bell Press.

Gregg, Michael L.
1986   An Overview of the Prehistory of Western and Central North Dakota: Class I Cultural Resources Inventory, Dickinson District, Bureau of Land Management, February 1984. Compiled by Michael L. Gregg; edited by Michael L. Gregg and Dale Davidson. U.S. Bureau of Land Management. Montana State Office. Cultural Resources Series 1. Billings, Mont.

1987   Archeological Excavation at the Naze Site (32SN246): Grand Forks. (Report Prepared for the U.S. Department of the Interior, Bureau of Reclamation, Missouri Basin Region, Department of Anthropology, University of North Dakota, Grand Forks.)

1987a   Knife River Flint in the Northeastern Plains. Plains Anthropologist 32(118):316–377.

1990   An Early Plains Woodland Structure in the Northeastern Plains. Plains Anthropologist 35(127):29–44.

1994   Archaeological Complexes of the Northeastern Plains and Prairie-Woodland Border, A.D. 500–1500. Pp. 71–95 in Plains Indians, A.D. 500–1500: The Archaeological Past of Historic Groups. Karl H. Schlesier, ed. Norman and London: University of Oklahoma Press.

Gregg, Michael L., and Paul R. Picha
1988   Synopsis of Cultural Developments in the Upper James River Valley, North Dakota (9000 B.C.–A.D. 1650). (Manuscript on file, Department of Anthropology, University of North Dakota, Grand Forks.)

Gregg, Michael L., Cynthia Kordecki, Fern Swenson, and Paul Picha
1986   Class I Cultural Resources Inventory for Nine OTH-B Radar Facility Study Areas in Eastern North Dakota, Western Minnesota, and Northeastern South Dakota. (Manuscript on file, Department of Anthropology, University of North Dakota, Grand Forks.)

Gregg, Michael L., David Meyer, Paul R. Picha, and David G. Stanley
1996   Archeology of the Northeastern Plains. Pp. 77–90 in Archeological and Bioarcheological Resources of the Northern Plains. George C. Frison and Robert C. Mainfort, eds. Arkansas Archeological Survey Research Series 47. Fayetteville.

Gregory, Hiram F.
1986   Introduction. Pp. xiii–xx in The Southern Caddo: An Anthology. Hiram F. Gregory, ed. New York: Garland Publishing.

Greiser, Sally T.
1981   Prehistoric Lifeways in the Tongue River Valley. Archaeology in Montana 22(3):27–74. Billings, [etc.].

1994   Late Prehistoric Cultures on the Montana Plains. Pp. 34–55 in Plains Indians, A.D. 500–1500: The Archaeological Past of Historic Groups. Karl H. Schlesier, ed. Norman and London: University of Oklahoma Press.

Greiser, Sally T., T. Weber Greiser, and Susan M. Vetter
1985   Middle Prehistoric Period Adaptations and Paleoenvironment in the Northwestern Plains: The Sun River Site. American Antiquity 50(4):849–877.

Greiser, Sally T., T. Weber Greiser, Susan M. Vetter, and Alan L. Stanfill
1983   Sun River (24CA74): A Stratified Pelican Lake and Oxbow Occupation Site Near Great Falls, Montana. (Report by Historical Research Associates to U.S. Army Corps of Engineers, Omaha, Nebr.)

Gresko, Jacqueline
1975   White Rites and Indian Rites: Indian Education and Native Responses in the West, 1870–1910. Pp. 163–181 in Western Canada: Past and Present. Western Canada Studies Conference, Calgary, Alta., 1974. Anthony W. Rasporich, ed. Calgary, Alta.: McClelland and Stewart West.

1986   Creating Little Dominions Within the Dominion: Early Catholic Indian Schools in Saskatchewan and British Columbia. Pp. 88–109 in Vol.1 The Legacy of Indian Education in Canada. Jean Barman, Yvonne Herbert, and Don McCaskill, eds. Nakoda Institute Occasional Paper 2. Vancouver: University of British Columbia Press.

Griffin, James B.
1937   The Archaeological Remains of the Chiwere Sioux. American Antiquity 2(3):180–181.

1942   On the Historic Location of the Tutelo and the Mohetan in the Ohio Valley. American Anthropologist 4(2):275–280.

1943   The Fort Ancient Aspect: Its Cultural and Chronological Position in Mississippi Valley Archaeology. Ann Arbor: University of Michigan Press.

1946   Cultural Change and Continuity in Eastern United States Archaeology. Pp. 37–95 in Man in Northeastern North America. Frederick Johnson, ed. Papers of the Robert S. Peabody Foundation for Archaeology 3. Andover, Mass.: Phillips Academy. (Reprinted: AMS Press, New York, 1980.)

1952   Some Early and Middle Woodland Pottery Types in Illinois. Pp. 95–129, 266–270 in Hopewellian Communities in Illinois. Thorne Deuel, ed. *Illinois State Museum Scientific Papers* 5(3). Springfield.

1960   A Hypothesis for the Prehistory of the Winnebago. Pp. 809–865 in Culture in History: Essays in Honor of Paul Radin. Stanley Diamond, ed. New York: Columbia University Press.

1965   Prehistoric Pottery from Southeastern Alberta. Pp. 209–248 in An Introduction to the Archaeology of Alberta, Canada; by H.M. Wormington and Richard G. Forbis. *Proceedings of the Denver Museum of Natural History* 11. Denver, Colo.

Griffin, James B., Richard E. Flanders, and Paul F. Titterington
1970   The Burial Complex of the Knight and Norton Mounds in Illinois and Michigan. *University of Michigan. Museum of Anthropology. Memoirs* 2. Ann Arbor, Mich.

Grim, John A.
1996   Cultural Identity, Authenticity, and Community Survival: The Politics of Recognition in The Study of Native American Religions. *The American Indian Quarterly* 20(3–4):353–376. Berkeley.

Grimm, Thaddeus C.
1985   Time-Depth Analysis of 15 Siouan Languages. *Siouan and Caddoan Linguistics Newsletter* 5(June):11–27. Boulder, Colo.

1986   A Comparison of Catawba with Biloxi, Mandan and Dakota. *International Journal of American Linguistics* 53(2):175–182. Chicago.

Grinnell, George Bird
1889   Pawnee Hero Stories and Folk-tales; With Notes on the Origin, Customs, and Character of the Pawnee People. New York: Forest and Stream Publishing Company. (See also Grinnell 1890, ed.)

_____, ed.
1890   Pawnee Hero Stories and Folk-tales; With Notes on the Origin, Customs and Character of the Pawnee People. To Which Is Added a Chapter on the Pawnee Language by John B. Dunbar. New York: Scribner. (Reprinted: C. Scribner's Sons, New York, 1893, 1909, 1912, 1920, 1925, 1929; also, University of Nebraska Press, Lincoln, 1961, 1990.)

1891   Marriage among the Pawnees. *American Anthropologist,* o.s. 4(3):275–281.

1891a   The Young Dog's Dance. *Journal of American Folk-lore* 4(15):307–313.

1891b   Account of the Northern Cheyenne Concerning the Messiah Superstition. *Journal of American Folk-lore* 4(12):61–69.

1892   Blackfoot Lodge Tales: The Story of a Prairie People. New York: Charles Scribner's Sons. (Several reprints, incl.: 1903, 1907, 1913, 1920, 1925; also, University of Nebraska Press, Lincoln, 1962; and, Corner House Publishers, Williamstown, Mass., 1972.)

1892a   Early Blackfoot History. *American Anthropologist,* o.s. 5(2):153–174.

1892b   Development of a Pawnee Myth. *Journal of American Folk-lore* 5(17):127–134.

1893   A Blackfoot Sun and Moon Myth. *Journal of American Folk-lore* 6(20):44–47.

1893a   Pawnee Mythology. *Journal of American Folk-lore* 6(21):113–130.

1894   A Pawnee Star Myth. *Journal of American Folk-lore* 7(26):197–200.

1896   Childbirth among the Blackfoot. *American Anthropologist,* o.s. 9(8):286–287.

1898   The Story of the Indian. *The Story of the West.* New York: D. Appleton and Company.

1901   The Lodges of the Blackfeet. *American Anthropologist,* n.s. 3(4):650–668.

1901a   The Punishment of the Stingy and Other Indian Stories. New York: Harper and Brothers.

1905   Social Organization of the Cheyenne. Pp. 135–146 in *Proceedings of the 13th International Congress of Americanists, Held in New York in 1902.* Easton, Pa.: Eschenbach Printing Company.

1910   Great Mysteries of the Cheyenne. *American Anthropologist,* n.s. 12(4):542–557.

1913   Some Indian Stream Names. *American Anthropologist,* n.s. 15(2):327–331.

1913a   Blackfeet Indian Stories. New York: Charles Scribner's Sons.

1914   The Cheyenne Medicine Lodge. *American Anthropologist,* n.s. 16(2):245–256.

1915   The Fighting Cheyennes. New York: Charles Scribner's Sons. (Reprinted: University of Oklahoma Press, Norman, 1956.)

1920   When Buffalo Ran. New Haven: Yale University Press.

1920a   Who Were the Padouca? *American Anthropologist,* n.s. 22(3):248–260.

1923   The Cheyenne Indians: Their History and Ways of Life. 2 vols. New Haven, Conn.:Yale University Press. (Reprinted: Cooper Square Publishers, New York, 1962; also, University of Nebraska Press, Lincoln, 1972.)

1923a   Bent's Old Fort and Its Builders. *Collections of the Kansas State Historical Society [for]1919–1922,* 15:28–91. Topeka.

1926   By Cheyenne Campfires. With Photographs by Elizabeth C. Grinnell. New Haven: Yale University Press. (Reprinted in 1962; also, University of Nebraska Press, Lincoln, 1962, 1971.)

1928   Two Great Scouts and Their Pawnee Battalion: The Experiences of Frank J. North and Luther H. North, Pioneers in the Great West, 1856–1882, and Their Defence of the Building of the Union Pacific Railroad. Cleveland, Ohio: Arthur H. Clark.

_____ 1961 *see* 1889 (reprint info.)

Griva, Edward M.
[1894–1895]   [English-Assiniboine Dictionary; Catechism and Prayers in Assiniboine Indian Language; compiled at St. Paul's Mission, Fort Belknap Reservation, Mont.] (Manuscripts in Oregon Province Archives of the Society of Jesus, Gonzaga University, Spokane, Wash.)

Grobsmith, Elizabeth S.
1974   Wakunza: Uses of Yuwipi Medicine Power in Contemporary Teton Dakota Culture. *Plains Anthropologist* 19(63):129–133.

| 1976 | Lakota Bilingualism: A Comparative Study of Language Use in Two Communities on the Rosebud Sioux Reservation. (Ph.D. Dissertation in Anthropology, University of Arizona, Tucson.) |

| 1979 | The Lakhota Giveaway: A System of Social Reciprocity. *Plains Anthropologist* 24(84, Pt. 1):123–131. |

| 1981 | Lakota of the Rosebud: A Contemporary Ethnography. New York: Holt, Rinehart, Winston. |

| 1981a | The Changing Role of the Giveaway Ceremony in Contemporary Lakota Life. *Plains Anthropologist* 26(91):75–79. |

| 1994 | Indians in Prison: Incarcerated Native Americans. Lincoln: University of Nebraska Press. |

Grobsmith, Elizabeth S., and Beth R. Ritter
| 1992 | The Ponca Tribe of Nebraska: The Process of Restoration of a Federally-Terminated Tribe. *Human Organization* 51(1):1–16. |

| 1994 | Northern Ponca. Pp. 459–460 in Native America in the Twentieth Century: An Encyclopedia. Mary B. Davis, ed. *Garland Reference Library of Social Science* 452. New York: Garland. |

Gross, Emma R.
| 1989 | Contemporary Federal Policy Toward American Indians. *Contributions in Ethnic Studies* 25. New York: Greenwood Press. |

Grosscup, Jeffrey P.
| 1975 | William Illingworth: Stereoscopic Eye on the Frontier West. *Montana: The Magazine of Western History* 25(2):36–50. Helena. |

Grosser, Roger D.
| 1970 | The Snyder Site: An Archaic-Woodland Occupation in South-central Kansas. (M.A. Thesis in Anthropology, University of Kansas, Lawrence.) |

| 1973 | A Tentative Cultural Sequence for the Snyder Site, Kansas. *Plains Anthropologist* 18(61):228–238. |

| 1977 | Late Archaic Subsistence Patterns from the Central Great Plains: A Systemic Model. (Ph.D. Dissertation in Anthropology, University of Kansas, Lawrence). |

Gruhn, Ruth
| 1971 | Preliminary Report on the Mulbach Site: A Besant Bison Trap in Central Alberta. *National Museums of Canada Bulletin* 232. Contributions to Anthropology 8. Archaeology Paper 5(4):128–156. Ottawa. |

Gryba, Eugene Michael
| 1975 | The Stampede Site, DjOn-26, Cypress Hills Provincial Park, June, 1975. (Manuscript on file at the Provincial Museum of Alberta, Edmonton, Alta.) |

| 1976 | The Early Side-Notched Component at Site DjOn-26. Pp. 92–107 in Archaeology in Alberta 1975. J. Michael Quigg and W.J. Byrne, eds. *Archaeological Survey of Alberta. Occasional Paper* 1. Edmonton. |

| 1983 | Sibbald Creek: 11,000 Years of Human Utilization of the Southern Alberta Foothills. Appendix II: The Faunal Remains from the Sibbald Creek Site by Donald A. Barnett. *Archaeological Survey of Alberta. Occasional Paper* 22. Edmonton. |

| 1985 | Evidence of the Fluted Point Tradition in Alberta. Pp. 22–38 in Contributions to Plains Prehistory. David Burley, ed. *Archaeological Survey of Alberta. Occasional Paper* 26. Edmonton. |

Guidry, Marion A., et al.
| 1979 | An Environmental Profile of the Palo Duro Creek Basin. Kilgore Research Institute, West Texas State University. (Report, Contract No. DAC-W56-78-C-0203 submitted to the U.S. Army Corps of Engineers; Technical Library, Tulsa, Okla.) |

Gulick, Charles Adams, et al., eds. 1921–1927 *see* Lamar, Mirabeau Buonaparte 1921–1927

Gunn, Donald
| 1868 | Indian Remains Near Red River Settlement, Hudson's Bay Territory. Pp. 399–400 in *Smithsonian Institution Annual Report for 1867*. Washington: U.S. Government Printing Office. |

Gunnerson, Dolores A.
| [1949–1956] | [Fieldnotes and Reports on the Stanton Site, Near Stanton, Nebraska.] (Manuscripts in D.R. Henning's possession.) |

| 1956 | The Southern Athabascans: Their Arrival in the Southwest. *El Palacio* 63(11–12):346–365. Santa Fe. |

| 1974 | The Jicarilla Apaches: A Study in Survival. De Kalb, Ill.: Northern Illinois University Press. |

Gunnerson, James H.
| 1952 | Some Nebraska Culture Pottery Types. *Plains Archeological Conference News Letter* 5(3):34–44. Lincoln. |

| 1956 | Plains-Promontory Relationships. *American Antiquity* 22(1):69–72. |

| 1959 | Archaeological Survey in Northeastern New Mexico. *El Palacio* 66(5):145–154. Santa Fe. |

| 1960 | An Introduction to Plains Apache Archeology: The Dismal River Aspect. *Bureau of American Ethnology Bulletin* 173; *Anthropological Papers* 58. Washington: Smithsonian Institution; U.S. Government Printing Office. (Reprinted: J&L Reprint Company, Lincoln, 1978.) |

| 1968 | Plains Apache Archeology: A Review. *Plains Anthropologist* 13(41):167–189. |

| 1969 | Apache Archaeology in Northeastern New Mexico. *American Antiquity* 34(1):23–39. |

| 1969a | A Human Skeleton from an Apache Baking Pit. *Plains Anthropologist* 14(43):46–56. |

| | 1979 *see* Handbook Vol. 9 (1979:162–169) |

| 1984 | Documentary Clues and Northeastern New Mexico Archeology. Pp. 45–76 in Papers of the Philmont Conference on the Archeology of Northeastern New Mexico. Carol J. Condie, ed. *Proceedings of the New Mexico Archeological Council* 6(1). Albuquerque. |

| 1987 | Archaeology of the High Plains. *U.S. Bureau of Land Management. Colorado State Office. Cultural Resources Series* 19. Denver. |

| 1987a | Dismal River Gray Ware and Sangre de Cristo Micaceous Ware. (Manuscript on file at the University of Nebraska State Museum, Lincoln.) |

| 1988 | Archeological Investigations at the Cramer and Nearby Sites Along the Lower Apishapa Canyon. (Manuscript on file at the University of Nebraska State Museum, Lincoln.) |

| 1989 | Apishapa Canyon Archeology: Excavations at the Cramer, Snake Blakeslee and Nearby Sites. *Reprints in Anthropology* 41. Lincoln: J&L Reprint Company. |

Gunnerson, James H., and Dolores A. Gunnerson
1970   Evidence of Apaches at Pecos. *El Palacio* 76(3):1–6. Santa Fe.

1971   Apachean Culture: A Study in Unity and Diversity. Pp. 7–27 in Apachean Culture History and Ethnology. Keith H. Basso and Morris E. Opler, eds. *Anthropological Papers of the University of Arizona* 21. Tucson.

1988   Ethnohistory of the High Plains. *United States. Bureau of Land Management. Colorado State Office. Cultural Resources Series* 26. Denver.

Gunther, Richard L.
1970   The Santee Normal Training School. *Nebraska History* 51(3):359–378. Lincoln.

Gussow, Zachary, LeRoy R. Hafen, and Arthur A. Ekirch, Jr.
1974   Arapaho-Cheyenne Indians. *American Indian Ethnohistory: Plains Indians.* David Agee Horr, comp. and ed. New York and London: Garland Publishing.

Gustavson, Thomas C., et al.
1991   Quaternary Geology of the Southern Great Plains and an Adjacent Segment of the Rolling Plains. Pp. 477–501 in Quaternary Nonglacial Geology: Conterminous U.S. Roger B. Morrison, ed. *Geology of North America* K-2. Boulder, Colo.: Geological Society of America.

Guthe, Carl E.
1967   Reflections on the Founding of the Society for American Archaeology. *American Antiquity* 32(4):433–440.

Guthrie, Mark R., Thomas Pozorski, Sheila Pozorski, and Tommy Fulgham
1984   Pinyon Canyon Archeological Project: First Season. Pp. 313–346 in Papers of the Philmont Conference on the Archeology of Northeastern New Mexico. Carol J. Condie, ed. *Proceedings of the New Mexico Archeological Council* 6(1). Albuquerque.

Haas, Daniel R.
1982   Walker Gilmore: A Stratified Woodland Period Occupation in Eastern Nebraska. *University of Nebraska. Department of Anthropology. Division of Archeological Research. Technical Reports* 80–22. Lincoln.

Haas, Mary R.
1942   Comments on the Name "Wichita". *American Anthropologist,* n.s. 44(1):164–165.

1951   The Proto-Gulf Word for *Water* (With Notes on Siouan-Yuchi). *International Journal of American Linguistics* 17(2):71–79. Chicago.

1952   The Proto-Gulf Word for *Land* (With a Note on Proto-Siouan). *International Journal of American Linguistics* 18(4):238–240. Chicago.

1958   A New Linguistic Relationship in North America: Algonkian and the Gulf Languages. *Southwestern Journal of Anthropology* 14(3):231–264. Albuquerque.

1963   The Muskogean and Algonkian Words for *Skunk. International Journal of American Linguistics* 29(1):65–66. Chicago.

1964   Athapaskean, Tlingit, Yuchi, and Siouan. Pp. 495–500 in 35th Congreso international de Americanistas, México, 1962. Actas y Memorias 2. 3 vols. México: Editorial Libros de México.

1967   On the Relations of Tonkawa. Pp. 310320 in Studies in Southwestern Ethnolinguistics. Dell Hymes and William E. Bittle, eds. *Studies in General Anthropology* 3. The Hague: Mouton.

1968   The Last Words of Biloxi. *International Journal of American Linguistics* 34(2):77–84. Chicago.

1978   Language, Culture and History: Essays by Mary R. Haas. Anwar S. Dil, ed. Stanford, Calif.: Stanford University Press.

Haas, Theodore H.
1947   Ten Years of Tribal Government Under I.R.A.. Chicago: United States Indian Service.

Haberland, Wolfgang
1973   Die Oglala-Sammlung Weygold im Hamburgischen Museum für Völkerkunde (Teil 1). *Mitteilungen aus dem Museum für Völkerkunde Hamburg,* n.f. 3:79–106. Hamburg, Germany.

1981   Die Oglala-Sammlung Weygold im Hamburgischen Museum für Völkerkunde (Teil 7). *Mitteilungen aus dem Museum für Völkerkunde Hamburg,* n.f. 11:29–56. Hamburg, Germany.

Habicht-Mauche, Judith A.
1987   Southwestern-Style Culinary Ceramics on the Southern Plains: A Case Study of Technological Innovation and Cross-Cultural Interaction. *Plains Anthropologist* 32(116):175–189.

1992   Coronado's Querechos and Teyas in the Archaeological Record of the Texas Panhandle. *Plains Anthropologist* 37(140):247–259.

Hackett, Charles W., ed.
1923–1937 Historical Documents Relating to New Mexico, Nueva Vizcaya and Approaches Thereto, to 1773. Adolf F.A. Bandelier and Fanny R. Bandelier, colls. 3 vols. *Carnegie Institution of Washington Publication* 300. Washington.
_____, ed.
1931–1946 Pichardo's Treatise on the Limits of Louisiana and Texas. 4 vols. Austin: University of Texas Press. (Reprinted: Books for Libraries Press, New York, 1971.)

Hackett, F.J. Paul
1991   The 1819–20 Measles Epidemic: Its Origin, Diffusion and Mortality Effects upon the Indians of the Petit Nord. (M.A. Thesis, Department of Geography, University of Manitoba, Winnipeg, Man.)

Haddon, Alfred C.
1895   Evolution in Art: As Illustrated by the Life-Histories of Designs. London: Walter Scott, Ltd.

Hadley, Lewis F.
1882   [A Quapaw Vocabulary; and, the Quapaw and Ponca Compared. Also, the Mystery of the Ponca Removal and the Troubles Quapaws Were Subjected to on Account of the Mystery Underlying the Removal of the Poncas, by Ingonompishi, Late Clerk of the Quapaw Nation.] (Manuscript No. 918, National Anthropological Archives, Smithsonian Institution, Washington.)

1893   Indian Sign Talk: Being a Book of Proofs of the Matter Printed on Equivalent Cards Designed for Teaching Sign Language, by In-go-nom-pa-shi (pseud.). Chicago: Baker and Company.

Hafen, LeRoy R., ed.
1965–1972 The Mountain Men and the Fur Trade of the Far West: Biographical Sketches of the Participants by Scholars of the Subject and with Introductions by the Editor. 10 vols. Glendale, Calif.: Arthur H. Clark.

Hafen, LeRoy R., and Francis Marion Young
1938   Fort Laramie and the Pageant of the West, 1834–1890. Glendale, Calif.: The Arthur H. Clark Company. (Reprinted: University of Nebraska Press, Lincoln, 1984.)   *1163*

BIBLIOGRAPHY

Hagan, William T.
1961   American Indians. *Chicago History of American Civilization.* Chicago: University of Chicago Press. (Reprinted in 1979, 1993.)

1966   Indian Police and Judges: Experiments in Acculturation and Control. *Yale Western Americana Series* 13. New Haven, Conn.: Yale University Press.

1971   Kiowas, Comanches, and Cattlemen, 1867–1906: A Case Study of the Failure of U.S. Reservation Policy. *Pacific Historical Review* 40(3):333–355. Berkeley, Calif.

1976   United States-Comanche Relations: The Reservation Years. New Haven, Conn.: Yale University Press.

1985   Adjusting to the Opening of the Kiowa, Comanche, and Kiowa-Apache Reservation. Pp. 11–30 in The Plains Indians of the Twentieth Century. Edited and with an Introduction by Peter Iverson. Norman: University of Oklahoma Press. (Reprinted from: United States-Comanche Relations: The Reservation Years, pp. 262–285, 1976.)

1993   Quanah Parker, Comanche Chief. Norman: University of Oklahoma Press.

Hahn, Frida
1935   [Grammar of Ponca.] (Manuscript 30(X4a.2), Gordon Marsh Collection, in the Library of the American Philosophical Society, Philadelphia.)

Hail, Barbara A.
1980   Hau, Kòla! The Plains Indian Collection of the Haffenreffer Museum of Anthropology. *Studies in Anthropology and Material Culture* 3. Providence, R.I.: Brown University, Haffenreffer Museum of Anthropology. (Reprinted in 1983 and 1993, with revisions.)

Haines, Francis
1938   Where Did the Plains Indians Get Their Horses? *American Anthropologist,* n.s. 40(3):112–117.

1938a   The Northward Spread of Horses among the Plains Indians. *American Anthropologist,* n.s. 40(3):429–437.

1976   The Plains Indians: Their Origins, Migrations, and Cultural Development. New York: Thomas Y. Crowell.

Hairy Shirt, LeRoy, et al.
1973   Lakota Woonspe Wowapi. Aberdeen, S.Dak.: North Plains Press.

Hale, Horatio E.
1846   Ethnography and Philology. Vol. 6 of United States Exploring Expedition; During the Years 1838, 1839, 1840, 1841, 1842, Under the Command of Charles Wilkes, U.S.N. Philadelphia: C. Sherman. (Reprinted: Gregg Press, Ridgewood, N.J., 1968.)

1883   Indian Migrations, as Evidenced by Language: Comprising the Huron-Cherokee Stock, the Dakota Stock, the Algonkins, the Chahta-Muskoki Stock, the Moundbuilders, and the Iberians. *American Antiquarian* 5(1):18–28.

1883a   The Tutelo Tribe and Language. *Proceedings of the American Philosophical Society* 21(114):1–47. Philadelphia.

1885   Report on the Blackfoot Tribes. Pp. 696–708 in Report of the Committee ... Appointed for the Purpose of Investigating and Publishing Reports on the Physical Characters, Language, Industrial and Social Condition of the Northwestern Tribes of the Dominion of Canada. *Proceedings of the 55th Report of the British Association for the Advancement of Science for 1884.* London.

1886   Ethnology of the Blackfoot Tribes. *The Popular Science Monthly* 29(June):204–212. New York.

1890   Remarks on Ethnology of British Columbia: Introductory to the 2nd General Report of Franz Boas on the Indians of That Province. Pp. 173–200 in *Proceedings of the 57th Report of the British Association for the Advancement of Science for 1889.* London. (Reprinted in *Northwest Anthropological Research Notes* 8(1/2), Moscow, Idaho, 1974.)

Hale, Kenneth L.
1962   Jemez and Kiowa Correspondences in Reference to Kiowa-Tanoan. *International Journal of American Linguistics* 28(1):1–5. Chicago.

1967   Toward a Reconstruction of Kiowa-Tanoan Phonology. *International Journal of American Linguistics* 33(2):112–120. Chicago.

Hale, Kenneth L., and David Harris 1979 *see* Handbook Vol. 9 (1979)

Hales, Peter B.
1988   William Henry Jackson and the Transformation of the American Landscape. Philadelphia: Temple University Press.

Haley, J. Evetts
1935   The Comanchero Trade. *Southwestern Historical Quarterly* 38(3):157–176. Austin, Tex.

Hall, Charles L.
[1876– [Arikaree or Ree Phrases.] (Manuscript in Charles L. Hall
1890]   Collection, North Dakota State Archives and Historical Society Research Library, Bismarck.)

[1878– [Hidatsa Phrases.] (Manuscript in Charles L. Hall
1908]   Collecton, North Dakota State Historical Society Archives and Research Library, Bismarck.)

[1878– [Mandan Phrases.] (Manuscript in Charles L. Hall Collec-
1908a] tion, North Dakota State Historical Society Archives and Research Library, Bismarck.)

1891   Ree Cosmology. *The Word Carrier* 20(9):32. Santee, Nebr.: Santee Indian Training School.

1895   A Few Scripture Selections and Hymns in the Gros Ventre or Hidatsa Language. Elbowoods, N.Dak.: Fort Berthold Mission; also, Santee, Nebr.: Santee Normal Training School Press.

1900   A Few Bible Translations and Hymns in the Ree or Sani Language. Santee, Nebr.: Published by Santee Normal Training School Press for the Fort Berthold Mission, Fort Berthold, N.Dak. (Cover title reads: Nosuhihatauwhi cesu - May You Too Have Light.)

1905   Hymns and Scripture Selections in the Mandan Language. Elbowoods, N.Dak.: Fort Berthold Mission; also, Santee, Nebr.: Santee Normal Training School Press.

1906   A Few Scripture Selections and Hymns; in the Hidatsa or Gros Ventre Language. 2d ed. Elbowoods, N.Dak.: Published for the Fort Berthold Mission [by Santee Normal Training School Press, Santee, Nebr.].

1906a   Autobiography of Poor Wolf, Head Soldier of the Hidatsa or Grosventre Tribe (Eight-six years old in 1906). *Collections of the State Historical Society of North Dakota* 1:439–443. Bismarck.

Hall, D.J.
1977   Clifford Sifton and Canadian Indian Administration, 1896–1905. *Prairie Forum* 2(2):127–151. Regina, Sask.: Canadian Plains Research Center, University of Regina.

Hall, Edward T.
1944   Recent Clues to Athapascan Prehistory in the Southwest. *American Anthropologist,* n.s. 46(1):98–105.

Hall, Grant D.
1998   Prehistoric Human Food Resource Patches on the Texas Coastal Plain. *Bulletin of the Texas Archaeological Society* 69:1–10. Austin.

Hall, Mark A.
1978   Contemporary Stories of "Taku He" or "Bigfoot" in South Dakota as Drawn from Newspaper Accounts. *The Minnesota Archaeologist* 37(2):63–78. Minneapolis, Minn.

Hall, Robert L.
1961   An Archaeological Investigation in the Gavin's Point Area, Yankton County, South Dakota. *University of South Dakota. W.H. Over Museum. Museum News* 22(7):1–3. Vermillion, S.Dak.

1962   The Archeology of Carcajou Point; with an Interpretation of the Development of Oneota Culture in Wisconsin. 2 vols. Madison: University of Wisconsin Press.

1997   An Archaeology of the Soul: North American Indian Belief and Ritual. Urbana: University of Illinois Press.

Hall, Stephen A.
1988   Environment and Archaeology of the Central Osage Plains. *Plains Anthropologist* 33(120):203–218.

Hallenbeck, Cleve
1940   Alvar Nuñez Cabeza de Vaca, The Journey and Route of the First European to Cross the Continent of North America, 1534–1536. Glendale, Calif.

1950   Land of the Conquistadores. Caldwell, Idaho: The Caxton Printers.

Hallowell, A. Irving
1930   Was Cross-Cousin Marriage Practiced by the North-Central Algonkian? Pp. 519–544 in *Proceedings of the 23d International Congress of Americanists, Held at New York, September 17–22, 1928*. New York.

Hallowell, Benjamin, et. al.
1973   Quaker Report on Indian Agencies in Nebraska. *Nebraska History* 54(2):150–220. Lincoln.

Halvorson, Mark J.
1997   Historical Tracings: "Sacred Beauty: Quillwork of Plains Women." *Nebraska History* 64(3):30–32. Lincoln.

Hamblin, Nancy L.
1989   Analysis of the Cramer Site Fauna. Appendix IA in: Apishapa Canyon Archeology: Excavations at the Cramer, Snake Blakeslee and Nearby Sites, by James H. Gunnerson. *Reprints in Anthropology* 41. Lincoln, Nebr.

Hambridge, Gove, ed.
1941   Climate and Man. *Yearbook of Agriculture*. Washington: U.S. Department of Agriculture.

Hamilton, Candy
1995   Elder Recognized at Annual Powwow. *News from Indian Country* 9(18):21.

Hamilton, Henry W., and Jean Tyree Hamilton
1971   The Sioux of the Rosebud: A History in Pictures. Photographs by John A. Anderson; Text by Henry Ward Hamilton and Jean Tyree Hamilton. Norman: University of Oklahoma Press.

Hamilton, William
1843   Original Hymns in the Ioway Language, by the Missionaries to the Ioway and Sac Indians, Under the Direction of the Board of Foreign Missions of the Presbyterian Church. Includes Wv-ro-hae (Prayers), and We-vw-hae-kju (Catechism). Indian Territory: Ioway and Sac Mission Press.

1843a   An Elementary Book of the Ioway Language, With an

English Translation. Indian Territory: Ioway and Sac Mission Press.

1846–1847   Ce-sxs wo-ra-kae-pe ae-ta-wae, Mat-fu ae-wv-kv-hae-na-ha, a-rae kae (6 Chapters of the Gospel of St. Matthew.) Indian Territory: Ioway and Sac Mission Press.

1854   Remarks on the Iowa Language. Pp. 397–406 in Historical and Statistical Information Respecting the History, Condition and Prospects of the Indian Tribes of the United States, 1851–1857. 4 vols. Henry Rowe Schoolcraft, comp and ed. Philadelphia: Lippincott, Grambo.

1856   Account of Otoe Tribe. *Publications of the Nebraska State Historical Society* 1. Lincoln.

1868   Translations into the Omaha Language, with Portions of Scripture; also, A Few Hymns. New York: Edward O. Jenkins.

1885   Autobiography of Rev. William Hamilton. *Transactions and Reports of the Nebraska State Historical Society* 1:60–75. Lincoln.

1885a   Indian Names and Their Meaning. *Transactions and Reports of the Nebraska State Historical Society* 1:73–75. Lincoln.

1887   Hymns in the Omaha Language. Prepared by Rev. William Hamilton. New York: American Tract Society.

Hamilton, William, and Samuel McCleary Irvin
1843   Wv-wv-kv-hae e-ya e-tu u-na-ha Pa-hu cae e-cae ae-ta-wae, mv-he-hvn-yae e-cae ra prae-tae-kae. Indian Territory: Ioway and Sac Mission Press.

1843a   Ya-wae pa-hu-cae e-cae ae-ta-wae e-tu-hce wa-u-na-ha. Pa-hu-cae fa-kae-ku wv-kun-fae ae-tawae ae-wv-u-nye-kae. [Iowa Song Book.] Indian Territory: Iowa and Sac Mission Press.

1848   An Ioway Grammar, Illustrating the Principles of the Language Used by the Ioway, Otoe, and Missouri Indians. [Wolf Creek, Nebr.]: Ioway and Sac Mission Press.

1849   The Ioway Primmer [sic]; Composed of the Most Comon Words, and Arranged in Alphabetic Order. Indian Territory: Ioway and Sac Mission Press. (2d ed. publ. in 1850.)

1850   We-wv-hæ-kju. [Some Questions.] Wolf Creek, Nebr.: Ioway and Sac Mission Press (With their: Original Hymns in the Ioway Language. Indian Terr., Ioway and Sac Mission Press, 1843.)

1850a   Ce-sxs wo-ra-kæ-pe æ-ta wæ, Mat- fu æ-wv-kv-hæ-na-ha, a-ræ-kæ. Six Chapters of the Gospel of St. Matthew in the Iowa Language. Indian Territory: Ioway and Sac Mission Press.

Hammatt, Hallett H.
1976   The Gore Pit Site: An Archaic Occupation in Southwestern Oklahoma and a Review of the Archaic Stage in the Southern Plains. *Plains Anthropologist* 21(74):245–277.

Hammerschlag, Carl A.
1988   The Dancing Healers: A Doctor's Journey of Healing with Native Americans. San Francisco: Harper & Row. (Reprinted in 1989.)

Hammond, George P.
1927   Don Juan de Oñate and the Founding of New Mexico; A New Investigation into the early history of New Mexico in the Light of a Mass of new Materials recently obtained from the Archivo General de Indias, Seville, Spain. Santa Fe, N. Mex.: El Palacio Press. *Historical Society of New Mexico. 1165*

Publications in History II. (Originally published as author's Ph.D. Dissertation, University of California.)

Hammond, George P., and Agapito Rey
1927 The Rodriguez Expedition to New Mexico, 1581–1582. *New Mexico Historical Review* 2:239–268. Albuquerque.

_____
1927a The Gallegos Relation of the Rodríguez Expedition to New Mexico, 1581–1582. *Historical Society of New Mexico. Publications in History* 4. Santa Fe.

_____
1929 Expedition into New Mexico Made by Antonio de Espejo, 1582–1583, as Revealed in the Journal of Diego Pérez de Luxán, a Member of the Party. *The Quivia Society* 1. Los Angeles.

_____, eds. and trans.
1940 Narratives of the Coronado Expedition, 1540–1542. *Coronado Cuarto Centennial Publications* 2. Albuquerque: University of New Mexico Press. (Reprinted: AMS Press, New York, 1977.)

_____, eds. and trans.
1953 Don Juan de Oñate, Colonizer of New Mexico, 1595–1628. 2 vols. *Coranado Cuarto Centennial Publications 1540–1940, Vols. 5–6.* Albuquerque: University of New Mexico Press.

Hammond, Harmony, Lucy Lippard, Jaune Quick-to-See Smith, and Erin Younger
1985 Women of Sweetgrass, Cedar and Sage. New York: Gallery of the American Indian Community House.

Hamp, Eric P.
1958 Prosodic Notes: 1. On Comanche Voiceless Vowels. 2. Tone in Crow. 3. Length in Kutenai. *International Journal of American Linguistics* 24(4):321–322. Chicago.

Hanks, Lucien M., Jr., and Jane Richardson Hanks
1939–1942 [Papers.] (Manuscripts in Glenbow Archives, Calgary, Alta.)

_____
1945 Observations on Northern Blackfoot Kinship. *Monographs of the American Ethnological Society* 9. Seattle: University of Washington Press.

_____
1950 Tribe Under Trust: A Study of the Blackfoot Reserve of Alberta. Photographs by F. Gully. Toronto: University of Toronto Press.

Hanna, Warren Leonard
1986 The Life and Times of James Willar Schultz (Apikuni). (Based in part on a manuscript by Harry C. James.) Norman: University of Oklahoma Press.

_____, comp. and ed.
1988 Recently Discovered Tales of Life among the Indians [by] James Willard Schultz. Preface by John R. Mauff. Missoula, Mont.: Mountain Press Publishing Company.

Hannus, L. Adrien
1994 Cultures of the Heartland: Beyond the Black Hills. Pp. 176–198 in Plains Indians, A.D. 500–1500: The Archaeological Past of Historic Groups. Karl H. Schlesier, ed. Norman: University of Oklahoma Press.

Hannus, L. Adrien, and Timothy R. Nowak
1988 Avonlea: A Point Industry Surfaces in South Dakota or Archers on the March. Pp. 183–189 in Avonlea Yesterday and Today: Archaeology and Prehistory. Leslie B. Davis, ed. Saskatoon, Sask.: Saskatchewan Archaeological Society.

Hans, Frederic Malon
1907 The Great Sioux Nation: A Complete History of Indian Life and Warfare in America. Chicago: M.A. Donohue & Company.

Hanson, Charles E., Jr.
1955 The Northwest Gun. *Nebraska State Historical Society. Publications in Anthropology* 2. Lincoln.

Hanson, James A.
1965 The Oglala Sioux Sun Dance. *Museum of the Fur Trade Quarterly* 1(3):3–5. Chadron, Nebr.

_____
1975 Metal Weapons, Tools and Ornaments of the Teton Dakota Indians. Lincoln: University of Nebraska Press.

_____
1996 Little Chief's Gatherings: The Smithsonian Institution's G.K. Warren 1855–1856 Plains Indian Collection and The New York State Library's 1855–1857 Warren Expeditions Journals. Crawford, Nebr.: The Fur Press.

Hanson, Jeffrey R.
1979 Ethnohistoric Problems in the Crow-Hidatsa Separation. Pp. 73–85 in Symposium on the Crow-Hidatsa Separations. Leslie B. Davis, ed. *Archaeology in Montana* 20(3). Billings, [etc.].

_____
1983 Hidatsa Culture Change, 1780–1845: A Cultural Ecological Approach. Lincoln: National Park Service, Midwest Archaeological Center. *Reprints in Anthropology* 34. Lincoln: J&L Reprint Company.

_____
1986 Kinship, Marriage, and Residence Patterns in Hidatsa Village Composition. Pp. 43–63 in The Origins of the Hidatsa Indians: A Review of Ethnohistorical and Traditional Data, by W. Raymond Wood. *Reprints in Anthropology* 32. Lincoln: J&L Reprint Company.

_____
1998 The Late High Plains Hunters. Pp. 456–480 in Archaeology on the Great Plains. W. Raymond Wood, ed. Lawrence, Kans.: University Press of Kansas.

Harbeck, Warren A.
1969 [A Study in Mutual Intelligibility and Linguistic Separation among Five Siouan Languages.] (Manuscript No.10(74) in the Library of the American Philosophical Society, Philadelphia.)

_____
1973 The Stoney Cultural Education Program. (Paper presented at the Northern Cross-cultural Education Symposium: Needs and Resources. University of Alaska, Fairbanks, November 8, 1973.)

Harbeck, Warren A., Gerald Kaquitts, and Tom Snow
1980 Stoney Country 1970–1980: When the New and the Old Sang Together. Morley, Alta.: The Stoney Tribe, Department of Communication.

Hardisty, R.G.
1946 The Last Sun Dance. *Alberta Folklore Quarterly* 2:57–61. Edmonton.

Hardorff, Richard G., comp. and ed.
1997 Lakota Recollections of the Custer Fight: New Sources of Indian-Military History. Lincoln: University of Nebraska Press.

_____, comp. and ed.
1998 Cheyenne Memories of the Custer Fight: A Source Book. New Introduction by Robert Wooster. Lincoln: University of Nebraska Press.

Harkins, Arthur M.
1969 Public Education of the Prairie Island Sioux: An Interim Report. *National Study of American Indian Education Series* 1, *Vol.* 10. Chicago: University of Chicago Press.

Harkins, Arthur M., Mary L. Zemyan, and Richards G. Woods
1970 Indian Americans in Omaha and Lincoln. Minneapolis: University of Minnesota, Training Center for Community Programs.

Harlan, Theresa
1994 Watchful Eyes: Native American Women Artists. Phoenix: Heard Museum.

Harmon, Daniel Williams
1820   A Journal of Voyages and Travels in the Interiour of North
            America; between the 47th and 58th degrees of North
            Latitude, Extending from Montreal Nearly to the Pacific
            Ocean ..., Including an Account of the Principal Occur-
            rences, during a Residence of Nineteenth Years, in Differ-
            ent Parts of the Country. To Which Are Added, a Concise
            Description of the Face of the Country, Its Inhabitants ...
            and Considerable Specimens of the Two Languages, Most
            Extensively Spoken ...Illustrated by a Map of the Country.
            Andover, Mass.: Flagg and Gould. (Reprinted: Allerton
            Book Company, New York, 1911; also under title: Sixteeen
            Years in the Indian Country: The Journal of Daniel Will-
            iams Harmon, 1800–1816; edited with an Introduction by
            W. Kaye Lamb, Macmillan of Canada, Toronto, 1957.)

1911   A Journal of Voyages and Travels in the Interior of North
            America [1820]. New York: Allerton Book Company.

1957   Sixteen Years in the Indian Country: The Journal of Daniel
            William Harmon, 1800–1816. W. Kaye Lamb, ed. Toronto:
            Macmillan of Canada. (Originally publ. under title: A
            Journal of Voyages and Travels, [etc.]; Flagg and Gould,
            Andover, Mass., 1820.)

Harnish, H. Michael
1980   The Sand Creek Massacre: Toward a Settlement. (M.A.
            Thesis in History, Wichita State University, Wichita, Kans.)

Harper, Elizabeth Ann
1953   The Taovayas Indians in Frontier Trade and Diplomacy,
            1779–1835. Panhandle-Plains Historical Review 23:1–32.

1953a   The Taovayas Indians in Frontier Trade and Diplomacy,
            1719–1768. Chronicles of Oklahoma 31(3):268–289.
            Norman.

1953b   The Taovayas Indians in Frontier Trade and Diplomacy,
            1769–1779. Southwestern Historical Quarterly 57(2):181–
            201. Austin, Tex.

Harper, J. Russell, ed.
1971   Paul Kane's Frontier. Including Wanderings of an Artist
            among the Indians of North America. Edited with a Bio-
            graphical Introduction and a Catalogue Raisonné, by J.
            Russell Harper. Austin: The University of Texas Press for
            the Amon Carter Museum, Fort Worth, and the National
            Gallery of Canada, Ottawa.

Harper, J. Russell, and Stanley Triggs, eds.
1967   Portrait of a Period: A Collection of [William] Notman
            Photographs 1856 to 1915. Introduction by Edgar Andrew
            Collard. Montreal: McGill University Press.

Harpole, Patricia C., and Mary D. Nagle, eds.
1972   Minnesota Territorial Census, 1850. St. Paul: Minnesota
            Historical Society.

Harrell, Lynn L., and Scott T. McKern
1986   The Maxon Ranch Site: Archaic and Late Prehistoric Habi-
            tation in Southwest Wyoming. Archaeological Services,
            Western Wyoming College. Cultural Resource Manage-
            ment Report 18. Rock Springs, Wyo.

Harring, Sidney L.
1994   Crow Dog's Case: American Indian Sovereignty, Tribal
            Law, and United States Law in the Nineteenth Century.
            Cambridge Studies in North American Indian History.
            Frederick Hoxie and Neal Salisbury, eds. Cambridge and
            New York: Cambridge University Press.

Harrington, John Peabody
[1900]   [Pawnee Word List.] (Manuscript in John Peabody
            Harrington Papers, National Anthropological Archives,
            Smithsonian Institution, Washington.)

1910   On Phonetic and Lexic Resemblances between Kiowan and

Tanoan. American Anthropologist, n.s. 12(1):119–123. (Is-
            sued also in Papers of the School of American Archaeology
            12. Santa Fe, N.Mex., 1910.)

1928   Vocabulary of the Kiowa Language. Bureau of American
            Ethnology Bulletin 84. Washington: Smithsonian Institu-
            tion; U.S. Government Printing Office.

1936–1941   [Informants, Addresses, etc. in Navajo Fieldnotes.] (Manu-
            script in John Peabody Harrington Papers, National Anthro-
            pological Archives, Smithsonian Institution, Washington.)

1939–1945   [Apache and Kiowa Apache.] (Manuscripts in John
            Peabody Harrington Papers, National Anthropological Ar-
            chives, Smithsonian Institution, Washington.)

1940   Otoe Vocabulary [from Mr. and Mrs. M. Springer]. (Manu-
            script No. 6031, National Anthropological Archives,
            Smithsonian Institution, Washington.)

1940a   Southern Peripheral Athapaskawan Origins, Divisions, and
            Migrations. Pp. 503–532 in Essays in Historical Anthropol-
            ogy of North America. Smithsonian Miscellaneous Collec-
            tions 100. Washington: Smithsonian Institution; Government
            Printing Office.

Harrington, Marc R.
1913   A Visit to the Otoe Indians. University of Pennsylvania.
            Museum Journal 4(3):107–113. Philadelphia.

1920   A Sacred Warclub of the Oto. Indian Notes and Mono-
            graphs 10(2):25–27. New York: Museum of the American
            Indian. Heye Foundation.

Harris, C.A. 1837 see ARCIA 1824–1848

Harris, John
1705   Navigantium atque itinerantium bibliotheca; or, a
            Compleat Collection of Voyages and Travels. 2 vols. Lon-
            don: T. Bennet [etc.].

Harris, LaDonna Crawford
1956   Tabbytite. Chronicles of Comanche County 2(2):78–84.
            Lawton, Okla.

Harris, R. Cole, and Geoffrey J. Matthews
1987   Historical Atlas of Canada. Vol. 1: From the Beginning to
            1800. Toronto: University of Toronto Press.

Harris, R.K.
1945   Bone Implement Burial, Collin County, Texas. Bulletin of
            the Texas Archeological and Paleontological Society
            16:84–89. Abilene.

1959   C-14 Data on Henrietta Focus in Texas. Oklahoma Anthro-
            pological Society Newsletter 8(3):2. Norman.

Harris, R.K., Inus Marie Harris, Jay C. Blaine, and Jerrylee Blaine
1965   A Preliminary Archeological and Documentary Study of the
            Womack Site, Lamar County, Texas. Bulletin of the Texas
            Archaeological Society 36:287–364. Dallas.

Harris, Moira F.
1989   Between Two Cultures: Kiowa Art from Fort Marion. St.
            Paul, Minn.: Pogo Press.

Harris, Zellig, and Charles F. Voegelin
1939   Hidatsa Texts Collected by Robert H. Lowie with Gram-
            matical Notes and Phonograph Transcriptions. Indiana His-
            torical Society, Prehistory Research Series 1(6):173–239.
            Indianapolis.

Harrison, Benjamin
1890   Message from the President of the United States, Transmit-
            ting Reports Relative to the Proposed Division of the great
            Sioux Reservation, and Recommending Certain Legisla-
            tion. 51st Congress. 1st Session. Senate Executive Docu-
            ment 51. (Report and council proceedings of the Sioux *1167*

Commission sent to obtain consent from the Sioux for a division and reduction of the Great Sioux Reservation, and to secure the relinquishment of the Indian title to the remainder.) Washington: Government Printing Office. (Reprinted: Microfilm Reel 12 of 29, University Publications of America, Bethesda, Md., 1991.)

Harrison, Billy R., and B.T. Griffin
1973   An Infant Burial in the Texas Panhandle. *Bulletin of the Texas Archaeological Society* 44:61–48. Austin.

Harrison, Julia D.
1985   Métis: People between Two Worlds. [Calgary, Alta.]: The Glenbow-Alberta Institute in assoc. with Douglas & McIntyre, Vancouver/Toronto.

Harrod, Howard L.
1971   Mission among the Blackfeet. Norman: University of Oklahoma Press.

1987   Renewing the World: Northern Plains Indian Religion. Tucson: University of Arizona Press.

1995   Becoming and Remaining a People: Native American Religion on the Northern Plains. Tucson: University of Arizona Press.

1996   Death. Pp. 154–156 in Encyclopedia of North American Indians. Frederick E. Hoxie, ed. Boston: Houghton Mifflin.

2000   The Animals Came Dancing: Native American Sacred Ecology and Animal Kinship. Tucson: University of Arizona Press.

Hart, Jeffrey A.
1981   The Ethnobotany of the Northern Cheyenne Indians of Montana. *Journal of Ethnopharmacology* 4(1):1–55. New York, [etc.].

Hart, John B.
1950–1952   North Dakota Indian Commission: Reports. 2 vols. Rolla, N.Dak.: The Commission.

Hart, Sheila, and Vida F. Carlson
1948   We Saw the Sun Dance: A Story of the Ancient Religious Ceremonial Rite of the Shoshone and Arapaho Indians of Wyoming. Concord, Calif.: Concord Graphic Arts.

Hartle, Donald D.
1963   The Dance Hall of the Santee Bottoms on the Fort Berthold Reservation, Garrison Reservoir, North Dakota. *Bureau of American Ethnology Bulletin* 185; *River Basin Surveys Papers* 28. Washington: Smithsonian Institution; U.S. Government Printing Office.

Hartley, John D.
1974   The Von Elm Site: An Early Plains-Woodland Complex in North-central Oklahoma. *University of Oklahoma. River Basin Survey. Archaeological Site Report* 28. Norman.

Hartman, M. Clare
1984   As It Was: History of Mission High School. 2 vols. Chinook, Mont.: Chinook Opinion.

Hartmann, Horst
1963   George Catlin und Balduin Möllhausen: Zwei Interpreten der Indianer und des Alten Westen. *Baessler Archiv. Beiträge zur Völkerkunde. Neue Folge Beiheft* 3. Berlin: Dietrich Reimer.

1968   Die Berliner Mato-tope-Robe. *Tribus: Veröffentlichungen des Linden-Museums* 17(August): 93–104. Stuttgart, Germany.

1973   Die Plains- und Prärieindianer Nordamerikas. Berlin: Museum für Völkerkunde.

Harvey, Amy Evelyn
1971   Challenge and Response: Environment and Northwest Iowa Oneota. (Ph.D. Dissertation in Anthropology, University of Wisconsin, Madison.)

1979   Oneota Culture in Northwestern Iowa. *University of Iowa. Office of the State Archaeologist. Reports* 12. Iowa City.

Haskell, Daniel C., comp.
1968   The United States Exploring Expedition, 1838–1842, and Its Publications, 1844–1874: A Bibliography. With an Introductory Note by Harry Miller Lydenberg. New York: Greenwood Press.

Haspel, Howard, and Dale Wedel
1985   A Middle Plains Archaic Child Burial from the KcKean Site in Northeastern Wyoming. Pp. 105–108 in McKean/Middle Plains Archaic: Current Research. Marcel Kornfeld and Lawrence C. Todd, eds. *Occasional Papers on Wyoming Archaeology* 4. Laramie: Wyoming Recreation Commission.

Hasse, F.R.
1969   Sun Dance. *Royal Canadian Mounted Police Quarterly* 34(4):54–55. Ottawa.

Hassett, Nancy S.
1984   A Spatial Analysis of a Late Woodland Site in the Kansas City Locality (23JA85). (M.A. Thesis in Anthropology, University of Kansas, Lawrence.)

Hasskarl, Robert A., Jr.
1962   The Culture and History of the Tonkawa Indians. *Plains Anthropologist* 7(18):217–231.

Hassrick, Royal B.
1944   Teton Dakota Kinship System. *American Anthropologist,* n.s. 46(3):338–347.

1947   Assiniboin Succession. *North Dakota History* 14(2):146–167. Bismarck.

1964   The Sioux: Life and Customs of a Warrior Society. Royal B. Hassrick in collaboration with Dorothy Maxwell and Cile M. Bach. Norman: University of Oklahoma Press. (Several reprints, incl.: 1967, 1977, 1988, 1993.)

1986   The Culture of the Sioux. Pp. 71–77 in Vestiges of a Proud Nation: The Ogden B. Read Northern Plains Indian Collection. Glenn E. Markoe, ed. Burlington, Vt.: Robert Hull Fleming Museum.

Hatch, Thom
1997   Custer and the Battle of the Little Bighorn: An Encyclopedia. Jefferson, N.C.: McFarland and Company.

Hatcher, Mattie Austin, trans. 1919 *see* Padilla, Juan Antonio 1919

_____, trans. and ed. 1927 *see* Casañas de Jesus María, Fray Francisco 1927 and Hidalgo, Fray Francisco 1927

Hathcock, Roy
1983   The Quapaw and Their Pottery: A Pictorial Study of the Ceramic Arts of the Quapaw Indians, 1650–1750. Camden, Ark.: Hurley Press.

Hatt, Gudmund
1916   Moccasins and Their Relation to Arctic Footwear. *Memoirs of the American Anthropological Association* 3(3):149–250. (Reprinted: Kraus Reprint, New York, 1964, 1976.)

Hatt, Ken
1985   Ethnic Discourse in Alberta Land and the Métis in the Ewing Commission. Pp. 64–79 in The Métis: Past and Present. Thomas Flanagan and John Foster, eds. *Canadian Ethnic Studies* 17(2)[Special issue]. Toronto.

Hatton, Orin T.
1974   Performance Practices of Northern Plains Powwow Singing

Groups. *Yearbook for the Inter-American Music Research* 10. Austin, Tex.: University of Texas Press.

1986   In the Tradition: Grass Dance Musical Style and Female Pow-wow Singers. *Ethnomusicology* 30(2):197–221. Middletown, Conn. and Ann Arbor, Mich.

1988   "We Caused Them to Cry": Power and Performance in Gros Ventre War Expedition Songs. (M.A. Thesis in Anthropology, Catholic University of America, Washington. Published: *Canada. National Museum of Man. Mercury Series. Ethnology Service Paper* 114. Ottawa, 1990.)

1990   Power and Performance in Gros Ventre War Expedition Songs. *Canada. National Museum of Man. Mercury Series. Ethnology Service Paper* 114. Ottawa. (Orig. issued as the Author's M.A. Thesis in Anthropology, 1988.)

Havemeyer, Loomis
1916   The Drama of Savage Peoples. New Haven: Yale University Press.

Hawthorn, H.B., et al.
1967   A Survey of the Contemporary Indians of Canada. Ottawa: The Canadian and U.S. Government Printing Office. (2 vols.)

Hayden, Ferdinand Vandeveer
1862   Contributions to the Ethnography and Philology of the Indian Tribes of the Missouri Valley. Prepared under the Direction of Capt. William F. Raynolds, T.E.U.S.A., and Published by Permission of the War Department. *Transactions of the American Philosophical Society*, n.s. 12(2):231–461. Philadelphia: C. Sherman and Son. (Cover title reads: Article III: On the Ethnography and Philology of the Indian Tribes of the Missouri Valley; with a Map and Plates.)

1868   Brief Notes on the Pawnee, Winnebago, and Omaha Languages. *Proceedings of the American Philosophical Society* 10(78, i.e. 79):389–421. Philadelphia.

1868a   Notes on Indian History, etc. Pp. 411–412 in *Smithsonian Institution Annual Report for 1867*. Washington: U.S. Government Printing Office.

1873   Brief Notes on the Present Condition of the Otoe Indians [1867]. Pp. 32–35 in *First, Second and Third Annual Reports of the United States Geological Survey of the Territories for 1867, 1868, and 1869*. Washington.

Hayes, Alden C.
1981   Excavation of Mound 7, Gran Quivira National Monument, New Mexico. *U.S. National Park Service Publications in Archeology* 16. Washington: Government Printing Office.

1981a   Contributions to Gran Quivira Archeology, Gran Quivira National Monument, New Mexico. *U.S. National Park Service Publications in Archeology* 17. Washington: Government Printing Office.

Haynes, Sam J.
1937   [Interview.] *Indian and Pioneer History* 28:343. (Manuscript in Newspaper/Archives and Manuscripts Division, Oklahoma Historical Society, Oklahoma City.)

Hays, Joe S., Robert L. Brooks, and Jack L. Hofman
1989   Historical Archeology in the Southern Great Plains. Pp. 101–110 in From Clovis to Comanchero: Archeological Overview of the Southern Great Plains, by Jack L. Hofman, Robert L. Brooks, Joe S. Hays, Douglas W. Owsley, Richard L. Jantz, Murray K. Marks, and Mary H. Manhein. *Arkansas Archeological Survey Research Series* 35. Fayetteville.

Hays, Luke C.
1899   [Letter to M. Gates, November 16, 1899.] (Manuscript in Box 55, Fort Belknap Records, Records of the Bureau of Indian Affairs, Record Group 75, National Archives-Pacific Northwest Region, Seattle, Wash.)

Hazen, Reuben W.
1893   History of the Pawnee Indians. Fremont, Nebr.: Fremont Tribune.

Head, Thomas
1985   Northern Plains Prehistory: The Late Prehistoric Period as Viewed from the H.M.S. Balzac Site (EhPm-34). Pp. 100–115 in Contributions to Plains Prehistory. David Burley, ed. *Archaeological Survey of Alberta. Occasional Paper* 26. Edmonton.

Headley, Robert K., Jr.
1971   The Origin and Distribution of the Siouan Speaking Tribes. (M.A. Thesis in Anthropology, Catholic University of America, Washington.)

Heap-of-Birds, Edgar
1983   Introduction. In: Modern Native American Abstraction. Philadelphia: Philadelphia Art Alliance.

Heard, J. Norman
1993   Handbook of the American Frontier: Four Centuries of Indian-White Relationships. Volume III: The Great Plains. *Native American Resources Series* 1. Metuchen, N.J.: The Scarecrow Press.

Hedren, Paul L.
1985   With Crook in the Black Hills: Stanley J. Morrow's 1876 Photographic Legacy. Boulder, Colo.: Pruett Publishing Co.

Heffington, Douglas
1985   The Altithermal Side-notched Knife: A Northwest Plains and Eastern Great Basin Horizon Style. *Journal of Intermountain Archaeology* 4:35–46. Rock Springs, Wyo.

Heffner, Micheal L.
1974   Temporal Variability of Some Kansas City Hopewell Projectile Points. (Manuscript on file at the Museum of Anthropology, University of Kansas, Lawrence.)

Heidenreich, Charles Adrian
1967   Review of the Ghost Dance Religion of 1889–90 among the North American Indians and Comparison of Eight Societies which Accepted or Rejected the Dance. (M.A. Thesis in Anthropology, University of Oregon, Eugene.)

1971   Ethno-documentary of the Crow Indians of Montana, 1824–1862. (Ph.D. Dissertation in Anthropology, University of Oregon, Eugene.)

1976   The Persistence of Values among the Crow Indians. (Paper presented at the Annual Meeting of the American Anthropological Association, San Francisco.)

1979   The Bearing of Ethnohistoric Data on the Crow-Hidatsa Separation(s). Pp. 87–111 in Symposium on the Crow-Hidatsa Separations. Leslie B. Davis, ed. *Archaeology in Montana* 20(3). Billings, [etc.].

Heidenreich, Virginia L., ed.
1990   The Fur Trade in North Dakota. Bismarck: State Historical Society of North Dakota.

Heilbron, Bertha L.
1932   The Goucher College Collection of Mayer Water Colors. *Minnesota History* 13(4):408–414. St. Paul.

Hellson, John C.
1974   Ethnobotany of the Blackfoot Indians. *Canada. National Museum of Man. Mercury Series. Ethnology Service Paper* 19. Ottawa.

Hellwald, Friedrich von *see* Stanford, Edward 1878–1885

Henday, Anthony *see* Hendry, Anthony

Henderson, Harry McCorry
1951   The Magee-Gutierrez Expedition. *Southwestern Historical Quarterly* 55(1):43–61. Austin, Tex.

Henderson, Norman
1994   Replicating Dog Travois Travel on the Northern Plains. *Plains Anthropologist* 39(148):145–159.

Hendrick, Irving G.
1981   The Federal Campaign for the Admission of Indian Children into Public Schools, 1890–1934. *American Indian Culture and Research Journal* 5(3):13–32. Los Angeles.

Hendricks, Sterling Brown
1919   The Somervell Expedition to the Rio Grande, 1842. With introduction and editorial notes by E.W. Winkler. *Southwestern Historical Quarterly* 23(2):112–140. Austin, Tex.

Hendry, Anthony
1907   York Factory to the Blackfeet Country: The Journal of Anthony Hendry, 1754–55. Lawrence J. Burpee, ed. Pp. 307–364 in *Proceedings and Transactions of the Royal Society of Canada,* 3d Ser.,Vol. 1, Sect. 2. Ottawa.

Hendry, Mary H.
1983   Indian Rock Art in Wyoming. Lysite, Wyo.: M.H. Hendry.

Hennepin, Louis
1698   A New Discovery of a Vast Country in America; Extending Above Four Thousand Miles, between New France and New Mexico; with a Description of the Great Lakes, Cataracts, Rivers, Plants, and Animals; also, the Manners, Customs, and Languages of the Several Native Indians, and the Advantage of Commerce with Those Different Nations. With a Continuation ... to Which Is Added, Several New Discoveries in North-America, Not Publish'd in the French edition. 2 vols. London: M. Bentley, J. Tonson, H. Bonwick, T. Goodwin, and S. Manship. (Reprinted, 2 vols., with Introduction, Notes, and Index by Reuben G. Thwaites: A.C. McClurg, Chicago, 1903.)

1880   A Description of Louisiana. Translated from the edition of 1683, and compared with the *Nouvelle découverte,* the La Salle Documents and Other Contemporaneous Papers by John Gilmary Shea. New York: John Gilmary Shea. (Reprinted: University of Minnesota Press, Minneapolis, 1938.)

1903   A New Discovery of a Vast Country in America [1698]; Reprinted from the Second London Issues of 1698; with Facsimilies of Original Title-pages, Maps, and Illustrations. Reuben G. Thwaites, ed. 2 vols. Chicago: A.C. McClurg. (Reprinted, 2 vols.: Canadiana House, Toronto, 1969.)

Henning, Dale R.
1961   Oneota Ceramics in Iowa. *Journal of the Iowa Archeological Society* 11(2). Iowa City.

1967   Mississippian Influences on the Eastern Plains Border: An Evaluation. *Plains Anthropologist* 12(36):184–194.

_____, ed.
1968–1969   Climatic Change and the Mill Creek Culture of Iowa. 2 vols. *Journal of the Iowa Archeological Society* 15–16. Iowa City. (Originally ed. by David A. Baerreis and Reid A. Bryson, *Archives of Archaeology* 29, 1967.)

1969   Ceramics from the Mill Creek Sites. Pp. 192–280 in Vol. 2 of Climatic Change and the Mill Creek Culture of Iowa. Dale R. Henning, ed. *Journal of the Iowa Archeological Society* 16. Iowa City.

1970   Development and Interrelationships of Oneota Culture in the Lower Missouri River Valley. *The Missouri Archaeologist* 32(December [whole vol.]). Columbia.

1971   Great Oasis Culture Distributions. Pp. 125–133 in Prehistoric Investigations. Marshall B. McKusick, ed. Iowa City, Iowa: Office of the State Archaeologist.

1974   The Osage Nation: 1775–1818. Pp. 295–325 in Osage Indians IV. *American Indian Ethnohistory: Plains Indians.* David Agee Horr, comp. and ed. New York: Garland Publishing.

1982   Subsurface Testing Program: Proposed Perry Creek Dam and Reservoir Area, Plymouth County, Iowa. *University of Nebraska. Department of Anthropology. Division of Archeological Research. Technical Report* 82-05. Lincoln.

1982a   Evaluative Investigations of Three Landmark Sites in Northwest Iowa. Decorah, Iowa: Luther College Archaeological Research Center.

1991   Great Oasis and Emergent Mississippian: The Question of Trade. *Journal of the Iowa Archeological Society* 38:1–4. Iowa City.

1993   The Adaptive Patterning of the Dhegiha Sioux. *Plains Anthropologist* 38(146):253–264.

1995   Oneota Evolution and Interaction: A Perspective from the Wever Terrace, Southeast Iowa. In: Oneota Archaeology: Past, Present, and Future. William Green, ed. *University of Iowa. Office of the State Archaeologist. Report* 20. Iowa City.

1996   The Archeology of Two Great Oasis Sites in the Perry Creek Valley, Northwest Iowa. *Journal of the Iowa Archeological Society* 43:7–118. Iowa City.

1998   The Oneota Tradition. Pp. 345–414 in Archaeology on the Great Plains. W. Raymond Wood, ed. Lawrence, Kans.: University Press of Kansas.

Henning, Dale R., Amy E. Henning, and David A. Baerreis
1968   1963 Excavations in the Mill Creek Sites. Pp. 35–106 in Pt./Vol. 1 of Climatic Change and the Mill Creek Culture of Iowa. Dale R. Henning, ed. *Journal of the Iowa Archeological Society* 15. Iowa City.

Henning, Darrell D.
1965   The Alkire Mound (32SI200). *Plains Anthropologist* 10(29):146–151.

Henning, Elizabeth R.P.
1981   Great Oasis and the Middle Missouri Tradition. Pp. 33–38 in The Future of South Dakota's Past. Larry J. Zimmerman and Lucille C. Stewart, eds. *Special Publication of the South Dakota Archaeological Society* 2. Vermillion: University of South Dakota, Archaeology Laboratory.

Henning, Elizabeth R.P., and Dale R. Henning
1982   Great Oasis-Mill Creek Interrelationships. Pp. 10–14 in Interrelations of Cultural and Fluvial Deposits in Northwest Iowa. Elmer A. Bettis and Dean M. Thompson, eds. Iowa City: Association of Iowa Archeologists.

Henry, Alexander 1809 *see* 1901

1901   Travels and Adventures in Canada and the Indian Territories between the Years 1760 and 1776 by Alexander Henry, Fur Trader. Edited, with Notes, Illustratives, and Biography, by James Bain. Boston: Little, Brown. (Originally publ. in 2 Pts. by I. Riley, New York, 1809. Reprinted: Readex Microprint, New York, 1966, 1974; also, C.E. Tuttle Company, Rutland, Vt., 1969; and, Garland Publishing, New York, 1976.)

Henry, Alexander (the Younger)
1799–1814   Journal Across the Mountains to the Pacific. (Manuscript MG19, A13, Vol. 1, in Public Archives of Canada, Ottawa.)

Henry, Alexander (the Younger)
1988–1992 The Journal of Alexander Henry the Younger, 1799–1814. Edited with an Introduction by Barry M. Gough. 2 vols. *Publications of the Champlain Society* 56–57. Toronto: The Champlain Society.

Henry, Donald O.
1977 The Prehistory of Little Caney River, 1976 Field Season. Tulsa, Okla.: University of Tulsa, Laboratory of Archaeology.

Henry, James Pepper
1997 Historic Kaw Photographs To Be Restored/Documented. *Kanza News: Newsletter of the Kaw Nation of Oklahoma* 4:17. Kaw City, Okla.

1998 Kaw Historic Photographs Recorded/Preserved. *Kanza News: Newsletter of the Kaw Nation of Oklahoma* 5:13. Kaw City, Okla.

Herbort, Dale P.
1988 Rediscovering the Cobble Industry: A Case Study on the Northern Plains. *Archaeology in Montana* 29(1):23–79. Billings, [etc.].

1990 Investigations at the Palmer Chert Quarry. *Archaeology in Montana* 31(1):7–15. Billings, [etc.].

Herman, Jake
1963 The Sacred Pole. *The Masterkey* 37(1):35–37. Los Angeles.
_____, comp.
[1968] Pictorial Booklet: Legends and History of Oglala Sioux. [Pine Ridge, S.Dak.]

Herring, D. Ann
1992 Toward a Reconsideration of Disease and Contact in the Americas. *Prairie Forum* 17(2):153–165. Regina, Sask.: Canadian Plains Research Center, University of Regina.

Hertzberg, Hazel W.
1971 The Search for an American Indian Identity: Modern Pan-Indian Movements. Syracuse, N.Y.: Syracuse University Press.

Hesketh, John
1923 History of the Turtle Mountain Chippewa. *Collections of the North Dakota State Historical Society* 5:85–154. Grand Forks, N.Dak.

Heski, Thomas M.
1978 "Icastinyanka Cikala Hanzi," The Little Shadow Catcher: D.F. Barry, Celebrated Photographer of Famous Indians. Seattle: Superior Publishing Company.

Hester, James J.
1962 Early Navajo Migrations and Acculturation in the Southwest. (*Navajo Project Studies* 5). *Museum of New Mexico Papers in Anthropology* 6. Santa Fe.

Heth, Charlotte
1976 Songs of Earth, Wind, Fire, and Sky: Music of the American Indian. Sound Recording. Produced and Recorded by Charlotte Heth for *Recorded Anthology of American Music*. New York: New World Records.

1989 Introduction to Songs of Indian Territory. In: Songs of Indian Territory: Native American Music Traditions of Oklahoma. Willie Smyth, ed. Oklahoma City, Okla.: Center of the American Indian. (Book and Cassette.)

1994 This Precious Heritage. *Akwe:kon Journal: Native American Expressive Culture* XI (3 and 4):31–37. Ithaca, N.Y.

1999 Synthesis of Indian Music. (Manuscript in G. Young's possession.)

Heth, Charlotte, and Michael Swarm, eds.
1984 American Indian Arts: Sharing a Heritage. *Contemporary American Indian Issues Series* 5. Los Angeles: American Indian Studies Center, University of California.

Hewes, Gordon W.
1949 Burial Mounds in the Baldhill Area, North Dakota. *American Antiquity* 14(4):322–328.

Hewitt, J.N.B., ed. 1930 *see* Denig, Edwin Thompson 1930

_____,ed. 1937 *see* Kurz, Rudolph Friederich 1937

Hicherson, Harold E.
1962 The Southwestern Chippewa: An Ethnohistorical Study. *Memoirs of the American Anthropological Association* 92. Menasha, Wis.

1956 The Genesis of a Trading Post Band: The Pembina Chippewa. *Ethnohistory* 3(4):289–345.

1959 The Journal of Charles Jean Baptiste Chaboillez, 1797–1798. *Ethnohistory* 6(3):265–316, (4):363–427.

1965 The Virginia Deer and Intertribal Buffer Zones in the Upper Mississippi Valley. Pp. 43–65 in Man, Culture, and Animals. Anthony Leeds and Andrew P. Vayda, eds. *American Association for the Advancement of Science. Publication* 78. Washington.

1970 The Chippewa and Their Neighbors: A Study in Ethnohistory. New York: Holt, Rinehart and Winston.

1974 Sioux Indians I: Mdewakanton Band of Sioux Indians. *American Indian Ethnohistory: Plains Indians*. David Agee Horr, comp. and ed. New York: Garland Publishing.

Hickerson, Nancy Parrott
1994 The Jumanos: Hunters and Traders of the South Plains. Austin: University of Texas Press.

Hicks, George L.
1975 The Same North and South: Ethnicity and Change in Two American Indian Groups. Pp. 75–94 in The New Ethnicity. John W. Bennett, ed. St. Paul, Minn.: West Publishing Co.

Hidalgo, Fray Francisco
1927 Description of the Tejas or Asinai Indians 1691–1722. Part III: Fray Francisco Hidalgo to Fray Isidro Cassos, November 20, 1710. Translated from the Spanish [and ed.] by Mattie Austin Hatcher. *Southwestern Historical Quarterly* 31(1):50–62. Austin, Tex.

Higgins, Kathleen
1936 The Blackfeet Medicine Lodge Ceremony. *Indians at Work* 2(23):18–19. Washington: Bureau of Indian Affairs.

High Hawk
[1907] [Winter Count, 900 A.D. to 1907; 2 sheets of paper, collected by Aaron Baker Clark, Rosebud, S.Dak.] (Manuscript Collection "Indians", Accession No. 969, Feb. 5, 1909, Manuscript Division, Library of Congress, Washington.)

Highwalking, Belle, and Katherine M. Weist
1991 Belle Highwalking: The Narrative of a Northern Cheyenne Woman. Billings: Montana Council for Indian Education.

Highwater, Jamake
1977 Ritual of the Wind: North American Indian Ceremonies, Music and Dances. New York: Francis P. Harper.

Hilbert, Robert
1987 Contemporary Catholic Mission Work Among the Sioux. Pp. 139–147 in Sioux Indian Religion: Tradition and Innovation. Raymond J. DeMallie and Douglas R. Parks, eds. Norman, Okla.: University of Oklahoma Press.

Hildebrandt, Walter
1985 The Battle of Batoche: British Small Warfare and the *1171*

Entrenched Métis. *Environment Canada. Parks Service. Studies in Archaeology, Architecture and History.* Ottawa.

Hildebrandt, Walter, and Brian Hubner
1994   The Cypress Hills: The Land and Its People. Saskatoon, Sask.: Purich Publishing.

Hildreth, James
1836   Dragoon Campaigns to the Rocky Mountains; by a Dragoon. New York: Wiley and Long. (Reprinted: Arno Press, New York, 1973.)

Hilger, (Sister) Mary Inez
1946   Notes on Cheyenne Child Life. *American Anthropologist,* n.s. 48(1):60–69.

1951   Some Customs Related to Arikara Indian Child Life. *Primitive Man* 24(4):67–71. Washington: The Catholic University of America.

1952   Arapahoe Child Life and Its Cultural Background. *Bureau of American Ethnology Bulletin* 148.Washington: Smithsonian Institution; U.S. Government Printing Office.

1959   Some Customs of the Chippewa on the Turtle Mountain Reservation of North Dakota. *North Dakota History* 26(3):123–125. Bismarck.

Hill, A.T., and Paul L. Cooper
1937   The Schrader Site: Prehistoric Village in Lancaster County Nebraska. *Nebraska History* 17(4):222–252. Lincoln.

1937a   The Champe Site: Excavation of a Prehistoric House in Douglas County, Nebraska. *Nebraska History* 17(4):253–270. Lincoln.

1937b   Fremont 1: Prehistoric Village Site in Sarpy County, Nebraska. *Nebraska History* 17(4):271–292. Lincoln.

1938   The Archeological Campaign of 1937. *Nebraska History* 18(4):[237] 243–359. Lincoln.

Hill, A.T., and Marvin Kivett
1941   Woodland-like Manifestations in Nebraska. *Nebraska History* 21(3):147–243. Lincoln.

Hill, A.T., and George Metcalf
1942   A Site of the Dismal River Aspect in Chase County, Nebraska. *Nebraska History* 22(2):158–226. Lincoln.

Hill, A.T., and Waldo R. Wedel
1936   Excavations at the Leary Indian Village and Burial Site, Richardson County, Nebraska. *Nebraska History*17(1):2–73. Lincoln.

Hill, Edward E.
1974   The Office of Indian Affairs, 1824–1880: Historical Sketches. New York: Clearwater Publishing.

1981   Guide to Records in the National Archives of the United States Relating to American Indians. Washington: National Archives and Record Service.

Hill, George W.
1877   Vocabulary of the Shoshone Language. Salt Lake City: Desert News Steam Printing Establishment.

Hill, Matthew G., Vance T. Holliday, and Dennis J. Stanford
1995   A Further Evaluation of the San Jon Site, New Mexico. *Plains Anthropologist* 40(154):369–390.

Hill, Tom, and Kenneth L. Beals
1966   Some Notes on Kiowa Apache Peyotism with Special Reference to Ethics and Change. *University of Oklahoma. Papers in Anthropology* 7(1):1–24. Norman.

Hill, W.W.
1937   Navajo Pottery Manufacture. *Anthropological Series* 2(3); *University of New Mexico Bulletin* 317:7–23. Albuquerque.

Himmel, Kelly F.
1999   The Conquest of the Karankawas and the Tonkawas, 1821–1859. College Station, Tex.: Texas A&M University.

Hinchman, Lewis, and Sara Hinchman
1994   Western Reservations and the Politics of Water. Pp. 246–296 in Native American Resurgence and Renewal: A Reader and Bibliography. *Native American Resource Series* 3. Robert N. Wells, Jr., ed. Metuchen, N.J.: The Scarecrow Press.

Hind, Henry Youle
1859   North-West Territory: Reports of Progress; Together with A Preliminary and General Report of the Assiniboine and Saskatchewan Exploring Expedition, Made under Instructions from the Provincial Secretary, Canada. Toronto: John Lovell [for] the Legislative Assembly.

1860   Narrative of the Canadian Red River Exploring Expedition of 1857; and of the Assiniboine and Saskatchewan Exploring Expedition of 1858. 2 vols. London: Longman, Green, Longman, and Roberts. (Reprinted, 2 vols. in 1 under title: Narrative of the Canadian Exploring Expeditions; C.E Tuttle Co., Rutland, Vt., 1971.)

1863   Explorations in the Interior of the Labrador Peninsula, the Country of the Montagnais and Nasquapee Indians. 2 vols. London: Longman, Green, Longman, Roberts, and Green.

Hinman, Eleanor H.
1976   Oglala Sources on the Life of Crazy Horse. *Nebraska History* 57(1):1–51. Lincoln.

Hinman, Samuel Dutton
1864   Calvary Catechism, in the Dakota Language. Translated from the Mission of St. John. Fairbault, Minn.: Central Republican Book and Job Office.

1869   Dakota Indians, To the Friends of the Santee Indian Mission. Philadelphia: The Indian's Hope.

1871   Calvary Catechism in Santee Dakota: Translated by Permission for the Collegiate Mission. 2d ed. Revisions and Corrections by Samuel Dutton Hinman. Santee Agency, Nebr.: Mission Press, Archdeaconry of the Niobrara.

1871a   Hymns and Psalms in Santee Dakota. For the Collegiate Mission, to the Dakota Indians. Santee Agency, Nebr.: Mission Press, Archdeaconry of the Niobrara.

1871b   Okodakiciye wakan odowan kin: isanyati Dakota iyapi en: yewicoxipi okodakiciye. Hymns of the Church in Santee Dakota. 2d ed. rev. and enl. Santee Agency, Nebr.: Mission Press, Archdeaconry of the Niobrara.

1874   Hymns in Dakota, for the Use in the Missionary Jurisdiction of Niobrara. [No place]: Published by the Indian Commission of the Protestant Episcopal Church.

Hinsley, Curtis M.
1981   Savages and Scientists: The Smithsonian Institution and the Development of American Anthropology, 1846–1910. Washington: Smithsonian Institution Press. (Reprinted under title: The Smithsonian Institution and the American Indian: Making of a Moral Anthropology in Victorian America. Smithsonian Institution Press, Washington, 1994.)

Hirabayashi, James, William Willard, and Luis Kemnitzer
1972   Pan Indianism in the Urban Setting. Pp. 77–88 in The Anthropology of Urban Environments. Thomas Weaver and Douglas White, eds. *Society for Applied Anthropology Monograph* 11. Boulder, Colo.

Hirschfelder, Arlene, and Martha Kreipe de Montaño
1993   The Native American Almanac: A Portrait of Native America Today. New York: Prentice Hall.

Hjermstad, Benjamin Edward
1996   The Fitzgerald Site: A Besant Pound and Processing Area on the Northern Plains. (M.A. Thesis in Anthropology and Archaeology, University of Saskatchewan, Saskatoon.)

Hlady, Walter M.
1964   Indian Migrations in Manitoba and the West. *Papers Read before the Historical Society of Manitoba* 3(17–18):24–53. Winnipeg, Man.

1967   A Besant Phase Bison Kill Site in Southwestern Manitoba. *Manitoba Archaeological Society Newsletter* 4(2):3–10. Winnipeg.

———, ed.
1970   Ten Thousand Years: Archaeology in Manitoba. Commemorating Manitoba's Centennial 1870–1970. Winnipeg: Manitoba Archaeological Society.

1971   An Introduction to the Archaeology of the Woodland Area of Northern Manitoba. *Manitoba Archaeological Society Newsletter* 8(2–3). Winnipeg.

Hoag, Enoch
1872   [Letter to F.A. Walker, dated December 3, 1872] (Manuscript No. M234, Letters Received, Records of the Bureau of Indian Affairs, Record Group 75, National Archives, Washington.)

Hockley, Nancy Lucinda Clemens
1985   Une chanson de vérité; Songs of the Prairie Métis. Indian Head, Man.: The Other Opera Company.

Hodge, Frederick Webb
1895   [Tribal Names in the Languages of the Pueblos.] (Manuscript No. 65, National Anthropological Archives, Smithsonian Institution, Washington.)

———, ed.
1907–1910 Handbook of American Indians North of Mexico. 2 Pts./vols. *Bureau of American Ethnology Bulletin* 30. Washington: Smithsonian Institution; U.S. Government Printing Office. (Reprinted: Rowman and Littlefield, New York, 1971.)

Hodge, Frederick Webb, George P. Hammond, and Agapito Rey, eds. and trans. 1945 *see* Benavides, Fray Alonso de 1945

Hodges, Daniel Houston
1980   Transcription and Analysis of Southern Cheyenne Songs. (Ph.D. Dissertation in Anthropology, University of Oklahoma, Norman.)

Hoebel, E. Adamson
1933   [Comanche Fieldnotes.] (Uncatalogued manuscript in the Library of the American Philosophical Society, Philadelphia.)

1935   The Sun Dance of the Hekandika Shoshone. *American Anthropologist,* n.s. 37(4):570–581.

1939   Comanche and Hekandika Shoshone Relationship Systems. *American Anthropologist,* n.s. 41(3):440–457.

1940   Political Organization and Law-ways of the Comanche Indians. *Memoirs of the American Anthropological Association* 54. Menasha, Wis.

1941   The Comanche Sun Dance and Messianic Outbreak of 1873. *American Anthropologist,* n.s. 43(2):301–303.

1954   The Law of Primitive Man: A Study in Comparative Legal Dynamics. Cambridge, Mass: Harvard University Press.

1960   The Cheyennes: Indians of the Great Plains. New York: Holt, Rinehart and Winston. (Reprinted in 1978.)

1972   Anthropology: The Study of Man. 4th ed. New York: McGraw-Hill.

1980   The Influence of Plains Ethnography on the Development of Anthropological Theory. Pp. 16–22 in Anthropology on the Great Plains. W. Raymond Wood and Margot Liberty, eds. Lincoln: University of Nebraska Press.

Hoebel, E. Adamson, and Karen D. Petersen, eds.
1964   A Cheyenne Sketchbook, by [William] Cohoe. Norman: University of Oklahoma Press.

Hoffhaus, Charles E.
1964   Fort de Cavagnial, Imperial France in Kansas, 1744–1764. *Kansas Historical Quarterly* 30(4):425–454. Topeka.

Hoffman, Bernard G.
1961   The Codex Canadiensis: An Important Document for Great Lakes Ethnography. *Ethnohistory* 8(4):382–400.

Hoffman, Charles W.
1909   [Letter to the Commissioner of Indian Affairs, dated, Elbowoods, N. Dak., August 30, 1909.] (Manuscript in Letters Received, Records of the Bureau of Indian Affairs, Record Group 75, National Archives, Washington.)

Hoffman, John J.
1967   Molstad Village. *Smithsonian Institution. River Basin Surveys. Publications in Salvage Archeology* 4. Lincoln.

1968   The La Roche Sites. *Smithsonian Institution. River Basin Surveys. Publications in Salvage Archeology* 11. Lincoln.

Hoffman, Michael P.
1977   The Kinkead-Mainard Site, 3PU2: A Late Prehistoric Quapaw Phase Site Near Little Rock, Arkansas. *The Arkansas Archeologist* 16–18:1–41. Fayetteville.

——— 1985 *see* 1990

1985a   The Quapaw, an Enduring People. (Manuscript on file at Arkansas Archeological Survey, Fayetteville.)

1986   The Protohistoric Period in the Lower and Central Arkansas River Valley in Arkansas. Pp. 24–37 in The Mid-south, 1500–1700: Proceedings of the 1983 Mid-south Archaeological Conference. David H. Dye and Ronald C. Brister, eds. *Mississippi Department of Archives and History. Archaeological Report* 18. Jackson, Miss.

1990   The Terminal Period in the Arkansas River Valley and Quapaw Ethnogenesis. Pp. 208–226 in Towns and Temples along the Mississippi. David H. Dye and Cheryl A. Cox, eds. Tuscaloosa: University of Alabama Press.

1991   Quapaw Structures, 1673–1834, and Their Comparative Significance. Pp. 55–68 in Arkansas Before the Americans. Hester A. Davis, ed. *Arkansas Archeological Survey Research Series* 40. Fayetteville.

Hoffman, Robert S., and J. Knox Jones, Jr.
1970   Influence of Late Glacial and Post-Glacial Events on the Distribution of Recent Mammals on the Northern Great Plains. Pp. 355–394 in Pleistocene and Recent Environments of the Central Great Plains. W. Dort, Jr., J. Knox Jones, Jr., eds. Lawrence: The University of Kansas Press.

Hoffman, Walter J.
1883   Note sur les flèches empoisonnées des Indiens de l'Amérique du Nord. *Bulletin de la Société d'Anthropologie de Paris,* 3d sr., Vol. 6:205–208. Paris.

1886   Remarks on Indian Tribal Names. *Proceedings of the 1173*

American Philosophical Society, n.s. 23(122):294–303. Philadelphia.

1886a   Vocabulary of the Selish Language. *Proceedings of the American Philosophical Society*, n.s. 23(123):361–371. Philadelphia.

1896   The Menomini Indians. Pp. 3–328 in Pt. 1 of *14th Annual Report of the Bureau of American Ethnology [for] 1892–1893*. Washington: Smithsonian Institution; U.S. Government Printing Office. (Reprinted: Johnson Reprint, New York, 1970.)

Hoffmann, Gerhard
1993   The Art of Canada's Indians and the Modern Aesthetic. Pp. 165–196 in In the Shadow of the Sun: Perspectives on Contemporary Native Art. Hull, Que.: Canadian Museum of Civilization.

1993a   Postmodern Culture and Indian Art. Pp. 257–302 in In the Shadow of the Sun: Perspectives on Contemporary Native Art. Hull, Que.: Canadian Museum of Civilization.

Hofman, Jack L.
1978   The Development and Northern Relationships of Two Archeological Phases in the Southern Plains Subarea. Pp. 6–35 in The Central Plains Tradition: Internal Development and External Relationships. Donald J. Blakeslee, ed. *University of Iowa. Office of the Archaeologist, Reports* 11. Iowa City.

1984   The Western Protohistoric: A Summary of the Edwards and Wheeler Complexes. Pp. 347–362 in Prehistory of Oklahoma. Robert E. Bell, ed. Orlando, San Diego, San Francisco, [etc.]: Academic Press.

1989   Prehistoric Culture History—Hunters and Gatherers in the Southern Great Plains. Pp. 26–60 in From Clovis to Comanchero: Archeological Overview of the Southern Great Plains, by Jack L. Hofman, Robert L. Brooks, Joe S. Hays, Douglas W. Owsley, Richard L. Jantz, Murray K. Marks, and Mary H. Manhein. *Arkansas Archeological Survey Research Series* 35. Fayetteville.

_____, ed.
1996   Archeology and Paleoecology of the Central Great Plains. With Contributions by Mary J. Adair, [et al.]. *Arkansas Archeological Survey Research Series* 48. Fayetteville.

Hofman, Jack L., and Robert L. Brooks
1989   Prehistoric Culture History Woodland Complexes in the Southern Great Plains. Pp. 61–70 in From Clovis to Comanchero: Archeological Overview of the Southern Great Plains, by Jack L. Hofman, Robert L. Brooks, Joe S. Hays, Douglas W. Owsley, Richard L. Jantz, Murray K. Marks, and Mary H. Manhein. *Arkansas Archeological Survey Research Series* 35. Fayetteville.

Hofman, Jack L., and Russell W. Graham
1998   The Paleo-Indian Cultures of the Great Plains. Pp. 87–139 in Archaeology on the Great Plains. W. Raymond Wood, ed. Lawrence: University Press of Kansas.

Hofman, Jack L., Robert L. Brooks, Joe S. Hays, and Douglas W. Owsley
1989   Adaptation Types for the Southern Great Plains Region. Pp. 157–174 in From Clovis to Comanchero: Archeological Overview of the Southern Great Plains, by Jack L. Hofman, Robert L. Brooks, Joe S. Hays, Douglas W. Owsley, Richard L. Jantz, Murray K. Marks, and Mary H. Manhein. *Arkansas Archeological Survey Research Series* 35. Fayetteville.

Hofman, Jack L., Robert L. Brooks, Joe S. Hays, Douglas W. Owsley, Richard L. Jantz, Murray K. Marks, and Mary H. Manhein
1989   From Clovis to Comanchero: Archeological Overview of the Southern Plains. Prepared by the Oklahoma Archeological Survey of the University of Oklahoma and the Louisiana

State University, with the Arkansas Archeological Survey. Final Report submitted to the U.S. Army Corps of Engineers, Southeastern Division. Study Unit 5 of the Southwestern Division Archeological Overview. (Contract DACW63-84-C-0149.) *Arkansas Archeological Survey Research Series* 35. Fayetteville.

Hofmann, Charles
1966   The Sun Dance of the Plains. [Text with accompanying sound recording, 1 disc.] Pp. 54–57 in American Indians Sing, by Charles Hofmann. New York: The John Day Company.

Hoig, Stan
1961   The Sand Creek Massacre. Norman: University of Oklahoma Press. (Reprinted in 1990.)

1976   The Battle of the Washita: The Sheridan-Custer Indian Campaign of 1867–69. Garden City, N.Y.: Doubleday. (Reprinted: University of Nebraska Press, Lincoln, 1979.)

1980   The Peace Chiefs of the Cheyennes. Norman: University of Oklahoma Press.

1993   Tribal Wars of the Southern Plains. Norman: University of Oklahoma Press.

1998   Beyond the Frontier: Exploring the Indian Country. Norman: University of Oklahoma Press.

Hoijer, Harry
1933   Tonkawa, an Indian Language of Texas. Pp. 1–148 in Pt. 3 of Handbook of American Indian Languages. Franz Boas, ed. New York: Columbia University Press; J.J. Augustin.

1934   [Lipan Texts and Linguistic Material.] (Manuscripts in Harry Hoijer Collection, No. 497.3/H68, The Library of the American Philosophical Society, Philadelphia.)

1938   The Southern Athapaskan Languages. *American Anthropologist*, n.s. 40(1):75–87.

1938a   Chiricahua and Mescalero Apache Texts; with Ethnological notes by Morris E. Opler. Chicago: The University of Chicago Press.

_____, ed.
1946   Linguistic Structures of Native America. (Editor's Introduction, pp. 9–29.) *Viking Fund Publications in Anthropology* 6. New York: Wenner-Gren Foundation for Anthropological Research. (Reprinted: Johnson Reprint, New York, 1963, 1971.)

1946a   Tonkawa. Pp. 289–311 in Linguistic Structures of Native America. Harry Hoijer, ed. *Viking Fund Publications in Anthropology* 6. New York: Wenner-Gren Foundation for Anthropological Research. (Reprinted: Johnson Reprint, New York, 1963, 1971.)

1949   An Analytical Dictionary of the Tonkawa Language. *University of California Publications in Linguistics* 5(1):1–74. Berkeley.

1949a   Tonkawa Syntactic Suffixes and Anaphoric Particles. *Southwestern Journal of Anthropology* 4(1):37–55.

1956   The Chronology of the Athapaskan Languages. *International Journal of American Linguistics* 22(4):219–234. Chicago.

1956a   Athapaskan Kinship Systems. *American Anthropologist*, n.s. 58(2):309–333.

1962   Linguistic Sub-grouping by Glottochronology and by the Comparative Method: the Athapaskan Languages. *Lingua: International Review of General Linguistics* 11:192–198. Amsterdam.

1971   The Position of the Apachean Languages in the Athapaskan Stock. Pp. 3–6 in Apachean Culture, History and Ethnology. Keith H. Basso and Morris E. Opler, eds. *Anthropological Papers of the University of Arizona* 21. Tucson.

1972   Tonkawa Texts. *University of California Publications in Linguistics* 73. Berkeley.

1975   The History and Customs of the Lipan, as Told by Augustina Zuazua. *Linguistics: An International Review* 161:5–37.

Hoijer, Harry, and Janet Joël
1963   Sarsi Nouns. Pp. 62–75 in Studies in the Athapaskan Languages, by Harry Hoijer and others. *University of California Publications in Linguistics* 29. Berkeley.

Holden, William C.
1929   Some Recent Explorations and Excavations in Northwest Texas. *Texas Archeological and Paleontological Society. Bulletin* 1:23–25. Abilene.

1930   The Canadian Valley Expedition of March, 1930. *Texas Archeological and Paleontological Society* 2:21–32. Abilene.

Holder, Preston
1949   The Role of the Caddaon Horticulturalists in Culture History on the Great Plains. (Ph.D. Dissertation in Anthropology, Columbia University, New York City.)

1958   Social Stratification among the Arikara. *Ethnohistory* 5(3): 210–218.

1970   The Hoe and the Horse on the Plains: A Study of Cultural Development among North American Indians. Lincoln: University of Nebraska Press. (Reprinted in 1991.)

Holler, Clyde
1984   Black Elk's Relationship to Christianity. *The American Indian Quarterly* 8(1):37–49. Berkeley, Calif.

1995   Black Elk's Religion: The Sun Dance and Lakota Catholicism. Syracuse, N.Y.: Syracuse University Press.

Holliday, Vance T.
1997   Paleoindian Geoarchaeology of the Southern High Plains. Austin: University of Texas Press.

Hollow, Robert C., Jr.
1965–1975   [Mandan Linguistic Notes.] (Manuscript No. 10494 in State Historical Society Archives and Research Library of North Dakota, Bismarck.)

1970   A Mandan Dictionary. (Ph.D. Dissertation in Linguistics, University of California, Berkeley.)

1970a   A Note on Assiniboine Phonology. *International Journal of American Linguistics* 36(4):296–298. Chicago.

1978   Mandan [Texts]. Pp. 79–117 in Earth Lodge Tales from the Upper Missouri. Douglas R. Parks, A. Wesley Jones, and Robert C. Hollow, eds. Bismarck, N.Dak.: Mary College.

Hollow, Robert C., Jr., and A. Wesley Jones
1976   Mandan Teacher's Guide. Bismarck, N.Dak.: Mary College, Indian Languages Program.

Hollow, Robert C., Jr., and Douglas R. Parks
1980   Studies in Plains Linguistics: A Review. Pp. 68–97 in Anthropology on the Great Plains. W. Raymond Wood and Margot Liberty, eds. Lincoln: University of Nebraska Press.

Holm, Bill
1981   The Crow-Nez Perce Otterskin Bowcase-Quiver. *American Indian Art Magazine* 6(4):60–70. Scottsdale, Ariz.

Holm, Tom
1985   Fighting a White Man's War: The Extent and Legacy of American Indian Participation in World War II. Pp. 149–168 in The Plains Indians of the Twentieth Century. Edited and with an Introduction by Peter Iverson. Norman: University of Oklahoma Press. (Reprinted from: *Journal of Ethnic Studies* (Summer 1981):69–81.)

1996   Strong Hearts, Wounded Souls: Native American Veterans of the Vietnam War. Austin: University of Texas.

Holmer, Nils M.
1945   Sonant-surds in Ponca-Omaha. *International Journal of American Linguistics* 11(2):75–85. Chicago.

1947   An Ofo Phonetic Law. *International Journal of American Linguistics* 13(1):1–8. Chicago.

Holmes, Jack D.L.
1982   Andrés de Pez and Spanish Reaction to French Expansion into the Gulf of Mexico. Pp. 106–128 in La Salle and His Legacy: Frenchmen and Indians in the Lower Mississippi Valley. Patricia K. Galloway, ed. Jackson: University of Mississippi Press.

Holmes, William H.
1894   An Ancient Quarry in Indian Territory. *Bureau of American Ethnology Bulletin* 21. Washington: Smithsonian Institution; U.S. Government Printing Office.

1903   Flint Implements and Fossil Remains from a Sulphur Spring at Afton, Indian Territory. Pp. 237–252 in *Report of the U.S. National Museum for 1901*. Washington.

1903a   Aboriginal Pottery of the Eastern United States. Pp. 1–201 [pp. 203–237, Vol. Index] in *20th Annual Report of the Bureau of American Ethnology [for] 1898–'99*. Washington: Smithsonian Institution; U.S. Government Printing Office.

1903b   Classification and Arrangement of the Exhibits of an Anthropological Museum. Pp. 255–278 in the *Annual Report of the Board of Regents of the Smithsonian Institution... for the Year Ending June 30, 1901. Report of the U.S. National Museum*. Washington: U.S. Government Printing Office.

1907   Catlinite. Pp. 217–219 in Pt./vol. 1 of Handbook of American Indians North of Mexico. Frederick W. Hodge, ed. 2 Pts/vols. *Bureau of American Ethnology Bulletin* 30. Washington: Smithsonian Institution; U.S. Government Printing Office. (Reprinted: Rowman and Littlefield, New York, 1971.)

1914   Areas of American Culture Characterization Tentatively Outlined as an Aid in the Study of the Antiquities. *American Anthropologist*, n.s. 16(3):413–446.

1919   Handbook of Aboriginal American Antiquities. Part I. Introductory: The Lithic Industries. *Bureau of American Ethnology Bulletin* 60. Washington: Smithsonian Institution; U.S. Government Printing Office.

Holt, Roy D.
1966   Heap Many Texas Chiefs. San Antonio, Tex.: The Naylor Company.

Holy Dance, Robert
1970   The Seven Pipes of the Dakota Sioux. *Plains Anthropologist* 15(48):81–81.

Honigmann, John J.
1944   Morale in a Primitive Society. *Character and Personality* 12(3):228–236. Durham, N.C.

1945   Northern and Southern Athapaskan Eschatology. *American Anthropologist*, n.s. 47(3):467–469.

1175

1949   Parallels in the Development of Shamanism among Northern and Southern Athapaskans. *American Anthropologist,* n.s. 51(3):512–514.

1956   The Attawapiskat Swampy Cree: An Ethnographic Reconstruction. *Anthropological Papers of the University of Alaska* 5(1):23–82. College, Alaska.

1956a   Notes on Sarsi Kin Behavior. *Anthropologica* 2:17–38. Ottawa: University of Ottawa, The Research Center for Amerindian Anthropology.

Hoover, Herbert T.
1976   Yankton Sioux Tribal Claims Against the United States, 1917–1975. *Western Historical Quarterly* 7(2):125–142. Logan, Utah.

1979   The Sioux: A Critical Bibliography. Bloomington: Indiana University Press.

1988   The Yankton Sioux. In collaboration with Leonard R. Bruguier. New York: Chelsea House Publishers.

Hoover, Herbert T., and Leonard R. Bruguier
1989   The Pipestone Reservation: A History. *Coteau Heritage: Journal of the Pipestone County Historical Society* 2(1):9–12. Pipestone, Minn.

Hoover, Herbert T., and Karen P. Zimmerman, comps.
1993   The Sioux and Other Native American Cultures of the Dakotas: An Annotated Bibliography. *Bibliographies and Indexes in Anthropology* 8. Westport, Conn.: Greenwood Press.

Hopkins, E.C., and C.L. Hall
[1900]   Natchcitu Ninhatun - Lessons in the Path of Life, by A.L. Riggs, D.D. Arickaree Translation. Santee, Nebr.: Santee Normal Training School Press.

Hopkins, E. Washburn
1918   The History of Religions. New York: Macmillan.

Hopkins, Kenneth N.
1980   Temporary Refuge: Otoe-Missouria Indians on the Big Blue Reservation, 1854–1881. (M.A. Thesis in History, Texas Christian University, Fort Worth, Tex.)

Hornaday, William T.
1889   The Extermination of the American Bison. Washington: Smithsonian Institution.

Horse Capture, George P.
1977   The Camera Eye of Sumner Matteson and the People Who Fooled Them All. *Montana: The Magazine of Western History* 27(3):58–71. Helena.

————, ed.
1980   Fourth Annual Plains Indian Seminar: Ribbonwork and Cloth Applique. [Cover title:] Native American Ribbonwork: A Rainbow Tradition. Cody, Wyo.: Buffalo Bill Historical Center.

————, ed.
1980a   The Seven Visions of Bull Lodge; As Told by His Daughter, Garter Snake. Gathered by Fred P. Gone. Ann Arbor, Mich.: Bear Claw Press. (Reprinted: University of Nebraska Press, Lincoln, 1992.)

————, ed.
1993   Robes of Splendor: Native American Painted Buffalo Hides. With contributions by George P. Horse Capture, Anne Vitart, Michael Waldberg, and W. Richard West, Jr.; Photographs of the Hides by Daniel Ponsard. (Musée de l'homme, Paris, Catalog.) New York: New Press, distributed by W.W. Norton.

Hothem, Lar
1986   Indian Flints of Ohio. Lancaster, Ohio: Hothem House Books.

Hotopp, John
1977   Iowa's Great River Road Cultural and Natural Resources. Vol. II: Archaeology, Geology and Natural Areas, A Preliminary Survey. *University of Iowa. Office of the State Archaeologist. Contract Report* 108. Iowa City.

Hotz, Gottfried
1935   Vor hundert Jahren am Missouri. *Atlantis: Länder, Völker, Reisen* 11:673–680. Leipzig, Germany.

1937   Über eine Büffeldecke mit indianischen Bilderschriften. *Zeitschrift für Ethnologie* 69(1/3):27–30. Berlin.

1960   Indianische Ledermalereien: Figurenreiche Darstellungen von Grenzkonflikten zwischen Mexiko und dem Missouri um 1720. Berlin: D. Reimer. (English editions: *see* Hotz 1970, 1991.)

1970   Indian Skin Paintings from the American Southwest: Two Representations of Border Conflicts between Mexico and the Missouri in the Early Eighteenth Century. Johannes Malthaner, trans. Norman: University of Oklahoma Press. (Reprinted under title: The Segesser Hide Paintings. University of New Mexico Press, Santa Fe, 1991. German ed.: *see* Hotz 1960.)

1991   The Segesser Hide Paintings: Masterpieces Depicting Spanish Colonial New Mexico. Johannes Malthaner, trans. Rev. ed., with a New Foreword by Thomas E. Chávez. Santa Fe: Museum of New Mexico Press. (First English ed. publ. under title: Indian Skin Paintings from the American Southwest. University of Oklahoma Press, Norman, 1970. German ed.: *see* Hotz 1960.)

Houck, Louis, ed.
1909   The Spanish Regime in Missouri: A Collection of Papers and Documents Relating to Upper Louisiana Principally within the Present Limits of Missouri during the Dominion of Spain, from the Archives of the Indies at Seville, etc. 2 vols. Chicago: R.R. Donnelley and Sons. (Reprinted: 2 vols in 1, Arno Press, New York, 1971.)

Hough, Walter
1908   Otis Tufton Mason. *American Anthropologist,* n.s. 10(4):661–667.

Hourie, Audreen
1991   Struggle for Métis Recognition: Education and Survival. Pp. 133–143 in The Struggle for Recognition: Canadian Justice and the Métis Nation. Samuel W. Corrigan and Lawrence J. Barkwell, eds. Winnipeg, Man.: Pemmican Publications.

House, John H.
1991   The Mississippian Sequence in the Menard Locality, Eastern Arkansas. Pp. 6–39 in Arkansas Before the Americans. Hester A. Davis, ed. *Arkansas Archeological Survey Research Series* 40. Fayetteville.

House, John H., and Henry McKelway
1982   Mississippian and Quapaw on the Lower Arkansas. Pp. 41–57 in A State Plan for the Conservation of Archeological Resources in Arkansas. Hester A. Davis, ed. *Arkansas Archeological Survey Research Series* 21. Fayetteville.

Howard, James H.
1951   Notes on the Dakota Grass Dance. *Southwestern Journal of Anthropology* 7(1):82–85. Albuquerque.

1952   The Sun Dance of the Turtle Mountain Ojibwa. *North Dakota History* 19(4):249–264. Bismarck.

1954   Plains Indian Feathered Bonnets. *Plains Anthropologist* 2:23–26.

1954a   Yanktonai Dakota Eagle Trapping. *Southwestern Journal of Anthropology* 19(1):69–74. Albuquerque.

1955   The Pan-Indian Culture of Oklahoma. *The Scientific Monthly* 18(5):215–220.

1955a   Two Dakota Winter Count Texts. *Plains Anthropologist* 5:13–30.

1955b   The Tree Dweller Cults of the Dakota. *Journal of American Folk-lore* 68(268):169–174.

1956   An Oto-Omaha Peyote Ritual. *Southwestern Journal of Anthropology* 12(4):432–446. Albuquerque.

1956a   The Persistence of Southern Cult Gorgets among the Historic Kansa. *American Antiquity* 21(3):301–303.

1957   The Mescal Bean Cult of the Central and Southern Plains: An Ancestor of the Peyote Cult? *American Anthropologist,* n.s. 59(1):75–87.

1958   The Turtle Mountain "Chippewa." *The North Dakota Quarterly* 26(2):37–46. Grand Forks, N.Dak.

1960   The Cultural Position of the Dakota: A Reassessment. Pp. 249–268 in Essays in the Science of Culture in Honor of Leslie A. White. Gertrude E. Dole and Robert L. Carneiro, eds. New York: Thomas Y. Crowell.

1960a   Dakota Winter Counts as a Source of Plains History. *Bureau of American Ethnology Bulletin* 173; *Anthropological Paper* 61. Washington: Smithsonian Institution; U.S. Government Printing Office.

1960b   The Northern Style Grass Dance Costume. *American Indian Hobbyist* 7(1):18–27. Alton, Ill.

1960c   Butterfly's Mandan Winter Count: 1833–1876. *Ethnohistory* 7(1):28–43.

1961   The Identity and Demography of the Plains-Ojibwa. *Plains Anthropologist* 6(13):171–178. (Reprinted in: *Nachrichtenblatt der Völkerkundlichen Arbeitsgemeinschaft* 4:91–100. Hamburg, Germany, 1963.)

1962   Two War Bundles from the Bungi or Plains-Ojibwa. *American Indian Tradition* 8:77–79. Alton, Ill.

1962a   Report of the Investigation of the Tony Glas Site, 32EM3, Emmons County, North Dakota. *University of North Dakota. Anthropological Papers* 1. Grand Forks, N.Dak.

_____ 1963–1965 *see* 1977 (reprint info.)

1965   The Ponca Tribe. In collaboration with Peter Le Claire, Tribal Historian, and Other Members of the Tribe. *Bureau of American Ethnology Bulletin* 195. Washington: Smithsonian Institution; U.S. Government Printing Office. (Reprinted: University of Nebraska Press, Lincoln, 1995.)

1965a   The Plains-Ojibwa or Bungi: Hunters and Warriors of the Northern Prairie, with Special Reference to the Turtle Mountain Band. *University of South Dakota. South Dakota Museum. Anthropological Papers* 1. Vermillion, S.Dak.

1966   The Dakota or Sioux Tribe. *University of South Dakota. Museum News* 27(5–6):1–10, (7–8):1–9, (9–10):1–9. Vermillion, S.Dak. (See also Howard, James H. 1966a.)

1966a   The Dakota or Sioux Indians: A Study in Human Ecology. *Dakota Museum. University of South Dakota. Anthropological Papers* 2. Vermillion, S.Dak. (Orginially appeared in: *Dakota Museum. University of South Dakota Museum News* 27(5–10), 1966.) (Reprinted: *Reprints in Anthropology* 20, J&L Reprint Company, Lincoln, 1980.)

1968   Archeological Investigations at the Spawn Mound, 39LK201, Lake County, South Dakota. *Plains Anthropologist* 13(40):132–145.

1968a   The Warrior Who Killed Custer: The Personal Narrative of Chief Joseph White Bull. Lincoln: University of Nebraska Press. (Reprinted: see 1998.)

1970   Known Village Sites of the Ponca. *Plains Anthropologist* 15(48):109–134.

1970a   1969 Archaeological Investigations at the Weston and Hogshooter Sites, Osage and Washington Counties, Oklahoma. *Bulletin of the Oklahoma Anthropological Society* 19:61–99. Oklahoma City.

1970b   The Dakota or Sioux Tribe: A Study in Human Ecology. Part I: The Santee or Eastern Dakota. *Powwow Trails* 7(1):5–16. Somerset, N.J.

1971   The Ponca Shinny Game. *The Indian Historian* 4(3):10–15. San Francisco.

1971a   Grandpa Saul Remembers: A Sioux Indian Paints His People's Past. *Oklahoma Historical Society Newsletter* 19(1):3–16, (2):3–6, (3):23–28, (4):11–14, (5):5–10, (6):5–6, (7):8–9, (8):3–5, (9):5–6.

1972   Arikara Native-made Glass Pendants: Their Probable Function. *American Antiquity* 37(1):93–97.

1972a   John F. Lenger: Music Man among the Santee. *Nebraska History* 53(2):[194] 195–215. Lincoln.

1972b   Firecloud's Omaha or Grass Dance Costume, Part 2. *American Indian Crafts and Culture* 6(3):2–8.

1972c   Notes on the Ethnogeography of the Yankton Dakota. *Plains Anthropologist* 17(58, Pt. 1):281–307.

1974   The Arikara Buffalo Society Medicine Bundle. *Plains Anthropologist* 19(66):241–271.

1976   Yanktonai Ethnohistory and the John K. Bear Winter Count. *Plains Anthropologist* 21(73, Pt. 2), *Memoir* 11. Lincoln.

1976a   The Plains Gourd Dance as a Revitalization Movement. *American Ethnologist* 3(2):243–259.

1977   The Plains-Ojibwa or Bungi: Hunters and Warriors of the Northern Prairies with Special Reference to the Turtle Mountain Band. *Reprints in Anthropology* 7. Lincoln, Nebr.: J&L Reprint Company. (Reprinted with omissions. Originally publ.: *University of South Dakota. South Dakota Museum. Museum News* 24(11–12)–26(1–2). Vermillion, S.Dak., 1963–1965.)

1978   The Native American Image in Western Europe. *The American Indian Quarterly* 4(1):33–56.

1979   Some Further Thoughts on Eastern Dakota "Clans." *Ethnohistory* 26(2):133–140.

1979a   The British Museum Winter Count. *British Museum. Department of Ethnography. Occasional Papers* 4. London: The British Museum.

1980   Birch Bark and Paper Cutouts: An Art Form of the Northern Woodlands and the Prairie Border. *American Indian Art Magazine* 5(4):54–61, 86–87. Scottsdale, Ariz.

1983   Pan-Indianism in Native American Music and Dance. *1177*

Ethnomusicology 27(1):71–82. Middletown, Conn., and Ann Arbor, Mich.

1984   The Canadian Sioux. *Studies in the Anthropology of North American Indians.* Raymond J. DeMallie and Douglas R. Parks, eds. Lincoln: University of Nebraska Press.

1998   Lakota Warrior: Joseph White Bull. Lincoln and London: University of Nebraska Press. (Originally publ. in 1968.)

Howard, James H., and Robert D. Gant
1966   Archeological Salvage Investigations in the Gavin's Point Reservoir Area. *University of South Dakota. South Dakota Museum. Archeological Studies Circulars* 11. Vermillion, S.Dak.

Howard, James H., and Gertrude P. Kurath
1959   Ponca Dances, Ceremonies and Music. *Ethnomusicology* 3(1):1–14. Middletown, Conn., and Ann Arbor, Mich.

Howard, James H., and Alan R. Woolworth
1954   An Arikara Bear Society Initiation Ceremony. *North Dakota History* 21(4):168–179. Bismarck.

Howard, Joseph Kinsey
1952   Strange Empire: Louis Riel and the Métis People. (Bibliography compiled by Rosalea Fox.) New York: William Morrow. (Reprinted: J. Lewis and Samuel, Toronto, 1974; also under title: Strange Empire, a Narrative of the Northwest, with a New Introduction by Nicholas C.P. Vrooman: Minnesota Historical Society Press, St. Paul, 1994.)

Howard, Kathleen L., and Diana F. Pardue
1996   Inventing the Southwest: The Fred Harvey Company and Native American Art. Flagstaff, Ariz.: Northland Pub.

Howard, Maj.Gen. Otis
1907   Life among Our Hostile Indians: A Record of Personal Observations, Adventures, and Campaigns among the Indians of the Great West with Some Account of their Life, Habits, Traits, Religions, Ceremonies, Dress, Savage Instincts, and Customs in Peace and War. Hartford: A.D. Worthington & Company.

Howe, M.A. DeWolfe
1911   The Life and Labors of Bishop Hare: Apostle to the Sioux. New York: Sturgis and Walton.

Howling Wolf, Dan
1977   Grasshopper, Ant and Mosquito Go Hunting. Bismarck: Mary College.

Hoxie, Frederick E.
1984   A Final Promise: The Campaign to Assimilate the Indians, 1880–1920. Lincoln: University of Nebraska Press.

1984a   Building a Future on the Past: Crow Indian Leadership in an Era of Division and Reunion. Pp. 76–84 in Indian Leadership. Walter Williams, ed. Manhattan, Kans.: Sunflower University Press.

1985   From Prison to Homeland: The Cheyenne River Reservation before World War I. Pp. 55–75 in The Plains Indians of the Twentieth Century. Edited and with an Introduction by Peter Iverson. Norman and London: University of Oklahoma Press. (Reprinted from: *South Dakota History* (Winter 1979):1–24.)

1989   The Crow. New York and Philadelphia: Chelsea House Publishers.

1995   Parading through History: The Making of the Crow Nation in America, 1805–1935. *Cambridge Studies in North American Indian History.* Frederick Hoxie and Neal Salisbury, eds. Cambridge and New York: Cambridge University Press.

1996   The Reservation Period, 1880–1960. Pp. 183–258 in The Cambridge History of the Native Peoples of the Americas. Vol. 1: North America, Part 2. Bruce G. Trigger and Wilcomb E. Washburn, eds. Cambridge and New York: Cambridge University Press.

Hrdlička, Aleš
1907   Skeletal Remains Suggesting or Attributed to Early Man in North America. Prefatory Note by W.H. Holmes. *Bureau of American Ethnology Bulletin* 33. Washington: Smithsonian Institution; U.S. Government Printing Office.

1910   Report on Skeletal Material from Missouri Mounds, Collected in 1906–07 by Mr. Gerard Fowke. Pp. 103–112 in Antiquities of Central and Southeastern Missouri, by Gerard Fowke. *Bureau of American Ethnology Bulletin* 37. Washington: Smithsonian Institution; U.S. Government Printing Office.

Hubach, Robert R.
1961   Early Midwestern Travel Narratives: An Annotated Bibliography, 1634–1850. Detroit: Wayne State University Press.

Hubner, Brian
1995   Horse Stealing and the Borderline: The NWMP and the Control of Indian Movement, 1874–1900. *Prairie Forum* 20(2):281–300. Regina, Sask.: Canadian Plains Research Center, University of Regina.

Hudson, Charles
1985   De Soto in Arkansas: A Brief Synopsis. *Field Notes: Newsletter of the Arkansas Archeological Society* 205(July/August):3–12.

Hudson's Bay Company
1717   [Journal, June to July 1717.] (Manuscript b.239/d/9, June to July, Hudson's Bay Company Archives, Provincial Archives of Manitoba, Winnipeg.)

1789–1804   Untitled Indian Map in Peter Fidler's Journal of Exploration and Survey. (Maps E. 3/2 fos. 105d., 106, Hudson's Bay Company Archives, Provincial Archives of Manitoba, Winnipeg.)

1967   Saskatchewan Journals and Correspondence: Edmonton House 1795–1800; Chesterfield House 1800–1802. Alice M. Johnson, ed. *Publications of the Hudson's Bay Company Record Society* 26. London: Hudson's Bay Company Record Society.

Hudson's Bay Company Archives
1985   Guide to Research Tools in the Hudson's Bay Company Archives, Provincial Archives of Manitoba. [Typescript, rev. ed.] Winnipeg, Man.: Hudson's Bay Company Archives, Provincial Archives of Manitoba.

Huebner, Jeffrey A.
1991   Late Prehistoric Bison Populations in Central and Southern Texas. *Plains Anthropologist* 36(137):343–358.

Huel, Raymond J.A.
1989   The Oblates, the Métis, and 1885: The Breakdown of Traditional Relationships. *Canadian Catholic Historical Association. Historical Studies/Cahiers historiques* 56:9–29. Ottawa.

1996   Proclaiming the Gospel to the Indians and the Métis. Edmonton, Alta.: University of Alberta Press/Canadian Publishers.

Huemer, Alan Anthony
1976   The Primitive Politics of the Sun Dance Nation. (Ph.D. Dissertation in Political Science, University of Hawaii, Honolulu.)

Huenemann, Lynn
1978 Songs and Dance of Native America: A Resource Text for Teachers and Students. Tsaile, Ariz.: Education House.

Hughes, Andrew S.
1837 [Letter to William Clark, dated Great Nemahaw Subagency, August 26, 1837.] (Microfilm M234, Roll 751, Letters Received, the Bureau of Indian Affairs, St. Louis Superintendency, 1824–1851, Record Group 75, National Archives, Washington.)

Hughes, Anne E.
1914 The Beginning of Spanish Settlement in the El Paso District. *University of California. Publications in History* 1(5). Berkeley, Calif.

Hughes, David T.
1985 1985 Excavations in the Wolf Creek Valley, Ociltree County, Texas. (Paper presented at the Annual Meeting of the Texas Archeological Society, San Antonio, Tex.)

1986 The Courson 1986 Archaeological Project. (Paper presented at the Annual Meeting of the Texas Archeological Society, Laredo, Tex.)

Hughes, David T., and A. Alicia Hughes-Jones
1987 The Courson Archaeological Projects, 1985 and 1986: A Final Report of the 1985 Investigations and Preliminary Report of the 1986 Work. (Cover Title: The Courson Archaeological Projects, Final 1985 and Preliminary 1986.) Perryton, Tex.: Courson Archaeological Projects.

Hughes, Jack T.
1949 Investigations in Western South Dakota and Northeastern Wyoming. *American Antiquity* 14(4):266–277.

1962 Lake Creek: A Woodland Site in the Texas Panhandle. *Bulletin of the Texas Archeological Society* 32 (for 1961):65–84. Austin.

1968 Prehistory of the Caddoan-speaking Tribes. (Ph.D. Dissertation in Anthropology, Columbia University, New York City. Published: Garland, New York, 1974.)

Hughes, Thomas
1927 Indian Chiefs of Southern Minnesota: Containing Sketches of the Prominent Chieftains of the Dakota and Winnebago Tribes from 1825 to 1865. Illustrated by A. Anderson. Mankato, Minn.: Free Press Company.

1929 Old Traverse des Sioux. St. Peter, Minn.: Herald Publishing Company.

Huld, Martin E.
1983 Athapaskan Bears. *International Journal of American Linguistics* 49(2):186–195. Chicago.

Hultgren, Mary Lou, and Paulette Fairbanks Molin
1989 To Lead and To Serve: American Indian Education at Hampton Institute, 1878–1923. Charlottesville, Va.: Virginia Foundation for the Humanities and Public Policy in cooperation with Hampton University.

Hultkrantz, Åke
1952 Some Notes on the Arapaho Sun Dance. *Ethnos* 17(1/4):24–38. Stockholm: National Museum of Ethnography.

1960 Religious Aspects of the Wind River Shoshoni Folklore Literature. Pp. 552–569 in Culture in History: Essays in Honor of Paul Radin. Stanley Diamond, ed. New York: Columbia University Press.

1965 The Study of North American Indian Religion: Retrospect, Prospect, Current Trends and Future Tasks. *Temenos: Studies in Comparative Religion* 1:87–121. Helsinki: Suomen Uskontotieteellinen Seura.

1966 North American Indian Religions in the History of Research: A General Survey. *History of Religion* 6/7. Chicago.

1967 The Religions of the American Indians. Berkeley: University of California Press.

1968 Shoshoni Indians on the Plains: An Appraisal of the Documentary Evidence. *Zeitschrift für Ethnologie* 93(1–2): 49–72. Berlin.

1969 Yellow Hand, Chief and Medicine-man among the Eastern Shoshoni. Pp. 293–304 in Vol. 2 of *Verhandlungen des XXXVIII Internationalen Amerikanistenkongresses.* [*Proceedings of the 38th International Congress of Americanists*] *Stuttgart-Müchen 12. bis 18. August 1968.* 4 vols. München: Kommissionsverlag Klaus Renner, 1969–1972.

1971 The Structure of Theistic Beliefs among North American Plains Indians. *Temenos: Studies in Comparative Religion* 7: 66–74. Helsinki: Suomen Uskontotieteellinen Seura.

1973 Prairie and Plains Indians. Leiden, Netherlands: E.J. Brill.

1979 The Religions of the American Indian. Berkeley: University of California Press.

1979a The Traditional Symbolism of the Sun Dance Lodge among the Wind River Shoshoni. Pp. 70–95 in Religious Symbols and Their Functions. Haralds Biezais, ed. Stockholm: Scripta Instituti Donneriani Aboensis.

1980 The Development of the Plains Indian Sun Dance. Pp. 223–243 in Perennitas: Studi in onore di Angelo Brelich. Roma, [Italy]: Edizioni dell'Ateneo.

1981 Belief and Worship in Native North America. Syracuse, N.Y.: Syracuse University Press.

1986 Peril of Visions: Changes of Vision Patterns among the Wind River Shoshoni *History of Religions* 26(1):34–46. Chicago.

1990 Decade of Progress: Works on the North American Indian Religions in the 1980s. Pp. 167–201 in Religions in Native North America. Christopher Vecsey, ed. Moscow: University of Idaho Press.

Humboldt, Alexander von
1827 Essai Politique sur le Royaume de la Nouvelle-Espagne. 2 vols. Paris.

Humfreville, James Lee
1902 Twenty Years among our Hostile Indians. Describing the Characteristics, Customs, Habits, Religions, Marriages, Dances, and Battles of the Wild Indians in their Natural State. New York: Hunter & Co.

Humphrey, Seth K.
1906 The Indian Dispossessed. Rev. ed. Boston: Little, Brown.

Hundley, Norris, Jr.
1985 The *Winters* Decision and Indian Water Rights: A Mystery Reexamined. Pp. 77–106 in The Plains Indians of the Twentieth Century. Edited and with an Introduction by Peter Iverson. Norman: University of Oklahoma Press. (Reprinted from: *Western Historical Quarterly* (January, 1982):17–42.)

Hungry Wolf, Adolf
1975 Blackfoot People: A Tribal Handbook. *Good Medicine Books* 12. Invermere, B.C.: Good Medicine Books.

1977 Blood People: A Division of the Blackfoot Confederacy. New York: Harper and Row.

1987 Children of the Sun: Stories By and About Indian Kids. New York: William Morrow and Company.

Hungry Wolf, Beverly
1982   The Ways of My Grandmothers. New York: Quill.

1996   Daughters of the Buffalo Women: Maintaining Tribal Faith. Skookumchuck, B.C.: Canadian Caboose Press.

Hunt, Charles B.
1974   Natural Regions of the United States and Canada. San Francisco: W.H. Freeman.

Hunt, David C., Marsha V. Gallagher, William H. Goetzmann, and William J. Orr 1984 *see* Bodmer, Karl 1984

Hunt, Jerome
1907   Catholic *Wocekiye Wowapi*. Fort Totten, N.Dak.: Catholic Indian Mission.

Hunter, James
1875   A Lecture on the Grammatical Construction of the Cree Language [1862]. London: Printed for the Society for Promoting Christian Knowledge.

Hunter, John D.
1823   Memoirs of a Captivity among the Indians of North America, from Childhood to the Age of Nineteen.... London: Longman, Hurst, Rees, Orme and Brown.

Hunter, Sara
1977   Northern Arapahoe Grandparents: Traditional Concepts and Contemporary Socio-Economics. (M.A. Thesis in Anthropology, Indiana University, Bloomington.)

Hurt, Wesley R., Jr.
1950   Notes on the Dakota Indians. *University of South Dakota. W.H. Over Museum. Museum News* 11(12):1–30. Vermillion, S.Dak.

1951   Report on the Investigation of the Swanson Site, 39BrI6, Brule County, South Dakota, 1950. *South Dakota. State Archaeological Commission. Archaeological Studies Circulars* 3. Pierre, S.Dak.

1952   Report of the Investigation of the Scalp Creek Site 39GR1; and the Ellis Creek Site, 39GR2, Gregory County, South Dakota, 1941, 1951. *South Dakota. State Archaeological Commission. Archaeological Studies Circulars* 4. Pierre, S.Dak.

1952a   The Dakota "Give-Away" Ceremony. *University of South Dakota. W.H. Over Museum. Museum News* 13(1):1–3. Vermillion, S.Dak.

1953   Report of the Investigation of the Thomas Riggs Site, 39HU1, Hughes County, South Dakota. *South Dakota. State Archaeological Commission. Archaeological Studies Circulars* 5. Pierre, S.Dak.

1953a   House Types of the Santee. *State University of South Dakota. W.H. Over Museum. Museum Notes* 14(11):1–3. Vermillion, S.Dak.

1954   Pottery Types of the Over Focus, South Dakota. In Prehistoric Pottery of the Eastern United States. James B. Griffin, ed. Ann Arbor: University of Michigan, Museum of Archaeology.

1960   Factors in the Persistence of Peyote in the Northern Plains. *Plains Anthropologist* 5(9):16–27.

1960a   The Yankton Church: A Nationalistic Movement of the Northern Plains Indians. Pp. 269–287 in Essays in the Science of Culture in Honor of Leslie A. White. Gertrude E. Dole and Robert L. Carneiro, eds. New York: T.Y. Crowell.

1961   Archaeological Work at the Tabor and Arp Sites. *University of South Dakota. W.H. Over Museum. Museum News* 22(8):1–6. Vermillion, S.Dak.

1962   The Urbanization of the Yankton Indians. *Human Organization* 20(4):227–245. Washington.

1966   The Altithermal and the Prehistory of the Northern Plains. Pp. 101–114 in Proceedings of the VII Congress, International Association for Quaternary Research, INQUA; Boulder - Denver - Colorado U.S.A., August 14–September 19, 1965. Arranged by H.E. Wright, Jr., and F. Clark Howell. *Quaternaria: Storia Naturale e Culturale del Quaternario* VIII (Volume 15). Roma, [Italy].

1969   Seasonal Economic and Settlement Patterns of the Arikara. *Plains Anthropologist* 14(43):32–37.

1974   Sioux Indians II: Dakota Sioux Indians. *American Indian Ethnohistory: Plains Indians.* David Agee Horr, comp. and ed. New York: Garland Publishing.

Hurt, Wesley R., and James H. Howard
1952   A Dakota Conjuring Ceremony. *Southwestern Journal of Anthropology* 8(3):286–296. Albuquerque.

Hurt, Wesley R., Jr., and William E. Lass
1956   Frontier Photographer: Stanley J. Morrow's Dakota Years. Vermillion, S.Dak.: University of South Dakota.

Huscher, Betty H., and Harold A. Huscher
1942   Athapaskan Migration via the Intermontane Region. *American Antiquity* 8(1):80–88.

1943   The Hogan Builders of Colorado. Gunnison, Colo.: Colorado Archaeological Society. (Reprinted from *Southwestern Lore* 9(2), 1943.)

Huss, Peggy A.
1980   Quill and Beadwork of the Plains Indians: A Study of the Case Collection at the University of Colorado Museum. (M.A. Thesis in Anthropology, University of Colorado, Boulder.)

Husted, Wilfred M.
1965   The Meander Site (39LM201) in Fort Randall Reservoir, South Dakota. *Plains Anthropologist* 10(29):171–180.

1968   Wyoming. Pp. 63–68 in The Northwestern Plains: A Symposium. W.W. Caldwell, ed. *The Center for Indian Studies. Rocky Mountain College. Occasional Papers* 1. Billings, Mont.

1969   Bighorn Canyon Archeology. *Smithsonian Institution. River Basin Surveys. Publications in Salvage Archaeology* 12. Lincoln. (Reprinted: J&L Reprint Company, Lincoln, 1991.)

1978   Excavation Techniques and Culture Layer Analyses. Pp. 50–145 in The Mummy Cave Project in Northwestern Wyoming. Harold McCracken, ed. Cody, Wyo.: Buffalo Bill Historical Center.

Husted, Wilfred M., and Robert Edgar
1968   The Archaeology of Mummy Cave, Wyoming: An Introduction to Shoshonean Prehistory. (Manuscript in W.M. Husted's possession.)

Hutchinson, Gerald M. 1977 *see* Rundle, Robert Terrill 1977

Hutton, Paul Andrew
1985   Phil Sheridan and His Army. Lincoln: University of Nebraska Press.

Hyde, George E.
1937   Red Cloud's Folk: A History of the Oglala Sioux Indians. Norman: University of Oklahoma Press. (Rev. ed. 1957.)

1951   Pawnee Indians. Denver, Colo.: University of Denver Press. (Reprinted: University of Oklahoma Press, Norman, 1974.)

1951–1952   The Mystery of the Arikaras. [2 Pts.] *North Dakota History* 18(4):187–218, 19(1):25–58. Bismarck.

1952   Rangers and Regulars. Columbus, Ohio: Long's College Book Company.

1956   A Sioux Chronicle. Norman: University of Oklahoma Press.

1959   Indians of the High Plains: From the Prehistoric Period to the Coming of the Europeans. Norman: University of Oklahoma Press. (Reprinted in 1966.)

1961   Spotted Tail's Folk: A History of the Brulé Sioux. Norman: University of Oklahoma Press.

1968   Life of George Bent; Written from His Letters. Savoie Lottinville, ed. Norman: University of Oklahoma Press. (Reprinted in 1983.)

Hyer, Joseph K., and William S. Starring, comps.
1866   Lahcotah: Dictionary of the Sioux Language. Compiled with the Aid of Charles Guerreu, Indian Interpreter. Fort Laramie, Dakota [Terr.]: [The Authors]. (Facsimile reprint: Yale University Press, New Haven, Conn., 1968.)

Hyer, Sally
1990   One House, One Voice, One Heart: Native American Education at the Santa Fe Indian School. Santa Fe: Museum of New Mexico Press.

Hymes, Dell H.
1957   A Note on Athapaskan Glottochronology. *International Journal of American Linguistics* 23(4):291–297. Chicago.

1987   Tonkawa Poetics: John Rush Buffalo's "Coyote and Eagle's Daughter." Pp. 17–61 in Native American Discourse: Poetics and Rhetoric. Joel Sherzer and Anthony C. Woodbury, eds. *Cambridge Studies in Oral and Literate Culture* 13. Cambridge, Mass.

IHC = Illinois State Historical Library
1903–   Illinois State Historical Collections. [-vols.] Springfield, Ill.: Illinois State Historical Library.

Iapi Oaye
1871–1939   *Iapi Oaye/Word Carrier.* 68 vols. Greenwood, Dak.Terr. [S.Dak.]: Dakota Mission (1871–1887); Santee, Nebr.: Santee Normal Institute (1888–1939).

Imlay, Gilbert
1793   A Topographical Description of the Western Territory on North America; Containing a Succinct Account of Its Soil, Climate, Natural History, Population, Agriculture, Manners, and Customs, [etc.]. 2 vols. [Vol. 2 has title: The Discovery, Settlement, and Present State of Kentucky ... Being a Supplement to Imlay's Description of the Western Territory; by John Filson.] New York: S. Campbell. (Reprinted: Johnson Reprint Corporation, New York, 1968.)

Indian Arts and Crafts Board
1973   Painted Tipis by Contemporary Plains Indian Artists. With an Introduction by Myles Libhart and Rosemary Ellison. Blackfeet Tipi Legends by Cecile Black Boy. An Exhibition organized by the Indian Arts and Crafts Board of the U.S. Department of the Interior. Anadarko: Oklahoma Indian Arts and Crafts Cooperative.

Indian Association of Alberta
1970   Citizens Plus: A Presentation by the Indian Chiefs of Alberta to Right Honourable P.E. Trudeau, Prime Minister and the Government of Canada. Edmonton: Indian Association of Alberta.

Indian Country Today, July 28, 1997; June 8, 1999; January 31, 2000. Rapid City, S.Dak.

Indian Health Service
1996   Trends in Indian Health. Rockville, Md.: Indian Health Service.

Indians at Work
1942   Indian Soldiers Vow to Dance in Berlin. *Indians at Work* 10(1):16–17. Washington: Bureau of Indian Affairs.

1945   Ceremonial Dances in the Pacific [by Ernie Pyle.] *Indians at Work* 1945. Washington: Bureau of Indian Affairs.

Indian News 1992 *see* Bureau of Indian Affairs 1992

Innis, Ben
1994   Bloody Knife: Custer's Favorite Scout. Richard E. Collin, ed. Bismarck, N.Dak.: Smoky Water Press.

Investigation of the Bureau of Indian Affairs 1953, 1954 *see* U.S. Congress. House. Committee on Interior and Insular Affairs 1953, 1954

Iowa Chiefs
1864   [Petition of December 29, 1864, Asking Permission to Get Medicine and Help from Druggist in White Cloud, etc.] (Microfilm M234, Roll 312, Correspondence of the Office of Indian Affairs, Record Group 75, National Archives, Washington.)

Ireland, Stephen K.
1970   Purgatoire River Reservoir Salvage Archaeology, 1969: Sites TC:C9:4 and TC:C9:9. Trinidad, Colo.: Trinidad State Junior College, Department of Anthropology.

Irvin, Samuel McCleary
1841–1849   [Diary of a Journal Kept at Ioway Mission....] (Microfilm Box No. 89, Samuel M. Irvin Collection, Manuscripts Department, Kansas State Historical Society, Topeka.)

1846   [Report to Major W.E. Rucker, dated Iowa and Sac Mission, September 21.] Pp. 371–373 in Report of the Commissioner of Indian Affairs, War Department, for 1846. Washington.

1871   The Waw-ru-haw-a. The Decline and Fall of Indian Superstitions. Outline of a Talk to the Theological Students in the Western Theological Seminary, Allegheny City, Pa. Philadelphia: A. Martien.

Irvin, Samuel McCleary, and William Hamilton 1847 *see* ARCIA 1824–1848

Irvine, A.G.
1882   [Letter to White, dated Fort Walsh, 20 May 1882.] (Record Group 10, Vol. 3744, File 29506-2, National Archives of Canada, Ottawa.)

Irving, John Treat
1835   Indian Sketches; Taken During an Expedition to the Pawnee Tribes. 2 vols. Philadelphia: Carey, Lea and Blanchard. (Reprinted: John F. McDermott, ed., 2 vols., University of Oklahoma Press, Norman, 1955. Originally publ. also under title: Indian Sketches Taken During an Expedition to the Pawnee and Other Tribes of American Indians. 2 vols. John Murray, London, 1835.)

1837   The Hawk Chief: A Tale of the Indian Country. Philadelphia: Carey, Lea and Blanchard; also, under title: The Hunters of the Prairie: Or, The Hawk Chief: A Tale of the Indian Country. London: R. Bentley.

1955 *see* 1835 (reprint info.)

Irving, Washington
1868   Astoria; or, Anecdotes of an Enterprise Beyond the Rocky Mountains. New York: G.P. Putnam and Son.

Irwin, Henry J., and Cynthia Irwin
1959   Excavations at the LoDaisKa Site in the Denver, Colorado, Area. *Denver Museum of Natural History, Proceedings* 8. Denver.

1961   Radiocarbon Dates from the LoDaisKa Site, Colorado. *American Antiquity* 27(1):114–115.

Irwin, Lee
1994   The Dream Seekers: Native American Visionary Traditions of the Great Plains. Foreword by Vine Deloria, Jr. Norman: University of Oklahoma Press.

_____
1997   Freedom, Law, and Prophecy: A Brief History of Native American Religious Resistance. *American Indian Quarterly* 21(1):35–55. Hurst, Tex.

Irwin, William
1890–1900 [Photographs of Comanches.] (In Amon-Carter Museum, Fort Worth, Texas.)

Irwin-Williams, Cynthia, and Henry T. Irwin
1966   Excavations at Magic Mountain: A Diachronic Study of Plains-Southwest Relations. *Denver Museum of Natural History. Proceedings* 12. Denver.

Isenberg, Andrew C.
2000   The Destruction of the Bison: An Environmental History, 1750–1920. New York: Cambridge University Press.

Isham, James
1949   James Isham's Observations on Hudsons Bay, 1743; and Notes and Observations on a Book entitled *A Voyage to Hudsons Bay in the Dobbs Galley, 1749.* Edwin E. Rich, ed., assisted by A.M. Johnson. *Publications of the Champlain Society. Hudson's Bay Company Series* 12. London and Toronto: The Champlain Society. (Half-title: Isham's Observations and Notes, 1743–1749. Reprinted: Kraus Reprint, Nendeln, Lichtenstein, 1968.)

Iverson, Peter, ed.
1985   The Plains Indians of the Twentieth Century. Edited and with an Introduction by Peter Iverson. Norman: University of Oklahoma Press.

Ives, John C.
1955   Glenwood Ceramics. *Journal of the Iowa Archeological Society* 4(3 and 4). Iowa City.

_____
1962   Mill Creek Pottery. *Journal of the Iowa Archeological Society* 11(3):1–59. Iowa City.

Izard, George
1827   [French-Quapaw Vocabulary.] (Manuscript No. 185(34) in the Library of the American Philosophical Society, Philadelphia.)

JR = Thwaites, Reuben G. ed.
1896–1901 The Jesuit Relations and Allied Documents: Travel and Explorations of the Jesuit Missionaries in New France, 1610–1791. The Original French, Latin and Italian Texts, with English Translations and Notes. 73 vols. Cleveland, Ohio: Burrows Brothers. (Reprinted: Pageant, New York, 1959.)

Jablow, Joseph
1951   The Cheyenne in Plains Indian Trade Relations, 1795–1840. *Monographs of the American Ethnological Society* 19. Seattle: University of Washington Press. (Reprinted in 1966; also, with an Introduction by Morris W. Foster: University of Nebraska Press, Lincoln, 1994.)

_____
1974   Ponca Indians. *American Indian Ethnohistory: Plains Indians.* David Agee Horr, comp. and ed. New York: Garland.

Jacknis, Ira
1990   In Search of the Imagemaker: James Mooney as an Ethnogaphic Photographer. Pp. 179–212 in Picturing Cultures: Historical Photographs in Anthropological Inquiry. Joanna Cohan Scherer, guest ed. *Visual Anthropology* 3(2–3), Special Issue. Chur, London, [etc.]: Harwood Academic Publishers.

Jackson, Andrew
1832   Message from the President of the United States, in Compliance with a Resolution of the Senate Concerning the Fur Trade, and Inland Trade to Mexico; [dated] Washington, February 8, 1832. *22d Congress. 1st Session. Senate Executive Document No.* 90. (Serial No. 213). Washington.

Jackson, Curtis E., and Marcia J. Galli
1977   A History of the Bureau of Indian Affairs and Its Activities among Indians. San Francisco: R and E Research Associates.

Jackson, Donald D.
1960   Lewis and Clark among the Oto. *Nebraska History* 41(3):237–248. Lincoln.
_____, ed.
1962   Letters of the Lewis and Clark Expedition; With Related Documents, 1783–1854. Urbana: University of Illinois Press. (Reprinted, 2d ed., 1978.)
_____, ed.
1966   The Journals of Zebulon Montgomery Pike with Letters and Related Documents. 2 vols. Norman: University of Oklahoma Press. (Originally publ. under title: An Account of Expeditions to the Sources of the Mississippi; C&A Conrad, Philadelphia, 1810.)
_____, ed.
1978   Letters of the Lewis and Clark Expedition; With Related Documents, 1783–1854. 2d ed. 2 vols. Urbana: University of Illinois Press. (Reprinted in 1992.)

Jackson, Donald D., and Mary Lee Spence, eds.
1970   The Expeditions of John Charles Frémont. 2 vols. and map portfolio. Urbana: University of Illinois Press.

Jackson, Helen Hunt
1998   The Indian Reform Letters of Helen Hunt Jackson, 1879–1885. Valerie Sherer Mathes, ed. Norman: University of Oklahoma Press.

Jackson, John
1982   The Branden House and the Mandan Connection. *North Dakota History* 49(1):11–19. Bismarck.

Jackson, Royal G.
1987   An Oral History of the Battle of the Little Big Horn from the Perspective of Northern Cheyenne Descendants: Final Report. Corvallis, Oreg.: The University (University of Wyoming, National Park Service Research Center Contract # CX1200-4-A037. Cover Title: Custer Battlefield National Monument, Oral History Program: Final Report.)

Jackson, William H.
1877   Descriptive Catalogue of Photographs of North American Indians; by W.H. Jackson, Photographer of the Survey. *Department of the Interior. United States Geological Survey of the Territories. Miscellaneous Publications* 9. F.V. Hayden, U.S. Geologist. Washington: Government Printing Office.

_____
1940   Time Exposure: The Autobiography of William Henry Jackson. New York: G.P. Putnam's Sons.

Jacobs, Wilbur R.
1950   Diplomacy and Indian Gifts: Anglo-French Rivalry along the Ohio and Northwest Frontiers, 1748–1763. Stanford, Calif.: Stanford University Press.

Jacobsen, Claes-Håkan
[1990] Rosebud Sioux: Ett folk i förvandling. Stockholm: Förlag C-H Jacobsen Produktion AB.

Jacobson, Oscar Brousse
1929   Kiowa Indian Art: Watercolor Paintings in Color by the Indians of Oklahoma. Nice, France: C. Szwedzicki.

Jacobson, Oscar Brousse, and Jeanne d'Ucel
1950   Les peintres indiens d'Amerique. Nice, France: C. Szwedzicki.

Jahner, Elaine A.
1975   Spatial Categories in Sioux Folk Narrative. (Ph.D. Dissertation in Folklore, Indiana University, Bloomington.)

_____, ed. 1983 *see* Walker, James R. 1983

_____
1987   Lakota Genesis: The Oral Tradition. Pp. 45–65 in Sioux Indian Religion: Tradition and Innovation. Raymond J. DeMallie and Douglas R. Parks, eds. Norman: University of Oklahoma Press.

James, Edwin, comp.
1823   Account of an Expedition from Pittsburgh to the Rocky Mountains, Performed in the Years 1819 and '20; by Order of the Hon. J.C. Calhoun, Sec'y of War: Under the Command of Major Stephen H. Long. 2 vols. with an Atlas. Philadelphia: H.C. Carey and I. Lea. (Reprinted in Vols. 14–17 of Early Western Travels, 1748–1846. Reuben G. Thwaites, ed. Arthur H. Clark, Cleveland, Ohio, 1904–1907; also, University Microfilms, Ann Arbor, Mich., 1966.)

_____, ed. 1830, 1956 *see* Tanner, John 1830 and (reprint info.)

_____ 1904–1907 [in Thwaites, ed.] *see* 1823 (reprint info.)

James, Eli
1983   Pervasive Nasality in Lakhota. Pp. 5–7 in Proceedings of the Second Siouan Languages Conference, 1982. Mary C. Marino, ed. *Na'pāo: A Saskatchewan Anthropology Journal* 13(October): Special Issue. Saskatoon, Sask.

James, Thomas
1846   Three Years among the Indians and Mexicans. Waterloo, Ill.: Everett D. Graff. (Reprinted: Walter Bond Douglas, ed. Missouri Historical Society, St. Louis, 1916; also, *Annual Lakeside Classics* 51, Lakeside Press, Chicago, 1953; Citadel Press, New York, 1966; and University of Nebraska Press, Lincoln, 1984.)

_____
1984   Three Years among the Indians and Mexicans. Milo Milton Quaife, ed. Lincoln: University of Nebraska Press. (Originally publ.: Everett D. Graff, Waterloo, Ill., 1846. Reprinted: *Annual Lakeside Classics* 51, Lakeside Press, Chicago, 1953.)

Jameson, Sheilagh S.
1984   W.J. Oliver: Life Through a Master's Lens. Calgary, Alta.: Glenbow Museum.

Jamieson, Melvill Allan
1936   Medals Awarded to North American Indian Chiefs, 1714–1922, and to Loyal African and Other Chiefs in Various Territories within the British Empire. London, S.W.I.: Spink and Son, Ltd.

Jamison, John
1817   [Letter to the Secretary of War, dated Red River Indian Agency, Natchitoches, 10th June, 1817.] (Manuscript J129-10, Microfilm M221, Roll 74 in Letters Received by the Secretary of War, Series 1801–1860, National Archives, Washington.)

_____
1817a   [Letter to the Secretary of War, dated Red River Indian Agency, Natchitoches, 19th August, 1817.] (Manuscript J186-10, Microfilm M221, Roll 74 in Letters Received by the Secretary of War, Series 1801–1860, National Archives, Washington.)

Janson, Charles W.
1807   The Stranger in America: Continuing Observations Made During a Long Residence in That Country, [etc.]. London: Printed for J. Cundee. (Reprinted as: The Stranger in America, 1793–1806. B. Franklin, New York, 1971.)

Jayne, Mary P.
1907   [Diaries and Records of the Oto-Pawnee Church, and the Cluemet Indian Baptist Church, kept by Baptist Missionary Mary P. Jayne, 1898–1915.] (Microfilm No. 516, 2 Rolls, Western History Collections, University of Oklahoma, Norman.)

Jefferson, James, Robert W. Delaney, and Gregory C. Thompson
1972   The Southern Utes: A Tribal History. Ignacio, Colo.: Southern Ute Tribe.

Jefferson, Robert
1929   Fifty Years on the Saskatchewan: Being a History of the Cree Indian Domestic Life and the Difficulties Which Led to Serious Agitation and Conflict of 1885 in the Battleford Locality. As Written by Robert Jefferson, with a Foreword by James G. Gardiner. *Canadian North-west Historical Society Publications* 1(5). Battleford, Sask.

Jefferson, Thomas
[1803]   Jefferson's Instructions to Lewis (20 June 1803). Pp. 61–66 in Vol. 1 of Letters of the Lewis and Clark Expedition; With Related Documents, 1783–1854. Donald D. Jackson, ed. 2 vols. 2d ed. University of Illinois Press, Urbana, 1978.

_____
1804   Estimate of the Number of Indian Warriors in Louisiana [by Meriwether Lewis.] (Manuscript in Thomas Jefferson Papers, Series 1: Dec. 31, 1804 — March 23, 1805, Manuscripts Division, Library of Congress, Washington.)

_____ 1806, 1832 *see* Lewis, Meriwether, [and William Clark] 1832

_____
1825   Notes on the State of Virginia. (With "An appendix ... relative to the Murder of Logan's Family"). Philadelphia: H.C. Carey and I. Lea. (The "1st hot-pressed ed." publ. by R.T. Rawle, Philadelphia, 1801.)

Jefferys, Thomas
1761   The Natural and Civil History of the French Dominions in North and South America. 2 Pts. in 1 Vol. London: Printed for T. Jefferys.

_____
1776   The American Atlas; or, A Geographical Description of the Whole Continent of America.... London: R. Sayer and J. Bennett. (Reprinted: Theatrum Orbis Terrarum, Amsterdam, 1974.)

Jelinek, Arthur J.
1967   A Prehistoric Sequence in the Middle Pecos Valley, New Mexico. *University of Michigan. Museum of Anthropology. Anthropological Papers* 31. Ann Arbor.

Jelks, Edward B., ed.
1967   The Gilbert Site: A Norteño Focus in Northeastern Texas. *Bulletin of the Texas Archaeological Society* 37; *University of Texas. Department of Anthropology. Archaeology Series* 5. Dallas.

Jenkins, John Holland
[1958]   Recollections of Early Texas: The Memoirs of John Holland Jenkins, III. Austin: University of Texas Press.

Jenks, Tudor
1893   The Century World's Fair Book for Boys and Girls: Beginning the Adventure of Harry and Philip with Their Tutor, Mr. Douglass, at the World's Columbian Exposition. New York: The Century Co.

Jenness, Diamond
1932   The Indians of Canada. *Anthropological Series* 15, *National Museum of Canada Bulletin* 65. Ottawa. (Reprinted, 7th ed.: University of Toronto Press, Toronto, 1977.)

_____
1938   The Sarcee Indians of Alberta. *National Museum of Canada. Department of Mines and Resources. Bulletin* 90. Ottawa.

Jennings, Jesse D.
1974   Prehistory of North America. 2d ed. New York: McGraw-Hill.

1183

Jensen, Richard E.
1965   Archaeology of the Sommers Site (39ST56), Big Bend Reservoir, South Dakota. (Manuscript in the Midwest Archaeological Center, National Park Service, Lincoln.)

_____, ed. 1997 *see* Allen, Charles W. 1997

1998   The Wright-Beauchampe Investigation and the Pawnee Threat of 1829. *Nebraska History* 79(3):133–143. Lincoln.

1998a   The Fontenelle and Cabanné Trading Posts: The History and Archaeology of Two Missouri River Sites, 1822–1838. Lincoln: Nebraska State Historical Society.

Jensen, Richard E., R. Eli Paul, and John E. Carter
1991   Eyewitness at Wounded Knee. Lincoln: University of Nebraska Press.

Jerome Agreement 1892 *see* U.S. Senate 1893

Jeter, Marvin D.
1989   Protohistoric and Historic Americans. Pp. 221–248 in Archeology and Bioarcheology of the Lower Mississippi Valley and Trans-Mississippi South in Arkansas and Louisiana. M.D. Jeter, J.S. Rose, G.I. Williams, Jr., and A.M. Harmon, eds. *Arkansas Archeological Survey Research Series* 37. Fayetteville.

Jilek, Wolfgang G.
1982   Indian Healing: Shamanic Ceremonialism in the Pacific Northwest Today. Surrey, B.C., and Blaine, Wash.: Hancock House.

1992   The Renaissance of Shamanic Dance in Indian Populations of North America. *Diogenes* 158:87–100. New York.

Jobson, Valerie
1985   The Blackfoot and the Rationing System. *Alberta History* 33(4):13–17. Calgary: Historical Society of Alberta.

John, Elizabeth A.H.
1975   Storms Brewed in Other Men's Worlds: The Confrontation of Indians, Spanish, and French in the Southwest. College Station, Tex.: Texas A&M University Press. (Reprinted: University of Nebraska Press, Lincoln, 1985.)

1982–1983 Portrait of a Wichita Village, 1808. *Chronicles of Oklahoma* 9(4):412–437. Norman.

1985   An Earlier Chapter of Kiowa History. *New Mexico Historical Review* 60(4):379–397. Albuquerque.

1994   Inside the Comanchería: The Diary of Pedro Vial and Francisco Xavier Chaves. *Southwestern Historical Quarterly* 98(1):27–56. Austin, Tex.

Johnson, Alfred E.
1969   Archeological Investigations in the Clinton Reservoir Area, Eastern Kansas. Lawrence: University of Kansas, Museum of Anthropology.

1976   A Model of the Kansas City Hopewell Subsistence-settlement System. Pp. 7–15 in Hopewellian Archaeology in the Lower Missouri Valley. Alfred E. Johnson, ed. *University of Kansas. Publications in Anthropology* 8. Lawrence.

1979   Kansas City Hopewell. Pp. 86–93 in Hopewell Archaeology: The Chillicothe Conference. David S. Brose and N'omi Greber, eds. *MCJA Special Paper* 3. Kent, Ohio: Kent State University Press.

1983   Late Woodland in the Kansas City Locality. *Plains Anthropologist* 28(100):99–108.

_____, ed.
1983a   Phase IV Archaeological Investigation at El Dorado Lake, Butler County, Kansas, Summer 1980. Alfred E. Johnson,

John M. Parisi, Ricky L. Roberts, contributors; Paul E. Brockington, Jr., principal investigator. *University of Kansas. Museum of Anthropology. Project Report Series* 52. Lawrence.

1984   Temporal Relationships of Late (Plains) Woodland Components in Eastern Kansas. *Plains Anthropologist* 29(106):277–288.

1991   Kansa Origins: An Alternative. *Plains Anthropologist* 36(133):57–65.

Johnson, Alice M. 1967 *see* Hudson's Bay Company 1967

Johnson, Ann Mary
1977   The Dune Buggy Site, 24RV1, and Northwestern Plains Ceramics. *Plains Anthropologist* 22(75):37–49.

1977   Testing the Modified Initial Middle Missouri Variant. Pp. 14–20 in Trends in Middle Missouri Prehistory: A Festschrift Honoring the Contributions of Donald J. Lehmer. W. Raymond Wood, ed. *Plains Anthropologist* 22(78, Pt. 2); *Memoir* 13. Lincoln.

1979   Extended Middle Missouri Components in the Big Bend Region, South Dakota. *South Dakota Archaeological Society. Special Publications* 1. Vermillion, S.Dak.

1979a   The Problem of Crow Pottery. Pp. 17–29 in Symposium on the Crow-Hidatsa Separations. Leslie B. Davis, ed. *Archaeology in Montana* 20(3). Billings, [etc.].

1988   Parallel Grooved Ceramics: An Addition to Avonlea Material Culture. Pp. 137–143 in Avonlea Yesterday and Today: Archaeology and Prehistory. Leslie B. Davis, ed. Saskatoon, Sask.: Saskatchewan Archaeological Society.

Johnson, Ann Mary, and Alfred E. Johnson
1998   The Plains Woodland. Pp. 201–234 in Archaeology on the Great Plains. W. Raymond Wood, ed. Lawrence: University Press of Kansas.

Johnson, Bryan R.
1988   The Blackfeet: An Annotated Bibliography. *Garland Reference Library of Social Science* 441. New York: Garland Publishing.

Johnson, Craig M.
1977   Factor Analysis as a Technique for Exploring Patterned Variability in Archaeological Remains. Pp. 38–52 in Trends in Middle Missouri Prehistory: A Festschrift Honoring the Contributions of Donald J. Lehmer. W. Raymond Wood, ed. *Plains Anthropologist* 22(78, Pt. 2); *Memoir* 13. Lincoln.

1996   A Chronology of Middle Missouri Plains Village Sites. (Report prepared for the Department of Anthropology, National Museum of Natural History, Smithsonian Institution, Washington.)

1998   The Coalescent Tradition. Pp. 308–344 in Archaeology on the Great Plains. W. Raymond Wood, ed. Lawrence, Kans.: University Press of Kansas.

Johnson, Dorothy M.
1969   Warrior for a Lost Nation: A Biography of Sitting Bull. Philadelphia: The Westminister Press.

Johnson, Eileen M.
1972   An Analysis and Interpretation of Faunal and Floral Material from a Kansas City Hopewell Site. (M.A. Thesis in Anthropology, University of Kansas, Lawrence.)

1975   Faunal and Floral Material from a Kansas City Hopewell Site: Analysis and Interpretation. *Texas Tech University. The Museum. Occasional Papers* 36. Lubbock, Tex.

1977   Animal Food Resources of Paleoindians. Pp. 65–77 in Paleoindian Lifeways. Eileen M. Johnson, ed. *The Museum Journal* 17. Lubbock, Tex.

Johnson, Eileen M., and Vance T. Holliday
1986   The Archaic Record at Lubbock Lake. Pp. 7–54 in Current Trends in Southern Plains Archaeology. Timothy G. Baugh, ed. *Plains Anthropologist* 31(114, Pt.2); *Memoir* 21. Lincoln.

1995   Archeology and Late Quaternary Environments of the Southern High Plains. *Bulletin of the Texas Archeological Society* 66:519–540. Austin.

Johnson, Eileen M., Vance T. Holliday, Michael J. Kaczor, and Robert Stuckenrath
1977   The Garza Occupation at the Lubbock Lake Site. *Bulletin of the Texas Archeological Society* 48:83–109. Austin.

Johnson, Elden
1969   Decorative Motifs on Great Oasis Pottery. *Plains Anthropologist* 14(46):272–276.

1971   The Northern Margin of the Prairie Peninsula. *Journal of the Iowa Archeological Society* 18:13–21. Iowa City.

1991   Cambria and Cahokia's Northwestern Periphery. Pp. 307–317 in New Perspectives on Cahokia: Views from the Periphery. James B. Stoltman, ed. *Monographs in World Archaeology* 2. Madison, Wis.: Prehistory Press.

Johnson, Frederick
1966   Archaeology in an Emergency. The Federal Government's Inter-agency Archaeology Salvage Program Is 20 Years Old. *Science* 152(3729):1592–1597. Washington.

Johnson, Ian V.B.
1984   Helping Indians to Help Themselves, A Committee to Investigate Itself: The 1951 Indian Act Consultation Process. Ottawa: Treaties and Historical Research Centre, Indian and Northern Affairs Canada.

Johnson, LeRoy, Jr.
1994   The Life and Times of Toyah-Culture Folk as Seen from the Buckhollow Encampment, Site 41KM16, of Kimball County, Texas. Principal investigator Frank A. Weir. *Texas. Office of the State Archeologist. Report* 38. Austin.

1994a   Reconstructed Crow Terminology of the Titskanwatits, or Tonkawas, with Inferred Social Correlates. *Plains Anthropologist* 39(150):377–413.

Johnson, LeRoy, Jr., and Thomas N. Campbell
1992   Sanan: Traces of a Previously Unknown Aboriginal Language in Colonial Coahuila and Texas. *Plains Anthropologist* 37(140):185–212.

Johnson, LeRoy, Jr., and Glenn T. Goode
1994   A New Try at Dating and Characterizing Holocene Climates, as Well as Archaeological Periods, on the Eastern Edwards Plateau. *Bulletin of the Texas Archaeological Society* 65:1–51. Austin.

Johnson, LeRoy, Jr., and Edward B. Jelks
1958   The Tawakoni-Yscani Village, 1760: A Study of Archeological Site Identification. *The Texas Journal of Science* 10(4):405–422. San Angelo, [etc.], Tex.

Johnson, Michael G.
1993   The Native Tribes of North America: A Concise Encyclopedia. London: Windrow and Greene.

Johnson, Rufus David
1961   J.E.J. Trail to Sundown, Cassadaga to Casa Grande, 1817–1882: The Story of a Pioneer, Joseph Ellis Johnson. Salt Lake City: Joseph Ellis Johnson Family Committee.

Johnson, Stephen L.
1977   Guide to American Indian Documents in the Congressional Serial Set: 1817–1899. (A Project of the Institute for the Development of Indian Law.) New York: Clearwater Publishing Company.

Johnson, Troy, and Joane Nagel
1994   Remembering Alcatraz: Twenty-five Years After. *American Indian Culture and Research Journal* 18(4):9–23. Los Angeles.

Johnson, W. Fletcher
1891   The Red Record of the Sioux: Life of Sitting Bull and History of the Indian War of 1890–'91. A Graphic Account of the Life of the Great Medicine Man and Chief Sitting Bull; His Tragic Death; Story of the Sioux Nation; Their Manners and Customs, Ghost Dances and Messiah Craze; also, a Very Complete History of the Sanguinary Indian War of 1890–'91. Chicago: Edgewood Publishing Company.

Johnston, Alex
1987   Plants of the Blackfoot. *Lethbridge Historical Society. Occasional Paper* 15. Lethbridge, Alta. (Originally publ. as: *Provincial Museum of Alberta. Natural History Occasional Paper* 4. Edmonton, Alta., 1982.)

Johnston, Jim, and Maureen Johnston
1991   Jingle Dresses. Illustrated by Judie Aitken and Jeff Frye. *Whispering Wind* 24(2):[4] 5–14. New Orleans: Louisiana Indian Hobbyist Association.

Johnston, Richard B.
1967   The Hitchell Site. *Smithsonian Institution. River Basin Surveys. Publications in Salvage Archeology* 3. Washington.

Johnston, Richard B., and John J. Hoffman
1966   An Analysis of Four Survey Collections from Armstrong County, South Dakota, 39AR2 (No Heart Creek Site), 39AR4, 39AR5 and 39AR7. *Plains Anthropologist* 11(31):39–75.

Jones, A. Wesley
1978   Hidatsa [Texts]. Pp. 53–78 in Earth Lodge Tales from the Upper Missouri. Douglas R. Parks, A. Wesley Jones, and Robert C. Hollow, eds. Bismarck, N.Dak.: Mary College.

1979   Hidatsa-English/English-Hidatsa Wordlist. Bismarck, N.Dak.: Mary College, North Dakota Indian Languages Program.

1979a   Morphological Constellations in Hidatsa: Locative, Demonstrative, Relative. *International Journal of American Linguistics* 45(3):232–235. Chicago.

1983   Some Archaisms and Innovations in Hidatsa. Pp. 8–10 in Proceedings of the Second Siouan Languages Conference, 1982. Mary C. Marino, ed. *Na'pāo: A Saskatchewan Anthropology Journal* 13(October): Special Issue. Saskatoon, Sask.

1983a   On Proto-Siouan Ablaut and Nasalization. Pp. 29–30 in Proceedings of the Second Siouan Languages Conference, 1982. Mary C. Marino, ed. *Na'pāo: A Saskatchewan Anthropology Journal* 13(October): Special Issue. Saskatoon, Sask.

1991   The Case for Root Extensions in Proto-Siouan. Pp. 505–517 in 1990 Mid-America Linguistics Conference Papers. Frances Ingemann, ed. Lawrence: Department of Linguistics, University of Kansas.

1992   The Hidatsa Approximative: Morphology, Phonology, Semantics—and an Approximate Look at Ablaut. Pp. 324–337 in Florence M. Voegelin Memorial Volume: A Collection of Essays Dedicated to the Memory of the Founding Editor of Anthropological Linguistics. *Anthropo-* 1185 *logical Linguistics* 34. Bloomington, Ind.: American Indian Studies Research Institute, Indiana University.

Jones, Bruce A., and Thomas A. Witty, Jr.
1980   The Gilligan Site. Pp. 67–120 in Salvage Archeology of the John Redmond Lake, Kansas. Thomas A. Witty, Jr., ed. *Kansas State Historical Society Anthropological Series* 8. Topeka.

Jones, Charles T.
1997   Kiowa Elders Oppose Revival of Sun Dance. *The Plain Dealer*, 28 May:7E.

Jones, Christopher A.
1984   Prehistoric Sites on Carrizo Ranches, Southeastern Colorado. Pp. 293–312 in Papers of the Philmont Conference on the Archeology of Northeastern New Mexico. Carol J. Condie, ed. *Proceedings of the New Mexico Archeological Council* 6(1).

Jones, David E.
1972   Sanapia: Comanche Medicine Woman. New York: Holt, Rinehart and Winston. (Reprinted: Waveland Press, Prospect Heights, Ill., 1984.)

Jones, Douglas C.
1966   The Treaty of Medicine Lodge: The Story of the Great Treaty Council as Told by Eyewitnesses. Norman: University of Oklahoma Press.

Jones, John Alan
1950   The Role of the Sun Dance in Northern Ute Acculturation. (Ph.D. Dissertation in Anthropology, Columbia University, New York City.)

1955   The Sun Dance of the Northern Ute. *Bureau of American Ethnology Bulletin* 157; *Anthropological Paper* 47. Washington: Smithsonian Institution; U.S. Government Printing Office.

Jones, Oakah L., Jr.
1966   Pueblo Warriors and Spanish Conquest. Norman: University of Oklahoma Press.

Jones, Peter (Kahkewaquonaby)
1861   History of the Ojebway Indians; with Especial Reference to Their Conversion to Christianity. With a Brief Memoir of the Writer ... and Introductory Notice by G. Osborn. London: A.W. Bennett. (Reprinted: Canadiana House, Toronto, 1973.)

Jones, Rosalie May
1968   The Blackfeet Medicine Lodge Ceremony: Ritual and Dance-Drama. (M.A. Thesis in Anthropology, University of Utah, Salt Lake City.)

Jones, William K.
1968   Three Kwari Comanche Weapons. *Great Plains Journal* 8(1):31–47. Lawton, Okla.

1969   Notes on the History and Material Culture of the Tonkawa Indians. *Smithsonian Contributions to Anthropology* 2(5). Washington: Smithsonian Institution.

Jonker, Peter M., comp.
1983   Stoney History Notes: Chief John Chiniki, Chiniki Band, Stoney Indians. Morley, Alta.: Chiniki Band of the Stoney Tribe.

1988   The Song and the Silence, Sitting Wind: The Life of Stoney Chief Frank Kaquitts. Edmonton, Alta.: Lone Pine.

Jordan, Julia A.
1965   Ethnobotony of the Kiowa-Apache. (M.A. Thesis in Anthropology, University of Oklahoma, Norman.)

Jordan, Julia A., and William E. Bittle
1974   Ethnobotany of the Kiowa-Apache. (Manuscript in J.A. Jordan and W.E. Bittle's possession.)

Jorgensen, Joseph G.
1965   The Ethnohistory and Acculturation of the Northern Ute. (Ph.D. Dissertation in History, Indiana University, Bloomington.)

1972   The Sun Dance Religion: Power for the Powerless. Chicago: University of Chicago Press.

1985   Religious Solutions and Native American Struggle: Ghost Dance, Sun Dance and Beyond. Pp. 97–128 in Religion, Rebellion, Revolution: An Interdisciplinary and Cross-Cultural Collection of Essays. Bruce Lincoln, ed. New York: St. Martins Press.

1986   Federal Policies, American Indian Politics and the New Federalism. *American Indian Culture and Research Journal* 10(2):1–13. Los Angeles.

Josephy, Alvin M., Jr.
1965   Nez Perce Indians and the Opening of the Pacific Northwest. New Haven: Yale University Press.

1970   The Artist Was a Young Man: The Life Story of Peter Rindisbacher. Fort Worth, Tex.: Amon Carter Museum.

Josephy, Alvin M., Jr., Trudy Thomas, and Jeanne Eder
1990   Wounded Knee: Lest We Forget. Cody, Wyo.: Buffalo Bill Historical Center.

Josephy, Alvin M., Joane Nagel, and Troy Johson, eds.
1999   Red Power: The American Indians' Fight for Freedom. 2nd Edition. Lincoln: University of Nebraska. (Originally published: American Heritage Press, New York, 1971; Reprinted: University of Nebraska Press, Lincoln, 1985.)

Joslyn Art Museum
1963   Artist Explorers of the 1830's: George Catlin, 1796–1872; Karl Bodmer, 1809–1893; Alfred Jacob Miller, 1810–1874; also, Drawings by Plains Indians. Catalog, edited by Mildred Goosman. Omaha, Nebr.: Joslyn Art Museum.

1984 *see* Bodmer, Karl 1984

Josselin de Jong, Jan Petrus Benjamin de, ed. and trans.
1914   Blackfoot Texts from the Southern Peigans Blackfoot Reservation, Teton County, Montana. With the help of Black-Horse-Rider; collected and published with an English translation. *Verhandelingen der Koniklijke Akademie van Wetenschappen te Amsterdam. Afdeeling Letterkunde,* n.r. 14(4). Amsterdam: J. Müller.

Joutel, Henri
1714   A Journal of the Last Voyage Perform'd by Monsr. de La Sale, to the Gulph of Mexico, to Find out the Mouth of the Missisipi River... London: A. Bell, B. Litott, J. Baker.

1962   Joutel's Journal of La Salle's Last Voyage [1714]. Introduction by Darrett B. Ruthman. New York: Corinth Books.

Joyes, Dennis C.
1970   The Culture Sequence at the Avery Site at Rock Lake. Pp. 209–222 in Ten Thousand Years: Archaeology in Manitoba. Walter M. Hlady, ed. Winnipeg: Manitoba Archaeology Society.

1973   The Shippe Canyon Site. *Archaeology in Montana* 14(2):49–85. Billings, [etc.].

1988   A Summary and Evaluation of Avonlea in Manitoba. Pp. 227–236 in Avonlea Yesterday and Today: Archaeology and Prehistory. Leslie B. Davis, ed. Saskatoon: Saskatchewan Archaeological Society.

Joyes, Dennis C., and Tom Jerde
1970   Northeastern Montana Archaeology. *Archaeology in Montana* 11(4):1–14. Billings, [etc.].

Judy, Mark A.
1987   Powder Keg on the Upper Missouri: Sources of Blackfeet Hostility, 1730–1810. *The American Indian Quarterly* 11(2):31–48. Hurst, Tex.

Junkin, William
1889   [Inspection Report 4654, Fort Belknap Agency, Montana, dated July 27, 1889.] (Manuscript No. M1070, Roll 12, Records of the Bureau of Indian Affairs, Record Group 75, National Archives, Washington.)

Justice, Noel D.
1987   Stone Age Spear and Arrow Points. Bloomington: Indiana University Press.

Kaiser, Patricia L.
1984   The Lakota Sacred Pipe: Its Tribal Use and Religious Philosophy. *American Indian Cultural Research Journal* 8(3):1–26. Los Angeles.

Kan, Michael, and William Wierzbowski
1979   Notes on an Important Southern Cheyenne Shield. *Bulletin of the Detroit Institute of Arts* 57(3):124–133. Detroit, Mich. (Reprinted, abridged: Pp. 235–245 in Native North American Art History: Selected Readings. Zena P. Mathews and Aldona Jonaitis, comps. Peek Publications, Palo Alto, Calif., 1980.)

Kane, Lucile M., ed. and trans. 1951 *see* de Trobriand, Philippe Régis
1951

Kane, Lucile M., June D. Holmquist, and Carolyn Gilman, eds.
1978   Northern Expeditions of Stephen H. Long: The Journals of 1817 and 1823 and Related Documents. [St. Paul:] Minnesota Historical Society Press.

Kane, Paul
1859   Wanderings of an Artist among the Indians of North America; From Canada To Vancouver's Island and Oregon, Through Hudson's Bay Company's Territory and Back Again. London: Longman, Brown, Green, Longmans, and Roberts. (Reprinted, with Introduction and Notes by Lawrence J. Burpee: Radisson Society of Canada, Toronto, 1925; also, C.E. Tuttle, Rutland, Vt., 1967, 1968; Hurting Publishing, Edmonton, Alta., 1968, 1973; Dover Publications, Mineola, N.Y., 1996; see also J. Russell Harper, ed., 1971.)

_____   1967, 1968, 1973, 1996 *see* 1859 (reprint info.)

_____   1971 *see* Harper, J. Russell, ed. 1971

Kappler, Charles J., comp. and ed.
1904–1941 Indian Affairs: Laws and Treaties. 5 vols. (Vols. I–V). Washington: Government Printing Office. (Reprinted: AMS Press, New York, 1971; see also Kappler 1904–1979.)

_____, comp. and ed.
1904–1979 Indian Affairs: Laws and Treaties. 7 vols.: Vols. I–V, reprinted [plus:] Kappler's Indian Affairs: Laws and Treaties. 2 vols.: Vols. VI–VII, prepared under the direction of Deputy Solicitors Raymond C. Coutler and David E. Lindgren. Washington: U.S. Department of the Interior; U.S. Government Printing Office. (Reprinted, 7 vols.: William S. Hein, New York, [1990].)

Kardiner, Abram, et al.
1945   The Psychological Frontiers of Society. With the Collaboration of Ralph Linton, Cora Du Bois, and James West. New York: Columbia University Press. (Reprinted in 1956, 1963; also, Greenwood Press, Westport, Conn., 1981.)

Karlstrom, Eric T.
1977   Genesis, Morphology and Stratigraphy of Soils at the Laddle Creek Archeological Site, Bighorn Mountains, Wyoming. (M.A. Thesis in Geography, University of Wyoming, Laramie.)

Karol, Joseph S.
1974   Everyday Lakota: An English-Sioux Dictionary for Beginners. St. Francis, S.Dak.: Rosebud Educational Society.

Karson, Terry
1990   L.A. Huffman, Pioneer Photographer. Introduction by Donna M. Forbes. Billings, Mont.: Yellowstone Art Center.

Kaschube, Dorothea V.
1954   Examples of Tone in Crow. *International Journal of American Linguistics* 20(1):34–36. Chicago.

_____
1960   Structural Elements of Crow. (Ph.D. Dissertation in Anthropology, Indiana University, Bloomington.)

_____
1967   Structural Elements of the Language of the Crow Indians of Montana. *University of Colorado Studies. Series in Anthropology* 14. Boulder.

_____, ed.
1978   Crow Texts. *International Journal of American Linguistics. Native American Texts Monograph Series* 2. Chicago: The University of Chicago Press.

Kate, Herman Frederik Carel ten *see* ten Kate, Herman F.C.

Kavanagh, Thomas W.
1979–1987 [Ethnographic Notes from Fieldwork among the Comanche, Oklahoma.] (Manuscripts in T.W. Kavanagh's possession.)

_____
1980   Recent Socio-cultural Evolution of the Comanche Indians. (M.A. Thesis in Anthropology, George Washington University, Washington.)

_____
1982   The Comanche Pow-wow: Pan-Indianism or Tribalism. (Haliksa'i. U.N.M. Contributions to Anthropology) *Journal of the University of New Mexico Anthropological Society* 1:12–27. Albuquerque.

_____
1985   The Comanche: Paradigmatic Anomaly or Ethnographic Fiction. (Haliksa'i. U.N.M. Contributions to Anthropology) *Journal of the University of New Mexico Anthropological Society* 4:109–128. Albuquerque.

_____
1986   Political Power and Political Organization: Comanche Politics, 1786–1875. (Ph.D. Dissertation in Anthropology, University of New Mexico, Albuquerque.)

_____
1988   [Notes on the Comanche Sun Dance.] (Manuscript in T.W. Kavanagh's possession.)

_____
1989   Comanche Population Organization and Reorganization, 1869–1901: A Test of the Continuity Hypothesis. Pp. 99–111 in Plains Indian Historical Demography and Health: Perspectives, Interpretations, and Critiques. Gregory R. Campbell, ed. *Plains Anthropologist* 34(124, Pt. 2); *Memoir* 23. Lincoln.

_____
1991   Whose Village? Photographs by William S. Soule, Winter 1872–1873. *Visual Anthropology* 4(1):1–24. Chur, London, [etc.].

_____, comp.
1991a   A Comanche Sourcebook: Notes of the 1933 Laboratory of Anthropology Field Party Recorded by Waldo R. Wedel, E. Adamson Hoebel, and Gustav G. Carlson. (Manuscript in T.W. Kavanagh's possession.)

_____
1992   Southern Plains Dance: Tradition and Dynamics. Pp 105–123 in Native American Dance: Ceremonies and Social Traditions. Charlotte Heth, ed. Washington: Smithsonian Institution, National Museum of the American Indian.

_____
1996   Comanche Political History: An Ethnohistorical Perspective *1187*

1706–1875. *Studies in the Anthropology of North American Indians.* Lincoln: University of Nebraska Press. (Reprinted, rev. ed.,1999, under title: The Comanches: A History, 1706–1875.)

1996a   North American Indian Portraits: Photographs from the Wanamaker Expeditions. From the Wanamaker Collection at the William Hammond Mathers Museum, Indiana University. New York: Konecky & Konecky.

Kawecki, Patricia L., and Don G. Wychoff, eds.
1984   Contributions to Cross Timbers Prehistory. *University of Oklahoma. Oklahoma Archeological Survey. Studies in Oklahoma's Past* 12. Norman.

Kay, Marvin
1983   Archaic Period Research in the Western Ozark Highland, Missouri. Pp. 41–70 in Archaic Hunters and Gatherers in the American Midwest. James L. Phillips and James A. Brown, eds. New York: Academic Press.

1998   The Central and Southern Plains Archaic. Pp. 173–200 in Archaeology on the Great Plains. W. Raymond Wood, ed.; Maps by E. Stanley Wood. Lawrence, Kans.: University Press of Kansas.

Kealiinohomoku, Joann W.
1986   The Would-be Indian. Pp. 111–126 in Explorations in Ethnomusicology: Essays in Honor of David P. MacAllester. Charlotte J. Frisbie, ed. Detroit: Information Coordinators.

Keane, A.H.
1878   Ethnography and Philology of America. Pp. 443–561 (Appendix) in Central America, the West Indies, and South America. Henry W. Bates, ed. *Stanford's Compendium of Geography and Travel.* London: Edward Stanford.

Keating, William H., comp.
1824   Narrative of an Expedition to the Source of the St. Peter's River, Lake Winnepeek, Lake of the Woods, ... Performed in the Year 1823, by Order of the Hon. J.C. Calhoun...Under the Command of Stephen H. Long, U.S.T.E. Compiled from the Notes of Major Long, Messrs. Say, Keating, and Colhoun. 2 vols. Philadelphia: H.C. Carey and I. Lea. (Also publ. in England, 1825, 1828. American ed. reprinted: Ross and Haines, Minneapolis, Minn., 1959.)

———, comp.
1825   Narrative of an Expedition to the Source of the St. Peter's River, Lake Winnepeek, Lake of the Woods, ... Performed in the Year 1823, by Order of the Hon. J.C. Calhoun...Under the Command of Stephen H. Long, U.S.T.E. Compiled from the Notes of Major Long, Messrs. Say, Keating, and Colhoun. 2 vols. London: Geo. B. Whittaker. (Reprinted under title: Travels in the Interior of North America, [etc.]. 2 vols. London, 1828.)

Keeling, Henry C.
1910   My Experience with the Cheyenne Indians. *Collections of the Kansas State Historical Society [for] 1909–1910,* Vol. 11:306–313. Topeka.

Keeling, Richard
1997   North American Indian Music: A Guide to Published Sources and Selected Recordings. *Garland Library of Music Ethnology.* New York: Garland Publishing.

Keeney, Bradford, ed.
1999   Lakota Yuwipi Man, Gary Holy Bull. Philadelphia: Ringing Rocks Press.

Kehoe, Alice B.
1959   Ceramic Affiliations in the Northwestern Plains. *American Antiquity* 25(2):237–246.

1968   The Ghost Dance Religion in Saskatchewan, Canada. *Plains Anthropologist* 13(42 pt. 2):296–304.

1970   The Function of Ceremonial Sexual Intercourse among the Northern Plains Indians. *Plains Anthropologist* 15(48):91–103.

1970a   The Dakotas in Saskatchewan. Pp. 148–174 in The Modern Sioux: Social Systems and Reservation Culture. Ethel Nurge, ed. Lincoln: University of Nebraska Press.

1975   Dakota Indian Ethnicity in Saskatchewan. *Journal of Ethnic Studies* 3(2):37–42.

1976   Old Woman had Great Power. *Western Canadian Journal of Anthropology* 6(3): 68–76. Edmonton, Alta.

1980   The Giveaway Ceremony of Blackfoot and Plains Cree. *Plains Anthropologist* 25(87):17–26.

1981   North American Indians: A Comprehensive Account. Englewood Cliffs, N.J.: Prentice-Hall. (Reprinted, 2d ed., in 1992.)

1989   The Ghost Dance: Ethnohistory and Revitalization. New York: Holt, Rinehart and Winston.

——— 1992 *see* 1981 (reprint info.)

1995   Blackfoot Persons. Pp. 113–125 in Women and Power in Native North America. Laura F. Klein and Lillian A. Ackerman, eds. Norman: University of Oklahoma Press.

1995a   Introduction. Pp. i–xxxiii in Mythology of the Blackfoot Indians, by Clark Wissler and D.C. Duvall. Lincoln: University of Nebraska Press.

1996   Transcribing Insima, a Blackfoot "Old Lady". Pp. 381–402 in Reading Beyond Words: Contexts for Native History. Jennifer S.H. Brown and Elizabeth Vibert, eds. Peterborough, Ont. and Orchard Park, N.Y.: Broadview Press.

Kehoe, Alice B., and Thomas F. Kehoe
1979   Solstice-Aligned Boulder Configurations in Saskatchewan. *Canada. National Museum of Man. Mercury Series. Ethnology Service Paper* 48. Ottawa.

Kehoe, Thomas F.
1958   Tipi Rings: The "Direct Ethnological" Approach Applied to an Archaeological Problem. *American Anthropologist,* n.s. 60(5):861–873.

1960   Stone Tipi Rings in North-Central Montana and the Adjacent Portion of Alberta, Canada. Their Historical, Ethnological, and Archeological Aspects. *Bureau of American Ethnology Bulletin* 173; *Anthropological Paper* 62. Washington: Smithsonian Institution; U.S. Government Printing Office. (Reprinted: J&L Reprint Company, Lincoln, 1985.)

1965   'Buffalo Stones': An Addendum to 'The Folklore of Fossils.' *American Antiquity* 39(155):212–213.

1966   The Small Side-Notched Point System on the Northern Plains. *American Antiquity* 31(6):827–841.

1973   The Gull Lake Site: A Prehistoric Bison Drive Site in Southwestern Saskatchewan. *Milwaukee Public Museum. Publications in Anthropology and History* 1. Milwaukee, Wis.

1974   The Large Corner-Notched Point System of the Northern Plains and Adjacent Woodlands. Pp. 103–114 in Aspects of Upper Great Lakes Anthropology. Elden Johnson, ed. *Minnesota Prehistoric Archaeology Series* 11. St. Paul.

Kehoe, Thomas F., and Alice B. Kehoe
1968   Saskatchewan. Pp. 21–35 in The Northwestern Plains: A Symposium. W.W. Caldwell, ed. *The Center for Indian Studies. Rocky Mountains College. Occasional Papers* 1. Billings, Mont.

1974   The Identification of the Fall or Rapid Indians. *Plains Anthropologist* 19(65):231–232.

1977   Stones, Solstices and Sun Dance Structures. *Plains Anthropologist* 22(76):85–95.

Kehoe, Thomas F., and B.A. McCorquodale
1961   The Avonlea Point-Horizon Marker for the Northwestern Plains. *Plains Anthropologist* 6(13):179–188.

1961a   The Avonlea Projectile Point. *The Blue Jay* 19(3):137–139. Regina: Saskatchewan Natural History Society.

Kehoe, Thomas F., Bruce A. McCorquodale, and Alice B. Kehoe
1988   1984 Excavations at the Avonlea Type Site. Pp 11–23 in Avonlea Yesterday and Today: Archaeology and Prehistory. Leslie B. Davis, ed. Saskatoon, Sask.: Saskatchewan Archaeological Society.

Keim, De B. Randolph
1885   Sheridan's Troopers on the Borders: A Winter Campaign on the Plains. Philadelphia: D. McKay. (Reprinted in 1889 and 1891; also, Books for Libraries Press, Freeport, N.Y., 1970; Corner House Publishers, Williamstown, Mass., 1973; and, with a Foreword by Paul Andrew Hutton, University of Nebraska Press, Lincoln, 1985. Originally publ.: Claxton, Remsen, and Haffelfinger, Philadelphia, 1870.)

Keith, Kenneth D., and Clyde S. Snow
1976   The Gore Pit Skeleton: Earliest Dated Human Burial from Oklahoma. *Plains Anthropologist* 21(74):283–289.

Keller, Gordon
1961   The Changing Position of the Southern Plains in the Late Prehistory of the Great Plains Area. (Ph.D. Dissertation in Anthropology, University of Chicago, Chicago.)

Kelley, William F.
1971   Pine Ridge 1890: An Eye Witness Account of the Events Surrounding the Fighting at Wounded Knee. Alexander Kelley and Pierre Bovis, eds. San Francisco: Pierre Bovis. (Originally publ. in: *Nebraska State Journal*, November 24, 1890 to January 16, 1891, Omaha, Nebr.)

Kellogg, Louise Phelps, ed.
1917   Early Narratives of the Northwest, 1634–1699. New York: C. Scribner's Sons. (Reprinted: Barnes and Noble, New York, 1945, 1953, 1967.)

Kelly, Charles
1941   Ute Sun Dance. *The Desert Magazine* 5(1):22–24. El Centro, Calif.

Kelly, Fanny
1871   Narrative of My Captivity among the Sioux Indians. Cincinnati: Wilstach, Baldwin and Co.

Kelsey, Cynthia
1956   Changing Social Relationships in an Eastern Dakota Community. *Minnesota Academy of Science Proceedings* 24:12–19. Minneapolis.

Kelsey, Henry
1929   The Kelsey Papers; With an Introduction by Arthur G. Doughty and Chester Martin, eds. Ottawa: F.A. Acland, for The Public Archives of Canada and The Public Record Office of Northern Ireland. (Reprinted, with an Introduction by John Warkentin: Canadian Plains Research Center, University of Regina, Regina, Sask., 1994.)

Kemnitzer, Luis S.
1968   Yuwipi: A Modern Dakota Healing Ritual. (Ph.D. Dissertation in Anthropology, University of Pennsylvania, Philadelphia.)

1970   The Cultural Provenience of Objects Used in Yuwipi: A Modern Teton Dakota Healing Ritual. *Ethnos* 35:40–75. Stockholm: National Museum of Ethnography.

1970a   Familial and Extra-familial Socialization in Urban Dakota Adolescents. Pp. 246–267 in The Modern Sioux: Social Systems and Reservation Culture. Ethel Nurge, ed. Lincoln: University of Nebraska Press.

1976   Structure, Content, and Cultural Meaning of *yuwipi*: a Modern Lakota Healing Ritual. *American Ethnologist* 3(2):261–280.

1980   Research in Health and Healing in the Plains. Pp. 272–284 in Anthropology on the Great Plains. W. Raymond Wood and Margot Liberty, eds. Lincoln: University of Nebraska Press.

Kendall, Daythal L., comp.
1982   A Supplement to *A Guide to Manuscripts Relating to the American Indian in the American Philosophical Society. Memoirs of the American Philosophical Society* 65. Philadelphia.

Kendall, George W.
1844   Narrative of the Taxan Sante Fe Expedition. 2 vols. New York: Harper and Brothers.

Kennard, Edward
1936   Mandan Grammar. *International Journal of American Linguistics* 9(1):1–43. Chicago.

1936a   Mandan Folkloristic Texts. (Manuscript No. 30(X6.1) in The Library of the American Philosophical Society, Philadelphia.)

Kennedy, Dan Ochankugahe
1972   Recollections of an Assiniboine Chief. James R. Stevens, ed. Toronto and Montreal: McClelland and Stewart.

Kennedy, Fred
1946   The Indian Sun Dance of Today. *Canadian Cattlemen* 8(4): 180, 252–253. Winnipeg, Alta.

Kennedy, Michael Stephen, ed.
1961   The Assiniboines: From the Accounts of the Old Ones Told to First Boy (James Larpenteur Long). Edited and with an Introduction by Michael Stephen Kennedy. Drawings by William Standing. Norman: University of Oklahoma Press. (Originally publ. under title: Land of Nakoda; the Story of the Assiniboine Indians. From the Tales of the Old Ones Told to First Boy (James L. Long), with Drawings by Fire Bear (William Standing): Writers' Program, Montana. State Pub. Co., Helena, 1942. Reprinted: AMS Press, New York, 1975.)

_____, ed.
1965   The Red Man's West. New York: Hastings House.

Kennedy, Timothy F.
1997   Kaw Nation Environmental Department Report. *Kanza News: Newsletter of the Kaw Nation of Oklahoma* 4:18. Kaw City, Okla.

1998   Kaw Nation Environmental Activities. *Kanza News: Newsletter of the Kaw Nation of Oklahoma* 5:14. Kaw City, Okla.

1998a   Environmental Department Receives Compliments from Agency. *Kanza News: Newsletter of the Kaw Nation of Oklahoma* 6:18. Kaw City, Okla.

Kennedy, William
1841   Texas: The Rise, Progress, and Propects of the Republic of Texas. 2 vols. 2d ed. London: R. Hastings.

Kenner, Charles L.
1969   A History of New Mexican-Plains Indian Relations. Norman: University of Oklahoma Press.

1189

1994   The Comanchero Frontier: A History of New Mexican-Plains Indian Relations. Norman: University of Oklahoma Press.

Kenney, M.M.
1897   Tribal Society among Texas Indians. *Quarterly of the Texas State Historical Association* 1(1):26–33. Austin.

Kenney, William Fitch
1971   Pine Ridge 1890. San Francisco: Pierre Bovis.

Kercheval, George T.
1893   An Oto and an Omaha Tale. *Journal of American Folk-lore* 6(22):199–204.

Kermoal, Nathalie
1996   Le «temps de cayoge»: la vie quotidienne des femmes métisses au Manitoba de 1850 à 1900. (Ph.D. Dissertation in History, University of Ottawa, Ottawa.)

Kessell, John L.
1979   Kiva, Cross, and Crown: The Pecos Indians and New Mexico, 1540–1840. Washington: National Park Service.

Ketchum, Daniel
1827   [Letter to Henry Atkinson, dated March 3, 1827.] (Letters Sent 1824–33, U.S. Army Command, 6th Infantry Division at Fort Atkinson, War Department Records, National Archives, Washington.)

Keyes, Charles R.
1927   Prehistoric Man in Iowa. *The Palimpsest* 8(6):185–229. Iowa City.

1930   A Unique Survey. *The Palimpsest* 11(5):214–226. Iowa City.

1949   Four Iowa Archeologies with Plains Affiliations. Pp. 96–97 in Proceedings of the Fifth Plains Conference for Archeology. John L. Champe, ed. *University of Nebraska. Laboratory of Anthropology. Notebook* 1. Lincoln.

1951   Prehistoric Indians of Iowa. *The Palimpsest* 32(8):285–344. Iowa City.

Keyser, James D.
1977   Writing on Stone: Rock Art on the Northeastern Plains. *Canadian Journal of Archaeology* 1(1):15–80. Ottawa.

1979   Late Prehistoric Period Procurement on the Milk River in North-Central Montana. *Archaeology in Montana* 20(1). Billings [etc.], Mont.

1982   A Comparative Analysis of Two McKean Phase Occupations in the Grand River Drainage. *Journal of the North Dakota Archaeological Association* 1:31–42. Grand Forks, N.Dak.

1986   The Evidence for McKean Complex Plant Utilization. *Plains Anthropologist* 31(113):225–235.

Keyser, James D., and Carl M. Davis
1984   Lightening Spring: 4000 Years of Pine Parkland Prehistory. *Archaeology in Montana* 25(2–3):1–64. Billings, [etc.].

1985   Lightening Spring and Red Fox: McKean Research in the Grand River Drainage. Pp. 123–136 in McKean/Middle Plains Archaic: Current Research. Marcel Kornfeld and Lawrence C. Todd, eds. *Occasional Papers on Wyoming Archaeology* 4. Laramie, Wyo.

Khan, E.
1971   Suggestive Evidence for the Presence of Early Man. *Na'pāo: A Saskatchewan Anthropology Journal* 3(1):32–33. Saskatoon, Sask.

Kidd, Kenneth E.
1986   Blackfoot Ethnography. *Archaeological Society of Alberta*

Manuscript Series 8. Edmonton, Alta. (Originally presented as the Author's M.A. Thesis in Anthropology, University of Toronto, 1937.)

Kidd, Kenneth E., and Martha Ann Kidd
1970   A Classification System for Glass Beads for the Use of Field Archaeologists. Pp. 45–89 in *Canada Historic Sites. Occasional Papers in Archaeology and History* 1. Ottawa: National Historic Sites Service, National and Historic Parks Branch, Department of Indian Affairs and Northern Development.

Kidder, Alfred V.
1932   The Artifacts of Pecos. *Phillips Academy. Department of Archaeology. Papers of the Southwest Expedition* 6. New Haven, Conn. (Reprinted: Garland, New York, 1979.)

Kidder, Alfred V., and Anna O. Shepard
1936   The Pottery of Pecos. Vol. 2. New Haven, Conn.: Published for Phillips Academy by Yale University Press.

Kielman, Chester V., comp.
1967–1971 Guide to the Microfilm Edition of the Bexar Archives, 1717–1836. 3 vols. in 1. Austin: University of Texas, Archives Microfilm Production.

Killion, Thomas W., Scott Brown, and J. Stuart Speaker
1992   *Naevahoo'ohtseme* [We are going back home]. Cheyenne Repatriation: The Human Remains. Washington: Repatriation Office, National Museum of Natural History, Smithsonian Institution.

Kilpatrick, Jack F.
1946   The Possible Relationship of Content to Form in Certain Gros Ventre Songs. (M.A. Thesis in Music, The Catholic University of America, Washington.)

Kimball, Geoffrey D.
1994   Koasati Dictionary. *Studies in the Anthropology of North American Indians.* Lincoln: University of Nebraska Press.

Kimball, Harry
1872   [Report of Indians on the Kiowa, Comanche and Apache Reservation.] (Manuscript No. 1911, National Anthropological Archives, Smithsonian Institution, Washington.)

Kindscher, Kelly
1987   Edible Wild Plants of the Prairie: An Ethnobotanical Guide. Lawrence: University Press of Kansas.

King, D.R.
1961   The Bracken Cairn: A Prehistoric Burial. *The Blue Jay* 19(1):45–53. Regina: Saskatchewan Natural History Society.

King, Frances B.
1984   Plants, People, and Paleoecology: Biotic Communities and Aboriginal Plant Usage in Illinois. *Illinois State Museum. Scientific Papers* 20. Springfield.

King, James T.
1969   "A Better Way": General George Crook and the Ponca Indians. *Nebraska History* 50(3):239–256. Lincoln.

Kinglsey, John S., ed.
1885   The Standard Natural History. 6 vols. Boston: S.E. Casino and Company.

Kingsbury, George W.
1915   History of Dakota Territory. South Dakota: Its History and Its People. 5 vols. George Martin Smith, ed. Chicago: S. J. Clark Publishing Company. (Microfilm: *Cox Library. County, State, and Local Histories. Part* 3. Prairies and Plains Region. South Dakota. Reel 1–3, No. 3–7. Americana Unlimited, Tuscon, Ariz., 1974.)

Kingsbury, Lawrence A., and Lorna H. Gabel
1980   Eastern Apache Campsites in Southeastern Colorado. *Colo-*

rado *College Publications in Archaeology* 3. Colorado Springs, Colo.

Kingsbury, Lawrence A., and Michael Nowak
1980   Archaeological Investigations on Carrizo Ranches, Inc.: 1974–1979. *Colorado College Publications in Archaeology* 2. Colorado Springs, Colo.

Kinietz, W. Vernon
1942   John Mix Stanley and His Indian Paintings. Ann Arbor: University of Michigan Press.

Kinnaird, Lawrence, ed.
1946–1949 Spain in the Mississippi Valley, 1765–1794. [Translations of Materials from the Spanish Archives in the Bancroft Library.] 3 vols. Pt. 1: The Revolutionary Period, 1765–1781. Pt. 2: Post War Decade, 1782–1791. Pt. 3: Problems of Frontier Defence, 1792–1794. *Annual Report of the American Historical Association for the Year 1945,* Vols. 2, 3, 4. Washington: Government Printing Office.

_____, ed. and trans. 1958 *see* Lafora, Nicolás de 1958

Kinsey, Joni L.
1996   Plain Pictures: Images of the American Prairie. Washington: Published for the University of Iowa Museum of Art by the Smithsonian Institution Press.

Kiowa Tribe Enrollment Office
1990   [Letter to the *Handbook* Editors, regarding Tribal Enrollment.] (Original in *Handbook* Office, Kiowa Bibliographic File, Smithsonian Institution, Washington.)

Kipp, Darrell Robes
1996   Horses and Indians. Pp. 255–257 in Encyclopedia of North American Indians. Frederick E. Hoxie, ed. Boston: Houghton Mifflin.

Kipp, James
1873   On the Accuracy of Catlin's Account of the Mandan Ceremonies. Pp. 436–438 in *Smithsonian Institution Annual Report for 1872.* Washington: U.S. Government Printing Office.

Kiste, Robert
1965   Crow Peyotism. (Manuscript in F. Voget's possession.)

Kivett, Marvin F.
1949   A Woodland Pottery Type from Nebraska. Pp. 67–69 in Proceedings of the Fifth Plains Conference for Archeology. John L. Champe, ed. *University of Nebraska. Laboratory of Anthropology. Notebook* 1. Lincoln.

1949a   Archaeological Investigations in Medicine Creek Reservoir, Nebraska. *American Antiquity* 14(4):278–284.

1952   Woodland Sites in Nebraska. *Nebraska State Historical Society. Publications in Anthropology* 1. Lincoln.

1953   The Woodruff Ossuary, a Prehistoric Burial Site in Phillips County, Kansas. *Bureau of American Ethnology Bulletin* 154; *River Basin Surveys Papers* 3. Washington: Smithsonian Institution; U.S. Government Printing Office.

1959   Logan Creek Complex. *Nebraska State Historical Society. Publications in Anthropology [Report for 1959]*:1–5. Lincoln.

1960   Wolfe Creek Component of Crow Creek Site (39BF11). [Abstract]. P. 4 in *Proceedings of the 70th Annual Meeting of the Nebraska Academy of Sciences.* Lincoln.

1962   Logan Creek Complex. (Paper presented at the 20th Plains Anthropological Conference, Lincoln, Nebr., 1962.)

Kivett, Marvin F., and George S. Metcalf
1997   The Prehistoric People of the Medicine Creek Reservoir,

Frontier County, Nebraska: An Experiment in Mechanized Archaeology (1946–1948). *Plains Anthropologist* 42(162); *Memoir* 30. Lincoln.

Klassen, Rudolph W.
1972   Wisconsin Events and the Assiniboine and Qu'Appelle Valleys of Manitoba and Saskatchewan. *Canadian Journal of Earth Sciences* 9(5):544–560. Ottawa.

Klaudt Indian Family
1969   The Highest Hill: Gospel Music Performed by the Klaudt Family and by Ensembles drawn from the Family Members. [Sound recording, incl.: Amazing Grace / Newton, by Mrs. Klaudt, an Arikara Indian.] Los Angeles: Corner Stone Productions.

Klein, Alan M.
1980   Plains Economic Analysis: The Marxist Complement. Pp. 129–140 in Anthropology on the Great Plains. W. Raymond Wood and Margot Liberty, eds. Lincoln: University of Nebraska Press.

1983   Political-economy of Gender: A 19th Century Plains Indian Case Study. Pp. 143–179 in The Hidden Half: Studies of Plains Indian Women. Patricia Albers and Beatrice Medicine, eds. Washington, D.C.: University Press of America.

1993   Political Economy of the Buffalo Hide Trade: Race and Class on the Plains. Pp. 133–160 in The Political Economy of North American Indians. John H. Moore, ed. Norman: University of Oklahoma Press.

Kluckhohn, Clyde
1944   Navaho Witchcraft. *Papers of the Peabody Museum of American Archaeology and Ethnology, Harvard University* 22(2). Cambridge, Mass.

1968   The Philosophy of the Navajo Indians. Pp. 674–699 in Readings in Anthropology. Morton H. Fried, ed. New York: Thomas Y. Crowell.

Kluckhohn, Clyde, and Dorothea Leighton
1946   The Navaho. Cambridge, Mass.: Harvard University Press; London: G. Cumberlage, Oxford University Press.

Kluckhohn, Clyde, W.W. Hill, and Lucy W. Kluckhohn
1971   Navaho Material Culture. Cambridge, Mass.: Belknap Press of Harvard University Press.

Knauth, Otto
1963   The Mystery of the Crosses. *Annals of Iowa* 37(2):81–91. Des Moines.

Kneale, Albert H.
1950   Indian Agent. Caldwell, Idaho: The Caxton Printers.

Knight, Melanie
1998   Federal Programs, Grants and Contract News. *Kanza News: Newsletter of the Kaw Nation of Oklahoma* 6:6. Kaw City, Okla.

Knox, R.H., ed.
1980   Indian Conditions: A Survey. Ottawa: Department of Indian and Northern Affairs Canada.

Knudson, Ruth A.
1967   Cambria Village Ceramics. *Plains Anthropologist* 12(37):247–299.

Koltun, Lilly, ed.
1984   Private Realms of Light: Amateur Photography in Canada/ 1839–1940. Markham, Ont.: Fitzhenry and Whiteside.

Koontz, John E.
1980   The Proto-Siouan and Siouan Personal Pronouns. (Manuscript in J.E. Koontz's possession.)

1983   Siouan Syncopating *r-Stems. Pp. 11–23 in Proceedings of *1191* the Second Siouan Languages Conference, 1982. Mary C. Marino, ed. *Na'pāo: A Saskatchewan Anthropology Journal* 13(October): Special Issue. Saskatoon, Sask.

1985   On the Existence of the Mississippi Valley Subgroup in the Siouan Language Family. (Manuscript in J.E. Koontz's possession; copy at University of Arkansas, Fayetteville.)

1985a   The Typology of Mississippi Valley Siouan Pronouns. (Paper presented at the 24th Conference on American Languages, Washington.)

1986   Dakotan Nominal Ablaut and Proto-Mississippi Valley Problem Finals. (Manuscript in J.E. Koontz's possession.)

Kornfeld, Marcel, and George C. Frison
1985   McKean Site: A 1983 Preliminary Analysis. Pp. 31–44 in McKean/Middle Plains Archaic: Current Research. Marcel Kornfeld and Lawrence C. Todd, eds. *[Office of Wyoming State Archaeology.] Occasional Papers on Wyoming Archaeology* 4. Laramie: Wyoming Recreation Commission.

Kornfeld, Marcel, and M.L. Larson
1986   Identification and Characterization of Surfaces at the McKean Site. *The Wyoming Archaeologist* 29(1–2):69–82. Cheyenne, [etc.,] Wyo.

Kornfeld, Marcel, and Lawrence C. Todd, eds.
1985   McKean/Middle Plains Archaic: Current Research. *[Office of Wyoming State Archaeology.] Occasional Papers on Wyoming Archaeology* 4. Laramie: Wyoming Recreation Commission.

Kracht, Benjamin R.
1989   Kiowa Religion: An Ethnohistorical Analysis of Ritual Symbolism, 1832–1987. (Ph.D. Dissertation in Anthropology, Southern Methodist University, Dallas, Tex.)

1992   The Kiowa Ghost Dance, 1894–1916: An Unheralded Revitalization Movement. *Ethnohistory* 39(4):452–477. Lubbock, Tex.

1994   Kiowa Powwows: Continuity in Ritual Practice. *The American Indian Quarterly* 18(3):321–348. Los Angeles.

1994a   Kiowa Powwows: Tribal Identity Through the Continuity of the Gourd Dance. *Great Plains Research [Journal]* 4(2):257–269. Lincoln.

Kraft, Kenneth C.
1995   The Certain Site (34BK46): A Multi-Component Bison Kill in Western Oklahoma. Pp. 15–26 in Transactions of the 39th Regional Archeological Symposium for Southeastern New Mexico and Western Texas.

1997   The Distribution of Alibates Silicified Dolomite Clasts along the Canadian River. *Current Research in the Pleistocene* 14:106–109. Orono, Maine.

Kratz, F.C.
[1937–   [Field Notes, Twelve Mile Creek Site.] (Manuscripts on
1942]   file, W.H. Over Dakota Museum, University of South Dakota, Vermillion.)

Krause, Richard A.
1967   Arikara Ceramic Change: A Study of the Factors Affecting Stylistic Change in the late 18th and early 19th Century Arikara Pottery. (Ph.D. Dissertation in Anthropology, Yale University, New Haven, Conn.)

1969   Correlation of Phases in Central Plains Prehistory. Pp. 82–96 in Two House Sites in the Central Plains: An Experiment in Archaeology. W. Raymond Wood, ed. *Plains Anthropologist* 14(44, Pt.2). *Memoir* 6. Lincoln.

1192 1970   Aspects of Adaptation among Upper Republican Subsistence

Cultivators. Pp. 103–115 in Pleistocene and Recent Environments of the Central Great Plains. Wakefield Dort, Jr., and J. Knox Jones, Jr., eds. Lawrence, Kans.: University Press of Kansas.

1972   The Leavenworth Site: Archaeology of an Historic Arikara Community. *University of Kansas. Publications in Anthropology* 3. Lawrence, Kans.

1977   Taxonomic Practice and Middle Missouri Prehistory: A Perspective on Donald J. Lehmer's Contributions. Pp. 5–13 in Trends in Middle Missouri Prehistory: A Festschrift Honoring the Contributions of Donald J. Lehmer. W. Raymond Wood, ed. *Plains Anthropologist* 22(78, Pt. 2); *Memoir* 13. Lincoln.

1987   Archeology in the Midwest; a review of: *Central Plains Prehistory, Holocene Environments and Cultural Change in the Republican River Basin,* by Waldo R. Wedel. *Science* 236(4799):339–340. Washington.

1995   A Production Stage Grammar of Nollmeyer Potting Practices. *Archaeology in Montana* 36(2):19–44. Billings, [etc.].

1998   A History of Great Plains Prehistory. Pp. 48–86 in Archaeology on the Great Plains. W. Raymond Wood, ed. Lawrence, Kans.: University Press of Kansas.

Krech, Shepard, III
1994   Native Canadian Bibliography and History: A Selected Bibliography. Rev. ed. Foreword by Jennifer S.H. Brown. Norman: University of Oklahoma Press. (Originally publ.: Rupert's Land Research Centre, Winnipeg, Man., 1986.)

Krech, Shepard, III, and Barbara A. Hail
1999   Collecting Native America, 1870–1960. Washington: Smithsonian Institution Press.

Kress, Margaret Kenney, and Mattie Austin Hatcher
1932   Diary of a Visit of Inspection of the Texas Missions Made by Fray Gaspar José de Solis in the Year 1767–1768. *Southwestern Historical Quarterly* 35(1):28–76. Austin, Tex.

Krickeberg, Walter
1954   Ältere Ethnographica aus Nordamerika im Berliner Museum für Völkerkunde. *Baessler-Archiv, Neue Folge* 2:2–280. Berlin. (Reprinted: Johnson Reprint Company, New York, 1968.)

Krieger, Alex D.
[1947]   Culture Complexes and Chronology in Northern Texas; with Extension of Puebloan Datings to the Mississippi Valley. *The University of Texas Publication* 4640. Austin.

Kroeber, Alfred L.
1899   [Vocabulary of Nawathinehena.] (Manuscript No. 2560-a, 10:31v.–34v., National Anthropological Archives, Smithsonian Institution, Washington.)

1900   Symbolism of the Arapaho Indians. *Bulletin of the American Museum of Natural History* 13(2):69–86. New York. (Reprinted: Knickerbocker Press, New York, 1902.)

1901   Decorative Symbolism of the Arapaho. (Ph.D. Dissertation in Anthropology, Columbia University, New York City. Published: *American Anthropologist,* n.s. 3(2):308–336, 1901.)

1902–1907 The Arapaho. 4 Pts. I: General Description. II: Decorative Art and Symbolism. III: Ceremonial Organization. IV:Religion. *Bulletin of the American Museum of Natural History* 18(1):3–35, (1):36–150, (2):151–229, (4):279–454. New York. (Reprinted: Ye Galleon Press, Fairfield, Wash., 1975; also, University of Nebraska Press, Lincoln, 1983.)

1907   Gros Ventre Myths and Tales. *American Museum of Natural*

History Anthropological Papers 1(3):55–139. New York. (Originally publ. by Knickerbocker Press, New York, 1902.)

1907a   The Ceremonial Organization of the Plains Indians of North America. Pp. 53–64 in Pt. 2 of *Congrès International des Américanistes, 15 session.* 2 Pts. Québec.

1908   Ethnology of the Gros Ventre. *American Museum of Natural History Anthropological Papers* 1(4):141–281. New York. (Reprinted: AMS Press, New York, 1978.)

1916   Arapaho Dialects. *University of California Publications in American Archaeology and Ethnology* 12(3):71–138. Berkeley. (Reprinted: Kraus Reprint, New York, 1965.)

1928   Native Culture of the Southwest. *University of California Publications in American Archaeology and Ethnology* 23(9):375–398. Berkeley.

1931   The Culture-area and Age-area Concepts of Clark Wissler. Pp. 248–265 in Methods in Social Science. S. Rice, ed. Chicago: University of Chicago Press.

1939   Cultural and Natural Areas of Native North America. *University of California. Publications in American Archaeology and Ethnology* 38. Berkeley. (Reprinted: University of California Press, Berkeley, 1947, 1953, 1963; also, Kraus Reprint, Millwood, N.Y., 1976.)

1942   Franz Boas: The Man. Pp 5–26 in Franz Boas 1858–1942. Alfred L. Kroeber, et al., eds. *American Anthropological Association Memoir* 61; *American Anthropologist,* n.s. 45(3, Pt. 2). Menasha, Wis.

1948   Anthropology: Race, Language, Culture, Psychology, Prehistory. Rev. ed. New York: Harcourt, Brace and Co. (Reprinted in 1962.)

1955   Linguistic Time Depth Results So Far and Their Meaning. *International Journal of American Linguistics* 21(2):91–104. Chicago.

1958   Sign Language Inquiry. *International Journal of American Linguistics* 24(1):1–19. Chicago.

———   1947, 1976 *see* 1939 (reprint info.)

———   1983 *see* 1902–1907 (reprint info.)

Krouse, Susan Applegate
1990   Photographing the Vanishing Race. Pp. 213–233 in Picturing Cultures: Historical Photographs in Anthropological Inquiry. Joanna Cohan Scherer, guest ed. *Visual Anthropology* 3(2–3), Special Issue. Chur, London, [etc.].

Krozser, Kit
1991   Canid Remains at Kill Sites: A Case Study from the Oldman River Dam Project. Pp. 81–100 in Archaeology in Alberta 1988 and 1989. Martin Magne, ed. *Archaeological Survey. Provincial Museum of Alberta. Occasional Paper* 33. Edmonton.

Kruse, Babs.
1982   Arapaho Alphabet. Arapaho Language Student Workbook. Ethete, Wyo.: Wyoming Indian High School.

Krutz, Gordon W.
1973   Compartmentalization as a Factor in Urban Adjustment: The Kiowa Case. Pp. 101–116 in American Indian Urbanization. J.O. Waddell and O.M. Watson, eds. West Lafayette, Ind.: Purdue University Press.

Kuehn, David D., Carl R. Falk, and Amy Drybred
1982   Archeological Data Recovery at Midipadi Butte, 32DU2, Dunn County, North Dakota. *University of North Dakota. Department of Anthropology. Contribution* 181. Grand Forks.

Kuoni, Carin, et al.
1996   Red River Crossings: Contemporary Native American Artists Respond to Peter Rindisbacher (1806–1834). New York: The Swiss Institute.

Kupferer, Harriet J.
1988   Ancient Drums, Other Moccasins: Native North American Cultural Adaptation. Englewood Cliffs, N.J.: Prentice Hall.

Kurath, Gertrude P.
1957   Pan-indianism in Great Lakes Tribal Festivals. *Journal of American Folk-lore* 70(276):179–182.

Kurkiala, Mikael
1997   "Building the Nation Back Up": The Politics of Identity on the Pine Ridge Indian Reservation. (Ph.D. Dissertation in Anthropology, Uppsala University, Uppsala, Sweden.) Published: *Acta Universitatis Upsaliensis. Uppsala Studies in Cultural Anthropology* 22. Uppsala, Sweden.

Kurz, Rudolph Friederich
1937   Journal of Rudolph Friederich Kurz: An Account of His Experiences among Fur Traders and American Indians on the Mississippi and Upper Missouri Rivers during the Years 1846 to 1852. Myrtis Jarrell, trans.; John N.B. Hewitt, ed. *Bureau of American Ethnology Bulletin* 115. Washington: Smithsonian Institution; U.S. Government Printing Office. (Reprinted: University of Nebraska Press, Lincoln, 1970; also under title: The Journal of Rudolph Friederich Kurz, the Life and Work of This Swiss Artist: Ye Galleon Press, Fairfield, Wash, 1960.)

Kuykendall, J.H.
1903   Reminiscences of Early Texas: A Collection from the Austin Papers. *Quarterly of the Texas State Historical Association* 7(1):29–64. Austin.

Kvasnicka, Robert M., and Herman J. Viola, eds.
1979   The Commissioners of Indian Affairs, 1824–1877. Lincoln: University of Nebraska Press.

LR-NA = National Archives
1824–1881 [Correspondence of the Office of Indian Affairs, Central Office, Letters Received.] (Microfilm Publication M234, 962 Rolls, Letters Received, Records of the Bureau of Indian Affairs, Record Group 75, National Archives, Washington.)

LR-UA = Upper Arkansas Agency
1855–1874 [Correspondence of the Office of Indian Affairs, Upper Arkansas Agency, Letters Received.] (Microfilm Publication M234, Rolls 878–882, Letters Received, Records of the Bureau of Indian Affairs, Record Group 75, National Archives, Washington.)

La Barre, Weston
1938   The Peyote Cult. *Yale University. Publications in Anthropology* 19. New Haven, Conn.: Yale University Press. (Reprinted: Shoe String Press, Hamden, Conn., 1959; also, University of Oklahoma Press, Norman, 1989.)

1960   Twenty Years of Peyote Studies. *Current Anthropology* 1(1):45–60. Chicago.

1969   The Peyote Cult. Enlarged ed. New York: Schocken Books.

1975   The Peyote Cult. Enlarged 4th ed. Hamden, Conn.: Archon Books.

1989   The Peyote Cult. Enlarged 5th ed. Norman: University of Oklahoma Press.

1990   The Ghost Dance: Origins of Religion. Prospect Heights, Ill.: Waveland Press.

———, et al.
1935   [Kiowa Fieldnotes. Santa Fe Laboratory of Anthropology Expedition 1935.] (Manuscript [unnumbered] in Weston La *1193*

Barre Collection, Series 1, Boxes 1, 2, 3, 4, National Anthropological Archives, Smithsonian Institution, Washington.)

Lacombe, Albert
1874   Dictionnaire de la langue des Cris. Montréal: C.O. Beauchemin et Valois. (Inside title page reads: Dictionnaire de langue crise, par un missionnaire de la Saskatchiwan; imprint date: 1873.)

1874a   Grammaire de la langue des Cris. Montréal: Beauchemin et Valois.

1886   First Reader in the English and Blackfoot Languages, with Pictures and Words: Prepared by Order of the Department of Indian Affairs for the Use of Industrial Schools among the Blackfoot Tribes in the NorthWest Territories. Montreal: C.O. Beauchemin and Son.

La Farge, Oliver
1956   A Pictorial History of the American Indian. New York: Crown Publishers.

1957   Termination of Federal Supervision: Disintegration and the American Indians. *The Annals of the American Academy of Political and Social Science* 311:41–46. Philadelphia.

La Flesche, Francis
1885   The Sacred Pipes of Friendship. [Abstract.] Pp. 613–615 in *Proceedings of the American Association for the Advancement of Science, 33d Meeting, held at Philadelphia, Penn., September, 1884.* Salem, Mass.

1889   Death and Funeral Customs among the Omaha. *Journal of American Folk-lore* 2(4):3–11.

1890   The Omaha Buffalo Medicine-Men. *Journal of American Folk-lore* 3(10):215–221.

1900   The Middle Five: Indian Boys at School. Boston: Small, Maynard & Co. (Reprinted as: The Middle Five: Indian Schoolboys of the Omaha Tribe, University of Wisconsin Press, Madison, 1963; also, University of Nebraska Press, Lincoln, 1978.)

1914   Ceremonies and Rituals of the Osage. Pp. 66–69 in Explorations and Field-work of the Smithsonian Institution in 1913. *Smithsonian Miscellaneous Collections* 63(8). Washington: Smithsonian Institution; Government Printing Office.

1917   Omaha and Osage Traditions of Separation. Pp. 459–462 in *Proceedings of the 19th International Congress of Americanists, Held at Washington, December 27–31, 1915.* Frederick W. Hodge, ed. Washington.

1919   Researches among the Osage. *Smithsonian Miscellaneous Collections* 70:110–113. Washington: Smithsonian Institution; Government Printing Office.

1920   The Symbolic Man of the Osage Tribe. *Art and Archaeology* 9:68–72.

1921   The Osage Tribe: Rite of the Chiefs; Sayings of the Ancient Men. Pp. 37–640 in *36th Annual Report of the Bureau of American Ethnology [for] 1914–1915.* Washington: Smithsonian Institution; U.S. Government Printing Office. (Reprinted: Johnson Reprint, New York, 1970.)

1924   Omaha Bow and Arrow-Makers. Pp. 111–116 [117] in *Annaes do XX Congresso Internacional de Americanistas, Rio de Janeiro, Brasil, 20 a 30 de Agosto de 1922.* Rio de Janeiro, Brasil: Imprensa Nacional.

1925   Ethnology of the Osage Indians. *Smithsonian Miscellaneous Collections* 76:104–107. Washington: Smithsonian Institution; Government Printing Office.

1925a   The Osage Tribe: Rite of Vigil. Pp. 31–630 in *39th Annual Report of the Bureau of American Ethnology [for] 1917–'18.* Washington: Smithsonian Institution; U.S. Government Printing Office.

1928   The Osage Tribe: Two Versions of the Child-naming Rite. Pp. 23–164 in *43d Annual Report of the Bureau of American Ethnology [for] 1925–'26.* Washington: Smithsonian Institution; U.S. Government Printing Office.

1930   The Osage Tribe: Rite of the Wa-xo'Be. Pp. 529–833 in *45th Annual Report of the Bureau of American Ethnology [for] 1927–'28.* Washington: Smithsonian Institution; U.S. Government Printing Office.

1932   A Dictionary of the Osage Language. *Bureau of American Ethnology Bulletin* 109. Washington: Smithsonian Institution; U.S. Government Printing Office. (Reprinted: Scholarly Press, St. Clair Shores, Mich., 1976; also, Native American Publishers, Brighton, Mich., 1990.)

1939   War Ceremony and Peace Ceremony of the Osage Indians. *Bureau of American Ethnology Bulletin* 101. Washington: Smithsonian Institution; U.S. Government Printing Office.

1963   The Middle Five: Indian Schoolboys of the Omaha Tribe. Foreword by David A. Baerreis. Madison: University of Wisconsin Press. (Reprinted: University of Nebraska Press, Lincoln, 1978.)

1995   The Osage and the Invisible World: From the Works of Francis La Flesche. Garrick Bailey, ed. Norman: University of Oklahoma Press.

Lafora, Nicolás de
1958   The Frontiers of New Spain: Nicolás de Lafora's Description, 1766–1768. Lawrence Kinnaird, ed. and trans.; Translation of Nicolás de Lafora's *Relación del viaje que hizo a los presidios internos. Quivira Society Publications* 13. Berkeley, Calif.: The Quivira Society. (Reprinted: Arno Press, New York, 1967.)

La France, Joseph
1749   [Narrative.] Appendix II. Pp. 243–248 in Report from the Committee Appointed to Inquire into the State and Condition of the Countries Adjoining to Hudson's Bay, and of the Trade Carried on There. *Reports from Committees of the House of Commons, Which Have Been Printed by Order of the House and Are Not Inserted in the Journals,* Vol. 2. London, 1803.

Lagassé, Jean H.
1959   The People of Indian Ancestry in Manitoba. 3 vols. Winnipeg: Manitoba Department of Agriculture and Immigration.

Lah, Ronald L.
1980   Ethnoaesthetics of Northern Arapaho Indian Music. (Ph.D. Dissertation in Anthropology, Northwestern University, Evanston, Ill.)

La Harpe, Bénard de
1831   Journal historique de l'éstablissement des Français à la Louisiane. Nouvelle-Orléans: A.L. Boimare; Paris: H. Bossange. (English translation in: Historical Collections of Louisiana, Vol. 3, by B.F. French, New York, 1851; see also La Harpe 1971.)

1951   Exploration of the Arkansas River by Bénard de La Harpe, 1721–1722: Extracts from His Journal and Instructions. Translated and Annotated by Ralph A. Smith. *The Arkansas Historical Quarterly* 10(4):339–363. Fayetteville.

1959   Account of the Journey of Bénard de la Harpe: Discovery Made by Him of Several Nations Situated in the West. Ralph A. Smith, trans. and ed. 3 Pts. *Southwestern Historical Quarterly* 62(2):246–259, (3):371–385, (4):525–541. Austin, Tex.

1971   Historical Journal of the Settlement of the French in Louisiana. Virginia Koenig and Joan Cain, trans.; Glenn R. Conrad, ed. *The U.S.L. History Series* 3. Lafayette, La.: University of Southwestern Louisiana, Center for Louisiana Studies. (Originally publ. in French in 1831.)

Lahontan, Louis Armand de Lom d'Arce, Baron de
1703   New Voyages to North-America: An Account of the Several Nations of That Vast Continent ... a Geographical Description of Canada ... also a Dialogue between the Author and a General of the Savages ... to Which Is Added a Dictionary of the Algonkine Language, Which Is Generally Spoke in North-America. Written in French by Baron Lahontan; done into English in two volumes. London: Printed for H. Bonwicke, T. Goodwin, M. Wotton, B. Tooke, and S. Manship. (Reprinted, with Facsimilies of Original Title-pages, Maps, and Illustrations, and the addition of Introduction, Notes and Index by Reuben G. Thwaites: A.C. McClurg, Chicago, 1905; also, Burt Franklin, New York, 1970.)

_____ 1905 *see* 1703 (reprint info.)

Lahren, Larry A.
1971   Archeological Investigations in the Upper Yellowstone Valley, Montana. Pp. 168–182 in Aboriginal Man and Environments on the Plateau of Northwest America. Arnoud H. Stryd and Rachel A. Smith, ed. Alberta: University of Calgary Archaeological Association.

1976   The Myers-Hindman Site: An Exploratory Study of Human Occupation Patterns in the Upper Yellowstone Valley from 7000 B.C. to A.D. 1200. (Ph.D. Dissertation in Archeology, University of Calgary, Calgary, Alta. Microfiche: 28532, National Library of Canada, Ottawa, 1977.) Livingston, Mont.: Anthropologos Researches International Incorporated.

Laird, Mr.
1877   [Letter to the Minister of the Interior, dated Battleford, 19 November 1877.] (Manuscript in Group Record 10, Vol. 3656, File 9092, National Archives of Canada, Ottawa.)

Lamar, Howard R.
1977   The Trader on the American Frontier: Myth's Victim. College Station, Tex.: Texas A&M University Press.

Lamar, Mirabeau Buonaparte
1921–1927   The Papers of Mirabeau Buonaparte Lamar; Edited from the Original Papers in the Texas State Library. 6 vols. in 7. Vols. 1–3, ed. by Charles A. Gulick, Jr., and Katherine Elliott; Vol. 4, ed. by Charles A. Gulick, Jr., and Winnie Allen; Vols. 5–6, ed. by Harriet Smither. Austin, Tex.: A.C. Baldwin. (Vols. 3–6 printed by Von Boechmann-Jones. Reprinted: Pemberton Press, Austin, Tex., 1968; also, AMS Press, New York, 1973.)

Lamb, George F.
1932   Earth Lodge Ruins of Indian Habitation on Rose Creek in Thayer County. (Presumably Pre-historic). *Nebraska History* 13(3):169–172. Lincoln.

Lamb, W. Kaye, ed. 1957 *see* Harmon, Daniel Williams 1957

_____, ed. 1970 *see* Mackenzie, Alexander 1970

Lame Deer, Archie Fire *see* Fire/Lame Deer, Archie

Lame Deer, John Fire *see* Fire/Lame Deer, John

Landals, Alison J.
1990   The Maple Leaf Site: Implications of the Analysis of Small-Scale Bison Kills. Pp. 122–151 in Hunters of the Recent Past. Leslie B. Davis and Brian O.K. Reeves, eds. London: Unwin Hyman.

Landes, Ruth
1937   Ojibwa Sociology. *Columbia University Contributions to Anthropology* 29. New York.

1938   The Ojibwa Woman. *Columbia University Contributions to Anthropology* 31. New York.

1959   Dakota Warfare. *Southwestern Journal of Anthropology* 15(1):43–52. Albuquerque.

1968   The Mystic Lake Sioux: Sociology of the Mdewakantonwan Santee. Madison: University of Wisconsin Press.

1968a   Ojibwa Religion and the Midéwiwin. Madison: University of Wisconsin Press.

1970   Ojibwa Religion. Madison: University of Wisconsin Press.

Lanford, Benson L.
1980   Parflesche and Crow Beadwork Design. *American Indian Art Magazine* 6(1) [Special Crow Issue]:32–39. Scottsdale, Ariz.

Lang, Gottfried O.
1953   A Study in Culture Contact and Culture Change: The Whiterocks Utes in Transition. *University of Utah Anthropological Papers* 15. Salt Lake City: University of Utah Press.

Lang, Gretchen Chesley
1982   "Sugar" Is New to Indian People. *Plainswoman* 6(4):4–6. Grand Forks, N.Dak.

1989   "Making Sense" About Diabetes: Dakota Narratives of Illness. *Medical Anthropology* 11(3):305–327. Pleasantville, N.Y.

Lange, Charles H. 1979 *see* Handbook Vol. 9 (1979:201–205)

Lanning, C.M.
1882   A Grammar and Vocabulary of the Blackfoot Language; Being a Concise and Comprehensive Grammar for the Use of the Learner, to Which Is Added an Exhaustive Vocabulary. Compiled from Translations by Joseph Kipp and W.S. Gladstone, Jr. Fort Benton, Mont.: The Author.

Lanternari, Vittorio
1963   The Religions of the Oppressed: A Study of Modern Messianic Cults. Lisa Sergio, trans. New York: A. Knopf.

Lapham, Increase A., Levi Blossom, and George G. Dousman
1870   A Paper on the Number, Locality and Times of Removal of the Indians of Wisconsin; with an Appendix Containing a Complete Chronology of Wisconsin, from the Earliest Times down to the Adoption of the State Constitution, in 1848. Milwaukee: Starr's Book and Job Printing House.

Larkin, Georgia
1964   Chief Blue Cloud: Biography of the Yankton Sioux Chief. *The Blue Cloud Quarterly* 10(2):1–33. Marvin, S.Dak.: Blue Cloud Abbey.

Larmour, Jean
1970   Edgar Dewdney and the Aftermath of the Rebellion. *Saskatchewan History* 23:105–117. Saskatoon, Sask.

1980   Edgar Dewdney: Indian Commissioner in the Transition Period of Indian Settlement, 1879–1884. *Saskatchewan History* 33:13–24. Saskatoon, Sask.

Larner, John William, Jr.
1972   The Kootenay Plains (Alberta) Land Question and Cana-

dian Indian Policy, 1799–1947. (Ph.D. Dissertation in History, West Virginia University, Morgantown, W.Va.; Photocopy: University Microfilms, Ann Arbor, Mich., 1973.)

1976   The Kootenay Plains Land Question and Canadian Indian Policy, 1799–1949: A Synopsis. *The Western Canadian Journal of Anthropology* 6(2):83–92. Edmonton, Alta.

LaRocque, Emma
1983   The Métis in English Canadian Literature. *The Canadian Journal of Native Studies* 3(1):85–94. Brandon, Man.

1986   Conversations on Métis Identity. *Prairie Fire* 7(1):19–24. Winnipeg, Man.

Larocque, François-Antoine
1910   Journal of Larocque from the Assiniboine to the Yellowstone, 1805. L.J. Burpee, ed. *Canadian Archives Publications* 3. Ottawa.

1985   François-Antoine Larocque's "Yellowstone Journal." Pp. 156–220 in Early Fur Trade on the Northern Plains: Canadian Traders among the Mandan and Hidatsa Indians, 1738–1818. W. Raymond Wood and Thomas D. Thiessen, eds. Norman: University of Oklahoma Press.

Larpenteur, Charles 1898 *see* Coues, Elliott, ed. 1898

———— 1933 *see* Quaife, Milo Milton, ed. 1933

Larson, Daniel O.
1987   An Economic Analysis of the Differential Effects of Population Growth and Climatic Variability among Hunters and Gathers and Food Producers. (Ph.D. Dissertation in Anthropology, University of California, Santa Barbara.)

Larson, Mary Lou
1990   Early Plains Archaic Technological Organization: The Laddle Creek Example. (Ph.D. Dissertation in Anthropology, University of California, Santa Barbara.)

Larson, Mary Lou, and Julie E. Francis, eds.
1997   Changing Perspectives of the Archaic on the Northwestern Plains and Rocky Mountains. Vermillion: University of South Dakota Press.

Larson, Robert W.
1997   Red Cloud: Warrior-Statesman of the Lakota Sioux. Norman: University of Oklahoma Press.

La Salle, Nicolas de
1898   Relation of the Discovery of the Mississippi River, Written from the Narrative of Nicolas de La Salle, Otherwise Known as the Little M. de La Salle. Melville B. Anderson, trans. Chicago: The Caxton Club.

La Salle, Robert Cavelier, Sieur de
1876–1886 Lettre du Découvreur à un de ses associés; 1679. — 29 Septembre 1680. Pp. 32–93 in Vol. 2 of Découvertes et établissements des Français dans l'ouest et dans le sud de l'Amérique septentrionale (1614–1754); Mémoires et documents originaux. Pierre Margry, comp. and ed. 6 vols. Paris: D. Jouaust.

1876–   Voyage de M. de La Salle à la rivière Mississipi [1680a]. Pp.
1886a   93–102 in Vol. 2 of Découvertes et établissements des Français dans l'ouest et dans le sud de l'Amérique septentrionale (1614–1754); Mémoires et documents originaux. Pierre Margry, comp. and ed. 6 vols. Paris: D. Jouaust.

1876–   Lettre de Cavelier de La Salle; Au fort Frontenac, le 22
1886b   Aoust 1682 [i.e.1681]. Pp. 212–262 in Vol. 2 of Découvertes et établissements des Français dans l'ouest et dans le sud de l'Amérique septentrionale (1614–1754); Mémoires et documents originaux. Pierre Margry, comp. and ed. 6 vols. Paris: D. Jouaust.

1876–   Seconde lettre de Cavelier de La Salle à M. de La Barre. Du
1886c   portage de Checagou, 4 Juin 1683. Pp. 317–328 in Vol. 2 of Découvertes et établissements des Français dans l'ouest et dans le sud de l'Amérique septentrionale (1614–1754); Mémoires et documents originaux. Pierre Margry, comp. and ed. 6 vols. Paris: D. Jouaust.

La Société historique de Saint-Boniface
1991   Histoire de Saint-Boniface, tome 1: A l'ombre des cathédrales, les origines de la colonie jusqu'en 1870. Saint-Boniface, Man.: Les Éditions de Blé.

Lass, William E.
1994   The History and Significance of the Northwest Fur Company, 1965–1869. *North Dakota History* 61(3):21–40. Bismarck.

Lass, William E., and Wesley R. Hurt
1956   Frontier Photographer: Stanley Morrow's Dakota Years. Vermillion, S.Dak.: University of South Dakota.

Lassiter, Luke E.
1997   "Charlie Brown": Not Just Another Essay On The Gourd Dance. *American Indian Culture and Research Journal* 21(4):75–103. Los Angeles.

1998   The Power of Kiowa Song: A Collaborative Ethnography. Tucson: University of Arizona Press.

Latham, Robert Gordon
1854   On the Languages of New California. Pp. 72–86 in *Proceedings of the Philological Society [of London]* 6. London.

1856   On the Languages of Northern, Western, and Central America. Pp. 57–115 in *Transactions of the Philological Society [of London] for 1856*. London.

1860   Opuscula: Essays, Chiefly Philological and Ethnological. London: Williams and Norgate.

1862   Elements of Comparative Philology. London: Walton and Maberly.

Laubin, Reginald, and Gladys Laubin
1977   The Indian Tipi: Its History, Construction, and Use. With a History of the Tipi by Stanley Vestal. 2d ed. Norman: University of Oklahoma Press. (Reprinted in 1980 and 1989; originally publ.: Ballantine Books, New York, 1957.)

1977a   Indian Dances of North America: Their Importance to Indian Life. Norman: University of Oklahoma Press.

1980   American Indian Archery. Norman: University of Oklahoma Press. (Reprinted in 1990.)

Laughlin, William S.
1972   Ecology and Population Structure in the Arctic. Pp. 379–392 in The Structure of Human Populations. Geoffrey A. Harrison and Anthony J. Boyce, eds. Oxford, England: Clarendon Press.

Laurie, John L.
1957–1959 The Stoney Indians of Alberta. 4 vols. (Manuscripts in the Glenbow Foundation, Calgary, Alta.)

1959   A Grammar of the Stoney Language. (Manuscript in the Glenbow Foundation, Calgary, Alta.)

1959a   Dictionary of the Stoney Language. (Manuscript in the Glenbow Foundation, Calgary, Alta.)

Lavallée, Guy Albert Sylvestre
1986   A Profile of My Political Life. *Kerygma* 47(20):253–265. Ottawa: Institut des sciences de la mission, Université Saint-Paul.

1988   The Métis People of St. Laurent, Manitoba: An Introductory Ethnography. (M.A. Thesis in Anthropology, University of British Columbia, Vancouver, B.C.)

1990   The Michif French Language: A Symbol of Métis Group Identity and Solidarity at St. Laurent, Man. (Manuscript in G.A.S. Lavallée's possession.)

1992   Prayer of a Métis Priest [First Peoples and the Constitution Conference, Ottawa, March, 1992]. *Bulletin of Western Oblate History Project* 20(October):12–14.

1997   Prayers of a Métis Priest: Conversations with God on the Political Experience of the Canadian Métis, 1992–1994. Winnipeg, Man.: G. Lavallée / Kromar Printing.

Lavender, David S.
1954   Bent's Fort. Garden City, N.Y.: Doubleday (Reprinted: University of Nebraska Press, Lincoln, 1972.)

Laverdure, Patline, and Ida Rose Allard
1983   The Michif Dictionary: Turtle Mountain Chippewa Cree. John C. Crawford, ed. Winnipeg, Man.: Pemmican Publications.

La Vere, David
1998   Life among the Texas Indians: The WPA Narratives. *Elma Dill Russell Spencer Series in the West and Southwest* 18. College Station, Tex.: Texas A&M University Press.

La Vérendrye, Pierre Gaultier de Varennes, Sieur de
1927   Journals and Letters of Pierre Gaultier de Varennes de la Vérendrye and His Sons. With Correspondence between the Governors of Canada and the French Court, Touching the Search of the Western Sea. Edited with Introduction and Notes by Lawrence J. Burpee. *Publications of the Champlain Society* 16. Toronto: The Champlain Society.

Laviolette, Gontran
1944   The Sioux Indians in Canada. Regina, Sask.: The Marian Press.

1991   The Dakota Sioux in Canada. Winnipeg, Man.: DLM Publications.

Law, John 1720 *see* [Defoe, Daniel] 1720

Law, Laura T.
1953   History of Rolette County, North Dakota, and Yarns of the Pioneers. Minneapolis: The Lund Press. (Reprinted: Star Printing [for] Rolla Centennial Committee, Rolla Kiwanis Club, Rolla, N.Dak., 1989.)

Lawlor, Laurie
1994   Shadow Catcher: The Life and Work of Edward S. Curtis. New York: Walker; also, Vancouver: Douglas & McIntrye.

Lawrence, Deirdre E., and Deborah Wythe
1996   Guide to the Culin Archival Collection. Brooklyn, N.Y.: The Brooklyn Museum.

Lawson, Michael L.
1982   Dammed Indians: The Pick-Sloan Plan and the Missouri River Sioux, 1944–1980. Foreword by Vine Deloria, Jr. Norman: University of Oklahoma Press. (Reprinted: 1994.)

1982a   Federal Water Projects and Indian Lands: The Pick-Sloan Plan, A Case Study. *American Indian Culture and Research Journal* 6(4):23–40. Los Angeles.

Lawton, Sherman P.
1968   The Duncan-Wilson Bluff Shelter: A Stratified Site of the Southern Plains. *Bulletin of the Oklahoma Anthropological Society* 16:1–94. Oklahoma.

Lazarus, Edward
1991   Black Hills/White Justice: The Sioux Nation Versus the United States, 1775 to the Present. New York: Harper Collins.

Lea, Luke 1850, 1851 *see* ARCIA 1849–

Leach, Duane M.
1959   The Santee Sioux, 1866–1890. (M.A. Thesis in History, University of South Dakota, Vermillion.)

Le Boullenger, Jean-Baptiste
[1725]   [French and Miami-Illinois Dictionary.] (Manuscript in the John Carter Brown Library, Brown University, Providence, R.I.)

Leckie, William H.
1963   The Military Conquest of the Southern Plains. Norman: University of Oklahoma Press.

1967   The Buffalo Soldiers: A Narrative of the Negro Cavalry in the West. Norman: University of Oklahoma Press.

LeClaire, Nancy, and George Cardinal
1998   Alberta Elders' Cree Dictionary—alperta ohci kehtehayak nehiyaw otwestamâkewasinahikan. Earle Waugh, ed. Edmonton, Alta.: The University of Alberta Press.

Lecompte, Janet
1964   Gantt's Fort and Bent's Picket Post. *Colorado Magazine* 41(4):111–125. Denver.

1964a   Sand Creek. *Colorado Magazine* 41(4):314–335. Denver.

1972   Auguste Pierre Chouteau. Pp. 63–90 in Vol. 4 of The Mountain Men and the Fur Trade of the Far West. 10 vols. Leroy R. Hafen, ed. Glendale, Calif.: Arthur H. Clark Company.

1972a   Pierre Chouteau, Jr. Pp. 91–124 in Vol. 4 of The Mountain Men and the Fur Trade of the Far West. 10 vols. Leroy R. Hafen ed. Glendale, Calif.: Arthur H. Clark Company.

Lederman, Anne
1988   Old Indian and Métis Fiddling in Manitoba: Origins, Structure and Question of Syncretism. *The Canadian Journal of Native Studies* 8(2):205–230. Brandon, Man.

Lee, Dayna B., ed.
1995   Remaining Ourselves: Music and Tribal Memory; Traditional Music in Contemporary Communities. Oklahoma City: State Arts Council of Oklahoma.

Lee, Dorothy Sara D.
1952   The Religious Dimension of Human Experience Pp. 338–359 in Religious Perspectives in College Teaching. Hoxie N. Fairchild, ed. New York: The Ronald Press.

1959   Responsibility among the Dakotas. Pp. 59–69 in Freedom and Culture, by Dorothy Sara D. Lee. Englewood Cliffs, N.J.: Prentice-Hall.

1979   Native North American Music and Oral Data: A Catalogue of Sound Recordings, 1893–1976. Foreword by Willard Rhodes. Bloomington: Indiana University Press.

Lee, Dorothy Sara D., and Maria La Vigna, eds.
1985   Omaha Indian Music [Sound Recording]: Field recordings made by Alice Cunningham Fletcher and Francis La Flesche. 1 sound cassette/disc with booklet. Washington: Library of Congress, American Folklife Center.

Leforge, Thomas H. 1928, 1974 *see* Marquis, Thomas B. 1928 and (reprint info.)

Le Gardeur de Saint-Pierre, Jacques Repentigny
1887   Note C: Memoir or *Summary Journal of the Expedition of Jacques Repentigny Legardeur de Saint Pierre, Knight of the Royal and Military Order of Saint Louis, Captain of a* *1197*

Company of Troops detached from the Marine in Canada, Charged with the Discovery of the Western Sea.* [1752.] Pp. clviii–clxix in *Report on Canadian Archives by Douglas Brymner, Archivist, 1886.* Ottawa: MacLean, Roger and Co. (Originally publ. in French, pp. 637–652 in Vol. 6 of Découvertes et établissements des Français dans l'ouest et dans le sud de l'Amérique septentrionale, 1614–1754; Pierre Margry, ed.; D. Jouaust, Paris, 1886.)

Lehmer, Donald J.
1951   Pottery Types from the Dodd Site, Oahe Reservoir South, South Dakota. *Plains Archeological Conference News letter* 4(2). Omaha, Nebr.

1954   Archeological Investigations in the Oahe Dam Area, South Dakota, 1950–51. *Bureau of American Ethnology Bulletin* 158; *River Basin Surveys Papers* 7. Washington: Smithsonian Institution; U.S. Government Printing Office.

1963   The Plains Bison Hunt — Prehistoric and Historic. *Plains Anthropologist* 8(22):211–217.

1966   The Fire Heart Creek Site. Warren W. Caldwell, ed. *Smithsonian Institution. River Basin Surveys. Publications in Salvage Archeology* 1. Lincoln, Nebr.

1966a   Horizon and Tradition in the Northern Plains. *American Antiquity* 31(4):511–516.

1970   Climate and Culture History in the Middle Missouri Valley. Pp. 117–129 in Pleistocene and Recent Environments of the Central Great Plains. Wakefield Dort, Jr., and J. Knox Jones, Jr., eds. *University of Kansas. Department of Geology. Special Publication* 3. Lawrence: University Press of Kansas.

1971   Introduction to Middle Missouri Archeology. *U.S. Department of the Interior. National Park Service. Anthropological Papers* 1. Washington.

1977   The Other Side of the Fur Trade. Pp. 98–104 in Selected Writings of Donald J. Lehmer. *Reprints in Anthropology* 8. Lincoln: J&L Reprint Company.

1977a   Epidemics among the Indians of the Upper Missouri. Pp. 105–111 in Selected Writings of Donald J. Lehmer. *Reprints in Anthropology* 8. Lincoln: J&L Reprint Company.

Lehmer, Donald J., and Warren W. Caldwell
1966   Horizon and Tradition in the Northern Plains. *American Antiquity* 31(4):511–116.

Lehmer, Donald J., and David T. Jones
1968   Arikara Archeology: The Bad River Phase. *Smithsonian Institution. River Basin Surveys. Publications in Salvage Archeology* 7. Washington. (Reprinted: J&L Reprint Company, Lincoln, Nebr., 1978.)

Lehmer, Donald J., L.K. Meston, and C.L. Dill
1973   Structural Details of a Middle Missouri House. *Plains Anthropologist* 18(60):160–166.

Leighton, Dorothea, and Clyde Kluckhohn
1947   Children of the People: The Navaho Individual and His Development. Cambridge, Mass.: Harvard University Press.

Leman, Wayne E.
1980   A Reference Grammar of the Cheyenne Language. 2 vols. *University of Northern Colorado. Museum of Anthropology. Occasional Publications in Anthropology. Linguistic Series* 5. Greeley, Colo.

1981   Cheyenne Pitch Rules. *International Journal of American Linguistics* 47(4):283–309. Chicago.
———, ed.
1987   Náévåhóo'ôhtséme/ We Are Going Back Home: Cheyenne

History and Stories Told by James Shoulderblade and Others. *Algonquian and Iroquoian Linguistics Memoir* 4. Winnepeg, Man.

Lenius, Brian J., and Dave M. Olinyk
1990   The Rainy River Composite: Revisions to Late Woodland Taxonomy. Pp. 77–112 in The Woodland Tradition in the Western Great Lakes: Papers Presented to Elden Johnson. Guy E. Gibbon, ed. *University of Minnesota Publications in Anthropology* 4. Minneapolis.

Lent, D. Geneva
1973   West of the Mountains: James Sinclair and the Hudson's Bay Company. Seattle: University of Washington Press.

Leonard, Zenas
1904   Narrative of the Adventures of Zenas Leonard. Adventures of Zenas Leonard, Fur Trader and Trapper 1831–1836. Edited by W.F. Wagner; With Maps and Illustrations. Cleveland: The Burrows Brothers Company.

1934   Narrative of the Adventures of Zenas Leonard, Written by Himself. Milo M. Quaife, ed. Chicago: The Lakeside Press. (Reprinted: University of Nebraska Press, Lincoln, 1978.)

1959   The Adventures of Zenas Leonard, Fur Trader. Edited by John C. Ewers. New ed., 1st ed. Norman: University of Oklahoma Press.

Le Page du Pratz, Antoine Simeone
1758   Histoire de la Louisiane. 3 vols. Paris: De Bure.

1774   The History of Louisiana; or of the Western Parts of Virginia and Carolina; Containing a Description of the Countries That Lie on Both Sides of the River Mississippi; with an Account of the Settlements, Inhabitants, Soil, Climate, and Products. Translated from the French of M. Le Page Du Pratz, with Some Notes and Observations Relating to Our Colonies. New ed. London: Printed for T. Becket. (Reprinted: J.S.W. Harmanson, New Orleans, 1947; Claitor's Publishing Division, Baton Rouge, 1972; also, edited by Joseph G. Tregle, Jr.: Louisiana State University Press for the Louisiana American Revolution Bicentennial Commission, Baton Rouge, 1975.)

———   1947 *see* 1774 (reprint info.)

Le Raye, Charles
1908   The Journal of Charles Le Raye. *South Dakota Historical Collections* 4:150–180. Sioux Falls, S.Dak.

Leslie, Jean
1977   Victoria Whitney. *Heritage* 5(4):7–10.

Leslie, Robert H.
1979   The Eastern Jornada Mogollon, Extreme Southeastern New Mexico (A Summary). Pp. 179–199 in Jornada Mogollon Archaeology: Proceedings of the First Jornada Conference. Patrick H. Beckett and Regge N. Wiseman, eds. Las Cruces: New Mexico State University, Cultural Resources Management Division.

Lessard, F. Dennis
1980   Crow Indian Art: The Nez Perce Connection. *American Indian Art Magazine* 6(1) [Special Crow Issue]:54–63. Scottsdale, Ariz. (Reprinted: Chandler Institute, Missions, S.Dak., 1984.)

1984   Classic Crow Beadwork: Upper Missouri River Roots. Pp. 61–68 in Crow Indian Art: Papers Presented at the Crow Indian Art Symposium Sponsored by the Chandler Institute, April 1981, Pierre, South Dakota. F. Dennis Lessard, ed. Mission, S.Dak.: Chandler Institute.
———, ed.
1984a   Crow Indian Art: Papers Presented at the Crow Indian Art Symposium Sponsored by the Chandler Institute, April 1981, Pierre, South Dakota. F. Dennis Lessard, ed. Mission, S.Dak.: Chandler Institute.

1990   Pictographic Art in Beadwork from the Cheyenne River Sioux. *American Indian Art Magazine* 16(1):54–63. Scottsdale, Ariz.

1990a   Defining the Central Plains Art Area. *American Indian Art Magazine* 16(1):36–43. Scottsdale, Ariz.

1991   Pictographic Sioux Beadwork: A Re-examination. *American Indian Art Magazine* 16(4):70–74. Scottsdale, Ariz.

1992   Plains Pictographic Art: A Source of Ethnographic Information. *American Indian Art Magazine* 17(2):62–69, 90. Scottsdale, Ariz.

Lessard, Rosemary
1970   The Pine Ridge Sun Dance — A Description. *American Indian Crafts and Culture* 4(8):14–15, 20. Tulsa, Okla.

Lesser, Alexander
1928   Bibliography of American Folklore, 1915–1928. *Journal of American Folk-lore* 41(159).

1929   Kinship Origins in the Light of Some Distributions. *American Anthropologist,* n.s. 31(4):710–730.

1929–1930   [Kitsai Linguistic Fieldnotes.] (Copies of manuscripts in D.R. Parks's possession.)

1930   Levirate and Fraternal Polyandry among the Pawnees. *Man: A Monthly Record of Anthropological Science* 30(6):98–101. London.

1930a   Some Aspects of Siouan Kinship. Pp. 463–471 in *Proceedings of the 23d International Congress of Americanists held at New York, September 17–22, 1928.* Lancaster, Pa.: The Science Press Printing Company.

1933   The Pawnee Ghost Dance Hand Game: Ghost Dance Revival and Ethnic Identity. *Contributions to Anthropology* 16. New York: Columbia University Press. (Reprinted: AMS Press, New York, 1969; see also Lesser 1978.)

1933a   Cultural Significance of the Ghost Dance. *American Anthropologist,* n.s. 35(1):108–115.

1958   Siouan Kinship. (Ph.D. Dissertation in Anthropology, Columbia University, New York City.)

1961   Education and the Future of Tribalism in the United States: The Case of the American Indian. *Social Science Review* 35:135–143. (Reprinted: The Right Not to Assimilate. Pp. 583–593 in Readings in Anthropology, Vol. 2, Morton H. Fried, ed. New York: Thomas Y. Crowell.)

1968   The Right Not to Assimilate: The Case of the American Indian. Pp. 583–593 in Readings in Anthropology. Morton H. Fried, ed. New York: Thomas Y. Crowell.

_____   1969, 1996 *see* 1933, 1978 (reprint info.)

1977   Kitsai Texts. Pp. 44–64 Caddoan Texts. Douglas R. Parks ed. *International Journal of American Linguistics. Native American Text Series* 2(1). Chicago: The University of Chicago Press.

1978   The Pawnee Ghost Dance Hand Game: Ghost Dance Revival and Ethnic Identity. [Wisconsin ed.] Madison: University of Wisconsin Press. (Originally publ. as: *Contributions to Anthropology* 16. Columbia University Press, New York City, 1933. Reprinted, with an Introduction to Bison Books edition by Alice B. Kehoe: University of Nebraska Press, Lincoln, 1996.)

1979   Caddoan Kinship Systems. *Nebraska History* 60(2):260–271. Lincoln.

Lesser, Alexander, and Gene Weltfish
1932   Composition of the Caddoan Linguistic Stock. *Smithsonian Miscellaneous Collections* 87(6):1–15; (*Publication* 3141). Washington: Smithsonian Institution; Government Printing Office.

Lester, Patrick D.
1995   The Biographical Directory of Native American Painters. Tulsa, Okla.: SIR Publications.

Le Sueur, Pierre-Charles
1700   [Journal en forme de lettre de M. Le Sueur sur le Mississippi et l'intérieur des terres en 1700.] (Manuscript in Archives de la Marine, 4JJ14, No. 4, Archives Nationales, Paris.)

Letakots-Lesa (Eagle Chief)
1907   Introduction to the Pawnee Songs. Pp. 96–99 in The Indians' Book. Natalie (Curtis) Burlin, Recorder and ed. New York: Harper and Brothers.

Létourneau, Henri
1978   [Henri Létourneau] Raconte. Winnipeg, Man.: Editions Bois Brûlés. (Reprinted, 2d ed., 1980.)

Levathes, Louise E.
1988   The Man and the Myth: Remington. *National Geographic* 174(2):200–230. Washington.

Levin, Norman Balfour
1964   The Assiniboine Language. *Indiana University Research Center in Anthropology, Folklore, and Linguistics. Publication* 32; *International Journal of American Linguistics* 30(3, Pt.2). Chicago.

Levine, Frances
1991   Economic Perspectives on the Comanchero Trade. Pp. 155–169 in Farmers, Hunters, and Colonists: Interaction between the Southwest and the Southern Plains. Revised Papers from a Conference on the Plains-Pueblo Interaction held at the Fort Burgwin Research Center of Southern Methodist University, Ranchos de Taos, N.Mex., in September 1987. Katherine A. Spielmann, ed. Tucson: University of Arizona Press.

Levine, Frances, and Martha Doty Freeman
1982   A Study of Documentary and Archeological Evidence for Comanchero Activity in the Texas Pan-handle. Austin: Texas Historical Commission.

Levine, Frances, and Joseph C. Winter, eds.
1987   Investigations at Sites 48 and 77, Santa Rosa Lake, Guadalupe County, New Mexico: An Enquiry into the Nature of Archeological Reality. (Prepared under the Supervision of Joseph C. Winter, Principal Investigator for the U.S. Army Corps of Engineers, Contract No. DACW67-83-C-0013.) Albuquerque: University of New Mexico, Office of Contract Archeology.

Levine, Stuart, and Nancy O. Lurie, eds.
1968   The American Indian Today. Deland, Fla.: Everett/ Edwards, Inc. (Reprinted: Pelican Books, New York, 1970.)

Levy, Jerrold E.
1958   Kiowa and Comanche: Report from the Field. *Anthropology Tomorrow* 6(2):30–44.

1959   A Recent Revival of Some Kiowa Warrior Societies. (Paper read before the Central States Anthropological Society Meetings, Madison, Wis.)

1959a   After Custer: Kiowa Political and Social Organization from the Reservation Period to the Present. (Ph.D. Dissertation in Anthropology, University of Chicago, Chicago.)

1961   Ecology of the South Plains. Pp.18–15 in Symposium: Patterns of Land Utilization and Other Papers. *Proceedings of the 1961 Annual Meeting of the American Ethnological* *1199*

Society. Viola Garfield, ed. Seattle: University of Washington Press.

Lewallen, Arlene
1998   Nourishing Hearts, Creative Hands: Contemporary Art by Native American Women. Hampton, Va.: Hampton University Museum.

Lewis, Emily H.
1980   Wo'wakita: Reservation Recollections: A People's History of the Allen Issue Station District on the Pine Ridge Indian Reservation of South Dakota. Sioux Falls, S.Dak.: Augustana College, Center for Western Studies.

Lewis, G. Malcolm
1975   The Recognition and Delimitation of the Northern Interior Grasslands during the Eighteenth Century. Pp. 23–44 in Images of the Plains: The Role of Human Nature in Settlement. Brian W. Blouet and Martin P. Lawson, eds. Lincoln: University of Nebraska Press.

Lewis, Henry
1967   The Valley of the Mississippi Illustrated. Edited with an Introduction by Bertha L. Heilbron. A. Hermina Poatgieter, trans. St. Paul: Minnesota Historical Society.

Lewis, James Otto
1835–1836 The Aboriginal Portfolio; or, A Collection of Portraits of the Most Celebrated Chiefs of the North American Indians. Philadelphia: J.O. Lewis.

Lewis, Meriwether 1805, 1806, 1832 *see* Lewis, Meriwether, [and William Clark] 1832

Lewis, Meriwether, and William Clark
1809   The Travels of Capts. Lewis and Clarke, by Order of the Government of the United States; Performed in the Years 1804, 1805, and 1806; Being Upward of Three Thousand Miles, from St. Louis, by Way of the Missouri, and Columbia Rivers, to the Pacifick [sic] Ocean; Containing an Account of the Indian Tribes, Who Inhabit the Western Part of the Continent Unexplored, and Unknown Before; with Copious Delineations of the Manners, Customs, Religion, &c. of the Indians, Compiled from Various Authentic Sources, and Documents; to Which Is Subjoined, a Summary of the Statistical View of the Indian Nations, from the Official Communication of Meriwether Lewis. [Earliest American ed. of the spurious account of the Lewis and Clark expedition.] Philadelphia: Hubbard Lester. (Also publ. in England [under slightly different title]: Printed for Longman, Hurst, Rees, and Orme, London, 1809.)

1814   History of the Expedition under the Command of Captains Lewis and Clark, to the Sources of the Missouri; Thence Across the Rocky Mountains and Down the River Columbia to the Pacific Ocean; Performed during the Years 1804–5–6. By Order of the Government of the United States. Prepared for the Press by Paul Allen. [1st Nicholas Biddle edition.]. Philadelphia: Bradford and Inskeep; New York: Abm. H. Inskeep. (Reprinted in 1817; also A.C. McClurg, Chicago, 1902; and, J.B. Lippincott Company, Philadelphia, 1961. See also MacVickar, Archibald, 1842.)

Lewis, Meriwether, [and William Clark]
1832   Lewis and Clarke's Expedition. [Communicated to Congress by Thomas Jefferson, February 19, 1806; containing] Extract of a Letter from Meriwether Lewis to the President of the United States, dated Fort Mandan, April 7, 1805 [titled]: A Statistical View of the Indian Nations Inhabiting the Territory of Louisiana, and the Countries Adjacent to Its Northern and Western Boundaries. Pp. [705] 706–721 in *American State Papers. Documents, Legislative and Executive, of the Congress of the United States,* Vol. IV [i.e. I], *Class* II: Indian Affairs. Washington: Gales and Seaton. (Reprinted as: Estimate of Eastern Indians, pp. 386–450 in Vol. 3 of Journals of the Lewis and Clark Expedition. Gary

E. Moulton, ed. University of Nebraska Press, Lincoln, 1987. Pp. 721–725 in *American State Papers* is: Historical Sketches of the Several Indian Tribes in Louisiana [etc.], by John Sibley, 1805; see Sibley 1832.)

_____ 1893 *see* Coues, Elliott, ed. 1893

_____ 1904–1905 *see* Thwaites, Reuben Gold, ed. 1904–1905

_____ 1953 *see* DeVoto, Bernard, ed. 1953

_____ 1983– *see* Moulton, Gary E., ed. 1983–

Lewis, Oscar
1942   The Effects of White Contact Upon Blackfoot Culture, with Special Reference to the Role of the Fur Trade. *Monographs of the American Ethnological Society* 6. New York: J.J. Augustin; also, Seattle: University of Washington Press. (Originally presented as the Author's Ph.D. Dissertation in Anthropology, Columbia University, New York City, 1942. Reprinted in: Anthropological Essays, by Oscar Lewis, Random House, New York, 1970; also, University of Washington Press, Seattle, 1973.)

_____ 1970   Anthropological Essays. New York: Random House.

Lewis, Stuart, and Nancy Oestreich Lurie, eds
1968   The American Indian Today. Deland, Fla.: Evertee Edwards.

Lewis, Theodore H.
1890   Effigy Mound in the Valley of the Big Sioux River, Iowa. *Science* 15(378):275. Washington.

Lewis, Thomas H.
1968   The Oglala Sun Dance 1968. *Pine Ridge Research Bulletin* 5:52–64. Pine Ridge, S.Dak.

_____ 1972   The Oglala (Teton Dakota) Sun Dance: Vicissitudes of Its Structure and Function. *Plains Anthropologist* 17(55):44–49.

_____ 1987   The Contemporary Yuwipi. Pp. 173–187 in Sioux Indian Religion: Tradition and Innovation. Raymond J. DeMallie and Douglas R. Parks, eds. Norman: University of Oklahoma Press.

_____ 1990   The Medicine Men: Oglala Sioux Ceremony and Healing. Lincoln: University of Nebraska Press.

L'Heureux, Jean
1878   [English and Blackfeet Dictionary.] (Manuscript in the Glenbow-Alberta Institute, Calgary, Alta.)

Libby, Orin Grant
1906   Biography of Old Settlers. *Collections of the North Dakota Historical Society* 1:325–380. Bismarck.

_____ 1908   Bad Gun (Rushing-After-The-Eagle). *Collections of the State Historical Society of North Dakota* 2(1):464–470. Bismarck.

_____, ed.
1920   The Arikara Narrative of the Campaign Against the Hostile Dakotas, June 1876. *Collections of the State Historical Society of North Dakota* 6:1–276. Bismarck.

Libby, Willard F.
1955   Radiocarbon Dating. 2d ed. Chicago: Univesity of Chicago Press.

_____ 1968   Radiocarbon Dating. Pp. 450–459 in Vol. 1 of Readings in Anthropology. Morton H. Fried, ed. New York: Thomas Y. Crowell.

Liberty, Margot
1965   Suppression and Survival of the Northern Cheyenne Sun Dance. *Minnesota Archaeologist* 27(4):120–144. Minneapolis.

1967   The Northern Cheyenne Sun Dance and the Opening of the Sacred Medicine Hat 1959. *Plains Anthropologist,* n.s. 12(38):367–385.

1968   A Priest's Account of the Northern Cheyenne Sun Dance. *University of South Dakota. W.H. Over Museum. Museum Notes* 29(1–2):1–32. Vermillion.

1972   [Fieldnotes and from Interviews of 214 Omaha and Seminole Women during the Summer of 1972.] (National Institute of Child Health and Human Development, Center for Population Research, Grant No. 1R01-HD-06129-01.)

1973   The Urban Reservation. (Ph.D. Dissertation in Anthropology, University of Minnesota, Minneapolis.)

1973a   Population Trends among the Present-day Omaha Indians. (Paper read at the 72d Annual Meeting of the American Anthropological Association, New Orleans, La., Nov. 30, 1973.)

1978   Francis La Flesche: The Osage Odyssey—Omaha, 1857–1932. Pp. [44] 45–59 in American Indian Intellectuals. Margot Liberty, ed. *1976 Proceedings of the American Ethnological Society.* Robert F. Spencer, gen. ed. St. Paul, Minn.: West Publishing Co.

1980   The Sun Dance. Pp. 164–178 in Anthropology on the Great Plains. W. Raymond Wood and Margot Liberty, eds. Lincoln: University of Nebraska Press.

Libhart, Myles
1970   Contemporary Sioux Painting: An Exhibition Organized by the Indian Arts and Crafts Board of the United States Department of the Interior. Rapid City, S.Dak.: The Tipi Shop, Inc.

———, ed.
1972   Contemporary Southern Plains Indian Painting: An Exhibition Organized by the Indian Arts and Crafts Board of the U.S. Department of the Interior. With an Essay by Rosemary Ellison. Anadarko, Okla.: Oklahoma Indian Arts and Crafts Cooperative.

Libhart, Myles, and Rosemary Ellison
1973   Painted Tipis by Contemporary Plains Indian Artists. Anadarko: Oklahoma Indian Arts and Crafts Cooperative.

Liebe-Harkort, M.L.
1980   Recent Developments in Apachean Language Maintenance. *International Journal of American Linguistics* 46(2):85–91. Chicago.

Lieberkühn, Samuel
1888   The History of Our Lord and Savior Jesus Christ....Translated into the Language of the Otoe, Ioway and Missouri Tribes of Indians, by Moses Merrill and Louis Dorion [1837]. Pt. 1. Rochester, N.Y.: Shawanoe Baptist Mission.

Liette, Pierre-Charles de
1934   De Gannes Memoir. T.C. Pease and R.C. Werner, eds. *Collections of the Illinois Historical Society* 23:302–395. Springfield, Ill.

Liljeblad, Sven
1972   The Idaho Indians in Transition, 1805–1960. Pocatello: Idaho State Museum Special Publication.

Limp, W. Frederick
1989   The Use of Multispectral Digital Imagery in Archaeological Investigations. Final Report Prepared by the Arkansas Archeological Survey under U.S. Army Corps of Engineers, Southwestern Division, Dallas. (Contract DACW63-84-C-0149.) *Arkansas Archeological Survey Research Series* 34. Fayetteville.

Lincoln, Bruce
1994   Lakota Sun Dance and the Problematics of Sociocosmic Reunion. *History of Religions* 34(1):1–14.Chicago.

Lincoln, W.L.
1881   [Letter to H.M Black, dated March 16, 1881.] (Manuscript in Box 54, Fort Belknap Records, Records of the Bureau of Indian Affairs, Record Group 75, National Archives-Pacific Northwest Region, Seattle, Wash.)

1881a   [Letters to Commissioner of Indian Affairs, dated August 2 and September 3, 1881.] (Manuscripts in Box 17, Fort Belknap Records, Records of the Bureau of Indian Affairs, Record Group 75, National Archives-Pacific Northwest Region, Seattle, Wash.)

1883   [Letter to Commissioner of Indian Affairs, dated January 8, 1883.] (Manuscript in Box 17, Fort Belknap Records, Records of the Bureau of Indian Affairs, Record Group 75, National Archives-Pacific Northwest Region, Seattle, Wash.)

1884   [Letter to Commissioner of Indian Affairs, dated August 4, 1884.] (Manuscript in Box 17, Fort Belknap Records, Records of the Bureau of Indian Affairs, Record Group 75, National Archives-Pacific Northwest Region, Seattle, Wash.)

1884a   [Letter to Commissioner of Indian Affairs, dated February 6, 1884.] (Manuscript in Box 17, Fort Belknap Records, Records of the Bureau of Indian Affairs, Record Group 75, National Archives-Pacific Northwest Region, Seattle, Wash.)

1884b   [Letter to Commissioner of Indian Affairs, dated November 20, 1884.] (Manuscript in Box 17, Fort Belknap Records, Records of the Bureau of Indian Affairs, Record Group 75, National Archives-Pacific Northwest Region, Seattle, Wash.)

1885   [Report to Commissioner of Indian Affairs: Statistics for 1884–1885.] (Manuscript in Letters Sent, 1880–1888, p. 254, Box 17, Fort Belknap Records, Records of the Bureau of Indian Affairs, Record Group 75, National Archives-Pacific Northwest Region, Seattle, Wash.)

Linderman, Frank Bird
1930   American: The Life Story of a Great Indian, Plenty-Coups, Chief of the Crows. New York: John Day. (Reprinted: University of Nebraska Press, Lincoln, 1962.)

1931   Old Man Coyote (Crow). New York: John Day.

1932   Red Mother: The Life Story of Pretty-Shield, Medicine-woman of the Crows. Illustrated by Herbert Morton Stoops. Rahway, N.J.: The John Day Company. (Reprinted: University of Nebraska Press, Lincoln, 1974; also, Time-Life Books, Alexandria, Va., 1991.)

1962   Plenty-Coups, Chief of the Crows. Lincoln: University of Nebraska Press.

Linnamae, Urve
1990   The Heron-Eden Site: 1990 Up-date. *Saskatchewan Archaeological Society Newsletter* 11(4):82. Saskatoon, Sask.

Linton, Adelin, and Charles Wagley
1971   The Writings of Ralph Linton. New York: Columbia University Press. (Reprinted in 1972.)

Linton, Ralph
1922   The Thunder Ceremony of the Pawnee. *Department of Anthropology Leaflet* 5. Chicago: Field Museum of Natural History.

1922a   The Sacrifice to the Morning Star by the Skidi Pawnee. *Department of Anthropology Leaflet* 6. Chicago: Field Museum of Natural History.

1923   Purification of the Sacred Bundles: A Ceremony of the Pawnee. *Department of Anthropology Leaflet* 7. Chicago: Field Museum of Natural History.

1923a   The Annual Ceremony of the Pawnee Medicine Men. *Department of Anthropology Leaflet* 8. Chicago: Field Museum of Natural History.

1926   The Origin of the Skidi Pawnee Sacrifice to the Morning Star. *American Anthropologist,* n.s. 28(3):457–466.

1935   The Comanche Sun Dance. *American Anthropologist,* n.s. 37(3):420–428.

1936   The Study of Man: An Introduction. New York: Appleton-Century Co.

_____, ed.
1940   Acculturation in Seven Indian Tribes. New York: Appleton-Century Press.

1943   Nativistic Movements. *American Anthropologist,* n.s. 45(2):230–240.

Lintz, Christopher R.
1978   The Panhandle Aspect and Its Early Relationship with Upper Republican. Pp. 36–55 in The Central Plains Tradition: Internal Development and External Relationships. Donald J. Blakeslee, ed. *The University of Iowa. Office of the State Archaeologist. Report* 11. Iowa City.

1978a   [Review of]: Robert G. Campbell's *The Panhandle Aspect of the Chaquaqua Plateau. Plains Anthropologist* 23(82):341–344.

1979   The Southwestern Periphery of the Plains Caddoan Area. *Nebraska History* 60(2):161–182. Lincoln.

1984   The Plains Villagers: Antelope Creek. Pp. 325–346 in Prehistory of Oklahoma. Robert E. Bell, ed. Orlando, San Diego, San Francisco, [etc.]: Academic Press.

_____, ed.
1985   A Chronological Framework of the Fort Carson Pinon Canyon Maneuver Site, Las Animas County, Colorado. 3 vols. *U.S. Army. Fort Carson-Pinon Canyon Cultural Resources Project. Contribution* 2. Denver, Colo.: University of Denver, Center for Archeological Research.

1986   The Upper Canark Regional Variant: Comparisons and Contrast of the Antelope Creek and Apishapa Phases of the Southwestern Plains. (Paper presented at the 44th Annual Plains Conference, Denver, Colo., 1986.)

1986a   Architecture and Community Variability within the Antelope Creek Phase of the Texas Panhandle. *University of Oklahoma. Archeological Survey. Studies in Oklahoma's Past* 14. Norman. (Originally presented as the Author's Ph.D. Dissertation in Anthropology, University of Oklahoma, Norman, 1984.)

1991   Texas Panhandle-Pueblo Interactions from the Thirteenth through the Sixteenth Century. Pp. 89–106 in Farmers, Hunters, and Colonists: Interaction between the Southwest and the Southern Plains. Katherine A. Spielmann, ed. Tucson: University of Arizona Press.

Lintz, Christopher R., and Leon George Zabawa
1984   The Kenton Caves of Western Oklahoma. Pp. 161–174 in Prehistory of Oklahoma. Robert E. Bell, ed. Orlando, San Diego, San Francisco, [etc.]: Academic Press.

Lintz, Christopher R., Abby C. Treece, and Fred M. Oglesby
1995   The Early Archaic Structure at the Turkey Bend Ranch Site (41CC112), Concho County. Pp. 155–185 in Advances in Texas Archeology: Contributions from Cultural Resource Management. James E. Bruseth and Timothy K. Perttula, eds. *Cultural Resource Management Report* 5. Austin: Texas Historical Commission, Department of Antiquities Protection.

Lischka, Joseph J., Mark E. Miller, R. Branson Reynolds, Dennis Dahms, Kathy Joyner-McGuire, and David McGuire
1983   An Archaeological Inventory in North Park, Jackson County, Colorado. *Bureau of Land Management. Colorado State Office. Cultural Resources Series* 14. Denver.

L'Isle, Guillaume de
1702   Carte du Canada et du Mississippi. (Original map in Ministere des Affaires Etrangeres, Paris: Copy in Library of Congress, Map Division, Washington.)

Lismer, Marjorie
1974   Adoption Patterns of the Blood Indians of Alberta, Canada. *Plains Anthropologist* 19(63):25–33.

Lister, Robert H.
1948   Notes on the Archaeology of Watrous Valley, New Mexico. *El Palacio* 55(1):35–41. Santa Fe.

Little Big Horn College
1997   Little Big Horn College Catalog 1997–1998. Crow Agency, Mont.: Little Big Horn College.

1997a   Land Grant Extension Program Application of Little Big Horn College. (Grant Proposal, Little Big Horn College, Crow Agency, Mont.)

1997b   Little Big Horn/Dull Knife Memorial College School To Work Opportunities System Proposal. (Grant Proposal, Little Big Horn College, Crow Agency, Mont.)

1997c   The Learning Lodge Institute of the Montana Tribal Colleges. (Grant Proposal, Little Big Horn College, Crow Agency, Mont.)

Little Big Horn College. Rural Systematic Initiative Program Office
1998   [Crow Tribal ... Degree Report.] (Database of Higher Education Degrees Attained by Crow Indians, Rural Systematic Initiative Program, Little Big Horn College, Crow Agency, Mont.)

Little Coyote, Bertha, and Virginia Giglio
1997   Leaving Everything Behind: The Songs and Memories of a Cheyenne Woman. Norman: University of Oklahoma Press.

Little Eagle, Avis
1993   Non-Indian Sun Dancers Bring Ohio Indian Protest. *Lakota Times* 13(3):A1–A2. Pine Ridge, S.Dak.

Llewellyn, Karl N., and E. Adamson Hoebel
1941   The Cheyenne Way: Conflict and Case Law in Primitive Jurisprudence. Norman: University of Oklahoma Press.

Lobdell, John E.
1973   The Scoggin Site: An Early Middle Period Bison Kill. (MA Thesis in Anthropology, University of Wyoming, Laramie; published in:) *The Wyoming Archaeologist* 16(3):1–71. Cheyenne, [etc.,] Wyo.

Loeb, Barbara
1980   Mirror Bags and Bandolier Bags: A Comparison. *American Indian Art Magazine* 6(1) [Special Crow Issue]:46–53, 88. Scottsdale, Ariz.

Loendorf, Lawrence L.
1989   A Sequence of Archaic Petroglyphs from the Pinon Canyon Maneuver Site, Colorado. *University of North Dakota. Department of Anthropology. Contributions* 248. Grand Forks, N.Dak.

Loendorf, Lawrence L., and Joan L. Brownell
1980   The Bad Pass Train. *Archaeology in Montana* 21(3)11–102. Billings, [etc.].

Loendorf, Lawrence L., Stanley A. Ahler, and Dale Davidson
1984   The Proposed National Register District in the Knife River
        Flint Quarries in Dunn County, North Dakota. *North Da-
        kota History* 51(4):4–20. Bismarck.

Loendorf, Lawrence L., James C. Dahlberg, and Lori O. Western
1981   The Pretty Creek Archaeological Site, 24CB4 and 5. (Re-
        port prepared for the Department of the Interior, National
        Park Service, Midwest Archaeological Center; University
        of North Dakota, Grand Forks.)

Loftin, John D.
1989   Anglo-American Jurisprudence and the Native American
        Tribal Quest for Religious Freedom. *American Indian Cul-
        ture and Research Journal* 13(1):1–52. Los Angeles.

Logan, Brad
1995   Phasing White Rock: Archaeological Investigations of the
        White Rock and Warne Sites, Lovewell Reservoir, Jewell
        County, Kansas, 1994–1995. *University of Kansas. Mu-
        seum of Anthropology. Project Report Series* 90. Lawrence.

Logan, Michael H., and Douglas A. Schmittou
1995   The Origins of Tribal Styles: An Evolutionary Perspective
        on Plains Indian Art. *Reviews in Anthropology* 24:65–86.

1995a   With Pride They Made These: Tribal Styles in Plains Indian
        Art. *Frank H. McClung Museum. University of Tennessee.
        Occasional Paper* 12. Knoxville.

1996   Identifying Berdache Material Culture: An Anthropometric
        and Statistical Approach. *Tennessee Anthropologist* 21(1):67–
        78. Knoxville.

1998   The Uniqueness of Crow Art: A Glimpse into the History of
        an Embattled People. *Montana: The Magazine of Western
        History* 48(2):58–71. Helena.

Logan, Wilfred D.
1976   Woodland Complexes in Northeastern Iowa. *U.S. Depart-
        ment of the Interior. National Park Service. Publications in
        Archeology* 15. Washington: Government Printing Office.

Logan, William R.
1908   [Letter to the Commissioner of Indian Affairs, dated De-
        cember 15, 1908.] (Manuscript in Box 21, Fort Belknap
        Records, Records of the Bureau of Indian Affairs, Record
        Group 75, National Archives—Pacific Northwest Region,
        Seattle, Wash.)

Lomawaima, K. Tsianina
1994   They Called It Prairie Light: The Story of Chilocco Indian
        School. Lincoln: University of Nebraska Press.

Long, James Larpenteur
1942   Land of Nakoda; the Story of the Assiniboine Indians. From
        the Tales of the Old Ones Told to First Boy (James L.
        Long), with Drawings by Fire Bear (William Standing).
        Helena: Writers' Program, Montana. State Pub. Co. (Re-
        printed under title: The Assiniboines: From the Accounts of
        the Old Ones Told to First Boy (James Larpenteur Long).
        Edited and with an Introduction by Michael Stephen
        Kennedy: University of Oklahoma Press, Norman, 1961.
        Reprinted: AMS Press, New York, 1975.)

Long, John S.
1985   Treaty No. 9 and Fur Trade Company Families: Northeast-
        ern Ontario's Halfbreeds, Indians, Petitioners and Métis.
        Pp. 137–162 in The New Peoples: Being and Becoming
        Métis in North America. Jacqueline Peterson and Jennifer
        S.H. Brown, eds. *Manitoba Studies in Native History* 1.
        Winnipeg: University of Manitoba Press; Lincoln: Univer-
        sity of Nebraska Press.

Long, M.F.
1897   [Report on Indian Houses, dated August 21,1897.] (Manu-
        script in Kiowa Agency Records, Oklahoma Historical
        Society, Oklahoma City.)

Long, Stephen H. 1823 *see* James, Edwin, comp. 1823

_____ 1824 *see* Keating, William H., comp. 1824

1889   Voyage on a Six-oared Skiff to the Falls of St. Anthony in
        1817. *Collections of the Minnesota Historical Society* 2:7–
        88. St. Paul.

Long Lance, Buffalo Child
1923   Secrets of the Forbidden Sun Dance Are Revealed:
        Blackfeet Hold Ceremony in Defiance of the Police.
        Toronto Star Weekly, Nov. 17:1. Toronto.

1927   The Sun Dance. A Chief of the Blackfoot Tribe Describes
        This Spectacular Ceremony of His People, in Which a
        Woman Is the Central Figure. *Good Housekeeping* 85(Au-
        gust):64–65, 219–220. New York.

Looking Horse, Arvol
1987   The Sacred Pipe in Modern Life. Pp. 67–73 in Sioux Indian
        Religion: Tradition and Innovation. Raymond J. DeMallie
        and Douglas R. Parks, eds. Norman: University of Okla-
        homa Press.

Loomis, Noel M., and Abraham P. Nasatir
1967   Pedro Vial and the Roads to Santa Fe. Norman: University
        of Oklahoma Press.

Lopach, Lames J., Margery Hunter Brown, and Richmond L. Clow
1990   Tribal Governments Today: Politics on Montana Indian
        Reservations. Denver, Colo.: Westview Press.

Lopez, David R.
1970   The McLemore Cemetery Complex: An Analysis of Prehis-
        toric Burial Customs. *Bulletin of the Oklahoma Anthropo-
        logical Society* 19:137–150. [Oklahoma City.]

Lorrain, Dessamae
1969   Archaeological Excavations in the Fish Creek Reservoir.
        *Southern Methodist University. Contributions in Anthro-
        pology* 4. Dallas, Tex.

1974   The Glass Site. Pp. 24–44 in A Pilot Study of Wichita
        Indian Archeology and Ethnohistory, by Robert E. Bell,
        Edward B. Jelks, and W.W. Newcomb. *American Indian
        Ethnohistory: Plains Indians.* David Agee Horr, comp. and
        ed. New York: Garland Publishing. (Originally issued as:
        Final Report for National Science Foundation Grant GS-
        964, Washington, 1967.)

Lothson, Gordon A.
1972   Burial Mounds of the Mille Lacs Lake Area. (M.A.Thesis in
        Anthropology, University of Minnesota, Minneapolis.)

Loud Hawk, Russell, et al.
1969   [Letter to Senator Robert F. Kennedy Transmitting Proposal
        for Loneman Demonstration School, dated Oglala, S.Dak.,
        April 2, 1968.] Pp.1284–1297 in Hearings Before the
        Special Subcommittee on Indian Education of the Commit-
        tee on Labor and Public Welfare. *U.S. Senate. 90th Con-
        gress. 1st and 2d Sessions* (on the Study of the Education of
        Indian Children), Pt. 4. April 16, 1968, Pine Ridge, S.Dak.
        Washington: Government Printing Office.

Lounsbury, Floyd G.
1956   A Semantic Analysis of the Pawnee Kinship Usage. *Lan-
        guage: Journal of the Linguistic Society of America*
        32(1):158–193.

1964   The Formal Analysis of Crow- and Omaha-Type Kinship
        Terminologies. Pp. 351–394 in Explorations in Cultural
        Anthropology: Essays in Honor of Peter Murdock. Ward H.
        Goodenough, ed. New York: McGraw-Hill.

Lovett, John R., Jr., and Donald L. DeWitt, comps.
1998   Guide to Native American Ledger Drawings and Picto-
        graphs in United States Museums, Libraries, and Archives. *1203*

Bibliographies and Indexes in American History 39. Westport, Conn.: Greenwood Press.

Lowendorf, L.L.
1971   The Results of the Archeological Survey in the Pryor Mountain-Bighorn Canyon Recreation Area: 1969 Field Season. Columbia: University of Missouri.

Lowie Museum (Robert H. Lowie Museum of Anthropology)
1968   A Chronicle of the Kiowa Indians, 1832–1892. ("An expanded, more detailed, version of the caption appearing with it [the chronicle] in the exhibit *Treasures of the Lowie Museum.*") Berkeley: Robert H. Lowie Museum.

Lowie, Robert H.
1909   The Assiniboine. *American Museum of Natural History Anthropological Papers* 4(1):1–270. New York. (Reprinted: AMS Press, New York, 1975.)

1909a   The Northern Shoshone. *American Museum of Natural History Anthropological Papers* 2(2):165–206. New York. (Reprinted: AMS Press, New York, 1975.)

1912   Social Life of the Crow Indians. *American Museum of Natural History Anthropological Papers* 9(2):179–248. New York. (Reprinted: AMS Press, New York, 1976; and, University Microfilms, Ann Arbor, Mich., 1987.)

1912a   [Comanche Fieldnotes.] (Manuscript in Department of Anthropology Archives, American Museum of Natural History, New York.)

1913   Dance Associations of the Eastern Dakota. *American Museum of Natural History Anthropological Papers* 11(2):101–142. New York. (Bound with other monographs in: Societies of the Plains Indians, Clark Wissler, ed., New York, 1916. Reprinted: Lakota Books, Kendall Park, N.J., 1993.)

1913a   Societies of the Crow, Hidatsa and Mandan Indians. *American Museum of Natural History Anthropological Papers* 11(3):143–358. New York. (Bound with other monographs in: Societies of the Plains Indians, Clark Wissler, ed., New York, 1916.)

1913b   Military Societies of the Crow Indians. *American Museum of Natural History Anthropological Papers* 11(16):143–218. New York. (Bound with other monographs in: Societies of the Plains Indians, Clark Wissler, ed., New York, 1916.)

1914   Ceremonialism in North America. *American Anthropologist*, n.s. 16(4):602–631. (Reprinted: pp. 229–258 in Anthropology of North America, by Franz Boas, et al., G.E. Stechert & Company, New York, 1915.)

1914a   The Crow Sun Dance. *Journal of American Folk-lore* 27(103):94–96.

1914b   Crow Rapid Speech Puzzles. *Journal of American Folklore* 27(106):330–331.

1915   Societies of the Arikara Indians. *American Museum of Natural History Anthropological Papers* 11(8):645–678. New York. (Bound with other monographs in: Societies of the Plains Indians, Clark Wissler, ed., New York, 1916.)

1915a   Dances and Societies of the Plains Shoshone. *American Museum of Natural History Anthropological Papers* 11(10):803–835. New York. (Bound with other monographs in: Societies of the Plains Indians, Clark Wissler, ed., New York, 1916.)

1915b   The Sun Dance of the Crow Indians. *American Museum of Natural History Anthropological Papers* 16(1):1–50. New York. (Reprinted: AMS Press, New York, 1978.)

1915c   The Crow Indian Sun-Dance. *The American Museum Journal* 15(10):23–25. New York.

1916   Plains Indian Age-Societies: Historical and Comparative Summary. *American Museum of Natural History Anthropological Papers* 11(13):877–992. New York. (Bound with other monographs in: Societies of the Plains Indians, Clark Wissler, ed., New York, 1916.)

1916a   Societies of the Kiowa. *American Museum of Natural History Anthropological Papers* 11(10): 837–851. New York. (Bound with other monographs in: Societies of the Plains Indians, Clark Wissler, ed., New York, 1916. Reprinted: Lakota Books, Kendall Park, N.J., 1995.)

1917   Notes on the Social Organization and Customs of the Mandan, Hidatsa, and Crow Indians. *American Museum of Natural History Anthropological Papers* 21(1):1–99. New York. (Reprinted: AMS Press, New York, 1976.)

1917a   The Kinship Systems of the Crow and Hidatsa. Pp. 340–343 in *Proceedings of the 19th International Congress of Americanists, held in Washington, December 1915.* Washington.

1918   Myths and Traditions of the Crow Indians. *American Museum of Natural History Anthropological Papers* 25(1):1–308. New York. (Reprinted: AMS Press, New York, 1975; also, with an Introduction by Peter Nabokov: University of Nebraska Press, Lincoln, 1993.)

1919   The Hidatsa Sun Dance. *American Museum of Natural History Anthropological Papers* 16(5):411–431. New York.

1919a   The Tobacco Society of the Crow Indians. *American Museum of Natural History Anthropological Papers* 21(2):101–200. New York. (Reprinted: AMS Press, New York, 1975.)

1919b   The Sun Dance of the Shoshone, Ute, and Hidatsa. *American Museum of Natural History Anthropological Papers* 16(5):387–431. New York. (Reprinted: AMS Press, New York, 1975.)

1919c   The Sun Dance of the Wind River Shoshone, and Ute. *American Museum of Natural History Anthropological Papers* 16(10):387–431. New York. (Reprinted: AMS Press, New York, 1975.)

1920   Primitive Society. New York: Boni and Liveright. (Reprinted: G. Routledge & Sons, Ltd., London, 1921.)

1922   The Material Culture of the Crow Indians. *American Museum of Natural History Anthropological Papers* 21(3):201–270. New York. (Reprinted: AMS Press, New York, 1975; also, Lakota Books, Kendall Park, N.J., 1996.)

1922a   Crow Indian Art. *American Museum of Natural History Anthropological Papers* 21(4):272–322. New York.

1922b   The Religion of the Crow Indians. *American Museum of Natural History Anthropological Papers* 25(2):309–444. New York. (Reprinted: AMS Press, New York, 1976.)

1923   A Note on Kiowa Kinship Terms and Usages. *American Anthropologist*, n.s. 25(2):279–281.

1924   Minor Ceremonies of the Crow Indians. *American Museum of Natural History Anthropological Papers* 21(5):323–365. New York.

1924a   Notes on Shoshonean Ethnography. *American Museum of Natural History Anthropological Papers* 20(3):185–314. New York.

1924b   Primitive Religion. New York: Boni and Liveright Publishers. (Reprinted: George Routledge and Sons, London, 1925, 1936; also, Gosset & Dunlop, New York, 1952.)

1930   A Crow Text; with Grammatical Notes. *University of California Publications in American Archaeology and Ethnology* 29(2):155–175. Berkeley. (Reprinted: Kraus Reprint, New York, 1965.)

1930a   The Omaha and Crow Kinship Terminologies. Pp. 102–108 in *Sonderabdruck aus den Verhandlungen des 24 Internationalen Amerikanisten-Kongresses, Hamburg, 7 bis 13 September 1930.* [Hamburg, Germany.]

1932   Proverbial Expressions among the Crow Indians. *American Anthropologist,* n.s. 34(4):739–740.

1933   Crow Prayers. *American Anthropologist,* n.s. 35(3):433–442.

1935   The Crow Indians. New York: Farrar and Rinehart. (Reprinted: Holt, Rinehart and Winston, New York, 1956, 1966; also, University of Nebraska Press, Lincoln, 1983.)

1939   Hidatsa Texts; With Grammatical Notes and Phonological Transcriptions by Zellig Harris and Charles F. Voegelin. *Indiana Historical Society. Prehistory Research Series* 1(6):173–239. Indianapolis. (Reprinted: AMS Press, New York, 1975.)

1941   The Crow Language: Grammatical Sketch and Analyzed Text. *University of California Publications in American Archaeology and Ethnology* 39(1):1–142. Berkeley. (Reprinted in 1945; also, Kraus Reprint, New York, 1965.)

1942   Studies in Plains Indian Folklore. *University of California Publications in American Archaeology and Ethnology* 40(1):1–27. Berkeley. (Reprinted: Kraus Reprint, New York, 1965.)

1950   Observations on the Literary Style of the Crow Indians. Pp. 271–283 in Beiträge zur Gesellungs- und Völkerwissenschaft; Professor Dr. Richard Thurwald zu seinem achtzigsten Geburtstag gewidmet. Berlin: Gebr. Mann.

1953   Alleged Kiowa-Crow Affinities. *Southwestern Journal of Anthropology* 9(4):357–368. Albuquerque.

1953a   The Comanche, a Sample of Acculturation. *Sociologus,* n.s. 3:122–127.

1954   Indians of the Plains. *American Museum of Natural History. Anthropological Handbook* 1. Garden City, N.Y.: Published for the American Museum of Natural History [by] the Natural History Press [Doubleday]; New York: McGraw-Hill. (Reprinted in 1963; also, with a Preface by Raymond J. DeMallie: University of Nebraska Press, Lincoln, 1982.)

1955   The Military Societies of the Plains Cree. Pp. 3–9 in Vol. 1 of *Anais do XXXI Congresso Internacional de Americanistas [Proceedings of the 31st International Congress of Americanists], Sâo Paulo, 23 a 28 de agôsto de 1954.* 2 vols. Herbert Baldus, comp. and ed. Sâo Paulo, Brasil: Editoria Anhembi.

1955a   Reflections on the Plains Indians. *Anthropological Quarterly* (formerly *Primitive Man*) 28, n.s. 3, No. 2:63–86. Washington: The Catholic University of America.

1959   Crow Curses. *Journal of American Folk-lore* 72(284):105.

1959a   The Oral Literature of the Crow Indians. *Journal of American Folk-lore* 72(284):97–105.

1960   Crow Texts. Berkeley: University of California Press.

1960a   Crow Word List: Crow-English and English-Crow Vocabularies. Berkeley: University of California Press.

1960b   A Few Assiniboine Texts. Preface by Luella Cole Lowie. *Anthropological Linguistics* 2(8):1–30. Bloomington.

_____   1963, 1982 see 1954 (reprint info.)

1964   My Crow Interpreter. Pp. 427–237 in In the Company of Man. Joseph Casagrande, ed. New York: Harper and Row.

Ludwickson, John
1978   Central Plains Tradition Settlements in the Loup River Basin: The Loup River Phase. Pp. 94–108 in The Central Plains Tradition: Internal Development and External Relationships. Donald J. Blakeslee, ed. *University of Iowa. Office of the State Archaeologist. Report* 11. Iowa City.

1988   Variability in Omaha Subsistence Economy. (Paper Read at the 98th Annual Meeting of the Nebraska Academy of Sciences.)

1995   Blackbird and Son: a Note Concerning Late-Eighteenth- and Early-Nineteenth-Century Omaha Chieftainship. *Ethnohistory* 42(1):133–149.

Ludwickson, John, and Terry L. Steinacher
1972   The Central Plains Tradition Reappraised. (Manuscript on file at the Department of Anthropology, University of Nebraska, Lincoln.)

Lummis, Charles F., ed.
1894–1901 *The Land of Sunshine: The Magazine of California and the West.* Los Angeles, Calif.: Land of Sunshine Publishing Co.

Lurie, Nancy Oestreich
1957   The Indian Claims Commission Act. Pp. 56–70 in American Indians and American Life. George E. Simpson and J. Milton Yinger, eds. *The Annals of the American Academy of Political and Social Science* 311. Philadelphia.

1968   Culture Change. Pp. 274–303 in Introduction to Anthropology. James Clifton, ed. New York: Houghton Mifflin Co.

1968a   An American Indian Renascence? Pp. 187–208 in The American Indian Today. Stuart Levine and Nancy Oestreich Lurie, eds. Deland, Fla.: Everett/Edwards, Inc.

1978   The Indian Claims Commission. Pp. 97–110 in American Indians Today. J. Milton Yinger and George Eaton Simpson, eds. *The Annals of the American Academy of Political and Social Science* 436. Philadelphia.

Lurie, Nancy Oestreich, and Duane Anderson
1998   A Lost Art Form: A Case Study of 19th Century Feathered Capes Produced by American Indians in the Great Lakes Region. *Museum Anthropology: Journal of the Council for Museum Anthropology* 22(2):3–16. Washington.

Lussier, Antoine S.
1981   Les rapports entre les Bois-Brûlés et les Canadiens Français au Manitoba depuis 1900. Pp. 73–86 in Actes du Premier Colloque des Educators Franco-Canadiens de l'Ouest.

1984   Mgr Provencher et l'éducation des autochtones 1818–1851. Pp. 183–194 in La langue, la culture et la société des francophones de l'Ouest: les Actes du troisième colloque du Centre d'études franco-canadiennes de l'Ouest, tenu au Centre d'études bilingues, Université de Régina, les 25 et 26 novembre 1983. Textes établis par Pierre-Yves Mocquais, André Lalonde, Bernard Wilhelm. Regina, Sask.: Institut de recherche du Centre d'études bilingues, University of Regina.

Lussier, Antoine S., and D. Bruce Sealy, eds.
1978–1980 The Other Natives the—Les Métis. 3 vols. Winnipeg, Man.: Métis Federation Press.

Luttig, John C.
1920   Journal of a Fur Trading Expedition on the Upper Missouri, 1812–1813. Stella M. Drumm, ed. St. Louis, Mo.: Missouri Historical Society. (Reprinted, with Preface and Notes by Abraham P. Nasatir: Argosy-Antiquarian, New York, 1964, 1970.)

Lutz, John J.
1906   The Methodist Missions among the Indian Tribes in Kansas. George W. Martin ed. *Transactions of the Kansas State Historical Society* 9:160–235. Topeka.

Luxton, Eleanor G.
1983   Stony Indian Medicine. Pp. 101–122 in The Developing West. John Foster, ed. Edmonton: University of Alberta Press.

Lyford, Carrie A.
1933   Sioux Beadwork. Lawrence, Kans.: Haskell Institute.

1940   Quill and Beadwork of the Western Sioux. *U.S. Office of Indian Affairs. Indian Handicraft* 1. Willard W. Beatty, ed. Lawrence, Kans.: Haskell Institute Printing Department. (Reprinted: U.S. Office of Indian Affairs, Education Division, Washington, 1954; also, Johnson Publishing Co., Boulder, Colo., 1979; and, R. Schneider Publishers, Stevens Point, Wis., 1983.)

1953   Ojibwa Crafts. 2d ed. Washington: Branch of Education, U.S. Office of Indian Affairs. (Originally publ. under title: The Crafts of the Ojibwa (Chippewa). *U.S. Office of Indian Affairs. Indian Handicrafts* 5. Willard W. Beatty, ed., Phoenix Indian School, Printing Department, Phoenix, 1943. (Reprinted: R. Schneider Publishers, Stevens Point, Wis., 1982, 1999.)

Lyman, Christopher M.
1982   The Vanishing Race and Other Illusions: Photographs of Indians by Edward S. Curtis. Introduction by Vine Deloria, Jr. New York: Pantheon Books [...] with the Smithsonian Institution Press.

Lynd, James W.
1864   The Religion of the Dakotas: Chapter Six of Mr. Lynd's Manuscript. *Collections of the Minnesota Historical Society [for]1864* 2(2):150–174. St. Paul. (2d ed. 1881.)

Lynd, James W. 1865, 1865a see Riggs, Stephen R., ed. 1865, 1865a, (2d ed. in 1881)

Lynott, Mark J.
1979   Prehistoric Bison Populations of Northcentral Texas. *Bulletin of the Texas Archeological Society* 50:89–101. Austin.

MHS = Massachusetts Historical Society
1795–1915 Collections. 10 series. 70 vols. Boston: The Society.

McAllester, David P.
1949   Peyote Music. *Viking Fund Publications in Anthropology* 13. New York. (Reprinted: Johnson Reprint, New York, 1971.)

McAllister, J. Gilbert
1935   Kiowa-Apache Social Organization. (Ph.D. Dissertation in Anthropology, University of Chicago, Chicago.)

1949   Kiowa-Apache Tales. Pp. 1–141 in The Sky Is My Tipi. Mody C. Boatright, ed. *Publications of the Texas Folklore Society* 22. Dallas.

1955   Kiowa-Apache Social Organization. Pp. 97–169 in Social Anthropology of North American Tribes. Fred Eggan, ed. 2d ed. Chicago: University of Chicago Press.

1965   The Four Quarts Rocks Medicine Bundle of the Kiowa-Apache. *Ethnology* 4(2):210–224.

1970   Dävéko: Kiowa-Apache Medicine Man. *Bulletin of the Texas Memorial Museum* 17. Austin.

McAnulty, Sarah
1976   Angel DeCora: American Artist and Educator. *Nebraska History* 57(2):143–199. Lincoln.

McAuliffe, Dennis, Jr.
1994   The Deaths of Sybil Bolton: An American History. New York: Time Books/Random House.

McBride, Dorothy McFathridge
1970   Hoosier Schoolmaster among the Sioux. *Montana: The Magazine of Western History* 20(4):78–97. Helena.

McBurney, Charles R.
1948   Cache Creek Indian Mission: A Study in Religious Education among the Comanche, Apache, and Kiowa Indians of Southern Oklahoma. (M.A. Thesis in History, University of Kansas, Lawrence.)

McCann, Lloyd
1956   The Grattan Massacre. *Nebraska History* 37(1):1–25. Lincoln.

McCaskill, Joseph Clyde, and D'Arcy McNickle
1942   La política de los Estados Unidos sobre los gobiernos tribales y las empresas comunales de los indios. Josefina de Román, ed. Washington: The National Indian Institute, Department of the Interior.

McCleary, Timothy P.
1997   The Stars We Know: Crow Indian Astronomy and Lifeways. Prospect Heights, Ill.: Waveland Press.

McClintock, Walter
1900   Four Days in a Medicine Lodge. *Harper's Monthly Magazine* 101(94):519–532. New York.

1910   The Old North Trail; or, Life, Legends and Religion of the Blackfeet Indians. London: Macmillan. (Reprinted: University of Nebraska Press, Lincoln, 1977 and 1992.)

1927   A Blackfoot Circle Camp. *The Masterkey* 1(4):5–12. Los Angeles.

1930   The Tragedy of the Blackfoot. *Southwest Museum Papers* 3. Los Angeles.

1936   Painted Tipis and Picture-writing of the Blackfoot Indians. *Southwest Museum Leaflets* 6. Los Angeles.

1948   Blackfoot Medicine-Pipe Ceremony. *Southwest Museum Leaflets* 21. Los Angeles.

McClure, Charles W.
1882   [Report Relative to Indian Affairs in Montana dated Fort Assiniboine, Mt., June 3d, 1882.] (Manuscript Letter [Copy], File 1201–1882, NNRC13E, Letters Received, Records of the Bureau of Indian Affairs, Record Group 75, National Archives, Washington.)

McCoontz, Pete
1937   [Interview.] (Manuscript, *Indian and Pioneer History* 34:457, Newspaper/Archives and Manuscripts Division, Oklahoma Historical Society, Oklahoma City.)

M'Coy, Isaac see McCoy, Isaac

McCoy, Isaac
1835–1838 The Annual Register of Indian Affairs within the Indian (or Western) Territory. 4 vols. Shawanoe Baptist Mission, Indian Terr.: J. Meeker, Printer. (Vol. 4 publ. by P. Force,

Washington.) (Reprinted, enl. facsimile, 4 vols. in 1, under title: The Annual Register of Indian Affairs, in the Western (or Indian) Territory, 1835–1838; Particular Baptist Publishing, Enid, Okla., 1998.)

1840   History of Baptist Indian Missions: Embracing Remarks on the Former and Present Condition of the Aboriginal Tribes, Their Settlement within the Indian Territory, and Their Future Prospects. Washington: William M. Morrison; also, New York: H. and S. Raynor. (Reprinted: Johnson Reprint, New York, 1970.)

McCoy, Ronald
1987   Kiowa Memories: Images from Indian Territory, 1880. Santa Fe: Morning Star Gallery.

McCracken, Harold, ed.
1978   The Mummy Cave Project in Northwestern Wyoming. With Contributions by Harold McCracken, Waldo R. Wedel, [et al.]. Cody, Wyo.: The Buffalo Bill Historical Center.

McCrady, David G.
1993   Stopping the Americans: A Comment on Indian Warfare in Western Canada, 1850 to 1885. *Journal of the West* 32:47–53.

1998   Living with Strangers: The Nineteenth-Century Sioux and the Canadian-American Borderlands. (Ph.D. Dissertation in History, University of Manitoba, Winnipeg.)

McCullough, Edward J.
1982   Prehistoric Cultural Dynamics of the Lac La Biche Region. *Archaeological Survey of Alberta. Occasional Paper* 18. Edmonton.

McCusker, Philip
1866   [Letter to Thomas Murphy, dated Mouth of Little Arkansas, September 7, 1866.] (Microfilm No. M234, Roll 375, Frames 390–392, Letters Received, Kiowa Agency, 1864–1880, Records of the Bureau of Indian Affairs, Record Group 75, National Archives, Washington.)

McDermott, John F., ed. 1940 *see* Tixier, Victor 1940

1941   A Glossary of Mississippi Valley French, 1673–1850. *Washington University Studies. New Series. Language and Literature* 12. St Louis, Mo.

1950   Samuel Seymour: Pioneer Artist of the Plains and the Rockies. *Smithsonian Institution Publications* 4043. Washington.

1961   Seth Eastman: Pictorial Historian of the Indian. Norman: University of Oklahoma Press.

1965   The French in the Mississippi Valley. Urbana: University of Illinois Press.

1973   Seth Eastman's Mississippi: A Lost Portfolio Recovered. Urbana: University of Illinois Press.

1974   The Spanish in the Mississippi Valley, 1762–1804. Urbana: University of Illinois Press.

McDonald, A.
1882   [Letter to Edgar Dewdney, dated Fort Walsh, 11 November 1882.] (Manuscript in Record Group 10, Vol. 3744, File 29506-3, National Archives of Canada, Ottawa.)

McDonald, Jerry N.
1981   North American Bison: Their Classification and Evolution. Berkeley: University of California Press.

McDonnell, Anne, ed.
1940   The Fort Benton Journal, 1854–1856. Pp. 1–99 [plus, Appendices, pp. 191–236; Notes and References, pp. 249–305; Bibliography, pp. 307–310] in *Contributions to the Historical Society of Montana* 10. Helena.

1940a   The Fort Sarpy Journal, 1855–1856. Pp. 100–236 [plus, Appendices, pp. 191–236; Notes and References, pp. 239–305; Bibliography, pp. 307–310] in *Contributions to the Historical Society of Montana* 10. Helena.

McDougall, John
1911   On Western Trails in the Early Seventies: Frontier Life in the Canadian North-west. Toronto: W. Briggs.

1970   Opening the Great West: Experiences of a Missionary in 1875–76. Introduction by J. Ernest Nix. Calgary, Alta.: Glenbow-Alberta Institute.

MacDowell, Marsha L., and C. Kurt Dewhurst, eds.
1997   To Honor and Comfort: Native Quilting Traditions. Santa Fe: Museum of New Mexico Press in association with Michigan State University Museum.

McDowell, William L., Jr., ed.
1958–1970 Documents Relating to Indian Affairs. 2 vols. *The Colonial Records of South Carolina, Ser. 2: The Indian Books.* Columbia: South Carolina Archives Department.

Mace, Mariana
1998   Native American Saddle Blankets: a Study of Shape and Tribal Attribution. *American Indian Art Magazine* 24(1):60–67, 73. Scottsdale, Ariz.

McElhannon, Joseph Carl
1949   Imperial Mexico and Texas, 1821–1823. *Southwestern Historical Quarterly* 53(2):117–150. Austin, Tex.

MacEwan, J.W. Grant
1969   Tatanga Mani: Walking Buffalo of the Stonies. Edmonton, Alta.: Hurtig.

1971   Portraits from the Plains. Toronto: McGraw-Hill.

1973   Sitting Bull, The Years in Canada. Edmonton, Alta.: Hurtig.

McFarling, Lloyd, ed. 1955 *see* Brackenridge, Henry Marie 1955

McFee, Malcolm
1968   The 150 Percent Man: A Product of Blackfeet Acculturation. *American Anthropologist,* n.s. 70(6):1096–1107.

1972   Modern Blackfeet: Montanans on a Reservation. New York: Holt, Rinehart and Winston. (Reprinted: Waveland Press, Prospect Heights, Ill., 1972.)

McGaa, Ed Eagle Man
1990   Mother Earth Spirituality: Native American Paths to Healing Ourselves and Our World. San Francisco: Harper & Row, Publishers.

McGee, WJ
1897   The Siouan Indians: A Preliminary Sketch. Pp. 153–205 in *15th Annual Report of the Bureau of American Ethnology [for] 1893–'94.* Washington: Smithsonian Institution; U.S. Government Printing Office.

1898   Ponka Feather Symbolism. *American Anthropologist,* n.s. 11(5):156–159.

M'Gillivray, Duncan *see* McGillivray, Duncan

McGillivray, Duncan
1929   The Journal of Duncan M'Gillivray of the North West Company at Fort George on the Saskatchewan, 1794–1795. With Introduction, Notes and Appendix by Arthur S. Morton. Toronto: Macmillan of Canada.

McGillycuddy, Julia B.
1941   McGillycuddy, Agent: A Biography of Dr. Valentine T. McGillycuddy. Stanford, Calif.: Stanford University Press. *1207*

McGimsey, Charles R., III
1964   A Report on the Quapaw in Arkansas Immediately Prior to the Treaty of 1818. (Manuscript on file, Quapaw Tribe Business Office, Quapaw, Okla.)

McGinnis, Anthony
1990   Counting Coup and Cutting Horses: Intertribal Warfare on the Northern Plains, 1738–1889. Evergreen, Colo.: Cordillera Press.

McGinnis, Dale, and Floyd W. Sharrock
1972   The Crow People. *Indian Tribal Series* 106:68–99. Phoenix, Ariz.

MacGowan, D.J.
1865   [Comparative Vocabulary, collected at (Comanche) Treaty Council, Sept. 1865.] (Manuscript No. 754a, National Anthropological Archives, Smithsonian Institution, Washington.)

_____
1865a   [Notes on a Stay with the Comanche in 1865, Prepared at Treaty Council, Sept. 1865.] (Manuscript No. 754b, National Anthropological Archives, Smithsonian Institution, Washington.)

Macgowan, Ernest S.
1942   The Arikara Indians. *Minnesota Archaeologist* 8(3):85–122. Minneapolis.

McGregor, Daniel E., and James E. Bruseth, eds.
1987   Hunter-gatherer Adaptation along the Prairie Margin: Site Excavations and Synthesis of Prehistoric Archaeology. James E. Bruseth and Randall W. Moir, Principal Investigators. *Randall Creek Technical Series* 3. Dallas, Tex.: Archaeology Research Program, Institute for the Study of Earth and Man, Southern Methodist University.

Macgregor, Gordon
1946   Warriors Without Weapons: A Study of the Society and Personality Development of the Pine Ridge Sioux. With the Collaboration of Royal B. Hassrick and William E. Henry. Chicago: University of Chicago Press. (Reprinted in 1975.)

_____
1949   Attitudes of the Fort Berthold Indians Regarding Removal from the Garrison Reservoir Site and Future Administration of Their Reservation. *North Dakota History* 16(1):31–60. Bismarck.

MacGregor, James G.
1954   Behold the Shining Mountains: Being an Account of the Travels of Anthony Henday, 1754–55, the First White Man to Enter Alberta. Edmonton, Alta.: Applied Art Products, Ltd.

_____
1967   Edmonton, A History. Edmonton, Alta.: Hurtig.

_____
1972   A History of Alberta. Edmonton, Alta.: Hurtig.

_____
1978   John Rowand: Czar of the Prairies. Saskatoon, Sask.: Western Producer Prairie Books.

McGregor, James H.
1940   The Wounded Knee Massacre from the Viewpoint of the Sioux. Baltimore: Wirth Brothers.

Machaj, Bart F.
1977   The Ethnobotany of the Plains Indians. (M.S. Thesis in Biology, Northeastern Illinois University, Chicago.)

McHugh, Tom
1972   The Time of the Buffalo. New York: Alfred A. Knopf.

McIntyre, Michael L.
1978   Studies in Archaeology: Highway 1A, Coal Creek Revision, Alberta. *Archaeological Survey of Alberta. Occasional Paper* 7. Edmonton.

Mack, Liz
1999   The Thundercloud Site (FbNp-25): An Analysis of a Multi-component Northern Plains Site and the Role of Geoarchaeology in Site Interpretation. (M.A. Thesis in Anthropology and Archaeology, University of Saskatchewan, Saskatoon.)

Mackay, Douglas
1936   The Honourable Company: A History of the Hudson's Bay Company. Toronto: McClelland and Stewart.

McKay, James *see* Mackay, James Diego (McKay)

Mackay, James Diego (McKay)
1952   Captain McKay's Journal [1796]. Pp. 490–495 in Vol. 2 of Before Lewis and Clark. Abraham P. Nasatir, ed. 2 vols. St. Louis, Mo.: St. Louis Historical Documents. (Reprinted: University of Nebraska Press, Lincoln, 1990.)

McKay, John
1858   [Indian Summer Debt Book.] (Manuscript BBH869J, Saskatchewan Archives Board, Saskatoon.)

McKeand, Peggy
1995   A Comprehensive Faunal Analysis of the Bushfield West (FhNa-10), Nipawin, Saskatchewan. (M.A. Thesis in Anthropology and Archaeology, University of Saskatchewan, Saskatoon.)

McKenney, Edward
1850   Omaha Primer. [Ioway and Sac Mission, Nebraska Terr.]: Ioway and Sac Mission Press.

M'Kenney, Thomas L., and James Hall *see* McKenney, Thomas L., and James Hall

McKenney, Thomas L., and James Hall
1848–1850 History of the Indian Tribes of North America; With Biographical Sketches and Anecdotes of the Principal Chiefs, Embellished with One Hundred and Twenty Portraits, from the Indian Gallery in the Department of War, Washington. 3 vols. Philadelphia: J.T. Bowen. (Earlier eds. include: E.C. Biddle, Philadelphia, 1836–1844; D. Rice and J.G. Clark, Philadelphia, 1842–1844. Reprinted: D. Rice and A.N. Hart, Philadelphia, 1854–1858; J. Grant, Edinburgh, 1933–1934; EP Pub., East Ardsley, Engl., 1972; Scholarly Press, St. Clair Shores, Mich., 1970; Volair, Kent, Ohio, 1978.)

_____ 1854–1858 *see* 1848–1850 (reprint info.)

Mackenzie, Alexander
1801   Voyages from Montreal, on the River St. Laurence, Through the Continent of North America, to the Frozen and Pacific Oceans; in the Years 1789 and 1793; With a Preliminary Account of the Rise, Progress, and Present State of the Fur Trade of That Country. [Compiled by William Combe from Mackenzie's notes.] London: T. Cadell, Jr., and W. Davies & etc. (Reprinted: The Radisson Society of Canada, Toronto, 1927; also, R. Nobe, London, 1927; and, University Microfilms, Ann Arbor, Mich., 1966.)

_____
1802   Voyages from Montreal, on the River St. Laurence, Through the Continent of North America, to the Frozen and Pacific Oceans; in the Years 1789 and 1793. With a Preliminary Account of the Rise, Progress, and Present State of the Fur Trade of That Country. [Compiled by William Combe from Mackenzie's notes.] Philadelphia: Published by John Morgan; R. Carr, Printer.

_____
1802a   Voyages d'Alex.dre Mackenzie dans l'Intérieur de l'Amérique Septentrionale, faits en 1789, 1792 et 1793. J. Castéra, trans. Paris: Dentu.

_____
1802b   Reisen von Montreal durch Nordwestamerica nach dem Fismeer und der Süd-See in den Jahren 1789 und 1793. Hamburg, [Germany]: Benjamin Gottlob Hoffman.

_____ 1927 *see* 1801 (reprint info.)

1970   The Journals and Letters of Sir Alexander Mackenzie. W. Kaye Lamb, ed. *Hakluyt Society, Extra Series* 41. Cambridge: Cambridge University Press.

Mackenzie, Charles
1889–1890 The Missouri Indians: A Narrative of Four Trading Expeditions to the Missouri, 1804–1805–1806. Pp. 315–393 in Vol. 1 of Les bourgeois de la Compagnie du Nord-Ouest. 2 vols. Louis R. Masson, ed. Quebec: Impr. générale A. Coté et cie. (Reprinted, 2 vols.: Antiquarian Press, New York, 1960.)

McKenzie, Parker P., and John Peabody Harrington
1948   Popular Account of the Kiowa Indian Language. *Monographs of the School of American Research* 12. Santa Fe.

McKern, W.C.
1939   The Midwestern Taxonomic Method as an Aid to Archaeological Culture Study. *American Antiquity* 4(4):301–313.

McKibbin, Anne, Kevin D. Black, Ronald J. Rood, Margaret A. Van Ness, and Michael D. Metcalf
1988   Archaeological Excavations at 48CA1391, Campbell County, Wyoming. Eagle, Colo.: Metcalf Archaeological Consultants.

McKinley, Robert
1971   A Critique of the Reflectionist Theory of Kinship Terminology: The Crow/Omaha Case. *Man*, n.s. 6(2):228–247. London.

1971a   Why Do Crow and Omaha Kinship Terminologies Exist? A Sociology of Knowledge Interpretation. *Man*, n.s. 6(3):408–426. London.

MacKinnon, Neil A., and G.S.L. Stuart, eds.
1987   Man and the Mid-Holocene Climatic Optimum. Calgary: The University of Calgary Archaeological Association.

McLaird, James D.
1988   The Welsh, the Vikings, and the Lost Tribes of Isreal on the Northern Plains: The Legend of the White Mandan. *South Dakota History* 18(4):245–273. Pierre.

McLaughlin, Irene Castle
1993   Colonialism, Cattle, and Class: A Century of Ranching on the Fort Berthold Indian Reservation (North Dakota). (Ph.D. Dissertation in Anthropology, Columbia University, New York City.)

McLaughlin, James
1910   My Friend the Indian. Boston: Houghton Mifflin Company. (See also McLaughlin 1926, 1936.)

1911   The Sun Dance of the Blackfeet. *Canadian Magazine* 37:403–412. Toronto.

1926   My Friend the Indian. New ed.; with an Introduction by George Bird Grinnell. Boston and New York: Houghton Mifflin Company. (See also McLaughlin 1936.)

1936   My Friend the Indian; or, Three Heretofore unpublished chapters of the book published under the title My Friend the Indian; by Major James McLaughlin; Edited and Prefaced by Usher L. Burdick. Baltimore: The Proof Press.

McLaughlin, Marie L.
1916   Myths and Legends of the Sioux. Bismarck, N.Dak.: Bismarck Tribune Company. (Reprinted: Tumbleweed Press, Bismarck, N.Dak., 1974.)

M'Lean, John *see* Maclean, John

Maclean, John
1889   The Blackfoot Sun-Dance. *Proceedings of the Canadian Institute [for] 1887–'88*, 3d ser., Vol. 6(7):231–237. Toronto.

1895   Social Organization of the Blackfoot Indians. *Proceedings of the Canadian Institute [for] 1893–'94*, 3d ser., Vol. 4(2):249–260. Toronto.

1896   Canadian Savage Folk: The Native Tribes of Canada. Toronto: William Briggs; Montreal: C.W. Coates. (Reprinted: Coles Publishing Co., Toronto, 1971.)

1961   Blackfoot Medical Priesthood [1909]. *Alberta Historical Review* 14(1):11–21. Calgary.

McLeary, Timothy P.
1997   The Stars We Know: Crow Indian Astronomy and Lifeways. Prospect Heights, Ill.: Waveland Press.

McLeod, David K.
1987   Below the Forks: Archaeology, Prehistory and History of the Selkirk and District Planning Area. Winnipeg, Man.: Historic Resources Branch, Manitoba Culture, Heritage and Recreation.

MacLeod, Margaret Arnett, and William Lewis Morton
1974   Cuthbert Grant of Grantown: Warden of the Plains of Red River. With a New Introduction by W.L. Morton. *The Carleton Library* 71. Toronto: McClelland and Stewart. (Originally publ. in 1963.)

MacLeod, William Christie
1938   Self-Sacrifice in Mortuary and Non-Mortuary Ritual in North America. *Anthropos: Internationale Zeitschrift für Völker-und Sprachenkunds, Sonderabdruck* 33:349–400. St. Gabriel-Mödling bei Wien, Austria.

McMaster, Gerald
1993   Tenuous Lines of Descent: Indian Art and Craft of the Reservation Period. Pp. 93–120 in In the Shadow of the Sun: Perspectives on Contemporary Native Art. Hull, Que.: Canadian Museum of Civilization.

1995   Edward Poitras: Canada XLVI Biennale di Venezia. Hull, Que.: Canadian Museum of Civilization.

McMaster, Gerald, and Lee-Ann Martin
1992   Indigena: Contemporary Native Perspectives. Vancouver and Quebec: Canadian Museum of Civilization.

McMillan, Alan D.
1989   Native Peoples and Cultures of Canada: An Anthropological Overview. Vancouver: Douglas and McIntyre.

McMurtrie, Douglas C., and Albert H. Allen
1930   Jotham Meeker, Pioneer Printer of Kansas; With a Bibliography of the Known Issues of the Baptist Mission Press at Shawanoe, Stockbridge, and Ottawa, 1834–1854. Chicago: The Eyncourt Press.

1930a   A Forgotten Pioneer Press of Kansas. Chicago: John Calhoun Club.

McNaught, Kenneth William K.
1969   The Pelican History of Canada. Baltimore: Penguin Books. (Several reprints, incl.: 1971, 1978, 1982.)

McNeil, David E., and Edward A. Tennant
1979   Parí Pakuru': An Introduction to Spoken Pawnee. Albuquerque: Educational Research Associate.

MacNeish, Richard S.
1958   An Introduction to the Archaeology of Southeast Manitoba. *National Museum of Canada Bulletin* 157; *Anthropological Series* 44. Ottawa.

McNickle, D'Arcy
1946   Rescuing Sisseton. *The American Indian* 3(2):21–27.

Macrae, J.A.
1884   [Letter to Minister, dated 25 August 1884.] (Record Group

10, Vol. 3697, File 15423, National Archives of Canada, Ottawa.)

McQuesten, Calvin
1912   The Sun Dance of the Blackfeet. With 10 woodcuts. *Rod and Gun for Canada* 13(10):1169–1177. Woodstock, Ont.

McQuillan, D.A.
1980   Creation of Indian Reserves on the Canadian Prairies, 1870–1885. *The Geographical Review* 70(4):379–396. Toronto.

McVaugh, Rogers
1956   Edward Palmer: Plant Explorer of the American West. Norman: University of Oklahoma Press.

M'Vickar, Archibald, ed. *see* MacVickar, Archibald, ed.

MacVickar, Archibald, ed.
1842   History of the Expedition under the Command of Captains Lewis and Clarke, to the Sources of the Missouri, Thence across the Rocky Mountains, and Down the River Columbia to the Pacific Ocean: Performed during the Years 1804, 1805, 1806. Prepared for the Press by Paul Allen. 2 vols. [Rev. ed.] New York: Harper and Brothers.

McWilliams, Richebourg Gaillard, trans. and ed. 1953 *see* Pénigaut, André-Joseph 1953

Madill, Dennis
1983   Select Annotated Bibliography on Métis History and Claims. Ottawa: Treaties and Historical Research Centre, Indian and Northern Affairs Canada.

Madole, Richard F., C. Reid Ferring, Margaret J. Guccione, Stephen A. Hall, William C. Johnson, and Curtis J. Sorenson
1991   Quaternary Geology of the Osage Plains and Interior Highlands. Pp. 503–546 in Quaternary Nonglacial Geology: Conterminous U.S. Roger B. Morrison, ed. *Geology of North America* K-2. Boulder, Colo.: Geological Society of America.

Madsen, David B., and David Rhode, eds.
1994   Across the West: Human Population Movement and the Expansion of the Numa. Salt Lake City: University of Utah Press.

Maelen, Philippe Marie Guillaume van der
1827   Amérique Septentrionale: partie du Mexique. [Map, hand col.; leaf no. 47] in: Atlas universel de gographie physique, politique, statistique et minéralogique. Bruxelles.

Magnaghi, Russell M.
1970   The Indian Slave Trader: The Comanche; a Case Study. (Ph.D. Dissertation in History, Saint Louis University, Saint Louis, Missouri.)

Magne, Martin P.R., and John W. Ives
1991   The First Albertans Project: 1988 and 1989 Research. Pp. 101–112 in Archaeology in Alberta 1988 and 1989. Martin Magne, ed. *Archaeological Survey. Provincial Museum of Alberta. Occasional Paper* 33. Edmonton.

Mailhot, P.R., and D.N. Sprague
1985   Persistent Settlers: The Dispersal and Resettlement of the Red River Métis, 1870–85. Pp. 1–30 in The Métis: Past and Present. Thomas Flanagan and John E. Foster, eds. *Canadian Ethnic Studies* 17(2)[Special issue]. Toronto.

Mails, Thomas E.
1978   Sundancing at Rosebud and Pine Ridge. Sioux Falls, S.Dak.: The Center for Western Studies, Augustana College. (Reprinted under title: Sundancing: the Great Sioux Piercing Ritual, Council Oak Books, Tulsa, Okla., 1998.)

1984   [Sun Dance Manuscripts and Audiotapes.] (Center for Western Studies, Archives and Manuscripts Collection, Augustana College, Sioux Falls, S.Dak.)

Mails, Thomas E., and Dallas Chief Eagle
1979   Fools Crow. Garden City, N.Y.: Doubleday. (Reprinted: Avon Books, New York, 1980: University of Nebraska Press, Lincoln, 1990.)

Mainfort, Robert C., Jr., and Marvin D. Jeter, eds.
1999   Arkansas Archaeology: Essays in Honor of Dan and Phyllis Morse. Fayetteville: The University of Arkansas Press.

Makseyn-Kelley, Stephanie A.
1996   Inventory and Assessment of Associated Funerary Objects in the National Museum of Natural History Affiliated with the Assiniboine. Addendum to the 1993 Repatriation Office Case Report "With a Lock of Hair for Remembrance" [by Timothy G. Baugh, Stephanie A. Makseyn-Kelley, and John W. Verano]. Washington: Smithsonian Institution, National Museum of Natural History, Repatriation Office.

Malainey, Mary Evelyn
1991   Internal External Relationships of Saskatchewan Plains Pottery assemblages: Circa A.D. 1300 to Contact. (M.A. Thesis in Anthropology and Archaeology, University of Sasketchwan, Saskatoon.)

Malan, Vernon D.
1958   The Dakota Indian Family. *South Dakota State College. Rural Sociology Department Agricultural Experiment Station. Bulletin* 470. Brookings, S.Dak.

1963   The Dakota Indian Economy: Factors Associated with Success in Ranching. *South Dakota State College. Rural Sociology Department Agricultural Experiment Station. Bulletin* 487. Brookings, S.Dak.

Malan, Vernon D., and Clinton J. Jesser
1959   The Dakota Indian Religion: A Study of Conflict in Values. *South Dakota State College. Rural Sociology Department Agricultural Experiment Station. Bulletin* 473. Brookings, S.Dak.

Malan, Vernon D., and R. Clyde McCone
1960   The Time Concept, Perspective and Premise in the Socio-Cultural Order of the Dakota Indians. *Plains Anthropologist* 5(9):12–15.

Malan, Vernon D., and Joseph F. Powers
1960   The Crow Creek Indian Family. *South Dakota State College. Rural Sociology Department Agricultural Experiment Station. Bulletin* 487. Brookings, S.Dak.

Malan, Vernon D., and Ernest L. Schusky
1962   The Dakota Indian Community: An Analysis of the Non-Ranching Population of the Pine Ridge Reservation. *South Dakota State College. Rural Sociology Department Agricultural Experiment Station. Bulletin* 505. Brookings, S.Dak.

Malinowski, Sharon, ed.
1995   Notable Native Americans. Foreword by George H. Abrahams. Detroit, Mich.: Gale Research Inc.

Mallery, Garrick
1877   A Calendar of the Dakota Nation. *Bulletin of the United States Geological and Geographical Survey of the Territories* 3:3–25. F.V. Hayden, U.S. Geologist-in-Charge. Washington: Government Printing Office.

1878   The Former and Present Number of Our Indians. Pp. 340–366 in *Proceedings of the American Association for the Advancement of Science, Twenty-sixth Meeting, Held at Nashville, Tenn., August, 1877.* Salem, Mass.: The Salem Press.

1881   Sign Language among North American Indians Compared with That among Other Peoples and Deaf-Mutes. Pp. 263–552 in *1st Annual Report of the Bureau of [American]*

Ethnology [for] 1879–'80. Washington: Smithsonian Institution; U.S. Government Printing Office. (Reprinted with articles by Alfred L. Kroeber and Charles F. Voegelin in: *Approaches to Semiotics* 14. Mouton, The Hague, 1972.)

1886   Pictographs of the North American Indians: A Preliminary Paper. Pp. 3–256 in *4th Annual Report of the Bureau of [American] Ethnology [for] 1882–'83*. Washington: Smithsonian Institution; U.S. Government Printing Office.

1893   Picture-writing of the American Indians. Pp. 3–822 in *10th Annual Report of the Bureau of [American] Ethnology [for] 1888–'89*. Washington: Smithsonian Institution; U.S. Government Printing Office. (Reprinted, 2 vols.: Dover Publications, New York, 1972.)

Malouf, Carling
1962   Notes on the Logan Buffalo Jump. Pp. 12–15 (et al., pp. 40–56: Panel Discussion on Buffalo Jumps) in Symposium on Buffalo Jumps. Carling Malouf and Stuart Conner, eds. *Montana Archaeological Society. Memoir* 1. Missoula and Helena.

1963   Crow-Flies-High (32MZ1), a Historic Hidatsa Village in the Garrison Reservoir Area, North Dakota. *Bureau of American Ethnology Bulletin* 185; *River Basin Surveys Papers* 29. Washington: Smithsonian Institution; U.S. Government Printing Office.

Malouf, Carling, and Stuart Conner, eds.
1962   Symposium on Buffalo Jumps. *Montana Archaeological Society. Memoir* 1. Missoula and Helena.

Manchester House Journals
1786–1793 [Journals from 1786 to 1793.] (Hudson's Bay Company Collection, Reels 1M73 and 1M74, Public Archives of Canada, Ottawa.)

Mandan, Hidatsa, Arikara Times
1997   Holyday Greetings from TAT Chairman Russell D. Mason, Sr. *Mandan, Hidatsa, Arikara Times*, Dec. 17, 1997; IX(41):3. New Town, N.Dak.

Mandelbaum, David G.
1936   Changes in an Aboriginal Culture following a Change in Envirnoment, As Exemplified by the Plains Cree. (Ph.D. Dissertation in Anthropology, Yale University, New Haven, Conn.)

1940   The Plains Cree. *American Museum of Natural History Anthropological Papers* 37(2):155–316. New York. (Reprinted as Part I, pp. 1–258 in The Plains Cree: An Ethnographic, Historical, and Comparative Study. University of Regina, Regina, Sask., 1979; also: AMS Press, New York, 1979.)

1967   Anthropology and People: The World of the Plains Cree. *University of Saskatchewan. University Lectures* 12. Saskatoon.

1979   The Plains Cree: An Ethnographic, Historical, and Comparative Study. 2 pts. in 1 vol. *Canadian Plains Studies* 9. Regina, Sask.: Canadian Plains Research Center, University of Regina. (Pt. 1 originally publ. in 1940; Pt. 2, previously unpubl., comp. in 1935–1936.)

Mangum, Neil C.
1987   Battle of the Rosebud: Prelude to the Little Bighorn. El Segundo, Calif.: Upton.

Manitoba Culture. Heritage and Recreation
1989   A Glossary of Manitoba Prehistoric Archaeology. Winnipeg: Historic Resources Branch, Manitoba Culture, Heritage and Recreation.

Mann, Donna
1992   George Catlin (1796–1872). Washington: National Gallery of Art.

Mann, Henrietta
1997   Cheyenne-Arapaho Education 1871–1982. Boulder: University Press of Colorado. (Originally Presented as the Author's Ph.D. Dissertation in Anthropology, University of New Mexico, Albuquerque, 1982, under the name Henrietta Whiteman.)

Manuel, George, and Michael Posluns
1974   The Fourth World: An Indian Reality. Don Mills, Ont.: Collier-Macmillan.

Manypenny, George W.
1880   Our Indian Wards. Cincinnati: Robert Clarke and Co.

Manzanet, Fray Damian
1899   Carta de Don Damian Manzanet á Don Carlos de Siguenza sobre el Descrubrimiento de la Bahía del Espíritu Santo. [Facsimile]; Letter of Don Damian Manzanet to Don Carlos de Siguenza Relative to the Discovery of the Bay of Espiritu Santo. Lilia M. Casis, trans. *Texas State Historical Association Quarterly* 2(4):252–312. Austin.

Manzione, Joseph
1991   I Am Looking to the North for My Life: Sitting Bull, 1876–1881. Salt Lake City: University of Utah Press.

Marín del Valle, Francisco Antonio
1758   Descripcion de la Provincia del Nuevo Mexico, con un mapa que manifesta su situacion, y Pueblos. (AGN, Californias, 39:1.)

Marcy, Randolph Barnes
1853   Exploration of the Red River of Louisiana, in the Year 1852, by Randolph B. Marcy, Captain Fifth Infantry U.S. Army; assisted by George B. McClellan, Brevet Captain U.S. Engineers; with Reports on the Natural History of the Country and Numerous Illustrations. (Pp. 305–311, Appendix H: Vocabularies of the Comanches and Wichitas ..., With Some General Remarks by Prof. W.W. Turner.) *32d Congress. 2d Session. Senate Executive Document No. 54*. Washington: Robert Armstrong, Public Printer. (Published also as: *33d Congress. 1st Session. House Executive Document No. 33*. A.O.P. Nicholson, Public Printer, Washington, 1854.)

————— 1854 *see* 1853

1859   The Prairie Traveler: A Hand-book for Overland Expeditions; with Illustrations, and Itineraries of the Principal Routes between the Mississippi and the Pacific. New York: Harper and Brothers. (Reprinted: Appleton Books, Old Saybrook, Conn., 1989; also, Perigee, New York, 1994.)

1866   Thirty Years of Army Life on the Border. New York: Harper and Brothers.

Margolies, Susan
1973   Powwows and Peyote Help Indians Adjust to Life in the Big City. *Wall Street Journal*, June 5, 1973:1, 31. New York.

Margry, Pierre, comp. and ed.
1876–1886 Découvertes et établissements des Français dans l'ouest et dans le sud de l'Amérique Septentrionale (1614–1754). Mémoires et documents originaux. 6 Pts./vols. Paris: D. Jouaust. (Cover page of Vol. 1 has 1875 imprint date. See also the 1879–1888 ed.)

—————, comp. and ed.
1879–1888 Découvertes et établissements des Français dans l'ouest et dans le sud de l'Amérique Septentrionale (1614–1754). Mémoires et documents originaux. 6 Pts./vols. Paris: Maisonneuve et Cie. (Reprinted: AMS Press, New York, 1974.)

Marino, Mary C., ed
1983   Proceedings of the Second Siouan Languages Conference, 1982. *Na'pāo: A Saskatchewan Anthropology Journal* 13(October): Special Issue. Saskatoon, Sask.

Mark, Joan
1988   A Stranger in Her Native Land: Alice Fletcher and the American Indians. Lincoln: University of Nebraska Press.

Marken, Jack W., and Herbert T. Hoover
1980   Bibliography of the Sioux. *Native American Bibliography Series* 1. Metuchen, N.J.: The Scarecrow Press.

Markgraf, Vera, and Tom Lennon
1986   Paleoenvironmental History of the Last 13,000 Years of the Eastern Powder River Basin, Wyoming, and Its Implications for Prehistoric Cultural Patterns. *Plains Anthropologist* 31(111):1–12. Lincoln.

Markley, Elinor R., and Beatrice Crofts
1997   Walk Softly, This Is God's Country: Sixty-Six Years on the Wind River Indian Reservation; compiled from the Letters and Journals of The Rev. John Roberts, 1883–1949. Lander, Wyo.: Mortimore Publishing.

Markoe, Glenn E., ed.
1986   Vestiges of a Proud Nation: The Ogden B. Read Northern Plains Indian Collection. Burlington, Vt.: Robert Hull Fleming Museum.

Markowitz, Harvey
1987   Catholic Mission and the Sioux: A Crisis in the Early Paradigm. Pp. 113–137 in Sioux Indian Religion: Tradition and Innovation. Raymond J. DeMallie and Douglas R. Parks, eds. Norman: University of Oklahoma Press.

Marquis, Thomas B.
1928   Memoirs of a White Crow Indian (Thomas H. Leforge) as Told by Thomas B. Marquis. New York: The Century Company. (Reprinted, with an Introduction by Joseph Medicine Crow and Herman J. Viola: University of Nebraska Press, Lincoln, 1974.)

1931   A Warrior Who Fought Custer. Minneapolis: Midwest Company. (See also Marquis 1957.)

1933   She Watched Custer's Last Battle: The Story of Kate Bighead, Cheyenne Indian, Interpreted in 1927. Hardin, Mont.: Custer Battle Museum.

1957   Wooden Leg: A Warrior Who Fought Custer. Lincoln: University of Nebraska Press. (Originally publ. in 1931; reprinted in 1962, 1971.)

1973   Cheyenne and Sioux: The Reminiscences of Four Indians and a White Soldier. Ronald H. Limbaugh, ed. *University of the Pacific. Pacific Center for Western Historical Studies. Monograph* 3. Stockton, Calif.

1975   Custer, Cavalry & Crows; Being the Thrilling Account of the Western Adventures of William White; the Story of William White as Told to Thomas Marquis. Introduction by Hugh Scott; Annotated by John A. Popovich. Fort Collins, Colo.: Old Army Press.

1978   The Cheyennes of Montana. Edited, with an Introduction and a Biography of the Author by Thomas D. Weist. Algonac, Mich.: Reference Publications.

Marriott, Alice
[1936–   [Kiowa Fieldnotes.] (Manuscripts in J.E. Levy's posses-
1956]   sion.)

1945   The Ten Grandmothers. Norman: University of Oklahoma Press. (Several reprints, incl.: 1951, 1968, 1983, 1989.)

1947   Winter-telling Stories. New York: Thomas Y. Crowell. (Reprinted in 1969.)

1956   The Trade Guild of the Southern Cheyenne Women. *Bulletin of the Oklahoma Anthropological Society* 4:19–27.

Norman. (Reprinted, abrid.: Pp. 247–255 in Native North American Art History: Selected Readings. Zena P. Mathews and Aldona Jonaitis, comps. Peek Publications, Palo Alto, Calif., 1980.)

1959   Ribbon Applique Work of the North American Indians. *Oklahoma Anthropological Society Bulletin* 6:49–59.

1962   The Black Stone Knife. Illustrated by Harvey Weiss. Eau Claire, Wis.: E.M. Hale and Company.

1963   Saynday's People: The Kiowa Indians and the Stories They Told. Lincoln: University of Nebraska Press.

1968   Kiowa Years: A Study in Culture Impact. New York: Macmillan.

Marriott, Alice, and Carol K. Rachlin
1975   Plains Indian Mythology. New York: Thomas Y. Crowell.

1977   Dance Around the Sun: The Life of Mary Little Bear Inkanish: Cheyenne. New York: Thomas Y. Crowell.

1980   Southern Plains Ribbonwork Development and Diffusion. Pp. 23–29 in Fourth Annual Plains Indian Seminar: Ribbonwork and Cloth Applique. [Cover title:] Native American Ribbonwork: A Rainbow Tradition. George P. Horse Capture, ed. Cody, Wyo.: Buffalo Bill Historical Center.

Marsh, Gordon H.
1936   [Materials for a Study on the Iowa Language: Iowa Grammar and Vocabulary.] (Manuscript 497.3, B63c (X4a.2) [Kendall No. 4178] in the Library of the American Philosophical Society, Philadelphia.)

Marshall, Humphrey
1824   The History of Kentucky; [Containing] Ancient Annals of Kentucky; or, Introduction to the History and Antiquities of the State of Kentucky, by C.S. Rafinesque. 2d ed. 2 vols. Frankfort, Ky.: G.S. Robinson.

Marshall, James O.
1972   The Archeology of the Elk City Reservoir, a Local Archeological Sequence in Southeast Kansas. *Kansas State Historical Society. Anthropological Series* 6. Topeka.

Marshall, John T.
1927   [Statistical Report, Fort Belknap Agency, Montana, Year 1927.] (Manuscript No. M1011, Roll 65, Records of the Bureau of Indian Affairs, Record Group 75, National Archives, Washington.)

Marshall, Richard A.
1963   Archaeology of Jasper County, Missouri. *Plains Anthropologist* 8(19):1–16.

Marshall, Susan, and Jack Brink
1986   A Preliminary Test of the Calderwood Buffalo Jump (DkPj-27). Pp. 140–159 in Archaeology in Alberta 1985. John W. Ives, ed. *Archaeological Survey of Alberta. Occasional Paper* 29. Edmonton.

Martínez, Antonia Maria
1957   The Letters of Antonio Martínez, Last Spanish Governor of Texas, 1817–1822. Translated and edited from the original copies in the Texas State Archives by Virginia H. Taylor, assisted by Mrs. Juanita Hammons. Austin: Texas State Library.

Martel, Gilles
1984   Le messianisme de Louis Riel. Waterloo, Ont.: Wilfrid Laurier University Press.

Martin, Chester
1916   Lord Selkirk's Work in Canada. *Oxford Historical and Literary Studies* 7. Oxford: At the Clarendon Press.

1212

Martin, Christopher
1988   Native Needlework: Contemporary Indian Textiles from North Dakota. Fargo, N.Dak.: North Dakota Council for the Arts.

Martin, H.T.
1909   Further notes on the Pueblo Ruins of Scott County. *Kansas University Science Bulletin* 5(2):11–22. Lawrence.

Martin, James E., Robert A. Alex, and Rachel C. Benton
1988   Holocene Chronology of the Beaver Creek Shelter, Wind Cave National Park, South Dakota. *Proceedings of the South Dakota Academy of Science* 67. Vermillion.

Mason, J. Alden
1926   A Collection from the Crow Indians. *Museum Journal* 17:393–413. Philadelphia: University of Pennsylvania Museum.

1929   The Texas Expedition. *Museum Journal* 20:318–338. Philadelphia: University of Pennsylvania Museum.

Mason, Otis Tufton
1894   Ethnological Exhibit of the Smithsonian Institution at the World's Columbian Exposition. Pp. 208–216 in Memoirs of the International Congress of Anthropology. C. Staniland Wake, ed. Chicago: The Schulte Publ. Co.

1894a   Summary of Progress in Anthropology. Pp. 601–629 in *Annual Report of the Board of Regents of the Smithsonian Institution [...] to July, 1893.* Washington: U.S. Government Printing Office.

1896   Influence of Environment upon Human Industries or Arts. Pp. 639–665 in *Annual Report of the Board of Regents of the Smithsonian Institution [...] to July, 1895.* Washington: U.S. Government Printing Office.

1907   Environment. Pp. 427–430 in Pt./vol. 2 of Handbook of American Indians North of Mexico. Frederick W. Hodge, ed. 2 Pts./vols. *Bureau of American Ethnology Bulletin* 30. Washington: Smithsonian Institution; U.S. Government Printing Office. (Reprinted: Rowman and Littlefield, New York, 1971.)

Mason, Ronald J.
1993   Oneota and Winnebago Ethnogenesis: an Overview. *The Wisconsin Archaeologist* 74(1–4):400–421. Milwaukee.

Massignan, Marco
1996   La danza del sole dei Lakota. Milano: Xenia Edizioni.

Masson, Louis François Redrigue
1889–1890   Les bourgeois de la Compagnie du Nord-Ouest; récits de voyages, lettres et rapports inédits relatifs au Nord-Ouest canadien. Publiés avec une esquissee historique et des annotations par L.R. Masson. 2 vols. Quebec: Impr. générale A. Coté et cie. (Reprinted, 2 vols.: Antiquarian Press, New York, 1960.)

1960 *see* 1889–1890 (reprint info.)

Masson, Marilyn A., and Michael B. Collins
1995   The Wilson-Leonard Site (41WM235). *Cultural Resource Management News and Views* 7(1):6–10. Austin, Tex.

Mathes, Valerie S.
1982   Four Bears as Seen by His Artists: Catlin and Bodmer. *North Dakota History* 49(3):4–13. Bismarck.

Mathews, John Joseph
1934   Sundown. New York: Longmans, Green.

1961   The Osages: Children of the Middle Waters. Norman: University of Oklahoma Press.

Mathews, Zena Pearlstone, and Aldona Jonaitis, comps.
1982   Native North American Art History: Selected Readings. Palo Alto, Calif.: Peek Publications.

Mattern, Mark
1996   The Powwow as a Public Arena for Negotiating Unity and Diversity in American Indian Life. *American Indian Culture and Research Journal* 20(4):183–201. Los Angeles.

Mattes, Merrill J.
1960   The Enigma of Wounded Knee. *Plains Anthropologist* 5(9):1–11.

1971   John Dougherty. Pp. 113–141 in Vol.8 of The Mountain Men and the Fur Trade of the Far West. LeRoy R. Hafen, ed. 10 vols. Glendale, Calif.: Arthur H. Clark, 1965–1972.

Matteson, Sumner V.
1906   The Fourth of July Celebration at Fort Belknap. *Pacific Monthly* 16(1):93–103.

Matthews, G. Hubert
1955   Phonemic Analysis of a Dakota Dialect. *International Journal of American Linguistics* 21(1):56–59. Chicago.

1958   Handbook of Siouan Languages. (Ph.D. Dissertation in Linguistics, University of Pennsylvania, Philadelphia.)

1959   On Tone in Crow. *International Journal of American Linguistics* 25(2):135–136. Chicago.

1959a   Proto-Siouan Kinship Terminology. *American Anthropologist*, n.s. 61(2):252–278.

1965   Hidatsa Syntax. *Papers on Formal Linguistics* 3. The Hague: Mouton.

1970   Some Notes on the Proto-Siouan Continuants. *International Journal of American Linguistics* 36(2):98–109. Chicago.

1973   Thoughts on k-fronting in Crow. Pp. 153–157 in A Festschrift for Morris Halle. S. Anderson and Paul Kiparsky, eds. New York: Holt, Rinehart and Winston.

1979   Glottochronology and the Separation of the Crow and Hidatsa. Pp. 113–125 in Symposium on the Crow-Hidatsa Separations. Leslie B. Davis, ed. *Archaeology in Montana* 20(3). Billings, [etc.].

1981   Introduction to the Crow Language. 3d rev. ed. Bozeman, Mont.: Indian Bilingual Teacher Program, Center For Bilingual/Multicultural Education.

Matthews, Washington
1873–1874   Grammar and Dictionary of the Language of the Hidatsa (Minnetarees, Grosventres of the Missouri). 2 vols. *Shea's Library of American Linguistics,* ser. 2(1–2). New York: Cramoisy Press.

1877   Ethnography and Philology of the Hidatsa Indians. *United States Geological and Geographical Survey of the Territories. Miscellaneous Publications* 7. Washington. (Reprinted: Johnson Reprint, New York, 1971.)

Matthiessen, Peter
1980   In the Spirit of Crazy Horse. New York: Viking Press.

Mattina, Anthony
1987   Colville-Okanagan Dictionary. *University of Montana. Occasional Papers in Linguistics* 5. Missoula: Linguistics Laboratory, Department of Anthropology, University of Montana.

Mattison, Ray H.
1955   The Indian Reservation System on the Upper Missouri, 1865–1890. *Nebraska History* 36(3):141–174. Lincoln.

Matuz, Roger, ed.
1998   St. James Guide to Native North American Artists: With a preface by Rick Hill; and an Introduction by W. Jackson Rushing. Detroit, Mich.: St. James Press.

1213

Matzko, John
1997   Ralph Budd and Early Attempts to Reconstruct Fort Union, 1925–1941. *Nebraska History* 64(3):2–19. Lincoln.

Maurer, Evan M.
1977   The Native American Heritage: A Survey of North American Indian Art. Chicago: The Art Institute of Chicago.
_____, ed.
1992   Visions of the People: A Pictorial History of Plains Indian Life. With Essays by Evan M. Maurer, Louise Lincoln, George P. Horse Capture, David W. Penney, Father Peter J. Powell. Minneapolis and Seattle: Minneapolis Institute of Arts and University of Washington Press.

Maximilian, Alexander Philipp Prinz zu Wied
1839–1841 Reise in das innere Nord-America in den Jahren 1832 bis 1834. 2 vols. and Atlas. Coblenz, Germany: J. Hoelscher.

1843   Travels in the Interior of North America, 1832–1834. Translated from the German, by H. Evans Lloyd; To Accompany the Original Series of Eighty-one Elaborately-coloured Plates [...]. 2 vols. London: Ackermann and Co. (Originally publ. in German: J. Hoelscher, Coblenz, 1839–1841; English ed. reprinted in Vols. 22–24 [1906] of Early Western Travels, 1748–1846, Reuben G. Thwaites, ed., Arthur H. Clark, Cleveland, Ohio, 1904–1907.)

_____ [1904–1907] 1906 *see* Thwaites, Reuben G., ed. 1904–1907 (Vols. 22–24:1906)

1976   People of the First Man: Life among the Plains Indians in Their Final Days of Glory; the Firsthand Account of Prince Maximilian's Expedition Up the Missouri River, 1833–34. Watercolors by Karl Bodmer. Davis Thomas and Karin Ronnefeldt, eds. New York: E.P. Dutton.

Maxwell, Joseph A.
1971   The Development of Plains Kinship Systems. (M.A. Thesis in Anthropology, University of Chicago, Chicago.)

1978   The Evolution of Plains Indian Kin Terminologies: A Non-Reflectionist Account. *Plains Anthropologist* 23(79):13–29.

1986   The Conceptualization of Kinship in an Inuit Community: A Cultural Account. (Ph.D. Dissertation in Anthropology, University of Chicago, Chicago.)

1994   Biology and Social Relationship in the Kin Terminology of an Inuit Community. Pp. 25–48 in North American Indian Anthropology: Essays on Society and Culture. Raymond J. DeMallie and Alfonso Ortiz, eds. Norman: University of Oklahoma Press.

Mayer, Frank B.
1932   With Pen and Pencil on the Frontier in 1851: The Diary and Sketches of Frank Blackwell Mayer. Edited with an Introduction and Notes by Bertha L. Heilbron. (Pt.1.) *Publications of the Minnesota Historical Society. Narratives and Documents* 1. St. Paul. (Pt. 2: Frank B. Mayer and the Treaties of 1851. Edited with an Introduction and Notes by Bertha L. Heilbron. *Minnesota History* 22, 1941. Reprinted as a combined volume with a Foreword by Thomas O'Sullivan: Minnesota Historical Society Press, St. Paul, 1986.)

Mayer-Oakes, William J., ed.
1967   Life, Land, and Water. *University of Manitoba. Department of Anthropology. Occasional Papers* 1. Winnipeg.

Mayhall, Mildred P.
1962   The Kiowas. 1st ed. Norman: University of Oklahoma Press.

1971   The Kiowas. 2d ed. Norman: University of Oklahoma Press. (Reprinted in 1987.)

Maynard, Eileen
1968   Baseline Data Study-Preliminary Findings. *Pine Ridge Research Bulletin* 1(January):2–13. Pine Ridge, S.Dak.

Maynard, Eileen, and Gayla Twiss
1969   That These People May Live: Conditions among the Oglala Sioux of the Pine Ridge Reservation. Pine Ridge, S.Dak.: U.S. Public Health Service.

Mazakootemane, Paul
1880   Narrative of Paul Mazakootemane. S.R. Riggs, trans. *Collections of the Minnesota Historical Society* 3[1870–1880]:83–90. Saint Paul.

Mead, Barbara
1981   Seed Analysis of the Meehan-Schell Site (13BN110), a Great Oasis Site in Central Iowa. *Journal of the Iowa Archeological Society* 28:15–90. Iowa City.

Mead, Margaret
1932   The Changing Culture of an Indian Tribe. New York: Columbia University Press. (Reprinted: AMS Press, New York, 1969.)

1960   The Golden Age of American Anthropology. New York: George Braziller.

Meadows, William C.
1999   Kiowa, Apache, and Comanche Military Societies: Enduring Veterans, 1800 to the Present. Austin: University of Texas Press.

Means, Russell
1995   Where White Men Fear To Tread: The Autobiography of Russell Means. With Marvin J. Wolf. New York: St. Martin's Press.

Medicine, Beatrice
1970   The Use of Magic among the Stoney Indians. Pp. 283–292 in Vol. 2 of *Verhandlungen des XXXVIII. Internationalen Amerikanistenkongresses [Proceedings of the 38th International Congress of Americanists], Stuttgart-München 12. bis 18. August 1968.* 4 vols. München: Kommissionsverlag Klaus Renner, 1969–1972.

1975   Self-Direction in Sioux Education. *Integrated Education* 13(6):15–17. Chicago.

1978   The Native American Woman: A Perspective. Austin, Tex.: National Educational Laboratory Publishers.

1980   Ceremonial Networks on the Northern Plains. (Manuscript, copy in J. Archambault's possession.)

1981   Native American Resistance to Integration: Contemporary Confrontations and Religious Revitalization. *Plains Anthropologist* 26(94, Pt.1):277–285.

1987   Indian Women and the Renaissance of Traditional Religion. Pp. 159–171 in Sioux Indian Religion: Tradition and Innovation. Raymond J. DeMallie and Douglas R. Parks, eds. Norman: University of Oklahoma Press.

1997   Changing Native American Roles in an Urban Context and Changing Native American Sex Roles in an Urban Context. Pp. 145–155 in Two Spirit People: Native American Gender Identity, Sexuality, and Spirituality. Sue-Ellen Jacobs, Wesley Thomas and Sabine Lang, eds. Urbana, Ill.: University of Illinois Press.

1999   Ella Cara Deloria: Early Lakota Ethnologists (Newly Discovered Novelist). Pp 259–267 in Theorizing the American Tradition. Lisa Philips Valentine and Regna Darnell, eds. Toronto: University of Toronto Press.

Medicine Crow, Joseph
1962   The Crow Indian Buffalo Jump Legends. Pp. 35–39 (et al.

1214

pp. 40–56: Panel Discussion on Buffalo Jumps) in Symposium on Buffalo Jumps. Carling Malouf and Stuart Conner, eds. *Montana Archaeological Society, Memoir* 1. Missoula and Helena.

1979   The Crow Migration Story. Pp. 63–72 in Symposium on the Crow-Hidatsa Separations. Leslie B. Davis, ed. *Archaeology in Montana* 20(3). Billings, [etc.].

1979a   From M.M. to M.D.: Medicine Man to Doctor of Medicine. Pp. 81–85 in Lifeways of Intermontane and Plains Montana Indians. Leslie B. Davis, ed. *Occasional Papers of the Museum of the Rockies* 1. Bozeman, Mont.: Montana State University.

1992   From the Heart of the Crow Country: The Crow Indians' Own Stories. New York: Orion Books.

Medicine Crow, Joseph, and Charles C. Bradley, Jr.
1976   The Crow Indians: 100 Years of Acculturation. Wyola, Mont.:Wyola Bilingual Project.

Medicine Horse, Magdalene, and Tim Bernardis, comps.
1992   Crow Tribal Government and Little Big Horn College Records Survey: A Report to the Crow Tribe of Indians and Little Big Horn College. Crow Agency, Mont.: Little Big Horn College Archives.

Medicine Horse, Mary Helen, comp.
1987   A Dictionary of Everyday Crow: Crow-English / English-Crow. Rev. ed. Preface by G. Hubert Matthews. Crow Agency, Mont.: Bilingual Materials Development Center. (Originally comp. by Belva Tushka, with the assistance of G. Hubert Matthews and Robert Chadwick, Crow Agency, Mont., 1979.)

Medicus [Hiller, Wesley R.]
1951   Indian Village at Fort Berthold. *The Minnesota Archaeologist* 17(1):3–9. Minneapolis.

Medland, Wendy S.
1981   Henry Pollard, Photographer. *Alberta History* 29(2):20–28. Calgary.

Meister, Barbara, ed.
1996   Mending the Circle: A Native American Repatriation Guide. Understanding and Implementing NAGPRA and the Official Smithsonian and Other Repatriation Policies. Walter Echo-Hawk, Elizabeth Sackler, and Jack Trope, ed. committee; Introduction by Suzan Shown Harjo. New York: American Indian Ritual Object Repatriation Foundation.

Mekeel, H. Scudder
1932   A Modern American Indian Community in the Light of Its Past: A Study in Culture Change. (Ph.D. Dissertation in Anthropology, Yale University, New Haven, Conn.)

1932a   A Discussion of Culture Change as Illustrated by Material from a Teton-Dakota Community. *American Anthropologist,* n.s. 34(2):274–288. (Title in table of contents reads: A Discussion of Cultural Change... [etc.].)

1936   The Economy of a Modern Teton Dakota Community. *Yale University Publications in Anthropology* 3(6):3–14. New Haven, Conn.

1936a   An Anthropologist's Observation on Indian Education. *Progressive Education* 13(3):151–159. Washington.

1943   A Short History of the Teton-Dakota. *North Dakota Historical Quarterly* 10(3):137–205. Grand Forks and Bismarck.

1944   An Appraisal of the Indian Reorganization Act. *American Anthropologist* 46(2, Pt.1):209–217.

Meleen, Elmer E.
1938   A Preliminary Report of the Mitchell Indian Village Site and Burial Mounds on Firesteel Creek, Mitchell, Davison County, South Dakota. *University of South Dakota. Museum. Archaeological Studies Circulars* 2(Pt. 1). Vermillion.

Mellow, J. Dean
1989   A Syntactic Analysis of Noun Incorporation in Cree. (M.A. Thesis in Linguistics, McGill University, Montreal, Que.)

1990   Asymmetries between Compunding and Noun Incorporation in Plains Cree. Pp. 247–257 in Papers of the Twenty-first Algonquian Conference. William Cowan, ed. Ottawa: Carleton Press.

Melody, Michael Edward
1976   The Lakota Sun Dance: A Composite View and Analysis. *South Dakota History* 6(4):433–455. Pierre.

Meltzer, David J.
1991   Altithermal Archaeology and Paleoecology at Mustang Springs, on the Southern High Plains of Texas. *American Antiquity* 56(2):236–267.

Meltzer, David J., and Michael B. Collins
1987   Prehistoric Water Wells on the Southern High Plains: Clues to Altithermal Climate. *Journal of Field Archaeology* 14(1):9–28.

Mennonite General Conference
1887–1896 *The Mennonite.* Newton, Kans., [etc.]: General Board of the General Conference Mennonite Church, [etc.]. (Copies in Bethel College Library, Newton, Kans.)

Mennonite Indian Leaders Council
1982   Tsese-Ma'heone-Nemeotôtse: Cheyenne Spiritual Songs. Newton, Kans.: Faith and Life Press.

Mereness, Newton Dennison, ed.
1916   Travels in the American Colonies; Edited under the Auspices of the National Society of the Colonial Dames of America. New York: The Macmillan Company. (Reprinted: Antiquarian Press, New York, 1961.)

_____ 1961 *see* 1916 (reprint info.)

Meriam, Lewis
1928   The Problem of Indian Administration. Report of a Survey made at the Request of Honourable Hubert Work, Secretary of the Interior, and submitted to him, February 21, 1928. Baltimore, Md.: Johns Hopkins Press. (Reprinted: Johnson Reprint Corporation, New York, 1971. University Microfilms International, Ann Arbor, Mich., 1982.)

Meritt, E.B.
1916   [Letter to James Ahtone, dated June 27, 1916.] (Manuscript, Microfilm Publication KA, Roll 47, Frame 1059 in Kiowa Agency Records, Indian Archives Division, Oklahoma Historical Society, Oklahoma City.)

Merlan, Francesca C.
1975   Noun-verb Relationships in Arikara Syntax. (Ph.D. Dissertation in Linguistics, University of New Mexico, Albuquerque.)

Merriam, Alan P.
1968   The Purposes of Ethnomusicology: An Anthropological View. Pp. 779–790 in Readings in Anthropology. Morton H. Fried, ed. New York: Thomas Y. Crowell.

Merrill, Moses
1834   Wdtwhtl Wdwdklha Tva Eva Wdhonetl. Marin Awdofka. Otoe Hymn Book. Shawnee Mission, Kans.: J. Meeker, Printer.

1837   Mdkuntl Eeifa Cesus Kryst Wdwdklha Atva, Wdhseka Ukewyglhce Atvakineitlnl Wowdkowika Marin Wdtotl *1215*

Wdkwnga Atva. Shawnee Baptist Mission, Kans.: J. Meeker, Printer.

1892   Extracts from the Diary of Rev. Moses Merrill, a Missionary to the Otoe Indians from 1832 to 1840. *Nebraska State Historical Society. Transactions and Reports* 4:160–191. Lincoln.

Merrill, William L., Marian Kaulaity Hansson, Candace S. Greene, and Frederick J. Reuss
1997   A Guide to the Kiowa Collections at the Smithsonian Institution. *Smithsonian Contributions to Anthropology* 40. Washington: Smithsonian Institution Press.

Merritt, Ann
1988   Women's Beaded Robes: Artistic Reflections of the Crow World. Pp. 41–47 in To Honor the Crow People. (Father) Peter J. Powell, ed. Chicago: Foundation for the Preservation of Indian Art and Culture.

Messagge on the Fur Trade 1832 *see* Secretary of War 1832

Messer, James
1937   [Interview.] (Manuscript, *Indian and Pioneer History* 36:89–90, Newspaper Archives and Manuscript Division, Oklahoma Historical Society, Oklahoma City.)

Metcalf, George
1949   Three Pottery Types from the Dismal River Aspect. Pp. 73–78 In Proceedings of the Fifth Plains Conference for Archeology. John L. Champe, ed. *University of Nebraska. Laboratory of Anthropology. Note Book* 1. Lincoln.

1963   Small Sites On and About Fort Berthold Indian Reservation, Garrison Reservoir, North Dakota. *Bureau of American Ethnology Bulletin* 185; *River Basin Surveys Papers* 26. Washington: Smithsonian Institution; U.S. Government Printing Office.

Metcalf, Michael D.
1974   Archaeological Excavations at Dipper Gap: A Stratified Butte Top Site in Northeastern Colorado. (M.A. Thesis in Anthropology, Colorado State University, Fort Collins, Colo.)

1987   Contributions to the Prehistoric Chronology of the Wyoming Basin. Pp. 233–261 in Perspectives on Archaeological Resources Management in the "Great Plains". Alan J. Osborn and Robert C. Hassler, eds. Omaha, Nebr.: I&O Publishing Company.

Metcalf, Michael D., and Kevin D. Black
1988   The Yarmony Site, Eagle County, Colorado: A Preliminary Summary. *Southwestern Lore* 54(1):10–28. Boulder, Colo.

1997   Archaic Period Logistical Organization in the Colorado Rockies. Pp. 168–209 in Changing Perspectives of the Archaic on the Northwestern Plains and Rocky Mountains. Mary Lou Larson and Julie E. Francis, eds. Vermillion: The University of South Dakota Press.

Métis Association of Alberta 1981 *see* Sawchuk, Joe, Patricia Sawchuk, and Theresa Ferguson 1981

Mexican Border Commission
1875   Reports of the Committee of Investigation Sent in 1873 by the Mexican Government to the Frontier of Texas. Translated from the official edition made in Mexico. New York: Baker and Godwin, Printers.

Mexican Boundary Commission
1857–1859 Report on the United States and Mexican Boundary Survey: Made Under the Direction of the Secretary of the Interior, by William H. Emory. Major First Cavalry, and United States Commissioner. Washington: Cornelius Wendall, Printer.

Mexico, Republic of
1878   Tratados y convenciones concluidos y ratificados por la Republica Mexicana desde su independiencia hasta el año actual, acompañados de varios documentos qu le son referentes. Edicion oficial. Mexico, D.F.: Imprenta de Gonzalo A. Esteva. (Half-title: Derecho Internacional Mexicano: Primera parte.)

Meya, Wilhelm Krüdener
1999   The Calico Winter Count, 1825–1877: An Ethnohistorical Analysis. (M.A. Thesis in American Indian Studies, University of Arizona, Tucson.)

Meyer, David
1978   The Clearwater Lake Phase: A Saskatchewan Perspective. *Archae-facts* 5:27–42. Brandon, Man.: Archaeological Society of Southwestern Manitoba.

1983   The Prehistory of Northern Saskatchewan. Pp. 141–170 in Tracking Ancient Hunters: Prehistoric Archaeology in Saskatchewan. Henry T. Epp and Ian Dyck, eds. Regina: Saskatchewan Archaeological Society.

1983a   Comment on McCullough's View of Protohistoric Cree and Blackfoot in Alberta and Saskatchewan. *Saskatchewan Archaeology* 4:45–46. Saskatoon.

1984   Anent, the Pehonan Complex. *Saskatchewan Archaeology: The Journal of the Saskatchewan Archaeological Society* 5:43–46. Saskatoon.

1985   The Red Earth Crees, 1860–1960. Canada. *National Museum of Man. Mercury Series. Ethnology Service Paper* 100. Ottawa.

1985a   A Component in the Scottsbluff Tradition: Excavations at the Niska Site. *Canadian Journal of Archaeology* 9(1):1–37. Ottawa.

1988   The Old Women's Phase on the Sakatchewan Plains: Some Ideas. Pp. 55–63 in Archaeology in Alberta 1987. Martin Magne, ed. *Archaeological Survey of Alberta. Occasional Paper* 32. Edmonton.

Meyer, David, and Henry T. Epp
1990   North-South Interaction in the Late Prehistory of Central Saskatchewan. *Plains Anthropologist* 35(132):321–342.

Meyer, David, and Scott Hamilton
1994   Neighbors to the North: Peoples of the Boreal Forest. Pp. 96–127 in Plains Indians, A.D. 500–1500: The Archaeological Past of Historic Groups. Karl H. Schlesier, ed. Norman: University of Oklahoma Press.

Meyer, David, and Henri Liboiron
1990   A Paleoindian Drill from the Niska Site in Southern Saskatchewan. *Plains Anthropologist* 35(129):299–302.

Meyer, David, and Dale Russell
1987   The Selkirk Composite of Central Canada: A Reconsideration. *Arctic Anthropology* 24(2):1–31. Madison, Wis.

Meyer, David, and Paul C. Thistle
1995   Saskatchewan River Rendezvous Centers and Trading Posts: Continuity in a Cree Social Geography. *Ethnohistory* 42(3):403–444.

Meyer, David, Olga Klimko, and James Finnigan
1988   Northernmost Avonlea in Saskatchewan. Pp. 33–42 in Avonlea Yesterday and Today: Archaeology and Prehistory. Leslie B. davis, ed. Saskatoon: Saskatchewan Archaeological Society.

Meyer, Roy W.
1961   The Prairie Island Community: A Remnant of Minnesota Sioux. *Minnesota History* 37(6):271–282.

1962 The Iowa Indians, 1836–1885. *Kansas Historical Quarterly* 28(3):273–300. Topeka.

1964 The Establishment of the Santee Reservation, 1866–1869. *Nebraska History* 45(1):59–97. Lincoln.

1967 History of the Santee Sioux: United States Indian Policy on Trial. Lincoln: University of Nebraska Press.

1968 Fort Berthold and the Garrison Dam. *North Dakota History* 35(3–4):217–355. Bismarck.

1971 The Canadian Sioux, Refugees from Minnesota. Pp. 168–182 in The American Indian: Past and Present. R.L. Nichols and G.R. Adams, eds. Waltham, Mass.: Zerox Publishing.

1975 New Light on Lewis Garrard. *Western Historical Quarterly* 6(3):261–278. Logan, Utah.

1977 The Village Indians of the Upper Missouri: The Mandans, Hidatsas, and Arikaras. Lincoln: University of Nebraska Press.

1993 History of the Santee Sioux: United States Indian Policy on Trial. Rev. ed. Lincoln: University of Nebraska Press.

Michelson, Truman
1910 [Notes on Medicine Arrows of the Cheyenne, from Bull Thigh and William Somers, Sept. 7–13, 1910.] (Manuscript No. 2799, National Anthropological Archives, Smithsonian Institution, Washington.)

1911 Menominee Tales. *American Anthropologist,* n.s. 13(1):68–88.

1925 Notes on Fox Mortuary Customs and Beliefs. Pp. 351–496 in *40th Annual Report of the Bureau of American Ethnology [for] 1918–'19.* Washington: Smithsonian Institution; U.S. Government Printing Office.

1929 [Fieldnotes from Jesse Rowlodge.] (Manuscript No. 1791, National Anthropological Archives, Smithsonian Institution, Washington.)

1929a [Vocabulary, with Occasional Ethnographic Notes on "Doctors," "Shaking Lodge," Medicine Arrow, and Sun Dance Songs, etc.; Concho, Okla., July, 1929.] (Manuscript No. 3343, National Anthropological Archives, Smithsonian Institution, Washington.)

1932 The Narrative of a Southern Cheyenne Woman. *Smithsonian Michellaneous Collections* 87(5):1–13. (Publication 3140.) Washington.

1933 Narrative of an Arapaho Woman. *American Anthropologist,* n.s. 35(4):595–610.

1934 Some Arapaho Kinship Terms and Social Usages. *American Anthropologist,* n.s. 36(1):137–139.

1935 Phonetic Shifts in Algonquian Languages. *International Journal of American Linguistics* 8(3–4):131–171. Chicago.

1939 Linguistic Classification of Cree and Montagnais-Naskapi Dialects. *Bureau of American Ethnology Bulletin* 123; *Anthropological Paper* 8. Washington: Smithsonian Institution; U.S. Government Printing Office.

Michlovic, Michael G.
1983 The Red River Valley in the Prehistory of the Northern Plains. *Plains Anthropologist* 28(99):23–31.

Michlovich, Michael G., and Fred E. Schneider
1993 The Shea Site: A Prehistoric Fortified Village on the Northeastern Plains. *Plains Anthropologist* 38(143):117–137.

Michno, Gregory F.
1997 Lakota Noon: The Indian Narrative of Custer's Defeat. Missoula, Mont.: Mountain Press Publishing Co.

Middleton, Samuel H.
1953 Kainai Chieftanship: History, Evolution and Culture of the Blood Indians; Origin of the Sun-Dance. With a Foreword by His Excellency, Field Marshall, Rt. Hon. the Viscount Alexander of Tunis. Lethbridge, Alta.: The Lethbridge Herald. (Second impression, James Muir edition, 1954. Cover title: Blackfoot Confederacy, Ancient and Modern. Title on spine: Indian Chiefs.)

Mikkanen, Arvo Quoetone
1987 Skaw-Tow: The Centennial Commemoration of the Last Kiowa Sun Dance. *American Indian Journal* 9(4):5–9. Washington.

Mikkelsen, Glen
1987 Indians and Rodeo. *Alberta History* 35(3):13–19. Calgary.

Miles, Ellen G.
1988 Saint Mémin's Portraits of American Indians, 1804–1807. *The American Art Journal* 20(4):2–33.

Miles, John D.
1872 [Letter to Enoch Hoag, dated June 4th, 1872.] (Manuscript No. M234, Roll 127 Letters Received, Cheyenne River Agency 1871–1872, Records of the Bureau of Indian Affairs, Record Group 75, National Archives, Washington.)

1873 [Monthly Report for January–February 1873.] (Manuscript No. M234, Roll 128, Letters Received, Cheyenne River Agency 1873–1875, Records of the Bureau of Indian Affairs, Record Group 75, National Archives, Washington.)

1874 [Letter to E.P Smith, dated May 23, 1874.] (Manuscript No. M234, Roll 128, Letters Received, Cheyenne River Agency 1873–1875, Records of the Bureau of Indian Affairs, Records Group 75, National Archives, Washington.)

Miles, Nelson A.
1897 Personal Recollections and Observations of General Nelson A. Miles Embracing a Brief View of the Civil War; or, From New England to the Golden Gate: And the Story of His Indian Campaigns, with Comments on the Exploration, Development and Progress of Our Great Western Empire. Copiously Illustrated with Graphic Pictures by Frederic Remington and Other Eminent Artists. Chicago: Werner.

Millar, James F.V.
1978 The Gray Site: An Early Plains Burial Ground. 2 vols. *Parks Canada. Manuscript Report* 304. Ottawa.

1981 Mortuary Practices of the Oxbow Complex. *Canadian Journal of Archaeology* 5:103–117. Ottawa.

Millard, LeMoyne
1973 A Sioux Sun Dancer Recalls His Experience. *The South Dakota Museum* 1(2):9–10. Vermillion, S.Dak.

Miller, Alfred Jacob 1837 *see* Ross, Marvin C., ed. 1968

Miller, Carl F.
1964 Archeological Investigations at the Hosterman Site (39PO7) [in the] Oahe Reservoir Area, Potter County, South Dakota, 1956. *Bureau of American Ethnology Bulletin* 189; *River Basin Surveys Papers* 3. Washington: Smithsonian Institution; U.S. Government Printing Office.

Miller, David Humphreys
1959 Ghost Dance. New York: Duell, Sloan, and Pearce.

1973 A Prussian on the Plains: Balduin Möllhausen's Impressions. *Great Plains Journal* 12(2):174–193. Lawton, Okla. *1217*

Miller, David R.
1978   Charles Alexander Eastman, The "Winner": From Deep
          Woods to Civilization—Santee Sioux, 1858–1939. Pp. [60]
          61–73 in American Indian Intellectuals. Margot Liberty, ed.
          1978 Proceedings of the American Ethnological Society.
          Robert F. Spencer, gen. ed. St. Paul, Minn.: West Publish-
          ing Co.

1987   Montana Assiniboine Identity: A Cultural Account of
          American Indian Ethnicity. (Ph.D. Dissertation in Anthro-
          pology, Indiana University, Bloomington.)

1994   Definitional Violence and Plains Indian Reservation Life:
          Ongoing Challenges to Survival. Pp. 226–248 in Violence,
          Resistance, and Survival in the Americas: Native Americans
          and the Legacy of Conquest. William B. Taylor and Franklin
          Pease G.Y., eds. Washington: Smithsonian Institution.

Miller, Fred E. 1985 *see* O'Connor, Nancy Fields, comp. 1985

Miller, Frederick L.
1979   Tobacco and Smoking Phenomena in the Sun Dance Reli-
          gion of the Crow Indians of Montana: A Study in the
          Dynamics of the Sacred. (Ph.D. Disseration in Religion and
          Mythology, Temple University, Philadelphia.)

1980   The Crow Sun Dance Lodge: Form, Process, and Geometry
          in the Creation of Sacred Space. *Temenos: Studies in
          Comparative Religion* 16:92–102. Helsinki: Suomen
          Uskontotieteellinen Seura.

Miller, J.R., ed.
1989   Sweet Promises: A Reader in Indian-White Relations in
          Canada. Toronto: University of Toronto Press.

1991   Skyscrapers Hide the Heavens: A History of Indian-White
          Relations in Canada. Rev. ed. Toronto: University of
          Toronto Press.

1996   Shingwauk's Vision: A History of Native Residential
          Schools. Toronto: University of Toronto Press.

Miller, Mark E., and David J. McGuire
1997   Early Plains Archaic Adaptations: A View from the Medi-
          cine House Site in the Hanna Basin, South-central Wyo-
          ming. Pp. 368–392 in Changing Perspectives of the Archaic
          on the Northwestern Plains and Rocky Mountains. Mary
          Lou Larson and Julie E. Francis, eds. Vermillion: The
          University of South Dakota Press.

Miller, Mark E., Brian R. Waitkus, and David G. Eckles
1986   Butler-Rissler: A Plains Woodland Occupation Site Along
          the North Platte River in Central Wyoming. (Paper pre-
          sented at the 49th Annual Plains Conference, Denver,
          Colo.)

1987   Woodland-Besant Occurrence in Central Wyoming. *Plains
          Anthropologist* 32(118):420–423.

Miller, Wick R.
1959   A Note on Kiowa Linguistic Affiliations. *American Anthro-
          pologist,* n.s. 61(1):102–105.

1965   Acoma Grammar and Texts. *University of California Publi-
          cations in Linguistics* 40. Berkeley.

Milligan, Edward A.
1969   Sun Dance of the Sioux. Bottineau, N.Dak.: [privately
          printed.]

Milloy, John S.
1973   The Plains Cree: A Preliminary Trade and Military Chro-
          nology, 1670–1870. (M.A. Thesis in History, Carleton
          University, Ottawa.)

1988   The Plains Cree: Trade, Diplomacy, and War, 1790 to 1870.

          Manitoba Studies in Native History 4. Winnipeg: The
          University of Manitoba Press. (Reprinted in 1990.)

1991   Our Country: Significance of the Buffalo Resource for a
          Plains Cree Sense of Territory. In: Aboriginal Resource Use
          in Canada: Historical and Legal Aspects. Kerry Abel and
          Jean Friesen, eds. *University of Manitoba Studies in Native
          History* 6. Winnipeg: University of Manitoba Press.

1999   A National Crime: The Canadian Government and the
          Residential School System, 1879 to 1986. Winnipeg: Uni-
          versity of Manitoba Press.

Milne, Lourie Ann
1988   The Larson Site (D1On-3) and the Avonlea Phase in
          Southeastern Alberts. Pp. 43–66 in Avonlea Yesterday and
          Today: Archaeology and Prehistory. Leslie B. Davis, ed.
          Saskatoon: Saskatchewan Archaeological Society.

Milner, Clyde A., II
1982   With Good Intentions: Quaker Work among the Pawnees,
          Otos, and Omahas in the 1870s. Lincoln: University of
          Nebraska Press.

Milton, Viscount William Fitzwilliam, and Walter B. Cheadle
1865   The North-West Passage by Land: Being the Narrative of an
          Expedition from the Atlantic to the Pacific, undertaken with
          the View of Exploring a Route Across the Continent to
          British Columbia through British Territory by one of the
          Northern Passes in the Rocky Mountains. London: Cassell,
          Petter and Galpin. (Reprinted: Coles Pub., Toronto, 1970.)

Mindeleff, Cosmos
1898   Navaho Houses. Pp. 475–517 in Pt.2 of *17th Annual Report
          of the Bureau of American Ethnology [for] 1895–'96.*
          Washington: Smithsonian Institution; U.S. Government
          Printing Office.

Miner, H. Craig, and William E. Unrau
1978   The End of Indian Kansas: A Study of Cultural Revolution,
          1854–1871. Lawrence: The Regents Press of Kansas. (Re-
          printed: University of Kansas Press, Lawrence, 1990.)

Miner, Kenneth L.
1984   Winnebago Field Lexicon. (Manuscript in K.L. Miner's
          possession.)

Miner, William H.
1911   The Iowa. Cedar Rapids, Iowa: The Torch Press.

Minneapolis Star-Tribune, July 14, 1996. Minneapolis, Minn.

Minnesota. Governor's Human Rights Commission
1948   Race Relations in Minnesota: Reports of the Commission. 4
          Pts. in 1 Vol. St. Paul, Minn.: Governor's Human Rights
          Commission.

1952   The Indian in Minnesota: A Report to Governor C. Elmer
          Anderson of Minnesota, by the Governor's Interracial Com-
          mission. St. Paul, Minn.: Governor's Human Rights Com-
          mission.

1965   Minnesota's Indian Citizens, Yesterday and Today. St.
          Paul, Minn.: Governor's Human Rights Commission.

Minnesota Historical Society
1969   Chippewa and Dakota Indians: A Subject Catalog of Books,
          Pamphlets, Periodical Articles, and Manuscripts in the
          Minnesota Historical Society. James Taylor Dunn, Chief
          Librarian. St. Paul: Minnesota Historical Society.

Minnesota Territorial Census 1850 *see* Harpole, Patricia C., and Mary
D. Nagle, eds. 1972

Mirsky, Jeannette
1937   The Dakota. Pp. 382–427 in Cooperation and Competition
          among Primitive Peoples. New York: McGraw-Hill.

Mishkin, Bernard
1940   Rank and Warfare among the Plains Indians. *Monographs of the American Ethnological Society* 3. New York: J.J. Augustin.

Missionaries of the Society of Jesus
1891   Prayers in the Crow Indian Language Composed by the Missionaries of the Society of Jesus. De Smet, Idaho: De Smet Mission Print.

The Missouri Republican
1851   *The Missouri Republican*, Nov. 2. St Louis, Mo. (Microfilm: Bell and Howell, Wooster, Ohio.)

Missouri River Basin Investigations [Project] Staff
1949   Social and Economic Report of Fort Berthold Reservation, Supplement No. 1: A Summary of Data Obtained in the Fort Berthold Family Survey #2. *Bureau of Indian Affairs. Missouri River Basin Investigations. Report* 94. Billings, Mont.

Mitchell, Lynn Marie
1987   Shadow Catchers on the Great Plains: Four Frontir Photographers of American Indians. (M.A. Thesis in Liberal Studies, University of Oklahoma, Norman.)

Mithun, Marianne
1984   The Evolution of Noun Incorporation. *Language: Journal of the Linguistic Society of America* 60(4):847–894. Baltimore.

1991   Active/Agentive Case Marking and Its Motivations. *Language: Journal of the Linguistic Society of America* 67(3): 510–546. Baltimore.

Mixco, Mauricio J.
1997   Mandan. *Languages of the World Series. Materials* 159. Munich, Germany: Lincom Europa.

1997a   Mandan Switch Reference: A Preliminary View. *Anthropological Linguistics* 39(2):220–298. Bloomignton.

1999   Mandan Grammatical Sketch. (Manuscript in M. Mixico's possession.)

Mizen, Mamie
1966   Federal Facilities for Indians: Tribal Relations with the Federal Government. Committee Report on Appropriations, United States Senate. Washington: Government Printing Office.

Mocquais, Pierre-Yves, André Lalonde, and Bernard Wilhelm
1984   La langue, la culture et la société des francophones de l'Ouest. Les actes du troisième collogue du Centre d'études franco-canadiennes de l'Ouest tenu au Centre D'Études Bilingues, Université de Régina, les 25 et 26 novembre 1983. Régina, Sask.: Institut de recherche du Centre D'études Bilingues, The University of Regina.

Moffat, Charles R., et al.
1990   Archaeological Data Recovery at Five Prehistoric Sites, Lake Red Rock, Marion County, Iowa. Prepared for the U.S. Army Engeneer District, by American Resources Group, Ltd.; principal investigators, Michael J. McNerney and Charles R. Moffat; authors, Charles R. Moffat, [et al.]. 2 vols. *Cultural Resources Management Report* 133. Carbondale, Ill.: American Resources Group.

Mohatt, Gerald, and Joseph Eagle Elk
2000   The Price of a Gift: A Lakota Healer's Story. Lincoln , Nebr.: University of Nebraska Press.

Möllhausen, Baldwin
1858   Diary of a Journey from the Mississippi to the Coasts of the Pacific with a United States Government Expedition. With an Introduction by Alexander Von Humboldt, and Illustrations in Chromo-Lithography. Mrs. Percy Sinnett, trans. 2 vols. London: Longman, Brown, Green, Longmans, & Roberts.

Momaday, N. Scott
1967   The Journey of Tai-Me. Santa Barbara: University of California Press.

1968   House Made of Dawn. New York: Harper and Row; also, New York: New American Library; and, Harmondsworth, England: Penguin. (Several reprints, incl.: 1976, 1983, 1999.)

1969   The Way to Rainy Mountain. Illustrated by Al Momaday. Albuquerque: University of New Mexico Press; New York: Ballantine Books. (Reprinted in 1976, 1996.)

1974   Native American Attitudes to the Environment. Pp. 79–85 in Seeing with a Native Eye: Essays on Native American Religion. W. Capps, ed. New York: Harper and Row.

1974a   I Am Alive... Pp. 11–28 in The World of the American Indian. Jules B. Billard, ed. Washington: National Geographic Society.

1976   The Names: A Memoir. New York: Harper and Row. (Reprinted: University of Arizona Press, Tucson, 1987.)

1992   In the Presence of the Sun: A Gathering of Shields. Santa Fe, N.Mex.: The Rydal Press. (Reprinted in *Native Peoples* 11(1):56–61, Fall/Winter 1997.)

Montabé, Marie
1951   This Is the Sun Dance. [Privately printed.]

1962   Da-goo-win-net: Mystical Sun Dance of the Shoshones. [Art, design and printing by John Coulter.] [Privately printed.]

Montet-White, Anta
1968   The Lithic Industries of the Illinois Valley in the Early and Middle Woodland Period. *University of Michigan. Anthropological Papers of the Museum of Anthropology* 35. Ann Arbor.

Montgomery, Henry W.
1906   Remains of Prehistoric Man in the Dakotas. *American Anthropologist*, n.s. 8(4):640–651.

1908   Prehistoric Man in Manitoba and Saskatchewan. *American Anthropologist*, n.s. 10(1):33–40.

Montgomery, William B., and William C. Requa, comps.
1834   Washashe Wageressa Pahugreh Tse: The Osage First Book. Boston: Crocher and Brewster, for The American Board of Commissioners for Foreign Missions.

Montoya, Geronima Cruz
1995   Afterword. Pp. 165–166 in Modern By Tradition: American Indian Painting in the Studio Style, by Bruce Bernstein and W. Jackson Rushing. Santa Fe: Museum of New Mexico Press.

Moodie, D. Wayne
1985   Indian Map-making: Two Examples from the Fur Trade West. *Association of Canadian Map Libraries. Bulletin* 55(June):32–43.

Moodie, D. Wayne, and Barry Kaye
1977   The Ac Ko Mok Ki Map. *The Beaver: Magazine of the North* (Spring issue):4–15. Winnipeg, Man.

1982   Indian Agriculture in the Fur Trade Northwest. *Prairie Forum* 11(2):171–184. Regina, Sask.: Canadian Plains Research Center, University of Regina.

Mooney, James
1892   Eating the Mescal. *The Augusta Chronicle*, Jan. 24:11. Augusta, Ga.

1892a   A Kiowa Mescal Rattle. *American Anthropologist*, o.s. 5(1):64–65.

1219

1892b   Borrowed Ceremonials. *American Anthropologist,* o.s. 5(3):288.

1893   [Kitsai Vocabulary.] (Manuscript No. 2531, Vol.3, National Anthropological Archives, Smithsonian Institution, Washington.)

1896   The Ghost-dance Religion and the Sioux Outbreak of 1890. Pp. 641–1136 [pp. 1111–1136, Vol. Index] in Pt. 2 of *14th Annual Report of the Bureau of American Ethnology [for] 1892–'93.* Washington: Smithsonian Institution; U.S. Government Printing Office. (Reprinted: rev. ed., 1965; Dover Publications, New York, 1973; also, with an Introduction by Raymond J. DeMallie: University of Nebraska Press, Lincoln, 1991.)

1896a   The Messiah Religion and the Ghost Dance (Abstract). *Proceedings of the American Association for the Advancement of Science* 40(8):365–366. Washington.

1897   [Tribal Names and Divisions of Jicarilla, Lipan, and Mescalero Apaches.] (Manuscript No. 3785, Apache Catalog, National Anthropological Archives, Smithsonian Institution, Washington.)

1897a   [Comparative Vocabulary (Mescalero and Lipan); Peyote Notes and Songs.] (Manuscript No. 425, Apache Catalog, National Anthropological Archives, Smithsonian Institution, Washington.)

1898   Calendar History of the Kiowa Indians. Pp. 129–468 in Pt. 1 of *17th Annual Report of the Bureau of American Ethnology [for] 1895–'96.* Washington: Smithsonian Institution; U.S. Government Printing Office. (Reprinted, with an Introduction by John C. Ewers: *Classics of Smithsonian Anthropology,* Smithsonian Institution Press, Washington, 1979.)

1898a   The Jicarilla Genesis. *American Anthropologist,* o.s. 11(7):197–209.

1901   Our Last Cannibal Tribe. *Harper's Monthly Magazine* 103(Sept.):550–555. New York.

1902   [The Story of a Shield.] (Manuscript No. 1878, National Anthropological Archives, Smithsonian Institution, Washington.)

1907   The Cheyenne Indians. [Bound with: Sketch of the Cheyenne Grammar, by Rodolphe Petter.] *Memoirs of the American Anthropological Association* 1(Pt. 6):357–442 [443–478]. Menasha, Wis. (Reprinted: Kraus Reprint, New York, 1964.)

1907a   [Statistics and Notes on Population of Various Sections of North America.] (Manuscript No. 2535 [23 envelopes in 2 boxes], National Anthropological Archives, Smithsonian Institution, Washington.)

1907b   Cheyenne. Pp. 250–257 in Pt./vol. 1 of Handbook of American Indians North of Mexico. Frederick W. Hodge, ed. 2 Pts./vols. *Bureau of American Ethnology Bulletin* 30. Washington: Smithsonian Institution; U.S. Government Printing Office. Government Printing Office. (Reprinted: Rowman and Littlefield, New York, 1971.)

1907c   Dakota. Pp. 376–380 in Pt./vol. 1 of Handbook of American Indians North of Mexico. Frederick W. Hodge, ed. 2 Pts./vols. *Bureau of American Ethnology Bulletin* 30. Washington: Smithsonian Institution; U.S. Government Printing Office. (Reprinted: Rowman and Littlefield, New York, 1971.)

1907d   Kiowa. Pp. 699–701 in Pt./vol. 1 of Handbook of American Indians North of Mexico. Frederick W. Hodge, ed. 2 Pts./

vols. *Bureau of American Ethnology Bulletin* 30. Washington: Smithsonian Institution; U.S. Government Printing Office. (Reprinted: Rowman and Littlefiled, New York, 1971.)

1907e   Kiowa-Apache. Pp. 701–703 in Pt./vol. 1 of Handbook of American Indians North of Mexico. Frederick W. Hodge, ed. 2 Pts./vols. *Bureau of American Ethnology Bulletin* 30. Washington: Smithsonian Institution; U.S. Government Printing Office. (Reprinted: Rowman and Littlefield, New York, 1971.)

1907f   Arapaho. Pp. 72–74 in Pt./vol. 1 of Handbook of Americans North of Mexico. Frederick W. Hodge, ed. 2 Pts./vols. *Bureau of American Ethnology Bulletin* 30. Washington: Government Printing Office. (Reprinted: Rowman and Littlefield, New York, 1971.)

1907g   Indian Missions North of Mexico. Pp. 873–909 in Pt./vol. 1 of Handbook of American Indians North of Mexico. Frederick W. Hodge, ed. 2 Pts./vols. *Bureau of American Ethnology Bulletin* 30. Washington: Smithsonian Institution; U.S. Government Printing Office. (Reprinted: Rowman and Littlefield, New York, 1971.)

1910   Wichita. Pp. 947–950 in Pt./vol. 2 of Handbook of American Indians North of Mexico. Frederick W. Hodge, ed. 2 Pts./vols. *Bureau of American Ethnology Bulletin* 30. Washington: Smithsonian Institution; U.S. Government Printing Office. (Reprinted: Rowman and Littlefield, New York, 1971.)

1910a   Peyote. Pp. 237 in Pt./vol. 2 of Handbook of American Indians North of Mexico. Frederick W. Hodge, ed. 2 Pts./vols. *Bureau of American Ethnology Bulletin* 30. Washington: Smithsonian Institution; U.S. Government Printing Office. (Reprinted: Rowman and Littlefield, New York, 1971.)

1928   The Aboriginal Population of America North of Mexico. John R. Swanton, ed. *Smithsonian Miscellaneous Collections* 80(7); (*Publication* 2955). Washington: Smithsonian Institution; Government Printing Office.

_____ 1965, 1973, 1991 *see* 1896 (reprint info.)

Moore, Clarence B.
1908   Certain Mounds of Arkansas and of Mississippi. 3 Pts. *Journal of the Academy of Natural Sciences of Philadelphia,* 2d ser. 13:481–605. Philadelphia.

Moore, Darla Lee
1996   The Shoshone Sun Dance. (Website: www.shoshone.com/sundance.htm.)

Moore, Francis, Jr.
1965   Map and Description of Texas, Containing Sketches of Its History, Geology, Geography and Statistics [1850]. With an introduction by James M. Day. Waco: Texian Press.

Moore, John H.
1974   Cheyenne Political History, 1820–1894. *Ethnohistory* 21(4):329–359. Bloomington.

1974a   A Study of Religious Symbolism among the Cheyenne Indians. (Ph.D. Dissertation in Anthropology, New York University, New York City.)

1980   Aboriginal Indian Residence Patterns Preserved in Censuses and Allotments. *Science* 207(4427):201–202. Washington. (Addendum in Febr. 8, 1980 issue.)

1982   The Dynamics of Scale in Plains Indian Ethnohistory. *University of Oklahoma. Papers in Anthropology* 23(2):225–246. Norman.

1984   Cheyenne Names and Cosmology. *American Ethnologist* 11(2):291–312.

1987   The Cheyenne Nation: A Social and Demographic History. Lincoln: University of Nebraska Press.

1988   The Dialects of Cheyenne Kinship: Variability and Change. *Ethnology* 27(3):253–269.

1991   Developmental Cycle of Cheyenne Polygyny. *The American Indian Quarterly* 15(3):311–328.

1991a   Kinship and Division of Labor in Cheyenne Society. Pp. 135–158 in Marxist Approaches in Economic Anthropology. *Monographs in Economic Anthropology* 9. Lanham, Md.: University Press of America.

_____, ed.
1993   The Political Economy of North American Indians. Norman: University of Oklahoma Press.

1993a   How Pow-Wows and Giveaways Redistribute the Means of Subsistence. Pp. 240–269 in The Political Economy of North American Indians. John H. Moore, ed. Norman: University of Oklahoma Press.

1994   Ethnogenetic Theories of Human Evolution. The Cultural Results of Cladistic and Ethnogenetic Processes, an Addendum. *Research and Exploration: A Scholarly Publication of the National Geographic Society* 10(1):10–23, 24–37. Washington.

1996   The Cheyenne. Oxford, England, and Cambridge, Mass.: Blackwell Publishers.

Moore, Michael C.
1984   A Reconnaissance Survey of Quartermaster Creek. Pp. 51–214 in Archaeology of the Mixed Grass Prairie. Phase I: Quartermaster Creek. Timothy G. Baugh, ed. *Oklahoma Archeological Survey. Archeological Resource Survey Report* 20. Norman.

1988   Archeology of the Mixed Grass Prairie, Phases II and III: Hay and Cyclone Creeks Surveys and Predictive Modeling in the Quartermaster Watershed. *Oklahoma Archeological Survey. Archeological Resource Survey Report* 33. Norman.

Moorehead, Warren K.
1931   Archeology of the Arkansas River Valley. New Haven: Yale University Press.

Moorhead, Max L.
1968   The Apache Frontier: Jacobo Ugarte and Spanish-Indian Relations in Northern New Spain, 1769–1791. Norman: University of Oklahoma Press.

Moquin, Wayne, and Charles Van Doren, eds.
1995   Great Documents in American Indian History. Afterword by Robert Powless. New York: Da Capo Press.

Morantz, Toby
1982   Northern Algonquian Concepts of Status and Leadership Reviewed: A Case Study of Eighteenth-Century Trading Captain System. *Canadian Review of Sociology and Anthropology* 19:482–500. Toronto and Montreal.

Morehouse, George P.
1904   Along the Kaw Trail. *Transactions of the Kansas State Historical Society for 1903–1904*, Vol. 8:206–212. Topeka.(Reprinted: State Printing Office, Topeka, 1908.)

1908   History of the Kansa or Kaw Indians. *Transactions of the Kansas State Historical Society for 1907–1908*, Vol. 10:327–368. Topeka.

Morfi, Juan Agustín
1932   Excerpts from the Memorias for the History of the Province of Texas; Being a Translation of Those Parts of the Memorias Which Particulary Concern the Various Indians of the Province of Texas; Their Tribal Divisions, Characteristics, Customs, Traditions, Superstitions, and all Else of Interest Concerning Them. With a Prolog, Appendix, and Notes, by Frederick C. Chabot. Covering the Period from Earliest Times to the Close of the Memorias by Padre Fray Juan Agustín de Morfi. Translated and Annotated by Frederick C. Chabot. Translation revised by Carlos E. Castañeda. San Antonio, Tex.: Privately publ.; printed by the Naylor Printing Company. (Halt-title: Memorias for the History of Texas, by Father Morfi.)

1935   Historia de la Provincia de Texas, 1673–1779 / History of Texas, 1673–1779; Translated, with Biographical Introduction and Annotations, by Carlos Eduardo Castañeda. 2 vols. *Publications of the Quivira Society* 6. Albuquerque: The Quivira Society. (Reprinted in 1967.)

Morgan, Dale L.
1953   Jedediah Smith and the Opening of the West. New York: Bobbs-Merrill.

_____, ed.
1964   The West of William H. Ashley: The International Struggle for the Fur Trade of the Missouri, the Rocky Mountains, and the Columbia, with Explorations beyond the Continental Divide, Recorded in the Diaries and Letters of William H. Ashley and His Contemporaries, 1822–1838. Denver, Colo.: Old West Publishing Co.

Morgan, Lewis Henry
1848–1852 Copy of "Extracts from the Unpublished Journals of the Rev. William Hamilton, 1848–1852. (Lewis Henry Morgan Papers at the University of Rochester, N.Y., Library, Department of Rare Books and Special Collections.)

1851   League of the Ho-dé-no-sau-nee, or Iroquois. Rochester, N.Y.: Sage and Brother, Publishers. (Reprinted as: League of the Iroquois; with an Introduction by William N. Fenton. Secaucus, N.J.: Citadel Press; New York: Corinth Books, 1962.)

1869   The "Seven Cities of Cibola." *North American Review* 108(223):457–498. Cambridge: University Press.

1869a   Indian Migrations. [Pt. 1.] *North American Review* 109(225):391–442. Cambridge: University Press. (Reprinted with Pt. 2 [1870]: pp. 158–257 in The Indian Miscellany; William W. Beach, ed., J. Munsell, Albany, N.Y., 1877.)

1870   Indian Migrations. [Pt. 2.] *North American Review* 110(226):33–82. Cambridge: University Press. (Reprinted with Pt. 1 [1869]: pp. 158–257 in The Indian Miscellany; William W. Beach, ed., J. Munsell, Albany, N.Y., 1877.)

1871   Systems of Consanguinity and Affinity of the Human Family. *Smithsonian Contributions to Knowledge* 17. Washington. (Reprinted: Humanities Press, New York, 1966.)

1877   Ancient Society; or, Researches in the Lines of Human Progress from Savagery through Barbarism to Civilization. New York: Henry Holt. (Reprinted: University of Arizona Press, Tucson, 1985.)

1959   The Indian Journals, 1859–1862. Leslie A. White, ed. Ann Arbor: University of Michigan Press.

1963   The Stone and Bone Implements of the Arickarees. *North Dakota History* 30(2–3):115–135. Bismarck.

Morgan, R. Grace
1979   An Ecological Study of the Northern Great Plains as Seen Through the Garrett Site. *University of Regina. Department of Anthropology. Occasional Papers* 1. Regina, Sask.

Morgan, Thomas J.
1890   Indian Education. [Washington: U.S. Government Printing Office.]

Morier, Jan
1979   Métis Decorative Art and Its Inspiration. *Dawson and Hind* 8(1):28–32. Winnipeg, Man.

Morinis, Alan, ed.
1992   Sacred Journeys: The Anthropology of Pilgrimage. With a Foreword by Victor Turner. Westport, Conn.: Greenwood Press.

Morlan, Richard E.
1988   Avonlea and Radiocarbon Dating. Pp. 291–309 in Avonlea Yesterday and Today: Archaeology and Prehistory. Leslie B. Davis, ed. Saskatoon, Sask.: Saskatchewan Archaeological Society.

1992   Bison Size and Gender at the Gowen Sites. Pp. 203–208 in The Gowen Sites: Cultural Responses to Climatic Warming on the Northern Plains (7500–5000 B.P.), by Ernest G. Walker. *Canadian Museum of Civilization. Mercury Series. Archaeological Survey Paper* 145. Ottawa.

1993   A Compilation and Evaluation of Radiocarbon Dates in Saskatchewan. *Saskatchewan Archaeology* 13:3–84. Saskatoon, Sask.

1994   Oxbow Bison Procurement as Seen from the Harder Site, Saskatchewan. *Journal of Archaeological Science* 21(6): 757–777. London.

1999   Canadian Archaeological Radiocarbon Database: A Digital Database on the World Wide Web. (Internet site: *http://www.canadianarchaeology.com*.)

Morris, Alexander
1880   The Treaties of Canada with the Indians of Manitoba and the North-West Territories: Including the Negotiations on Which They Were Based, and Other Information Relating Thereto. Toronto: Belfords, Clarke, and Co. (Reprinted: Coles Publishing Company, Toronto, 1971; also, Fifth House Publishers, Saskatoon, Sask., 1980 and 1991.)

      1971, 1980, 1991 *see* 1880 (reprint info.)

Morris, Elizabeth A., Richard C. Blakeslee, and Kevin Thompson
1985   Preliminary Description of McKean Sites in Northeastern Colorado. Pp. 11–20 in McKean/Middle Plains Archaic: Current Research. Marcel Kornfeld and Lawrence C. Todd, eds. *Occasional Papers on Wyoming Archaeology* 4. Laramie.

Morrison, Bruce, and Roderick C. Wilson, eds.
1986   Native Peoples: The Canadian Experience. Toronto: McClelland and Stewart.

Morrow, Baker H. 1990 *see* Burton, Richard F. 1861 (reprint info.)

Morrow, Mable
1975   Indian Rawhide: An American Folk Art. Norman: University of Oklahoma Press.

Morse, Dan F.
1991   On the Possible Origin of the Quapaws in Northeast Arkansas. Pp. 40–54 in Arkansas Before the Americans. Hester A. Davis, ed. *Arkansas Archeological Survey Research Series* 40. Fayetteville.

Morse, Dan F., and Phyllis A. Morse
1983   Archaeology of the Central Mississippi Valley. New York: Academic Press.

Morse, Eric W.
1969   Fur Trade Canoe Routes of Canada: Then and Now. Ottawa: Queen's Printer. (Reprinted as 2d ed., University of Toronto Press, Toronto, 1979.)

Morse, Jedidiah
1776   The History of North America, Containing an Exact Account of Their First Settlements; ... with the Present State of the Different Colonies; and a Large Introduction. Illustrated with a Map of North America. London: Sold by Millar [etc.]. (Reprinted, micro-opaque: Lost Cause Press, Louisville, Ky., 1959.)

1822   A Report to the Secretary of War of the United States, on Indian Affairs, Comprising a Narrative of a Tour Performed in the Summer of 1820, Under a Commission of the President of the United States, for the Purpose of Ascertaining, for the Use of the Government, the Actual State of the Indian Tribes in Our Country. New Haven, Conn.: S. Converse. (Reprinted: Augustus M. Kelly, New York, 1970; also, Scholarly Press, St. Clair Shores, Mich., 1972.)

Morton, Arthur S., ed. 1929 *see* McGillivray, Duncan 1929

1973   A History of the Canadian West to 1870–71: Being a History of Rupert's Land (the Hudson's Bay Company Territory) and of the North-West Territory (including the Pacific Slope). 2d ed., Lewis G. Thomas, ed. Toronto: University of Toronto Press. (Originally publ.: T. Nelson and Sons, London and New York, 1939.)

Morton, Desmond
1972   The Last War Drum: The Northwest Campaign of 1885. *Canadian War Museum. Historical Publications* 5. Toronto: Hakkert.

Morton, William L., ed.
1956   Alexander Begg's Red River Journal and Other Papers Relative to the Red River Resistance of 1869–1870. Toronto: The Champlain Society.

1967   Manitoba: A History. 2d ed. Toronto: University of Toronto Press. (Originally publ. in 1957; reprinted in 1970, 1989.)

Moses, Lester G.
1984   The Indian Man: A Biography of James Mooney. Urbana: University of Illinois Press.

1996   Wild West Shows and the Images of American Indians, 1883–1933. 1st ed. Albuquerque: University of New Mexico Press. (Reprinted in 1999.)

Mott, Mildred
1938   The Relation of Historic Indian Tribes to Archaeological Manifestations in Iowa. *Iowa Journal of History and Politics* 36(3):227–314. Iowa City. (See also: Wedel, Mildred Mott.)

Moulton, Gary E., ed.
1983–   The Journals of the Lewis and Clark Expedition. [12 vols. through 1999.] Sponsored by the Center for Great Plains Studies, University of Nebraska, Lincoln, and the American Philosophical Society, Philadelphia. Lincoln: University of Nebraska Press.

Mountain Horse, Mike
1979   My People the Bloods. Calgary, Alta.: Glenbow Museum.

Muckleroy, Anna
1922   The Indian Policy of the Republic of Texas. *Southwestern Historical Quarterly* 25(4):229–260. Austin, Tex.

Mudge, B.F.
1896   Traces of the Moundbuilders in Kansas. *Kansas Academy of Science Transactions for 1873*, Vol. 2:69–71. Topeka.

Mulloy, William T.
1942   The Hagen Site: A Prehistoric Village on the Lower Yellowstone. *University of Montana. Publications in the Social Sciences* 1. Missoula.

1943   A Prehistoric Campsite near Red Lodge, Montana. *American Antiquity* 9(2):170–179.

1952   The Northern Plains. Pp. 124–138 in Archeology of Eastern United States. James B. Griffin, ed. Chicago: University of Chicago Press.

1953   The Ash Coulee Site. *American Antiquity* 19(1):73–75.

1954   Archaeological Investigations in the Shoshone Basin of Wyoming. *University of Wyoming Publications* 18(1):1–70. Laramie.

1954a   The McKean Site in Northeastern Wyoming. *Southwestern Journal of Anthropology* 10(4):432–460. Albuquerque.

1958   A Preliminary Historical Outline for the Northwestern Plains. *University of Wyoming. Publications in Science* 22(1–2):1–235. Laramie.

1959   The James Allen Site Near Laramie, Wyoming. *American Antiquity* 25(1):112–116.

1965   Archaeological Investigations Along the North Platte River in Eastern Wyoming. *University of Wyoming Publications* 31(1–3):23–51. Laramie.

Mulloy, William T., and Louis C. Steege
1967   Continued Archaeological Investigations Along the North Platte River in Eastern Wyoming. *University of Wyoming Publications* 33(3):169–233. Laramie.

Mun, Jules Louis René de
1928   The Journals of Jules de Mun. Nettie Harney Beauregard, trans.; Thomas M. Marshall, ed.; Genealogy of de Mun Family in France and America, compiled by Marquis de Mun and N.H. Beauregard. *Collections of the Missouri Historical Society* 5(3):167–208. St. Louis, Mo.

Munroe, Scott William
1969   Warriors of the Rock: Basic Social Structure of the Mountain Bands of Stoney Indians at Morley, Alberta. (M.A. Thesis in Anthropology, University of Calgary, Calgary, Alta.)

Munsell, Marvin R.
1961   Anthony: A Kansas-Oklahoma Border Site. *Plains Anthropologist* 6(12):112–114.

Munson, Patrick J.
1975   [Map of Proto-Siouan Homeland, Showing Proto-Dakota/Dhegiha/Chiwere Homeland.] (Copy in Raymond J. DeMallie's possession.)

Murdock, George Peter
1949   Social Structure. New York: Macmillan.

1965   Algonkian Social Organization. Pp. 24–35 in Context and Meaning in Cultural Anthropology; in Honor of A. Irving Hallowell. Melford E. Spiro, ed. New York: The Free Press.

1967   Ethnographic Atlas: A Summary Ethnology. *Ethnology* 6(2):222–225.

Murdock, George Peter, and Timothy J. O'Leary
1975   Ethnographic Bibliography of North America. 4th ed. 5 vols. New Haven, Conn.: Human Relations Area Files Press.

Murie, James R.
1914   Pawnee Indian Societies. *American Museum of Natural History Anthropological Papers* 11(7):543–644. New York. (Bound with other monographs in: Societies of the Plains Indians. Clark Wissler, ed., New York, 1916.)

1921   Ceremonies of the Pawnee. Edited by Clark Wissler. (Manuscript No. 2520, National Anthropological Archives, Smithsonian Institution, Washington.)

1981   Ceremonies of the Pawnee. 2 Pts. Part I: The Skiri; Part II: The South Bands. Edited with an Introducton by Douglas R. Parks. *Smithsonian Contributions to Anthropology* 27. Washington: Smithsonian Institution Press. (Reprinted: University of Nebraska Press for the American Indian Studies Research Institute, Indiana University; Lincoln, 1989.)

Murphy, Edmund R.
1941   Henry de Tonty Fur Trader of the Mississippi. Baltimore, Md.: Johns Hopkins University Press.

Murphy, Robert F.
1967   Tareg Kinship. *American Anthropologist,* n.s. 69(2):163–170.

Murphy, T.
1867   [Report to the Commissioner of Indian Affairs, dated Upper Arkansas Agency, December 23, 1867.] (Manuscript No. M234, Roll 879, Letters Received, Upper Arkansas Agency 1865–1867, Records of the Bureau of Indian Affairs, Record Group 75, National Archives, Washington.)

Murray, Sir Charles Augustus
1839   Travels in North America During the Years 1834, 1835, and 1836. Including a Summer Residence with the Pawnee Tribe of Indians, in the Remote Prairies of the Missouri, and a Visit to Cuba and the Azure Islands. London: R. Bently; New York: Harper and Brothers. (Reprinted: Da Capo Press, New York, 1974.)

Murray, Stanley N.
1984   The Turtle Mountain Chippewa, 1882–1905. *North Dakota History* 51(1):14–37. Bismarck.

Myer, William E.
1922   Archaeological Fieldwork in South Dakota and Missouri. Pp. 117–125 in Explorations and Field-work of the Smithsonian Institution in 1921. *Smithsonian Miscellaneous Collections* 72(15). Washington: Smithsonian Institution; U.S. Government Printing Office.

Myers, Thomas P.
1992   Birth and Rebirth of the Omaha. (Catalog to accompany an Exhibit entitled "Birth and Rebirth of the Omaha" presented by the University of Nebraska State Museum in cooperation with the Omaha Tribe of Nebraska.) Lincoln: University of Nebraska State Museum.

Myrick, David F.
1970   New Mexico's Railroads — A Historical Study. Golden, Colo.: Colorado Railroan Museum.

NAES = National Center for Educational Statistics
1998   American Indians and Alaska Natives in Postsecondary Education. *NAES* 98-291. Washington: U.S. Department of Education.

NARA = National Archives and Records Administration
1998   American Indians: A Select Catalog of National Archives Microfilm Publications. Washington, D.C.: National Archives Trust Fund Board, National Archives and Records Administration.

NYCD = O'Callaghan, Edmund B., ed. 1853–1887 *see* Brodhead, John R. 1853–1887

Nabokov, Peter, ed.
1967   Two Leggings: The Making of a Crow Warrior. (Based on a Field Manuscript prepared by William Wildschut for the Museum of the American Indian, Heye Foundation.) New York: Thomas Y. Crowell. (Reprinted in 1970. Also, with a Foreword by John C. Ewers: University of Nebraska Press, Lincoln, 1982.)

1988   Cultivating Themselves: The Inter-play of Crow Indian Religion and History. (Ph.D. Dissertation in Anthropology, University of California, Berkeley.)

———
1997   Native View of History. Pp. 1–59 in Cambridge History of the Native Peoples of the Americas, Volume 1: North America, Pt. 1. Bruce G. Trigger and Wilcomb E. Washburn, eds. Cambridge: Cambridge University Press.

Nabokov, Peter, and Robert Easton
1989   Native American Architecture. New York and Oxford: Oxford University Press.

Naef, Weston J., and James N. Wood
1975   Era of Exploration: The Rise of Landscape Photography in the American West, 1860–1885. With an Essay by Therese Thau Heyman. New York: Albright-Knox Art Gallery, The Metropolitan Museum of Art; distributed by New York Graphic Society, Boston.

Nagy, Imre
1994   A Typology of Cheyenne Shield Designs. *Plains Anthropologist* 39(147):5–36.

———
1994a   Cheyenne Shieds and Their Cosmological Background. *American Indian Art Magazine* 19(3):38–47, 104. Scottsdale, Ariz.

Nakoda Lodge Brochure
1998   [Stoney Reserve, Morley, Alta.]

Nance, Berta Hart
1952   D.A. Nance and the Tonkawa Indians. *West Texas Historical Association Yearbook* 28:87–95. Abilene.

Nance, Joseph Milton
1963   After San Jacinto: The Texas-Mexican Frontier, 1836–1841. Austin: University of Texas Press.

———
1964   Attack and Couterattack: The Texas-Mexican Frontier, 1842. Austin: University of Texas Press.

Narbona, Antonio
1826   [Letter to Augustín Duran, dated July 6, 1826.] (Manuscript 1826–654, Spanish Archives of New Mexico, State Archives and Records Center, Santa Fe.)

Nasatir, Abraham P., ed.
1930   An Account of Spanish Louisiana, 1785. *Missouri Historical Review* 24(4):521–536.

———
1931   John Evans, Explorer and Surveyor. 3 Pts. *Missouri Historical Review* 25(2):219–239, (3):432–460, (4):585–608.

———
1952   Before Lewis and Clark: Documents Illustrating the History of the Missouri, 1785–1804. 2 vols. St. Louis, Mo.: St. Louis Historical Documents Foundation. (Reprinted: University of Nebraska Press, Lincoln, 1990.)

Nash, Mrs. M.B.
1939   Painted Savages Writhe Through Sun Dance Test. *Idaho Statesman* (May 21). Boise, Idaho.

Nathan, Paul D., and Lesley Byrd Simpson, eds. and trans.
1959   The San Sabá Papers: A Documentary Account of the Founding and Destruction of the San Sabá Mission. San Francisco: J. Howell-Books.

National Geographic Society
1988   Historical Atlas of the United States. Washington, D.C.: National Geographic Society.

Nava, Pedro de
1793   [Letter to Governor Fernando de la Concha, dated Chihuahua, December 31, 1793.] (Manuscript, Twitchell No. II:1272 in Spanish Archives of New Mexico, State Archives and Records Center, Santa Fe.)

Neal, William L., and Richard R. Drass
1999   Middle Holocene Archeology in Northeastern Oklahoma.

Bulletin of the Oklahoma Anthropological Society 47(for 1998):39–66. Norman.

Neighbors, Robert S.
1847   Comanche and Other Indians. *29th Congress. 2d Session. House Document* 100. (Serial No. 500.) Washington.

———
1849   [Letter to Orlando Brown, dated October 18, 1849.] (Manuscript M-234, Roll 858, Frames 0415–0416, Letters, Texas Agency 1847-52, Records of the Bureau of Indian Affairs, Record Group 75, National Archives, Washington.)

———
1852   The NA-ü-ni, or Comanches of Texas: Their Traits and Beliefs, and Their Divisions and Intertribal Relations. Pp. 125–134 in Vol. 2 of Historical and Statistical Information Respecting the History, Condition and Prospects of the Indian Tribes of the United States. Henry Rowe Schoolcraft, comp and ed. 6 vols. Philadelphia: Lippincott, Grambo, 1851–1857.

———
1957   The Report of the Expedition of Major Robert S. Neighbors to El Paso in 1849. Kenneth F. Neighbours, ed. *Southwestern Historical Quarterly* 60(4):527–532. Austin, Tex.

———
1955   Robert S. Neighbors and the Founding of Texas Indian Reservations. *West Texas Historical Association Year Book* 31:65–74. Abilene, Tex.

———
1957   Chapters from the History of Texas Indian Reservations. *West Texas Historical Association Year Book* 33:3–16. Abilene, Tex.

———
1958   The Assassination of Robert S. Neighbors. *West Texas Historical Association Year Book* 34:38–49. Abilene, Tex.

———
1960   Indian Exodus Out of Texas in 1859. *West Texas Historical Association Year Book* 36:80–97. Abilene, Tex.

———
1975   Robert Simpson Neighbors and the Texas Frontier, 1836–1859. Waco: Texian Press.

Neihardt, John G.
1932   Black Elk Speaks: Being the Life Story of a Holy Man of the Ogalala Sioux. New York: William Morrow and Co. (Reprinted: University of Nebraska Press, Lincoln, 1961.)

———
1951   When the Tree Flowered: An Authentic Tale of the Old Sioux World. New York: Macmillan (Reprinted: University of Nebraska Press, Lincoln, 1970).

——— 1984 *see* DeMallie, Raymond J., ed. 1984

Neill, Edward D.
1858   The History of Minnesota, from the Earliest French Explorations to the Present Time. Philadelphia: J.B. Lippincott.

———
1872   A Sketch of Joseph Renville: A "Bois Brule". *Collections of the Minnesota Historical Society* 1:196–206. St. Paul.

———
1872a   Dakota Land and Dakota Life. *Collections of the Minnesota Historical Society* 1:254–294. St. Paul.

———
1876   Sieur de La Verendrye and His Sons the Discoverers of the Rocky Mountains, by Way of Lake Superior and Winnipeg, and Rivers Assiniboine and Missouri in 1743. *Contributions to the Historical Society of Montana* 1:302–316. Helena, Mont. (Originally publ.: Johnson and Smith, Printers, Minneapolis, 1875.)

———
1881   Early French Forts and Footprints of the Valley of the Upper Mississippi. *Collections of the Minnesota Historical Society* [1864], 2d. ed., Vol. 2(Pt. 2): 89–101. St. Paul.

———
1885   History of the Ojibways, and Their Connection with Fur Traders, Based upon Official and Other Records. *Collections of the Minnesota Historical Society* 5:395–510. St. Paul.

1890   Memoir of the Sioux: A Manuscript in the French Archives, Now First Printed, with Introduction and Notes. *Macalester College. Contributions of the Department of History, Literature and Political Science,* 1st ser., Vol. 1:223–240. St. Paul, Minn.

1892   The First Ioway Indians at Montreal. *Macalester College. Contributions of the Department of History, Literature and Political Science,* 2d ser., Vol. 5:109–112. St. Paul, Minn.

1892a   Visit of First White Men among the Mandans. *Macalester College. Contributions of the Department of History, Literature and Political Science,* 2d ser., Vol. 5:113–119. St. Paul, Minn.

Nellis, George W.
1913   [Letter to Commissioner of Indian Affairs, dated Pawnee Agency, September 29, 1913, re: Ghost Dancing.] (Manuscript in Pawnee Agency, Central Files 1907–1939, Records of the Bureau of Indian Affairs, Record Group 75, National Archives, Washington.)

Nelson, William
1974   The Sun Dance. Malspan, N.J.: Graphic House Atelier.

Nemiroff, Diana, Robert Houle, and Charlotte Townsend-Gault
1992   First Nations at the National Gallery of Canada. Ottawa: National Gallery of Canada.

Neog, Prafulla, Richard G. Woods, and Arthur M. Harkins
1970   Chicago Indians: The Effects of Urban Migration. Minneapolis: University of Minnesota.

Nero, Robert W., and Bruce A. McCorquodale
1958   Report of an Excavation at the Oxbow Dam Site. *The Blue Jay* 16(2):82–90. Regina: Saskatchewan Natural History Society.

Nespor, Robert P.
1984   The Evolution of the Agricultural Settlement Pattern of the Southern Cheyenne Indians in Western Oklahoma, 1876–1930. (Ph.D. Dissertation in Anthropology, University of Oklahoma, Norman.)

1989   Ecology of Malaria and Changes in Settlement Pattern on the Cheyenne and Arapaho Reservation, Indian Territory. Pp. 71–84 in Plains Indian Historical Demography and Health: Perspectives, Interpretations, and Critiques. Gregory R. Campbell, ed. *Plains Anthropologist* 34(124, Pt. 2); *Memoir* 23. Lincoln.

Nett, Betty R.
1952   Historical Changes in the Osage Kinship System. *Southwestern Journal of Anthropology* 8(2):164–181. Albuquerque.

Nettl, Bruno
1953   American Indian Music North of Mexico: Its Styles and Areas. (Ph.D. Dissertition in Anthropology, Indiana University, Bloomington.)

1953a   The Shawnee Musical Style: Historical Perspective in Primitive Music. *Southwestern Journal of Anthropology* 9(3):277–285. Albuquerque.

1954   Text-music Relationships in Arapaho Songs. *Southwestern Journal of Anthropology* 10(2):192–199. Albuquerque.

1954a   North American Indian Musical Styles. Philadelphia: American Folklore Society.

1955   Musical Culture of the Arapaho. *The Musical Quarterly* 41(3):325–331. New York.

1961   A Bibliographic Essay on Primitive, Oriental and Folk Music; Reference Materials in Ethnomusicology. *Detroit*

Studies in Music Bibliography 1:37–46. Detroit, Mich.

1967   Studies in Blackfoot Indian Musical Culture, Parts I and II. *Ethnomusicology* 11(2):141–160, (3):292–309. Middletown, Conn., and Ann Arbor, Mich.

1968   Studies in Blackfoot Indian Musical Culture, Parts III and IV. (Part IV with Stephen Blum.) *Ethnomusicology* 12(1):11–48, (2):192–207. Middletown, Conn., and Ann Arbor, Mich.

1989   Blackfoot Musical Thought: Comparative Perspectives. Kent, Ohio: Kent State University Press.

Neuman, Robert W.
1960   The Truman Mound Site, Big Bend Reservoir Area, South Dakota. *American Antiquity* 26(1):78–92.

1963   Check-stamped Pottery on the Northern and Central Great Plains. *American Antiquity* 29(1):17–26.

1967   Radiocarbon-dated Archaeological Remains on the Northern and Central Great Plains. *American Antiquity* 32(4):471–486.

1967a   Atlatl Weights from Certain Sites on the Northern and Central Great Plains. *American Antiquity* 32(1):36–53.

1975   The Sonota Complex and Associated Sites on the Northern Great Plains; With an Appendix on the Human Skeletal Remains by William M. Bass and Terrell W. Phenice. *Nebraska State Historical Society. Publications in Anthropology* 6. Lincoln.

Neville, G.W., comp. and ed.
1970   Linguistic and Cultural Affiliations of Canadian Indian Bands. Ottawa: Department of Indian Affairs and Northern Development, Indian Affairs Branch; Queen's Printer for Canada. (Reprinted, rev. ed.: Indian and Northern Affairs Canada, Ottawa, 1980.)

Nevin, Arthur
1916   Two Summers with the Blackfeet Indians of Montana. *Musical Quarterly* 2():257–270. New York.

New Mexico (Province)
1968   Calendar of the Spanish Archives of New Mexico, 1621–1821. Santa Fe: State of New Mexico Records Center.

1969   Guide to the Microfilm Edition of the Mexican Archives of New Mexico, 1821–1846. 42 Rolls. Myra E. Jenkins, ed. Santa Fe: State of New Mexico Records Center.

Newberry, Janice C., and Cheryl Harrison
1986   The Sweetwater Creek Site. *Cultural Resource Management Report* 19. Rock Springs, Wyo.: Western Wyoming College, Archaeological Services.

Newcomb, William W., Jr.
1950   A Re-examination of the Causes of Plains Warfare. *American Anthropologist* 52(3):317–330.

1955   A Note on Cherokee-Delaware Pan-Indianism. *American Anthropologist* 57(5):1041–1045.

1961   The Indians of Texas from Prehistoric to Modern Times. Austin: University of Texas Press. (Reprinted in 1969.)

1976   The People Called Wichita. Phoenix, Ariz.: Indian Tribal Series.

1993   Historic Indians of Central Texas. *Bulletin of the Texas Archeological Society* 64:1–63. Austin.

Newcomb, William W., Jr., and Thomas N. Campbell
1982   Southern Plains Ethnohistory: A Re-examination of the *1225*

Escanjaques, Ahijados, and Cuitoas. Pp. 29–43 in Pathways to Plains Prehistory: Anthropological Perspectives of Plains Natives and Their Pasts; Papers in Honor of Robert E. Bell. Don G. Wyckoff and Jack L. Hofman, eds. *Oklahoma Anthropological Society Memoir* 3; *The Cross Timbers Heritage Association Contributions* 1. Duncan, Okla.

Newcomb, William W., Jr., and W.T. Field
1967   An Ethnohistoric Investigation of the Wichita Indians in the Southern Plains. Pp. 240–395 in A Pilot Study of Wichita Indian Archaeology and Ethnohistory, Final Report. Robert E. Bell, E.B. Jelks, and W.W. Newcomb, eds. Washington: National Science Foundation.

Newcombe, Barbara T.
1976   "A Portion of the American People": The Sioux Sign a Treaty in Washington in 1858. *Minnesota History* 45(3):82–96. St. Paul.

Newell, Cicero
1912   Indian Stories. Boston: Silver, Burdett and Company.

Newhall, Beaumont, and Diana E. Edkins
1974   William H. Jackson. With a Critical Essay by William L. Broecker. Forth Worth, Tex.: Amon Carter Museum.

Newlin, Deborah Lamont
1982   The Tonkawa People: A Tribal History from Earliest Times to 1893. *West Texas Museum Association. The Museum Journal* 21. Lubbock. (Originally presented as the Author's M.A. Thesis in Anthropology, Texas Tech University, Lubbock, Tex., 1981.)

Newman, Marshall T.
1950   The Blond Mandan: A Critical Review of an Old Problem. *Southwestern Journal of Anthropology* 6(3):255–272. Albuquerque.

Nicandri, David L.
1986   Northwest Chiefs: Gustav Sohon's Views of the 1855 Stevens Treaty Councils. Seattle: Washington State Historical Society.

Nichols, Johanna
1992   Linguistic Diversity in Space and Time. Chicago: University of Chicago Press.

Nichols, John D., and Earl Nyholm
1995   A Concise Dictionary of Minnesota Ojibwe. Minneapolis: University of Minnesota Press. (Originally publ. under title: Ojibwewi-ikidowinan: An Ojibwe Word Resource Book. John D. Nichols and Earl Nyholm, eds. with word contributors, Maude Kegg, Earl Nyholm, and Selam Ross. *Occasional Publications in Minnesota Anthropology* 7. St. Paul.)

Nichols, Roger L., ed.
1963   General Henry Atkinson's Report of the Yellowstone Expedition of 1825. *Nebraska History* 44(2):65–82. Lincoln.

———
1984   Backdrop for Disaster: Causes of the Arikara War of 1823. *South Dakota History* 14(2):93–113. Pierre.

Nicholson, B.A.
1990   Ceramic Affiliations and the Case for Incipient Horticulture in Southwestern Manitoba. *Canadian Journal of Archaeology* 14:33–59. Ottawa.

Nickel, Robert K.
1977   The Study of Archaeologically Derived Plant Materials from the Middle Missouri Subarea. Pp. 53–58 in Trends in Middle Missouri Prehistory: A Festschrift Honoring the Contributions of Donald J. Lehmer. W. Raymond Wood, ed. *Plains Anthropologist* 22(78, Pt. 2); *Memoir* 13. Lincoln.

Nicks, Trudy
1980   The Iroquois and the Fur Trade in Western Canada. Pp. 85–101 in Old Trails and New Directions: Papers of the Third North American Fur Trade Conference. Carol M. Judd and Arthur J. Ray, eds. Toronto: University of Toronto Press.

———
1985   Mary Anne's Dilemma: The Ethnohistory of an Ambivalent Identity. Pp. 103–114 in The Métis: Past and Present. Thomas Flanagan and John Foster, eds. *Canadian Ethnic Studies* 17(2)[Special issue]. Toronto.

Nicollet, Joseph N.
[1836–   [Dakota Vocabularies and Grammatical Notes.] (Manuscript
1840]   in New York Historical Society, Albert Gallatin Collection, New York.)

[1838–   [French Names for American Indian Tribes.] (Manuscript in
1839]   Department of Anthropology, American Museum of Natural History, New York.)

1839   La Peuple Crole...[Manuscript concerning French knowledge of Indian tribes from historical and contemporary sources.] (Manuscript in Department of Anthropology, American Museum of Natural History, New York.)

1843   Report Intended to Illustrate a Map of the Hydrographical Basin of the Upper Mississippi River; Made by J.N. Nicollet, While in Employ under the Bureau of the Corps of Topographical Engineers. *26th Congress. 2d Session. Senate Executive Document* 237. Washington: Blair and Rives, Printers. (Issued also as: *28th Congress. 2d Session. House Document* 52. Washington, 1845.)

1970   The Journals of Joseph N. Nicollet: A Scientist on the Mississippi Headwaters, With Notes on Indian Life, 1836–37. Translated from the French by André Fertey. Martha Coleman Bray, ed. St. Paul: Minnesota Historical Society Press.

1976   Joseph N. Nicollet on the Plains and Prairies: The Expeditions of 1838–39, With Journals, Letters, and Notes on the Dakota Indians. Edmund C. Bray and Martha Coleman Bray, trans. and eds. Appendix 3: Nicollet's Notes on the Dakota, ed. by Raymond J. DeMallie. St. Paul: Minnesota Historical Society Press.

Niddrie, John W.
1992   Memories of Morley. J.W. Chalmers, ed. *Alberta History* 40(3):10–15. Calgary.

Nieberding, Velma S.
1976   The Quapaws: Those Who Went Downstream. Quapaw, Okla.: Quapaw Tribal Council.

Nix, James E.
1960   Mission among the Buffalo: The Labours of the Reverends George M. and John C. McDougall in the Canadian Northwest, 1860–1876. Toronto: The Ryerson Press.

Norall, Frank, ed.
1988   Bourgmont, Explorer of the Missouri, 1698–1725. Lincoln: University of Nebraska Press.

Norris, Mary Jane
1998   Canada's Aboriginal Languages. *Canadian Social Trends* (Winter). Ottawa and Toronto.

North Dakota Heritage Foundation
1983   The Fiske Portfolios. Bismarck, N.Dak.: North Dakota Heritage Foundation.

Northern Cheyenne Tribe
1996   Amended Constitution and ByLaws of the Northern Cheyenne Tribe of the Northern Cheyenne Indian Reservation. Lame Deer, Mont.: Northern Cheyenne Tribal Office.

Notzke, Claudia
1982   The Development of Canadian Indian Reserves; as Illustrated by the Example of the Stoney and Peigan Reserves. (Ph.D. Dissertation, University of Calgary, Calgary, Alta.;

Canadian Theses on Microfiche 60814; National Library of Canada, Ottawa, 1984.)

1985   Indian Reserves in Canada: Development Problems of the Stoney and Peigan Reserves in Alberta. *Marburger geographische Schriften* 97. Marburg/Lahn, Germany: Im Selbstverlag des Geographischen Instituts der Universität Marburg.

1987   Indian Land in Southern Alberta. Pp. 107–126 in A Cultural Geography of North American Indians. Thomas E. Ross and Tyrel G. Moore, eds. Boulder, Colo.: Westview Press.

1987a   The Past in the Present: Spatial and Landuse Change on Two Indian Reserves. Pp. 95–121, 187–189 in Essays on the Historical Geography of the Canadian West: Regional Perspectives on the Settlement Process. L.A. Rosenvall and S.M. Evans, eds. Calgary, Alta.: Department of Geography, University of Calgary.

Nowak, Michael, and Christopher A. Jones
1986   Archaeological Investigations in Southeastern Colorado. *Colorado College Publications in Archaeology* 9. Colorado Springs.

Nowak, Michael and John W. Kantner
1991   Archaeological Investigations in Southeastern Colorado. With Contributions by Christopher B. Doggett, Peter J. Gleichman. *Colorado College Publications in Archaeology* 16. Colorado Springs.

Nowak, Timothy R., L. Adrien Hannus, John M. Butterbrodt, Edward J. Lueck, and R. Peter Winham
1984   1981 and 1982 Survey and Testing at West Horse Creek Quarry, Site 39SH37; with Contributions by Steven Ruple. Submitted to Historical Preservation Center, Office of Cultural Preservation, Vermillion, South Dakota. *White River Badlands Regional Research Project Report* 2. Sioux Falls, S.Dak.: Augustana College, Archeology Laboratory of the Center for Western Studies.

Noyes, Stanley, and Daniel J. Gelo
1999   Comanches in the West, 1895–1908: Historic Photographs. Foreword by Larry McMurtry. Photos by Alice Snearly and Lon Kelley. *The Jack and Doris Smothers Series in Texas History, Life, and Culture* 1. Austin: University of Texas Press.

Núñez Cabeza de Vaca, Alvar
1871   Relation of Alvar Nuñez Cabeça de Vaca; Translated from the Spanish by Buckingham Smith. [Rev. ed.] New York. [Albany: Printed by J. Munsell for H.C. Murphy.]

1905   Relación y commentarios. [English]: The Journey of Alvar Núñez Cabeza de Vaca and His Companions from Florida to the Pacific, 1528–1536. Translated from His Own Narrative by Fanny Bandelier; Together with the Report of Father Marcos of Nizza and a Letter from the Viceroy Mendoza. Edited, with an Introduction, by Ad. F. Bandelier. New York: A.S. Barnes and Co. (Reprinted: Allerton Book Co., New York, 1922; also, Rio Grande Press, Chicago, 1964; and, AMS Press, New York, 1973.)

Nurge, Ethel D.
1964   The Sioux Sun Dance in 1962. Pp. 105–114 in Vol. 3 of *XXXVI Congreso Internacional de Americanistas, España, 1964. Actas y Memorias.* 4 vols. Sevilla: Editorial Católica Española.

_____, ed.
1970   The Modern Sioux: Social Systems and Reservation Culture. Lincoln: University of Nebraska Press. (Reprinted: 1975.)

Nute, Grace Lee
[1940] Sketch of the Life of Henry Benjamin Whipple, D.D., LL.D. (Manuscript in Minnesota Historical Society, St. Paul, Minn.)

_____, ed.
1942   Documents Relating to Northwest Missions, 1815–1827. Edited with Notes and an Introduction by Grace Lee Nute. *The Clarence Walworth Alvord Memorial Commission of the Mississippi Valley Historical Association. Publication* 1. St. Paul, Minn.: Published for the Clarence Walworth Alvord Memorial Commission by the Minnesota Historical Society.

Nuttall, Thomas
1980   A Journal of Travels into the Arkansas Territory During the Year 1819 [1821]. Savoie Lottinville, ed. Norman: University of Oklahoma Press.

Nye, Wilbur S.
1934   The Annual Sun Dance of the Kiowa Indians: As Related by George Hunt. *Chronicles of Oklahoma* 12(3):340–358. Norman.

1937   Carbine and Lance: The Story of Old Fort Sill. Norman: University of Oklahoma Press. (Reprinted in 1969.)

1962   Bad Medicine & Good: Tales of the Kiowas. With Drawing by Nick Eggenhofer. Norman: University of Oklahoma Press. (Reprinted in 1969.)

Oberste, William H.
1953   Texas Irish Empresarios and Their Colonies: Power & Hewetson, McMullen & McGloin. Refugio-San Patricio. Austin, Tex.: von Boeckmann-Jones Company.

O'Brien, Lynne Woods
1973   Plains Indian Autobiographies. *Boise State College Western Writers Series* 10. Boise, Idaho.

O'Brien, Patricia J.
1971   Valley Focus Mortuary Practices. *Plains Anthropologist* 16(53):165–182.

1979   The Schultz Phase. (Paper presented at the 1979 Kansas Anthropology Meeting, University of Kansas, Lawrence.)

1984   Archeology in Kansas. *University of Kansas Publications. Museum of Natural History. Public Education Series* 9. Lawrence.

1994   The Central Lowland Plains: An Overview A.D. 500–1500. Pp. 199–223 in Plains Indians, A.D. 500–1500: The Archaeological Past of Historic Groups. Karl H. Schlesier, ed. Norman: University of Oklahoma Press.

O'Brien, Sharon
1989   American Indian Tribal Governments. Norman: University of Oklahoma Press.

1991   A Legal Analysis of the American Indian Religious Freedom Act. Pp. 27–43 in Handbook of American Indian Religious Freedom. Christopher Vecsey, ed. New York: Crossroads Publishing.

O'Brodovich, L.
1969   Plains Cree Sun Dance, 1968. *Western Canadian Journal of Anthropology* 1(1):71–87. Edmonton, Alta.

O'Connell, Samuel
[1800] [Unpublished Papers.] (Manuscripts, Sc597, Montana Historical Society, Helena.]

O'Connor, Nancy Fields
1985   Fred E. Miller: Photographer of The Crows. 1st ed. Missoula, Mont.: University of Montana School of Fine Arts and [in cooperation with] Carnan VidFilm Inc. of Malibu, Calif.

O'Crouley, Pedro Alonso
1972   A Description of the Kingdom of New Spain, 1774. Séan Galvin, ed. and trans. New York: John Howell Books; also, *1227*

Dublin, Ire.: Allen Figgis. (Translation of: Idea compendiosa del Reyno de Nueva España, by Pedro Alonso O'Crouley. Original manuscript in Biblioteca Nacional, Madrid, Spain.)

Odell, George H.
1999   The Protohistoric Period in Eastern Oklahoma: Evidence from Lastley Vore Site. *Bulletin of the Oklahoma Anthropological Society* 47(for 1998):83–117. Norman.

Oehler, Gottlieb F., and David Z. Smith
1914   Description of a Journey and Visit to the Pawnee Indians, Who Live on the Platte River, a Tributary to the Missouri, Seventy Miles from its Mouth, . . . April 22–May 18, 1851, to Which is Added a Description of the Manners and Customs of the Pawnee Indians by Dr. D.Z. Smith. New York. (Reprinted from the *Moravian Church Miscellany*, 1851–1852; also, new ed.: Ye Galleon Press, Fairfield, Wash., 1974.)

_____   1974 *see* 1914 (reprint info.)

O'Fallon, Benjamin
1820   [Letter of May 10, 1820 to John C. Calhoun.] (Copy formerly in Mildred M. Wedel's possession.)

Office of Indian Affairs *see* Bureau of Indian Affairs

Officer, James B.
1971   The American Indian and Federal Policy. Pp. 8–65 in The American Indian in Urban Society. Jack O. Waddell and Michael O. Watson, eds. Boston: Little, Brown and Co.

Ogden, Peter Skene
1950   Snake country Journals, 1824–25 and 1825–26. E.E. Rich, ed.; assisted by A.M. Johnson, with an Introduction by Burt Brown Baker. *Publications of the Hudson's Bay Company Record Society* 13. London. (Reprinted: Kraus Reprint, Nendeln, Liechtenstein, 1979.)

Oglesby, Richard Edward
1963   Manuel Lisa and the Opening of the Missouri Fur Trade. Norman: University of Oklahoma Press. (Reprinted in 1984.)

O'Hanlon, T.
1881   [Letter to T. Powers, November 8, 1881.] (Manuscript in Box 103, MS 55, T.C. Powers Papers, Montana Historical Society, Helena.)

Oklahoma Indian Affairs Commission
1977   The Ponca World. Norman: University of Oklahoma Press.

_____   1977a   Quapaw. Norman: University of Oklahoma Press.

Old Coyote, Henry, and Barney Old Coyote, trans.
1985   Crow Stories: Stories of the Crow Tribe. [Montana: privately printed.]

Old Elk, Dan
1972   [Jacket Notes for "Crow Celebration," recorded live during the 1971 Crow Indian Fair and Celebration, Crow Agancy, Montana.] *Canyon Records* C-6103. Phoenix, Ariz.

Old Horn, Dale, and Timothy P. McCleary
1995   Apsaalooke Social and Family Structure. Crow Agency, Mont.: Little Bigh Horn College.

Olden, Sarah Emilia
1918   The People of Tipi Sapa (The Dakotas): Tipi Sapa Mitaoyate Kin. Milwaukee: Morehouse Publishing Co.

Oliver, Symmes C.
1962   Ecology and Cultural Continuity as Contributing Factors in the Social Organization of the Plains Indians. *University of California. Publications in American Archaeology and Ethnology* 48(1):1–90. Berkeley and Los Angeles.

Olson, James C.
1965   Red Cloud and the Sioux Problem. Lincoln: University of Nebraska Press.

Omaha World-Herald, April 8, 1999; Febr. 9, 2000. Omaha Nebr.

O'Malley, Nancy
1979   Subsistence Strategies at the Sperry Site, Jackson County, Missouri. (M.A. Thesis in Anthropology, University of Kansas, Lawrence.)

O'Shea, John M., and John Ludwickson
1992   Archeology and Ethnohistory of the Omaha Indians: The Big Village Site. Lincoln: University of Nebraska Press.

_____   1992a   Omaha Chieftanship in the Nineteenth Century. *Ethnohistory* 39(3):316–352.

Opler, Marvin K.
1940   The Southern Ute of Colorado. Pp. 119–207 in Acculturation in Seven American Indian Tribes. Ralph Linton, ed. New York: Appleton-Century Co.

_____   1941   The Integration of the Sun Dance in Ute Region. *American Anthropologist,* n.s. 43(4):550–572.

_____   1943   The Origins of Comanche and Ute. *American Anthropologist,* n.s. 45(1):155–158.

Opler, Morris E.
1931–1935 [Lipan Apache Fieldnotes.] (Manuscripts formely in M.E. Opler's possession.)

_____   1936   The Kinship Systems of the Southern Athabaskan-Speaking Tribes. *American Anthropologist,* n.s. 38(4):620–633.

_____   1936a   A Summary of Jicarilla Apache Culture. *American Anthropologist,* n.s. 38(2):202–223.

_____   1936b   An Interpretation of Ambivalence of Two American Indian Tribes. *Journal of Social Psychology* 7:82–116.

_____   1938   The Use of Peyote by the Carrizo and Lipan Apache Tribes. *American Anthropologist,* n.s. 40(2):271–285.

_____   1938a   Dirty Boy: A Jicarilla Tale of Raid and War. *Memoirs of the American Anthropological Association* 52. Menasha, Wis.

_____   1938b   Myths and Tales of the Jicarilla Apache Indians. *Memoirs of the American Folk-lore Society* 31. New York.

_____   1940   Myths and Legends of the Lipan Apache Indians. *Memoirs of the American Folk-lore Society* 36. New York.

_____   1941   An Apache Life-Way: The Economic, Social, and Religious Institutions of the Chiricahua Indians. Chicago: University of Chicago Press. (Reprinted: Cooper Square Publishers, New York, 1965.)

_____   1941a   The Integration of the Sun Dance in Ute Religion. *American Anthropologist,* n.s. 43(4):550–572.

_____   1942   Myths and Tales of the Chiricahua Apache Indians. *Memoirs of the American Folk-lore Society* 37. New York.

_____   1943   The Character and Derivation of the Jicarilla Holiness Rite. *University of New Mexico Bulletin* 390; *Anthropological Series* 4(3):1–98. Albuquerque.

_____   1944   The Jicarilla Apache Ceremonial Relay Race. *American Anthropologist,* n.s. 46(1):75–97.

_____   1945   The Lipan Apache Death Complex and Its Extensions. *Southwestern Journal of Anthropology* 1(1):122–141. Albuquerque.

_____   1946   An Application of the Theory of Themes in Culture. *Jour-*

nal of the Washington Academy of Sciences 36(5):137–166. Washington.

1946a   Childhood and Youth in Jicarilla Apache Society. *Publications of the Frederick Webb Hodge Anniversary Publication Fund* 5. Los Angeles.

1946b   Reaction to Death among the Mescalero Apache. *Southwestern Journal of Anthropology* 2(4):454–467. Albuquerque.

1959   Component, Assemblage, and Theme in Cultural Integration and Differentiation. *American Anthropologist*, n.s. 61(6):955–964.

1960   Myth and Practice in Jicarilla Apache Eschatology. *Journal of American Folk-lore* 73(288):133–153.

1969   Western Apache and Kiowa Apache Materials Relating to Ceremonial Payment. *Ethnology* 8(1):122–124.

1969a   Apache Odyssey: A Journey between Two Worlds. New York: Holt, Rinehart and Winston.

1971   Pots, Apache, and the Dismal River Culture Aspect. Pp. 29–33 in Apachean Culture, History, and Ethnology, Keith H. Basso and Morris E. Opler, eds. *Anthropological Papers of the University of Arizona* 21. Tucson.

1971a   Jicarilla Apache Territory, Economy, and Society in 1850. *Southwestern Journal of Anthropology* 27(4):309–329. Albuquerque.

1974   [Lipan Ethnology.] (Manuscript formerly in M.E. Opler's possession.)

1974a   Lipan and Mescalero Apache in Texas. In: Apache Indians X. *American Indian Ethnohistory: Indians of the Southwest.* David Agee Horr, comp. and ed. New York and London: Garland Publishing.

_____ 1983 see Handbook Vol. 10 (1983:401–418, 419–439)

Opler, Morris E., and William E. Bittle
1961   The Death Practices and Eschatology of the Kiowa Apache. *Southwestern Journal of Anthropology* 17(4):383–394. Albuquerque.

Opler, Morris E., and Harry Hoijer
1940   The Raid and War-path Language of the Chiricahua Apache. *American Anthropologist*, n.s. 42(4):617–634.

Oppelt, Norman T.
1984   The Tribally Controlled Colleges in the 1980s: Higher Education's Best Kept Secret. *American Indian Culture and Research Journal* 8(4):27–45. Los Angeles.

Oppenheim, J.S.
1989   Dancing with the Ancestors: Maryland Indians Renew Ties to Heritage. *The Washington Post*, Aug. 24:1, 7, 9. Washington.

Orata, Pedro T.
1953   Fundamental Education in an Amerindian Community. Pedro T. Orata and the Staff of the Little Wound Day School, Pine Ridge, S.D. "Condensation of a Four-volume Report [...] entitled: Democracy and Indian Education." Haskell, Kans.: U.S. Department of the Interior, Bureau of Indian Affairs, Haskell Institute Printing Department.

Orchard, William C.
1916   The Technique of Porcupine-Quill Decoration among the North American Indians. *Museum of the American Indian. Heye Foundation. Contributions* 4(1). New York. (Reprinted, 2d ed., 1971.)

1929   Beads and Beadwork of the American Indians: A Study Based on Specimens in the Museum of the American Indian, Heye Foundation. *Museum of the American Indian. Heye Foundation. Contributions* 11. New York. (Reprinted, 2d ed., 1975.)

Orchard, William J.
1946   Kitchen Middens: Prehistoric Campsites. Regina and Toronto: School Aids and Text Book Publishing Co.

Orozco y Berra, Manuel
1864   Geografía de las Lenguas y Carta etnográfica de México. México: J.M. Andrade y F. Escalante.

Orr, Ellison
1963   Iowa Archaeological Reports, 1934–1939; with an Evaluation and Index, by Marshall McKusick. 10 vols. *Archives of Archaeology* 20. [Madison, Wis.]

Orser, Charles E., Jr.
1984   Trade Good Flow in Arikara Villages: Expanding Ray's "Middleman Hypothesis." *Plains Anthropologist* 29(103):1–12.

1984a   Understanding Arikara Trading Behavior: A Cultural Case Study of the Ashley-Leavenworth Episode of 1823. Pp. 101–107 in Rendezvous: Selected Papers of the Fourth North American Fur Trade Conference, 1981. T.C. Buckley, ed. St. Paul, Minn: North American Fur Conference.

Orser, Charles E., Jr., and Douglas W. Owsley
1982   Using Arikara Osteological Data to Evaluate an Assumption of Fur Trade Archaeology. *Plains Anthropologist* 27(97):195–204.

Osborn, Alan J.
1983   Ecological Aspects of Equestrian Adaptations in Aboriginal North America. *American Anthropologist*, n.s. 85(3):563–591.

Osborn, Nancy M.
1982   The Clarkson Site (13WA2), an Oneota Manifestation in the Central Des Moines River Valley. *Journal of the Iowa Archeological Society* 29:1–121. Iowa City.

Osgood, Ernest S., ed.
1964   The Field Notes of Captain William Clark, 1803–1805. New Haven, Conn.: Yale University Press.

Osterkamp, Waite R., et al.
1987   Great Plains. Pp. 163–210 in Geomorphic Systems of North American. William L. Graf, ed. *Centennial Special Volume* 2. Boulder, Colo.: Geological Society of America.

Osterwald, Frank W., and Doris B. Osterwald
1952   Wyoming Mineral Resources. *University of Wyoming. Geological Survey. Bulletin* 45. Laramie.

Ottaway, Harold N.
1970   The Cheyenne Arrow Ceremony, 1968. *Oklahoma Anthropological Society Bulletin* 19. Norman.

1970   A Possible Origin for the Cheyenne Sacred Arrow Complex. *Plains Anthropologist* 15(48):94–99. Lincoln.

Over, William H.
1954   Woodland Burial Mounds. *University of South Dakota. Museum News* 15(12):3. Vermillion, S.Dak.

Over, William H., and Elmer E. Meleen
1941   A Report on an Investigation of the Brandon Village Site and the Split Rock Creek Mounds. *University of South Dakota. Museum. Archaeological Studies Circular* 3. Vermillion.

Overholt, Thomas
1974   The Ghost Dance of 1890 and the Nature of the Prophetic Process. *Ethnohistory* 21(1):37–63. Lubbock, Tex.

Overstreet, Charles M.
1993–1996 Plains Indian and Mountain Man Arts and Crafts: An Illustrated Guide. 2 vols. Liberty, Utah: Eagle's View.

Overton, Daniel W.
1993 Spending the Indians' Money: A Quantitative Case Study of Oto-Missouri Trust Fund Disbursements, 1855–1881. *Nebraska History* 74(2):72–81. Lincoln.

Owens, Brian M., and Claude M. Roberto
1989 A Guide to the Archives of the Oblates of Mary Immaculate: Province of Alberta-Saskatchewan. Edmonton, Alta.: The Missionary Oblates, Grandin Province.

Owsley, Douglas W.
1992 Demography of Prehistoric and Early Historic Northern Plains Populations. Pp. 75–86 in Disease and Demography in the Americas. John W. Verano and Douglas H. Ubelaker, eds. Washington: Smithsonian Institution Press.

———
1994 Warfare in Coalescent Tradition Populations of the Northern Plains. Pp. 333–343 in Skeletal Biology in the Great Plains: Migration, Warfare, Health, and Subsistence. Douglas W. Owsley and Richard L. Jantz, eds. Washington: Smithsonian Institution Press.

Owsley, Douglas W., and Richard L. Jantz, eds.
1994 Skeletal Biology in the Great Plains: Migrations, Warfare, Health, and Subsistence. Washington: Smithsonian Institution Press.

PLSBW = Participants of the Lake Superior Basin Workshop
1988 Desperately Seeking Siouans: The Distribution of Sandy Lake Ware. *The Minnesota Archaeologist* 47(1):43–48. Minneapolis.

Pénicaut/Pénicault, André *see* Pénigaut, André-Joseph

Pénigaut, André-Joseph
1869 Annals of Louisiana, from the Establishment of the First Colony Under M. d'Iberville, to the Departure of the Author to France, in 1722. Pp. 33–162 in Historical Collections of Louisiana and Florida. New ser., Vol. 1, by Benjamin F. French. New York: J. Sabin and Sons; Albert Mason [bound with Vol. 2, 2d ser., 1875.]

———
1953 Fleur de Lys and Calumet: Being the Pénicaut Narrative of French Adventure in Louisiana. Translated from the French Manuscripts and Edited by Richebourg Gaillard McWilliams. Baton Rouge: Louisiana State University Press. (Reprinted, with a Foreword by Robert R. Rea: University of Alabama Press, Tuscaloosa, 1981, 1988.)

Padilla, Juan Antonio
1919 Texas in 1820. I: Report on the Barbarous Indians of the Province of Texas. Mattie Austin Hatcher, trans. *Southwestern Historical Quarterly* 23(1):47–68. Austin, Tex.

Page, Vicki
1985 Reservation Development in the United States: Peripherality in the Core. *American Indian Culture and Research Journal* 9(3):21–35. Los Angeles.

Pagel, Jean
1996 Corps, Kaw Nation Work To Resolve Grave Situation. *The Ponca City News*, November 24, 1996:6–A. Ponca City, Okla.

Paige, Darcy
1979 George W. Hill's Account of the Sioux Sun Dance of 1866. *Plains Anthropologist* 15(84):99–112.

Paige, Harry W.
1970 Songs of the Teton Sioux. *Great West and Indian Series* 39. Los Angeles: Westernlore Press.

Palladino, Lawrence B.
1894 Indian and White in the Northwest; or, A History of Catholicity in Montana. Baltimore, Md.: John Murphy and Company.

Palliser, John
1863 Exploration: British North America. The Journals, Detailed Reports, and Observations Relative to the Exploration, by Captain Palliser, of That Portion of British North America, Which, in Latitude, Lies between the British Boundary Line and the Height of Land or Watershed of the Northern or Frozen Ocean Respectively, and in Longitude, between the Western Shore of Lake Superior and the Pacific Ocean during the Years 1857, 1858, and 1860. Presented to Both Houses of Parliament by Command of Her Majesty, 19th May, 1863. London: Printed by G.E. Eyre and W. Spottiswoode, for H.M. Stationery Off. (Atlas has 1865 imprint date and cover-title: Index and Maps to Captain Palliser's Reports.)

Palliser Expedition of 1857–1860 *see* Spry, Irene M., ed. 1968, 1973

Pannekoek, Frits
1990 The Flock Divided: Factions and Feuds at Red River. *The Beaver* 70(6):29–37. Winnipeg, Man.

———
1991 A Snug Little Flock: The Social Origins of the Riel Resistance of 1869–70. Winnipeg, Man.: Watson and Dwyer.

Pantaleoni, Hewitt
1987 One of Densmore's Dakota Rhythms Reconsidered. *Ethnomusicology* 31(1):35–55. Middletown, Conn.

Papen, Robert A.
1984 Un parler français méconnu de l'Ouest canadien: le Métis. Pp. 121–136 in La langue, la culture et la société des francophones de l'Ouest: les actes du troisième colloque du Centre d'études franco-canadiennes de l'Ouest tenu au Centre d'Études Bilingues, Université de Régina, les 25 et 26 novembre 1983. Textes établis par Pierre-Yves Mocquais, André Lalonde, Bernard Wilhelm. Régina, Sask.: Institut de recherche du Centre d'Études Bilingues, The University of Regina.

———
1987 Linguistic Variation in the French Component of Métif Grammar. Pp. 247–259 in Papers of the Eighteenth Algonquian Conference. William Cowan, ed. Ottawa: Carleton University.

Paredes, J. Anthony
1971 Toward a Reconceptualization of American Indian Urbanism: A Chippewa Case. *Anthropological Quarterly* 44(4):256–271. Washington.

Parish of Saint-Boniface (Manitoba)
1818–1860 [Parish Register, 1818–1860.] (Manuscript Registers in the Archives of Saint-Boniface, Man.)

Parish Register of St. Boniface 1818–1860 *see* Parish of Saint-Boniface (Manitoba) 1818–1860

Parker, Donald Dean, ed.
1966 The Recollections of Philander Prescott: Frontiersman of the Old Northwest, 1819–1862. Lincoln: University of Nebraska Press.

Parker, John, ed.
1976 The Journals of Jonathan Carver and Related Documents, 1766–1770. St. Paul: Minnesota Historical Society Press. (See also DeMallie, ed., 1976a.)

Parker, Nathan Howe
1857 The Minnesota Handbook for 1856–57. Boston: J.P. Jewett; New York: Sheldon, Blakeman. (Reprinted: Arno Press, New York, 1975.)

Parker, Patricia
1990 The Feather and the Drum: The History of Banff Indian Days, 1889–1978. Calgary, Alta.: Consolidated Communications.

Parker, Samuel
1842   Journal of an Exploring Tour Beyond the Rocky Mountains, Under the Direction of the A.B.C.F.M., in the Years 1835, '36, and '37; Containing a Description of the Geography, Geology, Climate, Productions of the Country, and the Numbers, Manners, and Customs of the Natives; with a Map of Oregon Territory. 3d ed. Ithaca, N.Y.: Mack, Andrus, and Woodruff; Boston: Crocker and Brewster; New York: Dayton and Saxton; [...] London: Wiley and Putnam.

Parker, Wayne
1982   Archeology at the Bridwell Site. Crosbyton, Tex.: Crosby County Pioneer Memorial in Cooperation with Crosby County Historical Commission.

Parker, William B.
1856   Notes Taken During the Expedition Commanded by Capt. R.B. Marcy, U.S.Army, Through Unexplored Texas, in the Summer and Fall of 1854. Philadelphia: Hayes and Zell.

Parkman, Francis
1883   The Oregon Trail: Sketches of Prairie and Rocky-Mountain Life. 8th ed., rev. Boston: Little, Brown, and Company.

1897   A Half-Century of Conflict. 2 vols. Boston: Little, Brown and Company. (Reprinted: AMS Press, New York, 1969.)

Parks, Douglas R.
1965–1999 [Pawnee Linguistic Fieldnotes, collected at Pawnee, Okla.] (Manuscripts in D.R. Parks's possession.)

1970–1990 [Arikara Fieldnotes, collected at Fort Berthold Reservation, N.Dak.] (Manuscripts in D.R. Parks's possession.)

———— 1972 *see* 1976

1976   A Grammar of Pawnee. *Garland Studies in American Indian Linguistics.* New York: Garland Publishing. (Originally presented as the Author's Ph.D. Dissertation in Linguistics, University of California, Berkeley, 1972.)

1977   Pawnee Texts: Skiri and South Band. Pp. 65–90 in Caddoan Texts, Douglas R. Parks ed. *International Journal of American Linguistics. Native American Texts Series* 2(1). Chicago: The University of Chicago Press.

————, ed.
1977a   Caddoan Texts. *International Journal of American Linguistics. Native American Texts Series* 2(1). Chicago: The University of Chicago Press.

1978   James R. Murie: Pawnee Ethnographer—Pawnee, 1862–1921. Pp. [74] 75–89 in American Indian Intellectuals. Margot Liberty, ed. *1976 Proceedings of the American Ethnological Society.* Robert F. Spencer, gen. ed. St. Paul, Minn.: West Publishing Co.

1979   The Northern Caddoan Languages: Their Subgrouping and Time Depths. *Nebraska History* 60(2):197–213. Lincoln.

1979a   Bands and Villages of the Arikara and Pawnee. *Nebraska History* 60(2):214–239. Lincoln.

1980   [Wichita Linguistic Fieldnotes, collected in Oklahoma.] (Manuscript in D.R. Parks's possession.)

————, ed. 1981 *see* Murie, James R. 1981

1982   [Mandan Census for 1982, reelicited at Mandan, N.Dak.] (Manuscript in D.R. Parks's possession.)

————, ed.
1984   Arikara Coyote Tales: A Bilingual Reader. Naa'iikawiš Sahniš. Illustrated by David J. Ripley. Roseglen, N.Dak.: White Shield School District No. 89, Bilingual Education Program.

1985   Alexander Lesser 1902–1982. *Plains Anthropologist* 30(107):65–71.

————, ed.
1986   An English-Arikara Student Dictionary. Roseglen, N.Dak.: White Shield School District No. 85, Bilingual Education Program.

1986a   Panian Dialects. (Paper presented at the Symposium "Linguistic Variability on the Northern Plains," University of Manitoba, Winnipeg, February 22, 1986.)

1987   [Mandan and Hidatsa Synonymy Fieldnotes, collected at Parshall, N.Dak.] (Manuscript in D.R. Parks's possession.)

1988   [Wichita, Otoe-Missouria and Ponca Synonymy Fieldnotes, collected in Oklahoma.] (Manuscripts in D.R. Parks's possession.)

1991   Traditional Narratives of the Arikara Indians. 4 vols. *Studies in the Anthropology of North American Indians.* Lincoln: University of Nebraska Press.

1991a   [Mandan and Hidatsa Synonymy Fieldnotes, collected at New Town, N.Dak.] (Manuscript in D.R. Parks's possession.)

1992   Introduction. Pp. ix–xxxvii in [reprint ed. of] Hidatsa Social and Ceremonial Organization by Alfred W. Bowers. Lincoln: University of Nebraska Press. (Originally publ. in 1965.)

————, ed.
1993   A Fur Trader among the Arikara Indians: Jean-Baptiste Truteau's Journal and Description of the Upper Missouri, 1794–1796. Mildred Mott Wedel, trans. (Pre-publication draft in D.R. Parks's possession.)

1994   Three Skiri Pawnee Stories. Pp. 377–402 in Coming to Light: Contemporary Translations of the Native Literatures of North America. Brian Swan, ed. New York: Random House.

————, ed.
1995   [Skiri Pawnee Texts dictated by Roaming Scout in 1906.] (Manuscripts in D.R. Parks's possession.)

1999   [Skiri Pawnee Multimedia Dictionary.] (Database and manuscript in American Indian Studies Research Institute, Indiana University, Bloomington.)

1999a   [South Band Pawnee Multimedia Dictionary.] (Database and manuscript in American Indian Studies Research Institute, Indiana University, Bloomington.)

1999b   George A. Dorsey, James R. Murie, and the Textual Documentation of Skiri Pawnee. Pp 227–244 in Theorizing the Americanist Tradition. Lisa Philips Valentine and Regna Darnell, eds. Toronto: University of Toronto Press.

1999c   [Arikara Multimedia Dictionary.] (Database and manuscript in American Indian Studies Research Institute, Indiana University, Bloomington.)

1999d   [Yanktonai Dakota Multimedia Dictionary.] (Database and manuscript in American Indian Studies Research Institute, Indiana University, Bloomington.)

Parks, Douglas R., and Janet Beltran
1976   Arikara Teacher's Guide: Secondary Level. Bismarck, N.Dak.: Mary College.

1999   Arikara Elementary Lessons: A Teacher's Guide. Bloomington, Ind.: American Indian Studies Research Institute.

Parks, Douglas R., and Raymond J. DeMallie
1983–1988 [Assiniboine Texts.] (Manuscript in D.R. Parks's and R.J. DeMallie's possession.)

1985   [Stoney Linguistic Fieldnotes, Stoney Reserve, Morley, *1231*

Alta.] (Manuscript in D.R. Parks and R.J. DeMallie's possession.)

1988   [Assiniboine Dictionary.] (Manuscript in D.R. Parks and R.J. DeMallie's possession; see also Parks and DeMallie 1996, 1999.)

1992   Sioux, Assiniboine, and Stoney Dialects: A Classification. *Anthropological Linguistics* 34(1–4):233–255. Bloomington.

1992a   Plains Indian Native Literatures. *Boundary 2*, 19(3):105–147. (Reprinted in: 1492–1992: American Indian Persistence and Resurgence. Karl Kroeber, ed. Durham, N.C.: Duke University Press, 1994.)

1996   [Assiniboine Dictionary. Updated and revised.] (Manuscript in American Indian Studies Research Institute, Indiana University, Bloomington.)

1999   [Assiniboine Multimedia Dictionary.] (Database and manuscript in American Indian Studies Research Institute, Indiana University, Bloomington.)

Parks, Douglas R., and Ruth E. Pathe
1985   Gene Weltfish 1902–1980. *Plains Anthropologist* 30(107):59–64.

Parks, Douglas R., and Waldo R. Wedel
1985   Pawnee Geography: Historical and Sacred. *Great Plains Quarterly* 5(3):143–176. Lincoln, Nebr.

Parks, Douglas R., Janet Beltran, and Ella P. Waters
1979   An Introduction to the Arikara Language. Bismarck, N.Dak.: North Dakota Indian Languages Program, Mary College.

1998   An Introduction to the Arikara Language: Sahni¹ Wakuunu'. Vol. 1. Roseglen, N.Dak.: White Shield School District No. 85, Bilingual Education Program.

1998a   An Introduction to the Arikara Language. Vol.1. (Compact disk version.) Bloomington: American Indian Studies Research Institute.

Parks, Douglas R., Salena Ditmar, and Mindy J. Morgan
1999   Nakoda Language Lessons: Preliminary Edition. Fort Belknap, Mont.: Fort Belknap College in association with American Indian Studies Research Institute, Indiana University, Bloomington.

Parks, Douglas R., A. Wesley Jones, and Robert C. Hollow, eds.
1978   Earth Lodge Tales from the Upper Missouri: Traditional Stories of the Arikara, Hidatsa, and Mandan. Bismarck, N.Dak.: North Dakota Indian Language Program, Mary College.

Parks, Douglas R., Margot Liberty, and Andrea Ferenci
1980   Peoples of the Plains. Pp. 284–295 in Anthropology on the Great Plains. W. Raymond Wood and Margot Liberty, eds. Lincoln: University of Nebraska Press.

Parks, John
1976   The Journals of Jonathan Carver and Related Documents, 1766–1770. St. Paul: Minnesota Historical Society Press.

Parmalee, Paul W.
1977   The Avifauna from Prehistoric Arikara Sites in South Dakota. *Plains Anthropologist* 22(77):189–222.

Parrilla, Diego Ortiz
1759   [Testimony, dated October 7, 1759.] (Archivio General de las Indias, Audiencia de Mexico, 92-6-22; William E. Dunn Transcripts, 1759–1761 in Archives of the University of Texas Library, Austin.)

Parry, William J., and John D. Speth
1984   The Garnsey Spring Campsite: Late Prehistoric Occupation in Southeastern New Mexico. *University of Michigan. Museum of Anthropology. Technical Reports* 15. Ann Arbor.

Parsons, Elsie Clews
1929   Kiowa Tales. *Memoirs of the American Folk-Lore Society* 22. New York. (Reprinted: Kraus Reprint, New York, 1969.)

1939   Pueblo Indian Religion. 2 Vols. Chicago: University of Chicago Press.

Parsons, Mark L.
1967   Archeological Investigations in Crosby and Dickens Counties, Texas, During the Winter, 1966–1967. *Texas State Building Commission. Archeological Program Reports* 7. Austin.

Parton, William J., Dennis S. Ojima, and David S. Schimel
1994   Environmental Change in Grasslands: Assessment Using Models. *Climatic Change* 28(1–2):111–141.

Patterson, Patience E.
1987   Archaeological Investigations at 41LL78, the Slab Site, Llano County, Texas. *Texas State Department of Highways and Public Transportation. Publications in Archaeology* 34. Austin.

Patterson, Trudi Alice
1990   Theoretical Aspects of Dakota Morphology and Phonology. (Ph.D. Dissertation in Linguistics, University of Illinois, Urbana-Champaign.)

Pauketat, Timothy R., and Thomas E. Emerson, eds.
1997   Cahokia: Domination and Ideology in the Mississippian World. Lincoln: University of Nebraska Press.

Paul, R. Eli
1994   An Early Reference to Crazy Horse. *Nebraska History* 75(2):189–190. Lincoln.

1994a   Wounded Knee and the "Collector of Curios". *Nebraska History* 75(2):209–215. Lincoln.

_____, ed.
1997   Autobiography of Red Cloud, War Leader of the Oglalas. Helena: Montana Historical Society Press.

_____, ed.
1998   The Nebraska Indian Wars Reader: 1865–1877. Lincoln: University of Nebraska Press.

Paul Wilhelm, Herzog von Württemberg
1835   Erste Reise nach dem nördlichen Amerika in den Jahren 1822 bis 1824. Stuttgart und Tübingen, [Germany]: J.G. Gotta. (Reprinted: Borowsky, München, [Germany], 1980.)

1973   Travels in North America, 1822–1824. W. Robert Nitske, trans. Savoie Lottinville, ed. Norman: University of Oklahoma Press. (Originally publ. in German under title: Erste Reise nach dem nördlichen Amerika in den Jahren 1822 bis 1824; J.G. Cotta, Stuttgart und Tübingen, [Germany] 1835.)

Paullin, Charles O., and John K. Wright
1932   Atlas of the Historical Geography of the United States: A Collection of Maps, Cartograms, and Reproductions of Early Maps on Many Different Scales, Illustrating the Natural Environment of the United States and Its Demographic, Economic, Political, and Military History. John K. Wright, ed. *Carnagie Institution of Washington Publication* 401. Washington and New York: Published jointly by Carnegie Institution of Washington and American Geographical Society of New York.

Pawnee Agency
1920   [Annual Report for the Year 1920.] (Microfilm M1011, Roll 100, Pawnee Agency, 1910–1923, Records of the Bureau of Indian Affairs, Record Group 75, National Archives, Washington.)

[Pawnee Indian Veterans]
1947   The Pawnee Indians' Second Homecoming Celebration: Pawnee, Oklahoma, July 5–6–7–8 1947. Souvenir Program. Stillwater, Okla.: Lithographed by Crossman's.

1963   17th Annual Pawnee Indian Homecoming, Pawnee, Oklahoma, July 5, 6, 7, 1963. Souvenir Program. [Pawnee, Okla.]

1991   45th Annual Pawnee Indian Homecoming & Powwow, July 4, 5, 6 & 7, 1991. Souvenir Program. Pawnee, Okla.: *The Pawnee Chief* Publishers, Printers.

1997   51st Annual Pawnee Indian Homecoming, July 3, 4, 5 & 6, 1997. [Pawnee, Okla.]

Payment, Diane Paulette
1979   Monsieur Batoche. *Saskatchewan History* 32(3):81–103. Saskatoon.

1980   Riel Family: Home and Lifestyle at St. Vital [Manitoba], 1860–1910. (Manuscript Report No. 379, Environment Canada, Parks Service, Ottawa.)

1986   Batoche After 1885: A Society in Transition. Pp. 173–187 in 1885 and After: Native Society in Transition. Laurie F. Barron and James B. Waldram, eds. Regina: Canadian Plains Research Centre, University of Regina.

1988   Native Society and Economy at The Forks, 1850–1900. (Manuscript Report No. 383b, Environment Canada, Parks Service, Ottawa.)

1990   "The Free People — Otipemisiwak", Batoche, Saskatchewan, 1870–1930. *Studies in Archaeology, Architecture and History.* Ottawa: National Historic Parks and Sits, Parks Service, Environment Canada. (Revised and augumented ed.of the Author's M.A. Thesis, publ. in French in 1983, Soleil Collection of Éditions du Blé, St-Boniface, under title: *Batoche, 1870–1910.*)

1991   The Willow Cree of One-Arrow Reserve and the Métis of Batoche, Saskatchewan: An Ambivalent Relationship. (Manuscript, Environment Canada, Parks Service, Prairie and Northern Region, Saskatoon, Sask.)

1996   «La vie en rose?» Métis Women at Batoche, 1870–1920. Pp. 19–37 in Women of the First Nations. Patricia Chuchryk and Christine Miller, eds. Winnipeg: The University of Manitoba Press.

Payno, Manuel
1869   Las bibliotecas de México. México: Impr. del Gobierno, en Palacio, á cargo de J.M. Sandoval.

1870   Compendio de la historia de Mexico, para el uso de los Establecimientos de instrucción primaria, por Manuel Payno. México: Impr. de F. Diaz de Leon y Santiago White.

Pazola, Ron
1994   Sacred Ground: What Native Americans Believe. *U.S. Catholic* 59(2):16–23. Chicago.

Peake, Ora B.
1954   A History of the United States Factory System, 1795–1822. Denver: Sage Books.

Peale, Titian R.
1978   The Use of Brain and Marrow of Animals among the Indians of North America. *The Minnesota Archaeologist* 37(2):56–58. Minneapolis.

Pearce, James E.
1932   The Present Status of Texas Archaeology. *Bulletin of the Texas Archaeological and Paleontological Society* 4:44–54. Abilene.

Pease, Eloise Whitebear, ed.
1968   Crow Tribal Treaty Centennial Issue, 1868–1968. [Crow Agency, Mont.: Crow Tribe.]

Pease, Theodore C., and Raymond C. Werner
1934   The French Foundations, 1680–1693. *Collections of the Illinois State Historical Library* 23. Springfield, Ill.

Peel, Bruce Braden
1973   A Bibliography of the Prairie Provinces to 1953; with Biographical Index. 2d [enl.] ed. Toronto: University of Toronto Press. (Originally publ. in 1956.)

Peers, Laura
1987   An Ethnohistory of the Western Ojibway, 1780–1830. (M.A. Thesis, University of Winnipeg and University of Manitoba, Winnipeg.)

1994   The Ojibwa of Western Canada, 1780 to 1870. *Manitoba Studies in Native History* 8. Winnipeg: The University of Manitoba Press.

Pelletier, Emile
1974   A Social History of the Manitoba Métis: The Development and Loss of Aboriginal Rights. Winnipeg: Manitoba Métis Federation Press.

1977   Le vécu des Métis. Winnipeg, Man.: Pemmican Publications.

Pelzer, Louis, ed. 1943 *see* Carleton, James Henry 1943

Pennanen, Gary
1970   Sitting Bull: Indian Without a Country. *Canadian Historical Review* 51(2):123–140. Toronto: University of Toronto Press.

Penney, David W.
1992   Art of the American Frontier: The Chandler-Pohrt Collection. With Essays by Richard A. Pohrt, Milford G. Chandler, and George P. Horse Capture. Seattle: University of Washington Press.

Pennington, Robert
1961   Oscar Howe: Artist of the Sioux. Sioux Fall, S.Dak.: Dakota Territorial Commission.

Pennington, William D.
1972   Government Policy and Farming on the Kiowa Reservation, 1869–1901. (Ph.D. Dissertation in History, University of Oklahoma, Norman.)

Pentland, David H.
1977   Nêhiyawasinahikêwin: A Standard Orthography for the Cree Language. Regina, Sask.: Saskatchewan Indian Federated College, Federation of Saskatchewan Indians.

1978   A Historical Overview of Cree Dialects. Pp. 104–126 in Papers of the 9th Algonquian Conference. William Cowan, ed. Ottawa: Carleton University.

1979   Causes of Rapid Phonological Change: The Case of Atsina and Its Relatives. *Calgary Working Papers in Linguistics* 5:99–137. Calgary, Alta.: Logos, Department of Linguistics, The University of Calgary.

1979a   An Early Iroquoian Loanword in Algonquian. *Algonquian Linguistics* 4(3):27–29. Thunder Bay, Ontario.

Pepper, George H., and Gilbert L. Wilson
1908   An Hidatsa Shrine and the Beliefs Respecting It. *Memoirs of the American Anthropological Association* 2(4):275–328. Menasha, Wis. (Reprinted: Kraus Reprint, New York, 1964.)

Perreault, Jeanne, and Sylvia Vance, eds.
1990   Writing the Circle: Native Women of Western Canada. Edmonton: NeWest Publishers.

Perrin du Lac, François-Marie
1802   Carte du Missouri, Levee ou Rectifiée dans toute son Etendue par F.ois Perrin du Lac. [Paris.] (Facsimile reprint in: *Missouri Historical Society Collections* 4(1). St. Louis, 1912.)

1805   Voyage dans les deux Louisianes, et chez les nations sauvages du Missouri, par les États Unis.... en 1801, 1802, et 1803. Paris: Capelle et Renand; [also] Lyon: Bruyset Ainé et Buynand.

1807   Travels Through the Two Louisianas, and among the Savage Nations of the Missouri; also in the United States, along the Ohio, and the Adjacent Provinces, in 1801, 1802, and 1803. London: Printed for Richard Phillips by J.G. Barnard.

Perrine, Fred S.
1927   Military Escorts on the Santa Fe Trail (Continued). *The New Mexico Historical Review* 2(3):269–304. Santa Fe.

Perrot, Nicolas
1864   Mémoire sur les moeurs, coustumes et religion des sauvages de l'Amérique septentrionale [1717]. R.P.J. Tailhan, ed. Leipzig and Paris: A. Franck. (Reprinted in part: Pp. 25–31 in The French Regime in Wisconsin, Pt. I: 1634–1727. Reuben G. Thwaites, ed. *Collections of the State Historical Society of Wisconsin* 16. Madison, 1902; also, Johnson Reprint, New York, 1968.)

Perttula, Timothy K.
1991   European Contact and Its Effects on Aboriginal Caddoan Populations between A.D. 1520 and A.D. 1680. Pp. 501–518 in Columbian Consequences, Vol. 3: The Spanish Borderlands in Pan-American Perspective. David Hurst Thomas, ed. Washington: Smithsonian Institution.

1992   The Caddo Nation: Archaeological and Ethnohistoric Perspectives. Austin: University of Texas Press.

1994   Material Culture of the Koasati Indians of Texas. *Historical Archaeology* 28(1):65–77.

Peters, Virginia Bergman
1995   Women of the Earth Lodges: Tribal Life on the Plains. North Heaven, Conn.: Archon Books.

Petersen, Karen Daniels
1964   Cheyenne Soldier Societies. *Plains Anthropologist* 9(25):146–172.

1968   Howling Wolf: A Cheyenne Warrior's Graphic Interpretation of His People. Palo Alto, Calif.: American West.

1971   Plains Indian Art from Fort Marion. Norman: University of Oklahoma Press.

Peterson, Hans
1978   Imasees and His Band: Canadian Refugees After the Northwest Rebellion. *Western Canada Journal of Anthropology* 8(1):21–37. Edmonton, Alta.

Peterson, Harold L.
1965   American Indian Tomahawks. *Museum of the American Indian. Heye Foundation. Contributions* 19. New York.
_____, ed.
1976   I Wear the Morning Star: An Exhibition of American Indian Ghost Dance Objects. Minneapolis Institute of Arts; co-sponsored by the Minneapolis Regional Native American Center, July 29–September 26, 1976. Minneapolis: Minneapolis Institute of Arts.

Peterson, Helen L.
1957   American Indian Political Participation. Pp.116–126 in American Indians and American Life. George S. Simpson and J. Milton Yinger, eds. *The Annals of the American Academy of Political and Social Science* 311. Philadelphia.

Peterson, Jacqueline C.
1985   Many Roads to Red River: Métis Genesis in the Great Lakes Region, 1680–1815. Pp. 37–71 in The New Peoples: Being and Becoming Métis in North America. Jacqueline Peterson and Jennifer S.H. Brown, eds. *Manitoba Studies in Native History* 1. Winnipeg: The University of Manitoba Press; Lincoln: University of Nebraska Press.

1990   Gathering at the River: The Métis of the Northern Plains. Pp. 47–64 in The Fur Trade in North Dakota. Virginia L. Heidenreich, ed. Bismarck: State Historical Society of North Dakota.

Peterson, Jacqueline C., and Jennifer S.H. Brown, eds.
1985   The New Peoples: Being and Becoming Métis in North America. *Manitoba Studies in Native History* 1. Winnipeg: The University of Manitoba Press; Lincoln: University of Nebraska Press.

Peterson, Lynelle A.
1986   An Attribute Analysis of Sandy Lake Ware from Norman County and North Central Minnesota. (M.A. Thesis in Anthropology, University of Nebraska, Lincoln.)

Petitot, Emile
1869   [Comparative Vocabulary of Chipewyan, Hare, Kutchin and Eskimo. Fort Norman-Franklin-Great Bear Lake, January 11, 1869.] (Manuscript No. 221, National Anthropological Archives, Smithsonian Institution, Washington.)

1883   On the Athabasca District of the Canadian North-West Territory. *Proceedings of the Royal Geographical Society* 5(11):633–655. London. (Reprinted in: *Canadian Record of Science* 1:27–53, Montreal, 1884–1885.)

1891   Autour du Grand Lac des Esclaves. Paris: A. Savine.

Petrone, Penny
1990   Native Literature in Canada from the Oral Tradition to the Present. Toronto: Oxford University Press.

Petter, Rodolphe C.
1907   Sketch of the Cheyenne Grammar. [Bound with: The Cheyenne Indians, by James Mooney.] *Memoirs of the American Anthropological Association* 1(Pt. 6):443–478, [357–442]. Menasha, Wis. (Reprinted: Kraus Reprint, New York, 1964.)

1913–1915 English-Cheyenne Dictionary. Printed Entirely in the Interest of the Mennonite Mission among the Cheyenne Indians of Oklahoma and Montana. Kettle Falls, Wash.: Valdo Petter.

1952   Cheyenne Grammar. Newton, Kans.: Mennonite Publication Office.

Pettipas, Katherine
1993   Severing the Ties That Bind: Government Repression of Indigenous Ceremonies on the Prairies. *Manitoba Studies in Native History* 7. Winnipeg: The University of Manitoba Press.

Pettipas, Leo
1985   Recent Developments in Paleo-Indian Archaeology in Manitoba. Pp. 39–63 in Contributions to Plians Prehistory. David Burley, ed. *Archaeological Survey of Alberta. Occasional Paper* 26. Edmonton.

Pettis, George H.
1908   Personal Narratives of the Battles of Rebellion: Kit Carson's Fight with the Comanche and Kiowa Indians [1878]. Max Frost, ed. *Historical Society of New Mexico [Publications]* 12. Santa Fe: New Mexican Printing Company.

Pfaller, Louis L.
1950   Catholic Missionaries and the Fort Berthold Indians Before 1889. (M.A. Thesis in History, Loyola University, Chicago.)

1978   James McLaughlin: The Man with an Indian Heart. New York: Vantage Press. (Reprinted: Assumption Abbey Press, Richardton, N.Dak., 1992.)

Phelp, Kenneth R.
1977   John Collier's Crusade for Indian Reform. Tuscon: University of Arizona Press.

Phenice, Terrell W.
1969   An Analysis of the Human Skeletal Material from Burial Mounds in North Central Kansas. *University of Kansas. Publications in Anthropology* 1. Lawrence.

Phenix, T.S.
1969   Melhagen Site Preliminary Report. *Saskatchewan Archaeology Society Newsletter* 24:13–15. Saskatoon.

Phillips, Donna, ed.
1979   Assiniboine Legends. Saskatoon, Sask.: Saskathchewan Indian Cultural College, Federation of Saskatchewan Indians, Curriculum Studies and Research Department.

Phillips, Paul C., ed. 1925 *see* Stuart, Granville 1925

1961   The Fur Trade. 2 vols. With Concluding Chapters by J. W. Smurr. Norman: University of Oklahoma Press.

Phillips, Philip
1970   Archeological Survey in the Lower Yazoo Basin, Mississippi, 1949–1955. 2 vols. *Papers of the Peabody Museum of Archaeology and Ethnology, Harvard University* 60. Cambridge, Mass.

Phillips, Philip, James A. Ford, and James B. Griffin
1951   Archeological Survey in the Lower Mississippi Alluvial Valley, 1940–1947. *Papers of the Peabody Museum of American Archaeology and Ethnology, Harvard University* 25. Cambridge, Mass.

Philp, Kenneth R.
1977   John Collier's Crusade for Indian Reform, 1920–1954. Tucson: University of Arizona Press.

1985   Stride Toward Freedom: The Relocation of Indians to Cities, 1952–1960. *Western Historical Quarterly* 16(2):175–190. Logan, Utah.

_____, ed.
1995   Indian Self-Rule: First-Hand Accounts of Indian-White Relations from Roosevelt to Reagan. Logan, Utah: Utah State University. (Originally printed: *Current Issues in the American West* 4, Howe Brothers, Salt Lake City, 1986.)

1999   Termination Revisited: American Indians on the Trail to Self-Determination, 1933–1953. Lincoln: University of Nebraska Press.

Picard, Marc
1975   The Phonological History of Arapaho: A Study in Linguistic Change. (Ph.D. Thesis in Linguistics, McGill University, Montreal. Microfiche: *Canadian Theses on Microfiche* 29425, National Library of Canada, Ottawa, 1977.)

1994   Principles and Methods in Historical Phonology: From Proto-Algonkian to Arapaho. Montreal and Buffalo: McGill-Queen's University Press.

1994a   On the Evidence of PA *s to Arapaho /n/. *International Journal of American Linguistics* 60(3):295–299. Chicago.

Picha, Paul R.
1996   Rivière á Jacques and the James River Dakota Rendezvous: An Exploratory Study of Dakota Sioux Ethnohistory. (M.A. Thesis in History, University of Missouri, Columbia.)

Pierce, Franklin
1855   Indian Hostilities: Message from the President of the United States, Transmitting a Letter from the Secretary of War on the Subject of Indian Hostilities; January 18, 1855. *33d Congress. 2d Session. House Executive Document No. 36.* Washington.

1856   Council with the Sioux Indians at Fort Pierre: Message from the President of the United States, Communicating Minutes of a Council Held at Fort Pierre with the Sioux Indians by General Harley with a Delegation from Nine Tribes of the Sioux Indians. *34th Congress. 1st Session. House Executive Document No.* 130 (July 25, 1856, Referred to the Committee on Indian Affairs). Washington. (Reprinted: Microfiche 31907, Research Publications, Woodbridge, Conn., 1988.)

Pierce, Joe E.
1954   Crow vs. Hidatsa in Dialect Distance and in Glottochronology. *International Journal of American Linguistics* 20(2):134–136. Chicago.

Pike, Albert
1833   [Letter to John Cass, dated Van Buran, Arkansas Territory, March 16, 1833.] (Microfilm Publication M234, Roll 921, Frames [166]167–168 in Office of Indian Affairs, Letters Recieved from the Western Superintendency, Record Group 75, National Archives, Washington.)

1861   Articles of a Convention...between the Confederate States of America...and the Pen-e-tegh-ca Band of the Ne-um or Comanches [etc.]. (Published in: The War of the Rebellion: A Compilation of the Official Records of the Union and Confederate Armies, Series IV, Vol. 1:542–548. Washington: U.S. Government Printing Office, 1900.)

1861a   Articles of a Convention...between the Confederate States of America...and the No-co-ni, Ta-ne-i-weh, Co-cho-tih-ca, and Ya-pa-rih-ca Bands of the Ne-um or Comanches [etc.]. (Published in: The War of the Rebellion: A Compilation of the Official Records of the Union and Confederate Armies, Series IV, Vol. 1:548–554. Washington: U.S. Government Printing Office, 1900.)

1861b   Message of the President, and Report of Albert Pike, Commissioner of the Confederate States to the Indian Nations West of Arkansas, of the Results of His Mission. Richmond, Va.: Enquirer Book and Job Press, Tyler, Wise, Allegre, and Smith. (Cover title: Report of Albert Pike on Mission to the Indian Nations. Reprinted by: Supreme Council, 33: Ancient and Accepted Scottish Rite, Washington, 1968.)

1861c   [Comparative Vocabulary of the Tonkawa Language; copy of the original manuscript, transcribed and arranged by J.H. Trumbull, Dec. 1874.] (Manuscript No. 1007, National Anthropological Archives, Smithsonian Institution, Washington.)

1866   [Comanche Bands and Other Indian Names.] (Manuscript No. 593a, National Anthropological Archives, Smithsonian Institution, Washington.)

Pike, James
1932   Scout and Ranger: Being the Personal Adventures of James Pike of the Texas Rangers, in 1859–60 [1865]. Carl L. Cannon, ed. Princeton, N.J.: Princeton University Press. (Reprinted: Da Capo Press, New York, 1932.)

Pike, Zebulon Montgomery
1810   An Account of Expeditions to the Sources of the Mississippi, and Through the Western Parts of Louisiana, to the Sources of the Arkansaw, Kans, La Platte, and Pierre Juan, Rivers ... Performed....during the Years 1805, 1806, and 1807 [etc.]. 3 Pts. Philadelphia: C. & A. Conrad. (Reprinted as: The Journals of Zebulon Montgomery Pike, Donald D. Jackson, ed. 2 vols. University of Oklahoma Press, Norman, 1966.)

1235

1811   Exploratory Travels Through the Western Territories of North America; Comprising a Voyage from St. Louis, on the Mississippi, to the Source of That River, and a Journey Through the Interior of Louisiana, and the North-Eastern Provinces of New Spain, Performed in the Years 1805, 1806, 1807....Thomas Rees, ed. London: Printed for Longman, Hurst, Rees, Orme, and Brown. (Reprinted: W.H. Lawrence, Denver, Colo., 1889.)

_____ 1966 *see* Jackson, Donald D., ed. 1966

Pillaert, E. Elizabeth
1963   The McLemore Site of the Washita River Focus. *Bulletin of the Oklahoma Anthropological Society* 11:1–113. Oklahoma City.

Pilling, James Constantine
1885   Proof-sheets of a Bibliography of the Languages of the North American Indians. (Distributed only to collaborators.) *Bureau of [American] Ethnology Miscellaneous Publication* 2. Washington: Smithsonian Institution; U.S. Government Printing Office. (Reprinted: Central Book Company, Brooklyn, N.Y., 1966.)

1887   Bibliography of the Siouan Languages. *Bureau of [American] Ethnology Bulletin* 5. Washington: Smithsonian Institution; U.S. Government Printing Office. (Reprinted as Vol. 1, Pt. 1 of 3 Vols.: AMS Press, New York, 1973.)

1891   Bibliography of the Algonquian Languages. *Bureau of [American] Ethnology Bulletin* 13. Washington: Smithsonian Institution; U.S. Government Printing Office. (Reprinted as Vol. 2, Pt. 5 of 3 Vols.: AMS Press, New York, 1973.)

Pimentel, Francisco
1862–1865 Cuadro descriptivo y comparativo de las lenguas indígenas de México. 2 vols. México [City]: Imprenta de Andrade y Escalante.

Pinckney, Pauline A.
1967   Painting in Texas: The Nineteenth Century. Introduction by Jerry Bywaters. Austin, Tex.: Published for the Amon Carter Museum of Western Art, Fort Worth, by the University of Texas Press.

Pink, William
1765–1768 [William Pink Journal, in York Factory Journal, 1765–1768.] (Hudson's Bay Company Collection, Reel 1M158, Public Archives of Canada, Ottawa.)

Pino, Pedro Baptista
1812   Exposición sucinta y sencilla de la provincia del Nuevo México. Cádiz, España: Imprenta del Estado-Mayor-General.

1995   The Exposition on the Province of New Mexico, 1812, by Don Pedro Baptista Pino. Translated, edited and with a Preface by Adrian Bustamante and Marc Simmons. Introduction by Eduardo Garrigues; Prefatory Letter by His Royal Highness Don Felipe de Borbón Prínce de Asturias. Santa Fe and Albuquerque: El Rancho de las Golondrinas and the University of New Mexico Press.

Piscataway News
1989   [July: Piscataway Sun Dance 4th Annual.] Accokeek, Md.: Piscataway Indian Nation.

Pitsula, James M.
1994   The CCF Government and the Formation of the Union of Saskatchewan Indians. *Prairie Forum* 19(2):131–151. Regina, Sask.: Canadian Plains Research Center, University of Regina.

1994a   The Saskatchewan CCF Government and Treaty Indians, 1944–1964. *Canadian Historical Review* 75(1):21–52. Toronto: University of Toronto Press.

1996   The Thatcher Government in Saskatchewan and Indian Treaties, 1964–71: The Quiet Revolution. *Saskatchewan History* 48(1):3–17. Saskatoon.

1997   Educational Paternalism Versus Autonomy: Contradictions in the Relationship between the Saskatchewan Government and the Federation of Saskatchewan Indians, 1958–1964. *Prairie Forum* 22(1):47–71. Regina, Sask.: Canadian Plains Research Center, University of Regina.

Pittman, Philip
1906   The Present State of the European Settlements on the Mississippi [1770]. Frank H. Haddor, ed. Cleveland, Ohio: Arthur H. Clark.

Platt, Elvira Gaston
1892   Reminiscences of a Teacher among the Nebraska Indians, 1843–1885. *Transcations and Reports of the Nebraska State Historical Society* 3:125–143. Fremont, Nebr.

1918   Some Experiences as a Teacher among the Pawnees. *Collections of the Kansas State Historical Society for the Years 1915–'18*, Vol. 14:784–794. Topeka.

Plaut, W. Gunther
1953   A Hebrew-Dakota Dictionary. *Publications of the American Jewish Historical Society* 42(4):361–370. Philadelphia.

Plummer, Norman B.
1974   The Crow Tribe of Indians. (Commission Findings: Indian Claims Commission Docket No. 54.) *American Indian Ethnohistory: Plains Indians* . David Agee Horr, comp. and ed. New York and London: Garland Publishing.

Pocaterra, George W.
1963   Among the Nomadic Stoneys. *Alberta Historical Review* 11(3):12–19. Calgary.

Pocklington, Thomas C.
1991   The Government and Politics of the Alberta Métis Settlements. Regina, Sask.: Canadian Plains Research Center, University of Regina.

Pohorecky, Zenon
1988   The Saskatoon Site-Paleontological or Archaeological? Pp. 47–64 in Out of the Past: Sites, Digs and Artifacts in the Saskatoon Area. Urve Linnamae and Tim E.H. Jones, eds. Saskatoon: Saskatchewan Archaeological Society.

Pohrt, Richard A.
1969   A Breastplate of Dragoons. *The Museum of the Fur Trade Quarterly* 5(4):5–6. Chadron, Nebr.

1978   Plains Indians Riding Quirts with Elk Antler Handles. *American Indian Art Magazine* 3(4):62–67. Scottsdale, Ariz.

1989   Tribal Identification of Northern Plains Beadwork. *American Indian Art Magazine* 15(1):72–79. Scottsdale, Ariz.

Point, Nicolas
1967   Wilderness Kingdom: Indian Life in the Rocky Mountains: 1840–1847; The Journal and Paintings of Nicolas Point, S.J.; Translated and introduced by Joseph P. Donnelly, S.J. With an Appreciation by John C. Ewers. New York, Chicago, San Francisco: Holt, Rinehart and Winston.

[Ponca Singers]
1967   War Dance Songs of the Ponca. Vol. II. [Record album No. 2002.] Taos, N.Mex.: Indian House.

Ponca Tribe of Oklahoma
1975   Ponca Tribal Handbook. Ponca City, Okla.: The Tribe.

Pond, Gideon H.
1854   Power and Influence of Dakota Medicine-men. Pp. 641–651 Vol. 4 of Historical and Statistical Information Respecting

the History, Condition and Prospects of the Indian Tribes of the United States. Henry Rowe Schoolcraft, comp. and ed. 6 vols. Philadelphia: Lippincott, Grambo, 1851–1857.

1867   Dakota Superstitions and Gods. *Collections of the Minnesota Historical Society* 2:32–62. St. Paul. (Reprinted: 1889, in vol 2:215–255 of the bound set. St. Paul.)

Pond, Samuel W.
1844   Dakota wiwangapi wowapi=Catechism in the Dakota or Sioux Language. New Haven, Conn.: Hitchcock & Stafford.

1880   Indian Warfare in Minnesota. *Collections of the Minnesota Historical Society* 3:129–138. St. Paul.

1908   The Dakotas or Sioux in Minnesota As They Were in 1834. *Minnesota Historical Society Collections* 12:320–501. St. Paul. (Reprinted, with an Introduction by Gary C. Anderson: Minnesota Historical Society Press, St. Paul, 1986.)

Pond, Samuel W., and Gideon H. Pond
1840   [Santee Dakota Texts. Trans. by Ella C. Deloria.] (Manuscript No. 30(X8a.17), Franz Boas Collection, the Library of the American Philosophical Society, Philadelphia. Original manuscripts in Archives of the Minnesota Historical Society, St. Paul.)

Ponziglione, Paul Mary
1878   [Letter from Osage Mission, Neosho County, Kansas, dated December 31st, 1877.] *Woodstock Letters* 7(2):99–105. Woodstock, Md.

1882   [Letter from Osage Mission, Neosho County, Kansas, dated July 1st, 1881.] *Woodstock Letters* 11(2):163–169. Woodstock, Md.

1883   [Letter from Osage Mission, Neosho County, Kansas, dated July 2, 1883.] *Woodstock Letters* 12(3):292–298. Woodstock, Md.

1889   Indian Traditions among the Osages. *Woodstock Letters* 18(1):68–76. Woodstock, Md.

1890   Father Schoenmakers and the Osage. (Manuscript in Jesuit Archival Collection, Vatican Film Library, St. Louis University, St. Louis, Mo.)

Poolaw, Linda
1990   Horace Poolaw: Kiowa Photographer. *Winds of Change: A Magazine of American Indians* 5(4):46–51. Boulder, Colo.

1990a   War Bonnets, Tin Lizzies, and Patent Leather Pumps: Kiowa Culture in Transition, 1925–1955. [Exhibition Catalogue]: The Photographs of Horace Poolaw; Oct. 5–Dec. 14, 1990. Stanford, Calif.: Stanford University.

Poole, Dewitt Clinton
1881   Among the Sioux of Dakota: Eighteen Months' Experience as an Indian Agent, 1869–70. New York: D. Van Nostrand. (Reprinted: Minnesota Historical Society Press, 1988.)

Poor Man, Mercy
1987   Christian Life Fellowship Church. Pp. 149–155 in Sioux Indian Religion: Tradition and Innovation. Raymond J. DeMallie and Douglas R. Parks, eds. Norman: University of Oklahoma Press.

Pope, Polly
1966   Trade in the Plains: Affluence and Its Effects. *Kroeber Anthropological Society Papers* 34:53–62. Berkeley: Department of Anthropology, University of California.

Porter, James W.
1962   Notes on Four Lithic Types Found in Archaeological Sites Near Mobridge, South Dakota. *Plains Anthropologist* 7(18):267–269.

Porter, Joseph C.
1986   Paper Medicine Man: John Gregory Bourke and His American West. Norman: University of Oklahoma Press.

Posada, Alonso de
1982   Alonso de Posada Report, 1686: A Description of the Area of Present Southern Unvited States in the Late Seventeenth Century. Alfred B. Thomas, ed. Pensacola, Fla.: Perdido Bay Press.

Potter, J. H.
1885   [Telegram to C.C. Augur, dated June 26, 1885.] (Manuscript No. 15102, Letters Received by the Office of Indian Affairs, 1881–1907, Records of the Bureau of Indian Affairs, Record Group 75, National Archives, Washington.)

Potvin, Annette
1966   The Sun Dance Liturgy of the Blackfoot Indians. (M.A. Thesis in Religious Sciences, University of Ottawa, Ottawa.)

Pouliot, Léon
1969   Le Roy de La Potherie, dit Bacqueville de La Potherie (La Poterie), Claude-Charles. Pp.421–423 in Vol.2 of the Dictionary of Canadian Biography, 1701–1740. Toronto: University of Toronto Press.

Powell, (Father) Peter J.
1958   Mahuts, the Sacred Arrows of the Cheyenne. *Westerners Brand Book* 15:35–40.

1960   Issiwun: Sacred Buffalo Hat of the Northern Cheyenne. *Montana: The Magazine of Western History* 10(1):24–40. (Reprinted in: The Red Man's West. Michael S. Kennedy, ed. Hastings House, New York, 1965.)

1969   Sweet Medicine: The Continuing Role of the Sacred Arrows, the Sun Dance, and the Sacred Buffalo Hat in Northern Cheyenne History. 2 vols. Norman: University of Oklahoma Press. (Reprinted in 1998.)

1975   Artists and Fighting Men: A Brief Introduction to Northern Cheyenne Ledger Book Drawing. *American Indian Art Magazine* 1(1):44–48. Scottsdale, Ariz.

1976   They Drew From Power: An Introduction to Northern Cheyenne Ledger Book Art. Pp. 3–54 in Montana, Past and Present: Papers Read at a Clark Library Seminar, April 5, 1975; by (Father) Peter J. Powell and Michael P. Malone. Los Angeles: William Andrews Clark Memorial Library, University of California.

1977   Beauty for New Life. Pp. 33–56 in The Native American Heritage. E. Maurer, ed. Chicago: Foundation for the Preservation of American Indian Art and Culture.

1980   The Cheyennes, Maheoo's People: A Critical Bibliography. Bloomington: Indiana University Press.

1981   People of the Sacred Mountain: A History of the Cheyenne Chiefs and Warrior Societies, 1830–1879; with an Epilogue 1969–1974. 2 vols. San Francisco: Harper and Row.

1985   A Report to the Keepers of the Sacred Arrows and the Sacred Buffalo Hut; the Chiefs, the Headmen, and the Men of the Warrior Societies; the Arrow Lodge Men and the Sun Dance Priests of the Cheyenne People. Chicago: Written at The Newberry Library and St. Augustine's Indian Center.

1985a   Power for New Days. Pp. 249–264 in The Plains Indians of the Twentieth Century. Edited and with an Introduction by Peter Iverson. Norman: University of Oklahoma Press. (Reprinted from: pp. 412–428 in Vol. 1, Pt.2 of Sweet Medicine: The Continuing Role of the Sacred Arrows, the Sun Dance, and the Sacred Buffalo Hat in Northern Cheyenne History, by Father Peter J. Powell. University of Oklahoma Press, Norman, 1969.)

1237

_____, ed.

1988   To Honor the Crow People: Crow Indian Art from the Goelet and Edith Gallatin Collection of American Indian Art. Chicago: Foundation for the Preservation of American Indian Art and Culture, and St. Augustine's Center for American Indians.

1994   The Killing of Morning Star's People. *Distinguished Lecture Series of the Mari Sandoz Heritage Society* 2. Chadron, Nebr.

Powell, John Wesley

1877   Introduction to the Study of Indian Languages, with Words, Phrases, and Sentences To Be Collected. [1st ed.] Washington: Government Printing Office.

1880   Introduction to the Study of Indian Languages, with Words, Phrases, and Sentences To Be Collected; 2d ed., with Charts. Washington: Government Printing Office.

1881   Report of the Director. Pp. xi–xxxiii in *1st Annual Report of the Bureau of [American] Ethnology [for] 1879–'80.* Washington: Smithsonian Institution; U.S. Government Printing Office.

1888   Work of Mr. A.S. Gatchet. Pp. xxxiii–xxxvi in *6th Annual Report of the Bureau of [American] Ethnology for 1884–'85.* Washington: Smithsonian Institution; U.S. Government Printing Office.

1891   Indian Linguistic Families of America North of Mexico. Pp. 1–142 [pp. 399–409, Vol. Index] in *7th Annual Report of the Bureau of [American] Ethnology for 1885–'86.* With Map. Washington: Smithsonian Institution; U.S. Government Printing Office. (Reprinted with Franz Boas's Introduction to *Handbook of American Indian Languages.* Preston Holder, ed. University of Nebraska Press, Lincoln, 1966.)

1891a   Study of Indian Languages. *Science* 17(418):71–74. Washington.

1894   Map of Linguistic Stocks of American Indians Chiefly Within the Present Limits of the United States. [Facing] p. 36 in Report on Indian Taxed and Indians Not Taxed in the United States (Except Alaska) at the Eleventh Census: 1890. Washington: Government Printing Office. (Reprinted: Norman Ross Publishing, New York, 1994.)

Powell, Vio Mae

1947   Dramatic Ritual as Observed in the Sun Dance. *The Quarterly Journal of Speech* (April):167–171.

Powers, John

1998   Coal Firm to Offer Crow $530 Million. *Big Horn County News,* May 6, 1998:1. Hardin, Mont.

Powers, Marla N.

1986   Oglala Women: Myth, Ritual and Reality. Chicago: Univeristy of Chicago Press.

1988   Symbolic Representations of Sex Roles in the Plains War Dance. *European Review of Native American Studies* 2(2):17–24. Vienna, Austria [etc.].

1990   A Century of Vision: The Star Quilt, A Symbol of Lakota Identity. Kendall Park, N.J.: Lakota Books.

1991   Dakota Naming: A Modern Day Hunka Ceremony. Kendall Park, N.J.: Lakota Books.

Powers, Ramon, and James N. Leiker

1998   Cholera among the Plains Indians: Perceptions, Causes, Consequences. *Western Historical Quarterly* 29(3):317–340.

Powers, William K.

1960   American Indian Music, Part 1: An Introduction. *American Indian Hobbyist* 7(1):5–7. Alton, Ill.

1961   American Indian Music, Part 3: The Social Dances. *American Indian Tradition* 7(3):97–104. Alton, Ill.

1961a   American Indian Music, Part 4: War Dance Songs. *American Indian Tradition* 7(4):128–134. Alton, Ill.

1961b   American Indian Music, Part 5: Contemporary Music and Dance of the Western Sioux. *American Indian Tradition* 7(5):158–165. Alton, Ill.

1961c   American Indian Music, Part 6: The Sioux Omaha Dance. *American Indian Tradition* 8(1):24–33. Alton, Ill.

1962   The Rabbit Dance. (American Indian Music Part VII: Contemporary Music and Dance of the Western Sioux.) *American Indian Tradition* 8(3):113–118. Alton, Ill.

1962a   Sneak-up Dance, Drum Dance, and Flag Dance. (American Indian Music Part VIII: Contemporary Music and Dance of the Western Sioux.) *American Indian Tradition* 8(4):166–171. Alton, Ill.

1965   Grass Dance Costume. *Powwow Trails* 2:1–16. Somerset, N.J. (Reprinted: Lakota Books, Kendall Park, N.J., 1994.)

1966   Feather's Costume. *Powwow Trials* 3(7–8):4–19. Somerset, N.J.

1967   Okan, Sun Dance of the Blackfoot (film review.) *American Anthropologist,* n.s. 69(5):561–562.

1968   Diffusion of the Plains War Dance. *Powwow Trails* 5(6):68–72. Somerset, N.J.

1968a   Contemporary Oglala Music and Dance: Pan-Indianism Verses Pan-Tetonism. *Ethnomusicology* 12(3):352–372. Ann Arbor, Mich.

1969   Indians of the Northern Plains. New York: G.P. Putnam's Sons. (Reprinted: Capricorn Books, New York, 1973.)

1970   Contemporary Oglala Music and Dance: Pan-Indianism versus Pan-Tetonism. Pp. 268–290 in The Modern Sioux: Social Systems and Reservation Culture. Ethel Nurge, ed. Lincoln: University of Nebraska Press.

1972   Indians of the Southern Plains. New York: Capricorn Books.

1972a   The Language of the Sioux. *Language in American Indian Education: A Newsletter of the Office of Education Program, Bureau of Indian Affairs* (Spring 1972):1–21. Washington: Bureau of Indian Affairs.

1975   Continuity and Change in Oglala Religion. (Ph.D. Dissertation in Anthropology, University of Pennsylvania, Philadelphia.)

1977   Oglala Religion. Lincoln: University of Nebraska Press.

1980   Plains Indian Music and Dance. Pp. 212–229 in Anthropology of the Great Plains. W. Raymond Wood and Margot Liberty, eds. Lincoln: University of Nebraska Press.

1980a   Oglala Song Terminology. Pp. 23–42 in *Selected Reports in Ethnomusicology* 3(2). Charlotte Heth, ed. Los Angeles: University of California Press.

1982   Yuwipi: Vision and Experience in Oglala Ritual. Lincoln: University of Nebraska Press.

1986   Sacred Language: The Nature of Supernatural Discourse in Lakota. Norman: University of Oklahoma Press.

1987   Beyond the Vision: Essays on American Indian Culture. Norman: University of Oklahoma Press.

1990   War Dance: Plains Indian Musical Performance. Tucson: University of Arizona Press.

1990a   Voices from the Spirit World. Kendall Park, N.J.: Lakota Books.

1994   American Indian Music. Kendall Park, N.J.: Lakota Books. (Originally publ. as separate articles in: *American Indian Tradition,* 1960–1962.)

Poynter, C.W.M.
1915   A Study of Nebraska Crania. *American Anthropologist,* n.s. 17(3):509–524.

Pratt, Grace Roffey
1981   [Running Eagle] Female War Chief of the Blackfeet. *The Piegan Storyteller* 6(1):3–5.

Praus, Alexis
1962   The Sioux, 1798–1922: A Dakota Winter Count. *Cranbrook Institute of Science. Bulletin* 44. Bloomfield Hills, Mich.

Prescott, Philander
1852   Contributions to the History, Customs, and Opinions of the Dacota Tribe. Transmitted from the St. Peters Agency. Pp. 168–199 Vol. II of Historical and Statistical Information Respecting the History, Condition and Prospects of the Indian Tribes of the United States. Henry Rowe Schoolcraft, comp. and ed. 6 vols. Philadelphia: Lippincott, Grambo, 1851–1857.

1853   The Dacotahs or Sioux of the Upper Mississippi. [Second Paper, continued from "Contributions," p. 199, Vol. II.] Pp. 225–246 in Vol. III of Historical and Statistical Information Respecting the History, Condition and Prospects of the Indian Tribes of the United States. Henry Rowe Schoolcraft, comp. and ed. 6 vols. Philadelphia: Lippincott, Grambo, 1851–1857.

1854   Manners, Customs and Opinions of the Dacotahs. Pp. 59–72 in Vol. IV of Historical and Statistical Information Respecting the History, Condition and Prospects of the Indian Tribes of the United States. Henry Rowe Schoolcraft, comp. and ed. 6 vols. Philadelphia: Lippincott, Grambo, 1851–1857.

1894   Autobiography and Reminiscences of Philander Prescott. *Collections of the Minnesota Historical Society* 6(3):475–691. St. Paul.

President of the United States 1890 *see* Harrison, Benjamin 1890

Prewitt, Elton R.
1981   Cultural Chronology in Central Texas. *Bulletin of the Texas Archeological Society* 52:65–89. Austin.

1982   Archeological Investigations at the Loeve-Fox Site, Williamson County, Texas. *Prewitt and Associates. Reprints in Anthropology* 1. Austin. (Originally publ.: *Texas Archeological Survey* 49, University of Texas, Austin, 1974.)

1985   From Circleville to Toyah: Comments on Central Texas Chronology. *Bulletin of the Texas Archeological Society* 54:201–238. Austin.

Price, Catherine
1996   The Oglala People, 1841–1879: A Political History. Lincoln: University of Nebraska Press.

Price, John A.
1968   The Migration and Adaptation of American Indians to Los Angeles. *Human Organization* 27(2):168–175. Washington.

1975   U.S. and Canadian Indian Urban Ethnic Institutions. *Urban Anthropology* 4(1):035–052. New York, [etc.]: Plenum Publishing.

1979   Indians of Canada: Cultural Dynamics. Scarborough, Ont.: Prentice-Hall of Canada.

Price, Monroe E.
1973   Law and the American Indians: Readings, Notes, and Cases. Indianapolis, Ind.: Bobbs-Merrill. (Reprinted: Michie Company, Charlottesville, Va., 1983.)

Price, Raymond S.
1956   Early Ceramic Period Sites in Northeastern Nebraska. (M.A. Thesis in Anthropology, University of Nebraska, Lincoln.)

Price, Richard, ed.
1987   The Spirit of the Alberta Indian Treaties. Edmonton, Alta.: Pica Pica Press. (Originally publ.: Butterworth and Co. Ltd., Toronto, 1979.)

Prichard, James C.
1847   Researches into the Physical History of Mankind. 5 vols. London: Houlston and Sons.

Prieto, Alejandro
1873   Historia geografía y estadística del Estado de Tamaulipas [etc.]. México: Tip. Escalerillas.

Prikryl, Daniel J.
1990   Lower Elm Fork Prehistory: A Redefinition of Cultural Concepts and Chronologies along the Trinity River, North-Central Texas. *Texas Historical Commission. Office of the State Archeologis.t Report* 37. Austin.

1993   Section III: Regional Preservation Plan for Archeological Resources, Prairie-Savanna Archeological Region. Pp. 191–204 in Archeology in the Eastern Planning Region, Texas: A Planning Document. Nancy A. Kenmotsu and Timothy K. Perttula, eds. *Texas Historical Commission. Department of Antiquities Protection. Cultural Resource Management. Report* 3. Austin.

Pringle, Robert M.
1958   The Northern Cheyenne Indians in the Reservation Period. (M.A. Thesis in History, Harvard College, Cambridge, Mass.)

Proulx, Paul
1989   A Sketch of Blackfoot Historical Phonology. *International Journal of American Linguistics* 55(1):43–82. Chicago.

Provincial Archives of Alberta
1989   C.W. Mathers' Vision, 1893–1905. Catalogue of the Exhibition "C.W. Mathers' Vision", 21 January – 2 April 1989, at the Provincial Museum of Alberta, presented by the Provincial Archives of Alberta. [Essay: "Charles Wesley Mathers", by Brock V. Silversides.] Edmonton, Alta.: Historical Resources Division, Alberta Culture and Multiculturalism.

Provinse, John H.
1937   The Underlying Sanctions of Plains Indian Culture. Pp. 339–374 in Social Anthropology of North American Tribes. Fred Eggan, ed. Chicago: University of Chicago Press.

Provinse, John H., and Ruth Hill Unseem
1954   The American Indian in Transition. *American Anthropologist,* n.s. 56(3):388–394.

Provo, Daniel J.
1984   Fort Esperance in 1793–1795: A North West Company Provisioning Post, with appendix by W. Raymond Wood: 1239

Journal of John Macdonell, 1793–1975. *Reprints in Anthropology* 28. Lincoln: J&L Reprint Company.

Prucha, Francis Paul (S.J.)
1962   American Indian Policy in the Formative Years: The Indian Trade and Intercourse Acts, 1790–1834. Cambridge, Mass.: Harvard University Press.

1964   A Guide to the Military Posts of the United States, 1789–1895. Madison, Wis.: The State Historical Society of Wisconsin.

1971   Indian Peace Medals in American History. Madison, Wis.: State Historical Society of Wisconsin.

1975   Documents of United States Indian Policy. Lincoln: University of Nebraska Press.

1976   American Indian Policy in Crisis: Christian Reformers and the Indian, 1865–1900. Norman: University of Oklahoma Press.

1977   A Bibliographical Guide to the History of Indian-White Relations in the United States. (A Publication of the Center for the History of the American Indian of the Newberry Library.) Chicago: The University of Chicago Press.

1979   The Churches and the Indian Schools, 1888–1912. Lincoln: University of Nebraska Press.

1984   The Great Father: The United States Government and the American Indians. 2 vols. Lincoln: University of Nebraska Press.

1990   Documents of United States Indian Policy. 2d ed., expanded. Lincoln: University of Nebraska Press.

1990a   Atlas of American Indian Affairs. Lincoln: University of Nebraska Press.

1994   American Indian Treaties: The History of a Political Anomaly. Berkeley, Calif.: University of California Press.

Prud'homme, L.A.
1905   Pierre Gaultier de Varennes, Sieur de la Vérendrye. *Transactions of the Royal Society of Canada* 1:9–57. Ottawa.

Pulford, Florence
1989   Morning Star Quilts. Los Altos, Calif.: Leone Publications.

Purrington, Burton L.
1971   The Prehistory of Delaware County, Oklahoma: Cultural Continuity and Change on the Western Ozark Periphery. (Ph.D. Dissertation in Anthropology, University of Wisconsin, Madison.)

Putnam, Frederic W.
1880   Report of the Curator. *13th Annual Report for 1879 for the Peabody Museum of American Archaeology and Ethnology* 2(4):709–755. Cambridge. Mass.

[Pyle, Ernie] 1945 *see Indians at Work* 1945

Pyszczyk, Heinz W.
1997   The Use of Fur Goods by the Plains Indians, Central and Southern Alberta, Canada. *Canadain Journal of Archaeology/Journal Canadien d'Archéologie* 21(1): 45–84. Ottawa.

Quaife, Milo Milton, ed.
1916   Extracts from Capt. McKay's Journal — and Others. *State Historical Society of Wisconsin Proceedings [for] 1915*:180–210. Madison: Cantwell Printing.

1933   Forty Years a Fur Trader on the Upper Missouri: The Personal Narrative of Charles Larpenteur, 1833–1872. Historical Introduction by Milo Milton Quaife. Chicago: The Lakeside Press; R.R. Donnelly and Sons. (Reprinted, with an Introduction by Paul H. Hedren: University of Nebraska Press, Lincoln, 1989.)

Quigg, J. Michael
1984   A 4700-Year-Old Tool Assemblage from East-Central Alberta. *Plains Anthropologist* 29(104):151–159.

1986   Ross Glen: A Besant Stone Circle Site in Southeastern Alberta. *Archaeological Survey of Alberta. Manuscript Series* 10. Edmonton.

1986a   The Crown Site (FhNa-86) Excavation Results. *Saskatchewan Research Council. Nipawin Reservoir Heritage Study* 8. Saskatoon.

1988   A Ceramic Bearing Avonlea Component in Southwestern Alberta. Pp. 67–79 in Avonlea Yesterday and Today: Archaeology and Prehistory. Leslie B. Davis, ed. Saskatoon: Saskatchewan Arcaeological Society.

1997   The Sanders Site (41HF128): A Single Event Late Archaic Camp/Bison Processing Site, Hanford County, Texas. *TRC Mariah Associates. Technical Report* 19751. Austin, Tex.
_____, et al.
1993   Historic and Prehistoric Data Recovery at Palo Duro Reservoir, Hansford County, Texas. *TRC Mariah Associates. Technical Report* 485. Austin, Tex.
_____, et al.
1996   Early Archaic Use of the Concho River Terraces: Cultural Resource Investigations of 41TG307 and 41TG309, Tom Green County, San Angelo, Texas. *TRC Mariah Associates. Techincal Report* 11058. Austin, Tex.

Quimby, George Irving
1965   Plains Art from a Florida Prison. *Chicago Natural History Museum. Bulletin* 36(10):[1–5]. Chicago.

Quintero, Carolyn
1995   Osage Dictionary. (Database and manuscript in C. Quintero's possession.)

1997   Osage Phonology and Verbal Morphology. (Ph.D. Dissertation in Linguistics, University of Massachusetts, Boston.)

1999   First Course in Osage. Tulsa, Okla.: [The Author.]

Raby, Stewart
1973   Indian Land Surrenders in Southern Saskatchewan. *Canadian Geographer* 17(1):36–52. Montreal.

Racette, Calvin
1987   Flags of the Métis. Regina, Sask.: Gabriel Dumont Institute.

Racette, Sherry Farrell
1991   The Flower Beadwork People. Regina, Sask.: Gabriel Dumont Institute.

Rachlin, Carol K.
1964   Native Americam Indian Church in Oklahoma. *Chronicles of Oklahoma* 42(2):262–272. Norman.

1965   Tight Shoe Night. *Midcontinent American Studies Journal* 6(2):84–100. Lawrence, Kan.

1968   Tight Shoe Night: Oklahoma Indians Today. Pp. 99–114 in The American Indian Today. Stuart Levine and Nancy O. Lurie, eds. Deland, Fla.: Everett/Edwards, Inc.

Radin, Paul
1911   The Ritual and Significance of the Winnebago Medicine Dance. (Ph.D. Dissertation in Anthropology, Columbia University, New York City. Published in:) *Journal of American Folk-lore* 24(92):149–208.

1919   The Genetic Relationship of the North Amerian Indian

Languages. *University of California Publications in American Archaeology and Ethnology* 14(5):489–502. Berkeley.

1921   A Sketch of the Peyote Cult of Winnebago: A Study in Borrowing. *Journal of Religious Psychology* 7:1–22. Worcester, Mass.

1923   The Winnebago Tribe. Pp. 35–350 [pp. 551–560, Vol. Index] in *37th Annual Report of the Bureau of American Ethnology [for] 1915–'16.* Washington: Smithsonian Institution; U.S. Government Printing Office. (Reprinted: Johnson Reprint, New York, 1970.)

Radisson, Pierre Esprit
1885   Voyages of Peter Esprit Radisson; Being an Account of His Travels and Experiences among the North American Indians, from 1652 to 1684; Transcribed from Original Manuscripts in the Bodleian Library and the British Museum; with Historical Illustrations and an Introduction, by Gideon D. Scull. *Publications of the Prince Society* 16. Boston: The Prince Society. (Reprinted: Burt Franklin, New York, 1971.)

1961   The Explorations of Pierre Esprit Radisson, from the Original Manuscript in the Bodleian Library and the British Museum. Arthur T. Adams, ed.; Modernized by Loren Kallsen. Minneapolis: Ross and Haines.

Rafinesque, Constantine Samuel 1824 *see* Marshall, Humphrey 1824

1832–1833   *Atlantic Journal, and Friend of Knowledge*, Vol. 1, Nos. 1–8: Containing about 160 Original Articles and Tracts on Natural and Historical Sciences, the Description of about 150 New Plants, and 100 New Animals or Fossils. Many Vocabularies of Languages, Historical and Geological Facts. Philadelphia: [C.S. Rafinesque.]

Rahill, Peter
1953   Catholic Indian Missions and Grant's Peace Policy. Washington: The Catholic University Press.

Raish, Carol B.
1979   King Hill (23BN1), Fanning (14DP1) and Leary (25RH1): A Study of Oneota Ceramic Variability. (M.A. Thesis in Anthropology, University of Nebraska, Lincoln.)

Ralph, Elizabeth K., Henry N. Michael, and and M.C. Han
1973   Radiocarbon Dates and Reality. *MASCA Newsletter* 9(1):1–9. Philadelphia: Applied Science Center for Archaeology, The University Museum, University of Pennsylvania.

Ramón, Domingo
1933   Captain Don Domingo Ramón's Diary of His Expedition into Texas in 1716. Translated by Paul J. Foik. *Preliminary Studies of the Texas Catholic Historical Society* 2 (April):2–28. Austin.

Ramenofsky, Ann F.
1987   Vectors of Death: The Archaeology of European Contact. Albuquerque: University of New Mexico Press.

Ramsay, Allyson M.
1991   The Melhagen Site: A Besant Bison Kill in South Central Saskatchewan. (M.A. Thesis in Anthropology and Archaeology, University of Saskatchewan, Saskatoon.)

Ramsay, Charles L.
1993   The Redtail Site: A McKean Habitation in South Central Saskatchewan. (M.A. Thesis in Anthropology and Archaeology, University of Saskatchewan, Saskatoon.)

Ramsey, Alexander
1872   Our Field of Historical Research. [Address of Gov. Alex. Ramsey, President of the Society, before Its Annual Meeting, Jan. 13, 1851.] *Collections of the Minnesota Historical Society* 1:43–52. St. Paul. (Republication of the orig. parts issued in 1850–1853, 1856.)

Randlett, James
1901   [Letter to the Commissioner of Indian Affairs, dated December 11, 1901.] (Manuscript, P-2186, Letters Received 1881–1901, Records of the Bureau of Indian Affairs, Record Group 75, National Archives, Washington.)

Randolph, Richard W.
1937   Sweet Medicine and Other Stories of the Cheyenne Indians, as Told to Richard W. Randolph. Illustrations by R.H. Hall. Caldwell, Idaho.: The Caxton Printers, Ltd.

Rankin, Charles E., ed.
1996   Legacy: New Perspectives on the Battle of the Little Bighorn. Proceedings of the Little Bighorn Legacy Symposium, Held in Billings, Montana, August 3–6, 1994. Billings: Montana Historical Society Press.

Rankin, Robert L.
1977   From Verb, to Auxiliary, to Noun Classifier and Definite Article: Grammaticalization of the Siouan Verbs Sit, Stand, Lie. Pp. 273–283 in Proceedings of the 1976 Mid-America Linguistics Conference. R.L. Brown, et al., eds. Minneapolis: University of Minnesota Linguistics Department.

1982   A Quapaw Vocabulary. *Kansas Working Papers in Linguistics* 7:125–152. Lawrence.

1985   On Some Ohio Valley Siouan and Illinois Algonquian Words for 'Eight'. *International Journal of American Linguistics* 51(4):544–547. Chicago.

1985a   Quapaw as a Historically Dhegiha Language: Grammar. (Manuscript in R.L. Rankin's possession, and at the University of Arkansas, Fayetteville.)

1986   Review: Paula Einaudi, A Grammar of Biloxi. *International Journal of American Linguistics* 52(1):77–85. Chicago.

1986a   Current Estimates of Number and Status of Speakers of Siouan Languages. (Manuscript distributed at the 1987 Siouan and Caddoan Linguistics Conference, Boulder, Colo.)

1987   Kansa-English, English-Kansa Lexicon. (Manuscript in R.L. Rankin's possession.)

1987a   Ponca, Biloxi, and Hidatsa Glottals and Quapaw Gemination as Historically Related Accentual Phenomena. Pp. 252–262 in *Proceedings of the 1985 Mid-America Linguistics Conference.* Columbia, Mo.: Linguistics Area Program, University of Missouri.

1988   Quapaw: Genetical and Areal Affiliations. Pp. 629–650 in In Honor of Mary Haas: From the Haas Festival Conference on Native American Linguistics. William Shipley, ed. Berlin: Mouton de Gruyter.

1991   [Quapaw Vocabulary.] (Manuscript in R.L. Rankin's possession.)

1991a   Quapaw-English, English-Quapaw Dictionary. (Manuscript in R.L. Rankin's possession.)

1994   On the Sources and Scope of Siouan Aspiration. Pp. 205–216 in *Proceedings of the 1993 Mid-America Linguistics Conference.* Jule Gómez de García and David S. Rood, eds. Boulder, Colo.: University of Colorado Department of Linguistics.

1994a   Absolute Dating of Siouan Linguistic Splits: Problems and Results. (Paper Presented at Comparative Linguistics Workshop, University of Pittsburgh, April 9, 1994.)

1994b   The Kansa Vocabulary of Maximilian of Wied. *Kansas Working Papers in Linguistics.* Lawrence.

1998   Grammatical Evidence for Genetic Relationship and the *1241*

Macro-Siouan Hypothesis. Pp. 20–44 in Actes du 21ieme Colloque annuel de l'Association de Linguistique des Provinces Atlantiques. Halifax, N.S.: Mount St. Vincent University.

1999 Quapaw. In: Studies in Southeastern Languages. Heather Hardy and Janine Scancarelli, eds. Lincoln: University of Nebraska Press.

Rankin, Robert L., Richard T. Carter, and A. Wesley Jones
1998 Proto-Siouan Phonology and Morphology. In: Proceedings of the 1997 Mid-America Linguistics Conference. Tom Stroik, et al., eds. Columbia, Mo.: Linguisitcs Area Program, University of Missouri.

Rasporich, Anthony W., ed.
1975 Western Canada: Past and Present. Western Canada Studies Conference, Calgary, Alta., 1974. Calgary: McClelland and Stewart West.

Ravoux, Augustin
1843 Wakantanka ti ki canku [Road to Heaven]. Written in French by Augustin Ravoux, translated into Dakota by David Alexander and Oliver Faribault. Saint Paul, Minn.: Joseph Cretin's Press. (Reprinted: Pioneer Press, Saint Paul, Minn., 1897.)

1863 Wakantanka ti ki canku [Road to Heaven]. 2d ed. St. Paul, Minn.: Pioneer Office.

1876 Katolik Wocekiye Wowapi Kin. [Rev. and publ. by Bishop Martin Mary, O.S.B., Vicar Apostolic of Dakota.] [St. Paul, Minn.]

1890 Katolik Wocekiye Wowapi Kin. Rev. ed. by Bishop Martin Marty. Sioux Falls, S.Dak.: Brown and Saenger.

1890a Reminiscences, Memoirs and Lectures. St. Paul, Minn.: Brown, Treacy, and Co.

Ray, Arthur J.
1974 Indians in the Fur Trade: Their Role as Trappers, Hunters, and Middlemen in the Lands Southwest of Hudson's Bay, 1660–1870. Toronto: University of Toronto Press. (Reprinted, with a New Introduction, 1998.)

1978 History and Archaeology of the Northern Fur Trade. American Antiquity 43(1): 26–34.

1987 The Fur Trade in North America: An Overview from a Historical Geographical Perspective. Pp. 21–30 in Wild Furbearer Management and Conservation in North America. James A. Baker, Martyn E. Obbard and Bruce Mallock, eds. Ottawa: Ontario Trappers Association and Ontario Ministry of Natural Resources.

1993 Some Thoughts about the Reasons for Spatial Dynamism in the Early Fur Trade, 1580–1800. Pp. 113–123 in Three Hundred Prairie Years: Henry Kelsey's "Inland Country of Good Report." Henry Epp, ed. Regina: Canadian Plains Research Center, University of Regina.

1996 I Have Lived Here Since the World Began: An Illustrated History of Canada's Native People. Toronto: Lester Publishing and Key Porter Books.

Ray, Arthur J., and Donald B. Freeman
1978 "Give Us Good Measure": An Economic Analysis of Relations between the Indians and the Hudson's Bay Company Before 1763. Toronto: University of Toronto Press.

Ray, Cyrus N.
1929 A Differentiation of the Prehistoric Cultures of the Abilene Section. Texas Archeological and Paleontological Society. Bulletin 1:7–22. Abilene.

1930 Report on Some Recent Archeological Researches in the Abilene Section. Texas Archeological and Paleontological Society. Bulletin 2:45–58. Abilene.

Ray, Dorothy Jean, ed.
1972 Contemporary Indian Artists: Montana, Wyoming, Idaho. An Exhibition Organized by the Indian Arts and Crafts Board of the U.S. Department of the Interior. Selected by Myles Libhart and Ramon Gonyea. With an Essay by Ramon Gonyea. Rapid City, S.Dak.: The Tipi Shop.

Ray, Verne F.
1974 Ethnohistorical Analysis of Documents Relating to the Apache Indians of Texas. Apache Indians X. American Indian Ethnohistory: Indians of the Southwest. David Agee Horr, comp. and ed. New York and London: Garland Publishing.

Rayburn, John C., and Virginia Kemp Rayburn, eds.
1966 Century of Conflict, 1821–1913: Incidents in the Lives of William Neale and William A. Neale, Early Settlers in the South West. Waco, Tex.: Texian Press.

Raynolds, William Franklin
1868 Report on the Exploration of the Yellowstone River; communicated by the Secretary of War in Compliance with a Resolution of Senate, February 13, 1866. 40th Congress. 1st [i.e. 2d] Session. Senate Executive Document 77. Washington: U.S. Government Printing Office. (Microfilm: Research Publications, New Haven, Conn., 1967.)

Read, John Arthur Stanley
1978 A Sociolinguistic Study of Crow Language Maintenance. (Ph.D. Dissertation in Education, Curriculum and Instruction, University of New Mexico, Albuquerque. Photocopy: University Microfilms International, Ann Arbor, Mich., 1989.)

Reading, Robert S.
1960 Arrows over Texas. San Antonio, Tex.: The Naylor Company.

Real Alencaster, Joaquin 1806 see Alencaster, Joaquin Real 1806

Real Bird, C. Lanny
1997 "Ashaammaliaxxia," The Apsaalooke Clan System: A Foundation for Learning. (Ed.D. Thesis in Education, Montana State University, Bozeman.)

[Records of the Office of Secretary of War]
1822 [Sixth Infantry, Orders and Letters, 1817–1826.] (Records of the Office of the Secretary of War, Record Group 107, National Archives, Washington.)

Red, William S., ed.
1913 Extracts from the Diary of W.Y. Allen, 1838–1839. Southwestern Historical Quarterly 17(1):43–60. Austin, Tex.

Redbird, Duke
1980 We Are Metis: A Metis View of the Development of a Native Canadian People. Willowdale, Ont.: Ontario Metis & Non Status Indian Association. (Originally presented as the Author's M.A. Thesis in History, York University, Ottawa.)

Redden, James E., ed.
1991 Papers from the American Indian Languages Conference held at the University of California, Santa Cruz, July and August 1991. Occasional Papers on Linguistics 16. Carbondale: Department of Linguistics, Southern Illinois University.

Reeve, Frank D.
1946 The Apache Indians in Texas. Southwestern Historical Quarterly 50(2):189–219. Austin, Tex.

Reeve, Stuart A., Gary A. Wright, and Priscilla Mecham
1979 Archeological Investigations of the Lawrence Site

(48TE509): Grand Teton National Park, Wyoming. (Manuscript on file, Midwest Archeological Center, Lincoln, Nebr.)

Reeves, Brian O.K.

1969 The Southern Alberta Paleo-Cultural Paleo-Environmental Sequence. Pp. 6–46 in Post Pleistocene Man and His Environment on the Northern Plains. R.G. Forbis, L.B. Davis, O.A. Christensen, and G. Fedirchuk, eds. Calgary, Alta.: University of Calgary Archaeological Association.

1970 Culture Change in the Northern Plains: 1000 B.C.–A.D. 1000. (Ph.D. Dissertation in Archaeology, University of Calgary, Calgary, Alta.; Microfilm: *Canadian Theses on Microfilm* 6862. Published: see Reeves 1983.)

1970a Culture Dynamics in the Manitoba Grasslands 1000B.C.–700A.D. Pp.153–174 in Ten Thousand Years: Archaeology in Manitoba. Commemorating Manitoba's Centennial 1870–1970.Walter M. Hlady, ed. Winnipeg: Manitoba Archaeological Society.

1972 The Archaeology of Pass Creek Valley, Waterton Lakes National Parks. 2 vols. *Canada. National and Historic Parks Branch. Manuscript Report* 61. Ottawa.

1973 The Concept of an Altithermal Cultural Hiatus in Northern Plains Prehistory. *American Anthropologist* 75(5):1221–1253.

1977 Conservation Excavations-Fh Qg-2 Robb Vicinity. *Archaeological Survey of Alberta. Occasional Paper* 5. Edmonton.

1977a Historical Site Report, Dome Petroleum Limited, Empress-Red Deer Ethane Pipeline. (Report on file at The Provincial Museum of Alberta, Edmonton.)

1978 Head-Smashed-In: 5500 Years of Bison Jumping in the Alberta Plains. Pp. 151–174 in Bison Procurement and Utilization: A Symposium. Leslie B. Davis and Michael C. Wilson, eds. *Plains Anthropologist* 23(82, Pt.2); *Memoir* 14. Lincoln.

1980 Fractured Cherts from Pleistocene Fossiliferous Beds at Medicine Hat, Alberta. Pp. 83–98 in Early Native Americans. The Hague [and] New York: Mouton.

1983 Culture Change in the Northern Plains: 1000 B.C.–A.D. 1000. *Archaeological Survey of Alberta. Occasional Paper* 20. Edmonton. (Originally presented as the Author's Ph.D. Dissertation in Archaeology, 1970.)

1983a General Remarks on Native Subsistence Adaptations in the Great Plains: A Symposium. Pp. 115–118 in Man and Changing Environments in the Great Plains. Warren W. Caldwell, Charles B. Schultz, and Thompson M. Stout, eds. *Transactions of the Nebraska Academy of Sciences* 11(Special issue). Lincoln.

1983b Six Millenniums of Buffalo Kills. *Scientific American* 249(4):120–122, 124, 124d, 124h, 128–130, 135. New York.

1988 Notes From Napi's World: Avonlea in Perspective. Pp. 311–313 in Avonlea Yesterday and Today: Archaeology and Prehistory. Leslie B. Davis, ed. Saskatoon: Saskatchewan Archaeological Society.

1990 Communal Bison Hunters of the Northern Plains. Pp. 168–194 in Hunters of the Recent Past. Leslie B. Davis and Brian O.K. Reeves, eds. London and Boston: Unwin Hyman.

Reff, Daniel T.

1991 Disease, Depopulation, and Culture Change in Northwest-ern New Spain, 1518–1764. Salt Lake City: University of Utah Press.

Rego, Mary

1977 First Thunder of the Rocky Boys. *The Indian Historian* 10(1):37–41. San Francisco.

Reher, Charles A.

1970 Population Dynamics of the Glenrock *Bison bison* Population. Pp. 51–55 in The Glenrock Buffalo Jump, 48CO304. George C. Frison, ed. *Plains Anthropologist* 15(50); *Memoir* 7. Lincoln.

1971 A Survey of Ceramic Sites in Southeastern Wyoming. (M.A. Thesis in Anthropology, University of Wyoming, Laramie.)

1983 Analysis of Spatial Structure in Stone Circle Sites. Pp. 193–222 in From Microcosm to Macrocosm: Advances in Tipi Ring Investigation and Interpretation. Leslie B. Davis, ed. *Plains Anthropologist* 28(102, pt. 2), *Memoir* 19. Lincoln.

Reher, Charles A., and George C. Frison

1980 The Vore Site, 48CK302: A Stratified Buffalo Jump in the Wyoming Black Hills. *Plains Anthropologist* 25(88, Pt. 2), *Memoir* 16. Lincoln.

Reichard, Gladys A.

1950 Navaho Religion: A Study of Symbolism. 2 vols. *Bollingen Series* 18. New York: Pantheon Books.

Reichart, Milton

1979 Bourgmont's Route to Central Kansas: A Reexamination. *Kansas History* 2(2):96–120. Lawrence.

Reid, Kenneth C.

1977 *Psoralea esculenta* as a Prairie Resource: An Ethnographic Appraisal. *Plains Anthropologist* 22(78, Pt. 1):321–327.

1983 The Nebo Hill Phase: Late Archaic Prehistory in the Lower Missouri Valley. Pp. 11–39 in Archaic Hunters and Gatherers in the American Midwest. James A. Brown and James L. Phillips, eds. New York: Academic Press.

1984 Nebo Hill and Late Archaic Prehistory on the Southern Prairie Peninsula. *University of Kansas Publications in Anthropology* 15. Lawrence.

Reid, T.R.

1998 Scots to Yield Sioux Relic: Native Americans' Dignity, Pleas Move Glasgow Council. *The Washington Post*, November 20, 1998:A44. Washington.

Reiger, John F., ed.

1972 The Passing of the Great West: Selected Papers of George Bird Grinnell. New York: Wincester Press.

Remele, Larry, ed.

1986 Fort Totten: Military Post and Indian School, 1867–1959. Bismarck, N.Dak.: State Historical Society of North Dakota.

1987 Fort Buford and the Military Frontier on the Northern Plains, 1850–1900. Bismarck, N.Dak.: State Historical Society of North Dakota.

Remington, Frederic

1976 The Sun Dance of the Sioux, Written and Illustrated by Frederic Remington. *South Dakota History* 6(4):421–432. Pierre.

Renaud, Abel Etienne B.

1930 Prehistoric Cultures of the Cimarron Valley, Northeastern New Mexcio and Western Oklahoma. *Colorado Scientific Society Proceedings* 12(5):113–150. Denver.

1931 Archaeological Survey of Eastern Colorado: [First Report]. Denver: University of Denver, Department of Anthropology. *1243*

1932   Archaeological Survey of Eastern Colorado: Second Report, Season 1931. Denver: University of Denver, Department of Anthropology.

1933   Archaeological Survey of Eastern Colorado: Third Report, Season 1932. Denver: University of Denver, Department of Anthropology.

1942   Indian Stone Enclosures of Colorado and New Mexico. *University of Denver. Department of Anthropology. Archaeological Series* 2. Denver.

Renville, Joseph, Sr., and Thomas S. Williamson, trans.
1837   Wiconi owihanke wannin tanin kin: Dr. Watt's Second Catechism for Children in the Dakota Language. Written by Dr. Isaac Watts; [etc.]. Boston: Crocker and Brewster, for the American Board of Commissioners for Foreign Missions.

_____, trans.
1842   Wicoicage wowapi, qa odowan wakan, hebri iapi etanhan kagapi pejihuta wicaxta, psincinca, qa tamakoce, okagapi kin hene eepi: The Book of Genesis, and a Part of the Psalms, in the Dakota Language. Translated from the Original Hebrew, by the Missionaries of the American Board of Commissioners for Foreign Missions, [etc.]. Cincinnati, Ohio: Kendall and Barnard, Printers; for the American Board of Commissioners for Foreign Missions. (Reprinted in 1843, with the Gospels of Luke and John.)

Report on Indian Affairs 1824–1831 *see* ARCIA 1824–1848 (inclusive)

Reyhner, Jon, and Jeanne Eder
1989   A History of Indian Education. Billings, Mont.: Eastern Montana College.

Reynolds, John D.
1977   Preliminary Report of Archaeological Investigations at Site 14ML307, the Range Mound, Glen Elder, Kansas. *Kansas Anthropological Association Newsletter* 23(2 and 3):1–11. Lawrence.

1979   The Grasshopper Falls Phase of the Plains Woodland. *Kansas State Historical Society. Anthropological Series* 7. Topeka.

1981   The Grasshopper Falls Phase: A Newly Defined Plains Woodland Cultural-historical Integration Phase in the Central Plains. *The Missouri Archaeologist* 42:85–95. Columbia, Mo.

Reynolds, Karen Dewees, and William R. Johnson 1982 *see* Tyler, Ron, ed. 1982

Rhoades, Marjorie A.
1989   Plains Archaeology: Finding the Grey Literature. (M.S. Thesis, Colorado State University, Ft. Collins, Colorado.)

Rhodes, Richard A.
1977   French Cree—A Case of Borrowing. Pp. 6–25 in Actes du huitième congrès des algonquinistes. William Cowan, ed. Ottawa: Carleton University.

1982   Algonquian Trade Languages. Pp. 1–10 in Papers of the Thirteenth Algonquian Conference. William Cowan, ed. Ottawa: Carleton University.

1986   Métchif — A Second Look. Pp. 287–296 in Actes du dixseptième congrès des algonquinistes. William Cowan, ed. Ottawa: Carleton University.

Rhodes, Richard A., and Evelyn M. Todd 1981 *see* Handbook Vol. 6 (1981:52–66)

Rhodes, Willard
1952   Acculturation in North American Indian Music. Pp. 127–132 in Acculturation in the Americas. Sol Tex, ed. *Proceed-*

ings of the International Congress of Americansists 29. Chicago: University of Chicago Press.

Rice, Julian
1989   Words for the Sun Dance: Pete Catches, 1969. *Melus: The Journal of the Society for the Study of the Multi-Ethnic Literature of the United States* 16(1):59–76. Los Angeles; with the Department of English, University of Massachusetts, Amherst.

1991   Black Elk's Story: Distinguishing Its Lakota Purpose. Albuquerque: University of New Mexico Press.

1992   Deer Women and Elk Men: The Lakota Narratives of Ella Deloria. Albuquerque: University of New Mexico Press.

1992a   Narrative Styles in *Dakota Texts*. Pp. 276–292 in On the Translation of Native American Literatures. Brian Swann, ed. Washington: Smithsonian Institution Press.

1993   Ella Deloria's *Iron Hawk*. Albuquerque: University of New Mexico Press.

1994   Ella Deloria's *The Buffalo People*. Albuquerque: University of New Mexico Press.

Rice, Julie A.
2000   The Cartographic Heritage of the Lakota Sioux. (M.A. Thesis in Geography, Kent State University, Kent, Ohio.)

Rich, Edwin E., ed. 1939 *see* Robertson, Colin 1939

_____, ed. 1949 *see* Isham, James 1949

_____, ed. 1950 *see* Ogden, Peter Skene 1950

_____, ed.
1951–1952 Cumberland House Journals and Inland Journal, 1775–82. Edited by E.E. Rich, assisted by A.M. Johnson. With an Introduction by Richard Glover. 2 vols. Vol. 1, First Series, 1775–79; Vol. 2, Second Series, 1779–82. *Publications of the Hudson's Bay Record Society* 14–15. London: Hudson's Bay Record Society.

Richardson, Jane Hanks
1940   Law and Status among the Kiowa Indians. *Monographs of the American Ethnological Society* 1. New York: J.J. Augustin.

_____, et al.
1935   [Notes on Kiowa Ethnography, Santa Fe Laboratory of Anthropology Expedition 1935.] (Manuscripts (unnumbered) in Weston La Barre Collection, Ser. 1, Boxes 1–4, National Anthropological Archives, Smithsonian Institution, Washington.)

Richardson, Rupert N.
1929   The Comanche Reservation in Texas. *West Texas Historical Association Year Book* 5:43–65. Abilene.

1933   The Comanche Barrier to South Plains Settlement. Glendale, Calif.: Arthur H. Clark.

Richardson, Sir John
1851   Arctic Searching Expedition: A Journal of a Boat-Voyage Through Rupert's Land and the Arctic Sea, in Search of the Discovery of Ships Under Command of Sir John Franklin with an Appendix on the Physical Geography of North America. [Pp. 363–402 in Vol. II: Vocabularies of North America.] 2 vols. London: Longman, Brown, Green, and Longmans. (Reprinted: Harper, New York, 1954.)

Richardson, William P.
1842   [Letter to D.D. Mitchell. dated Great Nemaha Sub-agency, September 16, 1842, Transmitting "Annual Report of the Condition of the Indians."] (Microfilm M234, Roll 307, Frames 0452–0457, Great Nemaha Agency, 1837–1847, Let-

ters Received, 1824–1880, Records of the Bureau of Indian Affairs, Record Group 75, National Archives, Washington.)

1843 A Map Showing the Location of the Principal Improvements within the Great Nemahaw Sub-agency, A.D. 1843. (Microfilm M234, Roll 307, Frame 0618, Great Nemaha Agency, 1837–1847, Letters Received, 1824–1880, Records of the Bureau of Indian Affairs, Record Group 75, National Archives, Washington.)

——— 1843a *see* ARCIA 1824–1848

Ricketts, MacLinscott
1973 Review of: *The Sun Dance Religion, Power for the Powerless* by Joseph G. Jorgensen, [1972]. *Journal of the American Academy of Religion,* 41(2):256–259. Missoula.

Ricklis, Robert A.
1992 The Spread of a Late Prehistoric Bison Hunting Complex: Evidence from the South-Central Coastal Prairie of Texas. *Plains Anthropologist* 37(140):261–273.

Ricklis, Robert A., and Michael B. Collins
1994 Archaic and Late Human Ecology in the Middle Onion Creek Valley, Hays County, Texas. *University of Texas. Texas Archeological Research Laboratory. Studies in Archeology* 19. Austin.

Ridington, Robin
1987 Omaha Survival: A Vanishing Indian Tribe That Would Not Vanish. *The American Indian Quarterly* 11:37–49.

1987–1988 A Tree That Stands Burning: Reclaiming a Point of Views as From the Center. *Journal of the Steward Anthropological Society* 17(1–2):47–75. Urbana, Ill.

1990 Receiving the Mark of Honor: An Omaha Ritual of Renewal. Pp. 20–35 in Religion in Native North America. Christopher Vecsey, ed. Moscow, Idaho: University of Idaho Press.

Ridington, Robin, and Dennis Hastings
1997 Blessing for a Long Time: The Sacred Pole of the Omaha Tribe. Lincoln: University of Nebraska Press.

Riggs, Alfred L.
1881 Wicoie Wowapi. Wowapi Pehanpi kin. [The Word Book Wall Roll.] New York City: Published for the Dakota Mission by the American Tract Society.

Riggs, Mary Ann Clark
1852 An English and Dakota Vocabulary. New York: American Board of Commissioners of Foriegn Missions.

Riggs, Mary B.
1928 Early Days at Santee. Santee, Nebr.: Santee Normal Training School Press.

Riggs, Stephen R.
1841 Sioux: Journal of a Tour from Lac Qui Parle to the Missouri River. *Missionary Herald* 37:179–186. Boston.

1852 Grammar and Dictionary of the Dakota Language. *Smithsonian Contributions to Knowledge* 4. Washington. (Reprinted, rev. ed. by James Owen Dorsey; see Riggs 1890.)

1855 Education among the Dakotas. Pp. 695–697 in Vol. 5 of Historical and Statistical Information Respecting the History, Conditions and Prospects of the Indian Tribes of the United States. Henry Rowe Schoolcraft, comp. and ed. 6 vols. Philadelphia: Lippincott, Grambo, 1851–1857.

1864 Dakota wiwicawangapi kin. Dakota Catechism. New York: The American Tract Society. (Reprinted in 1882.)

———, ed.
1865 History of the Dakotas: James W. Lynd's Manuscripts. *Minnesota Historical Collections [for] 1864,* Vol. 2(Pt. 2):143–149. St. Paul. (Reprinted, 2d ed., in 1881.)

———, ed.
1865a The Religion of the Dakotas: Chapter Six of Mr. Lynd's Manuscript. *Minnesota Historical Collections [for] 1864,* Vol. 2(Pt. 2):149–174. St. Paul. (Reprinted, 2d ed., in 1881.)

1869 Taĥ-koo Wah-kaṅ; or, The Gospel among the Dakotas. Boston: Congregational Sunday-School and Publishing Society.

1872 The Dakota Language. *Collections of the Minnesota Historical Society* 1:89–107. St. Paul. (Originally publ. under title: Address of S.R. Riggs in Annals of the *[Minnesota Historical] Society,* 1851; reprinted in 1902.)

1877 Jeremiah, Ezekiel, Daniel, qa wicásta wokcan toktokeca, Dakota iapi en = Jeremiah, Ezekiel, Daniel, and the Minor Prophets in the Dakota Language. Translated from the Hebrew by S.R. Riggs. New York: American Bible Society. (Title on cover: Wicásta Wokcan.)

1880 The Dakota Mission. *Minnesota Historical Society Collections* 3(1):115–128. St. Paul.

1881 Panka Oyate Qa Maste Makoce Kin. *Iapi Oaye* 10(2):10. Greenwood, Dak.Terr. [S.Dak.]: Dakota Mission.

1887 Mary and I: Forty Years with the Sioux. Enl. ed. Boston: Congregational Sunday-School and Publishing Society.

1889 Woonspe Itakihna: Percept upon Precept. Translated into the Dakota Language by Rev. John B. Renville. New ed. New York: American Tract Society.

1890 A Dakota-English Dictionary. James Owen Dorsey, ed. *Contributions to North American Ethnology* 7. Washington: Smithsonian Institution. (Reprinted: Ross and Haines, Minneapolis, 1968.)

1893 Dakota Grammar, Texts and Ethnography. James Owen Dorsey, ed. *Contributions to North American Ethnology* 9. Washington: U.S. Geographical and Geological Survey of the Rocky Mountain Region. (Reprinted: AMS Press, New York, 1976.)

1918 Dakota Portraits. Willoughby M. Babcock, ed. *Minnesota Historical Society Bulletin* 2(6):481–568. St. Paul.

Riggs, Thomas Lawrence
1997 Sunset to Sunset: A Lifetime with My Brothers, the Dakotas. New Introduction by Paula M. Nelson. Foreword by Theodore F. Riggs. Pierre, S.Dak.: South Dakota Historical Society Press. (Originally publ. in 1958.)

Riggs, Venda
1949 Alternate Phonemic Analyses of Comanche. *International Journal of American Linguistics* 15(4):229–231. Chicago.

Riley, Carroll L.
1987 The Frontier People: The Greater Southwest in the Protohistoric Period. Albuquerque: University of New Mexico Press.

Riley, Paul D.
1973 The Battle of Massacre Canyon. *Nebraska History* 54(2): 221–250. Lincoln.

Riney, Scott
1999 The Rapid City Indian School, 1898–1933. Norman: University of Oklahoma Press.

Risch, Barbara
2000 A Grammar of Time: Lakota Winter Counts, 1700–1900. *American Indian Culture and Research Journal* 24(2):23–48. Los Angeles.

Ritchie, J.C.
1983   Paleoecology of the Central and Northern Parts of the Glacial Lake Agassiz Basin. Pp. 157–170 in Glacial Lake Agassiz. J.T. Teller and L. Clayton, eds. *Geological Association of Canada. Special Paper* 26. St. Johns, N.S.

Ritzenthaler, Robert E. 1978 *see* Handbook Vol. 15 (1978:743–759)

Roaming Scout
1907   [Skiri Pawnee Texts; trans. and ed. by Douglas R. Parks, 1995.] (Manuscripts in D.R. Parks's possession.)

Robarchek, Clayton A.
1994   Plains Warfare and the Anthropology of War. Pp. 307–316 in Skeletal Biology in the Great Plains: Migration, Warfare, Health, and Subsistence. Douglas W. Owsley and Richard L. Jantz, eds. Washington: Smithsonian Institution Press.

Robert H. Lowie Museum of Anthropology *see* Lowie Museum (Robert H. Lowie Museum of Anthropology)

Roberts, Frank H.H., Jr.
1935   A Folsom Complex: Preliminary Report on Investigations at the Lindenmeier Site in Northern Colorado. *Smithsonian Miscellaneous Collections* 94(4). Washington: Smithsonian Institution; U.S. Government Printing Office.

———
1936   Additional Information on the Folsom Complex: Report on the Second Season's Investigations at the Lindenmeier Site in Northern Colorado. *Smithsonian Miscellaneous Collections* 95(10). Washington: Smithsonian Institution; U.S. Government Printing Office.

Roberts, John M.
1964   The Self Management of Cultures. Pp. 433–454 in Explorations in Cultural Anthropology. Ward Goodenough, ed. New York: McGraw-Hill.

Roberts, Robert B.
1988   Encyclopedia of Historic Forts: The Military, Pioneer, and Trading Posts of the United States. New York: Macmillan.

Roberts, William O.
1943   Dakota Indians: Successful Agriculture within the Reservation Framework. *Applied Anthropology* 2(3):37–44. Boston.

Robertson, Colin
1939   Colin Robertson's Correspondence Book, September 1817 to September 1822. Edwin E. Rich, ed. London: The Champlain Society. (Reprinted: Kraus Reprint, Nendeln, Liechtenstein, 1963.)

Robertson, Paul M.
1995   The Power of the Land: Identity, Ethnicity, and Class among the Oglala Lakota. (Ph.D. Dissertation in Cultural Anthropology, Union Institute, Cincinnati, Ohio; Reprinted: UMI, Ann Arbor, Mich., 2000.)

Robertson, Valerie
1992   Plains Ledger Art: The Demonstration of a Way of Life Through the Nineteenth Century Pictorial Account of an Unknown Assiniboine Artist. *Prairie Forum* 17(2). Regina, Sask.: Canadian Plains Research Center, University of Regina.

———
1993   Reclaiming History: Ledger Drawings by the Assiniboine Artist Hoṅgeeȳesa. With Essays by Valerie Robertson and Charlotte Nahbixie; Captions by John Haywahe. Calgary, Alta.: Glenbow-Alberta Institute.

Robin, Abbé
1807   Voyages dans l'intérieur de la Louisiane: de la Floride occidentale, et dans les isles de la Martinique et de Saint-Dominque, pendant les années 1802, 1803, 1804, 1805 et 1806; contenant de nouvelles observations sur l'historie naturelle, la géographie, les moeurs, l'agriculture, le commerce, l'industrie et les maladies de ces Contrées paticuliérement sur la fièvre jaune, et les moyens de la prévenir en outre, contenant ce qui s'est passé de plus intéressant, relativement à l'établissement des Anglo-Américains à la Louisiane; suivis de la flore louisianaise; avec une carte nouvelle, gravée en taille-douce. Paris: F. Buisson.

Robinett, Florence M.
1955   Hidatsa I: Morphophonemics; II: Affixes; III: Stems and Themes. *International Journal of American Linguistics* 21(1):1–7, (2):160–177, (3):210–216. Chicago. (Reprinted: Kraus Reprint, New York, 1965.)

Robins, Robert H.
1962   The Third Person Pronominal Prefix in Yurok. *International Journal of American Linguistics* 28(1):14–18. Chicago.

Robinson, Doane
1904   A History of the Dakota or Sioux Indians. *South Dakota Historical Society Collections* 2. Pierre. (Reprinted: Ross and Haines, Minneapolis, 1967.)

———
1913–1914   La Vérendrye's Farthest West. Pp. 146–150 in *Proceeding of the 61st Annual Meeting of the Wisconsin Historical Society*. Madison.

Robinson, Henry M.
1879   The Great Fur Land; or, Sketches of Life in the Hudson's Bay Territory. With numerous illustrations from designs by Charles Gasche. New York: G.P. Putnam's Sons. (Reprinted: Coles Pub., Toronto, 1972.)

Robinson, Lila Wistrand 1972 *see* Wistrand-Robinson, Lila 1972

Robinson, Lila Wistrand, and James Armagost
1990   Comanche Dictionary and Grammar. *Summer Institute of Linguistics and the University of Texas at Arlington. Publications in Linguistics* 92. Dallas, Tex.: Summer Institute of Linguistics.

Rodell, Roland L.
1991   The Diamond Bluff Site Complex and Cahokia Influence in the Red Wing Locality. Pp. 253–280 in New Perspectives on Cahokia: Views from the Periphery. James B. Stoltman, ed. *Monographs in World Archaeology* 2. Madison, Wis.: Prehistory Press.

Rodnick, David
1937   Political Structure and Status among the Assiniboine Indians. *American Anthropologist,* n.s. 39(4, Pt. 1):408–416.

———
1938   The Fort Belknap Assiniboine of Montana: A Study in Culture Change. New Haven, Conn.: [privately printed]. (Originally presented as the Author's Ph.D. Dissertation in Anthropology, University of Pennsylvania, Philadelphia, 1936. Reprinted: AMS Press, New York, 1978.)

Roe, Frank Gilbert
1951   The North American Buffalo: A Critical Study of the Species in Its Wild State. Toronto: University of Toronto Press. (Reprinted, 2d ed. 1970.)

Rogles, David, Lori A. Stanley, and Louanna Furbee
1989   Lack of Accommodation in a Dying Language. (Paper presented at the Annual Meeting of the American Anthropological Association for 1989.)

Rohn, Arthur H., C.M. Stein, and Gerold Glover
1977   Wolf Creek Archaeology, Coffey County, Kansas. (Report on file, Wichita State University Archaeology Laboratory, Wichita, Kans.)

Rohrbaugh, Charles L., ed.
1974   Kaw Reservoir, the Central Section. *University of Oklahoma. River Basin Survey. Archaeological Site Reports* 27. Norman.

1982   An Hypothesis for the Origin of the Kichai. Pp. 51–63 in Pathways to Plains Prehistory: Anthropological Perspectives of Plains Natives and Their Pasts; Papers in Honor of Robert E. Bell. Don G. Wyckoff and Jack L. Hofman, eds. *Oklahoma Anthropological Society. Memoir* 3; *The Cross Timbers Heritage Association Contributions* 1. Duncan, Okla.

Roll, Tom E.
1979   Additional Archaeological Assessment on the Fisher River Site (24LN10), Northwestern Montana. *Archaeology in Montana* 20(2):79–106. Billings, [etc.].

1988   Focus on a Phase: Expanded Geographical Distribution and Resultant Taxonomic Implications for Avonlea. Pp. 237–250 in Avonlea Yesterday and Today: Archaeology and Prehistory. Leslie B. Davis, ed. Saskatoon: Saskatchewan Archaeological Society.

Rollings, Willard H.
1992   The Osage: An Ethnohistorical Study of Hegemony on the Prairie-Plains. Columbia and London: University of Missouri Press.

Rollins, Philip Ashton, ed.
1935   The Discovery of the Oregon Trail: Robert Stuart's Narratives. New York: Charles Scribner's Sons.

Ronda, James P.
1984   Lewis and Clark among the Indians. Lincoln: University of Nebraska Press. (Reprinted in 1988.)

1990   Astoria and Empire. Lincoln: University of Nebraska Press.

1990a   Westering Captains: Essays on the Lewis and Clark Expedition; Editorial Introduction by Robert E. Lange. Portland, Oreg.: Lewis and Clark Trail Heritage Foundation.

1997   Exploring the American West in the Age of Jefferson. Pp. 9–7 in North American Exploration, Vol. 3: A Continent Comprehended. John Logan Allen, ed. 3 vols. Lincoln: University of Nebraska Press.

Rondeau, Clovis, and Adrien Chabot
1970   Histoire de Willow-Bunch, Saskatchewan, 1870–1979. 2d ed. 2 vols. in 1. Vol. 1: La montagne de Bois, 1870–1920, par C. Rondeau; Vol. 2: Willow Bunch, 1920–1970, par A. Chabot. Gravelbourg, Sask.: [privately printed.] (Originally publ. in 1923.)

Rood, David S.
1971   Wichita: An Unusual Phonology System. (Mimeograph.) *Colorado University Research in Linguistics* 1:R1–R24. Boulder.

1971a   Agent and Object in Wichita. *Lingua: International Review of General Linguistics* 28(1–2):100–107. Amsterdam, The Netherlands.

1973   Swadesh's Keres-Caddo Comparison. *International Journal of American Linguistics* 39(3):189–190. Chicago.

1975   Implications of Wichita Phonology. *Language: Journal of the Linguistic Society of America* 51(2):315–337. Baltimore.

1975a   Wichita Verb Structure: Inflectional Categories. Pp. 121–134 in Studies in Southeastern Indian Languages. James M. Crawford, ed. Athens: University of Georgia Press.

1976   Wichita Grammar. New York: Garland Publishing. (Originally presented as the Author's Ph.D. Dissertation in Linguistics under title: Wichita Grammar, a Generative Semantic Sketch; University of California, Berkeley, 1969.)

1977   Wichita Texts. Pp. 91–128 in Caddoan Texts. Douglas R.

Parks, ed. *International Journal of American Linguistics. Native American Texts Series* 2(1). Chicago: The University of Chicago Press.

1979   Siouan. Pp. 236–298 in The Languages of Native America. Lyle Campbell and Marianne Mithun, eds. Austin: University of Texas Press.

1983   A Preliminary Consideration of Proto-Siouan Ablaut. Pp. 24–28 in Proceedings of the Second Siouan Languages Conference, 1982. Mary C. Marino, ed. *Na'pāo: A Saskatchewan Anthropology Journal* 13(October): Special Issue. Saskatoon.

1989   Code Switching in a Wichita Text. Pp. 101–113 in Papers from the Twenty-third Annual Mid-America Linguistics Conference, 1988. John A. Dunn, comp. Norman: Department of Modern Languages, Literatures, and Linguistics, University of Oklahoma.

Root, Matthew J.
1981   The Milbourne Site: Late Archaic Settlement in the Southern Flint Hills of Kansas. (M.A. Thesis in Anthropology, University of Kansas, Lawrence.)

Roper, Donna C., ed.
1989   Protohistoric Pawnee Hunting in the Nebraska Sand Hills. Grand Island, Nebr.: United States Bureau of Reclamation.

1990   Artifact Assemblage Composition and the Hunting Camp Interpretation of High Plains Upper Republican Sites. *Southwestern Lore* 56(4):1–19. Boulder, Colo.

1992   Documentary Evidence for Changes in Protohistoric and Early Historic Pawnee Hunting Practices. *Plains Anthropologist* 37(141):353–366.

Roscoe, Will
1990   "That Is My Road": The Life and Times of a Crow Berdache. *Montana: The Magazine of Western History* 40(1):46–55. Helena.

Rosenvall, Lynn A., and Sara M. Evans, eds.
1987   Essays on the Historical Geography of the Canadian West: Regional Perspectives on the Settlement Process. Calgary, Alta.: Department of Geography, University of Calgary.

Rosier, Paul
1999   "The Old System Is No Success": The Blackfeet Nation's Decision to Adopt the Indian Reorganization Act of 1934. *American Indian Culture and Research Journal* 23(1):1–37. Los Angeles.

Ross, Alexander
1849   Adventures of the First Settlers on the Oregon or Columbia River; Being a Narrative of the Expedition Fitted Out by John Jacob Astor, to Establish the "Pacific Fur Company", with an Account of Some of the Indian Tribes of the Coast of the Pacific. London: Smith, Elder and Co. (Reprinted: Citadel Press, New York, 1969.)

1856   The Red River Settlement: Its Rise, Progress and Present State. With Some Account of the Native Races and Its General History to the Present Day. London: Smith, Elder. (Reprinted: Ross and Haines, Minneapolis, 1957; also, Hurtig Publishing, Edmonton, Alta., 1972; and, C.E. Tuttle, Rutland, Vt., 1972.)

_____ 1957, 1972 *see* 1856 (reprint info.)

Ross, John W.
1998   LBHC Graduates Given Advice for " The Real World." *Big Horn County News,* June 10, 1998:10. Hardin, Mont.

Ross, Marvin C,. ed.
1968   The West of Alfred Jacob Miller (1837), From the Notes and Water Colors in the Walters Art Gallery. With an

Account of the Artist by Marvin C. Ross. Rev. and enl. ed. Norman: University of Oklahoma Press. (Originally publ. under title: Sketches and Notes, Illustrating an Expedition to the Rocky Mountians in 1837, by Alfred J. Miller. Conducted by William Drummond Stewart, Walters Art Gallery, Baltimore, Md. 1899.)

Ross, Norman A., ed.
1973   Index to the Decisions of the Indian Claims Commission. New York: Clearwater Press.

Rossignol, M.
1938   Cross-cousin Marriage among the Saskatchewan Cree. *Primitive Man* 11(1–2):26–28. Washington: The Catholic University of America.

1938a   Religion of the Saskatchewan and Western Manitoba Cree. *Primitive Man* 11(3–4):67–71. Washington: The Catholic University of America.

1939   Property Concepts among the Cree of the Rocks. *Primitive Man* 12(3):61–70. Washington: The Catholic University of America.

Roth, H. Ling
1908   Moccasins and Their Quill Work. *The Journal of the Royal Anthropological Institute of Great Britain and Ireland* 38, n.s. 11:47–57. London.

1923   American Quillwork: A Possible Clue to Its Origin. *Man: A Monthly Record of Anthropological Science* 23(72):113–116. London.

Rowand, John
1830   [Letter to George Simpson, January 8, 1830.] (Manuscript No. D53 folios 430–433, George Simpson Inward Correspondence, 1830–1844, Hudson's Bay Company Archives, Provincial Archives of Manitoba, Winnipeg.)

Rowlison, Don
1977   A Preliminary Report of the 1976 Big Hill Reservoir Project. *Newsletter of the Kansas Anthropological Association* 22(6):1–12. Topeka.

Royal Commission on Aboriginal Peoples 1996 *see* Canada. Royal Commission on Aboriginal Peoples 1996

Royce, Charles C., comp.
1899   Indian Land Cessions in the United States. Pp. 521–997 in *18th Annual Report of the Bureau of American Ethnology for 1896–'97*. Washington: Smithsonian Institution; U.S. Government Printing Office. (Reprinted: AMS Press, New York, 1973.)

Ruíz, José Francisco 1840 *see* Lamar, Mirabau Buonaparte 1921–1927 (Vol. 4, Pt. 1)

1972   Report on the Indian Tribes of Texas in 1828. (Facsimile.) Edited with an Introduction by John C. Ewers. Translated from the Spanish by Georgette Dorn. *Western Americana Series* 5. New Haven, Conn.: Yale University Library.

Ruby, Jay
1981   Photographs of the Piegan by Roland Reed (Photo Essay). Editor's Introduction: Jay Ruby. *Studies in Visual Communication* 7(1):48–62. Philadelphia.

Ruby, William K.
1955   The Oglala Sioux: Warriors in Transition. New York: Vantage Press.

Ruebelmann, George N.
1983   An Overview of the Archaeology and Prehistory of the Lewistown BLM District, Montana. *Archaeology in Montana* 24(3):1–165. Billings, [etc.].

1988   The Henry Smith Site: An Avonlea Bison Procurement and Ceremonial Complex in Northern Montana. Pp. 191–202 in Avonlea Yesterday and Today: Archaeology and Prehistory. Leslie B. Davis, ed. Saskatoon: Saskatchewan Archaeological Society.

Ruggles, Mary Jo
1995   Songs of the Peoples of the North American Plains Pp. 27–30 in Remaining Ourselves: Music and Tribal Memory. Dayna Bowker Lee, ed. Oklahoma City: State Arts Council of Oklahoma.

Ruis, José Francisco *see* Ruiz, José Francisco

Rundle, Robert Terrill
1977   The Rundle Journals, 1840–1848. Introduction and Notes by Gerald M. Hutchinson; Hugh A. Dempsey, ed. *Historical Society of Alberta* 1. Calgary: Alberta Records Publications Board, Historical Society of Alberta.

Rupp, Isaac Daniel
1846   Early History of Western Pennsylvania and of the West....from MDCCLIV to MDCCCXXXIII. Pittsburgh, Pa.: D.W. Kaufman.

Ruppé, Reynold J.
1956   Archaeological Investigations of the Mill Creek Culture of Northwestern Iowa. Pp. 335–339 in *American Philosophical Society Yearbook for 1955*. Philadelphia.

Ruppert, Michael E.
1974   Analysis of the Vertebrate Faunal Remains from the King Hill Site, 23BN1. (M.A. Thesis in Anthropology, University of Nebraska, Lincoln.)

Rusco, Mary Kiehl
1960   The Whiterock Aspect. *University of Nebraska. Laboratory of Anthropology. Notebook* 4. Lincoln.

Rush Fair (Oklahoma)
1927   [Premium Booklet.] (Anadarko Agency, Central Files 1907–1939, Decimal File .047, No. 8105–1927, Records of the Bureau of Indian Affairs, Record Group 75, National Archives, Washington.)

1929   [Premium Booklet.] (Anadarko Agency, Central Files 1907–1939, Decimal File .047, No. 8105–1929, Records of the Bureau of Indian Affairs, Record Group 75, National Archives, Washington.)

Rushing, W. Jackson
1992   Marketing the Affinity of the Primitive and the Modern: René d'Harnoncourt and "Indian Art of the United States". Pp. 191–236 in The Early Years of Native American Art History: The Politics of Scholarship and Collecting. Janet Catherine Berlo, ed. Seattle: University of Washington Press.

1992a   Critical Issues in Recent Native American Art. *Art Journal* 51(3):6–14. New York.

1995   Native American Art and the New York Avant-Garde: A History of Cultural Primitivism. Austin: University of Texas Press.

Russell, Dale R.
1991   Eighteenth-Century Western Cree and Their Neighbours. *Canadian Museum of Civilization. Mercury Series. Archaeological Survey Paper* 143. Ottawa.

Russell, Don
1970   The Wild West: A History of Wild West Shows. Fort Worth, Tex.: Amon Carter Museum of Western Art.

Russell, Frank
[1898]   [Jicarilla Apache Vocabulary. Vocabulary listed according to categories in Powell's printed outline with added information on culture, customs, and religion.] (Manuscript No. 1302-a, Apache Catalog, National Anthropological Archives, Smithsonian Institution, Washington.)

Russell, Osborne
1914   Journal of a Trapper; or, Nine Years in the Rocky Mountains, 1834–1843. Being a General Description of the Country, Climate, Rivers, Lakes, Mountains, etc., and a View of the Life Led by a Hunter in Those Regions. Edited from the Original Manuscript by L.A. York. Boise, Idaho: Syms-York. (2d ed. repr. in 1921.)

1955   Journal of a Trapper. Edited from the Original Manuscript in the William Robertson Coe Collection of Western Americana in the Yale University Library. With a Biography of Osborne Russell and Maps of His Travels While a Trapper in the Rocky Mountains, by Aubrey L. Haines. Portland, Oreg.: Oregon Historical Society. (Reprinted: University of Nebraska Press, Lincoln, 1965; also, MJF Books, New York, 1996.)

Ruxton, George F.
1848   Adventures in Mexico and the Rocky Mountains. [1st American ed.] New York: Harper and Brothers. (Originally publ.: John Murray, London, 1847. Several reprints, incl.: Lost Cause Press, Louisville, Ky., 1960; Rio Grande Press, Glorieta, N.Mex. 1973.)

SA-C = Superintendents' Annual Narrative and Statistical Reports
1913–1923 Superintendents' Annual Narrative and Statistical Reports from Field Jurisdictions of the Bureau of Indian Affairs: Cantonment. (Microfilm M1011, Roll 8, Records of the Bureau of Indian Affairs, Record Group 75, National Archives, Washington.)

SA-CA = Superintendents' Annual Narrative and Statistical Reports
1916–1929 Superintendents' Annual Narrative and Statistical Reports from Field Jurisdictions of the Bureau of Indian Affairs: Cheyenne-Arapaho Agency. (Microfilm M1011, Rolls 14–15, Records of the Bureau of Indian Affairs, Record Group 75, National Archives, Washington.)

Sabo, George, III
1989   Enemies and Allies: The Quapaw and Their Neighbors. (Paper presented at the Annual Meeting of the American Society for Ethnohistory, Nov. 1989.)

1991   Inconsistent Kin: French-Quapaw Relations at Arkansas Post. Pp. 105–130 in Arkansas Before the Americans. Hester A. Davis, ed. Arkansas Archeological Survey Research Series 40. Fayetteville.

Sage, Rufus B.
1846   Scenes in the Rocky Mountains, and in Oregon, California, New Mexico, Texas, and the Grand Prairies; or, Notes by the Way, during an Excursion of Three Years, with a Description of the Countries Passed Through, Including Their Geography, Geology, Resources, Present Condition, and the Different Nations Inhabiting Them. Philadelphia: Carey and Hart.

Saint Ann's Centennial
1985   100 Years of Faith. Rolla, N.Dak.: Star Printing.

St. Clair, Harry H.
1909   Shoshone and Comanche Tales. Robert Lowie, ed. Journal of American Folk-lore 22(85):265–282.

St. Clair, Lynn, and Herman St. Clair
1977   Shoshone Indian Religion. American Indian News 1(2–3, 5).

St. John, Percy B.
1844   The Death Blanket. Chamber's Edinburgh Journal, n.s. 1(24):373–376. Edinburgh.

St-Onge, Nicole J.M.
1985   The Dissolution of a Métis Community: Pointe à Grouette [Ste. Agathe, Man.], 1860–1885. Studies in Political Economy 18(Autumn):149–172. Ottawa.

1989   Race, Class, and Marginality in a Manitoba Settlement, 1850–1950. Pp. 116–132 in Race, Class, Gender: Bonds and Barriers. Jesse Vorst, ed. Socialist Studies/Etudes Socialistes 5. Toronto.

1992   Variations in Red River: The Traders and Freemen Métis of Saint Laurent, Manitoba. Canadian Ethnic Studies 14(2):1–21. Calgary, Alta.

Salvatori, Giorgio
1991   Il Cerchio Sacro dei Sioux. [Libro e videocassetta Si-Tanka Wokiksuye.] Firenze [Italy]: Vallecchi Editore.

Salzano, Francisco M.
1972   Genetic Aspects of the Demography of American Indians and Eskimos. Pp. 234–251 in The Structure of Human Populations. Geoffery A. Harrison and Anthony J. Boyce, eds. Oxford: Clarendon Press.

Salzmann, Zdeněk
1950   An Arapaho Version of the Star Husband Tale. Hoosier Folklore 9(2):50–58. Indianapolis, Ind.

1951   Contrastive Field Experience with Language and Values of the Arapaho. International Journal of American Linguistics 17(2):98–101. Chicago.

1956   Arapaho I: Phonology. International Journal of American Linguistics 22(1):49–56. Chicago.

1956a   Arapaho II: Texts. International Journal of American Linguistics 22(2):151–158. Chicago.

1956b   Arapaho III: Additional Texts. International Journal of American Linguistics 22(4):266–272. Chicago.

1957   Arapaho Tales III. Midwest Folklore 7: 27–37. Bloomington, Ind.

1959   Arapaho Kinship Terms and Two Related Ethnolinguistic Observations. Anthropological Linguistics 1(9):6–10. Bloomington, Ind.

1960   Two Brief Contributions toward Arapaho Linguistic History. Anthropological Linguistics 2(7):39–48. Bloomington, Ind.

1961   Arapaho IV: Interphonemic Specification. International Journal of American Linguistics 27(2):151–155.Chicago.

1961a   Concerning the Assumed L-sound in Arapaho. Plains Anthropologist 6(14):270–271.

1963   A Sketch of Arapaho Grammar. (Ph.D. Dissertation in Linguistics, Indiana University, Bloomington.)

1965   Arapaho V: Noun. International Journal of American Linguistics 31(1):34–49. Chicago.

1965a   Arapaho VI: Noun. International Journal of American Linguistics 31(2):136–151. Chicago.

1967   Arapaho VII: Verb. International Journal of American Linguistics 33(8):209–223. Chicago.

1967a   Some Aspects of Arapaho Morphology. Pp. 128–134 in Contributions to Anthropology: Linguistics I (Algonquian). National Museum of Canada. Bulletin 214; Anthropological Series 78. Ottawa.

1967b   On the Inflection of Transitive Animate Verbs in Arapaho. Pp. 135–139 in Contributions to Anthropology: Linguistics I (Algonquian). National Museum of Canada. Bulletin 214; Anthropological Series 78. Ottawa.

1969   Salvage Phonology of Gros Ventre (Atsina). International Journal of American Linguistics 35(4):307–314. Chicago. *1249*

1980   Arapaho Stories. Anchorage, Alaska: National Bilingual Materials Development Center.

_____, comp.
1983   Dictionary of Contemporary Arapaho Usage. *Arapaho Language and Culture Instructional Materials Series* 4. William J. C'Hair, gen. ed. Wind River Reservation, Ethete, Wyo.

_____
1987   [Arapaho Songs, Transcribed by Bruno Nettl.] (Manuscript in Z. Salzmann's possession.)

_____, comp.
1988   The Arapaho Indians: A Research Guide and Bibliography. *Bibliographies and Indexes in Anthropology* 4. New York: Greenwood Press.

_____, comp.
1994   Arapaho Bibliographic Addenda. *Plains Anthropologist* 39(150):465–473.

Samarin, William J.
1987   Demythologizing Plains Indian Sign Language History. *International Journal of American Linguistics* 53(1):65–73. Chicago.

Samek, Hana
1987   The Blackfoot Confederacy, 1880–1920: A Comparative Study of Canadian and U.S. Indian Policy. Albuquerque: University of New Mexico Press.

Sample, James
1900   [Report to M.L. Bridgeman, dated August 1, 1900.] (Manuscript in Box 32, Fort Belknap Records, Records of the Bureau of Indian Affairs, Record Group 75, National Archives—Pacific Northwest Region, Seattle, Wash.)

Sánchez, José María
1926   A Trip to Texas in 1828. Carlos E. Castañeda, trans. *Southwestern Historical Quarterly* 29(4):249–288. Austin, Tex.

Sánchez, Joseph P.
1997   Explorers, Traders, and Slavers: Forging the Old Spanish Trail, 1678–1850. Salt Lake City: University of Utah Press.

Sanderson, Sol
1984   Preparations for Indian Government in Saskatchewan. Pp. 152–158 in Pathways to Self-Determination: Canadian Indians and the Canadian State. Leroy Little Bear, Menno Boldt, and J. Anthony Long, eds. Toronto: University of Toronto Press.

Sanderville, Richard
1934   [The Religion of the Blackfeet Indians.] (Manuscript.)

Sandoz, Mari
1942   Crazy Horse: Strange Man of the Oglalas. New York: Alfred A. Knopf. (Reprinted, with an Introduction by Stephen B. Oates: University of Nebraska Press, Lincoln, 1992.)

_____
1953   Cheyenne Autumn. New York: McGraw-Hill. (Reprinted: University of Nebraska Press, Lincoln, 1992.)

_____
1954   The Buffalo Hunters: The Story of the Hide Men. New York: Hastings House. (Reprinted: University of Nebraska Press, Lincoln, 1978.)

_____
1961   These Were the Sioux. New York: Hastings House. (Reprinted: Dell Publishing, New York, 1967.)

Sanford, Margaret S.
1971   Present Day Death Practices and Eschatology of the Kiowa Apache. *University of Oklahoma. Papers in Anthropology* 12(2):81–134. Norman. (Originally presented as the Author's M.A. Thesis in Anthropology, The Catholic University of America, Washington, 1966.)

1971a   Pan-Indianism, Acculturation and the American Ideal. *Plains Anthropologist* 16(53):222–227.

Sangiacomo, Michael
1993   New Agers Abuse Sun Dance Ceremony, Say Native Protesters. *News from Indian Country* 7(14):9. Hayward, Wis.

Sansom-Flood, Renée
1986   Lessons from Chouteau Creek: Yankton Memories of Dakota Territorial Intrigue. *Augustana College. Center for Western Studies. Dakota Series* 1. Sioux Falls, S.Dak.

1995   Lost Bird of Wounded Knee: Spirit of the Lakota. New York: Scribner. (Reprinted: Da Capo Press, New York, 1998.)

Sansom-Flood, Renée, and Shirley A. Bernie
1985   Remember Your Relatives: Yankton Sioux Images, 1851–1904. Vol. 1. Leonard R. Bruguier, ed. Introduction by Herbert T. Hoover. Marty, S.Dak.: Marty Indian School.

Santos, Richard G.
1968   Santa Ana's Campaign Against Texas, 1835–1836. Waco, Tex.: Texian Press.

Sapir, Edward
1916   Time Perspective in Aboriginal Culture: A Study in Method. *Geological Survey of Canada. Department of Mines. Memoir* 90; *Anthropological Series* 13. Ottawa.

_____
1920   The Hokan and Coahuiltecan Languages. *International Journal of American Linguistics* 1(4):280–290. Chicago.

_____
1921   A Bird's Eye View of American Languages North of Mexico. *Science*, n.s. 54(1400):408. Washington.

_____
1924   Personal Names among the Sarcee Indians. *American Anthropologist*, n.s. 26(1):108–119.

_____
1925   The Hokan Affinity of Subtiaba in Nicaragua. *American Anthropologist*, n.s. 27(3):402–435, (4):491–527.

_____
1929   Central and North American Languages. Pp. 138–141 in Vol. 5 of Encyclopaedia Britannica, 14th ed. London and New York: Encyclopaedia Britannica Company. (Reprinted: Pp. 169–178 in Selected Writings of Edward Sapir in Language, Culture, and Personality. David G. Mandelbaum, ed. University of California Press, Berkeley and Los Angeles, 1949, 1963; also, Johnson Reprint Corporation, New York, 1968.)

_____
1930–1931 The Southern Paiute Language. 3 Pts. *Proceedings of the American Academy of Arts and Sciences* 65(1–3). Boston.

_____
1936   Internal Linguistic Evidence Suggestive of the Northern Origin of the Navaho. *American Anthropologist*, n.s. 38(2):224–235.

Sarcee Executive Staff
1983   The Sarcee Nation: Future Aspiration. In Tsu T'ina K'osa. Calgary: JBC and Associates.

Saskatchewan (Province of)
[1974– [*Sweet Grass Transcript.*] Regina, Sask.: Department of
1975]   Culture and Youth.

Saskatchewan Treaty Land Entitlement
1992   Saskatchewan Treaty Land Entitlement Framework Agreement among: Her Majesty the Queen in Right of Canada, as Represented by the Prime Minister of Canada and the Minister of Indian Affairs and Northern Development, and: The Entitlement Bands, and: Her Majesty the Queen in Right of Saskatchewan, as Represented by the Premier of Saskatchewan and the Minister Responsible for the Indian and Métis Affairs Secretariat (22 September). Regina: Saskatchewan Indian and Métis Affairs Secretariat.

Sasso, Robert F.
1993   La Crosse Region Oneota Adaptations: Changing Late Pre-
            historic Subsistence and Settlement Patterns in the Upper
            Mississippi Valley. *The Wisconsin Archaeologist* 74:324–
            369. Milwaukee.

Saul, John M.
1969   Study of the Spanish Diggings, Aboriginal Flint Quarries of
            Southeastern Wyoming. Pp. 183–199 in *National Geo-
            graphic Society Research Reports, 1964 Projects.* Wash-
            ington: National Geographic Society.

Savage, Sheila B.
1995   Bison Procurement and Processing Strategies: Contrasts in
            Two Non-Kill Sites on the Southern Plains. (Ph.D. Disserta-
            tion in Anthropology, University of Oklahoma, Norman.)

Sawchuck, Joe
1985   The Métis: Non-Status Indians and the New Aboriginality:
            Government Influence on Native Political Alliances and
            Identity. Pp. 135–146 in The Métis: Past and Present.
            Thomas Flanagan and John Foster, eds. *Canadian Ethnic
            Studies* 17(2)[Special issue]. Toronto.

Sawchuk, Joe, Patricia Sawchuk, and Theresa Ferguson
1981   Métis Land Rights in Alberta: A Political History.
            Edmonton, Alta.: Métis Association of Alberta.

Saxton, Rufus
1855   Report of Lieutenant R. Saxton, U.S.A., of His Trip in a
            Keel-boat from Fort Benton to Fort Leavenworth, and of the
            Navigability of the Missouri River by Steamer; [dated]
            Washington, D.C., June 8, 1854. Pp. 249–269 in Report of
            Explorations for a Route for the Pacific Railroad, near the
            Forty-seventh and Forty-ninth Parallels of North Latitude,
            from St. Paul to Puget Sound, by I.I. Stevens. In: Vol. 1 of
            Reports of Explorations and Surveys to Ascertain the Most
            Practicable and Economical Route for a Railroad from the
            Mississippi River to the Pacific Ocean; Made....in 1853–4.
            33d Congress. 2d Session. Senate Executive Document 78.
            Washington: Beverly Tucker.

Scaglion, Richard
1980   The Plains Culture Area Concept. Pp. 23–34 in Anthropol-
            ogy on the Great Plains. W. Raymond Wood and Margot
            Liberty, eds. Lincoln: University of Nebraska Press.

Scanlan, Peter L.
1998   Prairie du Chien: French, British, American. Prairie du
            Chien, Wis.: Prairie du Chien Historical Society. (Origi-
            nally publ. in 1937; reprinted, 2d ed., 1949; 3d ed., 1985.)

Schaafsma, Curtis F.
1987   [Letter to James H. Gunnerson, dated April 24, 1987.]
            (Original in J.H. Gunnerson's possession.)

Schaeffer, Claude E.
[1948–   [Papers.] (Manuscripts in Glenbow Archives, Calgary,
1969]   Alta.)

1962   The Bison Drive of the Blackfeet Indians. *Museum of the
            Plains Indian. Information Leaflet Series.* Browning,
            Mont.: Department of the Interior, Bureau of Indian Affairs.
            (Published also, pp. 28–34; et al. pp. 40–56: Panel Discus-
            sion on Buffalo Jumps) in Symposium on Buffalo Jumps.
            Carling Malouf and Stuart Conner, eds. *Montana Archaeo-
            logical Society. Memoir* 1. Missoula and Helena, Mont.,
            1962. See also Schaeffer 1978.)

1965   The Kutenai Female Berdache: Courier, Guide, Prophetess,
            and Warrior. *Ethnohistory* 12(3):193–236.

1969   Blackfoot Shaking Tent. *Glenbow-Alberta Institute. Occa-
            sional Paper* 5. Calgary.

1978   The Bison Drive of the Blackfeet Indians. Pp. 243–248 in
            Bison Procurement and Utilization: A Symposium. Leslie

B. Davis and Michael Wilson. *Plains Anthropologist*
23(82, Pt. 2), *Memoir* 14. Lincoln.

Scheans, Daniel J.
1957   The Archeology of the Battle-Porcupine Creek Area, Sioux
            County, North Dakota. (Manuscript at the North Dakota
            State Historical Society, Bismarck; copy at the National
            Park Service, Midwest Archaeological Center, Lincoln,
            Nebr.)

Scheiber, Laura L., and George W. Gill
1996   Bioarcheology in the Northwestern Plains. Pp. 91–119 in
            Archeological and Bioarcheological Resources of the
            Northern Plains. George C. Frison and Robert C. Mainfort,
            eds. *Arkansas Archeological Survey Research Series* 47.
            Fayetteville.

Scherer, Joanna Cohan
1997   A Preponderance of Evidence: The 1852 Omaha Indian
            Delegation Daguerreotypes. *Nebraska History* 78(3):116–
            121. Lincoln.

1998   A Preponderance of Evidence: The 1852 Omaha Indian
            Delegation Daguerreotyoes Recovered. [Rev. ed.] Pp. 146–
            158 in *The Daguerreian Annual [for] 1997.* Mark S.
            Johnson, gen. ed. Pittsburgh, Pa.: The Daguerreian Society.

1999   W.H. Boorne's Photos of the Medicine Lodge Ceremony:
            The Construction of an Icon. *European Review of Native
            American Studies* 13(2):37–46. Vienna, Austria [etc.].

Scherer, Mark R.
1999   Imperfect Victories: The Legal Tenacity of the Omaha
            Tribe, 1945–1995. *Law in the American West* 6. Lincoln:
            University of Nebraska Press.

Schermerhorn, John F.
1814   Report to the Society for Propagating the Gospel among the
            Indians and Others in North America. Report Respecting
            the Indians, Inhabiting the Western Parts of the United
            States, Communicated by John F. Schermerhorn to the
            Secretary of the Society for Propagating the Gospel among
            the Indians and Others in North America. *Collections of the
            Massachusetts Historical Society,* 2d ser., Vol. 2:1–45.
            Boston. (Reprinted: Charles C. Little and James Brown,
            Boston. 1846.)

Schilz, Thomas F.
1987   The Lipan Apaches in Texas. El Paso, Tex.: Texas Western
            Press, University of Texas at El Paso.

1990   Robes, Rum, and Rifles: Indian Meddlemen in the Northern
            Plains Fur Trade. *Montana: The Magazine of Western
            History* 40(1):2–13. Helena.

Schimmel, Julie
1991   Inventing "the Indian". Pp. [148] 149–189 in The West as
            America: Reinterpreting Images of the Frontier, 1820–
            1920. William H. Truettner, ed. Washington and London:
            Smithsonian Institution Press for the National Museum of
            American Art.

Schlesier, Karl H.
1974   American Indian Action. Action Anthropology and the
            Southern Cheyenne. *Current Anthropology* 15(3):277–283.
            Chicago.

1987   The Wolves of Heaven: Cheyenne Shamanism, Ceremonies,
            and Prehistoric Origins. Norman: University of Oklahoma
            Press.

1990   Rethinking the Midewiwin and the Plains Ceremonial
            Called the Sun Dance. *Plains Anthropologist* 35(127):1–
            27.

_____, ed.
1994   Plains Indians, A.D. 500–1500: The Archaeological Past of
            Historic Groups. Norman: University of Oklahoma Press.   *1251*

1994a   Commentary: A History of Ethnic Groups in the Great Plains A.D. 150–1550. Pp. 308–381 in Plains Indians, A.D. 500–1500. Karl H. Schlesier, ed. Norman: University of Oklahoma Press.

Schmidt, Louis
1912   [Mémoirs.] (Unpublished transcription, Manuscript Group 9, A31, Provincial Archives of Manitoba, Winnipeg.)

Schmits, Larry J.
1978   The Coffey Site: Environment and Cultural Adaptation at a Prairie Plains Archaic Site. *MidContinental Journal of Archaeology* 3(1):69–185. Kent, Ohio.

1980   Holocene Fluvial History and Depositional Environments at the Coffey Site, Kansas. Pp. 79–105 in Archaic Prehistory on the Prairie-Plains Border. Alfred E. Johnson, ed. *University of Kansas. Publications in Anthropology* 12. Lawrence.

1980a   The Williamson, Salb and Dead Hickory Sites. Pp. 79–106 in Salvage Archeology of the John Redmond Lake, Kansas. Thomas A. Witty, Jr., ed. *Kansas State Historical Society. Department of Archeology Division. Anthropological Series* 8. Topeka.

1987   The Williamson Site: Late Archaic Settlement in the Southern Flint Hills of Kansas. (M.A. Thesis in Anthropology, University of Kansas, Lawrence.)

Schmits, Larry J., and B.C. Bailey
1986   Prehistoric Chronology and Settlement-Subsistence Patterns in the Little Blue Valley, Western Missouri. In: Prehistory of the Little Blue River Valley, Western Missouri: Archaeological Investigations at Blue Springs Lake. Larry J. Schmits, ed. (Report submitted to the U.S. Army Corps of Engineers, Kansas City District, Kans.)

Schmitt, Karl
1950   Wichita-Kiowa Relations and the 1874 Outbreak. *Chronicles of Oklahoma* 28(2):154–160. Norman.

1950a   The Lee Site, Gv3, of Garvin County, Oklahoma. *Bulletin of the Texas Archeological and Paleontological Society* 21:69–89. Lubbock.

1952   Wichita Death Customs. *Chronicles of Oklahoma* 30(2):200–206. Norman.

Schmitt, Karl, and Iva O. Schmitt
1951   [Fieldnotes on Arikara Kinship.] (Manuscript in Western History Collections, University of Oklahoma, Norman.)

1952   Wichita Kinship, Past and Present. Norman: University [of Oklahoma] Book Exchange.

Schmitt, Martin Ferdinand, and Dee Alexander Brown
1948   Fighting Indians of the West. New York: C. Scribner's Sons.

Schneider, David M.
1968   American Kinship: A Cultural Account. Chicago: University of Chicago Press.

1972   What is Kinship All About? Pp. 32–63 in Kinship Studies in the Morgan Centennial Year. Priscilla Reining, ed. Washington: Anthropological Society of Washington.

1976   Notes Toward a Theory of Culture. Pp. 197–220 in Meaning in Anthropology. Keith H. Basso and Henry A. Selby, eds. Albuquerque: University of New Mexico Press.

Schneider, Fred E.
1969   The Roy Smith Site, Bv-14, Beaver County, Oklahoma. *Bulletin of the Oklahoma Anthropological Society* 18:119–179. Norman.

1982   A Model of Prehistoric Cultural Developments in the James River Valley of North Dakota. *Journal of the North Dakota Archaeological Association* 1:113–133. Grand Forks, N.Dak.

Schneider, Fred E., and Jeff Kinney
1978   Evans: A Multicomponent Site in Northwestern North Dakota. *Archaeology in Montana* 19(1–2):1–39. Billings, [etc.], Mont.

Schneider, Mary Jane
1980   Plains Indian Art. Pp. 197–211 in Anthropology on the Great Plains. W. Raymond Wood and Margot Liberty, eds. Lincoln: University of Nebraska Press.

1981   Economic Aspects of Mandan/Hidatsa Giveaways. *Plains Anthropologist* 26(91):43–50.

1982   Connections: Family Ties in Kiowa Art. Pp. 7–18 in Pathways To Plains Prehistory: Anthropological Perspectives of Plains Natives and Their Pasts; Papers in Honor of Robert E. Bell. Don G. Wyckoff and Jack L. Hofman, eds. *Oklahoma Anthropological Society. Memoir* 3; *The Cross Timbers Heritage Association Contributions* 1. Duncan, Okla.

1983   Woman's Work: An Examination of Woman's Roles in Plains Indian Arts and Crafts. Pp. 101–121 in The Hidden Half: Studies of Plains Indian Women. Patricia C. Albers, Beatrice Medicine, eds. Washington, D.C.: University Press of America.

1984   An Investigation into the Origin of the Arikara, Hidatsa, and Mandan Twilled Basketry. *Plains Anthropologist* 2(106):265–276.

1986   North Dakota Indians: An Introduction. Dubuque, Iowa: Kendall/Hunt. (Reprinted in 1994.)

1989   The Hidatsa. New York and Philadelphia: Chelsea House.

1990   North Dakota's Indian Heritage. Grand Forks: University of North Dakota Press.

1994   Three Affiliated Tribes. Pp. 633–634 in Native America in the Twentieth Century: An Encyclopedia. Mary B. Davis, ed. *Garland Reference Library of Social Science* 452. New York and London: Garland Publishing.

Scholes, France V., and H.P. Mera
1940   Some Aspects of the Jumano Problem. *Carnegie Institution of Washington Publication* 523; *Contributions to American Anthropology and History* 6(34). Washington.

Scholtz, James A.
1969   A Summary of Prehistory in Northwest Arkansas. *Arkansas Archeologist* 10(1–3)51–60. Fayetteville.

Schoolcraft, Henry Rowe
1821   Narrative Journal of Travels Through the Northwestern Regions of the United States; Extending from Detroit, Through the Great Chain of American Lakes to the Sources of the Mississippi River, Performed as a Member of the Expedition Under Governor Cass in the Year 1820. Albany: E. & E. Hosford. (Reprinted, ed. by Mentor L. Williams: Michigan State College Press, East Lansing, 1953; Michigan State University Press, East Lansing, 1992; also, Arno Press, New York, 1970.)

————, comp. and ed.
1851–1857 Historical and Statistical Information Respecting the History, Condition and Prospects of the Indian Tribes of the United States; Collected and Prepared Under the Direction of the Bureau of Indian Affairs, per Act of Congress of March 3d, 1847. S[eth] Eastman, illus. 6 vols. Philadelphia: Lippincott, Grambo and Co. (Published also under title: Information Respecting the History, Condition and Prospects [etc.]; 1852–1860. Reprinted: Arno Press, New York, 1969.)

_____, comp. and ed.
1860   Archives of Aboriginal Knowledge. Containing All the Original Paper Laid Before Congress Respecting the History, Antiquities, Language, Ethnology, Pictography, Rites, Superstitions, and Mythology, of the Indian Tribes of the United States. Philadelphia: J.B. Lippincott and Co. (This work is a reissue of Vol. VI of: Information Respecting the History, Condition and Prospects [etc.]; 1851–1857.)

Schrader, Robert Fay
1983   The Indian Arts and Crafts Board: An Aspect of the New Deal Indian Policy. Albuquerque: University of New Mexico Press.

Schroeder, Albert H.
1959   A Study of the Apache Indians: Part II: The Jicarilla Apache. [Mimeograph.] (Manuscript prepared for Jicarilla Apache Lands Claim Hearing, U.S. Department of Justice, Santa Fe, N.Mex.)

1962   A Re-analysis of the Routes of Coronado and Oñate into the Plains in 1541 and 1601. *Plains Anthropologist* 7(15):2–23.

1968   Shifting for Survival in the Spanish Southwest. *New Mexico Historical Review* 43(4):291–310. Albuquerque.

1973   The Changing Ways of Southwestern Indians: A Historical Perspective. Glorieta, N.Mex.: The Rio Grande Press.

1974   A Study of the Apache Indians. Pts. 1–3. *American Indian Ethnohistory. Indians of the Southwest: Apache Indians* 1. David Agee Horr, comp. and ed. New York and London: Garland Publishing.

_____ 1979 *see* Handbook Vol. 9 (1979:236–254)

Schubert, Frank N.
1993   Buffalo Soldiers, Braves and the Brass: The Story of Fort Robinson, Nebraska. Shippensburg, Pa.: White Mane Publ. Co.

Schubert, Melvin Frank
1954   An Analysis of Certain Similarities between the City Dionysia and the Fort Hall Sun Dance. (M.A. Thesis in Drama, University of Southern California, Los Angeles.)

Schudel, Emily
1997   Elicitation and Analysis of Nakoda Texts from Southern Saskatchewan. (M.A. Thesis in Linguistics, University of Regina, Sask.)

Schukies, Renate
1993   Red Hat: Cheyenne Blue Sky Maker and Keeper of the Sacred Arrows. Prepared using the Words of Arrow Keeper Edward Red Hat and Bill Red Hat. Muenster: Lit. (Originally presented as the author's Thesis, Universität Hamburg, Germany.)

Schulenberg, Raymond F.
1956   Indians of North Dakota. *North Dakota History* 23(3–4):119–230. Bismarck.

Schuler, Harold H.
1990   Fort Pierre Chouteau. Vermillion: University of South Dakota Press.

Schultz, Duane P.
1990   Month of the Freezing Moon: the Sand Creek Massacre, November 1864. New York: St. Martin's Press.

Schultz, George A.
1972   An Indian Canaan: Isaac McCoy and the Vision of an Indian State. Norman: University of Oklahoma Press.

Schultz, Jack M.
1992   The Use-Wear Generated by Processing Bison Hides. *Plains Anthropologist* 37(141):333–351.

Schultz, James Willard (Apikuni)
1907   My Life As an Indian: The Story of a Red Women and a White Man in the Lodges of the Blackfeet. Illustrated from Photographs, mostly by George Bird Grinnell. New York: Doubleday, Page and Co.; Boston: Houghton Mifflin. (Reprinted, illustrated with photographs by Roland Reed: Confluence Press, Lewiston, Idaho, 1983.)

1919   Rising Wolf, the White Blackfoot: Hugo Monroe's Story of His First Year on the Plains. Boston: Houghton Mifflin Company.

1988   Recently Discovered Tales of Life among the Indians. Missoula, Mont.: Mountain Press Publishing Co.

Schultz, James Willard (Apikuni), and Jessie Louise Donaldson
1930   The Sun God's Children; With Portraits of Blackfeet by Winold Reiss. Boston and New York: Houghton Mifflin.

Schulze-Thulin, Axel
1979   Prairie and Plains Collections of the Linden-Museum, Stuttgart. *American Indian Art Magazine* 4(3):52–55, 90. Scottsdale, Ariz.

1987   Indianer der Prärien und Plains: Reisen und Sammlungen des Herzogs Paul Wilhelm von Württemberg (1822–24) und des Prinzen Maxmilian zu Wied (1832–34) im Linden-Museum Stuttgart. [2d ed. rev. and enl.] *Bildhefte des Linden-Museums Stuttgart. Staatliches Museum für Völkerkunde. Abteilung Amerika* 2. Stuttgart, Germany: Linden Museum. (Cover title: Prärie-Indianer. Originally publ., 1st ed., 1976.)

Schuon, Frithjof
1990   The Feathered Sun: Plains Indians in Art and Philosophy. Bloomington, Ind.: World Wisdom Books

Schusky, Ernest L.
1963   Mission and Government Policy in Dakota Indian Communities. *Practical Anthropology* 10(3):109–114. Tarrytown, N.Y.

1965   The Right To Be Indian. University of South Dakota, Institute of Indian Studies and United Presbyterian Church, Board of National Missions. (Reprinted: The Indian Historian Press, San Francisco, 1970.)

1975   The Forgotten Sioux: An Ethnohistory of the Lower Brule Reservation. Chicago: Nelson-Hall. (Reprinted in 1977.)

1975a   Development by Grantmanship: Economic Planning on the Lower Brule Sioux Reservation. *Human Organization* 34(3):227–236. Washington.

1979   Political Constraints on Economic Development: The Dakota Reservations. Pp. 337–362 in Currents in Anthropology: Essays in Honor of Sol Tax. Robert Hinshaw, ed. New York: Mouton.

1986   The Evolution of Indian Leadership on the Great Plains, 1750–1950. *The American Indian Quarterly* 10(1):65–82. Hurst, Tex.

Schwartz, Marion
1997   A History of Dogs in the Early Americas. New Haven: Yale University Press.

Schwartz, O. Douglas
1981   Plains Indian Theology: As Expressed in Myth and Ritual, and in the Ethics of Culture. (Ph.D. Dissertation in Religion and Mythology, Fordham University, New York.)

Schwartz, Warren E.
1989   The Last Contrary: The Story of Wesley Whiteman (Black Bear). Sioux Falls, S.Dak.: The Center for Western Studies, Augustana College.

1253

Schwatka, Frederick
1890   The Sun-Dance of the Sioux. *Century Magazine* 39(5):739–759. New York.

Schwechten, John L.
1972   Epilogue in Spite of the Law: A Social Comment on the Impact of Kennerly and Crow Tribe. *Montana Law Review* 33(2):317–320. Missoula.

Schweger, Charles
1987   A Critical Appraisal of the Altithermal and Its Role in Archaeology. Pp. 371–378 in Man and the Mid-Holocene Climatic Optimum. Neil A. MacKinnon and G.S.L. Stuart, eds. Calgary: The University of Calgary Archaeological Association.

Schweitzer, Marjorie M.
[1974–   [Ethnographic, linguistic fieldnotes and photographs.]
1998]   (Manuscripts in M. Schweitzer's possession.)

1981   The Otoe-Missouria War Mothers: Women of Valor. *Moccasin Tracks* 7(1): 4–6 Keshena, Wis.

1983   The Elders: Cultural Dimensions of Aging in Two American Indian Communities. Pp. 168–78 in Growing Old in Different Cultures: Cross-cultural Perspectives Jay Sokolovsky, ed. Belmont, Calif.: Wadsworth.

1983a   The War Mothers: Reflections of Space and Time. *Papers in Anthropology* 24(2):157–171.

1985   Giving Them a Name: An Otoe-Missouria Ceremony. *Moccasin Tracks* (April) 4–7. Keshena, Wis.

Scoggin, William E.
1978   The Sand Creek Burial from Central Wyoming. *The Wyoming Archaeologist* 21(3):10–20. Cheyenne, [etc.,] Wyo.

Scollon, Ronald, and Suzanne B.K. Scollon
1979   Linguistic Convergence: An Ethnography of Speaking at Fort Chipewyan, Alberta. New York: Academic Press.

Scott, Douglas D.
1998   Euro-American Archaeology. Pp. 481–510 in Archaeology on the Great Plains. W. Raymond Wood, ed. Lawrence: University Press of Kansas.

Scott, Hugh L.
[1890–   [Ledger Book.] (Manuscript in Fort Sill Museum Archives,
1900]   Fort Sill, Okla.)

_____ 1893 *see* 1898

1898   The Sign Language of the Plains Indians. *Archives of the International Folk-lore Association* 1:1–206. Chicago: Charles H. Sergel Company.

1907   The Early History and the Names of the Arapaho. *American Anthropologist,* n.s. 9(3):545–560.

1911   Notes on the Kado, or Sun Dance of the Kiowa. *American Anthropologist*, n.s. 13(3):345–379. (Reprinted: New Era Printing Company, Lancaster, Pa., 1911.)

1912–1934 [Notes on Plains Indian Sign Language and Miscellaneous Ethnographic Notes.] (Manuscript No. 2932 [4 boxes], National Anthropological Archives, Smithsonian Institution, Washington.)

1928   Some Memories of a Soldier. New York: The Century Company.

Scott, Linda J.
1982   Pollen and Fiber Analysis of the McEndree Ranch Site, 5BA30, Southeastern Colorado. *Southwestern Lore* 48(2): 18–24. Boulder, Colo.

Scott, Patricia, comp.
1976   Chippewa and Cree: A Bibliography of Books, Newspaper Articles, Government Documents and Other Printed and Written Matter in Various Libraries of the United States and Canada. Rocky Boy, Mont.: The Rocky Boy School.

Scott-Cummings, Linda
1996   Paleoenvironmental Interpretations for the Mill Iron Site: Stratigraphic Pollen and Phytolith Analysis. Pp. 177–193 in The Mill Iron Site. George C. Frison, ed. Albuquerque: University of New Mexico Press.

Scriver, Bob
1990   The Blackfeet: Artists of the Northern Plains. The Scriver Collection of Blackfeet Indian Artifacts and Related Objects, 1894–1990. Kansas City, Kans.: The Lowell Press, Inc.

Sealy, D. Bruce
1975   Staturory Land Rights of the Manitoba Métis. Winnipeg, Man.: Manitoba Métis Federation Press.

Sealy, D. Bruce, and Antoine S. Lussier
1975   The Métis: Canada's Forgotten People. Winnipeg, Man.: Pemmican Publications.

Secoy, Frank R.
1951   The Identity of the "Paduca": An Ethnohistorical Analysis. *American Anthropologist,* n.s. 53(4):524–542.

1953   Changing Military Patterns on the Plains (17th Century Through Early 19th Century). *Monographs of the American Ethnological Society* 21. Locust Valley, N.Y.: J.J. Augustin. (Reprinted: University of Washington Press, Seattle, 1966.)

Secretary of War
1824   Letter from the Secretary of War, to the Chairman of the Committee on Indian Affairs, in Relation to Indian Agencies, &c. [...]; February 2, 1824. *18th Congress. 1st Session. House Document No.* 56. Washington: Gales and Seaton.

1826   Indian Treaties, and Laws and Regulations Relatig to Indian Affairs; To Which Is Added and Appendix, Containing the Proceedings of the Old Congress, and Other Important State Papers, in Relation to Indian Affairs. (Compiled by Chief Clerk Samuel S. Hamilton at the direction of Secretary of War John C. Calhoun and Thomas L. McKenney, [...], War Department.) Washington: Way and Gideon.

1829   Letter from the Secretary of War, Transmitting the Information Required by a Resolution of the House of Representatives of the 15th ultimo, in Relation to Our Indian Affairs Generally. *20th Congress. 2d Session. House Document No.* 117 (War Department: Indian Affairs). Washington.

1832   Remarks Concerning the Indian Trade, and the Inland Trade to Mexico: [dated] Department of War, February 8th, 1832. Pp. 1–86 in Message from the President of the United States, in Compliance With a Resolution of the Senate Concerning the Fur Trade, and Inland Trade to Mexico; [dated] Washington, February 8, 1832. *22d Congress. 1st Session. Senate Executive Document No.* 90. (Serial No. 213). Washington.

Seger, John H.
1934   Early Days among the Cheyenne and Arapahoe Indians. Stanley Vestal [i.e. Walter Stanley Campbell], ed. Norman: University of Oklahoma Press. (Originally publ. as: *University of Oklahoma Bulletin. University Series* 281; *University Studies* 19. W.S. Campbell, ed. Norman, 1924.)

Seldon, Ron
1999   TAAMS Rollout to 'Square up' Troubled Trust Accounts. *Indian Country Today,* July 12–19. Rapid City, S.Dak.

Sellards, Elias H.
1940   Early Man in America: Index to the Localities and Selected

Bibliography. *Geological Society of America. Bulletin* 51(3):373–432. Washington.

1952   Early Man in America. Austin: University of Texas Press.

Seton, Ernest Thompson
1918   Sign Talk; A Universal Signal Code, Without Apparatus, for Use in the Army, the Navy, Camping, Hunting and Daily Life. The Gesture Language of the Cheyenne Indians, with Additional Signs Used by Other Tribes; also a Few Necessary Signs from the Code of the Deaf in Europe and America, and Others That Are Established among Our Policemen, Firemen, Railroad Men, and School Children, in All 1,725. Prepared with Assistance from General Hugh L. Scott, U.S.A. The French and German Words Added by Lillian Delger Powers, M.D. Garden City, N.Y.: Doubleday, Page and Co.

Seymour, E. Sandford
1850   Sketches of Minnesota, the New England of the West; With Incidents of Travel in That Territory during the Summer of 1849. In Two Parts [1 vol.]. New York: Harper and Brothers.

Shaeffer, James B.
1958   The Alibates Flint Quarry, Texas. *American Antiquity* 24(2):189–191.

Shakespeare, Tom
1971   The Sky People. New York: Vantage Press.

Shane, Ralph M.
1956   Short History of Fort Berthold. New Town, N.Dak.: Fort Berthold Indian Agency

Sharp, Paul Frederick
1954   Massacre at Cypress Hills. *Montana Magazine of History* 4(1):26–41. Helena. (Published also in: *Saskatchewan History* 7:81–99, 1954. Saskatoon.)

1955   Whoop-Up Country: The Canadian-American West, 1865–1885. With Drawings by Charles M. Russell. Minneapolis: University of Minnesota Press. (Reprinted: Historical Society of Montana, Helena, 1960; also, University of Oklahoma Press, Norman, 1973.)

Sharrock, Floyd W.
1961   The Grant Site of the Washita River Focus. *Bulletin of the Oklahoma Anthropological Society* 9:1–66. Oklahoma City.

1966   Prehistoric Occupation Patterns in Southwest Wyoming and Cultural Relationships with the Great Basin and Plains Culture Areas. *University of Utah Anthropological Papers* 77. Salt Lake City.

Sharrock, Floyd W., and Susan R. Sharrock
1974   History of the Cree Indian Territorial Expansion From the Hudson Bay Area to the Interior Saskatchewan and Missouri Plains. Pp. 183–402 in Chippewa Indians VI. *American Indian Ethnohistory: North Central and Northeastern Indians.* David Agee Horr, comp. and ed. New York and London: Garland Publishing.

Sharrock, Susan R.
1974   Crees, Cree-Assiniboines, and Assiniboines: Interethnic Social Organization on the Far Northern Plains. *Ethnohistory* 21(2):95–122.

Shaw, P.C.
1976   I Saw the Last Brave. *Alberta History* 24(4):28–29. Calgary.

Shaw, Patricia A.
1976   Dakota Phonology and Morphology. (Ph.D. Dissertation in Linguistics, University of Toronto, Toronto.)

1980   Theoretical Issues in Dakota Phonology and Morphology.

Outstanding Dissertations in Linguistics. New York: Garland Publishing.

1985   Coexistent and Competing Stress Rules in Stoney (Dakota). *International Journal of American Linguistics* 51(1):1–18. Chicago.

1985a   Modularisation and Substantive Constraints in Dakota Lexical Phonology. *Phonology Yearbook* 2:203–224. Cambridge [and] New York.

Shay, C. Thomas
1971   The Itasca Bison Kill Site: An Ecological Analysis. *Minnesota Historical Society Prehistorical Archaeology Series.* St. Paul: Minnesota Historical Society.

Shea, John Gilmary
1852   Discovery and Exploration of the Mississippi Valley; With the Original Narratives of Marquette, Allouez, Membré, Hennepin, and Anatase Douay. New York: J.S. Redfiled. (Reprinted, 2d ed.: J.M. McDonough, Albany, N.Y., 1903.)

1855   History of the Catholic Missions among the Indian Tribes of the United States, 1529–1854. New York: T.W. Strong.

1861   Early Voyages Up and Down the Mississippi, by Cavelier, St. Cosme, Le Sueur, Gravier, and Guignas. Albany, N.Y.: J. Munsell.

_____, trans. and ed. 1880 *see* Hennepin, Louis 1683, 1880

_____ 1882 *see* Freytas, Nicolas de

1903   Discovery and Exploration of the Mississippi Valley; With the Original Narratives of Marquette, Allouez, Membré, Hennepin, and Anatase Douay. 2d ed. Albany, N.Y.: J.M. McDonough. (Originally publ.: J.S. Redfield, New York, 1852.)

Shea, Kathleen Dorette
1984   A Catawba Lexicon. (M.A. Thesis in Linguistics, University of Kansas, Lawrence.)

Sheldon, Addison E., ed.
1923   New Chapter in Nebraska History. *Nebraska History and Record of Pioneer Days* 6(1):1–31. Lincoln.

Shelford, Victor E.
1963   The Ecology of North America. Urbana: University of Illinois Press. (Reprinted in 1978.)

Sheridan, Susan Guise, Jeannette L. Mobley-Tanaka, Dennis P. Van Gerven, and William Lane Shields
1992   A Case of Late Prehistoric Mutilation on the Northwest Plains. *Plains Anthropologist* 37(141):289–298.

Sherman, Bob
1980   The News: A History of AIM. *American Indian Journal* 6(1):3–9. Washington.

Shields, Rev. Joseph M., Sr., and Duane L. Shields, Sr.
1983   Songs of the Native American Church. Recorded at Lake Andes, South Dakota, June 29, 1979. Recording and notes by Tony Isaacs. [Sound cassette.] Taos, N.Mex.: Indian House.

Shields, William L.
1980   Preliminary Investigations at the McEndree Ranch Site. *Southwestern Lore* 46(3):1–17. Boulder, Colo.

Shimkin, Demitri Boris
1941   The Uto-Aztecan System of Kinship Terminology. *American Anthropologist*, n.s. 43(2):223–245.

1942   Dynamics of Recent Wind River Shoshone History. *American Anthropologist*, n.s. 44(3):451–462.

1947   Wind River Shoshone Ethnogeography. *University of California. Anthropological Records* 5(4):245–288. Berkeley. *1255*

1953   The Wind River Shoshone Sun Dance. *Bureau of American Ethnology Bulletin* 151; *Anthropological Papers* 41. Washington: Smithsonian Institution; U.S. Government Printing Office.

Shindler, Antonio Zeno
[1869]   Photographic Portraits of North American Indians in the Gallery of the Smithsonian Institution. *Smithsonian Miscellaneous Collections* 14(216). (Incorrectly dated 1867 on the title page.) Washington: Smithsonian Institution; Government Printing Office.

Shippee, James M.
1967   Belated Archaeological Investigation on King's Hill, St. Joseph, Missouri. *(St. Joseph) Museum Graphic* 19(1):5–9. St. Joseph, Mo.

Shoemaker, Nancy
1988   Urban Indians and Ethnic Choices: American Indian Organizations in Minneapolis, 1920–1950. *Western Historical Quarterly* 19(4):431–447. Logan, Utah.

Shonle, Ruth
1925   Peyote, The Giver of Visions. *American Anthropologist,* n.s. 27(1):53–75.

Shore, Frederick J.
1991   The Canadian and the Métis: The Re-Creation of Manitoba, 1858–1872. (Ph.D. Dissertation in History, University of Manitoba, Winnipeg.)

Shorris, Earl
1971   The Death of the Great Spirit. New York: Simon and Schuster.

Shunatona, Richard
1922   Otoe Indian Lore. *Nebraska History and Record of Pioneer Days* 5(4):60–64. Lincoln.

Sibley, George C.
1927   Extracts from the Diary of Major Sibley. *Chronicles of Oklahoma* 5(2):196–218. Norman.

Sibley, Henry Hastings
1874   Reminiscences of the Early Days of Minnesota. *Collections of the Minnesota Historical Society* 3(Pt. 2):242–277. St. Paul.

1950   Iron Face: The Adventures of Jack Frazer, Frontier Warrior, Scout and Hunter. Theodore C. Blegen and Sarah A. Davidson, eds. Foreword by Stanley Vestal. Chicago: The Caxton Club.

Sibley, John 1806 *see* 1832

1832   Historical Sketches of the Several Indian Tribes in Louisiana, South of the Arkansas River, and between the Mississippi and River Grande [dated] Natchitoches, April 5, 1805. [Communicated to Congress by Thomas Jefferson, February 19, 1806.] Pp. 721–730 in *American State Papers. Documents, Legislative and Executive, of the Congress of the United States,* Vol. IV [i.e. I]; *Class* II: Indian Affairs. Washington: Gales and Seaton.

1922   A Report from Natchitoches in 1807. Edited, and with an Introduction, by Annie Heloise Abel. *Museum of the American Indian. Heye Foundation. Indian Notes and Monographs [Miscellaneous 25].* New York. (Reprinted: Evangeline Genealogical and Historical Society, Ville Platte, La., 1987.)

Siebert, Frank T., Jr.
1945   Linguistic Classification of Catawba I, II. *International Journal of American Linguistics* 11(2):100–104, (4):211–218. Chicago.

1967   The Original Home of the Proto-Algonquian People. Pp. 13–47 in Contributions to Anthropology: Linguistics I (Algonquian). *National Museum of Canada. Bulletin* 214; *Anthropological Series* 78. Ottawa.

1967a   Discrepant Consonant Clusters Ending in *-k in Proto-Algonquian, a Proposed Interpretation of Saltatory Sound Changes. Pp. 48–59 in Contributions to Anthropology: Linguistics I (Algonquian). *Anthropological Series* 78; *National Museum of Canada. Bulletin* 214. Ottawa.

1989   A Note on Quapaw. *International Journal of American Linguistics* 55(1):471–476. Chicago.

1996   Proto-Algonquian *na:tawe:wa 'massasauga': Some False Etymologies and Alleged Iroquoian Loanwords. *Anthropological Linguistics* 38(4):635–642. Bloomington.

Sifton, John B.
[1895]   An English—Aáni (Gros Ventres) Dictionary. (Manuscript, Microfilm Reel 8, Frames 385–536, Oregon Province Archives of the Society of Jesus Indian Language Collection, Gonzaga University, Spokane, Wash.)

[1895a]   Grammar of the Aánai or Gros Ventres Language. (Manuscript, Microfilm Reel 8, Frames 577–698, Oregon Province Archives of the Society of Jesus Indian Language Collection, Gonzaga University, Spokane, Wash.)

[1895b]   Elements of the Gros Ventres Language. (Manuscript, Microfilm Reel 8, Frames 699–741, Oregon Province Archives of the Society of Jesus Indian Language Collection, Gonzaga University, Spokane, Wash.)

1977   An English-Aa'ni Dictionary. George P. Horse Capture, ed. Great Falls, Mont.: [Mimeograph.]

Siggins, Maggie
1994   Riel: A Life of Revolution. Toronto: HarperCollins.

Sigstad, John S.
1969   Mowrey Bluff and Nuzum Pottery. Pp. 17–23 in Two House Sites in the Central Plains: An Experiment in Archaeology. W. Raymond Wood, ed. *Plains Anthropologist* 14(44, Pt. 2); *Memoir* 6. Lincoln.

Silberman, Arthur
1978   100 Years of Native American Painting. March 5 – April 16, 1978; The Oklahoma Museum of Art, Exhibition Catalogue. Oklahoma City: Oklahoma Museum of Art.

Silversides, Brock V.
1994   The Face Pullers: Photographing Native Canadians 1871–1939. Saskatoon, Sask.: Fifth House Publishers.

Simmons, Marc
1966   New Mexico's Smallpox Epidemic of 1780–1781. *New Mexico Historical Review* 41(4):319–326. Albuquerque.

1973   The Mysterious A Tribe of the Southern Plains. Pp. 73–89 in The Changing Ways of Southwestern Indians: A Historical Perspective. Albert H. Schroeder, ed. Glorieta, N.Mex.: The Rio Grande Press.

1991   Coronado's Land: Essays on Daily Life in Colonial New Mexico. Albuquerque: University of New Mexico Press.

Simms, Stephen C.
1903   Traditions of the Crows. *Field Columbian Museum Publication* 85; *Anthropological Series* 2(6). Chicago.

1903a   A Wheel-Shaped Stone Monument in Wyoming. *American Anthropologist,* n.s. 5(1):107–110.

1904   Cultivation of "Medicine Tobacco" by the Crows. *American Anthropologist,* n.s. 6(2):331–335.

1904a   Traditions of the Sarcee Indians. *Journal of American Folklore* 17(66):180–182.

Simms, Thomas
1980   Sun Dance Equipment and Dress. *Sinte Gleska College News* 2(6):1, 8–9. Rosebud, S.Dak.

Simon, Arleyn
1979   Pottery Manufacture Analysis: Experimental Assessment of Technological Continuity in the Altamont Region. *Archaeology in Montana* 20(2):1–78. Billings, [etc.].

Simon, (Brother) C.M. (S.J.)
1992   Five Families of Sioux Artists. In: Five Families Art Exhibition; Organized by The Heritage Center Inc., Red Cloud Indian School [and] The University Art Galleries, University of South Dakota. [Pine Ridge, S.Dak.: Red Cloud Indian School.]

Simon, Steve
1995   Healing Waters: The Pilgrimage to Lac Ste. Anne. Edmonton, Alta.: University of Alberta Press.

Simons, Helen, and William E. Moore, comps.
1997   Archeological Bibliography for the Central Region of Texas. *Office of the State Archaeologist. Special Report* 36. Austin: Texas Historical Commission.

Simpson, George Eaton, and Milton Yinger, eds.
1957   American Indians and American Life. *Annals of the American Academy of Political and Social Science* 311. Philadelphia. (Reprinted: Kraus Reprint, Millwood, N.Y., 1973; also, Russell and Russell, New York, 1975.)

Simpson, Sir George
1841   Governor George Simpson's Journal 1841. (Hudson's Bay Company Collection, Reel 3M2, Public Archives of Canada, Ottawa.)

1847   An Overland Journey Round the World, during the Years 1841 and 1842. 2 vols. London: Henry Colburn. (Published also, American ed.: Lea and Blanchard, Philadelphia, 1847.)

1931   Fur Trade and Empire: George Simpson's Journal ... 1824–1825 [etc.]. Frederick Merk, ed. Cambridge, Mass.: Harvard University Press. (Reprinted: Belknap Press, Cambridge, Mass., 1968.)

1984   Population Dynamics of Mule Deer. Pp. 1–2 in The Dead Indian Creek Site: An Archaic Occupation in the Absaroka Mountains of Northwestern Wyoming. George C. Frison and Danny N. Walker, eds. *The Wyoming Archaeologist* 27. Cheyenne, [etc.,] Wyo.

Šina Sapa Wocekiye Taeyanpaha
1892–1939 *Šina Sapa Wocekiye Taeyanpaha/The Catholic Sioux Herald*. Fort Totten, N.Dak. [etc.]: Rev. Jerome Hunt, O.S.B. [etc.].

Sioui, Anne-Marie
1979   Qui est l'auteur du Codex canadiensis? *Recherches amérindiennes au Québec* 8(4):271–279. Montréal.

Sioui, Georges
1992   For an Amerindian Autohistory. Toronto-Montréal: McGill-Queen's.

Sjoberg, Andrée F.
1953   The Culture of the Tonkawa: A Texas Indian Tribe. *The Texas Journal of Science* 5(3):280–304. San Angelo, [etc.], Tex.

1953a   Lipan Apache Culture in Historical Perspective. *Southwestern Journal of Anthropology* 9(1):76–98. Albuquerque.

Skinner, Alanson B.
1914   Notes on the Plains Cree. *American Anthropologist*, n.s. 16(1):68–87.

1914a   Political Organization, Cults and Ceremonies of the Plains-Cree. *American Museum of Natural History Anthropological Papers* 11(6):513–542. New York. (Bound with other monographs in: Societies of the Plains Indians, Clark Wissler, ed., New York, 1916. Reprinted: Inter Documentation, Zug, Switzerland, 1976.)

1914b   The Cultural Position of the Plains Ojibway. *American Anthropologist*, n.s. 16(2):314–318.

1914c   Political and Ceremonial Organization of the Plains-Ojibway. *American Museum of Natural History Anthropological Papers* 11(6):475–511. New York. (Bound with other monographs in: Societies of the Plains Indians, Clark Wissler, ed., New York, 1916.)

1915   Societies of the Iowa, Kansa, and Ponca Indians. *American Museum of Natural History Anthropological Papers* 11(9):679–801. New York. (Bound with other monographs in: Societies of the Plains Indians, Clark Wissler, ed., New York, 1916.)

1915a   Ponca Societies and Dances. *American Museum of Natural History Anthropological Papers* 11(9):777–801. New York. (Bound with other monographs in: Societies of the Plains Indians, Clark Wissler, ed., New York, 1916. Reprinted: Lakota Books, Kendall Park, N.J., 1998.)

1915b   Kansa Organizations. *American Museum of Natural History Anthropological Papers* 11(9):741–755. New York. (Bound with other monographs in: Societies of the Plains Indians, Clark Wissler, ed., New York, 1916.)

1919   The Sun Dance of the Plains-Cree. *American Museum of Natural History Anthropological Papers* 16(4):283–293. New York.

1919a   The Sun Dance of the Plains-Ojibway. *American Museum of Natural History Anthropological Papers* 16(4):311–315. New York.

1919b   Notes on the Sun Dance of the Sisseton Dakota. *American Museum of Natural History Anthropological Papers* 16(4):381–385. New York. (Reprinted: Lakota Books, Kendall Park, N.J., 1993.)

1919c   A Sketch of Eastern Dakota Ethnology. *American Anthropologist*, n.s. 21(2):164–174.

1920   Medicine Ceremony of the Menomini, Iowa, and Wahpeton Dakota, with Notes on the Ceremony among the Ponca, Bungi Ojibwa, and Potawatomi. *Indian Notes and Monographs* 4. New York: Museum of the American Indian. Heye Foundation. (Reprinted: AMS Press, New York, 1984.)

1921   Material Culture of the Menomini. New York: Museum of the American Indian, Heye Foundation.

1922   Notes on the Museum's Collecting Expeditions in 1922: A Summer among the Sauk and Ioway Indians. *Public Museum of the City of Milwaukee. Yearbook* 2:6–22. Milwaukee, Wis.

1923   Some Unusual Ethnological Specimens. *Public Museum of the City of Milwaukee. Yearbook* 3:103–109. Milwaukee, Wis.

1925   Remarkable Oto Necklace. *Indian Notes* 2(1):36–38. New York: Museum of the American Indian. Heye Foundation.

1925a   Traditions of the Iowa Indians. *Journal of American Folklore* 38(150):425–506.

1925b   Tree-Dweller Bundle of the Wahpeton Dakota. *Indian 1257*

Notes 2(1):66–73. New York: Museum of the American Indian. Heye Foundation.

1926   Ethnology of the Ioway Indians. *Bulletin of the Public Museum of the City of Milwaukee* 5(4):181–352. Milwaukee, Wis.

Slattery, Richard G., George A. Horton, and Michael E. Ruppert
1975   The McKinney Village Site: An Oneota Site in Southeastern Iowa. *Journal of the Iowa Archeological Society* 22:35–61. Iowa City.

Slobodin, Richard 1981 *see* Handbook Vol. 6 (1981:361–371)

Slotkin, James S.
1956   The Peyote Religion: A Study in Indian White Relations. Glencoe, Ill.: The Free Press. (Reprinted: Octagon Books, New York, 1956, 1975.)

1957   The Menomini Powwow: A Study in Cultural Decay. *Milwaukee Public Museum Publictions in Anthropology* 4. Milwaukee, Wis.

Slotkin, Richard
1974   Regeneration through Violence: The Mythology of the American Frontier, 1600–1860. Middletown, Conn.: Wesleyan University Press.

Sluman, Norma, and Jean Goodwill
1982   John Tootoosis: A Biography of a Cree Leader. Ottawa: Golden Dog Press.

Small, Alan A.
1958   The Nation of the Missouris. (M.A. Thesis in History, St. Louis University, St. Louis, Mo.)

Smet, Pierre-Jean de
1843   Letters and Sketches: With a Narrative of a Year's Residence among the Indian Tribes of the Rocky Mountains. Philadelphia: M. Fithian.

1847   Oregon Missions and Travels Over the Rocky Mountains, in 1845–46. New York: E. Dunigan. (Reprinted: Ye Galleon Press, Fairfield, Wash., 1978.)

1848   Missions de l'Orégon et voyages aux Montagnes Rocheueses aux sources de la Colombie, de l'Athabasca et du Sascatshawin, en 1845–46. Gand: Gand, Impr. & Lith. de V. Van der Scheldon.

1863   Western Missions and Missionaries: A Series of Letters. New York: James B. Kirker.

1905   Life, Letters, and Travels of Father Pierre-Jean De Smet, S.J. 1801–1873; Missionary Labors and Adventures among the Wild Tribes of the North American Indians, Embracing the Minute Description of Their Manners, Customs, Games, Modes of Warfare and Torture, Legends, Tradition, etc. Edited from the Original Unpublished Manuscript Journals and Letter Books and from His Printed Works with Historical, Geographical and Other Notes; Also a Life of Father De Smet. Hiram Martin Chittenden and Alfred Talbot Richardson, eds. 4 vols. New York: Francis P. Harper. (Reprinted: Arno Press, New York, 1969.)

Smith, Brian J., and E.G. Walker
1988   Evidence for Diverse Subsistence in an Avonlea Component. Pp. 81–88 in Avonlea Yesterday and Today: Archaeology and Prehistory. Leslie B. Davis, ed. Saskatoon: Saskatchewan Archaeological Society.

Smith, Buckingham
1857   Coleccion de varios documentos para la historia de la Florida y tierras adyacentes. Tomo I. Londres [i.e. London]: Trübner. (Only one vol. published.)

Smith, Carlyle S.
1949   Archaeological Investigations in Ellsworth and Rice Counties, Kansas. *American Antiquity* 14(4):292–300.

1959   The Temporal Relationships of Coalescent Village Sites in Fort Randall Reservoir, South Dakota. Pp. 111–123 in Vol. 2 of *Actas del XXXIII Congreso Internacional de Americanistas, San Jose, 20–27 Julio 1958; Bajio el patrocinio del Gobierno de Costa Rica*. 2 vols. San Jose, Costa Rica: Lehman.

1977   The Talking Crow Site: A Multi-Component Earthlodge Village in the Big Bend Region, South Dakota. With Appendices by: Rupert I. Murrill, Ricky L. Roberts, Nancy J. Fix, Hugh C. Cutler, Leonard W. Blake. *University of Kansas Publications in Anthropology* 9. Lawrence.

Smith, Carlyle S., and Roger T. Grange, Jr.
1958   The Spain Site (39LM301), a Winter Village in Fort Randall Reservoir, South Dakota. *Bureau of American Ethnology Bulletin* 169; *River Basin Surveys Papers* 11. Washington: Smithsonian Institution; U.S. Government Printing Office.

Smith, Cecil Bernard
1928   Diplomatic Relations between the United States and Mexico concerning Border Disturbances during the Díaz Regime, 1876–1910. (M.A. Thesis in History, University of Texas, Brownsville.)

Smith, Duane A.
1992   Rocky Mountain West: Colorado, Wyoming, and Montana, 1859–1915. Albuquerque: University of New Mexico Press.

Smith, F. Todd
1995   The Caddo Indians: Tribes at the Convergence of Empires, 1542–1854. *Texas A&M University. The Centennial Series of the Association of Former Students* 56. College Station, Tex.

1996   The Caddos, the Wichitas, and the United States, 1846–1901. *Texas A&M University. The Centennial Series of the Association of Former Students* 64. College Station, Tex.

Smith, G. Hubert
1972   Like-a-Fishhook Village and Fort Berthold, Garrison Reservoir, North Dakota. *U.S. Department of the Interior. National Park Service. Anthropological Papers* 2. Washington.

1973   Notes on Omaha Ethnohistory, 1763–1820. *Plains Anthropologist* 18(62):257–270.

1974   Ethnohistorical Report on the Omaha People. *American Indian Ethnohistory: Plains Indians*. David Agee Horr, comp. and ed. New York and London: Garland Publishing.

1980   The Explorations of the La Vérendryes in the Northern Plains, 1738–43. W. Raymond Wood, ed. Lincoln: University of Nebraska Press.

Smith, Harlan I.
1910   An Unknown Field in American Archeology. *American Geographic Society Bulletin* 42:511–520. Washington.

Smith, Helen, and Mickey Old Coyote
1992   Apsaalooka: The Crow Nation Then and Now. Greensburg, Pa.: McDonald Sward.

Smith, J.L.
1970   The Sacred Calf Pipe Bundle: It's [*sic*] Effect on the Present Teton Dakota. *Plains Anthropologist* 15(48):87–93.

Smith, James G.E.
1976   On the Territorial Distribution of the Western Woods Cree. Pp. 414–435 in Papers of the 7th Algonquian Conference, 1975. William Cowan, ed. Ottawa: Carleton University.

1987   The Western Woodlands Cree: Anthropological Myth and Historical Reality. *American Ethnologist* 14(3):434–448.

_____ 1981 *see* Handbook Vol. 6 (1981:256–270)

1988   Canada—The Lubicon Lake Cree. *Cultural Survival Quarterly* 11(3):61–62. Cambridge, Mass.

Smith, John L.
1967   A Short History of the Sacred Calf Pipe of the Teton Dakota. *University of South Dakota. W.H. Over Museum. Museum News* 28(7–8). Vermillion.

Smith, Jaune Quick-to-See
1992   The Submuloc Show/Columbus Wohs: A Visual Commentary on the Columbus Quincentennial from the Perspective of America's First People. Phoenix: Atlatl.

Smith, Marian W.
1938   The War Complex of the Plains Indians. *Proceedings of the American Philosophical Society* 78(3):425–464. Philadelphia.

1960   Mandan "History" as Reflected in Butterfly's Winter Count. *Ethnohistory* 7(3):199–205.

Smith, Maurice Greer
1924   The Political Organization of the Plains Indians. *University Studies of the University of Nebraska* 24(Jan.–April). Lincoln. (Reprinted: AMS Press, New York, 1978.)

Smith, Ralph A., ed. 1951, 1959 *see* La Harpe, Bénard de 1951, 1959

1970   The Comanche Sun Over Mexico. *West Texas Historical Association Year Book* 46:25–62. Abilene.

1972   The Fantasy of a Treaty to End Treaties. *Great Plains Journal* 12(1):26–51. Lawton, Okla.

Smith, William
1765   An Historical Account of the Expedition Against the Ohio Indians in the Year MDCCLXIV. Under the Command of Henry Bouquet, Esq. Philadelphia: W. Bradford. (Reprinted: T. Jefferies, London, 1766; also, R. Clarke, Cincinnati, Ohio, 1907.)

_____ 1766 *see* 1765 (reprint info.)

Smithsonian Institution
1940   Essays in Historical Anthropology of North America: Published in Honor of John R. Swanton in Celebration of His Fortieth Year with the Smithsonian Institution. [Essays by A.L. Kroeber, J.H. Steward, et al.] *Smithsonian Miscellaneous Collections* 100; (*Publication* 3588). Washington: Smithsonian Institution; Government Printing Office.

Smithsonian Institution. Bureau of [American] Ethnology
1885   Linguistic Families of the Indian Tribes North of Mexico, with Provisional List of the Principal Tribal Names and Synonyms. [Pt. 1: Henry W. Henshaw, comp.; Pt. 2: James Mooney and Henry W. Henshaw, comps.] *[Smithsonian Institution.] Miscellaneous Publication* 3. Washington: U.S. Government Printing Office.

Smithwick, Noah
[1900]   The Evolution of a State; or, Recollections of Old Texas Days. Austin: Gammel Book Company.

Smyth, David
1976   The Fur Trade Posts at Rocky Mountain House. *Parks Canada. Manuscript Report Series* 197. Ottawa.

1984   The Struggle for the Piegan Trade: The Saskatchewan Versus the Missouri. *Montana: The Magazine of Western History* 34(2):2–15. Helena.

Smyth, Willie, ed.
1989   Songs of Indian Territory: Native American Music Traditions of Oklahoma. Oklahoma City, Okla.: Center of the American Indian. (Book and Cassette.)

Smythe, Charles W., and Priya Helweg, comps.
1996   Summary of Ethnological Objects in the National Museum of Natural History Associated with the Sioux Culture. Washington: Repatriation Office, National Museum of Natural History, Smithsonian Institution.

_____, comps.
1996a   Summary of Ethnological Objects in the National Museum of Natural History Associated with the Arapaho Culture. Washington: Repatriation Office, National Museum of Natural History, Smithsonian Institution.

_____, comps.
1996b   Summary of Ethnological Objects in the National Museum of Natural History Associated with the Cheyenne Culture. Washington: Repatriation Office, National Museum of Natural History, Smithsonian Institution.

Snelling, William Joseph
1830   Tales of the Northwest; or, Sketches of Indian Life and Character, by a Resident Beyond the Frontier. Boston: Hilliard, Gray, Little, and Wilkins. (Reprinted under title: William Joseph Snelling's Tales of the Northwest; with an Introduction by John T. Flanagan: University of Minnesota Press, Minneapolis, 1936, 1964; also, Ross and Haines, Minneapolis, 1971; Garland, New York, 1976; Dorset Press, [Minneapolis], 1985.)

_____ 1936, 1964, 1971, 1976, 1985 *see* 1830 (reprint info.)

Sneve, Virginia Driving Hawk
1977   That They May Have Life: The Episcopal Church in South Dakota, 1959–1976. New York: Seabury Press.

Snodgrass, Jeanne O.
1968   American Indian Painters: A Biographical Dictionary. *Museum of the American Indian. Heye Foundation. Contributions* 21(1): New York.

Snow, Chief John
1977   These Mountains Are Our Sacred Places: The Story of the Stoney Indians. Toronto and Sarasota: Samuel Stevens.

1985   Identification and Definition of Our Treaty and Aboriginal Rights. Pp 41–46 in The Quest for Justice: Aboriginal Peoples and Aboriginal Rights. Menno Boldt and J. Anthony Long, in assoc. with Leroy Little Bear, eds. Toronto: University of Toronto Press.

Snow, E.P.
1895   The Hartville Iron Ore Deposits in Wyoming. *The Engineering and Mining Journal* 60(14):320–321. New York.

Snyder, A.R.
1928   [Letter to Commissioner of Indian Affairs, dated Pawnee, Oklahoma, October 26, 1928. re Ponca Dance Hall.] (Manuscript, Central Files 1907–1939, Pawnee Agency, Decimal File .047, No. 33600–1928, Records of the Bureau of Indian Affairs, Record Group 75, National Archives, Washington.)

Snyder, Walter W.
1969   The Native American Church: Its Origin, Ritual, Doctrine, and Ethic. *Oklahoma Anthropological Society. Bulletin* 18:13–38. Oklahoma City.

Sociedad de Geografía y Estadística de la República Mexicana
1869–1872   *Boletín de la Sociedad de Geografía y Estadística de la República Mexicana, Segunda época* 1–4. México: La Sociedad. (Microfilm: Harvard College Library Imaging Services, Cambridge, Mass., 1999.)

Solecki, Ralph, and Charles Wagley
1963   William Duncan Strong 1899–1962. *American Anthropologist*, n.s. 65(5):1102–1111.

Sooktis, Rubie
1976   The Cheyenne Journey. Ashland, Mont.: Religion Research Center.

Sooktis, Rubie, and Anne Terry Straus
1981   A Rock and a Hard Place: Mineral Resources on the Northern Cheyenne Reservation. *Chicago Anthropology Exchange* 14(1–2):27–35. Chicago.

Sorkin, Alan L.
1978   The Urban American Indian. Lexington, Mass.:Lexington Books.

Soule, William S.
1868–1874   [William S. Soule Photographs, ca. 1867–1874 (some earlier).] (Manuscript No. 4791, National Anthropological Archives, Smithsonian Institution, Washington. Prints received from Barker Texas History Library, Austin, Tex., Dec. 1966.)

South Dakota Writer's Project
1941   Legends of the Mighty Sioux. Chicago: Albert Whitman and Company.

Southesk, James Carnegie, Earl of
1875   Saskatchewan and the Rocky Mountains: A Diary and Narrative of Travel, Sport, and Adventure, during a Journey Through the Hudson's Bay Company's Territories in 1859 and 1860. Edinburgh: Edmonston and Douglas. (Reprinted: C.E. Tuttle, Rutland, Vt., 1969.)

Sowell, Andrew Jackson
1964   Rangers and Pioneers of Texas [1884]. New York: Argosy-Antiquarian.

_____
1964a   Early Settlers and Indian Fighters of Southwest Texas [1900]. 2 vols. New York: Argosy-Antiquarian.

Spang, Bentley, and Jessica Hunter
2000   Material Culture: Innovation in Native Art. Great Falls, Mont.: Paris Gibson Square Museum of Art.

Spaulding, Albert C.
1956   The Arzberger Site, Hughes County, South Dakota. *University of Michigan. Museum of Anthropology. Occasional Contributions* 16. Ann Arbor.

Speaker, Stuart, Thomas W. Killion, and John W. Verano
1993   Arapaho Repatriation: Human Remains. Washington: Repatriation Office, National Museum of Natural History, Smithsonian Institution.

Speck, Frank G.
1907   Notes on the Ethnology of the Osage Indians. *University of Pennsylvania. Transactions of the Free Museum of Science and Art* 2(2):159–171. Philadelphia.

_____
1928   Notes on the Functional Basis of Decoration and the Feather Technique of the Oglala Sioux. *Indian Notes* 5:1–42. New York: Museum of the American Indian. Heye Foundation.

Spector, Janet
1985   Etnoarchaeology and Little Rapids: A New Approach to 19th Century Eastern Dakota Sites. Pp. 167–203 in Archaeology, Ecology and Ethnohistory of the Pairie-Forest Border Zone of Minnesota and Manitoba. Janet Spector and Elden Johnson, eds. Lincoln: J&L Reprint Company.

Spencer, Joab
1908   The Kaw or Kansas Indians: Their Customs, Manners and Folk-lore. *Transactions of the Kansas State Historical Society for 1907–1908*, 10:373–382. Topeka.

Sperry, James E.
1968   Excavations at the Havens Site, 32EM1, Emmons County, North Dakota. (Manuscript on file at the State Historical Society of North Dakota, Bismarck.)

_____
1968a   The Shermer Site (32EM10). *Plains Anthropologist* 42(2); *Memoir* 5. Lincoln.

Speth, John D.
1979   The Garnsey Bison Kill Site, Chaves County, New Mexico. Pp. 143–158 in Jornada Mogollon Archaeology Patrick H. Beckett, and Regge N. Wiseman, eds. Las Cruces, N.M.: New Mexico State University Press.

_____
1983   Bison Kills and Bone Counts: Decision Making by Ancient Hunters. Chicago: University of Chicago Press.

Speth, John D., and William J. Parry
1978   Late Prehistoric Bison Procurement in Southeastern New Mexico: The 1977 Season at the Garnsey Site. *University of Michigan. Museum of Anthropology. Technical Reports* 8. Ann Arbor.

_____
1980   Late Prehistoric Bison Procurement in Southeastern New Mexico: The 1978 Season at the Garnsey Site (LA-18399). *University of Michigan. Museum of Anthropology. Technical Reports* 12. Ann Arbor.

Spicer, Edward H., ed.
1961   Perspectives in American Indian Culture Change. Chicago: University of Chicago Press.

_____
1982   The American Indians. Cambridge, Mass.: Harvard University Press.

Spider, Emerson, Sr.
1987   The Native American Church of Jesus Christ. Pp. 189–209 in Sioux Indian Religion: Tradition and Innovation. Raymond J. DeMallie and Douglas R. Parks, eds. Norman: University of Oklahoma Press.

Spielmann, Katherine A.
1983   Late Prehistoric Exchange between the Southwest and Southern Plains. *Plains Anthropologist* 28(102, Pt. 1):257–272.

_____
1991   Interdependence in the Prehistoric Southwest: An Ecological Analysis of Plains-Pueblo Interaction. New York: Garland Publishing. (Revision of the Author's Ph.D. Dissertation in Anthropology, University of Michigan, Ann Arbor, 1982.)

_____
1991a   Coercion or Cooperation? Plains-Pueblo Interaction in the Protohistoric Period. Pp. 36–50 in Farmers, Hunters, and Colonists: Interaction between the Southwest and the Southern Plains. Katherine A. Spielmann, ed. Tucson: University of Arizona Press.

Spier, Leslie 1920 *see* 1921

_____
1921   The Sun Dance of the Plains Indians: Its Development and Diffusion. *American Museum of Natural History Anthropological Papers* 16(7):451–527. New York. (Originally presented as the Author's Ph.D. Dissertation in Anthropology, Columbia University, New York City, 1920.)

_____
1921a   Notes on the Kiowa Sun Dance. *American Museum of Natural History Anthropological Papers* 16(6):433–450. New York.

_____
1924   Wichita and Caddo Relationship Terms. *American Anthropologist*, n.s. 26(2):258–263.

_____
1935   The Prophet Dance of the Northwest and Its Derivatives: The Source of the Ghost Dance. *General Series in Anthropology* 1. Menasha, Wis.: George Banta Publishing Co. (Reprinted: AMS Press, New York, 1979.)

1961 Sun Dance. Pp. 565 in Encyclopaedia Britannica, Vol. 21. London and New York: The Encyclopaedia Britannica.

Spindler, Will H.
1955 Tragedy Strikes at Wounded Knee. Gordon, Nebr.: Journal Publishing Company.

Spitzer, Allen
1960 Religious Structure in Mexico. *Alpha Kappa Delta. Sociological Journal* 30(1):54–58. Claremont, Calif.

Sprague, Douglas N.
1988 Canada and the Métis, 1869–1885. Waterloo, Ont.: Wilfrid Laurier University Press.

_____
1991 Dispossession vs. Accommodation in Plaintiff vs. Defendant Accounts of Métis Dispersal from Manitoba, 1870–1881. *Prairie Forum* 16(2):137–155. Regina, Sask.: Canadian Plains Research Center, University of Regina.

_____
1992 Métis Land Claims. Pp. 195–213 in Aboriginal Land Claims in Canada. Ken Coates, ed. Toronto: Copp, Clark and Pitman.

Sprague, Douglas N., and R.P. Frye, comps.
1983 The Genealogy of the First Métis Nation: The Development and Dispersal of the Red River Settlement, 1820–1900. Winnipeg, Man.: Pemmican Publications.

Sprenger, George H.
1972 An Analysis of Selective Aspects of Métis Society, 1810–1870. (M.A. Thesis in Anthropology, University of Manitoba, Winnipeg.)

_____
1987 The Métis Nation: Buffalo Hunting versus Agriculture in the Red River Settlement, 1810–1870. Pp. 120–135 in Native People, Native Lands. Bruce Alden Cox, ed. *Carleton Library Series* 12. Ottawa: Carleton Library.

Springer, James Warren, and Stanley R. Witkowski
1983 Siouan Historical Linguistics and Oneota Archaeology. Pp. 69–83 in Oneota Studies. Guy E. Gibbon, ed. *University of Minnesota. Publications in Anthropology* 1. Minneapolis. (Title page has 1982 imprint date.)

Springer, Patrick
1998 Métis Work to Preserve Historic Cemetery. *Fargo Forum*, A1, A15, A18. Fargo, N.Dak.

Springer, William F.
1976 The Omaha Indians: What They Ask of the United States Government. *The Indian Historian* 9(Winter):30–33. San Francisco.

Sproat, Gilbert Malcom
1868 Scenes and Studies of Savage Life. London: Smith, Elder. (Reprinted: Sono-Nis Press, Victoria, B.C., 1987.)

Spry, Irene M., ed.
1968 The Papers of the Palliser Expedition, 1857–1860. Edited with an Introduction and Notes by Irene M. Spry. *Publications of the Champlain Society* 44. Toronto: The Champlain Society.

_____
1968a The Transition from a Nomadic to a Settled Economy in Western Canada, 1856–96. *Transactions of the Royal Society of Canada*, 4th ser., Vol. 6:187–201. Ottawa.

_____
1973 The Palliser Expedition: An Account of John Palliser's British North American Exploring Expedition, 1857–1860. Toronto: Macmillan of Canada. (Originally publ. in 1963.)

_____
1976 Buffalo Days and Nights: Reminiscences of Peter Erasmus as Told to Henry Thompson. Calgary, Alta.: Glenbow Alberta Institute.

_____
1976a The Great Transformation: The Disappearance of the Commons in Western Canada History. Pp. 19–27 in Man and Nature on the Prairies. Richard Allen, ed. *Canadian Plains Studies* 6. Regina, Sask.: Canadian Plains Research Center, University of Regina.

_____
1985 The Métis and Mixed-bloods of Rupert's Land Before 1870. Pp. 95–118 in The New Peoples: Being and Becoming Métis in North America. Jacqueline Peterson and Jennifer S.H. Brown, eds. *Manitoba Studies in Native History* 1. Winnipeg: The University of Manitoba Press; Lincoln: University of Nebraska Press.

_____
1985a The "Memories" of George William Sanderson, 1846–1936. Pp. 115–134 in The Métis: Past and Present. Thomas Flanagan and John E. Foster, eds. *Canadian Ethnic Studies* 17(2)[Special issue]. Toronto.

_____
1991 Aboriginal Resource Use in the Nineteenth Century in the Great Plains of Modern Canada. Pp 81–92 in Aboriginal Resource Use in Canada: Historical and Legal Aspects. Kerry Abel and Jean Friesen, eds. Winnipeg: University of Manitoba Press.

Squier, Ephrain G., and Edwin H. Davis
1848 Ancient Monuments of the Mississippi Valley. *Smithsonian Contributions to Knowledge* 1. Washington.

Stabler, Eunice W.
1943 How Beautiful the Land of My Forefathers. [Wichita, Kans.: Privately printed.]

Stallcop, Emmett A.
1968 The So-called Sun Dance of the Gros Ventre. *Plains Anthropologist* 13(40):148–151.

Standing Bear, Luther
1928 My People the Sioux. Earl A. Brininstool, ed. Boston: Houghton Mifflin Company. (Reprinted: University of Nebraska Press, Lincoln, 1975.)

_____
1931 My Indian Boyhood; by Luther Standing Bear, Who Was the Boy, Ota K'te (Plenty Kill). Boston: Houghton Mifflin Company. (Reprinted: University of Nebraska Press, Lincoln, 1988.)

_____
1933 Land of the Spotted Eagle. Boston: Houghton Mifflin Company. (Reprinted, with Foreword by Richard E. Nellis: University of Nebraska Press, Lincoln, 1978.)

_____
1934 Stories of the Sioux. With Illustrations by Herbert Morton Stoops. Boston: Houghton Mifflin Company. (Reprinted: University of Nebraska Press, Lincoln, 1988.)

Stands in Timber, John, and Margot Pringle Liberty
1967 Cheyenne Memories. New Haven, Conn.: Yale University Press.

Stands in Timber, Josephine Glenmore *see* Glenmore, Josephine Stands-in-Timber

Stanford, Edward
1878–1885 Stanford's Compendium of Geography and Travel for General Reading; Based on Hellwald's "Die Erde und ihre Völker." Translated, with Ethnographic Appendix by A.H. Keane. 6 vols. [Vol. 6: North America.] London: E. Stanford.

Stanley, George F.G., ed.
1960 The Birth of Western Canada: A History of the Riel Rebellions. Toronto: University of Toronto Press. (Originally publ. by Longmans, Greens and Company, Ltd., London and New York, 1936. Reprinted with maps by C.C.J. Bond in 1961, 1970, and as 2d ed. in 1992.)

_____, ed.
1963 Louis Riel. Toronto: McGraw-Hill Ryerson Press. (Reprinted in 1972, 1985; also, *Conference donnee à la*

Société historique de St-Boniface, le 17 janvier 1970. St. Boniface, Man.: Société historique de St. Boniface, 1970.)

_____, ed.
1985   The Collected Writing of Louis Riel/ Les ecrits complets de Louis Riel. 5 vols. Edmonton, Alta.: The University of Alberta Press.

Stanley, Lori A.
1993   The Indian Path of Life: A Life History of Truman Washington Dailey of the Otoe-Missouria Tribe. (Ph.D. Dissertation in Anthropology, University of Missouri, Columbia.)

Stanley, Samuel, ed.
1978   American Indian Economic Development. The Hague: Mouton.

Stanley, Samuel, and Robert K. Thomas
1968   The North American Indians:1950 Distribution of Descendants of the Aboriginal Population of Alaska, Canada and the United States. Washington: Center for the Study of Man, Smithsonian Institution.

Stanton, James B.
1972   The Plains Buffalo: The Staff of Life. Illustrated by Larry Jamieson. Winnipeg, Man.: Manitoba Museum of Man and Nature. [Juvenile lit.]

Starita, Joe
1995   The Dull Knives of Pine Ridge: A Lakota Odyssey. New York: Putnam.

Starkloff, Carl F.
1974   The People of the Center: American Indian Religion and Christianity. *A Crossroad Book.* New York: Seabury Press.

Starlight, Bruce
1983   Sarcee Indian Days. In Tsu T'ina K'osa. Calgary: JBC and Associates.

Starr, Edward
1994   Dictionary of Modern Lakota. Kendall Park, N.J.: Lakota Books.

Starr, Frederick
1889   Mound Explorations in Northwestern Iowa. *Proceedings of the Davenport Academy of Natural Sciences [for] 1884–1889,* Vol. 5(1):110–112. Davenport, Iowa.

Statistics Canada
1994   Aboriginal Data: Canada's Aboriginal Population by Census Subdivisions and Census Metropolitan Areas. Ottawa: Statistics Canada.

Stead, Robert
1987   Traditional Lakota Religion in Modern Life. Pp. 211–216 in Sioux Indian Religion: Tradition and Innovation. Raymond J. DeMallie and Douglas R. Parks, eds. Norman: University of Oklahoma Press.

Stearn, Esther Wagner, and Allen E. Stearn
1945   The Effect of Smallpox on the Destiny of the Amerindian. Boston: B. Humphries. (Reprinted: Brown Book Company, Deer Park, N.Y., 1971.)

Stecker, Ernest
1910   [Narrative and Statistical Report for the Year 1910, Kiowa Agency, Anadarko, Okla.] (Microfilm M-1011, Roll 70, Frames 815–855, Superintendents' Annual Narrative and Statistical Reports from Field Jurisdictions of the Bureau of Indian Affairs, 1907–1938, Records of the Bureau of Indian Affairs, Record Group 75, National Archives, Washington.)

1912   [Letter to Cantonment School Superintendent, dated Kiowa Agency, August 14, 1912, re. dances.] (Manuscript, Microfilm CA45, Frame 886, Cheyenne and Arapaho: Indian History, Culture and Acculturation, Newspapers/Archives and Manuscript Division, Oklahoma Historical Society, Oklahoma City.)

Steege, Louis C.
1960   A Probable Middle Period Burial in Wyoming. *Plains Anthropologist* 5(10):82–84.

Steele, C. Hoy
1975   Urban Indian Identity in Kansas: Some Implications for Research. Pp. 167–178 in The New Ethnicity. John W. Bennett, ed. St. Paul, Minn.: West Publishing Co.

Steele, Sir Samuel Benfield
1915   Forty Years in Canada: Reminiscences of the Great North-West with Some Account of His Service in South Africa, by Colonel S.B. Steele, C.B., M.V.O., [etc.]. Toronto: McClelland, Goodchild and Stewart; London: Hervert Jenkins. (Reissued: *The Ryerson Archive Series,* McGraw-Hill Ryerson Limited, Toronto, 1972.)

Steele, William
1849   [Letter to George Deas, dated September 22, 1849.] (Microfilm M234, Roll 858, Frames 441–442, Letters Received, Texas Agency 1847–52, Records of the Bureau of Indian Affairs, Record Group 75, National Archives, Washington.)

Stegler, Robert
1949   [Fieldnotes Regarding Excavation of the Snake Blakeslee Site.] (On file at the Department of Anthropology, University of Denver, Denver.)

Steiger, Brad
1974   Medicine Power. Garden City, N.Y.: Doubleday and Company.

Stein, Wayne J.
1992   Tribally Controlled Colleges: Making Good Medicine. New York: Peter Lang.

Steinacher, Terry L., and Gayle F. Carlson
1998   The Central Plains Tradition. Pp. 235–268 in Archaeology on the Great Plains. W. Raymond Wood, ed. Lawrence: University Press of Kansas.

Steinbring, Jack H. 1981 *see* Handbook Vol. 6 (1981:244–255)

Steiner, Stan
1968   The New Indians. New York: Harper and Row.

Steinmetz, Paul B. (S.J.)
1984   The Sacred Pipe in American Indian Religions. *American Indian Culture and Research Journal* 8(3): 27–80. Los Angeles.

_____
1990   Pipe, Bible, and Peyote among the Oglala Lakota: A Study in Religious Identity. Knoxville: University of Tennessee Press.

Steltenkamp, Michael F.
1982   The Sacred Vision: Native American Religion and Its Practice Today. New York: Paulist Press.

_____
1993   Black Elk: Holy Man of the Oglala. Norman: University of Oklahoma Press.

Stenberg, Molly Peacock
1946   The Peyote Cult among Wyoming Indians: A Transitional Link Between an Indigenous Culture and an Imposed Culture. *University of Wyoming Publications* 12(4): 85–156. Laramie.

Stephenson, Robert L.
1954   Taxonomy and Chronology in the Central Plains-Middle Missouri Area. *Plains Anthropologist* 1(1):15–21.

_____
1962   Three Smithsonian Salvage Sites. *Plains Anthropologist* 7(16):80–81.

_____
1969   Blue Blanket Island (39WW9): An Historic Contact Site in the Oahe Reservoir Near Mobridge, South Dakota. *Plains Anthropologist* 14(43):1–31.

1971   The Potts Village Site (39CO19), Oahe Reservoir, North Central South Dakota. *The Missouri Archaeologist* 33. Columbia.

Stern, Theodore
1996   Tradition and Change: Kiowa Indian Art. Pp. 1–7 in Chin Hills to Chiloquin: Papers Honoring the Versatile Career of Theodore Stern. With A Note of Personal Appreciation by Patrick M. Haynal. Don E. Dumond, ed. *University of Oregon Anthropological Papers* 52. Eugene.

Stern, Theodore, Martin Schmitt, and Alphonse F. Halfmoon
1980   A Cayuse-Nez Percé Sketchbook. *Oregon Historical Quarterly* 81(4):341–376.

Sterns, Frederick H.
1914   Ancient Lodge Sites on the Missouri in Nebraska. *American Anthropologist*, n.s. 16(1):135–137.

1915   The Archaeology of Eastern Nebraska, with Special Reference to the Culture of the Rectangular Earth Lodges. 2 vols. (Ph.D. Dissertation in Anthropology, Harvard University, Cambridge, Mass.)

1915a   A Stratification of Cultures in Eastern Nebraska. *American Anthropologist*, n.s. 17(1):121–127.

Stevens, Hazard
1900   The Life of Isaac Ingalls Stevens, by His Son, Hazard Stevens. Boston and New York: Houghton, Mifflin and Company.

Stevens, Isaac Ingalls
1859   Reports of the Explorations and Surveys, To Ascertain the Most Practicable and Economical Route for a Railroad from the Mississippi River to the Pacific Ocean. Made under the Direction of the Secretary of War, in 1853–5, according to Acts of Congress of March 3, 1853, May 31, 1854, and August 5, 1854. *35th Congress. 2d Session. Senate Executive Document 46*. Vol. 1. Washington: William A. Harris.

1860   Reports of Explorations and Surveys, To Ascertain the Most Practicable and Economical Route for a Railroad from the Mississippi River to the Pacific Ocean. Made under the Direction of the Secretary of War, in 1853–5, according to Acts of Congress of March 3, 1853, May 31, 1854, and August 5, 1854. *36th Congress. 1st Session. House Executive Document 56*. Vol. 2. Washington: Thomas H. Ford, Printer.

Stevens, Jedediah Dwight
1836   Sioux Spelling-Book, Designed for the Use of Native Learners. Boston: The Board of Commissioners for Foreign Missions.

Stevenson, Winona
1996   The Journals and Voices of a Church of England Native Catechist: Askenootow (Charles Pratt). Pp. 304–329 in Reading Beyond Words: Contexts for Native History. Jennifer S.H. Brown and Elizabeth Vibert, eds. Peterborough, Ont.: Broadview Press.

Steward, Julian H.
1934   The Blackfoot. Berkeley, Calif.: National Park Service, Field Division of Education.

1937   Ancient Caves of the Great Salt Lake Region. *Bureau of American Ethnology Bulletin* 116. Washington: Smithsonian Institution; U.S. Government Printing Office.

1938   Basin-Plateau Aboriginal Sociopolitical Groups. *Bureau of American Ethnology Bulletin* 120. Washington: Smithsonian Institution; U.S. Government Printing Office. (Reprinted: University of Utah Press, Salt Lake City, 1970.)

1940   Native Cultures of the Intermontane (Great Basin) Area. Pp. 445–502 in Essays in Historical Anthropology of North America. *Smithsonian Miscellaneous Collections* 100. Washington: Smithsonian Institution; Government Printing Office.

1943   Culture Element Distributions, XXIII: Northern and Gosiute Shoshoni. *University of California Anthropological Records* 8(3):263–392. Berkeley.

1955   Theory of Culture Change: The Methodology of Multilinear Evolution. Urbana: University of Illinois Press.

Stewart, Edgar I.
1955   Custer's Luck. Norman: University of Oklahoma Press.

Stewart, Frank H.
1974   Mandan and Hidatsa Villages in the Eighteenth and Nineteenth Centuries. *Plains Anthropologist* 19(66, Pt.1):287–302.

1975   [Hidatsa Population Figures in David Thompson.] (Typescript, copy in *Handbook* Office, Smithsonian Institution, Washington.)

1975a   [Village Movements of the North Horticulturalists (Mandan and Hidatsa) 1675 to 1860.] (Manuscript in National Park Service, Midwest Archaeological Center, Lincoln, Nebr.)

1976   Hidatsa Origin Traditions Reported by Lewis and Clark. *Plains Anthropologist* 21(72):89–92.

1977   Fundamentals of Age-Group Systems. New York: Academic Press.

Stewart, Jeffrey C.
1989   To Color America: Portraits by Winold Reiss. With an Essay by John C. Ewers. Washington City: Smithsonian Institution Press for the National Portrait Gallery.

Stewart, Omer C.
1944   Washo-Northern Paiute Peyotism: A Study in Acculturation. Berkeley: University of California Press.

1952   Southern Ute Adjustment to Modern Living. Pp. 80–87 in Acculturation in the Americas, Sol Tax, ed. Chicago: University of Chicago Press.

1960   [Sun Dance Fieldnotes.] (Manuscript, University of Colorado, Boulder.)

1962   [Fieldnotes, on the Sun Dance, Ignacio, 4–9 July 1962.] (Manuscript, University of Colorado, Boulder.)

1966   Ute Indians: Before and After White Contact. *Utah Historical Quarterly* 34:38–61. Salt Lake City.

1977   Contemporary Document on Wovoka (Jack Wilson) Prophet of the Ghost Dance in 1890. *Ethnohistory* 24(3):219–222.

1978   The Western Shoshone of Nevada and the U.S. Government, 1863–1950. Pp. 77–114 in Selected Papers from the 14th Great Basin Anthropological Conference, September 14, 1974. Donald R. Tuohy, ed. *Ballena Press Publications in Archaeology, Ethnology and History* 11. Ramona, Calif.

1979   A New Look at Cree Peyotism. Pp. 151–155 in Lifeways of Intermontane and Plains Montana Indians: In Honor of J. Verne Dusenberry. Leslie B. Davis, ed. *Occasional Paspers of the Museum of the Rockies* 1. Bozeman, Mont.: Montana State University.

1980   The Ghost Dance. Pp. 178–187 in Anthropology on the

Great Plains. W. Raymond Wood and Margot Liberty, eds. Lincoln: University of Nebraska Press.

1980a   Peyotism and Mescalism. *Plains Anthropologist* 25(90): 297–301.

1987   The Peyote Religion: A History. Norman: University of Oklahoma Press.

Stewart, Rick, Joseph D. Ketner, II, and Angela L. Miller
1991   Carl Wimar: Chronicler of the Missouri River Frontier. Fort Worth, Tex.: Amon Carter Museum; New York: Distributed by Harry N. Abrams.

Stewart, T. Dale
1954   Appendix: The Lower Level Human Skull. Pp. 457–459 in The McKean Site in Northeastern Wyoming, by William T. Mulloy. *Southwestern Journal of Anthropology* 10(4):432–460. Albuquerque.

Stewart, Tyrone, and Jerry Smith
1973   The Oklahoma Feather Dancer. Tulsa, Okla.: American Indian Crafts and Culture.

Stillman, Pamela
1994   Tipis, Tipis Everywhere; Crow Fair Attendance an Estimated 30,000. *Indian Country Today,* Aug. 3:A6. Rapid City, S.Dak.

Stinchecum, C.V.
1917   [Letter to Commissioner of Indian Affairs; dated 19 September, 1917.] (Manuscript, file 067, "Business Committee 1916–1922" in Federal Records Center. Fort Worth, Tex.)

1917a   [Narrative Report to the Commissioner of Indian Affairs; dated Kiowa Indian Agency, Anadarko, Okla., August 23d, 1917.] (Document in Microfilm M-1011, Roll 70, Superintendents' Annual Narrative and Statistical Reports from Field Jurisdictions of the Bureau of Indian Affairs, 1907–1938, Records of the Bureau of Indian Affairs, Record Group 75, National Archives, Washington.)

Stiner, Mary C., ed.
1991   Human Predators and Prey Mortality. Boulder, Colo.: Westview Press.

Stipe, Claude E.
1968   Eastern Dakota Acculturation: The Role of Agents of Culture Change. (Ph.D. Dissertation in Anthropology, University of Minnesota, Minneapolis.)

1971   Eastern Dakota Clans: The Solution of a Problem. *American Anthropologist,* n.s. 73(5):1031–1035.

Stirling, Matthew W.
1924   Archeological Investigations in South Dakota. Pp. 66–71 in Explorations and Field Work of the Smithsonian Institution in 1923. *Smithsonian Miscellaneous Collections* 76(10). Washington: Smithsonian Institution; Government Printing Office.

1938   Three Pictographic Autobiographies of Sitting Bull. *Smithsonian Miscellaneous Collections* 97(5):1–57. Washington: Smithsonian Institution; Government Printing Office.

1947   Arikara Glassworking. *Journal of the Washington Academy of Sciences* 37(8):257–263. Washington.

Stocking, George W., Jr., ed.
1974   The Shaping of American Anthropology, 1883–1911: A Franz Boas Reader. New York: Basic Books.

Stolzman, William First Eagle
1986   How to Take Part in Lakota Ceremonies. Pine Ridge: Heritage Center, Red Cloud Indian School. (Reprinted in 1988; and, Tipi Press, Chamberlain, S.Dak., 1995.)

Stone, Tammy
1999   The Prehistory of Colorado and Adjacent Areas. Salt Lake City: University of Utah Press.

Stonechild, Blair
1986   The Indian View of the 1885 Uprising. Pp. 155–170 in 1885 and After: Native Society in Transition. Regina, Sask.: University of Regina.

Stonechild, Blair, and Bill Waiser
1997   Loyal Till Death: Indians and the North-West Rebellion. Calgary, Alta.: Fifth House Publishers.

Stoney Cultural Education Program
1973   The Stoney Alphabet. [9–73 ed.] Morley, Alta.: Stoney Cultural Education Program.

Stoney News
1981–   *Stoney News: Newspaper of the Stoney Tribe.* Morley, Alta.: The [Stoney] Tribe.

Stoney Tribal Administration (S.T.A.)
1986   A New Path in the Mountains: A Financial Report to Stoney Members on Major Expeditures 1976–1985. Morley, Alta.: Stoney Tribal Council.

Storck, Peter L.
1973   A Description of Some Paleo-Indian and Archaic Projectile Points and Knives from Saskatchewan, Manitoba and Alberta in Collections of the Royal Ontario Museum, Toronto. *Saskatchewan Archaeology Society Newsletter* 44:1–28. Saskatoon.

Story, Dee Ann, and S. Valestro, Jr.
1977   Radiocarbon Dating and the George C. Davis Site, Texas. *Journal of Field Archaeology* 4(1):63–89.

Straffin, Dean
1971   Wolfe Havana Hopewell Site. Pp. 53–65 in Prehistoric Investigations. Marshall McKusick, ed. *University of Iowa. Office of the State Archaeologist. Report* 3. Iowa City.

Straus, Anne S.
1976   Being Human in the Cheyenne Way. (Ph.D. Dissertation in Anthropology, University of Chicago, Chicago.)

1977   Northern Cheyenne Ethnopsychology. *Ethos* 5(3):326–357. Ames, Iowa, [etc.]

1978   The Meaning of Death in Northern Cheyenne Culture. *Plains Anthropologist* 23(79):1–6.

1994   Northern Cheyenne Kinship Reconsidered. Pp. 147–171 in North American Indian Anthropology: Essays on Society and Culture. Raymond J. DeMallie and Alfonso Ortiz, eds. Norman: University of Oklahoma Press.

Strauss, Joseph H., and Bruce A. Chadwick
1979   Urban Indian Adjustment. *American Indian Culture and Research Journal* 3(2):23–38. Los Angeles.

Strickland, Rennard
1992   The Santa Fe Indian Studio: Traditional Indian Painting of the Santa Fe Studio. Norman: Fred Jones, Jr., Museum of Art.

Strickland, Rennard, and Margaret Archuleta
1991   "The Way People Were Meant To Live". Pp. 5–11 in Shared Visions: Native American Painters and Sculptors in the Twentieth Century, by Margaret Archuleta and Rennard Strickland. Essays by Joy L. Gritton [and] W. Jackson Rushing. Phoenix: Heard Museum.

Strong, William Duncan
1932   An Archeological Reconnaissance in the Missouri Valley. Pp. 151–158 in *Explorations and Field-work of the Smithsonian Institution in 1931.* Washington: Smithsonian Institution.

1933   The Plains Culture Area in the Light of Archaeology. *American Anthropologist,* n.s. 35(2):271–287.

1935   An Introduction to Nebraska Archeology. *Smithsonian Miscellaneous Collections* 93(10):1–323. Washington: Smithsonian Institution; U.S.Government Printing Office.

1940   From History to Prehistory in the Northern Great Plains. Pp. 353–394 in Essays in Historical Anthropology of North America, Published in Honor of John R. Swanton in Celebration of His Fortieth Year with the Smithsonian Institution. *Smithsonian Miscellaneous Collections* 100; (*Publication* 3588). Washington: Smithsonian Institution; Government Printing Office. (Reprinted in: *Plains Anthropologist* 17(57):353–388, 1972.)

Strout, Clevy Lloyd
1971   Flora and Fauna Mentioned in the Journals of the Coronado Expedition. *Great Plains Journal* 11(1):5–40. Lawton, Okla.

Stuart, Glenn S.L.
1990   The Cranford Site (DlPb-2): A Multicomponent Stone Circle Site on the Oldman River. *Archaeological Survey of Alberta. Manuscript Series* 17. Edmonton.

Stuart, Granville
1865   Montana As It Is: Being a General Description of Its Resources both Mineral and Agricultural, Including a Complete Description of the Face of the Country, Its Climate, etc.; Illus. with A Map of the Territory Drawn by Capt. W.W. DeLacey, Showing the Different Roads and the Location of the Difference Mining Districts. To Which Is Appended a Complete Dictionary of the Snake Language, and also of the Famous Chinook Jargon, with Numerous Critical and Explanatory Notes, Concerning the Habits, Superstitions, etc., of These Indians, with Itineraries of All the Routes across the Plains. New York: C.S. Westcott & Co. (Reprinted: Arno Press, New York, 1973.)

1925   Forty Years on the Frontier as Seen in the Journals and Reminiscences of Granville Stuart, Gold-miner, Trader, Merchant, Rancher and Politician. Paul C. Phillips, ed. Cleveland, Ohio: Arthur H. Clark.

Stuart, Robert
1935   The Discovery of the Oregon Trail: Robert Stuart's Narrative of His Overland Trip Eastward from Astoria in 1812–1813. New York: Charles Scribner's Sons.

Stubbendieck, James L., Stephan L. Hatch, and Charles H. Butterfield
1992   North American Range Plants. 2d ed. Lincoln: University of Nebraska Press.

Stuiver, Minze, and Gordon W. Pearson
1986   High-precision Calibration of the Radiocarbon Time Scale, AD 1950–500BC. *Radiocarbon* 28(2B):805–838. New Haven, Conn.

Stuiver, Minze, and P.J. Reimer
1986   A Computer Program for Radiocarbon Age Calibration. *Radiocarbon* 28(2B):1022–1030. New Haven, Conn.

Stuiver, Minze, and Hans E. Suess
1966   On the Relationship between Radiocarbon Dates and True Sample Ages. *Radiocarbon* 8:534–541. New Haven, Conn.

Sturm, J.J.
1875   [Notes of Travel in Search of the Quah-de-ru Band of Comanches.] (Manuscript S248/2 in Letters Received, Department of the Missouri, Record Group 98, National Archives, Washington.)

Sturtevant, William C., and June Helm 1981 *see* Handbook Vol. 6 (1981:xii–xvi)

Subcommittee on Indian Affairs
1950   Compilation of Material Relating to the Indians of the United States and the Territory of Alaska, Including Certain Laws and Treaties Affecting Such Indians. Subcommittee on Indian Affairs of the Committee on Public Lands, House of Representatives. *81st Congress. 2d Session. House Report No.* 66. Washington: U.S. Government Printing Office.

Suhm, Dee A., Alex D. Krieger, and Edward B. Jelks
1954   An Introductory Handbook of Texas Archeology. *Bulletin of the Texas Archeological Society* 25. Austin.

Summreby, Janice
1993   Native Soldiers, Foreign Battlefields. Ottawa: Communications Division, Veteran Affairs Canada; Minister of Supply and Services Canada.

Sunder, John E.
1965   The Fur Trade on the Upper Missouri, 1840–1865. Norman: University of Oklahoma Press. (Reprinted in 1993.)

1968   Joshua Pilcher: Fur Trader and Indian Agent. Norman: University of Oklahoma Press.

Sundstrom, Linea
1989   Culture History of the Black Hills with References to Adjacent Areas of the Northern Great Plains. *Reprints in Anthropology* 40. Lincoln: J&L Reprint Company.

1997   Smallpox Used Them Up: References to Epidemic Disease in Northern Plains Winter Counts, 1714–1920. *Ethnohistory* 44(2):305–343. Bloomington.

1997a   The Sacred Black Hills: An Ethnohistorical Overview. *Great Plains Quarterly* 17(3–4):185–212. Lincoln, Nebr.

Supree, Burton, and Ann Ross
1971   Bear's Heart: Scenes from the Life of a Cheyenne Artist One Hundred Years Ago with Pictures by Himself. Philadelphia: J.B. Lippincott.

Sutherland, Edwin V.
1964   The Diaries of John Gregory Bourke: Their Anthropological and Folkloric Content: A Dissertation in Folklore. (Ph.D. Dissertation in Folklore, University of Pennsylvania, Philadelphia.)

Svaldi, David
1989   Sand Creek and the Rhetoric of Extermination: A Case Study in Indian-White Relations. Lanham, Md.: University Press of America.

Svingen, Orlan J.
1993   The Northern Cheyenne Indian Reservation, 1877–1900. Niwot, Colo.: University Press of Colorado. (Reprinted in 1997.)

Svoboda, Joseph G., comp.
1983   Guide to American Indian Resource Materials in Great Plains Repositories. Lincoln: Center for Great Plains Studies, University of Nebraska.

Swadesh, Morris
1958   Some New Glottochronological Dates for Amerindian Linguistic Groups. Pp. 670–674 in *Proceedings of the 32nd International Congress of Americanists, Copenhagen, 8–14 August 1956.* Copenhagen: Munksgaard.

1967   Linguistic Classification in the Southwest. Pp. 281–309 in Studies in Southwestern Ethnolinguistics. Dell Hymes and William E. Brittle, eds. The Hague: Mouton.

Swagerty, William R.
1980   Marriage and Settlement Patterns of Rocky Mountain Trappers and Traders. *Western Historical Quarterly* 11(2):159–180. Logan, Utah.

_____ 1988 *see* Handbook Vol. 4 (1988:351–374)

1991   Protohistoric Trade in Western North America: Archaeological and Ethnohistorical Considerations. Pp. 471–499 in Columbian Consequences, Vol. 3: The Spanish Borderlands in Pan-American Perspective. David Hurst Thomas, ed. Washington: Smithsonian Institution Press.

1994   The Upper Missouri Outfit: The Men and the Fur Trade in the 1830s. Pp. 25–42 in Fort Union Fur Trade Symposium Proceedings, September 13–15, 1990. Williston, N.Dak.: Friends of Fort Union Trading Post for the National Park Service.

_____, ed. 1997 *see* Chardon, Francis A. 1932 (reprint info.)

Swan, Daniel C.
1998   Early Osage Peyotism. *Plains Anthropologist* 43(163):51–71.

1999   Peyote Religious Art: Symbols of Faith and Belief. Jackson, Miss.: University Press of Mississippi.

Swanson, Earl H., Jr., and Paul G. Sneed
1966   The Archaeology of the Shoup Rockshelters in East Central Idaho. *Occasional Papers of the Idaho State University Museum* 17; *Birch Creek Papers* 3. Pocatello.

Swanson, Earl H., Jr., B. Robert Butler, and Robson Bonnichsen
1964   Natural and Cultural Stratigraphy in the Birch Creek Valley of Eastern Idaho. *Occasional Papers of the Idaho State University Museum* 14; *Birch Creek Papers* 2. Pocatello.

Swanton, John R.
1909   A New Siouan Dialect. Pp. 477–486 in Putnam Anniversary Volume: Anthropological Essays Presented to Fr. W. Putnam in Honour of his Seventieth Birthday. Franz Boas, ed. New York: G.E. Stechert.

1911   Indian Tribes of the Lower Mississippi Valley and Adjacent Coast of the Gulf of Mexico. *Bureau of American Ethnology Bulletin* 43. Washington: Smithsonian Institution; U.S. Government Printing Office. (Reprinted: Johnson Reprint, New York, 1970; also, Dover Publications, Mineola, N.Y., 1998.)

1915   Linguistic Position of the Tribes of Southern Texas and Northeastern Mexico. *American Anthropologist*, n.s. 17(1):17–40.

1921   [Pawnee Word List.] (Manuscript in National Anthropological Archives, Smithsonian Institution, Washington.)

1923   New Light on the Early History of the Siouan Peoples. *Journal of the Washington Academy of Sciences* 13(3):33–43. [Publ. by Williams & Wilkins, Baltimore, for the Washington Academy of Sciences.]

1936   Early History of the Eastern Siouan Tribes. Pp. 371–381 in Essays in Anthropology Presented to A.L. Kroeber. Robert H. Lowie, ed. Berkeley: University of California Press.

1940   Linguistic Material from the Tribes of Southern Texas and Northeastern Mexico. *Bureau of American Ethnology Bulletin* 127. Washington: Smithsonian Institution; U.S. Government Printing Office.

1942   Source Material on the History and Ethnology of the Caddo Indians. *Bureau of American Ethnology Bulletin* 132. Washington: Smithsonian Institution; U.S. Government Printing Office. (Reprinted, with a Foreword by Helen Hornbeck Tanner: University of Oklahoma Press, Norman, 1996.)

1943   Siouan Tribes and the Ohio Valley. *American Anthropologist*, n.s. 45(1):49–66.

1952   The Indian Tribes of North America. *Bureau of American Ethnology Bulletin* 145. Washington: Smithsonian Institution; U.S. Government Printing Office. (Reprinted: Smithsonian Institution Press, Washington, 1969, 1995.)

_____, ed.
1985   Final Report of the United States De Soto Expedition Commission [1939]. With an Introduction by J.P. Brain and Foreword by W.C. Sturtevant. *Classics of Smithsonian Anthropology Series*. Washington: Smithsonian Institution Press.

Swenson, Fern E.
1986   A Study in Cultural Adaptation to Climatic Shifts on the Southern Plains: Washita River Phase and Edwards Complex Cultural Complexity. (M.A. Thesis in Anthropology, University of Oklahoma, Norman.)

Swenson, Fern E., and Michael L. Gregg
1988   A Devils Lake-Sourisford Mortuary Vessel from Southeastern North Dakota. *Journal of the North Dakota Archaeological Association* 3:1–15. Grand Forks.

Swetland, Mark J., comp.
1977   Umoⁿhoⁿ iye of Elizabeth Stabler: A Vocabulary of the Omaha Language. Winnebago, Nebr.: Nebraska Indian Press.

Switlo, Janice G.A.E.
1997   Gustafsen Lake: Under Siege: Exposing the Truth Behind the Gustafsen Lake Stand-off. Peachland, B.C.: TIAC Communications Ltd.

Sword, George
1909   [Lakota Texts; Written for James R. Walker.] (Manuscript in Department of Anthropology Archives, American Museum of Natural History, New York.)

1998   [Lakota Texts by George Sword.] (Edited by Raymond J. DeMallie from manuscripts in the Colorado Historical Society, Denver, and the American Museum of Natural History, New York.)

Syms, E. Leigh
1969   The McKean Complex as a Horizon Marker in Manitoba and on the Northern Great Plains. (M.A. Thesis in Anthropology, University of Manitoba, Winnipeg.)

1970   The McKean Complex in Manitoba. Pp. 123–138 in Ten Thousand Years: Archaeology in Manitoba. Walter M. Hlady, ed. Winnipeg: Manitoba Archaeological Society.

1972   The 1971 Field Season in the Southwestern Manitoba Research Area. (Archaeology Manuscript No. 750, Library of the Canadian Museum of Civilization, Hull, Que.)

1977   Cultural Ecology and Ecological Dynamics of the Ceramic Period in Southwestern Manitoba. *Plains Anthropologist* 22(76, Pt. 2); *Memoir* 12. Lincoln.

1978   Aboriginal Mounds in Southern Manitoba: An Evaluative Overview. *Parks Canada. Manuscript Report* 323. Ottawa.

1979   The Devil's Lake-Sourisford Burial Complex on the Northeastern Plains. *Plains Anthropologist* 24(86):283–308.

1980   A Description and Analysis of the Nash Random Survey Sample, Southwestern Manitoba, 1972–1973. *Brandon University. Southman Human Adaptation and Paleo-environmental Explorations. Data Log* 1. Brandon, Man.

Szabo, Joyce M.
1992   Howling Wolf: An Autobiography of a Plains Warrior-Artist. *Allen Memorial Art Museum. Bulletin* 46(1):4–87. Oberlin, Ohio: Oberlin College.

1266

1994   Howling Wolf and the History of Ledger Art. Albuquerque: University of New Mexico Press.

Szasz, Margaret Connell
1974   Education and the American Indian: The Road to Self-Determination Since 1928. Albuquerque: University of New Mexico Press.

1975   Thirty Years Too Soon: Indian Education under the Indian New Deal. *Integrated Education* 13(4):3–9. Chicago.

Szasz, Margaret Connell, and Carmelita Ryan 1988 *see* Handbook Vol. 4 (1988:284–300)

Tabeau, Pierre-Antoine
1939   Tabeau's Narrative of Loisel's Expedition to the Upper Missouri. Annie Heloise Abel, ed.; Translated from the French by Rose Abel Wright. Norman: University of Oklahoma Press. (Reprinted in 1968.)

Taft, Robert
1953   Artists and Illustrators of the Old West, 1850–1900. New York: Scribner. (Reprinted in 1970.)

Takahashi, Junichi
1984   Case Marking in Kiowa: A Study of Organization of Meaning. (Ph.D. Dissertation in Linguistics, City University of New York, New York.)

Talks and Councils
1910   Papers Relating to Talks and Councils Held with the Indians in Dakota and Montana Territories in the Years 1866–1869. Washington: Government Printing Office.

Tallbull, Henry, and Tom Weist
1971   The Turtle Went to War: Northern Cheyenne Folk Tales. Illustrated by Rebekah Knows Gun [et al.]. *Indian Culture Series. Series of the Northern Cheyenne* BB-12. Billings, Mont.: Montana Reading Publications.

Tallbull, Richard
1988   We Are the Ancestors of Those Yet To Be Born: Northern Cheyenne History and The Battle of 100-in-Hand (The Fetterman Battle). Sheridan, Wyo.: Bozeman Trail Association.

Tambiah, Stanley J.
1965   Kinship Fact and Fiction in Relation to the Kandyan Sinhalese. *Journal of the Royal Anthropological Institute of Great Britain and Ireland* 95(2):131–173. London.

Tamplin, Morgan
1977   Prehistoric Occupation and Resource Exploitation on the Saskatchewan River at The Pas, Manitoba. (Ph.D. Dissertation in Anthropology, University of Arizona, Tucson.)

Tannenbaum, Joan S.
1992   "They Count the Years by Winters": Mandan-Hidatsa Lifeways as Related in Butterfly's Winter Count and Accompanying Commentary by Buffalo Bird Woman. (M.A. Thesis in Anthropology, Hunter College, The City University of New York, New York.)

Tanner, Beccy
1996   Kaw Nation Wants To Log Artifacts. *The Wichita Eagle,* Oct.18:13-A.

Tanner, Helen Hornbeck
1972   The Territory of the Caddo Tribe of Oklahoma. Indian Claims Commission Docket 226. (Reprinted as pp. 66–104 in Caddo Indians IV. David Agee Horr, comp. and ed. Garland, New York, 1974.)

1994   The Career of Joseph La France, *Courer de Bois* in the Upper Great Lakes. Pp. 171–187 in The Fur Trade Revisited: Selected Papers of the Sixth North American Fur Trade Conference, Mackinac Island, Michigan, 1991. Jennifer S.H. Brown, W.J. Eccles, and Donald P. Heldman, eds. East Lansing/Mackinac Island: Michigan State University Press and Mackinac State Historic Parks.

_____, et al., eds.
1987   Atlas of Great Lakes Indian History. Carthography by Miklos Pinther. Norman: University of Oklahoma Press for the Newberry Library.

Tanner, John
1830   Narrative of Captivity and Adventures of John Tanner ... during Thirty Years' Residence among the Indians in the Interior of North America. Edwin James, ed. New York: G. and C. and H. Carvill. (Reprinted: Ross and Haines, Minneapolis, 1956.)

Tarasoff, Koozma J.
1980   Persistent Ceremonialism: The Plains Cree and Saulteaux. *Canada. National Museum of Man. Mercury Series. Ethnology Service Paper* 69. Ottawa.

Tardif, Émile
1961   St-Albert. Edmonton, Alta.: La Survivance.

Tate, Michael L.
1971   Frontier Defense on the Comanche Ranges of Northwest Texas, 1846–1860. *Great Plains Journal* 11(1):41–56. Lawton, Okla.

1986   The Indians of Texas: An Annotated Research Bibliography. *Native American Bibliography Series* 9. Metuchen, N.J., and London: The Scarecrow Press.

1991   The Upstream People: An Annotated Research Bibliography of the Omaha Tribe. *Native American Bibliography Series* 14. Metuchen, N.J., and London: The Scarecrow Press.

1994   Comanche Captives: People Between Two Worlds. *Chronicles of Oklahoma* 72(3):228–263. Norman.

Tatum, Lawrie
[1870]   [A Nominal List Containing the Name of Each Head of Band in the Comanche and Kiowa Tribes of Indians.] (Manuscript, microfilm publication KA, Roll 1A, frame 15 in Kiowa Agency Records, Oklahoma Historical Society, Oklahoma City.)

1872   [Letter to Enoch Hoag, dated Kiowa Agency, I.T., November 15, 1872; Enclosure in Letter to Cyrus Beede to F.A. Walker, 22 November, 1872.] (Microfilm M234, Roll 377, Frames 842–845, Letters Received, Kiowa Agency, 1864–1880, Records of the Bureau of Indian Affairs, Record Group 75, National Archives, Washington)

Tax, Sol, et al.
1960   The North American Indians: 1950 Distribution of Descendants of the Aboriginal Population of Alaska, Canada, and the United States. Map, prepared under the direction of Sol Tax. 5th printing. ("The data for the United States were compiled by Samuel Stanley and Robert K. Thomas in 1956, for correction. In 1957 Bruce MacLachlan added the data for Canada, and Stanley for Alaska. The composite map was then made by MacLachlan and Myron Rosenberg, and finally revised and corrected by Stanley.") Chicago: University of Chicago, Department of Anthropology.

1978   The Impact of Urbanization on American Indians. *Annals of the American Academy of Political and Social Science* 436:121–136. Philadelphia.

Taylor, Allan R.
1963   The Classification of the Caddoan Languages. *Proceedings of the American Philosophical Society* 107(1):51–59. Philadelphia.

1267

1963a   Comparative Caddoan. *International Journal of American Linguistics* 29(2):113–131. Chicago.

1967   Some Observations on a Comparative Arapaho-Atsina Lexicon. Pp. 113–127 in Contributions to Anthropology: Linguistics I. *National Museum of Canada. Bulletin* 214; *Anthropological Series* 78. Ottawa.

1969   A Grammar of Blackfoot. (Ph.D. Dissertation in Linguistics, University of California, Berkeley.)

1976   On Verbs of Motion in Siouan Languages. *International Journal of American Linguistics* 42(4):287–296. Chicago.

1977   Arikara Texts. Pp. 20–26 in Caddoan Texts. Douglas R. Parks, ed. *International Journal of American Linguistics. Native American Texts Series* 2(1). Chicago: The University of Chicago Press.

1978   Blackfoot Historical Phonolgy: A Preliminary Survey. (First version 1960; one-page addendum dated 1978; Manuscript on deposit in the Survey of California and Other Indian Languages, Dwinelle Hall, University of California at Berkeley.)

1978a   Nonverbal Communication in Aboriginal North America: The Plains Sign Language. Pp. 223–244 in Vol. 2 of Aboriginal Sign Language of the Americas and Australia. D. Jean Umiker-Sebeok and Thomas Sebeok, eds. 2 vols. New York: Plenum Press.

1981   Indian Lingua Francas. Pp. 175–195 in Language in the USA. Charles A. Ferguson and Shirley B. Heath, eds. Cambridge, Mass.: Cambridge University Press.

1981a   Variation in Canadian Assiniboine. *Siouan and Caddoan Linguistics Newsletter,* July (1981):9–16.

1982   "Male" and "Female" Speech in Gros Ventre. *Anthropological Linguistics* 24(3):301–307. Bloomington.

_____, comp. and ed. 1983 [Atsina-English / English-Atsina Dictionary] *see* 1994

1983a   The Many Names of the White Clay People. *International Journal of American Linguistics* 49(4):429–434. Chicago.

1983b   Old Vocabularies and Linguistic Research: the Case of Assiniboine. Pp. 31–44 in Proceedings of the Second Siouan Languages Conference, 1982. Mary C. Marino, ed. *Na'pāo: a Saskatchewan Anthropology Journal* 13(October):Special Issue. Saskatoon, Sask.

1989   Review Essay: Two Decades of Ethnobotany in the Northern Plains. *International Journal of American Linguistics* 55(3):359–381. Chicago.

1990   A European Loanword of Early Date in Eastern North America. *Anthropological Linguistics* 32(3–4):187–210. Bloomington.

1994a   [Notes on Blackfoot Band Names.] (Manuscript sent to Douglas R. Parks.)

_____, comp. and ed.
1994   Gros Ventre Dictionary: English to Gros Ventre with an Index of Gros Ventre Stems. 4 vols. Vol. 1: A–L; Vol. 2: M–Z; Vol. 3: Gros Ventre Stem Index; Vol. 4: Index Verborum Dictorumque Prohibitorum. Boulder, Colo.: University of Colorado, Department of Linguistics, Center for the Study of the Native Languages of the Plains and Southwest; [copyright] Gros Ventre Treaty Committee.

Taylor, Colin F.
1973   The O-Kee-Pa and Four Bears: An Insight into Mandan Ethnology. *The Band Book* 15(3):37–56. London.

1981   Crow Rendezvous. *English Westerners Society. American Indian Studies Series* 1:1–37. [London.]

1987   Early Nineteenth Century Crow Warrior Costume. *Jahrbuch des Museums für Völkerkunde zu Leipzig* 37:302–319. Berlin: Akademie-Verlag.

1994   The Plains Indians: A Cultural and Historical View of the North American Plains Tribes of the Pre-Reservation Period. London: Salamandar Books.

1996   Catlin's O-Kee-Pa: Mandan Culture and Ceremonial. The George Catlin O-Kee-Pa Manuscript in the British Museum. With a foreword by W. Raymond Wood. Translated into German by Wolfgang Nuehaus. Wyck auf Foehr, Germany: Verlag für Amerikanistik.

1996a   Wapáha: The Plains Featherhead Head-dress = Die Plains-Federhaube. Wyk auf Foehr, Germany: Verlag für Amerikanistik.

Taylor, Colin F., and Hugh Dempsey
1999   With Eagle Tail: Arnold Lupson and 30 Years among the Sarcee, Blackfoot and Stoney Indians on the North American Plains. London: Vega, an Imprint of Salamander Books Limited.

Taylor, Graham D.
1980   The New Deal and American Indian Tribalism: The Administration of the Indian Reorganization Act, 1934–1945. Lincoln: University of Nebraska Press.

Taylor, John F.
1977   Sociocultural Effects of Epidemics on the Northern Plains: 1734–1850. *Western Canadian Journal of Anthropology* 7(4):55–81. Edmonton, Alta.

1979   Tenting on the Plains: Archaeological Inferences about the Awatixa Hidatsa—Mountain Crow Schism from the Missouri River Trench. Pp. 31–41 in Symposium on the Crow-Hidatsa Separations. Leslie B. Davis, ed. *Archaeology in Montana* 20(3). Billings, [etc.].

1989   Counting: The Utility of Historic Population Estimates in the Northwestern Plains, 1800–1880. *Plains Anthropologist* 34(124):17–30.

Taylor, John L.
1976   The Development of an Indian Policy for the Canadian North-west, 1869–79. (Ph.D. Dissertation in History, Queen's University, Kingston, Ont.)

1977   Canada's North-west Indian Policy in the 1870s: Traditional Premises and Necessary Innovations. Pp. 104–110 in Approcahes to Native History in Canada. D.A. Muise, ed. *Canada. National Museum of Man. Mercury Series. History Division Paper* 25. Ottawa.

1984   Canadian Indian Policy During the Inter-War Years, 1918–1939. Ottawa: Department of Indian and Northern Affairs.

Taylor, Walter Willard
1948   A Study of Archaeology. *American Anthropological Association. Memoir* 69 [*American Anthropologist*, n.s. 50(3, Pt. 2)]. Menasha, Wis. (Reprinted, with a Foreword by Patty Jo Watson: Southern Illinois University, Center for Archaeological Investigations, Carbondale, 1983.)

Tefft, Stanton K.
1960   Cultural Adaptation: The Case of the Comanche Indians. (Ph.D. Dissertation in Anthropology, University of Minnesota, Minneapolis.)

1960a   Sociopolitical Change in Two Migrant Tribes. *Proceedings of the Minnesota Academy of Science* 28:103–111. Minneapolis.

1961   The Comanche Kinship System in Historical Perspective. *Plains Anthropologist* 6(14):252–263.

1965   From Band to Tribe on the Plains. *Plains Anthropologist* 10(29):166–170.

Teilhet-Fisk, Jehanne, and Robin Franklin Nigh
1998   Dimensions of Native America: The Contact Zone. Tallahasse: Florida State University Museum Press.

Teit, James A.
1930   The Salishan Tribes of the Western Plateaus. Franz Boas, ed. Pp. 23–396 [pp. 835–857, Vol. Index] in *45th Annual Report of the Bureau of American Ethnology [for] 1927–'28.* Washington: Smithsonian Institution; U.S. Government Printing Office. (Reprinted: Shorey Book Store, Seattle, Wash., 1973.)

Teller, James T., and Lee Clayton, eds.
1983   Glacial Lake Agassiz. *Memorial University of Newfoundland. Department of Geology. Geological Association of Canada Special Paper* 26. St. John's, Nfld.

Temple, Wayne C.
1975   Indian Villages of the Illinois Country. *Scientific Papers of the Illinois State Museum* 2(1): *Atlas Supplement.* Springfield, Ill.

ten Kate, Herman F.C.
1884   Sur la synonymie ethnique et la toponymie chez les Indiens de l'Amérique du Nord. Amsterdam: J. Müller.

1885   Notes ethnographiques sur les Comanches. *Revue d'Ethnographie* 4(2):120–136. Paris.

1885a   Reizen en onderzoekingen in Noord-Amerika. Leiden, The Netherlands: E.J. Brill. (Microfilm: Louisville Microfilms, Louisville, Ky., 1966; also, New York Public Library for The New-York Historical Society, New York, 1986.)

Terrell, John Upton
1974   Sioux Trail. New York: McGraw-Hill.

1975   The Plains Apache. New York: Crowell.

Testerman, Karen L.
1998   Religious Freedom: Voice from the Past. *Indian Country Today* 18(Sept. 14–21).

Textor, Lucy E.
1896   Official Relations Between the United States and the Sioux Indians. Palo Alto, Calif.: Leland Stanford University Publications.

Thayer, Burton W.
1961   The Sioux Quill Iron. *The Minnesota Archaeologist* 23(2):33–37. Minneapolis, Minn.

The Editors of Time-Life Books
1995   Tribes of the Southern Plains. *The American Indians.* Henry Woodhead, series ed. Alexandria, Va.: Time-Life Books.

The Otoe-Missouria Tribe
1979   Otoe-Missouria Indian Tribal Specific Health Plan. Red Rock, Okla.: Otoe-Missouria Tribe.

1981   The Otoe-Missouria Elders: Centennial Memoirs (1881–1981). Red Rock, Okla.: Otoe-Missouria Tribe.

Theisz, R.D.
1988   Multi-faceted Double Woman. *European Review of Native American Studies* 2(2):9–16. Vienna, Austria [etc.].

Thies, Randall M.
1990   The Archeology of the Stigenwalt Site, 14LT351. *Kansas State Historical Society. Contract Archeology Series Publication* 7. Topeka, Kans.

Thiessen, Thomas D.
1977   A Tentative Radiocarbon Chronology for the Middle Missouri Tradition. Pp. 59–82 in Trends in Middle Missouri Prehistory: A Festschrift Honoring the Contributions of Donald J. Lehmer. *Plains Anthropologist* 22(78, Pt. 2); *Memoir* 13. Lincoln.

1999   Emergency Archeology in the Missouri River Basin: The Role of the Missouri Basin Project and the Midwest Archeological Center in the Interagency Archeological Salvage Program, 1946–1975. *U.S. Department of the Interior. National Park Service. Midwest Archeological Center. Special Report* 2. Lincoln.

Thistle, Paul C.
1986   Indian-European Trade Relations in the Lower Saskatchewan River Region to 1840. *Manitoba Studies in Native History* 2. Winnipeg: The University of Manitoba Press.

Thomas, Alfred B., ed. and trans.
1929   An Eighteenth Century Comanche Document. *American Anthropologist,* n.s. 31(2):289–298.

_____, ed. and trans.
1932   Forgotten Frontiers: A Study of the Spanish Indian Policy of Don Juan Bautista de Anza, Governor of New Mexico, 1777–1787. Norman: University of Oklahoma Press.

_____, ed. and trans.
1935   After Coronado: Spanish Exploration Northeast of New Mexico, 1696–1727; Documents from the Archives of Spain, Mexico and New Mexico. Norman: University of Oklahoma Press. (Reprinted in 1969.)

_____, ed. and trans.
1940   The Plains Indians and New Mexico, 1751–1778: A Collection of Documents Illustrative of the History of the Eastern Frontier of New Mexico. *Coronado Cuatro Centennial Publications, 1540–1940, Vol. 11.* Albuquerque: University of New Mexico Press.

_____, ed. and trans.
1941   Teodoro de Croix and the Northern Frontier of New Spain, 1776–1783, from the Original Document in the Archive of the Indies, Seville. Norman: University of Oklahoma Press.

Thomas, Cyrus
1873   Ancient Mounds of Dakota. Pp. 655–658 in the *Sixth Annual Report [of the] U.S. Geological [and Geographical] Survey of the Territories for the year 1872.* Washington.

1894   Report on the Mound Explorations of the Bureau of Ethnology. Pp. 3–742 in *12th Annual Report of the Bureau of [American] Ethnology for 1890–'91.* Washington: Smithsonian Institution; U.S. Government Printing Office.

1910   Quapaw. Pp. 333–336 in Pt./vol. 2 of Handbook of American Indians North of Mexico. Frederick W. Hodge, ed. 2 Pts./vols. *Bureau of American Ethnology Bulletin* 30. Washington: Smithsonian Institution; U.S. Government Printing Office. (Reprinted: Rowman and Littlefield, New York, 1971.)

Thomas, David Hurst
1978   Arrowheads and Atlatl Darts: How the Stones Got the Shaft. *American Antiquity* 43(3):461–472.

_____, ed. 1986 *see* Wissler, Clark 1986

Thomas, Davis, and Karin Ronnefeldt, eds. 1976 *see* Maximilan, Alexander Philipp, Prinz zu Wied 1976

Thomas, Diane
1978   The Southwest Indian Detours: The Story of the Fred Harvey—Santa Fe Railway Experiment in "Detourism". Phoenix: Hunter Publishing. *1269*

Thomas, Lewis H.
1978 The Struggle for Responsible Government in the North-West Territories, 1870–1897. 2d ed. Toronto: University of Toronto Press.

1982 Riel, Louis. Pp. 736–752 in Dictionary of Canadian Biography, Vol. XI: 1881 to 1890. Toronto: University of Toronto Press.

Thomas, Prentice M., Jr.
1972 Ecological and Social Correlates of Religious Movements among North American Indians. (Ph. D. Dissertation in Anthropology, Anthropology Department, Tulane University, New Orleans.)

Thomas, Robert K.
1968 Pan-Indianism. Pp. 77–86 in The American Indian Today. Stuart Levine and Nancy O. Lurie, eds. Deland, Fla.: Everett Edwards, Inc. (Reprinted: Penguin Books, Baltimore, 1970.)

Thomas, Sidney J.
1941 A Sioux Medicine Bundle [Calf Pipe Bundle]. *American Anthropologist* n.s. 43(4, Pt. 1):605–609.

Thompson, Albert E.
1973 Chief Peguis and His Descendants. Winnipeg, Man.: Peguis Publishers. (Reprinted in 1974.)

Thompson, David
1916 David Thompson's Narrative of His Explorations in Western America, 1784–1812. Joseph B. Tyrrell, ed. *Publications of the Champlain Society* 12. Toronto: The Champlain Society. (Reprinted: Greenwood Press, New York, 1968.)

1962 David Thompson's Narrative, 1784–1812. New edition. Richard Glover, ed. *Publications of the Champlain Society* 40. Toronto: The Champlain Society.

Thompson, Erwin N.
1968 Fort Union Trading Post: Historic Structures Report, Part I: Historical Data Section. Washington: Office of Archaeology and Historic Preservation, National Park Service. (Reprinted as Fort Union Trading Post: Fur Trade Empire on the Upper Missouri, Theodore Roosevelt Nature and History Association, Medora, N.Dak., 1986.)

Thompson, Francis M.
1912–1914 Reminiscences of Four-Score Years: Including His Narrative of Three Years in the New West, During which He Took in 1862 a 3000 Mile Trip from St. Louis Up the Missouri, and Thence down the Snake and Columbia Rivers to Portland, and to San Francisco, Returning in 1863. *Massachusetts Magazine* 5:123–167. Salem, Mass.

1944 In Old Wyoming. *Wyoming State Tribune*, Aug. 8. Cheyenne, Wyo.

Thompson, George Alexander 1812–1815 *see* Alcedo, Antonio de 1812–1815

Thompson, John H.
1998 Forging the Prairie West. Toronto: Oxford University Press.

Thompson, Judy
1977 The North American Indian Collection: A Catalogue. *Sonderdruck aus dem Jahrbuch des Bernischen Historichen Museums* 53. und 54. *Jahrgang*, 1973/1974. Bern, Switzerland: Bernisches Historisches Museum.

Thompson, Laura H.
1982 Historical Translation of the Antoine Barraque Manuscript. (M.A. Thesis in History, University of Arkansas, Fayetteville.)

Thompson, Thomas, ed.
1978 The Schooling of Native America. Washington: American Association of Colleges for Teacher Education.

Thompson, Vern E.
1955 A History of the Quapaw. *Chronicles of Oklahoma* 33(3):360–382. Norman.

Thomson, Gregory E.
1978 The Origin of Blackfoot Geminate Stops and Nasals. Pp. 249–254 in Linguistic Studies of Native Canada. Eung-Do Cook and Jonathan D. Kaye, eds. Vancouver: University of British Columbia Press.

Thornbury, William D.
1965 Regional Geomorphology of the United States. New York: John Wiley and Sons.

Thorne, Tanis C.
1984 The Chouteau Family and the Osage Trade: A Generational Study. Pp. 109–120 in Rendezvous: Selected Papers of the Fourth North American Fur Trade Conference, 1981. T.C. Buckley, ed. St. Paul, Minn.: North American Fur Trade Conference.

1993 Black Bird, "King of the Mahars:" Autocrat, Big Man, Chief. *Ethnohistory* 40(3):410–437.

1996 The Many Hands of My Relations: French and Indians on the Lower Mississippi. Columbia and London: University of Missouri Press.

Thornton, Russell
1986 We Shall Live Again: The 1870 and 1890 Ghost Dance Movements As Demographic Revitalization. New York: Cambridge University Press.

1987 American Indian Holocaust and Survival: A Population History since 1492. Norman: University of Oklahoma Press.

Thrall, Homer S.
1897 A Pictorial History of Texas from the Earliest Visits of European Adventurers, to A.D. 1897. St. Louis: N.D. Thompson & Co.

Thunder, Mary Elizabeth
1995 Thunder's Grace: Walking the Road of Visions with My Lakota Grandmother. Augusta Ogden, ed. Barrytown, N.Y.: Station Hill Press.

Thurman, Melburn D.
1970 The Skidi Pawnee Morning Star Sacrifice of 1827. *Nebraska History* 51(3):269–280. Lincoln.

1980 Comanche. Pp. 4–13 in Vol. 5 of Encyclopedia of Indians of the Americas. Keith Irvine, ed. St. Clair Shores, Mich.: Scholarly Press.

1982 Nelson Lee and the Green Corn Dance: Data Selection Problems with Wallace and Hoebel's Study of the Comanches. *Plains Anthropologist* 27(97):239–243.

1987 Reply to Gelo. *Current Anthropology* 28(4):552–555. Chicago.

1988 On the Indentity of the Chariticas: Dog Eating and Pre-horse Adaptations on the High Plains. *Plains Anthropologist* 33(120):159–170.

Thurmond, J. Peter
1988 The 1988 Society Field School: The Beaver Dam Site, 34RM208. *Oklahoma Anthropological Society Newsletter* 36(4):2–5. Norman.

1988a An Update on Investigations at the Beaver Dam Site (34RM208), Roger Mills County. *Oklahoma Anthropological Society Newsletter* 36(6):3–9. Norman.

1989 An Accelerator Mass Spectrometry Date from a Late Archaic Component in Roger Mills County, Oklahoma. *Oklahoma Anthropological Society Newsletter* 37(8):3–4. Norman.

Thwaites, Reuben G., ed.
1896–1901 The Jesuit Relations and Allied Documents: Travels and Explorations of the Jesuit Missionaries in New France, 1610–1791; the Original French, Latin, and Italian Texts, with English Translations and Notes. 73 vols. Cleveland, Ohio: Burrows Brothers. (Reprinted: Pageant, New York, 1959.)

_____, ed.
1904–1905 Original Journals of the Lewis and Clark Expedition, 1804–1806. Printed from the Original Manuscripts in the Library of the American Philosophical Society and by Direction of Its Committee on Historical Documents, together with Manuscript Material of Lewis and Clark from Other Sources, Including Note-Books, Letters, Maps, etc., and the Journals of Charles Floyd and Joseph Whitehouse. 8 vols. New York: Dodd, Mead. (Reprinted: Antiquarian Press, New York, 1959; also, Arno Press, New York, 1969.)

_____, ed.
1904–1907 Early Western Travels, 1748–1846: A Series of Annotated Reprints of Some of the Best and Rarest Contemporary Volumes of Travel, Descriptive of the Aborigines and Social and Economic Conditions in the Middle and Far West, during the Period of Early American Settlement. With Notes, Introduction, Index, etc. 32 vols. Cleveland, Ohio: Arthur H. Clark. (Reprinted: AMS Press, New York, 1966; also, Arthur H. Clark, Cleveland, 1974.)

_____, ed.
1906 The French Regime in Wisconsin, II: 1727–1748. *Collections of the State Historical Society of Wisconsin* 17. Madison.

_____, ed.
1908 1757 Memoir of Bougainville. *Collections of the State Historical Society of Wisconsin* 18:167–195. Madison, Wis.

_____, ed.
1908a The French Regime in Wisconsin, III: 1743–1760, [and] The British Regime in Wisconsin, 1760–1800. *Collections of the State Historical Society of Wisconsin* 18:1–222; 223–468. Madison.

_____, ed. 1959, 1969 *see* 1904–1905 (reprint info.)

_____, ed. 1966, 1974 *see* 1904–1907 (reprint info.)

Tibbles, Thomas H.
1957 Buckskin and Blanket Days. Garden City, N.Y.: Doubleday.

1972 The Ponca Chiefs: An Account of the Trial of Standing Bear [1880]. Kay Graber, ed. Lincoln: University of Nebraska Press. (Originally publ. : Lockwood, Brooks and Co., Boston, 1880.)

Tidzump, Malinda
1970 Shoshone Thesaurus. Grand Fork, N.Dak.: Summer Institute of Linguistics.

Tiffany, Joseph A.
1977 Artifacts from the Sharp's Site: A Sterns Creek omponent in Southwestern Iowa. *Journal of the Iowa Archeological Society* 24:84–124. Iowa City.

1978 Middle Woodland Pottery Typology from Southwest Iowa. *Plains Anthropologist* 223(81):179–181.

1979 An Overview of Oneota Sites in Southeastern Iowa: A Perspective from the Ceramic Analysis of the Schmeiser Site, 13DM101, Des Moines County, Iowa. *Proceedings of the Iowa Academy of Science* 86(3):89–101. Des Moines.

1979a An Archaeological Survey of the Bastian Oneota Site (13CK28), Cherokee County, Iowa. *University of Iowa. Office of the State Archaeologist. Report* 1. Iowa City.

1982 Chan-ya-ta: a Mill Creek Village. *University of Iowa. Office of the State Archaeologist. Report* 15. Iowa City.

1983 An Overview of the Middle Missouri Tradition. Pp. 87–108 in Prairie Archaeology: Papers in Honor of David A.

Baerreis. Guy E. Gibbon, ed. *University of Minnesota. Publications in Anthropology* 3. Minneapolis.

1983a Site Catchment Analysis of Southeast Iowa Oneota Sites. Pp. 1–13 in Oneota Studies. Guy E. Gibbon, ed.*University of Minnesota. Publications in Anthropology* 1. Minneapolis. (Title page has 1982 imprint date.)

1988 Preliminary Report on Excavations at the McKinney Oneota Village Site (13LA1), Louisa County, Iowa. *Wisconsin Archeologist* 69:228–312. Milwaukee.

1991 Modeling Mill Creek-Mississippian Interaction. Pp. 319–347 in New Perspectives on Cahokia: Views from the Periphery. James B. Stoltman, ed. *Monographs in World Archaeology* 2. Madison, Wis.: Prehistory Press.

1991a Models of Mississippian Culture History in the Western Prairie Peninsula: A Perspective from Iowa. Pp. 183–192 in Cahokia and the Hinterlands: Middle Mississippian Cultures of the Midwest. Thomas E. Emerson and R. Barry Lewis, eds. Urbana and Chicago: University of Illinois in coop. with the Illinois Historic Preservation Agency.

1997 Oneota Ceramics from the Kelley Site. *Plains Anthropologist* 42(160):206–236.

Tiffany, Joseph A., and Duane Anderson
1993 The Milford Site (13DK1): A Postcontact Oneota Village in Northwest Iowa. Pp. 283–306 in Prehistory and Human Ecology of the Western Prairies and Northern Plains. Joseph A. Tiffany, ed. *Plains Anthropologist* 38(145); *Memoir* 27. Lincoln.

Tiller, Veronica E. Velarde, comp. and ed.
1996 American Indian Reservations and Trust Areas. Washington: U.S. Department of Commerce, Economic Development Administration. (Published also under title: Tiller's Guide to Indian Country: Economic Profiles of American Indian Reservations. BowArrow Publishing Company, Albuquerque, 1996.)

Tims, John W.
1889 Grammar and Dictionary of the Blackfoot Language in the Dominion of Canada. For the Use of Missionaries, Schoolteachers, and Others. Comp. by the Rev. John W. Tims, C.M.S. Missionary. London: Society for Promoting Christian Knowledge.

Tims, Winifred A.
1929 The Interesting Origin of the Sarcee Indians of Canada. *The American Indian* 4(2):7.

Tisdale, Mary Ann
1978 Investigations at the Scott Site: A Review of Research from 1947 to 1977. *Papers in Manitoba Archaeology. Final Report* 5. Winnipeg.

Titley, E. Brian
1983 W.M. Graham: Indian Agent Extraordinaire. *Prairie Forum* 8(1):25–41. Regina, Sask.: Canadian Plains Research Center, University of Regina.

1986 A Narrow Vision: Duncan Campbell Scott and the Administration of Indian Affairs in Canada. Vancouver: University of British Columbia.

1991 The Fate of the Sharphead Stoneys. *Alberta History* 39(1):1–8. Calgary.

1992 Transition to Settlement: The Peace Hills Indian Agency, 1884–1890. *Canadian Papers in Rural History* 8:175–194. Gananoque, Ont.: Langdale Press.

1993 Hayter Reed and Indian Administration in the West. Pp. 109–147 in Swords and Ploughshares: War and Agriculture *1271* in Western Canada. R.C. Macleod, ed. Edmonton: University of Alberta Press.

1997   Unsteady Debut: J.A.N. Provencher and the Beginnings of Indian Administration in Manitoba. *Prairie Forum* 22(1):21–46. Regina, Sask.: Canadian Plains Research Center, University of Regina.

Tixier, Victor
1940   Tixier's *Travels on the Osage Prairies*. John F. McDermott, ed.; Translated from the French by Albert J. Salvan. Norman: University of Oklahoma Press. (Originally publ. in French in 1844.)

Tobias, John L.
1976   Protection, Civilization, Assimilation: An Outline History of Canada's Indian Policy. *Western Canadian Journal of Anthropology* 6(2):13–29. Edmonton, Alta.

1983   Canada's Subjugation of the Plains Cree, 1879–1885. *Canadian Historical Review* 64(4):519–548. Toronto: University of Toronto Press.

1986   The Origins of the Treaty Rights Movement in Saskatchewan. Pp. 241–252 in 1885 and After: Native Society in Transition. F. Laurie Barron and James B. Waldram, eds. Regina, Sask.: Canadian Plains Research Center, University of Regina.

1991   Indian Reserves in Western Canada: Indian Homesteads or Devices for Assimilation. Pp. 148–157 in Native People, Native Lands: Canadian Indians, Inuit and Métis. Bruce Alden Cox, ed. Ottawa: Carleton University Press.

Todd, J.E.
1888   Some Ancient Diggings in Nebraska. *American Antiquarian* 100(6):374–376.

Toll, Oliver W.
1962   Arapaho Names and Trails: A Report of a 1914 Pack Trip. [Privately published.]

Tonti, Enrico (Henri de)
1697   Dernières découvertes dans l'Amérique septentrionale de M. de La Salle. Paris: Chez J. Guignard. (Spurious work; trans. in English in 1698.)

1698   An Account of Monsieur de La Salle's Last Expedition and Discoveries in North America. Presented to the French King, and Published by the Chevalier Tonti, Governour of Fort St. Louis, in the Province of the Illinois; [etc.]. London: J. Tonson, S. Buckley and R. Knaplock. (Spurious work, orig. publ. in French in 1697.)

1876   Relation de Henri de Tonty: Entreprises de M. de La Salle, de 1678 a 1683. Relation écrite de Québec, le 14 novembre 1684, par Henri de Tonty. Pp. 573–616 in Vol. 1 [Première partie, 1614–1684] in Découvertes et établissements des Français dans l'Ouest et dans le Sud de l'Amérique septentrionale (1614–1754); Mémoires et documents originaux. Pierre Margry, ed. 6 vols. Paris: D. Jouaust, 1876–1886. (Cover page of Vol. 1 has 1875 imprint date.)

1898   Relation of Henri de Tonty Concerning the Explorations of La Salle from 1678 to 1683. Melville B. Anderson, trans. Chicago: The Caxton Club.

Tonty, Henri/Henry de *see* Tonti, Enrico (Henri de)

Toom, Dennis L.
1992   Early Village Formation in the Middle Missouri Subarea of the Plains. Pp. 131–191 in Long-Term Subsistence Change in Prehistoric North America. Dale R. Croes, Rebecca A. Hawkins, and Barry L. Isaac, eds. *Research in Economic Anthropology. Supplement* 6. Greenwich, Conn.: JAI Press.

1996   Archeology of the Middle Missouri. Pp. 56–76 in Archeological and Bioarcheological Resources of the Northern Plains. George C. Frison and Robert C. Mainfort, eds. *Arkansas Archeological Survey Research Series* 47. Fayetteville.

Torrence, Gaylord
1994   The American Indian Parfleche: A Tradition of Abstract Painting. Seattle: University of Washington Press, in association with the Des Moines Art Center.

Tough, Frank
1996   Métis Aboriginal Title. Pp. 114–132 in 'As Their Natural Resources Fail': Native Peoples and the Economic History of Northern Manitoba, 1870–1930. Vancouver: University of British Columbia Press.

Tousey, Thomas G.
1939   Military History of Carlisle and Carlisle Barracks. Richmond, Va.: Dietz Press.

Toussaint, A.
1833   Carte de l'Amérique septentrionale et méridionale avec cartes particulières des iles et des cotes environantes. [Map.] Paris: Turgis.

Townsend, [E.]
1871   [Report to the Commissioner of Indian Affairs, dated Upper Arkansas Agency, November 13, 1871.] (Manuscript in Letters Received, Upper Arkansas Agency, Records of the Bureau of Indian Affairs, Record Group 75, National Archives, Washington.)

Townsend, John Kirk
1839   Narrative of a Journey Across the Rocky Mountains to the Columbia River.... Philadelphia: H. Perkins. (Reprinted under title: Across the Rockies to the Columbia, with an Introduction by Donald D. Jackson: University of Nebraska Press, Lincoln, 1987.)

Territorial Papers of the United States *see* Carter, Clarence Edwin, comp. and ed. 1934–1962

Trémaudan, Auguste Henri de
1982   Hold High Your Heads: History of the Métis Nation in Western Canada. Elizabeth Maguet, trans. Winnipeg, Man.: Pemmican Publications. (Originally publ. in French under title: Histoire de la nation métisse dans l'ouest canadien; A. L'Evesque, Montreal, 1935, 1936.)

Trager, George L., and Edith C. Trager
1959   Kiowa and Tanoan: Reply to a Note on Kiowa Linguistic Affiliations by Wick R. Miller. *American Anthropologist*, n.s. 61(6):1078–1083.

Tranholm, Virginia C.
1970   The Arapahoes, Our People. Norman: University of Oklahoma Press.

Tratebas, Alice M.
1985   McKean Settlement Patterns in the Black Hills: Suggestions for Future Research. Pp. 137–145 in McKean/Middle Plains Archaic: Current Research. Marcel Kornfeld and Lawrence C. Todd, eds. *Occasional Papers on Wyoming Archaeology* 4. Laramie.

Tratebas, Alice M., and Kristi Vagstad
1979   Archaeological Test Excavations of Four Sites in the Black Hills National Forest, South Dakota. *South Dakota Archaeological Research Center. Contract Investigations Series* 6. Fort Meade, S.Dak.

Trautman, Milton A.
1963   Isotopes, Incorporated: Radiocarbon Measurements, III. *Radiocarbon* 5:62–79. New Haven, Conn.

Treat, John
1807   [Arkansas Trading House Letterbook, 1805–1810.] (Micro-

film M142, U.S. Office of Indian Trade, Records of the Bureau of Indian Affairs, Record Group 75, National Archives, Washington.)

Treaty No.7 Elders and Tribal Council, with Walter Hildebrandt, Dorothy First Rider, and Sarah Carter
1996   The True Spirit and Original Intent of Treaty 7. Montreal: McGill Queen's Press.

Trechter, Sara
1995   The Pragmatic Functions of Gender Clitics in Lakhota. (Ph.D. Dissertation in Linguistics, University of Kansas, Lawrence.)

Treece, Abby C., Christopher R. Lintz, W. Nicholas Trierweiler, J. Michael Quigg, and K.A. Miller
1993   Cultural Resource Investigations in the O.H. Ivie Reservoir, Concho, Coleman, and Runnels Counties, Texas. Vol. 3: Data Recovery Results from Non-Ceramic Sites. *Mariah Associates. Technical Report* 346-3. Austin. Tex.

Trenholm, Virginia Cole
1964   The Shoshonis: Sentinels of the Rockies. Norman: University of Oklahoma Press.

_____
1970   The Arapahoes, Our People. Norman: University of Oklahoma Press.

Trennert, Robert A., Jr.
1975   Alternative to Extinction: Federal Indian Policy and the Beginnings of the Reservation System, 1846–1851. Philadelphia: Temple University Press.

Trimble, Bessie
1934–1935 Sioux Give-Away Ceremony. *Indians at Work* 2(24):38–39. Washington: Bureau of Indian Affairs.

Trimble, Michael K.
1979   An Ethnohistorical Interpretation of the Spread of Smallpox in the Northern Plains Utilizing Concepts of Disease Ecology. (M.A. Thesis in Anthropology, University of Missouri, Columbia. Published: see Trimble 1986.)

_____
1985   Epidemiology on the Northern Plains: A Cultural Perspective. (Smallpox, Great Plains, Ethnohistory, Fort Clark, North Dakota.) (Ph.D. Dissertation in Anthropology, University of Missouri, Columbia.)

_____
1986   An Ethnohistorical Interpretation of the Spread of Smallpox in the Northern Plains Utilizing Concepts of Disease Ecology. *Reprints in Anthropology* 33. Lincoln: J&L Reprint Company.

_____
1988   Chronology of Epidemics among Plains Village Horticulturalists: 1738–1838. *Southwestern Lore* 54(4):4–31. Boulder, Colo.

_____
1989   Infectious Disease and the Northern Plains Horticulturalists: A Human Behavior Model. Pp. 41–59 in Plains Indian Historical Demography and Health: Perspectives, Interpretations, and Critiques. Gregory R. Campbell, ed. *Plains Anthropologist* 34(124 pt. 2); *Memoir* 23. Lincoln.

_____
1994   The 1837–1838 Smallpox Epidemic on the Upper Missouri. Pp. 81–90 in Skeletal Biology in the Great Plains: Migration, Warfare, Health, and Subsistence. Douglas W. Owsley and Richard L. Jantz, eds. Washington and London: Smithsonian Institution Press.

Troike, Rudolph C.
1964   A Pawnee Visit to San Antonio in 1795. *Ethnohistory* 11(4):380–393.

_____
1969   Prehistoric Tonkawa-Caddo Acculturation: An Ethnological and Linguistic Reconstruction. (Paper presented at the American Anthropological Association Annual Meeting, New Orleans, Nov. 1969; copy in I. Goddard's possession.)

_____
1970   Evidence for Change in the Tonkawa Kinship System. Pp. 319–325 in Vol. 2 of *Verhandlungen des XXXVIII. Internationalen Amerikanistenkongresses, [Proceedings of the 38th International Congress of Americanists] Stuttgart-München 12. bis 18. August 1968.* 4 vols. München: Kommissionsverlag Klaus Renner, 1969–1972.

Trudeau, Jean-Baptiste *see* Truteau, Jean-Baptiste

Truettner, William H.
1979   The Natural Man Observed: A Study of Catlin's Indian Gallery. Washington: Smithsonian Institution Press.

Trumbull, Henry
1851   History of the Indian Wars; to which is Prefixed a Short Account of the Discovery of America by Columbus... Philadelphia: Thomas, Cowperthwait for James A. Bill.

Truteau, Jean-Baptiste
1912   Journal of Jean Baptiste Trudeau among the Arikara Indians in 1795. Translated by Mrs. H.T. Beauregard. [With facsimile reprint of: Carte du Missouri; Levee ou Rectifée dans toute son Etendue par F.ois Perrin du Lac, 1802.] *Missouri Historical Society Collections* 4(1):9–48. St. Louis.

_____
1921   Remarks on the Manners of the Indians Living High Up the Missouri. Translated from a Manuscript of Jean Baptiste Trudeau, Put into the Possession of Dr. Mitchell, by Mr. Nicholas Boilvin. (Microfilm No. T-11, Ayer Collection, The Newberry Library, Chicago.)

_____   1993 *see* Parks, Douglas R., ed. 1993

Tsa To Ke, Monroe
1957   The Peyote Ritual: Visions and Descriptions. San Francisco: Grabhorn Press.

Tucker, Sara Jones, comp.
1942   Indian Villages of the Illinois Country. Part 1: Atlas. *Illinois State Museum Scientific Papers* 2(1). Springfield.

Tunnell, Curtis D., and William W. Newcomb, Jr.
1969   A Lipan Apache Mission: San Lorenzo de la Santa Cruz, 1792–1771. *Texas Memorial Museum. Bulletin* 14. Austin: The University of Texas.

Turgeon, Donna D., et al.
1988   Common and Scientific Names of Aquatic Invertebrates from the United States and Canada: Mollusks. *American Fisheries Society. Special Publication* 16. Bethesda, Md. (Reprinted, 2d ed., 1998.)

Turley, Frank
1961   Ponca Fair and Powwow. *American Indian Tradition* 7(5):180–181. Alton, Ill.

Turner, Alvin O.
1992   "Journey to Sainthood": David Pendleton Oakerhater's Better Way. *Chronicles of Oklahoma* 70(2):116–143. Norman.

Turner, Christy G., II
1980   Suggestive Dental Evidence for Athabascan Affiliation in a Colorado Skeletal Series. Appendix I in: Trinidad Lake Cultural Resource Study. Pt. II: The Prehistoric Occupation of the Upper Purgatoire River Valley, Southeastern Colorado, by Caryl E.Wood and Gerald A. Bair. Trinidad, Colo. Trinidad State Junior College, Laboratory of Contract Archeology.

Turpin, Solveig A.
1987   Ethnohistoric Observations of Bison in the Lower Pecos River Region: Implications for Environmental Change. *Plains Anthropologist* 32(118):424–429.

Turtle Mountain Indian Reservation (Belcourt, N.Dak.)
1985   St. Ann's Centennial: 110 Years of Faith, 1885–1995. Rolla, N.Dak.: Star Printing.

Tushka, Belva
1979   A Dictionary of Everyday Crow: Crow-English, English-Crow. Crow Agency, Mont.: Crow Agency Bilingual Program.

Twitchell, Ralph E., comp.
1914   The Spanish Archives of New Mexico. 2 vols. Cedar Rapids, Iowa: The Torch Press.

Tyler, George W.
1966   The History of Bell County. Edited by Charles W. Ramsdell. Belton, Tex.: Dayton Kelley.

Tyler, Kenneth J., and Roland A. Wright
1978   The Alienation of Indian Reserve Lands during the Administration of Sir Wilfrid Laurier, 1896–1911: Pheasant's Rump Reserve #68. Ocean Man Reserve #69. Report Prepared for the Federation of Saskatchewan Indians. Ottawa: Tyler and Wright Research Consultants.

Tyler, Ron, ed.
1982   Alfred Jacob Miller: Artist on the Oregon Trail: With a Catalogue Raisonné by Karen Dewees Reynolds and William R. Johnson. Fort Worth, Tex.: Amon Carter Museum.

Tyler, S. Lyman
1973   A History of Indian Policy. Washington: United States Department of the Interior, Bureau of Indian Affairs.

Tyler, S. Lyman, and H. Darrel Taylor, trans.
1958   The Report of Fray Alonso de Posada in Relation to Quivira and Teguayo. *New Mexico Historical Review* 33(4):285–314. Albuquerque.

Tyrrell, Joseph B., ed. 1916, 1968 *see* Thompson, David 1916 (reprint info.)

Tyson, Carl N.
1976   The Pawnee People. Phoenix: Indian Tribal Series.

U.S. Army
1882   Record of Engagements with Hostile Indians Within the Military Division of the Missouri from 1868 to 1882; Lientenant-General P.H. Sheridan, Commanding. Compiled at Headquarters, Military Division of the Missouri, from Offical Records. Washington: Government Printing Office.

U.S. Army. Corps of Topographical Engineers 1875 *see* Warren, Gouverneur K. 1875

U.S. Bureau of Indian Affairs *see* Bureau of Indian Affairs

U.S. Bureau of the Census
1915   Indian Population in the United States and Alaska, 1910. 13th Census. Washington: Department of Commerce; U.S. Government Printing Office.

1937   The Indian Population of the United States and Alaska, 1930. Washington: U.S. Government Printing Office.

1973   1970 Census of Population, Subject Reports PC(2)-1F: American Indians. Washington: U.S. Department of Commerce, Social and Economic Statistics Administration, Bureau of the Census; U.S. Government Printing Office.

1986   1980 Census of Population. Subject Reports PC80-2-1D: American Indians, Eskimos, and Aleuts on Identified Reservations and in the Historic Areas of Oklahoma (Excluding Urbanized Areas). Issued January 1986. 2 Pts. Washington: U.S. Department of Commerce, Bureau of the Census; U.S. Government Printing Office.

1989   1980 Census of Population. Subject Reports PC80-2-1C: Characteristics of American Indians by Tribes and Selected Areas: 1980. Issued September 1989. 2 Pts. Washington: U.S. Department of Commerce, Bureau of the Census; U.S. Government Printing Office.

1991   American Indian and Alaska Native Areas: 1990. Edna Paisano, Joan Greendeer-Lee, June Cowles, and Debbie CarRoll, comps. Washington: Bureau of the Census, Population Division, Racial Statistics Branch; U.S. Government Printing Office.

1992   American Indian Population by Tribe for The United States, Regions, Divisions, and States: 1990. Prepared by: Edna Paisano, June Cowles, Deborah Caroll, and Ann Robinson, Racial Statistics Division, [etc.]. Washington: Bureau of the Census, Population Division; U.S. Government Printing Office.

1993   1990 Census of the Population, Social and Economic Statistics: North Dakota. Washington: U.S. Department of Commerce, Bureau of the Census / U.S. Government Printing Office.

U.S. Census Office (Department of the Interior. Census Office)
1894   Report on Indians Taxed and Indians Not Taxed in the United States (Except Alaska) at the Eleventh Census: 1890. Washington: U.S. Government Printing Office. (Reprinted: AMS Press, New York, 1973; also, Norman Ross Publishing, New York, 1994.)

U.S. Commission to the Columbian Exposition at Madrid
1895   Report of the United States Commission to the Columbian Exposition at Madrid, 1892–93. Washington: U.S. Government Printing Office.

U.S. Congress
1832   American State Papers. Documents, Legislative and Executive, of the Congress of the United States, from the First Session of the First to the Third Session of the Thirteenth Congress, Inclusive: Commencing March 3, 1789, and Ending March 3, 1815. Class II. Indian Affairs. Vol. IV [i.e. I.]. Washington: Gales and Seaton. (Reprinted: William S. Hein and Co., Buffalo, N.Y., 1998.)

1834   American State Papers. Documents, Legislative and Executive, of the Congress of the United States, from the First Session of the Fourteenth to the Second Session of the Nineteenth Congress, Inclusive: Commencing December 4, 1815, and Ending March 3, 1827. Class II. Indian Affairs: Vol. II. Washington: Gales and Seaton. (Reprinted: Willliam S. Hein and Co., Bufalo, N.Y., 1997.)

1873   A Compilation of All the Treaties between the United States and the Indian Tribes Now in Force as Laws. Washington: U.S. Government Printing Office.

1994   Crow Boundary Settlement Act of 1994. (Public Law 103-444, 108 U.S. Stat. 4632, Washington.)

U.S. Congress. House. Committee on Indian Affairs
1876   [Province of Oklahoma, Report: To Accompany H.R.2823.] *44th Congress. 1st Session. House Report No. 299* (Serial No. 1708). Washington.

U.S. Congress. House. Committee on Interior and Insular Affairs
1950   Compilation of Material Relating to the Indians of the United States and the Territory of Alaska, Including Certain Laws and Treaties Affecting Such Indians; by Subcommittee on Indian Affairs of the Committee on Public Lands, House of Representatives, Making Study of Problems in Connection with the Public Lands of the United States pursuant to H. Res. 66, 81st Cong., 2d Sess. June 13, 1950. *81st Congress. 2d Session. House Report* 30. Washington: U.S. Government Printing Office.

1953   Report With Respect to the House Resolution Authorizing the Committee on Interior and Insular Affairs To Conduct an Investigation of the Bureau of Indian Affairs. Pursuant to H. Res. 698 (82d Congress). *82d Congress. 2d Session. House Report* 2503. (Serial No. 11582). *Union Calendar* 790. Washington: U.S. Government Printing Office.

1954   Report With Respect to the House Resolution Authorizing the Committee on Interior and Insular Affairs to Conduct an Investigation of the Bureau of Indian Affairs, Pursuant to House Resolution 89 (83d Congress). *83d Congress. 2d Session. House Report No.* 2680. (Union Calendar No. 925). Washington: U.S. Government Printing Office.

U.S. Court of Claims
1937   Plaintiffs Statement of Fact. Case No. C-531-(7): The Sioux Tribe of Indians v. The United States. (Document filed in U.S. Court of Claims, Washington.)

U.S. Department of Agriculture 1941 *see* Hambridge, Gove, ed. 1941

U.S. Department of Commerce
1971   Federal and State Indian Reservations: An EDA Handbook. Washington: U.S. Department of Commerce, Economic Development Administration; U.S. Government Printing Office.

1974   Federal and State Indian Reservations and Indian Trust Areas. Washington: U.S. Government Printing Office.

U.S. Department of Health, Education and Welfare
1959   Indians on Federal Reservations in the United States — A Digest. Aberdeen Area: Nebraska, North Dakota, South Dakota, Iowa, Michigan, Minnesota, Wisconsin. *Public Health Service Publication* 615. Washington: U.S. Department of Health, Education, and Welfare; Public Health Service; Division of Indian Health; U.S. Government Printing Office.

1960   Indians on Federal Reservations in the United States: A Digest. Pt. 5: Oklahoma City Area and Florida. *Public Health Service Publications* 615(5). Washington: U.S. Government Printing Office.

U.S. Department of the Interior. Bureau of Indian Affairs *see* Bureau of Indian Affairs

U.S. Geological Survey
1970   The National Atlas of the United States of America. Washington: Department of the Interior; U.S. Government Printing Office.

U.S. Indian Claims Commission
1974   Commission Findings on the Sioux Indians. New York: Garland Publishing.

1980   United States Indian Claims Commission, August 13, 1946 – September 30, 1978: Final Report. Washington: U.S. Government Printing Office.

U.S. Mint (Treasury Department)
1914   Catalogue of Coins, Tokens, and Medals in the Numismatic Collection of the Mint of the United States at Philadelphia, Pa. 3d ed. *Treasury Department. Document* 2612. Washington: U.S. Government Printing Office.

U.S. National Museum
1895   Part I: Report upon the Condition and Progress of the U.S. National Museum ... by G. Brown Goode, Assistant Secretary of the Smithsonian Institution, in Charge of the U.S. National Museum. Pp. 1–263 in *Annual Report of the Board of Regents of the Smithsonian Institution... for the Year Ending June 30, 1893: Report of the U.S. National Museum.* Washington: U.S. Government Printing Office.

U.S. Office of Indian Affairs *see* Bureau of Indian Affairs

U.S. Secretary of the Interior
1888   Letter from the Secretary of the Interior, Transmitting, in Response to Senate Resolution of December 13, 1888, Report Relative to Opening Part of the Sioux Reservation. *50th Congress, 2d Session, Senate Executive Document No.* 17. Washington.

U.S. Senate
1893   Message from the President of the United States, Transmitting an Agreement with the Comanche, Kiowa, and Apache Indians for the Cession of Certian Lands, and for other Purposes, in the Territory of Oklahoma; January 4, 1893. *52d Congress. 2d Session. Senate Executive Document* 17. (Serial No. 3055). Washington: U.S. Government Printing Office.

U.S. Supreme Court
1988   Montana v. Crow Tribe of Indians. (Number 87-343, Supreme Court Affirmation of Judgment of 9th Circuit Court of Appeals CA 9, 819 F2d 895, Washington.)

1998   Montana et al. v. Crow Tribe of Indians et al. (Number 96-1829, U.S. Supreme Court, Washington.)

Ubelaker, Douglas H.
1976   The Sources and Methodology for Mooney's Estimates of North American Indian Populations. Pp. 243–292 in The Native Population of the Americas in 1492. William M. Denevan, ed. Madison: University of Wisconsin Press.

1992   North American Indian Population: Changing Perspectives. Pp. 169–176 in Disease and Demography in the Americas. John W. Verano and Douglas H. Ubelaker, eds. Washington: Smithsonian Institution Press.

Ubelaker, Douglas H., and William M. Bass
1970   Arikara Glassworking Techniques at Leavenworth and Sully Sites. *American Antiquity* 35(4):467–475.

Ubelaker, Douglas H., and Richard L. Jantz
1979   Plains Caddoan Relationships: The View from Craniometry and Mortuary Analysis. *Nebraska History* 60(2):249–259. Lincoln.

Ubelaker, Douglas H., and Waldo R. Wedel
1975   Bird Bones, Burials, and Bundles in Plains Archeology. *American Antiquity* 40(4):444–452.

Udden, Johan A.
1900   An Old Indian Village. *Augustana Library Publications* 2. Rock Island, Ill.: Lutheran Augustana Book Concern.

Ugarte y Loyola, Jacobo
1787   [Letter to Juan Bautista de Anza, dated Febuary 8, 1787.] (AGN, PI, Tomo 65, exp. 2.)

Uhde, Adolf
1861   Die länder am untern Rio Bravo del Norte. Geschichtliches und erlebtes von Adolf Uhde... Mit einer uebersichtskarte. Pp. 411–422 in "Verzeichniss der vice-könige Neu-Spaniens, sowie der präsidenten der republik Mexico..." 1518–1861: "Verzeichniss der gouverneure von Texas..." 1685–1861.

Uhlenbeck, Christian C.
1911   Original Blackfoot Texts from the Southern Piegans, Blackfoot Reservation, Teton Country, Montana; with the help of Joseph Tatsey, collected and published with an English translation. *Verhandelingen der Koninklijke Akademie van Wetenschappen te Amsterdam. Afdeeling Letterkunde*, n.r. 12(1). Amsterdam: J. Müller.

1912   A New Series of Blackfoot Texts from the Southern Piegans, Blackfoot Reservation, Teton Country, Montana; with the help of Joseph Tatsey. *Verhandelingen der Koninklijke Akademie van Wetenschappen te Amsterdam. Afdeeling Letterkunde*, n.r. 13(1). Amsterdam: J. Müller. (Reprinted: AMS Press, New York, 1978.)

1938   A Concise Blackfoot Grammar, Based on Material from the Southern Piegans. *Verhandelingen der Koninklijke Akademie van Wetenschappen te Amsterdam. Afdeeling Letterkunde*, n.r. 41. Amsterdam: J. Müller. (Reprinted: AMS Press, New York, 1978.)

Uhlenbeck, Christian C., and R.H. van Gulik

1930   An English-Blackfoot Vocabulary; Based on Material from the Southern Piegans. *Verhandelingen der Koninklijke Akademie van Wetenschappen te Amsterdam. Afdeeling Letterkunde*, n.r. 33(2). Amsterdam: J. Müller. (Reprinted: AMS Press, New York, 1984.)

1934   A Blackfoot-English Vocabulary; Based on Material from the Southern Piegans. *Verhandelingen der Koninklijke Akademie van Wetenschappen te Amsterdam. Afdeeling Letterkunde*, n.r. 33(2). Amsterdam: J. Müller. (Reprinted: AMS Press, New York, 1984.)

Umfreville, Edward

1790   The Present State of Hudson's Bay: Containing a Full Description of that Settlement, and the Adjacent Country; and Likewise of the Fur Trade, with Hints for Its Improvement. To Which Are Added, Remarks and Observations Made in the Inland Parts, During a Residence of Near Four Years; a Specimen of Five Indian Languages; and a Journal of a Journey from Montreal to New York. London: Charles Stalker. (Reprinted: see Umfreville 1954.)

1954   The Present State of Hudson's Bay: Containing a Full Description of that Settlement, and the Adjacent Country; and Likewise of the Fur Trade, with Hints for Its Improvement, etc. [1790]. Ed. with an Introduction and Notes by W. Stewart Wallace. Toronto: Ryerson Press.

Underhill, Ruth Murray

1965   Red Man's Religion: Beliefs and Practices of the Indians North of Mexico. Chicago: University of Chicago Press. (Reprinted in 1974.)

Underwood, McLellan, and Associates Ltd.

1970   A Program for the Stoney People. Morley Indian Reserve, Alta.: Stoney Recreation Resource Study.

University of Colorado Lakhota Project

1976   Beginning Lakhota. 2 vols. Vol. 1: Lessons 1–10; Vol. 2: Lessons 11–20. Boulder, Colo.: Department of Linguistics, University of Colorado Press.

1976a   Elementary Bilingual Dictionary: English-Lakhóta, Lakhóta-English. Boulder, Colo.: Department of Linguistics, University of Colorado Press.

1976b   Lakhóta Wayáwapi/Lakhota Reader. Boulder, Colo.: Department of Linguistics, University of Colorado Press.

Unrah, John D., Jr.

1979   The Plains Across: The Overland Emigrants and the Trans-Mississippi West, 1840–1860. Champaign: University of Illinois Press.

Unrau, William E.

1962   Indian Water Rights To the Middle Arkansas: A Case for the Kaws. *Kansas History: A Journal of the Central Plains* 5(1):52–69. Topeka.

1971   The Kansa Indians: A History of the Wind People, 1673–1873. Norman: University of Oklahoma Press.

1975   The Kaw People. Phoenix, Ariz.: Indian Tribal Series.

1976   Removal, Death, and Legal Reincarnation of the Kaw People. *The Indian Historian* 9(1):2–9. San Francisco.

1979   The Emigrant Indians of Kansas: A Critical Bibliography. Bloomington: Indiana University Press.

1989   Mixed-bloods and Tribal Dissolution: Charles Curtis and the Quest for Indian Identity. Lawrence: University Press of Kansas.

1996   White Man's Wicked Water: The Alcohol Trade and Prohibition in Indian Country, 1802–1892. Lawrence: University Press of Kansas.

Upton, L.F.S.

1973   The Origins of Canadian Policy. *Journal of Canadian Studies* 8(4):51–61. Brandon, Man.

Urban, Greg

1994   The Social Organizations of the Southeast. Pp. 172–193 in North American Indian Anthropology: Essays on Society and Culture. Raymond J. DeMallie and Alfonso Ortiz, eds. Norman: University of Oklahoma Press.

Urciuoli, Bonnie

1988   A Catalog of the C.F. and F.M. Voegelin Archives of the Languages of the World. Bloomington: Archives of Traditional Music, Indiana University Press.

USA Today, May 13, 1994. Arlington, Va.

Useem, John, Gordon Magregor, and Ruth Hill Useem

1943   Wartime Employment and Cultural Adjustments of the Rosebud Sioux. *Applied Anthropology* 2(2):1–9. Boston.

Useem, Ruth Hill, and Carl K. Eicher

1970   Rosebud Reservation Economy. Pp. 3–34 in The Modern Sioux: Social Systems and Reservation Culture. Ethel Nurge, ed. Lincoln: University of Nebraska Press.

Usner, Daniel H., Jr.

1992   Indians, Settlers, & Slaves in a Frontier Exchange Economy: The Lower Mississippi Valley before 1873. Chapel Hill: University of North Carolina Press.

Utley, Robert M.

1963   The Last Days of the Sioux Nation. New Haven, Conn.: Yale University Press.

1967   Frontiersmen in Blue: The United States Army and the Indian, 1848–1865. New York: Macmillan.

1973   Frontier Regulars: The United States Army and the Indian, 1866–1891. New York: Macmillan.

1984   The Indian Frontier of the American West, 1846–1890. Albuquerque: University of New Mexico Press.

1993   The Lance and the Shield: The Life and Times of Sitting Bull. New York: Henry Holt and Company.

1996   The Encyclopedia of the American West. New York: Wings Books.

Végrevile, Valentin

1875–1881 [Dictionnaire français-assiniboine.] (Manuscripts in University of Manitoba Archives, Winnipeg, and in Provincial Archives of Alberta, Oblate Collection, Edmonton.)

Vaillant, George C.

1939   Indian Arts in North America. New York: Harper and Brothers.

Valentine, J. Randolph

1986   A Survey of (Canadian) Ojibwa Dialects. (Paper presented at the 1986 Algonquian Conference; manuscript in J.R. Valentine's possession.)

Vallentine, John F.

1989   Range Development and Improvements. 3d ed. San Diego: Academic Press. (Originally publ.: Brigham Young University Press, Provo, Utah, 1971.)

Valliere, Frank, and Vida Valliere

1937   [Interview.] (Manuscript: *Indian and Pioneer History* 48:33–34, at Newspaper/Archives and Manuscripts Division, Oklahoma Historical Society, Oklahoma City.)

Vance, Robert E., Don Emerson, and Thelma Habgood
1983   A Mid-Holocene Record of Vegetative Change in Central Alberta. *Canadian Journal of Earth Sciences* 20(3):364–376. Ottawa.

Vance, Robert E., R.W. Matthews, and J. Clague
1992   7000 Year Record of Lake-Level Change on the Northern Great Plains: A High Resolution Proxy of Past Climate. *Geology* 20(10):879–882. Boulder, Colo.

Vander, Judith
1988   Songprints: The Musical Experience of Five Shoshone Women. Urbana and Chicago: University of Illinois Press.

Van Dyke, Stanley, and S. Stewart
1985   Hawkwood Site (EgPm-179): A Multicomponent Prehistoric Campsite on Nose Hill. *Archaeological Survey of Alberta. Manuscript Series* 7. Edmonton.

Van Dyke, Stanley, Sharron Hanna, Wendy Unfreed, and Barbara Neal
1991   That Dam Archaeology: Campsites in the Oldman River Reservoir. Pp. 25–65 in Archaeology in Alberta, 1988 and 1989. Martin Magne, ed. *Archaeological Survey of Alberta. Occasional Paper* 33. Edmonton.

Van Kirk, Sylvia
1980   "Many Tender Ties," Women in Fur Trade Society, 1670–1820. Winnipeg, Man.: Watson and Dwyer.

VanStone, James W.
1983   The Simms Collection of Plains Cree Material Culture from Southeastern Saskatchewan. *Fieldiana: Anthropology*, n.s. 6 (Publication 1342). Chicago: Field Museum of Natural History.

_____   1989   Indian Trade Ornaments in the Collections of Field Museum of Natural History. *Fieldiana: Anthropology*, n.s. 13 (Publication 1404). Chicago: Field Museum of Natural History.

_____   1991   The Isaac Cowie Collection of Plains Cree Material Culture from Central Alberta. *Fieldiana: Anthropology*, n.s. 17 (Publication 1427). Chicago: Field Museum of Natural History.

_____   1992   Material Culture of the Blackfoot (Blood) Indians of Southern Alberta. *Fieldiana: Anthropology*, n.s. 19 (Publication 1439). Chicago: Field Museum of Natural History.

_____   1996   Ethnographic Collections from the Assiniboine and Yanktonai Sioux in the Field Museum of Natural History. *Fieldiana, Anthropology,* n.s. 26 (Publication 1476). Chicago: Field Museum of Natural History.

Van Valin, Robert D., Jr.
1977   Aspects of Lakhota Syntax: A Study of Lakhota (Teton Dakota) Syntax and Its Implications for Universal Grammar. (Ph.D. Dissertation in Linguistics, University of California, Berkeley.)

_____   1985   Case Marking and the Structure of the Lakhota Clause. Pp. 363–413 in Grammar Inside and Outside the Clause. Johanna Nichols and Anthony C. Woodbury, eds. Cambridge, Mass.: Cambridge University Press.

Vater, Johann Severin
1821   Analekten der Sprachenkunde. Leipzig [Germany]: Dyksche Buchhandlung.

Vatter, Ernst
1927   Historienmalerei und heraldische Bilderschrift der nordamerikanischen Präriestämme. *IPEK: Jahrbuch für prähistorische und ethnographische Kunst, 1927*:46–81. Leipzig, Germany.

Vaughan, Alfred J. 1848 *see* ARCIA 1824–1848

Vaughn, Jesse Wendell
1956   With Crook at the Rosebud. Harrisburg, Pa.:The Stackpole Company.

_____   1961   The Reynolds Campaign on Powder River. Norman: University of Oklahoma Press.

Vazeilles, Danièle
1977   Le cercle et le calumet: ma vie avec les Sioux d'aujourd'hui. Préf. de Jacques Soustelle. Toulouse, France: Privat.

_____   1996   Chamanes et visionnaires sioux. Monaco: Éditions du Rocher/Le Mail. Jean-Paul Bertrand.

Vazulik, Johannes W.
1997   Peter Rindisbacher's Red River Watercolors at the West Point Museum. *Nebraska History* 64(3):20–29. Lincoln.

Vecsey, Christopher
1983   Emergence of the Hopi People. *The American Indian Quarterly* 7(3):69–92. Berkeley, Calif.

Vehik, Susan C.
1982   A Model for Prehistoric Cultural Change in North-Central Oklahoma. Pp. 65–75 in Pathways to Plains Prehistory: Anthropological Perspectives of Plains Natives and Their Pasts; Papers in Honor of Robert E. Bell. Don G. Wyckoff and Jack L. Hofman, eds. *Oklahoma Anthropological Society. Memoir* 3; *The Cross Timbers Heritage Association Contributions* 1. Duncan, Okla.

_____   1984   The Woodland Occupations. Pp. 175–197 in Prehistory of Oklahoma. Robert E. Bell, ed. Orlando, San Diego, San Francisco, [etc.]: Academic Press.

_____   1986   Oñate's Expedition to the Southern Plains: Routes, Destinations, and Implications for Late Prehistoric Cultural Adaptations. *Plains Anthropologist* 31(111):13–33.

_____   1988   Late Prehistoric Exchange on the Southern Plains and Its Periphery. *Midcontinental Journal of Archaeology* 13:41–68. Kent, Ohio.

_____   1989   Problems and Potential in Plains Indian Demography. Pp. 115–125 in Plains Indian Historical Demography and Health: Perspectives, Interpretations and Critiques. Gregory R. Campbell, ed. *Plains Anthropologist* 34(124 pt. 2); *Memoir* 23. Lincoln.

_____   1992   Wichita Culture History. *Plains Anthropologist* 37(141):311–332.

_____   1993   Dhegiha Origins and Plains Archaeology. *Plains Anthropologist* 38(146):231–264.

_____   1994   Cultural Continuity and Discontinuity in the Southern Prairies and Cross Timbers. Pp. 239–263 in Plains Indians, A.D. 500–1500: The Archaeological Past of Historic Groups. Karl H. Schlesier, ed. Norman and London: University of Oklahoma Press.

Vehik, Susan C., and Kenneth A. Ashworth
1983   Kaw Lake Hydropower: Further Archaeological Investigations at the Uncas Site (34KA172). (Report submitted to the U.S. Army Corps of Engineers, Tulsa District, Tulsa, Okla.)

Vehik, Susan C., and Timothy G. Baugh
1994   Prehistoric Plains Trade. Pp. 249–274 in Prehistoric Exchange Systems in North America. Timothy G. Baugh and Jonathon E. Ericson, eds. New York: Plenum Press.

Vehik, Susan C., and Peggy Flynn
1981   Archaeological Excavations at the Early Plains Village Uncas Site (34KA172). (Report submitted to the U.S. Army Corps of Engineers, Tulsa District, Tulsa, Okla.)

Vennum, Thomas, Jr.
1982   The Ojibwa Dance Drum: Its History and Construction. *Smithsonian Folklife Series* 2. Washington: Smithsonian Institution Press.

——— 1988   Wild Rice of the Ojibway People. St. Paul, Minn.: Minnesota Historical Society Press.

Verbicky-Todd, Eleanor
1984   Communal Buffalo Hunting among the Plains Indians: An Ethnographic and Historic Review. *Archaeological Survey of Alberta. Occasional Paper* 24. Edmonton: Alberta Culture, Historical Resources Dvision.

Vestal, Paul A., and Richard E. Schultes
1939   The Economic Botany of the Kiowa Indians, As It Relates to the History of the Tribe. Cambridge, Mass.: Botanical Museum of Harvard University. (Reprinted: AMS Press, New York, 1981.)

Vestal, Stanley (Walter Stanley Campbell)
1932   Sitting Bull, Champion of the Sioux. Boston and New York: Houghton Mifflin Company.

——— 1934   Warpath: The True Story of the Fighting Sioux Told in a Biography of Chief White Bull. Boston: Houghton Mifflin Company. (Reprinted, with a Foreword by Raymond J. DeMallie: University of Nebraska Press, Lincoln, 1984.)

——— 1934a   New Sources of Indian History, 1850–1891: The Ghost Dance—The Prairie Sioux: A Miscellany. Norman: University of Oklahoma Press.

——— 1948   Warpath and Council Fire: The Plains Indian's Struggle for Survival in War and in Diplomacy, 1851–1891. New York: Random House.

——— 1957   Sitting Bull, Champion of the Sioux. Revised edition. Norman: University of Oklahoma Press. (Originally published 1932.)

Vial, Pedro, and Francisco Xavier de Chaves
1785   [Diary of Trip from San Antonio to the Comanche Villages to Treat for Peace, Nov. 15, 1785.] (AGI, Guadalajara, Legajo 286; Microfilm copy in Western History Collection, University of Oklahoma, Norman.)

Vickers, J. Roderick
1986   Alberta Plains Prehistory: A Review. *Archaeological Survey of Alberta. Occasional Paper* 27. Edmonton.

——— 1994   Cultures of the Northwestern Plains: From the Boreal Forest Edge to Milk River. Pp. 3–33 in Plains Indians, A.D. 500–1500: The Archaeological Past of Historic Groups. Karl H. Schlesier, ed. Norman: University of Oklahoma Press.

Vickers, J. Roderick, and Alwynne B. Beaudoin
1989   A Limiting AMS Date for the Cody Complex Occupation at the Fletcher Site, Alberta, Canada. *Plains Anthropologist* 34(125):261–264.

Viers, Margaret
1983   A Linguistic Comparison of Quapaw and Osage. (Manuscript in Department of Anthropology, University of Arkansas, Fayetteville.)

Vigorelli, Leonardo
1987   Gli oggetti indiani raccolti da G. Costantino Beltrami. Fotografie di Franco Zaina. Bergamo: Ikonos Editore; Civico Museo E. Caffi.

Villaseñor y Sánchez, José Antonio de
1746–1748 Theatro americano: descripcion general de los reynos y provincias de la Nueva-España, y sus jurisdicciones: dedicala al rey nuestro señor El Señor D. Phelipe Quinto, Monarca de las Españas. 2 vols. México: La Viuda de Joseph Bernardo

de Hogal. (Reprinted: Familia Cortina del Valle, Mexico, 1987; Editorial Trillas, Mexico, 1992.)

Villiers du Terrage, Marc de
1921   Le Massacre de l'expedition espagnole du Missouri (11 aôut 1720). *Journal de la Société des Americanistes de Paris,* n.s. 13:239–255. Paris.

——— 1925   La Découverte du Missouri et l'histoire du Fort d'Orléans (1673–1728). Paris: Librairie Ancienne Honore Champion.

Vincent, Joan
1990   Anthropology and Politics: Visions, Traditions, and Trends. Tucson: University of Arizona Press.

Viola, Herman J.
1974   Thomas L. McKenney: Architect of America's Early Indian Policy, 1816–1830. Chicago: Swallow Press.

——— 1976   The Indian Legacy of Charles Bird King. Washington: Smithsonian Press; New York: Doubleday.

——— 1981   Diplomats in Buckskins: A History of Indian Delegations in Washington City. Washington: Smithsonian Institution Press. (Reprinted, with a Foreword by Ben Nighthorse Campbell: Rivilo Books, Bluffton, N.C., 1995.)

——— 1998   Warrior Artists: Historic Cheyenne and Kiowa Indian Ledger Art Drawn by Making Medicine and Zotom. With Commentary by Joseph D. and George P. Horse Capture. Washington: National Geographic Society.

Vis, Robert B., and Dale R. Henning
1969   A Local Sequence for Mill Creek Sites in the Little Sioux River Valley. *Plains Anthropologist* 14(46):253–271.

Vissier, Paul
1827   Histoire de la tribu des Osages, peuplade sauvage de l'Amérique Septentrionale, dans l'état du Missouri, l'un des États-Unis d'Amérique [etc.]. Paris: Chez C. Béchet.

Vitart, Anne, ed.
1993   Parures d'Histoire: Peaux de bisons peintes des Indianes d'Amérique du Nord. Paris: Musée de l'Homme and Réunion des Musées Nationaux.

Vivian, R. Gwinn
1960   The Navajo Archaeology of the Chacra Mesa, New Mexico. (M.A. Thesis in Anthropology, University of New Mexico, Albuquerque.)

Voegelin, Charles F.
1938–1940 Shawnee Stems and the Jacob P. Dunn Miami Dictionary. 5 Pts. *Indiana Historical Society. Prehistory Research Series* 1(3):63–108, (5):135–167, (8):289–341, (9):345–406, (10):409–478. Indianapolis.

——— 1939   Ofo-Biloxi Sound Correspondences. *Proceedings of the Indiana Academy of Science* 48:23–36. Indianapolis.

——— 1941   Internal Relationships of Siouan Languages. *American Anthropologist,* n.s. 43(2, Pt. 1):246–249.

——— 1941a   Historical Results of Crow-Hidatsa Comparisons, According to Three Methods. *Proceedings of the Indiana Academy of Science* 50:39–42. Indianapolis.

Voegelin, Erminie W.
1933   Kiowa-Crow Mythological Affiliations. *American Anthropologist,* n.s. 35(3):470–474.

——— 1954   A Note from the Chairman, The History of the OVHIC (Ohio Valley Historic Indian Conference). *Ethnohistory* 1(1):1–6.

Voegelin, Erminie W., and Harold Hickerson
1974   The Red Lake and Pembina Chippewa. Chippewa Indians I.

American Indian Ethnohistory: North Central and North-eastern Indians. David Agee Horr, comp. and ed. New York and London: Garland Publishing.

Voget, Fred W.
1939   [Crow Fieldnotes.] (Manuscripts in F.W. Voget's possession.)

1948   Individual Motivation in the Diffusion of the Wind River Shoshone Sundance to the Crow Indians. *American Anthropologist,* n.s. 50(4, Pt.1):634–646.

1950   A Shoshone Innovator. *American Anthropologist,* n.s. 52(1):53–63.

1950a   The Diffusion of the Wind River Sundance to the Crow Indians of Montana. (Ph.D. Dissertation in Anthropology, Yale University, New Haven, Conn.)

1952   Crow Socio-Cultural Groups. Pp. 88–93 in Acculturation in the Americas. Sol Tax, ed. Chicago: University of Chicago Press.

1953   Current Trends in the Wind River Shoshone Sun Dance. *Bureau of American Ethnology Bulletin* 151; *Anthropological Paper* 42. Washington: Smithsonian Institution; U.S. Government Printing Office.

1956   The American Indian in Transition: Reformation and Accommodation. *American Anthopologist* 58(2):249–263.

1964   Warfare and the Integration of Crow Culture. Pp. 483–509 in Explorations in Cultural Anthropology: Essays in Honor of George Peter Murdock. Ward B. Goodenough, ed. New York: McGraw-Hill Book Company.

1980   Tradition, Identity, and Adaptive Change among the Crow of Montana. Pp. 163–187 in Political Organization of Native North Americans. Ernust L. Schusky, ed. Washington: University Press of America.

1984   The Shoshoni-Crow Sun Dance. Norman: University of Oklahoma Press.

1987   The Crow Indian Give-Away: A Primary Instrument for Cultural Adaptation and Persistence. *Anthropos* 82(1–3): 207–214. Salzburg, Austria.

1987a   [Crow Fieldnotes.] (Manuscript in F.W. Voget's possession.)

1987b   [Comes-Out-of-the-Water: Life History of a Crow Indian Woman.] (Manuscript in F.W. Voget's possession.)

1995   They Call Me Agnes: A Crow Narrative Based on the Life of Agnes Yellowtail Deernose. (With the assistance of Mary K. Mee.) Norman: University of Oklahoma Press.

1996   Religion in Crow Indian Culture and Culture History. Pp. 87–102 in Chin Hills to Chiloquin: Papers Honoring the Versatile Career of Theodore Stern. With a Note of Personal Appreciation by Patrick M. Haynal. Don E. Dumond, ed. *University of Oregon Anthropological Papers* 52. Eugene.

Vogt, Evon Z.
1957   The Acculturation of American Indians. Pp. 137–146 in American Indians and American Life. George E. Simpson and J. Milton Yinger, eds. *Annals of the American Academy of Political and Social Science* 311. Philadelphia.

1961   Navaho. Pp. 278–336 in Perspectives in American Indian Culture Change, Edward H. Spicer, ed. Chicago: University of Chicago Press.

Voisine, Nive
1969   Robutel de La Noue, Zacharie. P. 581 in Canadian Biography, Vol. 2, 1701 to 1710. Toronto: University of Toronto Press.

von Kittlitz, Hans-Wernher
1998   Karl Bodmer: A Biographical and Bibliographical Survey. *European Review of Native American Studies* 12(1):19–34. Vienna, Austria [etc.].

Voorhis, Paul H.
1971   New Notes on the Mesquakie (Fox) Language. *International Journal of American Linguistics* 37(2):63–75. Chicago.

1977   A Saulteaux (Ojibwe) Phrase Book based on the Dialects of Manitoba. A Compilation of Material from the Course "Introduction to the Saulteaux Language" developed in the IMPACTE Programme at Brandon University and First Taught in the Fall of 1972. Contributors, Native Speakers of Saulteaux: Charles Bittern, Florence Bone, Karen Bunn, [et al.]. Brandon, Man.: Brandon University, Department of Native Studies.

1988   Kickapoo Vocabulary. *Algonquian and Iroquoian Linguistics. Memoir* 6. Winnipeg, Man.

Vore, Jacob
1919   The Omaha Indians Forty Years Ago. Addendum by Albert Watkins. *Publications of the Nebraska State Historical Society* 19:114–125. Lincoln.

Vorst, Jesse, et al.
1989   Race, Class, Gender: Bonds and Barriers. *Socialist Studies/Études socialistes* 5. Toronto: Published by Between the Lines in Co-operation with the Society for Socialist Studies.

Voth, Henry R.
1912   Arapaho Tales. *Journal of American Folk-lore* 25(95):43–50. Philadelphia.

WHC = Wisconsin Historical Society Collections
1855–1911 Collections of the State Historical Society of Wisconsin. Lyman C. Draper and Reuben G. Thwiates, eds. 21 vols. Madison: The Society.

Waddell, Jack O., and O. Michael Watson, eds.
1973   American Indian Urbanization. West Lafayette, Ind.: Purdue Research Foundation.

Wade, Mason, ed.
1947   The Journals of Francis Parkman. 2 vols. New York: Harper and Brothers Publishers. (Reprinted: Kraus Reprint, New York, 1969.)

Wagner, Glendolin D., and William A. Allen
1987   Blankets and Moccasins: Plenty Coups and His People, the Crows. Lincoln: University of Nebraska Press.

Wagoner, Paula
1998   An Unsettled Frontier: Land, Blood, and U.S. Federal Policy. Pp. 124–141 in Property Relations: Renewing the Anthropological Tradition. C.M. Hann, ed. London: Cambridge University Press.

1997   Ambivalent Identies: Land, Blood, and U.S. Federal Policy in Bennett County, South Dakota. (Ph.D. Dissertation in History, Indiana University, Bloomington.)

Wagoner, Paula L., and Mindy J. Morgan, eds.
1999   Interpreting Cultures: A Symposium. Bloomington: Indiana University, Department of Anthropology.

Wakefield, Sarah F.
1864   Six Weeks in the Sioux Tepees: A Narrative of Indian Captivity. Second edition. Shakopee, Minn.: Argus Book and Job Printing Office. (Reprinted, Edited and Annotated, and with an Introduction by June Namias: University of Oklahoma Press, Norman, 1997.)

1279

Walde, Dale Allen
1994 The Mortlach Phase. (Ph.D. Dissertation in Archaeology, University of Calgary, Calgary, Alta.)

Waldram, James B.
1997 The Way of the Pipe: Aboriginal Spirituality and Symbolic Healing in Canadian Prisons. Peterborough, Ont.: Broadview Press.

Walker, Danny N.
1975 A Cultural and Ecological Analysis of the Vertebrate Fauna from the Medicine Lodge Creek Site (48BH499). (M.A. Thesis in Anthropology, University of Wyoming, Laramie.)

1982 Cultural Modification of Bone from Pronghorn (*Antilocapra americana*) and Other Small Mammals. Pp. 270–274 in The Agate Basin Site: A Record of the Paleoindian Occupation of the Northwestern High Plains. George C. Frison and Dennis Stanford, eds. New York: Academic Press.

Walker, Danny N., and Julie E. Francis
1989 Legend Rock Petroglyph Site (48HO4), Wyoming: 1988 Archaeological Investigations. (Manuscript on file, Office of State Archaeologist, Department of Anthropology, University of Wyoming, Laramie.)

Walker, Ernest G.
1982 The Bracken Cairn: A Late Middle Archaic Burial from Southwestern Saskatchewan. *Saskatchewan Archaeology* 3(1–2):8–35. Saskatoon.

1983 The Woodlawn Site: A Case for Interregional Disease Transmission in the Late Prehistoric Period. *Canadian Journal of Archaeology* 7(1):49–59. Ottawa.

1984 The Graham Site: A McKean Cremation from Southern Saskatchewan. *Plains Anthropologist* 29(104):139–150.

1986 Human Skeletal Remains from the Crown Site. Pp. 247–261 in The Crown Site (FhNa86) Excavation Results, by J. Michael Quigg. *Saskatchewan Research Council. Nipawin Reservoir Heritage Study* 8. Saskatoon, Sask.

1988 The Archaeological Resources of the Wanuskewin Heritage Park. Pp. 75–89 in Out of the Past: Sites, Digs and Artifacts in the Saskatoon Area. Urve Linnamae and Tim E.H. Jones, eds. Saskatoon, Sask.: Saskatoon Archaeological Society.

1992 The Gowen Sites: Cultural Reponses to Climatic Warming on the Northern Plains (7500–5000 B.P.). *Canadian Museum of Civilization. Archaeological Survey of Canada. Mercury Series Paper* 145. Hull, Que.

Walker, Henry P., ed.
1963 William McLane's Narrative of the Magee-Gutierrez Expedition, 1812–1813. *Southwestern Historical Quarterly* 66(4):569–588. Austin, Tex.

Walker, James R.
1914 Oglala Kinship Terms. *American Anthropologist*, n.s. 16(1):96–109.

1917 The Sun Dance and Other Ceremonies of the Oglala Division of the Teton Dakota. *American Museum of Natural History Anthropological Papers* 16(2):51–221. New York. (Reprinted: Lakota Books, Kendall Park, N.J., 1993.)

1960 The Sun Dance of the Oglala. Pp. 377–391 in The Golden Age of American Anthropology. Margaret Mead and Ruth L. Bunzel, eds. New York: George Braziller.

1980 Lakota Belief and Ritual. Raymond J. DeMallie and Elaine A. Jahner, eds. Lincoln: University of Nebraska Press.

1982 Lakota Society. Raymond J. DeMallie and Elaine A. Jahner, eds. Lincoln: University of Nebraska Press.

1983 Lakota Myth. Elaine A. Jahner, ed. Lincoln: University of Nebraska Press.

Wallace, Anthony Francis Clarke
1956 Revitalization Movements. *American Anthropologist,* n.s. 58(2):264–281.

1966 Religion: An Anthropological View. New York: Random House.

Wallace, Edward S.
1951 General John Lapham Bullis, the Thunderbolt of the Texas Frontier. *Southwestern Historical Quarterly* 54(4):452–461; 55(1):77–85. Austin, Tex.

1953 General Ranald Slidell Mackenzie, Indian Fighting Cavalryman. *Southwestern Historical Quarterly* 56(3):378–396. Austin, Tex.

Wallace, Ernest
1953 The Comanches on the White Man's Road. *West Texas Historical Association Year Book* 29:3–32. Abilene, Tex.

1954 David G. Burnet's Letters Describing the Comanche Indians. *West Texas Historical Association Year Book* 30:115–140. Abilene, Tex.

1964 Ranald S. Mackenzie on the Texas Frontier. Lubbock, Tex.: West Texas Museum Association.

_____, ed.
1967 Ranald S. Mackenzie's Official Correspondence Relating to Texas, 1871–1873. Lubbock, Tex.: West Texas Museum Association.

_____, ed.
1968 Ranald S. Mackenzie's Official Correspondence Relating to Texas, 1873–1879. Lubbock, Tex.: West Texas Museum Association.

Wallace, Ernest, and E. Adamson Hoebel
1952 The Comanche: Lords of the South Plains. Based on Field Work 1933–1945. *Human Relations Area Files* 6(3). Norman: University of Oklahoma Press. (Reprinted in 1954, 1958, 1969, 1982, 1986, 1988.)

Wallace, Karen Kay
1993 Verb Incorporation and Agreement in Crow. (Ph.D. Dissertation in Linguistics, University of California, Los Angeles.)

Wallis, Ruth S.
1954 The Overt Fears of Dakota Indian Children. *Child Development* 25:185–192.

1955 The Changed Status of Twins among the Eastern Dakota. *Anthropological Quarterly* 28(3):116–120. Washington: The Catholic University of America.

Wallis, Ruth S., and Wilson D. Wallis
1953 The Sins of the Fathers: Concept of Disease among the Canadian Dakota. *Southwestern Journal of Anthropology* 9(4):431–436. Albuquerque.

Wallis, Wilson D.
1918 Messiahs: Christian and Pagan. *World Worship Series.* Boston: R.G. Badger.

1919 The Sun Dance of the Canadian Dakota. *American Museum of Natural History Anthropological Papers* 16(4):317–380. New York. (Reprinted in 1921; also, Lakota Books, Kendall Park, N.J., 1993.)

1923 Beliefs and Tales of the Canadian Dakota. *Journal of American Folk-lore* 36(139):36–101. Washington.

1947 The Canadian Dakota. *American Museum of Natural History Anthropological Papers* 41(1):1–225. New York.

Walton, Ann T., John C. Ewers, and Royal B. Hassrick
1985   After the Buffalo Were Gone: The Louis Warren Hill, Sr., Collection of Indian Art. St. Paul, Minn.: Northwest Area Foundation, in cooperation with the Indian Arts and Crafts Board [...] and the Science Museum of Minnesota.

Wanica, A.O.J. Selitch
1970   The Dakota Sun Dance. *Expedition* 13(1):17–23. Philadelphia: University Museum of the University of Pennsylvania.

Wapp, Edward, Jr.
1984   The American Indian Courting Flute: Revitalization and Change. In: Sharing a Heritage: American Indian Arts. Charlotte Heth and Michael Swarm, eds. *Contemporary American Indian Issues Series,* 5. Los Angeles: American Indian Studies Center. (Originally presented as the Author's M.A. Thesis in History, and published under title: The Sioux Courting Flute: Its Traditions, Construction, and Music. University of Washington, Seattle, 1984.)

WarCloud, Paul
1967   Dakotah Sioux Indian Dictionary. Sisseton, S.Dak.: Paul WarCloud.

Warden, Cleaver
1903–1906 [Notebooks.] (Manuscripts in Field Columbian Museum Archives, Chicago.)

Wardwell, Allen, ed.
1998   Native Paths: American Indian Art from the Collection of Charles and Valerie Diker. Janet Catherine Berlo ... [et al.]. Catalog of an Exhibition held at the Metropolitan Museum of Art, May 7, 1998–January 2, 2000. New York: Metropolitan Museum of Art.

Ware, Eugene F.
1911   The Indian War of 1864, Being a Fragment of the Early History of Kansas, Nebraska, Colorado and Wyoming. Topeka, Kans.: Crane.

Warkentin, Germaine
1996   Discovering Radisson: A Renaissance Adventurer between Two Worlds. Pp. 43–70 in Reading Beyond Words: Contexts for Native History. Jennifer S.H. Brown and Elizabeth Vibert, eds. Peterborough, Ont.: Broadview Press.

Warkentin, John
1994   Introduction to the 1994 Edition. Pp. vi–xxvi in The Kelsey Papers. Regina, Sask.: Canadian Plains Research Center, University of Regina.

Warkentin, John, and Richard I. Ruggles, eds.
1970   Manitoba Historical Atlas: A Selection of Facsimile Maps, Plans, and Sketches from 1612 to 1969. Winnipeg: Historical and Scientific Society of Manitoba.

Warner, John Anson
1975   The Life and Art of the North American Indian. London: The Hamlyn Publishing Group Ltd.; New York: Crescent Books.

1990   Nature and Spirit in Contemporary Native Manitoba Painting. *American Indian Art Magazine* 15(2):38–47. Scottsdale, Ariz.

Warren, Gena
1998   Wanda (Kekabah) Stone. *Kanza News: Newsletter of the Kanza Nation of Oklahoma* 5:9–11. Kaw City, Okla.

Warren, G.K. (Gouverneur Kemble)
1856   Explorations in the Dacota Country, in the Year 1855; By Lieut. G.K. Warren, Topographical Engineer of the "Sioux Expedition." *34th Congress. 1st Session. Senate Executive Document* 76. Washington: A.O.P. Nicholson.

1875   Preliminary Report of Explorations in Nebraska and Dakota, in the Years 1855–'56–'57; by Lieut. G.K. Warren, Topographical Engineers. Washington: Government Printing Office. ("This Report was originally printed in the Appendixes [sic] to the Report of the Secretary of War, in the President's Message and Documents, Dec. 1858.")

Warren, William W.
1885   History of the Ojibways, Based Upon Traditions and Oral Statements. *Collections of the Minnesota Historical Society* 5(24):21–394. St. Paul, Minn. (Reprinted under title: History of the Ojibway People; with an Introduction by W. Roger Buffalohead: Minnesota Historical Society Press, St. Paul, Minn., 1957, 1970, 1984.)

1946   Sioux and Chippewa Wars. *The Minnesota Archaeologist* 12(4):95–107. Minneapolis, Minn. (Originally publ. in *The Minnesota Chronicle and Register*, June 3 and 10, 1850.)

_____ 1957, 1970, 1984 *see* 1885 (reprint info.)

Warrior, Robert Allen
1996   Clyde Warrior. Pp. 665–666 in Encyclopedia of North American Indians. Frederick E. Hoxie, ed. Boston: Houghton Mifflin.

Washakie, Dick
1973   The Sun Dance. Pp. 74–76 in Great Documents in American Indian History. Wayne Moquin and Charles Van Doren, eds. New York: Praeger Publishers.

Washburn, Wilcomb E.
1973   The American Indian and the United States: A Documentary History. 4 vols. New York: Random House. (Reprinted, Greenwood Press, New York, 1979.)

_____, ed.
1984   A Fifty-Year Perspective on the Indian Reorganization Act. *American Anthropologist,* n.s. 86(2):279–289.

_____, vol. ed. 1988 *see* Handbook Vol. 4 (1988)

Watembach, Karen
1996   St. Xavier Mission: A Century of Catholicism among the Crow People, 1888–1988. 1st ed. [Ashland, Mont.]: Published by St. Labre Mission.

Waters, William T.
1984   Otoe-Missouria Oral Narratives. (M.A. Thesis in Anthropology, University of Nebraska, Lincoln.)

Watkins, Arthur V.
1957   Termination of Federal Supervision: The Removal of Restrictions Over Indian Property and Person. Pp. 47–55 in American Indians and American Life. George E. Simpson and J. Milton Yinger, eds. *The Annals of the Academy of Political and Social Science* 311. Philadelphia.

Watkins, Edwin A., comp.
1865   A Dictionary of the Cree Language, as Spoken by the Indians of the Hudson's Bay Company's Territories. Part I: English-Cree; Part II: Cree-English. London: Society for Promoting Christian Knowledge. (See also Faries, Richard, ed., 1938.)

Watkins, Laurel J.
1984   A Grammar of Kiowa. With the Assistance of Parker P. McKenzie. *Studies in the Anthropology of North American Indians.* Lincoln: University of Nebraska Press.

Watrall, Charles R.
1968   An Analysis of the Bone and Shell Materials from the Cambria Focus. (M.A. Thesis in Anthropology, University of Minnesota, Minneapolis.)

1968a   Virginia Deer and the Buffer Zone in the Late Prehistoric-Early Protohistoric Periods in Minnesota. *Plains Anthropologist* 13(40):81–86.

Watson, George D., Jr.
1993   The Oglala Sioux Tribal Court: From Termination to Self- *1281*

Determination. *Great Plains Research [Journal]* 3(1):61–93. Lincoln, Nebr.

Watson, Virginia D.
1950   The Optima Focus of the Panhandle Aspect: Description and Analysis. *Bulletin of the Texas Archeological and Paleontological Society* 21:7–68. Lubbock.

Watt, Frank H.
1969   The Waco Indian Village and Its Peoples. *Central Texas Archeologist. Bulletin* 9:187–243. Waco, Tex.: Reprinted by TEXANA for the Central Texas Archeological Society.

Wax, Murray L.
1971   Indian Americans: Unity and Diversity. Englewood Cliffs, N.J.: Prentice-Hall.

Wax, Murray L., and Rosalie H. Wax
1978   Religion among American Indians. *Annals of the American Academy of Political and Social Science* 436:27–39. Philadelphia.

Wax, Murray, Rosalie Wax, and Robert V. Dumont, Jr.
1964   Formal Education in an American Indian Community. *Social Problems* 11(4). Kalamazoo, Mich.

Wax, Rosalie
1971   Doing Field Work: Warnings and Advice. Chicago: University of Chicago Press.

Weakly, Ward F.
1965   1964 Archeological Salvage in the Elk City Reservoir. *Newsletter of the Kansas Anthropological Association* 10(6):1–4. Topeka.

1971   Tree-ring Dating and Archaeology in South Dakota. *Plains Anthropologist* 16(54, Pt. 2); *Memoir* 8. Lincoln.

Weathers, Winston
1970   Indian and White: Sixteen Eclouges. Lincoln: University of Nebraska Press.

Weaver, John E., and Frederick W. Albertson
1956   Grasslands of the Great Plains: Their Nature and Use. Lincoln: Johnsen Publishing.

Webb, H.G.
1894   The Dakota Sun Dance of 1883. (Manuscript No. 1394a, National Anthropological Archives, Smithsonian Institution, Washington.)

Webb, Walter Prescott
1931   The Great Plains. Boston: Ginn & Company.

1965   The Texas Rangers: A Century of Frontier Defense. Austin: University of Texas Press.

Webber, Charles W.
1849   The Gold Mines of the Gila: A Sequel to Old Hicks the Guide. 2 vols. New York: Dewitt and Davenport.

Weber, David J.
1971   The Taos Trappers: The Fur Trade in the Far Southwest, 1540–1846. Norman: University of Oklahoma Press.

Webster, John Clarence
1946   Catalogue of the John Clarence Webster Canadiana Collection (Pictorial Section) New Brunswick Museum. *The New Brunswick Museum. Catalogue* 2. Saint John, N.B.

Webster, Sean Michael
1999   Interpreting Northern Plains Subsistence Practices: An Analysis of the Faunal and Floral Assemblages from the Thundercloud Site (FbNp-25). (M.A. Thesis in Anthropology and Archaeology, University of Saskatchewan, Saskatoon.)

Weddle, Robert S.
[1964]   The San Sabá Mission, Spanish Pivot in Texas. Austin: University of Texas Press.

_____, ed.
1987   La Salle, the Mississippi, and the Gulf: Three Primary Documents. College Station: Texas A&M University Press.

Wedel, Mildred Mott
1959   Oneota Sites on the Upper Iowa River. *The Missouri Archaeologist* 21(2–4). Columbia.

1961   Indian Villages on the Upper Iowa River. *The Palimpsest* 42(12):561–592. Iowa City.

1971   J.-B. Bénard, Sieur de la Harpe: Visitor to the Wichitas in 1719. *Great Plains Journal* 10(2):37–70. Lawton, Okla. (Reprinted in: The Wichita Indians, 1541–1750: Ethnohistorical Essays. *Reprints in Anthropology* 38. J&L Reprint Company, Lincoln, 1988.)

1972   Claude-Charles Dutisné: A Review of His 1719 Journeys. [Pt.1.] *Great Plains Journal* 12(1):[4]5–25. Lawton, Okla. (See 1973a for Pt. 2. Pt. 1 and Pt. 2 reprinted, pp. 74–130 in The Wichita Indians, 1541–1750: Ethnohistorical Essays. *Reprints in Anthropology* 38. J&L Reprint Company, Lincoln, 1988.)

1973   The Identity of La Salle's *Pana* Slave. *Plains Anthropologist* 18(61):203–217. Lincoln, Nebr.

1973a   Claude-Charles Dutisné: A Review of His 1719 Journeys. [Pt. 2.] *Great Plains Journal* Pt. 1, 12(1):4–25; Pt. 2, 12(2):147–173. Lawton, Okla. (See 1972 for Pt. 1. Pt. 1 and Pt. 2 reprinted: pp. 74–130 in The Wichita Indians, 1541–1750: Ethnohistorical Essays. *Reprints in Anthropology* 38. J&L Reprint Company, Lincoln, 1988.)

1974   The Prehistoric and Historic Habitat of the Missouri and Oto Indians [1950]. Pp. 25–76 in Oto and Missouri Indians. *American Indian Ethnohistory: Plains Indians*. David Agee Horr, comp. and ed. New York and London: Garland Publishing.

1974a   Le Sueur and the Dakota Sioux. Pp. 157–171 in Aspects of Upper Great Lakes Anthropology: Papers in Honor of Lloyd A. Wilford. Elden Johnson, ed. *Minnesota Prehistoric Archaeology Series* 11. St. Paul: Minnesota Historical Society.

1976   Ethnohistory: Its Payoffs and Pitfalls for Iowa Archaeologists. *Journal of the Iowa Archeological Society* 23:1–44. Iowa City.

1978   A Synonymy of Names for the Ioway Indians. *Journal of the Iowa Archeological Society* 25:49–77. Iowa City.

1979   The Ethnohistoric Approach to Plains Caddoan Origins. *Nebraska History* 60(2):183–196. Lincoln. (Reprinted: pp. 1–37 in The Wichita Indians, 1541–1750: Ethnohistorical Essays. *Reprints in Anthropology* 38. J&L Reprint Company, Lincoln, 1988.)

1981   The Ioway, Oto, and Omaha Indians in 1700. *Journal of the Iowa Archeological Society* 28:1–13. Iowa City.

1981a   The Deer Creek Site, Oklahoma: A Wichita Village Sometimes Called Ferdinandia. An Ethnohistorian's View. *Oklahoma Historical Society. Series in Anthropology* 5. Oklahoma City.

1982   The Wichita Indians in the Arkansas River Basin. Pp. 118–134 in Plains Indian Studies: A Collection of Essays in Honor of John C. Ewers and Waldo R. Wedel. *Smithsonian Contributions to Anthropology* 30. Douglas H. Ubelaker and Herman J. Viola, eds. Washington: Smithsonian Institution. (Reprinted: Pp. 13–37 in The Wichita Indians, 1541–1750, by Mildred Mott Wedel. J&L Reprint Company, Lincoln, 1988.)

1986   Peering at the Ioway Indians through the Mist of Times:

1650–Circa 1700. *Journal of the Iowa Archeological Society* 33:1–74. Iowa City.

1988
The Wichita Indians, 1541–1750: Ethnohistorical Essays. *Reprints in Anthropology* 38. Lincoln: J&L Reprint Company.

Wedel, Mildred Mott, and Raymond J. DeMallie
1980
The Ethnohistorical Approach in Pawnee Archaeology. Pp. 110–128 in Anthropology on the Great Plains. W. Raymond Wood and Margot Liberty, eds. Lincoln: University of Nebraska Press.

Wedel, Waldo R.
1933
[Comanche Notes, Drafts, Photos, and Negatives, Field Notebooks, Maps, Specimen Catalog; Fieldnotes of San Francisco Bay (while Wedel was a Graduate Student).] (Waldo R. Wedel Collection, Box # 108, National Anthropological Archives, Smithsonian Institution, Washington.)

1934
Preliminary Notes on the Archaeology of Medicine Valley in Southwestern Nebraska. *Nebraska History* 14(3):144–166. Lincoln.

1935
Contributions to the Archaeology of the Upper Republican Valley, Nebraska. *Nebraska History* 15(3):132–209. Lincoln.

1935a
Minneapolis 1: A Prehistoric Village Site in Ottawa County, Kansas. *Nebraska History* 15(3):210–237. Lincoln.

1935b
Preliminary Classification for Nebraska and Kansas Cultures. *Nebraska History* 15(3):251–255. Lincoln.

1936
An Introduction to Pawnee Archeology. *Bureau of American Ethnology Bulletin* 112. Washington: Smithsonian Institution; U.S. Government Printing Office. (Reprinted: J&L Reprint Company, Lincoln, 1977.)

1938
The Direct-historical Approach in Pawnee Archeology. *Smithsonian Miscellaneous Collection*s 97(7):1–21. Washington: Smithsonian Institution; U.S. Government Printing Office. (Reprinted: J&L Reprint Company, Lincoln, 1976.)

1940
Culture Sequences in the Central Great Plains. Pp. 291–352 in Essays in Historical Anthropology of North America: Published in Honor of John R. Swanton in Celebration of His Fortieth Year with the Smithsonian Institution. *Smithsonian Miscellaneous Collections* 100; (*Publication* 3588). Washington: Smithsonian Institution; U.S. Government Printing Office. (Reprinted in: *Plains Anthropologist* 17(57):291–352, 1972.)

1941
Environment and Native Subsistence Economies in the Central Great Plains. *Smithsonian Miscellaneous Collections* 101(3):10–290. Washington: Smithsonian Institution; U.S. Government Printing Office.

1942
Archeological Remains in Central Kansas and Their Possible Bearing on the Location of Quivira. *Smithsonian Miscellaneous Collections* 101(7). Washington: Smithsonian Institution; Government Printing Office.

1943
Archeological Investigations in Platte and Clay Counties, Missouri. *United States National Museum Bulletin* 183. Washington.

1946
The Kansa Indians. *Transactions of the Kansas Academy of Science* 49(1):1–35. Lawrence.

1947
Prehistory and Environment in the Central Great Plains. *Transactions of the Kansas Academy of Sciences* 50(1):1–18. Topeka.

1947a
Culture Chronology in the Central Great Plains. *American Antiquity* 12(3):148–156.

1947b
Note on Some Potsherds from Northeastern Wyoming. *Journal of the Washington Academy of Sciences* 37(5):157–159. Washington.

1950
Notes on Plains-Southwestern Contacts in the Light of Archeology. Pp. 99–116 in For the Dean: Essays in Anthropology in Honor of Byron Cummings on his Eighty-Ninth Birthday, September 20, 1950, Erik K. Reed and Dale S. King, eds. Tucson, Ariz.: Hohokam Museums Association; Santa Fe, N.M.: Southwestern Monuments Association.

1951
The Use of Earth-moving Machinery in Archaeological Excavations. Pp.17–33 in Essays on Archeological Methods: Proceedings of a Conference Held under the Auspices of the Viking Fund. James B. Griffin, ed. *University of Michigan. Museum of Anthropology. Anthropological Papers* 8. Ann Arbor.

1953
Some Aspects of Human Ecology in the Central Plains. *American Anthropologist*, n.s. 55(4):499–514.

1953a
Prehistory and the Missouri Valley Development Program: Summary Report on the Missouri River Basin Archeological Survey in 1948. *Bureau of American Ethnology Bulletin* 154; *River Basin Surveys Papers* 1. Washington: Smithsonian Institution; U.S. Government Printing Office.

1953b
Prehistory and the Missouri Valley Development Program: Summary Report on the Missouri River Basin Archaeological Survey in 1949. *Bureau of American Ethnology Bulletin* 154; *River Basin Surveys Papers* 2. Washington: Smithsonian Institution; U.S. Government Printing Office.

1954
Earthenware and Steatite Vessels from Northwestern Wyoming. *American Antiquity* 19(4):403–409.

1955
Archeological Materials from the Vicinity of Mobridge, South Dakota. *Bureau of American Ethnology Bulletin* 157; *Anthropological Papers* 45. Washington: Smithsonian Institution; U.S. Government Printing Office. (Reprinted: J&L Reprint Company, Lincoln, 1976.)

1959
An Introduction to Kansas Archeology. With Description of the Skeletal Remains from Doniphan and Scott Counties, Kansas, by T.D. Stewart. *Bureau of American Ethnology Bulletin* 174. Washington: Smithsonian Institution; U.S. Government Printing Office.

1961
Prehistoric Man on the Great Plains. Norman: University of Oklahoma Press.

1961a
Plains Archaeology, 1935–60. *American Antiquity* 27(1):24–32.

1963
The High Plains and Their Utilization by the Indians. *American Antiquity* 29(1):1–16.

1964
The Great Plains. Pp. 193–220 in Prehistoric Man in the New World. Jesse D. Jennings and Edward Norbeck, eds. Chicago: University of Chicago Press for William Marsh Rice University.

1967
The Council Circles of Central Kansas: Were They Solstice Registers? *American Antiquity* 32(1):54–63.

1967a
Salvage Archeology in the Missouri River Basin. *Science* 156(3775):589–597. Washington.

1968
After Coronado in Quivira. *Kansas Historical Quarterly* 34(4):369–385. Topeka.

1968a
Some Thoughts on Central Plains-Southern Plains Archaeological Relationships. *Great Plains Journal* 7(1):53–62. Lawton, Okla.

1283

1969   Washington Matthews: His Contribution to Plains Anthropology. *Plains Anthropologist* 14(45):175–176.

1970   Some Observations on: *Two House Sites in the Central Plains: An Experiment in Archeology.* W. Raymond Wood, ed. *Nebraska History* 51(2):225–252. Lincoln.

1970a   Coronado's Route to Quivira, 1541. *Plains Anthropologist* 15(49):161–168.

1975   Chalk Hollow: Culture Sequence and Chronology in the Texas Panhandle. Pp. 271–278 in Vol. 1 of *Actas del XLI Congreso Internacional de Americanistas, México, 2 al 7 de septiembre de 1974.* México: Instituto Nacional de Antropología e Historia.

1975a   Chain Mail in Plains Archeology. *Plains Anthropologist* 20(69):187–196.

1977   Native Astronomy and the Plains Caddoans. Pp. 131–145 in Native American Astronomy. Anthony F. Aveni, ed. Austin: University of Texas Press.

1978   Notes on the Prairie Turnip (*Psoralea esculenta*) among the Plains Indians. *Nebraska History* 59(2):154–179. Lincoln.

1979   Some Reflections on Plains Caddoan Origins. Pp. 272–293 in Toward Plains Caddoan Origins: A Symposium. *Nebraska History* 60(2). Lincoln.

1979a   Introduction. Pp. 131–133 in Toward Plains Caddoan Origins: A Symposium. *Nebraska History* 60(2). Lincoln.

1981   Towards a History of Plains Archaeology. *Great Plains Quarterly* 1(1):16–38. Lincoln.

1983   Native Subsistence Adaptations in the Great Plains. Pp. 93–110 in Man and the Changing Environments in the Great Plains. Warren W. Cadwell, C. Bertrand Schultz, and T. Mylan Stout, eds. *Transactions of the Nebraska Academy of Sciences and Affiliated Societies* 11(Special issue). Lincoln.

————, ed.
1985   The Dunbar-Allis Letters on the Pawnee. New York: Garland Publishing.

————, ed.
1985a   A Plains Archaeology Source Book: Selected Papers of the Nebraska State Historical Society. New York: Garland Publishing.

1986   Central Plains Prehistory: Holocene Environments and Culture Change in the Republican River Basin. Lincoln: University of Nebraska Press.

Wedel, Waldo R., and Marvin F. Kivett
1956   Additional Data on the Woodruff Ossuary, Kansas. *American Antiquity* 21(4):414–416.

Wedel, Waldo R., Wilfred M. Husted, and John H. Moss
1968   Mummy Cave: Prehistoric Record from Rocky Mountains of Wyoming. *Science* 160(3824):184–186. Washington.

Weekes, Mary
1994   The Last Buffalo Hunter; as Told to Her by Norbert Welsh. Saskatoon, Sask.: Fifth House Publishing. (Originally publ.: T. Nelson and Sons, New York, 1939.)

Wehrkamp, Tim
1978   Manuscript Sources in Sioux Indian History. *South Dakota History* 8(1):143–156. Pierre.

Weir, Frank A.
1976   The Central Texas Archaic. (Ph.D. Dissertation in Anthropology, Washington State University, Pullman.)

Weist, Katherine M.
1970   The Northern Cheyennes: Diversity in a Loosely Structured Society. (Ph.D. Dissertation in Anthropology, University of California, Berkeley.)

1973   Giving Away: The Ceremonial Distribution of Goods among the Northern Cheyenne of Southeastern Montana. *Plains Anthropologist* 18(60):97–103.

1977   An Ethnohistorical Analysis of Crow Political Alliances. *The Western Canadian Journal of Anthropology* 7(4):34–54. Edmonton, Alta.

1983   Beasts of Burden and Menial Slaves: Nineteenth Century Observations of Northern Plains Indian Women. Pp. 29–52 in The Hidden Half: Studies of Plains Indian Women. Patricia Albers and Beatrice Medicine, eds. Washington: University Press of America.

Weist, Katherine M., and Susan R. Sharrock
1985   An Annotated Bibliography of Northern Plains Ethnohistory. *University of Montana Contributions to Anthropology* 8. Missoula.

Weist, Tom.
1977   A History of the Cheyenne People. Billings, Mont.: State Council for Indian Education.

Weitzner, Bella
1979   Notes on the Hidatsa Indians Based on Data Recorded by the Late Gilbert L. Wilson. *American Museum of Natural History Anthropological Papers* 56(2). New York.

Wells, Robert N., Jr., ed.
1994   Native American Resurgence and Renewal: A Reader and Bibliography. *Native American Resources Series* 3. Metuchen, N.J.: The Scarecrow Press.

Welsch, Roger L.
1981   Omaha Tribal Myths and Trickster Tales. Athens, Ohio: Ohio University Press.

Welsh, Christine
1992   Women in the Shadows. Episode 1 of a two-part Series: Keepers of the Nation. Written and Produced by Christine Welsh. Directed by Norma Bailey. Produced for Studio D by Signe Johansson. Montréal: Studio D of the National Film Board of Canada; also, Toronto: Direction Films.

Welsh, Peter H.
1986   "Taking Care of Our Own": Identity and Dependency among the Northern Arapahoe. (Ph.D. Dissertation in Anthropology, University of Pennsylvania, Philadelphia.)

Welsh, William
1870   Sioux and Ponca Indians: Reports to the Missionary Organizations of the Protestant Episcopal Church and to the Secretary of the Interior, on Indian Civilization. Philadelphia: M'Calla & Staveley, Printers.

Weltfish, Gene
1930   Coiled Gambling Baskets of the Pawnees and Other Plains Tribes. *Indian Notes and Monographs* 7(3):277–295. New York: Museum of the American Indian. Heye Foundation.

1930a   Prehistoric North American Basketry Techniques and Modern Distributions. *American Anthropologist*, n.s. 32(3, Pt. 1):503–521.

1936   The Vision Story of Fox-Boy, a South Band Pawnee Text. (With Translation and Grammatical Analysis.) *International Journal of American Linguistics* 9(1):44–75. Chicago.

1937   Caddoan Texts: Pawnee, South Band Dialect. *American Ethnological Society Publication* 17. New York.

1940   Morphology of the Pawnee Language. (Manuscript 30[C1.1] in the Library of the American Philosophical Society, Philadelphia.)

1965   The Lost Universe: Pawnee Life and Culture. Lincoln: University of Nebraska Press. (Reprinted in 1977. Published also under title: The Lost Universe; With a Closing Chapter on The Universe Regained. Basic Books, New York, 1965; Reprinted: Ballantine Books, New York, 1971.)

Wendland, Wayne M.
1978   Holocene Man in North America: The Ecological Setting and Climatic Background. *Plains Anthropologist* 23(82, Pt. 1):273–287.

Wendorf, Fred, and James J. Hester
1962   Early Man's Utilization of the Great Plains Environment. *American Antiquity* 28(2):159–171.

1975   Late Pleistocene Environments of the Southern High Plains. *Fort Burgwin Research Center Publication* 9. Ranchos de Taos, N.Mex.

Wentworth, Edward N.
1957   Dried Meat—Early Man's Travel Ration. Pp. 557–571 in *Annual Report of the Smithsonian Institution for the Year 1956.* Washington: U.S. Government Printing Office.

Wessel, Thomas R.
1982   Political Assimilation on the Blackfoot Indian Reservation, 1887–1934: A Study in Survival. Pp. 59–72 in Plains Indian Studies: A Collection of Essays in Honor of John C. Ewers and Waldo R. Wedel. Douglas H. Ubelaker and Herman J. Viola, eds. *Smithsonian Contribution to Anthropology* 30. Washington.

West, Elizabeth Howard
1905   De Leon's Expedition of 1689. *Texas Historical Association Quarterly* 8(3):199–224.

West, Elliott
1998   The Contested Plains: Indians, Goldseekers, and the Rush to Colorado. Lawrence: University Press of Kansas.

West, LaMont, Jr.
1960   The Sign Language: An Analysis. (Ph.D. Dissertation in Anthropology, Indiana University, Bloomington. Xerographic reprint: University Microfilms International, Ann Arbor, Mich., 1977.)

West, Martin L., et al.
1873   [Petition Address to Alexander Morris, dated 4 March 1873.] (Record Group 10, Vol. 3600, file 1567, microfilm reel C-10104 in The National Archives of Canada, Ottawa.)

Wetsit, Lawrence D.
1982   Assiniboine Claims History. *Wotanin Wowapi* 30(14) (July 30, 1982):6. Poplar, Mont.: Fort Peck Tribal Executive Board.

Wettlaufer, Boyd N.
1955   The Mortlach Site in the Besant Valley of Central Saskatchewan. (With a Chapter on Soils Report: Physical Features and Soils of the Mortlach Archaeology Area, by Harold C. Moss.) *Saskatchewan Museum of Natural History. Anthropological Series* 1. Regina, Sask.

Wettlaufer, Boyd N., comp., and William J. Mayer-Oakes, ed.
1960   The Long Creek Site. *Saskatchewan Museum of Natural History. Anthropological Series* 2. Regina, Sask.

Wharton, Clifton
1925   The Expedition of Major Clifton Wharton in 1844. *Collections of the Kansas State Historical Society for the Years 1922–1925,* vol. 16:272–305. Topeka.

Wheat, Carl I.
1957–1963   Mapping the Transmississippi West, 1540–1861. 5 vols. in 6 [vol. 5 in 2 pts.]. San Francisco: The Institute of Historical Cartography.

Wheeler, Charles W., and Gary Martin
1982   The Granby Site: Early-Middle Archaic Wattle and Daub Structures. *Southwestern Lore* 48(3):16–25. Boulder, Colo.

Wheeler, Richard P.
1952   A Note on the "McKean Lanceolate Point." *Plains Anthropological Conference Newsletter* 4(4):39–44.

1954   Two New Projectile Point Types: Duncan and Hanna Points. *Plains Anthropologist* 1(1):7–14.

1957   Archaeological Remains in Three Reservoir Areas in South Dakota and Wyoming. (Manuscript on file at the National Park Service, Interagency Archaeological Services, Denver, Colo.)

1985   The Middle Prehistoric Period in the Central and Northern Plains. Pp. 5–10 in McKean/Middle Plains Archaic: Current Research. Marcel Kornfeld and Lawrence C. Todd, eds. *Occasional Papers on Wyoming Archaeology* 4. Laramie: Wyoming Recreation Center.

1996   Archeological Investigations in Three Reservoir Areas in South Dakota and Wyoming. *Reprints in Anthropology* 47. Lincoln: J&L Reprint Company.

Wheeling, F.J., and J.E. Johnson
1852   [Abstract of Expenses of the Om-Ma-Ha Indian Delegation now in Washington, conducted in part by F.J. Wheeling and J.E. Johnson. Company consisting of nineteen. Letter to Luke Lea, Commissioner of Indian Affairs, dated Febrary 9, 1852.] (Microcopy 234, Roll 218, Letters Received by the Office of Indian Affairs from the Council Bluff Agency, 1824–1881, Records of the Bureau of Indian Affairs, Record Group 75, National Archives, Washington.)

Wheelock, Thompson B.
1835   Journal of Colonel Dodge's Expedition from Fort Gibson to the Pawnee Pict Village. Pp. 70–91 in Message from The President of the United States....*23d Congress. 2d Session. House Executive Document,* Vol. 1, No. 2. (Serial No. 271) Washington: Gales and Seaton.

Wheelwright Museum of the American Indian, comp.
1985   Guide to the Microfilm Edition of the Washington Matthews Papers. 10 rolls. Albuquerque: University of New Mexico Press.

Whelan, Mary K.
1987   The Archaeological Analysis of a 19th Century Dakota Indian Economy. (Ph.D. Dissertation in Anthropology, University of Minnesota, Minneapolis.)

Whidden, Lynn
1993   Métis Songs: Visiting Was the Métis Way. Regina, Sask.: Gabriel Dumond Institute of Native Studies and Applied Research.

1995   A Métis Suite: Video and Guide. Brandon, Man.: All Media Musics.

Whidder, Keith C., ed.
1999   Battle for the Soul: Métis Children Encounter Evangelical Protestants at Mackinaw Mission, 1823–1837. East Lansing, Mich.: Michigan State University Press.

Whipple, Amiel Weeks
1856   Report of Explorations and Surveys, To Ascertain the Most Practicable and Economical Route for A Railroad from the Mississippi River to the Pacific Ocean. Made under the Direction of the Secretary of War, in 1853–4, According to Acts of Congress of March 3, 1853, May 31, 1854, and August 5, 1854. 2 vols. [Report of the Secretary of War Communicating the Several Pacific Railroad Explorations, Volumes 3–4.] *33d Congress. 2d Session. House Executive Document* 91; [issued also as] *Senate Executive Document* 78. Washington: A.O.P. Nicholson Printer; [also] Beverly Tucker Printer.

1285

Whipple, Amiel Weeks, Thomas Ewbank, and William W. Turner 1855 *see* 1856

1856   Report Upon the Indian Tribes. (Incl., Chapter I: Remarks Regarding the Localities, Numbers, Modes of Subsistence, &c., of the Various Tribes upon the Route; and Chapter V: Vocabularies of North American Languages, collected by A.W. Whipple; classified, with accompanying remarks, by Wm. W. Turner.) Explorations and Surveys for a Railroad Route from the Mississippi River to the Pacific Ocean. War Department: Route Near the Thirty-Fifth Parallel, Under the Command of Lieut. A.W. Whipple, Topographical Engineers, in 1853 and 1854. [This Report has imprint date: Washington, D.C., 1855.] In: Vol. III of Reports of Explorations and Surveys to Ascertain the Most Practicable and Economical Route for a Railroad Route from the Mississippi River to the Pacific Ocean. Made under the Direction of the Secretary of War, in 1853–4. *33d Congress. 2d Session. House Executive Document No. 91.* Washington: A.O.P. Nicholson, Printer.

Whipple, Henry Benjamin
1899   Lights and Shadows of a Long Episcopate: Being Reminiscences and Recollections of the Right Reverend Henry Benjamin Whipple, D.C., L.L.D., Bishop of Minnesota. New York: Macmillan.

White, Anta Montet *see* Montet-White, Anta

White, Benjamin, and John C. Baine
1919   St. Joseph Okolakiciye Ta Olowan. Bismarck, N.Dak.: B. White.

White, Donny
1998   In Search of Geraldine Moodie. Regina, Sask.: University of Regina, Canadian Plains Research Center.

White, Eugene E. 1893 *see* 1965

1965   Experiences of a Special Indian Agent. Norman: University of Oklahoma Press. (Originally publ. under title: Service on the Indian Reservations; Arkansas Democrat Company, Little Rock, Ark., 1893.)

White, Leslie A., ed. 1959 *see* Morgan, Lewis Henry 1959

White, M. Catherine, ed.
1950   David Thompson's Journals Relating to Montana and Adjacent Regions, 1808–1812. Transcribed from a Photostatic Copy of the Original Manuscripts and Edited with an Introduction by M. Catherine White. Missoula: Montana State University Press.

White, Phillip M., comp.
1998   The Native American Sun Dance Religion and Ceremony: An Annotated Bibliography. *Bibliographies and Indexes in American History* 37. Westport, Conn.: Greenwood Press.

White, Richard
1978   The Winning of the West: The Expansion of the Western Sioux in the Eighteenth and Nineteenth Centuries. *The Journal of American History* 65(2):319–343. Bloomington, Ind.

1983   The Roots of Dependency: Subsistence, Environment, and Social Change among the Choctaws, Pawnees, and Navajos. Lincoln: University of Nebraka Press. (Reprinted 1988).

1991   "It's Your Misfortune and None of My Own": A History of the American West. Norman: University of Oklahoma Press.

White, Robert J.
1970   The Lower Class "Culture of Excitement" Among the Contemporary Sioux. Pp. 175–197 in The Modern Sioux: Social Systems and Reservation Culture. Ethel Nurge, ed. Lincoln: University of Nebraska Press.

White, William 1975 *see* Marquis, Thomas B. 1975

White Hat, Albert, Sr.
1999   Reading and Writing the Lakota Language = Lakȟota Iyapi uŋ Wowapi nahaŋ Yawapi. Edited by Jael Kampfe. Foreword by Vine Deloria, Jr. Salt Lake City: The University of Utah Press.

White Weasel, Charlie 1900, 1995 *see* Gourneau, Charles J. 1989 (reprint info.)

Whitebear Pease, Eloise, ed.
1968   *Absaraka*: Crow Tribal Treaty Centennial Issue. Crow Agency, Mont.: Crow Tribe.

Whitehouse, Joseph (Lewis and Clark Expedition) *see* Thwaites, Reuben G., ed. 1904–1905

Whitewell, J.
1902   [Letter to Cheyenne and Arapaho Agency, dated Hammond, Oklahoma Territory, September 3, 1902. re. Elk City Dance.] (Manuscript in Cheyenne and Arapaho: Indian History, Culture and Acculturation, Archives of the Oklahoma Historical Society, Oklahoma City.)

Whitewolf, Adeline
1991   Revision of "Northern Cheyenne Reservation." Lame Deer, Mont. Northern Cheyenne Planning Office.

Whitewolf, Jim 1969 *see* Brant, Charles S., ed. 1969

Whiting, William Henry Chase
1850   Report of the Secretary of War, Enclosing the Report of Lieutenant W.H.C. Whiting's Reconnaissance of the Western Frontier of Texas. Pp. 235–250 in *31st Congress. 1st Session. Senate Executive Document* 64. (Serial No. 562.) Washington.

Whitman, William
1937   The Oto. *Columbia University Contributions to Anthropology* 28. New York. (Reprinted: AMS Press, New York, 1969.)

1938   Origin Legends of the Oto. *Journal of American Folk-lore* 51(200):173–205.

1939   Xube, a Ponca Autobiography. *Journal of American Folk-lore* 52(204):180–193.

Whitman, William
1947   Descriptive Grammar of Ioway-Oto. *International Journal of American Linguistics* 13(4):233–248. Chicago.

Whittaker, Fredrick
1876   A Complete Life of General George Custer. New York: Sheldon and Company.

Whittlesey, Charles, trans.
1855   Green Bay in 1726: Memoir Concerning the Peace Made by Monsieur De Ligney.... *First Annual Report and Collections of the State Historical Society of Wisconsin for the Year 1854,* Vol. 1:21–33. Madison.

Whittlesey, Col. Charles
1871   Ancient Earth Forts of the Cuyahoga Valley, Ohio. *Western Reserve and Northern Ohio Historical Society* 1(5):1–40. Cleveland.

Whorf, Benjamin L., and George L. Trager
1937   The Relationship of Uto-Aztecan and Tanoan. *American Anthropologist,* n.s. 39(4):609–624.

Wied-Neuwied, Maximilian Alexander Philipp Prinz von *see* Maximilian, Alexander Philipp, Prinz zu Wied

Wiedman, Dennis, and Candace C. Greene
1988   Early Kiowa Peyote Ritual and Symbolism: The 1891 Drawing Books of Silverhorn (Haungooah). *American Indian Art Magazine* 13(4):32–41. Scottsdale, Ariz.

Wiegers, Robert P.
1985   Osage Culture Change Inferred from Contact and Trade with the Caddo and the Pawnee. (Ph.D. Dissertation in Anthropology/Archaeology, University of Missouri, Columbia.)

Wilbarger, John Wesley
1889   Indian Depredations in Texas: Reliable Accounts of Battles, Wars, Adventures, Forays, Murders, Massacres, etc., etc., Together with Biographical Sketches of Many of the Most Noted Indian Fighters and Frontiersmen of Texas. Austin: Hutchings Printing House. (Reprinted: The Steck Company, Austin, 1935; also, Pemberton Press, Austin, 1967.)

Wilcox, David R.
1988   Avonlea and Southern Athapaskan Migrations. Pp. 273–280 in Avonlea Yesterday and Today: Archaeology and Prehistory. Leslie B. Davis, ed. Saskatoon: Saskatchewan Archaeological Society.

Wilcox, David R., and W. Bruce Masse, eds.
1981   The Protohistoric Period in the North American Southwest, A.D. 1450–1700. *Arizona State University. Anthropological Research Papers* 24. Tempe, Ariz.

Wilcox, Lloyd
1942   Group Structure and Personality Types among the Sioux Indians of North Dakota. (Ph.D. Dissertation in Anthropology, University of Wisconsin, Madison.)

Wildhage, Wilhelm
1988   Die Winterzählungen der Oglala. Wyk auf Foehr, Germany: Verlag für Amerikanistik.

_____
1990   Material on Short Bull. *European Review of Native American Studies* 4(1):35–42. Vienna, Austria, [etc.].

Wildschut, William
1924   Blackfoot Beaver Bundle. *Indian Notes* 1(3):138–141. New York: Museum of the American Indian. Heye Foundation.

_____
1925   Crow Love Medicine. *Indian Notes* 2(3):99–107. New York: Museum of the American Indian. Heye Foundation.

_____
1925a   A Crow Shield. *Indian Notes* 2(4):315–320. New York: Museum of the American Indian. Heye Foundation.

_____
1925b   The Crow Skull Medicine Bundle. *Indian Notes* 2(2):119–122. New York: Museum of the American Indian. Heye Foundation.

_____
1926   Crow Sun-Dance Bundle. *Indian Notes* 3(2):99–107. New York: Museum of the American Indian. Heye Foundation.

_____
1926a   A Cheyenne Medicine Blanket. *Indian Notes* 3(1):33–36. New York: Museum of the American Indian. Heye Foundation.

_____
1926b   A Crow Pictographic Robe. *Indian Notes* 3(1):28–32. New York: Museum of the American Indian. Heye Foundation.

_____
1926c   Moccasin-bundle of the Crows. *Indian Notes* 3(3):201–205. New York: Museum of the American Indian. Heye Foundation.

_____
1927   Arapaho Medicine-mirror. *Indian Notes* 4(3):252–257. New York: Museum of the American Indian. Heye Foundation.

_____
1928   Blackfoot Pipe Bundles. *Indian Notes* 5(4):419–433. New York: Museum of the American Indian. Heye Foundation.

_____
1960   Crow Indian Medicine Bundles. John C. Ewers, ed. *Contributions from the Museum of the American Indian Heye Foundation*, Vol. 17. New York: Heye Foundation. (Reprinted 2d ed., 1975.)

Wildschut, William, and John C. Ewers
1959   Crow Indian Beadwork: A Descriptive and Historical Study. *Museum of the American Indian. Heye Foundation. Contributions* 16. New York. (Reprinted: Eagle's View Publishing, Ogden, Utah, 1985.)

Wilford, Lloyd A.
1941   A Tentative Classification of the Prehistoric Cultures of Minnesota. *American Antiquity* 6(3):231–249.

_____
1945   Three Village Sites of the Mississippi Pattern in Minnesota. *American Antiquity* 11(1):32–40.

_____
1946   Fox Lake Village Site. (Manuscript on file at the Department of Anthropology. University of Minnesota, Minneapolis.)

_____
1949   Archeological Field Work in Minnesota, 1941–1947. Pp. 34–36 in *Notebook* 1. Lincoln: University of Nebraska, Laboratory of Anthropology.

Wilford, Lloyd A.
1955   A Revised Classification of the Prehistoric Cultures of Minnesota. *American Antiquity* 21(2):130–142.

Wilhelm, Paul Duke of Württemberg *see* Paul Wilhelm, Herzog von Württemberg

Wilkes Expedition *see* Haskell, Daniel C., comp. 1968

Wilkinson, Glen A.
1966   Indian Tribal Claims Before the Court of Claims. *Georgetown [University] Law Journal* 55(4):511–528. Washington.

Wilkinson, James
1805   [An Enumeration of Some of the Indian Nations South West of the Missouri River.] (Microfilm Reel No. 32, Folio No. 25409, Library of Congress, Manuscript Division, Washington.)

Will, George F.
1906–1951 [Mandan Linguistic Notes and Word Lists.] (Manuscript No. 10190, State Historical Society of North Dakota Archives, Bismarck.)

_____
1917   Criticism of 'Some Vérendrye Enigmas.' *American Anthropologist,* n.s. 19(2):291–297.

_____
1921   An Unusual Group of Mounds in North Dakota. *American Anthropologist,* n.s. 23(1):175–179.

_____
1924   Archaeology of the Missouri Valley. *American Museum of Natural History Anthropological Papers* 22(6):285–344. New York.

_____
1934   Notes on the Arikara Indians and Their Ceremonies. *Old West Series* 3. Denver, Colo.: John VanMale.

Will, George F., and Thad. C. Hecker
1944   Upper Missouri River Valley Aboriginal Culture in North Dakota. *North Dakota Historical Quarterly* 11(1–2). Grand Forks and Bismarck.

Will, George F., and George E. Hyde
1917   Corn among the Indians of the Upper Missouri. St. Louis, Mo.: William Harvey Miner. (Reprinted: University of Nebraska Press, Lincoln, 1964.)

_____
1964 *see* 1917 (reprint info.)

Will, George F., and Herbert J. Spinden
1906   The Mandans: A Study of Their Culture, Archaeology and Language. *Papers of the Peabody Museum of American Archaeology and Ethnology* 3(4):81–219. Cambridge, Mass: Harvard University. (Reprinted: Kraus Reprint, Millwood, N.Y., 1974.)

1287

Willcomb, Roland H.
1970   Bird Rattle and the Medicine Prayer. *Montana: The Magazine of Western History* 20(2):42–49. Helena.

Willey, Gordon R.
1966   An Introduction to American Archaeology. Volume One: North and Middle America. Englewood Cliffs, N.J.: Prentice-Hall.

Willey, Gordon R., and Philip Phillips
1958   Method and Theory in American Archaeology. Chicago: University of Chicago Press. (Reprinted in 1962.)

Willey, Gordon R., and Jeremy Sabloff
1974   A History of American Archaeology. London: Thames and Hudson; also, San Francisco: W.H. Freeman. (Reprinted, 2d ed. in 1980.)

Willey, P.
1990   Prehistoric Warfare on the Great Plains. New York: Garland Publishing.

_____
1996   "The bullets buzzed like bees": Gunshot Wounds in Skeletons from the Battle of the Little Bighorn. *International Journal of Osteoarchaeology* 6(1):15–27. Chichester.

Williams, Amelia W., and Eugene C. Barker
1938–1943 The Writings of Sam Houston, 1813–1863. Austin: University of Texas Press.

Williams, Barry G.
1986   Early and Middle Ceramic Remains at 14AT2: A Grasshopper Falls Phase House and Pomona Focus Storage Pits in Northeastern Kansas. *Kansas State Historical Society. Contract Archeology Publication* 4. Topeka.

Williams, Ezekiel
1913   Ezekiel Williams' Adventures in Colorado. *Missouri Historical Society Collections* IV:194–208. St. Louis, Mo. (Originally publ. in *The Missouri Gazette*, Sept. 14, 1816.)

Williams, Glyndwr, ed.
1969   Andrew Graham's Observations on Hudson's Bay, 1767–1791. *Hudson's Bay Company Record Society* 27. London: Hudson's Bay Company Record Society.

_____
1978   The Puzzle of Anthony Henday's Journal, 1754–55. *The Beaver* 309(3):41–56. Winnipeg, Man.

Williams, J.W.
1962   New Conclusions on the Route of Mendoza, 1683–1684. *West Texas Historical Association Year Book* 38:111–134. Abilene.

Williams, John
1996   Bioarcheology of the Northeastern Plains. Pp. 120–149 in Archeological and Bioarcheological Resources of the Northern Plains. George C. Frison and Robert C. Mainfort, eds. *Arkansas Archeological Survey Research Series* 47. Fayetteville.

Williams, L.H.
1849   [Letter to R.S. Neighbors, dated October 9, 1849.] (Microfilm M-234, Roll 858, Frames 0413–0414 in Letters Received by the Office of Indian Affairs, 1824–80: Texas Agency 1847–52, Records of the Bureau of Indian Affairs, Record Group 75, National Archives, Washington.)

Williams, Mrs. W.K.
1930   Sun Dance of the Teton Dakota Was Very Trying Ordeal. *América indígena* 5(1):10–11, 15. México.

Williams, Patricia McAlister
1795   The Williams Site (13PM50): A Great Oasis Component in Northwest Iowa. *Journal of the Iowa Archaeological Society* 22:1–33. Iowa City.

Williams, Roger
1643   A Key into the Language of America, or an Help to the Language of the Natives in that Part of America Called New-England; Together with Briefe Observations of the Customs, Manners, and Worship, etc. of the Aforsaid Natives, in Peace and Warre, in Life and Death. On all of Which are Added Spiritual Observations Generall and Particular.... London: Gregory Dexter. (Reprinted: Pp. 17–163 in *Collections of the Rhode Island Historical Society* 1., Providence, 1827.)

Williamson, Andrew W.
1885   Minnesota Geographical Names Derived from the Dakota Language, with Some that are Obsolete. Pp. 104–112 in *13th Annual Report of the Geological and Natural History Survey of Minnesota for 1884*. St. Paul.

Williamson, Janis Shirley
1984   Studies in Lakhota Grammar. (Ph.D. Dissertation in Linguistics, University of California, San Diego.)

Williamson, John P. , comp.
1886   English-Dakota School Dictionary. Yankton Agency, Dakota Terr.: Iapi Oaye Press.
_____, comp.
1902   An English-Dakota Dictionary = Wašicun ḳa Dakota ieska wowapi. New York: American Tract Society; Yankton, S.Dak.: Pioneer Press.

Williamson, John W.
1922   The Battle of Massacre Canyon: The Unfortunate Ending of the Last Buffalo Hunt of the Pawnees. Trenton, Nebr.: Republican Leader. (Reprinted 1930.)

Williamson, Thomas S.
1872   Who Were the First Men? *Collections of the Minnesota Historical Society* 1:295–301. St. Paul: Ramaley, Chaney and Company. (Republication of the original parts issued in 1850–1853, 1856.)

_____
1880   The Sioux or Dakotas. A Sketch of Our Intercourse with the Dakotahs on the Missouri River, and Southwest of That Stream. *Minnesota Historical Collections* 3(Pt. 3):283–294. St. Paul.

Williamson, Thomas S., and Stephen R. Riggs
1880   Dakota Wowapi Wakan. The Holy Bible, in the Language of the Dakotas: Translated Out of the Original Tongues. New York: American Bible Society.

Williston, Samuel W.
1899   Some Prehistoric Ruins in Scott County, Kansas. *Kansas University Quarterly*, Series b.7(4):109–114. Topeka.

_____
1902   An Arrowhead Found with Bones of *Bison Occidentalis* Lucas, in Western Kansas. *American Geologist* 30:313–315.

Williston, Samuel W., and H.T. Martin
1900   Some Pueblo Ruins in Scott County, Kansas. *Kansas Historical Collections* 6:124–130.

Wilmeth, Roscoe
1960   Kansa Village Locations in the Light of McCoy's 1828 Journal. *Kansas Historical Quarterly* 26(2):152–157.

Wilmsen, Edwin N., and Frank H.H. Roberts, Jr.
1978   Lindemeir, 1934–1974: Concluding Report on Investigations. *Smithsonian Contributions to Anthropology* 24. Washington: Smithsonian Institution; U.S. Government Printing Office.

Wilson, Carrie Vee
1978   The Peyote Religion among the Quapaws. (M.A. Thesis in Anthropology, University of Arkansas, Fayetteville.)

Wilson, Charles Banks, comp. and ed.
1947   Quapaw Agency Indians. [Quapaw, Okla.:] Charles Banks Wilson.

Wilson, Charles C.
1908 The Successive Chiefs Named Wabasha. *Minnesota Historical Society Collections* 12:504–512. St. Paul.

Wilson, Edward F.
1888 Report on the Blackfoot Tribes. Pp. 183–197 in Third Report [...] on the North-Western Tribes of the Dominion of Canada. *57th Annual Report of the British Association for the Advancement of Science [for] 1887.* London. (Also issued as a separate, with new pagination.)

1889 Report on the Sarcee Indians. Pp. 242–253 in Fourth Report [...] on the North-Western Tribes of the Dominion of Canada. *58 Annual Report of the British Association for the Advancement of Science [for] 1888.* London. (Also issued as a separate, with new pagination.)

Wilson, Gilbert L.
1908–1918 [Fieldnotes on the Ethnography of the Hidatsa.] (Manuscripts on file at the American Museum of Natural History, New York City.)

1910 Report on Mandan-Hidatsa Work, Fort Berthold Reservation, North Dakota. (Microfilm No. 460, Roll 1, [Vol. 9], in Minnesota Historical Society, St. Paul.)

1911 Report on Mandan-Hidatsa Work, Fort Berthold Reservation, North Dakota. (Microfilm, No. 460, Roll 2, [Vol.10], in Minnesota Historical Society, St. Paul.)

_____, ed. 1914 *see* Goodbird, Edward 1914

1917 Agriculture of the Hidatsa Indians: An Indian Interpretation. *University of Minnesota. Studies in the Social Sciences* 9. Minneapolis.

1921 Waheenee: An Indian Girl's Story Told by Herself to Gilbert L. Wilson. St. Paul, Minn.: Webb Publishing. (Reprinted: University of Nebraska Press, Lincoln, 1981.)

1924 The Horse and the Dog in Hidatsa Culture. *American Museum of Natural History Anthropological Papers* 15(2):127–311. New York. (Reprinted: *Reprints in Anthropology* 10. J&L Reprint Company, Lincoln, 1978; also, AMS Press, New York, 1980.)

1928 Hidatsa Eagle Trapping. *American Museum of Natural History Anthropological Papers* 30(4):99–245. New York. (Reprinted: *Reprints in Anthropology* 13. J&L Reprint Company, Lincoln, 1978.)

1934 The Hidatsa Earthlodge. Bella Weitzner, ed. *American Museum of Natural History Anthropological Papers* 33(5):341–420. New York. (Reprinted: *Reprints in Anthropology* 11. J&L Reprint Company, Lincoln, 1978.)

1977 Mandan and Hidatsa Pottery Making. W. Raymond Wood and Donald J. Lehmer, eds. *Plains Anthropologist* 22(76, Pt. 1):97–105.

1978 The Ordeal of Getting Civilized: Troubles of an Indian Treading the White Man's Path. *The Minnesota Archaeologist* 37(2):79–83. Minneapolis.

_____ 1979 *see* Weitzner, Bella 1979

Wilson, Michael Clayton
1976 In the Lap of the Gods: Archeology and Ethnohistory in the Big Horn Mountains. *Archeology in Montana* 17:33–34.

1978 Archaeological Kill Site Populations and the Holocene Evolution of the Genus *Bison.* Pp. 9–22 in Bison Procurement and Utilization: A Symposium. Leslie B. Davis and Michael Wilson, eds. *Plains Anthropologist* 23(82, Pt. 2), *Memoir* 14. Lincoln.

1981 Megaliths to Medicine Wheels. Calgary, Alta.: University of Calgary Archaeological Association.

1981a Sun Dances, Thirst Dances and Medicine Wheels: A Search for Alternative Hypotheses. Pp. 333–370 in Megaliths to Medicine Wheels. Michael C. Wilson ed. Calgary, Alta.: University of Calgary Archaeological Association.

1983 Once Upon a River: Archaeology and Geology of the Bow River Valley at Calgary, Alberta, Canada. *Canada. National Museum of Man. Mercury Series. Archaeological Survey Paper* 114. Ottawa.

1990 Archaeological Geology in Western Canada: Techniques, Approaches, and Integrative Themes. Pp. 61–86 in Archaeological Geology of North America. N. P. Lasca and J. Donahue, eds. *Geological Society of America Centennial Special Volume* 4. Boulder.

Wilson, Michael Clayton, J. Roderick Vickers, Arthur C. MacWilliams, Alwynne B. Beaudoin, and Ian G. Robertson
1991 New Studies at the Fletcher Palaeo-Indian Bison Kill (Alberta/Scottsbluff), Southern Alberta. Pp. 127 –134 in Archaeology in Alberta 1988 and 1989. Martin Magne, ed. *Archaeological Survey. Provincial Museum of Alberta. Occasional Paper* 33. Edmonton.

Wilson, Raymond
1983 Ohiyesa: Charles Eastman, Santee Sioux. Urbana: University of Illinois Press.

Wilson, Terry P.
1981 Osage Oxonian: The Heritage of John Joseph Mathews. *Chronicles of Oklahoma* 59(3):264–293. Norman.

1982 Osage Indian Women During a Century of Change, 1870–1980. *Prologue: Journal of the National Archives* 14(4):185–201. Washington.

1985 The Underground Reservation: Osage Oil. Lincoln: University of Nebraska Press.

1985a Bibliography of the Osage. *Native American Bibliography Series* 6. Metuchen, N.J.: The Scarecrow Press.

1988 The Osage. New York: Chelsea House.

Winchell, Newton H.
1908 Habitations of the Sioux in Minnesota. *Wisconsin Archaeologist* 7(4):155–164.

1911 The Aborigines of Minnesota: A Report Based on the Collections of Jacob V. Brower, and on the Field Surveys and Notes of Alfred J. Hill and Theodore H. Lewis; collated, augumented, and described by N.H. Winchell. St. Paul, Minn.: The Pioneer Company.

1913 A Consideration of the Paleoliths of Kansas. The Weathering of Aboriginal Stone Artifacts 1. *Minnesota Historical Society Collections* 16:(1). St. Paul.

Windy Boy, Jonathan, et al., (singers)
1997 Haystack: Live at Piapot. [Audiocassette: record. live at Piapot Reserve, Sask., Aug. 16–18, 1996.] Taos, N.Mex.: Indian House.

Winfrey, Dorman H., and James M. Day, eds.
1959–1966 The Indian Papers of Texas and the Southwest, 1825–1916. 5 vols. Austin: Pemberton Press. (Vols. 1–4 originally publ. as: Texas Indian Papers; Texas State Library, Austin, 1959–1961.)

Winham, R. Peter, and Francis A. Calabrese
1998 The Middle Missouri Tradition. Pp. 269–307 in Archaeology on the Great Plains. W. Raymond Wood, ed. Lawrence: University Press of Kansas.

Winham, R. Peter, and Edward J. Lueck
1994   Cultures of the Middle Missouri. Pp. 149–175 in Plains Indians, A.D. 500–1500: The Archaeological Past of Historic Groups. Karl H. Schlesier, ed. Norman and London: University of Oklahoma Press.

Winship, George P., trans. and ed.
1896   The Coronado Expedition, 1540–1542. Pp. 329–613 [Vol. Index, pp. 615–637] in Pt.1 of *14 Annual Report of the Bureau of American Ethnology [for] 1892–'93*. Washington: Smithsonian Institution; U.S. Government Printing Office. (Reprinted: Rio Grande Press, Chicago, 1964; see also Winship 1990.)

_____, trans. and ed.
1990   The Journey of Coronado, 1540–1542. Translated and edited by George Parker Winship; Introduction by Donald C. Cutter. Golden, Colo.: Fulcrum Press.

Winsor, Justin, ed.
1884–1889 Narrative and Critical History of America. 8 vols. Boston and New York: Houghton, Mifflin and Company.

Wintemberg, William John
1928   Artifacts from Ancient Graves and Mounds in Ontario. Ottawa: Royal Society of Canada.

Winterhalder, Bruce
1981   Optimal Foraging Strategies and Hunter-gatherer Research in Anthropology: Theory and Models. Pp. 13–35 in Hunter-gatherer Foraging Strategies. Bruce Winterhalder and Eric A. Smith, eds. Chicago: University of Chicago Press.

Wishart, David J.
1976   Cultures in Co-operation and Conflict: Indians in the Fur Trade on the Northern Great Plains, 1807–1840. *Journal of Historical Geography* 2(4):311–328. London and New York: Academic Press.

1979   The Fur Trade of the American West, 1807–1840: A Geographical Synthesis. Lincoln: University of Nebraska Press.

1979a   The Dispossession of the Pawnee. *Annals of the Association of American Geographers* 69(3):382–401. Washington.

1985   The Pawnee Claims Case, 1947–64. In: Irredeemable America: The Indians' Estate and Land Claims. Imre Sutton, ed. Albuquerque: University of New Mexico Press.

1990   Compensation for Dispossession: Payments to the Indians for Their Lands on the Central and Northern Great Plains in the 19th Century. *National Geographic Research* 6(1):94–109. Washington.

1994   An Unspeakable Sadness: The Dispossession of the Nebraska Indians. Lincoln: University of Nebraska Press.

Wissler, Clark
1904   Decorative Art of the Sioux Indians. *Bulletin of the American Museum of Natural History* 18(3):231–277. New York. (Reprinted: Lakota Books, Kendall Park, N.J., 1998.)

1905   The Whirlwind and the Elk in the Mythology of the Dakota. *Journal of American Folk-lore* 18(71):257–268.

1905a   Symbolism in the Decorative Art of the Sioux. Pp. 339–345 in *Proceedings of the 13th International Congress of Americanists, Held in New York in 1902*. Easton, Pa.: Eschenbach Printing Company.

1907   Some Protective Designs of the Dakota. *American Museum of Natural History Anthropological Papers* 1(2):19–53. New York. (Reprinted: Lakota Books, Kendall Park, N.J., 1998.)

1907a   Diffusion of Culture in the Plains of North America. Pp. 39–52 in Vol. 2 of *Congrès International des Américanistes, XV*

Session, tenue à Québec en 1906. Québec: Dussault et Proulx.

1907b   Some Dakota Myths. 2 Pts. *Journal of American Folk-lore* 20(77):121–131, (78):195–206.

1908   Ethnographical Problems of the Missouri Saskatchewan Area. *American Anthropologist*, n.s. 10(2):197–207.

1910   Material Culture of the Blackfoot Indians. *American Museum of Natural History Anthropological Papers* 5(1):1–175. New York. (Reprinted: AMS Press, New York, 1975; also in: A Blackfoot Source Book: Papers by Clark Wissler; Garland Publishing, New York, 1986.)

1911   The Social Life of the Blackfoot Indians. *American Museum of Natural History Anthropological Papers* 7(1):1–64. New York. (Pt. 1 of volume titled: Social Organization and Ritualistic Ceremonies of the Blackfoot Indians. 2 Pts. in 1 Vol.; Pt. 2 is Wissler 1912.) (Reprinted: AMS Press, New York, 1975; also in: A Blackfoot Source Book: Papers by Clark Wissler; Garland Publishing, New York, 1986.)

1912   Ceremonial Bundles of the Blackfoot Indians. *American Museum of Natural History Anthropological Papers* 7(2):65–284. New York. (Pt. 2 of volume titled: Social Organization and Ritualistic Ceremonies of the Blackfoot Indians. 2 Pts in 1 Vol.; Pt. 1 is Wissler 1911.)

1912a   Societies and Ceremonial Associations in the Oglala Division of the Teton-Dakota. *American Museum of Natural History Anthropological Papers* 11(1):1–99. New York. (Bound with other monographs in: Societies of the Plains Indians, Clark Wissler, ed., New York, 1916. Reprinted with cover title: Societies of the Oglala: Lakota Books, Kendall Park, N.J., 1993.)

1912b   North American Indians of the Plains. *Handbook Series* 1. New York: American Museum of Natural History.

_____, ed.
1912–1916 Societies of the Plains Indians. *American Museum of Natural History Anthropological Papers* 11. New York. (Reprinted: AMS Press, New York, 1975.)

1913   Societies and Dance Associations of the Blackfoot Indians. *American Museum of Natural History Anthropological Papers* 11(4):359–460. New York. (Bound with other monographs in: Societies of the Plains Indians, Clark Wissler, ed., New York, 1916; Reprinted in: A Blackfoot Source Book: Papers by Clark Wissler; Garland Publishing, New York, 1986.)

1914   Material Cultures of the North American Indians. *American Anthropologist*, n.s. 16(3):447–505.

1914a   The Influence of the Horse in the Development of the Plains Culture. *American Anthropologist* n.s. 16(1):1–25. (Reprinted: Pp. 252–259 in Source Book in Anthropology. Alfred L. Kroeber ed. A.L. &Waterman, T.T. Company, New York, 1931; also pp. 505–512 in a rev. ed., 1931; and, pp. 155–173 in Readings in Anthropology. E. Adamson Hoebel, et al., eds. Thomas Y. Crowell Company, New York, 1955.)

1915   Costumes of the Plains Indians. *American Museum of Natural History Anthropological Papers* 17(2):39–91. New York. (Reprinted, together with "Structural Basis to the Decoration of Costumes among the Plains Indians": AMS Press, New York, 1975.)

1915a   Riding Gear of the North American Indians. *American Museum of Natural History Anthropological Papers* 17(2):39–91. New York.

_____, ed.
1915–1921 Sun Dance of the Plains Indians. *American Museum of Natural History Anthropological Papers* 16. New York.

1916 General Discussion of Shamanistic and Dancing Societies. *American Museum of Natural History Anthropological Papers* 11(12):853–876. New York. (Bound with other monographs in: Societies of the Plains Indians, Clark Wissler, ed., New York, 1916. Reprinted: Lakota Books, Kendall Park, N.J., 1993.)

1916a Structural Basis to the Decoration of Costumes among the Plains Indians. *American Museum of Natural History Anthropological Papers* 17(3):93–114. New York. (Reprinted, together with "Costumes of the Plains Indians": AMS Press, New York, 1975.)

1917 The American Indian: An Introduction to the Anthropology of the New World. Tables of Linguistic Stocks (pp. [369]–385), Bibliography (pp. [387]–411) and Index, compiled by Miss Bella Weitzner. New York: D.C. McMurtrie. (Reprinted: 2d ed., Oxford University Press, New York, London, [etc.], 1922; 3d ed., 1938.)

1918 The Sun Dance of the Blackfoot Indians. *American Museum of Natural History Anthropological Papers* 16(3):223–270. New York. (Reprinted in: A Blackfoot Source Book: Papers by Clark Wissler; Garland Publishing, New York, 1986.)

1920 The Sacred Bundles of the Pawnee. *Natural History* 20(5):569–571.

_____ 1922 *see* 1917 (reprint info.)

1926 The Relation of Nature to Man in Aboriginal North America. New York: Appleton. (Reprinted: AMS Press, New York, 1971.)

1927 Distribution of Moccasin Decorations among the Plains Tribes. *American Museum of Natural History Anthropological Papers* 29(1):1–23. New York (Microfilm: Harvard University Library Photographic Services, Cambridge, Mass., 1998.)

1936 Population Change among the Northern Plains Indians. *Yale University Publications in Anthropology* 1:1–20. New Haven, Conn.

1938 Indian Cavalcade; or, Life on the Old-Time Indian reservations. New York: Sheridan House.

1940 Indians of the United States. New York: Doubleday. (Reprinted in 1945, 1948, 1949, 1953, 1954; 1967; and, with Revisions by Lucy Wales Kluckhohn: Anchor Books, New York, 1966, 1989.)

1941 North American Indians of the Plains. 3d ed. *American Museum of Natural History. Handbook Series* 1. New York. (Originally publ. in 1912; reprinted: *Burt Franklin Research & Resource Works Series. American Classics in History and Social Science* 253; B. Franklin Reprints, New York, 1974.)

1986 A Blackfoot Source Book: Papers by Clark Wissler. Edited with an Introduction by David Hurst Thomas. *The North American Indian.* New York: Garland Publishing.

Wissler, Clark, and D.C. Duvall
1908 Mythology of the Blackfoot Indians. *American Museum of Natural History Anthropological Papers* 2(Pt. 1):1–163. New York. (Reprinted: AMS Press, New York, 1975; also, University of Nebraska Press, Lincoln, 1995.)

Wissler, Clark, and Herbert J. Spinden
1916 The Pawnee Human Sacrifice to the Morning Star. *American Museum Journal* 16(1):49–55. New York.

Wistrand-Robinson, Lila
1972 An Iowa/Otoe - English Dictionary. Manhattan, Kans.: [Kansas State University.]

Wistrand-Robinson, Lila, and Otoe and Iowa Language Speakers
1977 Otoe and Iowa Indian Language. Jiwele - Baxoje Wan'shige Uk'enye Ich'e. Book 1: Alphabet, Conversational Phrases, and Drills. Park Hill, Okla.: Jiwere-Baxoje Language Project.

1978 Otoe and Iowa Indian Language. Book 2: Simple, Compound, and Complex Sentences; Songs and Stories for Practice. Park Hill, Okla.: Jiwere-Baxoje Language Project.

Withers, Arnold M.
1954 University of Denver Archaeological Fieldwork. *Southwestern Lore* 19(4):1–3. Boulder, Colo.

Withrow, Randall M.
1988 Archaeological Manifestations of the 17th Century Ioway in the Upper Mississippi River Valley. (Paper presented at the Ethnohistory Symposium, 46th Plains Anthropological Conference, Wichita, Kans., Nov. 1988.)

Withrow, Randall M., and Roland L. Rodell
1984 Archaeological Investigations in Southeastern Minnesota: The 1984 Root River Survey. (Mimeo.) *University of Wisconsin-LaCrosse. Mississippi Valley Archaeology Center. Report of Investigations* 29. LaCrosse, Wis.

Witmer, Robert
1973 Recent Change in the Musical Culture of the Blood Indians of Alberta, Canada. *Yearbook for the Inter-American Musical Research* 9. Austin: University of Texas.

1982 The Musical Life of the Blood Indians. *Canada. National Museum of Man. Mercury Series. Canada. Ethnology Service Paper* 86. Ottawa. (Originally issued as the Author's M.M. Thesis under title: The Musical Culture of the Blood Indians, University of Illinois, Urbana-Champain, 1970.)

Witty, Thomas A., Jr.
1962 Archeological Investigations of the Hell Creek Valley in the Wilson Reservoir, Russel and Lincoln Counties, Kansas. *Kansas State Historical Society. Anthropological Series* 1. Topeka.

1966 The West Island Site, 14PH10: A Keith Focus Plains Woodland Site in Kirwin Reservoir, Phillips County, Kansas. *Plains Anthropologist* 11(32):127–135.

1967 The Pomona Focus. *Kansas Anthropological Association Newsletter* 12(9):1–5. Topeka.

1969 The Caldwell Dig. *Kansas Anthropological Association Newsletter* 15(2):1–3. Topeka.

1969a The K.A.A. Fall Dig, 1969. *Kansas Anthropological Association Newsletter* 15(3):1–3. Topeka.

1970 K.A.A. Fall Dig, 1970. *Kansas Anthropological Association Newletter* 16(3):1–3. Topeka.

1975 Report of the 1975 Lake Scott Kansas Anthropological Association Dig and Kansas Archeology Training School Activities. *Kansas Anthropological Association Newsletter* 21(1–2):1–9. Topeka.

1978 Along the Southern Edge: The Central Plains Tradition in Kansas. Pp. 56–66 in The Central Plains Tradition: Internal Development and External Relationships. Donald J. Blakeslee, ed. *The University of Iowa. Office of the State Archaeologist. Reports* 11. Iowa City.

1982 The Slough Creek, Two Dog and William Young Sites *1291*

Council Grove Lake, Kansas. *Kansas State Historical Society. Anthropological Series* 10. Topeka.

1983 An Archeological Review of the Scott County Pueblo. *Bulletin of the Oklahoma Anthropological Society* 32:99–106.

Witzner, Bella, ed.
1979 Notes on the Hidatsa Indians Based on Data Recorded by the Late Gilbert L. Wilson. *American Museum of Natural History Anthropological Papers* 56(2):181–322. New York.

Wolfart, H. Christoph
1973 Plains Cree: A Grammatical Study. *Transactions of the American Philosophical Society* 63(5). Philadelphia.

_____ 1996 *see* Handbook Vol. 17 (1996:390–439)

Wolfart, H. Christoph, and Freda Ahenakew, eds. and trans.
1992 Kôhkominawak Otâcimowiniwâwa=Our Grandmothers' Lives, as Told in Their Own Words. Told by Glecia Bear et al. Saskatoon, Sask.: Fifth House Publishers.

_____, eds. and trans.
1993 Kinchiyawiwininaw nehiyawewin=The Cree Language Is Our Identy: The La Ronge Lectures of Sarah Whitecalf. Winnipeg: University of Manitoba Press.

_____, eds. and trans.
1997 Kwayask e-ki-kiskinowapahtihicik=Their Example Showed Me the Way: A Cree Woman's Life Shaped in Two Cultures. Edmonton: University of Alberta Press..

_____, eds. and trans.
1998 Ana ka-pimwewehahk okakeskihkemowina=The Counseling Speeches of Jim Ka-Nipitehtew. Winnipeg: University of Manitoba Press.

_____, comps. and eds.
1998a The Student's Dictionary of Literary Plains Cree. *Algonquian and Iroquoian Linguistics Memoir* 15. Winnipeg: University of Manitoba.

Wolfart, H. Christoph, and Janet F. Carroll
1981 Meet Cree: Guide to the Cree Language. New and completely rev. ed. Edmonton: University of Alberta Press / Lincoln: University of Nebraska Press. (Originally publ. under title: Meet Cree, A Practical Guide of the Cree Language. University of Alberta Press, Edmonton, 1973.)

Wolff, Hans
1950–1951 Comparative Siouan, I, II, III, IV. *International Journal of American Linguistics* 16(2):61–66, (3):113–121, (4):168–178; 17(4):197–204. Chicago.

1952 Osage I: Phonemes and Historical Phonology. *International Journal of American Linguistics* 18(1):63–68. Chicago.

1952a Osage II: Morphology. *International Journal of American Linguistics* 18(4):231–237. Chicago.

1958 An Osage Graphemic Experiment. *International Journal of American Linguistics* 24(1):30–35. Chicago.

Wolvengrey, Arok
1997 "Iyiniwak ekwa itawina." *Ahkami-nehiyawetan* 1(1):22–23.

Wonderly, William L., Lorna F. Gibson, and Paul L. Kirk
1954 Number in Kiowa: Nouns, Demonstratives, and Adjectives. *International Journal of American Linguistics* 20(1):1–7. Chicago.

Wong, Hertha Dawn
1992 Sending My Heart Back Across the Years: Tradition and Innovation in Native American Autobiography. New York and Oxford: Oxford University Press.

Wood, Caryl E., and Gerald A. Bair
1980 Trinidad Lake Cultural Resource Study. Pt. II: The Prehistoric Occupation of the Upper Purgatoire River Valley, Southeastern Colorado. Trinidad, Colo.: Trinidad State Junior College, Laboratory of Contract Anthropology.

Wood, John J.
1967 Archaeological Investigations in Northeastern Colorado. (Ph.D. Dissertation in Anthropology, University of Colorado, Boulder.)

Wood, W. Raymond
1956 A Woodland Site Near Williston, North Dakota. *Plains Anthropologist,* [o.s.] 6:21–24.

1959 Notes on Ponca Ethnohistory, 1785–1804. *Ethnohistory* 6(1):1–27.

1960 The Boundary Mound Group (32 SI-1): An Eastern Woodland Complex in North Dakota. *Plains Anthropologist* 5(10):71–78.

1962 A Stylistic and Historical Analysis of Shoulder Patterns on Plains Indian Pottery. *American Antiquity* 28(1):25–40.

1965 The Redbird Focus and the Problem of Ponca Prehistory. *Plains Anthropologist* 10(28); *Memoir* 2. Lincoln.

1967 An Interpretation of Mandan Culture History. *Bureau of American Ethnology Bulletin* 198; *River Basin Surveys Papers* 39. Washington: Smithsonian Institution; U.S. Government Printing Office.

1968 Mississippian Hunting and Butchering Patterns: Bone from the Vista Shelter, 23SR-20, Missouri. *American Antiquity* 33(2):170–179.

1969 The Middle Missouri Region: Typology and Concepts. *Plains Anthropologist* 14(44, Pt.1):144–148.

_____, ed.
1969a Two House Sites in the Central Plains: An Experiment in Archaeology. *Plains Anthropologist* 14(44, Pt. 2); *Memoir* 6. Lincoln.

1971 Pottery Sites Near Limon, Colorado. *Southwestern Lore* 37(3):53–85. Boulder, Colo.

1971a Biesterfledt: A Post-Contact Coalescent Site on the Northeastern Plains. *Smithsonian Contributions to Anthropology* 15. Washington: Smithsonian Institution; U.S. Government Printing Office.

1972 Contrastive Features of Native North American Trade Systems. Pp. 153–169 in For the Chief: Essays in Honor of Luther S. Cressman. Fred W. Voget and Robert L. Stephenson, eds. *University of Oregon Anthropological Papers* 4. Eugene.

1973 Culture Sequence at the Old Fort Saline County, Missouri. *American Antiquity* 38(1):101–111.

1974 Northern Plains Village Cultures: Internal Stability and External Relationships. *Journal of Anthropological Research* 30(1):1–16.

_____, ed.
1976 Fay Tolton and the Initial Middle Missouri Variant. *Missouri Archaeological Society. Research Series* 13. Columbia, Mo.: College of Arts and Sciences, University of Missouri-Columbia.

1977 David Thompson at the Mandan-Hidatsa Villages, 1797–1798: The Original Journals. *Ethnohistory* 24(4):329–342.

_____, ed.
1977a Trends in Middle Missouri Prehistory: A Festschrift Honoring the Contributions of Donald J. Lehmer. *Plains Anthropologist* 22(78, Pt. 2); *Memoir* 13. Lincoln.

1292

1980   Plains Trade in Prehistoric and Protohistoric Intertribal Relations. Pp. 98–109 in Anthropology on the Great Plains. W. Raymond Wood and Margot Liberty, eds. Lincoln: University of Nebraska Press.

1983   An Atlas of Early Maps of the American Midwest. *Illinois State Museum Scientific Papers* 18. Springfield.

———, ed.
1986   Ice Glider 320L110: Papers in Northern Plains Prehistory and Ethnohistory. *South Dakota Archaeological Society. Special Publication* 10. Sioux Falls, S.Dak.: Archaeological Laboratory, Augustana College.

———, ed.
1986a   The Origins of the Hidatsa Indians: A Review of Ethnohistorical and Traditional Data. *Reprints in Anthropology* 32. Lincoln: J&L Reprint Company.

1990   Early Fur Trade on the Northern Plains. Pp. 2–16 in The Fur Trade in North Dakota. Virginia L. Heidenreich, ed. Bismarck: State Historical Society of North Dakota.

1990a   The Role of the Romantic West in Shaping the Third Reich. *Plains Anthropologist* 35(132):313–319.

1993   Integrating Ethnohistory and Archaeology at Fort Clark State Historic Site, North Dakota. *American Antiquity* 58(3):544–559.

———, ed.
1998   Archaeology on the Great Plains. Introduction by W. Raymond Wood. Maps by E. Stanley Wood. Lawrence, Kans.: University Press of Kansas.

Wood, W. Raymond, and Alan S. Downer
1977   Notes on the Crow-Hidatsa Schism. Pp. 83–100 in Trends in Middle Missouri Prehistory: A Festschrift Honoring the Contributions of Donald J. Lehmer. W. Raymond Wood, ed. *Plains Anthropologist* 22(78, Pt. 2); *Memoir* 13. Lincoln.

Wood, W. Raymond, and Ann M. Johnson
1973   High Butte, 32ME13: A Missouri Valley Woodland-Besant Site. *Archaeology in Montana* 14(3):35–83. Billings, [etc.].

Wood, W. Raymond, and Margot Liberty, eds.
1980   Anthropology on the Great Plains. Lincoln: University of Nebraska Press.

Wood, W. Raymond, and Thomas D. Thiessen, eds.
1985   Early Fur Trade on the Northern Plains: Canadian Traders among the Mandan and Hidatsa Indians, 1738–1818; the Narratives of John Macdonell, David Thompson, François-Antoine Laroque, and Charles McKenzie. Norman: University of Oklahoma Press.

Wood, W. Raymond, and Alan R. Woolworth
1964   The Paul Brave Site (32S14), Oahe Reservoir Area, North Dakota. *Bureau of American Ethnology Bulletin* 189; *River Basin Surveys Papers* 31. Washington: Smithsonian Institution; U.S. Government Printing Office.

Woodcock, George
1976   Gabriel Dumont: The Métis Chief and His Lost World. Edmonton, Alta.: Hurtig Publishers. (Reprinted, French ed.: Pierre Desruisseaux and François Lanctôt, trans.: VLB, Montréal, 1986.)

Woodward, Grace Steele
1963   The Cherokees. Norman: University of Oklahoma Press.

Wooley, David L.
1988   Waw-no-she's Dance. *American Indian Art Magazine* 14(1): 36–45. Scottsdale, Ariz.

Wooley, David L., and Joseph D. Horse Capture
1993   Joseph No Horns, He Nupa Wanica. *American Indian Art Magazine* 18(3):32–43. Scottsdale, Ariz.

Woolworth, Alan R.
1956   Archeological Investigations at Site 32ME59 (Grandmother's Lodge). *North Dakota History* 23(2):79–102. Bismarck.

1956a   A Historical Study of the Oto with Some Reference to Other Chiwere Siouan Tribes. (M.A. Thesis in History, University of Minnesota, Minneapolis.)

1960   Some Aspects of Indian Trade Post Design and Construction on the Missouri River, ca. 1720–1870. (Manuscript on file, Minnesota Historical Society, St. Paul.)

1974   Ethnohistorical Report on the Yankton Sioux. Pp. 9–245 in Sioux Indians III. *American Indian Ethnohistory: Plains Indians.* David Agee Horr, comp. and ed. New York and London: Garland Publishing.

———, ed.
1983   The Red Pipestone Quarry of Minnesota: Archaeological and Historical Reports. *Minnesota Archaeologist* 42(1–2). Minneapolis.

——— 1987 *see* Gilmore, Melvin R. 1929b (reprint info.)

Woolworth, Alan R., and W. Raymond Wood
1964   The Demery Site (39CO1), Oahe Reservoir Area, South Dakota. *Bureau of American Ethnology Bulletin* 189; *River Basin Surveys Papers* 34. Washington: Smithsonian Institution; U.S. Government Printing Office.

Woolworth, Alan R., and Nancy L. Woolworth
1980   Eastern Dakota Settlement and Subsistence Prior to 1851. *Minnesota Archaeologist* 39(2):70–89. Minneapolis.

Woolworth, Nancy L.
1961   Captian Edwin V. Sumner's Expedition to Devil's Lake in the Summer of 1845. *North Dakota History* 28(2–3):79–81. Bismarck.

1975   Gingras, St. Joseph and the Métis of the Red River Valley, 1843–1873. *North Dakota History* 42(4):16–27. Bismarck.

Wooster, Robert
1988   The Military and United States Indian Policy, 1865–1903. New Haven, Conn.: Yale University Press.

Wooten, Dudley G., ed.
1898   A Comprehensive History of Texas, 1685–1897. 2 vols. Dallas, Tex: William G. Scarff. (Reprinted: Texas State Historical Association in cooperation with the Center for Studies in Texas History, The University of Texas, Austin, 1986.)

Worcester, Donald E.
1941   The Beginnings of the Apache Menace of the Southwest. *New Mexico Historical Review* 16(1):1–14. Albuquerque.

1944   The Spread of Spanish Horses in the Southwest. *New Mexico Historical Review* 19(3):225–232. Albuquerque.

1947   Early History of the Navajo Indians. (Ph.D. Dissertation in History, University of California, Berkeley.)

———, ed. and trans.
1949   Advice on Governing New Mexico, 1794 [by Don Fernando de la Concha]. *New Mexico Historical Review* 24(3):236–254. Albuquerque.

1951   The Navaho during the Spanish Regime in New Mexico. *New Mexico Historical Review* 26(2):101–118. Albuquerque.

Word, James H.
1963   Floydada Country Club Site. *Bulletin of the South Plains Archeological Society* 1:37–63 Floydada, Tex.

1965   The Montgomery Site in Floyd County, Texas. *Bulletin of the South Plains Archeological Society* 2:55–102. Floydada, Tex.

1970   Excavations at Baker Cave, Val Verde County, Texas: The Archeological Investigation, by James H. Word. Analysis of the Faunal Remains, by Charles L. Douglas. *Bulletin of the Texas Memorial Museum* 16. Austin.

1994   Coronado's Route in the Texas Panhandle. (In: Programs and Abstracts of the 52d Annual Plains Anthropological Conference, Lubbock, Tex.)

Wormington, Hannah M.
1957   Ancient Man in North America. *Denver Museum of Natural History, Popular Series* 4. (Fourth Edition.) Denver.

Wormington, Hannah M., and Richard G. Forbis
1965   An Introduction to the Archaeology of Alberta, Canada. *Denver Museum of Natural History. Proceedings* 11. Denver.

Wozniak, John S.
1978   Contact, Negotiation and Conflict: An Ethnohistory of the Eastern Dakota, 1819–1839. Lanham, Md.: University Press of America. (Orginially presented as the Author's Ph.D. Dissertation in Anthropology, University of Texas at Austin, 1974.)

Wright, C.M.
1982   An Archaic Site in Osage County, Kansas. *Journal of the Kansas Anthropological Association* 3(1):7–9. Topeka.

Wright, Gary A.
1978   The Shoshonean Migration Problem. *Plains Anthropologist* 23(80):113–137.

Wright, Gwendolyn, ed.
1996   The Formation of National Collections of Art and Archaeology. *Studies in the History of Art* 47; *Center for Advanced Study in the Visual Arts. Symposium Papers* 27. Washington: National Gallery of Art.

Wright, H.E., Jr.
1982   Holocene Chronostratigraphy for United States and Southern Canada. Pp. 53–55 in Chronostratigraphic Subdivision of the Holocene. Jan Mangerud, H.J.B. Birks, and K.-D. Jäger, eds. *Striae* 16. Uppsala, Sweden: Societas Upsaliensis pro Geologia Quaternaria.

Wright, J.C.
1980   Archeological Investigations in the Proposed Blue Springs Lake Area, Jackson County, Missouri: The Early Woodland Period. (Manuscript on file at the Museum of Anthropology, University of Kansas, Lawrence.)

Wright, James V.
1968   The Boreal Forest. Pp. 55–68 in Vol. 1 of Science, History and Hudson Bay. 2 vols. C.S. Beals, ed. Ottawa: Queen's Printer [for the] Department of Energy, Mines and Resources .

1971   Cree Culture History in the Southern Indian Lake Region. *Anthropological Series* 87; *National Museum of Canada. Bulletin* 232:1–31. Ottawa.

       1981 *see* Handbook Vol. 6 (1981:86–96)

Wright, Muriel H.
1946   Pioneer Historian and Archeologist of the State of Oklahoma. *Chronicles of Oklahoma* 24(4):396–413. Norman.

1951   A Guide to the Indian Tribes of Oklahoma. Norman: University of Oklahoma Press. (Reprinted in 1986.)

1967   Chief Moses George Harragarra, Last Medal Chief of the Oto and Missouri Tribe. *Chronicles of Oklahoma* 45(2):220–222. Norman.

Writer's Program. Montana 1942, 1961, 1975 *see* Kennedy, Michael Stephen, ed. 1961

Wurtzburg, Susan, and Lyle Campbell
1995   North American Indian Sign Language: Evidence of Its Existence Before European Contact. *International Journal of American Linguistics* 61(2):153–167. Chicago.

Wyckoff, Don G.
1992   Archaic Cultural Manifestations on the Southern Plains. *Revista de arqueología americana* 5:167–199. México, D.F.: Instituto Panamericano de Geografía e Historia.

1993   Gravel Sources of Knappable Alibates Silicified Dolomite. *Geoarchaeology: An International Journal* 8(1):35–58.

Wyckoff, Don G., and Robert L. Brooks
1983   Oklahoma Archeology: A 1981 Perspective of the State's Archeological Resources, Their Significance, Their Problems and Some Proposed Solutions. *University of Oklahoma. Oklahoma Archeological Survey. Resource Survey Report* 16. Norman.

Wyckoff, Don G., and Jack L. Hoffman, eds.
1982   Pathways To Plains Prehistory: Anthropological Perspectives of Plains Natives and Their Pasts. Papers in Honor of Robert E. Bell. *Oklahoma Anthropological Society Memoir* 3; *The Cross Timber Heritage Association Contributions* 1. Duncan, Okla.: The Cross Timbers Press.

Wyckoff, Don G., and Charles Rippey
1999   Late Pleaistocene-Early Holocene People and Animals in Tulsa County: Some Preliminary Insights. *Bulletin of the Oklahoma Anthropological Society* 47(for 1998):5–37. Norman.

Wyckoff, Don G., and Lyonel Taylor
1971   The Pumpkin Creek Site, an Early Archaic Site in the Southern Plains Border. *Plains Anthropologist* 16(51):20–50.

Wyckoff, Don G., D. Morgan, and L.Woodward
1994   Calf Creek on the Cherokee Prairie, Part 1: The Arrowhead Ditch Site (34MS174). *Bulletin of the Oklahoma Anthropological Society* 40:307–328. Norman.

Wyckoff, Lydia L., ed.
1996   Visions and Voices: Native American Paintings from the Philbrook Museum of Art. Tulsa, Okla.: Philbrook Museum of Art.

Wyeth, Nathaniel J.
1899   The Correspondence and Journals of Captain Nathaniel J. Wyeth, 1831–6; A Record of Two Expeditions for the Occupation of the Oregon Country, with Maps, and Introduction to Index. Edited by Frederick G. Young. *Sources of the History of Oregon* 1(3–6). Eugene, Oreg. (Reprinted: Lost Cause Press, Louisville, Ky., 1968; also, Arno Press, New York, 1973; and, under title: The Journals of Captain Nathaniel J. Wyeth's Expeditions to the Oregon Country, 1831–1836. Edited by Don Johnson. Ye Galleon Press, Fairfield, Wash., 1984.)

Wyman, Leland C., W.W. Hill, and Iva Osanai
1942   Navajo Eschatology. *University of New Mexico Bulletin* 377. *Anthropological Series* 4(1). Albuquerque: University of New Mexico Press.

Yarrow, H.C.
1881   A Further Contribution to the Study of the Mortuary Customs of the North American Indians. Pp. 87–205 in *1st Annual Report of the Bureau of [American] Ethnology [for] 1879–'80*. Washington: Smithsonian Institution; U.S. Government Printing Office.

Yellen, John and Henry Harpending
1972   Hunter-gatherer Populations and Archaeological Inference. *World Archaeology* 4(2):244–253. Derek Rowe, ed. London: Routledge and Kegan Paul.

Yellowtail, Thomas 1991 *see* Fitzgerald, O. Michael 1991

Young Bear, Severt, and R.D.Theisz
1994   Standing in the Light: A Lakota Way of Seeing. Lincoln: University of Nebraska Press.

Young, David, Grant Ingram, and Lise Swartz
1989   Cry of the Eagle: Encounters with a Cree Healer. Toronto: University of Toronto Press.

Young, Gloria A.
1972–1989 [Fieldnotes from Fieldwork conducted in Northeastern Oklahoma.] (Manuscripts in G.A. Young's possession.)

1978   Negotiating a Musical Event: The Modern American Indian Powwow. (Manuscript in G.A. Young's possession.)

1981   Powwow Power: Perspectives on Historic and Contemporary Intertribalism. (Ph.D. Dissertation in Anthropology, Indiana University, Bloomington.)

1983   Play as Power: The Policitical Aspects of Native American Games. Pp. 209–220 in North American Indians: Humanistic Perspectives. *Papers in Anthropology* 24. James S. Thayer, ed. Norman: University of Oklahoma Department of Anthropology.

1986   Aesthetic Archives: The Visual Language of Plains Ledger Art. Pp. 45–63 in The Arts of the North American Indians: Native Traditions in Evolution. Edwin L. Wade, ed. New York: Hudson Hill Press, in assoc. with Philbrook Art Center, Tulsa.

1989   The Dream Dance and Ghost Dance in Oklahoma. Pp. 18–25 in Songs of Indian Territory: Native American Music Traditions of Oklahoma. Willie Smyth, ed. Oklahoma City: Center of the American Indian.

1994   Dance as Communication. Pp. 9–15 in Native American Expressive Culture. *Akwe:kon Journal* 11(3–4). Ithaca, N.Y.: Akwe:kon Press and National Museum of the American Indian.

Young, Gloria A., and Michael P. Hoffman
1993   The Expedition of Hernando de Soto West of the Mississippi, 1541–1543. Fayetteville, Ark.: University of Arkansas Press.

Young, John
1994   Opponents Charge Political Purge on Crow Reservation. *Indian Country Today* May 25:A1. Rapid City, S.Dak.

Young, Robert W.
[1968]   The Role of the Navajo in the Southwestern Drama. Gallup, N.Mex.: The Gallup Independent.

_____ 1983 *see* Handbook Vol. 10 (1983:393–400)

Young, Robert W., and William Morgan, Sr.
1980   The Navajo Language: A Grammar and Colloquial Dictionary. A Revision and Expansion of the Authors': The Language and a Vocabulary of Colloquial Navaho. Albuquerque: University of New Mexico Press.

1992   Analytical Lexicon of Navajo. Albuquerque: University of New Mexico Press.

Young, Wayne C.
1978   Kaw Reservoir — The Northern Section, Part II: Report of Phase Va Research of the General Plan for Investigation of the Archaeological Resources of Kaw Reservoir, North-Central Oklahoma. *University of Oklahoma. Oklahoma River Basin Survey. Archaeological Site Report* 33. Norman.

Zárate-Salmerón, Gerónimo de
1856   Relaciones de Todas las Cosas que en el Nuevo-Mexico se han visto y Sabido, assi por Mar como por Terra desde el año de 1538 hasta el de 1626. Por el Padre Gerónimo de Zárate-Salmerón Predicado de la Orden de los menores de la Provincia del Santo Evangelio: Dirigidas a Nro. Rmo. Pe. Fr. Franco de Apodaca Padre de la Provincia de Cantabria, y Comisario General de todas las de esta Nueva España. *Documentos para la Historia de Mexico* 3 (1, Pt. 2):1–55. Madrid. (Reprinted, Alicia Ronstadt Milich, trans.: Horn and Wallace, Albuquerque, 1966.)

Zalucha, L. Anthony
1982   Methodology in Paleoethnobotany: A Study of Vegetational Reconstruction Dealing with the Mill Creek Culture of Northwestern Iowa. (Ph.D. Dissertation in Anthropology, University of Wisconsin, Madison.)

Zeilig, Ken, and Victoria Zeilig
1987   Ste. Madeleine: Community Without a Town; Métis Elders in Interview. Winnipeg, Man.: Pemmican Publications.

Zeimens, George M., Danny Walker, Thomas K. Larson, John Albanese, and George W. Gill
1978   The Dunlap-McMurry Burial (48NA67) Natrona County, Wyoming. *The Wyoming Archaeologist* 22(1):15–40. Cheyenne, [etc.,] Wyo.

Zelitch, Jeffrey
1970   The Lakota Sun Dance. *Expedition* 13(1):17–23. Philadelphia.

Zier, Christian J., and Stephen M. Kalasz
1991   Recon John Shelter and the Archaic-Woodland Transition in Southeastern Colorado. *Plains Anthropologist* 36(135):111–138.

Zier, Christian J., Denise P. Fallon, and Michael D. Metcalf
1983   Riley Ridge Natural Gas Project. (Cultural Resource Technical Report.) Eagle, Colo.: Metcalf-Zier Archaeologists.

Zier, Christian J., S.M. Kalasz, A.H. Peebles, M.A. Van Ness, and E. Anderson
1988   Archaeological Excavation of the Avery Ranch Site (5PE56) on the Fort Carson Military Reservation, Pueblo County, Colorado. (Report submitted to the National Park Service and the U.S. Army by Centennial Archaeology, Fort Collins, Colo.)

Zimmerly, David W.
1968   When the People Gather: Notes on the Teton Dakota Sun Dance. *Pine Ridge Research Bulletin* 6(December):35–42. Pine Ridge, S.Dak.: Public Health Service, Division of Indian Health, Community Mental Health Program.

1969   On Being an Ascetic: Personal Document of a Sioux Medicine Man. *Pine Ridge Research Bulletin* 10(August):46–71. Pine Ridge, S.Dak.: Public Health Service, Division of Indian Health, Community Mental Health Program.

Zimmerman, Larry J.
1985   Peoples of Prehistoric South Dakota. Lincoln: University of Nebraska Press.

1995   We Do Not Need Your Past! Politics, Indian Time, and Plains Archaeology. Pp. 28–45 in Beyond Subsistence: Plains Archaeology and the Postprocessual Critique. Philip Duke and Michael C. Wilson, eds. Tuscaloosa: University of Alabama Press.

Zimmerman, Mark E.
1918   The Ground-House Indians and Stone-Cist Grave Builders of Kansas and Nebraska. *Collections of the Kansas State Historical Society* 14:471–487. Topeka.

Zitkala-Ša [Gertrude Bonnin]
1901   Old Indian Legends. Boston: Ginn and Company. (Reprinted: University of Nebraska Press, Lincoln, 1985.)

——
1921   American Indian Stories. Washington: Hayworth Publishing House. (Reprinted: University of Nebraska Press, Lincoln, 1985.)

Zoltai, Stephen C., and Dale H. Vitt
1990   Holocene Climatic Change and the Distribution of Peatlands in Western Interior Canada. *Quaternary Research: An Interdisciplinary Journal* 33(2):231–240. [Seattle, Wash.]

Zoltvany, Yves F.
1969   Greysolon Dulhut, Daniel. Pp. 261–264 in Dictionary of Canadian Biography, Vol. II: 1701 to 1710. Toronto: University of Toronto Press.

——
1974   Gaultier de Varennes et de la Verendrye, Pierre. Pp. 246–253 in Dictionary of Canadian Biography, Vol. III: 1741 to 1770. Toronto: University of Toronto Press.

Zurburg, Suzanne Caroline
1991   The Norby Site: A Mummy Cave Complex Bison Kill on the Northern Plains. (M.A. Thesis in Anthropology and Archaeology, University of Saskatchewan, Saskatoon.)

Zweiner, Dan
[1970]   Gardens of the Ioway. (Typescript; prepared for the Iowa Natural Heritage Foundation, Des Moines, Iowa.)

Index

Ahtone, Vernon Burr: *921*
Ahuachés; synonymy: 544
Ahwahha(r)ways; synonymy: 346
Ähyä´to; synonymy: 861
Aiaoüa; synonymy: 445
Ai-dĭk-a-da-hu; synonymy: 388
Aiiaes; synonymy: 544
Aijados; synonymy: 966
Aijaos; synonymy: 966
Aijaoz; synonymy: 965
Aijoues; synonymy: 445
Aiken site: *197*
a-i-nun´; synonymy: 714
Aïouez; synonymy: 445
Aitche jibbla minnach Baga; synonymy: 623
Aitché shilbisha wrach baga; synonymy: 623
Aixaos; synonymy: 965–966
Aixas; synonymy: 966
ai´yue; synonymy: 445
ai´yuwe; synonymy: 445
Ajaouez; synonymy: 445
Ajouas; synonymy: 445
Akamsians; synonymy: 512
Akancas; synonymy: 512
A Kancea; synonymy: 512
Akansas; synonymy: 511, 512
Akanscas; synonymy: 512
Akansea; synonymy: 512
Akanzas; synonymy: 512
aka·sa; synonymy: 475
Akepa: *771*
Aker site: *160–161*
Akinsaws; synonymy: 512
á·k̓ɔpʰà·gɔ; synonymy: 460
akparea·šú·paško; synonymy: 751
Akwech; synonymy: 566
akʷi·c; synonymy: 566
Akwits; synonymy: 566
Alähó; synonymy: 475, 513
áláhô·gɔ́; synonymy: 513
A-lân-sâr; synonymy: 692
Alberts Creek site: *188*
Albion Boardinghouse complex: 144
Alcedo; synonymy: 754
alcohol: 621, 622. abuse: 318, 326, 441, 442,
    454, 618, 620, 621, 622, 779, 942, 956.
    bootleggers: 411. sales to Indians: 295, 296,
    315, 324, 367, 391, 411, 436, 441, 635, 779,
    916. trade: 277, 315, 499, 574, 585, 635,
    678, 734, 782, 787, 890
alcoholism: 299, 318, 621, 956
Alderin Creek site: *246*
Alexis: 599
Algonquian languages: 61–63, *62–63,* 71–79,
    638, 677, 974. borrowings: 77. comparative
    vocabulary: 64–66. diffusion among: 76–77.
    geographic incidence: 71. prehistoric: 77–78.
    survival: *78,* 78–79. and tribal classification:
    2. vowel system: 78
Algonquians, in 17th century: 301
Aliatans; synonymy: 903
Alibates 28 site: *210–211*
Alicara; synonymy: 388
alik̓awàho: 470
Alitanes; synonymy: 903
Alkansas; synonymy: 512
Alkire site: *160–161*

Alkire variant: 169
All, Barbara: *961*
Al-la-ka-we-ah; synonymy: 716
Allis, Samuel: 28, 520
Allison, E. H.: 98
Allison, Fred J.: *288*
allotment. *See* land
Allouez, Jean Claude: 23, 301
All Over Black: 785
Altithermal period: 19
Always Calling: *984–985*
Amahami; synonymy: 346
Amahami site: *246*
Amatiha; synonymy: 346
Amatiha; synonymy: 346
Amatsichá; synonymy: 346
Ambrose: *279*
American Board of Commissioners for Foreign
    Missions: 393, 520
American Chief: 471
American Crow Creek site: *197*
American Fur Company: 266, 276, 277, 309,
    367, 574, 662, 678, 697, *733*
American Horse: 799
American Horse, Ben: *836*
American Indian Exposition: 1013–1015
American Indian Higher Education Consortium:
    827
American Indian Movement: 299, 833, 835–
    836, *836,* 853, 989, 990, 992, 993, 994, 1010
American Indian Religious Freedom Act: 831–
    833
American Museum of Natural History: 2, 29,
    33, 34, 35, 82
American Society for Ethnohistory: 40
American War Mothers Association: 459, *459*
A-me-she´; synonymy: 346
Amiotte, Arthur: 994, 1060, *1060–1061*
Amisk site: *116*
Amkepatines; synonymy: 755
Amos Shields site: *246*
Ampapa; synonymy: 758
Ampapes; synonymy: 758
Amparacs; synonymy: 904
Ana; synonymy: 650
Anahō; synonymy: 475, 513
Anahons; synonymy: 475, 494
Anahous; synonymy: 475, 494
Ánahú; synonymy: 475
Ancavistis; synonymy: 905
Anderson, John A.: 28
Anderson, Phyllis Hawley: *588*
Anderson phase: 188, 192
André, Louis: 432
Andrews, A. Joseph: *31*
Angallas; synonymy: 757
Angel, Louis: 506
Anibishiwininiwak; synonymy: 753
ani·hwsa·si; synonymy: 494
animals. *See* buffalo; dogs; environment;
    fishing; horses; hunting
A´nipahu; synonymy: 860
anišsina·pe·; synonymy: 659
ani·wahsa·si; synonymy: 494
Anjoues; synonymy: 445
Ankima: *916*
Anko: 1068, *1068–1069*

Ankora; synonymy: 388
Annach bogu minnarch baga; synonymy: 363
Annah; synonymy: 650
Annahawas; synonymy: 346
An *nah* hose; synonymy: 971
Annaho; synonymy: 475, 494
annual cycle: 1011. Archithinue: 678. Arikara:
    248, 381. Assiniboine: 577–578. Blackfoot:
    609–610. Cheyenne: 875. Crow: 707, 713.
    Gros Ventre: 678, 679. Hidatsa: 248, 332–
    333. High Plains tribes: 974, 977, 978. Iowa:
    440. Kiowa: 908. Kitsai: 569. Mandan: 248.
    Omaha: 403. Osage: 477, 479–480. Pawnee:
    248–249, 526. Plains Cree: 640. Plains
    Métis: 667. Plains Ojibwa: 653. Plains
    Village tradition: 248–249. Ponca: 418.
    Prairie Plains: 975–976. prehistoric: 60, 248–
    249. Quapaw: 507. Santee Sioux: 729.
    Sarcee: 630–631. Teton Sioux: 731–732.
    Wichita: 249, 552. Yankton-Yanktonai: 789,
    791
ano´s-anyotskano; synonymy: 861
Anquoe, Mary Ann: *1031*
Antelope, Joe: 879
Antelope Creek phase: 154, 155, 156, 182, 207,
    212, 213–216, 219, 220, 234
Antelope Creek site: *188*
Antelope Creek 22 site: *210–211*
Antelope Creek 24 site: *210–211*
Anthontans; synonymy: 755
Anthoutantas; synonymy: 460
Anton Rygh site: *197, 246*
Aovages; synonymy: 544
Aovajes; synonymy: 544
Aowias; synonymy: 445
Apache; art: 241, *909.* Carlana: 244, 926.
    ceremonies: 1004, 1005. classification: 4.
    disease: 257. dogs: 260. external relations:
    262, 569, 905. Faraon: 926, 972. history:
    266. horses: 260. migrations: 239. origins:
    127. prehistory: 242–243, 244. slavery: 239–
    240, 264, 518. subsistence: 53, 241.
    synonymy: 938. trade: 67, 262. warfare: 266,
    518, 550, 846. *See also* Chiricahua Apache;
    Jicarilla Apache; Lipan Apache; Mescalero
    Apache; Plains Apache; Plains Apacheans
Apachean (language). *See* Plains Apache
    language
Apache Ben: *934*
Apache Jim: *931*
Apache John: *289, 931*
Apacheria Lipana; synonymy: 951
Apaches del Norte; synonymy: 928
Apaches Lipanes (de Abajo); synonymy: 951
Apaches Lipanes de Arriva; synonymy: 951
Apaches of the Arkansas River; synonymy: 938
Apache Tribe of Oklahoma; synonymy: 938
apa·ni·ha; synonymy: 543
Apeatone: *289,* 1004, 1007
Apishapa phase: 155, 212, 234–239, 243
api·wišé; synonymy: 694
Appaches of the Plains; synonymy: 938
Apsáalooke; synonymy: 715
Ap sair-e-ca; synonymy: 715
Apsarechas; synonymy: 715
apsâ·ro·ke; synonymy: 715
Apsar(r)uka; synonymy: 715

Alkire site: *160–161*

INDEX

466, 577, 581, 789, 867, 945
Bowwetegoweninnewug; synonymy: 693
The Boy: *681*
Boyer variant: 165
Boysen Reservoir site: *132–133,* 139, 141, *142*
Bozeman Trail: 282, 781, *794,* 796
Bozner site: *132–133,* 135
Brace, Ned: *289*
Brackenridge, Henry M.: 26, 390
Bradbury, John: 26, 390
Braden site: *210–211*
Bradley, James H.: 28, 1070
Bradwell site: *116,* 122
Brady, Jim: *664, 666*
Brandon House: *259,* 268, 308, 309
Brandon phase: 222
Brandon site: *223,* 227
Brass, Alex: *322*
Bratley, Jesse Hastings: 28
Brave Bear: 786
Brave Wolf: *68*
breed; synonymy: 675
Breeden site: *197*
Bremner, Joseph: *323*
Bremner, Tom: *323*
Bremner, William: *323*
Brewer site: *160–161,* 171, 208, *210–211*
Brewster site: *223,* 235
Bridwell site: *147,* 157
Brochet; synonymy: 677, 968–969
Brockie, Clarence: *294*
Brockie, Victor: *294*
Brockinton site: *116*
Broken Kettle site: *223,* 226
Broken Kettle West site: *223,* 224, 225, *225, 226*
Brotherhood of Christian Unity: 792
Brother-of-All Spring site: *197*
Broulé; synonymy: 675
Brous site: *160–161*
Brown, George: *298*
Brown, Howard: *298*
Brown, Joseph R.: *783*
Brown, Kenneth L.: 18
Brown, Lamont: *1032*
Brown, Lionel A.: 17
Brown, Sugar: 1013
Brown Bull, Jerome: *822*
Brown Hat: 1070, 1071, *1071*
Brown site: *210–211*
Brulé Dakotas; synonymy: 756
Brulees; synonymy: 756
Brule Flat Village site: *197*
Brule Sioux; synonymy: 756. *See also* Teton Sioux
Brulies; synonymy: 756
Bruner, Edward: 39
Bruyère, André Fabry de la: 568
Bryan site: *223,* 232
Bryson-Paddock site: 550
The Buck: *781*
Buckhollow Encampment site: *147,* 156
Buckman, John: *294, 681*
Buechel, Eugene: 99, 1072
buffalo: 1, 115, 119–120, 149, 315. as cultural focus: 1, 2, 6, 7, 12. disappearance: 309, 310, 312, 315, 317, 331, 487, 507, 521, 559, 585,

596, 619, 635, 641, 657, 667, 678, 686, 729, 763, 782, 785, 786, 788, 794, 797, 812, 842, 847, 849, 889, 893, 999, 1000, 1001. as food: 55, 56, 117–118, 403, 789, 867. hunting: 6, *7,* 10, 56, 60, 263, 309, 332, 463, 477, 480, 482, 575, 577, 605–607, 609, 619, 629–630, 634, 640–641, 642, 653, 654–655, 657, 666, *666,* 678, 679, 695, 698, 719–720, 725–726, 729, 730, 731–732, 767, 768, 769, 777, 779, 780, 788, 797, 803, 805, 847, 863, 889, 908, 911, 926, 928, 945, 955, 974, 978, 979, 996. migrations: 609. prehistoric role: 117–118, 119–120, 122, 124, 125, 130, 131, 135, 136, 138, 142, 144, 145, 149, 150, 151, 153, 154, 155, 156, 158, 175–176, 208, 209, 220, 222, 225, 233, 236, 244. processing of: 6–7, *8–9,* 9, *10–11, 34,* 175–176, 183, 185, 251, 277, 500, 575–576, *576,* 577, 680, 699–700, 725, 789, 805, 928–929, 945. range: 908. religious role: 336. uses: 6, 477, 517, 526, 527, 605, 630, 698–699, 725, 803, 929, 945–946. *See also* fur trade
Buffalo, Sam: 1004
Buffalo Bird Woman: *251*
Buffalo Black: 1005
Buffalo Calf site: *197*
Buffalo Chief: *711*
Buffalohead, Harry: *1032*
Buffalohead, Robert: 428
Buffalo Indians; synonymy: 860
Buffalo Nation; synonymy: 750
Buffalo Pasture site: *246*
Buffalo Paunch: *392*
bugji wrach baga; synonymy: 881
Bulger, Andrew: 309
Bull Against Wind: *392*
Bull Child, George: *617*
Bull Child, Percy: *1068–1069*
Bull Head: 635
Bull Lodge: 42, *1029*
Bull's Ghost: 787
Bungays; synonymy: 659
Bungees; synonymy: 659
Bungi; synonymy: 659
Burdick, Usher L.: *1073*
Bureau of American Ethnology: 28, 29–32, 35, 39, 82
Bureau of Indian Affairs: 271, 823, 825. agencies: 213, 258, *283,* 284, 331, 351, 367, 385, 391–393, 401, 425, 427, 436, 441, 444, 454, 471, 473, 474, 488, 521, 539, 540, 569, 575, 583, 585, 707, 734, 782, 783, 784, 787, 797, 799, 812, 823, 842, 849, 850, 888, 916, 919, *919,* 933, 955. commissioners: 284, 290, 292, 296, 297, 821, 837, 988, 1004, 1011, 1013, 1056, 1057. education: 385, 387, 396, 1057, 1059. management: 28, 39, 271, 284–286, 292, 293, 295, 297, 298, 387, 394, 396, 412, *412,* 459, 509, 521, 539, 540, 541, 559, 561, 586, 686, 689, 690, 713, 782, 796, 797, 812, 823, 825, 827, 828, 830, 853, 877, 899, 918, 919, 920. paternalism: 817–818, 828, 829–830. policies: 520, 815, 824, 837, 899, 900. reservations and removals: 824, 866. termination: 296, 297, 325, 411, 427, *474,* 620, 823–824, 835
Buresh site: *210–211,* 218

burial. *See* death practices
Buried City complex: 154–155, 212, 216, 219, 220
Burke, Charles H.: *294,* 988, 1013
Burke Act (1906): 290, 291, 457, 816
Burland, Thomas: *294*
Burleigh, Walter A.: 779–780
Burned arms; synonymy: 884
burned thighs; synonymy: 756
Burnette, Robert: 835
Burnham, Harry Lawson Webster Levy, Lord: *314*
Burning Woods; synonymy: 756
Burnt; synonymy: 756
Burnt Hip Brulé; synonymy: 756
Burnt Prairie: *783*
Burnt Prairie site: *197*
Burnt-Thighs; synonymy: 756
Burnt-woods; synonymy: 756
Bushfield West site: *116*
Bushotter, George: 31, 99, 993, 1072
Bushyhead, Allan: *1014–1015, 1029*
Butler, Toney: *466*
Butler, William: 313
Butler phase: 153, 165
Butterfly: *1068*
Bwoi(r)nug; synonymy: 750

C
C.B. Smith site: *197*
ca baʔkuš; synonymy: 751
Cabanne's Post: *259,* 277
Cabeza de Vaca, Álvar Núñez: 67, 256, 257
Cable, Greg: *298*
Cable site: *197*
Cacawguieohninnewog; synonymy: 714
caches: 150, 479. box: 217. construction: 217. pits: 131, 133, 135, 150, 157, 162, 164, 165, 166, 168, 171, 172, 174, 176, 177, 178, 179, 183, 184, 185, 188, 192, 198, 208, 209, 213, 217, 219, 225, 226, 229, 232, 249, 251, 353, 368, 369, 402, 418, 419, 436, 523, 526, 552, 724–725, 789. platform: 217. scaffold: 217, 251
Cactus Flower site: *116,* 120, 121, *121*
Caddo; ceremonies: 1004, 1034. classification of: 4. contact: 24, 263, 264. disease: 257, 269. external relations: 568. history: 282. music and dance: 1034. origins: 245. Plains bands: 40. political organization: 282. religion: *1006–1007,* 1007. reservations: 281, 558, 568–569. social organization: 10–12. subsistence: 53. trade: 264, 266, 928. warfare: 281, 916
Caddoan languages: 61–63, *62–63,* 80–93, 517, 974. borrowings: 90–91. characteristics: 88–90. classification of: 105. comparative vocabulary: 64–66. dating of: 84–85. external relationships: 85–86. geographical incidence: 80. historical changes: 78. influence: 70. internal relationships: 83–85. languages: 80–83. phonology: 86–88. subgroupings: 84, *85.* survival: *91,* 91–93, *92,* 93. and tribal classification: 2
Caddoans; characteristics of: 974. migrations: 256, 476–477. trade: 476. warfare: 476

Cadell Homestead site: *186–187, 188*
Cadohadacho; alliances: 567. external relations: 568. treaties: 568
Cadotte site: *246*
Caesar, Julius: *1058–1059*
Cagua: 70
Cahcahkewahchow; synonymy: 714
Cahi(a)guas; synonymy: 922
Cah-tah-kahs; synonymy: 939
Cai-a-was; synonymy: 923
Caigua; synonymy: 922
Calahorra, Fray Joseph de: 550
Calderwood site: *116*, 124
Caldwell, Warren W.: 17
calendrical systems: 381, 908, 1043, 1068, *1068–1069*, 1070–1072
Calf Creek tradition: 149–150
Calf Robe, Ben: *617*
Calgary Indian Industrial School: *73*
Calgary Treaty Urban Alliance: 649
Calhoun, John C.: 270, *436*
Calihoo, Félix: *664*
Calihoo, Johnny: 648
Callinglast, George: *324*
Camanche; synonymy: 902
Camarena, Richard A.: *298*
Cambria phase: 186, 222, 228
Cambria site: *223, 228*
Cameron, Duncan: 306
Caminanbiche; synonymy: 840, 860
camp criers: 375, 533, 556, 615, 796, 801, 805, 949, *1032*
Camp Holmes: *259*
Camp Holmes Treaty (1835): 272, 274, 551, 888
Camp Poplar River: 788, 812
Camp Rankin: 796
Camp Robinson: *259*, 799
camps: *487, 711*, 801, 848, *990, 1044*. hunting: 245, 332, 356, 448, 479, 534. seasonal: 55–56, 120, 125, 137, 156, 248, *250*, 277, 332–333, 428, 609, 630–631, 662, 663, 768, 788, 791, *894*, 908, 930, 934, 945, 978, 983
Camp Supply: *259, 287*
Camuches; synonymy: 902
Canada, government of: 313–315, 316. agricultural program: 316. army: 665. assimilation policy: 315–316, 319–321, *321*, 323, 324–325. benefits: 648. civil rights: 324–325. Department of Indian Affairs: 28, 270, 317, 318, 319, 320–321, 325, 326, 586, 599, 649. Department of the Interior: *668*. education: 319, *320*, 322, 323. financial aid: 620, 668. food crisis of 1870s-80s: 315–318. gifts and annuities: *326*. land transfers: 312, 313–314. North West Half Breed Commission: *668*. North West Mounted Police: 313, 317, 318, 585, 618, 619, 635, 665, 988. and Plains resources: 311–312. Royal Commission on Aboriginal Peoples: 674. self-government policies: 600. termination: 325. treaties: 314–316. voting rights: 319, 324, *324*. White Paper: 325, 666. *See also* reservations and reserves
Canadian Assiniboine; synonymy: 585
Canadian Cree, economy: 668
Canas; synonymy: 963

Cancer(es); synonymy: 939
Cances; synonymy: 939
Canchez; synonymy: 475
Canchy; synonymy: 939
Cancis; synonymy: 939
Cancy; synonymy: 475, 939. warfare: 927–928
Caneenawees; synonymy: 860
Ca-ne-na-vich; synonymy: 860
Caneninavish; synonymy: 860
Caninanbiches; synonymy: 860
cànnànà; synonymy: 751
Can nar vesh; synonymy: 971
Cannecis; synonymy: 939
Cannecy; synonymy: 939
cannibalism: 548, 550, 557, 567, 569, 950, 962. prehistoric: 180
Cannon, T.C.: 1060, *1060–1061*
canoes: 302, 303, 500, 574, 640, 652, 655, 724, 729
Canpocksa: *786*
Cans; synonymy: 475
Canseres; synonymy: 939
Canses; synonymy: 475
Cansis; synonymy: 939
Cantcy; synonymy: 939
Canterbury site: *235*, 237
Cantey; synonymy: 939
Canyon City site: *210–211*
Canz(er)es; synonymy: 939
Canzez; synonymy: 475
Cap(p)as; synonymy: 511
Capture, John: *691*
carara·t; synonymy: 751
Carbella site: *132–133*, 137
Cardinal, Harold: *324, 632*, 648
Cargua; synonymy: 922
Caricara; synonymy: 388
Caricoë; synonymy: 962
Carlana Apache. *See* Plains Apacheans
Carleton, James Henry: 519
Carlisle Indian School: 288, *291*, 539, 708, 814, 875, 1057
Carondelet, Francisco de: *267*
Carpenter site: *197*
Carr, Eugene A.: 865
Carrington, Henry B.: 796
Carrion, Joe: 541
Carrizo: 951
Carrizo Creek sites: *235*
Carry the Kettle: 586
Carson, Christopher (Kit): 889, 915
Carson, Linda: *298*
Carter, Sybil: *775*
Carver, Jonathan: 42, 97, 727, 729, *730*
Caschotethka; synonymy: 904
Case, H. W.: *395*
Case, Ralph: 838
Cashen, Will: *710–711*
casinos: 398, 589, 658, 824, 826
Cassia; synonymy: 570
Castahana; synonymy: 971
Castañeda, Pedro de: 1
Castihania; synonymy: 971
Castillo, Diego del: 966
Castor Creek site: *116*, 119
Castors de Prairies; synonymy: 636
Castro, Cuelgas de: 943, 945

Cat, Rosa: *792*
Cataha; synonymy: 939
Cataka; synonymy: 937, 939
Ca-ta-ka tribe of Pado; synonymy: 939
catarax: 549
Catarkas; synonymy: 939
Catawba language: 103. classification of: 103, 105
Catches, Peter: *832–833*, 993
Catlin, George: 26, *27*, 81, 277, *278*, 347, 350, *354, 358*, 364, 390, *420, 436*, 440, *442, 730, 760*, 983
Cat-tar-kah; synonymy: 939
cattle. *See* livestock
Cattle Oiler site: *197*
Cauchon, Joseph: 316
Caunouche; synonymy: 902
Caunzie; synonymy: 714
Cauzes; synonymy: 475
Cava. *See* Tonkawa
Cavayo: *898*
Caw; synonymy: 475
cawí·ʔa; synonymy: 545
cawí·ʔi; synonymy: 545
Caw-mainsh; synonymy: 902
Cawri; synonymy: 714
Cayanwa; synonymy: 923
Cay-au-wa; synonymy: 970
Caygüa; synonymy: 922, 923
Cayohuas; synonymy: 922
Cayou, Frank, Jr.: *1017*
Cayowa; synonymy: 923
Cayugas; synonymy: 922
ccamí; synonymy: 545
ccawí; synonymy: 545
Cedar Point Village site: *235*, 239
Cedar Wood Feather: *392*
Ceetshongos; synonymy: 756
čeinówu·hunóʔ: 854
celts: 153
Centennial Exposition: 29, *30*
cé·ptití·menin̊; synonymy: 881
ceremonies: 6, 10, 81, 82, *267*, 269, 338, 421, 726, 1011, 1015. adoption: 297, 409, 424, 440, 470, 502, 538, 697, 706, 713, 726–727, 807, 1011, 1023, *1024*, 1035. age-group: 334. agricultural: 355, 356, *361*, 381, 404, 437, 448, 502, 558, 634, 1007. All Smoke ceremony: *617*. alówapi: 1035. Animal Dance: 873, *874*. Anointing the Pole: 409. Baby Grass dance: 386. Back to Batoche Days: 674. Ball ceremony: 808. baptismal ceremony: *380*. Bear Dance: 424, 438. Bear Song ceremony: 707. Beaver ceremony: 892–893. Beaver Dance: 713. Big Moon ceremony: 1007. Big Sleight of Hand: 998. birth: 338, 407, 450, 808. Blue-Bead ceremony: 790. Bone Dance: 440. Braves Dance: 438, 440. Buffalo Calf Pipe ceremony: 1034. Buffalo Calling ceremony: *1000*. Buffalo Dance: 438, 541, 647, 893. Buffalo dreamers: 769. Buffalo Sing: 807, 809. Bull Dance: *358*. bundle: 335–336, 355–356, 362, 687–688, 692, 932, 1033, *1033*, 1062, 1063, 1065, 1066. Calumet ceremony: 372, 378, 379, *380*, 440, 470, 502–503, 538, 546, 549–550, 556, 558, 726– *1305*

Chárata-numangkä; synonymy: 544

Charbonneau, Toussaint: 268

Chardon, Francis A.: 25

Charette, Guillaume: 673

Charger: 784

Charging, Francis: *395*

Charging, Kenneth: *397*

Chariticas; synonymy: 861

Charity Red Gun: *327*

Charles II: 300

charms and amulets: *1029*

Chase Bench site: *235*

Chase Orchard site: *235*

čʰatʰókapina; synonymy: 637

Chats; synonymy: 881

Chau-i; synonymy: 545

Chä´-we; synonymy: 545

Chawi Pawnee; synonymy: 545. *See also* Pawnee

Chayennes; synonymy: 880, 881

Chayon; synonymy: 880

Cheaun; synonymy: 880

Che che ree; synonymy: 756

Cheeons; synonymy: 880

Chelsea phase: 144, 150

Chêniers; synonymy: 495

Cherokee; ceding of land: 281. Chickamauga: 478. external relations: 273. language: 105. migrations: 271–272. relocations: 273. reservation: 281. territory: 478. warfare: 273, 275, 478, 551

Cherokee Commission: 473, 488, 559–560, 918, 956

Cherokee Sewer site: *132–133,* 144

Chetopah: *483*

Che-ve-te Pu-ma-ta: *699*

Cheyenne: *33,* 863–885, 888. agriculture: 863, 865, 867, 877. alliances: 840, 841, 842, 863, 926, 928, 971, 972. allotment: 865–866, 877. annual cycle: 875. art: 867–868, *868, 869,* 873, 1039, *1044,* 1045, 1046, 1047, *1047,* 1051. ceremonies: 35, *852,* 863, 873–875, *874,* 876–877, 983, 984, *986,* 988, 989, 994, 996, *998,* 999, 1000, 1001, *1002–1003, 1003,* 1004, 1011, 1018, 1034. clothing and adornment: 868, *869,* 870. contact: 24, 27, 28, 270, 865. cosmology: 873. curing: 874, 875, 1032. disease: 258, 865, 879. division of labor: 867–868. dogs: 260. economy: 284, 292, 293, 878, 879. education: 877–878, 879. external relations: 77, 270, 349, 727, 863, 865, *870.* fairs and celebrations: 1013. games and toys: 509, 868–869, 869, *869, 871,* 1025. history: 79, 284, 291–292, 295, 863–866. horses: 12. income: 878. kinship: 872–873, 878, 978. life cycle: 870–873, *873.* migrations: 256, 270, 734, 797–799, 840, 863, *864,* 865, 888. music and dance: 32, 1028, 1029, *1029,* 1030, 1032, 1034, 1035, 1036. mythology: 1051, 1065. Northern: 37, 41, 42, 43, 282, 283, 284, 293, 295, 843, 865, 877–878, 882–883, *998,* 1001, 1009. oral tradition: 1067. political organization: 866, 875–876, 877, 878–879. population: 879–880. religion: 863, 873–875, *874,* 876–877, 1001, 1004, *1006–1007,* 1009. reservations: 282, 283–284, 284–285, *864,*

582. burials: 535, 950. ceremonies: 378–379, 407, 422, 451, 492, 507, 769, 790, 850, 870–871, 950. clothing: 378, *869,* 891. custody: 297, 408, 895, 959. death practices: 807–808, 950. discipline: 339, 582. games: 703, *703,* 808. grandchildren: 534, 555, 569, 646, 809, 856, 950. illegitimate: 646. infanticide: 581. infants: 895. mortality rates: 296, 322, 444. naming: 306, 337, 361, 378, 386, 407, 422, 439, 449, 451, 467, 470, 485, 492, 507, 509, 534, 555, 581, 612–613, 631, 646, 702, 703, 726, 769, 808. nursing: 378, 534, 582, 646, 703, 808, 849. orphans: 334. socialization: 361, 449, 467, 769, 931. training: 534–535, 555, 569, 582, 610, 613–614, 631, 646, 656, 663, 769, 806, 808, 809, 895, 929, 950, 977, 1049–1050. transport: 811. travel: *598–599. See also* cradles and cradleboards; puberty; toys

Chilocco School: 288

Chimney Creek site: *210–211*

Chiⁿchakiⁿze; synonymy: 939

Chiouitounes; synonymy: 693

Chioutoumes; synonymy: 693

Chippewa: *309.* alliances: 720. education: *320.* external relations: 349, 384, 573, 721, 729. migrations: 720. political organization: 720. synonymy: 659. territory: 668. trade: 720. treaties: 727, 729. warfare: 720, 721–722, 722, 727, 729, 761. *See also* Ojibwa

Chiricahua Apache: *909,* 941, 944. synonymy: 951

cʰišé; synonymy: 952

chisels, prehistoric: 224

Chíshí; synonymy: 951

Chiwere language: 102, 447. classification of: 102, 103. comparative studies: 105. consonant system: 432. dialects: 432. education: 112. Oneota tradition and: 232. orthography: 432, 447. phonology: 105, 432, 447. revival programs: 112. survival: 112. vowel system: 432

Chiwere Siouans; migrations: 1067. origins: 447, 718

Choctaw; language: 105. migrations: 271–272. territory: 560

Chokitapix; synonymy: 622

choppers, prehistoric: 171, 224, 229, 241

Chouta; synonymy: 73

Chouteau, Auguste: *505,* 519, 915

Chouteau, Forrest: *466*

Chouteau, Frederick: 471

Chouteau, Pierre: 269, 471, 543

Chouteau, Pierre, Jr.: 276

Chouteau family: 266, 269, 888

Chowees; synonymy: 545

Chrétien, Jean: 325

Christianity: 311, *395,* 775, 792, *792,* 814, *835, 857,* 875, 877, 960. Bible: *72,* 770. burials: 588. education: 288, 311, 319, 323, 385, 394, 401, 487, 506, 520, 588, 619, 635, 669, 686, 708, 734, 780, 783, 784, 786, 792, 814, *814,* 850, 854, 856. impact of: 394. indigenization of: 287, *289,* 311, 394, 442, 469, 488, 507, 542, 597, 601, 649, 669, *674,* 711, 774, 817, 834, 851, 854, 856, 875, 877, 917, 934, 937, 999, 1005, *1006–1007,* 1007–

865, 875–879, 877, 928. shamans: 1001. social organization: 5, 12, 284, 878, 879, 882–883, 884, 980, 1053. societies: *870,* 875, 876, 877, 879, 1036, 1051. Southern: 9, 43, 273, 282, 283, 513, 865, 883, *1003, 1029.* structures: 727, 863, *867,* 868, *868, 872,* 873. subsistence: 9, *10–11,* 53, 56, *57, 59,* 282, 283, 284–285, 863, 867. synonymy: 751, 880–884, 971. technology: 868–870. territory: 291, 292, 863, *864,* 865. trade: 10, 248, 276–277, 278, 370, 707, 863, 865, 867. transport: 863. treaties: 273, 280, 282, 284, 794–795, 842–843, 843, 865, 879, 889, 915–916. Two Moons band: 865. warfare: 270, 273, 279, 281, 282, 283–284, 284, 295, 416, 425, 478, 521, 641, 652, 698, 732, 796, 797, 841, 843, 863, *864,* 865, 888, 916. wealth: 292, 877

Cheyenne Agency Village site: *197*

Cheyenne language: 73–74, *74,* 76, 77, 863, 878. classification: 71. classification of: 102. comparative vocabulary: 63, 64–66, 75. dialects: 61, 73. education: 79. historical changes: 63, 78. hymns: *74* orthography: 79. phonology: 73–74, 77–78, 863. survival: 79, 879. vowel systems: 73

Cheyenne River site: *186–187, 197, 246, 263*

Cheyennes; synonymy: 880

Chi8; synonymy: 750

Chibitty, Charles: *510*

Chibitty, Pam: *510*

cʰicakize; synonymy: 939

cʰicak ize; synonymy: 939

Chickasaw; migrations: 271–272. territory: 560. warfare: 499, 916

Chicken Creek site: *210–211*

chicots; synonymy: 675

The Chief: *426*

Chief Friday: 855

Chiefly Fox: *522–523*

Chief Masketo: *584–585*

chieftainship: 12, 332, 405–407, 422, 556–557. authority: 286, 292, 374, 405, 406–407, 421, 442, 450, 501, 540, 685, 686, 698, 735, 767, 782, 788, 812, 854, 879, 895–896, 896–898, 949. ceremonial functions: 419, 439, 507, 509. clothing and adornment: *341,* 354, *354,* 422, *443, 529,* 576, *584–585, 598–599, 612, 732, 760, 931, 933* judicial functions: 482, 609, 615, 895. message runners: 375. restrictions: 424, 450. rewards: 482. selection of officials: 375, 450. shamans: 768. societies: 410, 411. spokesmen: 615. succession: 332, 422, 437, 450, 470–471, 471, 481, 501, 530, 531, 533, 576, 609, 704, 705, 735, 767, 851, 875, 896, 911, 949, 960, 977. task roles: 337, 342–343, 360, 405, 422, 423, 450, 471, 501, 525, 531, 556, 609, 645, 801–802, 847, 875–876, 877, 896, 911. wealth: 540, 576, 609

Chien; synonymy: 880, 881

Chienne; synonymy: 880

Chihuahua: 902

Chikĭkaíyú; synonymy: 881

Chikovi, Frank: *891*

children: 32, 39, 337–338, 582. adoption: 334, 357, 362, 379, 663, 767, 807. adornment:

Crow Dog, Henry: 990
Crow Dog, Leonard: 990, 992, 994
Crow Dog, Mary: 994
Crowes; synonymy: 715
Crowfeather: 998
Crow Flies High: *331, 393*
Crowfoot: 315, 316, 641
Crow Ghost: 386
Crow language: 329, 695. bilingualism: 111.
    characteristics: 103, 108. classification: 63.
    classification of: 102, 103. comparative
    vocabulary: 63, 64–66. dating of: 104.
    education: 111–112. historical changes: 63.
    orthography: 695. phonology: 64–67, 103,
    106, 695. revival programs: 111–112. studies
    on: 94. survival: 112–113, 713
Crow Mountain Indians; synonymy: 716
Crown site: *116,* 120
Crow People; synonymy: 716
Crows Breast: 393
Crows Heart: 38, *38, 353, 392*
Crozat, Antoine: 264
Crumbo, Woody: 1057
Cruzat, Francisco: 518
Cuampas; synonymy: 972
Cuampe: 888. synonymy: 940, 971, 972
Cuampis; synonymy: 972
Cuartelejo. *See* Plains Apacheans
Cuchanec; synonymy: 904
Cuchan Marica; synonymy: 904
Cuchantica; synonymy: 904
Cuchunticas; synonymy: 904
Cuerbos; synonymy: 714
Cuerno Verde: 262
Cuesta variant: 162, *163*
Cuhtzuteca; synonymy: 904
Cuitoa; synonymy: 966
Culbertson, Thaddeus: 390
Culin, Stewart: 32
Cumanche; synonymy: 902
Cumancias; synonymy: 902
Cumberland House: 262, *301,* 303, 305
Cumeehes; synonymy: 902
Cummins, John: 994
curing: 360, 393, 421, 422, 482, 502, 507,
    532–533, 537–538, *578,* 587, 610–612, 649,
    669, 683, 684–685, 688, 706–707, 774, 850,
    929. bloodletting: 684. ceremonies: 410, 440,
    532, 579, 647, *686,* 790, 808, *834, 874,* 875,
    932, 951, 961, 962, 984, 996–997, 1007,
    1009, 1034. massage: 707. medicinal plants:
    209, 410, 421, 422, 440, 442, 452, 578, 587,
    684, 685, 696, *706,* 707, 768, 892, 932, 934,
    1032. medicine bags: *578, 598–599,* 789–
    790, 843, *997.* medicine bundles: 9–10, 36,
    185, *251,* 270, 281, 322, 357, 361, 408, 423,
    439, 440, 452, *452,* 462, 466, 481, 502, 559,
    578, *611,* 615, 616, 633, 634, *634,* 683–684,
    697, 701, 705, *706,* 707, 911, 951, 971,
    1033, *1033.* medicine men: 9, 10–12, 42,
    440, 442, *442,* 558, 578, *578,* 581, *598–599,*
    633, *656,* 726, *760,* 768, 774, 784, *834,* 851,
    913, 992. medicine pipes: *358,* 621.
    medicine songs: 1032–1033. singing method:
    410, 440, 784, 1032–1033. sucking: 410,
    656, 685, 707, 892, 932. sweatbaths: 578,

685. thermotherapy: 684–685. *See also*
    health care; shamans
Curly Hair: *870*
Curly Head: *681, 1029*
Currie site: 208, *210–211*
Curtis, Charles: 473–474, *491,* 1013
Curtis, Edward S.: 33, 81, 94, 96, 377, 386, *689*
CuschuTexca; synonymy: 904
Custer, George A.: 27, 32, 284, 368, *374,* 386,
    483, 698, 797, 865, *870, 916*
Custer phase: 155, 182, 208–209, 219, 220
Cut arms; synonymy: 884
Cut Beards; synonymy: 755
Cutfoot: 996
Cut Hair: 848, *986*
Cut heads; synonymy: 755
Cut Nose: *772*
Cuttako; synonymy: 939
Cutter, Rosie: *1033*
Cutthroats; synonymy: 751
Cut wrists; synonymy: 884
cúùɫínà; synonymy: 637
Cuytoas; synonymy: 966
Cypress Hills Massacre: 585

D

Dacorta; synonymy: 750
Dacota; synonymy: 750
Dacotas of the St. Peter's; synonymy: 752
dadíšʔišą́; synonymy: 938
daggers. *See* knives
Dahcotah; synonymy: 750
Dahcotas; synonymy: 750
Dailey, George Washington: *458*
Daingkau, Clyde: *921*
dakʰóta; synonymy: 718, 750
dakʰóta čʰįča; synonymy: 676
dakkó·te·; synonymy: 750
Dakota; social organization: 974. synonymy:
    718, 750. warfare: 303
Dakotan language; classification: 63. classifica-
    tion of: 103
Dakotha; synonymy: 750
Damhorst, Joseph: *289*
dams: *391,* 394–396, 474, 599, 600–601, 620,
    709. fish traps: 789. impact of: 387, 391,
    395, 396, 474, 599, 600–601, 823. irrigation:
    814
Dance Flag: *392*
Danemme; synonymy: 904
Daniels, John: *656*
Daniels, Lee: *15*
Dar co tar; synonymy: 750
Datami: 61. synonymy: 969
Datamixes: 61. synonymy: 969
Datekan: 1000, *1000,* 1007
Datŭmpa´ta; synonymy: 924
Daugherty Cave site: *132–133,* 140
Daveko: 932, *933,* 1007
Davin, Nicholas Flood: 319
Davis Creek sites: 176, 177
Dawes Severalty Act (1887): 289–290, 391,
    393, 394, 401, 507, 539, 559–560, 707, 773,
    865
Daychief, George: *323*
Day Child: *294*

Day Walker: *322*
Dead Indian Creek site: *116, 132–133,* 136,
    137, *138,* 142
Dead Indian Land Act (1902) : 290, 291
Deadman Wash phase: 131
Deadman Wash site: *132–133,* 135
Deaf Bull: *289*
Deane, William: *288*
Deapolis site: 350
death practices: 337, 339–340, 362, 408, *688,
    813,* 932. burials: 254, 339–340, 362, 368,
    379, 408, 422, 450, 451, 468, 485, 556, 582,
    588, 646, 704, 726, 786, 810, 872, 895, 932,
    950, 960. cairns: 122, 143, *143,* 151, 155.
    cemeteries: 119, 153, 155, 178, 181, 185,
    224, 225, 232, 254, 353, 368, 474, 525, *647,*
    817. ceremonies: 340, 450, 458, 459, 485,
    491, 536, 556, 588, *588,* 656, 769, 776, 807–
    808, 808, 817, 834, 856, 960, 1024. children:
    950. corpse treatment: 308, 339, 379, 408,
    422, 439, 451, 468, 485, 535, 582, 632, 645,
    704, 810, 872, 960. cremation: 151, 162,
    172, *588,* 726. disposal of property: 340,
    362, 422, 423, 468, 536, 556, 615, 704, 808,
    849, 872, 895, 913, 950, 1024. grave
    monuments: 408, 485, 556, *647, 704,* 846.
    graves and grave goods: 162, 368, 408, 439,
    468, 485, 492, 535–536, 556, 578, 582, 615,
    646, 810, 872, 960. house abandonment and
    destruction: 582, 615, 632. mourners: 340,
    362, 379, 408, 422, 439, 451, 468–469, 492,
    536, 556, 581, 582, 615, 632, 646, 704, 705,
    810, 872, 895, 929, 951, 960, 1024, 1030–
    1031. prehistoric: 118, 119, 120, 122, 123,
    124–125, 126, 127, 128, 129, 142, 150, 151,
    153, 154, 155, 162, 164, 166, 167, 168, 169,
    170, 172, 174, 176, 178, 180, 181, 184, 188,
    201, 208, 209, 213, 216, 224, 225, 228, 230,
    232, 233, 240, 254. purification rites: 950.
    reburial: 178, *691.* relocation of camp: 615.
    sacrifices: 408, 439, 451, 468, 502, 582, 615,
    810, 872, 960. scaffold burials: 254, 353,
    393, 422, 439, 582, 615, 632, 646, 704, *704,*
    726, 810. taboos: 615, 704
Debois-B-ruly; synonymy: 756
Déchêne, Joseph Mirville: *664*
Deckett, Reuben: *290*
De Cora-Dietz, Angel: *773,* 1057
De Cora-Dietz, William: 1057
DeCory, Sam: 994
de Croix, Teodoro: 266
Deep Creek Village site: *197*
Deer Creek site: *173,* 550
Deerfly site: *197*
D'Église, Jacques: 268
DeGrey site: *197*
Dehit; synonymy: 431
Deister site: *160–161*
Delaware; art: 910. ceremonies: 999. external
    relations: 1024. migrations: 271–272.
    museum exhibits: 2. religion: *1006–1007.*
    reservations: 558
Delegation of 1852: *402*
Deleware A phase: 170
Deleware B phase: 170
Delisle, Claude: *722*
Delisle, Guillaume: 518, *722*

Dubois, Verlin: *658*
Duck Chief: *73*
Duffy Village #2 site: *246*
Dulhut, Daniel Greysolon: 301, 573, 720
Dull Knife: 865, *870*
Dull Knife Memorial College: 878, 879
Dumont, Gabriel: 665, 669
Dumoulin, Sévère: 675
Dunbar, John B.: 28, 81, 520
Duncan, Charley: *457*
Duncan site: *147*, 156
Duncan-Wilson site: *160–161,* 171, *210–211*
Dune Buggy site: *235*
Dunlap-McMurry site: *116*, 118
Dunn, Dorothy: 1057
Dupuis, Caville: *294*
Durfee and Peck Co.: 583
Dutisné, Claude-Charles: 24, 264, 550, 563, 566
Duvall, David C.: 35
Dzitsi′stäs; synonymy: 881

E

Eads, Lucy Tayiah: 474
Eagle, Frank: 428
Eagle Chief: *530,* 542, 1038
Eagle Creek site: *160–161,* 166
Eagle Dog: 786
Eagle Feather: *832–833*
Eagle Flying Above: 542
Eagleman, Paul: *649*
Eagle Nose site: *351*
Eagle of Delight: *454*
Eagle plume: *466*
Eagle Robe: 635
Eagles brich Indians: 302
Ear, George: *601*
Ear, Peter: *598–599*
Earchethinues; synonymy: 623, 973
earchithinues; synonymy: 677, 973
Early Plains Archaic period; archeology: 133–136. defined: 131
ear piercing. *See* adornment
earsheadeneys; synonymy: 973
Earthboy, James: 68
Earth Walker: *322*
Eastern Comanches; synonymy: 902
Eastern Shoshone; ceremonies: 988, *990.* external relations: 310, 384, 698, 843, 973. history: 304, 797. horses: 607. hunting: 56. kinship: 981. migrations: 256, 304. reservations: 843. synonymy: 303. trade: 695, 696–697. treaties: 794–795. warfare: 304, 310, 846. wealth: 608
Eastern Swampy Cree language: 638
Eastman, Charles A.: 993, 1072
Eastman, Devere: 993
Eastman, Mary H.: 27, 983
Eastman, Seth: 27, *730, 765*
East Village; synonymy: 363
Ecanazeka: *786*
Eche-has-ka: *699*
Echiwaudah, Tennyson: *1008*
Echo Hawk: *530*
Economic Opportunity Act (1964): 297
1312 economy. *See* employment; trade

Ecueracapa: 262, 893
ʔeda; synonymy: 650
Edmonds, Randlett: 1034
Edmonton Native Communications Society: 649
education: 110, 292, 295, 298, 325, 326, 331, 393, 394, 396–397, 411, 412, 492, 505, 620, 649, 674, 690–692, 782, 825, 829, 853. adult: 824, 825. agricultural: 315, 618, 814. art: 920, 1049, 1050, 1051, 1052, 1056, *1056,* 1056–1059. bicultural: 297, 601, 659. bilingual: 79, 111, 297, 440, 659, 712, *773, 827, 858.* boarding schools: 288–289, 295, 311, 318, 319, 322, 368, 385, 394, 401, 411, 427, 440, 456, 473, 539, 559, 561, 619, 649, 669, 686, 708, 780, 782, 783, 784, 786, 792, 814, 827, *835, 850,* 854, 878, *1056,* 1057. Bureau of Indian Affairs schools: 385, 387, 396. in Canada: 310–313, 318, 319, *320,* 322, 323. Christian: 288, 311, 319, 323, 385, 394, 401, 487, 506, 520, 588, 619, 635, 669, 686, 708, 734, 780, 783, 784, 786, 792, 814, *814,* 850, 854, 856. college: 297, 326–327, 588, 620, 649, *710–711,* 712, 714, 827, 879, 1057. community colleges: 297, 588, 620, 674, 878. community-run schools: 440. day schools: 288. government schools: 783, 1057. Headstart: 877, 879. Indian language: 112, 326–327, 396–397, 474, 588, 649, 659, 714. industrial schools: *73,* 288, *291,* 319, *320,* 323, 385, 401, 427, 442, 539, 814. literacy: 110–111, 442, 478, 734, *773,* 780, 1070, 1072–1073. missionaries and: 311, 319, *320,* 442. mission schools: 288, 311, 319, 323, 385, 394, 401, 487, 506, 520, 588, 619, 635, 669, 686, 708, 734, 780, 783, 784, 786, 792, 814, *814,* 850, 854, 856. Native American Studies: 298–299, 326–327, 396–397, 588, 601, 620, 621, 649, 659, 714, 962, 1057. public schools: 295, 319, 326, 396, 473, 492, 635, 649, 879, 919. reservation and reserve schools: 288, 289, 295, 385, 393, 394, 401, 425, 487, 539, 540, 620, *621,* 635, 782, 793, 814, 827, 850, 877–878, 879, *1056.* treaties and agreements: 520, 618. tribal colleges: 326, 397, 588, 620, 649, 674, 712, 714, 827, 828, 878, 879. tribal schools: *291,* 297, 351, 385, *474,* 588, 601–602, *814,* 827, *835, 858* vocational: 288, 296, *320,* 397, 440, 444, 478, 521, *521,* 539, 559, 600, *773,* 814, *814,* 815, 827, *919*
Edwards I site: *147,* 156, *210–211,* 220, *235,* 242
Edwards II site: 208, *210–211*
Edwards Plateau sites: 149
Edwardsville phase: 165
Eeaiska; synonymy: 602
Ee-ta-si-shov; synonymy: 758
Eeyaythka; synonymy: 602
Egberts, William H.: *31*
Eggan, Fred: 37, 38, *38,* 43
Ehanktonwanna; synonymy: 754
E-hank-to-wana; synonymy: 754
E-hârt′-sâr; synonymy: 716
E-hawn-k'-t'-wawn-nah; synonymy: 754
E-hawn-k'-t'-wawns; synonymy: 754
Eidelbrook site: *188*

18 mile phase: 153
Eirichtih-Äruchpága; synonymy: 861
elderly; care of: 292, 334, 339, 422, 663, 712, 805. domestic role: 341. respect for: 855–856, 878. transport: 811
Elder Osages; synonymy: 495
elders, councils of: 332, 501, *518,* 705
El Dorado phase: 144, 150
Elementary and Secondary Indian Education Act (1972): 297
Elizabeth II: *632*
Elk Head: 817
Elkin, Stanley: 39
Elk Shoulder, Eva: *867*
Ella-causs-se: *699*
Ellis, C. Douglas: 638
Ellis Creek site: *160–161,* 166
Ellsworth, H. E.: 519
Elma Thompson site: *116,* 124
El Ronco: 888
Emessourita; synonymy: 461
Emet. *See* Tonkawa
Emil Afraid-of-Hawk: 111
Emilies I Village site: *246*
Emissourita; synonymy: 461
employment: 292, 293, 297, 396, 397, 412, 428, 444, 459, 586, 622, 657–658, 666, 668, 690, 713, 821–822, 919, 934. casinos: 826. Civilian Conservation Corps: 816, 825, 866. crafts: 774. farming: *285,* 325, 391–393, 396, 398, 442, 486, 619, 635, 636, 668, 690, 713, 825, 850, 853. firefighters: *298.* fishing: 668. forced labor: 707, 792. government: 825, 878, 919. Great Depression and: 293, 474, 825. gristmill: 473. guiding: 282–283, 284, 362, 368, *374,* 384, 386, 502, 521, 549, 568, 600, 666, 668, 955. hauling: 284, 393, 442, 473, 784, 813, 850. hunting: 368, 393. interpreters: 666, 779. logging: 690, 784. mail carriers: *368.* messengers: 393. migrant labor: 652, 879. military: 821, 850–851, 900, 918, 919. mining: 713, 878. post-1960s: 298. professional: 397, 444, 492. ranching: *285,* 393, 396, 442, 473–474, 486, 538, 600, 619, 620, 635, 636, 688, 690, 711, 713, *773,* 780, 782, 784, 825, 853. reservation and reserve: 298, 322, 325, 327, 428, 442, 506, 586, 587–588, 589, 600, 619, 620, 622, 635–636, *658,* 668, 690, 816, 850–851, 853, 878, 879. sawmill: 473. scouts: 281, 780, 900, 943. tourism: 600, 601, 620, 668, 826, 1054, 1056. training: 288, 296, *320,* 397, 428, 440, 444, 478, 521, *521,* 539, 559, 600, *773,* 814, *814,* 815, 827, *919* trapping: 305, 657, 774. tribal system: 428. wage work: 284, 325, 442, 444, 473, 635, 652, 657, 668, 686, 774, 784, 815–816, 816, 824, 825, 852. white-collar: 657, 690. women: 690. woodcutting: 393, 411, 774, 813, 850. Works Progress Administration: 866
ʔená; synonymy: 650
Ena-sa; synonymy: 345
E-na-ta; synonymy: 345
Enemy Heart: 386, 1012
Enemy Heart, Winnie: 386
Enepiah(o)es; synonymy: 963
Energy Park site: *223, 232*

Gibbon, John: 797

gíćaži; synonymy: 570

gift exchange: 300, 397, *454*, 549–550, 686, 711, 784, 1012, 1048, 1053. adoption ceremony: 379, 538. and authority: 405. ear-piercing: 378. between friends: 809. marriage: 809, 849, 850, 1053. wedding: 361–362, 379, 408, 422, 439, 451, 468, 485, 502, 535, 536, 555, 582, 614, 631, 646, 682, 686, 711, 726, 871, 895, 929, 949–950, 960

gifts: 502, 872, *980*, 1023, 1048, 1070. birth: 895. at ceremonies: 689, 932. funeral: 960. from war parties: 893. from Whites: 264, 266, 268, 331, 499, 503, 504, 567, 569, 678, 732, 733, 795, 888, 891, 943. *See also* ceremonies, disposition of goods at

Giglio, Virginia: *1031*

Gihchaitsá; synonymy: 716

Gilder, Robert F.: 14

Gill, DeLancey: 28

Gillette, Maude: *372*

Gillette Village site: *197, 246*

Gillett Grove site: *223*, 232

Gillingham, T. T.: 401

Gilmore, G. H.: 15

Gilmore, Melvin R.: 36, *36*, 81

Gilpin, Lawrence: *1017*

gimǎ·čiš; synonymy: 902

Gingras, Antoine: 667

Giroux, Léonidas Alcidas: *664*

giveaways: 394, *395*, 397, *397*, 429, *429*, 458, 459, 473, *489*, 492, 510, 556, 579, 586, 588, *588, 612, 621*, 686, *688*, 689, 692, 702, 704, 708, *710–711*, 711, 790, 791, *792*, 808, *813*, 815, 829, *837*, 844, 850, 856, *859*, 877, 920, *936–937, 984–985*, 1013, 1023–1024, 1025, 1053

Gladstone, James: 324, *324, 612*

Glass, Anthony: 25

glass, beads: 230, 233, *263*, 355, 372, 583, 610, *656*, 790, 1039–1041

Glasscock site: *235*

Glass site: *210–211*, 217

Glen Elder site: *173*, 176, 177–178

Glenmore, Ava Moss: *980*

Glenmore, Mylan, Jr.: *980*

Glenmore, Mylan, Sr.: *980*

Goddard, Pliny E.: 34

Godlp'äk'i; synonymy: 751

Goes Ahead, Carlson: *703*

Goes Along Good: *392*

Goff, Orlando Scott: 28

Gofroth, Ernest: *322*

Goggles, Ben, Jr.: *859*

Goggles, Merle: *859*

Goinkee, Sarah Longhorn: *936–937*

Gokey, Olin: *511*

Golden Eagle: *980*

*gołdi*ⁿ*di²į·lí;* synonymy: 951

gołgaʰį; synonymy: 951

Gone, Fred P.: 42

gonįčé²íšįna; synonymy: 564

Gonzalez, Joyce: *961*

Good Assiniboine: *392*

Good Bear: *392*

Goodbear, Paul: 1059

1316 Goodbird, Charles: 290

Goodbird, Edward: *333*

Goodbird, Emery, Sr.: *397*

Goodbird, John: *395*

Goodbird, Mrs.: *395*

Goodbird, Raymond: *34*

Good Chief: *529*

Gooderham, George H.: *323*

Goodman site: *160–161*

Goodman I site: 171, *210–211*

Goodman II site: *210–211*

Good Medicine Pipe: *699*

Goodwin-Baker site: *147, 157*

Good Worker: *392*

Goon-saudl-te: *917*

Gore Pit site: *147*, 149

Gothier site: *223*

gouges, prehistoric: 129, 149, 150, 152, 153, 154, 168

Gouladdle, Horace: *921*

Gouladdle, John: *921*

Gould Ruins site: *210–211*, 216

Goulet, Louis: 673

government. *See* Canada, government of; political organization; United States government

Governor Joe: *483*

Gowen 1 and 2 sites: *116*, 117, 118

goži; synonymy: 624

Grady, Charles: *288*

Graham, Andrew: 303

Graham, William Morris: 320, *322*

Graham Ossuary site: *173*, 179

Granby site: *132–133*

Grand Detour phase: 188, 192

Grand(es) Eaux; synonymy: 495

Grandes Osage; synonymy: 495

Grandmother's Lodge site: *186–187*

Grand Osage: 269. synonymy: 495

Grand Osarge; synonymy: 495

Grand Pana; synonymy: 545

Grand par; synonymy: 545

Grand Pawnee; synonymy: 545

Grands; synonymy: 545

Grands Osage; synonymy: 495

Grands Parleurs; synonymy: 967

Grand Tuc; synonymy: 495

Grand Zo; synonymy: 495

Graneros phase: 234

Granny Two Hearts site: *197*

Grant, Cuthbert, Jr.: 307, 308, 664

Grant, Ulysses S.: 281, 351, 368, 391, 506, 521

Grant site: *210–211, 212, 213, 223*

Grass, John: 786

Grasshopper Falls phase: 167–168

Grattan, John L.: 795

gravers, prehistoric: 119, 120, 124, 224

Gray site: *116*, 119, *173*, 185

Great Belly Indians; synonymy: 345, 693

Great Bend phase: 183–185, 220, 245, 246, 250–251, 548

Great Chief: *420*

Great Oasis phase: 186, 190, 222, 224–226

Great Oasis site: 224

Great Os(s)age; synonymy: 495

Great Ozages; synonymy: 495

Greatwalker, Joseph: *1014–1015*

Green, Albert: 455

Greenbelt site: *147*

Green Horn: 262

Greenwood phase: 165

Gregg, Josiah: 83

Gregg site: *197*

Griffin, Victor: 507, 509

Griffing site: *173*, 180

grinding implements: 149, 150. basins: 208, 209, 211, 214, 218, 239. hammers: 119, 120, 149, *162*, 171, 183, 189, 211, 214, 218, 224. manos: 134, 137, 138, 140, 141, *141*, 152–153, 157, 208, 209, 211, *213*, 214, 218, 224, 228, 229, 239. metates: 137, 138, 140, 141, *141*, 152–153, 157, 208, 211, 224, 229, 239, 241. mortar and pestle: *59*, 154, 211, 368, 372, *372*, 419, 436, *525*, 527, *553*, 789. mullers: 181, 211. prehistoric: 134, 137, 141, *141*, 149, 150, 151, 152–153, 153, 154, 155, 157, *162*, 164–165, 166, 168, 169, 171, 174, 176, 181, 183, 208, 211, *213*, 214, 218, 224, 228, 239, 241. slabs: 134, 166, 169, 171, 181, 183, 241. stones: 141, 150, 151, 153, 155, *162*, 164, 166, 168, 169, 171, 183

Grinnell, George Bird: 32, *33*

Griva, Edward M.: 94

Grorud, A. A.: *294*

Grosbeck, Felix: *859*

Groseilliers, Médard Chouart, sieur des: 256, 300, 722

Gross Vintres; synonymy: 345

Gros Ventre: *294*, 583, 585, 677–694. agriculture: 685. alliances: 604, 678, 842. allotment: 689, 690. annual cycle: 678, 679. art: *679*, 680, *680*, 683, 685, *687*, 1046, 1047. bands: 681–682, 694. ceremonies: 586–587, 679, *681*, 683, 684, 685–686, 687, *687*, 687–688, *688*, 688–689, 690, *691*, 692, 983, 988, 996, 1001, 1012, 1025. clothing and adornment: 680, *681*, *687* contact: 24, 27, 28, 267–268, 678. curing: 683–684, *684*–685, 686, 688. death practices: *688*. disease: 304, 678. economy: 686, 688, 689–690, 690–692. education: 686, 687–688, 690–691, 690–692. external relations: 270, 283, 305, 573, 575, 678, 686–687. firearms: 268. games: 587, 1025. health care: *691*. history: 303, 677–678, 678, 685–690, 686. kinship: 682, 978. migrations: 256, 304, 604, 677, 678, 679. music and dance: 685, *687*, 692, *1029*. mythology: 682, 683, 1065. origins: 256. political organization: 589, 679, *679*, *681*, 683–684, 685, 687, 689, *689*, 690–692. population: 690, 692. religion: 292, 682–684, 685–686, 687–688, 692, 1001. reservations and reserves: 283, 677, 678, 685–686, 685–692, 689–690, 690–692. social organization: 5, 12, 679, 681–682, 685, 686, 688–689. societies: 683–684, *684*, 685, *687*, 1012, 1051. structures: 679, *680*, 682, 686, *687*. subsistence: 678, 679–680, 686. synonymy: 303, 344, 345, 677, 692–694, 973. territory: 289, 677, *677*, 678, 686, 687. trade: 268, 574, 617, 678. treaties: 280, 618, 678, 685. warfare: 283, 304, 305, 574, 575, 640, 652, 677, 678, 679, 685, *689*, 697, 797, 842. wealth: 678–679, 688, 690

Gros Ventre, William: *711*

1321

786, 794–795. villages: 247, 249, *330*, 331, 349–350, *351*, 353. warfare: 281, 362, 641, 731, 734. *See also* Three Affiliated Tribes
Mandan, Arthur: *392*
Mandani; synonymy: 363
Mandan Lake site: *246*
Mandan language: 349. borrowings: 109. characteristics: 103–104, 107. classification of: 102, 103. comparative vocabulary: 63, 64–66, 67. dialects: 95, 349. education: 110, 112. historical changes: 63, 67. history of: 63, 67, 95. hymns: 95. phonology: 63–67, 103, 106, 349. preservation of: 112, *291*. studies on: 95–96. survival: 112
Mandanne; synonymy: 363
Mandas, migrations: 329
Mandeouacantons; synonymy: 752
Mandians; synonymy: 363
Ma-ne-to-par; synonymy: 593
Mangus site: *132–133*
Manihaut; synonymy: 966
Manitarres; synonymy: 345
Manitoba Act of 1870: 665, 668
Manitoba Métis Foundation: 661
Manouri, Charles: *392*
Manrhoat; synonymy: 966. trade: 927
Manrhout; synonymy: 966
Manruth; synonymy: 966
Mantannes; synonymy: 363
Mantons; synonymy: 363, 566
Mantou; synonymy: 566
Manwell site: *210–211*, 219
Man Who Took the Coat: 585, 586
Man With Legs Wide Apart: *779*
Many Bears: *260*
Many Bears, Al: 622
Many Growths: *339*
Many Guns: *612*
Many Hides, Philip: *621*
Many Horses: 618, 635
Many Lodges; synonymy: 716
Manypenny, George: 280
Many Wounds: *632*
Mapleleaf site: *116*
Maquetantala; synonymy: 460
Marais des Cygnes Post: *259,* 270
mar-an-sho-bish-ko; synonymy: 751
Marcy, Randolph B.: 569
Marest, Gabriel: 517
Marhout; synonymy: 966
Marion, Narcisse: 663, 665
Marion, Roger: 666
Markle, W.A.: 320
Marlain Indians; synonymy: 860
Marlin; synonymy: 860
Marquette, Jacques: 256, 399, 447, 462, 497–498, 499, 500, 517
Marquette, Pierre: 23
marriage: 306, 339–340, 361–362, 379, 407–408. adultery: 339, 379, 408, 424, 440, 485, 582, 632, 646, 704, 726, 766, 808, 849, 950, 960. age at: 339, 422, 467, 484–485, 555, 582, 726, 895. arranged: 339, 361, 408, 439, 451, 484, 490, 535, 555, 569, 614, 655, 682, 686, 703, 849, 850, 929, 949–950. betrothal: 379. bride price: 277, 304, 339, 379, 439, 451, 614, 686, 703, 782, 871. ceremonies:
361–362, 408, 422, 439, 451, 468, 485, *486,* 502, 555, 588, 646, 682. chastity: 703. courtship: 407–408, 422, 467–468, 535, 582, 614, 631, 646, 703, 726, 809, 871, *873,* 895, 1053. cross-cousin: 645–646, 978. divorce: 306, 339, 408, 422, 439, 468, 485, 555, 582, 614–615, 632, 646, 655, 704, 726, 766, 809–810, 849, 871, 895, 950, 959, 960, 1035. elopement: 408, 451, 703, 766, 849, 850, 929. endogamous: 332, 530. exogamous: 405, 407, 436, 449, 485, 614, 630, 681, 701, 711, 735, 766, 801, 809, 896. and fur trade: 277. gifts: 361–362, 379, 408, 422, 439, 451, 468, 485, 502, 535, 536, 555, 582, 614, 631, 646, 682, 686, 726, 809, 849, 850, 871, 895, 929, 949–950, 960, 1053. incest: 681–682, 929. intermarriage: 276, 277, 281, 297, 302, 305–307, 306, *307,* 311, 349, 350, 351, 398, 401, 462, 464, 486, 490, 506, 510, 572, 583, 618, 622, 638, 652, 657, 661–662, 663, 720, 729, 730–731, 734, 756, 772, 865, 879, 888, 943, 962, 1048. levirate: 337, 379, 422, 468, 485, 536, 569, 614, 631, 766, 809, 849, 910, 929, 950. monogamy: 451, 766. polyandry: 535, 569, 977. polygamy: 766. polygyny: 338, 339, 379, 399, 407, 411, 438, 451, 468, 485, 569, 614, 631, 682, 686, 726, 782, 784, 809, 849, 850, 871, 894, 910, 959, 978, 981. purchase: 809. qualifications for: 341, 485, 535, 579, 614, 682, 703, 726, 809, 871, 895, 1049. remarriage: 337, 536, 582, 766, 849, 871, 929. reservation and reserve: 541, 686, 818, 850. residence: 338, 362, 378, 451, 468, 478, 485, 534, 535, 555, 569, 582, 614, 630, 655, 681, 703, 735, 809, 849, 854, 871, 872–873, 911, 949, 975, 977, 978. sororate: 338, 362, 378, 407, 422, 438, 533, 555, 569, 582, 614, 631, 703–704, 766, 809, 849, 910, 929, 950, 959. taboos: 338, 439, 614. and trade: 661–662. widowhood: 468, 536, 582, 663, 766, 929. wife exchange: 646, 663, 809
Marriott, Alice L.: 38
Marsh, John: 97
Martín, Hernando: 966
Mar-too-ton-ha; synonymy: 364
Marty, Martin: 786
Mary Day Sun site: *197*
Mascouteins Nadouessi; synonymy: 756
Mascouten; synonymy: 756. warfare: 434
Mascoute(i)ns nadoessi; synonymy: 446
Mascoutens-Nadouessians; synonymy: 756
Mascoutens Nadouessioux; synonymy: 446
Mash Creek site: *246*
Maskepetoon: 309, 310
Masketo: *584–585*
maškote-aniššina·pe·; synonymy: 659
masks: *580, 833.* shell: 230, 232
Maskwa: *39*
Masohan; synonymy: 460
Mason, Otis T.: 2, *3,* 5
massasauga; synonymy: 749
Massourites; synonymy: 461
maštíca oyate; synonymy: 650
maštíca wicʰaša; synonymy: 650
Mathers, Charles W.: 28
mato-htata; synonymy: 460
matoʔkata; synonymy: 460
Matootonha; synonymy: 364
Ma-too-ton-ka; synonymy: 364
mató tópa: 27
Mato-tope: *354*
Matoutenta; synonymy: 460
Mattaugwessawacks; synonymy: 749
Matteson, Sumner: 28, *29*
Matthews, Washington: 28, 95, 347
máttowe; synonymy: 566
mauls, prehistoric: 183, 189, 199, 200, 224, 228, 229
Maurie, James R.: 91
Mavrakais-Bentzen-Roberts site: *132–133*
Maw-dân; synonymy: 363
Mawtawbauntowahs; synonymy: 752
Maxaxa; synonymy: 347
Maxent, Laclède and Co.: 266
Maximilian, Prince of Wied-Neuwied: 26, 74, 80–81, 94, 95, 98, 100, 101, 102, *262,* 347, 350, *354,* 364, 367, 377, 700
maxíriwiac: 34
Maxon Ranch site: *132–133*
maxpíato; synonymy: 860
maxpiattą; synonymy: 860
maxpiattu; synonymy: 860, 924
maxpíyatʰo; synonymy: 860
Max Thomas site: *210–211*
máxude; synonymy: 446
Maye(c)es; synonymy: 963
Mayer, Frank Blackwell: 27, *672–673*
Mayes; synonymy: 963
Mayeye; synonymy: 963. *See also* Tonkawa
Mayoahc; synonymy: 966
Mazzakootemanee: *771*
Mazzomanee: *771*
M'daywawkawntwawns; synonymy: 752
Mdewakanton; synonymy: 752. *See also* Santee Sioux
Mdewakantonwan-nan; synonymy: 752
Mead, Margaret: 38
Meandans; synonymy: 363
Meander site: *197*
Means, Russell: 835
Mechkadewikonaié: *308*
Mecoethinnuuck; synonymy: 624
Medawakantons; synonymy: 752
Medawakantwan; synonymy: 752
Me-da-we-con-tong; synonymy: 752
Med-ay-wah-kawn-t'waw; synonymy: 752
Mede-wakant'wan; synonymy: 752
Medford Ranch site: *210–211*
Medicine, Beatrice: 994
Medicine, John: 509
Medicine Bear: 781, 786, 787, 788, 791
Medicine Creek sites: 51, 59–60, *175,* 176, 177, *177, 179, 197,* 203
Medicine Crow: *710–711*
Medicine Crow, Joseph: 712, 994, 1067
Medicine Crow site: *132–133,* 145, *246*
Medicine Horse: 455
Medicine Knoll site: *197*
Medicine Lodge Creek site: 131–133, *132–133, 133, 133,* 134, 139
Medicine Lodge Creek Treaty (1867): 282
Medicine Rocks: *259*
Medicine Stone, Darcy: *397*
Medicine Tail: *709*

Mediwanktons; synonymy: 752
Meehan-Schell site: *223, 224*
Mee-ne-cow-e-gee; synonymy: 757
Meethno-thinyoowuc; synonymy: 624
Meghey; synonymy: 963
Meghty; synonymy: 963
Mehoja, Jesse: *466*
Mehojah family: 474
Meihites; synonymy: 963
Meintens; synonymy: 566
Mekeel, H. Scudder: 38
Meldrum, Robert: 695
Melhagen site: *116,* 124
Melody, G. H. C.: 440, *442*
Memacanjo; synonymy: 757
me·mahkate·wanasite·ha; synonymy: 623
men; activities: 340–341, 534. art styles: 9.
  clothing: *331,* 340, 353, *354, 355,* 373, *373,*
  404, *420, 426, 441, 452, 455,* 464–465, *465,*
  479, 501, 527–528, *529, 553,* 553–554, *570,*
  583, 584–585, 587, 610, *611, 613,* 643, *644,*
  655, 670, 672–673, 680, *681,* 700, *701, 730,*
  732, 760, 765, 766, 779, *784, 787,* 790, *803,*
  810, 868, *870,* 891. domestic role: 338.
  societies: 5–6, 10, 34, 35, *376, 401,* 410–
  411, 423–424, 597, 633, 655, 844–846, 850,
  875, 876, 879, 893, 912–913, 931, 935, 977,
  978, 998, 1036. warfare: 10. *See also*
  division of labor
Ménard (French trader): 268
Menard-Hodges site: 497
Menchokatonx; synonymy: 752
Menchokatoux; synonymy: 752
Mencouacantons; synonymy: 752
Mendanne; synonymy: 363
Mendeouacantons; synonymy: 752
Mendewacantongs; synonymy: 752
Mende Wahkan toan; synonymy: 752
Mendewakantoan; synonymy: 752
Mende-Wakan-Toann; synonymy: 752
Mendouca-ton; synonymy: 752
Mendoza, Domíngues de: 966
Me-ne-tar-re; synonymy: 345
Me-ne-tar-re Me-te-har-tar; synonymy: 346
Men-i-cou-zha; synonymy: 757
Menitares; synonymy: 345
Mennetarries; synonymy: 345
Mennitarris; synonymy: 345
Men of the River; synonymy: 753
Menoken site: *186–187*
Menominee; ceremonies: 998. external
  relations: 761. synonymy: 750
Menowa Kautong; synonymy: 752
menstrual practices: 682. restrictions: 420, 422,
  555. ritual observances: 451, 769. seclusion:
  535, 582, 646, 707, 809, 849, 871, 895, 960,
  1050. taboos: 960. *See also* puberty;
  structures, menstrual
Mento; synonymy: 566
Mentous; synonymy: 566
Mercredi, Tony: *324*
Merill, Moses: 454
Merriam v. *Jicarilla Apache Tribe:* 297
Merrick, Eustace: *898*
Merrill, Moses: 454
Merritt, Wesley: 799
Mescalero Apache; alliances: 926, 928.

religion: 951. territory: 886. warfare: 943,
  944
Messorites; synonymy: 461
metal: 908. adornment with: 124–125, 129,
  252, *263, 283, 405, 420, 438,* 464, 465, *465,*
  479, *480, 482, 483, 493,* 530, *570,* 583, *611,*
  612, 634, 656, 728–729, *765, 766,* 779, *784,*
  810, 891, *892,* 909, *910, 914,* 948, 949, 958,
  959, 1044–1045. beads: 124–125, 129, *263,*
  341, 342, 656. introduction of: 252, 329–
  331, 847, 1044, 1045, 1048. tools: *8–9, 10–*
  11, 228, 303, 1044, 1045, 1048. trade: 123,
  172, 189
Metcalf, George S.: *20*
Métchif; synonymy: 71
Métif; synonymy: 71, 675
métif; synonymy: 675
Métis. *See* Plains Métis
Métis Association of Alberta: 648, *664,* 666
Métis National Accord: 674
meto·htat; synonymy: 460
Me-too´-ta-häk; synonymy: 363
Metotantes; synonymy: 460
Métsai; synonymy: 905
Metutahanke; synonymy: 363
Métutahanke; synonymy: 364
MévavEheo²o; synonymy: 963
Mévaveo²o; synonymy: 963
Mexican Boundary Commission: 26
Mexican period. *See* History
Mexkemauastan: *679*
Méye; synonymy: 963
Meyer, Julius: *795*
Meyer site: *197*
Miami; ceremonies: 996. history: 996. warfare:
  434
Michif. *See* Mitchif
Micoby, Maude: *936–937*
Middle Park sites: 143
Middleton, Frederick D.: 665
Midewakantonwans; synonymy: 752
Miditadi; synonymy: 345
Midway site: *223*
Midwestern Taxonomic System: 15, 17
migrations: 281, 657. historic: 61, 80, 81, 83,
  94, 95, 96, 97, 100, 102, 312, 315, *662.*
  leadership: 802. prehistoric: 61, 80, 171, 183,
  196, 201, 205, 206, 220, 222, 229, 233, 234,
  239, 243, 974. protohistoric: 245, 256, 261,
  302, 304, 305–306. seasonal: 60, 156, 170,
  248, 300, 353, 368–369, 371, 403, 448, 464,
  477, 479, 526, 609–610, 629, 662, 678, 679,
  721, 724, 725, 767, 779, 802, 847, 849, 854
Miguel: 549
mihko·wiyiniw; synonymy: 624
Míhtichare; synonymy: 346
Mih-Tutta-Hangkusch; synonymy: 364
Mike: *786*
Miles, George: *957*
Miles, Nelson A.: 788, 799, 812
Milford site: 232
Mill Creek phase: 186, 192, 222, 226–228
Miller, Alfred Jacob: 26
Miller, George: *406*
Miller, Mr. and Mrs.: *554*
Millford site: *223*
milling; carpet mills: 711. gristmills: 454, 473.

sawmills: 454, 473, 599, 779, 784, 786, 878
Mills, Anson: 799
mi·mi·maxpâ·ge; synonymy: 602
Mindawarcarton; synonymy: 752
Mindewacantons; synonymy: 752
Minecogue; synonymy: 757
Minecosias; synonymy: 757
MineKanhini-yojou; synonymy: 757
Mi-ne-kaŋ´-žūs; synonymy: 757
minésepēre; synonymy: 716
Mine-set-peri; synonymy: 715
Mĭnĕsupĕ´rik; synonymy: 715
Minetare language, classification of: 102
Minetaries of Fort de Prairie; synonymy: 693
Minican-hiniyojou; synonymy: 757
Minican-hojou; synonymy: 757
Mini-con-gaha; synonymy: 757
Miniconjou Sioux: 97
Minicoughas; synonymy: 757
Mini-kan-jous; synonymy: 757
Minikanoju; synonymy: 757
Minikanye oju; synonymy: 757
Minikanyes; synonymy: 757
mínikʰąyewožupi; synonymy: 757
mínikʰóožu; synonymy: 757
Minikiniad-za; synonymy: 757
mining: 48, 49, *50,* 366, 435, 506, 720. coal:
  712–713. gold: 585. gold rushes: 282, 618,
  687, 734, 797, 842. lead: 506, 508. stone:
  774, 792, 793. zinc: 508, 1013
Minitari; synonymy: 344, 345
Minnake-noz(z)o; synonymy: 757
Minneapolis site: 180
Minnecarguis; synonymy: 757
Minnecaushas; synonymy: 757
Minnecogoux; synonymy: 757
Minnecongew; synonymy: 757
Minnecongou; synonymy: 757
Minneconjou Sioux: 97. synonymy: 757. *See*
  also Teton Sioux
Minneconjoux; synonymy: 757
Minne Con-ojus; synonymy: 757
Minne Coujou(x) Sioux; synonymy: 757
Minnecowzues; synonymy: 757
Minneh-sup-pay-deh; synonymy: 715
Min-ne-kaŋ´-zu; synonymy: 757
Minnekonjo; synonymy: 757
Minnetarees of the Prairie; synonymy: 693
Minnicongew; synonymy: 757
Minnikan-jous; synonymy: 757
Minnitarees; synonymy: 345
Minnitarees Metaharta: 345. synonymy: 346
Minnitarees of the Willows: 345
Minnitarries of the north; synonymy: 693
Minowakanton; synonymy: 752
Minoway-Kantong; synonymy: 752
Minoway-Kautong; synonymy: 752
Minow Kantong; synonymy: 752
Miró, Esteban Rodriguez: 366, 519, 543
mi´sis; synonymy: 883
Misquoeninnewog; synonymy: 624
missionaries: 28, 74, 81, 97–98, 110, *279,* 287,
  288, 292, 310–311, 311, 313–314, 318–319,
  320, 331, 359, 391, 734, 770, *773,* 852, 934,
  965, 988, 1072. Anglican: 311, 635, 638,
  648, 877. Baptist: 275, 471, 478, 561, 917,
  937. Church of England: 311. Congrega-

Ghost Dance songs: 1034. Grass Dance songs: 1037. hand game songs: 1024–1025, 1033, 1034, 1036. hunting songs: 1030. hymns: *74, 91,* 92, 95, 110, 114, 597, 669, 899, 1030. and language survival: 113, 114. love songs: 1030, 1031–1032. lullabies: 1030. medicine songs: 1032–1033, *1033.* men's societies songs: 1036. mourning songs: 1030–1031. mystery songs: 1030. name songs: 451. Native American Church/Peyote songs: 1034–1035. Omaha Dance songs: 1037. power songs: 1035. prayer songs: 1035. recordings of: *36,* 81, 82. rhythms: 1018, 1034, 1037. songs: 336, 375, 386, 429, 451, 485, 509, 542, 581, 587, 616, 633, 634, 668, 684, 685, *687,* 692, 790, 818, 829, 984, 994, 997, 998, 1001, 1003, 1004, 1005, *1008,* 1009, 1010, 1011, 1012, 1018, 1019, 1024, 1026, 1028, 1029, 1030–1031, *1032.* songs of thankfulness: 1026, 1030. song types: 1030–1038. story songs: 1032. Sun Dance songs: 1034. as symbol of identity: 92. War Dance songs: 1037–1038. war songs: 581, 1035–1036, 1037. woman songs: 1030

musical instruments: 375, 869–870, 1028–1030, 1034. Apache violins/fiddles: 1028. bells: 1012, 1013, 1029. construction and materials: *872.* drums: *30,* 357, 359, *380, 381, 401, 413,* 442, 466, *489,* 502, *587, 590, 598–599, 617, 621, 656,* 692, *709, 759,* 790, *834,* 869, *872,* 958, 961, *961, 986, 991, 997,* 998, 999, 1005, *1006–1007, 1008,* 1009, 1012, 1015, 1016, *1017,* 1018, 1023, 1026, *1026–1027,* 1028, 1029, 1037. European: 671, *673.* flageolets: 703, 870. flutes: 466, 502, *503,* 1028, *1029,* 1044. prehistoric: 208. rasps: 961, 1012, 1029. rattles: *27, 401,* 424, *444,* 466–467, *469,* 502, *508,* 617, 684, *687,* 727, *759,* 790, *834, 844–845,* 869, 946, 958, 961, *961, 1006–1007, 1008,* 1009, 1019, *1021,* 1028–1029, *1029, 1033,* 1036. striking sticks: 1028–1029. whistles: *27,* 424, *687,* 707, *844–845, 990, 1006–1007, 1029,* 1030

Muskogean language: 85. classification of: 105

Mustang Springs site: *147,* 149

muʹtsanɛ; synonymy: 905

Mutsha; synonymy: 905

Mútsíănă-tăníu; synonymy: 940

Muvinábore; synonymy: 905

Muvínavore; synonymy: 905

Muzzahshaw: *771*

Myer, Dillon S.: 296

Myer, William E.: 14, 15, 33

Myers-Hindman site: *132–133,* 139

mythology: 337, 356–357, 420, 449, 450, *617,* 727, 789, 1064. Buffalo Cow Pipe: 799. Buffalo People: 356. Buffalo Wife: 1051. Changing Woman: 951. Charred Body: 338, 1066. Chief Above: 379, 381, 1065. Cold: 1064. Corn Husk Earrings: 356. Corn People: 356, 1066. Coyote: 931, 932, 1064. Crazy Bull: 1064. creation: 337, 356, 423, 469, 530, 557, 616, 633, 646, 683, 707, 794, 892, 951. Double Woman: 1052. earth-diver: 1065. Earthmaker: 683, 1065. Exodus: 337. Fire Boy: 931–932. First Creator: 337, 338, 356, 1065, 1066. First Man: 706. First

Woman: 706. Flat Pipe: 843, 1065. floods: 557. Good Furred Robe: 356, 1066. Great Holy One: 381. Great Spirit: 557, 1065. Helldiver: 706. He Who Starved To Death: 683. Iktomi: 1064. Inktomi: 579. *isčkíkʰeː* 409. *ištínikʰeː* 409. Iya: 1064. Killer of Enemies: 951. Lodge Boy: 338, 1066. Lone Man: 337, 356, 357, *392,* 1066. Long Arm: 336. Man Never Known on Earth: 557. Man Whistles: 683. *m̥sčiŋe:* 409. Morning Star: 707. Mother Corn: 379, 381, 1065. Napi: 1065. Nihahat: 1065. Nih'atah: 682, 683. Nuakolahe: 931. Old Man: 706, 1065. Old Man Coyote: 706, 1065. Old Woman Who Never Dies: 336, 356. origin myths: 10, 336, 356, 359, 379–380, 383, 706, 794, 799, 803, 806–807, 843, 892, 961–962, 974, 977, 987, 1062–1063, 1065–1066, 1067. Our Father Above: 381. Rabbit: 409. Sacred Arrows: 337, 338, 340, 863, 873, 875, 1064, 1066. Sendeh: 915. songs: 1032. Spider Old Woman: 913, 915. spirits: 1065. Split Boys: 913, 915. Spring Boy: 336, 338, 1066. Star Husband: 913, 1066. Sun: 706. Sweet Medicine: 863, 873, 875. Tirawahat: 1066. tobacco: 356. tricksters: 10, 409. Turtle: 1065. Twin Boys: 987. Twins: 1066. Uses His Head for a Rattle: 356. Village Old Woman: 337. Wakanda: 480. Wakan Tanka: 1065. Water Boy: 931–932. Whirlwind Woman: 1051. White Buffalo Woman: 799, 1071, *1071.* White men: *706.* Witch: 1064. Yellow-Haired girl: 874. *See also* cosmology; oral tradition; supernatural beings

N

Nâ. câ. rê kâ; synonymy: 389

naatání; synonymy: 903

Nabedache, alliances: 567

Nacion qu'on nomme du Boeuf; synonymy: 750

Nacoghoche, alliances: 567

Na-co-ta Mah-ta-pa-nar-to; synonymy: 593

Na-co-ta O-ee-gah; synonymy: 593

Nad8echi8ec; synonymy: 749

Nad8esseronons sédentaires; synonymy: 752

Naddouwessces; synonymy: 749

Naddouwessiou; synonymy: 749

Nadeicha; synonymy: 938

nạdíʔị·šạ·; synonymy: 938

naʔdíʔįšáʔ; synonymy: 938

Nadîsha-déna; synonymy: 938

Nadioussioux; synonymy: 749

Nadoessious; synonymy: 749

Nadonaisioug; synonymy: 749

Nadonechiouk; synonymy: 749

Nadonessis; synonymy: 749

Nadooessis of the Plains; synonymy: 756

Nadouags; synonymy: 749

Nadouagssioux; synonymy: 749

Nadouaissious; synonymy: 749

Nadouaissioux; synonymy: 749

Nadouayssioux; synonymy: 749

Nadouechiouek; synonymy: 749

Nadoüechiowec; synonymy: 749

Nadoüecious; synonymy: 749

Nadouesans; synonymy: 749

Nadouesciouz; synonymy: 749

Nadouesiouek; synonymy: 749

Nadouesioux; synonymy: 749

Nadouessans; synonymy: 749

Nadouessies; synonymy: 749

Nadouessi maskoutens; synonymy: 446

Nadoüessioüak; synonymy: 749

Nadouessiouek; synonymy: 749

Nadouessious; synonymy: 749

Nadouessioux; synonymy: 749

Nadoüessis; synonymy: 749

Nadouessons; synonymy: 749

Nadoussians; synonymy: 749

Nadoussiens; synonymy: 749

Nadoussieux; synonymy: 749

Nadouwesis; synonymy: 749

Nadowassis; synonymy: 749

Nadsnessiouck; synonymy: 749

Naduesiu; synonymy: 572

Nadvesiv; synonymy: 749

Nadwechiwec; synonymy: 749

na-e-ca; synonymy: 938

náʔ̯ɛša; synonymy: 938

Nagle, Mrs. John: *392*

Nahcotah; synonymy: 750

Nahkawe·wiyiniwak; synonymy: 659

Nahkawiyiniwak; synonymy: 659

Nahokáhta; synonymy: 389

náhtovonaho; synonymy: 752

nAhuukaátA; synonymy: 389

Nailati phase: 188, 192, 193

náʔị·ša; synonymy: 938

nạʔišá; synonymy: 938

Naʹisha; synonymy: 938

Na-i-shan-dina; synonymy: 938

Na-ishi Apache; synonymy: 938

Naitanes; synonymy: 903

Naʹ-izhăʹñ; synonymy: 951

Nakaásh: *986*

na·karíkA; synonymy: 389

Nakasinéna; synonymy: 862

na-ka-siʹ-nin; synonymy: 862

Nakhaseinena: 840

nakʰóta; synonymy: 592, 602, 750

nakʰóta wičʰjčana; synonymy: 593

nakkawininiwak; synonymy: 659

Nakoda; synonymy: 602

nakóda iyéθka; synonymy: 602

Nakota; synonymy: 718

námasɛnɛ; synonymy: 905

names: 407, 439, 451. additional: 386, 631. ceremonies for: 386, 407, 422, 449, 451, 467, 485, 492, 502, 507, 588, 613, 692. of deceased: 960. native-language: 92, 492. nicknames: 451

Nänăbineʹnaⁿ; synonymy: 862

Naʹnita; synonymy: 903

Năⁿk'hăaⁿsēineʹnaⁿ; synonymy: 862

Năⁿwaçinähăⁱᵃ̈ænaⁿ; synonymy: 861

Naⁿwuineʹnaⁿ; synonymy: 861

Napao site: *116*

napɫwa·htɫ; synonymy: 905

Napuat No Shoes; synonymy: 905

Narcotah; synonymy: 750

Nardichia; synonymy: 938

Nash, Philleo: 297

1331

Naskapi, museum exhibits: 2
Nasseniboines; synonymy: 591
ná·ta·ʔáh; synonymy: 903
Natagé: 926
natara·kó·čI; synonymy: 388
Natchez language: 85, 105
Natchininga: *443*
Natchitoches: *259,* 266, 270
Natenéhima; synonymy: 749
Nat-e-ne´-hin-a; synonymy: 749
Natewa, Bob: *1032*
National Congress of American Indians: 295,
    296, 835
National Indian Brotherhood: 328
National Indian Youth Council: 428
National Museum of the American Indian Act
    of 1989: 22
nation du Corbeau; synonymy: 714
Nation of Braux Hommes: 303
Nation of the Beef; synonymy: 750
Native Action: 878
Native American Educational Services College:
    588
Native American Graves Protection and
    Repatriation Act (1990): 13, 22, *182,* 299,
    510, *511*
Natni; synonymy: 749
Nàtovona; synonymy: 752
*na·toweo·wa; synonymy: 749
na·towe·ssi(wak); synonymy: 749
Nátuesse; synonymy: 749
Nátuessuag; synonymy: 749
natural disasters: 309. drought: 280, 293, 309,
    455, 521, 538, 559, 561, 619, 667, 690, 770,
    780, 782, 788, 790–791, 813, 816, 817, 825,
    908, 919, 999. floods: 309, 505, 559, 620,
    667. frost: 309, 790–791. hail: 538, 780.
    insects: 309, 455, 521, 538, 559, 667, 780,
    782, 790–791, 813
Natwesix; synonymy: 749
Natyinéhĭn; synonymy: 592
Naudawissees; synonymy: 749
Naudouisioux; synonymy: 749
Naudouisses; synonymy: 749
Naudowessies; synonymy: 749
Nauduwassies; synonymy: 749
Näünë; synonymy: 902
Na-ü-ni; synonymy: 902
Nau´niĕm; synonymy: 905
Naut te nay in; synonymy: 592
Nava, Pedro de: 543
Navajo; origins: 127. warfare: 517
Navajo language, education: 110–111
Nawathi´nĕha; synonymy: 861
Nawathíneha; synonymy: 861
Nawathinehena; synonymy: 861. *See also*
    Arapaho
Nawathinehena language: 74, 75, 76, 840
Naw cotch is seen in nin nin; synonymy: 840
Naw cotch is seen in nin nin Blue Mud;
    synonymy: 862
Nawdowessie; synonymy: 749
náwinatyiné; synonymy: 751
Nawunena; synonymy: 861
na-wuth´-i-ni-han; synonymy: 861
Nayhaythaway; synonymy: 302. trade: 302
Naytane; synonymy: 903

Naywatame Poets: 302
Naze site: *116,* 123, *124, 160–161,* 170
nɔ́ɔ́kinéhinɔh; synonymy: 592
nɔ́ɔ́kinéíh; synonymy: 592
Ndakotahs; synonymy: 750
Nebo Hill complex: 144
Nebraska phase: 173, 178–180, *179*
Necklace, Mark: *288*
Neckless people; synonymy: 751
needles, prehistoric: 128, 176, 185, 224
Nee Koo chis ak kā: 861
ne·hiyawak; synonymy: 650
Neighbors, Robert S.: 944
Nellis, George: 1005
Nelson, E. Benjamin: *430*
Nelson, George: 306
Nemekaiwane; synonymy: 905
Némĕréxka; synonymy: 963
Nemousin: 76. synonymy: 861
nenebî·nennó·ʔ; synonymy: 862
Neo-Atlantic climatic episode: 190, 196
Neodesha "fort" site: *173*
Ne-o-ge-he; synonymy: 461
Ne-o-ta-cha; synonymy: 461
Ne Perce; synonymy: 446
ne persa; synonymy: 446
Ner-mon-sin-nan-see; synonymy: 861
Nest that Wears a Face: 781
Netsepoyè; synonymy: 623
Ne-u-cha-ta; synonymy: 461
Neum; synonymy: 902
Neu-mon-ya: *442*
Ne-u-tach; synonymy: 461
Neu-ta-che; synonymy: 461
New-dar-cha; synonymy: 461
Newella: *491*
New Holy, Sophie: *1017*
New Smith site: *210–211,* 216
New Town: *259*
Ne-yu-ta-ca; synonymy: 461
Nez Perce; art: 1046. classification: 3, 4.
    disease: 258. external relations: 698. history:
    2. trade: 260, 276, 695, 697. treaties: 618.
    wealth: 608
Nhutú; synonymy: 751
Nḣutuḣitú; synonymy: 650
Niakĕtsikûtk; synonymy: 751
Niă´rharĭ´s-kûrikiwă´s-hûski; synonymy: 861
Nichols site: *235*
ni·či·héhi·nén; synonymy: 924
Nickerson, William: 14
Nicollet, Joseph N.: 26, 42, 97, 735
Nicúdje; synonymy: 461
Night Gun, Mrs.: *617*
Nightwalker: *330*
ni·hit; synonymy: 431
ní·hitA; synonymy: 431
ni·ho·nihté·no·tinei; synonymy: 592
niihʔɔ́tɔɔhéíhích; synonymy: 602
nííkinʔihíhkʔi; synonymy: 602
níkkaðatʰe; synonymy: 963
níkkawaðatʰe; synonymy: 963
Niménim; synonymy: 902
Nimĕtéka; synonymy: 963
nimikaiwa; synonymy: 905
nimini·; synonymy: 902
Ni-mi-ou-sin; synonymy: 861

nimirika; synonymy: 963
Nimmetuhka; synonymy: 963
Nimoussines: 840. synonymy: 861
Niⁿam; synonymy: 902
Nines, Charles: 35
Nines, Richard: 35
Niniwi-nátyinéhĭn; synonymy: 602
ninoniks-skarĕnĭki; synonymy: 881
Niscaniche; synonymy: 565
niscéhiinennoʔ: 854
Nishkuntu: 1007
Niska site: *116*
ni·tsiʔpoyiwa; synonymy: 623
ni·tsísina·wa; synonymy: 592
nitsí-sĭnna; synonymy: 592
Ni'tsíssinaia; synonymy: 592
Ni-ú-t´a-tcí; synonymy: 461
Ni-úî-ati´; synonymy: 461
Nixaoxcexháes; synonymy: 758
Nixon, Richard M.: 297
niye·re·rikwa·ckannikih; synonymy: 881
Noble Starr: *934*
Nobows; synonymy: 758
Nocomies; synonymy: 904
Noconee; synonymy: 904
No-co-ni; synonymy: 904
No Heart Creek site: *197, 202, 203*
No Heart of Fear: 441, *443*
No-ho-mun-ya: *442*
Les Noire Indians; synonymy: 623
Noisy Pawnee; synonymy: 546
no·khô·seinénnó·ʔ; synonymy: 862
Nōk ko nē; synonymy: 904
Nokoni; synonymy: 904, 905. *See also*
    Comanche
No-ko-nies; synonymy: 904
no·kúhnen; synonymy: 650
Nollmeyer site: 202
No Milk in Breast: *392*
No-na-um; synonymy: 905
Nonĕm; synonymy: 905
no·nó·ʔowú·ʔunennó·ʔ: 854
nɔ́ɔ́chɔh; synonymy: 650
nɔɔcih; synonymy: 650
Noo´-ta; synonymy: 716
Noo-tar-wau; synonymy: 971
nɔ́ɔ́wunɔ́ɔ́kinéíhinɔh; synonymy: 751
Nopauwoi: 470
Norby site: *116,* 117
Norman, Charles: *961*
Norman, Jack: *961*
Norman, Lisa: *961*
Norman, Madaline: *961*
Norman, Toni: *961*
Norris, Malcoln F.: *664, 666*
Norse, Raphael: *857*
North, Frank: 521
North American Indian Brotherhood: 322
North Cannonball site: *186–187,* 188
Northern Arapahoe; synonymy: 862. *See also*
    Arapaho
Northern Axe: *1026–1027*
Northern Brule; synonymy: 756
Northern Caddoan languages: 548. bilingual-
    ism: 91. phonology: 86–88. survival: 91–93.
    vowel system: 87–88
Northern Cheyenne. *See* Cheyenne

411. population: 412, 415. religion: 286, 408–409, 411, 412, *414,* 1009. reservations: 100, 281, *400,* 401–402, 411–412. settlement pattern: 100. shamans: 410. social organization: 5, 9, 404–405, 410–411, 974, 975. societies: *401,* 410–411, 996, 997–998, 1012, 1036. structures: 400, 401, 402–403, *403,* 404. subsistence: 281, 401, 402, 403–404. synonymy: 399, 413–415. technology: 404. termination: 411. territory: 281, 400, *400,* 411. trade: 399–400, 403, 404, 732. treaties: 273, 274, 280, 401, 733–734. villages: 400, 401. warfare: 400, 401, 409–410, 416, 418, 734. wealth: 412

omąhą; synonymy: 413
Omahahcaka; synonymy: 414
Omahahs; synonymy: 415
Omaha language: 100, 399, 416. borrowings: 109. characteristics: 108, 109. classification: 63. classification of: 102. comparative vocabulary: 64–66. education: 110. orthography: 399. phonology: 106, 399. survival: 112, 412, 428. vowel system: 109
O-maŋ-ha; synonymy: 414
O-maŋ-ha-ȟca; synonymy: 414
Omans; synonymy: 415
Omauç-hau; synonymy: 415
Omawhaw; synonymy: 415
O'mĭ´sĭs; synonymy: 883
Omnibus Act (1910): 290
ǫmǫhǫ; synonymy: 413
ómɔ̀hɔ̀·gɔ̀: 414
Omouhoa; synonymy: 414
Oñate, Juan de: 244, 246, 260, 548, 563, 926, 954, 965
Oncapapas; synonymy: 759
Onch-pa-pah; synonymy: 758
Onco, Bobby: *836*
Oncpahpah; synonymy: 759
Oncpapa; synonymy: 758
One always foremost: *442*
One Gun: *73, 617*
Oneha; synonymy: 414
Onehao; synonymy: 414
onéhaoʔo; synonymy: 414, 431
One Horn: 795
Oneota Orr focus: 432
Oneota tradition: 222, 229–233
One who gives no attention: *442*
One Who Leads the Old Dog: *699*
Ongotoya: *30*
Oníhaeo; synonymy: 414
Onion Creek site: *210–211*
Onkpapa(h); synonymy: 758
ónoneoʔ; synonymy: 389
ónoneoʔO; synonymy: 363
O-no´-ni-o; synonymy: 389
Onyapes; synonymy: 512
óoetaneoʔo; synonymy: 714
Oo-gwapes; synonymy: 512
Oohenoupa; synonymy: 758
oʔóhenupa; synonymy: 758
oohkóheinénnoʔ; synonymy: 940
Oóȟithítaneo; synonymy: 495
ooʔkóhtAxétaneoʔO; synonymy: 475, 495
ooʔkótAxétaneoʔO; synonymy: 513
1334 Oo-ma-ha; synonymy: 415

ʔɔɔʔȥ́ȥ́ȥ́niinéninɔh; synonymy: 692
O-óqt-qitä´n-eo; synonymy: 513
ʔóóúnéninɔh; synonymy: 714
ʔóounénnɔh; synonymy: 715
Oo-yapes; synonymy: 512
Oo´-zâ-tâu; synonymy: 495
opwa·si·mo·w; synonymy: 591, 602
O-qua-pas; synonymy: 512
Orages; synonymy: 494
oral traditions: 311, 399, 402, 405, 427, 450, 459, 497, 629, 664, 695, 891–892, 913, 932. classification of: 1062–1065. comic: 1064. etiological narrative: 1064. fairy tales: 1062, 1064. fictional stories: 1062, 1064. functions of: 1062. hunting: 1064. legends: 329, 341, 352, 383, 1064. migration stories: 1067–1068. myths: 341, 1063–1064, 1064. narratives: 383, 1064. sacred tales: 1062–1064. secular stories: 1062, 1064. storytelling: 341, 383–384, 1062, *1063*. tales: 383. war stories: 1064. *See also* mythology
Oregon Trail: 280, 519, 795, 796, 842, 865
Orejones: 888. synonymy: 940, 972
Oriental Comanche; synonymy: 902
Ortiz, Francisco Xavier: 568
Os; synonymy: 494
Osage: 476–496. agriculture: 57, 60, 476, 477, 478, 479. allotment: 488, 490. annual cycle: 477, 479–480. art: 484, *484, 486, 493,* 1047–1048. bands: 481–483. ceremonies: 31, 35, 480, 481, *483,* 485, *486,* 487, 488, *489,* 490, *491,* 492, 999, 1004, 1009, 1011, 1013, 1018. clothing and adornment: 479, *480, 482,* 486, *491* contact: 26, 263, 264, 476. curing: 482. death practices: 485, 492. disease: 269. divisions: 495. economy: 478, 481, 491, *493.* education: 478, 487, 492. external relations: 233, 273, 477, 480, *491,* 557, 567, 569, 915, 1012, 1024. firearms: 476. Gaus: 23. history: 269, 271–272, 273, 275, 282, 476–478, 478, *483,* 485–492, 490. horses: 476. intermarriage: 486, 490. kinship: 485. knowledge: 481. language: 100. leadership: *483* life cycle: 485, *486.* migrations: 233, 273, 281, 399, 462, 476, 478, 1067. mixed blood band: 485–486, 488. music and dance: 485, 490, *491,* 492. mythology: 476, 1066. origins: 256, 476, 1067. orthography: 476. political organization: 478, 481–483, *484,* 487, 488, 491–492. population: 485–486, 487, 490, 492–493. prehistory: 476. religion: 480–481, 486, 490, 492, 1004, 1007, 1009. reservations: 281, 477, *477,* 478, 486–488, 488. rituals: 31. settlements: 486. slavery: 264. social organization: 5, 478, *479,* 480–481, 483–484, 484–485, 492, 975. societies: 492. structures: 476, 478–479, 480, 486, *487,* 488, *489, 490,* 492. subsistence: 476, 478, 479–480, 486, 487. synonymy: 493–495. technology: *486* termination: 296. territory: 212, 281, 292, 476, 477, *477,* 477–478, 478, 490, 886. trade: 252, 264, 266, 476, 477, 478, 479. treaties: 272–273, 273, 435, 477, 478. villages: 476–477, *477,* 479, *479,* 481, 484. warfare: 266, 272, 273, 281, 282, 464, 476, 478, 483–484, 499. wealth: 487, 488–

491, 1013
Osage, Joe David: *872*
Osage Allotment Act (1906): 488, 491
Osage language: 100–101, *101.* classification: 63. comparative vocabulary: 64–66. education: *101,* 110, 112. literacy: 478. phonology: 101, 106, 476. structural characteristics: 107. survival: 112, 492
Osage National Council: 487
Osage National Organization: 491–492
Osages des Chênes; synonymy: 495
Osages of the Oaks; synonymy: 495
Osages Pequeños; synonymy: 495
Osarge; synonymy: 494
Osark; synonymy: 512
O-saw-ses; synonymy: 494
Osayes; synonymy: 494
Osborne, Billie: *522–523*
Ose; synonymy: 494
Osier Tribe; synonymy: 345
Osinipoilles; synonymy: 591
Osniboine; synonymy: 591
Osotonoy; synonymy: 513
Osotoug; synonymy: 512–513
Osotouy; synonymy: 512–513
Osotteoez; synonymy: 513
Ospekakaerenousques; synonymy: 969
ospikay-iriniwak; synonymy: 969
ospike-kan-iriniwak; synonymy: 969
Ossage; synonymy: 494
Ossiniboins; synonymy: 591
Ossoteoez; synonymy: 513
Ossotoues; synonymy: 513
Ossoztoues; synonymy: 513
Osutuys; synonymy: 513
O-taski-wikamikwe·w; synonymy: 389
Ot Cemetery site: *223*
ɔtéta'o; synonymy: 905
Otetaone; synonymy: 905
Other Day, John: *771*
Others, Anna Collum: *486*
Otho; synonymy: 460
Othoc(a)tatas; synonymy: 460
Othouez; synonymy: 460
Othoves; synonymy: 460
oti taʔó·ʔ; synonymy: 905
Oto; ceremonies: 999. trade: 725
Otoctatas; synonymy: 460
Otoe; synonymy: 459–461. *See also* Otoe and Missouria
Otoe and Missouria: 447–461. agriculture: 57, 448, 454–455, 456. allotment: 456–457. art: 451, 1047–1048. ceremonies: 449, 450, 451, 458, *458,* 459, 996, 999, 1004, 1005, 1012, 1018. clothing and adornment: *452, 455, 456, 457.* contact: 263–264, *264,* 447. Coyote band: 455, 456. curing: 451–452, *452,* 456. death practices: 450, 451. disease: 269, 448, 454. division of labor: 448. economy: 457. employment: 459. external relations: 233, 453, *454,* 458–459, 463, 1012. games: 450, 457, 458. history: 281, 447–448, 452–459, 455–456, 459. kinship: 449, 459, 977. life cycle: 450–451. migrations: 102, 233, 281, 448, 453, 454, 455–456. Missouria: 256, 263–264, 272, 280, 281, 975, 1012. music and dance: 458,

509, 1029. mythology: 449, 450. origins: 232, 256, 447. Otoe: 256, 263–264, 264, 269, 272, 280, 281, 435, 975, 977, 996, 999, 1004, 1005, *1006–1007*, 1009, 1012, 1029. political organization: 449–450, *454*, 457. population: 447–448, 452–453, 454, 455. prehistory: 230, 232. Quaker Band: 455–456. religion: 450, 458, *458*, 999, 1004, 1005, *1006–1007*, 1009. reservations: 102, *448*, 454–456, 457. settlement pattern: 102. social organization: 5, 449–450, 455, 459, 975. societies: 449, 451–452, 459. structures: 448, 449, 450, 455, 456, 457, 459. subsistence: 448, *453*, 455. synonymy: 459–460, 460, 461. territory: *274*, 448, 453, 455–456. trade: 435, 447, 448. treaties: 272, 273, 274, 280, 453, 454, 733–734. villages: *274*, 447, *448*. warfare: 281, 447–448, 452, 453, 464
Otoe language: 102, 447. classification of: 102. education: *103*, 110. historical changes: 63. survival: 112, 447
Otoetata; synonymy: 460
O-tōh´-sōn; synonymy: 757
Otontanta; synonymy: 460
Ototenta; synonymy: 460
Otoutanta; synonymy: 460
Otsotchaué; synonymy: 513
Otsotchoué; synonymy: 513
Otsotchove; synonymy: 513
Otsoté; synonymy: 513
Ottawa; ceremonies: 300. external relations: 720. migrations: 720. trade: 301. warfare: 720
Ottawa Kwowahtewug; synonymy: 363
Otter Creek site: *246, 351*
Ottoe; synonymy: 460
Ottoos; synonymy: 460
Ottos; synonymy: 460
Ouacee; synonymy: 544
ouachipouanne; synonymy: 363–364
Ouachitas; synonymy: 563
Ouadbatons; synonymy: 753
Ouadebatons; synonymy: 753
Oua de Battons; synonymy: 753
Ouapeontetons; synonymy: 755
Ouasicontetons; synonymy: 755
Ouasoys; synonymy: 494
Ouass; synonymy: 544
Ouatabatonha; synonymy: 753
Ouchage; synonymy: 494
Ouckidoat: *308*
Ouedsitas; synonymy: 563
8emess8rit; synonymy: 461
Oue-ta-pa-ha-to; synonymy: 970
Ougapa; synonymy: 511
Ouguapas; synonymy: 512
Ouisy: 73. synonymy: 882
Ouitcitas; synonymy: 563
Ouitigami, external relations: 1024
8missouri; synonymy: 461
Ous; synonymy: 494
Ousasons; synonymy: 494
Ousasoys; synonymy: 494
Ousita; synonymy: 563
Ouyopetons; synonymy: 753
Ovacs; synonymy: 544
Ovadebathons; synonymy: 753

Ovagitas; synonymy: 563
Ovedsitas; synonymy: 563
ovens: 149, 150, 152. pits: 134, 137, 140, 141, *141*, 154, 155, 240
Over, William H.: *15*
Overhead site: *223*
ówahą; synonymy: 414
O'Watch, Joe: *590*
owe·liliniwak; synonymy: 715
Owen, Amos: *837*
Owilinioek; synonymy: 715, 967
Owings, Stuart: *562*
Owl Woman: *59, 333, 339*
Oxbow complex: *116, 119*, 119–120, *120*, 136
Oxbow Dam site: *116*, 119
óʔxevéhóʔE; synonymy: 675
oyáte nųpa; synonymy: 415
oyáte yámni; synonymy: 431
Oyesna: *786*
Ozages; synonymy: 494
Ozanges; synonymy: 494
Ozark; synonymy: 512
Ozas; synonymy: 494
Ozotheoa; synonymy: 513
Ozotoues; synonymy: 513
ozóttióhi; synonymy: 513
ozóttiowé; synonymy: 513

P
Pa-a-bo; synonymy: 905
Pabaksa; synonymy: 754–755
Pächarabó; synonymy: 881
Pacer: 930, *931*, 938
Packineau, David: *288*
Packineau, Joseph: *290, 392*
Packs Arrows: *709*
Packs Hat: *709*
Padani Mašteta; synonymy: 544
Páda^nka; synonymy: 903
Padaws; synonymy: 939
Padberg, John: *289*
Padduca; synonymy: 939
pádi piza; synonymy: 389
Pado; synonymy: 939
Pádǫkà; synonymy: 903
Padokas; synonymy: 939
padoo; synonymy: 939
Pados; synonymy: 928, 939, 969, 970
Padouca: *400*. contact: 24. synonymy: 24, 903, 938, 939. villages: 928. warfare: 416, 462, 927–928
Padoucas Orientaux; synonymy: 939
Padoucies; synonymy: 939
Padouka; synonymy: 939
Padouka blanc; synonymy: 939
Padouka Noirs; synonymy: 939
Paducar; synonymy: 939
Paducas; synonymy: 939
Pádu^nka; synonymy: 903
Paegan; synonymy: 627
Pägänävo; synonymy: 881
Pag-a now; synonymy: 881
Pagans; synonymy: 627
Págatsu; synonymy: 905
Pagazaurtundúa: *946*

Pa-ha-cae; synonymy: 445, 446
Pa-ha-sca; synonymy: 495
Pah Baxa(h); synonymy: 755
Pahdawy: *894*
Pah kah nahvo; synonymy: 881
Pah kee; synonymy: 627
Pah-ko-to-quoddle: *898*
páhkuta; synonymy: 446
pahneug; synonymy: 543
pahnIšúkAt; synonymy: 751
Páhoak-sá; synonymy: *592*
Pa-ho-cha; synonymy: 446
Pah8tet; synonymy: 446, 517
Pahtocahs; synonymy: 903
páhuxaix; synonymy: 905
Paikanavos; synonymy: 881
Paikandoos; synonymy: 881
Paingya: 1000, 1004
Pain-pe-tse-menay; synonymy: 751
Paint Creek site: *173, 185*
Painted Woods site: *246*
Paints Himself Red: 781
Paiute, museum exhibits: 2
páka; synonymy: 431
Pá ka na no; synonymy: 881
Pá-ka-na-wa; synonymy: 881
pakan napo·; synonymy: 881
pakan napo·ni·; synonymy: 881
Pak´ an navo; synonymy: 881
Pak´ke nah; synonymy: 627
Palliser, John: 311
Palmer, Erwin: *298*
Palmer, Gus: *920*
Palmer site: 519
Palo Duro complex: 154, 155
Paloma. *See* Plains Apacheans
Pambizimina; synonymy: 751
Pámpe Chyimina; synonymy: 751
pampiciminah; synonymy: 751
Pana: 517. synonymy: 544, 564
pánaixtɛ; synonymy: 905
Pana Maha; synonymy: 544
Panana; synonymy: 389, 544
Panane; synonymy: 544
Panani; synonymy: 389, 544
Panas; synonymy: 431
Pancassa; synonymy: 564
Paneas; synonymy: 544
Paneassa; synonymy: 564
Pânee; synonymy: 544
Panhandle aspect: 182, 211
Pani; synonymy: 544, 564
pa·ní; synonymy: 543
pānia; synonymy: 543
Pania Loup; synonymy: 545
Pania Pickey; synonymy: 564
Pania Proper; synonymy: 545
Panias; synonymy: 431
Pānias picqué; synonymy: 564
Pānias proper; synonymy: 544
Panias propres; synonymy: 545
Pānias Republican; synonymy: 545
Paniassa. *See* Wichita
Paniboucha; synonymy: 389
Panibousa; synonymy: 389
Panies; synonymy: 564

1338

457, 473, 474, 478, 487, 488, 491–492, 506, 508, 509, 540–541, 561, 586, 589, 600–602, 619, 621, 648–649, 658, 713, 791–792, 816, 850, 853, 934. tribal constitutions: 292–293, 294, 296, 411, 428, 443, 457, 474, 487, 540, 561, 586, 589, 619, 689, 709, 851, 853, 877, 879, 899–900, 900. tribal government: 292–293, 293–295, 294–295, 297, 298, 298, 298–299, 323, 327, 331, 394–396, 398, 405–407, 428, 444, 473, 509, 540, 586, 658, 712, 783, 825, 826, 829–830, 851, 866, 878–879, 895–896, 935, 944. villages: 7–9, 12, 356, 404, 420–421, 448, 470, 576, 609, 615, 630, 681, 777, 801, 843, 865, 875, 911, 930, 974, 975–977, 977, 990. *See also* chieftainship; social organization

Pomona phase: 172, 173, 181

Ponarak; synonymy: 750

Ponca: 416–431. agriculture: 57, 281, 418, 426, 427. alliances: 418. allotment: 426, 427. annual cycle: 418. art: 420, 1047–1048. ceremonies: 35, 286, 421, 422, 424, 425, 428, 429, 429, 983, 988, 996, 999, 1004, 1018, 1028, 1030, 1035. clothing and adornment: 420, 420. component groups: 416. contact: 31, 416. curing: 421, 422, 423. death practices: 422–423. disease: 269, 418, 422, 426, 430. division of labor: 418. economy: 428, 430. education: 425, 428. external relations: 384, 418, 788. games: 428, 429, 1036. health care: 430. history: 281, 416–418, 424–426, 424–431, 426–427. intermarriage: 427. kinship: 420, 977. life cycle: 422–423. migrations: 100, 233, 281, 416, 1067. music and dance: 423, 425, 427, 428, 429, 429, 1028, 1032, 1032, 1035, 1036, 1038. mythology: 423. Northern bands: 296, 426–427. origins: 256, 416, 1067. political organization: 422, 428. population: 281, 418, 430–431. prehistory: 416. religion: 286, 422–423, 423, 427, 428, 1004, 1009. reservations: 100, 417, 425–429. settlement pattern: 100. shamans: 421, 422, 423, 424. social organization: 5, 420–421, 420–422, 428, 429, 975. societies: 423–424, 428–429, 999. Southern bands: 427–429, 429. structures: 419–420, 420–421, 424, 427, 428. subsistence: 281, 416, 418–419, 424–425. synonymy: 431. technology: 419. termination: 296, 427. territory: 416, 417, 425, 426. trade: 416–417, 418, 419, 430, 732. treaties: 272, 273, 418, 425. villages: 399, 418. warfare: 400, 416, 418, 421, 424–425

Ponca House: 416

Ponca language: 100. borrowings: 109. characteristics: 108, 109. classification: 63. classification of: 102. comparative vocabulary: 64–66. education: 110, 112. phonology: 106. survival: 112. vowel system: 109

Ponca Post: 259, 268

Poncara(r)s; synonymy: 431

Poncârs; synonymy: 431

Ponckais; synonymy: 431

Pond, Doreen: 878

Pond, Gideon H.: 97, 734

Pond, Peter: 305, 727, 731

Pond, Samuel W.: 28, 97, 734

La Pong; synonymy: 431

Pongkaws; synonymy: 431

les Pongs; synonymy: 431

Poniars; synonymy: 431

Ponkas; synonymy: 431

Ponkaws; synonymy: 431

pónki; synonymy: 431

Po-no-í-ta-ní-o; synonymy: 883

Pons; synonymy: 431

Ponsars; synonymy: 431

Poolaw, Horace: 920

Poolaw, Irene: 933

pó-o-mas; synonymy: 624

Póomŭ´ts; synonymy: 624

Poor Dog, Henry: 792

Poor Elk: 870

Poorman: 585

Poor Wolf: 392

population: 247, 415, 543, 570, 590, 658, 978. band: 518, 583, 585. birth statistics: 780, 783, 784. blood quantum statistics: 296, 296. censuses: 344, 352, 493, 675, 898, 921–922, 1068–1069 decline: 281, 304, 309, 344, 350, 412, 418, 430, 441, 444, 447–448, 472, 473, 493, 501, 519, 520, 539, 543, 551, 563, 568, 574, 575, 590, 599, 602, 618, 635, 640, 650. 18th century: 344, 412, 430, 636. environmental limits: 285. historic: 281, 304, 412. mortality statistics: 296, 322, 444, 780, 783, 784, 851, 921. nadir: 344, 350–351, 352, 635, 879, 901, 956–957. 19th century: 344, 387, 412, 430, 444, 445, 453, 454, 472, 485–486, 492–493, 501, 543, 570, 583–585, 590, 622, 636, 650, 675, 692, 714, 748, 761, 797, 830, 848, 857–858, 879, 880, 900–901, 911, 920–921, 937–938, 945, 953, 955, 956–957, 970, 971. pre-1800: 245, 247, 256, 304, 344, 387–388, 430, 444, 445, 452–453, 472, 492, 501, 543, 548, 550, 551, 563, 570, 590, 622, 650, 674–675, 714, 748, 880, 900, 928, 942, 945, 956, 965. reservation and reserve: 296, 326, 352, 387, 396, 397, 415, 430–431, 444–445, 472, 473, 474, 485–486, 487, 506, 507, 522, 543, 590, 591, 599, 602, 635–636, 650, 690, 714, 782, 783, 784, 786, 787, 788, 823, 830, 850, 858–859, 879, 880, 938, 955. 20th-century: 296, 326, 344, 387, 430–431, 445, 453, 472, 490, 493, 501, 543, 563, 622, 636, 650, 675, 692, 714, 830, 853, 880, 901–902, 921–922, 938. White admixture: 291, 850

Porcupine: 1001

Porcupine Creek site: 160–161

Porcupine Creek variant: 169

Porcupine Woman: 1033

Porncases; synonymy: 431

Porter, N. S.: 788

Posada, Alonso de: 926

Potawatomi; ceremonies: 996, 998, 999. history: 996. migrations: 271–272. warfare: 434, 720

pottery: 372, 789, 1039, 1050. decoration: 526–527, 1045. manufacture of: 340, 354–355, 526–527, 730. prehistoric: 18, 123, 124, 125, 126, 126, 127, 128, 129–130, 139, 145, 151, 152, 153, 154, 155, 156, 157, 159, 160, 160–

161, 162, 163, 164, 164, 166, 166, 167, 167, 168, 168, 169, 170, 171, 171, 174, 176, 177, 177, 178, 179, 179, 180, 181, 182, 182, 183–184, 184, 185, 189–190, 190, 192, 193, 194, 195, 200–201, 201, 202, 204, 205, 208, 211, 213, 215, 216, 217, 218, 219, 224, 226, 226, 226–227, 227, 228, 228, 229, 230, 232, 233, 234, 237, 238, 238, 239, 240–241, 242, 242, 243. protohistoric: 250, 252, 497. shapes: 526–527. types and uses: 948, 1045

Pottorff site: 160–161, 173, 182

Potts site: 197, 202, 203

Poualac; synonymy: 750

Poualak; synonymy: 750

Pouanak; synonymy: 750

Poulak; synonymy: 750

Poundmaker: 316, 317, 318, 641, 648

Powderface: 850

Powder River site: 132–133

Powell, John Wesley: 29

Powell, Joseph: 455

power: 9–10, 339, 357, 361, 423, 450, 452, 533, 711, 806, 843, 855, 874, 913, 932, 933, 937, 1070. acquisition: 335–336, 337, 341, 343, 357, 383, 407, 421, 422, 423, 451, 633, 646–647, 683, 684, 687, 689, 705, 706, 706, 707, 733, 768, 790, 807, 851, 873, 892, 895, 913, 917, 932, 951, 962, 1050, 1064. curing: 844. importance of: 696. loss of: 335, 357, 362, 407, 424. songs: 1035. spiritual: 9–10. transfer of: 357, 360, 450, 451, 452, 499, 684, 702, 705, 706–707, 846, 892, 913–914, 1052. uses of: 790, 914–915, 932, 951, 1050, 1051, 1053. *See also* dreams and visions; shamans

Powers-Yonkee site: 132–133, 138

Powestic-Athinuewuck; synonymy: 693

Powestoc-Athinuewuck; synonymy: 303

ppáddąkka; synonymy: 903

ppádi; synonymy: 543

ppáðimąhą; synonymy: 543

ppáðimąhą; synonymy: 545

ppádi wasábe; synonymy: 564

ppádokka; synonymy: 903

ppaj; synonymy: 543

ppájmąhą; synonymy: 543

ppákka; synonymy: 431

ppánimáha; synonymy: 545

ppápawaxǫ; synonymy: 751

ppápaxǫ; synonymy: 751

ppátakka; synonymy: 903

ppátǫkka; synonymy: 903

ppattokka; synonymy: 903

ppaxáci; synonymy: 495

ppáxocce; synonymy: 446

ppáxoje; synonymy: 446

ppáyi; synonymy: 543

ppáyimąhą; synonymy: 545

ppayíxci; synonymy: 545

ppe·gázaje; synonymy: 715

ppǫ́kka; synonymy: 431

Prairie Apache; synonymy: 938

Prairie Farm Rehabilitation Act: 668

Prairie Gros Ventres; synonymy: 693

Prairie Indians; synonymy: 756

Prairie Kickapoo, warfare: 434

Prairie Owl site: 197

1339

794, 798–799, 823, 824, 831, 993, 1001, 1020. Star Blanket Reserve: 639. Stoney Reserve: 301, 325, 596, 597. Stony Plain Reserve: 639. Sturgeon Lake Reserve: 325, 639. Sucker Creek Reserve: 639. Sunchild Reserve: 639 Swan River Reserve: 639. Sweet Grass Reserve: 639. Tall Cree Reserve: 639. termination: 296, 297, 325, 411, 427, 474, 620, 620 823–824, 823–824, 835. Texas Kickapoo Reservation: 259 Thunderchild Reserve: 639. Tohono O'odham: 992. Tongue River Reservation: 41. Tonkawa Reservation: 953, 957. treaties: 27, 280, 282, 283, 284, 351–352, 367, 585, 586, 698, 771, 777, 779, 781, 791, 796–797, 798–799, 815, 842–843, 847, 865, 886, 889, 915, 928. trespass: 284, 788, 792–793, 797, 842, 843, 898, 916. Turtle Mountain Reservation: 259, 638, 639, 654, 657, 658, 658, 661, 665, 668, 674. Unipouheos Reserve: 639. Upper Sioux Reservation: 259, 762, 831. Utikoomak Lake Reserve: 639. Wabamun Reserve: 597, 639. Wabasca Reserve: 639. Wahpeton Reserve: 114, 301, 326, 762, 772, 831. Walker River Reservation: 1001. White Bear Reserve: 96, 109, 572, 573, 586, 588, 589, 591, 639, 762. White Cap Reserve: 762, 772, 831, 1001. White Fish Lake Reserve: 639. Wichita Reservation: 549, 567 William McKenzie Reserve: 639. Wind River Reservation: 79, 259, 289, 290, 293, 841, 843, 847, 854, 879, 988. Winnebago Reservation: 259, 400, 401, 411. Witchekan Lake Reserve: 639 Wood Mountain Reserve: 794, 831. Yankton Reservation: 114, 259, 289, 293, 295, 777, 778, 779, 780, 792, 823, 824, 831, 1009

Revard, Francis: 491
Reynolds, Joseph J.: 865
Rhoades, Everett: 920
Rhoads, Charles: 1057
Rhodes, Ernest Sun, Sr.: 289
Riana; synonymy: 923
Ribs, Lucy C. F.: 1032
Ricara band of Panies; synonymy: 388
Ricaris; synonymy: 388
Riccari; synonymy: 388
Riccarree; synonymy: 388
Rice, Lynn: 299
Rice, Norman Ross: 542
Rice Indians; synonymy: 388
Richard, Louis: 798–799
Richards, Fanny Goodeagle: 510
Richards Kill site: 116, 124
Richards Mounds site: 116, 125
Richland Creek phase: 155
Rickara language: 83
Rickarees; synonymy: 388
Rickerees; synonymy: 388
rickeries; synonymy: 388
Ricora; synonymy: 388
Ricrerees; synonymy: 388
Rider, Jonas: 991
Rides a Black Horse: 711
Rides at the Door: 294
Rides-at-the-Door, Mrs.: 1033
Ridgely, Lucille Goggles: 859
Riel, Louis, Jr.: 312, 313, 664, 664, 665, 669,

673, 674, 675
Riel, Louis, Sr.: 664, 665
Riel family: 670–671
Riggs, Alfred L.: 98, 773
Riggs, Frederick B.: 773
Riggs, Stephen Return: 28, 31, 97
Rigler Bluffs site: 132–133, 137
rí·hita; synonymy: 431
Rih's; synonymy: 388
Riis; synonymy: 388
Rikkara; synonymy: 388
Riks; synonymy: 388
Rindisbacher, Peter: 7, 26, 306, 309, 655, 672–673, 760
Ripley, David J.: 658
Ris; synonymy: 388
Ritchot, Noel-Joseph: 669
Ríu, Francisco: 518
River Crow: 585. synonymy: 715–716
River People; synonymy: 753
Riverside Indian School: 93
Rivet, Rick: 1060–1061
Roadmaker: 341
Roaming Chief: 542
Roaming Scout: 35, 43, 82, 83, 83, 528, 531
Roanhorse: 491
Roanhorse, Mrs.: 491
Roasters; synonymy: 750
La Robe Noire: 308
Roberts, Rush, Sr.: 522–523, 542
Roberts, Stephen Cornelius: 430
Robidoux trading house: 436
Robinson, Fred: 586–587
Robinson site: 197
rock art: 1042–1043, 1043. petroglyphs: 142–143. pictographs: 142–143, 237, 604. styles: 1042–1043
rockshelters: 120, 133, 136, 137, 140, 144, 151, 154, 168, 170, 209, 239, 243
Rocky Mountain House: 309, 323, 596, 597, 608, 631, 674
Rocky Mountain Indians; synonymy: 715
Rocky Mountain Sioux; synonymy: 602
Rocky Mountain Stoney Indians; synonymy: 602
rodeos: 327, 386, 587, 620, 633, 635, 688, 711, 713, 775, 818, 1020, 1023
Rolette, Joseph, Jr.: 667
Roman Nose: 865, 875
Roman Nose, Larry: 872
Rood, David S.: 93
Roop-tar ha; synonymy: 364
Roop-tar-hee; synonymy: 364
Roosevelt, Franklin Delano: 292, 540, 919
Roper site: 210–211
Rosa site: 246
Rosebud Tribal Land Enterprise (TLE): 828
Ross, Alexander: 311
Ross Glen site: 116, 124
Rotten Belly: 270, 697, 705
Roubideaux, Robert: 436, 444
Roulston-Rogers site: 147, 152, 160–161, 171
Roundface, Daniel E.: 298
Round Face, Theodore: 298
Round Prairie phase: 155
Rowand, John: 610
Rowe, Walt: 429

Rowell, Charles E.: 1068–1069
Rowell, Dorothy: 910
Rowell, James: 910
Rowell, Maude: 909, 910
Rowland, William: 1063
Rowland, Willis T.: 870
Roy Smith site: 210–211
Rubí, Marqués de: 943
Ruby Bison Pound site: 116, 124, 125, 132–133, 139–140
rú·ʔeta; synonymy: 363, 364
Ruhptare; synonymy: 364
Ruiz, José Francisco: 26
Ruling-His-Son: 522–523
Rundle, Robert T.: 307, 311, 596
Rundle Technology: 127
Runnels, H. R.: 569
Running Antelope: 732
Running Bear: 781, 782
Running Eagle: 610
Running Fisher, Jerry: 689
Running Horse, Jessie: 1020
Running Pit House site: 147
Running Rabbit: 1063
Running Rabbit, Houghton: 1063
Running Rabbit, Rosa: 613
Running toward the Enemy: 932
Rupert's Land: 300, 301, 313, 661, 665
rúpta·; synonymy: 364
Ruptare; synonymy: 364. See also Mandan
rúpta·re; synonymy: 364
Rùptari; synonymy: 364
Rush, Don, Jr.: 1014–1015
Rush, Joe H.: 1032
Rush, Russell: 1032
Rustler, George: 584–585
rû·swače·; synonymy: 924
Ruton-we-me: 442
Ruton-ye-we-ma: 442
rųwáʔka·ki; synonymy: 363
Ryuwas; synonymy: 923

sa·si·w; synonymy: 636

Saskatchewan Indian Federated College: 326–327, 649

Saskatchewan Métis Association: 666

Saskatchewan River Cree: 315

Sassee; synonymy: 636

Sassewuck; synonymy: 303

Sassis; synonymy: 636

Satank: 914

sá·tl; synonymy: 752

sati·tikkati; synonymy: 860

Satrahe; synonymy: 389

Satsikaa; synonymy: 623

Sau'hto; synonymy: 903

Sauk; ceremonies: 996, 997, 999. external relations: 464, 729. history: 996. treaties: 733–734. warfare: 401, 434, 453, 761

Saukamapee: 304

Saulteaux; agriculture: 315–316. migrations: 256, 261. synonymy: 659

Saulteaux language: 71, 72. classification: 71. comparative vocabulary: 63, 64–66. education: 79. historical changes: 63, 67. phonology: 652. survival: 79

Saussetons; synonymy: 753

Saux; synonymy: 750

Saux of the Woods; synonymy: 752

Savansa; synonymy: 512

sawí·ʔAt; synonymy: 545

Sawketakix; synonymy: 622

Sawons; synonymy: 758

sáw·ʔt'uh; synonymy: 940

sáw·ʔiuh; synonymy: 903

Saxoe-koe-koon; synonymy: 623

sa·xsáso·kitaki; synonymy: 602

saxsí(ua); synonymy: 636

saxsísokitaki; synonymy: 602

Say, Thomas: 26, 81, 94, 95, 98, 101, 102, 469

Sáyădĩ; synonymy: 880

šayánį; synonymy: 880

Sáyen; synonymy: 880

ša·ye·na; synonymy: 880

ša·ye·ni; synonymy: 880

Sayer, Pierre-Guillaume: 309, 664, 667

sá·yi·koana; synonymy: 650

Sayíw; synonymy: 650

Scalp Creek site: 116, 160–161, 166, 197, 202

Scarlet Plume: 771

Scarred Arms; synonymy: 884

Scattered Village: 392

Scattered Village site: 246, 351

Sceouex; synonymy: 750

Schahswintowaher; synonymy: 753

Schartzer, Shane Grant: 298

Scheyenne; synonymy: 881

Schianese; synonymy: 880

Schians; synonymy: 880

Schiffer Cave site: 132–133, 133

Schiffer Ranch Trail site: 132–133, 143

Schikoí; synonymy: 627

Schildt, Gary: 622

Schk̲waíshĩni; synonymy: 624

Schmidt, Louis: 673

Schmidt site: 160–161

Schmidt variant: 169

Schmitt site: 116, 132–133

Scholder, Fritz: 1059, 1060

Schrader site: 173, 181

Schultz phase: 165, 172

Schultz site: 160–161, 165

Schwarzfüssige; synonymy: 623

Schweigman, William: 832–833, 993

sčidi; synonymy: 544

Scieux; synonymy: 750

sčili; synonymy: 544

Sciou; synonymy: 749, 750

Scious of the Prairies; synonymy: 756

Scioux; synonymy: 749, 750

Scioux of the East; synonymy: 752

Scioux of the West; synonymy: 756

Scioux of the Woods; synonymy: 752

sči·ri; synonymy: 544

Scoggin site: 116, 132–133, 137, 144

Scollen, Constantine: 313

Scott, Hugh Lenox: 28, 918, 1004

Scott, Marion: 859

Scott County Pueblo site: 235, 242

sčq̓ʷáyšin; synonymy: 624

sčq̓ʷe; synonymy: 624

scrapers: 8–9, 10–11, 126, 434, 868, 958, 1045. postcontact: 268. prehistoric: 117, 119, 120, 123, 124, 126, 126, 128, 130, 149, 150, 151, 152, 153, 154, 155, 156, 157, 162, 163, 164, 164, 166, 168, 169, 170, 171, 174, 183, 185, 189, 191, 199, 208, 209, 212, 214, 217–218, 218, 224, 224, 228, 239, 241, 605. protohistoric: 631

Se ah sap pas; synonymy: 758

Searces; synonymy: 636

Se-ä´-sä-pä; synonymy: 758

Se-ash-ha-pa; synonymy: 758

Seauex; synonymy: 750

Se-ɔaŋ´-ɔos; synonymy: 756

Se chong hhos; synonymy: 756

Secundine, Tehi: 510

Seehasap; synonymy: 624

See-oo-nay; synonymy: 758

Seepans; synonymy: 952

Sees Pretty: 709

See with His Ears: 710–711

Segesser I: 242

Seissitons; synonymy: 736–737, 753

Seksekai; synonymy: 623

Selkirk, Thomas Douglas, earl of: 307, 308, 308

Selkirk composite: 128–129

Sells, Cato: 284, 290, 837

Semät; synonymy: 924

sémhát; synonymy: 924, 939

Semple, William: 307

Senipoetts; synonymy: 591

Se-non-ty-yah: 442

Seraticks; synonymy: 860

Seratics; synonymy: 861

Serre, Pierre Guillaume: 667

Sesabeithi: 849

Se-see-toans; synonymy: 753

Se-see-t'wawns; synonymy: 753

séʔsenovotsétaneoʔo; synonymy: 902

Sesetons; synonymy: 753

Se-si-toons; synonymy: 753

Sessatone; synonymy: 753

Sesseu; synonymy: 636

Sessews; synonymy: 636

settlement pattern: 432, 974. postcontact: 249.

prehistoric: 10, 117, 152, 155, 157, 162, 167, 170, 174, 177, 181, 185, 186, 192, 193, 198, 201, 202, 205–206, 207, 209, 213, 216, 217, 218, 219–220, 225, 227, 228, 230, 234, 235, 236, 240, 246–247, 254. seasonal: 55–56, 120, 125, 137, 156, 248, 250, 277, 332–333, 428, 609, 630–631, 662, 663, 768, 788, 791, 894, 908, 930, 934, 945, 978, 983. See also camps

settlements; fortified villages: 156–157, 185, 186, 188, 192–193, 194–195, 196–197, 198, 202–203, 206, 220, 226, 227, 228, 232, 236, 237, 242, 246–247, 249–250, 250–251, 352, 368, 399, 416, 479, 550, 551, 553, 654, 724, 928. gateway communities: 262. villages: 767, 778–779, 780. winter: 55–56, 120, 125, 137, 156, 248, 250, 277, 332–333, 428, 609, 630–631, 662, 663, 768, 786, 788, 791, 894, 908, 930, 934, 945, 978, 983

Seuser site: 210–211

Seven Bear: 392

Seven Council Fires: 6

Seven Years' War: 303

sexual practices and beliefs: 337, 339, 357, 360, 378, 383, 408, 534, 535, 582, 610, 614, 631, 645, 646, 682, 706–707, 726, 808, 809, 871, 1049–1050

se·yé·rih; synonymy: 880

Seymour, Samuel: 266, 454, 469

shaft smoothers: 241. prehistoric: 183, 199

Shahan I site: 210–211

Shahan II site: 210–211

Shahí; synonymy: 650

Shah-Ke-Wahpe: 493

Shahsweentowahs; synonymy: 753

šhaí; synonymy: 675

shamans: 410, 537–538, 913, 1001, 1004, 1007. curing: 410, 502, 507, 532, 790, 874, 932, 934, 951, 962, 996–997. death practices: 423, 913. functions: 357, 422, 424, 502, 805, 806, 807, 808, 817, 932, 934, 945, 948, 951, 1000. malicious actions: 962. naming of children: 646. paraphernalia: 932. performances: 382–383, 421, 424, 532, 538, 558, 790. power acquisition: 423, 768, 806. societies: 410, 424, 502, 532, 996, 997. songs: 538. women: 646, 951, 962. See also curing

Shane, Frank: 710–711

Shane, Pierre: 699

Shan-ke-t'wans; synonymy: 754

Shank't'wannons; synonymy: 754

Shank-t'wans; synonymy: 754

Shannon, George: 95

Sharas; synonymy: 881

Shar-ha; synonymy: 881

Sharphead: 599. synonymy: 599

Sharphead, Joseph: 599

Sharp Nose: 854, 855

Sharp's site: 160–161, 167

Sharshas; synonymy: 881

Shaumonekusse: 454

Shaved Heads; synonymy: 545

Shaw(h)ays; synonymy: 881

Shawnee; art: 910. ceremonies: 999. classification of: 4. external relations: 1024. reservations: 558

Tuxaxa; synonymy: 963
Túyĕchískĕ; synonymy: 751
Twelve: *392*
Twelve Mile Creek site: *223,* 227
25BD1 site: *197*
25FT13 site: *173, 179*
25FT18 site: 168
25FT28 site: *173*
25FT35 site: *173*
25FT70 site: *160–161,* 168, 169, *173, 177*
25HN12 site: *160–161,* 169
25HN36 site: *173, 177*
25HN44 site: *173, 175*
23JA41 site: *160–161*
23PL10: *160–161*
23PL44: *160–161*
23PL46: *160–161*
23PL53: *160–161*
23PL61 site: *160–161*
23PL62 site: *160–161*
23PL63: *160–161*
Twin Buttes Elementary School: 112
Twiss, Theodore: *822*
Two Bears: 781, 782, 785, 786, 787
Two Cauldrons; synonymy: 758
Two chief: *392*
Two Crow, John: *290*
Two Deer site: *147,* 153, *160–161*
Two Kettles Sioux; synonymy: 758. *See also*
   Teton Sioux
Two Leggings: 42, 705, *706, 710–711*
Two Rille band; synonymy: 758
Two Sisters site: *210–211*
Two Teeth site: *246*
Twoyoungmen, Isaac: *598–599*
Tyakmani: *786*
Tyler, Leonard: *289*

U
Û. tâ. wâ; synonymy: 971
ubðaða; synonymy: 757
ücétta; synonymy: 495
U-dse´-ta; synonymy: 495
Ugaχ-πáχti; synonymy: 512
Ugakhpa; synonymy: 512
U-gá-qpa-qti; synonymy: 512
ugáxpa; synonymy: 512
ugáxpe; synonymy: 512
úkahpa; synonymy: 512
Ŭ-kăh-pû; synonymy: 512
Ukaqpaqti; synonymy: 512
Úkasa; synonymy: 475
ukwáhpah; synonymy: 512
Ulibarrí, Juan de: 242, 518
’uma:ha; synonymy: 414
umáhą; synonymy: 413
Umaⁿhaⁿ; synonymy: 413
Umfreville, Edward: 96
umoⁿçhoⁿ; synonymy: 413
Umpedutokechaw: *771*
Uncas site: *210–211,* 219
Unc-pah-te; synonymy: 755
Uncpap(p)as; synonymy: 759
Uncpatina; synonymy: 755
Union Nationale Métisse de Saint-Joseph: 666,
   673

Union of Saskatchewan Indians: 322, 323
United Foreign Missionary Society: 275
United States government; archeology and: 20–
   22. Army: 270, 281, 282, 284, 316, 367, 368,
   426, 521, 558, 618, 697, 698, 733, 770, 780,
   781, 782, 787, 788, 793, 795, 796, 799, 815,
   842, 865, 889, 899, 915, 917, 944, 955, 988,
   1000, 1001. Army Corps of Engineers: 394,
   822–823. assimilation policy: 280, 284–292,
   1057. assistance programs: 293, 295, 296,
   297–299, 427, 428, 453, 690, 774, 825, 853,
   937, 962. Board of Indian Commissioners:
   619. and Canadian Indians: 316. citizenship:
   290, 505, 539–540, *773,* 821. civil rights:
   295, 297, 299, 426, *430,* 665, 988.
   Department of Commerce: 589. Department
   of Defense: 589. Department of Housing and
   Urban Development: 297, 588, 829.
   executive orders: 21, 281, 284, 368, 391,
   393, 618, 657, 782–783, 791, 842, 843.
   fixing of Canadian border: 308. food rations:
   287, 487, 538, 583, 585, 619, 678, 686, *708,*
   780, 782, 783, 784, 785, 787, 788, 790, 797,
   812, 815, 816, 850, 851, 898, 916, 933, 935–
   937, 955. Indian Health Service: 296, 297.
   Indian policy: 270–275, 280, 289–292, 291–
   292, 292–295, 296. Indian Services: 110.
   land allotments: 281, 284–285, *285,* 289–
   292, 292–295, 296, 320, 331, 385, 393, 394,
   401–402, 411, 426, 427, 442, 443, 456–457,
   473–474, 488, 490, 506, 507, 509, 521, 538–
   539, 559–560, 560, 586, 619, 657, 665, 669–
   670, 689, 690, 707, 708–709, *771,* 773, 791,
   797, 816, 850, 855, 865–866, 877, 886, 899,
   918–919, 934, 956. Office of Economic
   Opportunity: 825. Office of Indian Affairs:
   32, 385, 520, 539, 688, 796. Office of Indian
   Trade: 270–271. Peace Policy: 351, 368, 455,
   506, 521. relocation programs: 1016. Small
   Business Administration: 825. Supreme
   Court: 289, 290, 560, 712, 792, 793, 838,
   866, 918. Topographical Engineers: 26.
   voting rights: 295, 319, 324, 491–492, *598–*
   599, 709. War Department: 270, 796, 797.
   Works Progress Administration: 15, 20. *See*
   also Bureau of Indian Affairs; history; Indian
   Claims Commission; legislation, U.S.;
   litigation, U.S.; reservations and reserves;
   treaties and agreements, U.S.
United States v. *Means* (1988): 833
Unkepatines; synonymy: 755
Unkpapa Dakotas; synonymy: 759
Unmarked Human Burial Sites and Skeletal
   Remains Protection Act of 1989 (Nebraska):
   22
Upiyahideyaw: *771*
Upper Brule; synonymy: 756
Upper Canark variant: 154, 155, 156, 211–212
Upper Dakotas; synonymy: 752
Upper Missouri Company: 266
Upper Platte Bridge Fight (1856): 865
Upper Platte Indians; synonymy: 756
Upper Republican phase: 173–178, 234, 239–
   242. Graneros phase and: 234
Upper Sanger site: *246*
Upsàraukas; synonymy: 715
Up-sa-ro-ka; synonymy: 715

Useful Heart site: *197*
Ussinibwoinug; synonymy: 590
Ussinnewudj Eninnewug; synonymy: 637
Utasibaoutchactas; synonymy: 968
Ute: 851. ceremonies: 983, 988. classification:
   3, 5. external relations: 262. history: 2.
   migrations: 256. trade: 260, 262. warfare:
   846, 913
Uto-Aztecan language family: 69. comparative
   vocabulary: 64–66
Utsúshuat; synonymy: 513
Utz site: *223,* 230, *231,* 232, 447
uwá-ha; synonymy: 414
U-zu´-ti-u´-hi; synonymy: 513
U-zu´-ti-u´-wĕ; synonymy: 513

V
Vail Pass sites: 143
Valentine, Robert: 284, 290
Valley variant: *164,* 164–165
Valley View site: *223*
Valliere, Alphonsus: 507
Valverde, Antonio: 518
Van Dorn, Earl: 558
Vannerson, Julian: 28
váno²étaneo²o²; synonymy: 862
Van Schyver site: *210–211*
Vasāsan; synonymy: 494
Vaudreuil-Cavagnal, Pierre de Rigaud, marquis
   de: 434
Vaughan, Alfred D.: 777, 780
vault Indians; synonymy: 973
Ventrudos; synonymy: 345
Vermejo phase: 153
Vermillion Lakes site: *116*
Vermillion Post: *259,* 277
vétapAhaetó²eo²o; synonymy: 924
viajeros: 263
Vickery site: *160–161,* 170
Village de la feuille; synonymy: 753
Villasur, Pedro de: 264, *265,* 447, 518, 968
visions. *See* dreams and visions
Vitapāto; synonymy: 924
Vi´tāpä´tu´i; synonymy: 924
Voegelin, Erminie W.: 41
Voget, Fred: 39, *39*
vohkoohétaneo²o; synonymy: 650
Vohs site: *160–161,* 169
Vondrack site: *223*
Von Elm site: *160–161,* 170
Vonetonháes; synonymy: 756
Vosburg site: *223,* 232
Voxko; synonymy: 650
Voxkoeo; synonymy: 650
Vrebosch, Aloysius: 94

W
Wâ. hôô. kâ; synonymy: 389
Wa-ai´h; synonymy: 905
Waakpacootas; synonymy: 753
Wabipetons; synonymy: 753
Wa-çe´-toⁿ-hin-ga: *482*
Wachos; synonymy: 565
Wachpecoutes; synonymy: 752
Waco; synonymy: 564, 565. *See also* Wichita

1355

Wacoah; synonymy: 565
Waco language: 83, 84
waðáni; synonymy: 963
Wâd-doké-tâh-tâh; synonymy: 460
Wade, Margaret: 401
Wades-in-Water: *612*
Wades-in-Water, Julia: *612, 1060*
wadochtáta; synonymy: 460
Wa-dook-to-da; synonymy: 460
Wa-do-tan; synonymy: 460
wadóttadą; synonymy: 460
wadóttatta; synonymy: 460
waðúttada; synonymy: 460
Wa-ge´-ku-te; synonymy: 755
Wagh-toch-tat-ta; synonymy: 460
Wagon, Angelina: 994
Wahashas; synonymy: 494
Wahch-Pe-Kutch; synonymy: 753
Wahch-Pekuté; synonymy: 753
Wahkinny, Old Lady: *936–937*
Wahkpa Chu'gn site: *116*, 124
Wahkpakota; synonymy: 753
Wahkpa-toan; synonymy: 753
Wâh´-pa-coo-ta; synonymy: 752
Wahpacootay Sioux; synonymy: 753
Wahpakotoan; synonymy: 753
Wahpatoan Sioux; synonymy: 753
Wâh´-pa-tone; synonymy: 753
Wahpeconte; synonymy: 753
Wah-pee-ton; synonymy: 753
Wahpekute Sioux; synonymy: 752–753. *See also* Santee Sioux
Wahpetongs; synonymy: 753
Wahpeton Sioux; synonymy: 753. *See also* Santee Sioux
Wahpe-tonwans; synonymy: 753
Wahsash; synonymy: 494
Wahtee; synonymy: 973
Wah-toh-ta-na; synonymy: 460
Wah-tok-ta-ta; synonymy: 460
Wah too che work koo; synonymy: 970
Wah-tooh[-]tah-tah; synonymy: 460
wa·hú·kaxa; synonymy: 389, 592
Wahzecootai; synonymy: 755
Wah-zu-cootas; synonymy: 755
Waiwitchusha; synonymy: 626
Wajáje; synonymy: 493
Wakarusa phase: 165
Wakitamone: *453*
wá·kʷicinn; synonymy: 751
Walami: *931*
Wálaye; synonymy: 493
Walker, Jack: *322*
Walker, James R.: 35, 42, 99, *327*, 993, 1068, 1072
Walker, Robert, Sr.: *691*
Walker Gilmore site: *160–161*, 166–167, *168*
Walking Chief: *392*
Walking Eagle, Rae Jean: *837*
Walking Elk: *452*
Walking Horn: *482*
Walking in Light: *790*
Walking Rain: *442*
Walking Sun: *522–523*
Walks-at-Dusk: *330*
Walks Over Ice, Carson: *711*
Wallis, Wilson D.: 35, 36

Walnut phase: 144, 152
Walter Felt site: *116*, 121
Walter site: *160–161*, 169
Walth Bay site: *197*
Wamdupidutah: *771*
Wanak; synonymy: 750
Wananikwe: 998
Wanata: *759*, 784, *784*
Wa na tar wer; synonymy: 971
Wandering Spirit: 317
Wanikan complex: 129
wanmukantëk; synonymy: 627
Wanuĭ´tän-eo; synonymy: 862
wa-nuk´-e-ye´-na; synonymy: 346
Wáotănihtăts; synonymy: 623
Wapakotah; synonymy: 753
wapamathe; synonymy: 602
wàpe´maksa; synonymy: 602
Wapintowaher; synonymy: 753
Wappacoota; synonymy: 753
Wappitong; synonymy: 753
Wăqkotsi; synonymy: 446
waráš; synonymy: 493
wará·ye; synonymy: 493
WarCloud, Paul: 98
Wardell site: *116*, 125
Warden, Cleaver: *986*
War-doke-tar-tar; synonymy: 460
Ward site: *160–161, 246, 351*
warfare: 10, 24, 25, 341–343, 362, 375, 384–385, 409–410, 605, 631, *706, 866, 1044.* ambushes: 805. armor: 153, *163*, 184, 230, 550, 693, 731, 896, 958. braves: 438. captives: 971. casualties: 268, 343, 344, 362, 409, 410, 424, 478, 482, 581, 605, 616, 631, 678, 704, 705, 721, 788, 805, 815, 821, 843, 955. ceremonies: 273, 282, 283–284, 295, 362, 384–385, 424, 440, 470, 478, 484, 558, 581, 616, 685, 732, 841, 844, 875, 888, 893–894, 913, 915, 916–917, 950–951, 961, 984–987, 987, 1007, 1011–1012, 1012, 1020. clothing and adornment: 10, 343, *373, 374.452, 466, 484,* 527–528, 528, *528,* 581, 582–583, *584–585, 656, 732,* 803. counting coup: 616, 796, 805. dances: 384, 581. executions: 581, 943. honors: 410, 421, 423, *452,* 481, 554, 581, 685, 704–705, 805, 810, 846. intergroup: 10, 24, 25, *57,* 156, 206, 266, 268, 269, 270, 273, 275, 276, 277, 278, 279, *279,* 280, 281, 282, 283, 284, 295, 302, 304, 305, 309, 310, 313, 315, 317, 384, 400, 416, 418, 424, 425, 447, 452, 462, 464, 476, 478, 499, 521, 546, 549, 550, 557, 572, 574, 575, 585, 608, 616, 641, 663, 678, 697–698, 720, 721, 722, 731, 733–734, 788, 797, 805, 843, 846, 863, 865, 968. introduction of firearms: 233, *261,* 261–262, *262,* 304, 329–331, 370, 607, 863. introduction of horses: 608. leadership: 332, 342–343, 362, 384, 409, 421, 424, 469, 483, 501–502, 581, 609, 615–616, 645, 685, 704, 705, 726, 767–768, 801, 806, 846, 875, 876, 931. motives for: 10, 277–278, 384, 470, 501, 502, 574, 581, 608, 616, 685, 767, 950. music: 581. prisoners: 277–278, 478, 502, 517, *518,* 685, 697, 727, 750, 751, 770, 771, *772,* 805, 806, 812, 875, 888, 889, 908, 912, 917, *917,* 921,

950, 954, 1043. protohistoric: 23, 24, 267. raids: 262, 342, 362, 409–410, 462, 483–484, 579–581, 608, 615–616, 698, 705, 810, 842, 863, 865, 867, 888, 896, *907,* 908, 911, 915, 916, 941–942, 950–951, 955. ritualized face-to-face combat: 581. scalping: 304, 362, 384, 502, 581, 721, 805, 806, 896, 950–951. scouts: 281, 282–283, 284, 362, 368, *374,* 384, 386, 393, *483,* 521, *522–523,* 546, 581, 666, 698, 782, 797, 802, 806, 812, 955, *956.* songs: 1035–1036, 1037–1038. torture and desecration: 502, 557, 581, 721. warriors: *373, 374,* 438, 452, *452, 453, 466, 483, 484, 522–523,* 527–528, *528, 528,* 581, 582–583, *584–585,* 645, *656,* 698, 704–705, *711,* 803, *813, 866,* 894, 929, *931,* 958. warriors' societies: 615, 645, 769, 803, 893–894, 919, 931, *931,* 934, 998, 1011, 1012, 1018–1019, 1020. weapons: *139,* 140, 143, 304, *331, 373, 374,* 402, 404, *410,* 419, *419,* 450, 452, *452,* 466, *466,* 484, 502, *522–523, 529,* 550, 581, *584–585,* 604, *612,* 631, 640, 679, *681,* 705, *721,* 764, *779,* 811–812, *866,* 868, 950, 978, 1048. with Whites: 262, 264, *265,* 266, 267, 273, 276, 282, 283–284, 302, 303, 307–308, 309, 316, 317, 367, 447, 471, 478, 518, 521, 550, 551–552, 568, 585, 618, 647–648, 663, 664, 665, 678, 697, 698, 733, 762, 770, 771, 779, 781, 788, 795, 796, 797–799, 815, 836, 842, 843, 865, 886, 888, 889, 916–917, 941–943, 944, 954, 955
Warhpekute; synonymy: 753
Warhpeton; synonymy: 753
Warhpetonwan-nan; synonymy: 753
Wark-pay-ku-tay; synonymy: 753
Wark-pey-t'wawn; synonymy: 753
Warpecoutais; synonymy: 752
War-pe-kintes; synonymy: 753
Warpekute(y); synonymy: 753
Warpeton; synonymy: 753
War-pe-ton-wan; synonymy: 753
Warpetonwans; synonymy: 753
War-pe-t'wans; synonymy: 753
Warren, Philip: *859*
Warren, William: 77, 304, 305
Warrior, Brenda: *961*
Warrior, Clyde: 428
Warrior, Jeanette: *691*
Warrior, Mildred: *961*
Warrior, Sylvester: *1032*
Warteshe: 506
wasaasa; synonymy: 494
Wasache; synonymy: 494
Wasagè; synonymy: 494
wasa·ha; synonymy: 750
Wasas; synonymy: 494
waša·ša; synonymy: 494
Wä-sä-sa-o-no; synonymy: 751
Wä-sä´-seh-o-no; synonymy: 751
wasáse·onǫ; synonymy: 751
wasási; synonymy: 494
waʔsá·siʔ; synonymy: 494
waša·ši; synonymy: 494
Washakie, Dick: 994
Washásh; synonymy: 494
Washbashaws; synonymy: 494
Washita River phase: 182, 207, 209–211, *212,*

Handbook of

North American Indians

Handbook of North American Indians

WILLIAM C. STURTEVANT
General Editor